ENCYCLOPEDIA OF RHETORIC

ENCYCLOPEDIA OF
RHETORIC

Thomas O. Sloane

Editor in Chief

UNIVERSITY PRESS

2001

OXFORD
UNIVERSITY PRESS

Oxford New York
Athens Auckland Bangkok Bogotá Buenos Aires Calcutta
Cape Town Chennai Dar es Salaam Delhi Florence Hong Kong Istanbul
Karachi Kuala Lumpur Madrid Melbourne Mexico City Mumbai
Nairobi Paris São Paulo Shanghai Singapore Taipei Tokyo Toronto Warsaw
and associated companies in
Berlin Ibadan

Copyright © 2001 by Oxford University Press, Inc.

Published by Oxford University Press, Inc.
198 Madison Avenue, New York, New York 10016
www.oup.com

Oxford is a registered trademark of Oxford University Press

Library of Congress Cataloging-in-Publication Data

Encyclopedia of rhetoric / Thomas O. Sloane, editor in chief.
p. cm.
Includes bibliographic references and index.
ISBN 0-19-512595-9
1. Rhetoric—Encyclopedias. I. Sloane, Thomas O.
PN172 .E52 2001 808'.003—dc21 00-052870

Portions of "Feminist rhetoric" by Karlyn Kohrs Campbell previously appeared in Theresa Enos, ed.,
Encyclopedia of Rhetoric and Composition: Communication from Ancient Times to the Information Age
(Garland 1996); they are included here by permission of Routledge.

EDITORIAL AND PRODUCTION STAFF

Executive Editor: Christopher Collins
Development Editor: Mark Mones
Assistant Project Editor: Merilee Johnson
Copyeditors: Patricia Connolly, Alexa Firat,
Constantina Rhodes Bailly, Martha Goldstein
Manufacturing Controller: Donna Ng
Book Designer: Joan Greenfield
Managing Editor: Matthew Giarratano
Publisher: Karen Casey

1 3 5 7 9 8 6 4 2

Printed in the United States of America
on acid-free paper

Contents

◆

Editorial Board

Preface

◆

TEACHERS IN ANCIENT TIMES INSISTED THAT RHETORIC—ITS IDENTITY AS WELL as its nature—is best learned through practice, not through reading about it. Such doctrines, of course, keep teachers in business. Nonetheless, theories and manuals of rhetoric demonstrably fall short of the mark, and have done so for twenty-five hundred years. "For all a rhetorician's rules," wrote Samuel Butler in 1663, "[t]each nothing but to name his tools." Often called the world's second-oldest profession, the teaching of rhetoric has probably derived as little benefit from books as has the world's oldest profession. Readers, therefore, should not expect to find a "compleat rhetoric" within these covers. Rhetoric is a storehouse of communicative tactics: some are hoary and stale (e.g., "unaccustomed as I am to public speaking," which was identified in antiquity and preserved as a figure of speech); some are too new to be codified (like "emoticons" in e-mails); most are time-bound, dependent upon audience and occasion.

Given its great antiquity as well as the capriciousness of intellectual fashion, it is little wonder that our subject has been variously defined through the centuries: sophistry, queen of the liberal arts, oldest of the humanities, style, deception, specious reasoning, practical logic, loaded language, purple prose, what my opponent speaks, ad infinitum. Lately, rhetoric has been called "purposive communication"—a stunning neutrality. Our readers, we assume, will have at least some acquaintance with our subject's scarlet past, and will be neither astounded nor dismayed to discover that they have actually used its tactics from time to time. Indeed, our putative readers will in fact have moved beyond curiosity about such matters as a "simile" (which is nonetheless defined herein) to wondering what on earth a *hendiadys* might be, or how to conceive of a "virtual audience" or a "hypertext." Given the readers we have in mind, all recognizable words from antiquity have been left intact and more or less in their original Latin or Greek: *eloquentia*, for example, or *mythoi*; or for that matter *encyclopedia* and *rhetoric*.

The Synoptic Outline of Contents at the end of the book offers a quick and easy overview. Because the purpose of that outline was to help us plan this book and keep its parts from becoming disparate, it might prove useful to anyone wondering how some entry (e.g., "Questioning") fits in or if there is any coherence in a work like this, or in a subject like rhetoric. Obviously, as a glance at the outline will show, we treat our subject as something anchored in the past. At the same time, however, we treat it as something that has a place in the present and is not exactly limited to this or that culture. The history of the art from its origins in ancient Greece is recounted in these pages, in our longest single entry ("Classical rhetoric"). But we attempt also to track that history up to a possible postmodern era—when rhetoric's media extend from oratory to the Internet, its "commonplaces" encompass data storage and retrieval systems, and its *memoria* conceptualizes "space" on a "hard disk." Included too is recent work in comparative rhetoric, research into cultures that have not fully experienced the effects of our classical Western heritage. However pandemic rhetoric itself might prove to be, our subject nonetheless remains deeply ingrained within the academic worlds of Europe, England, and North America, where for centuries it has received its most explicit treatment—and where, moreover, scholarly interest in the subject has recently gained momentum and become a fully international enterprise. In North America, research in rhetoric is now bolstered by five journals, and well over a thousand students are enrolled in graduate programs in the subject. It is noteworthy, however, that our major entry on style and all the entries on figures of speech were composed by non-native speakers of English.

More than three-quarters of our 120 contributors are from the United States. Other contributors—who wrote almost half the articles—come from Austria, Belgium, Canada, the Czech Republic, Germany, Hong Kong, India, the Netherlands, South Africa, Spain, Switzerland, the United Arab Emirates, and the United Kingdom. Their departmental affiliations are primarily communications and secondarily English; classics is third; rhetoric is fourth, just ahead of philosophy. Other departments and disciplines include French, German, law, comparative literature, music, philology, theology, and sociology.

There are approximately two hundred entries in this volume, ranging in size from very short (about 100 words) for certain figures of speech to our longest entry (16,000 words) on classical rhetoric. Almost every entry emphasizes our common rhetorical tradition, partly as a result of the way this volume was planned. The three modes of proof, the five offices (or arts, or more loftily "canons") of rhetoric, and the traditional ends of eloquence and persuasion—these were the infrastructure of our project, the antique starting points of our Synoptic Outline, and in the editors' minds, the very requisites of rhetoric. Most of these matters move in directions unforeseen by our progenitors—eloquence and persuasion, for example. The former has to do with the beauty of an utterance, something that to modern readers might seem either quaint or much more at home in poetry than in rhetoric and something that in these pages just barely escapes its classical foundations. Persuasion, on the other hand, quickly flees those foundations and rushes headlong into the waiting arms of modern social scientists.

Too, in view of the experiential nature of rhetoric, the reader will find much overlapping between these entries. Plato seemed to think that the best rhetoric is a kind of love. Aristotle defined it as a kind of ability. In neither conception is the art itself clearly formulable, nor has it become so, and thus, virtually every entry offers a passage into a complex whole. One will find, for instance, that the entry on eloquence includes a discussion of *inventio*. Turning to the entry on invention, one finds a capsule history of classical rhetoric, where of course, everything seems either to belong or to have gotten started. The entry on persuasion, the other traditional end of rhetoric, leads one through an audience's emotions, a rhetor's credibility, and "message characteristics" at least part of the way back to traditional modes of proof, though with little dimming of persuasion's modernist sheen. The figures of speech, in the eyes of some the very essence of rhetoric, are treated in a long entry by that name; then again in the entry on style; once more in the entry on poetry; and then most are given individual treatment. Nor does the matter stop there: References to the figures, either collectively or individually, are sprinkled throughout this work, indicating their importance certainly, but also indicating the interlocking nature of rhetoric's pieces. Every entry, in short, could cross-reference every other entry, including our most defiantly modernist ones. When we came to consider "related subjects" (see the Synoptic Outline), we tried to keep from considering them simply as a miscellany, a nod in the direction of political correctness, or a scholarly appendix. But in order to keep the section from expanding exponentially, we selected subjects that seemed to have at least an indirect bearing on the identity of rhetoric—and wherein there are potential contributors whom we might recruit.

Long—for two and one-half millennia—considered the exclusive pursuit of white, classically-trained males preparing for careers in law, politics, or teaching, rhetoric once formed the very core of the educational curriculum, where it was linked closely with logic and grammar. The link with logic yet stands, but grammar seems to have bowed out in favor of linguistics, a discipline that pervades and gives a certain air to many definitions in this encyclopedia, particularly in that area mentioned earlier, the figures of speech, which rhetoric once shared with grammar. Old-school rhetoricians will surely be flabbergasted to read, for example, that *prolēpsis* is a "permutative metataxeme." At the same time, however, those same rhetoricians may be gratified to note that, given the many references throughout our entries to Plato's *Phaedrus*, Aristotle's *Rhetoric*, Cicero's *De oratore*, and Erasmus's *De copia*, there yet seems to be a rhetorical canon—perhaps made inescapable, like our tradition itself, by the way we planned this volume. Nonetheless, if the wisdom of that canon is attended to in all its impulses toward openness and experience, rhetoricians—old-school or otherwise—will welcome its inevitable expansion to include, say, the contributions from studies in African-American, communicationist, comparative, feminist, and queer rhetoric, all of which are already integral to our subject in a way that the word *related* in our Synoptic Outline might seem merely to patronize. Within this book, however, their contributions are encountered in alphabetical order as matters that seem to have an equally-significant bearing on the whole. The ostensible hierarchies of the Synoptic Outline merely locate what we take to be our foundations.

Those who believe they already know the subject sufficiently well may wonder why an encyclopedia about it has been published. These readers will, we hope, browse this work and find the answer the editors themselves found to their own similar inquiry. There are entries herein that might never have been written, or might not have been so succinctly put forth, without the prompting of a project like this. If some essays are reliquaries, others clearly move our subject toward its fourth millenium, in which it appears that rhetoric will continue to be as useful for analysis as for genesis; that is, as useful for the interpretation of discourse and phenomena as it is for their composition. Finally, although rhetoric is often thought of as a blend of literary and political interests, the subject itself is too seldom viewed discretely, as something that just might possibly stand alone. The "old rhetoric," one commentator observed, "has been spread over a multiplicity of disciplines"—but not, we believe, to such an airy thinness that something of its integrity cannot be restored.

There are other peculiarities, of course, one in particular: Although rhetoric is a people art, not one person is listed among the entries of this encyclopedia—not even Aristotle, not even Nietzsche. That decision was based on our effort to abstract rhetoric as far as we could, not only from this or that discipline but also from this or that theorist, time, place, culture, and to endeavor to search for its principles. We recognize the paradox, in view of what we take rhetoric to be. It is nearly impossible either to abstract a temporal cause from its effects or to look anew at a subject anchored in but not confined to an ancient tradition. But the attempt to do so, we believe, sets this work apart from other recent publications as the *Encyclopedia of Rhetoric and Composition* edited by Theresa Enos (1996) or Heinrich Lausberg's magisterial *Handbuch der literarischen Rhetorik* (1960).

There are oversights, no doubt, omissions and errors. But we have done what we could in chasing this Proteus, with more than a little help from Christopher Collins, Merilee Johnson, and Mark Mones at Oxford University Press, who were always ready with logistical support and advice. Oxford, moreover, was the "onlie begetter" of this work, though encouraged from the outset by scholars in the field. Those of us who were drawn to it, however reluctantly at first, gradually became enthusiastic participants, an attitude we hope we demonstrate.

Kenneth Burke dedicates his *Grammar of Motives* (1945) "To Elizabeth / Without Whom Not." I shall follow the example of this master rhetorician and offer similar praise of my colleagues on the editorial board—Shadi Bartsch, Tom Farrell, Heinrich Plett—and of our distinguished contributors. They are truly, in the language of Cicero, the *litterati sine quibus non* of this endeavor.

—THOMAS O. SLOANE
Berkeley, California
October 2000

ENCYCLOPEDIA OF RHETORIC

A–B

◆

ABOLITIONIST RHETORIC. *See* African-American rhetoric, *article on* Abolitionist rhetoric.

AD HOMINEM ARGUMENT. *Argumentum ad hominem* refers to a kind of argument in which the person is the focus of the argument, as opposed to objective evidence on which the argument may be based. *Argumentum ad hominem* has been prominently treated as a fallacy, in the logical tradition; however, recent work has shown that this type of argument is not always fallacious and that there is pervasive ambiguity in how it has been defined and what it has been taken to represent. [*See* Fallacies.]

The expression *argumentum ad hominem* is ambiguous. The main meaning it has in popular speech, as well as in the traditions of logic and rhetoric, is the use of personal attack as a way of refuting an argument. In its simplest form, this argument has the following schema : so-and-so is a person of bad (defective) character, therefore his argument should not be accepted. This simple form of argument is properly called *ad hominem*. It is also often called the "abusive" *ad hominem* argument in many modern logic textbooks. It could perhaps even be called the personal attack or character attack type of argument. However, not all attacks on character are *ad hominem* arguments. In order to be an *ad hominem* argument in the proper sense, the following conditions must be met. There must be two parties involved in disputation. The first party must have put a particular argument forward. The second party must then cite the bad character of the first party as a reason for concluding that the argument is no good. For a contrasting example, in a famous biography of the singer Frank Sinatra, the writer alleged that Sinatra was a person of bad character. But since no particular argument attributed to Sinatra was being attacked, the argumentation in the book would not properly be said to be *ad hom-*inem in the main sense appropriate for logic and rhetoric.

There is also another meaning of the expression *argumentum ad hominem* that has a place in traditional logic and rhetoric, as well as in everyday speech. This secondary meaning is not so dominant as the main meaning, but it is a fairly common usage in philosophical speech. According to this meaning, an argument is *ad hominem* if it is based on the other party's position in a dispute. For example, suppose that prolife Bob and prochoice Wilma are engaged in a dispute on the issue of abortion and that Wilma puts forward an argument based on the premise that human life is sacred. Let us say that she does not accept this premise, but she uses it to try to convince Bob to accept a conclusion because she knows that Bob accepts the premise. This form of argument is called "argument from commitment" in modern argumentation theory (Walton, 1996). Traditionally, it was called the *ex concessis* argument. But traditionally as well, in philosophy, it has often been called the *argumentum ad hominem.* However, the two kinds are distinct. Not all arguments from commitment (*ex concessis* arguments) are personal-attack arguments. And not all *ad hominem* arguments in the personal-attack sense are arguments from commitment (although many of them are, as will be shown below). How then, one might well wonder, did this ambiguity of terminology arise?

The answer, as Nuchelmans (1993) has shown, is that there are two separate lines of historical development of the phrase *argumentum ad hominem,* each having roots in the writings of Aristotle (384–322 BCE). The two kinds of argument not only share common features, but they are often referred to by similar or identical expressions. One root, coming from *On Sophistical Refutations* (165a37) and *Topics* (101a25), has been taken to refer to "arguments that are based on propositions which have been conceded by the adver-

1

sary" (Nuchelmans, 1993, p. 38). In other words, the one meaning that was taken from Aristotle and given the designation of *argumentum ad hominem* is that of the argument from commitment or *ex concessis* argument. This meaning was called *disputatio temptiva* by Boethius (480–524 CE). The other meaning is close to that of the personal attack type of argument described above. It was picked up by Aquinas (1225–1274) from passages in Aristotle's *Metaphysics,* (1005b35, 1062a2), where Aristotle distinguishes between proof in an absolute sense and proof relative to a particular person (Nuchelmans, 1993, p. 39). This meaning occurs in the works of Galileo (1564–1642) in several places (Finochiarro, 1980) and also in a well-known place in Locke's *Essay* (1690), as Hamblin (1970, p. 160) shows. This meaning also stems from ancient teachers of rhetoric, who distinguished between the substantive issues in a debate and the personal aspects that can also be involved. The two traditions of the meaning of *argumentum ad hominem* remained separate for a long time, but according to Nuchelemans (p. 44) they became intertwined in Rudolphus Agricola's *De inventione dialectica* (1479). It then became very tempting to treat the two different meanings of *ad hominem* as referring to essentially the same kind of argument. This temptation was made just too hard to resist any longer when Locke treated the *ad hominem* alongside other fallacies like the *ad verecundiam* and *ad ignorantiam,* but used the expression *argumentum ad hominem* in the argument from commitment sense.

The best solution to this confusing terminological problem is to use the expression *argumentum ad hominem* as a technical term of logic and rhetoric: it should refer to the personal attack kind of *ad hominem* argument. The other kind of argument should be called *ex concessis,* argument from commitment, to have an even better term for it.

Is *Ad Hominem* Fallacious? Traditionally in logic, *argumentum ad hominem* has been listed as a fallacy, but it has recently been acknowledged more and more that this type of argument (in either of its two meanings) can be reasonable in many instances (Walton, 1998). For example, in legal argumentation, it is recognized that attacking the character of a witness in court, called "im-

peachment of the witness," is sometimes quite a reasonable form of argument. Nonetheless, character attack is usually regarded as a dangerous form of argument in law, and attacks on the character of a defendant, a witness, or an attorney are sharply limited in trials by rules of evidence. The legitimacy of the character attack, the main meaning of *ad hominem,* has also been widely recognized in rhetoric, where *ēthos* or persuading an audience using argumentation based on the perceived character (good or bad) of a speaker, can be an acceptable form of argument. In political debate, for example, character is a relevant issue in a democratic system where voters cannot reasonably be expected to know all the facts on all issues, and will often vote on the basis of their perception of a candidate's character. [*See* Ēthos.]

On the other hand, *ad hominem* is an extremely powerful and slippery tactic of persuasion that often has a devastating effect in argumentation, especially when based on very little evidence, or on innuendo and no real evidence at all. Therefore, in some instances of its use, it is quite right to judge the argument to be fallacious. The fallacious cases tend to be the ones where the *ad hominem* argument is quite weak (from a logical point of view), or even irrelevant to the issue being discussed, but nevertheless works by a process of "where there's smoke there must be fire" to make the accused party seem guilty, and thus somehow in the wrong. Precisely because such arguments are based on suggestion and innuendo, it can be extremely difficult to reply to them successfully. The job of distinguishing between the reasonable and fallacious cases is further expedited by being aware of the various subtypes of the argument.

Subtypes of *Ad Hominem* Argument. The various subtypes of *ad hominem* argument have been classified in Walton (1998, pp. 248–263). In addition to the main meaning, defined above, three subtypes are especially common and important: circumstantial, bias, and poisoning the well. In the circumstantial *ad hominem,* the first party attacks the second party by alleging a practical inconsistency—claiming that she does not practice what she preaches—and then using this alleged contradiction to suggest that the second party is hypocritical, dishonest, confused, or otherwise has bad character and is therefore not a credible arguer. For example, a politician who argued long and hard that the opposition were wasteful spenders, may be attacked by alleging that he himself is acting like a "potentate" by flying around to exotic places with a huge staff of assistants, spending millions of dollars on excessive parties. In the bias type of *ad hominem* argument, the first party attacks the second party by alleging that the second party has some sort of personal interest that throws her credibility into doubt. For example, when the second party gives a speech claiming that environmentalists have exaggerated the problem of acid rain, the first party may reveal that the second party has a financial interest in a coal company. Again, such an allegation of bias, like any *ad hominem* argument, works by casting doubt on the credibility of an arguer. The attack is relevant, and can be especially powerful, in cases where the argument in question does depend for part of its support on the personal credibility of the arguer. For example, in witness testimony in a trial, it may be impossible to verify the facts directly, and therefore the testimony as evidence may depend very much on the credibility of the witness.

The final important subtype is poisoning the well. In this type of *ad hominem* argument, which may be seen as an extension of the bias subtype, the arguer is said to be so biased that he is permanently closed to any real, balanced consideration of the truth of a matter. The classic case is that of Cardinal Newman (1801–1890), who was attacked in the political arena on the grounds that, as a Catholic, he would always revert to the Catholic view, instead of really looking at both sides of any issue. Newman replied that this "poisoning of the well" prevented him from having any political voice that was not already discounted before he even said anything.

Are All Philosophical Arguments *Ad Hominem*? The weight of presumption in philosophy has generally been to consider *ad hominem* arguments as inherently fallacious, and to feature dramatic cases of their abuse in the logic textbooks. But very little serious attention was ever given to the possibility that these arguments could often be reasonable, as commonly used in everyday practices of argumentation. An exception to this neglect of taking a closer look at the *ad hominem* was the account given by Henry W. Johnstone, Jr., who combines an interest in logic with an interest in rhetoric. Johnstone (1978, p. 9) considered ordinary cases of the *ad hominem* argument, like the one cited by Schopenhauer (1788–1860). In this case, one man says, "Berlin is such a dreary place," and the other replies, "Why don't you leave then?" Johnstone compared everyday uses of the *ad hominem* argument like this one to cases of its use in philosophical controversies. In dispute between philosophers, this form of argumentation, where one arguer takes what she presumes to be the stated or implied positions of the other party, and then draws inferences from them, raising critical questions about the conclusions drawn, can be shown to be quite common. By studying cases of passages from philosophical writings, Johnstone shows that such *ad hominem* arguments are in fact typical of much philosophical argumentation. Thus, Johnstone posed an acute and provocative problem that woke philosophers out of their dogmatic slumbers on the subject of *ad hominem* arguments.

It would appear that what Johnstone primarily had in mind was the argument from commitment or *ex concessis*. If so, he was certainly right that this form of argument is not only quite often reasonable (nonfallacious), but is also very commonly found in historical and current texts of discourse of philosophical argumentation. Typically, for example, in the Platonic dialogues, the argumentation of Socrates is based on the expressed and implied positions of his interlocutors. Johnstone's view of such philosophical argumentation as commitment-based leads naturally to a certain metaphilosophy, or philosophy of philosophy. According to this view, philosophical arguments are different in nature from scientific or empirical arguments that are based on external and objective evidence. Instead, they represent a kind of rational persuasion that is based on premises that are the expressed or implied commitments of a party with whom one is engaged in a dialogue. By questioning and answering, the dialogue sharpens and refines these commitments, often in a critical way that probes into the reasons supporting them. So conceived, philosophical argumentation is based on the person of the arguer it is designed rationally to persuade. Philosophical argumentation, in this way of looking at it, does have an *ad hominem* aspect that makes it different from other kinds of argumentation with which it can easily be confused.

BIBLIOGRAPHY

Finochiarro, Maurice A. *Galileo and the Art of Reasoning.* Dordrecht, Netherlands, 1980.

Hamblin, C. L. *Fallacies.* London, 1970.

Johnstone, H. W., Jr. *Validity and Rhetoric in Philosophical Argument.* University Park, Pa., 1978.

Nuchelmans, Gabriel. "On the Fourfold Root of the *Argumentum ad Hominem.*" In *Empirical Logic and Public Debate.* Edited by Erik C. W. Krabbe, Rene Jose Dalitz, and Pier A. Smit, pp. 37–68. Amsterdam, 1993.

Walton, Douglas. *Argumentation Schemes for Presumptive Reasoning.* Mahwah, N.J., 1996.

Walton, Douglas. *Ad Hominem Arguments.* Tuscaloosa, Ala., 1998.

—DOUGLAS WALTON

AESTHETICS. *See* Eloquence; *and* Style.

AFRICAN-AMERICAN RHETORIC. [*This entry comprises four articles:*

> An overview
> Abolitionist rhetoric
> Double-consciousness
> Black Nationalism

The first article provides a brief overview of the problems black American speakers have faced in establishing an African-American rhetorical tradition. The second article describes the contribution of black abolitionists to abolitionist rhetoric. The third article explores the history and various uses of the term double-consciousness. *The fourth article addresses the evolving aims and strategies of black nationalism, as reflected in the rhetoric of various African-American leaders.*]

An overview

To speak of an African-American rhetorical tradition is at once to speak about the problems of speaking. Historically, black orators have instructed black folk about *how* to speak when one is not *supposed* to speak. Hence, African-American rhetoric has been engaged in a struggle with a profound paradox. In order to become a tradition, African-American rhetoric has had to overcome violent racist muting forces. It has filled an American silence regarding the immorality of slavery. And it has self-consciously constituted an African-American *ēthos*. When one thinks about black public speech, one must consider a cultural history wherein the very act of black speaking (and writing) was subject to severe censure. Attempting to keep black folks in their place, the institution of slavery was erected and sustained by strict regulations against the kinds of public rituals and practices that make an African-American rhetorical tradition possible. In the antebellum South, the very idea of an African-American "public" was a virtual oxymoron. In the North, African-American orators were often beaten and killed for attempting to exercise the liberty of free speech. Thus, to conceive of African-American rhetoric is to think first of all the ways that an American public tried to quash it.

In a similar fashion, a consideration of an African-American rhetorical tradition entails an exploration of a peculiarly American silence regarding the ills of slavery. The history of American slavery represents a moral crisis so acute that it still provokes inquiry. For black scholars like Alexander Crummell and W. E. B. Du Bois, the longtime enslavement of the African in America was empirical evidence of the moral failing of Victorian virtue (Zamir, 1995). The inability of America to suppress the slave trade, for example, represented for Du Bois a corruption that runs to the very heart of Anglo-European civilization. Moreover, this failing has not been spoken of directly in dominant American discourse. Rather, talk of abstract principles of "equality" (Condit and Loucaites, 1993) and references to dense legalese inscribed in "states' rights" conceal the error. Therefore, not only were black spokespersons consistently gagged by mob rule and the deformed rule of law, this particular failing of the civic good was exacerbated by a refusal to acknowledge it as such. In other words, this essential moral failing was prolonged by an American silence enveloping it.

But these silences beckon always for public speech, precisely because they call into question the capacity for public speech to provide for moral agency and social justice. Black public speech, therefore, always already asks and answers such a query. The story of an African-American rhetorical tradition not only depicts the transmutation and enactment of African styles, religions, and practices in America (Asante, 1987), but it specifies an American moral lack. Houston Baker Jr. (1987) refers to an African-American discursive "sounding" that ingenuously calls attention to such silences through an elaborate play of indirection and guile. By signifying (Gates, 1988) moral dramas for community contemplation, African-American rhetoric has advanced, in part, as a fulfillment of what Emmanuel Levinas refers to as a "call of conscience" (Hyde and Rufo, 2000). Marjorie Pryse (1985) has suggested that the activity of bringing voice out of an American abyss symbolizes a kind of black magic, hoodoo, or "conjure." As an act of resistance to racism through community renewal, African-American rhetoric can be thought of as a "conjuring" voice from within American spaces of negation and neglect. To conceive of African-American rhetoric as a "conjuring" voice constitutive of a "call" to America's conscience is to highlight its capacity for rhetorical invention and ethical action. This perspective makes salient the fact that African-American rhetoric must be understood as a transformative phenomenon in America.

Anthologies of African-American oratory capture the sense in which black public speech has sought to transform American racist and sexist practices, but also how black speech has been self-consciously reflexive. As a vital dimension of abolitionist discourse, for example, black speakers advanced the antislavery cause while providing through the sheer act of public speaking the warrant *for* black public speaking. Spokespersons like Cyrus Bustill, Richard Allen, William Hamilton, Maria Stewart, Charles Lenox Remond, Henry Highland Garnet, William Wells Brown, and Frederick Douglass take as one of their rhetorical objects the paradoxical activity of black speech itself. African-American eloquence is provocative and problematic in this regard. In the mid-nineteenth century, Douglass's power as a public speaker caused many northern white audiences to question his slave history (authenticity). Indeed, African-American eloquence has often been seen as a sign of the orator's (mimicked) "whiteness."

Historically, speaking on behalf of African-American freedom and dignity directly invoked this paradox. If black speakers were viewed as masterful orators, their artistry was often explained by referencing their perceived proximity to white culture. In this cultural dissociation, "blackness" is negated and made silent. The ground for establishing an African-American rhetorical tradition as such is denied. The abolition, women's suffrage, labor, and temperance movements were each infected by this form of racism. White movement organizers grudgingly allowed black speakers at civil rights and women's rights conventions, believing that for the most part white lecturers could better voice movement concerns. Thus, black speakers needed to negotiate this rhetorical dilemma—to provide powerful argument for movement issues and articulate moral critiques of the movements themselves (Foner and Branham, 1998).

Taken in full, African-American rhetoric is a brilliant and imaginative adaptation to a confluence of dynamic and shifting exigencies. The Reconstruction era in the United States, for instance, ushered in unprecedented black representation in the South, as well as a strident debate about what to do with all the freed slaves. Kirt H. Wilson (1998) has argued that the civil rights debate of 1874 to 1875 characterizes opposing notions of how race should matter in American politics. Analyses such as his also point out that American muting forces were constantly on the move against a "conjuring" African-American voice. Opponents of racial desegregation sought to arrest the debate by denying the harsh reality of racism. Thus, black speakers were challenged to fill in this void by supplying stark narratives about their daily lives.

The efficaciousness of African-American narrative is uncontested today. In a special sense, however, it took the Harlem Renaissance of the 1920s to introduce black folk sensibility to American literati. Also known as the "New Negro Movement," this post–World War I artistic explosion should be understood, in part, as a civil rights campaign designed to demonstrate a "modern" black subjectivity and constitute an African-American nationality. Although there has been much scholarly disagreement regarding the diverse influences sparking this Renaissance and about whether the character of the artistry warrants the term *Renaissance,* one interested in surveying the field of African-American rhetoric should be attentive to how black writing argued. That is, how black folk like James Weldon Johnson, Alain LeRoy Locke, Jesse Fauset, and W. E. B. Du Bois (to name a few) carefully managed the cultural resources of the "movement" so as to cultivate Harlem as a "race capital" and a resource for African-American rhetorical invention.

Central to this rhetorical inventive task was the negotiation and reinterpretation of "American" and "Negro." Harlem seemed to capture a rising black militancy, black pride, and the hopes that America would soon live up to its deferred promises of equality under the law. Housing the densest black population in the North, Harlem came geographically and emotionally to represent the "nation within a nation" that Martin Robinson Delany and Booker T. Washington characterized years earlier in quite different discourse and under different situations. On the one hand, the "race capital" signified a form of nationalism most clearly represented by Marcus Garvey and the Universal Negro Improvement Association. On the other hand, Alain LeRoy Locke's "New Negro" referred to a complex ideology and rhetorical strategy that transfigured both "race" and "American" identity. Public argument over how black art mediated these sorts of tensions are rich resources for appreciating the historical role that African-American cultural performance has always played in voicing a moral challenge to the ongoing constitution of America.

Almost as soon as the Harlem Renaissance was widely recognized, the Great Depression (1929–1941) diverted white America's gazing on the pages of blackness to green paper money and a "red menace." Concerns over the economic crisis, World War II, and communism had a divergent impact on African-American rhetors for decades. Artists, intellectuals, and activists, such as Marcus Garvey, A. Philip Randolph, W. E. B. Du Bois, Langston Hughes, and Paul Robeson, delivered potent addresses regarding the relation of race to labor, the role that black folk ought to play during the war, and how global imperialism warps Africa.

Specifically, after World War II, African Americans sought jobs and a greater freedom of movement across U.S. communities and across the nation. The doctrine of separate but equal was perceived to stand in the way of African-American economic and social progress. In a lecture at Dillard University in New Orleans on the night before his victory over Topeka, Kansas, in the famous desegregation case *Brown v. Board of Education* (1954), Thurgood Marshall asserted that segregation laws like the Black Codes of the Post-Reconstruction era concealed in legal garb the moral bankruptcy of a nation. Once again, African-American rhetoric voiced an ethical challenge to a peculiar American silence. This kind of rhetorical performance goes beyond the explication of bad law. By reinventing discrimination as a plague visited upon every American community, it issues a "call" to the transhistorical conscience of America.

Without a doubt, this African-American "call of conscience" has taken many forms over the generations; it has been sounded from the stages of convention platforms, and church pulpits, and it has reverberated off the pages of the black press. Du Bois posited it in spiritual terms in *The Souls of Black Folk* (1903) and Ralph Ellison transmuted it, ironically, into a faceless figure in *Invisible Man* (1952). During the turbulent 1960s, however, the "call" was registered in intense, explicit, moral, and confrontational tones (Scott and Smith, 1969). [*See* Social Movements.] When the Montgomery, Alabama, bus boycott was sparked by Rosa Parks's refusal to continue to be displaced and unheard, the ugly face of Southern hate filled America's television screens. Bull Connor's attack dogs, fire hoses, and billy clubs served as rhetorical resources and as amplifiers for the voices of the civil rights movement. Malcolm X turned the "call" into an ultimatum in the fiery "Ballot or the Bullet." Stokely Carmichael jolted America with a raised fist and his "Black Power" mantra. And Martin Luther King, Jr., orchestrated a national prayer for every American soul in magnificent utterances, such as "Letter From a Birmingham Jail" and "I Have a Dream."

The 1960s were a costly decade. Violence has

historically been a function of African-American rhetoric: to speak is to risk one's life. The paradox emerged here again because, as Audre Lorde has poignantly put it, silence is also a form of death. So, as Malcolm X, Medger Evers, and Martin Luther King, Jr., became black martyrs, cities burned. A rhetoric of rage and separation seemed to supplant a rhetoric of unification and transcendence. Black Panthers defended themselves against "whitey," and some members succumbed to brutal police tactics and hails of bullets. American moral silence was loudly punctuated by African-American rhetorical acts that literally cost (and saved) black life.

If it is reasonable to say that the twentieth century bore witness to African-American prophesy and sacrifice, then one might expect the twenty-first century to bring to fruition some of those prophetic fragments (West, 1999). This work is already underway, for example, in how Minister Louis Farrakhan's oratory not only forces African Americans to reconsider historic relations with Anglos and Jews but also compels some observers to reflect more fully on the black community's own complicity in the rhetoric of racism (McPhail, 1994). It also can be seen and heard in the cadence of the Rev. Jesse Jackson's presidential campaign rhetoric and in his delicate and skillful foreign diplomatic efforts. The pace and tone of African-American discursive soundings become frenetic and postindustrial if one listens to the "noises" of "hip-hop America" (George, 1998; Rose, 1994; Watts, 1997). These rhetorical forms vary widely, to be sure, but as "calls" to America's conscience, they are vital.

BIBLIOGRAPHY

Asante, M. K. *The Afrocentric Idea*. Philadelphia, 1987.

Baker, H. *Modernism and the Harlem Renaissance*. Chicago, 1987.

Condit, C. M., and J. L. Loucaites. *Crafting Equality: America's Anglo-African Word*. Chicago, 1993.

Foner, P. S. *The Voice of Black America*, vol. 1. New York, 1972.

Foner, P. S. *The Voice of Black America, 1797–1971*. New York, 1972.

Foner, P. S., and R. Branham. *Lift Every Voice: African American Oratory, 1787–1900*. Tuscaloosa, Ala., 1998.

Gates, H. L. *The Signifying Monkey: A Theory of Afro-American Literary Criticism*. New York, 1988.

George, N. *Hip Hop America*. New York, 1998.

Hyde, M., and K. Rufo. "The Call of Conscience, Rhetorical Interruptions, and the Euthansia Controversy." *Journal of Applied Communication Research* 28 (2000), pp. 1–23.

Locke, A. *The New Negro: An Interpretation*. New York, 1925.

Lorde, A. *Sister Outsider*. Trumansburg, N.Y., 1984.

McPhail, M. L. "The Politics of Complicity: Second Thoughts about the Social Construction of Racial Reality." *Quarterly Journal of Speech* 80 (1994), pp. 343–357.

Pryse, M. "Zora Neale Hurston, Alice Walker, and the Ancient Power of Black Women." In *Conjuring: Black Women, Fiction, and Literary Tradition*, edited by M. Pryse and H. J. Spillers, pp. 1–25. Bloomington, Ind., 1985.

Rose, T. *Black Noise: Rap Music and Black Culture in Contemporary America*. Hanover, N. H., 1994.

Scott, R. L., and D. K. Smith, "The Rhetoric of Confrontation." *Quarterly Journal of Speech* 55 (1969), pp. 1–8.

Watts, E. K. "An Exploration of Spectacular Consumption: Gangsta Rap as Cultural Commodity." *Communication Studies*, 48 (1997), pp. 42–58.

West, C. *The Cornel West Reader*. New York, 1999.

Wilson, K. H. "The Contested Space of Prudence in the 1874–1875 Civil Rights Debate." *Quarterly Journal of Speech* 84 (1998), pp. 131–149.

Zamir, S. *Dark Voices: W.E.B. Du Bois and American thought, 1888–1903*. Chicago, 1995.

—ERIC KING WATTS

Abolitionist rhetoric

In the introduction to *Abolitionism* (Boston, 1989), Herbert Aptheker declares that black abolitionists "were the first and most lasting Abolitionists." Rarely have historians granted the black community such authority, although some of its leaders, like Frederick Douglass, have received considerable attention since the revisionist histories of the 1960s. For scholars of rhetoric and U.S. history, the contribution of black abolitionists is profound. In fact, their rhetoric comprised the center of the U.S. antislavery struggle. They were the first to articulate the hypocrisy of early American "liberty." They persuaded white abolitionists to abandon gradualism and colonization. They helped abolitionism transform itself into a social movement, adopting the roles of advocate and internal critic. They insisted that freedom was not merely the absence of slavery but the affirmation of equality. As they pursued these activities, black abolitionists fostered an independent black community.

Black abolitionists in America occupied a complex position in the nineteenth century. They were outsiders marked by their race and political agitation, but they intentionally adopted aspects of British, New England, and Midwestern cultures. This is not to suggest that they repudiated their African past. Black abolitionists acknowledged their unique heritage; during the 1850s, nationalism was an important discursive theme. Some, like the radical Martin Delany, argued that people of color would enjoy freedom only if they emigrated to Africa. Black abolitionists were proud of their distinctiveness; nevertheless, most saw themselves as Americans with an African past. Henry Highland Garnet expressed this identity when he said, "Think of the undying glory that hangs around the ancient name of Africa—and forget not that you are native-born American citizens, and as such you are justly entitled to all the rights that are granted to the freest" ("Address to the Slaves of the United States of America," 16 August 1843).

The duality illustrated by Garnet influenced the rhetoric of black abolitionism. For example, African-American orators adopted the discursive standards of their day. Although some never received a formal education, they were accomplished at imitation and appropriation, and they created space for themselves in the rhetorical tradition. In a 22 June 1852 speech, William G. Allen, a professor at New York Central College, argued that Cicero, Demosthenes, Henry Clay, and Daniel Webster were exemplars of eloquence, but that Garnet and Frederick Douglass rivaled these archetypes. Furthermore, black abolitionists appropriated aspects of America's heritage. Before the formation of the American Anti-Slavery Society (1833), African Americans sought their freedom by co-opting the ideals of the American Revolution. For example, on 26 May 1774, several blacks petitioned Thomas Gage, governor of Massachusetts Colony, declaring that no one should have the authority to contravene the natural rights of a freeborn people. In a remarkable letter to Thomas Jefferson dated 19 August 1791, the self-taught astronomer Benjamin Banneker quoted from the *Declaration,* chiding Jefferson for not ex-

tending his principles to people of color. In *David Walker's Appeal to the Coloured Citizens of the World* (Boston, 1829), the radical activist condemned Southern slavery, the American Colonization Society, and the hypocrisy of white Christians. Blacks, he concluded, had more reason for revolution than had the nation's Founders. *Walker's Appeal* was too militant for most abolitionists, but his claims on liberty resonated in the black community. On 21 September 1832, Maria W. Stewart said that "whites have so long and loudly proclaimed the theme of equal rights and privileges, that our souls have caught the flame also."

The complexities of black identity are evident in the evolution of black abolitionist rhetoric. On 6 June 1831, African Americans from five states met in Philadelphia to institute a national convention movement against the American Colonization Society and slavery. Their efforts were assisted by a new newspaper, William Lloyd Garrison's *The Liberator.* Due in part to the persuasive efforts of black abolitionists, Garrison had abandoned gradualism. *The Liberator* supported immediate abolition and equal rights for free black citizens, and African Americans embraced the paper enthusiastically. They composed almost three-fourths of its subscribers; without their early patronage the most influential outlet for abolitionist thought might have failed. Blacks also applauded the creation of the New England Anti-Slavery Society (1832), and the 1833 formation of the American Anti-Slavery Association inaugurated a period of close cooperation between white and black abolitionists. Throughout the 1830s and early 1840s, leaders like William Whipper, James Forten, Jr., and Theodore S. Wright embraced the values of the reform era. In his presidential address to the Colored Temperance Society of Philadelphia (8 January 1834), Whipper argued that racial prejudice would end when blacks everywhere achieved a high moral character. Revival and the uplift of the race, he said, "would disperse slavery from our land." Daniel A. Payne, a Lutheran minister and later a preacher in the African Methodist Episcopal Church, turned the reform theme outward, arguing that slavery caused moral decay in European and African Americans.

When the role of women in abolitionism and the limitations of moral suasion fractured the movement in the 1840s, blacks affirmed their independence, but they also continued to identify with the country's ideals. On 16 August 1843, Henry Highland Garnet spoke before the National Convention of Negro Citizens. His immediate audience was composed of free blacks, but he addressed those in bondage. He said, "However much you and all of us may desire it, there is not much hope of redemption without the shedding of blood. If you must bleed, let it all come at once." In his peroration, he declared, "Let your motto be Resistance! *Resistance!* RESISTANCE! No oppressed people have ever secured their liberty without resistance." As with *Walker's Appeal*, Garnet's speech was both controversial and revealing. He advanced the claim that African Americans could only trust themselves to secure slavery's demise. At the same time, his arguments were familiar; even the text's call to arms was reminiscent of the American Revolution: "Rather die freemen than live to be slaves." The speech was not published until 1848, yet its presentation marked a shift in black abolitionist rhetoric. In the 1840s and 1850s, black abolitionists combined direct action and political agitation. The Underground Railroad freed as many slaves as possible, while black lecturers spoke for antislavery politicians, demanded emancipation legislation, and supported civil rights initiatives. They condemned the strengthened Fugitive Slave Law (1850), the policy of Popular Sovereignty, and the infamous *Dred Scott* decision (1857). Frederick Douglass in his "West India Emancipation" address (1857) expressed well the opinion of his colleagues: "The whole history of the progress of human liberty shows that all concessions yet made to her august claims have been born of earnest struggle. . . . Power concedes nothing without a demand. It never did and it never will."

As black abolitionism evolved, its speakers occupied the discursive center of abolitionism. That is, they used their identity as both Americans and Africans to become the movement's most successful evangelists. The earliest black agents, John Lewis, Jehiel Beman, Henry Highland Garnet, Samuel Ringgold Ward, and Charles Lenox Remond pursued exhausting lecture schedules. By the late 1830s, abolitionists recognized that first-hand testimonies of slavery were particularly effective. Sojourner Truth, Henry Bibb, William

Wells Brown, Henry "Box" Brown, and William and Ellen Craft became enormously popular. The success of their rhetoric resulted largely from their status as living examples of slavery's cruelty and the potential of African Americans once free. The testimony of escaped slaves led to a distinct literary genre, the slave narrative. The most famous of these is Harriet Ann Jacobs's *Incidents in the Life of a Slave Girl* (Boston, 1861) and Frederick Douglass's *Narrative of the Life of Frederick Douglass* (Boston, 1845) and *My Bondage and My Freedom* (New York, 1855). Many other narratives exist. *The History of Mary Prince* (London, 1831), *The Narrative of William W. Brown* (Boston, 1847), *The Narrative of the Life and Adventures of Henry Bibb* (New York, 1849), and William and Ellen Craft's *Running a Thousand Miles for Freedom* (London, 1860) were popular. These biographies established public personae that black abolitionists used to the fullest. [*See* Persona.] Speaking and writing were acts of courage. Not only did former slaves face hostile audiences, they also risked being returned to slavery. Maria W. Stewart, Sarah M. Douglass, Frances Ellen Walker Harper, and Mary Ann Shadd Cary faced additional obstacles. As black women, they had to negotiate the stigma of women speaking in public and the implications of race for the "cult of true womanhood."

Although the discursive role of African Americans provided opportunities, it also had limitations. Many white abolitionists came from New England's prosperous middle class; consequently, they benefited from the economics of slavery. Furthermore, despite a genuine abhorrence of the institution, some white abolitionists believed that African Americans were inferior. They resisted the participation of black abolitionists as leaders or independent agents, and sometimes they substituted their own voices for those of black speakers. Frederick Douglass was discouraged from assuming a leadership role, and he was advised to keep "a little of the plantation speech" in his lectures. Another instance of this subtle prejudice involves Sojourner Truth's famous speech, "Ar'n't I a Woman." The widely publicized version of this address was reported by the white abolitionist Frances Gage in *The Narrative of Sojourner Truth* (Battle Creek, 1878). The Gage text is dramatic; however, its language is colloquial in the extreme. Its introduction reads:

"Well, chilern, whar dar is so much racket dar must be something out o' kilter. I think dat 'twixt de niggers of de Souf and de women at de Norf all a talkin' 'bout rights, de white men will be in a fix pretty soon." A second version of Truth's speech appeared in the *Anti-Slavery Bugle,* 21 June 1851. It begins: "I want to say a few words about this matter. I am a woman's rights. I have as much muscle as any man, and can do as much work as any man. I have plowed and reaped and husked and chopped and mowed, and can any man do more than that?" Although the two texts contain similar themes and arguments, their styles differ greatly, giving rise to speculation that Gage imposed her own voice to make Truth's speech more "authentic" as the statement of a former slave. Unfortunately, this imposition denied the very identity that black abolitionists worked hard to create. The message of Truth's text was that she and the audience were more similar than different.

Black abolitionists recognized that white abolitionists sometimes viewed them as the Other; therefore, their rhetoric often challenged the abolitionist community. In a speech at the New York State Anti-Slavery Society (20 September 1837), Theodore S. Wright stated that his white colleagues "must annihilate in their own bosoms the cord of caste. . . . Let every man take his stand, burn out this prejudice, live it down, talk it down, everywhere consider the colored man as a man, in the church, the stage, the steamboat, the public house, in all places, and the death blow to slavery will be struck." Black abolitionists viewed slavery as a class system that abrogated the liberties of every person of color; subsequently, they declared themselves to be in a state of bondage. It is not surprising, then, that they objected when the American Anti-Slavery Society disbanded in 1870. So long as prejudice sustained racial hierarchies, work remained.

Frederick Douglass's "What to the Slave is the Fourth of July" (5 July 1852) is perhaps the best-known black abolitionist speech, and while it does not reflect the totality of this discourse, it illustrates how black identity affected its invention. The text first positions Douglass as an outcast from America's civic community. Next, it establishes the orator within a transcendent community dedicated to the principle that "all men are created equal." Douglass argues that his

community, the transcendent community, includes America's Founders. This spatial arrangement implies that European Americans are alienated from their own history. Because they support slavery, which is antithetical to the country's origins, America's civic life is no longer operating within the ideals of its Founders. Douglass, not his white audience, becomes the heir of Washington, Franklin, and Jefferson, and, in a deft twist, he is reconstituted as a truer citizen. Douglass's masterful appropriation and redirection reveals the genius of black abolitionist rhetoric. Through ironic reinvention, black abolitionists came to embody the spirit and principles of American republicanism. [*See* Irony.] They were more than the first and the last abolitionists; they were the concrete expression of the American experiment.

BIBLIOGRAPHY

Andrews, William L., and Henry Louis Gates, Jr., eds. *The Civitas Anthology of African American Slave Narratives.* Washington, D.C., 1999. Offers primary texts and commentary concerning slave narratives.

Bell, Howard Holman. *A Survey of the Negro Convention Movement, 1830–1861.* New York, 1969. Offers an account of the Negro conventions that played an important role in black abolitionism.

Blackett, R. J. M. *Building an Antislavery Wall: Black Americans in the Atlantic Abolitionist Movement, 1830–1860.* Baton Rouge, La., 1983. Offers an important account of black abolitionism and its relationship to Great Britain.

Foner, Philip S., and Robert James Branham, eds. *Lift Every Voice: African American Oratory, 1787–1900.* Tuscaloosa, Ala., 1998. An excellent compilation of nineteenth-century speeches by African Americans, including orations by black abolitionists.

Goodman, Paul. *Of One Blood: Abolitionism and the Origins of Racial Equality.* Berkeley, 1998. Offers an interesting investigation of abolitionism's origins and early evolution.

Pease, Jane H., and William H. Pease. *They Who Would Be Free: Blacks' Search for Freedom, 1830–1861.* New York, 1974. Offers an excellent discussion of black abolitionism's evolution.

Quarles, Benjamin. *Black Abolitionists.* New York, 1969. A groundbreaking interpretation of abolitionism from the perspective of African Americans.

Ripley, Peter, ed. *The Black Abolitionists Papers.* 5 vols. Chapel Hill, N.C., 1985–1992. An indispensable resource of primary materials including speeches, correspondence, and newspaper articles. Volumes 3–5 contain the texts of U.S. black abolitionists. Volume 3 pages 3–69 provides a concise history of black abolitionism.

Yee, Shirley J. *Black Women Abolitionists: A Study in Activism, 1828–1860*. Nashville, 1992. Focuses on the role of black women in abolitionism.

—KIRT H. WILSON

Double-consciousness

Also referred to as "two-ness," double-consciousness is an idea articulated by William Edward Burghardt Du Bois to describe the social and psychological struggles for inclusion in American culture that characterized African-American life at the beginning of the twentieth century. W. E. B. Du Bois (1868–1963) was an African-American intellectual and activist, and a major American race relations theorist and critic during much of the twentieth century. Du Bois contributed significantly to the establishment of the academic discipline of sociology in the United States, and was a founding member of the National Association for the Advancement of Colored People (NAACP).

Double-consciousness, Du Bois remarked, reflected "a sense of always looking at one's self through the eyes of others, of measuring one's soul by the tape of a world that looks on in amused contempt and pity. One ever feels his two-ness—an American, a Negro; two souls, two thoughts, two unreconciled strivings; two warring ideals in one dark body, whose dogged strength alone keeps it from being torn asunder" (1982, p. 45). His discussion of double-consciousness in *The Souls of Black Folk* (1903) is perhaps one of the most widely-cited passages from his extensive body of writings. The idea's origins have been the subject of scholarly debate, and the various ways in which it has been interpreted illustrate the diverse and complex ways in which African-American thought and culture has been conceptualized since Du Bois first coined the phrase in relation to racial identity and difference. Du Bois' fundamental concern, which has remained a common thread throughout the many interpretations of the concept, was with the tension between the social and central selves of people of African descent in the United States, the struggle to be both black *and* American at the same time. "The history of the American people is the history of this strife," he explains, "this longing to attain self-conscious manhood, to merge his double self into a better and truer self" (1982, p. 45). The idea had an important impact on African-American literary and rhetorical thought in the latter part of the twentieth century, and has influenced the thinking of theorists and critics in history, philosophy, and cultural studies.

While Du Bois may have been the first American writer to discuss double-consciousness in relation to racial matters, the phrase already had currency in various discursive communities in the early 1900s. Dickson D. Bruce, Jr. (1992) contends that the term "had a long history by the time Du Bois published his essay in 1897" (p. 299), an essay that first appeared in the *Atlantic*. Bruce suggests that Du Bois was influenced by the metaphorical use of the term produced by a union of European romanticism and American transcendentalism, as well as the clinical concept of "split personality" that had become part of both the technical and the popular discourse of the discipline of psychology. Ralph Waldo Emerson's figurative use of the term expressed the long-standing tension between the real and the ideal selves, and the conflict between the spiritual strivings of the individual and the pragmatic demands of society. In addition to the Emersonian influence, Bruce claims that Du Bois was also influenced by the psychological theories of the time, within which the term *double-consciousness* had been in use since at least 1817, and specifically notes that Du Bois was likely influenced by his Harvard University mentor William James.

In contrast to Bruce, Adolph Reed, Jr. (1997), whose explication of notions of double-consciousness is perhaps the most comprehensive account of the impact of these ideas on contemporary black intellectuals, argues that Du Bois's use of the term was applied specifically to the African-American experience. Emerson's use of the term, he argues, was generically applied to the human "race" and rested upon metaphysical assumptions that embraced eternal verities and ignored concrete realities. James's use of the term, while more complex, was no more influential than Emerson's. While noting some superficial similarities, Reed concludes that James's use of the term differed markedly from that of Du Bois:

"James saw the divided self as alternately a psycho-physiological and a spiritual or mystical phenomenon; for Du Bois the idea was sociological and historical" (p. 105). Reed does suggest that "two-ness" was a prominent idea among Du Bois's European-American contemporaries, a *"problematique"* that surfaced in the discourses of a number of progressive era intellectuals concerned with cultural phenomena such as social fragmentation, overcivilization, and gender identity. While these were issues with which Du Bois was also concerned, his intellectual project was more than academic; its major focus was on characterizing the material social conditions that defined African-American consciousness, culture, and communication.

That focus, Reed suggests, has had a significant impact on African-American intellectuals with diverse and sometimes divergent critical and theoretical agendas. Reed notes that Du Bois's use of the term has been appropriated by various thinkers over the course of the century whose projects have been characterized by three dominant ideological projects: "an integrationist–therapeutic motiv [sic] from the 1920s to the mid-1960s, a nationalist–therapeutic one from the mid-1960s to the early 1980s, and an academic race celebratory one since" (p. 92). From the 1920s to the 1960s, writers who invoked Du Bois's idea tended to focus on double-consciousness as an expression of an assimilationist impulse repulsed by a dominant white culture. Writers during that nationalist–therapeutic period between the 1960s and the 1980s alternately saw double-consciousness as the epitome of "blackness" and as a mentality in need of negation and destruction. Since the 1980s, many African-American intellectuals have invoked double-consciousness as an authentic characterization of the social realities of black life in America. Despite their different emphases, each of these projects has embraced the idea that the notion of double-consciousness was central to Du Bois's intellectual agenda, was a uniquely African-American theoretical construct, and reflected a way of being that was peculiar to the African-American experience. Such readings of double-consciousness, Reed suggests, distort the historical and intellectual contexts within which Du Bois articulated the term, and place an emphasis on it that obscures the empirical fact that

the idea largely disappears from Du Bois's later writings and is, in fact, not mentioned again in *The Souls of Black Folk*. He claims that the idea was embedded in many mainstream academic conceptual currents of the time, and reflected thinking on issues of racial identity that Du Bois revised shortly after 1903. Reed concludes, however, that the "double-consciousness idea's apparent resonance is, nevertheless, a revealing facet of contemporary black intellectual discourse" (p. 125). Double-consciousness reveals how African-American discourse and thought have always been inextricably linked to the conflicts and contradictions that have historically circumscribed black experience: in short, how black rhetoric has always embodied both the essential and the existential. Although the idea of double-consciousness is, as Reed notes, mentioned only once in *Souls*, the idea has had an important impact on contemporary black thought in general, and the areas of rhetorical theory and criticism in particular. For Reed, double-consciousness reveals the racial anxiety of African-American intellectuals working itself out within political, literary, and psychological contexts. Rhetorical scholars have drawn upon Du Bois's work to examine the discursive dimensions of this anxiety as well as to suggest its generative and transformative potential.

Du Bois's general influence is readily apparent, both implicitly and explicitly, in rhetorical and literary studies of African-American thought and discourse published since the 1960s. Several scholars note Du Bois's impact on African-American rhetoric, and place him within a discursive trajectory grounded in political critique and social action in contrast to conciliation and acquiescence. Arthur Smith (Molefi Kete Asante) describes Du Bois as "the most productive source for the secular themes in the rhetoric of the black revolution" (1969, p. 47). James L. Golden and Richard D. Rieke (1971) critically assess his influence as well as his oratory, juxtaposing his discourse and philosophy to that of his contemporary Booker T. Washington at several points in their study, even while suggesting that both men were "assimilationists." Other rhetorical scholars have followed a similar line of inquiry. Thomas E. Harris and Patrick C. Kennicott (1972) begin their critique of Washington's rhetoric with an observation from Du Bois, and Robert

Terrill and Michael Leff (1995) offer an analysis of Du Bois as a polemical artist in their examination of his critique of Washington and other African-American rhetors. Brian R. McGee (1998) explores Du Bois's rhetoric about "the other" as a starting point for the theorizing of otherness, and Kirt Wilson (1999), in theorizing a discursive conceptualization of racial identity, reads Du Bois's *The Souls of Black Folk* as a rhetorical response to biological determinism in the nineteenth century.

Wilson explicitly discusses Du Bois's double-consciousness, arguing that it "foreshadows the post structural critique of subjectivity, but that it does not lead to a complete dissolution of agency" (p. 207). Wilson's study is one of the few in the published literature that actually engages the notion of double-consciousness in terms of its rhetorical implications. Geneva Smitherman (1977) notes in passing that double-consciousness is reflected in the "'push–pull' syndrome in black America, that is *pushing* toward white American culture while simultaneously *pulling* away from it" (pp. 10–11), and Aaron David Gresson (1995) references Du Bois's notion of double-consciousness in his discussion of African-American recovery and identity formation. Stephen H. Browne (1998) provides an extended discussion of double-consciousness in his analysis of the rise of the modern American city at the turn of the century. Browne claims that double-consciousness "describes not only a condition of being but also a means to imagine, structure, and express a certain view of the world. It thus projects itself from a state of mind to a practice of reading" (p. 76). Like Wilson, Browne appropriates Du Bois's notion in order to amplify and extend the theoretical and critical possibilities of contemporary rhetorical inquiry that has traditionally focused on speech and oratorical studies. Smitherman and Gresson, on the other hand, read double-consciousness within the explicitly racialized context of African-American culture, an approach that aligns their projects more closely with the rhetorical interests of literary scholars. [*See* Criticism.]

Gresson argues, for example, that two leading African-American literary scholars, Houston Baker and Henry Louis Gates, are both "engulfed in the ambivalence and double-blinds implicit in the two-ness of which Du Bois wrote in 1903 and so many have echoed since" (p. 187). While this analysis buttresses Gresson's larger project of racial recovery, it does not address the extent to which Baker, Gates, and other African-American literary scholars have drawn upon Du Bois's ideas. Some literary scholars during the period defined above by Reed as "nationalist–therapeutic," called for the "death" of double-consciousness and the birth of a uniquely black sense of self. Hoyt Fuller, for example, notes that some African-American literary theorists "felt that the new black literature aims at nullifying the influence of the white image by destroying the 'double-consciousness' of black people—the dilemma of being both black and American" (1972, p. 329). Baker concurred, observing that Du Bois's notion of "two-ness" was "fast disappearing" with the emergence of black nationalist consciousness (1972, p. 17). During the period that Reed describes as "race celebratory," African-American literary scholars continued to appropriate the idea of double-consciousness in terms of its implications for African-American identity. Henry Louis Gates (1987) accentuated the metaphorical implications of Du Bois's idea, both as "a trope of dualism figured initially in black discourse," and also as a literary device. Literary theorist Michael Awkward also invokes double-consciousness as a figure for the integration of spirit and matter in African-American thought, and also as an anticipation of discursive tensions between the narrator and protagonist in Toni Morrison's *The Bluest Eye*. Barbara Johnson, while critical of Du Bois's gender bias, nonetheless subscribes to the importance of the idea of double-consciousness as a mark of racial distinctiveness (Reed, p. 221). In addition to literary theory and criticism, the concepts of two-ness and double-consciousness have also influenced numerous African-American cultural theorists in the disciplines of history, philosophy, and cultural theory.

African-American folk historian Lawrence W. Levine (1978) suggests that Du Bois's notion of "two-ness" increased African-American concerns about, and opposition to, assimilation in the decades following Reconstruction (p. 151). Philosopher Cornel West (1982) sees Du Bois as the progenitor of a distinctively African-American philosophical project, and extends the notion of double-consciousness to the idea of a "threeness," a "triple crisis of self-recognition" that reflects the essence of black identity and existence in American society (p. 30). Cultural theorist Paul Gilroy further expands West's analysis to suggest that double-consciousness reflects a fundamental principle of African diasporic thought. Gilroy explains that double-consciousness resolves "the core dynamic of racial oppression as well as the fundamental antinomy of diaspora blacks," and notes that the effect of the idea "has had extensive consequences in African American analyses of Du Bois's work" (pp. 30, 136). Gilroy's observation is confirmed by Reed, who observes that the ideas of double-consciousness and "two-ness" were not, for Du Bois, metaphorical, but represented an attempt to account for the actual historical circumstances of African-American life at the turn of the century. The diverse appropriations of this account by scholars in a number of disciplines suggest that Du Bois's idea might be understood not as more than psychological condition, literary trope, or sign of racial anxiety, but also as evidence of a critical hermeneutic, a mode of rhetorical invention capable of not only describing but also generating the social and symbolic possibilities of the souls of black folk.

BIBLIOGRAPHY

Baker, Houston A., Jr. *Long Black Song: Essays in Black American Literature and Culture.* Charlottesville, Va., 1972.

Browne, Stephen H. "Du Bois, Double-Consciousness, and the Modern City." In *Rhetoric and Community: Studies in Unity and Fragmentation.* Edited by J. Michael Hogan, pp. 75–92. Columbia, S.C., 1998.

Bruce, Dickson D., Jr. "W. E. B. Du Bois and the Idea of Double Consciousness." *American Literature* 64 (1992), pp. 299–309.

Du Bois, William Edward Burghardt. *The Souls of Black Folk.* New York, 1982. First published 1903.

Fuller, Hoyt. "The New Black Literature: Protest or Affirmation." In *The Black Aesthetic.* Edited by Addison Gayle, Jr., pp. 326–348. New York, 1972.

Gates, Henry Louis, Jr. *Figures in Black: Words, Signs and the 'Racial' Self.* New York, 1987.

Gilroy, Paul. *The Black Atlantic: Modernity and Double Consciousness.* Cambridge, Mass., 1993.

Golden, James L., and Richard Rieke. *The Rhetoric of Black Americans.* Columbus, Ohio, 1971.

Gresson, Aaron David, III. *The Recovery of Race in America.* Minneapolis, 1995.

Harris, Thomas E., and Patrick C. Kennicott. "Booker T.

Washington: A Study of Conciliatory Rhetoric." In *Language, Communication, and Rhetoric in Black America,* edited by Arthur L. Smith, pp. 124–140. New York, 1972.

Levine, Lawrence, W. *Black Culture and Black Consciousness: Afro-American Folk Thought From Slavery to Freedom.* Oxford, 1978.

Reed, Adolph, Jr. "Du Bois's 'Double Consciousness': Race and Gender in Progressive-Era American thought." In *W. E. B. Du Bois and American Political Thought: Fabianism and the Color Line,* pp. 91–125. New York, 1997.

Smith, Arthur. *Rhetoric of Black Revolution.* Boston, 1969.

Smitherman, Geneva. *Talkin and Testifyin: The Language of Black America.* Boston, 1977.

Terrill, Robert, and Michael Leff. "The Polemicist as Artist: W. E. B. Du Bois' 'Of Mr. Booker T. Washington and Others.'" In *Argumentation and Values: Proceedings of the Ninth SCA/AFA Conference on Argumentation.* Edited by Sally Jackson, pp. 230–236. Annandale-on-Hudson, N.Y., 1995.

West, Cornel. *Philosophy Deliverance!: An Afro-American Revolutionary Christianity.* Philadelphia, 1982.

Wilson, Kirt H. "Toward a Discursive Theory of Racial Identity: *The Souls of Black Folk* as a Response to Nineteenth-Century Biological Determinism." *Western Journal of Communication* 63 (1999), pp. 193–215.
—MARK LAWRENCE MCPHAIL

Black Nationalism

Black Nationalism is an umbrella term, encompassing back-to-Africa movements, efforts to lay claim to a portion of the continental United States as a separate black nation, proposals to establish all-black political parties, and various artistic and cultural endeavors to claim African and African-American culture as sources of racial pride and solidarity. The history of black nationalism is a contentious one, marked by much disagreement about aims and strategy. In general, this rhetoric is informed by a conviction that the dominant white culture of the United States is fundamentally corrupt and that integration into such a culture would be dangerous and self-defeating, even if it were possible. As a result, black nationalist rhetoric is directed primarily to African Americans. It does not ask whites to change, but rather, assuming that white attitudes toward blacks will remain unchanged, it demands that blacks reassess their relationship to whites and to white culture. Historically, black nationalist rhetoric has appealed especially to the poorest segments of the African-American population, those most alienated from and least invested in the dominant culture of the United States.

Through time, the cultural salience of black nationalist rhetoric has varied according to the virulence of explicit racism. For example, in 1829, David Walker, the owner of a small used-clothing shop in Boston, published his *Appeal to the Coloured Citizens of the World* because he was critical of such white-led emigration schemes as the American Colonization Society. His pamphlet, written in the voice of a prophet, foretold the end of white supremacy and urged armed slave revolt. Yet it did not advocate a return to Africa, because Walker wanted African Americans to claim their rightful place in the United States.

The Compromise of 1850, the Kansas–Nebraska Act of 1854, and the Dred Scott decision in 1857 each increased the weight of white oppression and fomented a pre-Civil War crescendo of separatist interest. Martin Delany, called by some the "Father of Black Nationalism," was at first an integrationist and coeditor of Frederick Douglass's newspaper, *The North Star*. In 1852, Delany published *The Condition, Elevation, Emigration and Destiny of the Colored People of the United States*. While this book advocated emigration to east Africa, Delany was always somewhat ambivalent about such a program. During the post-Civil War Reconstruction period, Delany, like many African Americans, regained hope for the prospects for black life in the United States.

With the end of Reconstruction and a concomitant rise in white racist violence, black nationalism underwent a renaissance. By far, the most important black nationalist during this period was Bishop Henry McNeal Turner. Turner's message, which he spread tirelessly throughout the southern United States, entailed both cultural nationalism and back-to-Africa emigration. He envisioned an emigrationist program completely controlled by blacks, but this plan was hobbled from its start because of the traditional audience for nationalist rhetoric—those least able to command the considerable financial reserves such an operation would require. This was to be a recurring stumbling block in the development of black nationalist thought until the emergence of the Nation of Islam.

At the dawn of the twentieth century, elements of nationalism surfaced in the rhetoric of Booker T. Washington and his most famous critic, W. E. B. Du Bois. Washington declared in his "Atlanta Exposition Address" of 1895 that the races might remain socially separate but economically linked, and this was interpreted by some as a concession of civil rights and by others as an economic black separatism with the long-range goal of subverting Southern institutions. Du Bois read Washington as a sellout, criticizing him as representing an outdated attitude of assimilation and adjustment. As for Du Bois himself, in 1897 he delivered an address entitled "The Conservation of Races," a scholarly explication and defense of cultural black nationalism. Washington and Du Bois carried on a public rhetorical duel until Washington's death in 1915, but both were interested in cultivating a black elite rather than in inciting nationalist–separatist fervor among the masses.

Between 1900 and 1920, the promise of increased respect, freedom, and opportunity in the North redirected emigrationist impulses into the "Great Migration" of black people out of the South, and the northern cities became the center of black nationalist thought in the United States. In 1916, Marcus Garvey traveled from his native Jamaica to New York, where he began to exploit the nationalist impulses among newly urban African Americans. Garvey admired and emulated Booker T. Washington, and initially came to the United States to meet Washington, but unlike Washington, Garvey's rhetoric featured both the conviction that the white dominant culture of the United States was irredeemably corrupt and a rather romanticized notion of African culture. Garvey's rhetoric bears much similarity to Turner's— indeed, because of the Great Migration, Garvey's audience was in many ways similar to Turner's. Garvey, by all accounts a master orator, staged impressive parades and galas in Harlem; established over seven hundred official branches of his Universal Negro Improvement Association; and increased the circulation of his *Negro World* until it was the largest African-American newspaper. However, as with Turner, Garvey grossly overestimated the financial resources and political clout of his primary audience. Well-connected African Americans, including W. E. B. Du Bois, instigated a "Garvey Must Go" campaign, which at least in part was responsible for Garvey being deported in 1927, convicted of mail fraud in connection with his efforts to fund his Black Star Line of steamships.

The Nation of Islam (NOI) would avoid the problems of Turner and Garvey by positioning itself as a nationalist organization that refused to become involved in emigrationist schemes. It offered, instead, an eschatology that invited intellectual and cultural separation from the foundational beliefs of white Christian culture. The Nation of Islam rose out of the fragmented remains of Garveyism and other nationalist organizations that appeared and dissipated among African Americans living in Detroit in the 1920s and 1930s. It was through one of these groups, Noble Drew Ali's Moorish Science Temple, that an adulterated Islam was introduced as an important element of black nationalism. Some sources suggest that the leader of one of the splinter groups that emerged after Ali's death in 1929 was Mr. W. D. Fard (also called "Wallace Fard" and "Fard Muhammad").

Fard (pronounced "Far-rod") taught a rapidly growing constituency of followers a rather heady mixture of Islam, Christianity, Garveyist black nationalism, freemasonry, and apocalyptic prophecy that established blacks as fundamentally pure, whites as the dangerous product of a genetic experiment, and Allah as a racial savior who will one day destroy the white race. One of his especially eager followers—like many, a recent arrival from the South—was Elijah Poole of Sandersville, Georgia. Fard bestowed on Poole the name Karriem and then the name Muhammad, and together they began to build the Nation of Islam. After Fard vanished under mysterious circumstances in 1934, Muhammad assumed control of the majority of the sect and moved NOI headquarters from Detroit to Chicago.

Though Muhammad would head the Nation of Islam until his death in 1975, it was Malcolm X who was primarily responsible for building the Nation from a tiny, little-known group into a nationally recognized organization, and for bringing black nationalism into white consciousness. Malcolm became a member of the Nation of Islam while in prison, and Elijah Muhammad elevated him to second-in-command soon after his release in 1952. As was the case for all Black Muslim ministers, Malcolm's rhetoric was controlled tightly by Elijah Muhammad. Malcolm's speeches to his congregations and potential converts consisted primarily of repeating the teachings of Fard, as taught to him by Muhammad. This form of black nationalist prophecy was in the tradition of David Walker, and was well suited to Malcolm's northern, urban, lower-class, black audiences.

But as Malcolm's efforts to expand the Nation of Islam proved fruitful, he began to speak more often to other audiences; his comments appeared in the newspapers, he was a guest on radio interview shows, local and national television covered his activities, and at one point he was second only to U.S. Senator Barry Goldwater as a requested speaker on college campuses. While Malcolm X sometimes rehearsed parts of the Nation of Islam's apocalyptic vision for these primarily white, middle-class audiences, increasingly he provided instead pointed social and political critique. Chafing under the Nation of Islam's doctrine of noninvolvement (members were not even permitted to vote), disillusioned by his discovery of Elijah Muhammad's marital infidelity, and under increasing attack from within the organization for spending too much time speaking to whites, Malcolm left the Nation of Islam in March 1964. Most of the critical attention given to Malcolm concentrates on his post-NOI rhetoric, in part because of its importance in the continuing evolution of black nationalism.

Malcolm's best-known and most representative oration from that time period, "The Ballot or the Bullet," was delivered several times between his split with the Nation of Islam and his pilgrimage to Mecca in April 1964. It is completely devoid of those elements of NOI discourse that assigned all power to Allah; instead, this speech provides for his audience a critique of contemporary racial oppression and a model for how to respond to it. The speech ranges over domestic and international scenes, and characterizes both as similarly limited by the dominance and duplicity of whites. Throughout, Malcolm presents models to his audience for reacting to this oppression in ways well outside what would be accepted within the dominant white culture. Then, he outlines a program of "black nationalism" that entails a careful, reasoned judgment concerning the most prudent action to be chosen from among a broad spectrum of possibilities. This speech represents Malcolm X's most significant contribution to the history of black nationalism. He does not demand a separate land, like Bishop Turner; nor does he provide a set of beliefs completely separate from those of the dominant culture, like Elijah Muhammad, rather, Malcolm empowers his audience to critique and engage the dominant white culture from a perspective that is available to them only after they separate their sense of identity from the limitations of that culture.

Malcolm was assassinated on 21 February, 1965, and since his death no black nationalist leader has emerged to rival his influence. "Black Power," for example, is often positioned as a direct descendent of the rhetoric of Malcolm X, and there are similarities that place both Malcolm X and "Black Power" firmly within the black nationalist tradition, such as the rejection of white standards and the recovery of African and African-American culture as a source of racial pride. However, as Stokely Carmichael used "Black Power" in the summer of 1966, and later elaborated in his 1967 book with Charles V. Hamilton, it ultimately describes something quite different from what Malcolm X advocated. Carmichael and Hamilton's central argument involves defining black ghettos as "colonies" and urging their readers to develop separatist economic and social enterprises based upon this interpretation. "Black Power," then, often seems more the legacy of Booker T. Washington than of Malcolm X; it is not an invitation to reach an independent evaluation of white America, but rather a program of social reform.

Elijah Muhammad named Louis Farrakhan as Malcolm's successor in the Nation of Islam. Elijah Muhammad's son, Wallace, a close friend of Malcolm's, took control of the Nation of Islam after his father's death in 1975, renaming it and turning it toward orthodox Islam. Farrakhan eventually balked at the reforms and left Wallace's organization to rebuild the Nation of Islam and restore Elijah Muhammad's doctrines. Farrakhan has stayed more comfortably within a tradition of black nationalism than did Malcolm X, continuing to speak primarily to black audiences and to deliver sometimes esoteric discourses of racial pride and uplift. His endorsement of Jesse Jackson in the 1984 presidential campaign, and his 1995 Million Man March on Washington, show that both Farrakhan and the black nationalist tenets he represents continue to resonate strongly within the United States. While Wallace Muhammad's organization, the Muslim American Society (formerly the American Muslim Mission), remains far larger than Farrakhan's, it is Farrakhan who most vividly signifies the rhetoric of black nationalism today.

BIBLIOGRAPHY

Clegg, Claude Andrew III. *An Original Man: The Life and Times of Elijah Muhammad*. New York, 1997. An extensive biography of Elijah Muhammad; contains a detailed summary of early Nation of Islam doctrine.

Cronon, E. David. *Black Moses: The Story of Marcus Garvey and the Universal Negro Improvement Association*. Madison, Wis., 1969. A fair-minded and readable overview and assessment of Marcus Garvey.

Garvey, Marcus. *The Philosophy and Opinions of Marcus Garvey, or Africa for the Africans*. Compiled by Amy Jacques Garvey. 2d ed. 2 vols. in one. Totowa, N.J., 1967. The most exhaustive collection of Garvey's speeches and statements.

Hall, Raymond L. *Black Separatism in the United States*. Hanover, N.H., 1978. Out-of-print, but widely available in university libraries, this is a highly useful and broad-ranging overview of black nationalist thought.

Lewis, David L. *W. E. B. Du Bois: Biography of a Race, 1868–1919*. New York, 1993. The finest autobiography of Du Bois, with extensive coverage of his public debate with Booker T. Washington.

Lincoln, E. Eric. *The Black Muslims in America*. 3d ed. Grand Rapids, Mich., 1994. Originally published in 1961, this was the first major investigation of the Nation of Islam (Lincoln coined the term *Black Muslims*); contains a brief history of black nationalism in the United States.

Malcolm X. *Malcolm X Speaks*, edited by George Breitman. New York, 1989. Originally published in 1965, this is the best-known and most widely available collection of key speeches and statements from Malcolm X's last year; contains "The Ballot or the Bullet."

Malcolm X, and Alex Haley. *The Autobiography of Malcolm X*. New York, 1965.

Moses, Wilson Jeremiah. *The Golden Age of Black Nationalism, 1850–1925*. Hamden, Conn., 1978. Out of print, but widely available in university libraries; one of the most thorough historical studies of black nationalism.

Moses, Wilson Jeremiah. *Classical Black Nationalism: From the American Revolution to Marcus Garvey.* New York, 1996. Combines excerpts from major speeches and documents with background information in an anthology format.

Redkey, Edwin S. *Black Exodus: Black Nationalist and Back-to-Africa Movements, 1890–1910.* Out of print, but widely available in university libraries; one of the best resources on black nationalism during the post-Reconstruction era.

Ture, Kwame (Stokely Carmichael), and Charles V. Hamilton. *Black Power: The Politics of Liberation.* New York, 1967.

Turner, Henry McNeal. *Respect Black: The Writings and Speeches of Henry McNeal Turner,* edited by Edwin S. Redkey. New York, 1971. Out of print, but widely available in university libraries; the only compilation of Turner's rhetoric ever produced.

Van Deburg, William L., ed. *Modern Black Nationalism: From Marcus Garvey to Louis Farrakhan.* New York, 1997. Combines excerpts from major speeches and documents with background information in an anthology format.

Walker, David. *Appeal, in Four Articles; together with a Preamble, to the Coloured Citizens of the World, but in Particular, and Very Expressly, to Those of the United States of America.* Rev. ed. New York, 1995.
—ROBERT E. TERRILL

ALLEGORY (Lat. *inversio*) is a trope constituted by a semantic substitution. It can be realized as a metataxeme or as a metatexteme. It differs from metaphor in that the substitution does not involve one lexeme but a series of lexemes. While Quintilian's famous definition of allegory as a *"continua metaphora"* (*Institutio oratoria,* first century CE 8.6.4) implicitly acknowledges the textual character of the trope, Thomas Wilson in *The Arte of Rhetorique* (1553), expresses it more clearly when he defines allegory as "a Metaphore vsed throughout a whole sentence or oration" (Fol. 93).

Although as a mode of expression allegory has a much longer tradition, its origins as a rhetorical category date back to Roman antiquity. In *De oratore* (55 BCE), Cicero mentions a special form of *translatio* consisting of "a chain of words linked together, so that something other than what is said has to be understood," but he does not refer to this form as "allegory" (3.41.166). The following nominal definition, however, can be found in Quintilian: *"Allegory,* which is translated in Latin by *inversio,* either presents one thing in words and another in meaning, or else something absolutely opposed to the meaning of the words" (8.6.44). According to Quintilian, the first variant is used for the purpose of illustration, while the second involves irony and is used for mockery (8.6.54–59). [*See* Irony.]

A distinction is commonly drawn between pure and mixed allegory. Whereas in the former all the central terms are to be taken in an allegorical sense, in the latter some keep their original meaning. Quintilian gives the following example of a mixed allegory: "I always thought that Milo would have other storms and tempests to weather, at least in the troubled waters of political meetings" (8.6.48). Here, the explicit reference to the sphere of politics represents a *verbum proprium* that helps the addressee gather the intended meaning. Generally, mixed allegories meet the demands of perspicuity but run the risk of being uninteresting; pure allegories may be more charming but are in danger of becoming obscure. If a point of reference cannot be established by a recipient, the allegory assumes the nature of an enigma. Quintilian, therefore, formulates the following restriction: "When, however, an allegory is too obscure, we call it a riddle: such riddles are, in my opinion, to be regarded as blemishes, in view of the fact that lucidity is a virtue" (8.6.52).

Allegory and Allegoresis. Whereas allegory refers to the process of encoding meaning, allegoresis is related to the process of decoding meaning. As an integral part of religious discourse, allegorical interpretations have been in use from early cultural stages. Several instances of allegoresis are to be found in the Bible, for example, in Joseph's interpretation of the Pharaoh's dreams in the Old Testament (*Gn.* 1.40–41), or in Saint Paul's interpretation of Old Testament figures and events as "types" prefiguring the Gospel (*1 Cor.* 10.1–11; *Gal.* 4.22–29). Although, ideally conceived, allegory and allegoresis correspond with each other by sharing a common cultural background, the intended meaning of a text and later attributions of allegorical meanings need not necessarily coincide (Lausberg, 1998, section 900). Accordingly, allegorical readings of traditional texts, such as the ancient myths, Homer's epic poems, or the Bible have been divergent, even contradictory, in former centuries. For literary critics, the problem of the adequacy of allegorical interpretations has always been a major concern. Herman Melville's novel *Moby Dick* (1851), for example, is open to several allegorical readings, including religious, psychological, and political ones. The latter may regard Ahab's destructive drive as forming a parallel to the unrestrained geographical expansion of the United States in the nineteenth century. Pointing to the fact that literary interpretations normally involve a translation of one meaning into another, the American critic Northrop Frye (1912–1991) wondered if all textual interpretations could, in a sense, be characterized as allegorical (*Anatomy of Criticism*, 1957, pp. 89–91).

Refering to *2 Corinthians* 3.6 ("The letter killeth, but the spirit giveth life"), Saint Augustine (354–430 CE) introduced allegoresis to early Christianity. In the following centuries, it was developed into a relatively standardized system of interpretation (Freytag, 1992, p. 342). In the Middle Ages, the quest for an allegorical interpretation of Scripture gave rise to the system of a fourfold meaning, which included: (1) the literal or historical level (*sensus litteralis*); (2) an allegorical level (*sensus allegoricus*); (3) a moral level (*sensus moralis / tropologicus*); and (4) a mystical or eschatological level (*sensus anagogicus*). In a distich attributed to Nicholas of Lyra (died 1349), these are explained as follows: "The letter teaches deeds, allegory what you should believe, / The moral what you should do, anagogy where you are going" (Rollinson, 1981, p. 78). As an example, "Jerusalem" represents the historical city (literal level), the Church of Christ (allegorical level), the human soul (moral level), and the Heavenly City (anagogical level).

Renaissance Allegory. During the Renaissance, which has been characterized as a period of allegorical syncretism (Fletcher, 1973, p. 43), allegory assumed the quality of an overall cultural paradigm (Plett, 1979, p. 310). After the revival of Neoplatonism in the School of Florence, the allegorical mode became associated with a number of theories and disciplines that rested on the epistemological assumption that the cosmos was pervaded with "secret analogies." In this context, one may refer to the idea that nature represents an allegorical text written by God, the theory of a correspondence between microcosm and mac-

rocosm, the alchemical tradition with its personified representations of elements and celestial bodies, the *magia naturalis* propagated by Henry Cornelius Agrippa (1486–1535), and Paracelsian medicine with its doctrine of signatures. Inspired by the *Hieroglyphica* of Horapollo, a Greek manuscript that had been discovered in 1419, the terms *allegory* and *hieroglyphic* were often used interchangeably (Dieckmann, 1970.) "Hieroglyphic" could denote the allegorical character of a text, a pictorial representation, or an individual symbol like the *Monas Hieroglyphica* (1564) by John Dee (1527–1608), to which its author attributed magical qualities.

Francis Bacon's (1561–1626) theory of allegory represents a watershed between the Renaissance and the Age of Reason. Classifying "Parabolical Poesy" as one of three principal poetical genres in *The Advancement of Learning* (1605) and in *De Augmentis Scientiarum* (1623), Bacon attributed to it the two opposing functions of "illustration" and "enfoldment" (*Works* 4. 317). Although Bacon repeated the Renaissance idea that the ancient myths were inscribed with secret philosophical knowledge, in his *De Sapientia Veterum* (1609) he dealt with them, first of all, as a means of pedagogical instruction. Bacon's attitude stands in contrast to that of Henry Reynolds, who regarded the ancient myths as sacred texts in his *Mythomystes* (1632) and criticized Bacon for his pragmatical approach.

Allegorical Practice. A text that had a considerable influence on the later development of allegorical literature is the philosophical poem *Psychomachia* by Prudentius (348–after 405 CE). Outstanding examples of allegory in medieval literature are the *Roman de la Rose* (c.1230–c.1275), *Piers Plowman* (c.1332–1400) by William Langland, and the *Divinia Comedia* (c.1307–1321) by Dante Alighieri. Another allegorical genre of medieval origin is the morality play, which had a considerable impact on the development of English drama. The most famous example is the anonymously published *Everyman* (c.1509–1519), which includes as characters personified abstract concepts like Virtue or Vice who are engaged in disputes over the human soul, thus demonstrating the temptations of mortal man and his possible redemption from sin.

An outstanding example of Renaissance allegorical practice is Edmund Spenser's epic poem *The Faerie Queene* (1590–1596), which was written to glorify Queen Elizabeth I. In an introductory letter, Spenser outlines the allegorical functions of his poem and speaks of his work as "a continued Allegory, or darke conceit." The predominant role that allegory played during the Renaissance period is also apparent in the popularity of genres and art forms that are qualified by their allegorical character. Among these are the emblem book, which comprises both pictorial and textual representations (e.g., Andreas Alciatus, *Emblematum liber*, 1531; Francis Quarles, *Emblems*, 1635); the many allegorical engravings and copperplates (e.g., by Robert Fludd); and, finally, the court masque with its combination of text, music, and dance (Ben Jonson, Inigo Jones).

Although allegory became a target of the antirhetorical movement of the seventeenth century, which was philosophically motivated by rationalism and empiricism and theologically fostered by Puritanism, its lasting attraction was evident in a number of important allegorical works. Literary examples are John Bunyan's prose narrative *Pilgrim's Progress* (1678), which describes the Christian way to salvation in allegorical terms, and John Dryden's political allegory *Absalom and Architophel* (1681). As regards philosophy, one may refer to the preface of Thomas Hobbes's *Leviathan* (1651) which, in connection with the book's famous frontispiece, depicts the author's idea of the Commonwealth in an allegorical way. During the eighteenth century, allegory remained important as an instrument of satire and political criticism, a famous example being Jonathan Swift's *Gulliver's Travels* (1726).

Johann Wolfgang von Goethe's (1749–1832) depreciation of allegory in favor of the symbol in *Maximen und Reflexionen* (1809–1829) corresponded to the general decline of rhetorical theory in the late eighteenth and early nineteenth centuries. The English Romanticist Samuel Taylor Coleridge (1772–1834) followed Goethe in *The Statesman's Manual* (1816), when he contrasted allegory with the symbol and regarded the latter as a more genuine poetical device. Whereas the symbol was viewed as being "characterized by a translucence of the Eternal through and in the Temporal," allegory represented "but a translation of abstract notions into a picture-language"

(*Collected Works* 6. 30). Despite these claims, however, allegory has continued to occupy a prominent place in both literary theory and practice, examples of the latter being George Orwell's *Animal Farm* (1945) or Thomas Pynchon's *Gravity's Rainbow* (1973).

[*See also* Figures of speech; *and* Style.]

BIBLIOGRAPHY

Bacon, Francis. *The Works of Francis Bacon.* Edited by James Spedding, Robert L. Ellis, and Douglas D. Heath. 14 vols. (1858–74). Reprint, Stuttgart, 1961–1963.

Coleridge, Samuel Taylor. *The Collected Works of Samuel Taylor Coleridge,* edited by R. J. White (1816). Reprint, London, 1972.

Dieckmann, Lieselotte. *Hieroglyphics: The History of a Literary Symbol.* Saint Louis, 1970.

Fletcher, Angus. *Allegory: The Theory of a Symbolic Mode.* 3d ed. New York, 1967.

Fletcher, Angus. "Allegory in Literary History." In *Dictionary of the History of Ideas,* edited by Philip P. Wiener, vol. 1, pp. 41–48. London, 1973.

Freytag, Wiebke. "Allegorie, Allegorese." In *Historisches Wörterbuch der Rhetorik,* edited by Gert Ueding, vol. 1, pp. 330–392. Tübingen, 1992.

Haug, Walter, ed. *Formen und Funktionen der Allegorie: Symposion Wolfenbüttel 1978.* Stuttgart, 1979.

Lausberg, Heinrich. *Handbook of Literary Rhetoric: A Foundation for Literary Study.* Translated by Matthew C. Bliss, Annemiek Jansen, David E. Orton; edited by David E. Orton and R. Dean Anderson. Leiden, 1998. English translation of *Handbuch der literarischen Rhetorik,* first published in 1960.

Lewis, C. S. *The Allegory of Love.* Oxford, 1936.

MacQueen, John. *Allegory.* London, 1970.

Madsen, Deborah L. *Rereading Allegory: A Narrative Approach to Genre.* New York, 1994.

Murrin, Michael. *The Veil of Allegory: Some Notes Toward a Theory of Allegorical Rhetoric in the English Renaissance.* Chicago, 1969.

Plett, Heinrich F. "Konzepte des Allegorischen in der englischen Renaissance. In *Formen und Funktionen der Allegorie-Symposion Wolfenbüttel,* edited by W. Haug, pp. 310–335. Stuttgart, 1979.

Rollinson, Philip. *Classical Theories of Allegory and Christian Culture.* London, 1981.

Whitman, Jon. *Allegory: The Dynamics of an Ancient and Medieval Technique.* Oxford, 1987.

—RICHARD NATE

ALLITERATION is an isophoneme that repeats an identical consonant at the beginning of successive words, thus creating a flow of similar sound structure. "Upon a *g*reat adventure was he bond / That *g*reatest *G*loriana to him *g*ave / That *g*reatest *G*lorious Queene of Faerie lond / to *w*inne him *w*orship, and her *g*race to have" (Edmund Spenser, *The Faerie Queene,* 1590). It is also used to give the text an archaic touch. Alliteration is a stylistic device typical of old Germanic poetry and its imitations. Alliteration is frequently used for emphasis and memorability in slogans: "*Fifty-four Forty, or Fight!*" (U.S. Senator William Allen of Ohio, 1844).

[*See also* Figures of speech; *and* Gorgianic figures.]

— ANDREA GRÜN-OESTERREICH

AMBIGUITY. As this term's everyday use implies, ambiguity centers on uncertainty. The "ambiguous," according to the Oxford English Dictionary, "drives both ways" at once, while "ambiguity" is the state of simultaneously admitting multiple plausible interpretations or explanations, thus permitting double meanings that "drive both ways." Initially, ambiguity is related to rhetoric as both a property of human experience and a quality of symbols in general. Together, experiential and symbolic ambiguities make rhetoric—defined by Kenneth Burke as, the use of symbols to "induc[e] cooperation in beings that by nature respond to symbols" (1969a, p. 43)—both possible and unavoidable. Rhetorical meaning making depends on a Burkean "paradox of substance":

> [T]he word "substance," used to designate what a thing *is,* derives from a word designating something that a thing *is not.* That is, though used to designate something *within* the thing, *intrinsic* to it, the word etymologically refers to something *outside* the thing, *extrinsic* to it. Or otherwise put: the word in its etymological origins would refer to an attribute of the thing's *context,* since that which supports or underlies a thing would be a part of the thing's context. And a thing's context, being outside or beyond the thing, would be something that the thing is *not.* (1969b, p. 23)

The paradox of substance also applies to both experience and symbols, implying that their mutual ambiguities must collaborate to produce socially plausible meanings capable of fostering people's cooperation. While rhetoric thus fundamentally depends on experiential and symbolic ambiguities' interaction to move people to shared interpretations, numerous specific persuasive strategies lean particularly heavily on ambiguity as a resource. After elaborating rhetoric's relationship to the general dynamic linking experiential ambiguity and symbolic ambiguity, this article surveys several such strategies.

Experiential and Symbolic Ambiguities. The fifth-century Greek Sophists were first to recognize formally experiential ambiguity. [*See* Sophists.] They concluded that, since it is impossible for humans to know with certainty (despite their continuing need to make decisions), the best practicable alternative is to equip skilled rhetors to argue competently on all sides of a probable issue. In an inherently indeterminate world, the Sophists reasoned, this approach, formally termed *dissoi logoi,* offered a better chance to make tested, shared decisions on contingent affairs than either uncritically following an individual who (necessarily falsely) claimed certain knowledge, or deciding in a random fashion.

In his *Rhetoric,* Aristotle (384–322 BCE) built on and yet attenuated the Sophists' view. [*See* Classical rhetoric.] He distinguished realms of the necessary, the certain, and the impossible from those of the contingent, the uncertain, and the probable; the latter realms are rhetoric's proper arena (1357a; 1359a–1359b). Rhetoric's object, Aristotle argued, is judgment on situated, probable issues of shared concern (1377b). Following Aristotle, Thomas B. Farrell (1993) elaborated: "[T]he very meaning of rhetoric's materials—the probable or contingent, what may be one way or another—derives from rhetoric's characteristic approach to appearances. Rhetorical questions thus offer a provisional, but engaged, sense of meaning in particular to a changing complex of appearances" (pp. 27–28). Aristotle believed that the better or more probable option usually will be both easier to prove rhetorically and to believe. So, provided that advocates defending the various options argue fairly and are equally rhetorically skilled, situated general audiences "naturally" should be persuaded to prefer that option (1355a). In classically based theories, rhetoric's purpose is to facilitate a meaningful choice, though tentative and for the moment, among the different directions that a probable matter drives. Experiential ambiguity thus becomes an invitation to rhetoric and a justification for teaching it, not an excuse for indecision.

Like human experience, symbols too are inherently ambiguous and subject to the paradox of substance. A symbol is anything that meaningfully "stands in" for a referent other than itself; language is an obvious, though by no means the only, example. By definition, symbols *are* something other than what they *represent*. The positive potential that a symbol's inescapable distance from its referent creates has not always been welcomed by rhetorical scholars. From classical times through the nineteenth century, ambiguity itself was viewed narrowly as an avoidable stylistic fault or deceptive device; clarity and precision were rhetorical ideals, and ambiguity their absence (Tashiro, 1968). As an adjective, *ambiguity* even came to designate an entire set of rhetorical fallacies (Broyles, 1975, p. 108). [*See* Fallacies.] In the twentieth century, however, some scholars began to appreciate ambiguity's potential. For example, as Sapir notes (1934), the symbolists acknowledged symbolic ambiguity's inevitability but designated its relative degree by distinguishing "referential" symbols (those with less distance between symbol and referent, admitting less interpretive license) from "condensational" ones (those admitting multiple emotionally charged, often incompatible concurrent interpretations). Later, in *The Philosophy of Rhetoric* (New York, 1936), I. A. Richards persuasively refuted eighteenth-century doctrine that every word has a single "right" or "good" use, proposing instead that a word's discursive and situational contexts inflect its symbolic ambiguity when making meaning. With C. K. Ogden (*The Meaning of Meaning*, London, 1923), he had developed a complex theory of the connections among words, thoughts, and referents, a theory admittedly necessitated by the intersection of experiential and symbolic ambiguities.

In *Seven Types of Ambiguity* (1953, p. 1), William Empson developed the sweeping position that "any verbal nuance, however slight, which gives room for alternative reactions to the same piece of language" constitutes ambiguity; even when one does not perceive his or her own sym-

bol use as multivocal, argued Empson, it legitimately may be labeled "ambiguous" if anyone else "might be puzzled" (p. x). Empson used this assumption not to deny the possibility of shared meaning, but to justify the rich potential of symbolic ambiguity for literary contexts. Finally and least conventionally, deconstructionists, such as Jacques Derrida (*Writing and Difference,* 1978), argued that experiential and symbolic ambiguities entail textual negations exceeding even those summarized by Burke's paradox of substance; deconstruction proposes that texts innately negate themselves and what their constituent symbols ostensibly affirm about indeterminate experience, affirming instead meanings that they seem at first glance to reject.

Debate raged over such challenges to ambiguity's traditional place in rhetorical theory. Some contended that the theoretical innovations merely reversed ambiguity's rhetorical valence, changing it from a symbolic vice to an unqualified virtue. For example, M. H. Abrams objected that Empson's text encouraged "over-reading: ingenious, overdrawn, and sometimes self-contradictory explications that violate the norms of the English language and ignore the controls upon reference exerted by the [discursive] context" (1971, p. 9). The embrace of ambiguity prompted concern, especially for symbol use outside the genre of poetry (Fowler, 1987). Some twentieth-century thinkers explicitly invoked classical and later pretwentieth century notions to reassert "ambiguity" as a pejorative label for particular acts of public advocacy (Tashiro, 1968). Struggling to establish a rhetorical middle ground in this contentious context, Roger Hufford's "The Dimensions of an Idea: Ambiguity Defined" (1966) attempted to make some measure of ambiguity in public discourse palatable by proposing conditions under which its presence is ethical. As of this writing, communication scholars largely agree that some degree of experiential and symbolic ambiguities are inevitable—though they disagree on what constitutes that degree—and that rhetors can be held responsible for their strategic exploitation of ambiguity in particular rhetorical acts (Hufford, 1966; Eisenberg, 1984). Postmodern critiques did less to deny this understanding than to modulate it by underscoring assumptions compatible with the foregoing reading: human experience is fragmented as well as ambiguous, and any symbolic interpretation is incomplete, tentative, and open to challenge.

Among twentieth-century theorists, Kenneth Burke (1897–1993) most comprehensively negotiated the importance of experiential and symbolic ambiguities as grounds for rhetoric. [*See* Modern rhetoric.] In his *Rhetoric of Motives,* Burke eloquently explained how the human condition of division, when addressed via strategic rhetorical management of ambiguity, might promote unity or "consubstantiality" (1969, p. 55) [*See* Identification.]:

> In pure identification there would be no strife. Likewise, there would be no strife in absolute separateness, since opponents can join battle only through a mediatory ground that makes their communication possible, thus providing the first condition necessary for their interchange of blows. But put identification and division ambiguously together, so that you cannot know for certain just where one ends and the other begins, and you have the characteristic invitation to rhetoric. (p. 25)

Ambiguity provides the "mediatory ground" facilitating competing interpretations of a perceived contingency or rhetorical exigence—a problem marked by urgency that might be mitigated if an advocate persuades empowered auditors (Bitzer, 1968). Significantly, experiential ambiguity also allows competing advocates to countermand a proposed interpretation and defend as superior an alternative that drives a different direction (Olson, 1989), as well as to revise or reevaluate interpretations as circumstances change (Olson, 1993). The possibility of promoting varying rhetorical characterizations, without deception or hypocrisy, depends on the interpretive range that experiential and symbolic ambiguities together provide.

In *Language as Symbolic Action* (1966) and *A Grammar of Motives* (1969), Burke playfully explored the ways that symbols support internally consistent terministic screens through which people make sense of ambiguous occurrences as well as the ambiguous relationship of symbols to conceptual and concrete referents. An advocate's interpretive faculties are engaged necessarily in the process of even selecting and interpreting an ambiguous experience as a problem worth ad-

dressing (Vatz, 1971). To facilitate conjoined action, people use rhetoric to promote identification by symbolically naming and framing shared experience in ways that coach shared attitudes and concerted action. Though indeterminate in meaning, experience simultaneously shapes and limits the range of credible symbol use. Selecting, reflecting, and deflecting ambiguous experiential aspects using symbols inevitably communicates attitudes or motives (Burke, *Language,* 1966, p. 45, *Philosophy,* 1973, pp. 1, 20). Consistent with Burke's dramatistic perspective, Murray Edelman (1971) noted that shared experiences are so ambiguous that "situations" are "largely the creations of the language used to describe them" (1971, p. 65). Characterizing occurrences symbolically involves the "magical decree . . . implicit in all language; for the mere act of naming an object or situation decrees that it is to be singled out as such-and-such rather than as something other" (Burke, *Philosophy,* 1973, p. 4). For example, a particular act of killing might plausibly admit such apparently inconsistent characterizations as "cold-blooded murder," "an accident," "self-defense," "justice," "a redemptive sacrifice," or "a prelude to the afterlife," each implying a different evaluation and course of action.

Rhetorical Strategies. As the ground of specific rhetorical strategies, ambiguity finds "its legitimate sphere of action in speeches to persuade" (Hufford, 1966, p. 5). Because Burke's explanation of "persuasion" constructs the field of ambiguity so broadly, for the sake of completeness, I will rely on it: "Wherever there is persuasion, there is rhetoric. And wherever there is 'meaning,' there is 'persuasion'" (*Rhetoric,* 1969a, p. 172). The implication is that all symbolic strategies, however subtly, trade on ambiguity to perform persuasive work. However, certain strategies very evidently exploit the nexus of experiential and symbolic ambiguities as a rhetorical resource. For instance, condensation symbols, a strategic concept that David Zarefsky proposed based on Sapir's symbolism commentary, "designate no clear referent but serve to 'condense' into one symbol a host of different meanings and connotations which might diverge if more specific referents were attempted" (1986, pp. 10–11). Because they remain at a relatively high level of abstraction, condensation symbols, such as a flag or the American Dream, can coalesce diverse emotions and create identification among even those whose specific meanings for these symbols may be incompatible. Similarly, nondiscursive rhetoric, such as the Vietnam Veterans Memorial, promotes identification even as it invites diverse interpretations (Foss, 1986, p. 337).

Discursive documents designed to unite a group across time, in spite of members' divergent tendencies, also depend on persuasively encompassing competing values at a sufficiently abstract level. For example, the U.S. Constitution and many diplomatic agreements depend on their ambiguities to provide flexibility without sacrificing unity (Hufford, 1966, p. 4). Like rhetorical tropes, especially irony, humor and puns rely on their measure of ambiguity to advance strategically a point or to inspire consubstantiality (Hufford, 1966, p. 5). [*See* Humor; Irony; *and* Paronomasia.]

Argumentative strategies, such as association and dissociation, operate by maneuvering ambiguous interpretive boundaries. Association attempts to link meaningfully referents formerly viewed as unrelated and thus create a fresh interpretive and evaluative context for the issue at hand. Dissociation strategically divides that which is interpreted currently as unitary into distinct parts that invite divergent evaluations (C. Perelman and L. Olbrechts-Tyteca, *The New Rhetoric,* Notre Dame, Ind., 1969). Transcendence and transformation operate similarly, strategically changing the scope and circumference of a phenomenon's interpretive borders and so redefining meaning (Burke, *Grammar,* 1969b).

Another Burkean concept, perspective by incongruity, strategically presents evidence that things "appearing" to be unrelated and so passing as consistent, "actually" are related and so inconsistent, thus inviting some sort of redress to avoid hypocrisy (Burke, *Permanence,* 1984). [*See* Perspective by incongruity.] Still another rhetorical use of ambiguity is to deny its presence. Declaring that a purportedly ambiguous issue actually is not so may be designed to convince auditors to support the *rhētōr* as a leader clear-sighted and determined enough to steer them effectively through this troubling "apparent" indeterminacy (Edelman, *Politics,* 1971, pp. 80–81). Finally, a rhetor strategically may highlight ambiguity's

presence, then argue that it is impossible to resolve it satisfactorily, even temporarily. This tactic serves to block agreement on a proposed judgment or course of action (Perelman and Olbrechts-Tyteca, 1969, p. 122). Readers interested in discovering additional rhetorical strategies using ambiguity as a resource should follow Burke's advice to examine critically "not terms that avoid ambiguity, *but* terms that clearly reveal the strategic spots at which ambiguities necessarily arise" (*Grammar,* 1969b, p. xviii).

BIBLIOGRAPHY

Abrams, M. H. "Ambiguity." In *A Glossary of Literary Terms,* 3d ed., pp. 8–10. New York, 1971.

Bitzer, Lloyd F. "The Rhetorical Situation." *Philosophy and Rhetoric* 1 (1968), pp. 1–14. Denies legitimate ambiguity in rhetorical situations; argues that a rhetorical situation prescribes its appropriate response and that a rhetor's success depends on "reading" and "filling" that prescription precisely. Contrast with Vatz.

Broyles, James E. "The Fallacies of Composition and Division." *Philosophy and Rhetoric* 8 (1975), pp. 108–113.

Burke, Kenneth. *Language as Symbolic Action: Essays on Life, Literature, and Method.* Berkeley, 1966.

Burke, Kenneth. *A Rhetoric of Motives.* First published in 1950. Berkeley, 1969a.

Burke, Kenneth. *A Grammar of Motives.* First published in 1945. Berkeley, 1969b.

Burke, Kenneth. *The Philosophy of Literary Form: Studies in Symbolic Action.* 3d ed. Berkeley, 1973.

Burke, Kenneth. *Permanence and Change: An Anatomy of Purpose.* 3d ed. Berkeley, 1984.

Derrida, Jacques. *Writing and Difference.* Translated by Alan Bass. Chicago, 1978. English translation of *L'écriture et la différence,* first published 1967.

Edelman, Murray. *Politics as Symbolic Action: Mass Arousal and Quiescence.* New York, 1971. In spite of its heavy cognitive bias, usefully discusses symbolic strategies for shaping perceptions and organizing concerted action in ambiguous political situations.

Eisenberg, Eric M. "Ambiguity as Strategy in Organizational Communication." *Communication Monographs* 51 (1984), pp. 227–242. Defends ambiguity as a legitimate and ethical alternative to clarity in organizational communication and explores its defensible uses.

Empson, William. *Seven Types of Ambiguity.* 3d ed. Norfolk, Va., 1953. Widely recognized as the twentieth-century's landmark work defending and systematizing legitimate literary uses of ambiguity.

Farrell, Thomas B. *Norms of Rhetorical Culture*. New Haven, 1993. Using a combination of theoretical argument and textual critique, this source recovers classically grounded rhetoric to promote contemporary practical reason and civic participation.

Foss, Sonya K. "Ambiguity as Persuasion: The Vietnam Veterans Memorial." *Communication Quarterly* 34 (1986), pp. 326–340. Critically investigates the symbolic features through which the memorial inspires emotional reactions and reverence among visitors despite wide variance among their interpretations of its meaning.

Fowler, Roger. "Ambiguity." In *A Dictionary of Modern Critical Terms*, rev. ed., pp. 7–8. New York, 1987.

Hufford, Roger. "The Dimensions of an Idea: Ambiguity Defined." *Today's Speech* 14 (April 1966), pp. 4–8. Attempts to rehabilitate "ambiguity" as a legitimate persuasive (versus philosophical) strategy; distinguishes ethical and unethical rhetorical uses based on whether or not the rhetor's concern for the auditors' well-being is "a prominent goal."

McKeon, Richard. "Creativity and the Commonplace." *Philosophy and Rhetoric* 6 (1973), pp. 199–210. Traces the efforts to "fix" the meaning of rhetorical "creativity" from classical times to the present; concludes that such attempts cannot succeed, because as soon as the notion's meaning is settled, it is no longer "creative" and that accepting creativity's productive systematic ambiguity is both more accurate and heuristic.

Olson, Kathryn M. "The Controversy over President Reagan's Visit to Bitburg: Strategies of Definition and Redefinition." *Quarterly Journal of Speech* 75 (1989), pp. 129–151. Argues that experiential ambiguity makes possible varying plausible rhetorical characterizations of events and demonstrates different audiences' active roles in fostering or refusing identification.

Olson, Kathryn M. "Completing the Picture: Replacing Generic Embodiments in the Historical Flow." *Communication Quarterly* 41 (1993), pp. 299–317. Examines the potential importance of historical distance and motivation in persuasively reinterpreting ambiguous events.

Sapir, Edward. "Symbolism." In *Encyclopaedia of the Social Sciences*, edited by Edwin R. A. Seligman, vol. 14, pp. 492–495. New York, 1934.

Tashiro, Tom. "Ambiguity as Aesthetic Principle." In *Dictionary of the History of Ideas: Studies of Selected Pivotal Ideas*, vol. 1. Edited by Philip P. Wiener, pp. 48–60. New York, 1968. Conceives "ambiguity" broadly enough to justify tracing indeterminacy's relationships to ontology and epistemology across two dozen centuries of Western experience. Includes a discussion of shifting allegiances to absolute and relative truth, illustrated with particular cultural expressions, as well as minicritiques of numerous plastic and performing art selections.

Vatz, Richard E. "The Myth of the Rhetorical Situation." *Philosophy and Rhetoric* 6 (1973), pp. 154–161. Takes the position that human experience is so relative that experiences' meanings legitimately may be construed with few or no interpretive limits. Contrast with Bitzer.

Zarefsky, David. *President Johnson's War on Poverty: Rhetoric and History*. University, Ala., 1986. Critically analyzes this administration's public discourse regarding its War on Poverty to demonstrate how rhetoric and experiential developments interact to shape policy.

—KATHRYN M. OLSON

AMPLIFICATION has a qualitative and a quantitative variant: vertical amplification and horizontal amplification.

Vertical amplification (Gk. *auxēsis;* Lat. *amplificatio*) serves the qualitative purpose of elevating or magnifying the subject in hand. Quintilian (*Institutio oratoria* 8.3.90) mentions four figures that help to achieve this end: (1) *auxēsis/incrementum,* (2) *comparatio*, (3) *ratiocinatio*, and (4) *congeries*. An illustration of the procedure is provided by Henry Peacham (1593, p. 167): "In praising, as to call an honest man a Saint, a faire Virgine an Angell, good musicke heavenly harmonie." [*See* Auxēsis.]

Horizontal amplification (Lat. *amplificatio, dilatatio*) denotes the enlargement of a proposition or, more generally, the extension of a text by the multiplication and variation of its constituents (places, circumstances) in order to heighten the rhetorical effect. Amplification in this broader sense refers to textual constituents such as subject matter (e.g., love in poetry), action (e.g., revenge in tragedy), character (e.g., the clown in comedy), genre (e.g., the letter in the epistolary novel). Amplification is achieved by dividing a statement into its parts or splitting up a whole into concrete phenomena. The procedure is thus one of expanding by means of diversified details. The most significant work to deal with this kind of amplification and the one that inaugurated a rhetorical practice that lasted for a long time was Erasmus's treatise *De duplici copia verborum ac rerum*, dealing not only with the abundance of words (*elocutio*) but also with that of ideas (*inventio*). Originally composed for John Colet's Saint Paul's School, London, it was after its *editio princeps* (1512) reprinted in numerous editions all over Europe. Erasmus, who justifies his method of creating resourcefulness of words and ideas by referring to Quintilian (*Institutio oratoria* 8.2; 12.1), connects the idea of *copia* with that of *varietas*. In the first book of *De copia,* he describes many techniques of variation: *Synonymia* (chap. 11), *Enallagē* (chap. 13), *Antonomasia* (chap. 14), *Periphrasis* (chap. 15), Metaphor (chap. 16), *Allegory* (chap. 18), *Catachrēsis* (chap. 19), Metonymy (chap. 22), Synecdoche (chap. 23), Comparatives (chap. 25), and Hyperbolē (chap. 28). By these figures he creates 147 variations of the statement "Your letter pleased me very much." Erasmus enumerates many classical authors who practiced the principle of *copia* and achieved an ornate style. The opposite procedure is abbreviation; the contrast to the ornate style is the plain style that strives toward the ideal of a total congruence of matter and manner: *quot res tot verba.* [*See* Copia.]

The various methods of vertical and horizontal amplification appeal to the *ēthos* and *pathos* of the recipients. Peacham (1593, p. 121) makes no clear distinction between the two kinds of amplification, and describes its effects in the following manner: "It is full of light, plenty and variety causing the Orator to teach and tell things plainly, to amplify largely, and to proue and conclude mightily." The very wording of this passage demonstrates the procedure of amplifying one term, amplification itself, and that with the purpose of catching the reader's attention.

[*See also* Ēthos; Figures of Speech; *and* Pathos.]

BIBLIOGRAPHY

Cave, Terence. *The Cornucopian Text: Problems of Writing in the French Renaissance.* Oxford, 1979.

Eramus of Rotterdam, Desiderius. *On Copia of Words and Ideas* (De Utraque Verborum ac Rerum Copia). Translated from the Latin with an Introduction by Donald B. King and H. David Rix. Milwaukee, 1963.

Peacham, Henry. *The Garden of Eloquence* (1593). Edited with an introduction and commentary by B.-M. Koll. Frankfurt, 1996.

Sloane, Thomas O. "Schoolbooks and Rhetoric: Erasmus's *Copia.*" *Rhetorica* 9.2 (Spring 1991), pp. 113–129.

Sloane, Thomas O. "Copiousness." In *On the Contrary: The Protocol of Traditional Rhetoric,* Chap. 3. Washington, D.C., 1998.

—HEINRICH F. PLETT

ANADIPLŌSIS (Lat. *reduplicatio*), called by Puttenham (*The Arte of English Poesie,* 1589) "redouble," is an isomorpheme that repeats the last word or words of a clause, sentence, or verse at the beginning of the following line, thus coupling together the two textual units. This may emphasize a central term: "I will lift my eyes unto the hills, from whence cometh *my help. My help* cometh from the Lord . . ." (*Ps(s).* 121.1.2). The combination of semantically disparate members can produce a comic effect: "So shall you share all that he doth possess, / By having him making yourself *no less.*" / "*No less!* Nay bigger; women grow by men" (Shakespeare, *Romeo and Juliet* 1.3.93–95).

[*See also* Figures of speech; Gorgianic figures; Gradatio; *and* Style.]

—ANDREA GRÜN-OESTERREICH

ANALOGY. *See* Casuistry; *and* Metaphor.

ANAPHORA (Lat. *relatio*), called by Puttenham (*The Arte of English Poesie,* 1589) "figure of report," is an isomorpheme that repeats one or more words at the beginning of successive clauses, sentences, or verses, thus enhancing the importance of the repeated element. "Wha will be a traitor knave? / Wha can fill a coward's grave? / Wha sae base as be a slave? / Let him turn and flee!" (Robert Burns, *Scots Wha Hae*). The repetition of rather irrelevant morphemes may have a comic effect. "Four other Oysters followed them, / *And* yet another four; / *And* thick and fast they came at last, / *And* more, and more, and more" (Lewis Carroll, *Through the Looking Glass,* 1872).

[*See also* Figures of speech; Poetry; Style; *and* Symplocē.]

—ANDREA GRÜN-OESTERREICH

ANASTROPHĒ (Lat. *inversio;* Engl. reversal) is a deviation from grammatical word order in that the sequence of any two words is reversed, an *ordo* *praeposterus* (Bede, pp. 672–735). The reversal of noun and adjective is one form of realization, as in "Speak from your lungs military" (Shakespeare, *Merry Wives of Windsor* 4.5.13); the reversal of subject and object is another: "Then none have I offended" (Shakespeare, *Julius Caesar* 3.2.39). Though considered an error, *anastrophē* can on occasion help, as Quintilian points out (*Institutio oratoria* 1.5.40; 9.3.27), to rouse a flagging audience. Frequently employed to adapt a phrase to the rhythmic pattern of a clause, its effect is generally to slow down the flow of words and ideas.

[*See also* Figures of speech; *and* Hysteron prōteron.]

BIBLIOGRAPHY

Arbusow, Leonid. *Colores rhetorici.* Göttingen, 1963.
Beda Venerabilis. In *Rhetores latini minores,* edited by C. Halm. Leipzig, 1863.
Plett, Heinrich F. *Systematische Rhetorik.* Munich, 2000.
— HEINER PETERS

ANTANACLASIS (Lat. *reflexio*), called "The Rebounde" by Puttenham (*The Arte of English Poesie,* 1589, p. 207), the repetition of a word in a different sense, a metasememe, so called by Dubois et al. (*Rhétorique générale.* Paris, 1970); for example, "and let the dead bury their dead" (*Mt.* 8.22). The repeated word need not be identical in form nor even etymologically related, "Not on thy sole, but on thy soul, harsh Jew, / Thou mak'st thy knife keen" (Shakespeare, *Merchant of Venice* 4.1.123f.). *Antanaclasis* serves as a useful distinction of meanings, whereby one hopes to make an opponent's hidden motives appear. It is criticized by classicists for its display of wit at the cost of perspicuity.

[*See also* Figures of speech; *and* Paronomasia.]
— HEINER PETERS

ANTISTHECŌN (Gk., also *antistoecon,* "standing opposite in pairs"; Lat. *littera pro littera* "letter for letter"), a metaplasm by substitution of a letter or sound within a word. It may be a mistake or a permanent dialectal or personal variant ("Veller" for "Weller" in Dickens's *Pickwick Papers*). Employed as a figure, *antisthecōn* produces archaisms

(e.g., "mote" for "may" in Spenser's *Faerie Queene,* canto 3.258), marks etymologies ("okecorne," erroneously, for "acorn"), or helps to make puns— as when, to Claudius's suggestion, Shakespeare's Hamlet retorts that he is "too much in the sun," that is, "son" (1.2.67). Richard Sherry (*Treatise of Schemes,* 1550) also subsumes permutations of letters ("cham*b*re" for "chamber") under this heading.

[*See also* Figures of speech.]

BIBLIOGRAPHY

Lausberg, Heinrich. *Handbook of Literary Rhetoric: A Foundation for Literary Study.* Translated by Matthew T. Bliss, Annemiek Jansen, David E. Orton; edited by David E. Orton and R. Dean Anderson. Leiden, 1998. English translation of *Handbuch der literarischen Rhetorik,* Munich, 1960.
— HEINER PETERS

ANTITHESIS. Under the general denomination of antithesis (Gk. *antithesis, antitheton;* Lat. *contentio, contrapositum*), authors usually gather together a varied and complex collection of discursive phenomena, which has as its main foundation the link in the space of a statement, or in different segments of it, of at least a pair of lexical units whose meanings are or can be opposite.

Since this figure was mentioned in Aristotle's *Rhetoric* (1410a24), the characterization usually provided by authors throughout the continuing classical tradition presents different degrees of explicitness. Of all the classical works, perhaps the *Rhetorica ad Herennium* (4.15.21) and, above all, Quintilian's *Institutio oratoria* (9.3.81–86) best synthesize the features of this family of figures that authors and treatises will go on repeating with little variation.

From the observations of those writers and treatises, the following aspects may be summarized:

1. The consideration of the statement—or different parts of it—as a framework in which the antithesis is developed.
2. The contribution of a typology of opposition between lexical units, a typology that comes from the field of Classical dialectic. [*See* Dialectic.] They are the types of oppositions between: (a) "terms of relation" (*father* / *son, dou-*

ble / half); (b) "contraries" (*good / evil, joy / sorrow, love / hate, heat / coldness, heaven / hell*); "privatives" (*death / life, sight / blindness, sanity / madness*); and (c) "contradictories" (*to be / not to be* at the same time), as established by Aristotle in his *Categories* (11b–14a). It should be noted that the great majority of those pairs of antonymous lexical units that constitute the base of antithesis are closely linked with the different tendencies, movements, and schools that comprise Western poetic traditions.

3. The proposal of a scale of different degrees of structural complexity in the use of antithetic phenomena in any statement, according to the number of pairs of elements implied in each case.

To these aspects the following formal features might be added:

4. That the antonymous lexical units implied in the figure antithesis should belong to the same grammatical category, a fact that conveys the presence of the same flexive and derivative morphemes.

5. That the respective sentence structures in which the antonymous words are integrated as syntagmatic constituents should carry out the same syntactic function.

6. That antonymous units tend to occupy identical distributional places in the respective sequences of elements to which they belong, in agreement with the laws of symmetry and proportion operative in both poetic discourse and "artistic prose," whose basic distributional scheme will be an (a) parallelistic, or (b) specular or chiasmic ordering. [*See* Chiasmus; *and* Parallelism.]

[*See also* Figures of speech; Gorgianic figures; *and* Thesis and antithesis.]

BIBLIOGRAPHY

Lanham, R. A. *A Handlist of Rhetorical Terms.* Berkeley, 1991.
Lausberg, H. *Handbuch der literarischen Rhetorik.* pp. 787–807. Munich, 1960.
Mayoral, J. A. *Figuras retóricas.* Pp. 262–274. Madrid, 1994.
Morier, H. *Dictionnaire de poétique et de rhétorique.* Paris, 1981.

—JOSÉ ANTONIO MAYORAL
Translated by A. Ballesteros

APHAERESIS (Lat. *detractio initii*) is a subtractive metaphoneme that omits sounds at the beginning of a word. It is often used for meeting metrical or rhythmical requirements. "You shall find / Some that will thank you, making just report / Of how unnatural and bemadding sorrow / The King hath cause to plain [instead of: complain]" (Shakespeare, *King Lear* 3.1.36–39). It can also bestow a colloquial touch on the flow of speech: "Use every man after his desert, and who should 'scape [instead of: escape] whipping?" (Shakespeare, *Hamlet* 2.2.529–530).

[*See also* Figures of speech.]

—ANDREA GRÜN-OESTERREICH

APOCOPĒ (Lat. *detractio finis*) is a subtractive metaphoneme that omits sounds at the end of a word. This may be for reasons of meter, rhythm, or rhyme. "First kill *th'* enormous giant, your Disdain, / And let *th'* enchantress Honour, next be slain" (Donne, *The Damp*). Furthermore, this sort of effective mispronunciation can add a colloquial tinge to the speech, especially if used in combination with *aphaeresis* or *syncopē*: "What are these, / So wither'd and so wild in their attire, / That look not like *th'* inhabitants *o' th'* earth, / And yet are on' t?" (Shakespeare, *Macbeth* 1.3. 39–42).

[*See also* Aphaeresis; Figures of speech; *and* Syncopē.]

—ANDREA GRÜN-OESTERREICH

APORIA (Lat. *addubitatio*), which Puttenham (*The Arte of English Poesie,* 1589) calls "The Doubtful," is a pragmatic figure of speech that states the author's pretended inability to speak competently about a certain topic. Aporia is often used as a topos of affected modesty, especially at the exordium of an oration or epic poem: "Of what shall I first complain . . . or where shall I first begin? Of what or of whom shall I call for help?" (Cicero, *Pro Sexto Roscio Amerino* 11.29). If the object of the text surpasses the possibilities of language, aporia is used to emphasize its greatness: "Who will make known to the world the . . . secret cause?" / "O king, I cannot tell you, and what you ask you can never hope to know" (Wagner, *Tristan and Isolde,* 2.3).

[*See also* Figures of speech.]

—ANDREA GRÜN-OESTERREICH

APOSIŌPĒSIS (Lat. *interruptio*) is a pragmatic figure, signifying a sudden disruption of discourse by omitting the expected end of a clause or sentence, as if the speaker/writer were unable or unwilling to proceed. Hence, this figure has a histrionic quality. It can simulate the impression of a speaker so overwhelmed by emotions that he or she is unable to continue speaking, as in Mark Antony's break during his funeral oration: "Bear with me, / My heart is in the coffin there with Caesar, / And I must pause till it come back to me" (Shakespeare, *Julius Caesar* 3.2.105–107). It can also convey a certain pretended shyness toward obscene expressions or even an everyday casualness. "My sister, I dare say, added he, does not care to let a man come so near her—I will not say whether my uncle Toby had completed the sentence or not" (Sterne, *Tristram Shandy*).

[*See also* Figures of speech; *and* Style.]

—ANDREA GRÜN-OESTERREICH

APOSTROPHĒ. Traditionally, the Greek term *apostrophē* (Lat. *aversio*) has designated the rhetorical device that indicates the momentary interruption of discourse, in order to address—often in a vehement tone—a real or imaginary, present or absent, human or nonhuman, living or dead addressee, different from the original addressee of that discourse. This interruption is characterized linguistically by a change from one discursive type to another—as when, for example, one inserts in an expositive–narrative modality, modalities associated with the expressive and appellative functions of language.

[*See also* Figures of speech; *and* Style.]

BIBLIOGRAPHY

Lanham, R. A. *A Handlist of Rhetorical Terms.* Berkeley, 1991.
Lausberg, H. *Handbuch der literarischen Rhetorik.* Pp. 762–765. Munich, 1960.
Mayoral, J. A. *Figuras retóricas.* P. 113. Madrid, 1994.
Morier, H. *Dictionnaire de poétique et de rhétorique.* Paris, 1981.

—JOSÉ ANTONIO MAYORAL
Translated by A. Ballesteros

ARABIC RHETORIC. The Arabic term *balāghah* covers rhetoric, eloquence, and *faṣāḥah,* or purity and perfection of language. Since its pre-Islamic usage, it has never lost its inclusiveness of manner and matter, clarity and brevity of address for the purpose of communicative efficacy. Its very etymology implies both attainment and effect (Ṣammūd, 1994, pp. 100–113). While its Western origination as a term "is linked to political notions of debate and dialogue" (Smyth, 1992, p. 243), its growth into an Arabic science of eloquence, ʿilm al-balāghah, is closely tied to Islam as religion and culture in a specifically Arabic context. To preserve ancient tradition, enhance mastery and influence among Islamized cultures, and resist cultural subversion, pre-Islamic poetry and oratory were to become, since the ninth century CE, a domain of study for philologists, theologians, and grammarians. [*See* Panegyric.] The study was intended for argumentation and debate on a large scale. Subsumed into Qurʾānic exegesis in response to opposition, the effort soon grew into a large corpus of writing on poetics and rhetoric whose primary purpose was, in al-Jāḥiẓ's words (died 255 H.; 868 CE), to prevent opposition from winning over "the young and the shallow-minded," a case that prompted other scholars and rhetors to embark on similar projects. "Had this not been the case," says al-Jāḥiẓ (1933), "we would not have taken the pains to clarify the obvious, highlight the visible, and argue for the evident."

To provide interpretations for the most anthropomorphic verses in the Qurʾān and to argue for its inimitability, *iʿjāz,* became the foremost concern of these scholars, grammarians, and critics. But the effort was never homogeneous or smooth. Some members of the Muʿtazilite school of theology, especially al-Naẓẓām, believed in the Ṣirfah principle, for although opponents to the word of God were incapacitated, Ṣirufū, the language is imitable. Others among them argued for the total inimitability of the Qur'ān. To balance these positions, it was also argued that whenever a "surface meaning runs counter to reason, interpretation is to bypass this, if it is so, in line with rational evidence," as al-Sharīf al-Murtaḍa (died 436 H.) contends (see Ṣammūd, 1994, p. 41). These issues had become the staples for the very theory of Arabic rhetoric and culture. But the precise concern with Qur'ānic exegesis entailed not only a hermeneutics of figurative style, but also a preoccupation with the book industry, to defy distortion, revive tradition, forestall oblivion, sustain identity, and ensure publicity. Al-Jāḥiẓ sums up this transfer to inscription by praising the book for being available, to be "read everywhere, studied always," as long as it is "low-priced and accessible" (al-Jāḥiẓ, n.d., vol. 1, pp. 80, 471). This transfer means that reading and understanding put specific demands on rhetoric, transforming it, to use the articulation of Hans-Georg Gadamer (1982, p. 123), "from the art of making speeches into the art of following discourses with understanding, which means into hermeneutics." [*See* Hermeneutics.]

The Tradition. Dichotomous divisions between ancients and moderns, literary and scholastic, left their imprint on the nature and directions of Arabic *balāghah*. As "meanings are to be found in the highways and byways," says al-Jāḥiẓ (Abū Deeb, 1990, p. 354), it was style as craft, or *elocutio*, that drew the foremost attention. Abu 'Ubayda (died 209 H.; 824–825 CE) wrote *Majāz al-Qur'ān*, treating *majāz* not only as a tropical element but also as "any deviation from the norm" (p. 362), to be followed, among others, by Ibn Qutaybah (died 276 H.; 889 CE) in his *Ta'wīl Mushkil al-Qur'ān* (Interpreting Qur'ānic Problematics), who relates the issue of tropics to Arabic language, enumerating many of these under the heading of *majāzāt*, or tropes. Rather than specific metaphors, his tropes include ones based on contiguity, syntactic transference, ellipsis, pleonasm, and periphrasis, along with grammatical slippage. Grammarians participated in these, for Ibn Jinnī (died 392 H.; 1002 CE) coined *al-'udūl* to indicate deviation from the factual or the literal, a point that was followed up by al-Zamakhsharī later (538 H.; 1144 CE) in his *al-Kashshāf* (Cairo,

1948, vol. 3, p. 133) when coining *al-laḥn,* meaning directing speech so as to draw the addressee's attention through parables, riddles, puns, and so on. But explanations for the nonliteral, *majāz,* abound, albeit with agreement on nonsurface meanings, as 'Abd al-Qāhir al-Jurjānī (died 471 H.; 1078 CE) stipulates (1969, pp. 262–263). Confronted by a surplus of words, argues Ishāq bin Ibrāhīm bin Wahab (died 335 H.; 946–947 CE) in his *Kitāb al-Burhān fi-Wujūh al-Bayān* (Evidence for Levels of Unhiddenness; Baghdad, 1967, p. 143), Arabs "resorted to metaphor," a point that Ibn Rashīq (died 456 H.; 1063 CE) also accepts in *al-'Umdah* (The Pillar; Cairo, 1972, vol. 1, p. 274). Central to discussions of *balāghah,* this surprising tropical richness impelled the philosopher al-Fārābī (died 389 H.) to argue the case in socio-structural terms, for "whenever words settle on their meanings as signs" there will follow "duplication and license in expression so as to reach meaning under another naming" (see Ṣammūd, 1994, p. 405). He sums up the whole tendency as a transfer from the literal to the tropical, *al-khaṭībah* to *al-shi'riyah,* or the message to the poetic (al-Fārābī, 1970).

Originating in Qur'ānic exegesis, many contributions on the literal and the tropical take the whole cultural milieu as context, not only in such readings of Qur'ānic inimitability in comparison to the poetry of the moderns, as al-Bāqillānī (died 403 H.; 1013 CE) argues for instance, but also in the very analysis of eloquence. Overlapping with rhetoric and oratory, eloquence for al-Jāḥiẓ demands a specific usage of discourse, suiting a certain milieu, while keeping in mind its target. Hence, "management of eloquence is harder than eloquence" (al-Jāḥiẓ, n.d., vol. 1, p. 162). Oratory for a Mu'tazilite like him is needed to persuade and influence others. But, it is not accessible to all, for its "head is nature [not artifice], its pillar is practice, its wings acquaintance with tradition, its ornament is grammar, and its glory is the choice of words" (vol. 1, p. 44). Wherever specifically concerned with *bayān,* or modes of representation in eloquent expression, al-Jāḥiẓ collapses rhetoric onto eloquence, for, as his use of the Mu'tazilite Bishr bin al-Mu'tamir's treatise shows, there is a focus on argumentation with a goal to know and to let others share that understanding (al-Jāḥiẓ, n.d., vol. 1, pp. 43, 76).

Although not prone to systematization, al-Jāḥiẓ views became common knowledge among two growing tendencies in rhetoric and eloquence: the purely literary on the one hand and the scholastic on the other, with their specific registers and schema to engage the *pathos* of audiences. On occasion, a critic like ʿAbd al-Qāhir al-Jurjānī would have a foot in each. Belonging to the first were the poet and critic Ibn al-Muʿtazz (died 296 H.; 908 CE), Abu Hilāl al-ʿAskarī (died 400 H.; 1010? CE), Ibn Rashīq (died 456 H.; 1063 CE), al-Jurjānī in *Asrār al-Balāgha* (Mysteries of Eloquence), Usāma bin Munqdh (died 584 H.), and Ibn al-Athīr (died 638 H.; 1239 CE), among many others. The scholastic trend could include Qudāmah bin Jaʿfar (died 337 H.; 968 CE), Ibn Wahab, al-Jurjānī in *Dalāʾil al-Iʿjāz* (Proofs of Inimitability), al-Khaṭṭābī (died 388 H.; 988 CE), al-Bāqillānī, al-Rummānī (died 386 H.; 996 CE), al-Sharif al-Raḍī (died 406 H.; 1016 CE), al-Razī (died 606 H.; 1209 CE), al-Sakkākī (died 626 H.; 1228 CE), al-Qazwīnī (died 739 H.; 1338 CE) al-Taftazānī (died 792 H.; 1389 CE), along with a large number of philologists and scholars.

Ibn al-Muʿtazz's *Kitāb al-Badīʿ* (Book of the New) gave impetus to a committed concern with rhetorical strategies and principles of address, especially "figures of speech and stylistic devices," as Bonebakker (1990, p. 390) rightly notices, along with issues "that were closer to grammar than to literary theory." His was a culmination of views already forwarded by others like ʿAmr bin al-ʿAlāʾ (died 154 H.; 770 CE), Khalaf al-Aḥmar (died 180 H.; 796 CE), Yūnus bin Habīb (died 182 H.; 798 CE), Thʿalab (died 291 H.; 904 CE), and al-Asmaʿī (died 828 CE) (see Bonebakker, 1990, p. 405). The actual significance of his work lies in the timing, organization, and articulation of a rhetorical principle and position, away from al-Jāḥiẓ's broad interdisciplinary spectrum. Here *elocutio* is given precedence, and the text gains greater recognition against context (Ṣammūd, 1994, p. 381). The book came out when there was a raging controversy over the poetry of the moderns, *al-muḥdithūn*, their elaborate use of figurative language. Especially regarding Abū Tammān's poetry (died 231 H.; 845 CE), there was a heated debate on poetry at large between *al-maṭbūʿ* (natural) and *al-maṣnūʿ* (artificial). Abū Tammam's innovation was criticized by some while

others argued that *al-badīʿ* (ornamentation and new figures) in his poetry is not foreign to tradition, including the Qurʾān. Critics wrote treatises that have formed the canon in rhetoric and criticism since then, establishing a tendency towards *wasāṭah* (mediation), and *muwāzanah* (balancing). In these writings by al-qaḍī ʿAbd al-ʿAzīz al-Jurjānī (392 H.; 1001 CE), Ibn Tabātabā (died 322 H.; 934 CE), al-Āmidī (died 370 H.; 981 CE), al-Ḥatimī (388 H.; 998 CE) among others, rhetorical devices are highlighted to bring about *ighrāb* (unusual rendition) and *taʿjīb* (surprise). Although Ibn al-Muʿtazz and his followers used antecedent authority, especially the Qurʾān, to corroborate the new, their argument is geared towards improvisation, where rhetoric becomes the domain of research.

Evolving through deliberate usage as "a principle of art" (Heinrichs, 1973, p. 25), *badīʿ* as rhetorical ornamentation was not systematically included in the science of rhetoric or eloquence before al-Qazwīnī's (died 739 H.; 1338 CE) *Talhkīṣ al-Miftāḥ* (Summation of the Key), which briefly organized al-Sakkākī's *Miftaḥ al-ʿUlūm* (Key to Sciences), and added *badīʿ* to its two other constituents: the science of *maʿānī* (notions, syntactic usage, and meanings), and the science of *bayān* (representational modes and eloquent expression). In other words, al-Razī (606 H.; 1209 CE), al-Sakkākī, and al-Qazwīnī, among others, made ʿAbd al-Qāhir al-Jurjānī's contribution to rhetoric as discipline more accessible and rewarding.

ʿAbd al-Qāhir Al-Jurjānī wrote *Asrār al-Balaghā* (Mysteries of Eloquence) as taxonomy for figurative stylization whereby *majāz* stands for tropical similarity among things, separate from nontropical devices already included by antecedent authority, such as Qudāmah in his *Jawāhir al-Alfāẓ* (Verbal Jewels). His *majāz mursal*, conceit, derives from contiguity in its deep structure, but is also based on incongruity among disparate elements, in a complementary relationship, a supplementation, whereby periphrasis, *kināyah*, among other tropes, suggests a hidden connection, a "meaning of meaning" that is inaccessible to surface reading. In *Dalāʾil al-Iʿjāz*, al-Jurjānī (1969, pp. 262–263) specifies a link, or medium, that leads to this hidden meaning, which unassisted verbalization cannot reach. The argument presupposes a reader-response, for al-Jurjānī (1954,

p. 8), in H. Ritter's stipulation, worked out "an aesthetic criticism justified by psychological argumentation." Distinguishing simile from analogy to advance his theory of *majāz* in its verbal and mental dimensions, al-Jurjānī contends that discourse derives eloquence from its tropical elements, including phantastic etiology with its reader-response, as the figure finds "an interesting fictitious cause for a fact in reality" (Heinrichs, 1998, p. 657). Metaphors displacing the metaphorical (see al-Jurjānī, 1954, p. 21) draw al-Jurjānī's attention, too, for his primary interest lies with "mysteries" of eloquence.

Although in tune with the notion of al-Jāḥiẓ (n.d., vol. 1, p. 75) of *bayān* as "conspicuous signification for a hidden meaning," and Qudāmah's notion of poetry as at its best when "the most lying" (Bonebakker, 1956, p. 36), ʿAbd al-Qāhir al-Jurjānī carries investigation and analysis beyond general rhetoric into domains of psychological interaction. Indeed, if both Qudāmah and Ibn al-Muʿtazz established a discipline of stylistic analysis that "resulted in . . . superfluous and affected embellishments" (Bonebakker, 1956, p. 46), al-Jurjānī raised questions in *Asrār al-Balaghā,* stimulated interest in tropics of discourse, and gave impetus, in his *Dalāʾil al-Iʿjāz,* to semantics as integral to rhetoric. It is in this last book that al-Jurjānī, the scholastic, towering over the scene, redirected the whole controversy over the *Qurʾānic majāz* into his theory of *naẓm,* structure or composition, whereby structural relations rather than words offer meanings.

Precursors and contemporaries, especially al-Rummānī, al-Bāqillānī, and al-Khaṭṭābī, offered significant contributions. Al-Rummānī divides rhetoric into ten parts, including compression, simile, metaphor, proportion, and so on, whereas al-Bāqillānī looks upon *naẓm* in view of poetic genres. The closest to ʿAbd al-Qāhir al-Jurjānī was al-Khaṭṭābī, who thinks of *naẓm* as placing words in their specific position. But al-Jurjānī (1372 H., p. 96) thinks that interrelatedness is a semantic aspect, for "words take a certain structure as servants and subordinates to meaning."

Such a concern with textual analysis implies a great shift of attention to writing. Rhetoric thereby assumed a status of its own, independent from eloquence. It should not surprise us that Ibn

Sinān al-Khafājī (died 466 H.; 1072 CE), a contemporary of ʿAbd al-Qāhir al-Jurjānī, specifies eloquence as prone to "description and depiction of words," whereas "rhetoric is both a description of words and meanings" (1932). Ahead in time, Abu Hilāl al-ʿAskarī (died 400 H.; 1010? CE) argued that "eloquence is a trait for the speaker not the speech" (1971).

The Twentieth Century. The amount of sophistication in rhetoric as science has impelled twentieth-century Arab intellectuals to search for a Hellenizing influence, based on comments and allusions to Greek *rhētors* and philosophers. Taha Hussein, Amīn al-Khūlī, Shukrī ʿAyād, and ʿAbd al-Rahmān Badawī spent effort and time to trace that influence; in subordination to Western tradition, they have bypassed the Indian and Persian (see Ṣammūd, 1994, p. 75–81; Bonebakker, 1990, p. 408). Yet al-Jāḥiẓ (n.d., vol. 3, pp. 27–28) had already criticized what he understood as the Greek lack of rhetorical output in contrast to their philosophy. With the exception of Qudāmah, argues G. E. von Grunebaum (1986, p. 983) on the basis of Bonebakker's study and edition of *Kitāb Naqd al-Shiʿr* (Book of Assaying Poetry), Greek presence is too thin to warrant discussion, for "Aristotle's ideas remained alien to the medieval Muslim." Aristotle's *Rhetoric* and *Poetics* had induced scholars like al-Ḥatimī (died 388 H.; 998 CE), for instance, to draw comparisons and to trace influences in al-Mutanabbī's poetry, as his *al-Risalah al-Hatimiyah* intends to demonstrate. In the main, as Heinrichs (1998, p. 654) contends, Aristotle's works "remained in the domain of philosophers for a long time while the literary theorists did not pay any attention." Bonebakker (1990, p. 408) is even more certain that the latter "were dealing with categories of literature quite different from those discussed by Aristotle."

As evidence of this particular nature of Arabic rhetoric, textbooks still retain al-Qazwinī's and al-Sakkākī's models of rhetorical classification. Along with al-Zamakhsharī's *al-Kashshāf,* these continue to provide popular textbooks, like ʿAlī al-Jarm's and M. Amīn's *al-Balāghah al-Wāḍihah* (Plain Rhetoric; Cairo, 1948), with methodology, systematization, and examples. But in an ironic reversal, and regardless of early twentieth-century efforts by Arab scholars to establish a connection with Greek rhetoric, twentieth-century Arabic rhetoric has been making achievements through deliberate recourse to tradition, resurrecting manuscripts and re-editing others. To challenge modernism, perhaps, or to face up to state manipulation of oratory, scholars have carried out extensive studies of rhetoric, in its scholastic, literary, and philological dimensions, as if to counteract both fusion into mass culture and state or political polemics of expediency and urgency. Between oratory for mass communication and rhetoric for the established cultured groups, many bygone arguments regain their validity and relevance.

BIBLIOGRAPHY

Abū Deeb, Kamal. "Literary Criticism." In *Abbasid Belles-Lettres*, edited by Julia Ashtiany, et. al., pp. 339–387. Cambridge, U.K., 1990. Coverage of literary criticism is provided, with a bias toward formalism.

Al-ʿAskarī, Abū Hilāl. *Kitāb al-Ṣināʿatayn* (Book of the Two Crafts, i.e., Poetry and Prose). P. 14. Cairo, 1971.

Bonebakker, S. A. *The Kitāb Naqd al-Šir of Qudāma b. Ǧaʿfar.* Leiden, Netherlands, 1956. The introduction is of some value, as it places the text (original translation) within the context of literary criticism.

Bonebakker, S. A. "Ibn al-Muʿtazz and Kitāb al-Badīʿ." In *Abbasid Belles-Lettres*, edited by Julia Ashtiany, et al., pp. 388–411. Cambridge, U.K., 1990. This reading attempts to explain the significance of the book; it is a careful, well-documented study.

Al-Fārābī. *Al-Ḥurūf*, edited by Muhsin Mehdi, p. 141. Beirut, 1970.

Gadamer, Hans-Georg. *Reason in the Age of Science*, translated by Frederick G. Lawrence, 1981; Cambridge, Mass., 1982.

Grunebaum, G. E. von. "Arabic Literary Criticism in the 10th Century." In *Themes in Medieval Arabic Literature*, edited with a foreword by D. S. Wilson, preface by S. Vryonis, Jr. London, 1981. A valid analysis, with the author's known taste for comparison with other cultures, especially Greek literature.

Grunebaum, G. E. von. "Balāgha." In *Encyclopedia of Islam*, new ed., edited by A. R. Gibb, et. al., pp. 981–983. Leiden, 1986. This is one of the main brief contributions on the subject.

Heinrichs, W. P. "Literary Theory: The Problem of Its Efficiency." In *Arabic Poetry: Theory and Development*, edited by G. E. von Grunebaum and Otto Harrassowitz. Wiesbaden, 1973. This contribution raises questions; it is well acquainted with Arabic criticism.

Heinrichs, W. P. "Rhetoric and Poetics." In *Encyclopedia of Arabic Literature*, edited by Julie Scott Meisami and Paul Starkey, vol. 2, pp. 651–662. London, 1998. Careful analysis, well-informed, leaning toward literary tradition.

Ibn Jinnī. *Al-Khaṣāʾiṣ.* Beirut, n.d.

Al-Jāḥiẓ. *Al-Bayān wa-al-Tabyīn*, edited by ʿAbd al-Salām Hārūn, 4 vols. Cairo, n.d.

Al-Jāḥiẓ. *Rasāʾil* (Epistles), edited by Ḥassan al-Sandūbī, p. 119. Cairo, 1933.

Al-Jāḥiẓ. *Al-Ḥaywān*, edited by ʿAbd al-Salām Hārūn. Cairo, 1969.

Al-Jurjānī, ʿAbd al-Qāhir. *Dalāʾil al-Iʿjāz.* Cairo, 1372 H.; also edited by A. M. Khafājī. Cairo, 1969.

Al-Jurjānī, ʿAbd al-Qāhir. *Asrār al-Balaghā* (Mysteries of Eloquence), edited by H. Ritter. Istanbul, 1954. Also edited by A. M. Khafājī. Cairo, 1972.

Al-Khafājī, Ibn Sinān. *Sirr al-Faṣāḥah* (Secret of Eloquence). Pp. 3–4. Cairo, 1932.

Kratchkovsky, Ignatius, ed. *Kitāb al-Badīʿ of ʿAbd Allāh Ibn al-Muʿtazz.* London, 1935.

Al-Sakkākī. *Miftāḥ al-ʿUlūm.* Cairo, 1937.

Ṣammūd, Hammādī. *Al-Tafkīr al-Balāghī ʿinda al-ʿArab* (Arab Rhetorical Thought). 1981; reprinted Tunis, 1994.

Smyth, William. "Rhetoric and ʿIlm al-Balāgha: Christianity and Islam." *Muslim World* 82. 3–4, (July–October 1992), pp. 242–255. An attempt to compare and to specify difference; it may prove useful to nonspecialists.

Smyth, William. "The Making of a Textbook." *Studia Islamica* (Paris) (1993), pp. 99–115. General survey, with good listing of primary material for the nonspecialist.

—MUHSIN J. AL-MUSAWI

ARGUMENTATION

ARGUMENTATION is the study of reasoning-giving used by people to justify their beliefs and values and to influence the thought and action of others. Its central concern is with the rationality or reasonableness of claims put forward in discourse. This, in turn, depends on whether the claims are warranted, or grounded in evidence and inference that are themselves acceptable and hence constitute good reasons for the claim. [*See* Inference.] There is a strong normative or evaluative component to argumentation, and a strong pedagogical dimension to its study, although there are also many descriptive studies that identify what people take to be good reasons for claims in various contexts and situations.

The scope of argumentation studies is vast. Argumentation can be conceived as a particular type of discourse or as a perspective that might be applied to any discourse, focusing on its reason-giving dimension. The former approach would distinguish argumentation from genres such as description and narration that are not overtly about making claims and giving reasons. The latter approach, however, might identify implicit reasoning structures in stories or in the selection of elements in a description, and might even examine nonverbal or nondiscursive "texts" as exercises in making and defending claims.

Similarly, the unit of analysis in argumentation might vary anywhere from the components of an individual argument to a social controversy that develops over time. "Micro" level studies examine individual claims, describe how they work, and assess their strength. Midrange studies examine the assembly of claims into larger units such as a speech or an essay. "Macro" level studies explore the dynamics of controversy in which multiple advocates participate and which is likely to extend across time.

Even this description, however, does not capture the diversity of argumentation studies. There are differences in belief about the fundamental characteristics of argument and the perspective from which it is studied. Daniel J. O'Keefe (1982) distinguished between "making an argument" and "having an argument," the former designating a kind of text and the latter, a kind of interaction. From this work came the distinction between argument as product and as process. Joseph Wenzel (1992) proposed an influential tripartite division of product, procedure, and process. "Procedure" refers to regulative conventions such as those characterizing courtroom argument or legislative debate, whereas "process" identifies the emergence, management, and resolution of disagreements in ordinary, informal interaction. The product/procedure/process distinction has become commonplace. A fourth perspective, identified most notably with the work of Dale Hample (1992), regards argumentation as a cognitive process that occurs within the individual prior to interaction. This orientation, however, has not attracted the same degree of scholarly attention as have the three approaches identified by Wenzel.

Argumentation also has been classified as representing the perspectives of logic, dialectic, and rhetoric. This is a useful category scheme but it does not map directly onto Wenzel's categories of product, procedure, and process. For example, texts can be the product of dialectic or rhetoric as well as of logic. For that matter, the term *logic* embraces both the tradition of formal logic and the work of informal logicians who have embraced concepts of procedure that are akin to dialectic. [*See* Dialectic; *and* Logic.]

Argumentation as Product. Until recently, argumentation studies were dominated by studies of texts, whether individual claims or larger units of discourse. Argumentative discourse is distinguished from narration, description, and exposition by the fact that it makes claims on the audience and seeks to justify them. Textual studies were guided primarily by the standards of logic, and the principal purpose of such studies was to assess whether the arguments were valid. They were if the conclusion followed inescapably from the premises. This did not mean that the conclusions were true, but that *if* the premises were true, then the conclusion had to be. The model logical form is the syllogism, a series of propositional claims, with identifiable premises that entail the conclusion. [*See* Syllogism.] If the form of the argument is not correct, so that the conclusion is not entailed, then the syllogism is invalid. Validity, then, is a test of form that is unrelated to the content of the argument. The principal types of syllogisms are the categorical (containing statements about categories), the conditional (containing an if–then statement), and the disjunctive (with either–or statements and conclusions about the presence or absence of one of the alternatives). The syllogism was taken as the model for argumentation and less structured arguments sometimes were described as "applied formalism." The assumption was that they aspired to but fell short of the standards of the syllogism.

During the twentieth century, groups of scholars questioned the prominent position of the syllogism in argumentation studies. These critics included, among others, philosophers Stephen Toulmin and Chaim Perelman and logicians C. L. Hamblin and Douglas Walton. Their most basic position is that the syllogism is an inappropriate paradigm for argument. It describes a very atypical mode of reasoning, that which occurs within a closed system where the conclusion merely rearranges information already implicit in the premises. Reasoning about matters of human affairs, critics suggested, could not and should not approach this standard. Whereas formal logic is deductive, most instances of reasoning are inductive, making (and justifying) an inferential leap from what is already known to the conclusion one wishes to establish. Toulmin (1958) proposed an alternative structure of argument encompassing elements of probability rather than certainty. In addition to the data, warrant (the major premise of the syllogism), and claim, he added qualifiers, rebuttals, and backing. With these additional elements, he regards the strength of an argument as a matter of degree. His model has been used widely in the teaching of argumentation, although some critics maintain that *any* model or schematic representation of argument is a distortion of the processes of inference and reasoning that naturally occur. Perelman (1963) proposed the rule of justice as the most basic standard of validity: essentially similar beings should be treated in the same way. Informal logicians such as Hamblin (1970) and Walton (1995) have concentrated on argument patterns that formal logic would regard as fallacies. To the informal logicians, though, many of these reasoning patterns are sometimes perfectly reasonable. Whether they are fallacious or not depends on more than just the form of the argument; it also involves assumptions underlying the context in which they are used. Their work takes into account human experience, differences in meaning, and conventions of language use, rather than just matters of form, in order to determine whether arguments are valid.

Scholars in rhetoric also have questioned the appropriateness of the syllogism as the central model for reasoning. To them, an arguer seeks not to repeat what is already known but to move an audience from its starting point to acceptance of the position he or she wishes to advance. Rhetorical scholars therefore call attention not to the syllogism, but to its close relative the enthymeme, as described in the work of Aristotle (384–322 BCE). Rather than being merely a syllogism with a premise missing, the enthymeme takes its premises—whether explicit or implicit—from the accepted beliefs of the audience. [*See* Enthy-

meme.] These beliefs form the audience's stock of social knowledge and frame the test of valid rhetorical arguments. The assumption is that the rhetor reasons with an audience and cannot compose a valid argument except in cooperation with the audience. [*See* Social knowledge.]

Argument as Procedure. Studies of argument as procedure begin with the assumption that argumentation differs from other modes of expressing disagreement (taunts, epithets) by the presence of rules or norms that regulate the conduct of discourse. At the most basic level, the presence of an adversary itself imposes norms on argumentation. Since one's arguments are open to scrutiny or refutation by a counterarguer, one has every incentive to put forward strong and compelling arguments; weak or fallacious ones will be less likely to withstand the scrutiny of an interlocutor. This competitive character of argumentation is sometimes criticized as undermining respect for persons and interpersonal sensitivity, but this will not be the case if arguers recognize that the reciprocal nature of their relationship—as advocates and interlocutors simultaneously—helps to regulate their disagreement and contributes to the quality of their discourse.

In some settings, more explicit rules and conventions exist. Legal and scientific argumentation are perhaps the most obvious examples, but within most professions there are established modes for characterizing evidence and reasoning from it. [*See* Politics, *article on* The personal, technical, and public spheres of argument.] Legislative settings and many public debates are also guided by procedural conventions. These include not only superficial matters such as the equal division of time between advocates but also more basic issues such as the assignment of the burden of proof and specification of what counts as discharging this burden. The purpose of procedural regulations is the same as that of the construct of validity in formal logic: to increase the chance of obtaining sound conclusions and to minimize the risk of accepting unsound ones. The justification for any particular procedure is either that over time it has led to these results or that, because of something in its nature, it is likely to do so.

In recent years, the argument-as-procedure perspective also has been applied to more informal arguments. An approach known as pragma-dialectics has been developed by scholars at the University of Amsterdam under the leadership of van Eemeren and Grootendorst. Their work relies on speech-act theory, which proposes "felicity conditions" or states to be achieved for an utterance to count as a speech act of a given type—a threat or a promise, for example. Applying this approach to argumentative discussions, they identify standards that they believe help to establish how well the discourse meets the conditions of the ideal discourse for resolving the dispute at hand. These range from the rule that the parties in an argumentative discussion must not prevent each other from advancing or casting doubt on standpoints, to the rules that neither party may use formulations that are insufficiently clear, and that one must interpret the other party's formulations as carefully and accurately as possible. The framework of rules can function both as an evaluative tool for the analyst of argument and as guidance for the arguers themselves. [*See* Speech acts, utterances as.]

The work of Douglas Walton is also relevant here. Walton's analyses of various formal fallacies are rooted in the assumption that people engage in dialogues of different types and functions—information-seeking dialogue and persuasion dialogue, for example. What determines whether an argument really is fallacious or whether it is valid is the dialogue context in which it is used. Hence the identification of the dialogue type in which arguers are engaged helps to clarify the procedural conventions regulating the use of argument in dialogues of that type. [*See* Fallacies.]

Argument as Process. The focus on argument as process has emerged primarily since about 1970 within studies in interpersonal communication. Here the focus is on how people engaged in everyday argument—"naive social actors," as they often are described in the literature—conduct and seek to resolve disagreement. The primary data for scholars come from naturally occurring talk in which overt opposition is present. Opposition develops when two or more people maintain what they take to be incompatible statements. By analyzing transcripts of conversation, scholars explore how the disagreement is expanded or narrowed and whether or how it is resolved. Sally Jackson and Scott Jacobs (1982; 1992) are the scholars most associated with the conversational analysis of arguments. Drawing on personal construct theory, Charles Willard (1989) has theorized about the implications of regarding argumentation primarily as a type of interaction. There are close parallels between conversational analysis and pragma-dialectics. In a collaborative project, van Eemeren, Grootendorst, Jackson, and Jacobs (1993) undertook both to reconstruct naturally occurring arguments through conversational analysis and to evaluate them by applying the standards of pragma-dialectics.

A particular application of the argument-as-process perspective has focused on how children are socialized into the speech-act conventions of arguing—how they come to understand the nature of claims and inferences, and what form their own argumentative exchanges take. Among the scholars pursuing this line of inquiry are Barbara J. O'Keefe and Pamela Benoit (1982). Argumentative competence, in their studies, has been found to relate to one's developing general knowledge about language, interaction, and conversational structure.

[*See also* Argument fields; *and* Logos.]

BIBLIOGRAPHY

Benoit, William L., Dale Hample, and Pamela J. Benoit, eds. *Readings in Argumentation*. New York, 1992. Reproduces major articles on argumentation theory that originally appeared in scholarly journals.

Brockriede, Wayne. "Where is Argument?" *Journal of the American Forensic Association* 11 (Spring 1975), pp. 179–182. Identifies defining characteristics of argumentative discourse.

Cox, J. Robert, and Charles A. Willard, eds. *Advances in Argumentation Theory and Research*. Carbondale, Ill., 1982. Original essays examining the scope of argumentation and the state of research in the field.

Ehninger, Douglas. "Argument as Method: Its Nature, Its Limitations, and Its Uses." *Communication Monographs* 37 (June 1970), pp. 101–110. Develops the idea that argumentation is a self-regulating procedure.

Hamblin, C. L. *Fallacies*. London, 1970.

Hample, Dale. "A Third Perspective on Argument." In *Readings in Argumentation*, edited by William L. Benoit, Dale Hample, and Pamela J. Benoit, pp. 91–115. New York, 1992.

Jackson, Sally, and Scott Jacobs. "Conversational Argument: A Discourse Analytic Approach." In *Advances in Argumentation Theory and Research*, edited by J. Robert Cox and Charles A. Willard, pp. 205–237. Carbondale, Ill., 1982.

Jackson, Sally, and Scott Jacobs. "Structure of Conversational Argument: Pragmatic Bases of the Enthymeme." In *Readings in Argumentation,* edited by William L. Benoit, Dale Hample, and Pamela J. Benoit, pp. 681–706. New York, 1992.

O'Keefe, Barbara J., and Pamela Benoit. "Children's Arguments." In *Advances in Argumentation Theory and Research,* edited by J. Robert Cox and Charles A. Willard, pp. 154–183. Carbondale, Ill., 1982.

O'Keefe, Daniel J. "The Concepts of Argument and Arguing." In *Advances in Argumentation Theory and Research,* edited by J. Robert Cox and Charles A. Willard, pp. 3–23. Carbondale, Ill., 1982.

Perelman, Chaim. *The Idea of Justice and the Problem of Argument.* Translated by J. Petrie. London, 1963.

Toulmin, Stephen. *The Uses of Argument.* Cambridge, U.K., 1958. Includes a presentation of the model Toulmin offers as an alternative to the syllogism.

van Eemeren, Frans H., Rob Grootendorst, Sally Jackson, and Scott Jacobs. *Reconstructing Argumentative Discourse.* Tuscaloosa, Ala., 1993. Integrates the perspectives of pragma-dialectics and conversation analysis.

van Eemeren, Frans H., Rob Grootendorst, Francisca Snoeck Henkemans, et al. *Fundamentals of Argumentation Theory: A Handbook of Historical Backgrounds and Contemporary Developments.* Mahwah, N.J., 1996. Overview essays of major current approaches to argumentation studies with a special emphasis on pragma-dialectics and related theories.

Walton, Douglas. *A Pragmatic Theory of Fallacy.* Tuscaloosa, Ala., 1995. Demonstrates that whether many argument forms are fallacious depends on the context in which they are used.

Wenzel, Joseph W. "Perspective on Argument." In *Readings in Argumentation,* edited by William L. Benoit, Dale Hample, and Pamela J. Benoit, pp. 121–143. New York, 1992.

Willard, Charles Arthur. *A Theory of Argumentation.* Tuscaloosa, Ala., 1989. Elaborates the perspective of argumentation as a kind of interaction, studied as a process.

Williams, David Cratis, and Michael David Hazen, eds. *Argumentation Theory and the Rhetoric of Assent.* Tuscaloosa, Ala., 1990. Collected essays addressing what counts as a warrant for inferences in argumentation.
— DAVID ZAREFSKY

ARGUMENT FIELDS. Argument fields are subdivisions of rhetorical argument according to its subject matter or context. [*See* Argumentation.] The assumption is that different norms characterize argument practice and evaluation in different fields. The concept of fields stands in opposition to the belief, often thought to characterize formal logic, that there are universal standards for evaluating an argument's strength. During the twentieth century, scholars in both rhetoric and informal logic increasingly held that the quest for universal, formal standards made impossible the assessment of argument in the practical realm of human affairs, where the purity of formal logic could not be achieved. [*See* Logic.] Rather than limit the applicability of argumentation only to formal, closed systems, and consign human affairs to the unreasonable, scholars saw context-based systems of argument evaluation as an attractive alternative.

The term *fields* is associated with the work of Stephen Toulmin. In *The Uses of Argument* (1958, p. 14), he wrote that "two arguments will be said to belong to the same field when the data and conclusions in each of the two arguments are, respectively, of the same logical type." Within a given field, there are accepted standards, drawn from the practice of that field, for assessing arguments. By making fields the arbiters of their own reasoning practices, Toulmin pointed to a middle ground between universal, formal validity, and utter relativism.

Approaches to Classifying Fields. The demarcation of an argument field, however, proved to be a frustrating exercise, because there was little or no understanding of what made data and conclusions of the same "logical type." Accordingly, the literature is replete with efforts to describe fields in different ways and with case studies purporting to identify distinct argument fields. While this work emphasizes the richness of context in understanding and interpreting arguments, it has not established the particular utility of the concept of fields as categories into which arguments may be placed.

Toulmin did not develop the field idea further in 1958, but in a later work, *Human Understanding* (1972), he treats fields as "rational enterprises" and largely equates them with academic disciplines. In contrast to his earlier work, which implied that "logical types" were prepositional forms, he now seemed to suggest that fields were occupied not by arguments but by people. In doing so, he shifted the focus from types of *text* or *inference* to types of *activity* or *procedure.* Other writers have followed in this tradition.

In *Human Understanding*, Toulmin contends that reasoning practices in "compact" disciplines such as atomic physics are different from those in "diffuse" disciplines such as history, different from those in "would-be" disciplines such as literary criticism, and different from those in "undisciplined" areas such as communication, and "undisciplinable" areas such as the arts. On this reading, it would appear that an argument's subject matter determines what field it is in, because thinkers in different disciplines make different assumptions or reason in different ways.

An alternative understanding, though, would equate fields not with particular academic disciplines but with general worldviews or frameworks that cross disciplinary boundaries. So, for example, behaviorist, Freudian, Marxist, or feminist arguments could each be seen as being of the same logical type regardless of the specific content or the disciplines in which they arise. On this view, too, arguments in critical legal studies, critical rhetoric, and some varieties of political economy, for example, would be seen as being of the same logical type.

Yet another approach to classifying arguments into fields is to group them according to the purpose of the arguers. Arguers who share the same purpose will produce discourse that differs from that produced by arguers with a different purpose. Those whose goal is problem solving, for example, will argue differently from those whose goal is persuasion or from those whose goal is exploration of new ideas. This view of argument fields closely resembles the classification by Douglas Walton (1999) of types of dialogue. Walton, for instance, distinguishes persuasion dialogue (including critical discussion) from negotiation or from eristic (argument for argument's sake). This approach recognizes that purpose may be a key determinant of the rhetorical situation and of the type of dialogue that ensues. Yet attempts to classify fields by purpose have encountered difficulties. Arguers often have multiple purposes; reduction to a single purpose is both unrealistic and unfaithful to context. Meaningful discussion does occur among people who have widely different purposes. Many political arguments, for example, result in compromises among arguers with different goals who reach the same conclusion for different reasons. Arguers may not always know their own purposes, and even when they do, the analyst or critic may not.

Are All Arguments in Fields? These three examples of classification illustrate the difficulties of moving from a general notion that arguments may vary by context, to the specific task of determining what field encompasses the argument and arguers in a given case. An even more fundamental question is whether all arguments lie within one or more fields, or whether there are reasoning structures that do not belong to a field. This question emerges with particular force when one seeks to examine arguments cast very broadly and addressed to the general public. Is public argument a separate field, or is there some qualitative difference between arguments located in the public forum and those set in the more limited context of a particular field? This question is sharply posed in a contrast between the work of Charles Arthur Willard (1990) and that of G. Thomas Goodnight (1982). For Willard, the public is a space in which arguments occur, and it is characterized by interfield borrowing—discourse in which the reasoning structures of one field come up against those of another. Willard's frequently cited example is the interaction that results when advocates of creationism and evolution come together to engage each other across field boundaries.

Goodnight, on the other hand, *contrasts* public argument with field-specific argument. Indeed, he moves beyond the concept of fields to talk about *spheres* of argument. Arguments addressed to people in general fall within the public sphere; those that occur within a specific field are grouped into the technical sphere (Goodnight also discusses a personal sphere of argument). [*See* Politics, *article on* The personal, public, and technical spheres of argument.] For Goodnight, the claim to specialized expertise may give one standing to make and settle arguments within a given field (in the technical sphere) but there is no such preference within the public sphere. Indeed, the public sphere is the place where citizens participate on equal grounds. In the public sphere, meaningfulness is not derived from any special feature of the argument known to experts but from the common judgment and accumulated "social knowledge" of citizens. Although the analogy is hardly perfect, Goodnight's distinction is like that which Perelman and Olbrechts-Tyteca invoke in *The*

New Rhetoric (Notre Dame, Ind., 1969) between two ideal notions of audience: the particular and the universal. The former consists of people who share a common framework, however it is defined. The latter, however, is imagined as a congress of all reasonable people—not all of whom would accept the specific judgments of a particular field. Similarly, for Goodnight, arguments in the public sphere must transcend the limits imposed by people in a particular field. What defines reasonableness in the public sphere, on this view, is a culture's accumulated store of knowledge and experience. This "social knowledge," rather than either formal logic or field-specific assumptions, becomes the standard for argument evaluation and critique. [*See* Social knowledge.]

Goodnight's particular concern is the shifting relationship between the technical and the public sphere. In his opinion, the technical sphere is eclipsing the public. That is, discourse that ought to engage the broad public sphere is instead defined as a technical matter to be discussed within a particular field. This has the effect of removing significant voices from discussion and employing a restricted perspective for argument evaluation. This is a special danger when the subject of the argument is complex, such as nuclear power, economics, or foreign policy.

The difference between Goodnight and Willard is not unlike that between classical liberalism and civic republicanism, and it at least obliquely raises the question, "who decides who decides" the appropriate standards that rhetorical arguments should meet. The liberal view would hold that this is an empirical question to be determined by the clash between opposing advocates in an unregulated marketplace under the assumption of equal access. The civic republican view, in contrast, would hold that a priori assumptions come into play about the need for public virtues to counter private vices.

Do Differences among Fields Matter? Among fields—whether they are thought to comprise only the technical sphere or all of argumentation—the assumption is that there are differences in one or more significant aspects of the interaction or of the discourse it produces. These differences could relate to the structure of underlying assumptions—what is taken as a given, what is rejected out of hand, and what must be proved. Or they could relate to preferences among the types of evidence—whether expert testimony or experimental data carries more probative force, for example. Or fields might differ as to the preferred mode of reasoning, such as the deductive application of "covering laws" versus inductive generalization. Or the difference might relate to the level of confidence required in order to accept a conclusion, such as the difference between "prevalence of the evidence" and "significant at the 0.01 level." Unless fields are shown to differ in some respect other than just by definition, then the identification of fields—particularly subject-matter fields—may be a distinction without a difference. In the existing literature, however, there are far more attempts to define fields or to locate specific arguments within a field than comparative assessments of how fields differ.

Likewise, it is difficult to make inferences from a field to its characteristics or vice versa. If distinctions among fields matter, then the knowledge that one is in the field of law, for instance, should make it possible to predict the characteristics of the argument and to distinguish them from arguments in a different field. Conversely, from the characteristics of a given argument, one should be able to predict what field it is in. But there is little evidence that this is the case. Arguments from precedent, from testimony, and from similarity and difference—typical examples of legal argument—frequently are found in nonlegal controversies as well. And if the suggestion is that fields differ in validity standards rather than in the components of argument, the same problem presents itself. Although it is widely accepted that an argument's validity depends on context as interpreted by people, there are few attempts to map these standards onto fields (or other categories of argument that transcend individual cases). To suggest, for example, that cost-benefit analysis is the appropriate standard for assessing public policy arguments, invites challenge on two levels. It is neither the appropriate standard for *all* public policy arguments nor the standard *exclusively* for public policy arguments. The same problems emerge with other proposed field-dependent (rather than situation-specific) standards.

McKerrow (1980) uses the term *argument communities* in approximately the same sense that other writers use the term *fields*. But there is an important, though perhaps subtle, difference. A field might be thought of as existing in the natural world, whereas a community is clearly constituted by people. Despite Toulmin's early statement that fields differ by the "logical type" of their arguments, fields really are not logical or rational categories. They are constructed by people in dialectical and rhetorical situations and hence are primarily sociological or cultural. Because people wish to convince others, they reject sheer relativism and recognize the need for an impartial standpoint of rationality to which they and others can subscribe. Because people recognize the inadequacies of formal logic in the realm of practical affairs, they seek a standard that is intersubjective rather than objective. These basic principles, buttressed by case studies of actual argumentative situations, explain the usefulness and the appeal of the concept of argument fields. But beyond this fundamental level of understanding, field theory has not progressed very far.

[*See also* Logos.]

BIBLIOGRAPHY

Farrell, Thomas B. "Knowledge, Consensus, and Rhetorical Theory." *Quarterly Journal of Speech,* 62 (February 1976), pp. 1–14. Distinguishes between technical knowledge and social knowledge.

Goodnight, G. Thomas. "The Personal, Technical, and Public Spheres of Argument: A Speculative Inquiry into the Art of Public Deliberation." *Journal of the American Forensic Association* 18 (Spring 1982), pp. 214–227. Distinguishes the nature of arguing within each sphere.

McKerrow, Ray E. "Argument Communities: A Quest for Distinctions." *Proceedings of the [First] Summer Conference on Argumentation*, pp. 214–227. Falls Church, Va., 1980.

Rowland, Robert C. "The Influence of Purpose on Fields of Argument." *Journal of the American Forensic Association* 18 (Spring 1982), pp. 228–245. Suggests that fields should be defined by the purpose of the arguers.

Toulmin, Stephen E. *Human Understanding*, vol. 1. Princeton, 1972. Explores how the process of coming to know varies across disciplines.

Toulmin, Stephen E. *The Uses of Argument*. Cambridge, U.K., 1958. Pleads for a nonformal sense of argument and develops a model for it.

Walton, Douglas. *One-Sided Arguments: A Dialectical Analysis of Bias*. Albany, N.Y., 1999. Chapter 2 offers a succinct classification of dialogue types.

Willard, Charles Arthur. "Argument Fields and Theories of Logical Types." *Journal of the American Forensic Association* 17 (Winter 1981), pp. 129–145. Regards fields as sociological entities whereas types are logical forms.

Willard, Charles Arthur. *A Theory of Argumentation*. Tuscaloosa, Ala., 1990. Develops the case for a sociological conception of argument.

—DAVID ZAREFSKY

ARRANGEMENT. [*This entry comprises two articles. The first article describes the traditional theory and practice of the parts of oratory from Aristotle through the Hellenistic treatises to Cicero and beyond. The second article examines modern arrangement and discusses the place of form in the composition and analysis of discourse, with particular attention to strategies of arrangement in composition and to formalism in criticism.*]

Traditional arrangement

The study of classical rhetoric is often introduced by citing the five canons of rhetoric: invention, arrangement, style, memory, and delivery. Approaching the discipline of rhetoric by arranging it into discrete components reveals, indirectly, how endemic taxonomy was to the discipline and, directly, how important the canon of arrangement (Gk. *taxis;* Lat. *dispositio*) was to classical rhetoric. It sustained the attention of both theoreticians and practitioners of rhetoric because its functions and benefits were manifold, both in the classical period and beyond.

Arrangement in Greek Rhetoric. By the fifth century BCE, rhetoric had begun to evolve into a formal discipline, and it had become clear during that time that arrangement could be a *dynamis,* a source of power in persuasion. That is, the earliest efforts to structure language to enhance persuasion reveal that arrangement could be used as a heuristic device for argumentative effect. By legend, Corax and Tisias are credited with the discovery of rhetoric as a "discipline" because they offered a systematic approach to arguing civil cases in Syracuse in the early fifth century BCE (Enos, 1993). These "stories" of the origins of rhetoric as a formal discipline are contested on many fronts, ranging from the very existence of Corax to the dating of "rhetoric" as a discipline (Schiappa, 1999). Yet, the extant accounts all assert that one of the earliest features of rhetoric was that Corax advanced both the notion of probability *and* patterns of arranging speeches. If we are to believe these early accounts, there is a clear recognition of the relationship between the creation of probable arguments and the patterns of arrangement to structure those probable arguments.

Although Plato (c.429–347 BCE) was one of rhetoric's strongest critics, he nonetheless recognized the importance of arrangement in rhetoric. In his *Phaedrus*, Plato has his dialogue-character Socrates examine the merits of rhetoric in order to consider its legitimacy as a discipline worthy of study. During this interrogation, Socrates asserts that rhetoric must attend to arrangement if it is to meet the tests of a true *technē* or art. For Socrates (as Plato has him say), arrangement is both a natural and an important feature of language. Plato believed that discourse should be arranged like a natural, living creature, with a body and component parts (264C). For Plato, however, this natural pattern of arrangement was not for the purpose of sophistic euphony of juxtaposing ideas, even through probable argument, but rather to facilitate the analysis and synthesis of ultimate causes and essences.

Plato challenged the legitimacy of sophistic rhetoric, in part, because of its limited use of arrangement as an expedient method of packaging argument. [*See* Sophists.] Aristotle (384–322 BCE), however, saw arrangement as meeting the pragmatic needs of sophistic rhetoric, but also as a heuristic for facilitating judgment (*krisis*) through rational deliberation (*phronēsis*). [*See* Judgment; *and* Phronēsis.] Aristotle's discussion of arrangement comes late in the *Rhetoric* (3.13 ff.). In Book 3 (13.4), Aristotle states that a speech should only need two parts: the first to advance a thesis (*prothesis*), and the second to offer proofs (*pisteis*). At this level, Aristotle claims, rhetorical argument is akin to its counterpart, dialectic, which requires the statement of a problem and demonstration (13.2–3). Yet, Aristotle goes on to assert, the very nature of rhetoric requires at least four components: an *exordium* or introduction (*prooimion*), an advanced thesis (*prothesis*), proofs (*pisteis*), and a

conclusion (*epilogos*). Aristotle realized that audiences determine the reasonableness, and therefore the saliency, of an argument. In order, then, for auditors and readers to render a positive judgment, the rhetor must arrange the discourse in harmony with the mentalities, and even the appetites, of his listeners.

Hellenistic and Roman Notions of Arrangement. The principles of arrangement developed in early Greek rhetoric became a part of advanced education in later antiquity (post fifth century BCE to fifth century CE). Two extant manuals of rhetoric reflect how arrangement was viewed in Hellenistic education and in early Roman schools of rhetoric: the *Rhetorica ad Alexandrum* (c.340 BCE) and the *Rhetorica ad Herennium* (c.86–82 BCE). Both works reflect an orientation to *declamatio*, the advanced study and practice of oral and written persuasion, which was popularized in the Hellenistic period and later solidified in the educational practices of the Roman Empire. In both works, the emphasis is on preparation for civic functions, which is especially evident in their treatment of arrangement. [*See* Declamation.]

The *Rhetorica ad Alexandrum* is an extant *technē* of rhetoric that is complete to the extent that it offers us a substantial artifact of sophistic rhetoric. Intended as a practical text, the *Rhetorica ad Alexandrum* is oriented toward the direct application of rhetorical principles in civic functions and, in this respect, is different from its later Roman counterpart, the *Rhetorica ad Herennium*, which is clearly directed toward schools of declamation. The *Rhetorica ad Alexandrum* treats three types of civic rhetoric: deliberative, epideictic, and forensic (1421b). [*See* Deliberative genre; Epideictic genre; *and* Forensic genre.] While arrangement is treated in each of these three types of rhetoric, it is most fully explicated in the first area, deliberative rhetoric, under the conventional parts of introduction, narration, proof (affirmative and refutative), and a summary that often concludes with an emotional appeal. The four parts of arrangement are modified when epideictic and forensic rhetoric are treated. In epideictic rhetoric, for example, attention is given to the topic selection of the ceremonial occasion. In forensic rhetoric, attention is given to confirming proofs and to anticipating and refuting opposing arguments. In the *Rhetorica ad Alexandrum*, the modifications for adapting arrangement are driven by the more macroscopic expectations of the genres of civic rhetoric and not, as we shall see in later Roman works, to the more microscopic (and localized) relationship between invention and arrangement in each part of the discourse. We may infer, if primacy reveals importance, that the *Rhetorica ad Alexandrum* was a pragmatic manual composed with the intent of laying out the procedural expectations of topics and their patterns of explication for immediate application to civic purposes. Later *technai* will stress a more pedagogical focus rather than an immediate application, particularly how arrangement can nurture creativity and cogent argument.

The *Rhetorica ad Herennium* is a highly prescribed and complicated *technē* (or in Latin, *ratio*). As Harry Caplan comments in the introduction to his translation of the text, the *Rhetorica ad Herennium* reflects Hellenistic rhetorical teaching, is oriented toward the schools of declamation and the study of models, and is in effect "Greek art in Latin dress, combining a Roman spirit with Greek doctrine" (vii, xvii). The unknown author of the *Rhetorica ad Herennium* maintains that *inventio* is inherent in all six parts of rhetorical discourse: *exordium, narratio, divisio, confirmatio, confutatio,* and *conclusio* (1.3.4; 3.9.16). The author offers a detailed analysis of the constituents of these six parts to show how an argument's structure is to be modified to accommodate *inventio*. As Caplan observes, this pattern of arrangement is a departure from the scheme prescribed by Aristotle in his *Rhetoric* and is closer to the Stoic format that included refutation, which is here labeled *confutatio* (8–9, n.a; Diogenes Laertius 7.43).

Another important feature of arrangement in the *Rhetorica ad Herennium* is the incorporation (and Latinization) of the Greek concept of *stasis,* or identification of the essential disagreement, into the structure of the argument, principally in the *confirmatio* where the point at issue (*constitutio causa*) is put forth. [*See* Stasis.] Modifications to the schemes of arrangement are discussed in Book 3 under deliberative and epideictic rhetoric, but these adaptations are treated as derivative to the detailed explication given in Book 1. The author, in fact, underscores the importance of flexibility by recalling the two general methods of arrangement. The first is an adherence to the six

parts set forth in the precepts of rhetoric discussed in Book 1. The second genera of arrangement is one that must be *ad hoc;* that is, arrangement dictated by the context and circumstances of the particular situation (3.9.16). In this latter, "natural" mode, the order prescribed by the rules of the *ratio* must accommodate to conditions (3.9.17). In the *Rhetorica ad Herennium,* we see a manual that is highly prescriptive yet inclusive enough to encourage modification, and even the abandonment of schemes of arrangement, if the situation so dictates.

Marcus Tullius Cicero (106–43 BCE)—Roman statesman, orator, and rhetorician—offered what would become the most popularized pattern of arrangement in the West with his first work on rhetoric, *De inventione* (86 BCE). In his later *De oratore* (55 BCE), Cicero urged readers to dismiss what he wrote in his first effort as the writings of a youthful schoolboy. Despite his request, Cicero's *De inventione* became a major rhetorical text used throughout the Middle Ages. His comments on arrangement persisted through the Renaissance, serving as a guide not only for argument but also in the epistolary manuals of *ars dictaminis* or the art of letter writing. Cicero put forth a seven- (not six-) part pattern for arranging compositions: *exordium, narratio, partitio, confirmatio, reprehensio,* an optional *digressio,* and *conclusio* (*De inventione* 1.19–109; the discussion on the optional *digressio* as the seventh component can be seen in 1.97). As even a cursory reading of *De inventione* reveals, within each of these seven divisions are internal heuristics to further aid rhetors in creating and structuring arguments for each respective division. As mentioned above, however, *De inventione* was composed when Cicero was quite young, and he modified his views and patterns of arrangement significantly in his later *Partitiones oratoriae* (c.50 BCE), encouraging much greater flexibility in structuring compositions to the context of the situation (*Partitiones oratoriae* 9.27). Cicero's modifications to the patterns of arrangement underscore his belief that these schemes of arrangement are intended to aid in both the structure and the invention of discourse, a theme which Quintilian was later to pursue in his *Institutio oratoria* (c.94–95 CE). [*See* Invention.]

The relationship of arrangement to invention is evident in Cicero's other rhetorical works. Cicero's most detailed statement on invention is his *Topica* (44 BCE). As the opening passages of this work reveal, any system of discourse must consider invention and, to that end, *topoi* or "places" are discussed to facilitate the creation of ideas (*Topica* 97–99). Throughout his career, Cicero saw arrangement as central to rhetoric. Believing that invention is localized in rhetoric, he argued that ideas must be appropriate not only to the situation but also to the appropriate "place" within the discourse. For Cicero, invention occurs within a domain; arrangement provides a structure, an heuristic, for the creation of ideas. In this respect, Ciceronian patterns of arrangement, with highly defined and localized schēmata, are intended to stimulate effective and responsive rhetoric.

Cicero's views on the interrelationship between invention and arrangement are in harmony with those of other Roman rhetoricians, especially Marcus Fabius Quintilian (35–c.95 CE). His comments on arrangement in the *Institutio oratoria* are especially important, occupying major portions of Books 4 to 6. Quintilian draws his views on arrangement from two primary sources: Greek rhetorical theory, especially the works of Aristotle and Isocrates, and the theory and practice of his Roman model, Cicero. In his introduction to Book 7, Quintilian claims that without arrangement, invention would be "nothing" (*Prooemium* 2). Consistent with Cicero's views, Quintilian's notion of invention within arrangement became a fundamental precept for his writings on rhetoric. To illustrate his point, Quintilian compares the relationship of arrangement to invention with the construction of a building, claiming that without skilled, prior organization the most elegant material would be little more than rubble (*Prooemium* 1). In some respects, Quintilian's views on arrangement are conventional. He repeatedly stresses a five-part pattern of arrangement: *prooemium* or *exordium, narratio, probatio, refutatio* and *peroratio* (3.9.1; 4.3.15; 5. *Prooemium* 11). As with his model, Cicero, Quintilian believes that arrangement must be flexible to the demands of the situation and the disposition of the audience. Quintilian is explicit in his belief that invention can only be creative when structured (7. *Prooemium* 1–2), but the structure must be malleable. In fact, Quintilian is so flexible with his views of arrangement that he asserts that

actually any of the five parts of arrangement can be abandoned except *probatio* or proof (5. *Prooemium* 5). Quintilian believed that the coexistence and interplay between invention and arrangement is so strong that one cannot function without the other, since both (together) are essential for structuring and expressing thoughts and sentiments.

The Appropriation of Classical Arrangement in the Middle Ages and Renaissance. The canon of arrangement continued well past the classical period. In the Middle Ages, the classical principles of arrangement were the basis for letter writing that evolved into *ars dictaminis*. [See Ars dictaminis.] Similarly, the patterns of arrangement that were the basis for oral argument and literary composition persisted into the Renaissance, where the highly stylized protocol of form based on classical precepts ensured that arrangement would remain a dominant feature of rhetoric. The principles of classical arrangement, for example, are clearly apparent in Sir Philip Sidney's late sixteenth-century treatise, *A Defence of Poetry*. Perhaps the reason for the endurance of the principles of classical arrangement is that its benefits remained obvious across both time and cultures. Arrangement served as an aid to memory when oral discourse was emphasized. Arrangement was also used to facilitate understanding between rhetor and auditor by structuring discourse that conformed to the conventional patterns and expectations of listeners and readers. Arrangement also had a civic and jurisprudential function, serving as a heuristic for deliberative, epideictic, and forensic rhetoric. The Renaissance mentality that saw rhetoric and poetics as indistinguishable also saw arrangement as inherent in the art of urbane, stylized expression. Arrangement remained a persistent and essential feature of rhetoric not only in classical curricula but also as a modified feature of medieval and Renaissance rhetoric. [*See overview article on* Medieval rhetoric; Nineteenth-century rhetoric; *and overview article on* Renaissance rhetoric.]

[*See also* Classical rhetoric.]

BIBLIOGRAPHY

Ad C. Herennium de Ratione Dicendi (Rhetorica ad Herennium). Translated by Harry Caplan. Cambridge, Mass., 1954. A thorough treatment of the *Rhetorica ad Herennium* that includes the Latin text with an English translation, an introduction to classical rhetoric, a dated but valuable bibliography, and an excellent analysis of the text.

Aristotle. *On Rhetoric: A Theory of Civic Discourse.* Translated by George A. Kennedy. New York, 1991. A very readable translation of Aristotle's *Rhetoric* with instructive notes and appendices.

Aristotle. *Problems.* Books 22–38. Translated by W. S. Hett. *Rhetorica ad Alexandrum.* Translated by H. Rackham. Cambridge, Mass., 1937. The Loeb series places Anaximenes's *Rhetorica ad Alexandrum* in the corpus of Aristotle's works. An introduction and helpful outline of the treatise is provided with the Greek text and an English translation.

Cicero, Marcus Tullius. *De inventione—De optimo genere oratorum—topica.* Translated by H. M. Hubbell. Cambridge, Mass., 1949. Contains the Latin texts with English translations, along with helpful introductions.

Cicero, Marcus Tullius. *De oratore.* Books 1–2. Translated by E. W. Sutton and H. Rackham. Revised edition. Cambridge, Mass., 1948. First published 1942. *De oratore.* Book 3. *De Fato—Paradoxa stoicorum—De partitione oratoria.* Translated by H. Rackham, 1942. These volumes contain the Latin texts with English translations. These two volumes provide the reader with Cicero's philosophy of rhetoric in the *De oratore* as well as more technical comments on topics such as arrangement.

Enos, Richard Leo. *Greek Rhetoric Before Aristotle.* Prospect Heights, Ill., 1993. An introduction to the emergence of Greek rhetoric with some helpful comments on early notions of arrangement.

Enos, Richard Leo. *The Literate Mode of Cicero's Legal Rhetoric.* Carbondale, Ill., 1988. A study of Cicero's application of his own rhetorical theory in his legal arguments with a detailed treatment of his views on, and practice of, arrangement.

Murphy, James J. *Rhetoric in the Middle Ages: A History of Rhetorical Theory from Saint Augustine to the Renaissance.* Berkeley, 1974. An excellent explanation of the transformation of classical canons of rhetoric into the medieval arts of rhetoric. The detailed treatment of *ars dictaminis* is especially helpful in understanding its evolution from classical systems of arrangement.

Plato. *Phaedrus.* Translated with an Introduction and Commentary by R. Hackforth. Cambridge, Mass., 1972. Offers detailed biographical information on Plato and an explanation of the issues behind his critique of rhetoric.

Quintilian, Marcus Fabius. *The institutio oratoria of Quintilian.* Translated by H. E. Butler. 4 vols. Cambridge, Mass., 1920–1922. Offers the Latin text with an English translation. A synopsis of each of the twelve books is an aid to the reader, as well as important background material on Quintilian, including a letter to his publisher, Trypho.

Schiappa. Edward. *The Beginnings of Rhetorical Theory in Classical Greece.* New Haven, 1999. A strong argument that challenges conventional claims about the origins of rhetoric. Rhetoric's origin as a discipline in Greece is viewed not by performance but by the articulation of theory.

Vickers, Brian. *In Defence of Rhetoric.* Oxford, 1988. A good overview of the history of rhetoric with a discussion of *dispositio* throughout the volume.

—RICHARD LEO ENOS

Modern arrangement

Arrangement concerns how parts of a text (whether spoken, written, or visual) can be defined, how they can be related to each other in a hierarchy, and how they can be ordered so that an audience experiences them in a certain sequence or configuration. From a rhetorical perspective, emphasizing the role of discourse in a situation, arrangement is considered a controllable variable that influences an audience's response to a text. In other words, the same material might be more or less understandable or persuasive depending on how it is placed on a page or computer screen or sequenced in its delivery to an audience. Though arrangement was one of the five major divisions of classical rhetoric, it has not received the attention given to invention or style in the twentieth-century revival of rhetoric. Even the term *arrangement* (or the Latin *dispositio* or Greek *taxis*) is rarely used. Instead the terms *form, structure,* or *organization* usually appear when issues of arrangement are discussed.

Attention to arrangement requires deciding, first of all, what is being arranged. What "parts" can or should be identified, and how can the boundaries between different parts of texts in different media be constructed or perceived? Once the parts or units of analysis have been defined, discussions of their order, their relative size, and their relation to each other can follow. What options are available to describe the parts of texts and their arrangement? In the following discussion, the term *text* can stand not only for spoken or written (including printed) discourse but also for nonverbal visual and video texts, and for texts that mix modes of presentation.

Rationales by Content. The arrangement of a text can be thought of in terms of how its subject matter is divided into topics, how these are sequenced, what relative amounts of space (for visual and verbal texts) or time (for aural texts) they receive, and what relations of hierarchy (subordination) or equality (coordination) are established among them. Schemes for arranging the content of a text are usually based on some rationale, conventional or presumably natural, for dealing with a subject. For example, verbal descriptions of a physical location often adopt some strategic ordering of details in a visual field, such as left to right or foreground to background, presumably recreating the order in which the observer would take in the scene. Biographies also follow the "natural order" of the chronological sequence of events in the subject's life (though they may open with a dramatic or famous moment in a person's career).

The headings and subheadings in a text represent its arrangement as a sequence hierarchically ordered; some parts are presented as more general and inclusive than others. In the past, the concern of sixteenth-century rhetoricians like Ramus with "Method," with the successively branching divisions of a subject, was also a concern to find the optimal way to arrange material based on inherent divisions in it. Such divisions and subdivisions, even when they are presented in hypertext formats on a Web site, can be highly conventional. For example, an encyclopedia article on a country will routinely include sections on its geography, history, economy, and culture; within a single encyclopedia, these sections will usually be sequenced in the same way, imposing the same order on every similar entry. How an item is perceived as distinct from another topic, so that it can be labeled as a separate section and placed in some scheme of arrangement, obviously depends on decisions by the producers of a text (authors, editors, book or Web-site designers), but these decisions are also constrained by cultural or social conventions. Hence the way a content area is defined and partitioned, and its parts then sequenced, can suggest the knowledge-forming routines of a culture.

Rationales by Acts or Effects. The arrangement of a text can be described as the sequence of acts its author performs, intentionally or not, or as the sequence of effects the text has, or might have, on its audience. (In terms of speech–act theory, these correspond to the illocutionary and perlocutionary acts accomplished by the text.) [*See* Speech acts, utterances as.] A "negative news" letter in business, for example, has the overall goal of maintaining a good relationship with an addressee while denying a request. To achieve that overall goal, the letter attempts a sequence of acts. Such letters may start out with an attempt to placate the addressee by acknowledging the original complaint or request in a positive way. Then the negative news will be delivered, followed by some positive closing message, such as the offer of a discount coupon for a disgruntled consumer or a wish for success to the disappointed job candidate.

Reciprocally, the arrangement of a piece can be described in terms of the series of effects it presumably has on an audience; for example, first frightening or worrying them, and then reassuring them. When a question-and-answer arrangement strategy is used, an audience is first puzzled or made curious, and then relieved or satisfied with a surprising but plausible answer. (Nature stories are often treated this way, especially when written for children. "How do elephants drink water?" the opening asks, and the text goes on to answer.) Arguments that propose a course of action have a fairly fixed order of effects; they usually begin by creating or increasing anxiety or outrage about a problem in the audience, then offer hope with the proposed solution, and end by arousing a commitment to act.

Rationales by Formal Features. The arrangement of a text can also be described in terms of the placement and sequencing of various formal features. Different type fonts and sizes, mixtures of prose and dialogue, paragraphs of different lengths, boxed or highlighted text, and unusual margins, all of these are formal features that can be altered and sequenced in a printed text. In the case of an aural text, sections can be formally differentiated by pauses and by changes in the speaker's pitch, volume, or speed of articulation. [*See* Delivery.] The arrangement of formal elements becomes crucial when the text is either entirely visual (a photograph, a diagram, a single video image) or a mixture of the visual and verbal like a magazine advertisement, or of the verbal, visual, and audio like a hypermedia Web site.

Formally distinct sections in a text can also be identified by changes in the language used. Classical rhetorical theory recommended that the different parts of the six-part oration use different levels of style and different densities of figuration and changes in delivery—middle style for the *narratio* and grand style for the *peroratio*. [See Style.] Contemporary stylistics would describe such differences as changes in register (e.g., colloquial language versus legalese) or, in the characterization of Russian critic M. M. Bakhtin (1895–1975), as changes in primary speech genres, the language patterns characteristic of distinct verbal activities like military commands or friendly letters (*Speech Genres and Other Late Essays,* Austin, 1986). Changes in register or speech genre may reflect the rhetor's awareness of different segments of the audience addressed. So, for example, a scientific popularization may repeat the same material in different registers, not changing the content but changing the level of accessibility. What constitutes a significant shift in register, where these shifts occur, and how they are sequenced are arrangement issues.

The formal linguistic markers of arrangement may also involve *metadiscourse,* language about language that includes the devices writers and speakers use to signal how their texts are organized. The phrase "in conclusion" is an example of metadiscourse that signals to an audience where a speaker is in a text. Other examples include initiation cues ("Let us first consider") and transitional devices ("Now I want to turn to"). These verbal devices have visual analogs (e.g., the border around an image, the fadeout). Even in the absence of a strong preexisting pattern for a text shared by its author and audience, a sense of its arrangement can be communicated with such devices.

While arrangement strategies based on ordering the content, the acts or effects, and the formal features can be described independently, theories of arrangement, whether developed for analysis or pedagogy or both, usually concern the overlay or compatibility of divisions based on these three rationales. Thus the sequencing or configuration of formal features can reflect or reinforce the sequencing or configuration of the content or the acts/effects. Acts of interpretation often depend on deciphering one arrangement strategy in terms of another. In the case of a sonnet, for example, formal divisions created by patterns of rhyming within the fourteen lines are used to make and mark movements in the content (e.g., stages of thought or thematic development) or in the effects. Formal divisions marked by subheadings or hypertext links are taken to represent different aspects or parts of the content. Sections defined by the acts they perform can also be marked by content shifts and layout differences; so, for example, the "negative news" letter, which performs at least three speech acts, might segregate each in a separate paragraph. Then, too, a text representing a sequence of voices might give each a formally distinct section in a text by manipulating indentation, spacing, type font, and so on. Among twentieth-century rhetoricians, Kenneth Burke (1897–1993) paid special attention to the interconnections between form, content, and effect. He pointed out that when audiences expect a text to conform to a certain formal pattern (whether they derive that expectation from the text itself or from elsewhere), and then have that expectation fulfilled, they are more likely to be persuaded by the content that completes the form.

Updating Traditional Schemes of Arrangement. In classical rhetoric, the arrangement of a typical courtroom speech was described as a sequence of six parts: an introduction, statement of facts, partition, confirmation of the case, refutation of opponents, and conclusion (see above). These parts were distinguished on the basis of what effects they were supposed to have on the audience. This traditional arrangement scheme is still current in the common advice that a speech, and many kinds of written texts, should have an introduction, some kind of body that delivers the author's arguments in an effective sequence, and a conclusion. According to classical and early modern rhetorical manuals, the options for sequencing one's arguments depend on their "strength," their persuasiveness with the intended audience. Rhetors were advised to order arguments according to their increasing or decreasing strength, or to place their weakest arguments in the middle, and open and close with stronger ones. While the notion of the "strength" of an argument depends on an assessment of its force for a particular audience, the Belgian rhetoricians Chaim Perelman and Lucie Olbrechts-Tyteca questioned whether the "strength" of an argument can be independently assessed (*The New Rhetoric*, Notre Dame, Ind., 1969). They pointed out that an argument's strength for an audience may in fact be created by its position. Researchers in psychology and speech communication have attempted to find empirical bases for various strategies of arrangement, devising experiments to test such issues as whether "primacy" (coming first) or "recency" (coming last) were more effective strategies for competing arguments. But the large number of variables involved in human communicative situations makes it difficult to generalize from such studies.

Modern mass media (print journalism, radio, TV, the Internet) present special complications for the study of arrangement because the sequencing of information and arguments, the order in which certain appeals reach an audience, is very difficult to predict, particularly because of the "boundary" problem mentioned above. Marshall McLuhan (1911–1980), a communication theorist, stressed the differences imposed by newer communication media, arguing that newspapers and television broke with the linear arrangement of written and spoken discourse by presenting messages all at once or in mosaic fashion. Though McLuhan's more extreme characterizations are not followed today, it is true that the contemporary media consumer may glimpse headlines in a newspaper, catch soundbites on television news, read banners on a Web site, or hear part of a radio talk show and subsequently form opinions from a chaos of fragmented impressions and bits of information. Hence saturation and sheer quantity of exposure to a "message" given in single bursts may count for more than the interrelationship of parts of a single message achieved by its carefully crafted arrangement.

Among newer media, the Internet and webbed environments in particular have brought about speculation on new modes of arrangement. First, the mixing of aural, verbal, visual, and video elements on the same screen presents arrangement options unique to this medium. Second, hypertext links create "multidimensional" hierarchical or branching schemes of arrangement. Third, the possibility of wandering from option to option, forward and backward, presumably gives the user of a webbed environment more control of the sequence of inputs. Theories of arrangement with these new technologies are the subject of recent scholarly attention, with disagreements over how much is really new in these new media.

Arrangement and Genre. Observations on arrangement—on the length, sequence, and relation among parts of a text—can often be found in critical analyses of individual works. Stanley Fish's analysis of Freud's case study of "The Wolf Man," for example, points out the rhetorical effectiveness of Freud's delayed disclosure of the meaning of the dream (*Doing What Comes Naturally*, Durham, N.C., 1989). However, more systematic observations about arrangement can be found in discussions of genres, recurring types of texts (e.g., the inaugural address, the TV news broadcast, the comedy of manners). Indeed, a typical arrangement strategy can be one of the distinguishing features of a genre, whether the parts being arranged are defined in terms of content, act/effect, formal feature, or some combination of the three. Once the typical arrangement strategy of a genre is defined, it then becomes possible to discuss how individual examples add to, delete from, or alter the typical configuration of elements.

The metagenre "narrative" illustrates how variations on a standard arrangement strategy can reflect the rhetorical situation of a text. In the most general sense, a text is a narrative when its parts are episodes or events (whether external or psychological). Histories, biographies, news stories, movies, and novels all fall under this broad classification. The default arrangement strategy for a narrative is chronological sequence, but the events constituting a narrative, real or fictional, do not necessarily have to be arranged in the order in which they presumably occurred. The possibility of rearranging the same basic narrative in different ways is aptly illustrated in the first of the progymnasmatic exercises in classical rhetoric, the fable, where students were directed to take a simple narrative and retell it in different ways, first starting at the beginning, then in the middle, then at the end. The typical newspaper story reflects yet another narrative arrangement strategy:

a highly condensed version of events is followed by a retelling in greater detail. The fact that the same basic sequence of events can nevertheless be arranged in different representations illustrates how narratives can be strategically shaped for different rhetorical effects.

While literary genres (e.g., *Bildungsroman,* film noir, haiku) are described by their content and/or formal devices, rhetorical genres (e.g., funeral orations, documentaries, summations before a jury) are more typically described in terms of the presumed acts performed or accomplished. Work on rhetorical genres flowered in the 1970s, stimulated by the criticism of Kathleen Jamieson (1975) who expanded the notion of rhetorical situation defined by Lloyd Bitzer (1968) to include among the constraints facing a *rhētōr* the available "antecedent genres." Even in novel situations, a rhetor is nevertheless likely to adopt and adapt forms of communication (genres) already used in similar situations. (Cases made for such precursors do not, however, always involve a discussion of the arrangement strategies typical in the borrowed genre.) [*See* Hybrid genres.]

Genre has also proved to be a useful concept in studies of the psychology of reading, or text consumption in general. Theorists often distinguish "bottom up" strategies of comprehension (where an understanding of a text's overall structure is built up from its parts) from "top down" strategies (where understanding is based on a prior model in the reader's mind). Psycholinguists have established that decisions about genre facilitate comprehension. A reader's (or viewer's or user's) familiarity with a genre, and with its typical arrangement strategy, is a kind of background knowledge; such background knowledge is often characterized in terms of its organization into chronological or hierarchical configurations known as "scripts" or "schemata." Highly conventional genres (e.g., recipes, weather reports, introductions of keynote speakers) are in effect *formal schēmata,* familiar patterns of arrangement, that assist readers in assimilating new content.

Arrangement and Functional Genres: Heuristic Approaches to Arrangement. Interesting work on genre and formal schemes of arrangement has been done by scholars who focus on professional and technical communication. This work aims to teach students and workplace professionals how to produce texts of a certain kind, especially in business and institutional settings where documents are valued for their efficiency and effectiveness. Advice on how to write functional genres (like resumes, business plans, or progress reports) is often given in the form of an ideal scheme of organization that is then filled in with content appropriate to the writer's immediate circumstances.

Among the most orderly of genres in terms of its arrangement is the scientific research report with, typically, the following fixed sequence of sections: Introduction, Materials and Methods, Results, and Discussion (IMRD). Scholars in the history and rhetoric of science have investigated the evolution and epistemology of this form, which presumably reflects the ideal order of experimental design, but which has also been criticized for misrepresenting the often chaotic nature of research procedures. Much work has also been done on the optimal internal arrangement of the individual sections of the research article, especially its introduction, which, according to John Swales (1990) and others, tends to follow a fixed series of moves to achieve the rhetorical goal of creating and occupying a research space.

Arrangement Below the Level of the Whole Text. While classical rhetoric concerned itself with the arrangement of a whole speech, it also paid attention to smaller textual units and their internal ordering. So, for example, a single line of argument in a speech could take the form of an *epicheirēme,* a five-part argument with claim, reason, proof of reason, embellishment, and resume. Some modern rhetoricians and composition theorists have also tried to define formal units smaller than a whole text that might appear in any genre or concern any subject matter.

The traditional "modes of development," once a staple of writing textbooks and now much criticized, can be described as arrangement strategies that involve smaller segments of a text and that are not bound to a particular genre or subject matter. The all-purpose modes include patterns such as narration (arrangement by sequence), classification (enumeration of the subgroups in a large group), analysis (presenting the hierarchical divisions in a subject), description (rendering a scene or object according to a principle of spatial ordering), cause and effect (linking antecedents and consequents), and comparison-contrast (deploying likenesses and differences between two entities either feature by feature or whole by whole). The arrangement strategy of a single text can be described as the sequence of the different modes of development it uses.

In the late nineteenth century, the Scottish psychologist Alexander Bain (1818–1903) nominated the paragraph as the key structural unit below the level of the whole text (*English Composition and Rhetoric,* enlarged edition, London, 1901), identifying principles of paragraph construction such as the "topic sentence," consecutive arrangement, and marked subordination. Composition theorists in the twentieth century continued this work by identifying types of paragraphs and describing their internal organization. The arrangement of a text could then be described as the sequence of items taken up in the sequence of its paragraphs using different methods. *Designs in Prose* (London, 1980) by Walter Nash is another attempt to define compositional units of roughly paragraph length. Behind this work is the notion that similar arrangement strategies can be imposed on textual units of different length. So one can have an antithesis (the deployment of opposites or contraries) at the sentence level, the paragraph level, and even across several paragraphs. [*See* Antithesis; *and overview article on* Composition.]

A smaller-scale theory of arrangement concerns "given/new" or "topic/comment" organization in groups of sentences. Building on the observation that sentences in Indo-European languages tend to put old or given information, material already known to the audience, in the beginning of a sentence, and new information, the "news" in the sentence, toward the end, patterns of organization can be investigated across passages of several sentences. So, for example, a passage can maintain the same topic in a series of sentences, or the new information in one sentence can become the given information in the next.

Arrangement in Visual Rhetoric. Arrangement in the sense of the disposition of static parts, rather than the sequencing of effects in time, becomes salient in the creation and interpretation of visuals such as illustrations, photographs, diagrams, emblems, drawings, or computer screens. The study of arrangement in visual texts has been enriched by the considerable body of knowledge on the physiology and psychology of perception. There are well-established principles on, for example, what the eye can distinguish and how perceivers can fill in a visual field according to their expectations. At the same time, unique cultural conventions also inform the configuration of parts of a visual; in Western iconography, a circle around a head can stand for holiness and the left to right ascension of a line graph can represent an increasing quantity.

Scholars debate the applicability of principles of arrangement derived from verbal texts to visual texts. Gunther Kress and Theo van Leeuwen's *Reading Images: the Grammar of Visual Design* (London, 1996) does use analogies drawn from verbal arrangement to identify the underlying arrangement strategies in visuals. For example, Kress and van Leeuwen apply the principle of given/new organization (see above) to the spatial arrangement of visual elements, arguing that what appears to the left in a visual is offered as the familiar, established, or orginary, and what appears to the right is the new, the created, the outcome.

[*See also* Hypertext.]

BIBLIOGRAPHY

Becker, Alton. "A Tagmemic Approach to Paragraph Analysis." *College Composition and Communication* 16 (1965), pp. 237–242. An identification of recurring patterns of paragraph arrangement such as TRI (topic, restriction, illustration).

Bitzer, Lloyd, F. "The Rhetorical Situation." *Philosophy and Rhetoric* 1.1 (1968), pp. 1–14.

Bolter, Jay David, and Richard Grusin. *Remediation: Understanding New Media.* Cambridge Mass., 1998. Makes the case that new media (e.g., webbed environments) "remediate" or extend earlier media but are not radically new.

Burke, Kenneth. *Counter-Statement.* New York, 1931. Burke's first work, contains a discussion of three types of form (arrangement): conventional, repetitive, progressive. References to the same concept appear in later works.

Campbell, Karlyn Kohrs, and Kathleen Hall Jamieson, eds. *Form and Genre: Shaping Rhetorical Action.* Falls Church, Va., 1978. Introductory essay by the editors defines rhetorical genres; discussions of genres in subsequent essays occasionally mention arrangement.

Clark, Herbert H., and Susan E. Haviland. "Comprehension and the Given-New Contract." In *Discourse Pro-*

duction and Comprehension. Edited by Roy O. Freedle. Norwood, N.J., 1977. An investigation of the assumptions and reasoning processes used to make sense of strings of clauses.

Dillon, George. *Constructing Texts.* Bloomington, Ind., 1981. Chapter 3 contains a discussion of organization in terms of schema; that is, structures of information or presumptions about the normal that readers bring to a text.

Hovland, Carl I., Irving Janis, and Harold H. Kelley. *The Order of Presentation in Persuasion.* New Haven, 1957. The classical account of empirical studies by psychologists on the position of arguments and their comparative persuasiveness.

Jamieson, Kathleen. "Antecedent Genre as Rhetorical Constraint." *Quarterly Journal of Speech* 61 (1975), pp. 406–415. Makes the case that in novel rhetorical situations, rhetors draw on earlier genres used in similar situations.

Jamieson, Kathleen. *Eloquence in an Electronic Age.* New York, 1988. Claims that informal conversational structure has replaced formal argument in televised political exchanges.

Landow, George P. *Hypertext 2.0: The Convergence of Contemporary Critical Theory and Technology.* 2d ed. Baltimore, 1977. Argues that the linear arrangement of individual literary texts will be replaced by continuous webs of text.

Larsen, Richard. "Toward a Linear Rhetoric of the Essay." *College Composition and Communication* 22 (1971), pp. 140–146. An application of speech act theory to arrangement, seeing a text as a sequence of acts to achieve a goal.

McLuhan, Marshall. *The Gutenberg Galaxy: The Making of Typographic Man.* Toronto, 1962. Argues for differences between linear and nonlinear media.

Meyer, Bonnie J. F. *The Organization of Prose and Its Effects on Memory.* Amsterdam, 1975. A psycholinguistic approach to the hierarchical organization of information in a text.

Pitkin, Willis. "Discourse Blocs." *College Composition and Communication* 20 (1969), pp. 138–148. An attempt to define units of arrangement according to their discourse function (coordination, complementation, subordination, superordination).

Snyder, Ilana. *Hypertext: The Electronic Labyrinth.* New York, 1997. A discussion of how reading and writing practices are changed in hypertext environments.

Swales, John M. *Genre Analysis: English in Academic and Research Settings.* Cambridge, U.K., 1990. Includes a useful summary of approaches to genre and a detailed discussion of the typical arrangement of sections in the academic/scientific research report, with special attention to introductions.

VandeKopple, William. "Some Exploratory Discourse on Metadiscourse." *College Composition and Communication* 36 (1985), pp. 82–93. Contains a survey of many possible types of metadiscourse, including those devices that signal arrangement.

Van Dijk, Teun. *Macrostructures.* Hillsdale, N.J., 1979. From the perspective of text linguistics, a discussion of how passages entail propositions at higher levels of generality.

—JEANNE FAHNESTOCK

ARS DICTAMINIS. The *ars dictaminis* is the variety of medieval rhetoric that provided instruction in the composition of letters and other epistolary documents. Between 1077 and 1085, Alberic of Monte Cassino produced the first textbooks of medieval rhetoric that incorporated explicit instruction on letter writing. Within a generation, Adalbert of Samaria and Hugh of Bologna had taken Alberic's innovation a step farther by developing textbooks that focused exclusively on letter writing, drawing their theory from the technical rhetorics of Cicero (*De inventione*) and pseudo-Cicero (*Rhetorica ad Herennium*) and the commentaries on them. [*See* Classical rhetoric.] Adalbert's and Hugh's textbooks and those of their contemporaries at Bologna in the first half of the twelfth century established a genre that eventually spread throughout Europe and is represented by hundreds of treatises in thousands of manuscripts. In longevity and influence, the *ars dictaminis* was the most successful of the medieval adaptations of classical rhetoric.

The typical treatise, called an *ars dictandi* or *summa dictandi,* combined a fairly standard range of precepts, concerned chiefly with arrangement and style, and illustrative examples or models for imitation. [*See* Arrangement: Traditional arrangement; Imitation; *and* Style.] Dictaminal teaching clearly reflects a fundamental conception of letters as official, public, and spoken texts. That letters are understood as quasi-orations can be seen from the treatment of their component parts, which is modeled on Cicero's analysis of forensic speeches. By the mid-twelfth century, most teachers of the *ars dictaminis* recognized five basic parts of a letter: (1) the *salutatio* or "greeting"; (2) the *captatio benevolentiae* or "securing of goodwill," which alternatively was called the *exordium,* the *arenga* ("harangue"), or even the *proverbium* (since proverbs often were used for this part); (3) the *narratio* or "statement of facts"; (4) the *petitio* or "request"; and (5) the *conclusio* or "summation or complimentary close." Of these, only the *salutatio* is particular to a letter: the remaining four derive from Cicero's six parts of an oration.

Medieval epistolary theory consisted primarily of the doctrine of these five parts of a letter. Because epistolary communication functioned within an explicitly hierarchical social system, the first two parts of a letter generally received the most extensive treatment in letter-writing manuals. Together, the *salutatio* and *captatio benevolentiae* ensured that the letter would be heard and in the right way. The *salutatio* was governed by a precisely calibrated ranking of persons according to a strict decorum. In letters addressed to persons of superior or even equal rank, the *captatio benevolentiae* provided a favorable context within which to view the specific circumstances about to be recounted and the request about to be made. The remaining three parts are almost never treated in comparable detail, perhaps not only because their contents are more variable but also because they are perceived as less crucial to a letter's rhetorical effectiveness. Many textbooks also discuss the varieties of letters and the circumstances under which it is permissible to omit one or more of the standard parts.

Like the overall structure of the letter, the stylistic elements of dictaminal instruction also point to the underlying model of an oration. The *cursus*, the rhythmical clause endings that had characterized artful prose since antiquity, became a standard part of the *ars dictaminis* in the late twelfth century. The use of *distinctiones*, that is, the construction of sentences in three sharply distinguished units, called *comma, colon,* and *periodus*, also depends on aural reception for its maximum effect. The same might be said of the figures of speech, which are the next most common stylistic component in treatises on the *ars dictaminis*. [*See* Figures of speech.]

Long before the emergence of the *ars dictaminis*, letter writing had been taught by means of formularies and collections of model letters, and dictaminal treatises preserve this pedagogy of imitation. Generally, the *salutatio* is taught more by example than by precept, which also helps account for the amount of space devoted to it. Like-

wise, many treatises include collections of model proverbs suitable for use as the second part of a letter. Separate examples of the other three parts are rarer. More common is the practice of including examples of entire letters, often paired with responses. Important collections of letters, such as those of Peter of Vinea and Richard of Pofi, often served as textbooks on the *ars dictaminis* in their own right.

The introduction of theoretical rigor into long-standing pedagogical practices that resulted in the *ars dictaminis* was a response to the need for more efficient training of functionaries. In northern Italy, the struggles between the papacy and the emperor, the expansion of commerce, and the development of communal forms of government all resulted in an unprecedented demand for trained clerks to serve in roles ranging from municipal notaries to papal secretaries and imperial chancellors. The emergence of Bologna as the premier center for legal studies helps to explain why the *ars dictaminis* flourished there and why the works of northern Italian teachers such as Bernard of Bologna in the twelfth century and Guido Faba in the thirteenth century set the standard for the *ars dictaminis* throughout Europe. Although the association between the *ars dictaminis* and legal studies was not equally strong everywhere, throughout Europe the *ars dictaminis* derived its strength from its practical utility in training the "bureaucrats" without whom neither secular nor ecclesiastical government could function. As medieval social and economic power structures grew more complex and more text-dependent, medieval teachers responded with a flexible and efficient means of preparing the literate class that kept the necessary documents flowing. So effective was the *ars dictaminis* in meeting such needs that it continued to be taught and practiced for more than a century alongside the Humanist epistolography that ultimately would displace it. [*See* Humanism.]

[*See also* Epistolary rhetoric; *and overview article on* Medieval rhetoric.]

BIBLIOGRAPHY

Anonymous of Bologna. "The Principles of Letter-Writing (1135 CE)." Translated by James J. Murphy. In *Three Medieval Rhetorical Arts*. Edited by James J. Murphy, pp. 1–25. Berkeley, 1971. English translation of the first part of a seminal treatise, probably written at Bologna by "Master Bernard."

Camargo, Martin. *Ars Dictaminis, Ars Dictandi*, vol. 60, *Typologie des sources du moyen âge occidental*. Turnhout, Belgium, 1991. Defines the genre and sketches its history.

Faulhaber, Charles B. "The *Summa dictaminis* of Guido Faba." In *Medieval Eloquence: Studies in the Theory and Practice of Medieval Rhetoric*. Edited by James J. Murphy, pp. 85–111. Berkeley, 1978. Analyzes what was probably the most influential treatise on the art, written at Bologna c. 1228–1229.

Murphy, James J. *Rhetoric in the Middle Ages*. Berkeley, 1974. See especially chapter 5, pp. 194–268. "*Ars dictaminis:* The Art of Letter-Writing." Still the fullest survey in English, with summaries of several treatises.

Patt, William D. "The Early *Ars dictaminis* as Response to a Changing Society." *Viator* 9 (1978), pp. 133–155. Argues that the *ars dictaminis* was not "invented" suddenly but rather evolved from existing pedagogical traditions in response to important cultural changes.

Transmundus. *Introductiones dictandi*. Text edited and translated with annotations by Ann Dalzell. Toronto, 1995. Edition and English translation of an important treatise, written in the early thirteenth century by a monk of Clairvaux who had earlier been a notary in the papal chancery.

Witt, Ronald. "Medieval *Ars dictaminis* and the Beginnings of Humanism: A New Construction of the Problem." *Renaissance Quarterly* 35 (1982), pp. 1–35. Describes the complex and shifting nature of rhetoric in Italy, from the late thirteenth through the fifteenth centuries, when the *ars dictaminis* continued to be taught and practiced, often by the very exponents of the Humanist eloquence that ultimately supplanted it.

—MARTIN CAMARGO

ART. Only occasionally, and only indirectly does classical rhetoric touch on issues relating to pictorial art. When it does so, it is as an art of oral declamation; that is, in order to clarify properly rhetorical issues by reference to presumably more familiar and better understood notions from the visual realm in the broadest sense of that term. References to pictorial and mental images, to the manner in which the pictorial images are produced, perceived, remembered, and evaluated, and in which mental images are caused and experienced, therefore belong primarily on the side of the *explanans* rather than the *explanandum* of rhetorical analysis. Thus Cicero, in order to be able to clarify the notion of propriety (*quid deceat, decorum*) reminds his readers of Apelles' remarks on painters "who do not know when they have done enough" (*qui non sentirent quid esset satis*), and of Timanthes of Cythnos's decision to depict Agamemnon's head as veiled when he painted the sacrifice of Iphigenia "because the supreme sorrow could not be portrayed by his brush" (*quoniam summum illum luctum penicillo non posset imitari*) (Cicero, *Orator* 21.72–74).

Quintilian, in his discussion of the place of memory (*memoria*) in the art of the orator (*Institutio oratoria* 11.2.17–20; 21–22; 23–26) offers an account of the role of both mental images (*imagines*) and pictorial images (*picturae, simulacra*), the latter in the sense of artifacts produced for the purpose of arresting, holding onto the former. The focus in this case is on the mental image rather than on an actual picture, which in this context is viewed by Quintilian as only one of several ways of locating and fixing the former. In the same vein, Quintilian's elaboration of *ekphrasis*, the type of description (*descriptio*) that aims at graphic clarity (*evidentia, enargeia*) of the described object, rather than only at thorough familiarity (*perspicuitas*) with that object (4.2.120; 123–124; 6.1.28; 31; 8.3.63–71) involves a detailed analysis of the manner in which listening to or reading such descriptions, thanks to the tropes and figures present, produces a sense of seeing what is being described with one's inner eye, and thereby a feeling of being turned from a listener or reader into a spectator of a theatrical performance. [*See* Descriptio.] Here, too, it is the mental image called up by what is described, rather than a pictorial representation of an object, that serves as an *explanans*. Elsewhere, it is the pictorial rather than the mental image that serves as a point of departure, as in the case of the familiar experience of being able to guess the eventual outcome of the drawing of a picture from a few outlines, which serves to elucidate the manner in which the outcome of a narrative can be anticipated (4.2.120) on the basis of just a few remarks. Even Quintilian's analysis of the role of affective gestures in the orator's attempt at persuasion, a subject that one would imagine to be more familiar from oratory than from the visual arts, has recourse to the familiarity with such gestures as presented in a silent picture (*pictura tacens*) (11.3.67).

Besides such explicit references to mental or pictorial images as familiar from everyday experience for the purpose of clarifying a number of rhetorical concepts, a number of the terms employed by classical rhetoric were themselves originally metaphors from visual experience; thus diction could be described as *translucidus* or as *versicolor* (Baxandall, 1986, p. 17). But here, too, the proper understanding of the visual was presupposed rather than thematic.

All in all, then, classical rhetoric did not branch out into a full-fledged rhetoric of visual art, occasional references to mental and pictorial images and metaphorical borrowings from visual experience notwithstanding. In fact, the very possibility of such a step could not be entertained seriously until well into the fifteenth century, for only then did the old division of the arts into *artes liberales* and *artes mechanicae* begin to lose its binding character. Until that point, the painter had been ranked with the carpenter, the blacksmith, and the weaver among the craftsmen of the *artes mechanicae,* but could now aspire to the status of the *artes liberales* worthy of a free man. Since Plato's time, there had been no doubt that both the orator and the painter possessed a teachable and learnable *technē*. The orator's *technē* could be related conceptually to the notion of affecting the emotions of the listener and persuading him of the rightness of a cause. By contrast, the painter's *technē,* like that possessed by the carpenter, the blacksmith, and the weaver, was thought to terminate in the production of a useful artifact. Undoubtedly, that was the case, but in terms of painting, understood to be mimetic, it could not as yet be conceptualized along the lines of a speech or a tragedy. [*See* Imitation.] The art of rhetoric, by contrast, together with grammar, dialectic, music, arithmetic, geometry, and astronomy, had been a discipline of the *artes liberales* or *studia liberalia* since classical antiquity. Raising the status of the painter and the sculptor to that of a representative of the liberal arts was thus tantamount to the possibility of lifting their *technē* out of the simple means-to-ends scheme of the mechanical arts, and reconstructing it along the conceptual and argumentative lines familiar from one or other of the disciplines of the *trivium* and the *quadrivium*. [*See* Trivium.]

Seen in that light, a Quattrocento treatise on art, such as Leon Battista Alberti's *De pictura* (1540), was not just an attempt at demonstrating that an art such as painting was something to be taught by precepts. That had been demonstrated sufficiently by numerous treatises conceived of within the framework of the *artes mechanicae,* without, however, contributing in the least to the improvement in social status of the craftsman-artist in question. What was essentially new in Alberti's *De pictura* was that here a rigorous attempt had been made to describe the *technē* of the painter on the model of that of the orator. Constructing, as Alberti did, an art of painting, not along the lines of one of the *artes mechanicae* but along those of rhetoric, one of the *artes liberales,* therefore amounted to such a radical breach with the older scheme of the arts that the use of the modern term *paradigm shift* would seem justified. Pictures, Alberti assumed, are capable of moving and persuading in ways similar to speeches. Hence, it should be possible to develop a descriptive apparatus for art theory similar to that of rhetoric. From Alberti's *De pictura* onward, it is therefore possible to speak of a rhetoric of art in a rather strict sense of that term, and to raise the kind of questions about art that are familiar from rhetoric proper: What does artistic persuasion mean? What are the activities that the painter must carry out in order to produce a pictorial work capable of persuasion? A treatise on art capable of answering these questions could therefore hope to achieve two goals at once: conceptualizing art for the lettered and along the most advanced lines of theorizing available at the time, and, in doing so, conceptualizing art in such a way that henceforth it could claim a dignity on a par with that of any of the liberal arts. Aiming for its first, strictly theoretical goal placed Alberti's treatise in the context of a whole number of contemporary attempts at theorizing about art, music, and literature under the auspices of classical rhetoric. Aiming for its second, pragmatic goal placed it in the context of fifteenth- and sixteenth-century debate about the ranking of the arts, for which the title of Leonardo da Vinci's treatise on painting, *Paragone* (1482–1500), was to supply the collective proper name.

Classical rhetoric is omnipresent in Alberti's *De pictura,* but the two concepts that most clearly show the direction in which a rhetoric of painting could be developed, are the concepts of *inventio* and *compositio.* [*See overview article on* Composition; *and* Invention.] In classical rhetoric, as in Alberti's enterprise, *inventio* serves as the term for both a fundamental activity of the rhetorician and the painter, and for an essential "part" of the art of rhetoric *qua* art. *Compositio,* by contrast, in both cases refers to the method and manner in which larger textual or pictorial wholes are put together from their constitutive elements. It is, in Alberti's words the "method of painting through which the parts are put together in the work of art" (*pingendi ratio qua partes in opus picture componuntur*; cited in Baxandall, 1986, p. 130). But it also refers to the manner in which those larger wholes can be analyzed into their constituent elements.

The transfer of the concept of *inventio* from rhetoric proper to a rhetoric of art is rather straightforward: both the orator and the painter need reason, art, diligence, and ingenuity if they wish to succeed, and therefore both need to be familiar with the requisite commonplaces (*loci*). [*See* Commonplaces and commonplace books.] Like the orator, the painter was viewed as a "professional visualizer of the holy stories" (Baxandall, 1988, p. 45), who could achieve internal representations of the stories in the form of sequences of mental images of the story he was going to depict. Hence, the painter's attempt at visualizing could be analyzed along the same lines as the laying out of the memory places by the orator; hence, the assumed similarity between the orator's and the painter's *inventio.* [*See* Memory.]

The transfer of the concept of *compositio* from rhetoric proper to a rhetoric of art in the making, by contrast, is considerably more involved; it also shows up the conceptual limitations, not only of Alberti's attempt at such a rhetoric, but of any such attempt. Wishing to identify a pictorial counterpart for the breakdown of the verbal whole of an *oratio* into periods, clauses, phrases, and words, that is, wishing to transfer a model of organization from rhetoric to painting, Alberti suggests a series made up of "plane" (*superficies*), "member" (*membrum*), "body" (*corpus*) "story" (*historia*), and "picture" (*pictura*) (Alberti, *De pic-* *tura,* Bk. 2). The suggestion that presenting a *historia* involving the bodies of people rather than the statue of a person (*colossus*)—narration rather than description, that is—should be considered the most important work of the painter (*amplissimum pictoris opus non colossus, sed historie*), may well have been prompted by the rhetorical model itself. In offering that listing of constituent elements, Alberti clearly did not consider it a problem that, depending on whether you adopt the painter's or the art theorist's perspective, the upward move from "plane" to "part" (in the sense of "part of the represented body") or the downward move from "part" to "plane," involves a categorial shift from the signifier to the signified or vice versa. A similar shift occurred with the upward move from *historia* to *pictura* or the downward one from *pictura* to *historia.* The rhetorical series, as envisaged by Alberti in accordance with tradition, by contrast, is categorially homogeneous throughout, and one would have to go a step lower to the phonetic or the phonemic level of analysis—a level never seriously contemplated by classical rhetoric—before one would reach a level containing semantically uninterpreted elements that might be compared to the lines and planes of a picture. This suggests that the transfer of the rhetorical model of composition to the art of painting apparently only works successfully so long as its scope is restricted to the content plane of a picture; to the stretch of the compositional elements ranging from "member" (*membrum*) via "body" (*corpus*) to "story" (*historia*). The analysis of what happens at both ends of the list (i.e., the question how the fact was to be explained that plane surfaces could be made to "mean" members, bodies, and stories, and how exactly the phrase *partes in opus picture componuntur* was to be understood), had to wait until the advent of a full-fledged comparative semiotics of the verbal and the pictorial text.

Apart from large-scale transfers of elements of the conceptual framework of classical rhetoric to painting in the manner of Alberti's treatise, classical rhetoric also offered what one might wish to call piecemeal transfers. These were facilitated by the references to visual experience mentioned earlier on, that is, classical rhetoric's characteristic practice of using references to the visual or pictorial realm for the purpose of clarifying issues of oratory and verbal art. That practice obviously did not preclude the possibility of reversing the order of *explanans* and *explanandum*. When that happened, the readily available rhetorical analysis of *ekphrasis* as a form of description capable of achieving *enargeia* could be used as an analytical tool for analyzing "ekphrastic" texts. These were texts not only thought to be descriptive so as to produce *evidentia*, but were now understood as texts describing pictorial works of art (e.g., Achilles' shield; John Keats' *Ode on a Grecian Urn*), in such a way that something akin to a mental image of the pictorial work of art in question was experienced by the reader of such descriptions. But this shift in the understanding of ekphrasis, which can be traced back to the educational programs (*progymnasmata*) of the second century CE, did not necessarily lead to the development of a rhetoric of art, not even a rhetoric of art description. For what the beginning orator was taught in those *ekphrases* of the progymnasmata was not the description of a bust of Cicero as a representational work of art, but as a simulacrum of Cicero.

Another context in which Renaissance attempts at a rhetoric of art could draw on extant analyses involving references to visual experience, this time that of a *pictura* in the sense of an artifact rather than a mental *imago,* can be found in the extended debate about the precise meaning of a phrase from Horace: *ut pictura poesis* (*Ars poetica,* p. 361), and on the implications of that comparison of picture and poem for the writing of (descriptive) poetry. [*See* Poetry.] The phrase was intended by Horace rather innocently as a comparison between different viewer positions demanded by different types of painting and different ways of reading demanded by different kinds of poems, and thus not at all referring to comparable properties of the poem and the picture itself. Especially if read in conjunction with the equally notorious statement of Simonides of Keos (first quoted in the anonymous *Rhetorica ad Herennium* (4.39) and mentioned by Plutarch (*De gloria Athenensium* 3.347a), that "poetry is a speaking picture, painting mute poetry," the Horatian formula opened another avenue for discussing the semantic properties to be shared by poem and picture, first in terms of the desirable descriptive properties of a poem, and subse-

quently, now in the context of an attempt at a rhetoric of art, the desirable narrative properties of a picture. The notion of *ut pictura poesis,* once elaborated in the context of rhetorical analysis as involving the demand that a descriptive text should possess certain pictorial qualities, could readily be inverted so as to allow for the identification and analysis of "poetic" (i.e., primarily "narrative") qualities of pictorial representations. Hence the insistence on *historia* as a feature of pictorial art; hence the introduction of the term *historia* into the terminological repertoire of Renaissance discourse on pictorial art. Alberti's insistence on *historia* as *amplissimum pictoris opus* was perhaps in part motivated by the contemporary *ut pictura poesis* debate.

It now also became possible to employ the rhetorically clarified references to the similarities between verbal and pictorial art polemically in the context of the Renaissance debate on the relative merits of the arts (Leonardo da Vinci's *Paragone*), as well as comparatively, especially during the eighteenth century, in investigations into the similarity of the arts (*Sister Arts*). The *Paragone* was to achieve its intended (but not openly acknowledged) purpose of raising the social status of the visual artist to that of the poet. In the wake of this upward move socially, it was intended to move the arts of painting and sculpture from the realm of the *artes mechanicae* or *sordidae* to that of the *artes liberales*. However, the debate in the wake of the Horatian *ut pictura poesis* was shown up as ultimately irrelevant for an understanding of the arts as a result of Lessing's insistence that painting should be understood as a spatial and poetry as a temporal art (*Laokoon oder Über die Grenzen der Malerei und Poesie,* Berlin, 1766). With this distinction, the visual arts were once again removed from the domain of objects of rhetoric proper, which, though it had at its disposal a clear distinction between various sorts of temporal ordering (*ordo naturalis, ordo artificialis*) of events to be reported or to be told by means of verbal texts, did not, and, within the boundaries of sets by its discourse could not, develop the idea of a nontemporal ordering needed for the description of the surfaces of pictorial works of art.

Viewed in historical perspective, Renaissance to Enlightenment attempts at developing some of the elements of a "rhetoric of art" on the model of classical rhetoric, thus appear as characteristic of a period of theorizing about the arts in general and the visual arts in particular, which did not yet have at its disposal reliable semiotic distinctions between the arts in terms of the different artistic media (symbol systems) employed. [*See overview article on* Renaissance rhetoric.] Whenever such elements of a rhetoric of art were identified, the similarity between the (mental) activities of orator (poet) and painter had to be tacitly assumed, or the existence of a shared semantics of verbal and pictorial art (*historia, imitatio naturae*) or the applicability of the same stylistic concepts (*humile, mediocris, sublime*) to both arts, or, finally, a similarity in communicative intent (*delectare, movere*). [*See* Style; *and* Sublime, the.] In addition, the theorizing in question was of a type that aimed at training the orator and the painter respectively. Its ultimate goal was not, it should not be overlooked, a theory of the verbal or the pictorial text. Instead, its focus on the orator and the painter, and on making their activities teachable and learnable, meant that issues like the relation of verbal sound and word (in the case of the orator's dealing with language), and the relation of plane surfaces and lines on the one hand and members, bodies, and stories on the other (in the case of the painter's work on pictorial surfaces), could be safely ignored. Those were issues falling into the domain of an aesthetics yet to be developed, rather into that of an art of declaiming or an art of painting. They would only present themselves for discussion once the theoretical focus was no longer on the training of the orator or the painter but on the verbal and the pictorial text itself. With the advent of a full-fledged semiotics of art in the second half of the twentieth century that shift in focus did indeed take place. With that shift came the realization that the aims of a rhetoric of visual art as envisioned by Renaissance art theorists like Alberti could best be realized in the form of the pragmatic component of a comprehensive semiotics of art, by that part of semiotics that addresses questions relating to the producer and the recipient of art.

Another issue, which also could only surface once a clear distinction between the verbal medium used by declamation and the pictorial one used by painting had been achieved, was that of the difference between a rhetoric of art and a rhetoric of art criticism. Only the latter, in contrast to the former, falls within the object domain of rhetoric proper. Texts of art criticism have a propositional content; they offer descriptions and evaluations of works of the visual arts, suggest specific ways of looking and seeing, and advise against others. Here, then, questions regarding persuasion and the means by which it is achieved can be raised directly and straightforwardly, rather than only by way of an ultimately problematic and unconvincing transfer of concepts of rhetorical analysis from verbal to pictorial art. [*See* Criticism; *and* Persuasion.]

[*See also* Classical rhetoric; *and* Color.]

BIBLIOGRAPHY

Barasch, Moshe. *Theories of Art: From Plato to Winckelmann.* New York, 1985. See especially chapters 3–5.

Baxandall, Michael. *Giotto and the Orators: Humanist Observers of Painting in Italy and the Discovery of Pictorial Composition 1350–1450.* Oxford, 1986. First published 1971.

Baxandall, Michael. *Painting and Experience in Fifteenth Century Italy: A Primer in the Social History of Pictorial Style.* 2d ed. Oxford, 1988. First published 1972.

Blunt, Anthony. *Artistic Theory in Italy 1450–1660.* Oxford, 1964. First published 1940.

Chambers, David. "'A Speaking Picture': Some Ways of Proceeding in Literature and the Fine Arts in the Late-Sixteenth and Early-Seventeenth Centuries." In *Encounters: Essays on Literature and the Visual Arts.* Edited by John Dixon Hunt, pp. 28–57. London, 1971.

Dolders, Arno. "Ut Pictura Poesis: A Selective, Annotated Bibliography of Books and Articles, Published between 1900 and 1980." *Yearbook of Comparative and General Literature* 32 (1983), pp. 105–124.

Farago, Claire. *Leonardo da Vinci's Paragone: A Critical Interpretation with a New Edition of the Text in the Codex Urbinas.* Leiden, 1992.

Gent, Lucy. *Picture and Poetry 1560–1620: Relations between Literature and the Visual Arts in the English Renaissance.* Leamington Spa, U.K., 1981.

Hagstrum, Jean H. *The Sister Arts: The Tradition of Literary Pictorialism and English Poetry from Dryden to Gray.* Chicago, 1987. First published 1958.

Heffernan, James A. W. "Speaking for Pictures: The Rhetoric of Art Criticism." *Word & Image* 15.1 (1999), pp. 19–33.

Kemp, Martin. "From Mimesis to Fantasia: The Quattrocento Vocabulary of Creation, Inspiration, and Genius in the Visual Arts." *Viator* 8 (1977), pp. 347–398.

Kristeller, Paul O. "The Modern System of the Arts: A Study in the History of Aesthetics." In *Renaissance*

Thought and the Arts: Collected Essays. First published 1965 as *Renaissance Art.* Princeton, 1980.

LeCoat, Gerard. *The Rhetoric of the Arts, 1500–1650.* Bern, Switzerland, 1975.

Lee, Rensselaer W. "Ut pictura poesis: The Humanistic Theory of Painting." *The Art Bulletin* 22 (1940), pp. 197–269. Reprint *Ut Pictura Poesis.* New York, 1967.

Scholz, Bernhard F. "*Ekphrasis* and *Enargeia* in Quintilian's *Institutionis oratoriae libri xii.*" In *Rhetorica Movet. Studies in Historical and Modern Rhetoric in Honour of Heinrich F. Plett.* Edited by Peter L. Oesterreich and Thomas O. Sloane, pp. 3–24. Leiden, 1999.

Spencer, John R. "Ut rhetorica pictura. A Study of Quattrocento Theory of Painting." *Journal of the Warburg and Courtauld Institutes* 20 (1957), pp. 26–44.

— BERNHARD F. SCHOLZ

ASSONANCE is a vocalic isophoneme that consists of corresponding similarity in repeated vowel-sounds, as in the 1896 poem "*I* heard a fl*y* buzz when *I* d*ie*d" by Emily Dickinson. Assonance is often used to give the text a lyrical quality.

[*See also* Alliteration.]

— ANDREA GRÜN-OESTERREICH

ASYNDETON (Lat. *dissolutio*), which Puttenham (*The Arte of English Poesie,* 1589) calls "loose language," an isotaxeme that lists clauses or single words by omitting an expected conjunction. Its effect is a staccato-like rhythm that results in clear-cut brevity and celerity of speech. Hence, it can be used, for example, in laconic military language: "Veni, vidi, vici" ("I came, I saw, I conquered." [Caesar]), as well as in pathetic outburst: "I love you more than words can wield the matter; / Dearer than eye-sight, space, and liberty / . . . No less than life, with grace, health, beauty, honour" (Shakespeare, *King Lear* 1.1.55–58). Its opposite is *polysyndeton.*

[*See also* Figures of speech; Polysyndeton; *and* Style.]

— ANDREA GRÜN-OESTERREICH

ATTICIST–ASIANIST CONTROVERSY. The terms *Atticist* and *Asianist* were employed over a period of several centuries (starting probably in the third century BCE) in a debate that was concerned as much with ideology and literary identity as it was with style and language. Developed in the Greek world, the terminology was taken up by the Romans at a critical point in their literary history. It would be a mistake to look for unity in a debate that spanned so many centuries and two different literary cultures.

In the second half of the first century BCE, we find at Rome a bad-tempered argument among writers and orators over how the appellation *Attic* was to be employed. This purely Roman debate, like much of the literary and intellectual revolution at Rome, was conducted in terminology taken over from Greek. Insofar as *Attic* had any meaning, it denoted a plain and unadorned style of composition; but its more important function was evaluative. It was used by the self-proclaimed Atticists as a term of approbation for the Roman heirs of the great figures of the classical Greek tradition (particularly Lysias, Demosthenes, Xenophon, and Isocrates): Attica is the region of Greece in which Athens is located. The antonym of Attic, on this view, was *Asianist,* a term best defined negatively; it denoted all the bad qualities that a dedicated Atticist should avoid. The principal object of this needling was Cicero (106–43 BCE), the most famous orator of his day. Roman Atticism was thus in part a normal literary reaction to a familiar and prestigious style, described by Quintilian as "full" (Cicero's sentences are often long and complex, characterized by attention to balance, rhythm, and rhetorical effect). Much of our insight into this ephemeral dispute comes from Cicero's *Brutus* and *Orator* (both composed in 46 BCE), in which he discusses style and replies to his opponents. He argues, with some justification, that it is absurd to restrict the term *Attic* to a single style (it was identified with the simple and unaffected style of Lysias by the Atticists), since a whole range of styles and registers are found in the Athenian orators. Part of Cicero's irritation seems to stem from the implicit threat by the Atticists to deny him the title of the Roman Demosthenes. Since Demosthenes was generally held to represent the acme of Athenian rhetoric, Cicero would become ineligible for this position if he were proven to be un-Attic. The name most associated with the Atticists is G. Licinius Calvus (82–47 BCE), and it is unlikely to be a coincidence that Calvus was a friend of the neoteric poet Catullus: both men championed the Callimachean literary aesthetic, which rejected the swollen and the large-scale in favor of the "slender Muse"— in other words, a smaller-scale and restrained style of composition.

The debate in Rome seems to presuppose an argument using the same terms in the Hellenistic schools of rhetoric. There is, unfortunately, a gap in our Greek sources between the end of the fourth century BCE and the time of Cicero, which makes it difficult to understand what exactly the debate was and what force the terms *Atticist* and *Asianist* may have had. After the end of the fourth century, the Greeks seem increasingly to have looked back to the "classical" period as a literary and linguistic high point, deviation from which could only mean decline. The establishment of a classical canon led to a conception of stylistic and linguistic norms, which affected almost the entire subsequent history of the Greek language (this linguistic insecurity coincided with the collapse of Greek political autonomy following the Macedonian conquest). It is likely, then, that Atticism had its roots in a Hellenistic tradition of declamation that looked back to the great masters of classical rhetoric and insisted on rigid adherence to the lexicon, syntax, and style of a period of the language that was increasingly remote. The requirement for "correct Greek" (*Hellēnizein*) is laid down in Aristotle's *Rhetoric,* and was reiterated by Stoic writers. At this early stage, the emphasis seems to have been on clarity, for which correct diction (grammar and syntax) was necessary: the choice of vocabulary is, of course, a gray area between diction and style. The Attic movement during the Hellenistic period was probably marked by an increasing emphasis on stylistic conformity.

The antonym *Asianism* is more difficult to unravel. There is some evidence that at the end of the fourth century, a separate tradition of rhetoric evolved in the eastern Mediterranean. This tradition to some extent loosened the stranglehold of classicism and encouraged a greater degree of creativity and innovation in composition. To this extent, the term had a geographical content, and its most famous exponent was Hegesias of Magnesia in Lydia. By the first century BCE, however, the terms *Attic* and *Asianic* denoted the style that a speaker adopted rather than his geographical provenance, and even from a stylistic perspective were often devoid of useful descriptive content

about a particular orator's technique. Cicero mentions two different rhetorical techniques, which he calls *Asianic* (he is talking of Greek, but then moves without a break to talking of Latin): one was "pointed and epigrammatic," and the other was "passionate and rapid." Cicero's attitude toward Asianic style is ambiguous: while he does not condemn it outright (just as he refuses to endorse a simplistic view of Atticism), most of the orators to whom he applies the designation are criticized for their excesses. Much of the point of the opposition was in fact ideological, stemming from a long tradition of viewing Asia Minor and the East as a repository of anticlassical values: corrupt, barbarian, and effeminate. This favored the eventual disappearance of the term *Asianic* (since there was reluctance to apply it to one's own side); but it does not mean that the Asianic style (as defined, and perhaps occasionally exemplified, by Cicero) was uninfluential in the subsequent development of prose style in Rome.

In the Greek world, the aspiration to Atticize enjoyed a new vogue in the period known as the Second Sophistic (c.60–230 CE), in which the ability to reproduce the Greek of the Athenian masters was a hallmark of education that was indispensable for civic prestige and political power.

[*See also* Classical rhetoric; *and* Style.]

BIBLIOGRAPHY

Cicero, Marcus Tullius. *Brutus* and *Orator.* Text and translation by G. L. Hendrickson and H. M. Hubbell. Loeb Classical Library. Cambridge, Mass., 1939.

Fairweather, Janet. *Seneca the Elder.* Cambridge, U.K., 1981. Contains a useful review of the Roman sources in section IV. 1, "Asianism, Atticism, and the Style of the Declaimers," pp. 243–303.

Flashar, H. *Le Classicisme à Rome aux Iers siècles avant et après J.-C.* Geneva (Entretiens Hardt 25), 1979. A collection of nine essays in English, French, and German by leading scholars in the field.

Kennedy, George A., ed. *The Cambridge History of Literary Criticism,* vol. 1, *Classical Criticism.* Cambridge, U.K., 1989. See especially E. Fantham, "The Growth of Literature and Criticism at Rome," pp. 220–244, and D. C. Innes, "Augustan Critics," pp. 245–273.

Wilamowitz-Moellendorf, U. von. "Asianismus und Atticismus." *Hermes* 35 (1900), 1–52. Reprinted in his *Kleine Schriften,* vol. 3, pp. 223–273, Berlin, 1969. A classic discussion that reviews (and corrects) previous scholarly interpretations.

—STEPHEN C. COLVIN

AUDIENCE. [*This entry comprises three articles:*
An overview
Mass audiences
Virtual audiences
The first article provides an overview of the audience as a constitutive element of and agency for rhetorical practice. The second article explores mass audiences from Ancient Greece and Rome to modern day, with its communication methods that reach an audience not necessarily unified in place. The third article discusses virtual audiences and the significance of disembodied audiences united and "interfaced" by computer technology.]

An overview

The audience has long been central to the rhetorical tradition. Definitions of this term usually refer to a real person or collection of people who see, hear, or read an event or work. A key assumption in rhetoric is that discourse is composed in light of those who will hear or read it. Because of this, many believe that rhetors must contemplate the needs of their audiences while speaking or writing. Just how they should do so, however, is a matter of some debate.

A History of Audience. The charge to writers and speakers to "consider the audience" is a venerable one, dating back to before the fifth century BCE. For instance, in the fourth century BCE, Plato's "Socrates" noted that one must understand the nature of the audience if one hopes to be a competent speaker. [*See* Classical rhetoric.] While Plato (c.428–c.347 BCE) and his contemporaries were largely interested in oral rhetoric, recent scholars stress that rhetors crafting other types of messages (written, nonverbal, visual, mass mediated, virtual) should also take the audience into account. It has been argued that if any feature of rhetoric and composition can be taken as axiomatic, it is the audience—an entity related to many factors involved in a rhetorical occasion, including subject matter, invention, argumentative strategy, arrangement, enthymemes, topics,

genres, ethics, style, medium, and even, punctuation (Porter, 1992).

In classical times, the audience was a physical gathering located in a specific place. Although contemporary theorists extend the definition to consider the many audiences that experience a text (i.e., individuals who witness a speech in real time as well as those who read, hear, or see a recorded version of that speech), the early audience was primarily associated with listeners witnessing an oratorical event or occasion. These groups were much smaller and more public than modern audiences, which because of advances in communication technologies, are often dispersed, fragmented, and privatized. Subject matter for early audiences varied according to social class and status; educated groups met for literary and musical works, and larger ones attended fights, races, games, comedies, and circuses.

Evolving terminology. The term *audience* first appeared in the English language in the fourteenth century, and its original use referred to a hearing. Its etymological roots derive from face-to-face communication contexts, interactions that were hierarchically organized; indeed, to be granted an audience was to be given listeners, to be considered an authoritative source. Over time, the word has grown to represent an assembly of listeners, including readers or viewers of particular authors, speakers, or publications. With the advent of electronic media in the twentieth century, the word expanded to include individuals who experience radio, film, television, and the Internet from a distance.

The exact terms used to refer to the audience can lead to confusion. For example, the words *audience* and *reader* are generally employed to refer to the persons who read a piece of writing (i.e., an identifiable real reader). At other times, however, these terms carry more specific meanings. In some cases, the "reader" may refer to the person in the act of reading and responding to a written work (i.e., reader-reading, audience-reading), whereas the "audience" can refer to (1) the imaginative construction a writer uses while composing a text; (2) something that the writer places in the discourse itself; or (3) a combination of these. Over the years, other terms have also been used to refer to the audience, such as *receivers, decoders, users, consumers, communities,* and *forums.*

Scholarly attention has also focused on what the audience is not. Efforts to formulate a proper definition of the term have resulted in the labeling of particular groups with certain characteristics as "audiences" and the excluding of all other groups of auditors. Groups that have not met these criteria are labeled by some as "mobs," "small groups," "crowds," aggregations," or the like and are excluded as objects of audience analysis. Features used in the past to distinguish certain types of audiences from others include, but are not limited to: *plurality*—when two or more listeners are jointly present and become a source of stimuli for each other; *size*—the number of individuals receiving a message; *homogeneity*—the extent to which members of the group share a common background of experience, attitudes, habits of thought, and other traits; *group feeling*—the extent to which the members of the audience are aware of and responding to one another; *orderliness*—the state or context of the listeners; *preliminary tuning*—the degree to which the listeners are prepared for a message; *common focus of attention*—the extent to which the individuals are attending to the same message; and *polarization*—a condition when audience members assume a listening attitude and regard the speaker as separate and apart from their own situation.

Audience as centerpiece. Several academic communities consider the audience to be central to their work; for example, the areas of rhetoric and composition, reading theory, literary theory and criticism, and rhetoric and philosophy; areas related to communication studies, oral performance, and debate; the disciplines of film, theater, radio, television, journalism, mass communication, and advertising; critical approaches including those in critical studies, cultural studies, and political economy; and such applied areas as telecommunications, public policy, law, marketing, and business.

Given such widespread interest in this concept, perhaps it is not surprising that the term has been conceptualized in divergent ways. For instance, scholars in the past have viewed the audience as sets of individuals and as collective groups; as passive entities and as active participants in meaning making; as fundamentally similar and as idiosyncratic group members; as located in physical space and as residing primarily

in an author's imagination; as something to be written for and something that gets in the way of writing; as something that should be catered to and—recently from the poststructuralist position—something that should be questioned. Moreover, another communication-oriented encyclopedia, the *International Encyclopedia of Communication* (Oxford, 1989), does not feature a single entry for audience but encourages readers to consult a variety of articles, including the following entries: crowd behavior, diffusion, interactive media, mass communications research, mass media effects, models of communication, persuasion, social cognitive theory, taste cultures; the measurement issues of consumer research, evaluation research, opinion measurement, poll, print audience measurement, rating systems, radio and television; and the societal concerns of agenda setting, bandwagon effects, cultivation analysis, cultural indicators, entertainment, leisure, opinion leader, political communication, politicization, public opinion, sleeper effect, and violence. In observing this range of meanings, Anderson (1996) notes that most definitions of the audience account for these criteria: exposure, content, interpretation, relationships, the individual, and the collective.

Although the rhetorical tradition has long been informed by the concept of audience, this essay will limit itself to the consideration of elaborated contemporary forms of audience types and styles of engagement. To provide a map of contributions on this topic, this entry considers both work conducted inside the rhetorical tradition (English, composition studies, speech communication, reader response work, postmodern and critical work) as well as in neighboring areas (mass communication, telecommunications, political science, marketing). Ideas from all of these fields help to shape the current state of audience research.

Attention to the Readers. In the early twentieth century, speech departments and then English departments began to emphasize rhetorical studies and courses that would train students how to communicate. As a result of these courses, as well as the work of philosophers, literary critics, and educators of the day, modern rhetoricians began to shift their attention from the speaker or writer to the auditor or reader. [*See* Criticism.] In the 1950s and 1960s, the audience enjoyed renewed interest as a result of the "New Rhetoric," an approach espoused by a group of theorists in speech communication, philosophy, composition, and English, which revived principles from classical rhetorical theory (mainly those associated with Aristotle) and integrated them with insights from modern philosophy, linguistics, and psychology. [*See* Modern rhetoric.]

Types of audience. This movement went beyond analyzing the form or content of discourse to consider elements of philosophy and sociology, and it led to a central concern with the audience. For instance, Perelman and Olbrechts-Tyteca (1969) suggest that all argumentation must be adapted to an audience and based on beliefs accepted by them. In this text, they describe three types of audiences: self as audience (arguing or questioning oneself); a universal audience (an ideal audience); and a particular audience (a real audience). In distinguishing between the universal and particular audience (the two which have been of greatest interest to rhetorical theorists), Perelman and Olbrechts-Tyteca draw on Immanuel Kant's notions of conviction (a judgment grounded in objectivity, valid for every rational being) and persuasion (a judgment grounded in the character of the subject). They then expand these notions by associating persuasion with action, and conviction with intelligence. Perelman and Olbrechts-Tyteca suggest that the particular audience, which can be distinguished by character, persuasion, and action, is subject to persuasion, whereas the universal audience, depicted by objectivity, conviction and competence, holds to its convictions. They admit that the universal audience is both ideal, the incarnation of traditional reason, and yet unreal because it never really exists. Rhetors can create a construct of a universal audience in order to persuade a particular one (which will resemble the universal audience in some, but not all respects), while being guided by its presumptions. The construct of the universal audience can thus be used to help rhetors distinguish between good arguments (reasonable ones) that this objective group would accept, and bad ones (specious claims) with which this group would disagree. [*See* Conviction; *and* Persuasion.]

Attention to Authors and Texts. In the 1960s and 1970s, expressivist scholars, who were interested in writing as self-discovery and the development of "authorial voice," and aesthetic scholars, who were fascinated with stylistic concerns, turned their attention to authors and texts, believing that true and pure artists create for themselves, not others. Consequently, it became acceptable in these camps to focus scholarly attention on intriguing authors, or texts, or both at the expense of audience. Others at the close of the twentieth century, however, became increasingly interested in the audience, specifically researchers from these perspectives: reader-response critics, who see the audience as active in constructing the meaning of a text; social constructionists, who view reality or truth as created by the author, text, and reader; mass communication and cultural studies scholars, who measure and question the effects of media on the audience; telecommunications scholars, who investigate the size and scope of virtual audiences; and postmodern scholars, who encourage new conceptualizations of the audience as a community or forum. These groups advance differing ideas about the audience, but a key product from recent research is that scholars have imagined the audience as powerful, and not simply a receptacle of rhetoric. Even though the idea of a powerful audience is not universally accepted, this perspective has inspired a rigorous, self-conscious, and meaningful debate as to the nature and agency of the audience.

The Relationship between Speaker and Audience. Audience analysis is of interest to both scholars and students of oral and written rhetoric. With regard to oral rhetoric, the basic course in speech communication departments for the past century has been public speaking. [*See* Public speaking; *and* Speech.] Audience analysis—the process of examining information about the expected listeners for a speech—is a critical component of this course's curriculum and is viewed by many to be key to a speaker's success. Textbooks for this course draw on time-honored advice in encouraging novice speakers to locate common themes that would appeal to most of the listeners; attempt to understand the nature of listeners in order to comprehend their passions; and physically place themselves in the position of the listeners. More specifically, these textbooks underscore how the relationship between the speaker and the audience determines the success of the speech, and they encourage asking several questions about an audience, including: *general questions* (How receptive is the audience? What kind of audience is being addressed? How does the audience perceive the speaker's credibility?); *demographic questions* (How does the speaker relate to the audience in terms of social groupings such as age, sex, family identification, sexual orientation, race, ethnic background, social class, philosophical or political perspectives, or religious orientation?); and *psychographic questions* (How does the speaker relate to the audience in terms of attitudes, values, lifestyle, and ideology?). In other words, the questions stressed in contemporary speech courses are not too different from those asked by Greek and Roman *rhētors*.

The influence of audience upon the speaker. Although the majority viewpoint holds that ethical speakers consider the audience while crafting messages, recent scholars have questioned the ethics of this process (Porter, 1992). For instance, some doubt whether any particular speech can sufficiently address the diversity present in actual audiences. These scholars ask such questions as: Should audience influence a speaker's approach to the topic? Should it determine it? When in the process of developing a message should concern with the audience begin? While those who question the ethics of designing messages for audiences are not in the majority, their concerns call attention to how widespread the support for audience analysis has been in the rhetorical tradition.

IDENTIFICATION AND COOPERATION. The work of literary critic and theorist Kenneth Burke (1897–1993) also challenges the prevailing view of the audience, specifically in his notion of *identification*. [*See* Identification.] Drawing on Aristotle's notion of "common ground," Burke suggests that persuasion occurs when rhetors create connections with their audiences and speak to them in the audience's own language. Burke pushes the notion of common ground or identification further than Aristotle, however, because he believes that the process of identification actually changes the speaker. While it is traditionally believed that speakers should learn about audiences simply to persuade them, Burke believes that the process of identification allows speakers to learn from audiences; for him, persuasion is

not unidirectional (speaker to listener), but a "moralizing process" in which rhetors are changed as they try to resemble the actions, words, beliefs, and writings of their audiences. In Burke's mind, then, persuasion is not simply a linear process, but a cooperative activity in which the speaker and the listeners become "one in being" (or "consubstantial"; 1950). The notion of identification is employed in persuasion teaching and research, some viewing identification as the basic preparation for persuasion.

AUDIENCE INFLUENCE DURING THE COMPOSITION PROCESS. Like their colleagues studying oral communication, composition theorists have considered how much, and recently whether, attention should be paid to the audience while composing texts. [*See overview article on* Composition.] The traditional advice in this field, as in public speaking, has been to "consider the audience" and make adjustments with regard to the listeners, the occasion, and the desired response (Booth, 1963). Proponents of this view believe awareness and understanding of audience can improve the quality of prose produced, reminding writers to communicate something to people in a way that will really make them wish to read it. Audience analysis is more difficult for writers than speakers, however, for while audiences of oral rhetoric are regarded as stable entities that speakers can analyze, observe, and accommodate, audiences of written texts are much less predictable. Accordingly, composition instructors face several challenges while teaching composition, including: encouraging students to (1) avoid writing for the obvious or immediate readers (their teacher or classmates); (2) refrain from assuming familiarity with or special knowledge of their readers; (3) write for a broader educated audience; and (4) imagine an audience beyond the demographic audience to guide the invention process (Park, 1986).

Theorists have not, however, universally advocated writing for the audience or with the audience in mind. For instance, advocates of expressivist and aesthetic rhetorics have been distrustful of the audience. These scholars focus on the author (at the expense of the audience), contending that true or pure artists create for themselves, not others. Expressivists, particularly in the 1960s and 1970s, viewed writing as a means of self-discovery and preferred that writers develop their own voice rather than creating texts to please the political and cultural norms of an era. Traces of the twentieth-century aesthetics movement and its influence can be found in composition and text manuals encouraging writers to please and satisfy themselves, and in the work of literary critics who prefer to focus on intriguing authors or texts instead of considering how readers might approach or respond to these works.

Other critics believe that anticipating the likes and dislikes of an audience can interrupt the writing process by paralyzing and compromising the integrity of the writer (Elbow, 1987) and, sometimes, by encouraging writers to rely on stereotypes of specific demographic groups. One alternative to relying on these stereotypes while writing is to conceptualize the audience as capable of playing many different roles as they read the text, mindful that these roles are not always bound by the identifiable characteristics these readers had before they started reading. It seems logical to believe that authors change while writing a text; they may discover that they have too little information on a subject, or their attitude may change on a subject. Similarly, it makes sense that a reader may change while reading a text; they may be intrigued by, horrified by, or entertained by a certain subject. From this perspective, it is preferable to envision the audience-reading, or playing roles with a text, than to fixate on the pre- or post-reader (Long, 1990). In envisioning the reader-reading, it is important to note that readers vary, naturally, in their ability to interact with texts (adults and educated readers are better at spotting cues in texts than children or less-educated readers), and that readers of fiction are more likely to play a broader number of roles than readers of nonfiction (particularly when the nonfiction focuses on deeply-held opinions).

THE RHETORICAL SITUATION. The audience is a key component in Lloyd Bitzer's seminal essay "The Rhetorical Situation" (1968), in which he ponders the nature of those contexts in which speakers or writers produce rhetoric. [*See* Rhetorical situation.] Bitzer suggests that the rhetorical situation entails the nature and disposition of the audience, the exigence that impels the writer to enter the situation, the writer's goal or purpose, whatever else has already been said on the sub-

ject, and the general state of the world outside the more specific context of the issue at hand. Bitzer holds that rhetoric always requires an audience, and stresses that a rhetorical audience (one that is capable of serving as mediator of the change that discourse functions to produce) is different from other types of audiences (a scientific audience, consisting of persons capable of receiving knowledge, or a poetic audience, composed of persons capable of participating in aesthetic experiences induced by the poetry). Bitzer emphasizes that rhetoric exists in a context, in a historical, cultural, and temporal setting that influences how speakers and listeners understand discourse. Because rhetoric is never about discourse in the abstract, the notion of audience is central to the rhetorical situation.

The rhetorical situation has been employed to help students learn how to conduct rhetorical criticism. Attending to the situation of a speech encourages students to ask a series of questions, including: (1) *Bitzer's questions* (Was a speaker's response to a rhetorical situation "fitting"? Did a speaker respond appropriately to a particular exigence?); (2) *questions implied by his approach* (What issue led to the decision to speak? What was the specific occasion for the rhetorical act? Why was this an issue? What was the specific point of stasis? What were the prevailing opinions or oppositional arguments on the issue? Who were the prominent or implicit counteradvocates? How could the issue be resolved or determined through rhetoric?); and (3) *questions related to the immediate and secondary audiences of a text* (Were the audiences in a position to respond appropriately? Were the audiences receptive to persuasion through argument? What were the demographics of the audiences? What were the values, needs, biases, goals, fears, and motives of the audiences?).

INTENDED AUDIENCE. Edwin Black (1970) also focuses on the audience, but rather than examine whether a speech fits an audience, he assesses speeches to discover what audience is implied in the discourse. He notes that the ideology of the audience will appear in the language of a text and that the representation of this implied audience can and should be morally judged from a rhetorical perspective. Phillip Wander (1984), also searches for audiences in texts, specifically for those that are negated, alienated through language, negated in history, negated in silence. Wander suggests that groups that are historically left out of discourse tend to be acted upon as non-subjects in political life and have been discriminated against in the body politic (i.e., discrimination based on "negated" peoples of certain races, religions, ages, genders, sexual preference, and nationalities). Like Black, Wander believes that *rhētors* should advance moral judgments, in this case about the groups left out of texts and the consequences of such practices.

READER-RESPONSE CRITICISM. *Reader-response criticism* sees the audience, or reader, as powerful and involves a set of critical theories that began to appear in the late 1960s and 1970s, but whose roots have a long history (e.g., Aristotle's *Poetics*, fourth century BCE, regarding the cathartic response of audiences at tragic performances). [*See* Reception theory.] The work of reader-response critics is often associated with certain prominent figures (Wolfgang Iser, *The Act of Reading*, Baltimore, 1980, and *The Implied Reader*, Baltimore, 1984; Stanley Fish, *Is There a Text in This Class?* Cambridge, Mass., 1980; Norman Holland, *5 Readers Reading*, New Haven, 1975; and Jonathan Culler, *Structuralist Poetics*, Ithaca, N.Y., 1976), each of whom argue that the audience plays a key role in the construction of textual meaning. This branch of criticism has developed a vocabulary for distinguishing various types of reading presences, including the "implied reader" (Wolfgang Iser); the "writer's audience" (Walter Ong's argument for the roles that real readers can adopt or reject); "interpretive community" (Stanley Fish's notion that collectives of readers develop conventions within a discipline or field that direct how meaning is to be constituted and interpreted); "identity themes" (Norman Holland's understanding that interpretation is a function of identity); and "literary competence" (Jonathan Culler's idea of a grammar of literature, which is internalized in the same ways as a person's ability to speak and understand his or her language).

It might be misleading to characterize reader-response criticism as a school or movement, for critics have advanced distinct and sometimes contradictory views. It is fair, however, to assert that this approach is unified by a set of common questions, such as: To what extent does the written text "determine" the act of reading? What happens to the reader during this act? How do the structures of extratextual knowledge and understanding within the reader's mind inform the art-event? How is meaning made in the reading process, and to what end? Such questions characterize the central focus in reader-response criticism, and underscore their efforts to call special attention to the reader or listener roles provided by texts as well as how these roles shape or direct audience reactions.

Contributions from reader-response critics have made their way to composition studies and composition instruction. For example, teachers encourage students to consider both the audience as "out there" (a group of actual people) as well as "in there" (a construct of a given text). These concepts, too, appear in the scholarly literature, as academics debate whether audiences can be addressed or whether they are invoked. In their essay on this debate, Ede and Lunsford (1984) differentiate between readers as concrete realities whom discourse must address (real audiences) and readers as textual constructs that actual readers must negotiate and possibly identify with (implied audiences). They suggest that the "audience addressed" perspective has its roots in the influence of cognitive psychology, speech communication, and business practices (expectations from groups outside of the academy including marketers, politicians, and businesses). Proponents of this position believe that actual audiences should be measured and that persuasion is achieved by tailoring messages for specific groups. The "audience invoked" view finds its basis in textual analysis and argues that writers cannot know their audiences in the same way that speakers can know their listeners. Advocates of this perspective contend that beginning writers should examine how other authors have created audiences via cues in texts, and come to internalize their own sense of a reader. For their part, Ede and Lunsford prefer a synthesis of these two perspectives. They advance an approach that considers how the writer-in-the-act-of-writing manages different writer–reader roles, constructing audience "in the text" as well as addressing the audiences "out there."

The Audience in Communication Models. The audience appears as a fundamental concept of basic communication models, most of which recognize four basic entities: speaker, listener, message, and transmission. [*See* Communication.] Specifically, the audience is featured in key definitions in communication research. Harold Lasswell encouraged the question: who says what in which channel to whom with what effect? Claude E. Shannon and Warren Weaver advanced a linear model of communication envisioning a source who encodes or creates a message and transmits it through a channel to a receiver who decodes or recreates the message. David Berlo's model featured four elements, source, message, channel, and receiver, (SMCR), which attends to such topics as encoding and decoding as well as personal factors that affect communicators.

The audience as individuals. Mass communication scholars also view the audience as central to their field, as well as key to an understanding of media industries, public life, and popular culture. In their minds, modern media outlets would not have the economic and cultural power they enjoy today without receivers, also referred to as markets or consumers (James Ettema and D. Charles Whitney, *Audiencemaking: How the Media Create the Audience,* Thousand Oaks, Calif., 1994). Many mass communication scholars believe that their very field was founded to tell communicators whom they were talking to. Early research on media effects views the audience as isolated individuals easily manipulated by the media (Frankfurt school). By the 1950s, however, scholars began to suggest that audience members were resistant to mediated messages as a "limited effects" perspective became the dominant paradigm of the field. Recent scholarship questions the limited effects paradigm, suggesting that it underestimates media effects as well as overstates the power and autonomy of the audience. Contemporary media scholars are also split as to whether mass audiences should be viewed as active or passive. For instance, researchers have likened television viewing to a range of activities that require little to extreme effort from individuals. Those who view television watching as equivalent to daydreaming suggest viewers are relatively passive, whereas revisionist scholars who believe viewers conduct political work by reading texts oppositionally argue that viewers are active.

Advancements in communication technologies and the proliferation of media outlets encourage scholars to revisit the assumption that the mass media play a uniform presence in people's lives. Because individuals have the opportunity to create increasingly unique media environments for themselves (via cable programming, satellites, the Internet), the likelihood that a majority of individuals will read the same news article or view the same television program on any given day is greatly decreased—a pattern that causes some to wonder if the media are losing their ability to create a common "coin of exchange" for audiences. Additionally, the trend toward fragmentation may alter the types of content appearing in the media. Whereas traditional media outlets assume a broad audience and develop content accordingly, new competitive outlets may develop narrower programming to hold an audience, a step that could lead toward a type of social dispersion. Many believe that as a result of fragmentation, scholars must be more explicit about the place of audience (presumed or otherwise) in their own academic work.

The audience as institutions. While most mass communication researchers examine the effects the media have on individuals, James Webster and Patricia Phalen (1997) have explored the effects mass audiences wield on institutions. They advance the concept of the *presumed audience*— an audience that places pressure on public forums and figures. Because institutions in the public eye are aware that they are being watched, these institutions attempt to predict and or react to the positions this presumed audience holds. Webster and Phalen suggest that individual viewers are also savvy to the presumed audience, for they know that while they are watching a major media event, they are part of a much larger audience participating in a common ritual. In a sense, this awareness increases the appeal of such major events for both citizens and the media; citizens have the opportunity to become part of a larger audience witnessing a common cultural event, and the media are supplied with a sizable, and profitable, audience.

Recent communication research. The audience has enjoyed a renewed interest in the late 1980s and 1990s from students of popular culture who take a critical, often openly political, perspective on the meanings of this concept. Recent work questions both previously held assumptions (i.e., the very idea of a vast audience), and methodologies employed by mass communication scholars (i.e., the use of survey data to measure audiences). Many critics question the state of mass communication research, believing that quantitative work in this area is largely misguided, for audiences are not naturally-occurring facts to be measured, but rather social creations of discourse. For example, Ien Ang (1996) disputes the assumption that the audience can be accurately observed, described, categorized, systematized, and explained in an empirical fashion. Instead, she believes that such research produces historically- and culturally-specific findings that result from discursive encounters between researchers and their subjects and are not products to be generalized to other populations.

Conceptualizing audience as a community. New terms for the audience emerge from postmodern research, including the audience as subcultures, interpretive communities, and taste publics. These perspectives assume that the rhetor's use of speech or writing is not original, but borrowed from the texts present in the various communities in which he or she resides. The discourse patterns in those communities, in turn, construct the rhetor. In this interactive model, truth and knowledge are local and contingent, and created through rhetoric that is always social and contextual. The conceptualization of audience as a community provides a middle ground between perspectives that see audiences as homogenous (such as the universal audience) and those that see all audience members as idiosyncratic, autonomous individuals. This model, too, offers a way to characterize audiences generally, while at the same time accommodating differences between and within communities. Advocates of this model applaud it for recognizing differences between various types of groups; critics, however, challenge it as potentially constraining and oppressive, because some communities have been known to be hegemonic and intolerant of minorities or dissenters.

THE DEMOCRACY OF PUBLIC OPINION. Democratic theorists are also concerned with the audience (and its related term the *public*), and have been since the fifth century BCE, when persuasive speech established claims in civil courts, as well as determined public policy, helped to administer laws, and could lend support to, or remove, leaders. [*See overview article on* Politics.] Many attest that democracy rests upon public opinion—a concept that, like the audience, is difficult to define. Basic questions exist about who and what constitutes a public, and how best to measure its thoughts and passions. One widespread attempt at measuring the thoughts of audience is polling, a practice that gained institutional legitimacy in the 1930s and has become a prevalent, albeit recently contested, means of measuring opinion. It has been argued that public opinion is always shaped and organized by the very instruments that purport to measure it. No such instrument is neutral; for instance, surveys encourage respondents to consider questions they may not know anything about; the variations in the wording of survey items encourage some responses and discourage others; surveys give voice to certain ideas and silence others. It is argued, therefore, that public opinion polls give power to the already powerful (Susan Herbst, *Numbered Voices,* Chicago, 1993).

Even though it is fashionable to critique political polling, as Pierre Bordieu (1979) does when he observes that public opinion does not exist although its effects are real, political scientists find that aggregate opinion has real effects in the polity. Research in this area suggests that the role of public opinion varies from issue to issue, and is most influential at the local level where the pressure from communities is most immediate. In general, elected officials try to avoid decisions that are at odds with polling data. Citizens, too, seem to be affected by public opinion data, as it has been observed that the public tends to accept decisions, initially at least, that are supported by public opinion data.

AUDIENCE ANALYSIS. Business and public relations departments also focus on the audience. A common statement in technological writing textbooks is that audience analysis and adaptation are crucial to successful writing, particularly with regard to instructions. [*See* Technical communication.] These textbooks also note that not long ago, technical writing was performed after product development and almost as an afterthought. Now these messages are often crafted right alongside the product. Marketing scholars are busily studying the niches resulting from fragmented audiences appearing on the Internet, and training students to understand audience demographics in order to offer informed consulting services. Rather than becoming less important in today's new information (digital) economy, many argue that an awareness of audience has become even more critical, particularly because, from the marketing perspective at least, businesses must compete with each other for the consumer's attention. As technological innovations find their ways to more households, business scholars believe that persuaders must become more sophisticated in the practice of niche marketing.

TECHNOLOGIES. Moreover, the appearance of such technologies in homes, schools, universities, and libraries raises new issues about the rhetorical relationship between online message senders and receivers. For writers, messages can be sent immediately, with little cost, to one or many receivers, and with a host of visual and audio characteristics (i.e., color and size of text, quantity and quality of hyperlinks, audio and video attachments), and all of these aspects of a message have potential effects on the receiver or audience. For their part, audiences have unprecedented opportunities for involvement in many computer-mediated communication occasions, as they can respond to e-mails and interactive Web sites; engage in online chats, forums, and polls; and post messages on electronic bulletin boards. At the end of the twentieth century, scholars were in the early stages of researching the conventions of computer-mediated communication (CMC) and focused on such topics as anonymity (when social cues are absent in CMC, aggressive communication increases as does an orientation for self); egalitarianism (when social cues are absent, receivers feel free to contribute ideas, less dominated by those in power positions, and decreased status competition); and concerns with reception (CMC is regarded as a lean medium that offers fewer cues and greater uncertainty and equivocation than a richer medium such as face-to-face communication, which offers feedback and multiple processing cues). While there is much to learn about the audience in cyberspace, many believe that this audience is more active than that of the Greek *polis*.

Conclusion. In sum, the rhetorical occasion always includes an audience, and the audience has been of central concern to rhetorical theorists, critics, philosophers, and practitioners for centuries. Many believe that an awareness and understanding of the audience has the power to make a significant difference in the quality of prose produced, as a sense of audience makes rhetors aware of the power, versatility, and consequences of effective writing and speaking. Indeed, success in a variety of fields (writing, law, religion, politics, entertainment, education) relies on connecting with an audience for a simple reason: individuals are more likely to achieve their broad objectives of persuading an audience if they have recognized its needs and formulated an appeal or message that is familiar to them.

Over time, the audience has grown from listeners of a specific speech to a term of interest in a variety of academic disciplines, technologies, businesses, and practices. The expansion of the audience concept, along with its diverse manifestations, opens up a dialogue across subfields, points to shared questions, fosters future theoretical development, and reveals how the audience is currently, as it has long been, an area of great interest to rhetorical thought and practice.

BIBLIOGRAPHY

Anderson, James. "The Pragmatics of Audience in Research and Theory." In *The Audience and Its Landscape,* edited by James Hay, Lawrence Grossberg, and Ellen Wartella, pp. 247–262. Boulder, Colo., 1996.

Ang, Ien. "Wanted: Audiences. On the Politics of Empirical Audience Studies." In *The Audience and Its Landscape,* edited by James Hay, Lawrence Grossberg, and Ellen Wartella, pp. 247–262. Boulder, Colo., 1996. A critique of empirical approaches to the audience.

Bitzer, Lloyd. "The Rhetorical Situation." *Philosophy and Rhetoric* 1 (1969), pp. 1–15.

Bizzell, Patricia, and Bruce Herzberg. *The Rhetorical Tradition: Readings From Classical Times to the Present.* Boston, 1991.

Black, Edwin. "The Second Persona." *Quarterly Journal of Speech* 56 (1970), pp. 109–119.

Booth, Wayne. "The Rhetorical Stance." *College Composition and Communication* 14 (1963), pp. 139–145.

Bordieu, Pierre. "Public Opinion Does Not Exist." In *Communication and Mass Struggle,* edited by Armand Mattelart and Seth Siegelaub. New York, 1979.

Burke, Kenneth. *A Rhetoric of Motives.* New York, 1950.

Campbell, George. In *Philosophy of Rhetoric*. Edited by Lloyd Bitzer. Carbondale, Ill., 1963.

Ede, Lisa, and Andrea Lunsford. "Audience Addressed / Audience Invoked: The Role of Audience in Composition Theory and Pedagogy." *College Composition and Communication* 25 (1984), pp. 155–171. An excellent essay on the debate as to whether audiences are best understood as material and identifiable or constructs of a given text.

Elbow, Peter. "Closing My Eyes as I Speak: An Argument for Ignoring Audience." *College English* 49 (1987), pp. 50–69. Elbow encourages novice writers to ignore audience until the revision stage.

Golden, James L., Goodwin F. Berquist, and William E. Coleman. *The Rhetoric of Western Thought*. 5th ed. Dubuque, Iowa, 1992.

Kirsch, Gesa, and Duane H. Roen, eds. *A Sense of Audience in Written Communication*. Newbury Park, Calif., 1990. Sixteen essays examining audience from historical, theoretical, and empirical considerations. See Russell Long's essay "The Writer's Audience: Fact or Fiction?" (pp. 73–84) for an analysis of the writer–audience relationship, and Theresa Enos's essay "An Eternal Golden Braid: Rhetor as Audience, Audience as Rhetor" (pp. 99–114) for an application of the notion of identification to the writing process.

Long, Russell. "The Writer's Audience: Fact or Fiction?" In *A Sense of Audience in Written Communication*, edited by Gesa Kirsch and Duane H. Roen, pp. 73–84. Newbury Park, Calif., 1990.

McQuail, Denis. *Audience Analysis*. Thousand Oaks, Calif., 1997. The media scholar observes that much of the confusion surrounding the word *audience* stems from the fact that a single term is used to describe an increasingly diverse and complex entity that is open to many different theoretical formulations.

Ong, Walter, S. J. "The Writer's Audience Is Always a Fiction." *Proceedings of the Modern Language Association* 90 (1975), pp. 9–21.

Park, Douglas. "The Meanings of Audience." *College English* 44 (1982), pp. 247–257.

Park, Douglas. "Analyzing Audiences." *College Composition and Communication* 37 (1986), pp. 478–488.

Perelman, Chaim, and L. Olbrechts-Tyteca. *The New Rhetoric: A Treatise on Argumentation*. Notre Dame, Ind., 1969. English translation of *Traite de l'argumentation,* first published in 1958.

Porter, James, E. *Audience and Rhetoric: An Archaeological Composition of the Discourse Community*. Englewood Cliffs, N.J., 1992. Offers a historical survey of approaches to the concept of audience, and advocates a social view of the audience as a "discourse community."

Wander, Phillip. "The Third Persona: An Ideological Turn in Rhetorical Theory." *Central States Speech Journal* 35 (1984), pp. 197–216.

Webster, James G., and Patricia F. Phalen. *The Mass Audience: Rediscovering the Dominant Model*. Mahwah, N.J., 1997.

—SHARON E. JARVIS

Mass audiences

One of the most controversial words in the English language is "mass" (Williams, 1985). It is a term both of abuse and endearment. Since the French Revolution, "the masses" have been the focus of radical hopes, liberal anxiousness, and conservative fears about democratic politics. The term *mass audience* can reflect such implied judgments about social quantity and cultural quality. Though some have argued that the term is obsolete (since audiences in a narrowcast age are increasingly segmented) or ethically tainted (since it treats the audience not as an agent but as a commodity), it designates, whatever its shortcomings, a lasting and important part of human discourse: attention collectives so large that personalized address, interaction between speaker and audience, or mutual acquaintance among audience members are all but impossible. Mass audiences, despite their considerable diversity, are all large gatherings of strangers oriented to a common focus.

Ancient Assembled and Dispersed Audiences. Though mass audiences are sometimes thought unique products of the enormous expansion of communication via mass media such as the press, cinema, and broadcasting in the twentieth century, they date to the beginning of rhetorical theory and practice.

Physical assembly is, of course, the classic setting for any kind of audience. Ancient Greece and Rome had various sorts of assembled mass audiences, in courts, political assemblies, and theaters. Up to six thousand citizens could gather in the *ekklēsia* (assembly) of Athens. Though every citizen had the theoretical right to speak (*isēgoria*), few spoke and most listened, an asymmetry characteristic of mass audiences. Theaters had even greater capacities, though precise estimates are dubious. The Athenian theater of Dionysos after its remodeling in 330 BCE probably held up to nineteen thousand people. The theater at Ephesus was said to hold fifty-five thousand people, also the approximate range of the Roman Coliseum, but the largest audience in the classical world was the Roman Circus Maximus, an oval-shaped arena used for chariot races, which held up to 150,000 spectators. A listening audience (such as for drama and oratory) was necessarily smaller than one of spectators, given the limits on acoustic intelligibility for the unamplified voice. Audiences are always the results of social engineering, and architecture was one shaper of audience forms in antiquity.

Even in modern times, assembled audiences rarely exceed limits reached in the ancient world. Though one million protestors might fill the Mall in Washington, D.C. or London's Trafalgar Square, such rallies might be better understood as mass rhetors than mass audiences, since their aim is sending rather than receiving communication. Perhaps the largest assemblies in history have taken place in Beijing's Tiananmen Square, from the May Fourth movement of 1919 through the Cultural Revolution to the Democracy Uprising of 1989.

The Bible offers interesting, if untrustworthy, indications of ancient mass audiences; the *Book of Numbers* (ch. 1) reports that the whole "congregation" of the twelve tribes of Israel was assembled together on the first day of the second month, totalling 603,550 males over the age of twenty. Whatever that number's accuracy, the congregation seems more an army camp than a body assembled to hear speeches or see drama, though the *Exodus* narrative often portrays the camp of Israel as an audience of the spectacular events that occurred on Mount Sinai. Perhaps the grandest premodern vision of a mass assembly is found in John Milton's *Paradise Lost* (1667). A "thronging audience" of millions of fallen angels gathers at Pandemonium to harken to Satan's eloquence (2:555). Since the demonic spirit-bodies, Milton informs us, take no space, there is no crowding or limit to the gathering. The dream, at least, of a potentially limitless audience is much older than modern mass media!

Classical antiquity also recognizes dispersed rather than congregated audiences. Socrates in Plato's *Phaedrus* (275e) offers a negative view of them. Writing, he complains, sends forth thoughts into the world like orphans to encoun-

ter unknown and unprepared readers. Whereas Socrates treats promiscuous audiences and open-ended address as dangerous, other ancient thinkers celebrate their publicity and universality. Both Stoicism and Christianity developed notions of global solidarity among all human beings, using civic (world citizenship) and theological (divine kinship) arguments respectively, notions that reflect the historical development of polyglot empires and imperial forms of communication. A nice example is found in the biblical *Book of Daniel* (4.1), written in the second century BCE, which (anachronistically) represents King Nebuchadnezzar as sending a decree "to all people, nations, and languages that dwell in all the earth." A similar notion of messages addressed "to whom it may concern" occurs in the parable of the sower in the synoptic gospels of the New Testament (Peters, 1999). The idea of a universal address that includes all recipients is ancient.

There is something utopian about addressing worldwide audiences, ancient or modern, given the diversity of human languages and the difficulties of distribution. A founding insight of rhetorical theory is that communication is always constrained by particulars (Aristotle, *Rhetoric* 1355b14); any attempt to reach *all* will only reach *some*. For Perelman and Olbrechts-Tyteca (1958), the universal audience is more a regulative norm than an achievement. The effort to conjure a mass (universal) audience at best yields a mix of segmented (particular) audiences. Discourse *ad humanitatem* never catches all humans, even though it may inspire or discipline a speaker's imagination; mass address or dissemination does not always imply mass reception.

With the development of modern mass media, the internal variety of mass audiences was discovered anew. The trend in modern media history is to isolate some audience members for strategic (often, but not always pecuniary) purposes. The mid nineteenth-century enthusiasm about "news for all" in American journalism faded with the early twentieth-century discovery that some readers were more economically desirable than others (Leonard, 1995). Similarly, the trend in U.S. television programming and advertising since the 1960s is fragmentation into segmented instead of nationwide audiences (Turow, 1997). Here again, rhetorical theory anticipates modern developments. Socrates argues that a good speaker, like a good doctor, should not scatter treatments indiscriminately to an audience, but single out specific kinds of listeners (*Phaedrus* 271b–272b). Socrates' call to consider the diversity of audience types was often hailed by twentieth-century pioneers of empirical social research on mass audiences (e.g., Merton, 1946). Thus, though the dream of an all-inclusive audience is ancient, so is the more sober insight that any actual mass audience can be understood as a composite of distinct subgroups.

Modern mass audiences. In modern times, assembly continues to be important, though the huge growth has been in audience forms not unified in place. Though the simultaneous audiences of radio and television—which can spread across a time-zone, a nation, or occasionally the entire planet—are typical examples of noncontiguous attention collectives, print media led the way well before electronic media. Not least among the historical consequences of the printing press was the establishment of dispersed social collectives such as scientific "invisible colleges" and national "imagined communities" (Anderson, 1991). Medieval manuscript culture did sustain farflung diasporas among Jewish, Christian, and Muslim scholars, but print, combined with mass literacy, allows for a qualitative change in scale. In Northern Europe and in America for several centuries, the vernacular Bible has been a station broadcasting to congregations numbering in the millions on Sunday mornings. That the "message" has been received with such fractiousness (Protestantism) simply illustrates the gaps that exist between address and reception in interpretation. The recent notion of the virtual audience, an online collective unified not by contact but by common orientation, is anticipated in print, if not manuscript culture.

Though print clearly exemplifies key features of mass audiences, it was not until the late nineteenth century that dispersed mass audiences emerged on a modern scale. Newspapers were largely elite organs until the 1830s, and even the popular press of the 1830s and 1840s had circulations at most in the tens of thousands. The threshold of 1 million people was probably passed first in the 1890s in New York City, during Hearst's and Pulitzer's newspaper circulation wars. By the 1930s, radio audiences could count tens of millions in the industrial nations. By the late 1960s, simultaneous global audiences became possible, as in the televised moon landing, sports extravaganzas, or other "media events" (Dayan and Katz, 1992).

The mass audience of electronic broadcasting offers conceptual difficulties. Though it is tempting to think that electronic media finally made mass audiences possible, radio and television may in one sense mark their demise—not in size but in forms of address and reception. Broadcasting has become a cultural form overwhelmingly received in private. In theory, it could have taken cinema's path of congregated reception (an option favored by policy-makers in 1920s Germany, for instance). Broadcast programs and personnel assumed personal modes of address, mellow vocal styles, and conversational formats to make audiences comfortable with the personae they had invited into their homes. Older styles of oratory addressed to an impersonal public assembly fell by the wayside. In the 1930s, radio listeners in Britain and elsewhere were invited to perceive themselves not as a Miltonic pandemonium or thronging audience, but as a gathering of friends or family (Scannell, 1991). Here we find the mass audience as the sum of innumerable small gatherings. A mass audience is not the same as an audience of masses.

Obviously, the self-perception of the home audience of radio or television is incomplete. To the manager or researcher, ratings techniques offer different views. There is a disconnect between the millions of domestic scenes in which programs are received and the technical apparatus that sends, measures, and finances them. The audience is not only what people experience; it is an industrial object worth tens of billions of dollars. Much is known about aggregate audience behavior, from seasonal and daily viewing patterns to age, gender, race, and regional variations in composition (Webster and Phalen, 1997). The business of commercial broadcasting is selling audiences to advertisers, and these are products constituted by research techniques. When Raymond Williams (1983) said "There are no masses, only ways of seeing people as masses," he meant to criticize undemocratic habits of thought, but also provided a neat description of the epistemological construction of mass audiences. As a "way of seeing," statistics can make a mass audience intelligible. What architecture was to ancient assemblies, audience research is to modern broadcasting: the chief agency of audience engineering. The convening of audiences is an exercise of power; audience measurement research can serve as a form of social control (Ang, 1991). Several tensions mark broadcast mass audiences: concrete versus abstract, part versus whole, sensible versus intelligible, experiential versus industrial. The broadcast audience is a totality that presents a very different face to the lay participant and the expert observer.

In addition to assemblies, dispersed publics, summed microaudiences, and epistemological constructs, mass audiences can be written reflexively into texts. Viewers, listeners, and readers are often hailed as live coparticipants with their far-flung counterparts. Many broadcast programs offer various sorts of internal audiences. Sports coverage, for instance, often shows spectators both at the game and watching it on television in homes, bars, and halls across the land. Laugh tracks in comedy programming imply a normative standard of audience response; studio audiences serve a similar function in talk shows. The pervasiveness of strategies that present media as sites of the amassed attention of internal audiences shows that assembly has not been outmoded by modern media; rather, its prestige and power are still actively invoked.

Finally, mass audiences can be dispersed across time as well as space. Millions have visited shrines such as Jerusalem's Holy Sepulcher or Lenin's Tomb, even though only few can be admitted at one time. Such audiences are pinpointed in space but dispersed in time, the precise inverse of broadcast audiences, which are dispersed in space but pinpointed in time. As in broadcasting, what we might call serial mass audiences are small experientially but enormous cumulatively. Such seems to be the predominant form of mass audience emerging around the Internet, with its geographical metaphor of visiting Web sites. A newspaper concentrates readers in one part of one day, though theoretically trailing off forever; temporally dispersed audiences require durable objects. New books, films, videos, and CDs may amass audiences across weeks or months, depending on

genre, marketing, and popularity, again trailing off forever in theory. Cultural monuments such as Homer or Shakespeare may accumulate mass audiences over centuries or even millennia. As Harold Adams Innis notes (1951), media that collect people across time generally have a more sacred status than those that collect people across space; it is no accident that shrines and classics provide the handiest examples of mass audiences dispersed across long periods of time.

BIBLIOGRAPHY

Anderson, Benedict R. O'G. *Imagined Communities: Reflections on the Origins and Growth of Nationalism.* 2d ed. New York, 1991. Suggestively connects history of print media and rise of nationalist consciousness.

Ang, Ien. *Desperately Seeking the Audience.* London, 1991. Critique of statistical measurement and ratings of mass audiences as social control and commodification.

Dayan, Daniel, and Elihu Katz. *Media Events: The Live Broadcasting of History.* Cambridge, Mass., 1992. Analysis of social consequences of live, participatory televised events involving mass audiences.

Innis, Harold Adams. *The Bias of Communication.* Toronto, 1951. Classic work on time and space as constituents of media of communication.

Leonard, Thomas. *News for All: America's Coming of Age with the Press.* New York, 1995. Lively treatment of U.S. press history.

Merton, Robert K, with Marjorie Fiske and Alberta Curtis. *Mass Persuasion: The Social Psychology of a War Bond Drive.* New York, 1946. Classic work drawing on both social theory and rhetorical theory.

Perelman, Chaim, and Lucie Olbrechts-Tyteca. *The New Rhetoric: A Treatise on Argumentation.* Translated by John Wilkinson and Purcell Weaver. Notre Dame, Ind., 1971; first published in 1958. Classic treatment of universal audience.

Peters, John Durham. *Speaking into the Air: A History of the Idea of Communication.* Chicago, 1999. Intellectual history of communication theory from Plato to radio.

Scannell, Paddy, ed. *Broadcast Talk.* Newbury Park, Calif., 1991. Essays suggesting that broadcasting involves not mass address but more subtle sorts of linguistic strategies.

Turow, Joseph. *Breaking Up America.* Chicago, 1997. Analysis of audience fragmentation in American advertising since the 1970s.

Webster, James G., and Patricia F. Phalen. *The Mass Audience: Rediscovering the Dominant Model.* Mahwah, N.J., 1997. The standard work, including comprehensive treatment of social research on mass audiences.

Williams, Raymond. *Culture and Society*. New York, 1983, first published 1958. Classic work on nineteenth- and twentieth-century British social thought.

Williams, Raymond. *Keywords*. Oxford, 1985. Dictionary of terms central to social analysis and cultural criticism.

—JOHN DURHAM PETERS

Virtual audiences

Virtual audiences are collectives of people who receive and send messages via Internet communication systems, including electronic distribution lists, Usenet news groups, electronic bulletin board systems, and the World Wide Web. Whereas the predominant use of computer-mediated communication is electronic mail between individuals, messages posted through these alternative channels reach many people at once. This development offers unique implications for audience making and rhetorical dynamics. The technical characteristics of these media are important, for they have a great deal to do with the way that computer-mediated communication transforms the nature of the audience, compared to audiences of speeches or traditional mass media.

An electronic distribution list is comprised of a computer file containing the mail addresses of numerous individuals who have subscribed to a given list. When an electronic message is sent to the list's address, that message is automatically regenerated via electronic mail to all subscribers, either immediately, or in a daily collection (or "digest"). The number of subscribers may range from a small group to thousands of individuals worldwide.

Usenet newsgroups are similar to lists, except that one need not be an ongoing subscriber in order to read messages. At its heart, Usenet news consists of a protocol for posting and appending messages, within topical categories, such that they are relayed among computer systems carrying Usenet "feeds" globally. In this case, messages are posted to the topic and relayed to distributed computers, where they are stored for varying periods of time. Subsequent readers may reply to previous messages (maintaining a "thread of con-

versation"), or may initiate a new subtopic. Since Usenet newsgroups are decentralized by their very nature (in contrast to distribution lists, which are owned or maintained by the specific entity that owns the subscription list), they are relatively anarchic. One cannot control communication within these groups, except by means of informal sanctioning through further replies (see McLaughlin, Osborne, and Smith, 1995), or, through a system administrator, by terminating access to some newsgroups for one's entire site.

Electronic bulletin board systems are among the oldest means of sharing comments with others via computer networks. Early versions predated the forerunners of the current Internet by allowing individuals to connect via modem and phone line to a privately-owned computer. Originally popular among hobbyists, such systems evolved into large groups such as the San Francisco area's WELL (Whole Earth Lectronic Link), made famous by journalist and essayist Howard Rheingold in 1993 as a "Virtual Community."

Most recently, the World Wide Web may be considered an interactive communication system. While most applications of the Web should be considered as publications rather than interactions, this consideration is tempered by several new developments, including (1) the increasingly easy and inexpensive ability for anyone to create a Web site of his or her own, which essentially puts a mass publication medium that can be changed continually, in the hands of many people, and (2) the development of chat-like and bulletin-board-like features within Web sites, where visitors can exchange comments.

The most dramatic way that the virtual audience differs from a traditional audience is in its potential interactivity. While it is theoretically possible for audience members of a speech, print, or broadcast message to attempt to talk back to, write, or call the original rhetor or medium owner (publisher or broadcast company), the auditor is in these cases less privileged than the original rhetor and may not be given the floor or recognized. In the case of computer-mediated communication, however, each reader is a writer. The same media that allow one to consume others' messages, easily allow one to send messages to the same audience. It is equally simple and no less costly whether one is contacting an entire audience or an individual. Each message appears in a recipient's queue, with no greater or lesser prominence than anyone else's, unless the recipient has personal familiarity with the senders' name or electronic address. Each auditor is aware of other auditors, and may communicate with them. This form of communication contrasts with familiar and traditional media, which offer one-to-one communication (face-to-face, in writing, or telephone), or one-to-many communication, where a rhetor, writer, or broadcaster transmits messages to a traditional, receiving audience. This new mode is referred to as many-to-many communication, where each auditor is a potential rhetor, and the audience communicates with itself, potentially eclipsing in frequency and volume any original message.

An additional aspect of computer-mediated communication is that there are no immediate signs of a messenger's status or expertise. This, according to some theorists, tends to "democratize" communication. That is, since one need not request the floor or buy space, and since no one is immediately perceived as any different until their text is read, writers are not subject to the inhibitions common in face-to-face interaction—due to lower social role, hierarchical position, or minority status—and therefore feel free to express themselves. From a reader's perspective, any person's posting is potentially as important or influential as anyone else's. At least, no judgments about a writer's authority can be made from extratextual circumstances; rather, one's credibility can only be established within the messages themselves. As William Mitchell, the former dean of Architecture at the Massachusetts Institute of Technology (MIT) argues, readers (and writers) do make social judgments and credibility assessments based on the implied status of one's electronic mail address that appears accompanying messages: "dean@mit.edu," Mitchell argues, has different connotations than "wjm@mit.edu," and "mit.edu" may carry its own connotations. Also, as researchers Jolene Galagher, Lee Sproull, and Sara Kiesler argue, given that there are no extrinsic cues to the writers' authority, nor does a physical presence indicate sincere commitment to discussion; writers themselves must establish the

importance of their contributions. They do so by making claims to legitimacy (displaying topicality, commonality, and need) and authority (they themselves have personal experience with the subject of the discussion). Third, experimental research has shown that, because of the relative lack of personal information transmitted in computer-mediated communication, subtle cues about social status or group membership transmitted by virtual participants or implied by the social context in which interactions take place, tend to have exaggerated value in the perceptions of readers, who make "overattributions" from the relatively sparse social information. These exaggerated perceptions may heighten ingroup/outgroup relations and tensions. They may even lead to misattributions and denigration of messages that seem inappropriate to the presumed (even falsely-presumed) role of the writer. Finally, despite the dearth of nonverbal cues as to personal identity online, users come to recognize and get to know one another over repeated interactions over time, within ongoing virtual affiliations, from which status may accrue, and through which friendships are commonly formed. [See Identification.]

Another difference between the virtual and traditional audience is the durability of auditors' responses. While a "live" audience member's response to a rhetor may be fleeting, remembered at most by those in immediate proximity, or recorded somehow if the rhetorical event is preserved, the virtual audience member's written response may be distributed much differently. A comment typed in regard to a specific stimulus—like anything shared on the Internet—may be forwarded by readers, in or out of context, to anyone else. Moreover, many communication systems are preserved (some, so far, indefinitely, such as the Dejanews—www.dejanews.com—searchable archive of Usenet postings), and may be searched by others who are entirely unfamiliar with the original rhetorical stimulus. Audience responses are relatively permanent, enduring, and potentially decontextualized. Rarely, elsewhere, might an audience respondent concern him or herself with the gravity that such permanence suggests.

A final characteristic of the virtual audience is

that individuals aggregate from all over the world, not on the basis of geography but on the basis of shared interests, as long as they share a common language (at least so far; efforts are being made to develop workable translation systems as well). In one sense, shared interests offer greater cohesion and expertise, and in larger numbers, than is typical of a nonelectronic group. On the other hand, there is more potential diversity of membership within ongoing bona fide groups that may span thousands of members and cross several continents. Each of these characteristics may be disruptive or beneficial. For instance, the audience for Usenet newsgroups focused on political issues is vast, and civility often gives way to polarization and hostility as people take sides, vociferously, on issues. Yet the newsgroups for exchanging information among depressed individuals, cancer patients, or other marginalized groups seem to benefit from the range of experience, expertise, and differences in perspective that a diverse yet involved and interactive audience offers. While many commentators raise serious concerns about whether individuals displace their time and attention from the "real" concerns of local communities, families, and friends offline by involving themselves in mediated groups—potentially weakening communities, disrupting relationships, and thereby reducing mental health—equally strong arguments can be made for the benefits that virtual participants are able to offer each other, in ways that are unavailable, too expensive, too remote, or too stigmatizing through traditional means (see Walther and Boyd, 2000). In corporate settings, it has been shown, individuals ask for strategic or technical advice "out in the air," that is, of the entire virtual audience, opening messages with "Does any one know . . . ," rather than targeting a specific source or series of sources, and this approach not only brings quick responses and is effective, but most frequently generates responses from sources who are not personally known by advice seekers.

Such connectivity at times suggests a "global village," allowing the virtual audience to take part, by reading others' immediate personal accounts, in momentous world events. For instance, the moment-by-moment activities of the failed Soviet coup attempt in 1991, blocked from traditional broadcast media, were transmitted all over the world by computer users in Russia. "Notes From a Sealed Room" became the byline of Israeli citizen Robert Werman, who transmitted narratives of the events and emotions experienced as he and his family took refuge from Iraqi SCUD missile attacks during the 1991 Persian Gulf War.

In addition to facilitating observation, however, the Internet can be used to mobilize the virtual audience into cooperative action. The passage of the U.S. 1996 Communications Decency Act (provisions of which, until set aside as unconstitutionally vague and restrictive, established penalties for Internet-based obscenity), for instance, was marked by thousands of Web site authors marking their Web pages black, in protest. Regarding more visible influence, rhetorical analyst Laura Gurak has detailed the rapid and vociferous self-organizing backlash in 1990 by Internet users to a prospective commercial product (Lotus Marketplace) that would have sold, on computer disk, demographic and financial information about U.S. citizens. Similarly, Gurak details how technologically sophisticated users with privacy concerns, beginning in 1993, continued to lobby the U.S. federal government over its intentions to regulate the use of data encryption technology in such a way that the government may be able to decode any scrambled electronic transmission. Focusing on the transformation of the canons of *ēthos* and *delivery* in cyberspace, she argues that *ēthos* is problematized by interaction that transpires with no physical basis, as through the Internet. A collective *ēthos,* implicit and reinforced among the technological elite online, both promotes persuasion and leads to uncritical acceptance of the veracity of facts and arguments. [*See* Ēthos.] *Delivery* is radically transformed, as the speed of the medium accelerates the dynamics of social movements, coupled with the Internet's ability for "narrowcasting," that is, broadcasting information and notable letters to thousands of like-minded individuals, through their use of electronic distribution channels such as specialized Usenet newsgroups, mailing lists, and bulletin boards. [*See* Delivery.] Such mechanisms facilitated more than thirty thousand complaints to Lotus, whose MarketPlace product was pulled from production. They also led to an electronic-mail based petitioning system, collecting numerous "signatures" for transmittal to government agencies, in addition to the volumes of protest e-mail sent directly to the addresses of the U.S. president and vice-president.

While the earliest research on computer-mediated communication viewed the impacts of the technology from a technical perspective, continuing development of sociotechnical approaches foster our evolving understanding of the virtual audience. The virtual audience differs from traditional audiences because of the sociotechnical impacts of the interaction of user motivations and the nature of the media.

Bibliography

Benson, Thomas W. "Rhetoric, Civility, and Community: Political Debate on Computer Bulletin Boards." *Communication Quarterly* 44 (Summer 1996), pp. 359–378. Critiques the Internet's ability to maintain a public sphere of civility, despite aggressiveness, angry assertion, insult, ideological abstraction, and humiliation of opponents. Method involved examination of a political Usenet newsgroup, in which discourse is marked by close attention to opposing arguments.

Bolter, Jay David. "Hypertext and the Rhetorical Canons." In *Rhetorical Memory and Delivery: Classic Concepts for Contemporary Composition and Communication.* Edited by John Frederick Reynolds, pp. 97–111. Hillsdale, N.J., 1993. Treats the transformation of the classical concept of delivery through electronic writing and transmission.

Galagher, Jolene, Lee Sproull, and Sara Kiesler. "Legitimacy, Authority, and Community in Electronic Support Groups." *Written Communication* 15 (October 1998), pp. 493–530. Examination of Usenet newsgroups shows how contributors establish credibility online, even through anonymous communication.

Gurak, Laura J. *Persuasion and Privacy in Cyberspace: The Online Protests over Lotus MarketPlace and the Clipper Chip.* New Haven, 1997. Rhetorical analysis of social movements conducted through Internet communication.

McLaughlin, Margaret L., Kerry K. Osborne, and Christine B. Smith. "Standards of Conduct on Usenet." In *Cybersociety: Computer-Mediated Communication and Community.* Edited by Steven G. Jones, pp. 90–111. Thousand Oaks, Calif., 1995. Identifies the communicative norms and sanctions evident through interchanges of messages posted to a variety of Usenet newsgroups.

Mitchell, William J. *City of Bits: Space, Place, and the Infobahn.* Cambridge, Mass., 1995. Chapters 1 to 3 in particular discuss the anonymity and alternative status symbols conferred by address in electronically networked communication. Also discusses prospective transformation of urban space due to "placeless" communication.

Postmes, Tom, Russell Spears, and Martin Lea. "Breaching or Building Social Boundaries? SIDE-Effects of Computer-Mediated Communication." *Communication Research* 25 (1998), pp. 689–715. Reviews series of experimental studies demonstrating overattribution of stereotyped impressions, similarity and dissimilarity in computer-mediated communication.

Rapaport, M. *Computer Mediated Communications: Bulletin Boards, Computer Conferencing, Electronic Mail, Information Retrieval.* New York, 1991. A primer on the development and characteristics of major types of electronic communication systems.

Rheingold, Howard. *The Virtual Community: Homesteading on the Electronic Frontier.* Reading, Mass., 1993. Popular, benchmark text discussing the history and benefits of online communities for social support, fans, social movements, and fantasy.

Howard, Tharon W. *A Rhetoric of Electronic Communities.* Greenwich, Conn., 1997. Argues for the democratizing effects of electronic writing and electronic publishing.

Walther, Joseph B., and Shawn Boyd. "Attraction to Computer-Mediated Social Support." In *Communication Technology and Society: Audience Adoption and Uses of the New Media.* Edited by Carolyn A. Lin and David Atkin. New York, forthcoming. Sociological and psychological investigation of the counterintuitive appeal to troubled and ill individuals of deeply personal advice and information from electronically linked anonymous and unknown sources.

Werman, Robert. *Notes from a Sealed Room: An Israeli View of the Gulf War.* Carbondale, Ill., 1993. Werman's frequent e-mail messages distributed worldwide, reprinted in book form, originally composed as he took shelter from potential nerve gas bombings during the Gulf War.

—JOSEPH B. WALTHER

AUXĒSIS (Lat. *incrementum*) is a figure of amplification, which by a progressive increase of words, clauses, or sentences puts a strong emphasis on the topic under discussion. If combined with morphological or syntactic figures of repetition, it enhances their pathetic effect, as in Cicero's oration *In Verrem* (Against Verres) (5.66.170): "It is a sin to bind a Roman citizen, a crime to scourge him, little short of the most unnatural murder to put him to death; what then shall I call this crucifixion?"

[*See also* Amplification; *and* Figures of speech.]

—ANDREA GRÜN-OESTERREICH

BELLES-LETTRES. *See overview article on* Composition; Eighteenth-century rhetoric; *and* Nineteenth-century rhetoric.

BLACK POWER MOVEMENT. *See* African-American rhetoric, *article on* Black Nationalism.

BYZANTINE RHETORIC. *See* Classical rhetoric; *and* Slavic rhetoric.

C

CAMPAIGNS. The twentieth century saw major changes in political campaign strategy and tactics. While campaigns were once dominated by party machines, ethnic politics, and self-developed promotions, the newer version reveals the impact of the modern media. In response to an increasingly media-savvy electorate, which has been influenced by radio, television, and now the Internet, campaigns of the twenty-first century will demand entertainment, expert advice, and transformation. The remainder of this article focuses on American political campaigns.

In the second half of the twentieth century, political campaigns began to look like product launches. This shift in style and substance was first evident in Dwight D. Eisenhower's presidential cámpaign of 1952, which took advantage of the picture and sound of television. The Eisenhower campaign used modern advertising techniques for the first time in response to the rapid increase in the television audience. The slogan "We Like Ike" was cycled through the electorate with the hammerlike repetition of the marketing of Rinso-White laundry soap and Buick's Dyna-Glide transmissions. The success of the Eisenhower campaign launched a flurry of techniques that transformed the entire political campaign landscape. It became clear that media exposure was rapidly approaching the importance of party backing, so a political campaign had to be fueled by the raising of large sums of money and the hiring of experts.

Radio was the first mass-market tool that enabled candidates to free themselves from the constraints of live performance. Until the emergence of radio in the 1920s, politicians were largely confined to public speeches in front of live audiences, one-on-one campaigning, appearances at parades, and quotations in newspapers. Theodore Roosevelt (1858–1919) had set the standard for that earlier model when, as assistant secretary of the Navy and later as president, he arranged for photographers and journalists to follow him on his hunts, nature expeditions, and military exploits. Radio, however, had the capacity for the first time to bring the voices of the politicians to the electorate in their homes and offices and in a real sense allow them to reach a mass audience in a personal way. Radio had the virtue of creating an intimacy and personal bond that had never been possible before. Innovative campaigners such as Louisiana governors Huey "Kingfish" Long in the 1930s and the singing, guitar-picking Jimmie Davis in the 1940s found the radio the cheapest and quickest route to the hearts and minds of the voters. At the national level, President Franklin Delano Roosevelt (1882–1945) used his Fireside Chats essentially to alter the relationship between the president and the public. The most effective politicians, such as Roosevelt, found that radio allowed them to use a conversational style that was personal and informal with an emotional quality not experienced before in American politics.

The success of radio and the subsequent explosion of television, cable, and the Internet requires an ever-increasing set of experts to guide a campaign. The modern campaign has become a combination of policy, image, and entertainment. The basic model combines the distribution systems of modern technology with the support strategies of the movie studios of the 1930s and 1940s, where experts were used to develop and market actors to a mass audience. This model not only moved into sports and business, but became the standard practice in politics. At the highest level of modern political campaigning, each portion of the campaign demands its own expert. In the early part of the twentieth century, these experts were drawn from party machines, friends, family, and volunteers loyal to the candidate. In the modern campaign there is still ideally a base of volunteers who will go door-to-door, make phone calls, and staff rallies. Because of compet-

itive pressures, however, it is increasingly necessary to hire specialized experts to guide the campaign. At the top of the hierarchy is the campaign
manager. Then, depending on budget and the
size of the campaign, he or she may hire a media
expert, pollster, fundraisers, speech writers and
debate consultants, opposition researchers, and
coordinators to organize volunteers. These experts are the "hired guns" of a campaign as opposed to the volunteers, who may be more ide-
alistic about the candidate, or in some cases, they
may be job-seekers who hope that volunteering
may lead to helpful contacts.

The real heart of the modern political campaign revolves around creating an electable candidate with a strong, differentiated image. While
the issues remain a staple of campaigns, the electorate, accustomed to fast-paced electronic messages, responds increasingly to highly visible candidates. The need for controlled exposure was
depicted memorably in the 1972 film *The Candidate*. Where the film was most prescriptive was in
the transformation of Bill McKay from a handsome, know-nothing, Jack Kennedy look-a-like
into a credible and electable victor in a California
senatorial race. The tension between the true Mc-
Kay and the transformed candidate was tellingly
portrayed in the film's last line, when McKay
turns to his manager after his victory and asks,
"What are we going to do now?" In that quandary lies the modern campaign dilemma. The
tallest and best-looking candidates may not be
the best public servants, while the shortest and
least photogenic may be admirable in the role.

Transforming the Candidate. There are three
typical approaches to choosing and developing
candidates in the modern political campaign. The
first is the fixed candidate approach: this candidate has all the attributes and requires little or no
transformation. In the fixed candidate approach,
the candidate is sold as-is. In the 2000 Republican
presidential primary, Senator John McCain made
his unbending positions and unyielding personality the cornerstone of his campaign. He lost.
The second is the improvement approach in
which a moderate amount of change will make
the candidate acceptable. In the same election cycle, the Democratic primary candidate, Vice-President Al Gore, modified his image as a wooden
policy specialist by donning sweaters instead of

jackets and ties, told personal stories, and used a
more direct and confrontative style when addressing his opponents. The third approach is the
candidate fulfillment approach, which surveys
the electorate to discover the archetypically ideal
candidate, who is then either drafted or reinvented to fill that mold. *The Candidate*'s Bill Mc-
Kay is a perfect example of drafting a candidate
to fit the political environment. All three approaches have their advocates, but the marketplace encourages a refinement or drafting model.

In the modern political campaign, candidate
transformation plays an essential role in the creation of a winning image. There are potentially
five steps in the process of candidate modification: concept generation, testing, refining, actualization, and distribution.

Generating Concepts. The first step, concept
generation, identifies a memorable persona that
can be easily understood by the electorate and
can serve as the backbone for the campaign and
issues. Traditionally, candidate archetypes such as
the Champion, Dark Horse, Favored Son, and Un-
derdog are used by the media to identify the campaign. These archetypes, if well chosen, can serve
as springboards to themes such as Senator Bob
Dole's hero typecasting in the 1996 campaign for
president, which emphasized his strength in
overcoming his personal war injuries. The development of a concept requires a survey of the competition leading to a differentiation of a candidate's traits from those of others. Richard Dyer in
his book *Stars* cites a number of characteristics
that can contribute to creating an effective and
believable character. For example, the candidate
should have characteristics that are distinct; the
candidate's traits should command attention; the
candidate should not be one-dimensional, but
have many traits, all of which are not immediately apparent. In this regard the managers might
decide their candidate should be warmer and
more playful than their opponent, and use public
appearances to emphasize this trait.

There are a number of techniques that can be
employed to generate a candidate's persona. In
many cases the pollster has access to material that
illuminates what electorates are responding to.
Polls using sophisticated phone banks among
other mechanisms are able to tease out subtle distinctions that indicate directions for behavior

change. While polls are useful for a general snapshot of the current position of the electorate, perceptions can and do change over time. Many modern candidates are then left in the unenviable position of appearing to waffle on their commitments and issues. In many campaigns when decisions are deadlocked, polling information usually serves as the final arbiter. Some campaign critics see this trend as encouraging middle of the road consensus campaigns.

Another technique is trend analysis, which scans popular culture, such as newspapers, books, films, and songs to discern what the electorate values. These media can offer clues not only to what the public is currently thinking but also to what might be the emerging trends. This method, drawn from product marketing methodology, can survey all aspects of the marketplace to provide useful avenues for the campaign to pursue. In the end, the concept that the candidate chooses must be viable and needs to be tested.

Testing. In the testing process, small markets where the risks are reduced are used by the campaign to evaluate the candidate's image and stance on issues. Venues for gauging reactions are fourfold. The first and most obvious site is a controlled audience situation, such as a focus group, in which likely voters can provide feedback on the candidate's attributes and issues. This technique, drawn from advertising, has become a useful device, particularly in the early stages of a campaign. One-on-one encounters, such as fundraisers, small-group meetings, meet-the-candidate teas, and other low-key but easily observed and monitored events are often used as testing grounds. Additional testing sites can include small-scale speeches to highly loyal groups at party events where the candidate's faults are likely to be overlooked. Radio or television appearances at off-hours are another testing area (e.g., Sunday morning at 7 A.M.) where the questions may well be softer and the audience smaller. All of these venues can serve as test beds for determining if changes are evoking a positive response from the voters.

Refining. If transformation of the candidate is necessary, then concept refinement becomes crucial to the campaign. In this stage of candidate and campaign development, the candidate is honed to meet the expectations of the concepts

and the voters. In the more sophisticated campaigns, a retinue of trainers, coaches, and consultants is retained for specific tasks. This advice is available to any candidate who can raise sufficient monies to fund his or her own image modeling. In a campaign, there are at least five major areas that traditionally are addressed to improve the candidate's voter appeal: signs and symbols, appearance, movement, behavior, and material.

Candidates in the media age find that signs such as clothing, gestures, facial expressions, walk, and other physical expressions of personality are important in effective communication. A candidate selection of appropriate signs signals to the audience his or her character and type and can be very powerful. When 1992 presidential candidate Bill Clinton would break off his afternoon jogs and duck into a McDonald's for a hamburger and fries or appear on late-night television playing a big band sound on his saxophone, he conveyed his accessible, personable, and contemporary character. Whether the candidate chooses to wear flannel shirts to communicate a frontier mentality or walk across the state to dramatically express physical fitness and a desire to listen to the constituency, signs and symbols are crucial tools in the modern campaign.

In the media age, much of a candidate's character comes from impressions of physical appearance. Appearance first became a real issue on television when Richard Nixon debated Jack Kennedy in 1960; because of Nixon's five-o'clock shadow and his refusal to wear makeup, he appeared to viewers to be less healthy and youthful than his opponent. Prior to television, the visible aspects of character were more easily concealed. While it cannot be proved that it was due to the absence of television that Franklin Delano Roosevelt's polio-related disability was concealed, there is no question that modern television coverage would have made that impairment more widely known. In the vernacular of the political business, certain appearance choices had become standard issue. In the 1988 *Des Moines Register* Democratic presidential primary debate, the overwhelming image was of a frieze of candidates wearing dark blue suits, red ties, and white shirts. As media scrutiny has intensified, candidate clothing has become more theatrical and less in lock step. There is an outfit for every emotion and occasion. While the standard attire for most candidates is still the business suit, indications are that physical presentation in future campaigns will reflect the effects of the entertainment industry. The new crop of candidates will take full advantage of appearance innovations, such as skin fresheners, teeth whiteners, hair transplants, tummy tucks, and liposuction. There are few modifications to a candidate's physical appearance that cannot be accomplished with the help of makeup artists, personal trainers, and plastic surgeons.

A candidate's body language can often be used to convey character. In the modern political age, the emphasis is on naturalness, control, and personal style. For example, John Kennedy had a brisk, youthful walk. He combined that apparent robustness with a preference for European style suits, and he chose not to wear a hat even on the coldest days—inadvertently damaging the hat industry. His movements symbolized a fresh start for America and the ascent of a new, younger group of leaders. Physical movement can appear in such subtle candidate situations as getting in and out of a car, or shaking hands at a rally. In classic campaign style, there are a number of greeting techniques that candidates adopt to convey their image. Audiences interpret these movements as portrayals of the candidate's fitness for office. A standard technique in preparing candidates is to catch them off guard with an unexpected question in settings such as exiting from an elevator. These simulations, usually videotaped and then analyzed with the candidate, are intended not only to improve the verbal style, but also to refine and eliminate movements that could be interpreted as detrimental to character and type.

It is essential that a candidate be able to portray his character both publicly and privately. It would be inexcusable for a candidate to swear, spit, or belch in a public setting. When in 1990 President George Bush vomited on the Japanese prime minister, it became international news and an embarrassment to the American public. While it is conceivable that anyone could have an upset stomach at a banquet, and find it impossible to restrain his or her own involuntary mechanisms, a politician cannot afford such accidental problems. Today's campaigns have to read the cultural trends carefully to monitor what range of behaviors are acceptable for their candidate. In the 1988 presidential primaries, married candidate Gary Hart was photographed with his girlfriend, Donna Rice, sitting on his lap on the yacht *Monkey Business*. His campaign was ruined with charges of womanizing and his presidential aspirations dashed. A decade later, President Bill Clinton weathered a seeming avalanche of revelations about his own sexual indiscretions. While it could be argued that Clinton was more adroit than Hart at dodging inquiries, it is probably more accurate to cite the public's changing expectations about a president or candidate's personal behavior.

It has become standard practice in campaigns to impose various tasks on candidates in order to expose aspects of their character in a positive light. In the 1980s, President Reagan was imaged as a cowboy/CEO who was always on the move and too busy and occupied with government matters to trouble himself with trivialities such as media questions. Recognizing his inability to answer questions on the fly, his aides turned this liability into a virtue by frequently adding background noise such as a loud, whirring helicopter. Reagan would wave off inquiries, gesturing that he could not hear reporter's questions. All the viewers saw was a dynamic, task-driven leader too busy to stop and chat. The staging of strong visual images for the benefit of media is now crucial to the development of a candidate's image. For example, if the candidate likes to play hockey three times a week or spends time teaching low-income children to read, these activities become essential to the campaign and are treated as important framing devices.

In the modern campaign, content is still important to a candidate's election. Politicians have a wide range of messages that must be developed by themselves or their advisors. The opportunities include speeches, press conferences, advertisements, direct mail pieces, Web sites, and billboards. In most cases the material reflects the messages that have been selected to portray the candidate's image and positions.

What will the candidate's material look like? In the media age there are limited opportunities for a candidate to make a lengthy speech. In most cases, a lengthy speech would be delivered before a live audience and if captured for television would be reduced to just fifteen or thirty seconds. In more and more campaigns, the emphasis is on developing short phrases and key ideas that are likely to be excerpted for the soundbite. As candidates figure out the realities of current media, the competition for coverage becomes increasingly intense, and the soundbytes need to be more controversial and colorful. The decrease in substantive argument has not gone unnoticed. In each election, public interest groups as well as the media criticize the absence of serious discussion of the issues and plead for a revival of Lincoln–Douglas style debates and forums.

In the early days of political campaigning, it was not uncommon for politicians to write their own material or rely on friends for advice. In today's campaigns, however, candidates often rely on speechwriters, debate consultants, and advertising professionals to provide counsel in their specific area of expertise. For example, in debate preparation a consultant will be hired to set up simulations of the actual debate. The candidate may be subjected to the identical rigors of the actual encounter. The material developed will often be a synthesis of campaign positions, consultant input, and polling results. In some cases the polished presentation is no longer a good measure of the candidate's skills, as the material, combined with appearance and other image-making strategies, has created a new character. All the refinement techniques are the result of increased media scrutiny and a public accustomed to professional levels of performance. Candidates who choose to ignore the refinement model are increasingly at a disadvantage.

Actualizing. In order for the changes to be credible in the eyes of the voters, the candidate's actions must fit the new image. In order to accomplish this, coaches use a number of techniques to transform the candidate. The most common and least expensive is behavior modification, which classically uses rewards and reinforcements to guide the candidate's future behaviors. When the candidate artfully answers a debate question or fails to use eye contact during a presentation, the reward system answers with applause or silence. In the short run, behavior

modification can be very effective; but unless the candidate is comfortable with the new self, the superficial nature of the technique can be counterproductive.

A more intensive method of training candidates involves hiring a mentor whose coaching and advising can be used to serve as a model for the candidate to emulate. The advantage of the mentoring system is that it usually moves at a slower pace, respects the interests of the candidate, and allows for the ups and downs of coming to grips with new ideas and techniques. The disadvantage is that it is expensive and time consuming, and under the pressure of launching a campaign, can easily be abandoned. Prior to the modern media age of political campaigns, it was common for candidates to self-mentor and study the speeches, styles, and manners of other candidates. President John Kennedy, for example, studied the speeches of British Prime Minister Winston Churchill (1874–1965) and became in turn, the model for President Bill Clinton.

Distribution. Once the image and the issues are delineated, political campaigns need to get their messages out to different audiences through a multiplicity of distribution channels. Depending on the scale of the race, decisions as to how to deliver the candidate's message and where to spend available money are crucial. There are four major areas in which the campaign's impressions are delivered to the voters, the first and most common being the candidate's public appearances when giving speeches, attending coffees and fundraisers, and touring communities. These efforts are often coordinated by a campaign scheduler who needs to be aware of a candidate's primary audiences, stamina, and strengths and weaknesses. A typical candidate might in a week speak at a synagogue, throw out the first pitch on opening day, address the local electrician's union at a dinner, and walk through an ethnic neighborhood, dropping in on local merchants.

In preparation for such intense and often diverse communication requirements, the candidate and advisors usually meet early in the day to discuss speeches and special voter interests and adapt arguments to press attention and deal with a competitor's charges. In these meetings, less attention is given to formal presentations, and more emphasis is placed on short comments and responses to questions from various audiences. The greatest danger for a candidate is to be caught off guard by a question that an opponent can use against him or her.

The second and most controllable area is the form of advertising used in a campaign, including direct mail, television and radio spots, Web sites, and pamphlets. While many local campaigns cannot afford television advertising, some effort is usually made to reach an audience beyond the candidate's live appearances. The strategies and tactics of the advertisements change from one campaign to another depending on voter reaction. Typically, advertisements emphasize a candidate's credentials, message, and promises. In the cluttered markets of modern media, however, candidates may turn to negative strategies, such as attacks on opponents, to differentiate themselves from their opponents, mobilize their support base, or in a desperate attempt to change the campaign's momentum. Much of advertising in political campaigns now resembles product advertising using comparisons, animation, catchy slogans, and jingles. An important development in campaigns is the use of Web sites to communicate with voters and address fast-changing issues. In Jesse Ventura's 1998 campaign for governor of Minnesota, his Web site reached out to disaffected voters and served as an inexpensive advertising vehicle and a thorn in the side of the competition.

The third area of public contact is planned and unplanned media appearances such as debates, interviews, press conferences, and general campaign coverage. These impressions are often the most telling because voters tend to hold the unpaid appearances as more representative of the candidate's true self than paid advertisements. Since the last half of the twentieth century, campaigns have recognized the impact of spontaneous appearances, and have tried to prepare the candidate for these experiences. For example, it is now customary after a debate for members of a candidate's staff—"spin doctors"—to make themselves available to the media to praise their candidate's performance in an attempt to influence the coverage. These public appearances require careful planning because the candidate may be on view at any time.

The fourth and final area is the campaign's use of traditional grassroots efforts to get out the vote. Some of the efforts used include volunteer phone banks and door-to-door appearances. If done successfully, the grassroots efforts match the image of the advertisements and media appearances. At the state and national levels, large databases are collected and sophisticated polling techniques are used to raise money and target voters. All of these candidate impressions, from formal speeches to campaign buttons, are ineffective unless the image has been carefully delineated, massaged, and consistently delivered. Web sites using spectacular graphics will eventually be coupled with telephone, television, and Internet delivery systems to provide new and potentially cheaper opportunities to reach voters.

The modern political campaign mirrors advances in entertainment, product marketing, and information technology. Increasingly, with the explosion in coaching and media technology and the corresponding pressures of information clutter and voters' media expectations, the candidate must adapt to these demands in order to compete. While there is still room at the local levels for the traditional campaign techniques of live appearances, unpaid volunteers, and the unhoned, natural candidate, the political marketplace has forever been altered by these quickly changing campaign strategies. Whether the democratic process is enhanced or diminished remains an open question.

[See also Ēthos; Persona; and Politics, article on Constitutive rhetoric.]

BIBLIOGRAPHY

Boorstin, Daniel. *The Image; A Guide to Pseudo-Events in America.* New York, 1992. The most frequently cited indictment of modern image making.

Dyer, Richard. *Stars.* London, 1979. A valuable and close examination of how images are produced.

Gamson, Joshua. *Claims to Fame: Celebrity in Contemporary America.* Berkeley, 1994. A comprehensive evaluation of the fame-building machine.

Jamieson, Kathleen Hall. *Packaging the Presidency: A History and Criticism of Presidential Campaign Advertising.* New York, 1996. A critical analysis of the strengths and weaknesses of political advertising.

Kurtz, Howard. *Spin Cycle: Inside the Clinton Propaganda Machine.* New York, 1998. A case-study of how the modern campaign controls information.

McDaniel, James P. "Fantasm: The Triumph of Form (An Essay on the Democratic Sublime)." *Quarterly Journal of Speech* 86 (2000), pp. 48–66. An insightful essay on how images, symbols, and the collective memory of Franklin Delano Roosevelt collide in the controversy over his memorial.

McGinniss, Joe. *The Selling of the President, 1968.* New York, 1970. How the Nixon campaign used television and advertising to influence voters.

Rein, Irving, Philip Kotler, and Martin Stoller. *High Visibility: The Making and Marketing of Professionals into Celebrities.* Chicago, 1997. An examination of how image concepts are manufactured and marketed.

Ritchie, Michael, dir. *The Candidate.* 1972. For Hollywood examples of earlier campaign models, see John Ford's 1958 film *The Last Hurrah,* which portrays Boston's big-city political machine, and Franklin Schaffner's 1964 film *The Best Man,* which captures smoke-filled room decision making.

Tye, Larry. *The Father of Spin: Edward L. Bernays and the Birth of Public Relations.* New York, 1998. Bernays laid the groundwork for many of the techniques used in the modern political campaign.
—IRVING J. REIN

CASUISTRY. Aristotle's characterization of rhetoric as a counterpart of both dialectic and ethics took on renewed importance with the publication of Albert Jonsen and Stephen Toulmin's *The Abuse of Casuistry* (Berkeley, 1988). Casuistry is an ancient art of case reasoning used to resolve moral dilemmas, whose "golden age" was the late Middle Ages. Jonsen and Toulmin sketch the contribution to casuistry of Cicero's topical system of invention, but, because of their historical focus in *Abuse,* Jonsen and Toulmin did not dwell at any length on the *why* and *how* of casuistry; opting rather to explain *what* it is, explore its development and abuses, and suggest both how it might be rehabilitated and, once rehabilitated, how it can serve clinical ethics today.

Jonsen and Toulmin present casuistry as one answer to the pressing need of medical practitioners for a rigorous method of rendering moral decisions. According to Jonsen, a moral dilemma is made of maxims in conflict. "Do no harm," "Patients ought to have autonomy in matters of treatment," and "Relieve suffering whenever possible" are examples of the type of maxims that reside in biomedical cases. So, for

example, in biomedical cases. So, for example, a medical dilemma could hinge on a conflict between the physician's obligation to "do no harm" and a patient's autonomous preference to discontinue a lifesaving treatment. Jonsen teaches clinicians how to conduct lines of inquiry, guided by topics, in order to discover the particular maxims that are in conflict at the heart of a given moral dilemma. Jonsen's topology (collection of special topics) is: Medical Indications, Patient Preferences, Quality of Life, and Context. Jonsen suggests how, in order to render a prima facie defense for a moral judgment in any given case in the care of patients in medicine and nursing, the arguer must address all four of these issues. Each issue, in turn, has attendant subtopics: For example, the issue of competency is an important subtopic of patient preferences because the preferences of an incompetent patient carry little weight compared with those of a fully competent one. The topology operates heuristically by prompting questions that, when taken together, constitute lines of practical inquiry. Such a method is a departure from the received approach to bioethics.

Jonsen and Toulmin discuss how modern moral philosophers privilege a rationalistic method that misuses principles and attempts to deduce from a single principle (autonomy, utility, sympathy, etc.) entire systems of moral philosophy. When "moral geometers" assume that only the knowledge deduced from a superprinciple is valuable knowledge, they deny forms of reasoning that are appropriate to the moral realm. Demonstrative reasoning has its place, but its limitations are underscored when one enters the moral realm. Jonsen and Toulmin contrast this habit of moral reasoning with those who take a rhetorical view, noting how the latter "do not assume that moral reasoning relies for its force on single chains of unbreakable deductions which link present cases back to some common starting point. Rather (they believe), this strength comes from accumulating many parallel, complementary considerations, . . . not like links to a chain but like strands to a rope or roots to a tree" (pp. 293–294).

Jonsen and Toulmin's critique is congruent with the work of many rhetorical theorists the past half-century, because both involve a defense of rhetorical reasoning against the hegemony of geometric or demonstrative reasoning. What is needed now is a fully-elucidated methodology of casuistry, because marking of boundaries (between rhetorical and demonstrative reasoning) is only a preliminary step in the advancement of rhetorical theory (which must eventually take a practical turn).

The methodology of casuistry (and, mutatis mutandis, of rhetorical reasoning) involves the identification and addressing of relevant issues by (1) recognizing and raising appropriate questions as they "issue" from the case, (special topics); (2) narrowing the field of inquiry until the question(s) upon which the case "hinges" comes clearly into view (stasis and maxims); and (3) building lines of argument congruent with and derived from the analysis of the case by turning to the common topics. [See Stasis.] Each of these components employs phronēsis because cases are situated in two ways: in real time and place, and relative to other similar cases. [See Phronēsis.] It takes practical wisdom to understand the relationship between analogous cases, and also to distinguish particulars that are relevant from those that are tangential to the heart of the case.

Rhetoricians will, of course, recognize the components identified above as the elements of the rhetorical method of case argument that was a staple of the forensic schools of antiquity. Given the importance of that doctrine in early systems of education, it is not surprising that the first casuists adopted rhetorical methods when faced with the need to render judgments in cases that involved difficult moral and theological dilemmas. They were schooled in the tradition of Cicero (106–43 BCE), Quintilian (c.35–c.100 CE), Augustine (354–430 CE), Boethius (480–524 CE) and Aquinas (1225–1274). Interestingly, the casuists never explicated their method; they simply went to work, determining appropriate amounts of penance for given sins and writing judgments on various moral and theological cases of conscience. Just after publication of Abuse in 1988, Albert Jonsen set about developing a fully-elucidated methodology of clinical casuistry. The following sketch of that methodology underscores what Jonsen means when he asserts "the form of reasoning constitutive of classical casuistry is rhetorical reasoning" ("Casuistry as Methodology in

Clinical Ethics," Theoretical Medicine 12, 1991, pp. 295–307; hereafter "Methodology."). This article focuses on Jonsen's casuistry because his conception of casuistry underscores the role of rhetoric in ethics like no other.

Albert Jonsen on Clinical Casuistry. Jonsen's more refined and nuanced account of clinical casuistry begins with "Methodology," which takes a step not taken in Abuse, according to Jonsen, because Abuse was primarily a historical account of casuistry. So, he and Toulmin did not there present casuistry as a technique for clinical ethics, although they did lay the groundwork for so doing.

Jonsen there describes the method of reasoning indigenous to casuistry by harkening back to Abuse, where casuistry is defined as:

> [T]he analysis of moral issues, using procedures of reasoning based on paradigms and analogies, leading to the formulation of expert opinion about the existence and stringency of particular moral obligations, framed in terms of rules or maxims that are general but not universal or invariable, since they hold good with certainty only in the typical conditions of the agent and circumstances of action. (Abuse, p. 257)

Jonsen posits that his reflections on the methodology of casuistry led him to the conclusion that the form of reasoning constitutive of classical casuistry is rhetorical reasoning. Whereas Abuse sketches how rhetorical doctrine contributed to the formulation of casuistry, "Methodology" explains how rhetorical reasoning drives its practice. This yeoman work advances the project begun in Abuse by highlighting how circumstances, topics, and maxims work in clinical judgments.

"A case," Jonsen writes, "derived from the Latin verb 'cadere,' is literally an event or a happening."

> The happening is a collection of circumstances and the circumstances, literally, "what surrounds or stands around," stands around the center of the case. That center is constituted of certain maxims, brief rule-like sayings that give moral identity to the case. A maxim was, for the rhetoricians, "maxima sententia," a leading or important proposition. Sometimes they referred to them as "gnomoi" or wise sayings, because they seemed to distill, in a pithy way,

experience reflected upon by wise men. ("Methodology," p. 298)

Casuistry then, works to order the circumstances of the case relative to the center (or crux) of the case, which is constituted of conflicting maxims. Thus, Jonsen takes a sharp rhetorical turn when revitalizing clinical casuistry. His reliance on classical rhetorical constructs to elucidate the methodology of casuistry bespeaks a deep and pervasive interrelatedness.

Considering his audience when his aim is to illustrate in practical terms how casuistry works, Jonsen employs three nonrhetorical constructs: morphology, taxonomy, and kinetics. In so doing, Jonsen's project contributes to rhetorical theorists' own understanding of the methods of rhetorical reasoning. Rhetoricians can learn a great deal by observing how this medical ethicist teases out the role of topical logic, of reasoning by analogy, of *stasis,* and of maxims in the resolution of moral dilemmas.

Morphology is a biological term having to do with form and structure. The analogy to case reasoning is that the "interplay of circumstances and maxims constitute the structure of a case" ("Methodology," p. 299). Hence, the first task of the casuist is to discern the structure of the case, or to "parse" it. Sound judgment is rendered relative to the center, but, in difficult cases, the center is not easily grasped. Jonsen further elucidates how the center is arrived at by means of special topics.

> Clinical–ethical activity has its proper special topics, the invariant constituents of that form of discourse. These consist of statements about the medical indications of the case, about the preferences of the patient, about the quality of the patient's life and about the social and economic factors external to the patient, but affected by the case. Mark Seigler, William Winslade and I originally proposed these as a means of analysis of a clinical case in our book, *Clinical Ethics.* I now believe that they represent the special topics of clinical medicine, always relevant to the clinical decision and with an invariant structure, although variable content. ("Methodology," p. 300)

When Jonsen writes "I *now* believe . . ." it is because he was beginning, by the late 1980s, to realize how utterly rhetorical is casuistry. Jonsen,

Siegler, and Winslade's *Clinical Ethics* (1982) is a practical handbook, that brings together practical moral guidelines (topically arranged) with pertinent medical principles and legal and professional precedents. Jonsen and his associates utilize there the four special topics of clinical medicine, without identifying them as such, because the link to rhetorical doctrine had not yet been firmly established in Jonsen's own mind. Jonsen's first attempt at explaining his topology in rhetorical terms appears in print in the debut issue of *The Journal of Clinical Ethics* ("Case Analysis in Clinical Ethics," 1990, pp. 63–65; hereafter "Case Analysis"). That explanation is noteworthy for the way it brilliantly explicates *how* topics work to guide inquiry.

After introducing classical lore on topics, and distinguishing between common and special topics, Jonsen writes, "It is my opinion that the method of analysis I am about to explain represents the 'special topics' of clinical ethics, that is, the concepts that are basic to, and indelibly present in, any ethical problem that presents itself in a clinical case" ("Case Analysis," p. 63). The topics may vary in degree of relevance, depending on the circumstances of the case, but they must be reviewed if an adequate analysis of the case is to be made. Jonsen then elucidates how each of the four topics works as a guide to moral inquiry. In so doing, he shows how the internal logic of each topic informs the discussion of the case and guides its direction.

Jonsen's treatment of Patient Preferences is illustrative in this regard. The patient's wishes are, of course, an ethically relevant component in all medical decisions. However, one must not only raise the question, "What does the patient want?" but the logic of this topic requires further questions: "Does the patient comprehend?" "Is the patient being coerced?" Each topic has an inner logic that suggests subtopics, and by following the lines of question suggested by the subtopics, the case analyst parses the case in order to reveal the issue. Jonsen then notes how "The ancient rhetoricians used the term *issue* in its literal sense, namely, the point at which various streams of logic, the topics, converge. The issue is the matter to be discussed in detail, the focus of attention, the knot that must be untied" ("Case Analysis," p. 65). Jonsen proceeds no further; however, rhetoricians will recognize that he has now hit upon the notion of *stasis*. Morphology may be understood, then, as parsing the case in order to discover its form and rhetorical structure. Jonsen then introduces another crucial component of the casuistic method: The lining up of relevant cases in a certain order, *taxis*.

Taxis is the Greek word meaning the marshaling of soldiers in a battle line. When offering a defense for a moral judgment in a difficult case, the casuist arranges cases from the least ambiguous paradigm case to the present case. The Holocaust is the prime example of a paradigm case for morally repugnant racial atrocities. It was clearly wrong for the Nazis to practice genocide, but, as one moves farther away from the paradigm case, one can arrive at cases that are not clear cut and, therefore, require the taxonomical move in order to contextualize them. *Taxis* in casuistry is vital because "it puts the instant case into its moral context and reveals the weight of argument that might countervail a presumption of rightness or wrongness" ("Methodology," p. 302). In short, taxonomy is the act of reasoning by analogy that saves casuistry from lapsing into mere situationism.

Jonsen offers an illustration from bioethics of how this interaction of paradigm and analogy provides a clear line of reasoning about the problem of foregoing life support. The determination of death by brain criteria initiates the taxonomy: one is not obliged to treat a dead body. Next come cases that involve persistent vegetative state, then cases of diminished mental capacity. As the case analyst moves by analogy from the paradigm to the less severe cases, the circumstances, coupled with their proximity to the paradigm, suggest the degree of obligation to provide medical care. At the beginning of the taxonomy, moral consensus prevails; as the analogous cases are lined up, more disagreement appears, and the taxonomy allows the differences between the instant case and the paradigm case to suggest which judgment is most appropriate.

A more germane feature of casuistic method is *how* the taxonomy is utilized to ground moral judgments. This dynamic Jonsen dubs "kinetics" in casuistry. Jonsen borrows the term *kinetics* from classical physics as he borrowed the term *morphology* from classical biology. Jonsen ob-

serves that, when rendering a moral judgment, the paradigm case imparts a kind of moral movement to the taxonomical line of cases, as a moving billiard ball imparts motion to the stationary one it hits. So casuistry relies upon a "moral movement" of certitude between paradigm and analogous cases. Jonsen associates kinēsis in casuistry fully with prudential reasoning, or *phronēsis*. The association between kinēsis in casuistry and *phronēsis* is complete because, in casuistry one reflects upon the relation between maxims (which are general rules of prudential conduct) and circumstances (which are the particulars that abide in the instant case) in light of analogous cases.

Phronēsis in Casuistry and Rhetorical Reason. In his *Rhetoric*, Aristotle (384–322 BCE) identifies the three canonical modes of artistic proof—*ēthos, pathos,* and *logos*—on grounds that, in order to persuade, one must evince good character, move the audience by appealing to emotions, and, of course, advance good reasons. [*See* Ēthos; Logos; *and* Pathos.] Aristotle further asserts that a trustworthy character is one of the requisites of persuading because persons are more readily persuaded by those whom they can trust. At the beginning of Book 2, Aristotle subdivides *ēthos* into *phronēsis, aretē,* and *eunoia* because, in order to establish credibility, the rhetor's words must project practical wisdom, virtue, and good sense. Aristotle discusses this tripartite division wholly in terms of the *technē* of rhetoric. However, despite Aristotle's limited aim in the *Rhetoric,* a fuller conception of *phronēsis* emerges in the course of the sort of nuanced reading, across the Aristotelian corpus, conducted by, among others, Hans-Georg Gadamer, Alisdaire MacIntyre, Martha Nussbaum, and Joseph Dunne. That is, when one reflects upon the dynamics of rhetorical reasoning, which constitutes the faculty of discovering the crux of the matter (*heurēsis*) that precedes the art of argumentation (*technē*) explicated in the *Rhetoric,* and simultaneously brings it to bear on the act of choosing the mean between extremes, elucidated in Aristotle's *Nicomachean Ethics,* one begins to appreciate the potential yield of understanding *phronēsis* and rhetorical reasoning in light of Jonsen's casuistry.

Phronēsis has not traditionally been associated

as directly with rhetoric as the concepts of *stasis* and topics, but, as the above sketch underscores, its role in rhetorical reasoning is ubiquitous indeed. Understood with precision, rhetorical reasoning guides and *phronēsis* drives moral inquiry. The aim of moral inquiry is to render sound judgment, but judgment in hard cases is frustrated because the crux of the matter is hedged in by a potentially limitless parade of particulars. Rhetorical reason manages particulars by systematically determining the relevance of issues and identifying the *stasis,* or the most relevant of the relevant issues. Now ascribing relevance, per se, is an act of *phronēsis.*

Phronēsis drives practical judgment in at least five distinct, discernible, and nuanced ways: (1) by bringing to bear ethical principles where appropriate; (2) by bringing to bear past experience on present situations; (3) by generalizing from analogous cases to present ones; (4) by working in tandem with special topics to guide inquiry by determining which issues are most relevant; and (5) by combining all four aspects above to bring together probabilities in their convergence in order to facilitate *praxis.* Enumerating these should clarify what Jonsen means when he writes, "above all, casuistic reasoning is prudential reasoning: appreciation of the relationship between paradigm and analogy, between maxim and circumstances, between the greater and less of circumstances as they bear on the claim and the rebuttals" ("Methodology," p. 306). Let us recall Jonsen's earlier statement, that "the form of reasoning constitutive of casuistry is rhetorical reasoning." These two statements suggest that, for Jonsen, rhetorical reasoning and *phronēsis* are nearly synonymous. By explicating the manner in which *phronēsis* accomplishes its work of "appreciating" the various issues that converge to facilitate moral judgment, we will better understand how rhetorical reasoning itself operates as a guide to judgment in the practical arena.

The casuistical view of the relation of rhetorical reasoning to *phronēsis,* then, is a valuable contribution to understanding the work of each as guides to moral judgment. But that is not all: The above also sheds light on why Aristotle considered rhetorical reason an antistrophe of dialectic.

Dialectic in Casuistry. Aristotle's *Topica* is about dialectical competition, or disputation. [*See* Dialectic.] However, his final exhortation to the would-be disputant indicates a concern that supersedes mere competition: "Moreover, as contributing to knowledge and to philosophic wisdom the power of discerning and holding in one view the results of either of two hypotheses is no mean instrument; for it only remains to make a right choice of one of them" (163*b* 9). Since virtue "is a state of character concerned with choice, lying in a mean" (*Nicomachean Ethics,* 1107a) dialectic, insofar as it provides clarity in deliberations, contributes a great deal to moral decision making. The distinction between dialectical disputation and dialectical inquiry obtains throughout Aristotle's *Topica.*

Dialectic is exemplified by the Socratic method. It is a three-step process: Socrates always begins with a proposition; pushes it to its conclusion, drawing out implications by means of question and answer; and applies the law of contradiction, which is later penned by Aristotle in *Metaphysics, 1011b,* "The most undisputable of all beliefs is that contradictory statements are not at the same time true." The law of contradiction is a statement about the manner in which the mind operates during the meaning-making process, and it is at the operational core of dialectical reasoning.

Let us take, for example, a certain case involving the wife of a man with a terminal heart condition. The particular situation that I have in mind was such that the husband was being kept alive on a ventilator, but the vent tube bothered him so much that he had to be heavily sedated. The doctors had tried unsuccessfully to wean him of the ventilator on a prior occasion, which precipitated cardiac arrest. Now, the attending physician explained, the wife had to decide whether she wanted to leave her husband in a heavily sedated (and incoherent) state to prolong his life, or allow him to live a few days in a state where he could communicate with his family. Her response to the physician is telling, and is based on an implicit dialectical distinction, one that helps illustrate how the law of contradiction works. After some deliberation with her son, she concluded that if her husband could speak for himself, he would choose to be removed from the ventilator and the sedation because "he's not really living, he's just existing." Implicit in the distinction is the premise that, for her husband, living entails the capacity to communicate with family and that any state of being that incapacitates one to such an extent is more like existing than living. In other words, merely existing contradicts the husband's likely preference for and understanding of life. So, the law of contradiction informs choice making by "holding in one view the results of either of two hypotheses," as Aristotle put it. It only remained for the wife to make a right choice of one of them.

Dialectical reasoning (as a mode of inquiry rather than as a method of disputation) parallels rhetorical reasoning. Robert Price (1968) argues, by exploring the parallel nature of Aristotle's *Analytics, Topics,* and *Rhetoric,* that analytic, rhetoric, dialectic, and deliberation all share a common methodology, but that they are concerned with varying degrees of abstractness. Hence, insofar as the woman in the above illustration was concerned with deciding on behalf of her husband, she exercises rhetorical reasoning, but is led to her decision based on a dialectical inference. Dialectic illumines the contraries among which she chooses. The above explication of Jonsen's casuistry illustrates how rhetorical reasoning situates her at a vantage point from which those contraries may be fully appreciated and also how *phronēsis* guides her choosing. And that is why Jonsen's casuistry helps one understand more fully why rhetoric is a counterpart of both dialectic and ethics.

BIBLIOGRAPHY

Dunne, Joseph. *Back to the Rough Ground: "Phronesis" and "Techne" in Modern Philosophy and in Aristotle.* Notre Dame, Ind., 1993. Dunne's reading of Aristotle and of modern practical philosophers. This work has not received the attention it deserves from rhetorical scholars.

Golden, James L., and Joseph J. Pilotta, eds. *Practical Reasoning in Human Affairs.* Dordrecht, Netherlands, 1986. Collection of illuminating essays on various aspects of practical wisdom.

Jonsen, Albert R. "Of Balloons and Bicycles—or—The Relationship between Ethical Theory and Practical Judgment." *The Hastings Center Report* 21 (1991), pp. 14–16.

Jonsen, Albert R., and Stephen Toulmin. *The Abuse of Casuistry.* Berkeley, 1988.

MacIntyre, Alisdaire. *After Virtue.* Notre Dame, Ind.,

1984. MacIntyre argues that the restoration of community, made necessary by the failure of the Enlightenment project to replace Aristotelian rationalism must entail, in part, the restoration of Aristotelian *phronēsis.*

MacIntyre, Alisdaire. *Whose Justice? Which Rationality?* Notre Dame, Ind., 1988. Argues for the need to recover the Thomistic tradition of practical rationality grounded in Aristotelian *phronēsis.* Refinement of the argument in *After Virtue.*

Miller, Carolyn R. "Aristotle's 'Special Topics' in Rhetorical Practice and Pedagogy." *Rhetoric Society Quarterly* 17 (1987), pp. 61–70. An excellent source for those interested in revitalizing topical logic.

Nussbaum, Martha C. *Love's Knowledge: Essays on Philosophy and Literature.* New York, 1990. See especially "The Priority of the Particular" and chapter 2.

Perelman, Chaim. *The Realm of Rhetoric.* Notre Dame, Ind., 1982. Trenchant examination of dialectic, practical argumentation and rhetoric.

Price, Robert. "Some Antistrophes to the *Rhetoric.*" *Philosophy and Rhetoric* 1 (1968), pp. 145–164.

Stump, Eleonore. *Boethius's De topicis differentiis.* Ithaca, N.Y., 1978. Boethius illuminates dialectic, rhetoric, and topics all at a glance.

Tallmon, James M. "How Jonsen Really Views Casuistry: A Note on the Abuse of Father Wildes." *The Journal of Medicine and Philosophy* 13 (1994), pp. 103–113.

Tallmon, James M. "Casuistry and the Role of Rhetorical Reason in Ethical Inquiry." *Philosophy and Rhetoric* 28 (1995), pp. 377–387.

Warnick, Barbara. "Judgment, Probability, and Aristotle's *Rhetoric.*" *Quarterly Journal of Speech* 9 (1989), pp. 299–311. One interested in pursuing further the relationship of rhetoric and *phronēsis* would do well to begin with Warnick's essay.

—JAMES M. TALLMON

CATACHRĒSIS (Lat. *abusio*) can be described as a "necessary metaphor" (Quintilian, *Institutio oratoria,* first century CE, 8.6.6), that is, a metasememe. Expressions like "the foot of a hill" or "the neck of a guitar" exist in a language because "there is no proper term available" (Quintilian, 8.6.35). Though often characterized as an abuse of language, the *catachrēsis* is an important means of adjusting the lexicon of a language to new areas of knowledge, as in the expression "genetic code." A rhetorical effect can be achieved by redirecting the addressee's attention to the substitutive character of a catachrēsis, thus creating an awareness that it is a metaphor after all.

[*See also* Figures of speech; *and* Metaphor.]

—RICHARD NATE

CHARACTER. *See* Ēthos; *and* Persona.

CHIASMUS. In the late rhetorical tradition, the Greek term *chiasmus* designates a device that has to do with a particular arrangement of the syntagmatic constituents of a statement, and it consists in the specular or "mirrorlike" distribution of pairs of elements formally and functionally equivalent. Thus, it is a variant of parallelism. [*See* Parallelism.]

For example, consider the following formula. Given the parallel sequences A and A', composed of the elements a, b (A) and a', b' (A'), elements formally and functionally equivalent, their distribution in the chain of discourse would be as follows:

Sequences:	A		/*/		A'	
Elements:	a	b	/*/	b'		a'
	Huye	la furia	y	el temor		espera.
						(F. de Quevedo)
	([He] Escapes	the rage	and	the fear		[he] awaits).

As can be observed, in the distribution of elements that constitute each sequence (A, A'), on the one hand, there is a positional correspondence between the elements located in the extreme places of the statement (a, a'), and, on the other hand, between the elements located in its central places (b, b').

[*See also* Antithesis; Epanodos; Figures of speech; Poetry; *and* Style.]

BIBLIOGRAPHY

Lanham, R. A. *A Handlist of Rhetorical Terms.* Berkeley, 1991.

Lausberg, H. *Handbuch der literarischen Rhetorik.* P. 723: Munich, 1960.

Mayoral, J. A. *Figuras retóricas.* Pp. 170–171. Madrid, 1994.

Morier, H. *Dictionnaire de Poétique et de Rhétorique.* Paris, 1981.

—JOSÉ ANTONIO MAYORAL
Translated by A. Ballesteros

CHINESE RHETORIC. If we define rhetoric as suasive discourse or symbolic inducement that is primarily language based, there is no one term in Chinese that exactly corresponds to this meaning. Nevertheless, the Chinese have practiced many types of suasive discourse and have produced essays, handbooks, and theoretical works that qualify as rhetorical. Research on the Chinese rhetorical tradition is in its very beginnings, and this essay reflects the uneven progress of the field in its concentration on earlier periods and dominant voices. As in other traditions, the existing corpus of materials on rhetoric in China reflects social groups' differential access to education, cultural capital, and power. The scholarly elite maintained a continuous set of histories and reproduced their classics, and the Buddhists and the Taoists printed and preserved their own histories, biographies, and sacred texts. Wealthy families might amass private libraries or publish the writings of a relative or friend. Other voices are sometimes heard echoing through these texts, or occasionally survive intact through historical accident.

Consistent with this bias, the first records of suasive discourse in China are speeches by kings and dukes found in the *Shang shu,* Book of History, (trans. Bernhard Karlgren, *The Book of Documents.* Göteborg, 1950), some of these as early as the first centuries of the Western Chou dynasty (1099–771 BCE). Legitimizing one's authority to rule and inducing the population to comply are pressing concerns that are already evident in these speeches, as the rulers harangue, cajole, and argue with their audiences.

During the periods known as Spring and Autumn (770–476 BCE) and the Warring States (475–221 BCE), the society of the central plain of China moved from a semifeudalist government to feuding city-states with rudimentary civil and military bureaucracies, urban life, some formal education, and circulation of texts, and lively controversies over political and ethical thought. Rhetoric emerged as a route for social mobility, and there appeared "roaming persuaders" (*yu-shui*) who traveled from court to court seeking employment as advisers. Some of the wandering persuaders, the *pien-che,* specialized in the language arts; they were both admired and castigated for their stylistic brilliance, for their ability to argue both sides and to prove paradoxes, and for their cosmological curiosity. These political and social conditions gave rise to several overtly persuasive genres that were used for centuries to come: the "memorial" (*piao/shang-shu*), a policy proposal addressed to those in power; face-to-face persuasions addressed primarily to one person (*shui*); debate on policy issues (*yi*); disputation on abstract themes (*pien*); and the argumentative essay (*lun*).

The paradigm of one-to-one persuasion received much attention from the Legalist Han-feitzu (c.280–233 BCE), who prescribed in-depth analysis of the audience, wholesale adaptation to its idiosyncrasies, and building long-term relations of trust. The most extensive and theoretical treatment of *shui* is the book *Kuei ku-tzu,* a work of uncertain date and authorship that is entirely devoted to this topic (trans. Thomas Cleary, *Thunder in the Sky: On the Acquisition and Exercise of Power,* Boston, 1993). In abstruse and elliptical language, the *Kuei ku-tzu* elaborates this audience-sensitive approach and also explicitly grounds it in an ontology based on alternating yin–yang cycles and in an epistemology based on recognizing patterns of change.

The early Confucian approach to suasion (from the fifth to third centuries BCE) also recommends adaptation, but along socially-regulated dimensions such as the status of both speaker and audience, the receptivity of the listener, the subject matter, and the occasion. But underlying all these gradations and distinctions was a deep commitment to the ethical dimension of human life. For the Confucians, moral principles inhered in the very structure of the universe, which translated into a rhetorical imperative that speakers have *ch'eng. Ch'eng* is often translated as sincerity or authenticity, but in this conceptual framework, it denotes the speaker's conformity to, and expression of, an inherently ethical reality. Rhetorical activities were not particularly different from most other human interactions in the need for decorum, propriety, and *ch'eng,* and Confucian reflections on rhetoric in this period tend not to be broken out from larger discussions of culture, ethics, politics, or epistemology (e.g., *Hsün-tzu,* chapters 21, 22, trans. John Knoblock, *Xunzi: A Translation and Study of the Complete*

Works, vol. 3, Stanford, 1988; and *Meng-tzu,* 2A.2, trans. D.C. Lau, *Mencius,* rev. ed., Hong Kong, 1984).

The Later Mohists (active during the late fourth and third centuries BCE) present a striking contrast to these two approaches to suasion. In a series of systematic treatises preserved in the book *Mo-tzu,* they laid down rigorous procedures for clarifying and resolving disagreements in disputation, naming, linguistic analysis, and ethical decision making, procedures that are entirely independent of particular audiences. These works apparently had limited influence, and within a few centuries, they were neglected and then corrupted to near unintelligibility, not to be readable again until A. C. Graham's magisterial reconstruction (*Later Mohist Logic, Ethics and Science,* Hong Kong, 1978).

The unification of the empire in 221 BCE marks the beginning of China's imperial age. For some two millennia, a centralized and increasingly complex bureaucracy administered a vast territory, leading to great reliance on written texts and formal channels of communication. Although in theory the emperor ruled absolutely, in reality each dynasty was deeply concerned with securing not just the ideological control of the masses, but also the assent and active cooperation of the elite. The elite exercised considerable political and cultural power, and as such, they were important rhetorically not only as audiences for, but also as producers of argumentation. For instance, during the Han dynasty (206 BCE–220 CE), the policy debates at court were institutionalized (as the *t'ing-yi;* for a well-preserved example from the first century BCE, see Huan K'uan, *Yen t'ieh lun,* trans. Gale Esson, *Discourses on Salt and Iron,* Taipei, 1967). The emperor's ruling on the debate was itself a persuasive document, outlining the reasons that supported his judgment. But even the emperor's decision was not the last word; these debates often continued informally in petitions and memorials to the emperor, further pronouncements from the emperor, and letters (*shu*) circulated among the literati.

With the gradual ascendance of the Confucian perspective during the Han dynasty, less overtly-argumentative genres were also generally conceived as suasive. History was to be written and read for its moral lessons, a view that persists to the present. Poetry, and especially the earliest collection of poems, the *Shih ching* (Book of Songs; trans. Arthur Waley, *The Book of Songs;* London, 1937), was also conceptualized as didactic, though views differed on exactly how it influenced its audience (see Stephen Owen, *Readings in Chinese Literary Thought,* Cambridge, Mass., 1992, chapter 2). This moralistic view of poetry and of literature more generally was first contested by Ts'ao P'i (187–226 CE), who presented writing as a way to achieve fame and immortality, and later writers proposed literature as a vehicle for original expression, but the view that literature should express and reinforce correct values remained the dominant position up into the twentieth century (and in this sense all literary production was, by nature, rhetorical).

During the Han dynasty, classical Chinese, which presumably was the vernacular of an earlier period, became fixed as a literary language. Until the early twentieth century, classical Chinese was usually the language for official documents and for elite literature throughout the empire, and education required mastering it. This linguistic continuity is one reason for the remarkable intertextuality of Chinese literature: other factors include the canonization of the classics, a process that stabilized in the eleventh century; the memorization of the classics as part of education; and the reliance on the classics for the civil service examinations, which began in the T'ang dynasty (618–907 CE). Paradoxically, this canonization of earlier works written in classical Chinese also opened up a space for argument over doctrine by creating a need for commentary and thus enabling reinterpretation.

One final rhetorical phenomenon that matured in the Han is the collection of model examples of a genre. For instance, the *Chan-kuo ts'e* (Records of the Warring States; trans. James Crump, *Chan-kuo ts'e,* Oxford, 1970) records hundreds of persuasions from the Warring States period. Admonitions, essays, witty remarks, and ministerial responses to imperial pronouncements were among the genres collected, and presumably studied down through the ages.

The Age of Disunion (221–589 BCE) after the fall of the Han dynasty, also called the Six Dynasties period, is conventionally described as an age of belletristic writing, evidenced in the evolution of an elaborate, highly parallelistic style of writing (*pian ti wen*), the development of critical literary terminologies and rankings of writers according to them, theories of prose, and anthologies such as Hsiao T'ung's *Wen hsüan* (*Wen xuan, or, Selections of Refined Literature,* trans. David R. Knechteges, Princeton, vol. 1, 1982; vol. 2, 1987; vol. 3, 1996). However, the rhetorical dimensions of these works are often seriously elided when they are regarded as purely literary. For instance, the *Wen fu* of Lu Chi (261–303 CE) (*The Art of Letters: Lu Chi's "Wen Fu," A.D. 302,* trans. E. R. Hughes, New York, 1951) is often presented as a treatise on poetics, but the essay itself addresses writing in all genres. The same applies to the book *Wen-hsin tiao-lung* by Liu Hsieh (c.465–523 CE), an anomalous and not especially influential work that has been rediscovered and even translated into English in the twentieth century (trans. and annotated by Vincent Yu-chung Shih, *The Literary Mind and the Carving of Dragons,* Taipei, 1975). Like other writers of the Six Dynasties and the T'ang, Liu acknowledged a general divide between rhymed and unrhymed writing, and, for the genres within them, he defined each type, listed criteria for criticism, and cited exemplary practitioners. By contrast, the latter half of the book discusses the inventional and compositional process and the modes of organization for all *wen* (literature, writing) without any differentiation.

Mention should be made here of the Buddhist contribution to Chinese rhetorical practices. Buddhism was brought to China sometime during the first century CE and reached its apogee during the T'ang. The Chinese Buddhists introduced several new persuasive genres, some of which were appropriated by the Confucians and Taoists; among their innovations were sermons (*t'an-yü*), sutra lectures (*chiang-ching wen*), storytelling with illustrations (*pien-wen*), formal religious disputation, and *yü-lu,* "records of conversations." These genres were recorded in the vernacular consistent with their oral origin.

For the T'ang and Sung (960–1279 CE) literati, however, the language issue was not vernacular versus classical Chinese, but rather whether to write classical Chinese in the prevailing "parallel prose" style (*p'ien-t'i wen*) or in the "ancient style" (*ku-wen*), as was so famously advocated by the literatus Han Yu (768–824 CE). For the Confucians of this period and later, this was a deeply ideological and even moral issue. Assuming, as they did, that the purpose of literature (*wen*) is to reveal the Tao, the (right) Way, that the way one writes expresses one's character and understanding, that the sages of the past wrote in *ku-wen,* and that literature affects its audience, then it follows that one must steep oneself in the *ku-wen* texts, internalize their prose style, use it in one's own writings, and in this way transform society.

Running parallel to the continuing debate over correct style was a more prosaic handbook tradition. From perhaps as early as the Chin dynasty (265–420 CE) down to the early twentieth century there have appeared treatises and manuals on how to write various kinds of prose and poetry. *Ars dictaminis* emerged, to meet the growing need, usually with model letters included. Instructions for producing such documents might also be incorporated in the books of "family instructions" that appeared from the T'ang dynasty on, just as advice on how to write official memoranda and informal reports might be appended to a guidebook for magistrates. Of course, there were also guides for composing the essays for the civil service examination (the so-called "eight-legged essay," *pa-ku wen*), as well as collections of successful essays for study and imitation. The abolition of the examination system in 1905, the popularity of the vernacular language (*pai-hua*) movement in the early twentieth century, and Western-style restructuring of the educational system weakened the influence of traditional Chinese rhetoric by making its texts less accessible for the average educated Chinese person than they had been.

Much work remains to be done on the Chinese rhetorical tradition, and there is not yet a comprehensive book-length overview. Those wishing to explore Chinese rhetoric should first consult the annotated bibliographies, and especially the bibliography on "rhetoric," in *The Indiana Companion to Traditional Chinese Literature* (ed. William Nienhauser, Bloomington, Vol. 1, 1986; Vol. 2, 1998). In addition, the individual entries in the *Companion* are a reliable source for locating Western-language translations and secondary scholarship. But the reader who relies on translations and consults secondary scholarship needs to keep in mind that sinologists may not be sensitive to the rhetorical dimensions of the Chinese texts, and also that they may define rhetoric quite narrowly, for instance, as tropes and figures. The reader also should be aware that sinology is a relatively new and rapidly evolving field, informed by new archaeological discoveries as well as advances in epigraphy, grammar, and textual studies.

[*See also* Comparative rhetoric.]

BIBLIOGRAPHY

Garrett, Mary M. "Reflections on Some Elementary Methodological Problems in the Study of Chinese Rhetoric." In *Rhetoric in Intercultural Contexts,* edited by Alberto Gonzalez and Dolores Tanno, pp. 53–63. International and Intercultural Communication Annual, vol. 22. Thousand Oaks, Calif., 1999.

Henderson, John B. *Scripture, Canon, and Commentary: A Comparison of Confucian and Western Exegesis.* Princeton, 1991. A detailed discussion of the evolution and functions of textual commentary, a significant rhetorical genre in the Chinese tradition.

Loewe, Michael, ed. *Early Chinese Texts: A Bibliographical Guide.* Berkeley, 1993. An excellent reference for the textual history as well as the translations and secondary scholarship for some sixty major pre-Han and Han texts.

Norman, Jerry. *Chinese.* Cambridge, U.K., 1988. An authoritative description of the historical development of the Chinese language and the writing system; also covers related language issues.

Lu, Xing. *Rhetoric in Ancient China, Fifth to Third Century B.C.E.: A Comparison with Classical Greek Rhetoric.* Columbia, S.C., 1998. A good introduction to the received Chinese view of pre-Han rhetoric.

Online Resources
Elman, Benjamin, comp. "Classical Historiography for Chinese History." *http://www.sscnet.ucla.edu/history/elman/ClassBib/.* Updated Summer 1999. An official Asian Studies WWW Virtual Associate Site. An excellent resource for locating bibliographies, translations, and scholarship for all periods of Chinese history.
—MARY M. GARRETT

CICERONIANISM. *See* Eloquence; *and* Renaissance rhetoric, *articles on* Rhetoric in Renaissance language and literature *and* Rhetoric in the age of Reformation and Counter-Reformation.

CLASSICAL RHETORIC, historically defined, is the total record—many thousands of printed pages—of Greek and Roman rhetorical teaching and practice from the time of the Homeric and Hesiodic epics to that of the Sophists, orators, dramatists, and philosophers of the fifth and fourth centuries BCE; to Roman speakers and writers beginning in the second century BCE; to speeches, sermons, rhetorical poetry, and handbooks of composition dating from the time of the Roman Empire. These practices and teaching can best be defined by comparison with rhetorical traditions of non-Western cultures or with rhetorical theories and practices in medieval, Renaissance, and modern cultures in the West that have departed from classical practice. [*See* Comparative rhetoric; *overview article on* Medieval rhetoric; Modern rhetoric; *and overview article on* Renaissance rhetoric.]

Theoretically defined, classical rhetoric is a systematic and comprehensive body of knowledge primarily intended to teach public speaking, which was conceptualized between the fourth century BCE and the early Middle Ages. This system has, to some extent, continued to be taught and practiced in Western civilization ever since, often extended from a focus on speaking to the teaching of written discourse and even poetry. The Sophists, Plato, Isocrates, Aristotle, philosophers of the Hellenistic period, and critics of the time of the Roman Empire made contributions to this theory, but the writings of Cicero, the anonymous *Rhetoric to Herennius,* and Quintilian's *Education of the Orator* have been the primary sources for this Western classical tradition. Although its main outlines, many of its precepts, and some of its technical terminology were largely consistent, there were numerous variations in detail among different authorities, and the version taught by Roman writers differed in some important ways from the theory of Greek rhetoricians that was transmitted to the Renaissance by Byzantine scholars. Classical rhetoric as a fully developed theory of human discourse has often been assumed by Westerners to be a universal rhetoric, applicable in all places and at all times, but it contains some features that are specific to the Greek- and Latin-speaking societies of antiquity and, conversely, ignores some rhetorical phenomena found in other cultures or periods. This article will trace the development of classical rhetorical teaching and practice in Greece and Rome, as well

as provide an account of rhetoric in the Ciceronian tradition and some of its major classical variations.

Classical rhetoric was largely a male phenomenon. Much valuable scholarship has recently been published about women in antiquity and their intellectual activities are now better understood, but there are no writings about rhetoric by women in antiquity. There were famous women poets, but only two are known to us from significant remains, the Greek Sappho, who wrote in the early sixth century BCE, and the Roman Sulpicia, of the Augustan period. Some women attended philosophical schools, but there is no known example of a woman studying or teaching rhetoric. Women were not allowed to speak in the law courts or political assemblies in Greece or Rome; public speaking by women was largely restricted to a few queens ruling in their own right in Greek-speaking portions of Asia Minor or in Egypt. There are numerous speeches attributed to women in imaginative literature in Greek and Latin, indicating some recognition by male authors that women could express themselves artistically and persuasively (women in Greek plays by Euripides and Aristophanes and in the Latin poetry of Ovid are especially effective speakers), and there are a few speeches attributed to women in writings of the historians, which may have a basis in what they actually said: examples include speeches attributed to Artemesia, Queen of Caria, by Herodotus (8.68 and 102) and to the Roman matron Hortensia by Appian (4.32.34). In Plato's *Menexenus,* Socrates quotes a funeral oration that he says is by Aspasia, the companion of Pericles, and in the *Symposium,* he reports an extended conversation on philosophical love that he claims to have learned from a priestess named Diotima; both of these may be Plato's own composition.

Greek literature of the archaic and early classical periods (eight to mid-fifth centuries BCE) reveals a society that put a high value on eloquent and persuasive public address and loved vigorous debate to the point of tolerating personal verbal attacks beyond what was acceptable in many other ancient societies.

The beginnings of classical rhetoric. Many of the conventions later formulated into precepts in handbooks of rhetoric were already in use at an early time, and examples from the early poets are cited by Aristotle and later writers as illustrations of the art. These include techniques of logical, ethical, and emotional appeal; the arrangement of formal speeches into logical parts; the use of different styles by different speakers or on different occasions; and the ornamentation of speech by tropes and figures. Among the most revealing passages are the speeches of the envoys to Achilles in *Iliad* 9, the assembly of the Ithacans called by Telemachus in *Odyssey* 2, the trial of Hermes for stealing cattle in the *Homeric Hymn to Hermes,* and the trial of Orestes for killing Clytemnestra in Aeschylus's *Eumenides.*

The Phoenician alphabet was adapted to the writing of Greek in the ninth century BCE, but until the fifth century BCE, the Greek literature we know is largely a written transcription of oral compositions that were "published" by oral performance. In the second half of the fifth century BCE, literacy became more general and composition in writing became the norm, facilitating the development of prose and the authorship of historical and philosophical works and technical writings on subjects such as medicine, rhetoric, and politics. This "literate revolution," as it is now called, like the invention of printing in the fifteenth century, had some effects on rhetoric in addition to making possible the composition of rhetorical handbooks and treatises for a growing literate readership. The spread of literacy in Greece contributed to setting linguistic standards and grammatical correctness; it facilitated understanding of complex logical argument that would have been difficult to grasp orally; and it probably encouraged the use of complex, periodic sentences, which began to appear at this time.

The word *rhētorikē* first appears in Plato's *Gorgias* (449a5), probably written about 385 BCE. In a conversation imagined to have taken place some thirty years earlier, the Sophist Gorgias describes himself there as a teacher of rhetoric. "Rhetoric" is literally the art of a *rhētōr,* a public speaker or politician, and it is viewed by Socrates with suspicion as involving flattery and deceit. It was not until Aristotle had given serious attention to the subject many years later that rhetoric, under that name, became a respected educational discipline, but the Greeks of the fifth century BCE and earlier were quite conscious of the phenomenon we call rhetoric, referring to it as *peithō,*

"persuasion"; *technē logōn,* the "art of speeches"; or in other terms. The word *logos* refers to anything "said" and can mean "word, speech, language, argument, reason," and related things, depending on the context.

Cicero (*Brutus,* section 44) and later writers, on the basis of statements in a now-lost work by Aristotle, credit the "invention" of an art of rhetoric to two Sicilians called Corax and Tisias. The alleged occasion was the need to provide some skill in public speaking to persons involved in litigation of property rights after the expulsion of the tyrants and establishment of democracy in Syracuse about 466 BCE *Corax* means "crow" in Greek, and it is probable that Corax and Tisias are the same person and that the nickname "Corax" was given to Tisias by those who resented his "cawing." Although details in the story are unreliable, two features of it seem important: the connection with litigation and the context of democracy. Classical rhetoric began and always remained primarily a system of training young men how to speak effectively in a court of law; and it was developed for the needs of participatory democracy, especially in Athens. Under the Athenian democracy, reaching its most radical form in the fifth and fourth centuries BCE, there was no public prosecutor and there were no professional lawyers; criminal indictments, like civil suits, were brought by an interested person. In both criminal and civil cases, prosecutor and defendant were ordinarily expected to speak on their own behalf, though if they were unable to do so an advocate could speak for them. Since women were not allowed to speak in court, they had to be represented by a male family member. Any evidence of witnesses was taken down in writing before the trial and read out by a clerk, and prosecutor and defendant were expected to deliver a carefully-planned speech, without interruption by the court. There was no presiding judge to ask questions, interpret the law, or establish relevance, only a clerk to organize proceedings; both fact and law were judged by a panel of jurors (*dikastai*) numbering at least 201 and, in some major cases, several thousand persons, chosen by lot from among male citizens. To make an effective case before such large juries required considerable rhetorical skill and confidence.

Someone needing to address a court of law

could turn to two sources for help, in addition to the possibility of securing an advocate in some cases. One source was to commission a *logographos,* or professional speech writer, who for a fee would write a speech. One would then try to memorize the speech and deliver it as best one could. Several famous orators in the fourth century BCE, including Lysias and Demosthenes, sometimes wrote speeches for pay, and they demonstrated great skill in portraying the character of their clients.

A second possibility was to study a handbook of judicial rhetoric, try to compose a speech following the outline it provided, and adapt its examples to the case at hand. Such a handbook, called a *technē logōn* or later *technē rhētorikē* (Lat. *ars rhetorica*) encapsulated and expanded the kind of advice Tisias the Crow was thought to have given. A number of handbooks were available in Athens by the late fifth and early fourth centuries BCE, and Plato gives a brief survey of them in *Phaedrus* (266d1–267d9). Two aspects of the advice found in these handbooks are especially important for the history of classical rhetorical teaching: the handbooks divided a judicial speech into a series of parts, each performing a specific function, and they showed how to construct a probable argument based on circumstantial evidence. The minimum number of parts of a judicial speech was considered to be four (some authorities identified more): a prooemion, to secure the attention, interest, and good will of the jury; a narration, to provide the facts of the case as the speaker wanted them to be understood; a proof of the speaker's contention, drawing on any witnesses, evidence, and probabilities; and an epilogue, recapitulating the speech and stirring the emotions of the jury to vote in the speaker's favor. Commonplaces (*topoi*), in the sense of examples of material useful in separate parts of the speech, probably constituted the greater part of a handbook, and Plato mentions other works containing collections of useful words, arguments, or emotional appeals that could be adapted by the speaker.

The classic example of argument from probability (*eikos*), cited by both Plato (*Phaedrus,* 273a–b) and Aristotle (*Rhetoric,* 2.2.11), is the case of a man charged with starting a brawl. If he is small or weak and his opponent is large or strong, he can argue that it is improbable he would have started the fight; conversely, if he is large or strong he can also argue that it is improbable, for he would have exercised restraint, knowing that he would be suspected. Surviving speeches of the Greek orators, as well as debates in Greek drama, often make use of arguments from probability, dependent on Greek views of human motivation and a feeling that moral character and motivation are often more valid bases of judgment than direct evidence, which could be, and often was, the result of bribes or faking.

No speeches by the great political figures of fifth-century BCE Athens—Themistocles, Aristides, Pericles, Nicias, Alcibiades, and others—survive in their original form. There are, however, testimonies to their eloquence, and Thucydides, who had heard many of them speak, includes speeches, which he attributes to Pericles and others in his *History of the Peloponnesian War.* The most famous, and most eloquent, is the version of a funeral oration (Thucydides, 2.35–46) given by Pericles in memory of those who died in the first year of the war.

The Sophists. Another form of rhetorical training was offered, for a fee, by traveling teachers called Sophists (i.e., "experts") who visited Athens in the second half of the fifth century BCE and attracted the interest of young aristocrats. Some Sophists are said to have written handbooks of the type described above, but their rhetorical teaching primarily took the form of epideictic demonstrations, which were elaborate show speeches on mythological, historical, or philosophical subjects, illustrating forms of argument and furnishing examples of stylistic experimentation. Students listened to these speeches, studied them in written form, and attempted to imitate them when they practiced speaking and writing. The Sophists sought to provide a kind of general education in knowledge and skills useful for an enterprising young man in a constitutional city in Greece, and they did not distinguish what came to be called rhetoric as a discipline from other potentially useful knowledge. [*See* Sophists.]

The two most famous Sophists are Protagoras (fl. c.445 BCE) and Gorgias (c.483–c.376 BCE). Plato's dialogue, *Protagoras,* contains an extended display by the Sophist that is doubtless Plato's composition but imitates the Sophist's methods and style. His writings are poorly preserved. One work began with the famous proclamation, "Man is the measure of all things: of those which that are, that they are; of those which are not, that they are not." This is usually taken as indicating philosophical relativism or skepticism, seen also in Gorgias's treatise *On Nature or That Which is Not.* This latter work survives in outline form and seeks to show, first, that nothing exists; second, that if anything does exist it cannot be apprehended by the human mind; and third, that if anything were apprehended, it could not be communicated by one person to another. Such ideas were exhilarating to some young radicals, shocking to some older conservatives, as dramatized in Aristophanes' comedy, *The Clouds,* originally produced in 423 BCE.

Two short speeches by Gorgias survive in complete form. They were perhaps first composed in the 420s BCE and may have been repeatedly revised and performed later. *The Defense of Palamedes* is an imaginary speech for a hero charged with treason in the Trojan war; the *Encomion of Helen,* despite the name, is not an encomion but a defense of Helen's actions in leaving her husband, Menelaus, and going to Troy with Paris, thus precipitating the war. Both speeches provide examples of the effective arrangement of separate parts, forms of argument, and devices of style. Gorgias argues that Helen must have eloped with Paris for one of four reasons: by fate and will of the gods, because she was taken by force, because she was persuaded by speech, or because she was overcome by love, and he seeks to show that in any of these cases, she should be held blameless. This involves arguing that speech is "a powerful lord," irresistible to the hearer, and Gorgias inserts a kind of prose hymn to speech (*logos*) that anticipates celebration of rhetoric found in later writers.

Gorgias's distinctive prose style gave the speeches their greatest interest; it created a sensation when he first came to Athens as an ambassador in 427 BCE. Gorgias introduced into oratory a poetic, rhythmical prose that makes repeated use of what came to be known as Gorgianic figures of speech. They include phrases or clauses with contrasting thought (antithesis), often of equal length (*parison*), rhyme at the ends of clauses (*homoeoteleuton*), and sound play of all sorts (*paronomasia*). [*See* Gorgianic figures.] Other writers of the time, including the historian Thucydides, imitate features of this style in a restrained way. Whether Gorgias ever used technical terms to describe figures or other aspects of rhetoric is unknown. Plato represented him as having little understanding of what he did, and Aristotle complained (*Sophistical Refutations,* 183b36–183b39) that his rhetorical and dialectical teaching was neither systematic nor analytical. A sophistic tradition can be traced in the history of rhetoric, characterized by celebration of the powers of speech, cultivation of epideictic in preference to other rhetorical genres, acute sensitivity to language usage and style, and teaching by example rather than by precept. From the second to the fifth century CE, what is known as the "Second Sophistic" flourished in the Greek-speaking cities of the Roman Empire. Great Sophists, including Dio Chrysostom (c.40–after 112 CE), Aelius Aristides (c.117–c.181 CE), Libanius (314–393 CE), and others attained fame and even political influence. Something analogous to Greek sophistry existed in ancient China and India, and seems to be a regular phenomenon in the intellectual development of sophisticated, literate societies.

Isocrates. Although Isocrates (436–338 BCE) criticized the Sophists and sought to distance himself from the movement (e.g., in the truncated speech *Against the Sophists*), he shares characteristics of sophistry listed above except for its philosophical relativism. About 392 BCE, he opened a school in Athens where for the rest of his long life he taught the arts of virtuous living, effective public speaking, and political leadership to large numbers of young men. He wrote and polished lengthy speeches on important issues of the time, which he read to his students—even inviting their criticisms—and which they were then expected to imitate in their own exercises. He himself lacked the self-confidence to speak in public and sought to influence public opinion by publication of his orations in pamphlet form. His amplification of every subject and his long periodic sentences are early examples of the effects of the "literate revolution" mentioned above. Isocrates' favorite theme was pan-Hellenism, the cultural unity of the Greeks despite their divisions into numerous quarreling states, and the need for union against barbarians, primarily the Persians, who had twice invaded Greece. This is the theme of his greatest work, *Panegyricus* (380 BCE), to which he returned in later orations.

Although Isocrates has much to say about speech, he does not use the word *rhētorikē*, preferring to call his teaching "philosophy." In some of his writing, there is an implied criticism of the teachings of his great contemporary, Plato (whom he never names), as abstruse and impractical. Plato mentions Isocrates only once, at the end of *Phaedrus,* where the compliment is probably ironic. There are, however, passages elsewhere that can be read as criticism of Isocrates, whom Plato doubtless regarded as too prone to smooth over the failings of Athenian democracy, too vague in his thinking, more concerned with appearance than with truth, and not a philosopher in any true sense.

Isocrates has often been viewed as the founding father of liberal arts education (*enkyklios paideia* in Greek, thus the English word *encyclopedia*). He taught composition, public speaking, logical reasoning, history, religion, mythology, and politics, primarily by providing examples, like the Sophists, not by analysis and conceptualization, as Aristotle was to do, and he did not distinguish rhetoric from other disciplines; but unlike fifth-century Sophists, his school was a continuing institution in one place. It ended with his death, however, and unlike the philosophical schools founded by Plato, Aristotle, Zeno, and Epicurus, it had no successor. Isocrates's bland and wordy writings have been read by students of rhetoric ever since his time, primarily as examples of smoothness in sound and prose rhythm, elaborated in lengthy periodic sentences.

The Attic orators. Isocrates is one of the so-called "Attic" orators, Athenian orators of the century between 430 and 330 BCE who came to be regarded by later teachers as employing the purest form of the Attic dialect of Greek and the best models for imitation by students. A canon of Ten Attic Orators was eventually created, possibly by Caecilius, a rhetorician of the late first century BCE—but the canon cannot be confidently dated before the second century CE, when it is found in *Lives of the Ten Orators,* preserved as part of Plutarch's *Moralia,* but by an unknown author. Works of the Ten were studied, copied, and, at

least in part, transmitted to Byzantine scholars and from them to the West. The Attic Orators are, in chronological order:

1. Antiphon (c.480–411 BCE). Athenian politician, executed for his role in the oligarchic revolution of 411; three logographic speeches on homicide cases are preserved, plus fragments of others and fragmentary philosophical writings. The *Tetralogies,* traditionally ascribed to him, were probably composed a generation after his death as models for argument in homicide cases.
2. Lysias (c.445–c.378 BCE). Thirty-four surviving speeches, of which three may be spurious, out of an original production of over two hundred. Most were written for clients to deliver in the law courts, but his most famous speech, *Against Eratosthenes* (no.12), concerns himself and his family. In the view of later critics, Lysias was the classic model of the simple style and of *ēthopoeia*, the artistic portrayal of the character of the speaker.
3. Andocides (c.440–c.390 BCE). Not a professional rhetorician; three speeches survive, all related to his political activities.
4. Isocrates (436–338 BCE). Discussed above.
5. Isaeus (c.420–c.350 BCE). Twelve extant speeches, all on testimentary cases.
6. Aeschines (c.397–c.322 BCE). Originally an actor, then a flamboyant political opponent of Demosthenes, and author of three long judicial speeches.
7. Hyperides (389–322 BCE). Portions of six speeches were recovered from papyri in the nineteenth century. A skilled logographer and minor political figure.
8. Demosthenes (384–322 BCE). The greatest Greek orator, in the opinion of many critics the greatest political orator of all time, famous for his versatility and *deinotēs* (fearful energy), finest master of the grand style. He was a conservative politician who tried to alert Athenians to the threat from Macedon in his *Olynthiacs* and *Philippics. On the Crown* is his eloquent defense of his policies against charges brought by Aeschines. Sixty extant speeches are attributed to him, of which forty-one judicial and deliberative speeches,

plus a collection of prooemia and some letters, are probably genuine.

9. Lycurgus (390–324 BCE). Conservative Athenian statesman and financial official, author of one surviving speech, *Against Leocrates,* on a charge of treason.

10. Dinarchus (c.360–c.290 BCE). Three speeches survive, prosecutions resulting from the alleged bribery of Demosthenes and others by Harpalus, treasurer of Alexander the Great.

Plato. Plato (c.428–347 BCE) was a consummate rhetorician as seen in the characterizations, speeches, and myths included in his dialogues. Many of his writings, including *Protagoras, Symposium, Menexenus, Republic,* and *Laws,* have relevance for rhetoric, and two dialogues, *Gorgias* (c.385 BCE) and *Phaedrus* (c.375 BCE or later) are focused primarily on that subject. In *Gorgias,* Plato's spokesman, Socrates, takes a highly critical view of contemporary rhetoric, describing it as a form of flattery and deceit, analogous to spicing up bad food to please the palate. In *Phaedrus,* however, a philosophical rhetoric is sketched which, if ever attained, would be an instrument of truth and moral instruction of an audience. To do that, the orator must know the truth and understand logical reasoning and human psychology, becoming a *psychagōgus,* or "leader of the soul," by adapting what is said to the minds of the audience. In a famous passage (264c6–264c9), Socrates argues that a good speech must be an organic unity like the human body, all the members cohering into one whole. The dialogue concludes with the myth of Theuth, describing the bad effects of writing, which will destroy memory and which, unlike an oral dialogue, cannot answer its critics.

Aristotle. Aristotle (384–322 BCE) was a native of Stagira in northern Greece and for twenty years, beginning in 367 BCE, a member of Plato's Academy, an institute of advanced philosophical studies on the outskirts of Athens. During that period, he composed some philosophical dialogues (all now lost), including one on rhetoric, *Gryllus,* which perhaps had some resemblance to Plato's *Gorgias,* and in the 350s BCE, he taught a public course on rhetoric. Some of the material that he prepared for the course can be identified in the text of his extant treatise *On Rhetoric.* Just

before Plato's death in 347 BCE, Aristotle left Athens and spent the next twelve years in Asia Minor and Macedon, devoting himself to scientific research, then from about 342 to 339 BCE, to supervising the education of the young Macedonian prince, Alexander. Philip of Macedon conquered the Greek city-states in 338 BCE. His son, Alexander, became king in 336 BCE, and the next year Aristotle returned to Athens, where he opened his own school, the Peripatetic school, at the gymnasium of the Lyceum and taught there for the next twelve years. After Alexander's death in 323 BCE, there were anti-Macedonian outbreaks in Athens and Aristotle withdrew to Chalcis, where he died the next year.

It was Aristotle, more than anyone, who was responsible for the creation of academic disciplines. Unlike previous teachers, he offered separate lecture courses on subjects specified as dealing with physics, metaphysics, politics, ethics, dialectic, poetics, rhetoric, and other subjects, and these lectures originated modern conceptions of the disciplines. In his lectures on public speaking, Aristotle adopted the word *rhetoric* as descriptive of the subject both generally and specifically. His work with Alexander may have directed his thinking back to public speaking; in any event, *On Rhetoric* as we know it seems to have been largely written in the years between 340 and 335 BCE, perhaps to become the basis of lectures on the subject in the event of his hoped-for return to Athens. Neither *On Rhetoric* nor Aristotle's other works as we know them today were published until the first century BCE, but the contents were known to his numerous students, including Theophrastus, his successor as head of the Peripatetic school, and by them given some dissemination through their own teaching and writing.

On Rhetoric was written at different times and never finally revised, resulting in some inconsistencies in audience, point of view, and terminology. Portions of the work, including the opening chapter, take an austere, rather Platonic view of rhetoric, while other parts (e.g., 1.9) read like a practical handbook and even give precepts for deceiving an audience. Aristotle may have thought future leaders of society among his students would need to know how to sway ignorant audiences in a badly-ordered state, as well as to recognize rhetorical tricks when used by others (*see* Carol Poster, "Aristotle's *Rhetoric* Against Rhetoric," *American Journal of Philology,* 1997, pp. 219–249). Some modern philosophers ignore signs of changes over time in Aristotle's thoughts about rhetoric, gloss over inconsistencies in the text of his lectures, and seek to force his views of rhetoric to agree in all respects with his ethical and political writings. This approach seriously distorts the meaning and significance of *On Rhetoric*.

Book divisions in *On Rhetoric* originated with Aristotle; chapter divisions were first made by George of Trebizond for his Latin translation in the fifteenth century. Scholars often refer to passages by page numbers, column letters, and line numbers (e.g., 1354a1) from the edition of the complete works of Aristotle by Immanuel Bekker (Berlin, 1831). The best modern edition of the Greek text is that by Rudolf Kassel (Berlin, 1976); there is a recent English translation, with notes (George A. Kennedy, New York, 1991).

Books 1 and 2 of *the Rhetoric* are concerned with what Aristotle calls *dianoia,* "thought," that is, the content of a speech, which later came to be known as rhetorical invention. Rhetoric, Aristotle says in the first chapter, is an *antistrophos,* or counterpart, to dialectic; both are useful arts with no specific content of their own, able to argue on either side of a question. At the beginning of the second chapter, rhetoric is defined as "an ability (*dynamis,* i.e., a faculty or power) in each case to see the available means of persuasion." Rhetoric thus deals with particular cases, not with general issues as does dialectic. [*See* Dialectic; *and* Inventory.]

Throughout the rest of this chapter (1.2), Aristotle lays out the whole subject of rhetorical invention as he understood it. Means of persuasion are either nonartistic—laws, witnesses, contracts, or oaths, used but not invented by the speaker—or artistic, the invention of the speaker. Artistic means of persuasion take three forms, which have come to be known as *ēthos,* the presentation of the character of the speaker as a person to be trusted; *pathos,* the emotions of the audience as stirred by the speaker; and *logos,* logical argument based on evidence and probability. There are two kinds of logical argument: paradigm, that is, inductive argument based on examples, implicitly or explicitly drawing a general conclusion and then applying this to a particular; and enthymeme (literally, "something in the mind"), that is, rhetorical syllogism, a deductive argument based on acceptance of premises. The conclusion of an enthymeme can in theory be valid if the premises are certain, but that is rarely true in rhetoric, where the subject matter is usually probable. Often, one premise of an enthymeme is omitted as easily supplied by the listener. Aristotle thinks of enthymemes as taking the form "if such and such is so, then it follows that something else is also so," or of a statement with a supporting clause giving a reason to believe the statement. The premises of enthymemes are derived from the specific propositions (*idia*) of bodies of knowledge such as politics or ethics, and also make use of topics, either *koina* ("commonalities," i.e., the possible or impossible, past fact, future fact, greater or smaller in magnitude or importance), or dialectical techniques, for which Aristotle usually reserves the term *topoi,* "topics" in the strict sense. These are discussed in detail in Book 2, chapter 23. [*See* Enthymeme; Ēthos; Logos; *and* Pathos.]

Aristotle's theory of the means of persuasion, and of paradigms, enthymemes, and various kinds of topics, differs somewhat from what is found in later classical rhetoric, but some features of his theory became permanent parts of the tradition. The most important of these was his definition of three species of rhetoric, based on the function of the audience (*On Rhetoric,* 1.3). An audience, he says, is either a judge or not a judge; that is, the audience is called upon to make a specific judgment about the subject under debate or no judgment or action is demanded. If the audience is asked to judge a fact in the past, as in a court of law, the species is *dikanikon* (judicial, forensic), and the basis of the judgment is determination of what is just (*to dikaion*); if the audience is asked to judge a proposed future action, as in a council or assembly, the species is *symbouleutikon* (deliberative), and the basis is determination of what is advantageous or expedient (*to sympheron*). If, on the other hand, no specific judgment or action is being demanded (other, perhaps, than a judgment that the speech is good), the species is *epideiktikon* (epideictic, demonstrative), which Aristotle viewed as concerned with praise or blame, as in a funeral oration or denunciation of an enemy or a speech at a festival, and the basis is the honorable (*to kalon*). *On Rhetoric* 1.4–8 describes the materials, methods, and goals of deliberative rhetoric, in which the most important subjects are said to be finances, war and peace, national defense, imports and exports, and legislation; chapter 9 deals with epideictic, chapters 10 to 15 with judicial rhetoric. [*See* Deliberative genre; Epideictic genre; *and* Forensic genre.] In Book 2, Aristotle resumes discussion of ēthos and pathos, discussing fourteen kinds of emotion and six kinds of character, and adds further details about paradigms, enthymemes, topics, and nonartistic proofs.

Book 3 of *On Rhetoric*, perhaps originally a separate work, begins with a brief discussion of rhetorical delivery, followed by a detailed consideration of prose style and of the parts of deliberative, epideictic, and judicial orations. The "virtue" (*aretē*) of style (3.2) is to be clear and neither flat nor above the dignity of the subject but appropriate to it. There are important chapters on word choice, including metaphor and simile, and features of composition, including prose rhythm and the periodic style. Aristotle had no concept of figures of speech, but he does discuss such matters as urbanities, visualization, and techniques later classified as figures. This part of the work ends (3.12) with a chapter on the differences between oral and written style. As for the parts of an oration, the only necessary parts, he says (3.13), are proposition and proof, but he then proceeds to discuss prooemion, ways of meeting a prejudicial attack, narration, proof, interrogation, and epilogue. [*See* Delivery; *and* Style.]

Although published in the first century BCE and known to Cicero and Quintilian, Aristotle's treatise on rhetoric was little-read throughout antiquity and the Middle Ages. Its neglect may be partly due to the rapid development between the fourth and second centuries BCE of aspects of rhetoric not discussed by Aristotle. Two Latin translations were made in the thirteenth century CE, followed by that of George of Trebizond in the fifteenth century CE, and a few Renaissance teachers lectured on the work or cited passages from it. It was not until the twentieth century, however, that the originality and brilliance of the treatise came to be fully appreciated.

Rhetoric to Alexander. In addition to the genuine treatise *On Rhetoric,* the Aristotelian corpus has transmitted a curious work believed by scholars to be a revision of a handbook of public speaking originally composed by Anaximenes of Lampsacus around the middle of the fourth century BCE, possibly before Aristotle's final revision of his lectures and perhaps known to him. At some time, this work, *Rhetoric to Alexander,* was revised by an unknown editor who prefixed an inept letter purporting to be a dedication by Aristotle to Alexander the Great; this forger, or someone else, then made a number of changes throughout to bring the work into somewhat closer harmony with Aristotle's genuine teaching. Originally, there seem to have been sections on protreptic and apotreptic oratory in public address (*dēmēgoria*) and accusation and defense in judicial oratory (*dikanikē*), to which a brief account of epideictic (here called *enkōmiastikon*) has been added. There are extended lists of things a speaker might say and arguments that might be used, discussion of the parts of each kind of oratory, and some remarks on devices of style. Except for some stylistic terms, the special rhetorical terminology used by Aristotle and that of later Greek rhetoric are largely lacking; "enthymemes," for example, are said (chapter 10) to be "things opposed to the speech or action in question or anything else." Unlike what is found in most other handbooks, no examples are cited from literature, though there are some examples from history (chapter 8). The work had little influence on the subsequent history of rhetoric.

Hellenistic rhetoric. Between the fourth and first centuries BCE, rhetoric, in name and in fact, was accepted throughout the Greek-speaking world—including cities in Asia Minor and North Africa, as a result of Alexander's conquests there—as the regular second stage in education, undertaken by boys in their early teens after several years of study in a grammar school. The primary function of rhetorical education was to provide skill in public speaking, especially speaking in courts of law, where this remained very useful. Opportunities for political oratory declined somewhat under the Hellenistic monarchies and later Roman rule, but individuals still needed to address state officials, orally or in writing; to plead cases in court; to judge speeches as delivered by others; and sometimes to speak themselves as members of local councils or assemblies. Despite the spread of literacy, ancient society remained strongly oral, and the study of rhetoric was regarded as enabling students to fully participate in their culture, distinguishing it from the life of barbarians. There are no surviving Greek speeches dating from this period. Later rhetoricians refer to it as a time when a highly artificial style was in vogue; they call this style "Asianism" and say that it flourished especially in rhetorical schools in Asia Minor, in contrast to the simpler "Attic" tradition of Athens, with its emphasis on a purer form of Greek, and an intermediate style taught on the island of Rhodes. [*See* Atticist–Asianist controversy.] As a young man in the early first century BCE, Cicero studied rhetoric in all three places; in *Brutus,* section 325, he describes Asianism, and in section 312, he credits his teacher on Rhodes, Apollonius Molon, with helping him control the youthful impetuosity of speech that had adversely affected his health.

Although these centuries were the time when classical rhetoric and rhetorical education assumed the form that it largely retained, primary sources are lacking for reconstruction of these developments. No rhetorical treatises have survived from the third and second centuries BCE, but from Cicero and other later writers, we know that rhetoric came to be taught as consisting of five subjects, usually called "parts" (*partes*) of rhetoric by the Romans. Quintilian (3.3.11–3.3.13) criticizes those who refer to them as "offices" or "elements." In modern times, they are sometimes called the "canons" (i.e., rules) of rhetoric. These parts or canons recapitulated the actions of planning, composing, and delivering a speech. These five parts (to be discussed in detail below) were invention (contents, arguments); arrangement (division of the speech into parts and arrangement of arguments); style (word choice, composition of sentences, tropes and figures); memory (mnemonic devices); and delivery (control of the voice, use of gestures). Additions made to earlier theories were most extensive in the case of invention and style. Hermagoras of Temnos in the second century BCE expounded a complex theory of the *stasis,* or definition of the question at issue in a speech, which remained a major concern to rhetoricians thereafter and which will be described later in this article. In the theory of style,

the major developments occurred in descriptions of separate kinds or "characters" of style and in the naming and definition of tropes and figures.

In the fourth and third centuries BCE, members of the Academic, Peripatetic, and Stoic philosophical schools in Athens all made contributions to rhetorical theory. In particular, Aristotle's successor as head of the Peripatetic School, Theophrastus, wrote numerous works on rhetoric, known to us only from later references, that further developed or revised Aristotelian concepts. He developed a theory of delivery and his theory of the "virtues (*aretai*) of style" went beyond Aristotle's original concept and was repeated in many later sources. These virtues he defined as correctness (purity of language, standard grammar), clarity, ornamentation (including figures of speech), and propriety (suiting style to speaker, subject, and audience). In the middle of the second century BCE, however, most philosophers in all the schools became hostile to rhetoric as a discipline and rejected its claims to being a reputable art, using arguments like those found in Plato's *Gorgias.* This attitude may, at least in some cases, have reflected a rivalry with rhetoricians for the attention of wealthy young Romans who were then beginning to study for a year or two in Athens or to patronize Greek teachers who visited Rome. The attitude of the ruling oligarchs in Rome toward rhetoric was long ambivalent; rhetoric appealed on the one hand to their practical and legalistic values, but rhetorical skills among the masses might constitute a threat to their dominance. In 161 BCE, the Roman senate authorized the expulsion of all philosophers and rhetoricians from Rome, and in 92 BCE, the censors issued an edict prohibiting the teaching of rhetoric in Latin but allowing Greek rhetoricians to continue to teach. Neither of these efforts was successful for long, and by the second decade of the first century BCE, many young Romans were studying rhetorical theory and practicing rhetorical exercises.

The Roman republican government, long dominated by members of aristocratic families, provided many opportunities for public address in the senate, in popular legislative assemblies, and in an extensive system of law courts. From the middle of the second century BCE until the establishment of the Roman Empire by Augustus after 30 BCE, political oratory of great eloquence flourished to an extent comparable only to Athens in the fifth and fourth centuries BCE and to eighteenth- and nineteenth-century CE Britain and America. Cicero's *Brutus* is a history of Greek and Roman oratory down to his own times.

Cicero's On Invention *and the Anonymous* Rhetoric to Herennius. There are references to discussions of rhetoric in Latin by Cato the Elder in the second century BCE and by Antonius in the early first century BCE, but these have not survived. The earliest Latin treatments of the subject are Cicero's *On Invention* (c.89 BCE), part of a never-completed comprehensive rhetorical handbook, and *Rhetoric to Herennius* (c.80 BCE), an anonymous work discussing all aspects of rhetoric as understood at the time. Where the two works overlap, their discussions are very similar, sometimes even verbally identical, and thus both authors seem to be drawing on the same Greek source or sources. Both present a version of Hermagoras's *stasis* theory. The anonymous author makes some minor adjustments of Greek theory for a Roman audience, Cicero none at all. Both works are dry, pedantic handbooks, but are of great historical importance. Not only do they set out rhetorical doctrine as it had come to exist by the early first century BCE, but from the fourth century CE until the Renaissance, they, rather than other more profound works, were the authoritative statements of classical rhetoric, the common basis of teaching the subject in schools and universities, the object of numerous commentaries by medieval and early Renaissance scholars, and the basic source of rhetoric as applied to letter writing and other medieval forms of composition. This was especially true of Cicero's *On Invention,* but *Rhetoric to Herennius,* commonly known as *Rhetorica Seconda,* was long attributed to Cicero and studied for its account of arrangement, style, memory, and delivery, subjects lacking in Cicero's own handbook. [*See* Arrangement, *article on* Traditional arrangement; *and* Memory.]

The content of these works will be summarized in the second part of this article, but a few special features should be noted here. Cicero's work is divided into two books, each with a preface. The preface to the first book, in particular, was to become famous and was frequently quoted or im-

itated by later writers on rhetoric. "Wisdom without eloquence," the young Cicero somewhat pompously asserts, "does too little to benefit states, but eloquence without wisdom does too much harm and is never advantageous." He then gives an account of the development of human society, probably derived from some Stoic philosopher. There must once have been a great leader with persuasive power who brought mankind out of primitive conditions, but such great men are not interested in the details of administration and a lesser class of those skilled at speech took over petty disputes. In the course of time, they became accustomed to defending falsehood. Strife resulted, and nobler souls withdrew into philosophical speculation The preface ends with a eulogy of eloquence resembling those by Gorgias and Isocrates:

> From it the greatest advantages come to the state, if wisdom is present as moderator of all things; from it, to those who have attained it, flow glory, honor, and prestige; from it also is secured the most certain and safe defense of one's friends. To me, it seems that although men are lower and weaker than the animals in many ways, they most excel them in that they are able to speak. Thus, the man seems to me to have gained something wonderful who excels other men in that very way in which mankind excels animals. Since it is acquired not only by nature and practice, but by some art, it is not irrelevant for us to see what they have to say who have left us precepts on the subject.

The author of *Rhetoric to Herennius* postponed his discussion of style to the fourth and last book of his work, apparently to give it specially extended treatment. He gives the earliest extant account (4.11–16) of a theory of three kinds of style, developed by Hellenistic Greek rhetoricians, calling them "figures" (*figurae*): the *gravis* or grand, *mediocris* or middle, and *adtenuata* or simple, and he supplies his own example of each as well as of the corresponding vitiated forms of style, the *sufflata* or swollen, *dissoluta* or slack, and *exile* or meager. His is also the earliest extant work to discuss rhetorical figures, here called "embellishments" (*exornationes*) and divided into those of words (*verborum*) (4.19–41) and those of thought (*sententiarum*) (4.47–69). Among verbal figures, he includes a group of ten devices, which in Greek would be called tropes (4.42–46). They include *denominatio* (metonymy), *superlatio* (hyperbolē), *intellectio* (synecdochē), *translatio* (metaphor), and others. Throughout, the author coins Latin names for the Greek terms, whereas later Roman rhetoricians often keep the Greek words, transliterated into the Latin alphabet. [*See* Figures of speech.]

Cicero. Marcus Tullius Cicero (106–43 BCE) was, like Demosthenes, a great orator and conservative politician who sought, unsuccessfully in the end, to preserve the traditional constitutional government of his city. He is the best known of all Romans, in large part because of the survival of over 900 of his personal letters. When not otherwise engaged, he wrote dialogues on rhetoric and philosophy, intended to inform Roman readers about issues as discussed in the Greek schools, and creating a Latin philosophical vocabulary in the process. In Roman legal procedure, individuals were not required to plead their own cases in court as they were in Greece; a *patronus,* like a barrister in British legal procedure, pleaded a case for a client. Cicero gained his greatest fame as a patron at the bar, most often speaking for the defense, and for speeches he delivered in the senate, including the four speeches delivered as part of his successful effort to thwart the conspiracy of Catiline in 69 BCE. Some fifty-eight of Cicero's speeches have survived, most in versions edited by himself, and have been studied throughout history as examples of powerful oratory, clever legal tactics, wit, and narrative skill. Among the most admired are his speeches for Roscius Amerinus, for Archias, for Caelius, for Cluentius, for Milo, and for Murena, and his fiery attacks on Mark Antony known as *Philippics* after their Demosthenic model.

The most important of Cicero's rhetorical works is the great dialogue *De oratore* (On the Orator, 55 BCE). The dramatic date of the dialogue is 91 BCE and the principal characters are major statesmen-orators of that time whom Cicero had known. Crassus is the spokesman for Cicero's own values: in Book 1, he argues for the citizen orator as the ideal civic model and demands of this ideal a wide and deep knowledge of philosophy, law, rhetoric, and other arts. Scaevola thinks this ideal unattainable and stresses an orator's need for a technical knowledge of law. Antonius takes an intermediate position about the orator's duties and needs; in Book 2 of the dialogue, he gives an account of rhetorical inven-

tion, arrangement, and memory in nontechnical terms. "The whole theory of speaking," he says (2.115), "is dependent on three sources of persuasion: that we prove our case to be true; that we win over those who are listening; that we call their minds to what emotion the case demands." Aristotle's *On Rhetoric* had been recently published, and Cicero adapts some ideas from it, including this version of Aristotle's three means of persuasion. In Book 3, Crassus is again the main speaker. He continues Antonius' nontechnical account of rhetoric with a long discourse on style, structured around the four virtues that Theophrastus had defined: correctness, clarity, ornamentation, and propriety.

Cicero's other major writings on rhetoric, both dating from 46 BCE, are *Brutus,* mentioned above for its history of oratory and including an interesting digression (sections 70–76) comparing the development of oratory to the history of sculpture and painting; and *Orator,* which gives a detailed account of rhetorical composition and enunciates (sections 69–99) an influential theory of the *officia oratoris,* the three "duties of an orator": to prove, to delight, and to stir, utilizing the plain, the middle, and the grand style, respectively. In both of these works, Cicero is concerned to defend his own expansive style against contemporary critics who called themselves "Atticists" and claimed to imitate the plain style of Lysias. It was Cicero's position that the Attic orators had used a wide variety of styles and that Demosthenes, the most versatile of them, was the finest model. Cicero had earlier written a kind of rhetorical catechism for his son, *Rhetorical Partitions,* as well as *De Optimo Genere Dicendi* (On the Best Kind of Speaking), which was the introduction to a never-completed translation of speeches of Demosthenes and Aeschines in the trial *On the Crown.* Finally, in 44 BCE, Cicero composed his *Topics,* a handbook of dialectical topics, which is an important link between Aristotelian and medieval dialectical teaching. [*See* Topics.]

Greek rhetorical teaching in the first century BCE. Lack of primary sources has made difficult a detailed knowledge of the development of Greek rhetorical teaching in the third and second centuries BCE, but several works survive from the first century BCE. The earliest of these may be the treatise *Peri Hermeneias* or *On Style,* attributed to someone named Demetrius, who was once thought to be Demetrius of Phaleron, statesman and orator of the late fourth century BCE. The actual author is unknown and the date of composition much debated: a time in the second quarter of the first century BCE is possible, since the author is familiar with Aristotle's *On Rhetoric*, not well known before then, and yet not concerned with the Atticism debate, which arose later in the century. "Demetrius"'s *On Style* is a perceptive piece of rhetorical criticism that discusses four "characters" of style (rather than the three commonly identified by others): the elevated, the plain, the elegant, and the forceful. They are identified on the basis of the thought, diction, rhythm, sentence structure, and figures and are illustrated by quotations from classical Greek prose and poetry. In contrast, there are also four defective styles: the frigid, the arid, the affected, and the graceless. A discussion of letter writing, unusual in a rhetorical treatise, is appended to the description of the plain style (sections 223–35). This implies a recognition that study of rhetoric applies to writing as well as speaking.

The Epicurean philosopher Philodemus (c.110–c.35 BCE) wrote treatises on a wide variety of subjects, including poetics and rhetoric. These partially survive on burned papyri from a library buried in the eruption of Mount Vesuvius in 79 CE. Philodemus's usual method was to criticize the views of earlier writers. Giving the fragmentary condition of the texts, reconstruction of his works is difficult (new editions are in progress), but he seems to have limited the art of rhetoric to sophistic or epideictic oratory, which, like poetry, he regarded as useless but pleasurable, a view consistent with his Epicurean principles.

We have some knowledge of the teachings of four Greek rhetoricians of the middle or late first century BCE. Gorgias of Athens, whom Cicero once employed as teacher for his son in Athens, wrote a brief handbook of figures of speech, which survives in a Latin translation by P. Rutilius Lupus. Apollodorus of Pergamum, one of the teachers of the future emperor Augustus, is frequently cited by later rhetoricians for his rigid views of the arrangement of an oration and is contrasted with Theodorus of Gadara, a teacher of the future emperor Tiberius, who is more flexible in some ways but dogmatic in others. The

schools of the Apollodoreans and Theodoreans long continued rancorous debate on pedantic details of rhetorical theory. A fourth rhetorician, famous at the time, was Caecilius of Calacte, whose handbook of figures is known from many later quotations. He seems to have been a proponent of Atticism and possibly originated the canon of the Ten Attic Orators. Among his works was a (lost) essay *On Sublimity,* criticized for its narrow approach at the beginning of the famous extant treatise on that subject commonly attributed to Longinus.

Best known of late-Hellenistic Greek rhetoricians is Dionysius of Halicarnassus, who can be approximately dated from his statement that he came to Rome after Augustus's victory in the civil wars (i.e., soon after 30 BCE). His extant works include a history of early Rome, a treatise *On the Ancient Orators* (with discussions of the style of Lysias, Isocrates, Isaeus, Demosthenes, and Dinarchus), an essay *On Thucydides,* three *Literary Epistles* (showing that Demosthenes could not have been influenced by Aristotle's *On Rhetoric,* defending Dionysius's preference for the style of Demosthenes over that of Plato, and continuing discussion of Thucydides), a lengthy and complex treatise *On Literary Composition,* and a fragmentary work *On Imitation.* In Dionysius's works are found descriptions of the evolution of classical Greek prose from what he calls a "rugged" style in the fifth century BCE to the "smooth" style of Isocrates and the "blended" style of Demosthenes, as well as theories of three "characters" of style, three "harmonies" of word order, and "virtues" of style, some necessary (i.e., correctness, clarity, conciseness), some supplementary (e.g., characterization, emotion, sublimity, elegance). He criticizes Asianism and is anxious to encourage the return to a chaster, purer Atticism, a reaction for which he gives much credit to the example of his Roman patrons.

Progymnasmata. "Preliminary exercises," *progymnasmata,* in prose composition were taught in ancient grammar schools and sometimes continued in rhetorical schools as well. They were regarded as "preliminary" to practice in declamation, which was the major activity of rhetorical schools. The earliest reference to such exercises occurs in *Rhetoric to Alexander* (28.1436a25) and the development of the traditional forms can probably be dated to the period between the fourth and first centuries BCE. Four Greek handbooks of progymnasmatic exercises survive from the time of the Roman Empire, and Quintilian (1.9 and 2.4) describes the exercises as used in Latin schools in his time. The handbooks outline a series of structured exercises in written composition by which a student progresses from simple restatement of a story or narrative to more complicated exercises using logical arguments, and they provide students with examples of topics to be employed in developing each of the compositions. These exercises heavily influenced the structure and style of literary composition, since most Greek and Roman writers of the Hellenistic and Roman periods had been practiced in them in their youth. Several of the exercises even became literary genres in their own right—for example, the *synkrisis* or comparison; the *ekphrasis* or vivid description; and the *ēthopoeia* or speech in character—and others are combined in different ways in composing epics, satires, occasional poetry, and prose romances.

The earliest and most thoughtful of the Greek handbooks is attributed to Aelius Theon of Alexandria, probably dating from the early or mid-first century BCE. It is unusual in being addressed to teachers rather than to students and in having chapters on teaching methods, which include requiring students to read passages of literature aloud, listen to passages read to them and reproduce the content from memory, write paraphrases, and elaborate or refute arguments. The Greek manuscripts of Theon's handbook do not preserve these chapters, which were long unknown but discovered in a classical Armenian version and have now been edited and published, with a French translation, by Michel Patillon and Giancarlo Bolognsi (Paris: Les Belles Lettres, 1997).

The second, and shortest, handbook of progymnasmata is attributed to Hermogenes of Tarsus, a Greek rhetorician of the second century BCE, to be discussed below, but its authenticity is doubtful. About 500 CE, a Latin adaptation of this work was made by the grammarian Priscian. This then found some use in medieval schools in western Europe. In the Greek-speaking East, however, a handbook by Aphthonius, a student of the great sophist Libanius in Antioch who wrote in the late

fourth century CE, became the standard authority. Aphthonius discusses fourteen exercises and provides a model for each: fable, narrative, chreia (or anecdote), maxim, refutation, confirmation, commonplace, encomion, invective, synkrisis (or comparison), ēthopoeia (or speech in character), ekphrasis (or description), thesis, and argument for or against a law. Aphthonius's work was used to teach Greek in Western schools in the Renaissance, Latin adaptations of it were made, as well as vernacular versions, and it was influential in teaching composition in Europe through the sixteenth and seventeenth centuries. The fourth surviving handbook is the work of Nicolaus of Myra, a Christian Platonist of the fifth century; he describes the same exercises as Aphthonius and gives special attention to how each relates to the genres of oratory and their traditional parts.

Declamation. Students of the early Sophists and of Isocrates developed their rhetorical skills by composing practice speeches on mythological, philosophical, or political subjects, some perhaps taking the form of imagary legal cases, like Gorgias's *Palamedes.* As rhetorical schools became common in the Hellenistic period, *meletai,* or practice speeches on subjects assigned by a teacher, became a regular feature of the curriculum. According to Quintilian (2.4.41), imaginary subjects in imitation of speeches in law courts and political assemblies came into common use in Greek schools at the end of the fourth century BCE and appeared in Rome about the beginning of the first century BCE, though they were probably not widely practiced there until the middle of the century. This seems to be confirmed by references in *Rhetoric to Herennius* and in Cicero's *On the Orator* and *Brutus,* as well as in the accounts of the beginnings of formal education in Rome in Suetonius's *Lives of the Grammarians and Rhetoricians.* [*See* Declamation.]

In Latin, practice in speaking was called *declamatio* and a practice speech is thus a "declamation." There were two kinds, a *suasoria,* the easier and less common exercise, was a mock deliberative speech on a mythological or historical theme; a *controversia,* the most common form in Roman schools, was a mock judicial speech. The subjects were intended to interest teenage boys, and thus sex and violence, war, pirates, ravished maidens, and difficult parents were favored themes. Declamation was not debate, as a modern teacher might expect; students were rarely, if ever, asked to take opposing sides and answer each other's arguments. Teachers announced a theme and gave suggestions for treatment or delivered a speech on the theme for students to imitate. Students then composed a speech, in writing, on the assigned subject, showing understanding of invention, arrangement, and style; their speeches were criticized by the teacher, and when a speech was approved, the student might be asked to memorize it and deliver it to the class or on one of the occasions when the school was open to parents and to the public. [*See* Controversia and suasoria.]

Our main source of information about Roman declamation in the late Republic and early Empire comes from a work in which Seneca the Elder (c.55 BCE–c.39 CE), father of the philosopher Seneca, describes the rhetorical schools of his youth in memoirs addressed to his sons. It carries the almost untranslatable title *Oratorum et rhetorum sententia, divisiones, colores*, which might be paraphrased as "A Collection of the Treatments of the Question, Arguments, and Clever Sayings of Orators and Teachers of Rhetoric." Seneca claims to remember verbatim many speeches he had heard spoken in the schools in his youth, especially on occasions when a school was open to the public, and he quotes extensively from them. By the Augustan period, these open sessions had become a kind of public entertainment and were often attended by the leaders of society, some of whom even participated in the declamation, as well as by professional rhetoricians, students, and students' families. Seneca's work, which is not preserved in its entirety, contained ten books on judicial themes and one book of ten deliberative themes. In introductions to the separate books, he gives his thoughts on the history and practice of declamation, which he loved and thought a valuable exercise, but which he saw growing morally and artistically decadent. In his first preface (section 7), he suggests three possible reasons for decline: the growth of luxury and laziness, less utility for rhetorical skills in real life, and the fatal cycles of history in which decline inexorably follows rise.

A number of other writers, including Philo, Velleius Paterculus, Petronius, Persius, Quintilian, and Tacitus, as well as the writer known as Longinus, comment on "the decline of eloquence" during the early centuries of the Roman Empire, often attributing it to similar causes and putting some of the blame on the practice of declamation for encouraging artificial stylistic affects and the use of clever figures of speech in unrealistic themes, rather than developing logical argument and clear and correct language use. Tacitus's *Dialogue on Orators*, written at the beginning of the second century CE, is an especially thoughtful discussion of the subject by speakers who viewed it from differing experiences and perspectives. Modern historians, following the lead of Tacitus in his later historical writings, have often blamed the restrictions placed on open debate and the loss of freedom of speech under the empire, an explanation more implied than stated by the ancient critics. There certainly was some repression of civic rights and some feeling of inhibition, especially in aristocratic social circles in the city of Rome. Even originally well-intentioned emperors, among them Augustus, Tiberius, and Claudius, were sometimes driven to desperate measures, including executions, exilings, and book burnings, by what they regarded as irresponsible or dangerous words and deeds or subversion of their rule, usually by the descendants of old republican families. The original and continuing rationale for imperial government, accepted by most Romans, was the inability of the republican government to control domestic and foreign affairs over the last century of its existence and the resulting destruction caused by civil war, as compared to the security and prosperity that Augustus and his successors had imposed on the state. Particularly in the provinces, and not least in Greece, the early empire was for ordinary free citizens one of the happiest periods in human history. The legislative assemblies of the Roman Republic had, however, ceased to meet; public officials were now elected by the senate, largely on nomination by the emperor. The senate, made up of former magistrates and imperial appointees, met regularly, debated questions of public policy referred to it by the emperors, who often took its advice, and acted as a court of offenses by its members. The system of law courts established under the Republic continued to exist, and patrons pleaded cases there for their clients, but the emperors sometimes intervened, either directly or indirectly, and tolerated or encouraged the notorious "informers" who sought favor or money by bringing indictments intended to please those on high. We can read in the writings of Quintilian, Tacitus, and Pliny about a number of famous orators and their speeches, and all three of these writers were themselves admired public speakers, but Latin oratory of the first century CE is known only at second hand and lacked the fiery earnestness of the time of Cicero. The situation is somewhat better in Greek, where the movement known as the "Second Sophistic," referred to above, was beginning to develop. The best-known Greek orator of the first century CE is Dio Cocceianus (c.40–after 112 CE), called *Chrysostomos,* the "Golden-Tongued." Eighty surviving speeches are attributed to him; some are display speeches on cultural themes, but there are also speeches on real situations delivered in the provincial assembly and council at Prusa in Asia Minor.

Quintilian. Marcus Fabius Quintilianus (c.39–c.96 CE), born in Spain but educated in Rome, was appointed by the emperor Vespasian about 71 CE to a salaried professorship of Latin rhetoric in the city. A Greek chair was apparently also created, but we know nothing about it or its holder. This was the first time the Roman government had made any provisions in support of public education, and the decision to do so seems to have been part of Vespasian's program to revive traditional cultural and moral values that had eroded during the troubled reign of his predecessor, Nero. In the next century, chairs in rhetoric were created in Athens, and imperial decrees ordered cities throughout the empire to subsidize the teaching of grammar and rhetoric.

Quintilian served in this official position for twenty years, occasionally also pleading cases in the law courts for clients, and toward the end of his tenure writing a treatise, now lost, *On the Causes of the Corruption of Eloquence.* He then retired and shortly after, began research on the great work for which he is known today, *Institutio oratoria,* a title usually translated as *The Education of the Orator.* In the course of its twelve books, Quintilian outlines his recommendations for the education of an upper-class Roman citizen, from his earliest studies in language and grammar (Books 1–2), through training in rhetorical the-

ory and exercises in declamation (Books 3–11), to a public career as an adult and even to retirement and postretirement activities (Book 12). It is a work rich in information about ancient education and about the history of rhetoric, for Quintilian often surveys the views of earlier authorities. It provides the fullest account of classical rhetorical theory that has survived. Although Quintilian makes some original suggestions based on his own experience and good sense, and although he vigorously combats affectation and artificiality in style, much of the time he restates earlier views with minor revisions or adaptations to circumstances of his time. His major source, in his view the greatest model for theory and practice and also for the life of an orator, is Cicero, whose fulsome prose had somewhat fallen out of favor in the three generations after his death. It is one of Quintilian's achievements to have restored Cicero's work to its rightful place as a rhetorical classic. An equally if not more important achievement was the propagation of the Ciceronian concept of the ideal citizen-orator, derived chiefly from *On the Orator,* as the highest civic goal for a Roman male. Quintilian was a loyal supporter of the imperial regime, including the difficult, touchy, and sometimes tyrannical emperor Domitian, and he gives little consideration to the affect on his ideal of the political changes from republic to empire. In the introduction to Book 4 of the *Institutio,* he reports on his appointment by Domitian to take charge of the education of the emperor's young heirs, and at times it seems as though Quintilian's *orator perfectus* can only be a future emperor. A major requirement for such a figure, however, or for any successful orator in Quintilian's view, is that he must be a *bonus vir,* "a good man." This requirement is made in the introduction to the whole work, rarely forgotten for long, and especially emphasized in the last book, where Quintilian begins (12.1.1) by quoting with approval the definition of an orator once given by Cato the Elder, venerable statesman of second century BCE Rome: *vir bonus, dicendi peritus,* "a good man, skilled in speaking." The definition is reflected in Quintilian's definition of rhetoric (2.15.34) as *bene dicendi scientia,* "the knowledge of speaking well," where *bene* carries moral as well as aesthetic and pragmatic connotations. Contrary to what has sometimes been assumed, Quintilian did not believe that the study of rhetoric would make a man morally good; moral standards in his opinion are largely derived from family values, good models, and the thoughtful study of ethically enlightened literature.

The part of Quintilian's work that is best known to Latin students is Book 10, a kind of supplement to his discussion of style in Books 8 and 9; here he raises the question of how to achieve *copia,* a supply or abundance of ideas and words. The answer he gives is to study and imitate great writers of the past. He provides a brief reading list of Greek authors (10.1.46–84), beginning with Homer and based on the canon of poets set out by Alexandrian grammarians in the third and second centuries BCE, to which he adds writers in the three prose genres of history, oratory, and philosophy. The account resembles that in Dionysius of Halicarnassus's fragmentary work *On Imitation.* Quintilian then follows this Greek canon with a longer Latin reading list (10.1.85–131), evaluating Roman writers in comparison to Greeks in the same genres, Virgil with Homer, Cicero with Demosthenes, and so on. In chapter 2 of Book 10, Quintilian continues with a discussion of imitation as a technique for improving rhetorical composition. [*See* Copia; *and* Imitation.]

Although Quintilian was always a respected authority to later writers on rhetoric, his work was more extended and detailed than many readers wanted and the ideal orator he described seemed less attainable as time passed. Throughout the Middle Ages, his work was known primarily from manuscripts that omitted large parts of the original. In 1416, Poggio Bracciolini discovered a manuscript with the complete text at Saint Gall. When copies of this text were circulated in Italy, they created a great sensation among the Humanists, and Quintilian reentered the tradition as major source on rhetoric side by side with Cicero, and on education as well. [*See* Humanism.]

There are two collections of declamations, compiled in the fourth or fifth century CE, which are attributed to Quintilian in the manuscripts. Those known as the *Major Declamations* are interesting as the only examples of complete Latin declamations, but they are certainly not by Quintilian. There is an English translation of them by Lewis A. Sussman (Frankfurt am Main, 1987). The excerpts, known as the *Minor Declamations,* of which there is no English translation, may include some themes once practiced in Quintilian's school.

Latin rhetoric after Quintilian. Pliny the Younger (c.61–c.113 CE) studied rhetoric with Quintilian and had a successful political career in Rome. He is known mostly for the collection of letters that he polished and published, including letters as governor of Bithynia, which include the earliest reference to Christians in Latin. His *Panegyricus,* a lengthy speech of thanks to the emperor Trajan on being appointed consul in 100 CE, survives as the earliest example of Roman ceremonial oratory. There are a number of later speeches of this genre, known collectively as *Panegyrici Latini.*

The most famous Roman orator of the middle of the second century CE was Marcus Cornelius Fronto (c.100–c.166 CE), who was the rhetoric teacher of the emperor Marcus Aurelius and author of a collection of letters written in a strongly archaizing style, popular in this period when the Greek Second Sophistic found some imitators among Latin writers. He has much to say about rhetoric, but readers have usually found it disappointing.

Rhetores Latini Minores, or *Minor Latin Rhetoricians,* is the name given the collected Latin writings on rhetoric dating from the third to the eighth century CE, as edited by Karl Halm (Leipzig, 1863). Included are several handbooks of tropes and figures; works discussing rhetoric as a whole by Fortunatianus, Sulpitius Victor, Julius Severianus, and others; Victorinus's commentary on Cicero's *On Invention;* the sections on rhetoric from early medieval encyclopedias of the liberal arts by Martianus Capella, Cassiodorus, and Isidore of Seville; Alcuin's *Dialogue on Rhetoric* with Charlemagne, and some other short texts. Some of these works have been published separately in more recent editions. Their chief importance is perhaps in showing the somewhat reduced form in which rhetoric was taught in those centuries and transmitted to the Middle Ages. It continued to be focused on judicial oratory, including an explanation of *stasis* theory.

Of the eight greatest Latin Fathers of the Church, five (Tertullian, Cyprian, Arnobius, Lactantius, and Augustine) were professional teachers of rhetoric before they became Christians, while the other three (Ambrose, Hilary, and Jerome) had been thoroughly trained in the rhetorical schools. Some early Christians were uncomfortable with rhetoric, Jerome in particular, but Lactantius (c.240–c.320 CE) attempted to reconcile pagan and Christian studies, and Augustine's treatise *On Christian Learning* contains the most important discussion of rhetoric written in Latin between Quintilian and the Renaissance humanists.

Later Greek Rhetoric. The teaching of rhetoric in Latin, derived from Cicero, *Rhetoric to Herennius,* and Quintilian, primarily discussed judicial oratory and was thus connected with the great intellectual achievement of the Romans in the development of a code of law and procedure. In contrast, later Greek rhetoric is characterized by a connection with the great intellectual achievement of the Greeks in philosophy. The study of rhetoric, accompanied by practice in declamation, came to be viewed by Greek philosophers and rhetoricians as primarily a form of training in logical thinking and expression, continuing what had begun in grammar school and preparing for the study of philosophy for those students who progressed that far. In later Greek times, philosophy meant Neo-Platonism; Neo-Platonists who wrote on rhetoric included Porphyry, Syrianus, Hermeias, and Olympiodorus, and Neo-Platonic influence is strong among the new Sophists as well. A good picture of Greek rhetorical and philosophical schools in the fourth century CE can be found in Eunapius's *Lives of the Philosophers.*

There is a significant amount of Greek writing about rhetoric, including handbooks of progymnasmata, *stasis* theory, invention, and style, surviving from the time of the Roman Empire, and a vast amount—thousands of pages—of speeches by Sophists and Christian preachers, with a wide range in style and rhetorical skill. The finest late Greek work on rhetoric is certainly the short treatise *Peri Hypseos,* or *On Sublimity,* attributed to Longinus. The author was long thought to be the famous rhetorician Cassius Longinus, who lived in the third century CE, the author of an *Art of Rhetoric,* which is partially preserved. *On the Sublime* (also called *On Sublimity*) is now generally regarded as a work of the first, or more probably the second, century CE by an unknown author variously referred to as Longinus, "Longinus," or Pseudo-Longinus, but the attribution to Cassius Longinus has been revived by Malcolm Heath in a 1999 article (*Proceedings of the Cambridge Philological Society,* vol. 45, pp. 43–77). The work is a sensitive study of the elevated style in prose and poetry, with well-chosen examples, employing a critical method derived from rhetoric. There are, the author says, five sources of the sublime: the power of conceiving impressive thoughts ("invention" in rhetoric); strong emotion (*ēthos* in rhetoric); and three parts of style as taught by rhetoricians: figures of thought and speech; nobility of diction, and composition (i.e., word order, rhythm, and euphony). This work, the text of which suffers from some lacunae, was not very widely known until a French translation with introduction and notes was published by Nicolas Boileau-Despréaux in 1674, followed by Boileau-Despréaux's essays on the subject. John Dryden popularized the subject in English, and a cult of "The Sublime" followed, with contributions by Edmund Burke, Immanuel Kant, and others. [*See* Sublime, the.]

Except for "Longinus," the most important later Greek writings on rhetoric are those by or attributed to Hermogenes of Tarsus (fl. c.180 BCE). His genuine works are treatises *On Stases* (or *On Issues:* English translation and commentary by Malcolm Heath, Oxford, 1995), which reorganized that complex subject into a series of logical divisions, and *On Ideas* (or *On Types of Style:* English translation by Cecil W. Wooten, Chapel Hill, N.C., 1987), which similarly reorganized the characters of style in a new and more readily-learned way. These two works became the core of a rhetorical compendium to which, probably in the fifth century CE, were added Aphthonius's *Progymnasmata* (see above), and two works by unknown authors: a treatise *On Invention,* discussing the parts of an oration and some devices of style; and an essay *On the Method of Forcefulness.* This compendium then became the basis of the curriculum in rhetoric throughout the Byzantine period and extensive commentaries were written on it. The "Hermogenic Corpus," as it is conventionally named, came to the attention of Italian Humanists in the fifteenth century CE, and Hermogenes' "ideas" in particular were then taken up with interest by Renaissance critics and teachers.

Among other late Greek rhetorical texts, two handbooks on epideictic attributed to Menander Rhetor are of special interest (text, translation, and commentary by D. A. Russell and N. G. Wilson, Oxford, 1981). Menander describes in detail the many different kinds of epideictic practiced in late Greek schools and delivered on public ceremonial occasions. Among these genres are prose hymns, encomia of places, addresses to emperors and other officials, speeches at weddings and funerals, speeches by ambassadors, and others.

A collection of Greek rhetorical texts was first printed by Aldus Manutius in Venice in 1508. Modern study of the Greek rhetoricians is still partially reliant on *Rhetores Graeci* in nine volumes as edited by Christian Walz (London, 1832–1836); some major texts were reedited by Leonard Spengel under the same title (Leipzig, 1853–1856). Several of the more important texts have, however, been reedited separately and provided with English translations and notes.

Classical Rhetoric Theoretically Defined. This section includes definitions and species of rhetoric, along with determination of the question at issue, the parts of a judicial oration, and other matters.

Definitions of rhetoric. Quintilian surveys (2.15), somewhat inaccurately, many definitions proposed by earlier Greek and Latin authorities on rhetoric. Whether rhetoric should be defined as a science, a virtue, an art, a faculty, a knack, or something else was much debated. His own definition, *bene dicendi scientia* ("knowledge of speaking well") was, as he acknowledges (2.15.34–35), similar to that of the Stoic philosophers Cleanthes and Chrysippus. Rather than defining rhetoric in a single phrase, many authorities preferred to describe it by considering its functions, purposes, materials, or parts, or the duties of an orator. This approach is found in Cicero, *On Invention* (1.6–7) and in *Rhetoric to Herennius* (1.2). Later Greek *prolegomena*, or "introductions" to the study of rhetoric prefixed to the Hermogenic Corpus, regularly use this approach but also offer versions of two definitions; one, ultimately derived from Aristotle by way of Hermagoras of Temnos, called rhetoric "an art in regard to a faculty concerning speech on a political matter, having the end of speaking persuasively in accordance with what is available"; another, attributed

to Dionysius of Halicarnassus (fragment 1 of *On Imitation*), called rhetoric "an artistic faculty of persuasive speech on a political matter, having speaking well as its end."

Species of rhetoric **(genera causarum).** All classical rhetoricians follow Aristotle in distinguishing three species or genres of rhetoric: judicial, deliberative, and epideictic. Post-Aristotelian handbooks discuss judicial rhetoric in detail, adding short chapters on the other two species. Progymnasmatic exercises (see above) offered training in the structure and topics of encomia and debate about legislation.

Determination of the question at issue. Before entering on the composition of an oration or declamation, it was thought essential for a speaker to determine the question at issue in the case. This was clearly needed in judicial rhetoric, but rhetoricians usually claimed it had some application to the other species as well. Aristotle refers to the subject briefly (*On Rhetoric*, 1.13.10; 3.17.1), using the term *amphisbētēsis* to mean "what is in doubt." The technical term *stasis* (literally "stance," as in boxing) was standardized in Greek by Hermagoras of Temnos (second century BCE), who discussed the subject in detail in an influential work, now lost. In Latin, the question at issue was at first called *constitutio,* later *status* or *stasis.* Variations on the system of Hermagoras are described by Cicero in *On Invention* (1.10–19; 2.11–154) and in *Rhetorical Partitions* (101–138), in *Rhetoric to Herennius* (1.18–25; 2.3–26), by Quintilian (3.6 and 11; 7.2–10), and by the Minor Latin Rhetoricians. The best account is the one found in Hermogenes' *On Stases,* but this Greek work, very influential throughout the Byzantine period, was largely unknown to Latin readers.

Generally, three forms of "rational" *stasis* were recognized. A person charged with a crime, or a patron representing a defendant, could deny any involvement in the act (e.g., deny he killed anyone). This is called *coniecturalis,* or (1) *stasis* of fact. The prosecution then has to show the probability of guilt by establishing a motive; by showing that no one else was likely to have done the deed; by reviewing the circumstances pointing to guilt (place, point of time, length of time, occasion, hope of success, hope of avoiding detection); by reviewing suspicious actions before, during, and after the crime; and by use of topics to confirm the allegation. These might include evidence from witnesses and arguments for or against their reliability. If the defense cannot expect successfully to question the fact, it can turn next to (2) *stasis* of definition (*finitivus*) or of law (*legalis*), claiming, for example, that the action does not meet the legal definition of murder and is, at most, homicide. The prosecution must define the crime, prove the definition, compare it with the act admitted, and can introduce commonplaces on the wickedness of the act and the need for punishment. The defense can attack these statements and can also attack the prosecutor and his motives. Another possible line of defense is (3) *stasis* of quality (*qualitas, generalis, iudicialis*). This is said to be "absolute" if the speaker admits the action and argues it was right in itself, that is, right in moral principle. Brutus is said (Quintilian 3.6.93) to have written a speech for Milo defending him from the charge of murdering Clodius on the grounds that Clodius well deserved to die. More common is "assumptive quality" in which the defense argues that the action was less evil than alternatives, or that it resulted from illegal actions by someone else, or that responsibility for the action lay with another (it was, perhaps, ordered by a superior); or the defendant may plead he acted out of ignorance or by accident or necessity and, in the final instance, may plead for mercy, perhaps bringing into court his distraught wife and weeping children.

Hermagoras's original system added a fourth *stasis*, "transference" (*translativus*), in which the defense argues that the judge or court lacks jurisdiction in the case. This is found in some later systems as well, but it was irrelevant in Roman legal procedure where jurisdiction was determined by the praetor in advance of a trial.

In addition to these forms of "rational" *stasis,* there are "legal" questions, which might apply to any of the four *stases* described above. They concern arguments about the letter and the intent of the law, or conflicts between laws, or the ambiguity of the law, or the need to reason by analogy if no law applies, or similar matters. [*See* Stasis.]

Canons of rhetoric. It was generally taught that instruction in rhetoric consisted of attention to offices invention, arrangement, style, memory, and delivery. Since in post-Aristotelian hand-

books discussion of invention (Gk. *heurēsis;* Lat. *inventio*) concerned what to say in each of the conventional parts of an oration, arrangement (Gk. *taxis;* Lat. *distributio*) was largely left with advice about the sequence of arguments: whether it was best to begin with the strongest arguments, or to leave them to the last, which depended largely on particular circumstances.

The parts of a judicial oration. Even from the beginning, rhetoricians made some additions to the four basic parts of introduction, statement of the case, proof, and conclusion. Quintilian (3.9.1) says most authorities divided a judicial speech into *exordium, narratio, probatio, refutatio,* and *peroratio,* and that some added (between narration and proof) a *partitio* and *propositio* and (between proof and peroration) an *excessus.* The function of an exordium (or prooemion), all agreed, was to make the hearers attentive, receptive, and well disposed; the common sources of an exordium are the person of the speaker, the opponents, the audience, and the facts of the case. If the case was disreputable, or the hearers seemed persuaded by a previous speaker, or were weary, it was necessary to employ *insinuatio,* an indirect approach (see *Rhet. to Herennius* 1.9–11). The *narratio,* or statement of facts, should be lucid, brief, and plausible (Quintilian 4.2.31). The *probatio,* perhaps preceded by a partition of the issues and a succinct statement of the speaker's proposition, presented the arguments (discussed below); a prosecutor might seek to anticipate and refute potential arguments of the defense, while the defense would consist in large part of a refutation of the arguments of the prosecution. In major judicial speeches, Cicero, like some of the Attic orators, often inserted an *excessus,* or "ethical digression," between the proofs and the conclusion; this was a description of the personal character of the principles in the case to support or discredit their claims or roles and has been discussed by James M. May, *Trials of Characters: The Eloquence of Ciceronian Ethos* (Chapel Hill, N.C., 1988). Finally, a peroration or epilogue summed up the speaker's case and might seek to stir the feelings of the hearers to pity, outrage, or other emotions. Quintilian devotes all of Book 5 of his *Institutio* to logical proof. He then discusses perorations in the first chapter of Book 6, followed by two lengthy chapters on *ēthos* and *pathos.* Aristotle had regarded *ēthos* as the presentation of a credible character by the speaker, who in a Greek court was often unknown to the jury. Cicero (in *On the Orator* and *Orator*) and Quintilian realized that in Roman procedure, where cases were pleaded by professional advocates, consideration of the character of the principles in the case, of their patrons, of witnesses, and even of the judges might contribute to success.

Proofs. Although the distinction between artistic and nonartistic proof, originally made by Aristotle, is noted by most classical rhetoricians, and, as stated above, some account of *ēthos* and *pathos* may be given, Aristotle's emphasis on logical proof is diluted in post-Aristotelian classical rhetoric. The strategies of argument that Aristotle discussed in *On Rhetoric* 2.23, called *loci argumentorum* in Latin, receive little attention in subsequent rhetorical treatises and were taught as part of dialectic. By the sixth century CE, rhetorical invention was sometimes treated as a part of dialectic (a view that recurs in the Renaissance); see, for example, Boethius's discussion of rhetoric in Book 4 of *De Topicis Differentiis*.

What Cicero had to say about argument in *On Invention* is part of his discussion of *stasis* theory. This includes (2.67–68) what he calls *ratiocinatio,* the five-part argument known to Greek rhetoricians as an *epicheirēme* (literally, "a handful"). In schools of declamation, the *epicheirēme* often became more a form of stylistic amplification than a device of reasoning; see especially the discussion in the Hermogenic treatise *On Invention* (3.5). Ratiocination, as described by Cicero (see also *Rhetoric to Herennius* 2.28), consists of a major premise, a supporting reason, a minor premise, a reason in support of the minor premise, and a conclusion. Quintilian devoted Book 5 of his *Education of the Orator* to the proof as a part of a judicial speech. Unlike the young Cicero in *On Invention* and the author of *Rhetoric to Herennius,* he reveals some knowledge of Aristotelian theories. Half of the book is devoted to nonartistic proofs, including legal precedents, rumors, and documentary evidence, with a unique chapter (5.7) on witnesses and cross-examination. There follows a series of chapters on artistic argument, including discussion of signs, argument from probability, and examples. A final chapter is devoted to the enthymeme and epicheireme. He notes (5.14.1)

two uses of the term enthymeme, apparently now acceptable in Latin: sometimes, he says, it is taken to mean an incomplete syllogism, sometimes an argument from incompatibles. As for an epicheireme, although some have held that it consists of four, five, or six parts, Quintilian regards it as usually consisting only of three parts (5.14.6). It is thus in form the same as a syllogism, but the syllogism has a larger number of species and infers truth from truth, while the epicheirēme is frequently concerned with statements that are only credible (5.14.14).

Style (lexis, phrasis, or hermēneia in Gk.; elocutio in Lat.). The classical theory of style has two parts: choice of words and their composition into phrases, clauses, and sentences. Theophrastus's theory of the virtues of style appears in Quintilian (without acknowledgement of its source) as the rule that single words should be good Latin, clear, ornate, and adapted to the desired effect; words in composition should be in the correct grammatical form for the context, aptly placed, and figured (8.1.1). His discussion of style consumes all of Books 8, 9, and 10, and the first chapter of Book 11. A major objective of the study of prose style in classical times, and in the Renaissance as well, was to learn how to amplify and lend variety to ideas, which in declamation, rhetorical poetry, and some other genres were often of a traditional sort, easily dismissed as trite and boring unless somehow dressed up. Quintilian discusses amplification and diminution of thoughts and expressions in chapter 4 of Book 8. Post-Ciceronian Latin gave vigor and point to style by the frequent use of *sententiae*—clever, sometimes epigrammatic, apothegmatic turns of phrase: "what oft was thought but ne'er so well express'd," as Alexander Pope was to put it. Quintilian devotes a chapter to *sententiae* (8.5), acknowledging that they had become a necessary part of the orator's art.

Ornamentation of style, a priority in declamation and important in literary prose as well, involved the use of tropes, figures, rhythms, and periods. Quintilian defines a *tropus* in 8.6.1 as the change of a word or phrase from its proper meaning to another. Metaphor, Latin *translatio,* is the most important trope, but Quintilian identifies six others that affect the meaning of a passage: synecdochē, metonymy, *antonomasia,* onomatopoeia, *catachrēsis,* and metalēpsis; in addition, there are tropes that he regards as useful only as ornaments: epithet, allegory, *periphrasis, hyperbaton,* and hyperbolē. A trope was usually thought of as substitution of one word or phrase for another or a change in the placement of a word or phrase. A figure (Gk. *schēma,* Lat. *figura*), in contrast, was a change in the configuration of a passage involving several words, and was divided into figures of word (*figurae verborum*), later often referred to as "grammatical figures," and figures of thought (*figurae sententiarum*). The earliest account is found in *Rhetoric to Herennius* (4.19–69), giving Latin names and defining forty verbal figures and nineteen figures of thought. In the more detailed account by Quintilian (Book 9, chapters 1–3), both Greek and Latin names are used, though the Greek terminology seems to have become standard in the schools. The classification of an artistic usage as a trope, a verbal figure, or a figure of thought was often arbitrary and differs in different handbooks.

Cicero took up the subject of prose rhythm and periodic sentences, neglected since Aristotle, in *Orator* and Quintilian discusses it in chapter 4 of Book 9. Rhythm in Greek and Latin prose, as in poetry, was determined by the pattern of long and short syllables, not by word accent. Rhetoricians agreed that it was desirable to achieve an overall rhythmical flow that, nevertheless, avoided regular sequences of poetic feet. Most important, however, was the *clausula,* the last few syllables of a periodic sentence, where a limited number of combinations of feet were preferred. Oddly, the recommendations of Cicero and Quintilian on this subject do not accord entirely with their own practice nor do their accounts of periodicity adequately describe the very long sentences that Cicero, in particular, often composed.

Classical rhetoric developed a theory of different kinds of style, known in Greek as *charactēres,* in Latin as *genera dicendi.* The theory of three styles described in *Rhetoric to Herennius* is noted above, as well as the theory of four styles found in the monograph *On Style* attributed to Demetrius and the more complex systems introduced by Dionysius of Halicarnassus and Hermogenes of Tarsus. There is, in addition, a treatise on this subject by an unknown rhetorician that was attributed to Aelius Aristides, a Sophist of the second century CE. In general, it can be said that a theory of three good styles—grand, middle, and plain, with corresponding faulty styles—prevailed in the Latin-speaking West; it was known in the Greek-speaking East as well, but there the "ideas of style" came to dominate discussion. These include clarity, grandeur, beauty, rapidity, character, sincerity, force, and subdivisions thereof. Quintilian discusses kinds of style in 12.10, drawing analogies to styles in sculpture and painting.

Memory (Gk. **mnēme,** *Lat.* **memoria***).* By far the best account of memory as the fourth part of classical rhetoric is to be found in *Rhetoric to Herennius* (3.28–40). Greek and Latin students were required to memorize a large amount of poetry and prose, even whole orations by the great masters; they had to rely on memory to a greater extent than is true in the modern world and, as a result, many individuals acquired what would seem today a remarkable ability to remember material. Natural memory skills were complemented by an artificial mnemonic system that involved imagining physical images suggestive of words or thoughts in a sequence against a familiar evolving background. This is what is described in the ancient texts; it continued to interest later thinkers and its history has been traced by Frances A. Yates in *The Art of Memory* (London, 1966).

Delivery (Gk. **hypokrisis,** *Lat.* **pronuntiatio** *or* **actio***).* Aristotle mentions the need for attention to this subject, vulgar though he thought it was, at the beginning of Book 3 of *On Rhetoric,* and his student Theophrastus wrote a treatise on it, now lost, that probably was the basis of later accounts. There is a discussion in *Rhetoric to Herennius* (3.19–27), and Cicero comments on it in several contexts, but the fullest account of how an ancient orator delivered a speech, including use of the voice, body movements, props, and gestures, is to be found in Quintilian 11.3. Later rhetorical handbooks largely omit the subject, though we know from descriptions of the speaking of Sophists and from Roman art that in real life, delivery remained important. The subject is discussed by Gregory S. Aldrete in *Gestures and Acclimations in Ancient Rome* (Baltimore, 1999).

The Relevance of Classical Rhetoric in the Modern World. Classical rhetoric, primarily the Latin tradition from Cicero and Quintilian, has been taught throughout Western history, even as new approaches to rhetoric appeared in the Renaissance and Early Modern period. Some falling off in study of it occurred in the nineteenth century, partly a result of the Romantic Movement, which reacted against rules for composition and preferred spontaneous expression, and this attitude continued into the early twentieth century. The "renaissance" of rhetoric that developed in the second half of the twentieth century redirected attention back to classical rhetoric and its basic texts. Often it has been rhetoric as understood by Plato or Aristotle that has most interested modern scholars and been most taught in English, speech communication, or other departments, but *Rhetoric to Herennius*—especially in the fine Loeb Library edition of Harry Caplin (Cambridge, Mass., 1954)—and rhetorical works by Cicero and Quintilian have had increased readership as well. *Classical Rhetoric for the Modern Student* by Edward P. J. Corbett (New York, 3d ed., 1990) has provided many students with a useful grasp of the subject. The extent to which rhetorical communication should be approached primarily through classical rhetoric, given the development of many new critical theories, is and will remain somewhat controversial. The issues are discussed by Kathleen E. Welch in *The Contemporary Reception of Classical Rhetoric: Appropriations of Ancient Discourse* (Hillsdale, N.J., 1990). It is certainly possible to learn effective public speaking from classical sources; once skill is attained, like the great orators of Greece and Rome, a speaker need no longer be bound by pedantic rules. [*See* Modern rhetoric; Nineteenth-century rhetoric; *and overview article on* Renaissance rhetoric.]

Cicero, Quintilian, and others drew analogies between rhetoric and the arts of painting and sculpture, with a few metaphors from architecture as well, and analogies between poetry and the visual arts are common throughout ancient criticism. [*See* Art.] From the point of view of modern times, the analogy between classical rhetoric and classical architecture as described by Vitruvius at the end of the first century BCE and writers on architecture in the Renaissance and Early Modern period is particularly apt. Both rhetoric and architecture have a concern with the building blocks and structure of their inventions. Classical architecture, like classical rhetoric, developed tradi-

tional styles and forms of ornamentation. The "orders" of classical architecture may be compared to the three kinds of style of classical rhetoric: Doric to the Plain Style, Ionic to the Middle Style, and Corinthian to the Grand Style. Both architecture and rhetoric make use of conventional ornaments that can be called tropes and figures, and both seek unity and rhythm in expression. The mnemonic system of classical rhetoric is analogous to an architectural frieze, and representations of delivery can be found in pedimental sculpture on classical buildings. The structures, motifs, and styles of both classical architecture and classical rhetoric have found expression throughout Western history, and both have proved versatile in creative new adaptations and variations.

BIBLIOGRAPHY

Texts and English translations of many authors discussed in this article can be found in volumes of *The Loeb Classical Library,* published over the course of the twentieth century by Harvard University Press, Cambridge, Mass., and often shelved as a series in libraries. Included are works by Aristotle, Cicero, Demosthenes and other Attic orators, Dionysius of Halicarnassus, Isocrates, Plato, Seneca, and Quintilian. Several of the older volumes have been recently revised or are scheduled for revision. Note that in the Loeb series, *Rhetoric to Alexander* is found in vol. 2 of Aristotle's *Problems;* Demetrius's *On Style* and Longinus's *On Sublimity* are with Aristotle's *Poetics;* and *Rhetoric to Herennius* is classed as a spurious work of Cicero.

L'Année philologique, an international bibliography of classical subjects published annually in Paris since 1924 under sponsorship of the Société internationale de bibliographique classique, includes comprehensive listings of books, articles (with abstracts), and reviews on rhetoricians and rhetorical topics. Recent volumes are also available on CD-Rom.

Bonner, S. F. *Education in Ancient Rome.* Berkeley, 1977.

Bonner, S. F. *Roman Declamation in the Late Republic and Early Empire.* Berkeley, 1949.

Bowersock, Glen. *Greek Sophists in the Roman Empire.* Oxford, 1969.

Carawan, Edwin. *Rhetoric and the Law of Draco.* Oxford, 1998. Examines the role of rhetoric in homicide cases in Greece from the beginning to the fourth century BCE.

Cole, Thomas. *The Origins of Rhetoric in Ancient Greece.* Baltimore, 1991. Critical of rhetoric as a deceptive art, but important for understanding of early Greek *tekhnai logōn.*

Dominik, William J., ed. *Roman Eloquence: Rhetoric in So-*

ciety and Literature. London, 1997. Fourteen essays on Roman rhetoric grouped under "Theories, transitions and tensions," "Rhetoric and society," and "Rhetoric and genre."

Fortenbaugh, William W., and David C. Mirhady, eds. *Peripatetic Rhetoric after Aristotle.* Rutgers University Studies in Classical Humanities, vol. 6. New Brunswick, N.J., 1994.

Guthrie, W. K. C. *A History of Greek Philosophy.* 6 vols. Cambridge, U.K., 1962–1981. On rhetoric, see especially, vol. 3, *The Fifth-Century Enlightenment;* vol. 4, *Plato, the Man and His Dialogues: Earlier Period;* and vol. 5, "The Later Plato and the Academy."

Kennedy, George A. *A New History of Classical Rhetoric.* Princeton, 1994. Provides an extensive bibliography.

Kennedy, George A. *Classical Rhetoric and Its Christian and Secular Tradition from Ancient to Modern Times.* 2d ed., revised and enlarged, Chapel Hill, N.C., 1999. Also with extensive bibliography.

Kinneavy, James L. *Greek Rhetorical Origins of Christian Faith: An Inquiry.* New York, 1987. Argues that the Christian concept of faith, *pistis,* is derived from rhetoric.

Lausberg, Heinrich. *Handbook of Literary Rhetoric: A Foundation for Literary Study.* Translated by Matthew T. Bliss, Annemiek Jansen, and David E. Orton; edited by David E. Orton and R. Dean Anderson. Leiden, 1998. English translation of *Handbuch der literarischen Rhetorik,* first published in 1960.

Leeman, A. D. *Orationis Ratio: The Stylistic Theories and Practice of the Roman Orators, Historians, and Philosophers.* 2 vols. Amsterdam, 1963.

Matsen, Patricia P., Philip Rollinson, and Marion Sousa, eds. *Readings from Classical Rhetoric.* Carbondale, Ill., 1990. Selections in English from important texts on rhetoric from Homer to Augustine.

O'Sullivan, Neil. *Alcidamas, Aristophanes, and the Beginnings of Greek Stylistic Theory.* Hermes Einzelschriften 60. Stuttgart, 1992.

Porter, Stanley E., ed. *Handbook of Classical Rhetoric in the Hellenistic Period, 330 B.C.–A.D. 400.* Leiden, 1997. Primarily intended to explain classical rhetoric to students of early Christianity; extensive bibliography.

Roberts, W. Rhys., ed. and trans. *Dionysius of Halicarnassus, On Literary Composition.* Cambridge, U.K., 1910. Contains explanatory notes and essays.

Romilly, Jacqueline de. *Magic and Rhetoric in Ancient Greece.* Cambridge, Mass., 1974.

Rorty, Amélie Oksenberg, ed. *Essays on Aristotle's Rhetoric,* largely from a philosophical point of view.

Russell, Donald A. *Greek Declamation.* Cambridge, U.K., 1983.

Schiappa, Edward. *Protagoras and Logos.* Columbia, S.C., 1991.

Sprague, Rosamond K., ed. *The Older Sophists: A Complete Translation by Several Hands.* Columbia, S.C., 1972.

Wisse, Jakob. *Ethos and Pathos from Aristotle to Cicero.* Amsterdam, 1989.

Worthington, Ian, ed. *Persuasion: Greek Rhetoric in Action.* London, 1994. Twelve essays on classical rhetoric grouped under "Communicating," "Applications," and "Contexts."

Yunis, Harvey. *Taming Democracy: Models of Political Rhetoric in Classical Athens.* Ithaca, N.Y., 1996. Special attention to Thucydides, Plato, and Demosthenes.

—GEORGE A. KENNEDY

COLOR. This article focuses on the word *color* in ancient Roman rhetoric as a technical term for a range of strategies supporting a particular line of argumentation, especially in the declamatory exercises known as *controversiae.* Discussed first, however, are wider usages of the word *color* in Latin, along with aspects of Greek rhetorical theory, which cast light on this technical usage. The most relevant ancient texts are Seneca the Elder's collection of *Controversiae (Cont.),* assembled in the 30s CE; Quintilian's *Institutio oratoria (Inst.),* written in the 90s CE; and two declamatory collections of uncertain date and authorship, but attributed to Quintilian in antiquity: the *Declamationes maiores (DMai.)* and *Declamationes minores (DMin.).*

The word *color* first appears in Latin writing regarding rhetoric and verbal art, in a group of rhetorical treatises dating from the early to middle first century BCE, those of the Roman orator and statesman Cicero (106–43 BCE) and the anonymous *Rhetorica ad Herennium.* In these treatises, the word does not yet label any particular technique or strategy of rhetoric itself, but rather participates in one of two metaphors by which rhetoric is commonly modeled. One of these metaphors is painting, verbal representation figured as pictoral representation. In Cicero's *De oratore* (3.96–100), rhetorical ornamentation is compared specifically to a painter's use of color. While colors are brighter and give more immediate pleasure in new paintings than old, in excess these can cause satiety, causing us to turn back to the faded austerity of older paintings. Likewise, in ornamenting our oratory, we should seek to give pleasure, but without causing satiety (cf. 3.217; *Brutus* 298; *Orator* 65, 169; *Rhetorica ad Herennium* 4.16). This rhetoric-as-painting metaphor is persistent, appearing in later texts such as *Institutio oratoria* (11.3.46), Fronto's *De Eloquentia* (4.7; mid-second century CE) and Gellius's *Noctes Atticae* (14.4; c.180 CE.) [*See* Art.]

The second metaphor, equally common, figures oratory as a human body. Here, *color* refers to skin tone or to the body's overall complexion, and serves as a metaphor for the general "cast" or "complexion" of a speech. Turning again to Cicero, in *De oratore* (2.60) one speaker says that, just as skin takes on color from being in the sun, so his oratory "takes on the color, so to speak" (*quasi colorari*) of books he reads. Later, another speaker remarks upon the "bearing and, so to speak, *color*" of a speech: it is "smooth and slim/plain (*teres et tenuis*), but not without muscles and strength" and it "should have a certain pleasing *color*—not smeared on with makeup (*fucus*), but infused with blood/vitality (*sanguis*)" (3.199, cf. *Brutus* 162; *De optimo genere oratorum* 8). In *Orator* 42, eloquence is said to be "raised upon the nourishment" provided by rhetorical exercises in school and "derives its *color* and strength" from them. This metaphor of speech (or text)-as-body also persists into the imperial age (cf. *Inst.* 8 pr. 18–20, 8.3.6). Perhaps related is the common use of *color* to mean directly the "overall complexion" or "style" or "tone" of speaking. Seneca says that Labienus spoke with the "*color* of old oratory, and the vigor of new" (*Cont.* 10 pr. 5); Quintilian likewise discusses how the *color* of a speech can be either varied or consistent throughout (*Inst.* 6.3.107, 110; 12.10.71). The painting metaphor, then, presents *color* as overtly added on, artificial, and ornamental, while the body metaphor usually presents it as (seemingly) inherent, natural, and essential—sometimes in contrast to *fucus*, "dye" or "makeup," that is applied on the surface.

Yet *color* is always recognized as a product of the orator's art, and acknowledged as being no less carefully contrived for a given rhetorical situation when it seems completely natural (as the body metaphor has it) than when it is more transparently added on (the painting metaphor). Consequently, *color* sometimes implies "falseness," indicating an appearance that is unrelated or contrary to an underlying reality. Quintilian notes that persons on trial must "have the *color* of worry," that they must appear thus, whatever their actual feelings (*Inst.* 11.1.49), and that a speaker must maintain a certain *color* throughout his speech "in order to appear not just to speak, but to speak truly" (11.1.58). Similarly, Apuleius (*Apologia* 19, c.160 CE) observes that the wealthy assume "the *color* of poverty" when they wish to seem down-to-earth.

In the large corpus of Greek-language declamations surviving from the second to fourth centuries CE, the word *chrōma* (color) is used in broadly the same ways as its Latin counterpart color. However, the technical usage of *color* to label specific argumentative strategies in declamation may have originated in Greek rather than Latin. For the acolytes of the rhetorician Hermagoras (c.150 BCE) are said to have used *chrōma* as a shorthand for "shift of cause" (*metathesis tēs aitias*)—the declaimer's attempt to mitigate the case against a defendant by arguing that his actions were morally right, or that he was seeking to forestall a worse outcome, or that he was retaliating for a previous injury, or that someone else was actually to blame (Matthes, 1962, pp. 25–30; Fairweather, 1981, pp. 166–167; Russell, 1983, pp. 48–49). Precisely such arguments are called *colores* in Roman declamation too, which took on its distinctive terminology a century later, in the 40s or 30s BCE (Fairweather, 1981, pp. 124–131; Bonner, 1949, pp. 20–31). This Latin usage, then, may derive most directly from the Hermagorean usage of *chrōma*, while also exhibiting features of the earlier, metaphorical Latin usages.

Color in its (Latin) technical sense first occurs in Seneca the Elder's collection of *controversiae*— fictive legal cases providing training in forensic oratory. [*See* Forensic genre.] In the 30s CE, Seneca (c.55 BCE–c.39 CE) assembled this collection from recollections of declamatory performances he had heard over his long life. He offers few transcripts of sustained declamation, but instead gathers the most striking expressions (*sententiae*) produced by the declaimers who spoke on a given theme, shows various ways they distinguished the issues at stake (*divisiones*), and lists the *colores* they used. *Controversia* 9.5 illustrates the meaning and function of *color* in Seneca. The *thema*, or "facts" of the case by which all declaimers must abide, is this: three boys live with their father and stepmother (their mother having died); two fall ill and die with symptoms indicating either indigestion or poison; the (natural) mother's father is excluded from visiting the sick children; he kidnaps the remaining boy; the father prosecutes him for perpetrating violence (*vis*). Arguing the father's side, the declaimer Porcius Latro uses this *color:* the father and his erstwhile father-in-law had always disliked one another, even when the boys' mother was alive; he was violent and abusive and couldn't be permitted to visit sick children (*Cont.* 9.5.9). Another declaimer's *color* is that the grandfather arrived inopportunely, and so was told "not now"; he then became abusive, but Latro criticizes this *color* for controverting the *thema,* which, he says, must be taken to mean that the grandfather was told "never," not merely "not now" (9.5.10). Still another *color* for the father is, "I turned him away, for I had been told that he came with the intention of kidnapping" (9.5.11). On the grandfather's side, one *color* is that he took the surviving boy to safety, since the stepmother had assuredly murdered the others (Roman stepmothers are stereotyped as hostile to their stepchildren); another is that the boy himself, fearing for his life, asked his grandfather to take him away (9.5.12).

The arguments labeled here as *colores* are clearly of the sort the Hermagoreans called *chromata:* retaliating for a previous injury, forestalling a worse outcome, shifting responsibility to another person. All such arguments involve inventing a "back story," a narrative of events preceding those specified in the *thema,* that explains the motivations of the defendant or plaintiff, thereby casting their actions as described in the *thema* in a more sympathetic or invidious light; for example, the grandfather had long been abusive and violent, or the boy asked to be taken. Inventions that contradict the *thema* are impermissible (cf. *Cont.* 2.3.11, 7.7.14; *Inst.* 4.2.28, 90; *DMin.* 316.3). Because *colores* involve invention, credibility and sustainability are crucial. Quintilian says that *colores* must suit the persons, times, and places involved in the case, and must never be mutually inconsistent (*Inst.* 4.2.89–91, cf. *DMai.* 1.14); moreover, in a real court case one must never invent something a witness can contradict (4.2.93).

Yet *colores* that cannot under any circumstances be contradicted, such as appealing to dreams or indications of divine will, are also unpersuasive because they are too easy (4.2.94; dreams: *Cont.* 2.1.33, 7.7.15; divine will: *Cont.* 1.3.8–9; *DMin.* 384.1). An effective, credible *color,* the critics say, requires careful, systematic development throughout the declamation: the renowned orator Asinius Pollio asserts (*Cont.* 4.3) that a *color* should be introduced in the *narratio* (the portion of the speech expounding what happened) and developed in the *argumenta* (the formal argument that "proves" the case one way or the other). [*See* Arrangement, *article on* Traditional arrangement.] Latro likewise says that over the full course of a speech even difficult, harsh *colores* can win acceptance (*Cont.* 10 pr. 15, cf. 7.1.20; *Inst.* 4.2.94). "Mixing" *colores*—using more than one in a given speech—is tricky: when speaking of yourself you should use only one (i.e., choose a single back story and consistently describe your motivations in that light), but when speculating on someone else's motivations you can propose several alternative stories (*Inst.* 4.2.90; *Cont.* 4.6). A well-developed *color,* then, appears to partake of the "body" metaphor more than of the "painting" metaphor, for it is an integrated, unitary, natural-seeming part of the argument that persuades by its appearance of truth (*Inst.* 11.1.58–59), while a speech whose *colores* are discernibly "added-on" and not integrated fails to persuade (*Inst.* 4.2.96, 11.1.58, 12.9.17). Indeed, a skilful *color* can save a difficult case when the *thema* is strongly biased in one direction, Seneca closely attends to the *colores* advanced for the harder side (*Cont.* 9.2.18–21; 10.4.15–18; cf. *Inst.* 4.2.100). Not every case requires one, however. Latro, declaring in *Controversia* (7.6.17) that "a defense, not a *color,* is needed," invents no back story but justifies the defendant's actions by enumerating advantages they entail, and adducing historical examples (cf. *Cont.* 7.5.8).

The criticism of *colores* evident in these passages was not merely in the service of rhetorical training. It was also a weapon in the competition for rank and status that was integral to the social dynamics of declamatory performance. Traces of such competition are manifest in Seneca's own connoisseurship: for instance, he declares that Latro and Otho achieved distinction in their virtuoso handling of certain *colores* (e.g., *Cont.* 10 pr. 15; 2.1.34–39), while Gargonius and Murredius are contemptible for their inappropriate, tasteless *colores* (e.g., *Cont.* 1.7.18; 9.4.22).

Because the back story introduces new events, *colores* may be productive, generating new declamations and even new history. Consider *Controversia* (2.4), which involves two brothers, one of whom is disinherited and dies. A common *color* for one side makes the brothers enemies: the one's accusations caused the other to be disinherited (2.4.7), and he even neglected to visit his brother on his deathbed (2.4.3). A declaimer arguing the other side answers these charges: the brothers were close; the one's disinheritance was due to the father's unreasonableness or insanity; the other failed to visit because the father concealed the crisis from him (2.4.10–11). This declaimer's *color* thus preempts the opposition's *color,* as if it were itself a "fact" to be addressed along with the "facts" specified in the *thema.* Such a *color* may eventually be fully incorporated into the *thema,* generating a variant declamation whose *thema* differs from the original only in this detail (compare *DMin.* 252 with 370, and *Cont.* 7.3 with *DMai.* 17; discussion in Roller, 1997, pp. 125–126; cf. *DMin.* 316.3, where a *color* is virtually amalgamated into the *thema*). When a declamatory theme is historical, such invention may (re)write history. For instance, back stories sometimes involve an invented earlier trial that affects the perception of the current case. In *Controversia* (7.2), where Popillius is on trial for killing Cicero, declaimers commonly use the *color,* damning to Popillius, that Cicero had once defended him successfully in court on a charge of parricide. Seneca declares the parricide charge a declamatory fabrication (*Cont.* 7.2.8), and indeed this entire back story is probably invented. Nevertheless, much of this material did enter the historical tradition, in part because the declamatory and historiographical traditions of Cicero's death evolved contemporaneously, and the historiographers, like all Roman aristocrats, were themselves trained in declamation (Roller, 1997). Invented trials are particularly common in declamations of the second to fourth centuries CE on Greek historical themes (Russell, 1983, pp. 117–120), but since these declamations were derivative of a long-established historical tradition, these inventions apparently did not infiltrate that tradition.

The technical usage of *color* is not restricted to declamation. Ovid, Seneca's contemporary, uses it to label an argument advanced in an altogether different setting (*Tristia* 1.9.63), and Quintilian speaks of certain arguments in real court cases as *colors* (*Inst.* 11.1.49, 81, 85; also Frontinus *De Aquis* 105, c.100 CE). The *Digest* of Justinian, compiled in the sixth century CE, also shows that the word labeled certain pleas in actual legal contexts during the imperial period (5.2.2.pr., 47.14.1.4). While this usage survives in medieval and Renaissance legal contexts, the more common usage in these periods makes *color* virtually synonymous with *figura* or *ornatus;* that is, it serves as an umbrella term encompassing a wide range of figural embellishments by which rhetoric is "adorned" (Arbusow, 1963). [*See* Style.]

[*See also* Art; Classical rhetoric; Controversia and suasoria; *and* Declamation.]

BIBLIOGRAPHY

Primary Sources
Cicero (Marcus Tullius Cicero). *De oratore.* 2 vols. Translated by E. W. Sutton and H. Rackham. Cambridge, Mass., 1942. The other works of Cicero cited in the text are also available in Loeb translations.

Seneca (Lucius Annaeus Seneca, also called "the Elder" or "Rhetor"). *The Elder Seneca.* 2 vols. Translated and edited by Michael Winterbottom. Cambridge, Mass., 1974. Valuable introduction and notes, and excellent indices.

Quintilian (Marcus Fabius Quintilianus). *The Institutio oratoria of Quintilian.* 4 vols. Translated by H. E. Butler. Cambridge, Mass., 1921–1922. Convenient Latin text and slightly old-fashioned English translation. The *Declamationes maiores* and *Declamationes minores* attributed to Quintilian are untranslated.

Secondary Sources
Arbusow, Leonid. *Colores Rhetorici.* Göttingen, 1963. First published 1948. A catalog of figures that go under the name *color* in medieval literature. Reprinted with corrections, indices, bibliography, and references to standard handbooks.

Bonner, Stanley F. *Roman Declamation in the Late Republic and Early Empire.* Liverpool, U.K., 1949.

Fairweather, Janet. *Seneca the Elder.* Cambridge, U.K., 1981. A detailed analysis of many aspects of Roman declamation, focusing on Seneca; the discussion of *color* is superb, and by far the most thorough available.

Matthes, Dieter, ed. *Hermagorae Temnitae Testimonia et Fragmenta.* Leipzig, 1962.

Roller, Matthew B. "*Color*-blindness: Cicero's death, declamation, and the production of history." *Classical Philology* 92 (1997), pp. 109–130.

Russell, Donald A. *Greek Declamation.* Cambridge, U.K., 1983.

—MATTHEW B. ROLLER

COMMONPLACES AND COMMONPLACE BOOKS.

In the Early Modern period, commonplaces were a universally understood mechanism for generating structured and amplified discourse (written and oral). It was only toward the end of that period that the term *commonplace* began to acquire connotations of banality and eventually became identical with "trite truism," a degenerate slide that paralleled the disgrace of "rhetoric" on its way to empty verbiage. Since Aristotle, however, in the fourth century BCE, commonplaces, topics, or *loci communes,* had been bound into the construction of cogent argument and the gathering of material to develop composition. For Aristotle, in his *Topics* and his *Rhetoric,* the "places" comprised the most effective ways of arguing from the basis of generally accepted opinions. They provided models for making deductions rigorous enough to satisfy the criteria of dialectic, while in rhetoric arguments could be as loosely formulated as audience response would tolerate. [*See* Dialectic.] "Commonplaces" were ratiocinative procedures, or "places," "common" to a range of disciplines of inquiry or lines of investigation. Cicero (106–43 BCE) also wrote a *Topics,* in which he accommodated Aristotle's commonplaces more specifically to rhetoric, particularly forensic rhetoric. Cicero codified the procedures and gave the Renaissance a language in which to talk about commonplaces. They were the "seats" of argument (*sedes argumentorum*), local habitations, places that anyone drafting a speech should "visit" in order to see whether his material could be effectively extended by drawing on the patterns of argument they contained in outline. Commonplace formulas included arguments to be drawn from definition, genus, species, enumeration of parts, etymology, conjugates, similarity, difference, contraries, adjuncts, antecedents, consequents, contradiction, cause, effect, comparison. These and various other stratagems for proving one's point were to constitute Renaissance descriptions of ways to argue convincingly, and thereby persuasively. They were the abstract formulation of "probable," that is to say "plausible," arguments intrinsic to the development of a speech on any topic. Among "places" to be incorporated into a speech from outside was one that in the future was to have as much importance as all the others, and that was the testimony of authoritative quotation from the writing of respected experts, orators, philosophers, poets, and historians. In Cicero's *De inventione,* as in the *Rhetorica ad Herennium,* foundation textbooks in rhetoric until well into the sixteenth century, commonplaces were fully acclimatized to the genres of oratory. In the process, they became not only templates for argument as yet empty of substance, but containers now filled with suggestions for very specific subjects to be incorporated into particular types of exposition. So an epideictic speech in praise of a person would run through places "common" to that genre—for example, birth, background, physical attributes, and moral qualities—with very precise indications of what topics should be included under each head. The concept of commonplace was clearly veering toward the notion of "general theme," and this was reinforced for the Renaissance when Humanists eagerly absorbed the newly discovered *Institutio oratoria* of Quintilian, which dates from the last years of the first century CE. From Quintilian they could learn that ancient orators were trained by doing written exercises on moral themes, such as denouncing typical instances of particular vices, and that they customarily made collections of such themes for all-purpose use. This sense of "commonplace," as a moral topic proposed for rhetorical amplification, was eventually transmitted to the humanist classroom. More influential in the immediate term, however, was the later *De differentiis topicis* of Boethius (c.480–524 CE). [*See* Classical rhetoric.]

It was primarily from Boethius that the Middle Ages got its concept of commonplaces. His sole focus was on seats of argument as a mechanism of proof. He tightened the mechanism considerably by defining *loci* in terms of maximal propositions, that is to say, the sort of self-evident truths that form the major premise of a syllogism, differentiated according to the rule of inference being employed in order to find the middle term for moving toward the conclusion of a watertight, syllogistic train of reasoning. [*See* Syllogism.] In the later Middle Ages, the topics of Boethius were more or less thoroughly absorbed into formal logic within the theory of consequents. Boethius had devoted the fourth and final book of his *De differentiis topicis* to the places of argument appropriate to rhetoric, a form of discourse that he distinguished from dialectic in so far as its reference was to particularities, and its mode of argument looser than the syllogism. Because of its concentration on the specific, its places of argument were very narrow in their application. The conclusion that medieval thinkers derived from this was that rhetoric was a subset of dialectic, and a rather poor relation, incapable as it was of rising from particular instances to universal truth. An important pointer toward the language that medieval logic and rhetorical theory were to develop was the fact that Boethius attached very little importance to argument from cited authorities. Indeed, his work on places has plenty of made-up examples, but no illustrative quotations from nonphilosophical sources, no obvious application to texts outside its own discipline. Nevertheless, medieval thinkers in pursuit of truth had a resource even more potent than pure reason. That was the Bible and other authors who expounded the Bible's message. Quotations from such texts had an authority not paralleled by any book known to the orators of antiquity. The place of argument from authority consequently acquired great force in all forms of disputation. In the particular spoken rhetoric of the church, in preaching, it was paramount. In the later Middle Ages, sermons acquired a highly systematized rhetoric of their own, generated from quotations. This was serviced by manuals and by compilations known as concordances, usually organized alphabetically by topic, in which preachers could find and match quotations from the Bible. Another feature of late medieval culture that encouraged quotation collections was the method for teaching Latin, often illustrating abstract grammatical precepts by short, morally edifying extracts from authors. Assemblies of such extracts, usually arranged by author, are known as *florilegia*. With the advent of Humanism in fifteenth-century Italy, there was a change in the environment in which the elements of the Latin language were learned. Students now learned their Latin from the practice of ancient writers, but this change stressed ever more urgently the need to collect extracts from authors. What was required were assemblies of phrases exemplifying authentic language use, every bit as valuable as any improving sentiments they might also contain. Typically, quotations might be arranged by topic, but principles of organization were fairly lax. [*See overview article on* Medieval rhetoric.]

By the end of the fifteenth century, volumes of collected excerpts, from both religious and classical sources, were being produced on an ever-growing scale made possible by the increased efficiency of the printing press. At a similar period, the Humanists' disdain for late medieval logic couched in the "barbaric" jargon of late medieval Latin, was taking them back to the argumentative procedures associated with the linguistic elegance of Cicero and Quintilian, back indeed to a dialectic and rhetoric based on commonplaces. The most noted example of this recovery of the *sedes argumentorum* was the *De inventione dialectica* of the Dutch Humanist, Rudolph Agricola, which did not appear in print until 1515, thirty years after the author's death. It is a systematic account of "heads" or "places" of argument. These were universally applicable stratagems for persuasive discourse based on a theory of commonplaces developed from Cicero and Boethius, and illustrated by worked examples of such stratagems operating in extracts from Cicero, Virgil, and other authors of impeccable Latinity. When it did finally appear, the *De inventione dialectica* gave a sharper focus to developments already in train at a more elementary level. One of the most crucial was the emergence of the commonplace book in the form it was to have for the hundred and fifty years or so of its effective implementation.

Commonplace books were collections of quotations, most frequently Latin quotations, arranged under heads in such a way as to combine the two features of the Early Modern mentality we have so far seen running in close parallel: on the one hand, the enthusiasm for collecting extracts; on the other hand, the notion of "places" or "heads" of argument, which by now had also gathered the sense of "general theme" to be found in Quintilian. Commonplace books had their antecedents, but they were more systematically organized than the phrase books of early Humanists, and much more closely geared to the imitation of the procedures of classical rhetoric than to the structures of the late medieval sermon (in whose manuals Humanists were loathe to recognize the forerunners of the tool they made their own). They were also a powerful formative influence on every schoolboy, for their original home was in the grammar classroom where boys learned their Latin from classical texts, retained the language forms they found there, and reproduced them in composition.

It was none other than the foremost Humanist of his day, Erasmus, in his *De copia* of 1512, who set the mold for making commonplace books, in a passage advising how to store collections of illustrative examples in retrievable form. One should make oneself a notebook divided by place-headings, then subdivided into sections. The headings should relate to "things of particular note in human affairs" or to the main types and subdivisions of vices and virtues, derived perhaps from Cicero, Aristotle's *Ethics,* the thirteenth century CE *Summa theologiae* of Saint Thomas Aquinas, or the examples collected by Valerius Maximus early in the first century CE. Extracted from the *De copia,* this advice was printed time and again for use in schools. The commonplace book thus mapped the moral universe of literate youths from a very early age and imprinted on their minds a morality of a particular stamp, pagan or Christian in its primary affiliation. Later, Protestants often used the Ten Commandments as their organizing principle. Roman Catholics preferred Saint Thomas Aquinus or the seven virtues and the deadly sins. Erasmus himself recommended an arrangement by similars and opposites, and did so because it replicates the way rhetorical discourse might be organized, engaging the recipients' attention and their eventual adherence by taking them through associations triggered by likenesses, affinities, and contraries. For Erasmus, not only was the arrangement of the heads thus related to rhetorical *dispositio,* but the

quotations they contained were agents of rhetorical invention. The commonplace book was a treasury of matter with which to enrich and amplify discourse. It collected witty, pregnant aphorisms, apposite metaphors, similitudes, examples, fables, and proverbial expressions for its owner to use in abundance. It also taught him by example how to formulate and manipulate these verbal ornaments in imitation of the stylistic virtuosity of the most admired ancient models.

That owner of a commonplace book was in the first instance a reader. With his notebook to hand, he probed his text, most often a Latin text, picking up notable passages and allocating them to his prepared heads. At school, he would probably do this under his teacher's guidance, but the habit was supposed to be acquired for life. The adult reader, still commonplacing, would develop a sense that reading was a very private activity, as he transferred texts from a book in the public domain to the notebook that he owned as he owned the contents of his own mind. Such reading also exercised his initiative. He had license to choose his own heads; he could fit his extracts wherever seemed appropriate to him; he could juxtapose contradictory excerpts on a single theme or put the same passage under different heads. He could be as skeptical or as conventional as he pleased. In practice, however, the heads, at least, tended to be much the same in all notebooks. This was partly because the printing industry quickly saw a market for mass production, and the headings used in printed commonplace books were generally taken over into manuscript ones. This was the case with the general commonplace books and their largely moral focus, but standardization was inevitably more marked once commonplace books became more ambitious in scope, as they very soon did. From 1519 onward, Philip Melanchthon (1497–1560), Martin Luther's close associate, began building on Erasmus's prescriptions for commonplace books and extended their application to the recognized disciplines of inquiry: politics, physics, theology, law, and so on. Each discipline was to be assigned its specific areas and subareas of investigation under their agreed heads. Within these parameters, there was no scope for free association. Erasmus had seen the commonplace book as harboring a restive flood of words. For Melanchthon, the heads of the commonplace book were much more tightly tied to systematic divisions latent in the universe of the knowable. He was also more interested than Erasmus in commonplaces as heads of argument. His commonplacing reader would not only collect potent expressions, but would note how a general theme or a place of argument gave rational coherence to a passage of writing and determined how it was to be understood. Commonplaces became tools of exegesis. Rhetoric, now virtually indistinguishable from dialectic on their common ground of commonplaces, became a hermeneutic, a science of interpretation. [*See* Hermeneutics.]

The commonplace book was not only a reading engine. It was also a production mechanism. The data it stored was meant to be retrieved and redeployed. However elaborate its organization, sometimes mapping a moral system, sometimes analyzing an intellectual discipline, sometimes even attempting to replicate the order of the universe and all things in it, there would always be a complementary index of its commonplace heads in alphabetical order. Whatever the subject, the writer could find matter to his purpose by looking up the heads in his commonplace book. He could also find ways to amplify and ornament his material. Rhetorical *inventio* and *elocutio* were equally well-served. The collected extracts in general commonplace books were meant to be striking: clever turns of phrase, adages, aphorisms, examples, metaphors, similitudes, and all forms of rhetorical figures. [*See* Figures of speech.] They could be retrieved, recycled, or remodeled, quoted in their original Latin, rendered into a vernacular, or transmogrified to fit a new context. Commonplace books supplied, and programmed, a culture of verbal discourse reveling in ornamentation, dilation, redundance. Being a resource shared by readers and writers, in an age when recognizable imitation was admired, commonplace books were also a cohesive factor, bonding an educated élite whose collective memory was stocked from classical texts packaged in labeled containers. Commonplace *inventio,* however, was not confined to rhetoric in its narrower sense of verbal variation. After the publication of Rudolphus Agricola's *De inventione dialectica* (1515) and the diffusion in schools of that and other more elementary manuals explaining the argumenta-

tive strategies using the "places," advice on making commonplace books not infrequently stipulated that they should introduce named places of argument as subheads or marginal notes. So the heads might be related to Aristotle's basic categories of definition, and the extracts might be accompanied with a signal for using them as places of division, cause, effect, adjuncts, circumstances, similars, opposites, and all the other stratagems appropriate to discourse designed to persuade. The commonplace book would thus provide its owner with dialectical operators for manipulating the general themes that comprised his headings and for bringing into strategic play the quotations he had collected under them. He was equipped to find material, to maneuver it in argument, and to deck it with verbal fluency. In other words, the commonplace book as agent of production fulfilled the aims of rhetoric: to teach, to move, and to delight.

The most widely-available printed commonplace books were those published for school use, and they were legion. Most frequently printed of all was the *Illustrium poetarum flores* (Flowers from Famous Poets), which had started life as a *florilegium,* but was rejigged as a commonplace book in handy format in 1538, with its extracts from poets distributed under alphabetically ordered heads and subheads. These were mostly moral in the broadest sense, including definitions of psychological characteristics, emotions, states of life, and human activities, as well as virtuous conduct and its opposite. The compilation started with "abstinence," "adolescence," "adversity," and "adulation," and such containers were filled exclusively by quotations from pagan classical poets. Still used in schools all over Western Europe in the early seventeenth century, the *Flores* were a young boy's first introduction to poetry. He learned to compose his first verses by imitating the lines he found there, and internalized not only a poetic language but a particular culture and moral perspective. The prose equivalent of the *Flores* was a volume of *Marci Tullii Ciceronis sententiae* (Quotable Quotes from Cicero), first published in the early 1540s, expanded several times, and used in parallel with the *Flores* for the next hundred years. Its headings would have reinforced the child's acquisition of a moral environment constructed from pagan literature, while the extracts from Cicero, to be transferred to his own composition or closely imitated, defined his style of writing as well as his cast of mind. Nearer the end of the sixteenth century, printed commonplace books grew to enormous size in large formats and became the chief rhetorical reference books. Sometimes they specialized in a particular formula for rhetorical persuasion, such as persuasion by force of example. This was the case with the 1565 *Theatrum vitae humanae* (Theater of Human Life) of Theodor Zwinger (1533–1588), that grew to eight volumes in the next fifty years or so. Its collected examples range well beyond classical literature, but Zwinger attempted to introduce some coherence into his printed universe by mapping the sequence of his heads onto logical connectives, such as genus and species, cause and effect. The most comprehensive rhetorical compilations of all were those by Josef Lang (1570–1615), an *Anthologia* in 1589 and a *Polyanthea* in 1604. Lang scoured all previous commonplace books for extracts and arranged them in classes under alphabetical heads. His classification system clearly pertained to forms of discourse that proceeded by argument from authority and by stratagems derived from rhetorical figures used persuasively. It consists of Biblical quotations, quotations from the Fathers of the Church, flowers from the poets, sayings from philosophers and orators, apothegms, similitudes, examples from sacred literature, examples from nonsacred literature, and emblems. By this period, the commonplace book was servicing every kind of composition, from pulpit rhetoric to private letters.

From the second half of the sixteenth century, the commonplace book also went outside the schoolroom and into vernacular speech. Printed vernacular commonplace books tended to be rather dishevelled replicas of the Latin ones, poorly edited, and almost always devoid of the references to original sources that generally accompanied Latin quotations. What they initially collected were translations of Latin texts, which in the process of translation naturally lost the stylistic specificity that had made the *Flores,* for example, an array of stylistic models as well as a collection of heterogeneous opinions. Their rather cheap production does suggest, however, that they aimed to sell as widely as possible in a market that did not have the bulk buying power of the schools. Styles of speaking and writing promoted in the classroom set the fashion for sophisticated manipulation of the vernaculars, and commonplace books were its resource. In English, French, and other languages, witty aphorisms, proverbial sayings, metaphors, similitudes, and examples were the stuff of cleverly- and prettily-turned speeches, while a close analysis will usually reveal a more or less rigorous structure that can be dismembered into the dialectical and rhetorical places of argument. In 1600, Robert Allott's *English Parnassus, or the Choysest Flowers of our Moderne Poets* provided the English speech community with a commonplace book to match the Latin ones, and advertised a change of masters of literary discourse. His alphabetical heads replicate Latin commonplace books, as does his subsequent section specializing in rhetorical set pieces, descriptions, comparisons, and similitudes. His excerpts, however, are now from Spenser, Shakespeare, Marlowe, and a host of lesser stars shining in the Elizabethan poetic firmament. Meanwhile, English readers assiduously penned their own commonplace books. As in other countries, as the seventeenth century progressed, there is evidence that the environment of the commonplace book began to expand beyond the confines of the schoolroom and the library. Experience, especially experience of foreign travel, but even day-to-day living could provide matter to be written up under suitable heads. Once again, the commonplace book could function as a conservative force, ensuring that all experience found its place in a preexisting mental culture, but, as ever, the manuscript commonplace book was always open to additional heads and to contents that could subvert as well as reaffirm the established order.

In the second half of the seventeenth century, the commonplace book in its Renaissance form began its long decline. Two reasons for this were connected with developments in rhetoric. On the one hand, the dialectic of places, to which the commonplace book had been so closely allied, fell into serious disrepute. The commonplaces of argument had always represented a form of reasoning that started from generally accepted opinions, not self-evident truth, and their target had been reasonable conviction, adequate persuasion, not by any means the inescapable logic of mathematical rigor. With the development of scientifically exact knowledge in the seventeenth century, the persuasive stratagems of dialectical rhetoric lost their hold on discourse that was not purely "literary," and the heads of commonplace books no longer mapped the universe of the knowable. Quotation, too, lost its charisma and its power to persuade. By the second half of the seventeenth century, vernacular authors had cut their umbilical ties to their Latin forebears. They proclaimed themselves sole progenitors of the texts they wrote, and works built out of retrieved and recycled excerpts were condemned as plagiarism, their producers reviled as mere hacks. The stylistic legacy of the commonplace book had been fully absorbed, but its mechanisms of production were not allowed to show.

The commonplace book survived but had an increasingly private life. There is evidence to suggest that authors habitually made classified repositories of information when preparing new work, more especially if that work required a degree of erudition. The philosopher, John Locke (1632–1704), published a *New Method of Making Common-Place-Books* in order to publicize his new, improved method of indexing. He, and subsequent improvers, clearly envisaged that compilers would be collecting recondite facts from their reading for the specific requirements of a book in preparation. There is no sense that their commonplace books were to have all-embracing heads or that the extracts were perceived to be culturally or stylistically formative. Rather more formative were commonplace books that exemplify a sense of the word recognizable to modern people, or more especially to women of a certain age. These were (perhaps still are) very private books indeed, uncoordinated collections of favorite passages from authors prized for sentiment and beauty, to be lingered over by, mainly, adolescent females. The practice of keeping these private volumes of personally chosen excerpts is very nurturing, but has little directly to do with the learned mechanisms of persuasive argument known to Renaissance schoolboys. Nevertheless, the commonplace book in its traditional, technical sense has recently reinvented itself to dramatic effect. We might attribute its initial con-

ception to the need to deal methodically with the mass of material flowing from the so-called "print explosion" of the early sixteenth century. That information overload is replicated on the World Wide Web. Contemporary data-storage and data-retrieval systems bear a not unexpected resemblance to the technology of the commonplace book. Whether they are equipped to produce effective rhetoric, and whether that rhetoric will be conservative or open, is a matter of no little interest.

[*See also* Amplification; Copia; Invention; *overview article on* Renaissance rhetoric; *and* Topics.]

BIBLIOGRAPHY

Boethius, Anicius Manlius Severinus. *De topicis differentiis.* Translated, with notes and essays on the text, by Eleonore Stump. Ithaca, N.Y., 1978.

Cicero, Marcus Tullius. *De inventione* and *Topica*, translated by H. M. Hubbell. Loeb Classical Library. Cambridge, Mass., 1949.

Cogan, Marc. "Rodolphus Agricola and the Semantic Revolutions of the History of Invention." *Rhetorica* 2 (1984), pp. 163–194. Very perceptive about the long-term consequences of Agricola's dialectic of places.

Erasmus, Desiderius. *Copia: Foundations of the Abundant Style.* Translated and annotated by Betty I. Knott. In *Collected Works of Erasmus*, edited by Craig R. Thompson, vol. 24, pp. 279–659. Toronto, 1978. Prescriptions for making a commonplace book, with examples of its application to composition, pp. 635–648.

Goyet, Francis. *Le sublime du "lieu commun": l'invention rhétorique dans l'Antiquité et à la Renaissance.* Paris, 1996. Essential complement to Moss, concentrates on commonplace rhetoric.

Mack, Peter. *Renaissance Argument: Valla and Agricola in the Traditions of Rhetoric and Dialectic.* Leiden, 1993. The most comprehensive analysis of Agricola's dialectic.

Meerhoff, Kees. "The Significance of Melanchthon's Rhetoric in the Renaissance." In *Renaissance Rhetoric*, edited by Peter Mack, pp. 46–62. London, 1994. The best introduction in English.

Moss, Ann. *Printed Commonplace-Books and the Structuring of Renaissance Thought.* Oxford, 1996. Contains an extensive bibliography of secondary sources on the subject.

Murphy, James J. *Rhetoric in the Middle Ages: A History of Rhetorical Theory from Saint Augustine to the Renaissance.* Berkeley, 1974.

—ANN MOSS

COMMUNICATION. Commonly defined as the transmission or exchange of ideas, communication relates to rhetoric in various small and large ways. Communication has long had a bit part in rhetoric as *communicatio,* a technique whereby the rhetor figuratively *deliberates* with the audience; for example, by asking and answering rhetorical questions ("Why now, you ask? I say, we dare not delay!"). In larger ways, communication as a whole can be nearly synonymous with rhetoric, subsume or be subsumed by rhetoric, or even play a costarring role—whether heroic or villainous—as rhetoric's archenemy. Communication relates to rhetoric in these diverse ways in part because communication, no less than rhetoric itself, has been conceptualized on radically different models.

Transmission and Constitutive Models. In the simplistic transmission model that is so often taken for granted in everyday discourse, communication is conceptualized as a process in which meanings, packaged in symbolic messages like bananas in crates, are transported from sender to receiver. Too often the bananas are bruised or spoiled in transport and so we have the ubiquitous problem of miscommunication: The message sent is not the message received, the sender's meaning does not come across. In order to improve communication, according to this model, we need better packaging and speedier transportation of messages. Good communication is basically a technical problem.

Sophisticated versions of the transmission model acknowledge that ideas cannot literally be put into words and transported. The English empiricist philosopher John Locke, in his *Essay Concerning Human Understanding* (1690), famously articulated the view, now regarded as a cliché, that meanings are in people, not in words. According to Locke, words have no natural meanings. The association of words with ideas in the mind is a voluntary act of the individual person. Although social convention establishes a rough correlation between words and ideas, however conscientiously we follow these conventional rules of language, we ultimately have no way of knowing whether the corporeal signs we choose to represent our thoughts will excite similar thoughts in the mind of another person. The inherent limitations of language thus make perfect communication well-nigh impossible. Yet, good communication is imperative; for communication is the bond that holds society together and the conduit through which knowledge is disseminated throughout society and conveyed to future generations. Locke warned against common abuses of language (such as confusing words with things) and proposed a series of remedies to improve communication. Except for the rhetorical principles of order and clarity, which promote understanding, Locke denounced rhetoric, especially the use of figurative language, as an "instrument of error and deceit." In this Lockean drama, then, rhetoric, unless it takes a deservedly minor role as communication's humble servant, can only play the villain as communication's archenemy.

Variations of the transmission model, whether simplistic or sophisticated, still typify everyday thinking and much of the academic literature about communication, but communication theorists recently have favored an alternative, the constitutive model. According to these critics, the transmission model misleadingly assumes that the essential elements of communication—distinct individuals, their private thoughts and feelings, and technical means of communication (e.g., shared codes, channels of transmission)—must all be fixed in place before the act of communication occurs. The constitutive model posits instead that the elements of communication, rather than being fixed in advance, are reflexively constituted within the act of communication itself. Communication is defined as an ongoing process that symbolically forms and re-forms our personal identities, our social relations, our common world of meaningful objects and events, our ideas and feelings, and our routine ways of expressing these socially constructed realities. No longer merely a technical question of how to get one's meaning across without distortion, the problem of communication has complex moral and political dimensions in a constitutive model. The field of communication expands to include all aspects of the creation and negotiation of meaning in society.

A constitutive model posits that the social practice of communication is ultimately inseparable from the ideas about communication embedded in ordinary language. The reality of communication as a distinct, meaningful kind of activity is socially created, shaped, and sustained by our routine ways of talking about communication. These ordinary ideas and ways of talking have emerged in history, and the traditions of intellectual thought now designated as "communication theory" have emerged along with them. Communication theory is thus inextricably bound up with the cultural evolution of communication as a social practice.

Formal theories of communication recurrently have drawn from, reflected upon, and influenced the vernacular language of communication, and so the everyday practice of communication. The idea of rhetoric emerged in ancient Greece as a reflection on practices of public speaking that were central to the life of citizens in the *polis*. Similarly, the idea of communication as transmission emerged in modern Europe as a reflection on practices (e.g., related to private property and trade, transportation, empire, the spread of literacy and print media) that were central to life in bourgeois society, and has been bolstered by subsequent advances in communication technology. Now, as communication theorists have recently argued, the idea of communication as a constitutive social process is emerging as a reflection on practices (e.g., related to global interdependence, cultural diversity, ideas of democracy and human rights) that are becoming central to life in our own world.

Rhetoric, as it was formally theorized, began to shape its own field of practices, which continued to play an important role in European education and public communication for many centuries after the demise of the Greek *polis*. Communication theory now shapes its own field of practices, which play an increasingly important role in education and other formal institutions of society. Communication skills, and a savvy awareness of communication techniques, are considered essential to success in business, the professions, public affairs, and personal relationships. We speak of communication in an eclectic terminology drawn from discourses of human relations and therapy, information processing, marketing, and entertainment, as well as rhetoric and the social sciences.

The subtext of current debates in communication theory is a dispute on how to shape the language that constitutes the field of communi-

cation practices in society. One of the virtues of the constitutive model is that it sensitizes us to the political stakes that are always involved in such debates. Every form of communicative practice, including ones that fly the banner of the constitutive model, reflects the perspectives of some social groups more than others. Cultural conservatives, for example, may understandably dislike the constitutive model with its overtones of cultural and moral relativism, while globalizing elites may like it for their own reasons.

In the expanded field of communication implied by the constitutive model, rhetoric, depending on how it is defined, may be subsumed as a particular kind of communication (rhetoric defined as persuasive or intentionally purposive communication), criticized as a misguided outgrowth of the transmission model (rhetoric defined as a manipulative technique for getting one's ideas across effectively), or identified with communication as a whole (rhetoric defined as a constitutive social process). [*See* Politics, *article on* Constitutive rhetoric.] Rhetorical theory under any of these definitions becomes a branch or tradition of communication theory.

Communication Theory. Communication theory emerged as a distinct intellectual topic only in the midtwentieth century. The term itself was first used in the 1940s by electrical engineers with reference to the mathematical analysis of signals. For many readers, Claude Shannon and Warren Weaver's *The Mathematical Theory of Communication* (Urbana, 1949), and Norbert Wiener's *Cybernetics* (New York, 1948) augured the dawn of a new science of communication. The technical vocabulary of information transmission and feedback entered the common language and was taken up by social scientists, especially in the booming interdisciplinary field of communication research.

The rapid spread of this vocabulary was one manifestation of a long crescendo of societal interest in problems of communication, punctuated by wars and technological advances, throughout the last century. Communication was recurrently at the center of public debates about democracy, propaganda, mass media, popular culture, and human relations. Early in the century, communication as a formal category of knowledge was still largely identified with commercial and military transportation. As late as 1928, the Library of Congress subject classification featured the word *communication(s)* in only two headings: "communication and traffic" and "communications, military." With the growth of electronic media, *communication(s)* more frequently referred to processes of information transmission through technological channels (the initial subject of communication theory). Around midcentury, however, as the quantity of published works on communication exploded, the emphasis in defining the term shifted decisively. *Communication* was now commonly defined as an interactive process that performs essential functions in every field of social practice. Subject categories related to communication now included communication in worship, communication in business, political communication, mass communication, communication in the family, and so on.

Communication theory, having germinated in the groves of academe in the late 1940s, grew like a weed by sinking roots into every intellectual tradition or trend in any way related to communication. Ideas from physical science and engineering, linguistics, anthropology, sociology, psychology, and philosophy were absorbed and reinterpreted as theories of communication. While continuing to grow in this fashion, the subject even now has not yet matured as a coherent body of thought. Unlike rhetorical theory, communication theory has not grown historically forward, out of its traditions, but, in a sense, historically backward, by retrospectively appropriating a series of traditions, one of which is rhetorical theory.

Currently, at least seven major traditions of communication theory can be distinguished, rhetoric being the oldest.

Rhetoric. From classical rhetoric comes the idea that communication can be studied and cultivated as a practical art of discourse. Whereas the art of rhetoric still refers primarily to the theory and practice of public, persuasive communication, the communication arts more broadly encompass the whole range of communication practices including interpersonal, organizational, and cross-cultural communication, technologically mediated communication, and practices specific to various professions and fields. Modern rhetorical theory has elaborated and problemati-

zed the epistemological, sociological, and political dimensions of the classical tradition in ways that further contribute to communication theory. In theories of epistemic and constitutive rhetoric, for example, rhetorical theory has developed its own versions of the constitutive model. From a communication theory point of view, this encyclopedia falls largely within the rhetorical tradition of communication theory.

Semiotics. A second tradition of communication theory, originated in its modern form by Locke, is semiotics, the study of signs. Semiotic theory conceptualizes communication as a process that relies on signs and sign systems to mediate across the gaps between subjective viewpoints. For semiotic theory, communication problems result from barriers to understanding that arise from the slippage between sign vehicles (physical signs such as spoken or written words, or graphic images) and their meanings, the structure of sign systems, and particular ways of using (or misusing) signs. Distinct traditions of semiotics grew from the late-nineteenth-century writings of the American pragmatist philosopher Charles Sanders Peirce (1839–1914), and the early-twentieth-century work of the Swiss linguist Ferdinand de Saussure (1857–1913). The Peirceian tradition analyzed the cognitive and mental functions of signs as a basis for distinguishing among types of signs (icon, index, symbol) and dimensions of semiosis (syntactics, semantics, pragmatics). The Saussurean tradition, which led to structuralist and poststructuralist theory, focused instead on the systematic structure of language and other sign systems. Although Locke's semiotic theory was the fountainhead of the transmission model, poststructuralist theories, such as Jacques Derrida's theory of deconstruction, conceptualize communication as a process in which meanings are not fixed by the linguistic system but billow up and float in shifting winds of discourse. In a poststructuralist view, we do not exist independently of signs, with our essentially real personal identities and subjective viewpoints, and "use" signs in order to communicate. Rather, we exist meaningfully only *in* and *as* signs. [*See* Linguistics.]

Phenomenology. A third, phenomenological tradition conceptualizes communication as the experience of self and other in dialogue. Such twentieth-century theorists of dialogue as Martin Buber, Hans-George Gadamer, Emanuel Levinas, and Carl Rogers (although Rogers was a psychologist rather than a philosopher) can be broadly identified with this tradition. The problem of communication for phenomenology, as for semiotics, is that of a gap between subjective viewpoints: one cannot directly experience another consciousness, and the potential for intersubjective understanding is thereby limited. The two traditions approach this problem in quite different ways, however. Whereas semiotics looks to the mediational properties of signs, phenomenology looks to the authenticity of our ways of experiencing self and other. The basis for communication lies in our common existence with others in a shared world that may be constituted differently in experience. Authentic dialogue requires open self-expression and acceptance of difference while seeking common ground. Barriers to communication can arise from self-unawareness, nonacceptance of difference, or a strategic agenda that precludes openness to the other. The phenomenological tradition in modern philosophy stems from Edmund Husserl's (1859–1938) transcendental phenomenology, which was an analysis of the essential structure of conscious experience. Husserl's protégé and critic Martin Heidegger, in *Sein und Zeit* (*Being and Time,* 1927/ 1962), held that our being has no essence apart from the interpretive self-understanding that unfolds through time as we engage with the particular world in which we find ourselves. This hermeneutic phenomenology influenced subsequent existentialist, hermeneutic, and poststructuralist theories that have emphasized the constitutive properties of dialogue. [*See* Hermeneutics.] In these theories, dialogue is not essentially a sharing of preexisting inner meanings, it is engagement with others to negotiate meaning.

Cybernetics. Fourth, a cybernetic tradition of communication theory grew from the midtwentieth century work of Shannon, Wiener, Gregory Bateson, and a host of other writers in many fields. This is actually one of the newest traditions of communication theory, although, as we have noted, it was the first communication theory explicitly named and widely known as such. Cybernetics conceptualizes communication as information processing. All complex systems, in-

cluding computers and telecommunication devices, DNA molecules and cells, plants and animals, the human brain and nervous system, social groups and organizations, cities, and entire societies, process information, and in that sense communicate. Cybernetic theory downplays the differences between human communication and other kinds of information processing systems. Information storage, transmission, and feedback, network structures, and self-organizing processes occur in every sufficiently complex system. Problems of communication can arise from conflicts among subsystems or glitches in information processing like positive feedback loops that amplify noise. Proponents of second-order cybernetics (such as Heinz von Forster, Klaus Krippendorff, and Paul Watzlawick) have recast cybernetic theory within a constitutive model of communication. Second-order cybernetics reflexively includes the observer within the system observed and emphasizes the necessary role of the observer in defining, perturbing, and often in unpredictable ways, changing a system by the very act of observing it.

Social psychology. A fifth tradition of communication theory, social psychology, conceptualizes communication as social interaction and influence. Communication always involves individuals with their distinctive personality traits, attitudes, beliefs, and emotions. Social behavior both displays the influence of these psychological factors and modifies them as participants influence each other, often with little awareness of what is happening. Influence can be essentially a transmission process from source to receiver. If, however, interaction reciprocally changes the participants and leads to collective outcomes that would not otherwise have occurred, communication becomes a constitutive social process. Whether conceived on a transmission or a constitutive model, the problem of communication from a sociopsychological perspective is how to manage social interaction effectively in order to achieve preferred and anticipated outcomes. This requires an understanding, solidly grounded in scientific theory and research, of how the communication process works. Social scientific communication research has always been closely identified with social psychology, so it is not surprising that classic mid-twentieth-century theories of group dynamics (Kurt Lewin), persuasion (Carl Hovland), and cognitive dissonance (Leon Festinger), were quickly absorbed into communication theory, and joined by many later theories in a flow of cross-disciplinary borrowing that continues unabated.

Sociocultural theory. Deriving from twentieth-century sociological and anthropological thought, sociocultural communication theory is a sixth tradition. Sociocultural theory conceptualizes communication as a symbolic process that produces and reproduces shared meanings, rituals, and social structures. As John Dewey noted in *Democracy and Education* (New York, 1916), society exists not only *by* but *in* communication. That is, society exists not only *by* using communication as a necessary tool for transmitting and exchanging information. To communicate as a member of society is to participate *in* those coordinated, collective activities and shared understandings that constitute society itself. There is a tension in sociocultural theory between approaches that emphasize macrosocial structures and processes and those that emphasize microsocial interaction. On the macro side, structural and functionalist views emphasize the necessary role of stable social structures and cultural patterns in making communication possible. On the micro side, interactionist views emphasize the necessary role of communication as a process that creates and sustains social structures and patterns in everyday contexts of social interaction. From either view, communication involves the coordination of activities among social actors, and communication problems are directly manifested in difficulties and breakdowns of coordination. Communication problems have apparently become more pressing and difficult under modern conditions of societal diversity, complex interdependence, and rapid change. A reasonable conjecture from a sociocultural point of view is that communication theory developed in modern society as a way of understanding and addressing this new condition in which communication seems to be at once the disease that causes most of our social problems, and the only possible cure.

A critical tradition. A seventh tradition of communication theory, and the last to be discussed here, is a critical tradition that defines communication as a reflexive, dialectical discourse essentially involved with the cultural and ideological aspects of power, oppression, and emancipation in society. Dialectic, like its counterpart rhetoric, was first conceptualized in ancient Greece. [*See* Dialectic.] In the philosophical practice of Socrates as portrayed in Plato's dialogues, dialectic was a method of argumentation through question and answer that, by revealing contradictions and clarifying obscurities, led the interlocutors to higher truth. The dialectical materialism of Karl Marx (1818–1883) initiated the modern conception of dialectic as an inherently social process connecting political economy to cultural practice. In orthodox Marxist theory, ideology and culture were determined by class interests, and dialectic at the level of ideas primarily reflected the underlying struggle between economic classes. Latter-day Marxism, notably in the midtwentieth-century critical theory of the Frankfurt School (a circle that formed in Frankfurt, Germany in the 1920s and migrated to the United States during the Nazi period), has tended to see a larger role, less directly dependent on economic class relationships, for cultural and ideological debate. The goal of critical theory is then to promote emancipation and enlightenment by lifting ideological blinders that otherwise serve to perpetuate ignorance and oppression. More recently, the German social theorist Jürgen Habermas has reconstructed critical theory around key concepts including *communicative action* and *systematically distorted communication*. Communicative action, or discourse that seeks mutual understanding, for Habermas inherently involves certain transcendental validity claims that social actors must be free to contest openly in order for authentic communication to occur. Communication is systematically distorted by power imbalances that affect participation and expression, and critical theory can serve emancipatory interests by reflecting upon the sources of systematically distorted communication. Recent movements in the critical tradition such as postmodernism and critical cultural studies tend to reject both Marxist economic determinism as well as Habermas's universalistic ideal of communicative action, but continue to conceptualize communication in ways that emphasize ideology, oppression, critique, and reflexivity. Postmodernist cultural

critique primarily addresses ideological discourses of race, class, and gender that suppress
differences, preclude or devalue the expression of
certain identities, and limit cultural diversity. In
postmodernist theory, ideal communication is
not, as it was for Plato, a dialectical discourse that
leads the way to higher, universal truths. Postmodernism nevertheless implies a similar model
of communication: that of a dialectical (that is,
critical) discourse that can, if only in limited
ways, liberate the participants and expand human possibilities.

These seven traditions include the most prominent intellectual sources that currently influence
communication theory, but the seven traditions
do not, of course, cover the field exhaustively.
Ideas about communication are too numerous,
diverse, and dynamically evolving to be captured
entirely by any simple scheme. The field could
certainly be mapped in other ways that would
distinguish the main traditions in a different
form. Moreover, no matter how the traditions
may be defined, they will not be found to have
developed independently of one another. Contemporary theory draws from all of the traditions
in various ways but is often hard to classify neatly
in any one of them. Blends and hybrid varieties
are common. Poststructuralist theory, for example, draws from both semiotics and phenomenology; is often regarded as a kind of rhetorical
theory; and has significantly influenced recent
sociocultural and critical theory. Similarly, traces
of every other tradition of communication theory
can be found in recent rhetorical theory. [See
Contingency and Probability; and Modern rhetoric.] The academic discipline of communication
studies has become like a cauldron in which ideas
from across the traditions of communication
theory are mixed and stirred in different combinations to make intellectual stock for current
debates.

Communication Studies. During the second
half of the twentieth century, academic studies of
human communication became the province of
a distinct academic discipline. Communication
research, which coalesced as an interdisciplinary
field in the 1940s, drew from research traditions
that had originated more or less independently
in many fields of behavioral and social science,

including sociology, political science, public opinion, propaganda analysis, education, advertising,
business, social psychology, linguistics, anthropology, and others. As this interdisciplinary movement grew to prominence, it influenced the intellectual identities of scholars in departments of
speech in U.S. universities. [See Speech.] By the
mid-twentieth century, speech departments had
become a primary academic home for rhetorical
studies. Because communication research was
identified with the behavioral and social sciences,
whereas rhetoric was considered to be a humanistic field, efforts to increase the presence of communication research in speech departments and
related professional organizations threatened the
dominant status of rhetoric. Intense institutional
conflict, along with some creative efforts at intellectual synthesis, resulted.

The development of communication studies
in speech departments (like the related evolution
of mass communication and media studies in
schools of journalism) was undoubtedly influenced by the growing prominence of communication as a theme in societal discourse. As evidenced, for example, by the proliferation of
communication-related topics we noted earlier
by the mid-twentieth century *communication* had
become a vogue word used to label an ever-wider
range of social problems and practices. Communication-related jobs and communication skills
in general were becoming more important in the
postindustrial economy that was beginning to
emerge. According to John Durham Peters (*Speaking into the Air,* Chicago, 1999), two themes predominated in the post–World War II discourse on
communication. One was a technological discourse associated with information theory and
cybernetics. The other was a therapeutic discourse associated with Carl Rogers and what was
later known as the human potential movement.
As Peters points out, the drive for communication
technology and therapy were both fueled by anxieties associated with the nuclear bomb and the
cold war against communism.

In light of these trends in society, it is not surprising that speech and eventually rhetoric increasingly were thought to fall naturally under
the general heading of communication. Beginning in the 1960s, communication gradually dis-

placed speech in the titles of academic departments, professional organizations, and scholarly journals, and the speech curriculum was accordingly transformed around a new focus on the theory and practice of communication. As communication became the accepted name of the field as a whole, communication studies ceased to be identified exclusively with the behavioral and social sciences. Although the old tensions between scientific and humanistic approaches continued in new forms in communication departments, and rhetoric itself rose to prominence as an interdisciplinary field, rhetorical studies became, among other things, a branch of communication studies, and rhetorical theory became a tradition of communication theory.

Communication studies currently range across a broad field, the boundaries and subdivisions of which resist stable definition. The traditions of communication theory provide one interesting approach to mapping the intellectual structure of communication studies, but several other approaches are more common and also continue to be useful. One common approach to classifying knowledge about communication is by discipline. Communication can be studied as a scientific or humanistic discipline, an art, or a professional field. As a multidisciplinary field of scholarship, communication extends into such traditional disciplines as sociology, psychology, and linguistics, as well as newer ones like cultural studies and information science. It includes, or is closely related to, professional and technical fields such as journalism, advertising, public relations, broadcasting, and telecommunications. Each of these disciplines contributes its own structure of knowledge, which we cannot begin to explore in this article. Knowledge in the discipline of communication studies is also conventionally classified according to certain conceptual schemes. Without attempting an exhaustive survey, we will briefly explore three of the most common conceptual schemes for mapping the field: functions; codes, media, channels; and levels and contexts.

Functions. Just as rhetoric can be adapted to the different ends of moving, instructing, or pleasing an audience, communication can perform a variety of different functions. Persuasion or social influence, socialization, social support, information processing, conflict, decision making, and entertainment are a few of the more widely studied functions of communication.

Persuasion, a large topic in itself, bonds communication studies to rhetoric in one important way. Aristotle (384–322 BCE) defined rhetoric as the art of discovering the available means of persuasion in any given case. Experimental social psychological research on persuasion and attitude change has often been linked to this Aristotelian tradition and characterized as "scientific rhetoric"—an effort to create a scientific basis for the art of persuasion. Numerous scientific experiments have investigated the persuasive effects of logical and emotional appeals, one-sided and two-sided arguments, source credibility (or *ēthos*), audience characteristics, media of transmission, and a host of other variables. Social psychological theories have been presented as scientific alternatives to traditional rhetoric. Leon Festinger's theory of cognitive dissonance, for example, not only offered a seemingly new explanatory principle for persuasion but opened entirely new fields of study such as selective exposure (the tendency to seek information that supports one's current attitudes) and self-persuasion (or counterattitudinal advocacy, as it was uncharmingly called). A more recent line of research has investigated "compliance-gaining" behavior, the strategies people use to influence each other in interpersonal situations. [*See* Persuasion.]

With the growing popularity of the human potential movement and associated therapeutic conceptions of communication in the 1960s and 1970s, the traditional focus of communication research on persuasion and social influence processes was criticized. As an alternative to such manipulative, "rhetorical" uses of communication, research was needed to promote more humane and therapeutic functions of communication such as interpersonal bonding, group cooperation, and conflict resolution. Lines of research have developed in each of these areas and have produced substantial bodies of knowledge. One such area, for example, is the study of social support and comforting communication. Some of these studies have investigated behaviors that function to express emotional supportiveness under given conditions, or variables that predict the ability to produce sophisticated comforting messages.

Social scientific communication researchers have often favored a functional approach because it focuses attention on measurable outcomes of communication, and attempts to explain how outcomes are influenced by variables and processes that occur across a wide range of communicative situations. For example, certain cognitive processes and message characteristics may help to explain the efficiency with which information is gained from communication, whether in the context of a political campaign in the mass media, the socialization of new members in an organization, a classroom lesson, or a group discussion among friends.

Codes, Media, and Channels. Another common way of classifying communication is according to the codes, media, or channels through which it occurs. Codes, media, and channels are not so much different kinds of things as they are different perspectives on the same range of phenomena. *Code* refers to the way a sign system is structured to constitute a particular correlation of signs to meanings. *Medium* (in current usage often confused with its Latinate plural form, *media*) refers to a particular configuration of physical, technological, and institutional characteristics that constitute a distinct form of communication such as face-to-face interaction, commercial television, or electronic mail. *Channel* refers to a selection from a particular array of options for sending and receiving information. One array of channels comprises the five senses of vision, hearing, touch, etc.; another array comprises the telephone, fax, postal letter, e-mail, or face-to-face interview as options for business communication; still another array might be a set of available television channels. The use of different channels may or may not involve the use of different media and codes for communication.

Language, of course, is a primary code (or, in different perspectives, a medium or channel) of human communication, and is a vast field of research in its own right. The commonplace distinction between verbal and nonverbal channels (or codes) is often criticized by experts in nonverbal communication, who point out that verbal and nonverbal behaviors are closely intertwined

and function together in the communication process. Kinesics (gesture, facial expression, and body movement), proxemics (the use of space), haptics (touch), and paralanguage (vocal pitch, intonation, etc.) are some codes of face-to-face communication that have been studied. On the wider scene of societal culture, every distinguishable field of cultural practice, insofar as it is meaningful, can be said to embody its own particular codes or sign system. Semiotic analysis reveals systematic codes that govern the social meaning of clothing, food, mythic stories, character types in television genres, or kinds of shots in film or video. For example, whether a television scene is filmed in close-up, medium, or long shots can contribute, in conjunction with other codes, to the portrayal of different kinds of social relationships (the longer the shot, the more public the relationship).

A branch of media theory known, in its more extreme formulations, as *technological determinism* holds that communication media shape our consciousness of the world, and that the dissemination of new media through society can bring about new forms of consciousness and culture. Marshall McLuhan (1911–1980), undoubtedly the most publicly famous technological determinist, popularized several catch phrases ("the medium is the message," "the Gutenberg galaxy," "the global village") that have persisted in common usage. McLuhan speculated that the new electronic media, especially television, were causing cultural and epistemological changes no less profound than the revolutionary changes in consciousness that came with the transition from oral to literate culture and the introduction of the printing press in earlier eras. The simplistic notion that changes in media technology directly cause changes in consciousness has never been widely accepted by communication theorists. McLuhan's ideas, however, along with the less popularized works of Harold Innis, Walter Ong, and other scholars of media history, continue to stimulate thought on the cultural implications of new communication media. The recent tidal waves of technological change in computing and telecommunications have triggered new waves of speculation on the changes in culture and consciousness that may come in the wake of this so-called digital revolution.

Levels and Contexts. A third, commonly used way of classifying communication is according to the context or situation in which it occurs. From the cybernetic tradition of general systems theory comes the idea of nested levels of systemic organization. Every complex system is composed of subsystems at lower levels and is itself a subsystem nested within some higher-level system. This idea has been applied by communication theorists to conceptualize levels of communication such as intrapersonal (within the person); interpersonal (between people); small group (among a set of individuals who are mutually aware and maintain a common focus of attention); organizational (within a complex network of individuals and groups having subgroups and differentiated functions); public (between a communication source and a large, copresent audience); and mass (from a communication source, through a technological medium, to a very large, anonymous audience).

Intrapersonal communication, which has never developed as a major research area within communication studies (perhaps because it seems well-enough covered by the discipline of psychology), in principle includes such topics as attention, perception, information seeking, cognitive processing, personality, and self-reflection. Interpersonal communication is a very broad research field that ranges from studies of the development, conduct, and dissolution of personal relationships (e.g., friendships, romantic relationships, family relationships), to studies of communicator traits such as communication apprehension and argumentativeness, to studies of the communication strategies and behaviors associated with social influence, deception, conflict, social support, impression management, and a myriad of other communication functions.

Small-group communication includes such topics as the effects of group composition on group outcomes; the functions of communication in groups (e.g., task-related versus group maintenance functions); group leadership and other group roles; stages and processes of group development and decision making; methods of group facilitation; and the characteristics of particular kinds of groups as in business, education, or therapy.

Organizational communication is a major field that includes, among other topics, studies of formal and informal communication networks, leadership, superior–subordinate relationships, power and control, decision making, socialization, identification, workplace democracy and participatory practices, organizational culture and change, and interorganizational and public relations.

Mass communication is an even vaster field that includes studies of media institutions, professions, law, economics, and history; the characteristics and behavior of media audiences; the effects of mass communication on audience knowledge and opinions, consumer and voting behavior, violence and perceptions of violence in society, public agendas and political processes; media formats, genres, and contents; and the role of media as producers of culture and agents of social change.

This "levels" scheme is thought by some to be especially useful because it provides distinct places for traditional subdisciplines of communication studies (such as interpersonal communication, organizational communication, and mass communication) while suggesting how these subdisciplines might work together to compose a coherent field of study. Rhetoric in this scheme can be conceived as the study of *public* communication. Understood in this way, rhetoric is naturally linked to the neighboring levels of mass communication (e.g., in studies of political campaigns and televised rhetoric), and organizational communication (e.g., in studies of organizational leadership and organizations as public actors).

From a strict, systems-theoretic standpoint, conventional versions of the levels scheme of communication are conceptually suspect. Whether intrapersonal processes constitute communication at all is a matter of dispute. It is equally questionable whether public communication is really a distinct systemic level nested between mass and organizational communication. Much of our public communication occurs via the mass media, yet individuals also interact in public (while walking on public streets, for example) without necessarily engaging in one-to-many public address. One also wonders what to do with an established field like intercultural communication (communication between members of different cultures). Sometimes intercultural communication is appended to the scheme as a level above mass communication, which makes little sense because much intercultural communication is also interpersonal, small group, and/or organizational. More generally, changes in media technology and practice are progressively blurring the boundaries between traditional levels of communication. Mass audiences are ever more finely segmented and play more interactive roles in the communication process. Individuals and groups interact through technological media, sometimes anonymously, and sometimes in public forums like virtual chat rooms or broadcast talk shows. Virtual organizations (such as agencies that manage temporary workers) become little more than loose networks of individuals connected by media. [*See* Audience, *articles on* Mass audiences *and* Virtual audiences.]

Apart from the levels model, there are other, less conceptually schematic ways of distinguishing contexts of communication. Intercultural communication, if not a distinct systemic level of organization, might be classified as a communication function, or perhaps simply as a particular kind of situation in which communication occurs. Every distinct social situation, field of activity, and cultural community has its own communication problems, practices, and ideals that need to be understood in their own terms. In this perspective, communication can be divided very finely into a myriad of overlapping contextual fields of religious communication, business communication, family communication, communication in education, communication in particular ethnic and cultural groups, and so on—finally, the innumerable, mundane categories of human interaction.

Current Trends. The discipline of communication has grown enormously in recent decades and continues to evolve. Some of the more important current trends in communication studies can be encapsulated in four emerging themes: technology, culture, discourse, and practice.

The first theme is technology. The present era is one of dizzying technological change, so rapid that we lack a conceptually stable language with which to describe it. Information has become a fungible commodity, transferable from any medium to any other. Twenty years ago, the television and the telephone were clearly two distinct technologies. Twenty years from now, the proliferating array of telecommunication devices may be classified quite differently. As we noted earlier, technological change is reshuffling the levels and functions of communication. Competence and critical awareness in the use of new media become important goals of communication education, but the contents of this learning are difficult to codify and expensive to keep up-to-date. Every tradition of communication theory is challenged to conceptualize new technology. The rhetoric of visual images, the phenomenology of virtual reality, the social psychology of e-mail, sociocultural community in cyberspace, and, perhaps most importantly, critical analysis and debunking of the ideology underlying much of the hype that currently surrounds technology, become topics for investigation.

A second emerging theme is culture. Culture converges with technology in critical cultural studies of technological practices, ethnographic studies of virtual communities, and so on. But culture is also an important theme in its own right. With increasing global interdependence, cultural diversity and change become visible everywhere and raise inescapable questions. Cross-cultural diffusion raises questions of neoimperialist cultural domination. Intercultural communication loses its distinct character as we become more aware of the interplay of cultural identity and difference in all communication. Gender, class, racial, ethnic, and national identities are always at stake, whether in media representations or workplace interactions. The performance of these identities, and their often subtle negotiation, become critical elements of communicative practice in multicultural societies. Much traditional communication theory and research has been implicitly ethnocentric and patriarchal. "We" studied the communication behavior of males, and occasionally of females in comparison with a male standard, and seldom questioned whether such categories might be defined differently except in "other" cultures. This approach is no longer intellectually or politically acceptable. Traditional ethnographic studies of communication in various cultural communities continue to be important. But every branch of communication studies is now challenged to address the cultural dimensions of communication and to recognize its own constitutive role in the production of culture.

A third trend is to conceptualize communication as discourse. Discourse is language in use, or more broadly, the interactive production of meaning. The theme of discourse is significant in several dimensions. In one dimension, it represents an effort to understand in greater detail the process by which communication actually occurs, beyond merely summarizing the process in abstract models and categories. It is no longer enough to count the number of experts who appear on television talk shows or to classify the types of advice they provide. The trend now is to ask exactly how "expertise" is constituted in the discourse among participants on stage and in the audience, and how this negotiation of the expert role relates to other discourses on matters such as legitimate knowledge and authority, selfhood, and the boundary between private and public spheres. In another dimension, discourse represents a point of convergence between rhetoric and other traditions of communication theory. It brings a rhetorical perspective to our understanding of forms of communication (such as personal interaction) that were not traditionally thought of as rhetoric. And it enriches the rhetorical perspective with insights and techniques from pragmatics, conversation analysis, cultural studies, and other fields. In a third dimension, discourse represents a movement toward understanding communication as practice; that is, as meaningful, situated, morally accountable action.

Practice, then, is a fourth theme that encapsulates current trends in communication. In recent years, it has become more academically respectable, and more intellectually interesting, to admit that communication is a practical discipline. Throughout the field, applied studies, critical studies, community-based action research, attention to normative, ethical, and educational issues, and, in general, the idea that academic work ought to address socially relevant practical concerns, are both more common and more esteemed in high places than they used to be. The forces that have contributed to this shift are numerous, but the tradition of rhetoric as a practical art within communication studies is surely one

of them. Contrary to what might be expected, the trend toward practice has not been accompanied by a rejection of theory. Communication theory is now flourishing as never before. Rather, the traditional separation of practice from theory has been challenged by alternative views. Some of those alternative views have been informed by an Aristotelian tradition of practical philosophy in which the art of rhetoric was closely associated with political *praxis*. In this tradition, practice requires judgment as well as skill, and both judgment and skill can be informed and cultivated with the help of theory that is specifically designed to serve those ends. The challenge to communication studies is not to elevate practice over theory, but to develop more practical theories for the cultivation of better and more reflective communication practices.

Metadiscourse, Theory, and Practice. Communication theory has sometimes aspired to transcend the mundane. Communication on a very abstract plane is universal. Planet and moon, flower and bee, lover and beloved, all communicate, all exist in reciprocal relations, all emit and respond to signals according to laws of physics and laws of information. Cybernetics reveled in such analogies, which inspired visions of a fundamental communication theory to rival the theories of Newton and Einstein.

If that mid-twentieth-century vision was grandiose, the reality has been grand enough in some ways. The abstract model of communication as information and signal transmission is a hallmark of the Information Age. It has been usefully applied in engineering and science, biology, psychology, and social science. Ironically, its role in the theory and practice of human discourse has been more limited and may even have diminished, relatively speaking, despite the current vogue of communication technology and the associated efflorescence of cybertalk. In a transmission model of communication, human interaction is merely one among many examples of information processing, less attractive to science than others, perhaps, because it is so complex and difficult to analyze. In the constitutive model that communication theorists now tend to prefer, information theory is merely one among many examples of *metadiscourse*, one way of constituting "communication" within the act of communication.

Practical metadiscourse, or reflexive discourse-about-discourse, occurs abundantly in human interaction. In everyday conversation, "the second point I want to make" could be a bit of metadiscourse used to bracket and introduce a segment of talk. "That's a promise" could be a bit of metadiscourse used to constitute what has just been said as a promise. "There was too much noise in the channel" could be a bit of metadiscourse used to make an excuse for a failure of communication. That last example happens to draw from the language of information theory. It illustrates one way in which theoretical metadiscourse, the formal discourse of communication theory, can be used in practical metadiscourse. Theory becomes a resource for constituting communication as an object of discussion in a particular way, for some practical purpose.

The entire field of communication—the discourse about models of communication, traditions of communication theory, disciplines, functions, codes, media, levels, contexts, technology, culture, discourse, and practice—is a vast metadiscourse that constitutes "communication" as an object for systematic study and critical reflection for many different purposes. Of the various ways in which rhetoric can be related to communication, one of the most currently useful may be to conceptualize communication theory as a *rhetoric of communication*. Classical rhetorical theory, as other articles in this encyclopedia amply demonstrate, provides a rich storehouse of topical categories, lines of argument, and figures of speech useful for crafting persuasive messages on public affairs. Rhetorical *stases* assist the communicator in defining the issues under dispute in a given situation, and rhetorical topics assist in finding arguments with which to address those issues. [*See* Stasis; *and* Topics.]

Just as rhetorical theory provides resources for participating in discourses on public affairs, communication theory provides resources for practical metadiscourse, that is, for participating in discourses on communication. This suggests one way of connecting communication theory to practice: Communication theory is to the practice of communication as rhetorical theory is to the practice of public affairs. Rhetorical theory

can affect public affairs indirectly, by informing what Thomas B. Farrell has called the norms of rhetorical culture (*Norms of Rhetorical Culture*, New Haven, 1993)—the climate of beliefs and habits that shapes the discourses in which we negotiate and conduct public affairs. So, communication theory can affect the practice of communication in society indirectly, by informing the practical metadiscourse in which we negotiate and conduct communication. Thus, academic communication studies, including rhetorical studies, can participate actively in societal discourses that ultimately constitute what we might call the norms of communicative culture.

BIBLIOGRAPHY

Arnold, Carroll C., and John Waite Bowers, eds. *Handbook of Rhetorical and Communication Theory*. Boston, 1984. Defines rhetoric as purposive communication. A functional approach with major review chapters on processing information, changing attitudes, pleasing, etc.

Barnouw, Erik, George Gerbner, Wilbur Schramm, Tobia L. Worth, and Larry Gross, eds. *International Encyclopedia of Communications*. 4 vols. New York, 1989. Comprehensive reference emphasizing media, history, and multidisciplinary perspectives.

Berger, Charles R., and Steven H. Chaffee, eds. *Handbook of Communication Science*. Newbury Park, Calif., 1987. Literature reviews, primarily of social psychological communication research, organized by levels, functions, and contexts. Includes a fine chapter by Delia on the history of the field.

Carey, James W. *Communication as Culture: Essays on Media and Society*. Winchester, Mass., 1989. Media history and cultural studies based on a ritual model of communication.

Deetz, Stanley A. *Democracy in an Age of Corporate Colonization: Developments in Communication and the Politics of Everyday Life*. Albany, N.Y., 1992. Critical theory of communication as a constitutive process, emphasizes organizational communication.

Ellis, Donald G. *Crafting Society: Ethnicity, Class, and Communication Theory*. Mahwah, N.J., 1999. Theoretical essays on the link between microcommunication activities and macrosocial categories such as race and class.

Hauser, Marc D. *The Evolution of Communication*. Cambridge, Mass., 1996. Excellent survey of the evolution of auditory and visual signals in a wide range of animal species, including humans.

Leeds-Hurwitz, Wendy. *Communication in Everyday Life: A Social Interpretation*. Norwood, N.J., 1989. Readable presentation of a sociocultural approach rooted in ethnography and microsociology.

Littlejohn, Stephen W. *Theories of Human Communication.* 6th ed. Belmont, Calif., 1999. Currently the most comprehensive textbook.

Mattelart, Armand. *The Invention of Communication.* Translated by Susan Emanuel. Minneapolis, 1996. Social history as an "archaeology of knowledge"; how communication came to be associated with the idea of progress.

McLuhan, Marshall. *Understanding Media: The Extensions of Man.* New York, 1964. Technological determinist media history and prophecy.

McQuail, Denis. *Mass Communication Theory: An Introduction.* 3d ed. London, 1994. Broad overview of media studies.

Pearce, W. Barnett. *Communication and the Human Condition.* Carbondale, Ill., 1989. Essay on forms of communication and ways of being, with "CMM" theory as a constitutive model.

Peters, John Durham. *Speaking into the Air: A History of the Idea of Communication.* Chicago, 1999. Beautifully written essay on the origins of communication as "a registry of modern longings."

Pilotta, Joseph J., and Algis Mickunas. *Science of Communication: Its Phenomenological Foundation.* Hillsdale, N.J., 1990.

Rogers, Everett M. *A History of Communication Study: A Biographical Approach.* New York, 1994. Twentieth-century founders and forerunners of social scientific communication research.

Rothenbuhler, Eric W. *Ritual Communication: From Everyday Conversation to Mediated Ceremony.* Thousand Oaks, Calif., 1998. Rituals and ceremonies as symbolic forms of communication linking individuals to the social order.

Schiller, Dan. *Theorizing Communication: A History.* New York, 1996. Critical history showing how communication theory has participated in the ideological split between intellectual and manual labor.

Taylor, Talbot J. *Mutual Misunderstanding: Scepticism and the Theorizing of Language and Interpretation.* Durham, N.C., 1992. Deconstruction of language theory since Locke as intellectual metadiscourse.

Watzlawick, Paul, Janet Helmick Beavin, and Don D. Jackson. *Pragmatics of Human Communication: A Study of Interactional Patterns, Pathologies, and Paradoxes.* New York, 1967. Influential cybernetic analysis of relational communication as a basis for therapeutic intervention.

—ROBERT T. CRAIG

COMPARATIVE RHETORIC is the cross-cultural study of rhetorical traditions, past or present, in societies around the world. Comparison of the rhetorical practices of two or more cultures can help identify features in one that might not be evident otherwise. The larger objectives of comparative study include trying to identify what is universal and what distinctive in any rhetorical tradition, including that of the West; formulating a general theory of rhetoric applicable to all societies and languages; testing structures and terminologies, Western or other, that can describe rhetorical practices cross-culturally; and applying what is learned to contemporary communication. Comparative rhetoric as an area of communication studies was a new development of the late twentieth century, when some students of rhetoric became concerned about the bias implicit in approaching rhetoric as an exclusively Western phenomenon. It remains, however, heavily dependent on fieldwork and other research by anthropologists, biologists, historians, and linguists that provide evidence for the forms and functions of speech in individual cultures around the world. Their publications describe and discuss political oratory, deliberation, judicial procedures, ceremonial rituals, and similar matters in which rhetoric is a factor, but often without using the word *rhetoric* in the descriptions and with only occasional comparison to practices elsewhere. Sensitivity on the part of a student of comparative rhetoric is needed to appreciate the values of societies in which technology has been little exploited and where cultural practices may seem strange to Western observers.

Rhetoric as a Natural Faculty. There are analogies to rhetoric in features of communication among nonhuman animals that live in groups and seek to influence each other's actions by utterance or gesture. Social animals, as they are called, use a variety of oral, visual, and chemical signs to persuade others to do what they want, primarily in connection with mating, dominating territory, securing food, and defense of the group. Intentionality in animal life covers a wide spectrum from virtually none in the simplest amebas to consciousness of self and of the motives of others in the higher apes. Examples of animal communication with rhetorical features, discussed by Dorothy L. Cheney and Robert M. Seyfarth in *How Monkeys See the World* (Chicago, 1990), are the six acoustically different alarm calls given by vervet monkeys, specifying potential danger to their group from leopards, eagles, snakes, smaller mammals, baboons, and humans; in addition, their grunts differ on the basis of whether addressed to a subordinate or a dominant monkey, or indicating movement into the open or warning that another group of monkeys is approaching. Animals in search of food or a mate also sometimes use vocal signs to deceive others of the same species. Acoustic virtuosity is extensive among birds, but the greatest development of mental skills in communication is found among apes, some of whom have been taught sign language or the use of a keyboard to communicate with human beings and each other. Chimpanzees and gorillas are closely related genetically to human beings; human language has probably evolved from the sounds made by common ancestors of apes and present-day humans.

Many animals perform epideictic rituals; there are examples among birds, and among mammals the morning duet of mated gibbons is a striking instance. It is important in the cohesion of the pair, who mate for life. Honey bees engage in a kind of deliberation when swarming in search of a new home. There is less evidence for judicial rhetoric on the part of animals, although some clearly engage in judgment of each other's activity and may succeed in driving a deviant animal from the group. Animal communication shares elements of invention, arrangement, style, and delivery with human rhetoric. Like monkeys, birds have different calls with different meanings and their songs follow a variety of arrangements, amplified by repetition, variation, combination, and substitution of themes. Among figures of speech heard in bird song are *anaphora, homoeoteleuton* (its opposite), and *paronomasia*. Some intelligent animals learn to understand and even to use metonymy, but metaphor, simile, and articulated logical arguments are distinctively human. [*See* Classical rhetoric; Figures of speech; *and* Style.]

Rhetoric in some form is thus a basic feature of human and nonhuman life, a tool in the survival of both species and individuals. It can be described as a form of mental and physical energy, reacting to a challenge, need, or desire by producing and transmitting signs to a real or imagined audience. The simplest natural rhetorical techniques, exploited by humans and other animals alike, are volume, pitch, and repetition in oral messages and the use of gestures.

Rhetoric in Societies without Writing. Ethnologists have collected much information about the forms and function of speech and techniques of persuasion in traditional societes of the recent past or present in Africa, Australia, the South Pacific, and the Americas. Most public speaking in traditional cultures can be classified as deliberative or epideictic; judicial oratory is largely undeveloped, except under Western influence, but a novel exception are the "song duels" used by Eskimos. The "songs," or speeches, are characterized by boasts of power and insults of the opponent and are used to settle quarrels over women without resorting to physical force. [*See* Epideictic genre; *and* Forensic genre.]

Formal deliberation is a regular feature of egalitarian societies, where some individuals gain reputations as orators, and in hierarchic societies recognized orators are employed as spokesmen for kings, chiefs, and priests. The goal of deliberation in traditional societies is usually consensus, real or imposed, and opponents are offered the opportunity to "save face" by seeming to compromise. Rhetoric in this context is ordinarily a conservative or corrective force, not an instrument of social or political change. [*See* Deliberative genre.]

The primary means of persuasion is the authority or *ēthos* of the speaker, deriving from age, sex, family, experience, and skill at speaking. [*See* Ēthos.] In some American Indian councils, almost the whole of a speech could be devoted to the speaker's deeds, thus establishing his right to give advice, with only a brief statement at the end of his specific proposal. The arrangement of content everywhere usually conforms to a pattern traditional for the particular kind of occasion or subject. There is much repetition in most traditional speeches and little explicit logical reasoning, though references to myth, legend, history, and proverbs may supply examples of what should be done in support of the speaker's proposition, and statements sometimes take enthymematic form (i.e., a conclusion with a reason for it), but often without inferential particles such as words meaning *because* or *therefore*. "Formal language" is required of speakers on official occasions everywhere and is learned by imitation of earlier speakers; it often has archaic elements of diction and grammar, as well as observing conventions of etiquette and arrangement, and makes use of proverbs, examples, and traditional metaphors.

Epideictic speech, as understood in the West, has its best non-Western parallels in religious rituals, where extreme forms of formal language, often archaic and incomprehensible to the general audience, are employed, frequently accompanied by music and dance. The use of Latin by the Roman Catholic Church and by scholars throughout the Middle Ages and Renaissance is a Western example of the use of a formal language. As it does in secular deliberations, a formal, ritual language seems to certify the authenticity or truth of what is said and helps chiefs and priests to perpetuate conservative social control over the society. Among many examples of formal discourse in non-Western societies, Aztec *huehuetlatolli* from Mexico show an unusually complex development of rhetorical artistry in a variety of epideictic speech genres, some analogous to those of Greco-Roman culture. Many examples of Aztec speeches were written down by Frey Bernardino de Sahagún and others in the sixteenth century, when the genre was still flourishing.

Indirect language and the use of allegory are features of public speaking in many cultures—sometimes used within a group that does not want outsiders to understand, sometimes used to protect personal space in situations where everybody knows everybody else. Allegory is sometimes cast in poetic form, using parallelism; in some cultures, such as that of the Cuna on the coastal islands of Panama, lengthy speeches are chanted by chiefs giving advice to the people in poetic form. [*See* Allegory.]

In most traditional cultures, sorcery and magic constitute a rhetorical genre, difficult to classify as deliberative or epideictic since speakers do not seek "persuasion" as it is usually understood. The words of a magical incantation, public or private, when properly performed are thought to control and constrain the activities of a spirit, a force of nature, other people, or physical objects, and sorcerers can, by secret words and actions, bring disease and death upon others living at a distance. From a scientific point of view, the rhetoric of magic works not on the nominal addressee but on the human participants and observers, in whom feelings of hope or revenge or other emo-

tions are instilled or strengthened. As such, magic should probably be regarded as a special kind of epideictic rhetoric. One of the few early ethnographers to make explicit reference to rhetoric and to use some rhetorical terminology was Bronislaw Malinowski in his classic work, *Argonauts of the Western Pacific* (London, 1922), which describes the culture of the Trobriand islanders, including rhetorical features of their magic.

A nonliterate culture, in which language and rhetoric have been extensively studied, is that of the aboriginal inhabitants of Australia. They had little or no contact with people outside their island continent for many thousands of years and continued to live in Stone-Age conditions until after British exploration of the interior in the nineteenth century. The aboriginals had little in the way of political structures: no regularly established councils, assemblies, or law courts, and unlike many other cultures they had no official orators. Formal language of an archaic sort, however, was highly developed among them and demanded in performances of myth and ritual. The primary means of persuasion was the authority of a speaker. Wisdom, based on age, experience, and knowledge of religious practices was a powerful influence, but this wisdom was not expressed in general terms; it was implied by citing specific instances. Logical argument took the form of the juxtaposition of a conclusion with a statement giving a reason, but without inferential particles. Metaphor was frequent, but explicitly stated similes seem to have been unknown. Australian myth and song exhibit a basic arrangement of beginning, middle, and end; parallelism, as known in the West from the Hebrew Psalms, was a regular feature of aboriginal poetic composition and is found in many other cultures as well.

There is a large amount of scholarship on American Indian rhetoric, some of it by students of speech communication using rhetorical concepts and based on speeches transcribed by explorers or settlers or on surviving Indian practices. Indian tribes were usually egalitarian; any man and sometimes women could speak in their assemblies, where the object of deliberation was consensus. Judicial rhetoric was undeveloped, but epideictic forms were practiced when war parties were sent out, at funerals, and on religious occasions. Use of formal language was largely restricted to medicine men and religious rites. Indian speakers sought persuasion primarily by the *ēthos* of the speaker. Although traditional analogies from nature and daily life were common, there was little use of metaphor in comparison to other cultures, nor did Indians traditionally use proverbs or oaths in their speeches.

The earliest versions of North American Indian oratory are found in *The Florida* by Garcilaso de la Vega, (Spain, 1605; translation by John G. and Jeanette J. Varner; Austin, 1951). Among famous examples of Indian rhetoric are the letter of the Mingo chief, Logan, to the governor of Virginia in 1774, quoted and praised by Thomas Jefferson as equal to the eloquence of Demosthenes or Cicero in Query VI of *Notes on the State of Virginia;* speeches by the Seneca chief Red Jacket (c.1756–1830), distinguished by his use of irony; and Chief Joseph's pathetic message to the federal commander after the Indian defeat at Eagle Creek, Montana, in 1877. Between 1745 and 1815, as Indian tribes were being pushed west by white settlement of eastern North America, a pan-Indian movement appeared in the Midwest and South; the most famous leaders were Pontiac in the eighteenth century and Tecumseh in the early nineteenth. Rhetorical themes in this movement included the need for Indians to redress the anger of the Great Spirit by ritual cleansing; the doctrine that Christianity had been given to the whites by the white god while the Indians had been separately created by the Great Spirit; and millenianism, found in other cultures when under stress, the promise of the coming of a savior and a return to the better conditions of the past. Indian messiahs appeared again at the end of the nineteenth century in the western United States, creating the Ghost Dance Religion, of which some features were revived in the twentieth century.

Rhetoric in Early Literate Societies. The invention of writing in Mesopotamia in the late third millenium BCE and its spread to Egypt, Greece, India, and elsewhere, as well as the unrelated invention of writing in China and its spread to Japan, clearly had some influence on rhetoric, though definition and proof of that influence is controversial. Scribes in Mesopotamia and Egypt celebrated their craft and obtained considerable power as necessary intermediaries between illiterate rulers and the general populace. Writing made possible communication over distance, record keeping, scientific and historical research, crystalization of oral poetic texts, creation of textbooks, and standardization of grammar. It probably facilitated thinking about abstractions, intricate logical argument, and the use of complex sentences. In contrast to references to writing, there is no explicit discussion of speech in Mesopotamian records, though there are many examples of speeches in the epic *Gilgamesh* and elsewhere.

The ancient Egyptians were more self-conscious about rhetorical composition. The story of "The Eloquent Peasant," for example, written in the early second millenium BCE, describes the case of a peasant who has been robbed of his goods and appeals to the high steward in a series of eloquent speeches combining ordinary language with elevated formal prose (translation in W. K. Simpson, ed. *The Literature of Egypt,* pp. 31–49. New Haven, 1972). *The Instructions* (or *Maxims) of Ptahhotep,* an example of wisdom literature dating from around 2000 BCE, has been called the oldest rhetorical handbook. It consists largely of unsystematic precepts about effective speech and about how people of different ranks should conduct themselves. Michael V. Fox has found in it five canons or rules of Egyptian rhetoric ("Ancient Egyptian Rhetoric." In *Rhetorica* 1, 1983, pp. 21–34): keeping silent, waiting for the right moment, restraining passion, speaking fluently with deliberation, and speaking the truth. Rather similar injunctions can be found in Hebrew in the biblical book of Proverbs. [*See* Hebrew rhetoric.]

Rhetoric in China and India. Of particular interest for comparative rhetoric is the study of rhetoric in China, where thousands of speeches, as well as handbooks of composition, rhetorical exercises, and critical, historical, and poetic writings, dating from antiquity to modern times, provide a rich source for comparative research. Confucianists, cosmologists, Mohists, Taoists, Legalists, and others expressed ideas about speech in the period between the sixth and third centuries BCE. One remarkable writer toward the end of this era was Han-fei-tzu (born about 280 BCE), sometimes called "the Machiavelli of China" because of his pragmatic, cynical teaching to rulers about how to employ rhetoric to solidify their power (*Basic Writings,* translated by Burton Watson. New York, 1967). In the early centuries of the common era, Chinese scholars produced moralizing and allegorizing commentaries on the Chinese classics that employ an extensive terminology, sometimes resembling but often differing from rhetorical concepts in the West. [*See* Chinese rhetoric.]

Comparable developments occurred in ancient India, where the early epics, *Mahabharata* and *Ramayana,* include speeches and debates analogous to those of the Homeric epic in Greece, and Brahmin and Buddhist philosophers later engaged in rhetorical contests. The *Arthashastra* of Kautilya (about 300 BCE; translated by Rudrapatna Shamasastry, Mysore, 1967) outlines a rhetoric of power and provides extensive technical terminology for teaching and criticizing rhetoric. Poetic and dramatic theory was later developed in India to a high degree of sophistication. [*See* Indian rhetoric.]

Western and Non-Western Rhetoric Compared. Societies all over the world have admired effective and eloquent orators. Rough approximations to the abstract term *rhetoric* can be found in Chinese, Egyptian, and a few other languages, but most of the world's languages have a word for *orator,* and almost everywhere orators have recognized functions in deliberation. Ability at speaking is partly a natural endowment, but enhanced by listening to older speakers to learn traditional techniques and topics, by imitating good speakers, and by opportunities to practice in private or in public.

In comparison with other traditions, Western rhetorical practice, beginning with the early Greeks as seen in the Homeric epics, has been more tolerant of contention, personal invective, and flattery, less insistent on consensus, politeness, and restraint than is commonly true elsewhere. Ancient Indian epics, however, show similar rivalries among the Aryan heroes, who were distant relatives of the argumentative Greeks, and there are a few societies, such as the Maori in New Zealand, noted for their ferocity or quarreling. Shouts of acclamation or a waving of hands as a show of unanimity are common tribal demonstrations; the Greeks, however, invented the actual counting of votes as a way of settling political and legal disputes, something unknown else-

where until modern times. Although voting can perform that function, its potential acceptance of a majority of one as determinative can sharpen disagreement and resentment. Artistic judicial rhetoric, with argument from probability and exploitation of circumstantial evidence in court, is largely a Western phenomenon; some examples of it can be cited from ancient Near Eastern texts, but it was principally developed in the law courts of democratic Athens in the fifth and fourth centuries BCE.

Although eloquent judicial oratory is thus a characteristic Western phenomenon, deliberative oratory has been practiced everywhere, as noted above. Epideictic oratory is also universal in the broad sense of speeches or rituals at festival or on ceremonial occasions. Formal oratory has usually required some degree of "formal language"; in a simple form this may be only an expectation that a speaker will use complete sentences, correct grammar and pronunciation, and polite titles in reference to others (e.g., "my honorable friend"), but the occasion may be thought to require the use of archaic language (e.g., "Four score and seven years ago. . . ."), and in extreme cases, a formal language may not be comprehensible to most in the audience. Formal languages have to be learned, and requirements for their use are often a form of social control by rulers or priests, limiting access to public opinion. The function of rhetoric in human society has been predominantly the preservation of the status quo, with only occasional exceptions, such as the efforts of the Buddhist king Asoka (c.274–234 BCE) in India to improve tolerance and understanding among his people. Even in the West, rhetoric was rarely a tool of political change until the revolutionary propagandists of the eighteenth century.

The Sophists in the fifth century BCE were among the earliest teachers of speaking skills in classical Greece. [*See* Sophists.] They celebrated the power of speech and expounded philosophical relativism or skepticism, questioning traditional beliefs and indulging a fascination with paradoxes and linguistic experimentation. They taught skills in public speaking, chiefly by composing and delivering speeches that illustrated forms of argument, arrangement, and style, which their students could imitate. Something analogous to Greek sophistry had appeared in India by the sixth century BCE, where it can be found in debates by Brahmins on metaphysical or religious issues. It appeared in China in the fourth and third centuries BCE in the logical wrangling of Mohist philosophers. Sophistry is unknown in nonliterate cultures. It seems to be a phenomenon of the development of literate and "sophisticated" cultures when there is wealth, leisure, and refinement of artistic taste, where there are competing philosophical schools, and where itinerant teachers seek to impress audiences with their verbal skills, to acquire followers, and to gain influence with rulers.

When rhetoric has been conceptualized and taught outside the West, as in China, India, and Egypt, it has been regarded as an aspect of politics, ethical philosophy, or literary criticism, and not as a separate discipline within a standard curriculum of the liberal arts, which has been its role in Western schools and universities. The Western approach to rhetoric as an academic discipline is an inheritance from the Greeks, for whom rhetorical skill was an essential feature of citizenship. Rhetoric was first treated as an academic discipline by Aristotle (384–322 BCE), who gave separate programs of lectures on rhetoric, politics, ethics, and other subjects. Rhetorical schools were a regular feature of Greek and Roman education from the fourth century BCE into the Byzantine period.

Greek and Latin rhetoricians divided their rhetorical precepts into five arts or canons that recapitulate the act of planning, composing, and delivering a speech. In English, these five arts are called invention, arrangement, style, memory, and delivery. This is a pedagogical approach, artificial especially in its separation of thought or content from words or style. There seems no exact parallel in non-Western thought or teaching.

Of the three means of persuasion identified by Aristotle, *ēthos, pathos,* and *logos, ēthos,* the character of the speaker, is the most prevalent everywhere. The extent to which *pathos,* stirring the emotions, is an acceptable speech technique varies widely with the culture and the occasion. Human beings, even in the most primitive conditions, have an understanding of cause and effect, but a complex chain of logical argument is not a feature of persuasion in nonliterate societies. Argument from examples—mythological, historical, experiential, or analogical—has probably

been the most common form of reasoning all over the world, and proverbs are a basis of demonstration in many cultures, though often universal propositions are not articulated. Argument from probability, arguing for the likelihood of an action on the basis of the character of a person or the circumstances, is occasionally found in ancient Near-Eastern texts but is rare or nonexistent elsewhere, except when introduced under Western influence. It was greatly exploited by the Greeks, especially for use in judicial rhetoric. [*See* Ēthos; Logos; *and* Pathos.]

The most natural and most universal rhetorical tropes are metaphor, synecdochē, and metonymy. The earliest form of metaphor was probably personification, including anthropomorphization of animals and natural objects, reflecting an animistic worldview. Most non-Indo-European languages do not, or have not traditionally, articulated similes, that is, they did not differentiate simile from metaphor by words of comparison. Figures of speech, such as *anaphora,* alliteration, or assonance, probably came to early human speech from song and are common in most cultures, as is parallelism in verse composition. Such devices impart emphasis, and like verse and prose rhythm, facilitate memorization of formulas and topics. Among figures of thought, the most common everywhere seems to be the rhetorical question, which, along with apostrophē, carries an especially high degree of rhetorical energy, originating in the emotion of the speaker and evocative of the emotion of the audience.

Comparative rhetoric is a difficult and can be a daunting field of study because of the amount of material deserving consideration and the diversity of languages and cultures involved. [*See* Arabic rhetoric; *and* Slavic rhetoric.] Western concepts and rhetorical terms are not always entirely applicable, but one objective of comparative study is to test them against non-Western practices. Although some conclusions about differences between European rhetorical traditions and practices elsewhere seem clear, the forms and functions of rhetoric in many of the world's cultures have not yet been systematically studied or the results of research have not yet been integrated into a total picture. In particular, central South America, parts of Africa, Central Asia, and Southeast Asia have been little studied, and Germanic, Scandanavian, Anglo-Saxon, and Icelandic rhetorics have not yet been brought into the general picture.

BIBLIOGRAPHY

Abbott, Don P. *Rhetoric in the New World: Rhetorical Theory and Practice in Colonial Spanish America.* Columbia, S.C., 1996.

Bloch, Maurice, ed. *Political Language and Oratory in Traditional Society.* London, 1975. Studies of deliberative rhetoric in Madagascar, parts of Africa, Indonesia, the Philippines, and Samoa.

Brendt, Ronald M., and Catherine H. Brendt. *The World of the First Australians.* 5th ed. Canberra, 1988.

Brenneis, Donald, and Fred. R. Myers, eds. *Dangerous Words: Language and Politics in the Pacific.* Prospect Heights, Ill., 1991. Studies reporting on rhetorical traditions in the South Pacific, including the use of indirect language.

Deeney, John J., ed. *Chinese-Western Comparative Literature: Theory and Strategy.* Hong Kong, 1980.

Dowd, Gregory E. *A Spirited Resistance: The North American Indian Struggle for Unity, 1745–1815.* Baltimore, 1992.

Graham, Angus C. *Disputers of the Tao: Philosophical Argument in Ancient China.* LaSalle, Ill., 1989.

Hoebel, E. Adamson. *The Law of Primitive Man: A Study of Comparative Legal Dynamics.* Cambridge, Mass., 1964.

Irvine, Judith T. "Formality and Informality in Communicative Events," *American Anthropologist* 81 (1979), pp. 773–790. Fundamental description and definition of the concept of "formal language."

Kennedy, George A. *Comparative Rhetoric: An Historical and Cross-Cultural Introduction.* New York, 1998. Contains chapters on rhetoric among social animals, in Australian and some other nonliterate cultures, among North American Indians, in the ancient New East, in China, in India, in Greece, with a concluding chapter comparing Western and non-Western rhetoric; extensive bibliography.

Kroeber, Karl, ed. *Traditional Literatures of the American Indian: Texts and Interpretations.* Lincoln, Nebr., 1981.

Lang, David. M., ed. *A Guide to Eastern Literatures.* London, 1971.

Lichtheim, Miriam, ed. *Ancient Egyptian Literature.* 2 vols. Berkeley, 1973, 1976. Translations of a variety of important texts from different periods.

Lu, Xing. *Rhetoric in Ancient China, Fifth to Third Century B.C.E: A Comparison with Classical Rhetoric.* Columbia, S.C., 1999.

Oliver, Robert T. *Communication and Culture in Ancient India and China.* Syracuse, N.Y., 1971.

Sherzer, Joel, and Anthony C. Woodbury. *Native American Discourse.* Cambridge, U.K., 1987.

— George A. Kennedy

COMPOSITION. [*This entry comprises two articles. The first article provides a brief overview. The second article describes a history of English departments in the United States.*]

An overview

Composition is literally a putting together of things. One of the earliest recorded uses of the word in English vernacular is in Thomas Wilson's *Arte of Rhetorique* (1553): "Composicion . . . is an apte joynyng together of wordes in suche order, that neither the eare shal espie any jerre, nor yet any man shal be dulled with overlong drawing out of a sentence . . ." (fol. 88). In practice, however, our understanding of composition is more capacious than any historically or etymologically specific definitions. Composition is more than a putting together of things.

Composition is an intellectual specialty for seeing, making, and doing—which encompasses processes as well as products. Although composition serves as a product of and for criticism, it also guides the processes through which invention and judgment are conducted. [*See* Invention; *and* Judgment.] Composition can proceed through and manifest itself in many media, forms, and genres, but here the focus is on speech and writing. These senses of the composition of writing and speech—seeing, making, and doing, as manifested in processes as well as products—are customarily disciplined and kept from one another; this entry endeavors to bring them together and to articulate composition's various liaisons with rhetoric. The historical, theoretical, and practical relationships of rhetoric to composition became *topoi* for scholarly argument in composition studies, conducted largely through departments of English in the last three decades of the twentieth century. Composition as a category, however, provides an important means of seeing past disciplinary distinctions among the production, reception, study, and teaching of historically distant texts, canonical and noncanonical literature, speech, writing, public discourse, and other forms of rhetoric.

In early Western practices of rhetoric, oral composition—motivated by various muses and conducted through commonplaces of invention and memory—actualized words and deeds. The composition of the rhapsode, the tales of the characters, and the social importance of the mythology revealed the inextricability of words and deeds. In Homeric traditions, composition was not simply a collection of concepts but rather a mode of action. Conversely, for the wordy Greek heroes, doing was meaningless; action was not fully human if it was not accompanied by composed words. The Sophists' oral compositions highlighted the centrality of *kairos*, or the opportune moment, as well as the incredible power (*dynamis*) of composed words and their ability to generate change through the embodied discourses of the speaker. [*See* Kairos; *and* Sophists.] Gorgias claimed in his *Helen* (c.425 BCE) that words appropriately composed could remove blame from Helen and ignorance from his hearers. Oral composition allowed for the composition of worlds, however ephemeral. Whether through mythopoesis or cosmology, humans practicing composition could understand themselves as the measure of all things. [*See* Orality and literacy.]

Plato's (c.428–c.347 BCE) preference for an already-formed, divinely-composed world manifested his ambivalence toward human compositions other than his own. The world-making powers of composition frightened Plato, though he used them masterfully in his own inventions. Indeed, Plato's *Gorgias, Phaedrus,* and *Republic* suggest that Plato understood composition as seeing, making, and doing. Plato's *Gorgias* posited dialectical composition as a means of seeing beyond convention. His *Phaedrus* first blamed and then praised composition; Plato's Socrates declared the composition of Lysias false, but Plato's own compositions of the world in the myth of the charioteer and the genesis of soul-memory reflected Plato's deep roots in a Greek culture that honored the power of mythopoesis in human affairs. The *Republic* composed Plato's insights on the power of human composition into a working model for bringing the city (*polis*) more into conformity with the world (*cosmos*)—a model for

both theory and practice. Additionally, Plato's fear of writing and its consequences for memory suggested how ways of knowing affected attitudes toward the powers of composition. [*See* Classical rhetoric.]

Aristotle's (384–322 BCE) entelechial world required human making in a way that Plato's did not. The causal force of the Homeric muse in oral composition, a *daimōn* beyond human control, was replaced for Aristotle by the definitively human arts of rhetoric, politics, and poetics—all of which involved composition and all of which could be taught. Aristotle defined rhetoric as both intellectual specialty (*technē*) and power (*dynamis*). This double definition combined a Platonic sense of ideal rhetoric as a means of knowing the types of souls, and tailoring one's compositions to the improvement of those souls, with a sophistic sense of the awesome power of composition. Rhetoric, as an art of seeing and doing within the realm of politics, involved composition for the purposes (*teloi*) of public judgment (*krisis*); whereas poetics, as an art of making things from language, concerned the composition of dramas and poems for the strengthening of public values. [*See* Poetry.] Aristotle's reformulation of character from *tropos* to *ēthos* set out to discipline the composition of public subjectivity. [*See* Ēthos.] Along with the relative potential of invention, the composition of subjectivity in the context of democracy or in its absence is a thread that can be traced through the history of rhetoric and composition.

Aristotle also systematized the commonplaces— used by both speakers and poets, doers and makers—as composition technologies. [*See* Commonplaces and commonplace books; *and* Topics.] Though the similarities between rhetoric and poetics are many and significant (e.g., *dianoia, eikos, ēthos, krisis, metaphora, mythos, pathos*), over the intervening millennia, Aristotle's separate treatment of the two robbed poetic composition of its persuasive resonances and rhetorical composition of its pathetic and ethical means and ends.

Slightly earlier than Aristotle, Isocrates (436– 338 BCE) was not subject to the rhetoric/poetic divorce. Isocrates practiced written composition, first through his work as logographer—a writer of speeches for others to deliver—and later through his treatises composed for reading rather than oral delivery. The most popular composition teacher in Athens, Isocrates understood the world in terms that were largely antithetical to those of Plato. For Isocrates, the *polis* was the *kosmos,* and human composition was the only means of making and knowing the world; what the gods knew, humans could not know. Rather than *technē, kairos* was Isocrates' muse, as suggested by his varying treatments of the Spartans in his different discourses. Like the earlier Sophists, Isocrates taught by example; however, he also relied on the innate talent of the student and the study of the art of composition. Isocrates taught that the study and practice of composition (*logos*) enabled individuals and communities to learn virtue itself, thus troubling the distinction between the public (*polis*) and private (*oikos*) realms. [*See* Logos.]

Isocrates' emphasis on the importance of composition pedagogy for public life manifested itself in his most famous student, Timoteus. In addition to composing discourses, teachers help compose students: the teachings of the Sophist Gorgias (c.480–c.376 BCE) helped produce Isocrates; the teachings of the gadfly Socrates (c.470–399 BCE) helped produce the idealist Plato; the teachings of the dialectician Plato helped produce the systematizer Aristotle; Aristotle's emphasis on rhetoric as a branch of politics helped produce the conquerer Alexander the Great (356–323 BCE); and the teachings of the pragmatist Isocrates helped produce the learned soldier-citizen Timoteus (died 354 BCE).

Cicero (106–43 BCE) was a master of various composition practices, processes, and products— speeches, dialogues, treatises, and poems. Following Isocrates and the Sophistic tradition, composing in language was for Cicero an act of world making; he used the Latin *ornatus,* cognate with Greek *kosmos,* to describe figured language that composes a world. Cicero also followed Isocrates in his pragmatic use of composition for public as well as private life. His concern with the *vir bonus* suggests that he took composition to be important not only as a means of seeing, making, and doing in public, but also as a means of composing the virtuous public man. Cicero was the last ancient champion of composition as a means of invention. The work of Quintilian (c.35–c.100 CE), who systematized much of Cicero's occasionally rambling and inconsistent works on composi-

tion, was taught instead of Cicero—or along with the latter's *De inventione*—for hundreds of years. Quintilian's conception of the good man speaking well, particularly when this conception was aligned with Christianity, conflated public composition with private goodness in a way that persisted for nearly two millennia. As Christianity and empire limited the uses of invention, teachers placed increasing emphasis on the figures and tropes as important ends in themselves rather than as means of seeing, making, and doing. [*See* Figures of speech.] In a way unknown since Plato's moment, worlds came to be understood as preformed and outside of the reach of human composition.

As the church and monarchy replaced civil society, composition generally became focused more narrowly on form and product than on invention and process. Since neither the church nor the empire was susceptible to public argument, invention lost its place as the central power of composition, and the formal genres of medieval composition—the arts of letter writing (*dictaminis*), preaching (*praedicandi*), courtiership, and rule—became the staples of rhetorical education. [*See* Ars dictiminis.] Invention of the printing press and improvements in paper making made textbooks more common and written composition easier to teach. As the power of composition to invent knowledge became limited, generic products of composition became the focus of language study, teaching, and practice. The *progymnasmata* or elementary exercises of composition, though first practiced through oral composition by the Sophists, reached their apex during the Middle Ages and early Renaissance. The *progymnasmata* were commonly associated more with grammar and literary criticism than with rhetoric, but they were powerful means of habituating the composing process, largely through *imitatio.* These formal, grammatical approaches to composition in school prefigured Renaissance school rhetorics and, later, English grammar schools that so influenced what would become the canonical literature of the English Renaissance. While play was encouraged in grammatical exercises—witness the baroque inventions of Erasmus (c.1466– 1536)—such play was unthinkable with regard to knowledge, at least as the emerging empiricists understood it. This bifurcation of invention from human composition reached its extremity in the writings of Ramus (1515–1572 CE), who understood probabilistic knowledge—the basis of and occasion for composition in ancient times—as essentially in error. Similarly, seventeenth-century Cartesian logic held any statement to be in error that could admit doubt or argument; the potential of composition was thus radically limited to the presentation of what was prediscovered or preformed. [*See overview articles on* Medieval rhetoric *and* Renaissance rhetoric.]

The Cartesian emphasis on clear and distinct language spun yet another important thread in the history of composition. The Royal Society's attempt to strip language of any ornamentation—to make language transparent—manifested the conflicting epistemologies of rationalism and empiricism and their attitudes to composition. Vico's (1668–1744) understanding of composition through language as the very material of thought is a counterstatement to Enlightenment conceptions of contingency as error. Making arguments similar to those of Isocrates and other Sophists, Vico argued that humans can know only what they themselves have composed, not what God has composed.

While the Royal Society's edicts culminated in dictionaries and a proliferation of usage rules in English and other vernaculars, usually aping Latin, the same impulses led to the elocution movement—all attempts to discipline subjectivities of the emerging bourgeoisie through prescriptive composition. This emphasis on correctness in composition also pervades Adam Smith's lectures (1748), though he is more tolerant of the composition—or at least the communication—of character through style. The emphasis on style would culminate also in a movement known as belles-lettres, which attempted to reconcile literature and composition, most pointedly through the complicit ideologies of sublimity and taste. [*See* Style; *and* Sublime, the.]

Three figures, bridging the eighteenth and nineteenth centuries, shared an epistemological commitment to absolute knowledge of human nature that manifested itself in their attitudes toward composition, belles-lettres, and religion. For George Campbell (1719–1796), Hugh Blair (1718–1800), and Richard Whately (1787–1863), rhetoric regained its place as an art of doing, as

well as making—if not yet of seeing. Campbell's point of departure into empiricism was articulated through the Scottish ideology of common sense. He valued rhetoric but understood it as subservient to, rather than productive of, truth—composition was to be the handservant to science. Blair's focus on belles-lettres was driven by concepts of taste and sublimity, which produced a formalist approach to composition. Taste was learned from form rather than through invention, and judgments of taste, once formed, were subsequently to be portrayed as self-evident, at least to members and aspiring members of a certain identifiable class. Whately, more concerned with orality and argumentation, applied composition to argumentative rhetoric. In light of this epistemology, invention took a particular shape, and written composition became a clearly disciplined form of rhetoric. Composition was narrowed to argumentation on the one hand and to writing about literature on the other hand. Both argumentation and belletristic composition were taught as means of entry into an already existing class structure rather than as a means of transforming it. Given an epistemology that separated facts from values architectonically, the distinction between argumentation and belles-lettres paralleled the schism between a scientific view of the world into which there was no human input and a humanistic of the world into which there was only human input. [*See* Argumentation; Eighteenth-century rhetoric; *and* Nineteenth-century rhetoric.]

In Campbell, Blair, and Whately's formalist rhetorics began a tradition that was continued in the work of Alexander Bain, Adams Sherman Hill, Barrett Wendell, John Genung, and Fred Newton Scott, and later instantiated in academic departments of English and speech. "English composition" was increasingly about canonical literature read out of its dynamic context. In the service of class structure, composition was separated from its publicly productive and practical powers. While in the Middle Ages composition was separated from those powers by God and the sword, now the separation was effected by clergy and a canon.

Understanding composition as both a practical and a productive art reveals how composition practices in the eighteenth and nineteenth centuries consistently outpaced rhetorical theory as represented by such figures as Hill, Genung, and Bain. The vernacular would not stay disciplined, particularly in the context of revolution and expansion of participatory democracy as composed by such people as Mary Wollstonecraft (1759–1797), Frederick Douglass (1817–1895), Frances Wright (1795–1852), Walt Whitman (1819–1892), Sojourner Truth (c.1797–1883), Ida B. Wells (1862–1931), Elizabeth Cady Stanton (1815–1902), and Susan B. Anthony (1820–1906). While Nietzsche (1844–1900) enlivened rhetorical theory by recovering the Sophists, his contribution was insufficient for comprehending composition's practical and productive powers. Matthew Arnold's (1822–1888) theoretical program, by contrast, was designed to save humanism by reinvigorating its connection to belles-lettres. Thus began remarkably privatizing critical traditions that extend in English studies to our own day.

The twentieth century saw the institutionalization in higher education of various attitudes toward composition. After the National Council of Teachers of English broke away from the Modern Language Association in 1911 to emphasize the teaching of writing, speech teachers formed their own organization—the National Association for Academic Teachers of Public Speaking—three years later, desiring to focus on instruction in speech. Across the century, public speaking as a category of composition became separated from rhetorical criticism, much as the teaching of written composition became separated from literary criticism in English studies. [See Public speaking.] The Conference on College Composition and Communication, founded in 1949, provided a professional locus for academics in English studies who were interested primarily in written composition, and cleared a path for composition studies to emerge as a discipline separate from, but until recently operating primarily within, English studies.

Yet the roots of these schisms were at least as deep in practice as they were in concept. Since Descartes's (1596–1650) theoretical innovations had translated themselves into the work of Campbell, Blair, and Whately, the epistemologies of science and modernism had dominated composition theory. With the emergence of the twentieth century, critics like Henry Adams (1838–1918)—writing histories of change rather than of unalterable, theoretical permanence—revealed the need for composition to reclaim its balance. One answer to this need was provided by William James (1842–1910) and John Dewey (1859–1952), whose pragmatism drew composition back toward practice. As the twentieth century faced the development of both democracy and technology, self-composed subjects—academic, public, corporate, and intimate—have had to act in worlds that are constantly remade. This pragmatic and processual sense of composition suggests how rhetoric can provide an antidote to humanism, a way of balancing Arnoldian with Deweyan pragmatism—humanism with public commitments.

Pragmatic teachers and scholars across the twentieth century reread the classical figures of rhetoric, poetics, and other intellectual specialties to the end of recomposing pedagogy and practice. The Chicago school of neo-Aristotelians, led by philosopher Richard McKeon (1900–1985) and critic R. S. Crane (1886–1967), created a discursive environment where ancient rhetorical theories formed the pedagogical basis for undergraduate writing. The Hutchins College at the University of Chicago featured the likes of Richard Weaver, Wayne C. Booth, Edward P. J. Corbett, Albert Duhamel, James Sledd, and Wilma Ebbitt. James Kinneavy's rereading of ancient rhetoric, particularly the Sophistic touchstone *kairos*, enriched instruction in written composition and, with the work of many others—Ross Winterowd, James Murphy, Winifred Bryan Horner—laid an intellectual groundwork for the interdisciplinary turn in composition that has been taken up by scholars in rhetoric and composition. Interest in composition across the curriculum has manifested itself in academic programs that study rhetorics of science and other specific fields, using the work of Kenneth Burke (1895–1993) as a means of understanding the world-making powers of composed language. Exacerbated by technologies that blur literacy and orality, institutional distinctions between oral and written composition are beginning to dissolve at both the graduate and undergraduate levels in the early twenty-first century. The Rhetoric Society of America, organized in 1968, provides an transdisciplinary locus for scholars in several fields to collaborate on studies of both oral and written composition as means of seeing, making, and doing.

The empiricism in the belletristic tradition assumed values of the white male landed gentry and those aspiring to that station in the social structure, with no attempt to challenge or recompose those values. Thus, it is not surprising that in the twentieth century, such practitioners as Cesar Chavez, Martin Luther King, Jr., and Andrea Dworkin, and such pragmatic theoreticians as Mary Daly, Cornel West, and bell hooks, opened composition to forms of authority different from taste and to regions of concern, word, and action more broadly transformative of society's composition. The practical and productive art they practiced and theorized put emphasis on the imperative for change, but in a vital collaboration with a commitment to do so thoughtfully in conversation with others who have a stake in the change. Such collaboration reflects an understanding of composition as a productive and practical as well as a theoretical art. [*See overview article on* African-American rhetoric; Feminist rhetoric; *and* Queer rhetoric.]

[*See also* Criticism; Law; *and* Speech.]

BIBLIOGRAPHY

Bizzell, Patricia, and Bruce Herzberg. *The Rhetorical Tradition: Readings from Classical Times to the Present.* Boston, 1990. This volume represents the first anthology of historical texts about rhetoric to address the concerns of composition in determining which texts to include.

Clark, Gregory, and S. Michael Halloran, eds. *Oratorical Culture in Nineteenth-Century America: Transformations in the Theory and Practice of Rhetoric.* Carbondale, Ill., 1993. This collection suggests how classical oratorical culture was transformed into the production of professional disciplinary discourses across the nineteenth century in the United States.

Connors, Robert J. *Composition-Rhetoric: Backgrounds, Theory, and Pedagogy.* Pittsburgh, 1997. This study of written composition in American colleges after 1780 discusses how rhetoric and composition have joined and parted ways and how nineteenth-century rhetoric and composition practices have often been excluded from histories of rhetoric and writing instruction.

Crowley, Sharon. *Composition in the University: Historical and Polemical Essays.* Pittsburgh, 1998. This book explores both the political positioning of composition

in the university and the implications for the present and future configurations of the field.

Horner, Winifred Bryan, and Michael Leff, eds. *Rhetoric and Pedagogy: Its History, Philosophy, and Practice: Essays in Honor of James J. Murphy.* Mahwah, N.J., 1995. This collection articulates themes and concerns common to scholars concerned with composition across the history of rhetoric.

Moss, Jean Dietz, ed. *Rhetoric and Praxis: The Contribution of Classical Rhetoric to Practical Reasoning.* Washington, D.C., 1986. Articles by teacher-scholars in communication and composition are featured in this collection, which includes essays reconsidering *topoi,* the enthymeme, and *kairos,* among other ancient concepts.

Murphy, James J., ed. *A Short History of Writing Instruction.* This survey of the ways in which writing has been taught in Western culture from ancient Greece to mid-twentieth-century America represents the first systematic view of composition instruction across the history of Western rhetoric.

Secor, Marie, and Davida Charney, eds. *Constructing Rhetorical Education: Essays in Honor of Wilma R. Ebbitt.* Carbondale, Ill., 1992. This collection of works suggests the range of meanings of composition late in the twentieth century, as well as the composition's relationship to rhetorical education.

—FREDERICK J. ANTCZAK AND ROSA A. EBERLY

History of English departments in the United States

College and university English departments in the United States came about through both evolution and revolution. The evolutionary process involved what might be called "psychological rhetoric," Romantic doctrines of imagination, and the influence of German universities on higher education in America. The revolution came about with the Morrill Act of 1862, creating land grant colleges and universities and thus democratizing higher education.

Psychological Rhetoric. As noted in the preceding overview essay, during the Enlightenment, two influential rhetoricians based their theories and dicta on their understanding of the human mind, George Campbell (1719–1796) and Hugh Blair (1718–1800).

In *The Philosophy of Rhetoric* (1776), Campbell's goal was to found a new rhetoric on the science of the human mind (i.e., faculty psychology), so that rhetoric becomes "That art or talent by which the discourse is adapted to its end" (p. 1), and

> All the ends of speaking are reducible to four; every speech being intended to enlighten the understanding, to please the imagination, to move the passions, or to influence the will.
> (p. 1)

Ultimately, a mode was associated with the faculties, giving us the familiar categories: exposition, argumentation, and persuasion, with the confusing addition of description and narration, which are not ends, but means of achieving those ends. (By *describing* the virtues of a product, one can influence another's will; by *narrating* an event, one can enlighten another's understanding.) This "psychologized" rhetoric, with its categories of discourse derived from faculty psychology, influenced composition in the United States throughout the nineteenth and well into the twentieth century.

Hugh Blair was the first Regius Professor of Rhetoric and Belles Lettres at Edinburgh University. His *Lectures on Rhetoric and Belles Lettres* (1783) had three purposes: to cultivate taste, to improve style, and to teach public speaking and composition. During the first half of the nineteenth century, the *Lectures* had perhaps the greatest influence on composition of any text, going through at least twenty-six editions in Great Britain, thirty-seven in the United States, and fifty-two abridged editions.

According to Blair, it is beyond the power of rhetoric to supply arguments on any subject whatever, and invention results from the natural genius of the writer or speaker, rhetoric's service being to guide the rhetor in managing his subject in the most effective way and helping gentlemen develop taste and refine their styles. Hence, with Blair rhetoric is managerial, no longer an architectonic, creative art.

The Romantic Imagination. During the Enlightenment, theorists such as the British physician and poet Mark Akenside (1721–1770) and Joseph Addison (1672–1719), the essayist whose work in *The Tatler* and *The Spectator* influenced British taste and style, speculated about the nature of imagination, as had George Puttenham (c.1529–1590) in his *The Arte of English Poesie* (1589). However, the influence of Samuel Taylor Coleridge (1772–1834), English poet, philosopher, and leader of the Romantic Movement, was one of the prime forces that brought about the split between "nonimaginative" literature (e.g., history, biography, the essay) and "imaginative" literature (i.e., poetry, prose fiction, and drama) and hence between composition and literature—a schism that was characteristic of English departments in the United States throughout the twentieth century.

In a new twist on the old faculty psychology, Coleridge divided the imagination into primary and secondary, explaining (in *Biographia Literaria,* 1817) that the primary imagination is "the living Power and prime Agent of all human Perception. . . . The secondary I consider as an echo of the former. . . ." After Coleridge, literature could be viewed as the product of the godlike primary imagination whereas composition results from the workings of the secondary imagination.

German Universities. As Albert R. Kitzhaber (1990, pp. 12–17) points out, prior to about 1870 graduate education was virtually nonexistent in the United States, and students were migrating in increasing numbers to German universities, where young scholars could pursue advanced studies in their fields of interest. Returning to the United States, they began to institute the German pattern of graduate education in American institutions.

Daniel Coit Gilman (1831–1908), first president of Johns Hopkins University, is typical of scholars of his day. After graduating from Yale, he served as an attaché in Saint Petersburg, Russia, and then did graduate work in Berlin (1854–1855). When he came to Hopkins in 1875, Gilman introduced sciences into the curriculum, emphasized graduate education, and created professional schools.

Hopkins was not the first university to institute graduate education; Yale established a graduate school in 1871, Harvard in 1872, and Michigan in 1876. Other universities followed, so that before the turn of the century, the graduate school and professional schools were part, in many ways the most important part, of higher education in the United States, thus devaluing undergraduate education and hence composition.

The Morrill Act. In 1862, President Lincoln signed the Morrill Act, giving public lands for the support of colleges and universities that would teach agriculture and "the mechanic arts." Now public colleges and universities entered the scene of higher education, alongside the privately endowed and inevitably elitist institutions such as Harvard and Yale. In all, sixty-nine land grant colleges were established, and education was open to great masses of students. The humanities, which had been the foundation of learning until the German model of higher education became widespread and land grant colleges were founded throughout the land, were no longer the central focus of the academic enterprise, but were relegated to a secondary status. This realignment of values created a hierarchy of educational pursuits in which, literature no longer stood at the pinnacle.

The English Department, 1900–1970. Altogether, the forces of psychologized rhetoric, the valuation of a more than questionable theory of imagination, the influence of German higher education, and the foundation of land grant colleges and universities (as well as other currents and tides, such as the movement for woman suffrage) resulted in the bifurcated English department, with literature as the goal and focus of the regular faculty and composition as the obligation undertaken, frequently, by part-time, nontenured faculty and graduate students. [*See* Criticism; *and* Modern rhetoric.]

In literature, theoretical fashions changed regularly: New Criticism, represented by René Wellek and Austin Warren (*Theory of Literature*, New York, 1949); structuralism (e.g., Roland Barthes, *Le Degré zéro de l'écriture*, 1953), translated by Annette Lavers and Colin Smith as *Writing Degree Zero*, London, 1967; myth criticism (e.g., Northrop Frye, *Anatomy of Criticism*, Princeton, 1957). Whatever the theory or method, the focus was sharply on literature, to the exclusion of composition.

By and large, composition was guided by what is now called *current traditionalism*, the kind of pedagogy that evolved from both psychologized rhetoric and Romanticism, represented by, for instance, Adams Sherman Hill, *The Principles of Rhetoric* (new edition, New York, 1895) or Frederick Crews, *The Random House Handbook* (New York, 1974). In these textbooks, rhetoric is form and style; that is, managerial; invention is not included. [*See* Invention.]

The English Department from 1970 to the Present. With the translation of Jacques Derrida's *De la grammatologie* into English as *Of Grammatology* (translated by Gayatri Spivak, Baltimore, 1967), *deconstruction* became the hegemonic theory in English departments. Deconstructive critics claim that because language is boundless in its signifying power, texts have not just one meaning, but an endless number of possible meanings. Whereas earlier interpreters such as the New Critics attempted to resolve ambiguities in texts, deconstructive critics use these *aporias* as the basis for their elaborations on the instability of texts. Thus, deconstruction is directly opposed to one of the goals of composition: teaching students to state their meanings as clearly as possible. (How can any meaning be clear when language signifies endlessly and indeterminately?)

In composition itself, three distinct movements came about as reactions against the *current traditionalism* that had evolved from psychological rhetoric during the Enlightenment: New Romanticism, New Classicism, and New Rhetoric.

The New Romanticism squares with current traditionalism in excluding invention from its canon and with Romanticism in its emphasis on self-expression and self-discovery. A representative text is Peter Elbow's *Writing With Power* (New York, 1981).

New Classicism is a modernization of ancient rhetoric, drawing on the doctrines of Aristotle, Roman statesman and orator Marcus Tullius Cicero, and Roman rhetorician Marcus Fabius Quintilian. A representative text is Edward P. J. Corbett's *Classical Rhetoric for the Modern Student* (New York, 1965).

New Rhetoric recovers invention as vital to the art and is heavily influenced by developments in linguistics and the social sciences and by the thought of the American philosopher and critic Kenneth Burke (1897–1993), who viewed language as symbolic action. This attitude (as Burke would have it) moves composition out of the academic cloister and solidly into the world of human affairs. An influential New Rhetorical text is Richard E. Young, Alton Becker, and Kenneth Pike's *Rhetoric: Discovery and Change* (New York, 1970).

[*See also* Nineteenth-century rhetoric.]

BIBLIOGRAPHY

Applebee, Arthur. *Tradition and Reform in the Teaching of English: A History.* Urbana, 1974.

Berlin, James. *Rhetoric and Reality: Writing Instruction in American Colleges, 1900–1985.* Carbondale, Ill., 1987.

Berlin, James. *Writing Instruction in Nineteenth-Century American Colleges.* Carbondale, Ill., 1984.

Connors, Robert. *Composition-Rhetoric: Backgrounds, Theory, and Pedagogy.* Pittsburgh, 1997.

Greenblatt, Stephen, and Giles Gunn, eds. *Redrawing the Boundaries: The Transformation of English and American Literary Studies.* New York, 1992.

Kitzhaber, Albert R. *Rhetoric in American Colleges, 1850–1900.* Dallas, Tex., 1990.

Miller, Thomas P. *The Formation of College English: Rhetoric and Belles Lettres in the British Cultural Provinces.* Pittsburgh, 1997.

Winterowd, W. Ross. *The English Department: A Personal and Institutional History.* Carbondale, Ill., 1998.

Young, Richard E. "Invention: A Topographical Survey." In *Teaching Composition: Ten Bibliographical Essays,* edited by Gary Tate, pp. 1–43. Fort Worth, Tex., 1976.

—W. Ross Winterowd

CONGERIES (Lat. *accumulatio*), Puttenham's "Heaping figure" (*The Arte of English Poesie,* 1589, p. 236), is a kind of enumeration that develops an idea by heaping together detailed aspects of the subject (synathroism). "I sing of *Brooks,* of *Blossomes, Birds,* and *Bowers*" announces and amplifies the theme of rural summer (Robert Herrick, *Hesperides,* 1648). Conversely, in the *peroratio* of a speech, *congeries* can recapitulate a number of points to remember. Though usually incremental or climactic, congeries can be (seemingly) chaotic or arbitrary, depending on the speaker's state of mind or simply on the wish to linger on the subject, by amassing, for example, maledictions extending to several pages, as in Sterne's *Tristram Shandy* (1760–1767, 3.1 Of.).

[*See also* Figures of speech.]

—Heiner Peters

CONSTITUTIVE RHETORIC. *See* Politics, *article on* Constitutive rhetoric.

CONTINGENCY AND PROBABILITY. For Aristotle (384–322 BCE), the contingent is the unproblematic scene of rhetoric. This Aristotelian connection between the scene and agency (or practice), originally put into play to blunt Plato's charge that rhetoric is a nomadic, hence unspecifiable discipline, persists to this day as a key, but largely unnoticed, assumption in contemporary rhetorical theory. In *Gorgias,* Plato (c. 428–c. 347 BCE) sets the "specifying" game in motion by demanding that rhetoric identify itself. He puts the identity question bluntly to Gorgias: "Who are you?" (447). "With what class of objects is rhetoric concerned?" (449). As the dialogue unfolds, Socrates poses a series of interrogatories regarding rhetoric's identity and domicile, and predictably, neither Gorgias nor Polus and Callicles who successively undertake to respond, give a satisfactory answer. It is not so much the amorality of rhetoric, but rather the inability of its teachers and practitioners to give a coherent account of it that finally delegitimizes rhetoric. Beneath Plato's ethical critique, which (in both *Gorgias* and *Protagoras*), functions more as a dramatic parody of sophistic pedagogic pretensions than as a determined scourging of evil, there is a more severe critique of rhetoric's lack of substance. In fact, one could read Plato as saying that rhetoric's moral deficiency springs from its nomadic quality, a quality accentuated by the itinerant character of its teachers. Rhetoric is amoral precisely because it is rootless.

Thus, on the manifest argumentative plane, Plato rejects rhetoric as a defective and incomplete art for the following reasons. First, rhetoric is rooted in a false ontology. It is content to deal with what appears to be true and good rather than inquire into what it is in reality. Second, rhetoric is epistemically deficient because it seeks to impart a mastery of common opinion rather than knowledge. Third, as an instrument of practical politics it exploits the resources of language to make the "weaker cause appear stronger" and to promote the acquisition of power as an end in itself without consideration for the well-being of the soul. Each of the three reasons for rejecting rhetoric—its reliance on appearance, its entanglement with opinion, and its linguistic opportunism—are marked, in Plato's imagination, by instability and danger. An art that engages such entities cannot possibly give a rational account of itself. However, at no point does Plato deny the sheer materiality or the "felt quality" of rhetoric and its objects, but he doubts that they constitute a specifiable domain. He recognizes that people are constantly involved in persuasive transactions that require them to negotiate a wide range of appearances and opinions, especially those sanctioned by common sense. But those persuasive negotiations are carried out not in accordance with the strictures of an art, but according to one's knack, a hit-or-miss procedure based on experience. Hence, the paradox of unspecifiability. On the one hand, rhetoric is very tangible, or as McGee (1982) puts it, it impinges on our consciousness as a "brute daily reality," but on the other hand, that reality is made up of appearances and opinions that cannot withstand critical scrutiny. No sooner does a dialectician try to seize upon that "brute daily reality," than it melts into thin air. One could theorize, as some contemporary rhetorical theorists have done (Hariman, 1986), about an epistemology of appearances and opinions that would anchor rhetoric, but Plato was too old fashioned to do it. He was content to dismiss rhetoric as unspecifiable.

Plato further elaborates on the unspecifiability thesis in *Phaedrus* where rhetoric is partially rehabilitated as a supplement to philosophical understanding. In the concluding sections of this dialogue, Plato states precisely the conditions rhetoric must meet to be regarded as a genuine art. Michael Cahn (1989) refers to Plato's specifications as the "dream of rhetoric," where the figure (linguistic strategy or utterance), soul (psychological state / disposition of audience), function (effect sought by the *rhētōr*, convictions he seeks implant) are perfectly coordinated. In short, rhetoric must supply a "gapless" causal model of persuasion, whose validity is to be established on the basis of its predictive capacity. But if rhetoric is unable to meet this demand, then it must be held under the supervision of philosophy. Thus in *Phaedrus,* Plato specifies conditions for freeing of rhetoric from the philosophical tutelage, but these conditions cannot be met. And insofar as these conditions cannot be met, rhetoric must remain in the margins of philosophy, held hostage in an eternal minority. At this point, rhetoric would have neither autonomy nor specificity. It would be parasitic on the prior philosophical achievement. Thus, Plato sets up an extraordi-

nary problematic. His challenge to the future champions of rhetoric is straightforward: "Unpack the riddle of rhetoric and it can go free." To free rhetoric, one must first give it a name, a domicile, and some specificity.

Aristotle and the "Contingency" Thesis. It is generally agreed that Aristotle's lectures on rhetoric were partly a response to Plato's critique. But Aristotle's text, by foregrounding the tripartite scheme, especially the tripartite theory of genre, obscures his response to Plato's charge of unspecifiability. Propelled by the tripartite scheme, the text moves swiftly into the pragmatics of oratory. Aristotle appears to be functioning in a different key from Plato. His initial claim that "it is possible to inquire the reason why some speakers succeed through practice and others spontaneously" and "that such an inquiry is a function of the art" (1354. 10), and his fourfold statement about the usefulness of rhetoric (1355a.20–1355b.5), pretty much ignore Plato's threefold critique about appearance, opinion, and linguistic opportunism.

However, if we foreground the contingency thesis, which tends to recede into the background in the glare of the tripartite scheme, we get a different reading of Aristotle. What is Aristotle's "contingency thesis"? To begin with, it involves a substitution. In order to specify the realm of rhetoric, Aristotle replaces Plato's binary opposition between reality and appearance with his own binary opposition between the necessary and the contingent. Once this seemingly unproblematic distinction is accepted, that is, once rhetoric is safely located in the realm of the contingent, Plato's charge of unspecifiability dissolves. By placing rhetoric (along with the dialectic) in the realm of the contingent, Aristotle gives it a domicile, a space within which it can manifest and contain itself. This is an extraordinarily cunning response to Plato's critique that rhetoric is homeless. This maneuver also takes the bite out of Plato's other two charges: rhetoric is epistemically deficient and linguistically opportunistic. Once rhetoric is placed in the realm of the contingent, it can be viewed not as epistemically deficient but as a medium/repository of a distinct type of knowledge—identified variously in contemporary rhetorical studies as "public knowledge" (Bitzer, 1978), or as "social knowledge" (Farrell, 1976), or as "prudential wisdom" (Leff,

1987)—in short, some sort of practical knowledge in use. Similarly, the charge of linguistic opportunism can be revalorized à la Kenneth Burke as a form of bricolage, an equipment for living in an inexact world.

The Aristotelian reading of the contingent has two main characteristics: First, the contingent is posited simultaneously as the opposite of the necessary (or necessarily true) and in conjunction with the "probable" or that about which one can generate probable proof. While the opposition to the necessary hugely expands the realm of rhetoric, the association with the probable makes it manageable. When the contingent is defined strictly in opposition to the necessary, it opens up a vast space of what is uncertain and indeterminate. But Aristotle and those who follow Aristotle do not allow us to peer too deeply into the abyss of the uncertain and the indeterminate. The contingent is immediately domesticated by its association with the probable. The probable here is not one derived from mathematical or statistical probability but one associated with the everyday (thus "ideological" in Barthes's 1972 sense of "anonymous ideology") notion of the "usual" or "things that normally or commonly happen." For Aristotle, at any rate, the idea of the contingent does not connote a Kafkaesque world of sheer uncertainty and terror, but rather a world made familiar by Emily Post—of gamesmanship and good manners displayed by those adept at ideological bricolage.

Second, the contingent is a mark of human actions because in any given situation, human beings can conceivably act in ways other than they do. According to Aristotle: "Most of the things about which we make decisions, and into which we therefore inquire, present us with alternative possibilities. For it is about our actions we deliberate and inquire, and all our actions have a contingent character; hardly any of them are determined by necessity (1357.23–27)." (The term *contingent* appears in W. Rhys Roberts's translation. Grimaldi in his commentaries also uses that word. However, George Kennedy 1991, p. 42, uses the phrase "[things] that are for the most part capable of being other than they are.") Thus, the contingent is the horizon within which human actions unfold and "deliberation," whose *telos* is judgment and choice, is the reflective mode of engaging in that unfolding. If human beings can act in more than one way (and if the outcome of their actions is uncertain, capable of unanticipated consequences), then it makes sense to deliberate and choose. Rhetoric is the discursive medium of deliberating and choosing, especially in the public sphere. Thus, the focus shifts imperceptibly from the scene of contingency to the agency of deliberation and decision making. That shift is made possible by a certain conception of the probable, the usual, and the normal—a generalized social epistemology—which domesticates and stabilizes the contingent. "A Probability," according to Aristotle, "is a thing that usually happens; not . . . anything whatever that usually happens, but only if it belongs to the class of the 'contingent' or 'variable'" (1357a35–1357b). In his commentary on that passage, Grimaldi, drawing on the other works of Aristotle, stresses that "stability" and "regularity" govern the relationship between contingency and probability:

> *Eikos* is not that which *simply* happens, for that equates it with sheer chance. *Eikos* possesses a note of stability and regularity which is intrinsic to the nature of the thing which is the ground for the *eikos* proposition derived from that nature. A stabilized, but contingent (i.e., not necessary), fact can be known (*Metaphysics* 1027a20–21), and it can even be used in a demonstrative syllogism (*Analytica priora* 32b20ff.). Obviously *eikos* is something relatively stabilized and knowable (*Analytica priora* 70a4ff.) and, as such, offers ground for reasonable inference to further knowledge. (Grimaldi, 1980, p. 62)

Thus, one begins to read the celebrated formulation regarding "the contingent and the probable" from the axis of the probable. Aristotle promotes such a reading by providing an elaborate account of probable reasoning based on enthymeme and *paradeigma* (example) and by calling enthymeme "the substance of rhetorical persuasion" (1354a. 12–14). [*See* Enthymeme; *and* Exemplum.] In this way, the contingent as the horizon of rhetoric recedes to the background and the probable as a mode of negotiating the contingent commands the center of attention.

The connection between rhetoric and contingency is rarely thematized as a theoretical issue in Aristotelian scholarship. To be sure, Grimaldi in his commentary explicates in detail the numerous ways in which the contingent is invoked and deployed in Aristotle's *Rhetoric* and in his other works. For Grimaldi, the contingent, however philologically complex, is not theoretically intriguing or problematic. It is part of the conceptual background that underwrites the rhetorical project.

The concept of contingency also gets some attention from scholars interested in Aristotle's logical works, especially in his pioneering account of the modal terms. In that account, the contingent is defined in terms of its difference from the two other modal operators—the "necessary" and the "possible." There is also a further distinction between the contingent as an event and the contingent as a property of propositions.

A contingent event is one that might or might not occur. Neither its occurrence nor its nonoccurrence is necessary. While a contingent event is possible, every possible event is not contingent because a necessary event is possible without being contingent. To put it simply, a contingent event is neither necessary nor impossible. From the standpoint of voluntary human agency, an event is necessary if it is not within anyone's power to prevent its occurrence and an event is impossible if it is not within anyone's power to bring about its occurrence. Hence, an event is contingent if it is within someone's power to bring about its occurrence and in someone's power to prevent its occurrence (see Cahn, 1967, pp. 24–27; Waterlow, 1982).

The distinction between necessary and contingent statements or truths is more complicated. There is no easy correspondence between events and statements. Moreover, Aristotle distinguishes between two types of necessary statements, relative and absolute, based on his metaphysical view, namely, that things have real essences. In an argument, when one claims that "something must be true," one is expected, if asked, to provide relevant reasons for that claim. In such a case, the truth of that claim is in an important sense necessitated by the reasons adduced in its support. Here the "necessarily true" is not a property of a given statement but obtains only in relation to supporting reasons. The force of that relation can be variable. A claim and its supporting

reasons (or a conclusion and its premises) might be so connected that one could only assert that "something is probably true or possibly true." Aristotle also regarded certain statements, such as the axioms of special sciences and general principles, say, the principles of contradiction, as absolutely necessary or true in themselves. An axiom expresses the essences of objects that constitute the province/field of a special science. Axioms are not derived from other propositions, but intuited. We see the truth of axioms in particular instances. According to such a theory of essences, a contingent statement would be one "whose truth is not determined by the essence of the thing about which it is asserted" (Hamlyn, p. 199). The necessary statement is concerned with "that which cannot be otherwise than it is" and the contingent statement is concerned with "that which can be otherwise and is so for the most part, only or sometime, or as it happens" (Hamlyn, 1967, pp. 198–205).

The logical explication of the contingent, as applied to events and statements, is carried out strictly in terms of its difference from the necessary. Since the concept of necessary statements/truths is a foundational topic in epistemology, there is a large and technically complex literature on it from Aristotle to the present. In that literature, the contingent stands in the shadow of the necessary, the explication of the former is a byproduct of the inquiry into the latter. It is difficult to connect what one has gleaned from a philosophical analysis of the contingent to its deployment as a generalized background assumption in rhetoric, except in the most obvious sense. The philosophical clarification of the contingent as an event (what might or might not happen) and of the contingent as a property of statements (what might or might not be true) has an obvious affinity to the sense in which the contingent ("things/matters that can be otherwise") is taken as the privileged object of rhetorical deliberation.

Aristotle states emphatically and repeatedly that no one wastes his time deliberating about things that are necessary or impossible (1357a. 1–8). But the characterization of the contingent as the scene of rhetoric is a much thicker notion, something more than the object and content of deliberative rationality. In my view, it signals the prefiguration of a certain vision of the human condition in general, and of political life in particular, which motivates and propels rhetoric. One of the pressing challenges of rhetorical theory today is to unpack that thicker notion of contingency.

One way to attend to that challenge is to track the career of the contingency thesis in rhetorical theory from Aristotle to the present. This would not be easy because that thesis functions as an implicit background assumption rather than as an explicit theoretical issue. One could surmount that difficulty by taking the indirect route of tracking the concept of "probable reasoning" after its initial formulation by Aristotle. Fortunately, Douglas Lane Patey provides such an account, which is brief but insightful, in the first two chapters of his *Probability and Literary Form* (1984). In that book, Patey is partly engaged in a polemic against what is known as the Foucault-Hacking Hypothesis regarding the sudden emergence of the modern concept of probability in the West around 1660. According to Hacking:

Probability has two aspects. It is connected with the degree of belief warranted by evidence, and it is connected with the tendency, displayed by some chance devices, to produce stable relative frequencies. Neither of these aspects was self-consciously and deliberately apprehended by any substantial body of thinkers before the time of Pascal. (p. 1)

Hacking refers to the two aspects as epistemic and aleatory. There is not much dispute about the aleatory aspect. However, Patey contests Hacking's claim that the epistemic aspect—"the degree of belief warranted by evidence"—was generally absent prior to 1660. Hacking's claim is based on the assumption that until the Renaissance, probability simply meant opinion supported by authority; and no notion of nondemonstrative evidence existed. Patey questions that assumption by noting that there are two ways to read the history of probability from Aristotle to Locke. In the first version, based on a selective reading of Aristotle common during the Middle Ages, probability is equated with opinion supported by authority. In the *Prior Analytics* (11.26.70a), Aristotle states that "A probability is a generally approved proposition"; and further, he states in the *Topics* (1.1.100b), that "opinions are 'generally accepted which are

accepted. . . . by all, or by the majority, or by the most notable and illustrious of them'" (Patey, p. 4). In such an equation of probability and "approved opinion," evidence is extrinsic to the claim. It is not what Hacking calls "inductive evidence" or "the evidence of things" in the modern sense. In the second version, which draws its orientation from the skeptics, especially Carneades (c.214–c.129 BCE) and Cicero (106–43 BCE), probability, still linked to opinion, is assessed on the basis of intrinsic as well as extrinsic criteria. According to Patey, Carneades' three tests for assessing "impressions" (of the external world on the mind)—"that they be credible, consistent, and proven in experience—are three criteria of probability" and constitute a putative "doctrine of evidence" (Patey, 1984, p. 15). Carneades also devised a practical method for establishing probabilities, the method of argument *in utramque partem,* which received its full articulation in Ciceronian theory and practice. Moreover, the canons of probability employed in the "topical" system (especially in Cicero's revision of Aristotle) draw on both extrinsic and intrinsic grounds of proof (*loci*); and, the latter are the seats of arguments grounded not in testimony but, in the words of Richard Sherry (1550), in "the thynge it selfe that is in question" (Patey, p. 21). To challenge Hacking's thesis, Patey adduces a wide range of additional historical and textual references that attest to the existence of the notion of nondemonstrative evidence prior to 1660. These references range from Cicero's notion of verisimilitude through the strictures of literary "decorum" in the Renaissance to Locke's claim that "probable and certain knowledge arise from the same kind of mental operation, and hence are epistemologically continuous."

Patey's account of the two versions of probability from Aristotle to Locke is interesting in itself. But it also gives some indication of the connection between the contingent and the probable during that period. In both versions, the contingent appears as the companion of opinion. In the first version, which draws heavily on the Aristotelian distinction between demonstrable knowledge and probable opinion (*endoxa*), opinion is denigrated precisely because it is contingent—sometimes true and sometimes false. Opinion is also associated with particular, perishable, and "changeable things" of which, being contingent, there can be no science. In the Christian imagination, man's exile from Eden reduces him to opinion. According to Aquinas, "'in Eden Adam had nearly no opinion ("penitus nulla opinio"); the Fall altered his mind, so that what once he could know, he could later only form opinions about'" (Patey, p. 12). And yet the practically minded Aquinas finds in rhetoric a postlapsarian crutch: "'In human affairs it is not possible to have demonstration and infallible proof; but it suffices to have some conjectural probability such as the rhetor uses to persuade'" (Patey, pp. 9–10). One can detect a similar ambivalence among the secular thinkers who simultaneously denigrate opinion as contingent and promote rhetoric as a mode of managing contingent opinion.

In the second version (what Patey calls an alternative history of probability), that ambivalence becomes more reflexive and productive. One no longer bemoans the fact that by the standards of *epistēmē* (demonstration and infallible proof) very little of what human beings know can count as true knowledge. One simply takes it, as with the Renaissance humanists, as an unavoidable feature of the human condition that demands an intelligent and practical response. Questions are now raised about privileging those "infallible" measures of knowledge that are so utterly irrelevant and inapplicable in practical affairs. Opinion, once derided as contingent, finally comes into its own as the inescapable scene and substance of human deliberation, judgment, and action. Treatises are composed as to how one might acquire, ascertain, and communicate "opinion" and what degrees of certitude and what modes of assent would accompany it. This attitude and sensibility, which can only be described as rhetorical, originates in the recognition of the contingency not only of opinion, but also of politics, of morals, and of history.

This is a thick notion of contingency that motivates and propels rhetoric. Faced with such a notion of contingency, one is no longer content to formulate the canons of probable reasoning, although that task remains important. On Patey's account, the career of probability prior to 1660, even as it moves through multiple tracks, remains legible and palpable. One such track develops into a highly elaborated and influential system known as casuistry (a form of moral reasoning based on the "case" method) between the fourteenth and the midseventeenth centuries. [*See* Casuistry.] Interestingly, according to Hacking, one of the enabling moments in the emergence of the modern notion of probability is Pascal's polemic (1656–1657) against casuistry (or its abuses), which decimated it. In recent years, there has been something of a revival of casuistry, especially among those interested in ethical questions in the practice of law, medicine, and public policy. It is equally interesting that Jonsen and Toulmin in their provocative book, *The Abuse of Casuistry* (1988), trace its intellectual roots back to Aristotle's notion of *phronēsis* and its embodiment in Cicero's oratorical practice; and thus, realign casuistry with rhetoric. [*See* Phronēsis.]

Tracking the career of probable reasoning alerts one to, but does not fully disclose, the various strands that are interwoven in the thick notion of contingency. Those strands link and place it in a web of concepts, of which "necessary" is only one. I will briefly identify two main strands that negotiate differently the encounter with those aspects of existence that elude human control. Each strand views contingency, to borrow John Kekes's (1995) phrase, as a "permanent adversity."

In the first strand, contingency is "external," something precipitated by chance, fate, or fortune, which eludes human comprehension and control. A contingent event in this sense has no definite cause. It is an effect, according to Aristotle, of an accidental or incidental cause. Take the famous example of the chance meeting of old friends, say at a theater, after a separation of many years. Here, two lines of action coincide and produce a specific result, which cannot be explained in terms of causes or purposes that triggered those actions. William James describes the world saturated with such events as a "concatenated universe" as opposed to a "block universe," which is fully determined. Contingency in this sense has a considerable hold on the rhetorical imagination (see *The Great Ideas: A Syntopican,* 1952, pp. 179–192). It casts a shadow over the human capacity to deliberate and to act on the basis probable reasoning. To some it is an encounter with the absurd, as in Sartre's short story, *The Wall* (1956), where a revolutionary facing imminent execution reveals to the police the whereabouts of his comrade by sheer coincidence and thus obtains a temporary reprieve. In a classic essay, Bernard Williams (1981) has revived this theme under the idea of "moral luck."

The second strand gives an "internal" anthropological view of contingency as something rooted in human nature and social life. Here contingency is linked, on the one hand, to concepts such as human "fallibility," and "incompleteness," which point to our epistemic deficiencies and moral shortcomings; and, on the other hand, to the phenomena of social conflict, competition, and ethical plurality. In this view, both the possibility and need for rhetoric are derived from the contingency of human nature and social life.

These two strands are closely intertwined. One can distinguish them only analytically. A number of contemporary scholars, mostly those who have some knowledge and affection for classical texts and traditions, have grappled with these two strands of contingency. The works of Pocock (1975), Nussbaum (1986), Struever (1970), and Garver (1987, 1994) are particularly relevant for a further unpacking of the connection between rhetoric and contingency. It is not possible to do that unpacking here. But it should be noted that these four scholars share a common set of texts, themes, and trajectories. They tend to map a line of thinking about practical reason or prudence that stretches from Aristotle through Cicero and the Renaissance humanists to Machiavelli. [See Prudence.] They are drawn to texts that are preoccupied with the play of chance, fate, and fortune in human affairs, especially in the moral and political spheres. And they are drawn to rhetoric, sometimes only implicitly and ambivalently, as an imperfect mode for managing contingency.

Contingency Thesis in Contemporary Rhetorical Theory. In this section, I will try to trace the career of the "contingency thesis" in contemporary rhetorical theory that generally adheres to Aristotle's reading of the contingent. This is not surprising since Aristotle dominated rhetorical studies in the twentieth century, especially within the disciplinary matrix of speech and communication studies. [See Communication; and Speech.] A careful reading of a series of key "field defining" essays from the time these studies, which became a distinct discipline in the United States from

around 1914 to the present, shows Aristotle's formulation regarding "the contingent and the probable" functions as a taken-for-granted background assumption. It is always presupposed, but rarely thematized. In a recent anthology of "contemporary rhetorical theory" consisting of thirty-four essays published since the 1960s, the term *contingency* appears barely two dozen times, and it is minimally thematized once. And yet that term figures prominently in the editors' introduction where they characterize rhetoric, following the classical tradition, as typically concerned with "the *public, persuasive,* and *contextual* characteristics of human discourse in situations governed by the problems of *contingency. Contingent* situations occur when decisions have to be made and acted upon, but decision makers are forced to rely upon probabilities rather than certainties" (Lucaites, Condit, and Caudill, 1999, p. 2).

There are, however, some notable exceptions, especially among those who view Aristotle's *Rhetoric* as the basic template for developing a contemporary rhetorical theory. Bryant, Bitzer, and Farrell are three prominent Aristotelians in whose work the contingency thesis is explicit and thematized to varying degrees. Their work, which taken collectively, spans the last half-century, represents a distinct and influential line of thinking. Moreover, one can chart the evolution of the contingency thesis from Bryant through Bitzer to Farrell as marking a significant shift from a "functionalist" to a "constitutive" view of rhetoric.

Bryant, Bitzer, and Farrell reiterate Aristotle's original formulation with the usual references to the contingent as something distinct from the necessary and the impossible, and as the domain of human affairs where one deliberates and decides about alternative possibilities of belief and action on the basis of informed opinion and probable reasoning. After rehearsing such Aristotelian notions, Bryant (1953) concludes: "In summary, rhetoric is the rationale of informative and suasory discourse, it operates chiefly in the area of the contingent, its aim is the attainment of maximum probability as a basis of public decision . . ." (p. 408).

One can locate similar passages in Bitzer and Farrell. The purpose of these reiterations is not to paraphrase but to modernize Aristotle's rhetoric. They show how the contingency thesis does not stand alone, rather it undergirds a cluster of concepts and propositions: First, rhetoric is a method for inquiring into and communicating about the realm of the contingent. Inquiry and communication are two facets of a single practice of managing contingency. Second, the inquiry into the contingent yields opinions of variable validity and utility, but not certain knowledge. Hence, opinion is the material with which rhetoric must work in the world of contingency. Third, the proper mode of working with opinion is deliberation (involving dialogue and debate) that relies primarily on probable reasoning to make decisions and to form judgments. Fourth, rhetorical deliberation and decision making is audience centered. It seeks to persuade or to gain adherence of an audience that is neither "universal" (as in philosophy) nor "imaginary" (as in poetry), but historically concrete and specific. Fifth, the deliberative engagement with the audience is temporally bound. The contingent world of human affairs is marked at every stage by the irreversible passing of time, whether one elects to discursively engage an audience or not, and if engaged whether one succeeds in persuading or not, and if successful whether it leads to intended consequences or not. Deliberation, enunciation, judgment, and action are continually held hostage by time.

These five propositions are not distinctive to rhetoric alone. Rhetoric shares some of them with its counterpart, dialectic. [See Dialectic.] "(F)or Aristotle," as Natanson notes, "both rhetoric and dialectic are concerned with world of probability, both begin with commonsense reality of contingency" (1955, p. 133); but they proceed differently. Without getting into the technical details of the two procedures as to how each finds and ascertains its premises and how each discursively moves from premises to conclusions with what degree of probability, one might note the obvious difference between dialectic and rhetoric in terms of the latter's inescapable entanglement with opinion, audience, and time. In a Socratic dialectic, opinion is not binding. One might begin with opinion, but only to cleanse it of error and prejudice and elevate it to the status, if not of truth, at least to one of critical and reflexive opinion. Nor is the audience sovereign in dialectic. The social profile of the interlocutors can be bracketed

and interlocutors can be addressed as if they were susceptible to reason, and reason alone. Nor is time of the essence. Faced with an *aporia*, the interlocutors can blithely defer judgment. [See Aporia.] One can reverse oneself and start afresh without damaging one's argument or one's character. Dialectic engages contingency reflectively and leisurely. Dialectic is detached. In rhetoric, on the other hand, opinion is binding, audience is sovereign, time is of the essence, and judgment is inescapable. This renders rhetoric's grasp of the contingent tenuous and fragile. There are too many variables thrown together that generate further contingencies. Rhetoric can never catch up with the unfolding chain of contingencies. The latter maintain an irreparable lead.

Such at least is the implication of a sheerly "functional" view of rhetoric as it negotiates the world of contingency. One might be tempted to recommend grounding rhetoric in dialectic, as Weaver (1953) and Natanson (1955) do. Neither Bitzer nor Farrell take that Platonic option of relegating rhetoric to a supplementary status. Instead they seek to fashion a constitutive view of rhetoric that engages contingency differently.

A subtle but recognizable terminological change occurs from Bryant to Bitzer. Rhetoric is still considered a method, but a greater stress is placed on "inquiry":

> [W]e regard rhetoric as a method of inquiry and communication which functions to establish judgments, primarily in areas of practical and human affairs, for ourselves and for the audience addressed. . . . It is obvious that we need to judge and persuade. . . . on the basis of purposeful deliberation which employs as much truth as the subject admits and proceeds systematically through methods of investigation, evaluation and communication suited to the subject, the audience, and the purpose. . . . rhetoric insists on rational justification. (Bitzer, 1981, p. 228)

Under Bitzer's version, opinion becomes "informed" by going through the process of critical deliberation and rational justification. The word *judgment* replaces *decision*, suggesting reflective rather than technical engagement. Audience is posited normatively as capable of rational persuasion and empowered to judge. Time, now subsumed under the term *exigence*, is radically particularized as a contingent set of constraints and opportunities. "Exigence" elicits reflection, both technical and normative, as to what is proper and fitting. Thus, a series of norms and strategies is generated, which attempts to stabilize one's rhetorical response to a given set of contingencies and their constituents—opinion, audience, and time. Bitzer's move toward a "constitutive" view of rhetoric is tentative. [*See* Politics, *article on* Constitutive rhetoric.] While he does not view the opinion/decision/audience string instrumentally, neither does he think of it dialogically. Bitzer places greater stress on the rational–critical aspect of the deliberative process than on the constitutive engagement with the audience. The focus is on the normativity and systemacity of rhetorical transaction among autonomous agents.

The shift to a "constitutive" view of rhetoric is relatively complete in Farrell. In his essay, "Knowledge, Consensus, and Rhetorical Theory," Farrell regards rhetoric as a practical art that employs "the common knowledge of a particular audience to inform and guide reasoned judgments about matters of public interest" (1976, p. 1). The key term here is *knowledge*—the type of knowledge pertinent to rhetorical practice. Farrell calls it "social knowledge," which now replaces Bryant's "opinion" and Bitzer's "informed opinion" in the conceptual set under review. [*See* Social knowledge.] "Social knowledge" is not exclusively agent centered, it requires the "collaboration of others" to materialize. According to Farrell, it is "a kind of knowledge which must be assumed if rhetorical discourse is to function effectively. . . . it is assumed to be shared by *knowers* in their unique capacity as audience. . . . social knowledge is actualized through the decisions and actions of an audience" (p. 4). Further, Farrell adds an inventional dimension to social knowledge when he claims that it "rests upon a peculiar kind of consensus. . . . which is attributed to an audience rather than concretely shared" (p. 6). Thus, Farrell repositions the audience as the co-producers at both ends of a rhetorical transaction, invention and judgment. [*See* Invention; *and* Judgment.]

Given Farrell's characterization of "social knowledge"—as attributed consensus, audience-centered, and generative—one might think that it would, unlike Bitzer's "informed opinion," elevate rather than attenuate the uncertainty and instability associated with the contingency of opinion. However, that possibility is obviated by emphasizing the rule-governed character of both rhetoric and its substance, social knowledge. As a mode of coordinating social conduct, rhetoric presupposes the existence of regularities:

> When we say, for instance, that, *as a rule,* politicians are not be trusted, or that, *as a rule,* people do not act against their own perceived interests, . . . each utterance points to an important similarity or regularity in the way human beings understand and act in their social world. . . . [T]his rule-like structure of social knowledge assumes that persons will regularly respond to problems in similar ways. (p. 5)

Thus, for Farrell, "social knowledge . . . is probable knowledge" and it is "confirmed through recurrent action" (p. 9).

In this essay, Farrell uses the word *contingent* only once to characterize a type of shared knowledge "consisting in signs, probabilities, and example" that forms the substance of rhetoric. However, it is explicitly thematized in his book, *Norms of Rhetorical Culture* (1993), where he calls for a "broader understanding of contingency," as something more than an event or a property of propositions. Here contingency refers to situations marked by social conflict and ethical choice where alternative construals are unavoidable. A rhetor must confront such a situation in the midst of "perishable circumstance, incomplete knowledge, and fallible human action" and render her judgment in the collaborative presence of an audience. That judgment and subsequent action, in all its contingency and irreversibility, will disclose and form the public character of the rhetor as well as her audience. A contingent situation sets in motion a constitutive rhetoric between character (*rhētōr*) and community (audience) that can give rise, under favorable conditions, to a collective moral agency, hence, to solidarity.

An examination of the theoretical trajectory moving from Bryant through Bitzer to Farrell shows that despite a significant shift from a "functional" to a "constitutive" view of rhetoric, the contingent remains the invariable scene of rhetoric. In these three writers, as in Aristotle, the abstract instability of the contingent is marvelously balanced by the substantive predictability of opinion and social action. And, rhetoric is seen as a discursive medium par excellence for managing the contingent.

Among scholars in communication studies who resist the Aristotelian domination (no one is fully immune from his overweening influence), which they do by invoking other theorists, both classical and modern, such as the Sophists (Poulakos, 1983), Plato (Natanson, 1955), Cicero (Leff, 1987), Kenneth Burke (Campbell, 1970), Stephen Toulmin (Scott, 1967), the contingency thesis is mostly implicit and rarely thematized. Nevertheless, it is possible to locate traces of contingency thesis when they try to characterize the specifity of rhetoric. For instance, Leff (1987) presupposes the contingent as the operative horizon when he characterizes rhetoric as a situated "local" practice that finds stability and intelligibility by meeting the standards of decorum such as "appropriateness" (*decorum*) and "timeliness" (*kairos*). [*See* Decorum; *and* Kairos.] That presupposition is also operative in the substantial body of literature that we have on "rhetoric as epistemic." In fact, Scott's inaugural essay on that topic briefly thematizes contingency by claiming that truth in human affairs is "not prior and immutable" but contingent (1967, p. 13). However, in those implicit references to the contingent as the scene of rhetoric it is no longer strictly yoked to the probable. That unyoking of the contingent from the probable, if rendered explicit and thematized in future studies, might produce new and challenging possibilities in our understanding of rhetoric.

The New Rhetoricians. Contemporary rhetorical theory has also evolved outside the disciplinary matrix of communication studies. In fact, a group of scholars generally referred to as the "new rhetoricians"—Burke (1897–1993), McKeon (1900–1985), Perelman (1912–1984), Richards (1893–1979), and Weaver (1910–1953)—were primarily responsible for keeping rhetoric alive on the broader cultural horizon in the three decades immediately following World War II. What these five scholars had in common was a commitment to refocus contemporary attention on rhetoric in a world increasingly dominated by science and scientific method. They were determined to challenge the modernist fact/value distinction which, they believed, severely attenu-

ated the possibility of the public use of reason in law, ethics, and politics. In rhetoric, they found not an alternative to reason but an enlarged version of it that could address and negotiate the vexing questions of public life. Apart from such broad affinities, the new rhetoricians did not share, nor did they generate, a common fund of ideas, principles, perspective, and whatever else it takes to be an intellectual movement. But they were highly influential as individual thinkers and their ideas dominated rhetorical theory in communication studies for a significant period of time. Burke continues to be influential to this day. The new rhetoricians also produced the two major texts in contemporary rhetorical theory: *The New Rhetoric: A Treatise on Argumentation* (1969) by Perelman and Olbrechts-Tyteca, and *A Rhetoric of Motives* (1962) by Kenneth Burke.

While none of the new rhetoricians explicitly thematized the contingency thesis, it is possible to show that it did operate as a taken-for-granted background assumption in their thinking. This holds true for the two major texts. Perelman's founding distinction between demonstration and argumentation is based on a further distinction between the necessary and the contingent as evident from his reiteration of the Aristotelian formulation:

> The very nature of deliberation and argumentation is opposed to necessity and self-evidence, since no one deliberates where the solution is necessary or argues against what is self-evident. The domain of argumentation is that of the credible, the plausible, the probable, to the degree that the latter eludes the certainty of calculation. (Perelman and Olbrechts-Tyteca, 1969, p. 1)

In a later work, Perelman claims that "the realm of action is the realm of the contingent," where dialectic and rhetoric are "essential in order to introduce some rationality into the exercise of the individual and the collective will" (1982, p. 155).

Burke may not explicitly subsume rhetoric under the sign of the contingent, but anyone familiar with Burke's "human barnyard" metaphor will quickly see its family resemblance to contingency: "The Rhetoric must lead us through the Scramble, the Wrangle of the Market Place, the flurries and flare-ups of the Human Barnyard, the Give and Take, the wavering line of pressure and counterpressure, the Logomachy, the onus of ownership, the War of Nerves, the War" (1962, p. 23). Moreover, Burke's maxim regarding "identification"—if men were not simultaneously consubstantial and divided, rhetoric would be neither possible nor needed to proclaim their unity—characterizes rhetoric as a constitutive but contingent movement between conflict and cooperation that sustains a community. [*See* Identification.]

Contingency in the Postfoundationalist Discourse. Finally, I want to briefly explore the sort of hermeneutic burden the term *contingent* is made to carry in contemporary postfoundationalist discourse. The story of the collapse of foundationalism in philosophy and its aftereffects in the humanities is well known. Scholars in various disciplines have meticulously mapped and documented how various intellectual movements (from poststructuralism through deconstruction to postmodernism and cultural studies)—consisting of a distinctive set of theoretical formulations, conceptual innovations, critical practices, and political positions—have emerged in the space created by that collapse. Some terms, *contingency, performance, rhetorical, articulation,* and *imaginary* among them, have become highly visible across many of those new intellectual formations. These are key terms with complex genealogies and contested meanings that are deployed in multiple contexts with such frequency and promiscuity that it is difficult to stabilize their range of meanings. This is particularly true in the case of *contingency,* which is rarely thematized by those who deploy it and whose Aristotelian/rhetorical genealogy is largely forgotten. Judith Butler titled her introductory essay to an edited volume on feminist political theory, "Contingent Foundations" (1992). This is only one of many instances of perplexing and paradoxical uses of the term, which is ubiquitous in virtually any postfoundationalist or postmodernist discourse/disciplinary formation. While the postfoundationalists are rarely aware of the rhetorical genealogy of *contingency,* that term is gradually being pulled into the gravitational field of rhetoric. This should not be surprising since the renewed interdisciplinary interest in rhetoric since the 1950s is also ignited by the collapse of foundationalism. Both rhetoric and contingency are finding nour-

ishment and renewal from the same intellectual soil. In fact, the interarticulation of the two terms could be beneficial for both: contingency could become more legible and readable (not just a suture or a floating signifier) by locating a genealogy within the rhetorical tradition, and rhetoric could become more reflexive about its "conditions of possibility" by thematizing contingency.

A detailed analysis of how contingency and rhetoric are linked in postfoundationalist thought would require a careful reading of the relevant works of five key authors: Judith Butler (1990, 2000), Stanley Fish (1989), Richard Rorty (1979, 1989), Jean-François Lyotard (1985, 1988), and Barbara Herrnstein Smith (1988). There are three reasons for this. First, each of these five thinkers deploys the term *contingency* at critical and strategic moments in their work, although they do not adequately thematize it. Second, they are familiar with the rhetorical tradition and relatively conscious of the elective affinity between contingency and rhetoric, although, once again, they don't adequately thematize that connection. Third, their work, generally perceived as friendly toward rhetoric, is familiar to students of rhetoric and has had a productive impact on their thinking. In short, it would be highly productive to chart the consequences of their reflections on contingency. They may contain the possibility of deeply destabilizing one of the taken-for-granted assumptions of traditional rhetoric regarding "the contingent and the probable."

However, it is not possible within the confines of this essay to undertake such an explication. Therefore, I will confine my observations to the works of just two authors: Rorty and Fish.

By the early 1970s, American scholars in the humanities had been exposed to the main currents of postfoundationalist thought through the writings of a group of continental thinkers, loosely known as the poststructuralists. Three of its best-known representatives—Foucault, Lacan, and Derrida—had just begun their enormously influential "American" careers, which radically transformed the shape and substance of the humanities research and teaching over the next two decades. However, it was the publication of Rorty's book *Philosophy and the Mirror of Nature* (1979) and the controversy it generated that firmly installed the postfoundationalist paradigm in the American academy. As an accomplished analytical philosopher, Rorty was in a unique position to mount an "internal" critique of the basic foundationalist assumptions of the dominant analytic school. Rorty's book and his subsequent essays, written in an engaging and accessible style (at least, in comparison with the poststructuralists) and drawing on his remarkable command of both philosophical cultures, analytic and continental, were highly influential in disseminating postfoundationalist thinking in the humanities.

One of Rorty's basic claims, the one most relevant to rhetorical studies, concerns the relation between language, truth, and reality. He flatly rejects the notion that language is a transparent medium for representing reality or for making true statements about an independent "world out there." Rorty asserts that it is impossible to say anything about the "world out there" apart from the words and sentences we use to describe it. There are no objective or extralinguistic tests to evaluate our claims and beliefs about the world. Truth is relative to the ways in which a given language embedded in a life-world is contextually deployed. Thus, Rorty emphasizes the radically temporal, local, and contingent character of patterns of thought and action that are intelligible only within a given language game or "form of life." According to Rorty: "[T]ruth and knowledge can only be judged by the standards of the inquirers of our own day. . . . nothing counts as justification unless by reference to what we already accept, and . . . there is no way to get outside our beliefs and our language so as to find some test other than coherence" (1979, p. 178). Rejecting both the foundationalist idea of mind as the "glassy essence" and its later replacement by "the logical structure of language" as the privileged objects of epistemological inquiry, Rorty proposes to examine knowledge-producing activities hermeneutically as a form of social practice.

It is easy to understand why Rorty's views would be highly attractive to the proponents of rhetoric who have, since the time of the older Sophists, recognized and emphasized the constitutive power of language and the social character of knowledge. [See Sophists.] In hermeneutics, as Rorty describes it, conversation is critical as interlocutors "play back and forth between guesses about how to characterize particular statements or other events" until they feel comfortable with "what was hitherto strange" or contentious and gradually come to an agreement (1979, p. 319). [See Hermeneutics.] A statement is accepted as true not because it accurately represents an aspect of the external world, but because it is recognized to cohere with the vocabulary shared by the interlocutors. This view clearly places persuasion and communication at the very center of what Rorty, borrowing a phrase from Michael Oakshott, calls "the conversation of mankind."

In his collection of essays, *Contingency, irony, and solidarity* (1989), Rorty further develops his constructivist views on language, selfhood, and community, which are tied to his notion of contingency. A brief account of the first essay, "The Contingency of Language," should suffice to show how Rorty's postfoundationalist view of contingency radically breaks from its Aristotelian/rhetorical genealogy. The essay has two aims: first, to dismantle the notion of language as a "medium" whose mission is to adequately represent the reality "out there" or to express the self "in here"; and second, to offer a theory of cultural change.

In a constructivist view, as noted earlier, language neither represents reality nor expresses the self. On the contrary, reality and self are effects of language, or more precisely, effects of vocabularies. There are a multiplicity of competing vocabularies and they are, à la Kuhn, strictly incommensurable. Why we choose or find ourselves held prisoner in one vocabulary rather than another (say, the rationalist as opposed to the pragmatist) is a matter of historical contingency. We simply happen to find ourselves in this one rather than that other. We might be able to give a causal account of how we got caught in a particular vocabulary, but that does not alter the fact that it is contingent. There is no necessary or demonstrable reason as to why we should remain within this or that vocabulary except that we are able do certain things with each. The world does not endorse one vocabulary over another: "[T]he fact that Newton's vocabulary lets us predict the world more easily than Aristotle's does not mean that the world speaks Newtonian" (1989, p. 6).

Nor does Rorty consider the choice of vocabulary to be arbitrary. The choice is neither objective nor subjective, it is not a choice at all; it is something that just happens:

Europe did not *decide* to accept the idiom of Romantic poetry, or of socialist politics, or of Galilean mechanics. This sort of shift was no more an act of will than it was a result of argument. Rather, Europe gradually lost the habit of using certain words and gradually acquired the habit of using others. (1989, p. 6)

According to Rorty, "a talent for speaking differently, rather than for arguing well, is the chief instrument of cultural change." Following Mary Hesse's (1980) characterization of scientific revolutions as "metaphorical redescriptions," Rorty argues that cultural change occurs when we start speaking "differently," that is, when we invest in a new description of our world. Here, what Rorty means by metaphor or by "metaphorical redescription" becomes critical. Rorty subscribes to Donald Davidson's view that dispenses with the traditional distinction between "literal" and "figural" meanings:

Davidson puts this point by saying that one should not think of metaphorical expressions as having meaning distinct from their literal ones. To have meaning is to have a place in a language game. Metaphors, by definition, do not. . . . In his view, tossing a metaphor into a conversation is like suddenly breaking off the conversation long enough to make a face, or pulling a photograph out of your pocket and displaying it, or pointing at a feature of the surroundings, or slapping your interlocutor's face, or kissing him. . . . All these are ways of producing effects on your interlocutor or your reader, but not ways of conveying a message. (1989, pp. 17–18)

Rorty's adherence to Davidson's view of metaphor indicates clearly what he means by contingency. It is something that is radically indeterminate, unanticipatable, hence random. If cultural change occurs through metaphorical redescription, and if that metaphorical redescription has no meaning within the existing language game, then there is no logic, except the logic of contingency, that can explain how we move from an old to a new language game. It is a happening, a contingent happening.

What role, if any, does rhetoric play in such an happening? If rhetoric is now imagined as a discursive practice that anchors or facilitates a putative metaphorical redescription, then rhetoric

itself becomes a contingent achievement as opposed to an art or practice of managing contingency. Although Rorty uses the term *contingency* so centrally and frequently, he rarely thematizes it. He is content to use the contingent as the opposite of the necessary, in fact as a suture, which brings under the former anything that is uncertain or indeterminate, an implication Aristotle sought to avoid by linking the contingent with the probable. Rorty is also not sufficiently interested in the fate of rhetoric to think through the implications as to how his views on language and contingency affect it or alter its course.

We have to turn to the work of Stanley Fish, a distinguished literary critic and legal scholar, to get a better grasp of how the postfoundationalist view of contingency affects the rhetorical project. Fish, unlike so many other postfoundationalist thinkers, is fluent in the rhetorical tradition and embraces rhetoric without reservation. In his major collection of essays, *Doing What Comes Naturally* (1989), *rhetorical* serves, by his own account, as a master word, and the conclusion the volume draws is that "we live in a rhetorical world" (p. 25). Fish also describes himself as "a card-carrying anti-foundationalist" and that partly explains his attraction to rhetoric. "Indeed," writes Fish, "another word for anti-foundationalism *is* rhetoric, and one could say without much exaggeration that modern anti-foundationalism is old sophism writ analytic" (p. 347).

Fish, like Rorty, regards human beings as situated selves always and already tethered to an "interpretive community." According to Fish:

Anti-foundationalism teaches that questions of fact, truth, correctness, validity, and clarity can neither be posed nor answered in reference to some extracontextual, ahistorical, nonsituated reality, or rule, or law, or value; rather, anti-foundationalism asserts, all these matters are intelligible and debatable only within the precincts of the contexts or situations or paradigms or communities that give them their local and changeable shape. (p. 344)

All practice is situated practice. Regardless of what we are doing—whether interpreting a literary text, making a legal argument, rendering a moral judgment, or opting for a political strategy—we cannot escape our situatedness.

What is provocative about Fish is the inferences he draws from the fact of our situatedness regarding the relationship between theory and practice, especially in interpretation. According to Fish, both friends and foes of antifoundationalism misunderstand its implications. Fish maintains that antifoundationalism has no consequences. The critics fear that an absence of any independent ground or neutral observation-language from which to assess and possibly modify our present beliefs and practices would lead to a world without controls—where unmoored subjects would act as though "anything goes" and where rational inquiry and communication would be impossible. For Fish, these dark forebodings are unwarranted. A situated self is not radically free and unencumbered, as the critics fear. Instead, it is massively bound and everything it does is a "function of the conventional possibilities built into this or that context." "Rather than unmooring the subject," Fish argues, "anti-foundationalism reveals the subject to be always and already tethered by the local community norms and standards that constitute it and enable its rational actions" (p. 346).

On the other hand, the proponents hope that once we recognize that we are always and already situated, this recognition would enable us to "become more self-consciously situated and inhabit our situatedness in a more effective way" (p. 347). Fish rejects that possibility because the recognition "that we are situated does not make us more situated," and it does not alter the way we know and act (p. 348). Besides, the act of recognition itself is situated, and therefore cannot become the object of reflexive attention. For Fish, the attempt to privilege the act of recognition is simply a symptom of the irrepressible longing to escape our situatedness; a sly maneuver to smuggle back foundationalism under the liberal disguise of reflexivity.

Fish, like Rorty, believes that the fundamental assumptions that structure our belief and behavior are contingent. They cannot be justified as necessary on transcendental or transhistorical grounds. This is one of the basic tenets of antifoundationalism. Here, once again, Fish insists that the recognition of the contingency of our fundamental beliefs and assumptions does not impair their hold over us. It is a mistake, says Fish:

[to turn] the recognition of contingency into a way of avoiding contingency, as if contingency acknowledged were contingency transcended. You may know *in general* that the structure of your convictions is an historical artifact, but that knowledge does not transport you to a place where those convictions are no longer in force. We remain embedded in history even when we know that it is history we are embedded in. . . . (pp. 523–524)

It seems that Fish, in a manner reminiscent of Aristotle, domesticates the contingent by linking it to our situatedness and to our embedding in history. Contingency becomes a distant horizon, which is powerless "in relation to particular convictions . . . by which we are now grasped and constituted" (pp. 523–524). Contingency so conceived is also not susceptible to rhetorical engagement.

But there is a catch. The contingent cannot be stabilized by our embedding in history, because the latter is also contingent and susceptible to rhetorical engagement. This is evident in Fish's account of the relationship between theory and practice. According to Fish, theory *qua* theory (that is, theory as a metadiscourse) has no consequences, it does not affect practice. But theory can be, and usually is, a certain type of practice. But, what is practice? Practice is an embedded activity, it is "doing what comes naturally" to situated selves. Fish, unlike Pierre Boudieu or the ethnomethodologists, does not offer a generalized account of everyday practice. He is specifically concerned with interpretive practice in law and literature. In this context, he describes himself as an antiformalist, an approach implicit in his antifoundationalism. The antiformalist begins by rejecting "literal meaning" as a constraint on interpretation. According to Fish, once that first step down the antiformalist road is taken, one inevitably runs into rhetoric and contingency. He schematically states the six subsequent steps as follows:

(1) relocating interpretive constraint in intention; (2) the realization that intention must itself be interpretively established, and that it can be established only through persuasion . . . (3) the characterization of persuasion as a matter entirely contingent, rational only in relation to reasons that have

themselves become reasons through the mechanism of persuasion; (4) the insight that contingency, if taken seriously, precludes the claims for theory as they are usually made; (5) the demoting of theory to a practice no different from any other; (6) the elevation of practice to a new, if ever-changing, universal in relation to which there is nothing higher . . . that can be invoked. (pp. 25–26)

Thus, the antiformalist road brings you to a point of *chiasmus* where the rhetoric of contingency (step 2) and the contingency of rhetoric (step 3) cross. In step 2, the contingency of alternative interpretations (as in Aristotle's deliberation) is closed for the moment by the force of rhetoric. In step 3, the achievement of rhetoric is contingently linked to what is always and already there (say, assumptions and vocabularies), the contingent products of prior persuasions. As for step 5, in another context Fish asserts that "theory is essentially a rhetorical and political phenomenon whose effects are purely contingent." And yet, Fish assures us that "these truths are the occasion neither of cynicism nor of despair" (p. 380). Here, as elsewhere, we are simply "doing what comes naturally." Thus contingency, once a sign of historical flux, becomes naturalized in some versions of postfoundationalist thought.

ACKNOWLEDGEMENTS: In writing this paper I have had numerous productive discussions with the following friends and colleagues: Sally Ewing, Jean Goodwin, James Jasinski, Christopher Kamrath, Benjamin Lee, Michael Leff, Thomas McCarthy, and Michael Pfau. I am particularly indebted to Jansinski for his detailed comments on an earlier version of this essay.

[*See also* Classical rhetoric; *and* Philosophy, *articles on* Perennial topics and terms *and* Rhetoric and philosophy.]

BIBLIOGRAPHY

Aristotle. *Rhetoric*. Translated by W. Rhys Roberts, pp. 1–218. In *The Rhetoric and the Poetics of Aristotle*. New York, 1954.

Aristotle on Rhetoric: A Theory of Civic Discourse. Translated with introduction, notes, and appendices by George A. Kennedy. New York, 1991.

Barthes, Roland. *Mythologies*. Selected and translated by Annette Lavers. New York, 1972. First published 1957.

Bitzer, Lloyd F. "Political Rhetoric." In *Handbook of Political Communication*. Edited by Dan Nimmo and Keith Sanders, pp. 225–248. Beverly Hills, Calif., 1981.

Bitzer, Lloyd F. "Rhetoric and Public Knowledge." In *Rhetoric, Philosophy and Literature: An Exploration*. Edited by D. M. Burks, pp. 67–93. West Lafayette, Ind., 1978.

Bryant, Donald C. "Rhetoric: Its Functions and Its Scope." *Quarterly Journal of Speech* 39 (1953), pp. 401–414.

Burke, Kenneth. *A Rhetoric of Motives*. Berkeley, 1962. First published 1950.

Butler, Judith. *Gender Trouble: Feminism and the Subversion of Identity*. New York, 1990.

Butler, Judith. "Contingent Foundations: Feminism and the Question of 'Postmodern'." In *Feminists Theorize the Political*. Edited by Judith Butler and Joan W. Scott, pp. 3–21. New York, 1992.

Butler, Judith, Ernesto Laclau, and Slavoj Zizek. *Contingency, Hegemony, Universality: Contemporary Dialogue on the Left*. New York, 2000.

Cahn, Michael. "Reading Rhetoric Rhetorically: Isocrates and the Marketing of Insight." *Rhetorica* 2 (1989), pp. 121–144.

Cahn, Steven M. *Fate, Logic, and Time*. New Haven, 1967.

Campbell, Karlyn Kohrs. "The Ontological Foundations of Rhetoric." *Philosophy and Rhetoric* 3 (1970), pp. 97–108.

Farrell, Thomas B. "Knowledge, Consensus, and Rhetorical Theory." *Quarterly Journal of Speech*, 62 (1976), pp. 1–14.

Farrell, Thomas B. *Norms of Rhetorical Culture*. New Haven, 1993.

Fish, Stanley. *Doing What Comes Naturally*. Durham, N.C., 1989.

Garver, Eugene. *Machiavelli and the History of Prudence*. Madison, Wis., 1987.

Garver, Eugene. *Aristotle's Rhetoric: An Art of Character*. Chicago, 1994.

Great Ideas: A Syntopicon, The. 2 vols. Chicago, 1952. See chapter 9 on "Chance," vol. 1, pp. 179–192; chapter 27 on "Fate," vol. 1, pp. 515–525; and chapter 61 on "Necessity and Contingency," vol. 2, pp. 251–269.

Grimaldi, William M.A., S.J. *Aristotle, Rhetoric I: A Commentary*. New York, 1980.

Hacking, Ian. *The Emergence of Probability: A Philosophical Study of Early Ideas about Probability, Induction and Statistical Inference*. New York, 1975.

Hamlyn, D. W. "Contingent and Necessary Statements." In *The Encyclopedia of Philosophy*, vol. 1. Edited by Paul Edwards, pp. 198–204. New York, 1967.

Hariman, Robert. "Status, Marginality, and Rhetorical

Theory." *Quarterly Journal of Speech* 72 (1986), pp. 38–54.

Hesse, Mary. *Revolutions and Reconstructions in the Philosophy of Science.* Bloomington, Ind., 1980.

Jonsen, Albert R., and Stephen Toulmin. *The Abuse of Casuistry: A History of Moral Reasoning.* Berkeley, 1988.

Kekes, John. *Moral Wisdom and Good Lives.* Ithaca, N.Y., 1995.

Leff, Michael. "The Habitation of Rhetoric." In *Contemporary Rhetorical Theory: A Reader.* Edited by John L. Lucaites, Celeste M. Condit, and Sally Caudill, pp. 52–64. New York, 1999. First published 1987.

Lucaites, John L., Celeste M. Condit, and Sally Caudill, eds. *Contemporary Rhetorical Theory: A Reader.* New York, 1999.

Lyotard, Jean-François, and Jean-Loup Thebaud. *Just Gaming.* Translated by Brian Massumi. Minneapolis, 1985. First published 1979.

Lyotard, Jean-François. *The Defferend: Phrases in Dispute.* Translated by Georges Van Den Abbeele. Minneapolis, 1988.

McGee, Michael C. "A Materialist's Conception of Rhetoric." In *Explorations in Rhetoric: Studies in Honor of Douglas Ehninger.* Edited by R. E. McKerrow, pp. 23–48. Glenville, Ill., 1982.

Natanson, Maurice. "The Limits of Rhetoric." *Quarterly Journal of Speech* 21 (1955), pp. 133–139.

Nussbaum, Martha C. *The Fragility of Goodness: Luck and Ethics in Greek Tragedy and Philosophy.* New York, 1986.

Patey, Douglas Lane. *Probability and Literary Form: Philosophical Theory and Literary Practice in the Augustan Age.* New York, 1984.

Perelman, Chaim. *The Realm of Rhetoric.* Translated by William Kluback. Notre Dame, Ind., 1982.

Perelman, Chaim, and Lucie Olbrechts-Tyteca. *The New Rhetoric: A Treatise On Argumentation.* Translated by John Wilkinson and Purcell Weaver. Notre Dame, Ind., 1969. First published 1958.

Plato. *The Collected Dialogues of Plato.* Edited by Edith Hamilton and Huntington Cairns. Princeton, 1961.

Pocock, J. G. A. *The Machiavellian Moment: Florentine Political Thought and the Atlantic Republican Tradition.* Princeton, 1975.

Poulakos, John. "Toward a Sophistic Definition of Rhetoric." *Philosophy and Rhetoric* 16 (1983), pp. 35–48.

Rorty, Richard. *Philosophy and the Mirror of Nature.* Princeton, 1979.

Rorty, Richard. *Contingency, irony, and solidarity.* New York, 1989.

Sartre, Jean Paul. "The Wall." In *Existentialism from Dostoevsky to Sartre.* Edited by Walter Kaufmann, pp. 223–240. New York, 1956.

Scott, Robert L. "On Viewing Rhetoric as Epistemic." *Central States Speech Journal* 18 (1967), pp. 9–17.

Smith, Barbara Herrnstein. *Contingencies of Value: Alternative Perspectives For Critical Theory.* Cambridge, Mass., 1988.

Struever, Nancy S. *The Language of History in the Renaissance: Rhetoric and Historical Consciousness in Florentine Humanism.* Princeton, 1970.

Waterlow, Sarah. *Passage and Possibility: A Study of Aristotle's Modal Concepts.* Oxford, 1982.

Weaver, Richard. *The Ethics of Rhetoric.* Chicago, 1953.

Williams, Bernard. *Moral Luck.* Cambridge, U.K., 1981.

—DILIP PARAMESHWAR GAONKAR

CONTROVERSIA AND SUASORIA. The *suasoria* and the *controversia,* both exercises in the composition and delivery of speeches on a given theme, formed the two constituent elements of the Roman rhetorical exercise called declamation (*declamatio*). [*See* Declamation.] This played an important part in the school curriculum at Rome from the first century CE onward and had a pedigree reaching back to exercises on abstract and specific themes (theses and hypotheses) in the Greek rhetorical tradition. The *suasoria* was deliberative in form, and addressed a great man at some critical period in his career; thus, in response to a historical fantasy such as "Alexander deliberates whether or not to cross the ocean," the speaker would offer Alexander advice on his course of action, speaking of him in the third person and occasionally addressing him directly. [*See* Deliberative genre.] The *controversia,* on the other hand, was a fictitious forensic speech that argued for or against an imaginary defendant. After the statement of a law and a summation of the facts of the case, the speaker would have to anticipate or rebut the arguments from the other side, concoct dialogues with witnesses or opponents, and create a narrative with various agents. The Roman rhetorician Quintilian indicated that by his day (c.35–c.100 CE), many rhetoricians specialized in the *controversia,* which was even performed as public entertainment by teachers of rhetoric and their students.

Of the two exercises, the *suasoria* was considered the simpler, and was often taught in the grammar schools. It shows many affinities with other exercises of the rhetorical and philosophical curriculum, and as a mode of deliberative oratory, ethical meditation, and biographical dramatization, the *suasoria* influenced popular and high literature from the diatribe to letter writing to epic poetry. [*See* Ars dictaminis.] The chief evidence for the Roman *suasoria* comes from the seven extant *suasoriae* in the elder Seneca's (c.55 BCE–c.39 CE) collection of excerpts from Roman declamations (*Oratorum et rhetorum sententiae divisiones colores*). These brilliant performances of the leading teachers, and indeed even of equestrian Romans (c.20 BCE to 40 CE), show a culture of wit, literary allusion, and high stylization, and so provide a fundamental insight into the literature of the Julio-Claudians, but, it must be said, they are polished, virtuoso performances to be appreciated by an audience who had all composed their own versions in school. The topics are quasi-historical: In Seneca, Alexander deliberates on whether to cross the ocean, whether to enter Babylon, the Spartans deliberate on whether to withdraw from Thermopylae, Agamemnon deliberates on whether to sacrifice Iphigenia, the Athenians whether to remove their victory monuments in order to forestall a second Persian invasion, Cicero whether to beg Antony for his life or whether to burn his writings in return for his life. Quintilian records other titles: Numa considers whether to be king, Cato considers whether to marry. The judgment of the arms of Achilles (whether to give them to Ajax or to Odysseus) seems to have been a favorite. In the *Lives of the Sophists,* Philostratus (third century CE) has recorded a number that indicate Greek practice: it is often the Spartans who deliberate whether to adopt some policy that might serve them well but perhaps contradicts the spirit of their traditions. The Scythians are made to wonder if they should give up the soft urban life and return to their ancestral nomadic ways.

The form of the title often requires the student to relate a general issue to a specific provocation: Agamemnon is moved to sacrifice his daughter because Calchas says otherwise it is not *fas* (religiously right or possible) to set sail for Troy. Cestius (first century BCE), perhaps the greatest Roman teacher after Quintilian, recognized that the *suasoria* constituted a useful exercise in the choice and practice of tone: giving advice to a tyrant required a tone different from giving advice to one's imagined peers in the senate hall or perhaps in the family council where one might set the exhortation to old Cato to marry. The *suasoria* thus provided first lessons in the relationships of speaker, audience, and style that the *controversia* would explore more systematically and with greater variation.

The *suasoria*, while occupied with flights of fancy of what might have been and the imaginative anachronism of placing oneself in history, also taught the rhetorical, logical, and compositional structure known as division. Division, and not simply the high stylization so palpable in the sentential and colorful Latin, was a mark of virtuosity. Teachers gave advice about it; audience members analyzed the performances in such terms. Fuscus, for instance, divided his argument so: Iphigenia should not be sacrificed because this was murder; further it was murder of kin. The act would lose more than it would profit, and in particular, it would lose Iphigenia to gain Helen. And now an additional point, a new species of division: the sacrifice was not needed, the Greeks were delayed at Aulis by the action of wind and sea; the gods are unknowable. Declaimers responded to prior treatments, and Seneca tells of the variations worked on this division, in particular on the alleged unknowability of the gods. Argument is thus advanced on several grounds at once, in ways reminiscent of ancient oratory and of abiding interest to the lawyer; for example, my client did not do it, even if he did, he is not guilty, even if he is guilty, he should not be punished. Where the *controversia* subjected law and the facts of a law case to such a division, the *suasoria* treated ethical argument and motive with a similar rhetorical categorization.

The *suasoria*'s philosophical affinities, if not exact origins, are clear. The philosophical thesis posed a general question, often ethical but also scientific (e.g., Aristotle *Nicomachean Ethics* 9.2.1: is it necessary to obey a father in all things?). The theses on whether a man should marry may date from Theophrastus (c.372–c.287 BCE). Quintilian (3.5.11) articulated the relationship of the thesis to *suasoria*: thesis changes to *suasoria* once a name or particular occasion is added; whether Cato should marry is thus a *suasoria*. Aristotle's query about obeying a father became hackneyed (Seneca 2.1.20 and *Declamationes minores* 257; Aulus Gellius, second century CE, connects this thesis to philosophical schools; cf. *Musonius Rufus* 16). The formal relationship is more interesting than the ancient theorists allow, driven as they were by a desire to isolate a single defining difference, for the ethical thesis turns on a paradox (should a father counseling evil be obeyed?), where competing ethical claims collide. At the heart of the *suasoria* is a similar paradox of definition or category: Cicero is a writer—how can he burn his writing? Alexander is an invader—how can he stop? Although the philosopher Fabianus was among the renowned declaimers approved by Seneca, the *suasoria* did more than transfer a philosophical question to the ancient schoolroom. Unlike the earlier school pieces in the rhetorical puzzle (e.g., *sententia, chreia,* commonplace), the *suasoria* required a unified speech that animated and moralized the past. This contributed to a moral and rhetorical understanding of history and human agency that is the hallmark of Plutarch (c.46–after 119 CE) and much of imperial literature.

The spur to the introduction or spread of the *suasoria* as a school form is unknown, but we do have the evidence of Cicero (106–43 BCE) himself practicing philosophical theses at a time and occasion where they look much like *suasoriae* addressed to the self. In his forced retirement as Caesar consolidated power, Cicero wrote to Atticus that he declaimed eight theses on tyranny. Elsewhere Cicero contrasts his philosophical practice to his son's preference for rhetorical themes. His own philosophical writings provided a thesaurus of moral arguments on social duties and constitute a strong impetus, if not a direct source, for the ethical moralizing in a rhetorical mode that so appealed to imperial Romans. The *suasoria* can then be seen (rather like the letter writing of Pliny and Seneca) as a literary mode of ethical address and training for one's self and one's friends.

The collections of declamations contain a larger number of *controversiae*, which formed the apex of rhetorical training, and so the importance of the *suasoria* has been eclipsed. The influence of the latter can be seen not simply in the school curriculum but in the literature of the empire. Despite the difficulty of demonstrating direct dependence (since the treatment of character that scholars at times call declamatory owes much to stock themes and persons of new comedy), *suasoria* contributed along with such rhetorical figures as *ēthopoeia, prosōpopoeia,* and *aporia* to a rhetorical understanding of character. [*See* Aporia; Ēthopoeia; *and* Prosōpopoeia.] Sulla confronting suicide, or Hamlet for that matter, engages in full-blown *suasoria.* Yet in its proper form, the *suasoria* is distinguished by the stance of the adviser; so the satellite addressing the king in Seneca's *Agamemnon* and certain of Ovid's *Heroides* or *Amores* (2.11), where the poet urges his wife not to sail, are directly inspired by the *suasoria.* Other dramatic monologues owe more to the Greek school exercise where the student writes the speech for a literary character (e.g., Achilles mourning Patroclus).

Still, it was in the *controversia* that the ancient rhetorician displayed his full mastery. In this final exercise of the rhetorical curriculum, the master set the facts of the case (*thema* or *propositum*) along with a relevant law; he might give advice (*sermo*) on the division of the case and the choice of *persona.* The extant collection of Minor Declamations from the school of Quintilian provides in addition sample treatments (the so-called Major Declamations are more showpieces and the collection of Calpurnius Flaccus are compressed excerpts). While the case could be argued from either side, themes were often designed for one side only. Having received the spare essentials of plot and law, the declaimer subjected the case to a division. The complexity of the structural system of argument and a greater range of situations and characters distinguished the *controversia* from the *suasoria.* While Hellenistic *stasis* theory was even more complex, Seneca remarks that a case could be considered from the point of view of law, justice, or fact; that is, did the law cited apply to the particular case, was there conflict between the letter and the spirit of the law, and, the option rarely used in declamation, did the crime occur or did the defendant commit the crime. The last, while useful in real law cases, did not suit declamation, which of course offered no witnesses or evidence, merely the brilliant arguing of the declaimer. *Stasis* theory, though confusing in its terms and classifications, was simply the reduction of the case at hand to essential questions; *stasis* in Greek, *status, constitutio,* or *quaestio* in Latin. [*See* Stasis.]

While this thinking underpinned the speech, the actual structure was determined by other conventions. Seneca makes clear a fourfold organization: proem, narrative, argumentation, epilogue. In practice, a most important consideration was the choice of *persona*. [*See* Persona.] Declamation was speech delivered in character, and the teachers spent much time instructing their pupils in the effective use of character. [*See* Ēthos.] Presented with a harsh script in which a severe father disowns a son for disobedience, (he has been kind to his father's enemy or married the wrong girl), the declaimer must create an attractive, sympathetic character. Son and father must be reconciled. The audience must be moved by the polished commonplace on fathers forgiving wayward sons, by a description of the place where the critical act of disobedience took place, and by the ethical argument, tied to the very language of the law, that the son's behavior did not in fact violate the father's injunctions or perhaps the spirit of the law. The rhetorical figures of commonplace and description, the *stasis* argument from definition or equity, must be ably subordinated to a narrative of a speech in the young man's character. [*See* Commonplaces and commonplace books; *and* Descriptio.] The elder Seneca's collection of the colors, maxims, and divisions of the famous declaimers reveal an expert audience appreciative but critical of the competitive display of declaimers and prone to retell or "borrow" the finest examples of these three parts of a declamation. [*See* Color.]

The *controversia* offered more than brilliant maxims for the excerptive listener. Declamatory plots turned on marriage, divorce, rape, adultery, abdication, parricide, tyrannicide, and insanity. The pirate, prostitute, freedman, military hero, the pair of the rich man and his poor friend and of severe father and errant son appear again and again. Declamation thus offered a public meditation on issues of loyalty within the family, between the family and the state, or the state and the gods. The son's maturing responsibilities to father, mother, stepmother, wife, and commander take center stage. This ethical reflection takes place in a customary context: the speaker treats stock themes and situations that have been exhausted. All have been treated before, and furthermore, the case seems hopeless, the young speaker powerless: the father has disowned his son, or the letter of the law seems unambiguous.

The schoolboy declaimer has the opportunity to resist this silencing. He is given the tools to speak, to make redress, and in this technical linguistic training he learns the upper-class "right" to speak for others, to represent their grievances. He also practices stylized accounts of how and why the father, the prostitute, and the freedman act as they do and begins to practice with versions of the law. The *suasoria* and *controversia* offer our best window into the playspeech of schooling and declamatory performance that formed the basis of an ancient rhetorical mentality.

[*See also* Classical rhetoric.]

BIBLIOGRAPHY

Bloomer, W. Martin. *The School of Rome*. Princeton, in press.

Bonner, S. *Roman Declamation in the Late Republic and Early Empire*. Liverpool, U.K., 1949. A fundamental work, especially strong on the relation of declamation to Roman law.

Fairweather, J. *Seneca the Elder*. Cambridge, U.K., 1981. A careful treatment not only of the life and work of Seneca but of the history of declamation and of stasis theory.

Russell, D. *Greek Declamation*. Cambridge, U.K., 1983. The best treatment of the subject.

Sussman, Lewis A. *The Major Declamations Ascribed to Quintilian*. Frankfurt a.M., 1987.

Sussman, Lewis A. *The Declamations of Calpurnius Flaccus*. Leiden, 1994. Text, translation, and commentary

Winterbottom, Michael. *The Elder Seneca*. Cambridge, Mass., 1974. Translation and introduction.

Winterbottom, Michael. *The Minor Declamations Ascribed to Quintilian*. Berlin, 1984. Text and commentary with thorough introduction.

— W. MARTIN BLOOMER

CONTROVERSY. What is involved when one is caught up in a controversy? How are controversies initiated, spread, and resolved? What are the stakes of controversy, and how can such stakes be clarified and critically engaged? These are important questions for a time when the tempo of contentious argumentation seems to be increasing. The Library of Congress has identified two types of traditional controversy: disputes over religious convictions and water rights. Today, sustained differences of opinion are conveyed across fields of knowledge, political systems, and alternative cultures. Controversy seems to be one of the defining features of the age, yet it remains one of the least studied or understood communication phenomena of our time.

There are several reasons for the prevalence of controversy. With the spread of modernist institutions came the development and use of technologies that challenged traditional forms of life, thereby destabilizing traditional forms of consensus. Modern medical science, for example, makes possible interventions that afford new choices relating to health that destabilize traditional norms regarding life-and-death situations. Second, the mass media seem to be centers of controversy. Human conflict appears as a dramatic form of gaining attention. The media endlessly pursue this form in putting contrasting opinions against one another. The media do more than report disputes, of course. Absent genuine conflict of opinions, the media conduct investigative reports, hold contentious interviews, or resurrect old disputes in the interest of gaining public attention while making themselves centers of controversy. Finally, a pluralistic society seems to be a breeding ground for dissensus: Pluralism encourages alternative lifestyles. While in theory such tolerance ought to underscore a flexible consensus pertaining to social norms, in practice pluralism generates controversy as each group affirms its own identity by commenting on the inappropriateness of others. To the extent, then, that the influence of modernist institutions, the mass media, and pluralism continue to grow, the domain of contemporary controversy is sure to expand across culture, generations, and epistemological fields.

Cultures generate controversies to the extent that norms of understanding and conduct remain contingent choices for individuals but are at the same time important to the collective wellbeing of society. Every culture's forms of communication find their way into useful social practice. Since practices are contestable, inconsistent, intertwined with special interest, or asserted as matters of individual or common preference, the "live" quality of a culture inevitably pits practices up against one another. The jostling among practices of communication generates contestation over claims to rightness, truthfulness, propriety, sincerity, and their opposites for any particular

claim. Disputation over such communication claims engenders several distinctive types of controversy.

For example, legitimization controversy tests claims to rightness made on behalf of institutions. [*See* Politics, *article on* Rhetoric and legitimation.] A controversy concerning authority pertains to contested hierarchies of command and control. Social and cultural controversies take on a temporal dynamic. If sufficiently widespread and important, a controversy can become a political marker event for a generation. The Vietnam War not only provided a focal point of disagreement with the mainstream for the sixties generation, it also afforded common grounds of agreement that forged a sustained identity for a cohort coming of age. So potent is the first political engagement, that even after the immediate cause of a dispute passes from the scene, the core issue itself may be reduplicated analogically, sustaining the controversy in different form. Thus, long after the Vietnam war had ended, the specter of a "new" Vietnam fueled debates over American foreign policy for decades.

Just as a controversy can define a political generation, so it can also sustain influence in an epistemological field. It may well be the case that special fields are definable as much by what is held in dispute as by field-oriented consensus. In one sense, sustained epistemic controversy is assured by scientific method itself. Even well-supported hypotheses are proven only by a preponderance of evidence, the null hypothesis remaining a statistical possibility. Additionally, scientific revolutions may generate fundamental disagreement over how nature itself is comported with the latest paradigms of knowledge. [*See* Science.] Finally, the claims of openness made by science itself give rise to a number of disputes. Creation science, for example, seizes upon specific scientific norms in its attempt to occupy a place alongside other theories that follow a more wholly scientific methodology. By manipulating public perception of the degree and kind of scientific consensus, controversies ranging from cancer caused by cigarette smoking to the effectiveness of missile defense, have been promoted as products of well-funded interest groups.

Controversy need not be the product of sustained disagreement across time or social venue.

Indeed, it is likely that most controversies are more or less short lived phenomena surrounding particular performances, services, or objects of consumption. Disputes concerning the quality of artistic performances are aesthetic controversies. In matters of taste, different evaluations of the quality of a performance may be advanced without stirring major disagreement—if parties agree to disagree. An aesthetic dispute becomes a controversy when a threshold is crossed that identifies the performances as having significant claims on an audience's appreciation or adherence. [See Criticism.] Performances are routinely criticized or championed based upon such evaluations. Services are objects of controversy as well. A service becomes controversial when it fails to meet state-of-the-art standards. Customary services that no longer meet standards, or new ones with high costs or unacceptable risks may be controversial. Public institutions routinely invite controversy when their services in providing education, medical care, public protection and so forth do not meet acceptable standards. Finally, objects of consumption may become the center of controversy. Blame and finger pointing may begin, for example, when the supply of some essential objects, such as food or fuel, is interrupted, or the goods become more expensive or scarce. Other objects may become controversial because of risks attached to their use. Whether risks are individually or collectively imposed is the basis of controversy over regulation of everything from seat belts to drug consumption. Together, performances, services, and consumer objects invite controversy in a consumer society.

So far, the pervasiveness of controversy as a cultural, social, and political phenomenon has been established. Despite the widespread appearance of such open disagreements, the subject of controversy itself has received little attention. Part of the problem is that the prevailing orientation toward argument has been to view controversy as a background context of disagreement that is resolved by appropriate reasoning techniques or dialogue. Since the costs of discord and the fruits of agreement are patent, advice on proper argumentation usually takes controversy as a starting point in the pursuit of resolution. Similarly, when controversy is studied, it is usually converted into its sister term *conflict* to ma-

terialize the stakes of disagreement. While controversial topics do engage conflict, controversies involve reflexive discourse that calls into question the very grounds of resolution or management. Exploration of the types, duration, consequences, and discursive and nondiscursive qualities of controversy require more study, but Edwin Black has given us a clue to their essential common property. For Black, controversy involves elements of persuasion and dissuasion. Such arguments are characterized as unique problems because not only is an audience addressed with the interests of gaining adherence to a particular viewpoint, but also the audience is instructed not to accept what otherwise might become a viable competing belief or supported action. To say that controversies are inherently complex problems should invite the study of how reason and action are culturally, temporally, and socially instantiated in each particular case. [See Deliberative genre; Epideictic genre; Forensic genre; Hybrid genres; and Law.]

[See also Logos.]

BIBLIOGRAPHY

Black, Edwin. *Rhetorical Criticism: A Study in Method.* Madision, Wis., 1965.

—G. THOMAS GOODNIGHT

CONVICTION. At the end of World War II, two scholars of argument, Chaim Perelman and Lucie Olbrechts-Tyteca, began collaborating on a project to study and theorize about the forms of argument used in daily deliberations in various fields such as law, religion, and politics. They became interested in this topic because they felt that their contemporaries were uninformed about practical argument, particularly in the public sphere. Having witnessed the excesses of Nazi propaganda and its horrible consequences in the Holocaust, the two Belgian scholars made a plan to study argument practices and generalize about them. During the period when they were collecting thousands of arguments produced by people in various fields, they also searched historical treatises for a theory that might explain the workings of these arguments. They found it in Aristotle's fourth-century BCE *Topics* and *Rhetoric*, works with which they had been unfamiliar, since their education in the European system had been limited to the study of stylistic tropes and figures in rhetoric and of formal validity in logic. Drawing upon Aristotle, as well as models in jurisprudence and the Talmudic tradition, they developed a theory of conviction based on justified belief that focused on the audience as an argumentative participant. After ten years of study, they published in French a treatise entitled *La Nouvelle Rhétorique: Traité de l'Argumentation* (1958); the English translation, *The New Rhetoric: A Treatise on Argumentation,* was published in 1969.

In developing his theory, Perelman rejected processes of reasoning and proof using a single kind of justification as models for argumentation. His theory made the idea of audience adherence central to every aspect of making arguments and providing justification. In *The New Rhetoric* and in *The Realm of Rhetoric* (1977, translated 1982), he began by contrasting analytical with dialectical reasoning. Analytical reasoning, such as that found in formal logic, is impersonal, demonstrative, and relies on formal rules for the validity of its inferences. Its premises function like axioms, and its conclusions are self-evident and compelling. Dialectical reasoning, such as that found in Aristotle's *Topics* and *Rhetoric,* is contextual and must be judged according to the extent to which it is adapted to its audience. Thus, it makes use of generally accepted opinions, is stated in natural language, and produces conclusions that are probable but not certain. Perelman emphasized that dialectical reasoning and argumentation take place in the realm of what is contestable (the "realm of rhetoric") in such fields as ethics, politics, and law. [*See* Dialectic; *and* Logic.]

Perelman believed that, in fields such as these, the epistemologies of the Enlightenment and the nineteenth and early twentieth centuries were insufficient to provide the means of reasoning and justification for deliberation and choice making. In "The New Rhetoric: A Theory of Practical Reasoning" (*Great Ideas Today,* Chicago, 1970), Perelman noted that empiricism cannot provide the basis for argumentation because it does not provide a theory of values and therefore does not enable us to justify choices and decisions. Cartesian rationalism likewise cannot be relied upon because it deals only with certainty and says nothing about speaker, audience, or culture. What was needed was a theory of argument that could be used to describe and study the processes people go through when they must deliberate in the realm of human affairs—the realm of the probable, the contestable, the uncertain. Perelman took jurisprudence as his model of argument because argument in law relies upon the practice of nested opposition in which claims are made, evidence is weighed, and the judge decides which side in a given context presents what is on balance the better case. [*See* Law.]

In *The New Rhetoric,* Perelman and Olbrechts-Tyteca also distinguish discourse designed to convince from that intended to persuade. They reject a traditional distinction between the two, which is based on the response the speaker or writer expects from the audience. Instead of identifying convincing discourse as that which seeks intellectual agreement and persuasion as that which moves the recipient to action, they differentiate the two based on the quality of audience envisioned by the speaker or writer. Speech intended to address the universal audience is speech intended to convince, whereas speech addressed to the particular audience is intended to persuade. Argumentation is associated with conviction, but persuasion takes the form of advertising and propaganda.

The distinction between the universal and the particular audience initially laid out in *The New Rhetoric* has caused a good deal of subsequent confusion among argument theorists and scholars. It is important to note that the "audience" to which Perelman refers is not an actual audience but rather one constructed by the speaker. In *The Realm of Rhetoric,* Perelman emphasized that "we must regard [audience] as *the gathering of those whom the speaker wants to influence by his or her arguments*" (p. 14). As we plan what we want to say, we can envision ourselves speaking to a particular audience—a particular individual or group that incarnates the people we think we are addressing. This audience is marked by a limited set of self-interested values. When we design what we say so as to move only this particular audience, we engage in persuasion.

Convincing speech, on the other hand, addresses the universal audience. A speaker or writer invoking the universal audience would design his or her message so as to meet the standards and expectations of an ideal audience. The posited universal audience is comprised of all those who are viewed as competent and reasonable. An appeal to the universal audience is an appeal to reason. When we design our arguments to meet the highest standards of proof and the best values in a society, we aim at conviction—the product of argumentation addressed to the universal audience. The idea of the universal audience is thus the normative standard in *The New Rhetoric*'s theory and is what distinguishes conviction from mere persuasion.

Since Perelman has rejected empirical proof and formal validity and instead emphasized audience adherence as the standard for judging argument, his theory is very much in need of this normative standard. Since argumentation is inherently an audience-focused activity, it makes sense to have recourse to audience as its raison d'être. The danger here, of course, is the danger of equating effectiveness in persuading an audience with the quality of an argument; the argument that is designed to be totally successful in changing the mind of the audience would be judged "best." But then there would be no safeguard to ensure that such argument is ethical and aims for the best. Interjecting the universal audience standard into his theory presumably enables Perelman to save it from an audience-dependent relativism.

The sympathetic reader of Perelman's theory may agree that the universal audience standard works well to set the qualitative standard for argumentation and conviction. In *The Realm of Rhetoric,* Perelman reminds us of an aspect of dialectical reasoning that originates in Aristotle—the idea that its premises rely upon opinions accepted by the majority, by philosophers, or by the most notable and illustrious among them. The universal audience thus invokes the judgment and wisdom of those in a society who are the best educated, the wisest, and the most experienced. Argumentation designed to meet the expectations of this group would surely be of high quality.

Another advantage of the idea of "universal audience" is that it is pluralistic. The term itself is misleading in that this audience is not really "universal;" rather it is universal within a particular culture or society. Perelman has noted that "the idea of a rational argumentation cannot be defined *in abstracto,* since it depends on the historically grounded conception of the universal audience" (*Great Ideas*, 1970, p. 1087). The "universal" audience, then, is specific to a historical epoch and to a culture. Perhaps the best way to describe it is as an imagined group of a society's better educated and more critical members to whom the arguer intends to direct his or her argumentation.

The universal audience is not the only guarantor of an argument's quality, however. Perelman and Olbrechts-Tyteca also stress the necessity of preconditions for argument that would lead to ethical deliberation and choice making. First, argumentation assumes a community of minds—a willingness to engage in discussion and to see things from the point of view of one's interlocutor. It thus enacts the practice of dialectic in its best sense. Second, ethical argumentation requires that its participants enter into intercourse with each other in good faith, renouncing deception and the manipulation of other participants. Third, it assumes freedom of speech and open channels of communication so that everyone has an opportunity to participate. Perelman and Olbrechts-Tyteca thus remind their readers that "the use of argumentation implies that one has renounced resorting to force alone, that value is attached to gaining the adherence of one's interlocutor by means of reasoned persuasion, and that one is not regarding him as an object, but appealing to his free judgment" (p. 55).

The universal audience construct has been widely criticized by philosophers and argument theorists. They have pointed out the tension between the concept's normative function and its variability. How can the universal audience set a standard when that standard varies so much with context? Critics also point out that the universal audience reflects a performative contradiction in Perelman's work, since he rejected formal logic and rationalism and at the same time incorporated a rationalistic standard into his theory. Others have observed that the universal audience is a tautology. It implies a rational standard without making a commitment to any phenomenon external to itself to explain what that standard is or how it functions.

One can come to an understanding of the universal audience function, however, if one considers what Perelman has to say elsewhere about the concepts of the rational and the reasonable. Applying these two standards to the practice of law in particular, Perelman notes how they exist in dialectic with each other. The rational coincides with strict conformity with law, precedent, and principle. The reasonable corresponds to common sense and common opinion. A court decision may be strictly rational and at the same time violate our sense of what is reasonable and fair. In such a case, the law (the system) is often changed so as to conform to what is reasonable. The rational provides stability and regularity to the system; the reasonable makes adjustments to keep the system in line with the changing mores of society. While the attributes of these two constructs are related to the context of the decision, the rational nonetheless can be viewed as corresponding to the universal audience.

In *The New Rhetoric* and subsequent works, Perelman and Olbrechts-Tyteca laid out a theory of argument that is consistent in its emphasis on audience as the adjudicator of an argument's quality and its success. They began by insisting that the object of the theory of argumentation must be to study how arguers work to induce or increase their recipients' adherence to the theses they have presented to them for their assent. If argumentation is by its very nature thoroughly oriented toward audience, then argumentation consists of a web of argument comprised of the premises, reasoning, and values acceptable to the audience. The starting points of argument are the facts the audience recognizes, the truths they accept, the presumptions to which they subscribe, and the values and value hierarchies that they hold. The inferences used must take the form of associative and dissociative reasoning patterns they recognize as common in their culture and as understandable to them. Only by use of such means can the arguer so craft his or her argument that acceptance or adherence is passed from one element of the argument to another in order to produce acceptance for the arguer's claim. Since argument is a historically and culturally grounded process enacted by human beings, it must have these rhetorical components. So long as arguers commit to appeals to reason rather than prejudice and self interest, and so long as they subscribe to good argumentation practices, Perel-

man's vision for a just society can be fulfilled. He described his view well when he said to the readers of *The Realm of Rhetoric:* "Let us recast our philosophy in terms of a vision in which people and human societies are in interaction and are solely responsible for their cultures, their institutions, and their future—a vision in which people try hard to elaborate reasonable systems, imperfect but perfectible" (p. 160).

[*See also* Argumentation; Audience; Identification; Judgment; *and* Persuasion.]

BIBLIOGRAPHY

Ede, Lisa S. "Rhetoric versus Philosophy: The Role of the Universal Audience in Chaim Perelman's *The New Rhetoric.*" *Central States Speech Journal* 32 (1981), pp. 118–125. Ede points to the universal audience as a sign that Perelman was unable to free himself from the assumptions of a conventional rationalist model of argumentation. She notes contradictions, such as the need to avoid self-evidence as a formal requirement while still retaining it as a characteristic of the universal audience. She notes that the universal audience presumably plays no role in the last two-thirds of *The New Rhetoric,* where its authors treat the techniques of argumentation.

Eemeren, Frans H. van, Rob Grootendorst, and Francisca Snoeck Honkemans. "Perelman and Olbrechts-Tyteca's New Rhetoric." In *Fundamentals of Argumentation Theory: A Handbook of Historical Backgrounds and Contemporary Developments* by Erick C. Krabbe et al. Mahwah, N.J., 1996. The chapter provides a lucid account of *The New Rhetoric's* theory of argumentation, in particular the concepts of conviction and the universal audience. The authors' criticisms of Perelman and Olbrechts-Tyteca's theory at the end of their essay are sometimes unfounded or based on a misunderstanding of some of Perelman's work.

Frank, David A. "The New Rhetoric, Judaism, and Post-Enlightenment Thought: The Cultural Origins of Perelmanian Philosophy." *Quarterly Journal of Speech* 83 (1997), pp. 311–331. This essay traces the influence of Judaism and Talmudic habits of thought on Perelman's theory. It incorporates the pluralism of Judaism and rejects scientific and mathematical reasoning where there is only one right answer to a given question. *The New Rhetoric* is said to favor the "truth" that emerges from community-based deliberation. Because *The New Rhetoric* views the community and the audience and not the individual as the arbiters of social values, Frank argues that its system offers a third way between Enlightenment metaphysics and postmodernism.

Golden, James L. "The Universal Audience Revisited." In *Practical Reasoning in Human Affairs,* edited by James L. Golden and Joseph J. Pilotta, pp. 287–304. Dordrecht, The Netherlands, 1986. This essay, one of the clearest on conviction and the universal audience, explains the concept so as to clear up confusion about it. Golden notes that the universal audience is a construct of the speaker that stresses an ideal appropriate for a given historical epoch, and he emphasizes the importance of its appeal to universal values. Golden distinguishes between conviction and persuasion and then concludes his article by examining universal audience appeals in Socrates' "Apology" and John F. Kennedy's 1960 address to the Houston ministers.

Gross, Alan. "A Theory of Rhetorical Audience: Reflections on Chaim Perelman." *Quarterly Journal of Speech* 85 (1999), pp. 203–211. This essay argues that appeals to the universal audience thematize the real (facts, truths, presumptions), whereas appeals to the particular audience thematize the preferable (values, hierarchies, loci of the preferable). Gross further argues that discourse thematizing values can never address a universal audience. Gross's interpretation is not in agreement with some others who hold that appeals to abstract values can be appeals to the universal audience.

Perelman, Chaim. "The Rational and the Reasonable." In *The New Rhetoric and the Humanities,* pp. 117–123. Dordrecht, The Netherlands, 1979. In this brief but profound essay, Perelman lays out his theory of the rational and the reasonable that he applies to law although it can apply in other fields. The rational corresponds to formal logic, coherence, conformity with precedent and rule, and principle. The reasonable corresponds to common sense, common opinion, and what is viewed as equitable. When a rational standard is applied strictly in such a way as to appear unreasonable, the standard is then altered to bring it into conformity with the reasonable. The dialectic between the rational and the reasonable forms the basis for the progress of thought.

Perelman, Chaim. *The Realm of Rhetoric.* Translated by William Kluback. Notre Dame, Ind., 1982. English translation of *L'Empire rhétorique: rhétorique et argumentation,* first published in 1977. This small book serves as an excellent summary of the sizable *New Rhetoric.* In 179 pages, it reviews *The New Rhetoric*'s theories of audience, premises, associative and dissociative forms, and argument order. It also explains the philosophical foundations for Perelman's theory of argument.

Perelman, Chaim. "The New Rhetoric and the Rhetoricians: Remembrances and Comments." *Quarterly Journal of Speech* 20 (1984), pp. 188–196. In this important essay written shortly before his death in 1983, Perelman notes that critics such as Ray and Ede have failed to distinguish between views in *The New Rhetoric* that he attributed to other people and his own views. Perelman emphasizes the role played by pluralism in his theory, and he maintains that the universal audience's function is to show how discourse aimed at the universal audience can transcend self-interest and particular values. He notes that jurisprudence plays a role in argumentation analogous to that played by mathematics in formal logic.

Ray, John W. "Perelman's Universal Audience." *Quarterly Journal of Speech* 64 (1978), pp. 361–375. Ray traces the development of the concepts of persuasion and conviction in Perelman's writings. He notes the apparent contradiction between the idea of a universal audience and its use by a particular audience in a specific cultural setting. He also maintains that the universal audience is a circular, tautological construct.

Scult, Alan. "A Note on the Range and Utility of the Universal Audience." *Journal of the American Forensic Association* 22 (1985), pp. 83–87. This essay explores the universal audience's potential to import into argument practices a standard for judging the quality and excellence of argumentation.

— BARBARA WARNICK

COPIA means "abundance," and all its connotations are with wealth, variety, fertility. It recurs frequently in the writings of ancient rhetoricians, not as a strict technical term, but as a way of describing stylistic fluency, and always in order to commend it. The negative counterparts of *copia* are poverty of linguistic resources and empty loquacity, or mere verbiage.

The Humanists' interest in recovering classical Latin in all its fullness of vocabulary and expressive techniques activated the first attempts to codify measures for ensuring the acquisition of an abundant style, both for speech and for written composition. In the earliest years of the fifteenth century, the Italian Gasparino Barzizza (1360–1430) probably supplemented his precepts for learning to write Latin like the ancients with lists of synonyms extracted from Cicero. Such collections of words and phrases proliferated in Italy over the next hundred years and were the means by which apprentice writers learned to mine classical Latin for vocabulary to vary their expression of ideas.

All culminated, however, in the book that fixed the image of copia for all time, and that was the *De duplici copia verborum ac rerum commentarii duo,* the so-called *De copia* that Erasmus first published in Paris in 1512. For pedagogic reasons, he put abundance of words and abundance of things in separate books, but both coalesce to form a generative mechanism for making speech "a magnificent and impressive thing, surging along like a golden river, with thoughts and words pouring out in rich abundance." The book of words provides a thesaurus of vocabulary on many and diverse subjects, hints for varying the structure of sentences, and ways of applying figures of speech to enhance expression. Its correlation is with grammar, rather than with rhetoric, but, taking grammar at the points where it overlaps with rhetoric, Erasmus turns the mechanics of correct speech into an engine of word power. The second book, on things, is more properly rhetorical, for Erasmus's "things" are mostly methods by which persuasive argument is reinforced or amplified: descriptions, accumulation of modes of proof, examples, likenesses, comparisons, maxims. The text of *De copia,* reveling in its own fertility of invention, unsystematized, mobile, is itself an example of the dynamic and exuberant manipulation of language it succeeded in promoting.

Words in abundance, however, had their critics. There were ethical objections to a profligate verbal luxuriance indifferent to moral discrimination, and a sense that *copia,* unalloyed, represented rhetoric's disturbing capacity to persuade against the truth. *De copia,* often in abbreviated forms, was destined for a long career as a school text, but usually in conjunction with manuals that encouraged students to direct their exploration of vocabulary and their flow of words along channels signaled by argumentative procedures that they were simultaneously learning in their dialectic classes. [*See* Dialectic.]

The most efficient and influential agent for organizing *copia* was the commonplace book, for which Erasmus had himself provided the blueprint in *De copia,* though as an agent for generating discourse, rather than as an organ to control it. In their commonplace books, students collected words, phrases, and quotations for recycling and imitating, and classified them under moral heads. [*See* Commonplaces and commonplace books.] Abundance of words was thus filled with matter. The exhilarating verbal energy of an Erasmus or a Rabelais was harnessed to the more rigorous persuasive strategies underlying Montaigne's abundant prose and giving their point to the golden words of Elizabethan poets.

In the case of *copia,* as all else, the qualities of style promoted in Latin writing became the qualities characteristic of the West European vernaculars, not only in writing but also in speech. Copiousness in speech ostentatiously drew on the resources of the cultural capital accumulated by a competitive elite. This is connected by some modern commentators to embryonic capitalism in the Early Modern period, although economic historians seem generally less convinced by such speculation than literary critics. A more general association of word power with political power at this time is easier to demonstrate.

In the seventeenth century, *copia* was gradually devalued. Erasmus had been able to match verbal diversity to nature's plenitude, because for him and his contemporaries, the universe delighted in variety. In the world of the seventeenth-century scientific revolution, variety was reduced to simple laws. Once clarity was prized above all else, abundance of words was viewed as an impediment to thought. Far from ornamenting and amplifying things perceived, language was now required to be transparent, mediating knowledge without verbal interference. Moreover, abundance of words lost the power to convince that it had acquired through its association with dialectic, once the argumentative strategies of dialectic were undone by the much more forceful logic of mathematics. *Copia* fell to the domain of literature, where verbal play was still licensed. Even there, it lost its status. The style of vernacular literary composition (with Latin now much diminished as a determining factor) was modeled on styles of polite behavior acceptable within the community that consumed it.

From the middle of the seventeenth century, the social style of France became the regulating type for Europe at large. What was admired was a behavior that was discreetly competent without display, and a command of words based on the pregnancy of understatement, as averse to the pedantry of bookish allusions as to the ostentation of redundant vocabulary. The French language itself was severely pruned, and even though English largely resisted such encroachment on its native fertility, it was responsive to the mood of the times. [*See* Style.]

Since the seventeenth century, the term *copia* has largely disappeared from critical discourse. It has remained to characterize the stylistic mannerisms of the Early Modern period, and has not figured greatly in the general rehabilitation of rhetoric since the 1950s. This is probably because it is a very diffuse term that only acquired some sharpness when contextualized in an era that used it with precision. *Copia* persists, however. It is most in evidence at the exuberant end of the stylistic spectrum, typified by the linguistic opulence of the novelists James Joyce and Marcel Proust. At the other end lies the minimalism of the novelist and playwright Samuel Beckett, but *copia* is all-inclusive. In the infinite riches of *De copia*, Erasmus found room for a very short chapter on brevity.

[*See also* Amplification.]

BIBLIOGRAPHY

Cave, Terence. *The Cornucopian Text: Problems of Writing in the French Renaissance*. Oxford, 1979. The seminal work on the topic, working within a context of literary history and literary theory.
Crane, Mary T. *Framing Authority: Sayings, Self, and Society in Sixteenth-Century England*. Princeton, 1993. Contextualizes *copia* within the political history of the period.
Erasmus, Desiderius. *Copia: Foundations of the Abundant Style*. Translated and annotated by Betty I. Knott. In *Collected Works of Erasmus*, edited by Craig R. Thompson, vol. 24, pp. 279–659. Toronto, 1978.
— ANN MOSS

CORRECTIO (Gk. *epanorthōsis*) is an amplifying figure of thought amending terms used, as Heinrich Lausberg shows, for two purposes. First, it specifies, corrects, or enhances what has been said, thus showing the speaker's precision or involvement in the subject matter, as when Shakespeare's Hamlet laments the short-lived memory of his father, "But two months dead, nay not so much, not two" (1.2.138). Second, *correctio* pays

respect to the audience's feelings by apologizing, before or after, for any form of moral or linguistic indecorum through such phrases as "If I may say so" or *Sit venia verbis*.

[*See also* Figures of speech.]

BIBLIOGRAPHY

Lausberg, Heinrich. *Handbook of Literary Rhetoric: A Foundation for Literary Study*. Translated by Matthew T. Bliss, Annemiek Jansen, David E. Orton; edited by David E. Orton and R. Dean Anderson. Leiden, 1998. English translation of *Handbuch der literarischen Rhetorik*, first published in 1960.
— HEINER PETERS

CREDIBILITY. We may understand credibility as the impression of trustworthiness that a speaker, or the arguments he or she uses, leaves with an audience. Credibility refers largely to the personal qualities of the orator, since from the outset, more than anything else, they affect the audience's perception of the speaker and the speech. The insight that someone who possesses good ethical qualities is more likely to speak the truth (Plato, *Republic* 1.331d2), and therefore to be more credible with an audience, seems self-evident. However, the potential of this idea as a powerful strategy for a speaker was not recognized at first by Greek orators or authors of technical treatises dealing with rhetoric.

In the *Encomium of Helen,* the orator Gorgias (c.483–c.376 BCE) described the overwhelming power of speech exclusively in terms of its ability to sway the emotions of the listeners so that they are, in Gorgias's account, left helpless and defenseless against the emotions by which they are completely overcome. A calm reasoning on the part of the audience, which could include a consideration of the credibility of the speaker or of his arguments, is not an aspect of the rhetorical approach presented by Gorgias. In this, Gorgias was no exception: There is evidence that other Greek orators of the fifth century BCE appealed mainly to the emotions. According to the Athenian historian Thucydides (c.460–c.401 BCE), the democratic politician Pericles possessed the power of reducing the Athenians to fear whenever he realized that they were too bold, as he was also able to restore their boldness when they fell victim to groundless fear (*Historia* 2.65.9). Plato (*Republic* 6.493a–b5), in his critical account of rhetoric as practiced by the Sophists, mentions as one feature the same power of arousing opposite emotions. That this was the practice used by orators is confirmed by Aristotle, who, in the very first chapter of his *Rhetoric,* stated that previous authors of rhetorical handbooks concentrated on playing on the emotions of the audience (1354a11–17). If he conceded that some of these earlier writers of rhetorical handbooks took notice of goodness of character as an element of the art of rhetoric, which is doubtful since the text (1.2.1356a11–12) is disputed, he expressed the view that in the opinion of these authors the quality of character did not contribute to bringing about persuasion in the audience.

Plato (c.428–c.347 BCE). The requirement that an orator in the true sense be a just person, is expressed by Socrates in Plato's *Gorgias* (508c), one of Plato's earliest dialogues. In this dialogue, Socrates does not perceive the quality of character as a rhetorical device that enhances the speaker's credibility with the audience; rather, Socrates' demand that the speaker possess justice reflects his rigorous moral standards, for he applied them in the same dialogue to Athenian politicians as well (politicians belong after all to the same group of people as orators, since rhetoric enables a man to *rule* over others in his city and to *persuade* in political assemblies [452d5–4]). Given the sort of society and power of political leadership that Plato envisions, the credibility of the orator cannot be an issue for him: the perfect statesman of the *Politicus* rules by persuasion or force, and Plato rejects the argument that this ruler should be blamed if he uses force instead of persuasion (296a4–e4). In the *Phaedrus,* Plato outlines an approach to rhetoric that meets philosophical standards. Here, rhetoric is the art of winning the souls of the audience (*psychagōgia*). In order to succeed, the expert has to study the soul and to learn how many kinds exist. He has to classify the different kinds of men and adapt the appropriate kind of speech to each of them (271a–273e). Here, Plato's focus is on the psychological makeup of the audience for which the orator has to compose a matching speech; however, Plato is not concerned with the qualities of the speaker.

Aristotle (384–322 BCE). His *Rhetoric* begins with very critical remarks about the preoccupation of orators and writers of rhetorical handbooks with a rhetorical strategy that relies mostly on the speaker's ability to influence the audience's emotions (1.1.1354b20). In his own rhetorical theory, he limits the role of emotions by adding, and assigning greater importance to, two other modes of persuasion: the rhetorical syllogism or enthymeme (1355a7), and the character (*ēthos*) of the speaker, which he calls the most important mode of persuasion (1.2.1356a13)—an assessment still cited by Quintilian (c.35–100 CE; 5.12.9). [*See* Enthymeme.] Playing on the emotions (*pathos*) of the audience is third in importance. Logical proofs and presentation of the speaker's character share the characteristic of causing the audience to believe the speaker (*Rhetoric* 2.1.1378a6–15)—*pathos* lacks this ability. [*See* Pathos.]

These three modes of persuasion are called "technical," which means that they are the product of the orator's creative mind or his mastery of the rhetorical art and its rules. They are distinguished from the nontechnical means, which are readily available for the orator's use, such as pieces of evidence, witnesses, or written accounts. In the judgment of Aristotle, the intellectual process of preparing a speech and providing and supplying any of the three modes of persuasion, ranks higher than using existing pieces of evidence. For Aristotle, however, the credibility of the speaker seems so important that he recommends that nontechnical means of persuasion should be employed for this purpose: an opportunity to present a witness to one's character should not be missed (1.15.1376a25). Yet, by including *ēthos* among the technical modes of persuasion, Aristotle focuses on the accomplishment of the speaker by virtue of his mastery of the rhetorical art, and no longer as previous rhetoric had done, on the qualities an orator possesses. This point is stressed by Aristotle (1.2.1356a8–10). As such, *ēthos* comes closer to an artistic creation by the orator of a certain character, who possesses the ability to convince the audience through his speech, so that he *appears* to have certain qualities—not that he actually has them. When Aristotle refers to the character of the speaker, it is usually with this qualification "as he appears" (e.g., 1.8.1366a11; 3.14.1415a38), regardless of his real qualities. This stress on making the orator appear in a certain way opens the door to the possibility that the character as presented by the speaker is almost fictional—the only limitation in this creative act of portraying a character consists in the fact that truth is by nature more credible (1.1.1355a37), so that an orator who presents himself with qualities he does not possess fights an uphill battle.

Persuasion by means of *ēthos* is accomplished if the speech is presented in such a way that it renders the speaker credible and trustworthy (1.2.1356a5). For Aristotle, this can be accomplished by means of three qualities: first, is the appearance of goodness of character (1.2.1356a6, a23; 9.1366a25–28); second of being well disposed (1.8.1366a11); third of possessing practical wisdom (2.1.1278a8). [*See* Practical wisdom.] Practical wisdom is obviously introduced, since this is the quality Aristotle expects a leading politician to possess (*Politics* 3.5.1277b25), and in the *Rhetoric* he mainly addresses the politician, because political or deliberative rhetoric is a higher form than that practiced in law courts (1.1.1354b22). The qualities falling under the technical mode of persuasion, *ēthos,* are, therefore, either of a moral or intellectual nature or concern the speaker's relationship with the audience. [*See* Deliberative genre; *and* Forensic genre.]

It has been argued that Aristotle did not owe his concept of *ēthos* in the *Rhetoric* to earlier rhetorical theories. Prose texts from the fifth century BCE show, however, that the qualities that fall under the Aristotelian *ēthos* were already being used in a rhetorical context. The historian Thucydides makes Pericles characterize himself in the same terms, referring to his intellectual abilities, his goodwill to the community, and his personal integrity, shown by the fact that he cannot be bribed (*Historia* 2.60.5). And in the anonymous *Constitution of the Athenians,* transmitted among the works of Xenophon (written c.425 BCE), the oligarchic author states that a member of his class would as speaker in a political assembly display "the good quality of a good man, knowledge, and ill will to the people." He contrasts him with a member of the Athenian demos who would lack the former two qualities but possess goodwill (1.7). The three qualities considered here are identical with those of the Aristotelian *ēthos*

(Schütrumpf, *Philogus* 137, 1993, pp. 12–17). The author of this anonymous pamphlet has no theoretical concept of rhetoric nor of the various means of being persuasive. He simply assumes that the audience trusts and supports the speaker because it knows his qualities, and not because the speaker creates the *impression* that he possesses them, as in Aristotle.

In classical Greek rhetorical theory, it was Aristotle who introduced the appearance of credibility of the speaker as one of the most important strategies to persuade an audience. He elevated *ēthos* to a mode of persuasion in its own right and coined the term *technicus* for it. A systematic treatment of *ēthos* is, however, absent in post-Aristotelian rhetorical treatises until the middle of the first century BCE.

Credibility in Roman Rhetoric. In contradistinction to court procedure in Athens, where defendants generally spoke on their own behalf, Roman defendants often had recourse to legal representation by an upper-class patron *(patronus),* whose authority and social standing lent both him and his client added credibility in a society that put great weight upon the respect due to such senatorial statesmen and orators. Nonetheless, rhetorical theory and instruction in Rome reveal the continued influence of Greek theory from both the Classical and Hellenistic eras, although now the inherited wisdom on *ēthos* was relevant to both the character of the defendant and that of his patron.

The Hellenistic manuals, written mainly for school rhetoric and instruction, are almost completely lost to us, although their influence is clear in the highly technical systems laid out in a number of first-century BCE treatises from Rome. But both the Roman statesman Cicero (106–43 BCE), who authored several of these, and the first-century CE rhetorician Quintilian in his *Institutio oratoria,* expand upon the mechanistic approach of the Hellenistic manuals by advocating an education of the future orator that aspires to the ideals of the Greek orators of the classical era and the principles outlined by Plato and Aristotle in their philosophical works on rhetoric.

Cicero (*De oratore* 2.115, 121) refers to the Aristotelian system of three modes of persuasion. Here, "to win over the audience" (*conciliare*) takes the place of the Aristotelian *ēthos.* Similarly,

Quintilian (6.2.8) uses the Greek word *ēthos* for the gentle emotions (*affectus*) evoked in the audience. It now signifies the sympathy the audience feels when "the character of the speaker shines clearly out of his speech." This *ēthos* affects the audience emotionally in a most gentle way and, by securing the listener's goodwill, helps to persuade him. Aristotle had referred to his treatment of emotions for an explanation of goodwill (*Rhetoric* 2.1.1278a19). However, such a link with emotions did not exist in the case of the other two elements of Aristotelian *ēthos*, moral goodness and practical wisdom. Cicero and Quintilian depart from Aristotle when they assume that the display of character has an emotional impact on the audience (W.W. Fortenbaugh, *Rhetorica* 6, 1988, pp. 259–273).

Credibility is an issue in all the parts of an oration. In the exordium, the speaker should stress that he has taken over the case out of a sense of moral obligation, and not for some personal gain (Quintilian 4.1.7). A speaker might choose to feign helplessness by pretending to be uncertain how to begin or proceed with his speech. This makes him appear, not so much as a skilled master of rhetoric, but as an honest man. This rhetorical device (called *dubitatio*) is supposed to inspire confidence in the truth of what he is saying (Quintilian 9.2.19). In addition to this, the speaker should present himself in the exordium as benevolent (Cicero *De inventione* 1.20; Quintilian 4.1.5). The exordium is also the most suitable place for an orator to anticipate the strategy of the opposing party and to respond to it (*praeparatio*). If one can assume that the credibility of a witness will be challenged, the orator should point out in advance that he deserves to be believed. Cicero (*De inventione* 2.50) lists this line of pleading under the generally valid areas of argument (*loci communes*).

There are three virtues that the account of events (*narratio*) should have: It must be short, lucid, and plausible (Lausberg, 1998, pp. 294–295). The orator has to present the events in a compelling way and to convince the audience that they truly happened in the way described. As a prosecutor, the speaker has to show that the defendant possesses a character prone to the kind of acts he is accused of (Quintilian 4.2.52). In case the events themselves are not favorable to the speaker's case,

he might choose a more biased presentation by retouching the account in a more favorable way (*color*, Quintilian 4.2.88). [*See* Color.] For this purpose, the use of psychological insights into expectations of the judge and related strategies are recommended (Lausberg, 1998, pp. 325–328).

In the proof (*probatio*), the orator uses instruction (*docere*) and reasoning (*ratiocinatio*) in order to convince the audience that the account presented is credible (Cicero *De inventione* 1.57). Achieving credibility ranks lower than proving that something is necessary, but is superior to establishing a course of events that is merely not at odds with ("*non repugnans*") the claims made (Quintilian 5.8.6; cf. Lausberg, 1998, p. 370). In the proof, an orator addresses issues of likelihood, which had been an important aspect in Greek rhetoric. He will raise the question whether it is credible that a father was killed by his son (Quintilian 5.10.19). An argument can be construed by referring to various conditions or circumstances of the person in question (*argumentum ad hominem*) and by pointing out that certain actions are likely, or unlikely, to be committed by a certain category of people. A wide array of arguments can be construed as well from the facts of the matter (Lausberg, 1998, pp. 377–399). Thus, showing that someone has the means and abilities to do certain acts makes allegations of that kind credible. [*See* Ad hominem argument.]

All in all, a presentation possesses credibility if it places the speaker, or the person on whose behalf he is speaking, in the best possible light, and meets in all points the expectations the common man has gained as experiences of his life. A credible speech avoids in all its parts everything that could raise doubts regarding any aspect of the account given by the speaker.

[*See also* Classical rhetoric; *and* Ēthos.]

BIBLIOGRAPHY

Gorgias. *Encomium of Helen.* Edited with introduction, notes, and translation by D. M. MacDowell. Bristol, U.K., 1982. Greek text and English translation.

Lausberg, Heinrich. *Handbook of Literary Rhetoric. A Foundation for Literary Study.* Translated by Matthew T. Bliss, Annemiek Jansen, and David E. Orton; edited by David E. Orton and R. Dean Anderson. Leiden, 1998. English translation of *Handbuch der literarischen Rhetorik,* first published in 1960. A systematic presentation of ancient rhetorical theory.

May, James M. *Trials of Character: The Eloquence of Ciceronian Ethos.* Chapel Hill, N.C., 1988. A study of the presentation of Cicero in his speeches.

Moore, John M. *Aristotle and Xenophon on Democracy and Oligarchy.* London, 1975. Translation of Greek texts on the constitution of Athens and Sparta.

Schütrumpf, Eckart. *Die Bedeutung des Wortes ethos in der Poetik des Aristoteles.* Zetemata 49 (1970). A monograph on the meaning of *ēthos* before Aristotle and its significance in his *Poetics.*

Wisse, Jakob. *Ethos and Pathos from Aristotle to Cicero.* Amsterdam, 1989. A comprehensive study of these two modes of persuasion.

— ECKART SCHÜTRUMPF

CRITICAL RHETORIC. *See* Politics, *article on* Critical rhetoric.

CRITICISM. The very notion of criticism has a long history of contrasting meanings. Originally, the critic was simply the medical doctor who was capable of judging matters of illness and health. By the seventeenth century, what that doctor did, criticism, had been expanded in England to include all judgments, in any field (the word did not catch on in French until the nineteenth century). For some, to do criticism was to engage in the most carefully informed, detailed judgment possible, for or against.

Since nobody likes to be criticized too much, it is not surprising that for many the term *criticism* quickly took on negative connotations: "Why are you always engaging in so much criticism?"— meaning destructive criticism. I can remember my own mother, when I was a teenager, shouting at me, "Wayne C., I just can't stand hearing so much criticism"—by which she meant, negative judgments on her own critical judgments and behavior.

As the term was adopted more and more by students of literature, for some it came to mean simply *literary* criticism: the judgment of literary quality. And since such judgments are always contested, many grappled with what makes good criticism and what bad. In one of the cleverest discussions of the subject ever, Alexander Pope's "An Essay on Criticism" (1711), Pope begins by taking on the critical problem that overlaps all study of rhetoric—how are we to develop the

kind of criticism that does not have bad effects on our readers by teaching the wrong valuations:

'Tis hard to say, if greater want of skill
Appear in writing or in judging ill;
But, of the two, less dang'rous is th' offence
To tire our patience, than mislead our sense.
Some few in that, but numbers err in this,
Ten censure wrong for one who writes amiss.
(1–6)

As more and more critics of literature adopted the term in its more favorable sense, as applying mainly to literary works—poems, plays, novels— it became the highest art of judging the difference between good works and bad. Matthew Arnold took it even further: Responding to those who saw it only as excessive negative judgment, Arnold said, "I am bound by my own definition of criticism: a disinterested endeavour to learn and propagate the best that is known and thought in the *world*" (*Essays in Criticism,* London, 1888). For some critics, then and now, Arnold's use of that word *propagate* proved troublesome, even offensive. For them, critics should do criticism not primarily to change or improve the world—that is what rhetoric does—but to *discover* the truth about artworks. To *propagate* the best is quite different from *disinterested* inquiry into what is in fact best. (In Arnold's time, the word *disinterested* meant something like unbiased, objective; most dictionaries today list that as only the second meaning; the first is "not interested," "not having the mind or feelings engaged"—a total contrast to Arnold's meaning.)

Debates about whether or how criticism is itself rhetorical, or whether it should deal with rhetoric, have thus flooded the world, from ancient times to the present. Indeed the relation of various definitions of "rhetoric" to various definitions of "criticism" are so complex that no brief account can avoid gross distortion. The ambiguity of both terms is so great that one is tempted to use those scare-quotes every time the words appear.

Many books have been written, and no doubt more will come, on a variety of contrasting relations or conflicts between criticism and rhetoric:

Between poetics and rhetoric. Poetics: the study of how literary works are made; rhetoric: the art of persuading, or as Aristotle (384–322

BCE) puts it, the faculty, the ability, of discovering "in any situation whatever" just what will persuade your audience (*Rhetoric* 1.2). Aristotle's *Poetics* and his *Rhetoric* were adopted as guides by thousands of thinkers from his time to ours.

Between beauty and usefulness. Many have seen all art as both pleasing and useful; as many Latin critics put it, it is both *dulce* and *utile* (Horace 65–8 BCE). Others have distinguished them sharply, especially by the time of the "art-for-art's-sake" movement, in which to talk of the usefulness of an artwork would be to corrupt it. The French phrase for it, *"l'art pour l'art"* was coined by Victor Cousin in the early nineteenth century, but it flourished only toward the end of that century.

Between aesthetic theory and utilitarian or political or social theory. Utilitarians like John Stuart Mill (1806–1873), even when deeply dependent, as he was, on the effects of literature, especially Wordworth's poetry, sharply distinguished practical theories from the arts.

Between varieties of formal or structural criticism (especially the so-called New Critics, midtwentieth century) and ethical or political issues;

Between rhetoric as the study of how to persuade, and criticism as the study of how to think about language—dialectics, hermeneutics, and various modes of deconstruction and cultural critique.

None of these pairings has any universally agreed-upon meaning, and most of them overlap with others. But anyone who explores rhetoric under its many synonyms, and literary criticism in its many guises, will inevitably encounter assertions ranging from total antipathy to total harmony. Defending "true poetry," for example, Paul Verlaine (1844–1896), taking poetry as the only true verbal art, said "Take Eloquence and wring his neck." John Stuart Mill (1806–1873), echoing an age-old identification of rhetoric with what orators, not writers, practice, and thus seeing eloquence as the heart of rhetoric, said, "Eloquence is written to be heard, poetry to be overheard." (quotations from Sloane 1993, p. 1046). Others have recently gone in the other direction, fusing the terms so completely as to suggest that all forms of effective communication, even nonver-

bal, are in some sense rhetorical: the very notion of effectiveness implies an audience and a purpose directed at that audience. Others have not gone that far but have simply said that all forms of communication, even the least rhetorical in intent, are dependent on rhetorical methods and devices.

This radically confusing scene would require a detailed history in itself. But here we must move quickly, after a somewhat extended but still inadequately brief historical account, to consider the major issues that are now faced by the many recent critics who have rediscovered the relevance of rhetorical studies to criticism.

Rhetoric's Historical Decline, Especially in Literary Criticism. According to the broader definitions of rhetoric—not mere oratory or argument but all modes of persuasion—literary critics have never been able to avoid practicing some form of rhetorical criticism. According to narrower and more popular definitions, however, rhetoric had almost completely disappeared from the literary scene by the end of the eighteenth century (see Genette, 1982). The very word *rhetoric* did not appear in most "literary" criticism through the nineteenth and early twentieth century. Even outside the field of literature, the status of rhetoric and rhetorical study had declined drastically from the Renaissance on, as various forms of "scientific" or "rational" proof (more scare-quotes required) took over the world of truth, and various celebrations of emotion and sentiment and romance took over the world of beauty. As Richard McKeon (1900–1985), perhaps the most profound student of the subject put it in 1942:

> The history of rhetoric as it has been written since the Renaissance is . . . in part the distressing record of the obtuseness of writers who failed to study the classics and to apply rhetoric to literature, and in part the monotonous enumeration of doctrines, or preferably sentences, repeated from Cicero or commentators on Cicero. ("Rhetoric in the Middle Ages," 1987, p. 121)

By the middle of the twentieth century, we find very little use of the word *rhetoric* by those overtly engaged in criticism. Its home was in politics, where it always meant something like "mere persuasion"—often even "mere tricky, dishonest persuasion." In the media, we find many quotations from politicians like "Let's drop the rhetoric and get down to serious talk." "Truth" (another necessary scare-quote), even truth about literature, was by then pursued with this or that version of "Cartesian" (René Descartes, 1596–1650) or positivistic or scientific or analytical rigor. Literature was studied either historically—who did what when and why?—or structurally, under a variety of names summarizable as formalism. The beauty of the work or its unique unity (or lack of it) became the center. But meanwhile, just as all philosophers were unconsciously but inevitably wrestling with rhetorical questions, all literary critics were in fact consciously or unconsciously practicing rhetorical criticism, in one or another of the broad definitions of rhetoric that have appeared in more recent times.

Before that fall and recovery, both the term *rhetoric* and the application of rhetorical methods to the "purer" territory of beauty or truth had an extraordinarily spotty history. Though the decline of the status of rhetoric from the Enlightenment to about fifty years ago was perhaps the sharpest ever, it was by no means unique. Rhetoric had always had its ups and downs as mate, handmaiden, or slave of either truth or the poetic, with ardent defenders and ardent opponents. Plato (c.428–c.347 BCE) and later Platonists and the Sophists quarreled about whether or how rhetoric corrupted or served truth and genuine inquiry. [*See* Classical rhetoric; *and* Sophists.] Thinking of how rhetoric might defend herself against the charges of truth-seekers like him, Plato, early in the *Phaedrus,* has Socrates say:

> But perhaps rhetoric has been getting too roughly handled by us, and she might answer: "What amazing nonsense you are talking! As if I forced any man to learn to speak in ignorance of the truth! Whatever my advice may be worth, I should have told him to arrive at the truth first, and then come to me. At the same time I boldly assert that mere knowledge of the truth will not give you the art of persuasion."
> (Jowett translation, 3d ed., vol. 1, 1892, p. 264)

Even Aristotle, who honored the rival powers of rhetoric and poetics more profoundly than Plato had dealt with the rivalry of rhetoric and truth, writes his *Poetics*—a work of *criticism* although the word did not yet exist—almost as if

his inquiry were totally separate from the problems faced in his *Rhetoric*. Rhetoric, his two key works suggest, is an entirely different "faculty" from the powers that enable a poet to produce a play or epic. Although in fact employing throughout the *Poetics* categories prominent in the *Rhetoric* (especially in the section on *ēthos* and *epideictic* rhetoric), Aristotle openly refers to rhetoric only when, while pursuing the elements constituting tragedies, he arrives at "thought"—and suddenly decides not to discuss it, because thought concerns the rhetorical way in which dramatized characters reveal their thought as they converse: "All that concerns Thought may be left to the [my] treatise on Rhetoric, for the subject is more proper to that inquiry" (*Poetics* 19.2–3). But for those who define rhetoric more broadly, it is clear that as the masterful analytical prober works on the other three primary elements of drama—plot, character, and diction—he inevitably employs the precise kind of rhetorical thinking that permeates the *Rhetoric* itself.

Such rhetorical reliance is inevitable, not just for him but for all critics, because he is thinking constantly of what poetic devices will produce the *proper,* the *best* effects on spectators. Again and again he uses words like *must* and *should* and *ought* as he instructs the "poet" in how to achieve maximum effects on the audience: "the poet must show invention [one of the most important concepts in the Rhetoric] and make a skilful use of the tradition. But we must state more clearly what is meant by 'skilful.'" (14.10–12). What could be more rhetorical, in the broader definition, than advice like the following:

> One *should* not seek from tragedy all kinds of pleasure but that which is peculiar to tragedy, and since the poet *must* by "representation" *produce the pleasure* which comes from feeling pity and fear, obviously this quality *must be embodied* in the incidents. (My italics. 14.4–5)

So we find in Aristotle a grand instance of what is revealed in every critic who openly or tacitly shoves rhetoric aside or puts it down: an inescapable reliance on rhetoric. Again and again through more than two millenia, critics have cited Aristotle's authority, often overstating his sharp distinction, and always revealing the paradox of his own "poetic" inquiry.

It is hardly surprising that from Aristotle on, many thinkers, in contrast to the Sophists and some other openly rhetorical movements, continued to treat rhetoric as in questionable relationship to genuine philosophical or dialectical or logical thinking, while literary criticism, sometimes called poetics, was ignored, or often shoved to the periphery, or even dismissed as not genuine thought. On the other hand, for some authors like Cicero (106–43 BCE), rhetoric was deemed of central importance to all human exchange, including discourse about poetry. It even became for some late medievalists and some Renaissance thinkers what was called the queen of the sciences: the master-study organizing and strengthening all the others. The central concept of rhetoric, *inventio* (which should be but is usually not translated as *discovery of good reasons*), became for some thinkers clearly essential in all serious writing and speaking, not just in dealing with poetry, fiction, and drama (the word *criticism* never appearing) but in philosophy, politics, and religion. [*See* Invention.] Even Saint Augustine (354–430 CE), having been converted from being a professional rhetorician to being a Christian priest and theologian, finally defended rhetoric as still an essential study for everyone: after all, if Satan has it available, those of us who oppose Satan must have it for our defense. Meanwhile almost the only criticism he practiced was of Bible stories, what some modern critics have called Biblical literature. [*See overview article on* Medieval rhetoric.] His discussions of other literatures were almost always appraisals of their likely moral effect on readers, as he practiced rhetorical analysis of the kind he had been trained professionally to do.

The Renaissance revived the status of rhetoric once granted by Cicero and Quintilian (c.35–c.100 CE). [*See overview article on* Renaissance rhetoric.] As Richard McKeon put the triumph of rhetoric in the Renaissance, in a masterful and much neglected essay, "Rhetoric and Poetics in the Philosophy of Aristotle"):

> Rhetoric, in the terms which Aristotle had used, but in an interpretation that owed much to Cicero and Quintilian, became in the Renaissance a discipline applicable to literature, to thought, and to life. It supplied the means by which to interpret poets, the criteria to regulate demonstration, and the technique for scientific inquiry and discovery. (*Selected Writings*, pp. 139–140, Chicago, 1998)

But this triumph was predictably followed by another decline, as devotees of rational or scientific certainty, following Descartes, tacitly used rhetoric to attack its powers, and devotees of poetic beauty rediscovered, as it were, Aristotle's distinction. As various forms of the Enlightenment took over, with more and more claims that only scientific thinking about hard facts produced real knowledge, rhetoric was narrowed down until it became, for most students, the mere icing on the cake: the study and practice of overt persuasion, performed after genuine hard thought had reached conclusions. [*See* Eighteenth-century rhetoric.] It was used either to deceive, or at best to convey a truth that one had discovered through some other, more respectable means. Socrates summarizes this version of rhetoric, a version which he himself repudiates, in the *Phaedrus*:

> [W]hen the question is of justice and good [or true art], or is a question in which men are concerned who are just and good, either by nature or habit, he who would be a skilful rhetorician has no need of truth—for that in course of law [and other oratorical scenes] men literally care nothing about truth, but only about conviction: and this is based on probability, to which he who would be a skilful orator should therefore give his whole attention. And they [the mere rhetoricians] say also that there are cases in which the actual facts, if they are improbable, ought to be withheld, and only the probabilities should be told either in accusation or defence, and that always in speaking, the orator should keep probability in view, and say good-bye to the truth. (Plato, 276)

Sometimes that kind of "oratorical" icing, mere probability or possibility, inevitably became identified with beauty or beautifying: the very kind of rhetoric that moved discourse into the aesthetic category. But usually genuine poetry, genuine "literature," was seen as an escape from the rhetorical.

Thus the role of rhetorical interests in literary studies sank lower and lower. Especially with the late-romanticist rise of art-for-art's sake, the very word *rhetoric* became for some, as we have seen, a term of abuse: when rhetoric entered the world of art, art was corrupted into cheap persuasion. The domain of usefulness, of practicality, of utility was the domain of rhetoric. Poetry, art, beauty: these were the escapes from the world of practical—that is, rhetorical—concerns. By the twentieth century, poets and critics were inventing epigrams like "Poetry makes nothing happen"—and therefore has nothing to do with rhetoric. "A poem should not mean but be"—and where there is no "meaning" rhetoric has no role. Rhetorical studies almost disappeared from the academic presses and from the curriculum, where they appeared if at all as confined to the teaching of "Rhetoric and Composition": how to write persuasive essays. For about one hundred and fifty years, one can find only a few scattered works directly applying rhetorical concepts to literary achievement (see Wightman, 1906; Talmor, 1984).

The prolonged movement to separate "rhetorical" (or historical) language from "poetic" or "aesthetic" or "critical" language, came to a climax with critical movements in mid-twentieth century. The *poem* was what you studied, not its history or its rhetorical (ethical, political) effects. Members of the Chicago school were often reductively called "neo-Aristotelians": Richard McKeon, Sheldon Sacks, Elder Olsen, Ronald Crane, Norman Maclean (Crane, 1952). The more famous New Critics (along with the Russian formalists and later the structuralists) concentrated on this or that aspect of literary structure, for the sake of structure. The New Critics included I. A. Richards, William Empson, John Crowe Ransom, Cleanth Brooks, and Allen Tate (Wimsatt, 1958).

The very word *rhetoric* does not even appear in most criticism from these two schools, as indeed it is still not found in many a critical work that is in fact laden with rhetorical analyses, but using other terms (see for an example of such a sharp divorce of criticism from rhetoric, the splendid book by philosopher Robert Pippin, *Henry James and Modern Moral Life*, Cambridge, U.K., 2000. Rhetoric is hardly mentioned.)

The New Critics even went so far as to attack "the affective fallacy"—the claim that criticism should give close attention to the emotional (rhetorical?) effect of literary works (Wimsatt, 1958). And though the Chicago-school critics did adopt Aristotle's notion that we must address the "end"

or purpose of the work—implying an audience to be affected in a given way, and thus moving toward openly-confessed rhetorical inquiry—the aim of the critic was still to discover the unique structure of the unique work, ruling rhetorical matters out not just because they were irrelevant but because they would poison the purity of the endeavor.

The Revival. The second half of the twentieth century experienced a radical and surprising resurrection of open use for rhetoric in criticism. [*See* Modern rhetoric.] Beginning with the publication of Kenneth Burke's *A Rhetoric of Motives* (Berkeley, 1950), James L. Guetti's *The Rhetoric of Joseph Conrad* (Amhurst, Mass., 1960), and on through Wayne Booth's *The Rhetoric of Fiction* (Chicago, 1961) and Kenneth Burke's *The Rhetoric of Religion* (Berkeley, 1961), the term *rhetoric* itself experienced an astonishing explosion, both in a broadening of its definition and in its quantitative entry into literary, political, and social studies. The phrase "The Rhetoric of . . ." in titles of books and articles soon outnumbered, especially in America, any other cliché. And such titles are still prominent: thousands of critics have been studying "the rhetoric of" this or that poet, novelist, or dramatist, and since rhetoric has become prominent in cultural and political studies, the relation of "criticism" and "rhetoric" has become more amorphous than ever.

That renaissance has not been merely a vocabulary shift. It is a rediscovery of what many a classical thinker had insisted on, the point tacitly illustrated in the *Poetics*. Despite what aestheticians claim, even the purest "literary" works succeed or fail by "rhetorically" addressing and capturing some audience. As Burke demonstrates, all language can be seen as "symbolic action" (1966). Though some authors do think of themselves as writing only for the joy of constructing beauty, thus totally purified of any rhetorical taint, whenever they in fact thoroughly engage any reader they have succeeded in one kind of rhetoric: the author who is implied by the very construction of the poem or novel or play has consciously or unconsciously employed the rhetorical strokes needed to win any reader.

Realization of this point is part of what has produced the rhetorical explosion of the last few decades. Supported in part by the postmodernist embrace of various ideologies, with the study of how literary works support or undermine belief systems, we now have, to repeat, a flood of rhetorical studies—not only hundreds of books and thousands of articles with rhetoric in the title, but also scores of responsible efforts to probe how those who think of themselves as critics simply cannot ignore rhetoric. Steven Mailloux's (1989) selected bibliography of "Rhetoric and Recent Critical Theory" offers more than a hundred works, most of them from the seventies, and eighties, purporting to grapple with some aspect of the relationship.

The Tension between Beauty, Goodness, and Truth. The historical explosion of rhetorical terms and concepts has by no means removed the ambiguities that the terms both create and disguise. Every serious writer of poetry or fiction encounters, consciously or unconsciously, a tension between the desire to be *effective*—accepted, attended to, moving, even morally transforming—and the desire to create a perfected object, a structure that is genuinely admirable, or even "beautiful," whether it captures readers or not. When an author thinks of himself or herself as writing a pure poem, the problem of audience may be totally suppressed; in contrast, when an author seeks a powerful practical effect, political or moral or scientific, thoughts about beauty of structure may never rise to the surface. Yet their goals overlap. As we have seen in Aristotle, even the purest, most *literary* work employs untold devices that scholars of rhetoric call rhetorical, and even the most polemical of practical oratory succeeds or fails depending on whether admirable structures have been created.

It is not surprising that many poets, novelists, and dramatists, ancient and modern, have seen themselves as driven by the desire to purge their practical motives and become purely aesthetic, pursuing the beauty of the work. Yet many poets and novelists have been, like Pope in his many satires, Wordsworth in his "The Prelude" (1850—begun many decades earlier), and George Orwell in *1984*, openly didactic, in the sense of clearly wanting to change readers' minds. Nobody could ever deal fully with such works without addressing their rhetorical purpose, if by rhetoric we mean, in Aristotle's definition, "the faculty of discovering the possible means of persuasion *in ref-erence to any subject whatever*" (1.1.2). Beautiful structure itself is one of the "means of persuasion"; excellent "persuasion" requires it, feeds upon it. Beauty of structure persuades, either to some truth or to some action, and is thus in this sense rhetorical.

It is not surprising, then, that the existence of the explosion has by no means simplified the critical quest of any serious student of rhetoric. The critical works are written from a threateningly broad range of theoretical perspectives: deconstructionists, philosophers attempting to rescue "sophistry," theologians, teachers of composition, passionate probers of the skills of individual writers, and so on.

The Six (and More?) Rhetorical Elements Found in All Criticism. What is unfortunately evident throughout too much of this flood is the temptation to reduce "rhetoric" to one or another narrow branch of its broad history. Every serious student, whether of Plato (see his summary in the epigraph above), or of Aristotle, with his four causes, or of Richard McKeon, with his sixteen-fold chart (*Selected Writings*, 1998, p. 218), or of Kenneth Burke (1966) with his "dramatistic pentad," knows that rhetorical effectiveness depends on many variables that are found not just in open argument or oratory but in every poem or novel or story or play. And yet many critics, whether consciously embracing rhetoric or not, chain themselves into one or another narrow element of literature—ironic structure, brilliance of style, emotional power, and so on—while ignoring other elements that serious rhetorical study would insist on including.

In short, a full rhetorical quest must always follow Aristotle and Cicero and Richard McKeon and Kenneth Burke by including attention to at least four or five or six elements influential in all authorial endeavors to attract or influence readers. For Aristotle, the elements sprang from his four causes, which in the *Poetics* yielded Object (plot = formal), Means (language = material), Manner (method = efficient), and End (purpose = final). Kenneth Burke's "dramatistic pentad," "act, agent, agency, purpose, scene," not only cannot be made strictly parallel to Aristotle's but adds an important element of "cause" that Aristotle just took for granted: *scene,* the whole range of cultural facts and forces that enter into any poetic encounter.

Burke's emphasis on scene moves him much more sharply toward the kinds of rhetorical inquiry about "culture" that have now sometimes become, destructively, the only element seriously addressed.

In one sense, this narrowing of "causes" to one is inevitable: no critic can at any one moment do full justice to all of the factors/elements/causes that every critic consciously or unconsciously faces. Indeed, some of the difficulties in reading Kenneth Burke's and Richard McKeon's seminal work spring from their passion for dealing with all of them. Sometimes Burke confuses readers by mixing his five together almost simultaneously. Sometimes McKeon puts off his readers by depending tacitly, in one essay, on readers' understanding that he is pursuing, for the time being, only one or another of the *sixteen* elements he considers pertinent to all inquiry.

For whatever reason, most critics still blindly and polemically talk as if only one or the other of the many elements, or variables, makes real "literary" or "theoretical" sense. Some members of the National Association of Scholars, breaking off from the Modern Language Association because of its hospitality to cultural studies and "theory," talk as if literature is doomed because critics have increasingly ignored the one element they think distinguishes genuine literature: admirable structure, sometimes called form, sometimes unity, sometimes beauty. For them, if you have a "beautifully structured" work, you have a true poem, or novel, or play. If you talk about that beauty, you are doing genuine criticism. But if you begin to talk about cultural and ethical effects and causes, you are doing rhetoric—as one of the founders of the deconstructionist movement openly states in the title of one of his works (de Man, 1983).

Opponents of such moves thus echo the formalists of the fifties, who, consciously or unconsciously repudiating rhetorical terminology, founded the journal *The Explicator*. In it, poem after poem was pursued, sometimes brilliantly, sometimes destructively, in the search of the "ironic" structure. One Chicago school professor spent one entire ten-week term teaching a seminar in which he and students pursued the one right conception of *the* unique "unity" of Browning's *My Last Duchess*. Others committed similar exaggerations and oversimplifications, placing literary works into other rhetorical categories, and sometimes placing all *good* works into a single category. Some, for example, seemed to pursue the one right kind of ironic intricacy as the one true mark of good poetic work—with never a word about rhetoric. For some, what was ruled out was not only the notion of rhetoric as persuasion but the entire rhetorical context in which any poem finds itself when written and published. One widely-used poetry anthology of the 1950s not only did not offer the date in which the poem was written but eliminated the author's name—except in a complex index at the back. The whole notion that a poem is written by an author at a cultural, rhetorical moment, addressing readers who will either understand or want to understand that moment as they address the poem—that was eliminated, "purifying" the scene into the totally "aesthetic." We should treat "the poem *as* poem and not another thing," they chanted (as a student at the time, I chanted it with them).

Some structural analysts narrowed even further to the study of syntax or prosody, as *the* literary center, sometimes reducing the full existence of the poem to the mere meaning of words in the poem. If the language worked, *that* was the true poem.

Such structural critics usually ignored, quite naturally, the second rhetorical element, the variety of *purposes* or *goals* or *ends* that poetic structure can pursue. No good rhetorical criticism can be conducted without two versions of the same goal question: both why is the author doing this and what is the intended effect on readers? Although the question of purpose was often implicit in structural analyses ("Why is this *part* here, if we consider the structure of the whole to be X, Y, or Z?"), to bring this rhetorical question to the surface was to commit the affective fallacy. It is true, however, that the neo-Aristotelians usually followed Aristotle in embracing this one, as they labored to do justice to his four causes.

They usually, therefore, also included the third major rhetorical element, method or means, not in the mere sense of syntax or style but the whole range of tools available to the artist. But like too many current critics who downplay that element, they often tended to take for granted a fourth variable: the definition of the subject at hand. Too often they assumed, as did the New Critics, that their readers would share a tacit notion of just what a "literary work" or a "true drama" would be. (The more perceptive of this group, like Ronald Crane, Sheldon Sacks, and Elder Olson, did make sharp distinctions of definition among works that produced an "action" or plot, works that aimed at satirical attack, and works called analogues: pursuing truth; Sacks, 1964.)

Some rhetoricians, on the other hand, have committed opposite oversimplifications: it's *all* purpose, the desired effect. They tend to ignore beauty of structure or style (the traditional end of eloquence), while the critical theorists ignore the excitement of literary–rhetorical engagement. [*See* Eloquence.] In many a book on rhetoric and politics, poetry or criticism is not even mentioned.

A fifth and sixth element, the "first principles" or deepest convictions of authors and readers, and the cultural scene in which authors and readers perform, have, unlike the others but like the language of rhetoric, exhibited an astonishing revival in literary criticism since the 1970s, partially as a result of the so-called postmodernist or poststructuralist movements. Led in part by French philosophers who, like Jacques Derrida and Roland Barthes, had been thoroughly trained in rhetoric, many postmodernists began focusing on both the general principles or deepest assumptions underlying all discourse, and on the differences between the cultural scenes in which all reading and writing and listening occur. [*See* Reception theory.] As the various movements of "reader-response criticism" have stressed, the scene in which any text is brought to life by a reader includes the very nature of that reader, of his or her culture, and of the *ēthos* the reader ascribes, rightly or wrongly, to the author. [*See* Ēthos.]

To repeat: too many critics untrained in rhetorical traditions tend to land on only one or two of these six, calling their focus "poetic" or "literary" or "linguistic," or "theoretical," or "new historical," or "cultural critique." While each of these directions can yield genuine critical truth about a literary work, the full literary–rhetorical truth about any text or collection of texts requires attention to all six. It is not that any one critic needs at any one moment to attend to them all;

that is always impossible. It is that critical warfare is pointless when it implies that only one or another selection from the six is legitimate. Rhetorical pluralism should provide attention to and respect for our many fruitful paths.

The Future. Implicit in this account has been a revival of the frequent medieval claim that rhetoric is the monarch overruling all disciplines—or at least the slave that all disciplines rely on for their roadwork. Also implicit is a kind of optimistic prediction: whatever happens to critical terminology over the next centuries, if literary criticism of any kind survives, if scholars continue to study what literature is for and how it works and what it achieves, the study of rhetoric will be found at its core.

There is obviously no way to predict the future relation of criticism and rhetoric. Some of the best students of rhetoric, like Steven Mailloux, are hoping that "English" Departments might see the value of renaming themselves as Departments of Cultural Rhetoric, departments that would still include literature as their center.

> I am not suggesting . . . that all English departments give up literature as their primary object of study or even that they necessarily need to scrap literary history as the organizational schema for their curricula. But I am arguing that using rhetorical study as an organizing framework makes room for a much wider range of interrelated scholarly activities than using a narrowly defined definition of literary studies. Work in this new rhetorical studies would not simply replace traditional interpretations of individual literary texts. Rather, I would incorporate such activities into a larger project of closely reading cultural practices, one that focuses on all the rhetorical events forming the cultural conversation at particular historical moments. . . . It's not that the "literary" drops out of such a project; it's just that this rhetorical study always historicizes the literary, showing how a text works rhetorically *when it is categorized* as literary within particular episodes of the cultural conversation and how the literary–nonliterary distinction functions differently in different contexts of reception. (1998, p. 191)

One can detect in the rhetoric of this passage considerable uneasiness about the age-old conflict between "criticism" and "rhetoric." Mailloux obviously fears that some readers will see him as downgrading literature and the truly "literary," and that fear is entirely justified. The conflict will almost certainly never go away. But meanwhile, everyone who believes in the importance of rhetorical studies can take comfort in the present moment of revival. Never since the sixteenth century have so many of those who are engaged in "criticism" seen themselves as working with traditional "rhetorical" questions and methods— even though the scare-quotes are still needed.

BIBLIOGRAPHY

Any complete bibliography of serious works relating criticism and rhetoric would require scores of pages. Depending on different definitions of rhetoric, it would include all important works on the ethical and moral effects of literature (see bibliography in Booth, *The Company We Keep*, 1988), and on the political consequences (Mailloux, *Reception Histories,* 1989), and on the relation to religion—and so on. It would also include all of the classical and Renaissance works on rhetoric, such as Quintilian's *Institutio oratoria,* Longinus's *On the Sublime,* Cicero's *De officiis,* and Sidney's *Defense of Poesie.* The following can only hint at the vast range of controversies from Plato and Aristotle to the present.

Altieri, Charles. "Plato's Performative Sublime and the Ends of Reading." *New Literary History* 16 (1985), pp. 251–273.

Angus, Ian, and Lenore Langsdorf, eds. *The Critical Term Rhetoric and Philosophy in Postmodern Discourse.* Carbondale, Ill., 1993.

Aristotle. *Poetics.* Translated by W. Hamilton Fyfe. London, 1973.

Aristotle. *Rhetoric.* Translated by J. H. Freese. London, 1957.

Bakhtin, M. M. *The Dialogic Imagination: Four Essays.* Edited by Michael Holquist; translated by Caryl Emerson and Holquist. Austin, 1981. Does not claim to be working primarily with rhetoric, but his emphasis on the notion of multiple voices, especially in fiction, transformed criticism of narrative.

Bialostosky, Don, ed. "Bakhtin and Rhetorical Criticism: A Symposium." *Rhetoric Society Quarterly* 22 (Fall 1992), pp. 1–28.

Booth, Wayne C. *The Rhetoric of Fiction.* Chicago, 1961. Though this work employs diverse definitions of rhetoric, it helped to turn fiction criticism from questions of formal structure to questions of rhetorical effect.

Booth, Wayne C. *A Rhetoric of Irony.* Chicago, 1974.

Booth, Wayne C. *The Company We Keep: An Ethics of Fiction.* Berkeley, 1988. From the perspective of this book, ethics could be considered an effort to harmonize rhetoric and criticism.

Burke, Kenneth. *Language as Symbolic Action: Essays on Life, Literature, and Method.* Berkeley, 1966. Burke is probably the most influential author in the "rhetorical revolution" of the 1960s to 1990s.

Burice, Kenneth. *The Philosophy of Literary Form: Studies in Symbolic Action.* Berkeley, 1973. First published 1941.

Burke, Sean. *The Death and Return of the Author: Criticism and Subjectivity in Barthes, Foucault and Derrida.* Edinburgh, 1998. First published 1992. A careful refutation of the popular postmodernist claim that the "author is dead": authorial intentions are irrelevant to criticism.

Chatman, Seymour. *Coming to Terms: The Rhetoric of Narrative in Fiction and Film.* Ithaca, N.Y., 1990. An influential extension of rhetorical interests to film criticism.

Clark, Donald Lemen. *Rhetoric and Poetics in the Renaissance: A Study of Rhetorical Terms in English Renaissance Literary Criticism.* New York, 1963. First published 1922.

Cooper, David. "Rhetoric, Literature and Philosophy." *The Recovery of Rhetoric: Persuasive Discourse and Disciplinarity in the Human Sciences.* Edited by R. H. Roberts and J. M. M. Good. Charlottesville, Va., 1993. A good survey of the immense number of questions raised by rhetorical study.

Crane, Ronald, ed. *Critics and Criticism, Ancient and Modern.* Chicago, 1952. Serious study of this neglected work might restore respect for the pluralism of critical methods that our current scene exhibits but seldom acknowledges.

de Man, Paul. *Blindness and Insight: Essays in the Rhetoric of Contemporary Criticism.* 2d ed. Minneapolis, 1983. A prominent representative of how the "deconstruction" movement joined rhetoric and criticism.

Fish, Stanley. *Is There a Text in This Class? The Authority of Interpretive Communities.* Cambridge, Mass., 1980. One of many works by Fish and others that over several decades questioned, often with absurd exaggeration, the rhetorical authority of any text, turning that authority over to the reader and the reader's culture.

Foucault, Michel. "What is an Author?" Translated by Donald F. Bouchard and Sherry Simon. Ithaca, N.Y., 1977. First published in *Bulletin de la Société française de Philosophie* 63.3(1969), pp 73–104. One of several strong statements about the "death of the author," challenged strongly by Sean Burke above.

Genette, Gerard. "Rhetoric Restrained." In *Figures of Literary Discourse.* Translated by Alan Sheridan, pp. 103–126. New York, 1982. A clear brief history of the decline of rhetoric's status through modern centuries.

Hernadi, Paul, ed. *The Rhetoric of Interpretation and the Interpretation of Rhetoric*. Durham, N.C., 1989.

Horace. *Art of Poetry (Ars Poetica)*. *Horace for English Readers*. Translated by E. C. Wickham. Oxford, 1903. Perhaps the most influential critical work until well into the eighteenth century.

Howell, Wilbur Samuel. *Poetics, Rhetoric, and Logic Studies in the Basic Disciplines of Criticism*. Ithaca, N.Y., 1975.

Jost, Walter, and Michael J. Hyde, eds. *Rhetoric and Hermeneutics: A Reader*. New Haven, 1997.

Kastely, James L. *Rethinking the Rhetorical Tradition: From Plato to Postmodernism*. New Haven, 1997. See especially "*Persuasion:* Jane Austen's Philosophical Rhetoric," pp. 145–167. A penetrating demonstration of how many "postmodernist" notions relate to or are derived from the rhetorical tradition.

Mailloux, Steven. *Rhetoric, Sophistry, Pragmatism*. New York, 1989.

Mailloux, Steven. *Reception Histories: Rhetoric, Pragmatism, and American Cultural Politics*. Ithaca, N.Y., 1998.

McKeon, Richard. *Rhetoric: Essays in Invention and Discovery*. Edited by Mark Backman. Woodbridge, Conn., 1987. Contains "Philosophy of Communications and the Arts," first published 1970; "Rhetoric in the Middle Ages," first published 1942; and "Poetry and Philosophy in the Twelfth Century: The Renaissance of Rhetoric," first published 1946.

McKeon, Richard. *Selected Writings of Richard McKeon*, vol. 1. Edited by Zahava K. McKeon and William G. Swenson. Chicago, 1998. Contains "Rhetoric and Poetics in the Philosophy of Aristotle."

Miller, J. Hillis. *The Ethics of Reading: Kant, de Man, Eliot, Trollope, James, and Benjamin*. New York, 1987. Without much explicit acknowledgement that he is "doing rhetoric," a challenging encounter with the rhetorical problem of good and bad kinds of reading.

Olson, Elder. *On Value Judgments in the Arts*. Chicago, 1976.

Phelan, James. "Character, Progression, and the Mimetic-Didactic Distinction: some Problems and Hypotheses." *Modern Philology* 84 (February 1987), pp. 282–299. A challenging demonstration of how the mimetic–didactic distinction parallels the poetic–didactic distinction.

Preminger, Alex, and T. V. F. Brogan, eds. *The New Princeton Encyclopedia of Poetry and Poetics*. Princeton, 1993. See especially the comprehensive Bibliography of Bibliographies, pp. 1050–1052.

Richter, David H. *Fable's End: Completeness and Closure in Rhetorical Fiction*. Chicago, 1974.

Richter, David H. *Falling into Theory: Conflicting Views on Reading Literature*. New York, 1984.

Ricoeur, Paul. *La metaphore vive*. Paris, 1975. English translation: *The Rule of Metaphor: Multidisciplinary Studies of the Creation of Meaning in Language*. Translated by Robert Czerny. Toronto, 1977. While not prominent in studies by rhetoricians, Ricoeur deserves to be.

Ricoeur, Paul. "Rhetoric—Poetics—Hermeneutics." Translated by Robert Harvey. In *Rhetoric and Hermeneutics: A Reader*. Edited by Walter Jost and Michael J. Hyde, pp. 60–72. New Haven, 1997.

Sacks, Sheldon. *Fiction and the Shape of Belief: A Study of Henry Fielding, with Glances at Swift, Johnson, and Richardson*. Berkeley, 1964.

Scholes, Robert. "Criticism: Rhetoric and Ethics." In *Protocols of Reading*. New Haven, 1989.

Sloane, Thomas O. "Rhetoric and Poetry." In *The New Princeton Encyclopedia of Poetry and Poetics*. Edited by Alex Preminger and T.V.F. Brogan, pp. 1045–1052. Princeton, 1993.

Springer, Mary Doyle. *A Rhetoric of Literary Character: Some Women of Henry James*. Chicago, 1978.

Talmor, Sascha. *The Rhetoric of Criticism: From Hobbes to Coleridge*. New York, 1984.

Vickers, Brian. *In Defense of Rhetoric*. New York, 1988.

Wightman, Melton. *The Rhetoric of John Donne's Verse*. London, 1906.

Wimsatt, William. "The Affective Fallacy." In *The Verbal Icon: Studies in the Meaning of Poetry*. New York, 1958.

—WAYNE C. BOOTH

D

DEBATE is a specific application of argumentation. [*See* Argumentation.] Although the term sometimes is used loosely to refer to any dispute or disagreement, the defining characteristic of a debate is the presentation of mutually exclusive claims by competing advocates to a decision maker for adjudication. Debate is inherently a rhetorical enterprise since the outcome depends on the judgment of an audience and the advocates seek to influence that judgment.

Elements of debate can be found in the writings of Homer, but the "father of debate" is considered to be Protagoras of Abdera (c.485–c.410 BCE), a Sophist best remembered for his statement that "man is the measure of all things." Protagoras believed that there were two sides to every question and taught his students to argue both sides. The skills that he and other Sophists taught were pragmatically valuable for Greek citizens who were expected to defend their own claims in assemblies and courts of law. [*See* Sophists.]

Debate skills remained useful during the Roman and early medieval periods, although they became more the tools of pedagogy than of citizenship. Students recited speeches, called *suasoriae* and *controversiae,* that argued opposing sides of fictitious legal cases. [*See* Controversia and suasoria.] During the Middle Ages and the Renaissance, public debates occurred concerning abstract theological questions.

Contemporary debate has several roots, among them the parliamentary tradition in Britain and in the United States Congress, the declamations featured in nineteenth-century literary societies in American colleges, and the emergence of debate contests in schools and colleges during the early twentieth century.

Components of a Debate. Any debate has three essential components, although any of them may be present implicitly rather than explicitly: the subject matter, the debaters, and the decision maker. Some debates also have estab- lished conventions of procedure, whereas in others the procedural rules are themselves subject to debate.

The subject matter. The subject of a debate is capable of being expressed as a resolution. In many public and contest debates, this is stated explicitly. For example, a public debate might be held on the resolution, "Resolved: That Congress should approve the North American Free Trade Agreement" (NAFTA). In other circumstances, the resolution is implicit. In a political campaign debate, it might be, "Resolved: That the Republocrat candidate should be elected to this office." Or in a debate among historians, taking place within the pages of a scholarly journal, it might be, "Resolved: That the Soviet Union rather than the United States was primarily responsible for the onset of the Cold War."

The aim of the resolution is to capture in a clear, precise, and unbiased statement just what is in dispute. It is intended to favor neither side and not to predetermine the outcome. Resolutions are grouped in various categories, with the most common distinction being one among resolutions of fact, value, and policy. Resolutions of fact actually tend to be concerned with disputes about interpretation, as in the example of the historians' debate about the Cold War, rather than with disagreements about claims that are susceptible to empirical or archival verification. Resolutions of value typically concern hierarchies of the preferable, such as the statement, "Resolved: That protecting the environment is more important than promoting economic growth." And resolutions of policy, like the NAFTA example above, are concerned with choices among courses of action. Some category systems include a fourth type of resolution, sometimes called definition or meaning. An example might be, "Resolved: That protecting Social Security means assuring that current benefit levels will not decrease." Resolutions of this type reflect the belief that definitions are not neutral and that competing notions of reality often contest for the same descriptors.

The purpose of classifying resolutions is that different types of resolutions suggest different issues, subsidiary questions that must be addressed satisfactorily if the resolution is to be sustained. For example, resolutions of value typically raise issues of criteria and application: by what criteria shall environmental protection and economic growth be compared, and what are the results of the comparison? In contrast, resolutions of policy raise issues of advantage and causality: Is there a substantial net benefit to liberalizing inter-American trade restrictions, and is NAFTA a necessary and sufficient means for doing so? (Some approaches to policy resolutions elaborate four issue categories: significance, inherency, efficacy, and disadvantage. The scheme here combines the first and fourth as "advantage" and the second and third as "causality." The two terms in each pair are opposite sides of the same coin.) The categories of issues arising from resolutions of a given type are called "stock issues" or *topoi*. [*See* Topics.] These are general topics or places one might go in search of the specific issues that must be addressed on a given resolution.

A skeptic might note, however, that the distinctions among types of resolutions are seldom so clear as the categories suggest. For example, the resolution pitting environmental protection against economic growth has clear policy implications, and the NAFTA resolution is rooted in questions about the value of liberalizing trade restrictions.

The debaters. A second essential component of a debate is the participants—the debaters themselves. Debaters play the role of committed advocates for or against the resolution. Often they are indeed expressing and defending their own sincere convictions. On other occasions, though, particularly in contest debates, the debater's position is stipulated or assigned, and it may or may not reflect personal conviction.

What makes the positions taken by the debaters mutually exclusive is the law of noncontradiction—in this case, that one cannot be both for and against the same resolution at the same time. Obviously, one can imagine complex resolutions that are supported in some respects and opposed in others. For this reason, the particular respects

that are in dispute should be identified at the outset and the debate should focus on those. For example, in the public debate that emerged in the United States during the late 1990s concerning the use of Federal budget surpluses, most participants agreed that the portion of the surplus produced by the Social Security trust fund should be earmarked for strengthening Social Security. That portion, though seemingly encompassed within a resolution referring to "the surplus," was removed from consideration. The debate over tax cuts versus public spending applied to the remainder of the surplus.

Since debaters maintain what they take to be mutually exclusive positions, one might surmise that they are fierce competitors. In fact, however, they operate from a posture that might better be characterized as restrained partisanship. The presence of an opponent who scrutinizes one's own statements and seeks to identify errors, creates incentives for debaters to be faithful to their evidence and to employ against an opponent only those methods and techniques of argument that they would be comfortable having an opponent use against themselves. Nor are debaters expected to disagree implacably over every possible subject. Some of an opponent's claims often can be granted without weakening one's own basic position, or may even be used to enhance one's own position. Finally, the inability to respond convincingly to an opponent's claims should be a powerful stimulus to reassess one's own position.

Debaters seek to convince decision makers by presenting a case. The case contains the supporting arguments and evidence to warrant affirmation or rejection of the resolution. By convention, those who favor the resolution speak first, so the organization of the affirmative case will have a major impact on the form of the overall debate. Sometimes the case will address each of the issues in turn. The drawback of this approach is that the loss of any major element of the case would doom the entire case. It has become more common for a case to consist of independent reasons to favor or oppose the resolution, with elements of the issues contained within each. If some but not all of these independent reasons are sustained, the decision maker still would have a reason to favor the resolution.

The judge. The final essential component of a

debate is the decision maker or judge. This term is sometimes isomorphic with the audience, but sometimes there will be a spectator audience above and beyond those who actually will choose between the contending claims and advocates.

The decision maker can be a third party uninvolved with any of the advocates, in which case the decision-making process is akin to binding arbitration. Often, however, the debaters will appeal to a larger audience of which they are a part. In a parliamentary debate, for example, senators might appeal for the support of the Senate as a whole. The fact that the debater is also part of the larger decision-making body is immaterial, since what is sought in such cases is a collective rather than an individual response.

On what basis do decision makers adjudicate debates? In contest settings, the focus is expected to be on the debate skills demonstrated by participants, such as analysis, reasoning, organization, use of evidence, and refutation. The decision maker is assumed to be indifferent regarding the debate's subject matter and to be influenced only by the claims presented in the debate and the skill with which they are put forth. In other settings, however, such as political campaign debates, the decision makers cannot be assumed to be indifferent. [*See* Campaigns.] Yet they are expected not just to vote their predispositions but to consider whether the debate justified them.

In reaching their decisions, debate judges sometimes are guided by considerations of presumption and burden of proof. These concepts determine which advocate has the ultimate responsibility to prevail and, reciprocally, which position can be presumed to be correct in the absence of a challenge. Should NAFTA be presumed unnecessary unless it is justified, for example, or should it be presumed to be desirable unless it is discredited? How this question is answered will determine the responsibilities of the two sides in the NAFTA debate.

Presumptions can be either natural (present in the world) or stipulated (set forward by convention). When people are happy with their lot, they are "naturally" resistant to change without good reason. On the other hand, the presumption in criminal law that a person is innocent until proven guilty is stipulated, regardless of what any audience actually believes, and it exists in order to reduce the likelihood that a truly innocent person would be convicted.

Determining where presumption lies in any given controversy, unless it is formally stipulated, is at least in part a political act; hence, it is a matter about which advocates jockey. If it is hard to prove the existence of racial discrimination, for example, then it matters a great deal whether discrimination is considered proved by statistical differences among races unless those differences can be otherwise justified, or whether the absence of discrimination is presumed unless evidence of a willful attempt to discriminate is provided. In other circumstances, however, presumption may have little weight, serving only to answer the utterly hypothetical question of how one would decide a debate in which everything ended up a tie. And in some circumstances, such as political campaign debates, when there is no incumbent, there may be no presumption at all—although some analysts hold that there is a presumption in favor of the political *party* that currently holds the office.

Not all debates result in an actual judgment. A nondecision debate can be useful in laying out competing positions and identifying principal points of disagreement. Even if no decision is rendered, knowing that there is a potential decision maker is important. It gives a sense of context to the debate by identifying the framework of assumptions and values within which the debaters must proceed. The assumption of a disinterested evaluator as well as a committed opponent helps to promote standards of fairness and rigor.

Implicit in a decision to debate, of course, is a commitment to abide by the outcome. Committed advocates are not required to surrender their convictions, and a dispute once settled may be reopened when time and circumstances change. But within the context of any given debate, the decision of the judges must be regarded as legitimate, final, and binding. Advocates choose to resolve disputes in this fashion because of their respect for the process of debate itself. They wish for their viewpoint to prevail, but only if it can do so through the rigorous and disciplined testing that a debate makes possible.

A Philosophy of Debate. Although sometimes seen as a combative activity, debate is primarily a method for collective decision making.

It rests on several philosophical assumptions; the first of which is that much in human affairs is uncertain and contingent, involving prediction, value, interpretation, and judgment. Decisions about such matters cannot be made with the precision of empirical measurement or the certainty of formal logic, but they are nonetheless important and often unavoidable. Rather than consign such choices merely to personal taste or to irrational forces, debate offers a means to ground them in good reasons. The rigorous testing of ideas through argument thus serves as a procedural analogue to formal logic and scientific method. [*See* Contingency and probablility.]

For the results of such a test to be reliable, the test should be truly rigorous, and the second philosophical assumption is that debate makes it so. The seemingly adversarial format means that any claim put forward may be subjected to scrutiny by an opponent whose role invites him or her to mount a challenge to it. This knowledge creates an incentive for debaters to eschew arguments that will not withstand scrutiny and to select those that will be more powerful. This is to say simply that with arguments as with products, competition is a stimulus to quality. It is important to stress, however, that the essential competition is between arguments rather than people. To be sure, one's identity as a person cannot be divorced from the arguments one makes, and one can lose face by repeatedly presenting arguments that do not survive challenge. But debaters willingly assume these risks for the sake of the larger goal of reaching decisions with confidence justified by the rigor of the test. In this sense, debate is fundamentally cooperative rather than competitive.

In the case of formal debates, rigor is promoted not only by the fact of competition but also by the specific procedures and conventions that regulate the event. These may include fixed time limits allocated equally between advocates, stipulations of what counts as proof and evidence, an explicit statement of the resolution, and the selection of judges with particular knowledge and skill.

Third, debate leads to decisions through a process of successive comparisons or tests. By its nature, debate is two-sided: one either supports or opposes the resolution. Yet the resolution will pose only one among many possible approaches for solving a problem or deciding what to do. It is sometimes said that debate is two-sided whereas reality is many-sided. This objection, though, fails to consider the successive nature of debate. To reject a resolution does not necessarily entail endorsing another; it keeps the controversy on the table. Additional resolutions are proposed and considered until finally a collective decision is made.

The successive nature of debate can be illustrated by the course of the controversy in the late 1990s over financing health care in the United States. A single-payer system offering universal coverage was effectively rejected during the debates within the Clinton administration leading to the design of its own proposal. That proposal, whose essential feature was managed competition, in turn was effectively rejected in the public forum in 1994. Thereafter, a series of less comprehensive health-care financing reforms were proposed and discussed. By the year 2000, although the issue was still far from resolved, the debate was tending in the direction of addressing health-care finance through incremental rather than comprehensive policies.

A fourth basic assumption is that debate generates and refines social knowledge. [*See* Social knowledge.] This term refers to the maxims, predispositions, preferences, and judgments that are widely accepted within a culture and acted upon as if they were truths. If the resolution prevails, its content becomes a social truth for those who adjudicated the debate; if it fails, its content is taken off the table. Informal logicians sometimes use the term *commitment set* to refer to the set of beliefs an individual is prepared to accept. These function as premises from which advocates can reason to conclusions that the individual likewise would be obliged to accept. Just so, the outcomes of debates represent the "commitment set" of a community or a society. Resolutions that withstand scrutiny are taken to be true by the community of advocates and therefore can serve as the premises for subsequent arguments.

Finally, debate is strongly related to the defense of freedom of expression on the basis that it is the system most likely to promote truth and justice. Aristotle (384–322 BCE) maintained that truth by nature is stronger than its opposite. If that is so, then truth should be more capable of surviving a fair and rigorous test such as debate provides. Democratic governance places confidence in the collective choices made in the cacophony of public discussion. A vigorous tradition and culture of debate help to justify that confidence.

Varieties of Debate. During the twentieth century, there were five major forms of debate: parliamentary debate, political campaign debate, specialized debate within particular fields, extended public debate, and academic contest debate.

Parliamentary debate. Debate is a major feature of legislative bodies, with procedures derived from law, tradition, and formal systems. Norms of debate in the British Parliament have evolved over time. In the United States, rules for Congressional debate derive from British precedents, from the U.S. Constitution, from the *Manual* written by Thomas Jefferson when he was vice president (and presiding officer of the Senate), and from rules adopted by each of the legislative branches for its own proceedings. Debates in parliamentary style, though less elaborate, also are a feature of state and local governments, annual meetings of organizations, and business meetings in the private sector. These groups may evolve their own procedural rules but frequently adopt an established codification. *Robert's Rules of Order,* compiled in 1876 by Henry M. Robert and later amended by him, is the most common system of parliamentary procedure, although competitive systems also exist.

Political campaign debate. Joint appearances by opposing candidates for office, dividing time in a debate format, became popular on the U.S. frontier during the early nineteenth century in order to reduce difficulties in transportation and communication for both candidates and voters. Among the most celebrated of these debates, though atypical, were the seven joint encounters between Abraham Lincoln and Stephen A. Douglas in the 1858 campaign for the U.S. Senate seat from Illinois. The first debates between presidential candidates of the two major parties occurred during the 1960 election campaign between John F. Kennedy and Richard M. Nixon. These debates were televised and also broadcast on radio, and they attracted wide attention. Each debate fea-

tured a brief opening and closing statement by each candidate, but most of the time was allotted for responding to questions posed by a panel of journalists. Although the research evidence is inconclusive, many believe that the debates, especially the visual comparison of the candidates, helped Kennedy.

Debates have been held in every U.S. presidential election since 1976, and debates have become a regular feature in state and local elections as well. Several other nations also have incorporated the tradition of political campaign debate. Debates have been promoted as a means of encouraging public interest in the political campaign; they have been criticized for the shallow and superficial comments they permit candidates to make. As with the 1960 debates, there is little research evidence to suggest that debates have a significant effect on people's voting decisions; their principal effect appears to be to reinforce the predispositions of audience members. In close elections, however, even small differences in turnout can affect the outcome.

Since 1988, U.S. presidential debates have been arranged under the auspices of a bipartisan Commission on Presidential Debates, which has proposed dates, sites, and formats to the candidates for their review. The journalist-panel format prevailed until 1992, when some of the debates employed a single-moderator format and one employed a "town hall" format in which questions were posed by citizens in the audience. The 1992 campaign also was the only time that the presidential debates included three candidates, because Reform Party candidate H. Ross Perot had achieved a 15 percent standing in major national polls—the benchmark established by the Commission on Presidential Debates for participation. To encourage citizen interest and involvement in the debates, the commission has developed a program called DebateWatch, in which individuals gather together to watch the presidential debates and then to discuss the issues afterward.

Specialized debates within fields. Debates within a special field—such as the example of the historians' debate over the origins of the Cold War—are conducted within the forums of the field, such as scholarly journals and professional meetings. The social knowledge on which they rely, evidence that they use, and reasoning patterns that they deploy may be field-specific rather than general. For a larger public, the outcomes may not matter although they are very important to those within the field. [*See* Argument fields.]

Extended public debate. Public debates concern controversies of widespread interest that develop over time. Many people are involved, numerous forums and media are employed, standards of evidence are highly variable, resolutions and norms of procedure are usually implicit, and it is often not clear when the debate begins or ends. Examples of extended public debate in the United States include the controversy over whether abortion should be legal, the dispute over whether race-conscious policies are appropriate to compensate for racial discrimination, and the previously mentioned debate over public financing of health care. Public debates may arise unpredictably and often terminate not because one set of arguments has clearly prevailed but because a compromise position emerges, because advocates run out of arguments and the dispute becomes stale, or because social or technological changes make the debate moot.

Academic contest debate. Since the late nineteenth century, debate contests have become prominent activities at universities, colleges, and high schools in the United States and in other countries as well. Debates had been an activity of the literary societies established in many American colleges and universities at midcentury. The first known intercollegiate debate took place on 29 November 1872 between the Hinman Society of Northwestern University and the Tri Kappa Society of the now defunct Chicago University, twenty years earlier than the 1892 Harvard–Yale debate that is often cited as the first intercollegiate match. During the late nineteenth and early twentieth centuries, schools scheduled single debates with contracts that specified, among other things, how teams and judges were to be selected. Two-year contracts provided that the debate would be held at one school the first year and at the other in the next. The first known extended tour, in which multiple debates were held on the same trip, was conducted by the University of Denver in 1913. In 1923, Southwestern College hosted the first intercollegiate debate tournament, and the tournament format has been dominant since that time. In the most common tour-

nament format, all teams have a certain number of debates, alternating between supporting and opposing the resolution, and the teams with the best composite records proceed into a single-elimination bracket. During the years after World War II, national competition developed; the National Debate Tournament began in 1947.

The first known international debate took place in 1921 between Bates College and the Oxford Union. International tours have become a regular part of the debate landscape, with participants from Australia, Great Britain, Japan, Russia, New Zealand, Israel, and other countries. Many of these tours are coordinated by the Committee on International Discussion and Debate under the auspices of the National Communication Association. At the high-school level, debate received a major boost from the formation of the National Forensic League (NFL) in 1925. In addition to many other services for high schools, the league has sponsored a national tournament annually since 1931 (except for the years during World War II).

BIBLIOGRAPHY

Branham, Robert James. *Debate and Critical Analysis: The Harmony of Conflict.* Hillsdale, N.J., 1991. A textbook that relates debate to critical thinking and analysis.

Ehninger, Douglas. "Debate as Method: Limitations and Values." *Speech Teacher* 15 (September, 1966), pp. 180–185. Suggests that debate is primarily a means of critical deliberation rather than a combative activity.

Ehninger, Douglas, and Wayne Brockriede. *Decision by Debate.* 2d ed. New York, 1978. Approaches to debate reflecting the argument theory of Stephen Toulmin and the belief that debate is a cooperative enterprise.

Freeley, Austin J., and David L. Steinberg. *Argumentation and Debate: Critical Thinking for Reasoned Decision Making.* 10th ed. Belmont, Calif., 2000. The most widely used textbook in debate.

Friedenberg, Robert V., ed. *Rhetorical Studies of National Political Debates, 1960–1992.* 2d ed. Westport, Conn., 1994. Studies of individual U.S. presidential debates in the campaigns between 1960 and 1992.

Jamieson, Kathleen H., and David Birdsell. *Presidential Debates: The Challenge of Creating an Informed Electorate.* New York, 1988. Examines the nature of argument in U.S. presidential debates and the expectations of the audience.

Kraus, Sidney, ed. *The Great Debates: Kennedy vs. Nixon, 1960.* Bloomington, Ind., 1977. First published

1962. Research studies of the first U.S. presidential debates.

Muir, Star A. "A Defense of the Ethics of Contemporary Debate." *Philosophy and Rhetoric* 26 (1993), pp. 277–295. Defends debate against various criticisms, especially the contention that debating both sides of a resolution is unethical.

Patterson, J. W., and David Zarefsky. *Contemporary Debate*. Boston, 1983. Approaches debate as an exercise in rigorous testing of hypotheses submitted to audiences for adherence.

Robert, Henry M. *The Scott, Foresman Robert's Rules of Order Newly Revised*. Glenview, Ill., 1990. The standard manual of parliamentary procedure.

Thomas, David A., and Jack P. Hart, ed. *Advanced Debate*. 4th ed. Lincolnwood, Ill., 1992. An anthology of articles about debate theory and practice that originally appeared in professional journals.

Ziegelmueller, George W., and Jack Kay. *Argumentation: Inquiry and Advocacy*. 3d ed. Boston, 1997. A mainstream textbook in argumentation and debate.

— DAVID ZAREFSKY

DECLAMATION was the practice speech on a fictitious deliberative or forensic theme that constituted the final stage of rhetorical education in the Roman Empire. [*See* Deliberative genre; *and* Forensic genre.] It was the most serious of the imaginative speaking and writing exercises that a student had begun by memorizing Cato or Menander's maxims and supplying voices in the retelling of a set fable. While always closely tied to the school, declamation eventually became a kind of speech concerto, akin, though remotely, to the performances of the original Sophists and the massed lectures of the Second Sophistic. As a ubiquitous school exercise in the empire, it was of great importance for literature, and indeed for the attitudes and mentality of the elite, because it trained competitive skills, and also skills in listening and comprehension as well as composition.

Having passed through a series of elementary exercises (the *progymnasmata*), which included fable, maxim, and *chreia*, grammar school students encountered the first stage of declamation, the *suasoria*. The first-century CE rhetorician Quintilian indicated that grammarians quite often took on this instruction, while many rhetoricians specialized in the more advanced *controversia*. [*See* Controversia and suasoria.] The *suasoria* offered the easier situation wherein the student plays adviser to some great man: Should Numa accept the kingship offered by the Roman people? Should Alexander set sail upon the ocean? The *controversia* presented a more challenging structure: the declaimer imagines himself as a lawyer in court. His teacher has provided a few sentences describing the (bizarre) situation and a law that stipulates dire punishment. The declaimer must compose and deliver a speech attacking or defending the allegedly chaste prostitute who wants to be a priestess or some young man who has run afoul of a severe father. Thanks to critics ancient and modern, declamation has been seen as impractical, fantastic, and overblown in style; its verbal pyrotechnics have long impressed or distressed readers. In fact, fantasy and an experimental categorization did mark this preparation for imperial life, and the ancient denigrators did not appreciate the usefulness of adolescent boys reflecting on stepmothers' actions, on fathers' drastic measures, or on sons' divided loyalties. Nonetheless, extant declamations provide a full course in the figures of ancient rhetoric. [*See* Figures of speech.] Imagined dialogue, anticipation of one's opponent's arguments, syllogistic arguments often *a fortiori*, commonplaces, maxims, descriptions, apostrophē, and *prosōpopoeia* abound. [*See* Apostrophē; Commonplaces and commonplace books; Descriptio; Prosōpopoeia; *and* Syllogism.] The imagination of what character to adopt receives specific, careful comment from the master in the declamations from the school of Quintilian. In detailing which persona will best win the audience's sympathies, and the instructions in what *color* to add (i.e., how to represent *animus*—intention, psychology of the defendant, or agents of the declamation), the instructor reveals the strong ethical preoccupation of declamation. [*See* Color.] The student constructs a narrative that explores the psychology of action and agent. The variety of perspective demanded by declamatory plots and the constant pressure to innovate, encouraged a facility in categorical thinking as well as rhetorical promptness. Quintilian and Latro, the declaimer most celebrated by the elder Seneca (c.55 BCE–c.39 CE), stressed division, which is both the reduction of the case to an essential issue or issues (is chastity simply virginity or the company one keeps; does the present case fit the spirit and not simply the letter of the law?) and the argumentative structure of the speech.

By considering the extreme expression of classes and by entertaining various explanations at the same time, declamation developed theory building. As the capstone of rhetorical education, declamation demanded that the young man present himself as an adult orator speaking on behalf of wronged sons, fathers, freedmen, or the maltreated freeborn girl. Parricide, rape, incest, kidnapping overabundantly supply violence that threatens the home and the state. To the rescue comes the student, sharpening his skills of advocacy and assuming the role of spokesman for the misjudged and the socially subordinate.

While born of the school, declamation's popularity as adult entertainment is well attested. Augustus (63 BCE–14 CE) and Maecenas visited performances. Seneca the Elder presents snippets from the contests of professionals and from the performances of famous teachers whose schools were open to visitors. The audience mercilessly pounces upon slips of taste, plausibility, or Latinity. For the performers, the declamatory milieu emerges as an extremely competitive verbal culture, whether the participants were schoolboys, freedmen, provincials, or equestrians. These were contests where aristocrats such as Messalla or Pollio could make or break a reputation with a pithily worded put-down.

Declamation, both the term and the practice, as described above, was current at Rome toward the end of Cicero's life (106–43 BCE). It persisted to the end of the empire—the young emperor-to-be Gratian was said to be good at the *controversia*—and beyond. Seneca the Elder believed declamation had grown up with him—a piece of ignorance that in its elimination of Greek precedent and preference for Latin sources no older than Cicero, presages the outlook of many an imperial, post-classical writer. As a species of eristic practice speaking, declamation has direct affinities to a long Greek intellectual heritage. [*See* Eristic.] In particular, the mid-fifth-century BCE tetralogies of Antiphon had established a training in mock judicial cases (though these followed the course of a real Athenian case with four speeches: contra, pro, contra, pro). Aristotle (384–322 BCE) and Theophrastus (c.371–c.288 BCE) are said to have introduced the philosophical thesis to the

schools (which proposes a general case; the hypothesis supplies names or a specific occasion or time). Philostratus maintained that Aeschines, driven from Athens by Demosthenes (330 BCE), initiated the Second Sophistic movement, which used hypotheses with the characters the poor man, the hero, and the tyrant known from later declamations. A certain amount of caution is called for since the sources indulge in an easy schematism—the real orator drives out the lesser who turns to school—and that vice of ancient intellectual history where every development is granted a famous name. Theophrastus and Menander were interested in a similar variety of ordinary people and extreme character types. The Hellenistic school remains in its actual practices somewhat murky and was no doubt far more varied than later accounts remember.

The early use of the verb *declamare* (often in the derogatory sense of overloud delivery) and a late gloss of *declamatio* as Greek *anaphōnēsis,* indicate an original meaning of voice training. The word could simply mean to practice or rehearse: Mark Antony and Pompey are each said to have "declaimed" in private as preparation for important cases. Cicero declaimed in Greek up to the time of his praetorship, in Latin throughout his life. He draws attention to the novelty of the word and refers humorously to his retirement practice of philosophizing in Greek as *senilis declamatio.* Cicero was out of step or sympathy with developments such as Plotius Gallus's school (early first century BCE), which modeled exercises on Roman cases and whose speakers were faulted for loud delivery.

Declamation in Greek flourished in the eastern portions of the empire (see especially the declamations on historical themes of Aristides and those of Libanius and Choricius of Gaza). The chief Latin collections are the excerpts made by Seneca the Elder, the major and minor declamations ascribed to Quintilian, and those of Calpurnius Flaccus. The fertile fictions of declamation provided a practical and ongoing myth making for the young.

[*See also* Classical rhetoric.]

BIBLIOGRAPHY

Bloomer, W. Martin. *Latinity and Literary Society at Rome.* Philadelphia, 1997. Chapter six treats the social role of declamation at Rome.

Bloomer, W. Martin. "Schooling in Persona." *Classical Antiquity* 16 (April 1997), pp. 57–78. A consideration of the place of declamation within Roman schooling.

Bonner, S. *Roman Declamation*. Berkeley, 1949. A fundamental work, especially strong on the relation of declamation to Roman law.

Fairweather, J. *Seneca the Elder*. Cambridge, U.K., 1981. A careful treatment not only of the life and works of Seneca but of the history of declamation and of *stasis* theory.

Russell, D. *Greek Declamation*. Cambridge, U.K., 1983. The best treatment of the subject.

Sussman, L. *The Declamations of Calpurnius Flaccus: text, translation, and commentary*. Leiden, 1994.

Sussman, L. *The Major Declamations Ascribed to Quintilian*. Frankfurt A.M., 1987.

Winterbottom, M. *The Minor Declamations Ascribed to Quintilian*. Berlin, 1984. Text and commentary with thorough introduction.

—W. MARTIN BLOOMER

DECONSTRUCTION. *See* Composition, *article on* History of English departments in the United States; Irony; *and* Politics, *article on* Constitutive rhetoric.

DECORUM. The classical concept of decorum embodies many of the paradoxical features of the art of rhetoric: It is at once antique and universal, a general maxim of composition and a richly inflected aesthetic sensibility, a radical assertion of the social character of language and a recipe for conventionality.

The basic idea of decorum is that speech will not be effective unless it fits in with the characteristic features of the speaker, subject, audience, occasion, or medium. The classical handbooks on rhetoric advised that one should not speak brashly if ashamed, or speak lightly of serious matters, or address the Senate the same way as the people, or argue in court as if before an assembly, or use the same sentence lengths when writing and speaking. Such advice does not guarantee persuasive success, but those who do otherwise are more likely to fail.

Decorum was identified in the classical texts as one of the four major virtues of style, and some writers featured it as the highest virtue. [*See* Style.] The concept was expressed in Greek as *to prepon*

(from *prepei*, it is fitting) and with other terms such as *harmottein* and *kairos* (which usually refers to appropriateness in respect to time). Originally referring to conspicuousness, *prepon* became a technical term referring to suitability and reflecting the society's social organization. Thus, in a civilized setting, we distinguish ourselves most effectively by fitting into received roles, and decorum becomes the aesthetic sense by which one masters this process. Latin usage included *decorum* (from *decet*, it is fitting, and also resonant with *decorare*, to adorn), along with *aptus, congruens, accommodatus,* and so forth. Decorum was a preoccupation of classical authors, any of whom could have understood Cicero's remark that "In an oration, as in life, nothing is harder than to determine what is appropriate" (*Orator* 70).

It is difficult for modern thinkers to imagine how decorum could sustain so much intellectual interest throughout antiquity. As Robert Kaster has summarized, in dealing with decorum:

> [W]e are dealing with a huge and very varied system of associations; but we are also dealing, ultimately, with a closed system. From reading the ancient opinions on the subject, one can conclude that it would be possible, in principle, to draw up a taxonomy that would co-ordinate all known persons, things, actions and thoughts in relation to all known nouns, verbs, adjectives and adverbs, as they could decorously be used by all possible speakers in all possible circumstances before all possible audiences.
> (p. 5)

Indeed, it was just this prospect that scared off Hermogenes (fl. 180 CE), whose treatise on types of style (*Peri ideōn*) deferred the subject to a later (unwritten) work:

> Anyone who has tried to deal with this topic will know what an overwhelming task it is. To treat all the problems involved in this subject in a systematic way seems almost beyond human ability and to require some divine power. One would have to deal with times, characters, places, causes, manners, and other such topics and to discuss all the possible cases, as well as the various forms that they can take and the ways in which they can be presented, and what kinds of sentiments are appropriate in each part of the speech. . . . It would be necessary to treat all the types of style and to discuss what kind of

style is generally appropriate to each particular problem, depending on the men involved and the character about whom they are talking and the moment at which they are speaking. . . . One would also have to discuss what sentiments can be used in each part of the speech. . . . It would also be necessary to deal with the best order in which to present the points that the orator has decided to make in one case or another; this too will depend on the circumstances of the case. One would also have to deal with how one point or another should be introduced and what thoughts should be expanded and what is the best way to do this, as well as which ones should be passed over as quickly as possible. (379)

Hermogenes' formalist intelligence requires the power of a supercomputer, and even then the prospect is not one that warms the imagination. Yet, his predecessors had claimed that this seemingly impossible task could be made manageable once it was recognized as an artistic process (Isocrates, *Against the Sophists* 12–13) requiring prudential intelligence (Cicero, *De oratore* 3.212) rather than methodical calculation.

These emphases on artistry and practical wisdom begin to account for the concept's persistent appeal in the classical world. [*See* Classical rhetoric.] There is another, complementary explanation as well, which is that the language of decorum carried a complex genealogy of aesthetic alternatives. Persistent recourse to this vocabulary reflected not a uniform reduction of varied experiences to the same categories, but rather the activation of a range of attitudes that could be adopted in turn toward a remarkably wide field of speech and conduct. The major developments in this genealogy are indicated in Figure 1.

This model is not strictly chronological, yet it is more than an ahistorical typology. Although the varied inflections of decorum were present from the onset, usually in somewhat fragmentary form, each received strong articulation in a particular order that reflects both logical and historical development of the concept. Individual authors were more or less precocious, but all of them were working out an aesthetic language in respect to both their predecessors and their own historical circumstances. History is inevitably less neat than any model, but generally we can place

the first set of alternatives amidst the political and cultural changes in the Greek world during the fifth and fourth centuries BCE, while the additional developments emerged or received their best statements in the Roman period ranging from the last days of the Republic (late first century BCE) through the first centuries of Empire. By identifying how a set of ideas became progressively available to the classical thinker, this genealogy reveals lines of influence and points of controversy that can be obscured by the scholarly habit of collating classical statements on decorum with little regard for periodization.

The original sense of appropriateness may be labeled a *sophistic* orientation: One persuades through creative adaptation to characteristic expectations, and the emphasis is almost entirely on a swift and timely response. Any sense of preferred form or character is subordinate to mastering the situation. The right action is the one that achieves the persuasive effect, and the speaker has to be continually alert to the ever-changing opportunities for success. One assumes a radically contingent world while looking for those moments when a relatively small initiative can transform the competitive field.

Gorgias (c.483–376 BCE) apparently wrote a study of *kairos,* and the Sophists are suitable representatives of this attitude (Untersteiner, 1954; Poulakos, 1995), in part because they were transitional figures who developed rhetoric out of an older logic of strategic action. This intelligence was both comprehensive and amoral: "capable of adapting to the most baffling of situations, of assuming as many faces as there are social categories and types of men in the city, of inventing the thousand ploys which will make his actions effective in the most varied of circumstances" (Detienne and Vernant 1978, pp. 39–40). Sophistic decorum refers to the artistic intuition for sizing up a situation, adapting to circumstances, and seizing the moment. This combination of discernment and brilliance was formidable, but thoroughly nomadic—and thus inadequate for those who have to operate in a more settled place. [*See* Sophists.]

The *organic* sense of decorum constitutes a significant reorientation of the concept. This mode focuses primarily on form and only then on func-

(a)

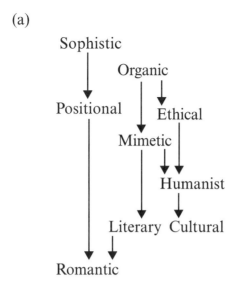

(b)

Sophists, Gorgias

Gorgias, Socrates/Plato

Isocrates   Socrates/Plato, Isocrates, Aristotle

Aristotle

Cicero

Horace/Dionysius   Quintilian

"Longinus"/"Demetrius"

Decorum. FIGURE 1. (a) *Classical Model of Decorum.* (b) *Exponents of the Modes.*

tion. Persuasive texts are conceived as made objects whose identity and value depend on both the relationship between the artifact and its purpose and the relationship among its parts. For example, Gorgias's *Encomium to Helen* (of Troy) features his artistic techniques (along with an obvious lack of practical exigency) while expressly aligning the form of his speech with his intention. Whereas the Sophistic sense of appropriateness was focused on doing whatever produced a desired effect in a given situation, the organic sensibility sees the relationship between purpose

and agency as a quality of the artifact itself. Socrates' (c.470–394 BCE) comparison of speech with other arts emphasizes this point:

Well now, the good man who speaks for the best surely will not say what he says at random but with some purpose in view, just as all other craftsmen do not each choose and apply materials to their work at random, but with the view that each of their productions should have a certain form. Look, for example, if you will, at painters, builders, shipwrights, and all other craftsmen—any of them you choose—and see how each one disposes each element he contributes in a fixed order, and compels one to fit and harmonize with the other until he has combined the whole into something well ordered and regulated. (Plato, *Gorgias* 503d–504a)

Form is defined with regard to universal relations of symmetry and harmony, and the artisan fashions the artifact by selecting and arranging materials in order to ensure that they "exhibit a proper relation to one another and to the whole of which they are parts" (Plato, *Phaedrus,* 268d). This association of internal coherence with expressive purpose creates a full-bodied articulation of an explicitly aesthetic sensibility, while focusing artistic interpretation on the "hermeneutical circle" of part and whole. It also introduced a fundamental ambiguity into interpretive judgment, particularly with regard to any practical art: Should the judgment of a work rest more on the relationship of its parts to its intrinsic intentionality, or on the relationship of any part or the whole composition to an extrinsic effect? This ambiguity remained within all subsequent developments of the idea of decorum.

Positional decorum tilts the composition of a text toward the social context supplied by the audience and other speakers. Persuasive artistry is now understood in terms of such considerations as social status, respect, deference, dignity, character by association, alliances, acknowledgments, insults, apologies, and many other such relational factors. One might say that this mode looks to what is characteristic, but without a strong sense of character. Positional decorum may be thought of as a domesticated version of the original, more nomadic sense of seizing the moment, though it is also a richer, more aesthetic sensibility that draws on and expands attention to textual form while still emphasizing persuasive effect. The fundamental orientation is to fit the artistic work into its context of reception. This sense of social context is both circumstantial and discursive: It refers to both the literal setting of the speech and its compositional field, which includes the relationship between the work and its artistic genre, competition with other speakers, debts owed to prior models, the search for both familiarity and novelty, and so forth.

As with harmonizing the parts of the composition, the classical writers were quick to declare that this positioning is not mechanical. Isocrates (436–338 BCE) emphasizes that this fitting of text to context (and work to genre) is the key to rhetorical invention (*Against the Sophists* 13–17). Interestingly, the better adjustment can include lesser violations of representational propriety, such that great things can be made to appear lowly and low things great (*Panegyricus* 8). These variations in magnitude subordinate the relationship between discourse and its subject matter to the ability to make strategic use of common materials in what is nonetheless a well-ordered manner (*Panegyricus* 9). Thus, positional decorum carries the fundamental insights that discourse has to be properly addressed to receive the desired response, and that the distinctiveness necessary for a strong response is derived from variations on received conventions. Though more committed to an artistic product and long-term reputation than the Sophistic mentality, this mode is not a completely settled thing: the speaker doesn't just assume a fixed position, but is always having to adjust to the other players in the rhetorical situation, "For what has been said by one speaker is not equally useful for the speaker who comes after him" (*Against the Sophists* 12). Appropriately, Isocrates' best examples of his aesthetic sense come from his own discourses, which are characterized by frequent and elaborate maneuvers for situating his words, arguments, reputation, and so forth in respect to real and imagined audiences and with an eye on questions of generic classification and judgment (*Antidosis* 45–46, *Panathenaicus* 1–2, 271).

As one positions oneself in respect to others, questions of morality soon arise. The mode of *ethical decorum* is similar to the positional mode, in that it orients the speaker toward others in respect to one's purpose, but it adds a much richer set of criteria for defining suitability. First, art and morality are joined organically in the objective of the harmonious, well-ordered soul (Plato, *Gorgias* 504b) that is reflected and maintained by right speech (Isocrates, *Antidosis* 255–256; Plato, *Phaedrus* 271b). Second, appropriateness itself is defined as a mean between two extremes. A sense of the mean is necessary because opposing variations in magnitude can be equally artistic (Aristotle, *Rhetoric* 3.2.14), and appropriateness itself is a qualitative judgment (Plato, *Statesman* 284e,

Laws 757) rather than something that can be measured like the length of an object. Therefore, the appropriate description has to be determined in respect to a range of possible alternatives and a sense of purpose that also can be judged more or less suitable to the occasion. Aristotle (384–322 BCE) concludes his discussion of style (*lexis*) with the rule that "the mean is suitable" (*to meson harmottei, Rhetoric* 3.12.16) and with the advice that the best results will come from a mixing of the several norms (i.e., in a balanced, harmonious manner).

It is a very short step from norming speech toward the mean to making moderate speech the measure of a balanced character. Thus, the ethical form of decorum becomes synonymous with a sense of tact (Aristotle, *Nicomachean Ethics* 1128a and Isocrates, *Panathenaicus* 30–32). In setting out the rules for conversation, for example, Aristotle counsels that one should always strive for the mean (for example, between excessive joking and persistent sternness), and that the free and responsible individual will only say or listen to what lies between the extremes discursively in order to exhibit and habituate oneself to moderation (*Nicomachean Ethics* 1128a, *Rhetoric* 3.2.15, *Poetics* 22.11). Because Aristotle also defines the virtues of character as means between extremes (*Nicomachean Ethics* 1107a), decorum then becomes the linchpin between the norms of style and the norms of right conduct (D'Alton, 1962). Decorum applies whenever language has the task of depicting character, while the society's conventions of expression can be used to regulate individual conduct.

The full statement of Aristotle's definition of decorum in the *Rhetoric* ties the ethical orientation to a deeper sense of appropriateness that undergirds the entire work: "The *lexis* will be appropriate if it expresses character and emotion and is proportionate to the subject matter" (3.7.1). With the addition of this norm of proportionality, the speech is more than a well-crafted artifact observing universal economies of craftsmanship or conduct; it is an imitation of other things. This *mimetic* mode of decorum is no less than a theory of representation of the social world, and it completes Aristotle's presentation of rhetoric as a rational process. [*See* Imitation.] Language should correspond to reality; discursive form should follow the outline of its subject. "Proof from signs is expressive of character, because there is an appropriate style for each genus and moral state" (3.7.6). Language can be used to provide an accurate depiction of who one is and what one ought to be doing, and it does this by correctly imitating the differences among the various elements of the moral world. Higher emotion requires higher intensity of expression or more excessive diction, pitiable circumstances are to be spoken of in a submissive manner, and so forth. We persuade when our discourse conforms most closely to the already existing configuration of social types and intelligible emotions—the more natural (3.2.4) and vivid (3.11) the imitation, the better. Mimicry is the source of the reality effect of a discourse, and it prompts an ethical caveat because audiences can be misled (3.7.4).

The significance of the mimetic mode of decorum within the rhetorical tradition is that it provides the basis for the architectonic expansion of the concept across all the elements of the art. Aristotle's discussion in Book 3 of the *Rhetoric* is illustrative: Appropriateness is first set out as a single term in a large system of concepts that comprise the art of rhetoric, but then it expands from its point of definition to produce a backward reassessment of the entire system. There is a style appropriate to each kind of rhetoric and to written as opposed to oral presentation, and to variations within these contexts in purpose and audience (3.12). The discussion of style concludes (3.12.6) by reaffirming only those norms that adhere to what is suitable, and it explicitly bonds the persuasiveness of a composition to its appropriateness (*to pithanon ek tou prepontos*). This schema is illustrated further by the example of the concluding discussion on arrangement: the appeals for the entire speech are organized according to what is appropriate for each type of oratory at each point in the speech, with additional illustration of suitable adjustments according to variations in emotion, purpose, and so forth.

From this vantage, one can see that Aristotle has been relying on a logic of suitability throughout the *Rhetoric*. The entire exercise in categorization has been oriented to identifying how persuasiveness follows from using the appropriate appeal in the specific place. This perspective does not supply the whole of Aristotle's observations, especially when he is discussing forms of proof and matters of diction, yet it controls the analysis of even the inner workings of the enthymeme and of metaphor. [*See* Arrangement, *article on* Traditional arrangement; Enthymeme; *and* Metaphor.] Indeed, rationality itself is defined within a logic of appropriateness: The level of precision should be adjusted to match the capability of the audience (*Rhetoric* 1.11.12) and the subject (*Nicomachean Ethics* 1094b25).

The architectonic expansion of decorum was not fully realized in Aristotle's use of it as a grammar of persuasive theory, however. That development was achieved by Roman writers, and Cicero (106–43 BCE) in particular, who drew on both the assimilation of Greek thought and a strong combination of personal interiority and social awareness. Cicero's *humanist* conception of decorum extends the idea across all social life:

> The universal rule, in oratory as in life, is to consider propriety. This depends on the subject under discussion, and the character of both the speaker and the audience. The philosophers are accustomed to consider this extensive subject under the head of duties . . . ; the literary critics consider it in connexion with poetry; orators in dealing with every kind of speech, and in every part thereof . . . it is important often in actions as well as words, in the expression of the face, in gesture and in gait. (*Orator* 71–74)

Decorum is not simply found everywhere, it is the quality whereby speech and thought, wisdom and performance, art and morality, assertion and deference, and many other elements of action intersect. The concept underwrites Cicero's alignment of the plain, middle, and elevated oratorical styles with the three functions of informing, pleasing, and motivating an audience (*Orator* 69), which in turn extends rhetorical theory across a wide range of human affairs. The scope of decorum also is evident in his examples, which include petty legal cases and affairs of state, poetic diction and philosophical method, the parts of a speech and the conduct of everyday life. This continuity acquires its full significance though the extended discussion of decorum in Cicero's treatise on ethics, *De officiis,* where the concept is grounded in a conception of human nature:

> We must realize also that we are invested by Nature with two characters, as it were: one of these is universal, arising from the fact of our being all alike endowed with reason and with that superiority which lifts us above the brute. From this all morality and propriety are derived, and upon it depends the rational method of ascertaining our duty. The other character is that which is assigned to individuals in particular. (1.107)

Development of the mature, fully formed human being consists of discerning what is appropriate for oneself in accord with these dual constraints of universal human nature and individual ability (1.110). Decorum is both the means and end of human development, the artistic measure for composing oneself in harmonious relationship with others. "Such orderliness of conduct is, therefore, to be observed, that everything in the conduct of our life shall balance and harmonize, as in a finished speech" (1.144).

As becomes evident from the subsequent exposition (through 1.130–132 and ff.), decorum becomes a disciplinary practice for which moral philosophy, the laws of the state, and rhetoric are accompanying bodies of knowledge. It also is clear that this humanist mode is a coherent assimilation of each of the prior modes of decorum; Cicero's speeches, for example, are masterpieces of positioning. Cicero deepens the concept, however, by focusing on the individual's self-conscious participation in the process of human development—and, not incidentally, with the hope of upward social mobility. The situation is seemingly paradoxical, in several senses: The individual realizes his or her potential by being aware of natural and social constraints (e.g., the proper dispositions for each period of life and the rules of propriety defining a class society). This inward attentiveness to all forms of conduct exists as a mentality of social performance, so that one always chooses with regard to how actions will be received by others. A general logic of suitability legitimates wide variance in choice; "Indeed, such diversity of character carries with it so great significance that suicide may be for one man a duty, for another (under the same circumstances) a crime" (1.112). Even the notion of tact is given more depth, elevated to the level of justice and made more a matter of empathy than self-interested moderation: "It is the function of justice not to do wrong to one's fellow-men; of considerateness, not to wound their feeling; and in this the essence of propriety is best seen" (1.99). No wonder that decorum is placed at the center of ethical study (1.98) and thought to be so difficult: it is the aesthetic sensibility that grounds moral life. So it is that Cicero discusses how propriety should guide everything from speech to one's choice of housing (1.138). His sense of decorum operates not merely as a set of rules but as the process of invention in the art of self-fashioning.

The humanist emphasis on cultivation allows easy extrapolation to the idea of a preferred culture. Although still focused on the individual's uniquely complicated determinations of appropriate speech and conduct, *cultural decorum* develops this sensibility within a more institutionalized context that emphasizes education, imitation of models, and association with other well-regulated people. Decorum becomes the chief virtue in a culture of taste that is the proper end of a liberal education. The major exemplar is the Roman educator Quintilian (c.35–c.100 CE), whose discussions of decorum make it a preoccupation for those assuming the increasingly professional and bureaucratic duties of Roman governance.

Quintilian's use of Cicero as his paragon of the educated person is indicative of the subtle alteration and expansion of the concept that characterizes cultural decorum. The Cicero to be imitated is not so much the orator capable of great emotional power, but rather a figure whose words reflect a life of self-control (*Institutio oratoria* 11.1.62–72). Likewise, Quintilian's inventory of the many elements of appropriateness—character, age, role, occasion, and so forth (Book 11)— imply a more settled world than the shifting allegiances of Cicero's forum. The common denominator for these changes is the larger shift from apprenticeship for and reflection on political life to an educational program that is to inculcate virtues of respectability and institutional competence. Decorum is learned by imitation, and Quintilian makes it clear that models such as Cicero are suitable because they embody qualities of moderation, tact, prudence, adaptability, and the like. What is insufficiently appreciated is how this recipe for hegemony is genuinely liberal by comparison to Plato's earlier, more authoritarian depiction of cultural norms (*Laws* 801d–803b): Unlike Plato, the Roman program of encultura-

tion does not emphasize rigid social stratification and state censorship.

An interesting element in Quintilian's work is his association of decorum with the practice of reading. Decorum is invoked in both of his accounts of reading: it supplies the rule for selecting and shaping literary study in the lower grades (1.8) and also for understanding the literary works that provide the models for the final development of the finished orator (10.1.8–9). This association gains additional significance from his parsing of decorum between stylistic maneuvers (8.2), largely at the level of diction, and a more general mentality of adaptation that reflects architectonic extension across the art of rhetoric (Book 11). Reading starts out as a storehouse of technical models, but it becomes a simulacrum of the entire rhetorical process in its now thoroughly domesticated form. As one reads the best works in a number of genres, one becomes capable of recognizing what would be suitably cultivated responses in a wide range of situations. Not incidentally, one also acquires the taste and character that now are the goal of the orator's education (cf. both Gadamer and Habermas for similar formulations in modern thought).

The "next" step in the genealogy of decorum developed in tandem with this shift from politics to culture. The constriction of public life encouraged a more thoroughgoing development of literary art than would have been the case while politics was the preoccupation of the elite and the end of rhetorical training. Rhetoric gradually was redefined from political persuasion to artistic expression, and rhetorical study was focused on developing critical discernment regarding matters of style (Kennedy, 1972, p. 363). One result was the mode of *literary decorum,* which was an adaptation of the norms of appropriateness to set out the structural principles for a distinctively literary art. Decorum became a question of what is suitable for the full realization of each artistic genre. The contemporaries Horace (65–8 BCE) and Dionysius of Halicarnassus exemplified this shift in sensibility, with Horace becoming a major influence in the subsequent development of Western literary study.

Horace's *Ars poetica* provides the best single statement of literary decorum. The work begins by ridiculing compositions that are patently indecorous because excessively inventive; for example, a painting of a man with a horse's mane (1–5). By contrast, good art follows the mimetic rule of painting life as it is (361–362). Diction should be suitable to the speaker (112–113), the ages and period of the subjects depicted (153–178), and so forth. One can be confident in the results because of the natural fidelity of our gestures and expressions to our emotions (108–111). The choice of the subject should be appropriate to the artist's abilities (14–15, 38–41), and ultimately the work has to reflect the cultivated tastes developed through education that characterize the socially elevated audience (188, 196–201, 212–213, 248–250).

The innovation within these conventional ideas comes through Horace's redefinition of the mimetic ideal. This ideal acquires more force than it had in the ethical and cultural modes, while it also is freed from Aristotle's epistemological assumptions. Horace reaffirms that mimesis is the dominant principle for artistic work, but he also argues strenuously against the norm of literal reproduction of phenomenal reality. Perfectly literal reproduction can be lifeless—more tellingly, artistically vapid (32–35)—while art requires a suitable distance from its objects (362). This sense of aesthetic distance gives an important inflection to the idea that mimetic art is an art of proportionate representation. Art captures the essential forms of experience, not the mere welter of experiences (312–318). When this attention to form is fused with an insistence on compositional exactitude (445–452), artistic reality emerges as the primary orientation of the artist. The details of the world don't matter so much, while the details of the artwork are exceedingly important. Likewise, the mimetic norm is invoked not so much because it is important to make accurate models of reality, but in order for the artist to gain control of the art. The first condition of art is the complete freedom of artistic expression (9–13, 378–382): the poet can literally say anything and call it poetry (and the more unrealistic it is, the more it will have to be called poetry rather than anything else). Horace sets poetry at a mean between wildness and pedantry, but the point is not so much moderation as it is identifying a new realm of artistic standards.

Despite his aesthetic innovation Horace remained wedded to the conventions of Roman society, but the development of art on its own terms leads logically to destabilization of the rules for matching speech to social type. The genealogy of decorum comes full circle, as artistic invention becomes something closer to amoral positioning and the attempt to seize the rare and fleeting moment when the artist can achieve a radical transformation of the audience. Ultimately, the pursuit of art's most powerful effects requires breaking with social norms and assumptions of mimetic fidelity. This *romantic decorum* is somewhat anachronistic, of course, for it is not only the "last" development of the classical world but also the most powerful conception of decorum in the modern era.

The classical work *On the Sublime* by "Longinus" (circa first century CE) epitomizes this final reassessment (and deconstruction) of the norms of decorum, while *On Style* by "Demetrius" (circa first century BCE) also should be mentioned. In each case, decorum remains a familiar grammar for aesthetic analysis, but the general thrust is toward a new understanding of aesthetic experience. This experience culminates in the "sublime"; that is, the awe-inspiring or transformative effect that characterizes the best works of art. [*See* Sublime, the.] One's sense of decorum is altered as well. On the one hand, the artist or critic still must consider place, manner, circumstances, and motive (*On the Sublime* 16.3), both the tone of an entire work and its diction must be suitable to author and subject, these things are acquired by imitation of historians and poets (13.2), and so forth. On the other hand, the whole point of verbal artistry now is the achievement of aesthetic transformation, and that is obtained by surpassing limits, breaking with conventions, going beyond the niceties of detailed accommodation to circumstances. Likewise, the sublime draws on artistic intuition rather than social knowledge. Homer's Battle of the Gods, for example, is said to be both a work of genius and one that shows "no sense of what is fitting" (9.6–7) since it treats gods as if they were humans. What had been a minor technique before—violating expectations for strategic effect (Aristotle, *Rhetoric* 3.18.7)—now has become an aesthetic principle.

This revaluation of decorum fixes a distinction between propriety and appropriateness. Social conventions in the romantic mode are the limits to be surpassed if one is to achieve the sublime; should the audience accept the violations of those conventions, it is because the work has the greater fullness of thought and emotion needed to speak to the soul (8.1). Just as the positional speaker need have no allegiance to a fixed idea of character, the romantic artist can dispense with a fixed idea of artistic form. *On the Sublime* strikes a new attitude toward the handbook tradition itself that is evident when the author dismisses the thousands of rhetorical techniques available for amplification (11.2, 12.1). What had been a comprehensive system of composition becomes a jangle of trivial distinctions and petty inhibitions. Even mistakes in usage are now acceptable, as long as they are due to the grand sweep of genius (33.2–4, 36). As with Horace, art is found between novelty and pedantry, but any sense of the mean is just about extinct. The artist will do anything that produces the highest effect, and if that includes risking harshness and bombast, so be it (32–33). Decorum remains alternately either as those conventions constraining artistic energy, or as the single rule that one should do whatever is appropriate to achieving the highest artistic effect.

Subsequent reference to decorum follows the history of rhetoric: In the Middle Ages, decorum was the guiding principle of the *ars dictaminis* (art of letter writing) and its mechanical application provided a map of medieval social order (Constable, 1977). [*See* Ars dictaminis.] It was revived as an important concept in the Renaissance, especially where Cicero was a model of imitation. One can argue that it was the master term of Renaissance humanism; it clearly played a central role in the development of humanist historiography (Struever, 1970), political thought (Kahn, 1985), ethics (Kahn, Struever), and poetics (Tuve, 1947, Plett, 1983). [*See* Humanism.]

In addition, decorum functioned as a code of conduct for several social orders, including the late-medieval and Renaissance courtier (Jaeger, 1985; Kahn, 1983; Whigham, 1984) and the Anglo-American gentlemen of the seventeenth and eighteenth centuries (Shapin, 1994). By the nineteenth century, that code had been replaced with the norms of bourgeois society; with that, mere propriety reigned while all traces of classical imitation disappeared. (The declension can be charted from the courtesy literature of the early modern era—Castiglioni, Puttenham—to the etiquette books of the ascendant middle class.) This social history parallels the modern intellectual history of decorum: by repudiating rhetoric and constructing a pure aesthetic, the Enlightenment severed essential connections between discursive artistry and action. Decorum became merely a compendium of manners. [*See* Eighteenth-century rhetoric.]

Within the critique of modernity developed in the late twentieth century decorum has been resuscitated as a significant term for understanding how discourse functions. [*See* Contingency and probability; Criticism; *and* Hermeneutics.] In rhetorical studies, Kenneth Burke provides the most thorough and original reformulation of rhetoric as a profoundly social practice; *A Rhetoric of Motives* (Berkeley, 1969) provides the sensibility of decorum without using the term: "Here is perhaps the simplest case of persuasion. You persuade a man only insofar as you can talk his language by speech, gesture, tonality, order, image, attitude, idea, identifying your ways with his" (p. 55). More recent attention to decorum includes both Sophistic (Poulakos, 1995) and humanist (Leff, 1990) variants. Each of these perspectives, along with corresponding interest in the classical concept of prudence, provides an opportunity to repair the schism between argument theory and stylistics that otherwise persists as a modernist legacy in both of those areas of inquiry (cf. *Institutio Oratoria* 11.1.7). More generally, the classical concept can be joined with contemporary political studies to understand how power is a byproduct of social performance (Hariman, 1995). Decorum has particular relevance for those who see the postmodern condition as a partial recuperation of premodern forms of symbolic action: For example, Richard Lanham argues that digital media are "deeply rhetorical" technologies that require a "bi-stable decorum" and sense of "balance" (*The Electronic Word: Democracy, Technology, and the Arts,* Chicago, 1993). In an intensively communicative environment characterized by cultural pluralism, multiple identities, decentered institutions, and smart machines, questions of decorum will acquire a renewed significance in the conduct of everyday life, while the concept could regain its early associations with both a sense of radical contingency and the definition of human being. The idea of decorum will never be settled, however, as it is itself "bi-stable." Whatever the situation, rules of appropriateness can appear either as opportunities for invention or as conformist constraints, as norms of ideological hegemony and cultural mediocrity or as resources for artistic representation and social change.

[*See also* Kairos; Phronēsis; *and* Prudence.]

BIBLIOGRAPHY

Constable, Giles. "The Structure of Medieval Society According to the Dictatores of the Twelfth Century." In *Law, Church, and Society: Essays in Honor of Stephan Kuttner,* edited by Kenneth Pennington and Robert Somerville, pp. 253–267. Philadelphia, 1977.

Cope, E. M. *An Introduction to Aristotle's Rhetoric.* London, 1867. Commentary on "propriety" provides still useful insights on *Rhetoric* 3.7; emphasizes the relationships with *ēthos* and *pathos.*

D'Alton, J. F. *Roman Literary Theory and Criticism: A Study in Tendencies.* New York, 1962. First published in 1931. Grounds classical literary theory in rhetoric and especially in decorum. Emphasis is on the relationship between speech and subject and in bringing a wide range of compositional questions under the rule of the "Golden Mean." Provides discussions of Cicero and Horace and extensive citations of classical texts.

Detienne, Marcel, and Jean-Pierre Vernant. *Cunning Intelligence in Greek Culture and Society.* Translated by Janet Lloyd. Chicago, 1978.

DeWitt, Helen. *Quo Virtus? The Concept of Propriety in Ancient Literary Criticism.* Dissertation, Oxford University, 1987. Review of the major sources with an eye to some of the controversies attending both classical and modern literary criticism.

Eden, Kathy. *Hermeneutics and the Rhetorical Tradition: Chapters in the Ancient Legacy and Its Humanist Reception.* New Haven, 1997. Demonstrates how the discipline of early modern hermeneutics was deeply grounded in classical rhetoric, particularly in Cicero's development of decorum as a principle of equitable accommodation to the particular circumstances of text and context.

Fantham, Elaine. "*Orator* 69–74." *Central States Speech Journal* 35 (1984), pp. 123–125.

Fantham, Elaine. "*Varietas* and *Satietas: De oratore* 3.96–103 and the limits of *ornatus.*" *Rhetorica* 6 (1988), pp. 275–290.

Gadamer, Hans-Georg. *Truth and Method.* 2d rev. ed. Translated by Joel Weinsheimer and Donald G. Marshall. New York, 1993.

Habermas, Jürgen. *The Structural Transformation of the Public Sphere: An Inquiry into a Category of Bourgeois Society.* Translated by Thomas Burger. Cambridge, Mass., 1989.

Hariman, Robert. *Political Style: The Artistry of Power.* Chicago, 1995.

Hermogenes. *Hermogenes' On Types of Style.* Translated by Cecil W. Wooten. Chapel Hill, N.C., 1977. His English translation of *Peri ideōn* (c. late second century CE).

Jaeger, C. Stephen. *The Origins of Courtliness: Civilizing Trends and the Formations of Courtly Ideals 939–1210.* Philadelphia, 1985. Argues that courtliness grew out of Ciceronian humanism, with emphasis on decorum as the ordering of one's self and relations with others.

Kahn, Victoria. *Rhetoric, Prudence, and Skepticism in the Renaissance.* Ithaca, N.Y., 1985. One of the best accounts of how Ciceronian decorum was central to the intellectual life and ethical sensibility of Renaissance humanism.

Kaster, Robert. "Decorum." Paper presented at the annual meeting of the American Philological Association, Philadelphia, December 1982.

Kennedy, George. *The Art of Persuasion in Greece.* Princeton, 1963.

Kennedy, George. *The Art of Rhetoric in the Roman World 300 B.C.–A.D. 300.* Princeton, 1972.

Kinneavy, James L. "Kairos: A Neglected Concept in Classical Rhetoric." In *Rhetoric and Praxis: The Contribution of Classical Rhetoric to Practical Reasoning.* pp. 79–105. Washington, D.C. 1986. Reviews the idea of appropriateness—defined by the two elements of right timing and proper measure—in antiquity and applies them to modern composition theory.

Lausberg, Heinrich. *Handbook of Literary Rhetoric: A Foundation for Literary Study.* Translated by Mathew T. Bliss, Annemiek Jansen, and David E. Orton; edited by David E. Orton and R. Dean Anderson. Leiden, 1998. English translation of *Handbuch der literarischen Rhetorik,* first published 1960. Categorized under *aptum,* Lausberg provides the best anatomy of the elements of decorum along with pertinent citations for each. The major distinction is between internal decorum (the relationships within the composition that produce a harmonious whole) and external decorum (the relationship between the text and its social circumstances of reception). The latter is primarily directed by the speaker's purpose, but also by ethical considerations.

Leff, Michael. "Decorum and Rhetorical Interpretation: The Latin Humanistic Tradition and Contemporary Critical Theory." *Vichiana* 1, 3rd series (1990), pp. 107–126. Argues that modernism has reduced the architectonic function of decorum in classical thought to its more narrow, technical function as one of the elements of style, which segregates argument from style and rhetoric from politics. By contrast, Cicero's *Orator* (69–74 and 122–125) presents a sophisticated account of the relationships among the function, form, content, and subject of persuasive discourse.

Plett, Heinrich F. "The Place and Function of Style in Renaissance Poetics." In *Renaissance Eloquence: Studies in the Theory and Practice of Renaissance Rhetoric,* edited by James J. Murphy, pp. 356–375. Berkeley, 1983.

Poulakos, John. *Sophistical Rhetoric in Classical Greece.* Columbia, S.C., 1995. Discusses the Sophists' sense of *kairos* as an alternative standard to the more fixed opposition between the appropriate and the inappropriate.

Puttenham, George. *The Arte of English Poesie.* Edited by Gladys Doidge Willcock and Alice Walker. Cambridge, Mass., 1936. Originally published anonymously in 1589 and widely influential. Sets out decorum as the common rule of poetry and courtliness.

Russell, D. A. *Criticism in Antiquity.* Berkeley, 1981. Claims that the classical theorists' emphasis on decorum limited their ability to "see their literature clearly," although it saved them from the opposite error of excessive appreciation of verbal euphony.

Shapin, Steven. *A Social History of Truth: Civility and Science in Seventeenth-Century England.* Chicago, 1994. Features the role played by decorum—particularly as it demarked truthtelling in respect to superiors, inferiors, and equals—in the code of conduct for the English gentlemen who were founding modern science.

Struever, Nancy S. *The Language of History in the Renaissance: Rhetoric and Historical Consciousness in Florentine Humanism.* Princeton, 1970. One of the best accounts of how Ciceronian decorum was central to the intellectual life and ethical sensibility of Renaissance humanism.

Trimpi, Wesley. *Muses of One Mind: The Literary Analysis of Experience and Its Continuity.* Princeton, 1983. An analysis of classical philosophy and rhetoric to identify and endorse a conception of decorum that balances literature's speculative, prudential, and productive functions.

Tuve, Rosemond. *Elizabethan and Metaphysical Imagery: Renaissance Poetic and Twentieth-Century Critics.* Chicago, 1947. "Propriety or decorum was the basic criterion in terms of which all the others were understood" by the Renaissance reader.

Untersteiner, Mario. *The Sophists.* Translated by Kathleen Freeman. Oxford, 1954. Established the centrality of *kairos/prepon* to Gorgias's radically situational epistemology and its extension across rhetoric, aesthetics, and ethics.

Whigham, Frank. *Ambition and Privilege: The Social Tropes of Elizabethan Courtesy Theory.* Berkeley, 1984.

White, Eric Charles. *Kaironomia: On the Will to Invent.* Ithaca, N.Y., 1987. Grounds a theory of literary invention in Gorgias's "radical principle of occasionality . . . a process of continuous adjustment to and creation of the present occasion, or a process of continuous *interpretation.*"

—ROBERT HARIMAN

DEDUCTION. *See* Syllogism.

DELIBERATIVE GENRE. In the field of rhetorical studies, deliberation is as old as the ancient Greeks and as new as the Internet. Throughout Western history, it has been an abiding act of faith that people acquit themselves best when (1) gathered together with their peers; (2) discussing important matters of the day; (3) in a nonautocratic atmosphere; (4) so that public policy can be changed in behalf of the commonweal. Such an arrangement has taken diverse forms—from the Greek *ekklēsia* to the Roman forum, from the Czech parliament to the Japanese Diet—but deliberation has long been the handmaiden of democracy. A second abiding assumption has been that democracy needs a handmaiden. Even in a democratic state, after all, leaders can become too fond of leading, bureaucracies can become calcified, voters can feel ignored, and pressing issues can go unaddressed. An elected body of representatives, meeting regularly and debating vigorously, has seemed the cure to such problems.

As with many things human, idealized models of deliberation have not always proved worthy. Deliberative bodies, even when chosen in free and open elections, have often lost their way, beset by monied interests and pressure groups, by the strictures of their own rules and procedures, by the whims of their leaders and would-be leaders, and by their own provincialisms and eccentricities. For these reasons, writers like Jürgen Habermas (1989) have argued that the public sphere has become cramped and sectarian in modern times, unable to sustain the pluralistic ideals a democracy needs to survive. [*See* Politics, *article on* The personal, technical, and public spheres of argument.] But even as this publication appeared, desperate boatloads were leaving Haiti for the United States, and citizens of former Iron Curtain countries flooded the streets of Berlin anxious to taste the fruits of democracy. Despite its infirmities, deliberation sings a siren song.

The History of Deliberation. The history of deliberation is the history of democracy itself. Deliberation has always flourished when freedom has flourished. When democracy disappeared, as it did in Germany in 1933, the burning of the Reichstag became a metaphorical reminder that deliberation is too unruly for a dictatorship. But as Aristotle (384–322 BCE) reminds us, unruliness lies at the heart of all deliberation since it treats means and not ends and because there are more of the former than the latter. [*See* Classical rhetoric.] Second, deliberation is unruly because it focuses on the future—on what should be done—and because the future is opaque; third, because it produces injunctive decisions that constrain an entire populace; and fourth, because it is polyvocal, because it must accommodate so many different voices.

Aristotle observed that there are five great matters about which people deliberate—ways and means, war and peace, national defense, imports and exports, and legislation. His list still seems reasonable, although "human rights" has since been added to the democratic agenda. But if "the Greeks invented rhetoric," say Golden and his colleagues (1997), "the Romans perfected it." In ancient Rome, citizens deliberated in one of two places: In the Commitia, where day-to-day laws were proposed and amended, and in the Senate, where issues pertaining to defense of the state were adjudicated. Cicero (106–43 BCE) observed that matters of such gravity were not merely utilitarian (Aristotle's model), but that they blended utility with honor. [*See* Utility.] Only such an admixture, said Cicero, can produce genuine eloquence.

Deliberation fell on hard times in the later republic of Rome (through 455 CE), as its emperors sought to concentrate power in their own hands. During this time dynasties alternated with despotisms and the public sphere inevitably diminished. To the extent that deliberation thrived in the Middle Ages, it thrived in ecclesiastical disputations, in forums where theological matters (heresies, scriptural interpretations, and modes of worship) were discussed by church fathers. These were truncated deliberations, to be sure, since who could speak, what they could speak about, and what resulted from their deliberations were carefully constrained by the papacy.

The Renaissance rediscovered the classical writers on rhetoric, even if it did not reproduce the political conditions necessary for a robust democracy. While epideictic speaking—the speech of remembrance—can flourish in any political culture (authoritarian or republican) and while forensic speech prospers wherever laws are applied, deliberation requires democracy for its perfectability. [*See* Epideictic genre; *and* Forensic genre.] Renaissance writers like Thomas Wilson (c.1525–1581) wrote about deliberation, but it was largely an academic matter. It would not be until the eighteenth century that the study of rhetoric would again become tripartite. Until then, deliberation would largely be an aesthetic inquiry—public language treated as an art form, not as an adjunct to civic life.

Deliberative oratory was reinvigorated with the rise of the British Parliament. After the Magna Carta was extracted from a reluctant King John in 1215, the House of Commons "became, inevitably and spontaneously, a permanent school of oratory" (Platz, 1935, p. 163). But the path of deliberation in England was often tortuous. Prior to the latter half of the seventeenth century, Parliament came into being only at the King's request and ended when he dissolved it (Oliver, 1986). The Revolution of 1688 and the passage of England's Bill of Rights in 1689, however, inaugurated parliamentary control of government, a development that may have prevented that nation from having its own version of the French Revolution. Thenceforth, the great moments in British political history would be parliamentary moments dominated by such names as Bolingbroke, Walpole, Chesterfield, Pitt, Gladstone, and Disraeli. Still, it would be many years before Parliament would adopt the full accouterments of deliberative government—enfranchisement without regard to caste, free and open elections, full transparency of all deliberations, a watchful and vigorous press.

The history of the United States also traverses an arc of deliberation. The Puritan and Anglican clergy dominated public discourse for that nation's first hundred years, but the eighteenth century ushered in colonial assemblies—democracy in its least genteel form. The New England town meetings also foreshadowed such developments, a possibility specified in the Body of Liberties granted to Massachusetts Bay in 1641 whereby "Everyone whether Inhabitant or Forreiner, free or not free, shall have libertie to come to any publique Court, Councel, or Town Meeting, and either by speech or writeing to move any lawfull, seasonable, and materiall question" (Oliver, 1965).

Thenceforth, each major moment of deliberation ensured further moments: The Constitution was fashioned in a deliberative body and, in turn, guaranteed a continuing, bicameral form of governance. Even then, however, it would take a series of state-by-state deliberations to ratify the Constitution, a process that strengthened local and national democracy simultaneously. Thenceforth, a considerable portion of the nation's history would be written in its assemblies: Henry Clay (1777–1852) on continental expansion, William Jennings Bryan (1860–1925) on nullification, Robert LaFollette (1855–1925) on progressivism, Lyndon Johnson (1908–1973) on civil rights, Newt Gingrich (1943–) on neoconservatism. Each of these moments was attended by great drama because each required the making of firm decisions about uncertain matters—the very essence of deliberation.

The Nature of Deliberation. History shows, then, that deliberation is distinct from the cabal, the rump session, the closed-door meeting, the conspiracy. "Every activity performed in public," declares Hannah Arendt (*The Human Condition,* 1958), "can attain an excellence never matched in privacy; for excellence, by definition, the presence of others is always required." John Stuart Mill (1806–1873) argues that the force of deliberation is its ability to call participants to account and that the need to preserve decency operates as a powerful constraint on those operating in the public sphere (1958). But publicity is a two-sided coin: Because deliberation lets diverse persons champion diverse agendas, it has an athletic quality; once a discussion is begun, it follows its own course, with the passion of ideas and the passion of human interaction often making individuals exceed their own, private imaginations.

Deliberation is also haunted by time. Critics of deliberation frequently complain about its sluggishness and its endless indulgences. The problem with deliberation is also the problem with socialism which, according to Oscar Wilde, took far too many evenings (Weale, 1989). Why so many evenings? Because deliberation is also haunted by the past or, more appropriately, by people's unique personal histories and preexisting allegiances. Moreover, as Aristotle observed, deliberation is haunted yet again by the future, by calculations of the probable and the improbable. As John Dewey (1859–1952) said, in most deliberations participants' anticipations of the future are based heavily on their recollections of the past (1991).

Ultimately, then, deliberation is also haunted by the present. Because the past speaks with so many voices and because the future speaks not at all, deliberative bodies are constantly caught in the turmoil of what to do. Not surprisingly, the language of time dominates these proceedings, as "temporary" alliances are formed, "stop-gap" measures adopted, "ad hoc" agreements and "eleventh hour" proposals fashioned. Deliberation is thus in a perpetually evanescent state; it never fully gets its work done. Human variability ensures that, as does the fragile nature of group coalitions and the uncertain matters about which deliberative bodies deliberate. As a result, most social agreements are provisional in a pluralistic democracy (Urbinati, 1998).

Because it is haunted by time, deliberation contributes to constitutive forms of government, not to essential forms. [*See* Politics, *article on* Constitutive rhetoric.] Its telos is the possibility of agreement, never its actuality. This makes democracy a largely methodological enterprise; it only ensures *a way* of making decisions, never a specific result. As a consequence, the mere agreement to deliberate on important matters can sometimes be newsworthy, a signal that longstanding rivals have chosen to submit themselves to the vagaries of human interaction. As philosopher J. L. Austin (1962) might say, the mere *act* of deliberation sends its own message, a message of possibility.

Deliberation is a hopeful enterprise because it is a procedural enterprise. For modern British parliamentarians, the rituals of interaction prize adversarial exchange, while the United States Congress runs itself by committee. In both cases, however, rules of order determine who will speak about what for how long. Admittedly, these procedures only forestall, never eliminate, the chaos to which human beings are prone. But because transcendent truths are so hard to determine and because ethics vary so widely from community to community, the "rules of discourse and forms of argumentation" (Habermas, 1989) become place holders for democracy. These rules of interaction make human decisions seem less capricious and give them legitimacy as a result. In the best of times, policies resulting from open deliberation are judged authoritative even when the decisions themselves remain controversial.

The Qualities of Deliberation. Today, deliberation is not what it was in ancient Greece. For Aristotle, it was inconceivable that a democracy larger than a small city-state like Athens could function properly. [*See* Oratory.] Even as late as the eighteenth century, observes J. H. Snider (1994), thinkers like Montesquieu (1689–1755) and Rousseau (1712–1778) continued to doubt the possibility of large-scale democracy. No less an authority than Hegel (1770–1831) argued that the United States could not become a "real republic" until all its space was occupied (Kemmis, 1990), so sure was he that deliberation required contiguity. The assumption undergirding such thinking, of course, was that only a face-to-face society could give citizens the sense of participation, and hence sense of control, needed in a republic. When a democracy's size exceeds the range of the human voice, the thinking went, deliberation is no longer possible. In most modern societies, says political scientist James Fishkin (1998), the three key requirements for deliberation are rarely present: messages exchanged (1) interactively, (2) at length, and (3) under conditions of studied reflection. Without such requisites, how can a nation survive?

The answer to that Question is through displacement. Modern forms of deliberation bear little resemblance to their forebears. [*See* Hybrid genres.] Today, largely because of the mass media, deliberation is part of the air we breathe, but it is also like a mist—felt but not seen, and only vaguely felt at that. The C-SPAN channel in the United States and the BBC in London bravely cover the national deliberations in toto, but most modern citizens catch mere snippets—a press conference here, a political debate there. Even more miss the oral experience entirely, following the nation's politics in the daily newspaper. Still others read nothing, getting the news third hand from their cohorts on the job or fourth hand from the late-night comedians. And yet many citizens feel part of the mix even when things do not go their way. This sense of involvement may be quite artificial, and there is danger in that. But countless polling studies find a pronounced sense of "political efficacy" among citizens in Western democracies. The largest of these democracies, the United States, often produces the highest scores of all. Somehow, displacement functions efficiently regardless of a nation's geography, even though it produces only functional certainty—truth for us, truth for this time and place.

Deliberative reason is thus a special kind of reason, the kind of sense people make when thinking aloud together. Any student of classical reasoning will immediately spot the problem with such an arrangement: People often flag in each other's presence, letting their insecurities, their prejudices, and their needs for approbation guide their thinking. Because of these shortcomings, public reason is often indecorous, trading in phantom facts and spurious assumptions. Perhaps in response, most democracies have placed an elected body of delegates between the people and their decisions, reasoning, as did Edmund Burke (1729–1797), that the average citizen should avoid the "overstimulating atmosphere of the political assembly" and "leave politics to someone less inclined to rashness" (Sanders, 1997).

Burke's exalted views sound foreign to modern ears, but he found the torpor of deliberative bodies to be their strength, a sign that no individual or dangerous faction was having an untoward influence. It is the deliberateness of deliberation that best recommended it to people like Burke. Because of such qualities, a deliberative body simultaneously increases options (by considering diverse points of view) and decreases options (by selecting only one of them). This gives deliberation a magnanimous quality, a signal that "your view, too, has been considered." At the same time, the *end-products* of deliberation almost always seem distorted, stripped of the marks of individual genius. A piece of legislation is typically shot through with compromises; its beauty lies in its complexity.

Deliberation, then, depends on displacement rather than direct involvement, socially constructed truths rather than political certainty, tested reason instead of sudden inspiration. Deliberation has such qualities, says Hannah Arendt (1958), not because people do not share a common world but because they see things from different locations in that world. When embraced fully, that is, deliberation almost always affects one's vision.

The Challenges to Deliberation. Despite its several strengths, deliberation has raised an army of critics. The complainants' charges are kaleidoscopic, but most center on the question of whether real deliberation is even possible today. Their worries range from the practical to the philosophical:

The declining space for deliberation. The importance of deliberation to Western peoples is perhaps best signaled by the democratic shrines they have erected. Italians take pride in their Chamber of Deputies and Israelis in their Knesset, not because politics is easy for Italians and Israelis but because it is not. As a result, these special, set-aside places take on added importance. But what about grassroots deliberation? Sociologists like Richard Sennett (1977) worry that modern individuals have come to fear open spaces, common spaces, and that they are losing their public skills as a result, which is to say, their ability to deal with strangers. Political scientist Robert Putnam (2000) adds to these worries when finding that Americans, especially, have sharply decreased their participation in voluntary associations during the past fifty years. Discoveries like these worry philosopher Thomas McCarthy (1994) who sees such cultural groupings as the very basis of self-governance and, hence, of political independence. Adding to the problem are the forces of capital which now superintend so many public gatherings, a point made by Peter Katz (1998) when warning that "free speech and soap boxes won't stand much of a chance in the corporate plazas and shopping malls of today. Uniformed security patrols would likely whisk an offending citizen away long before a sympathetic crowd could ever form" (p. 184).

Professionalizing deliberation. Some critics argue that deliberation began to collapse when the "chattering classes" came to power. Elected public officials, media personalities, academics, and professional activists now handle all the deliberative chores, these observers note, leaving the people with little to say and nowhere to say it. The deliberative bodies thereby formed inevitably ossify—the same sorts of people are elected and reelected, the public agenda shrinks, proceduralism reigns, and people lose touch with their leaders. Even worse, say critics like Kathleen Jamieson (1999), once in power the oligarchs behave badly, raising incivility to an art form and thereby making participation seem feckless and democracy a curse. But the greatest danger of all is that the people will lose their own deliberative competence. Like any skill, deliberation requires practice, not to mention patience, and so a disaffected electorate is doubly disadvantaged. Under such circumstances, warns Hannah Arendt (1958), the unsavory alternatives to deliberation are ever-present: "To be political, to live in a polis, meant that everything was decided through words and persuasion and not through force and violence" (pp. 26–27).

Deliberation and emotion. Some critics of deliberation argue that the Habermasian emphasis on rationality has left little room for people with strong views or for those who use incivility as a rhetorical weapon. The seventeenth century's James Harrington (1611–1677) captured this bias when maintaining that deliberation should be free of emotion because of the attendant possibilities of anarchy (Remer, 1995). Habermas "appears sometimes to prefer the rule of rationality," argues Peter Berkowitz (1996), "as opposed to the rule of real people." Some of these real people, of course, are those traditionally excluded from deliberative forums: women, racial minorities, recent immigrants, religious groups. All four challenge the Western, rationalist (some would argue, masculinist) assumptions and are plagued by a dilemma as a result: to abandon their natural voice to preserve their cause, or to react instinctively and thus risk being ineffective.

Deliberation as simulacrum. Another set of critics takes an entirely different tack, warning that the sheer frequency of formal deliberation makes people feel (falsely) empowered. By taking in so much political activity, especially through the electronic media, citizens can now feel informed when they are not and participatory when they have done nothing. According to Hart (1994), television in particular "creates a middle way between the active and dormant cultures." "By parading diverse political actors across the screen," says Hart, television transmutes professionals' words and activities into "emblems of involvement" for the citizenry. There is something of a dilemma here: No society can let everyone participate all the time, and yet no society can survive if the people abandon it. Some amount of deference to the state is always required, but too much of it leads to dominance and subordination, says Nancy Fraser (1989). As Jane Mansbridge (1990) argues, the transformation of "I" into "we" encouraged by political deliberation often masks subtle forms of control. And so the question becomes: Is virtual deliberation a worthy sort of deliberation? [*See* Audience, *article on* Virtual audiences.]

Deliberation and modernity. Today, time accelerates rapidly, new technologies goad us constantly, workplace pressures grow more complicated, cultural shifts torque the traditional family. "With politics occurring through media and information circuits," says philosopher Douglas Kellner (1988), "the time of deliberation and consensus is obliterated." With the public agenda now filled with such complexities as DNA research, nuclear throwweights, and global warming, the "knowledge class" threatens to dominate all public discussion, leaving the layperson bewildered. If hyperspecialization becomes central to all human decisions, worries rhetorical scholar Thomas Goodnight (1992), why should the average citizen bother to participate? Intellectual balkanization is not a new phenomenon, but its political implications have never been of greater consequence. It is one thing for a society to make a wrong choice, far worse when it cannot understand the choices it confronts. The more removed a nation is from its deliberative bodies, in short, the more it cedes power to those who may know ideas but who may not know people. [*See* Technical communication.]

The Possibilities of Deliberation. Formal deliberation has its critics, then, but few seem ready to abandon the project entirely. Indeed, one set of scholars (Frost and Makarov, 1998) finds considerable evidence that the Russian people craved political participation in the postcommunist era, while newly enfranchised South Africans demanded that democracy not be limited to the election cycle but be continued through popular forums and referenda (Nattrass and Seekings, 1998). In eastern Europe, too, scholars find renewed interest in parliamentary activities (Hibbings and Patterson, 1994). Anecdotes like these suggest that robust public deliberation is often taken for granted in societies having a long civic tradition, even as it is treated reverentially by those in aspiring democracies. There is little doubt, however, that the pressures of the age have taxed deliberation. Economic and cultural forces threaten to make it inconsequential, as does bureaucratization, as does science and technology.

Is deliberation still possible? Some say no, others find the question fatuous. In defense of deliberation, they point to democracies in which women were given the vote by men and in which blacks were enfranchised by whites. They find wars being stopped by college students, environmental laws passed by the children of corporation executives, and Nelson Mandela's cause assisted by a distant band of college professors. They point to an American president driven from office by a free press, a Russian president honored for dismantling a mighty Communist machine, and an Iraqi dictator stopped in his tracks by an unlikely coalition of United Nations forces. They could point, too, to gays suddenly being treated as full citizens, to a massive military establishment put on a short tether, and to educational possibilities abruptly made available to the handicapped. All of these changes came from deliberative work. Much of it took years to accomplish and some of it is not yet finished, but none of it could have been imagined outside of a deliberative framework. Without deliberation there would only have been continuity.

Choosing the path of deliberation is a hard choice for it means ceding power to others and embracing the unknown. Aristotle (*Politics*, p. 2034) framed the issue well when noting that "there is still a danger in allowing [the people] to share the great offices of the state, for their folly will lead them into error, and their dishonesty into crime." Alexander Hamilton (1755–1804) and Thomas Jefferson (1743–1826) argued over these same matters two hundred years ago in the United States when wondering if colonial ruffians could govern themselves. But Aristotle also had their answer: "there is a danger also in not letting them share [power], for a state in which many poor men are excluded from office will necessarily be full of enemies. The only way of escape is to assign to them some deliberative and judicial functions" (p. 2034). Pragmatism seems ugly when phrased this baldly, but deliberation makes little sense apart from pragmatism. Deliberation is to be preferred not because it is best but because there is no other choice when democrats choose to live with other democrats.

Not all deliberation, of course, is created equally. Ideally, deliberation should (1) *represent* the reigning public dialogue accurately so people can hear their voices being spoken; and (2) *improve* that dialogue so people can find a new political vision. Democracy depends on this reflexivity: too much "representation" makes elected officials mere pollsters, too little makes them autocrats. The people need to be "improved," yes, but only in their time and only when sufficient political skill exists to do the improving.

Ultimately, a democracy must find ways of teaching deliberative skills to its youth. That has been the purpose of rhetorical training since antiquity. At the very least, young democrats must be taught to listen—to sort the wheat of politics from its chaff—and also to speak. Deliberation thus requires both a judicial temperament and a flair for the imaginative. Without the former, a society loses its compass; without the latter, it goes only where it has gone before. But because these skills are often incommensurate, a democratic leader is always inadequate in some way—too far ahead of the people or too far behind. The more fully a society embraces democracy, the greater these tensions become.

Deliberation, then, is an occupation unsuited to either the neurotic or the reckless. The more pluralistic a deliberative body becomes, the less predictable its outcomes will be. "Managing deliberation" is therefore an oxymoron on most occasions, a high art on others. Because political matters inevitably border on the social, the psychological, the ideological, and the tribal, mastering the tools of deliberation has always been

hard. For some, however, deliverance is at hand. New modalities like the Internet, they argue, will finally provide deliberation without tears. The time has come, say the Electronic Democrats, to rescue deliberation from the formal bodies to which it has been historically entrusted. With the Internet, ordinary people can now have their say—unfettered, untransmogrified, twenty-four/seven. Because cyberspace transcends national boundaries, because its chat rooms require no pedigree of its participants, and because its anonymity is so emancipatory, True Deliberation is at hand.

Perhaps, but our suspicion is otherwise. No mere technology is likely to undo, or supplant, deliberative routines that have endured for centuries. The Internet makes processing information more efficient, but most political decisions, it seems clear, will continue to be made face-to-face. Deliberation puts people in close proximity on the assumption that political decisions are best made in the light of day with everyone watching. Deliberative bodies are often rancorous, and they play host to both horrific ideas and bestial personalities. Ultimately, though, these deliberative bodies tend democracy because it is there that the people's representatives decide what the people want. If their estimations are incorrect, they will be forced to continue their deliberations elsewhere. Democracy seems to prefer it that way.

[*See also* Expediency; *and* Invention.]

BIBLIOGRAPHY

Arendt, Hannah. *The Human Condition.* Chicago, 1958. A brilliant contrast of political assumptions in ancient Greece with those of modern societies.

Aristotle. "Magna Moralia." In *Aristotle: The Revised Oxford Translation.* 2 vols. Edited by Jonathan Barnes, pp. 868–1921. Princeton, 1984.

Aristotle. "The Politics." In *Aristotle: The Revised Oxford Translation.* 2 vols. Edited by Jonathan Barnes, pp. 1986–2129. Princeton, 1984.

Austin, J. L. *How to Do Things with Words.* Cambridge, U.K., 1962. A formative study of the social consequences of various speech acts.

Berkowitz, Peter. "The Debating Society." *The New Republic,* 25 November 1996, pp. 36–44. A review of the importance of deliberative democracy and the venues in which it occurs.

Dewey, John. *The Collected Works of John Dewey, 1882–1953: The Electronic Edition.* Charlottesville, Va.,

1991. Contains Dewey's works on a wide variety of topics including education, politics, and religion.

Fishkin, James. "Beyond Teledemocracy: America on the Line." In *The Essential Communitarian Reader.* Edited by Amitai Etzioni, pp. 55–60. New York, 1998. Discussion of the negative impact of uninformed democracy and the value of "deliberative opinion polling."

Fraser, Nancy. "Rethinking the Public Sphere: A Contribution to the Critique of Actually Existing Democracy." In *Habermas and the Public Sphere,* edited by Craig Calhoun, pp. 109–142. Boston, 1989. A bold reconsideration of Habermas's conception of a singular, unified public sphere.

Frost, S., and D. Makarov. "Changing Post-Totalitarian Values in Russia through Public Deliberation Methodology." *Political Science and Politics* 31(1998), pp. 775–782. A quantitative examination of political satisfaction levels among Russian citizens in the post-Soviet era.

Golden, J. L., G. F. Berquist, and W. E. Coleman. *The Rhetoric of Western Thought,* 6th ed. Dubuque, Iowa, 1997. An overview of rhetorical theory from ancient times to the present.

Goodnight, G. Thomas. "The Personal, Technical and Public Spheres of Argument: A Speculative Inquiry into the Art of Public Deliberation." *Journal of the American Forensic Association* 18 (1981), pp. 214–227. Keen analysis of various kinds of deliberative activity and their implications for political agency.

Habermas, Jürgen. *The Structural Transformation of the Public Sphere.* Translated by Thomas Burger with the assistance of Frederick Lawrence. Cambridge, Mass., 1989. An important chronicle of the emergence and decline of the public sphere in Western Europe.

Hart, Roderick P. *Seducing America: How Television Charms the Modern Voter.* New York, 1994. Broad-based examination of how the modern media falsely empower the electronic citizen.

Hibbings, John R., and Samuel C. Patterson. "Emergence of Democratic Parliaments in Central and Eastern Europe." In *Parliaments in the Modern World: Changing Institutions.* Edited by Gary W. Copeland and Samuel C. Patterson, pp. 129–150. Ann Arbor, 1994. A look at deliberative theory and parliamentary practices in a cross-national context.

Jamieson, Kathleen H. "Incivility and Its Discontents." *Carroll C. Arnold Distinguished Lecture Series.* Washington, D.C., 1999. A study of tact and tactlessness in the U.S. Congress through an investigation of the *Congressional Record.*

Katz, Peter. "What Makes a Good Urban Park?" In *The Essential Communitarian Reader.* Edited by Amitai Et-zioni, pp. 183–186. New York, 1998. A short but important essay connecting the availability of public space with citizen involvement.

Kellner, Douglas. "Virilio, War and Technology." *Theory, Culture and Society* 16 (1999), pp. 103–126. A criticism of technology's effects on political understanding and participation.

Kemmis, Daniel. *Community and the Politics of Place.* Norman, Okla., 1990. An argument for the importance of political involvement on the local level.

Mansbridge, Jane J. "Feminism and Democracy." *American Prospect* 1 (1990), pp. 126–139. Draws attention to the promise and pitfalls of deliberative democracy for women.

McCarthy, Thomas. "Kantian Constructivism and Reconstructivism: Rawls and Habermas in Dialogue." *Ethics* 105 (1994), pp. 44–63. A theoretical essay linking the philosophies of John Rawls and Jürgen Habermas to that of Immanuel Kant.

Mill, John Stuart. *Considerations on Representative Government.* Edited by Currin V. Shields. New York, 1958. First published 1861. Mill's trenchant commentary on how representative forms of government are best enacted.

Nattrass, Nicoli, and Jeremy Seekings. "Democratic Institutions and Development in Post-apartheid South Africa." In *The Democratic Developmental State,* edited by Mark Robinson and Gordon White. Oxford, 1998. An overview of South Africa's emerging democracy.

Oliver, Robert Tarbell. *History of Public Speaking in America.* Boston, 1965. A readable and fairly definitive history of political speechmaking in the United States.

Oliver, Robert Tarbell. *Public Speaking in the Reshaping of Great Britain.* Newark, Del., 1986. Historical analysis of how citizenship, political practice, and public discourse have been intertwined in English history.

Platz, M. *The History of Public Speaking: A Comparative Study of World Oratory.* New York, 1935. An early, and ambitious, overview of public speaking in Western democracies.

Putnam, Robert. *Bowling Alone: The Collapse and Revival of American Community.* New York, 2000. A landmark study of how modern politics has been compromised by citizens' withdrawal from group memberships.

Remer, Gary. "James Harrington's New Deliberative Rhetoric: Reflections of an Anti-classical Republicanism," *History of Political Thought* 16 (1995), pp. 532–557. An examination of the impact of classical theories of deliberation on the seventeenth century's James Harrington.

Sanders, Lynn. "Against Deliberation." *Political Theory* 25 (1997), pp. 347–377. A bold reanalysis of deliberation theory that calls into question a number of traditional assumptions.

Sennett, Richard. *The Fall of Public Man.* New York, 1977. An early warning about the modern individual's increasing discomfort with public interactions.

Snider, J. H. "Democracy On-line." *Futurist* 28 (1994), pp. 15–19. Brief article on how democracy and participation may be affected by the Internet.

Urbinati, Nadia. "Rhetoric and Representation: The Politics of Advocacy." Presented at the 1998 Annual Meeting of the American Political Science Association, September 3–6. A well-argued paper demonstrating why representative democracy is better than direct democracy for the average citizen.

Weale, A. "The Limits of Democracy." In *The Good Polity: Normative Analysis of the State,* edited by Alan Hamlin and Philip Pettit, pp. 39–44. Oxford, 1989.

—RODERICK P. HART AND COURTNEY L. DILLARD

DELIVERY, the fifth of the five classical canons (Gk. *erga;* Lat. *officia*) of rhetoric, offers instruction in bodily gesture, including manipulations of voice, breath, and rhythm, to help the orator communicate effectively in a given situation. Along with the other four canons (or offices) of rhetoric—invention, arrangement, style, and memory—it works to form a complex system that can be used to compose as well as analyze a speech. This canonical division of rhetoric was prominent in Roman rhetoric from the first century BCE *Rhetorica ad Herennium* onward (cf. 1.2.3, 3.11.19); so influential was this Latin text that some commentators have claimed that Greek rhetoric did not conceive of rhetoric as divided into five offices ending with delivery. However, based on extant references to now lost works on delivery, today scholars follow Scaglione in assuming that the fifth canon, as well as the other four canons, was a significant aspect of Greek rhetoric (1972, p. 14).

Delivery in Greek rhetoric receives its earliest extant treatment in Aristotle's *Rhetoric* (3.1), although Demosthenes, a contemporary of Aristotle (384–322 BCE) and a highly accomplished orator and influential political figure, is said (by Cicero and others) to have claimed that delivery was the first, second, and third most important aspects of a speech (cf. *De oratore,* 3.213). Aristotle does not go that far, but does assert that delivery (Gk. *hypokrisis*) is central to rhetoric and goes on

to treat volume, pitch, and rhythm in particular. He compares rhetorical delivery to theatrical performance and emphasizes the effect of delivery on different audiences; the effectiveness and appropriateness of delivery make a speech successful or not. Theophrastus, Aristotle's successor as leader of the Peripatetic School, wrote the lost *On Delivery,* a work that similarly stressed the power of good delivery and may have been influenced by Plato's demands for a psychologically oriented rhetoric (Kennedy, 1963, p. 283).

One of the works that Theophrastus influenced was the above-mentioned *Rhetorica ad Herennium,* whose writer is unknown to us. (The work was once attributed to Cicero because in some ways it resembles Cicero's youthful work on the first canon of rhetoric, *De inventione.*) The *Rhetorica ad Herennium* was very influential in the subsequent rhetorical tradition, and apparently synthesized historical delivery up to the time of the first century BCE while extending critical analysis of the canon. In his treatment of delivery (Lat. *actio*), the author delineates the figure of voice and the movement of the body during the presentation of a speech (Kennedy, 1999, p. 110). In this work, the three most important delivery aspects of voice are volume, stability, and flexibility. The author emphasizes that they all need to be practiced. Flexibility is further divided into three tones: (1) conversation; (2) debate; and (3) amplification. Gestures accompany the tones, and the author includes descriptions of the use of the body during the delivery of a speech. As with Aristotle's explanation of delivery, the author of the *Rhetorica ad Herennium* emphasizes that the skill in performing this canon of rhetoric can determine the success of the speech (3.11.19).

Cicero (106–43 BCE) emphasizes the power of delivery in a number of places, in particular *De oratore, Brutus,* and *Orator.* He too goes so far as to call it the most important aspect of a speech, claiming in *De oratore* that delivery is essential to the best speaking and that speakers with medium abilities can improve a speech's effect with the appropriate delivery, including the qualities of dignity and grace.

> But all these parts of oratory succeed according as they are delivered. Delivery . . . has the sole

and supreme power in oratory; without it, a speaker of the highest mental capacity can be held in no esteem; while one of moderate abilities, with this qualification, may surpass even those of the highest talent. (*De oratore,* 3.213)

Cicero, like Aristotle, links delivery with emotion, stating that each emotion brings with it a unique appearance, tone, and gesture, and links the tones of speaking to musical chords. [*See* Pathos.] Cicero then elaborates the linkage of vocal tone and emotion with the illustrations of anger, fear, violence, pleasure, and trouble. A practical discussion of voice as a key part of delivery concludes this significant section on the fifth canon. Tonal variation, gradation, and voice strengthening form central features of Cicero's program. Several of these points are stated in *Brutus,* where examples of orators and particular qualities are given, and *Orator,* in which language is linked to the body.

The last important classical source on the theory of delivery is Quintilian, who writes at the end of the first century CE, and treats delivery in Book 11 of the *Institutio oratoria.* Like Cicero, Aristotle, and others, he discusses the role of delivery and emotion, and emphasizes voice and gesture, linking one to the ear and the other to the eye. He writes:

For the nature of the speech that we have composed within our minds is not so important as the manner in which we produce it, since the emotion of each member of our audience will depend on the impression made upon his hearing. (11.3.2)

In addition, he quotes the story of Demosthenes and his belief that delivery constituted the first three most important aspects of a speech. Quintilian's consistent linking of effective rhetoric with moral qualities is further reflected in his comments on the fifth canon and in his linking of eloquence in general to the civic virtues of the speaker. [*See* Eloquence.]

During the medieval and Renaissance periods, delivery declined greatly because rhetoricians ignored it in favor of other rhetorical issues. [*See overview article on* Renaissance rhetoric.] The political and religious systems at work in this long period did not make delivery a compelling func-

tion of rhetoric. In the sixteenth century, Petrus Ramus, a French teacher and writer of rhetoric and dialectic, greatly influenced delivery by making it and the third canon, style, the parts of rhetoric; the other three canons, invention, arrangement, and memory, were placed by Ramus in the category of dialectic. [*See* Dialectic.] This division weakened not only delivery but rhetoric in general, and the persistent influence of Ramus's cordoning off of three of the five canons of rhetoric (in his university lectures and his publications, some with his collaborator Talaeus) is still felt. This change can still be seen in the very large number of writing textbooks (descendants of the handbooks toward which Plato and Aristotle were strongly opposed) that exerted power over rhetoric and writing practices in the twentieth century. This division began to be challenged in post-1980s textbooks.

Eighteenth- and early nineteenth-century English rhetoricians emphasized the fifth canon, reviving the importance of delivery. [*See* Eighteenth-century rhetoric; *and* Nineteenth-century rhetoric.] For example, Thomas Sheridan's a course of *Lectures on Elocution* (London, 1762) treated voice in ways that are similar to the precepts found in the *Rhetorica ad Herennium* and in Cicero: volume, stability, and flexibility in English are discussed, and significantly, ways of teaching these features are set forth. This emphasis on pedagogy reflects in part Quintilian's preoccupation with the nature and training of teachers. John Walker's *Elements of Elocution* (London, 1820) emphasized gesture and other physical movements. The waning of Latin as the dominant learned language and the rise of English as a central language contributed to this refocus on delivery; new needs had arisen, making spoken language more important than it had been for many centuries.

When print (especially after Gutenberg in the fifteenth century) competed with spoken delivery, the fifth canon underwent a number of changes and was weakened because of the transformations in seeing and hearing. Print removes the direct connection between the speaker and the hearer, making voice and gesture less important. With the medium of print, delivery comes to focus on presentation, typeface, ways of reading, and so on. Delivery received renewed attention in the late twentieth and early twenty-first century, as new forms of communication technologies have brought substantial attention to delivery as medium. While still including voice, gesture, and other bodily actions in a speaking situation, delivery has come to encompass the technology that transmits and in some sense forms a rhetorical event. Similarly, the current preoccupation with communication technology has enabled scholars to focus on the methods of transmission, so that delivery can be used to analyze the new and multiplying forms of electronic communication. [See Communication.]

Delivery also served as a locus for discussions about gender, both in antiquity and the present. The modern gender analyses of Ede et al., Gurak, and Gleason, for example, revivify delivery by thoroughly analyzing the traditional male sources, revealing the male dominance in the primary texts, and reinterpreting those texts in ways that illuminate current issues in gender scholarship, including the roles of women in the fifth canon. In antiquity, Roman orators in particular seemed to share a concern that the performative dimension of oratorical delivery might tarnish them via an association with the theater. Indeed, despite the dramatic particulars of a training in delivery and the use of an occasional analogy from the theater, Cicero and later rhetoricians would take care to distinguish training in delivery from acting on the stage. Cicero urges the orator to make his delivery strong and manly, and not to borrow his gestures from the stage and the lower class actors that populated it, but rather from the gymnasium (De oratore 3.220). Nonetheless, this was a slippage into the theatrical (and hence the unmanly) with which overly emotive orators could be branded, as happened to Cicero's contemporary, Hortensius (Aulus Gellius, Noctes Atticae 1.5).

Gender characteristics of delivery have also received attention in the last thirty years of Second Wave feminist scholarship in Anglo-North American studies of women and the twenty-five years of scholarship usually referred to as French feminisms. [See Feminist rhetoric; and Modern rhetoric.] Delivery has been seen by some as an issue of the distribution of power relations between males and females (and even among men of different sexual orientations, in antiquity; Gleason, 1995). The differences between female and male

voices and gestures suggest for many scholars, including scholars who focus on the body, some of the places to investigate the continuing power differentials between some groups of men and some groups of women and within genders as well. Delivery in its form as communication technology remains gendered as well, a point made by Walter J. Ong (1977) and others. In this stance, technology/delivery is not neutral in any sense; rather, the medium contains the gendered and other ideological issues of the people who devised the technologies as well as those of the people who interact with them.

The strong current scholarship on delivery, all connected to that canon's rich and multilayered history, demonstrates the lasting power of this canon and the remarkable uses it can be put to, including the oral, in-person communication events analyzed by Aristotle, the writer of the Rhetorica ad Herennium, Cicero, and Quintilian.

[See also Classical rhetoric.]

BIBLIOGRAPHY

Anonymous. Rhetorica ad Herennium. Translated by Harry Caplan. Cambridge, Mass., 1954. An anonymous first-century BCE Roman treatise in four books on the five canons of rhetoric. A very influential text attributed to Cicero until the fifteenth century.

Aristotle. On Rhetoric: A Theory of Civil Discourse. Translated by George A. Kennedy. New York, 1991. The standard English translation. Includes the earliest extant work on delivery in Book 3.

Cicero. On Oratory and Orators. Translated by J. S. Watson. Carbondale, Ill., 1970. Includes the full translations of De oratore (also referred to as On the Character of the Orator) and Brutus.

Cicero, De oratore. Translated by E. W. Sutton. Cambridge, Mass., 1979.

DuBois, Page. "Violence and the Rhetoric of Philosophy." In Rethinking the History of Rhetoric: Multidisciplinary Essays on the Rhetorical Tradition. Edited by Takis Poulakos, pp. 119–134. Boulder, 1993.

Ede, Lisa, Cheryl Glenn, and Andrea Lunsford. "Border Crossings: Intersections of Rhetoric and Feminism." Rhetorica 8.4 (1995), pp. 401–441. Uses the five canons of rhetoric to organize the interplay between rhetoric and feminism.

Enders, Jody. The Medieval Theatre of Cruelty: Rhetoric, Violence, and Representation in France. Ithaca, N.Y., 1998.

Gleason, Maud W. Making Men: Sophists and Self-Presentation in Ancient Rome. Princeton, 1995.

Gurak, Laura J. *Persuasion and Privacy in Cyberspace*. New Haven, 1997. Emphasizes delivery in electronic spaces and its relationship to Aristotle's conception of *ēthos* as it is set forth in *Rhetoric*.

Kennedy, George A. *The Art of Persuasion in Greece*. Princeton, 1963.

Kennedy, George A. *Classical Rhetoric and Its Christian and Secular Tradition from Ancient to Modern Times*. 2d ed. Chapel Hill, N.C., 1999.

Ong, Walter J. "Transformations of the Word." In *Interfaces of the Word*. Ithaca, N.Y., 1977.

Quintilian. *Institutio oratoria*. 4 vols. Translated by H. E. Butler. Cambridge, U.K., 1922–1933.

Reynolds, John Fredrick, ed. *Rhetorical Memory and Delivery: Classical Concepts for Contemporary Composition and Communication*. Hillsdale, N.J., 1993. Applies the fifth canon to a range of media, including print, digital media, and the ethics of delivery in a variety of media.

Scaglione, Aldo. *The Classical Theory of Composition from Its Origins to the Present: A Historical Survey*. Chapel Hill, N.C., 1972.

Welch, Kathleen E. *Electric Rhetoric: Classical Rhetoric, Oralism, and a New Literacy*. Cambridge, Mass., 1999. Examines delivery in the context of computers and television, analyzing screen literacy as a dominant rhetoric.

—KATHLEEN E. WELCH

DEMONSTRATIVE GENRE. *See* Epideictic genre.

DESCRIPTIO (Gk. *ekphrasis*) "is a generall name of many and sundry kindes of descriptions, and a description is when the Orator by a diligent gathering together of circumstances, and by a fit and naturall application of them doth expresse and set forth a thing so liuely that it seemeth rather painted in tables, then declared with words . . ." (Henry Peacham, 1593, p. 132). Originally a figure of thought, the *descriptio* was later regarded as a technique of amplification. As such, it is subdivided into diverse species according to the object described:

1. *Descriptio rei* (Gk. *pragmatographia*), the description of things, for example, the shield of Achilles in Homer's *Iliad,* or of actions, such as battles, conquests of cities (Quintilian, *Institutio oratoria* 8.3.67), natural catastrophes, plagues, feasts, or triumphal processions. This kind of description is frequent in epical digressions and re-

ports of messengers in drama. A Shakespearean example is Cominius's description of Coriolanus winning the city of Corioles single-handedly (*Coriolanus*, 2.2.112).

2. *Descriptio personae* (Gk. *prosōpographia*), the description of a person by means of "circumstances" (*loci*) as descent (country, town, social class, ancestry); external accomplishments (beauty, fortune, feats of chivalry, political career, reputation); internal accomplishments (education, virtues: magnanimity, prowess, etc.). This kind of description is often used for epideictic purposes, for example, in panegyrics, blazons, and verbal portraits of mythological and heroic figures. [*See* Epideictic genre; *and* Panegyric.]

3. *Descriptio loci* (Gk. *topographia, topothesia*), called "Counterfait place" by George Puttenham, (*The Arte of English Poesie,* 1589), the description: (a) of a real place (*topographia*) like a city, a palace, a garden, often employed as epic digressions; and (b) of an imaginary place (*topothesia*): an ideal pastoral scenery (*locus amoenus*) (Virgil, *Bucolica,* first century BCE; Sir Philip Sidney, *Arcadia,* 1580), and a utopian country or city (Sir Thomas More, *Utopia,* 1516; Tommaso Campanella, *Civitas Solis,* 1602; Francis Bacon, *Nova Atlantis,* 1627).

4. *Descriptio temporis* (Gk. *chronographia*), called "Counterfait time" by Puttenham (*The Arte of English Poesie,* 1589), the description of time, as of the seasons, for example, in James Thompson's poem (1726–1730) and Franz Joseph Haydn's oratorio *Die Jahreszeiten* (1801). In the exordia of medieval poetry, the description of spring is topical, for example, in the prologue to Chaucer's *Canterbury Tales* (1390s).

Under the impact of the Horatian dictum *ut pictura poesis* (first century BCE) and Simonides's similar and equally influential aphorism "painting is mute poetry and poetry a speaking picture" (fifth century BCE), poetry entered into a competition (*paragone*) with painting for the most prominent position in the hierarchy of the arts. This was the reason for the rise of ekphrastic literature and literary pictorialism, which became the predominant fashion from the Renaissance to neoclassicism. Thus, the late classical *Eikones,* a collection of descriptions of imaginary paintings by the two Philostrati (third century CE), found numerous imitations. In this ekphrastic concept of poetry, *descriptio* was not merely regarded as a

figure of speech but in connection with *enargeia/
evidentia* as a principle of mimesis, meaning such
a representation of an object that it appears to the
imagination as if it were present and even alive.
[*See* Imitation; *and* Style.] Thus, in "the speaking
picture" of poetry (Sir Philip Sidney, 1595) an
enargeiac *ekphrasis* is the source of illusion. Only
with Lessing's *Laokoon oder Über die Grenzen der
Malerei und Poesie* (1766), and its distinction between painting as a spatial art and poetry as a
temporal art, did the *paragone* of the verbal and
visual arts came to an end.

[*See also* Amplification; *and* Figures of speech.]

BIBLIOGRAPHY

Becker, Andrew Sprague. *The Shield of Achilles and the
Poetics of Ekphrasis.* Lanham, Md., 1995.
Boehm, Gottfried, and Pfotenhauer, Helmut, eds. *Bes-
cheibungskunst, Kunstbeschreibung: Ekphrasis von der
Antike bis zur Gegenwart.* Munich, 1995.
Borinski, Karl. *Die Antike in Poetik und Kunsttheorie.* 2
vols. Leipzig, 1914. Reprinted Darmstadt, 1965.
Faral, Edmond. *Les arts poétiques du XIIe et du XIIIe siècle.*
Paris, 1923. Reprinted in Paris, 1971.
Farmer, Norman K. *Poetry and the Visual Arts in Renais-
sance England.* Austin, Tex., 1984.
Gent, Lucy. *Picture and Poetry, 1560–1620.* Leamington
Spa, U.K., 1981.
Hagstrum, Jean H. *The Sister Arts: The Tradition of Literary
Pictorialism and English Poetry from Dryden to Gray.*
Chicago, 1958, 1968.
Peacham, Henry. *The Garden of Eloquence* (1593), edited
with an introduction and commentary by B.-M.
Koll. Frankfurt, 1996.
Scholz, Bernhard F. "*Ekphrasis* and *Enargeia* in Quintil-
ian's *Institutionis oratoriae libri xii.*" In *RHETORICA
MOVET: Studies in Historical and Modern Rhetoric in
Honour of Heinrich F. Plett,* edited by Peter L. Oester-
reich and Thomas O. Sloane. Leiden, 1999, pp. 3–
24.

—HEINRICH F. PLETT

DIALECTIC. In *Gorgias* (471e–472d), Plato
(c.428–c.347 BCE) has an exasperated Socrates attempt to explain to a particularly obtuse Polus
that there are two types of refutation. In one,
speakers seek through extended speeches to persuade a large group of the truth by an appeal to
existing opinion. These speakers assume that truth
lies in what the majority believes. Socrates, on the
other hand, calls on only one witness—the per-

son he is interrogating—and assumes that he will
have found a truth only if that interlocutor, un-
coerced, agrees with him. For Socrates, the attempt to secure truth through extended speeches
that confirm the opinion of the multitude exemplifies the inartistic and coercive tactics of
rhetoric. But the guided attempt to move to a
higher understanding by an engaged method of
question and answer in which the soul and opinions of a single interlocutor are probed, represents dialectic. Where rhetoric acknowledges the
authority of public opinion, dialectic begins in
opinion with the intent of transcending the
realm of empirical experience and arriving at
truths more securely grounded because they have
been purified by the operation of reason. Rhetoric
and dialectic would, thus, seem to offer two
deeply opposed approaches to securing the truth.

At the heart of the relationship between rhetoric and dialectic are questions of inference and
invention. [*See* Inference; *and* Invention.] For
some theorists, rhetoric and dialectic differ simply with respect to purpose or subject matter;
however, for others, rhetoric and dialectic are related hierarchically; and some theorists consider
either dialectic or rhetoric as an illegitimate art.
For Aristotle (384–322 BCE), dialectic and rhetoric
offer different modes of inference, addressing different subject matters, and following from different ends of inquiry. [*See* Casuistry; *and* Classical
rhetoric.] For theorists as different as Plato, Boethius (c.480–524 CE), Agricola (1444–1485 CE),
and Ramus (1515–1572 CE), the relationship between the two arts is hierarchical, with the hierarchy being a function of an underlying epistemology that bases knowledge either in certainty
or probability. [*See overview articles on* Medieval
rhetoric *and* Renaissance rhetoric.] Finally, theorists like Isocrates (436–338 BCE) and Cicero (106–
43 BCE) have challenged the legitimacy of dialectic, suggesting that it may not be a source of
genuine knowledge, while figures from Plato to
Kant (1724–1804) have criticized rhetoric as a deceptive and manipulative form of discourse.

Aristotle claimed that Zeno (c.495–c.430 BCE)
invented dialectic. Although the history is sketchy,
Zeno is credited with originating a method of arguing that rendered an opponent's position untenable by showing its logical impossibility. This
type of eristic reasoning became part of the train-

ing of students as skilled debaters. [*See* Eristic.] Sophists like Protagoras (485–410 BCE) used a variation of it when they taught their students to argue both sides of an issue. [*See* Sophists.] From this tradition of questioning a position until it displayed its incoherence emerged the practice that became Platonic dialectic.

In the *Phaedrus* (which is often read as Plato's revision of his earlier and more negative account of rhetoric in *Gorgias*), Plato has Socrates argue that dialectic allows its practitioner to make methodical distinctions of like from unlike and to use these dichotomies to discover an object's identity. Socrates argues that the true dialectician is like a skillful butcher who, through an artistic cleaving, is able to make divisions at the joints and not simply shatter the bones with random cuts. The two activities of the dialectician are collection and division, and through the practice of this art, a dialectician can discover the unity within multiplicity. For Socrates, if one wishes to practice an artful rhetoric, then one must first learn dialectic, for without such an art, rhetoric could not discover appropriate content for its speeches. Because it could not explore the nature of things, it would have no genuine power but simply be confined to the manipulation of commonplaces.

But if Socrates seems unqualified in his praise of dialectic, the dialogue suggests limits to its application. In his second speech, his palinode to Eros, for example, Socrates does not primarily use dialectic to develop his account of the soul but has recourse, instead, to extended figures of the soul as winged and the soul as a war chariot. So in the drama of the dialogue a dissonance develops between the laudatory account of dialectic and its actual performance. In addition to this tension surrounding the efficacy of dialectic in the *Phaedrus*, Plato further complicates dialectic in the *Meno* by claiming that it has two forms: a dialectic proper that is conducted among friends and an eristic form that is engaged in by adversaries. In eristic, opponents seek to destroy each other's position. Unlike dialectic, which is motivated by a concern with the interlocutors amicably contesting each other in pursuit of a mutual inquiry into the truth, the participants in eristic pursue a negative goal of simply obliterating each other's position. Eristic is verbal combat and

comes close to approaching the agonistic engagement of rhetoric. Its goal is not transcendance or truth but victory.

In a genuine dialectic, there is a winnowing of like from unlike in a movement from an empirically based opinion to an understanding of an underlying ideational structure that renders the world intelligible. The most famous account of this ascent is Plato's allegory of the cave (*Republic*, 7.514a–518d). Were dialectic to succeed, one could grasp those forms that have allowed one to function as an intelligent being. Such a grasping would be a recovery or recollection (an *anamnēsis*) of what we must have at some time known in order for the world to be even partially intelligible to us at present. The Platonic forms or ideas represent a logically prior condition that is necessary if we are to account for our ability to generalize from sensory experience. But as both the myth of the cave and the *Phaedrus* suggest, having dialectically arrived at an understanding of the ideas is no guarantee that someone could successfully communicate this understanding to another, not the least because very few are capable of the strenuous labor of dialectic. So it seems dialectic will inevitably need rhetoric to communicate its truths.

If there is tension in Plato's account of dialectic, Aristotle's account of the relation of rhetoric to dialectic has spawned a history of controversy. This controversy arises from the opening line of Aristotle's *Rhetoric:* "Rhetoric is an *antistrophos* (counterpart) to dialectic, for both are concerned with such things as are, to a certain extent, within the knowledge of all people and belong to no separately defined science" (1354a; Kennedy translation, pp. 28–29). Aristotle does not significantly elaborate on this statement, and commentators have been left to determine in what way Aristotle conceives of the antistrophic relationship between rhetoric and dialectic. He does, however, claim that both arts are held in common by the public and that both arts are used in the contesting of statements. One obvious question is: Are these two arts in a hierarchical relation, with one art providing the principles and justifications for the other art, or are these parallel forms of reasoning that can be distinguished because they deal with different types of statements? Aristotle seems to believe that they are both.

In explaining *logos* (argument) as a source of proof, Aristotle characterizes rhetoric not as an *antistrophos* to dialectic but as an offshoot (*paraphuēs*) of dialectic (1365a). [*See* Logos.] This would seem to argue that *dialectic* is the more inclusive term and that rhetoric can be understood as a particular instance of dialectic. But Aristotle never says that; instead, he situates rhetoric between dialectic and politics. Rhetoric is thus a distinct type of reasoning. What it shares with dialectic is its modes of inferential proceeding; what distinguishes it from dialectic is the type of propositions with which it works. Dialectic deals with universal propositions, while rhetoric deals with propositions whose truth holds good only for the most part. Aristotle further elaborates this contrast by pairing the deductive syllogism of dialectic reasoning with the enthymeme of rhetoric and the inductive reasoning of dialectic with rhetoric's reasoning from example. [*See* Enthymene; Exemplum; *and* Syllogism.] What unites dialectic and rhetoric is their involvement with inference. Both are ways of moving from current appearances or opinions to more securely held positions. In the case of dialectic, this procedure should lead to the universal propositions that form the basis of Aristotle's scientific reasoning. In rhetoric, these ways of making inferences should lead to the *logos* of the speech. This *logos* would represent how a particular situation should be understood by a particular audience given that audience's opinions and the various ways that the situation appears to them. Read this way, dialectic marks both the larger process of making inferences and also designates a particular type of inference. Rhetoric is then both a part of dialectic and separate from it.

Aristotle's complex if ambiguous delineation of dialectic and rhetoric can be read as his attempt to subordinate neither rhetoric to philosophy nor philosophy to rhetoric. Some commentators see his choice of the term *antistrophos* as a direct allusion to Plato in *Gorgias* characterizing rhetoric as the *antistrophos* of cooking. They thus see Aristotle's opening line as an attempt to resituate the relationship of rhetoric and philosophy and to argue for the legitimacy of rhetoric.

Aristotle's opening can also be read as a challenge to the tradition of Isocratean rhetoric that sought to deal with invention not by justifying a technical scheme of invention but by creating a broadly educated rhetor who could draw on a rich liberal education to discover what was appropriate to a particular speech. In this tradition, dialectic is suspect because it appears to degenerate into an empty formalism. In *De oratore,* for instance, Cicero, working within the Isocratean tradition, has the character of Crassus blame Socrates for severing wisdom and elegance and argue that the practice of dialectic is divorced from a concern with political responsibility, and, as such, it is a degenerate form of thought that had transformed serious thinking into the triviality of amusement (3.15).

Within the rhetorical tradition, a tension persists between those who would see *inventio* as tied to a rhetor's intellectual shaping by a rich liberal education, and those who argue that *inventio* is a technical matter and that what is crucial is that the form of the inference be guaranteed as valid. In *De differentiis topicis,* Boethius (early sixth century CE, a consul under the emperor Theodoric and author of *On the Consolation of Philosophy,* composed in prison while awaiting execution for conspiring against Theodoric) had challenged the view of dialectic espoused by Cicero's Crassus; he argued instead that dialectic is the crucial art because it governs the operations of inference. Boethius distinguishes dialectical and rhetorical topics, subordinating rhetoric to dialectic. This subordination is based on three factors: (1) dialectic deals with general questions and theses while rhetoric deals with specific questions and hypotheses; (2) dialectic proceeds through the use of a complete syllogism whereas rhetoric employs enthymemes, which are syllogisms that omit specific steps; and (3) in dialectic, disputants directly engage each other, while in rhetoric, the rhetor seeks to persuade a judge. Since dialectic designates the broader category of question and proceeds through the fuller chain of reasoning, it is logically prior to rhetoric. In effect, rhetoric, in its occupation with particular issues, is reduced to an instance of dialectic. What guarantees the conclusions of a rhetorical inquiry are the general rules of inference that are the province of dialectic.

Boethius's view of dialectic and invention prevailed through the Middle Ages. Yet, in a revolutionary redefinition of Boethius's account of *in-*

ventio, Rodolphus Agricola (a fifteenth-century Dutch scholar) reverses the hierarchy of dialectic and rhetoric. While Agricola's *De inventione dialectica* focuses exclusively on dialectical invention, he gave new meanings to key terms such as *dialectic, invention,* and *commonplace* that, in effect, return *inventio* to rhetoric. Agricola redefines the purpose of dialectic from providing a method of securing the logical validity of arguments to offering a method with which to inquire into questions that are disputed or doubtful. Agricola is concerned with the way that a predicate inheres in a subject, and he believes that knowledge about subjects and predicates comes from specialized fields of knowledge. What dialectic discovers are arguments that allow the two terms to be brought into meaningful relationship. This discovery or invention is concerned with particulars, for it is only through an investigation of particular points of agreement and disagreement that the relationship between a subject and predicate can be established. To discover these particulars, one needs to go to *loci* (places or topics). [*See* Topics.] Because of the large number of points of agreements and disagreement, knowledge, for Agricola, can never be certain but only probable. A proof, then, is not authorized by the validity of a syllogism, as in Boethius's system, but by the accumulation of particular evidence. So even if Agricola retains the term *dialectic* to designate this process, he has altered the meaning of the term and redefined dialectic as the rhetorical operation of topical invention.

Peter Ramus, a sixteenth-century French professor, thought that he was extending the argument of Agricola, but he again changed the relationship of rhetoric and dialectic. Ramus saw himself as an educational reformer whose task was to bring order into a chaotic and disorganized curriculum. He believed that Cicero and especially Quintilian (c.35–c.100 CE) had extended the scope of rhetoric beyond Aristotle's reasonable formulation and that the relationship of logic and rhetoric had to be reestablished. To effect this reorganization, Ramus removed invention from rhetoric and assigned it to dialectic. Rhetoric was limited to concerns of ornamentation (style) and delivery. The matter of a speech would be determined by logic. Through dialectic, one could discover truths that were universal and hence would command the mind's assent. Such a reformed art could have tremendous consequences in securing the mind to an understanding of God who was the author of these universal truths. It was this aspect that made Ramus's thought so appealing to Puritan *rhētors.* [*See* Homiletics; *and* Renaissance rhetoric, *article on* Rhetoric in the age of Reformation and Counter-Reformation.]

The limiting of rhetoric to the study of tropes and figures would eventually contribute to its decline. Rhetoric was seen increasingly by the developing positivist science and in Enlightenment critiques as a way to mislead audiences by deceptions of figurative language that worked *ultimately,* in Kant's terms, to obscure truth and enslave audiences (*Critique of Judgment,* section 53).

Kant was also ambivalent about dialectic. On the one hand, he considered a form of dialectic as falsely presenting itself as a logic that could derive truths that were independent of experience and based solely in the operation of reason; on the other hand, he used dialectical reasoning to display the antinomies of reason. The nineteenth-century German philosopher, G. W. F. Hegel (1770–1831) appropriated this latter sense of dialectic and claimed that history embodied the movement of reason through the resolution of contradictions. Karl Marx (1818–1883), in turn, applied the logic of dialectic not to contradictions within ideas but to contradictions within social structures that are embodied in the struggle of classes. Dialectic thus was no longer operating as a resource for the clarification of terms in an argument or as a source of invention or as the delineation of an inferential form, but rather it had detached from a moribund rhetorical tradition to become a method to locate contradictions within social organization. In the twentieth century, Kenneth Burke (1897–1993), a central figure in the recovery of rhetoric in the United States, would unite rhetoric and dialectic again, arguing that rhetoric marked the site of contending symbolistic actions and dialectic designated the transcendance of that contest by the discovery of a more general term that could embody and reconcile the opposing positions. [*See* Modern rhetoric.]

As a term deeply embedded in the quarrel between rhetoric and philosophy, *dialectic* is an ongoing site of contestation, and its use by a particular theorist is a good index as to how that thinker views invention and inference. [*See* Philosophy, *article on* Perennial topics and terms.] As its meaning has shifted during the history of rhetoric, dialectic has been used both to attack and limit rhetoric and to justify a probabilistic reasoning that is at the heart of rhetoric. But to recognize the instability of the term *dialectic* is itself to think rhetorically and to argue that its meaning is indeterminate, acquiring serious content only in the particularity of its use.

BIBLIOGRAPHY

Aristotle. *On Rhetoric: A Theory of Civic Discourse.* Translated with Introduction, notes, and appendixes by George A. Kennedy. New York, 1991. First published 330 BCE. Contains a good bibliography.

Boethius. *De topicis differentiis.* Translated, with notes and essays on the text by Eleonore Stump. Ithaca, N.Y., 1978.

Cicero, Marcus Tullius. *On the Making of an Orator.* Translated by E. W. Sutton and H. Rackham. 2 vols. Cambridge, Mass., 1942. First published c.55 BCE. English translation of *De oratore.*

Conley, Thomas M. *Rhetoric in the European Tradition.* New York, 1990. Excellent single-volume history of rhetoric.

Cogan, Marc. "Rodolphus Agricola and the Semantic Revolutions of the History of Invention." *Rhetorica* 2 (1984), pp. 163–194. An indispensable essay for understanding Agricola's contribution to the discussion of rhetoric and dialectic.

Duhamel, Pierre Albert. "The Logic and Rhetoric of Peter Ramus." *Modern Philology* 46 (1949), pp. 163–171.

Green, Lawrence D. "Aristotelian Rhetoric, Dialectic, and the Traditions of *Antistrophos*." *Rhetorica* 8 (1990), pp. 5–27. Good history of the commentary on the relationship of rhetoric and dialectic in Aristotle.

Isocrates. *Isocrates,* vol. 2, *Antidosis.* Translated by George Norlin, pp. 181–365. Cambridge, Mass, 1929. First published c.354–353 BCE.

Kennedy, George. *The Art of Persuasion in Greece.* Princeton, 1963.

Leff, Michael C. "Boethius and the History of Medieval Rhetoric." *Central States Speech Journal* 25 (1974), pp. 135–141. Excellent introduction to Boethius and his contribution to the history of rhetoric.

Ong, Walter J., S.J. *Ramus: Method and Decay of Dialogue.* Cambridge, Mass, 1958. Provides essential background material for appreciation of Ramus's redirection of rhetoric.

Plato. *Gorgias.* Translated by Donald J. Zeyl. In *Plato: Complete Works.* Edited, with an introduction and notes, by John M. Cooper; Associate Editor, D. S. Hutchinson, pp. 791–869. Indianapolis, 1997.

Plato. *Meno.* Translated by G. M. A. Grube, pp. 870–897. In *Plato: Complete Works.* Indianapolis, 1997.

Plato. *Phaedrus.* Translated by Alexander Nehamas and Paul Woodruff, pp. 506–556. In *Plato: Complete Works.* Indianapolis, 1997.

Ramus, Peter. *Arguments in Rhetoric against Quintilian.* Introduction by James J. Murphy; translation by Carole Newlands. Dekalb, Ill., 1986; translation of *Rhetoricae Distinctiones Quintilianum,* first published in 1549.

Ryle, Gilbert. *Plato's Progress.* Cambridge, U.K., 1966. A good discussion of Platonic and sophistic dialectic and of their pre-Socratic origins.

—JAMES L. KASTELY

DIGRESSIO (Gk. *parekbasis;* Lat. also *egressio, egressus*) is a textological figure of addition or an additive metatexteme, which is defined as an insertion of a longer and independent segment in a text to which it is thematically more or less connected. Both Cicero (*De oratore,* 55 BCE, 3.53.203) and Quintilian (Institutio oratoria, first century CE 4.3.12) group the *digressio* under the figures of sentences. Quintilian recommends the following persuasive functions and topics for this figure: praise of persons and places (*laus hominum locorumque*), description of regions (*descriptio regionum*), record of certain historical occurrences, even of legendary ones (*expositio quarundam rerum gestarum, licet etiam fabulosarum*). In Renaissance rhetoric (e.g., Erasmus's *De copia,* 1512), the principal function of the digression is the amplification of discourse. [*See* Amplification.] Digressions can be integral constituents of narrative fiction, which thus loses its structural unity in favor of exuberant subplots, authorial comments, and so on. At the turn of the sixteenth century, several oppositional forces rose against the dominance of *copia.* [*See* Copia.] Representatives of the classicist movement demanded a curtailment of such excesses in literature and a return to the Aristotelian ideal of the *hen kai holon* ("the one and whole"). Thomas Sprat in his *History of the Royal Society* (1667) demanded "a constant Resolution, to reject all the amplifications, digressions and swellings of style." Jonathan Swift, who made ample use of the digressive mode, parodied it in "A digression in praise of digressions," concerning his *A Tale of a Tub* (1704).

[*See also* Figures of speech.]

BIBLIOGRAPHY

Härter, Andreas. *Digressionen: Studien über das Verhältnis von Ordnung und Abweichung in Rhetorik und Poetik*. Munich, 2000. A monograph on the theory of digression in classical rhetoric and German poeti-

cal theory from the Renaissance through Romanticism.

—HEINRICH F. PLETT

DISSOI LOGOI. *See* Ambiguity; Judgment; Logos; Occasion; Persuasion; *and* Thesis and antithesis.

DRAMA. *See* Law; Pathos; *and* Poetry.

E

EDUCATION. *See* Classical rhetoric; Composition, *article on* History of English departments in the United States; Humanism; Imitation; Poetry; *overview article on* Renaissance rhetoric; *and* Speech.

EIGHTEENTH-CENTURY RHETORIC began with stylistic and neoclassical theories established in centuries past and ended with the redefinition of classical doctrines according to the "science of human nature." In the sixteenth-century, Protestant reformer Peter Ramus had defined logic as the art of disputation as well as reasoning, leaving rhetoric largely confined to style. In the seventeenth century, a more expansive sense of rhetoric had been reiterated by such neoclassical scholars as Gerardus Johannes Vossius. Stylistic and neoclassical rhetorics continued to appear in the eighteenth century, but rhetorical studies expanded to emphasize contemporary literary and psychological concerns. The most significant works on rhetoric were published in the decades when world empires were being established and traditional hierarchies were being challenged by revolutionary social change, creating rhetorical situations of historic proportions. The major rhetorical theorists of the Enlightenment remained aloof from the impassioned orations and pamphlets of their time and turned instead to philosophers of the new learning. Influenced by Newton, Descartes, Bacon, and Locke, rhetoric was reoriented to study the logic of the individual experience, the principles of correct English, and tasteful self-restraint.

While Descartes's *Discourse de la méthode* (1637) had dismissed rhetoric as an art concerned with mere probabilities rather than the self-evident certainties fundamental to real knowledge, British advocates of enlightenment grudgingly accepted that while logic could inform the reason, rhetoric was necessary to rouse the will to action. As propounded in Bacon's *Advancement of Learning* (1605), this model of the mental faculties established the general frame of reference for efforts to define rhetoric according to the workings of the individual consciousness. Bacon obviated Ramus's rigid distinctions between logic and rhetoric by defining the former as the art of learned inquiry and the latter as the art of inventing the materials needed for instruction and argument. Defining the genres of knowledge by the faculties addressed by each, Bacon identified philosophy with reason, poetry with imagination, history with memory, and rhetoric with the will. Like such successors as Locke, Bacon was a practicing rhetor active in the politics of his time, and his practical experience led him to recognize that rhetoric was an inevitable part of civic life. Although Locke's *Essay Concerning Human Understanding* (1690) criticized rhetoric for exploiting the artifices of language to promote factional divisions, Locke himself had lectured on rhetoric at Oxford in 1663, responding to the popular interest in the powers of persuasion that has often overcome philosophical reservations about rhetoric in periods of political change. [*See overview article on* Renaissance rhetoric.]

The eighteenth century was one such period, and Locke's *Essay Concerning Human Understanding* was a common source for rhetorical theorists. The redefinition of rhetoric and logic according to the methods and values of modern science is the central focus of the most comprehensive account of the period, W. S. Howell's *Eighteenth-Century British Logic and Rhetoric* (Princeton, 1971). Howell surveys a wide range of British and Continental works and then characterizes each according to whether it advanced beyond Aristotelian logics and Ciceronian rhetorics. According to Howell, seventeenth-century Aristotelians had viewed the deductive logic of the syllogistic disputation as the paradigm for both investigation and communication. The "old" logic assumed that reasoning from commonplace topics such as definition, classification, and comparison is the best way to examine whether disputed claims are consistent with established beliefs, and are therefore true. [*See* Dialectic.] The "new" logic distinguished observation and communication. Inductive generalizations from experiments became the model for scientific research that advances general truths from observable facts. Paralleling trends in logic, neoclassical rhetoric had concentrated on the art of speaking in forensic, deliberative, and ceremonial forums. This art used "artistic" modes of proof, such as the topics to invent arguments from received beliefs and develop them into enthymemes or abbreviated syllogisms, generally delivered in the form of highly figured and elaborately structured orations with six basic parts (introduction, narration, partition, proof, refutation, and peroration). [*See* Arrangement, *article on* Traditional arrangement; *and* Enthymeme.] The new rhetoric expanded study beyond popular persuasion to include informative and literary discourse. The facts of the issue gained priority over artistic proofs drawn from commonsense probabilities, and discourse was redefined according to the inductive logic, transparent form, and unadorned style of the sciences.

Other accounts such as Horner and Barton's useful bibliographical essay (1990) have surveyed eighteenth-century rhetoric using more multivalent categories. The rhetorical theories of the period have commonly been grouped into several overlapping categories: stylistic and neoclassical works that followed from established traditions, elocutionary manuals that responded to popular aspirations to speak with propriety, belletristic rhetorics that addressed the taste for refinement, and epistemological rhetorics that redefined classical assumptions according to the workings of mental faculties. These categories foreground eighteenth-century rhetoric's dynamic interactions with logic, speech, composition, and modern conceptions of literature and psychology. However, the epistemological emphases of the "new" rhetoric have tended to overshadow the civic relations of rhetoric and moral philosophy that remained significant into the eighteenth century. From a civic perspective, rhetoric is concerned with how citizens translate received beliefs into practical action to address public needs.

This perspective will serve as an appropriate point of reference when we shift from surveying the theories of the period to relating them to rhetorical practice, not merely in terms of their influence on practicing rhetoricians, but as a matter of how rhetoric was formalized and practiced in ways that set out the discursive conditions for modernity.

Stylistic and Neoclassical Rhetorics. Stylistic and neoclassical rhetorics were both Ciceronian, though they had different understandings of what that entailed. Elaborate lists of tropes and figures fill the pages of stylistic rhetorics such as John Stirling's *System of Rhetoric* (1733), Thomas Gibbons's *Rhetoric; or, a View of Its Principal Tropes and Figures* (1767), and Anthony Blackwall's *Introduction to the Classics* (1718). Stylistic rhetorics did not generally discuss the actual process of composing discourse, concentrating their attention instead on mechanical elaborations of a style that was understood to be Ciceronian, while ignoring the civic vision that had imbued Cicero's rhetoric with purpose. However, not all stylistic rhetorics ignored contemporary trends. César-Chesneau DuMarsais drew on the Port-Royalist disciples of Descartes to categorize tropes and figures according to principles of mental associations in his *Des Tropes* (1730). French neoclassical rhetorics were also more dynamically engaged with contemporary assumptions and tastes than British advocates of the ancients. Dominique Bonhours's *De la manière de bien penser dans les ouvrages de l'esprit* (1687) and Claude Buffier's *Traité de l'éloquence* (1728) used classical principles as practical aids to composing and provided modern literary examples along with classical models for imitation. Bonhours's text went through two dozen editions by 1800, while Buffier was an early proponent of the commonsense philosophy that influenced the epistemologically oriented rhetorics that will be discussed later. [*See* Style.]

British works that helped promote a fuller sense of classical rhetoric include John Ward's *System of Oratory* (1759), John Holmes's grammar school textbook *The Art of Rhetoric Made Easy* (1755), and John Lawson's more eclectic *Lectures Concerning Oratory* (1758). Ward provides eight hundred pages surveying classical theories of deliberative, forensic, and ceremonial discourse along with practical strategies for inventing, arranging, and delivering argument; aids for memorizing them; and extensive advice on style. [*See* Deliberative genre; Epideictic genre; *and* Forensic genre.] Holmes's text is a precis of Ciceronian rhetoric and Longinus's *On the Sublime* (first century CE), cast in rhyming couplets so that they could more readily be recited by rote. [*See* Sublime, the.] Lawson's text is the first published set of college lectures delivered in English on rhetoric and belles lettres. As professor of oratory and history at Trinity College, Dublin, from 1753 to 1759, Lawson reviewed classical theories but also taught English composition and commented upon English literature, while condemning the popular rage for modern studies. Lawson's ambivalence was due to the fact that he taught in an Irish bastion of Anglican culture that adhered to English educational traditions. Like Oxford and Cambridge, Trinity was closed to Catholics and Dissenters, and its curriculum was dominated by the classics. Its students were Irish, but they wanted to speak as Englishmen of taste. While Lawson's text thus touched on such contemporary concerns as English elocution, the book did not address popular tastes and needs as directly as textbooks that came from the first English courses in Scotland, and like Ward's *System,* Lawson's *Lectures* was not reprinted in the eighteenth century.

Though his neoclassical perspective on rhetoric was no more influential than those that appeared in Britain, Giambattista Vico (1688–1744) has today become the most widely studied eighteenth-century writer on rhetoric. While serving as professor of rhetoric at the University of Naples from 1699 to 1741, Vico published several works that responded to the Cartesian disdain for mere probabilities. In *Scienza nuova* (1725) and other writings, Vico rejected the new logic's pretension to be the method of nature and reiterated the classical sense of *logos* as the making of meaning in language. [*See* Logos.] From the assumption that humans can only understand what they have made together in civic life over time, Vico argues that only by studying the history of language, culture, and civic institutions can one understand human nature, and more importantly the nature of God. Representing prevailing tropes as the embodiments of the civic imagination of varied eras, Vico developed elaborate histories of the cyclical evolution of languages, social institutions, and cultural modes of understanding, moving from a poetic era when men lived as beasts and imagined the gods, through a heroic age when society gave rise to law, up to the times when civil society became valued and threatened by individualistic aspirations. Largely unread in his own time, Vico remained forgotten until cultural anthropology gave new meaning to his work and the tropes regained currency as characteristics of discourse, rather than aberrations from its referential nature. In his own time, Vico's critique of Descartes was dismissed as a reaction against the progress of knowledge, and his digressive and nonsystematic style reinforced the sense that he was writing for an audience that had passed into history.

Elocutionary Rhetorics. Elocutionary and belletristic rhetorics spoke directly to the practical aspirations of the reading public. Ironically, both drew on French sources to foster interest in English. French tastes set cosmopolitan standards across Europe, and the French language was the first to rival Latin as the international language of educated society. According to Conley (1990), French influences also contributed to works that advanced vernacular literacy and literary studies in Germany and Spain, most notably Johann Christof Gottsched's *Ausführliche Redekunst* (1736) and Gregorio Mayáns y Siscar's *Rhetorica* (1757). The British interest in elocution began with the introduction of Faucheur's *Traitté de l'action de l'orateur* (1657), which appeared in three separate translations and served as the basis for a fourth British work on elocution by the middle of the eighteenth century. Belles lettres, which mediated between a classical sense of the liberal arts and the modern conception of literature, gained currency in Britain with the translation of Charles Rollin's *De la maniére d'enseigner et d'étudier les belles letttres* (1726–1728). Rollin's textbook for teachers went through twenty-seven editions, including ten in English, with the first in 1734. Rollin was both a Ciceronian and an educational reformer. He included modern literature along with classical models because he assumed that the purpose of rhetorical studies is to prepare people to speak and write in a clear and direct manner from the pulpit and bar. To advance this purpose, he published an abridged translation of Quintilian's

Institutio oratoria in 1715. While he helped translate classical authorities into the public idiom, Rollin and his contemporaries were concerned that studies of the vernacular were so readily accessible that they would undermine the deference to the ancients that was inculcated through studies of classical languages.

English studies were spread by the establishment of elocution as a discipline with its own theories, methods, and manuals. The term *elocution,* which refers to the study of delivery, comes from the Latin *elocutio* or style, and like stylistic rhetorics, works on elocution tended to divorce form from content. The most influential include John Mason's *Essay on Elocution* (1748), James Burgh's *The Art of Speaking* (1761), Thomas Sheridan's *Lectures on Elocution* (1762), John Rice's *An Introduction to the Art of Reading* (1765), Joshua Steele's *An Essay towards Establishing the Melody and Measure of Speech to be Expressed and Perpetuated by Peculiar Symbols* (1775), William Cockin's *The Art of Delivering Written Language* (1775), and John Walker's *Elements of Elocution* (1781). These works provide elaborate directions on how to convey emotions by appropriate voice modulations, facial expressions, and hand gestures. Students were taught to deliver carefully controlled readings of texts, including popular anthologies of polite literature such as William Enfield's *The Speaker* (1774), Noah Webster's *An American Selection of Lessons in Reading and Speaking* (1785), and Mary Wollstonecraft's *The Female Reader* (published in 1789 under the pseudonym "Mr. Cresswick, teacher of elocution"). These works reached a very large audience: Webster's went through forty editions and Enfield's over sixty. Elocutionary manuals and anthologies helped spread educated tastes among the reading public by providing provincials, women, and other marginalized groups with lessons on how to read and speak with the self-control and moderate sentiment of a person of taste.

The elocutionary movement is the clearest example of how rhetoric was popularized by the spread of literacy beyond the learned. While leading elocutionists such as Thomas Sheridan invoked the authority of the classical tradition, they condemned the educational emphasis on classical languages as a barrier to the spread of knowledge, and to the upward mobility of provincials like themselves. Sheridan also criticized Locke

and other philosophers for concentrating on the communication of ideas through writing and ignoring speech—the natural language of the emotions. The elocutionary movement can be seen as the nostalgic idealization of orality in an era when print was coming to define public life. Although speech was represented as the natural mode of exchanging feelings, elocutionists paid far more attention to delivering readings than to extemporaneous debate or the composition of speeches. As the titles of several of the texts cited above indicate, elocutionists often equated public speaking with reading in public, and they methodically scripted speech with elaborate notations on written texts. Elocutionists such as Sheridan who advocated a more "natural" approach to delivery, have been contrasted with those who provided "mechanical" accounts of the emotions, but most elocutionists claimed to teach students how to speak naturally, while mechanically refashioning how they naturally spoke. The culmination of the elocutionary movement is Gilbert Austin's *Chironomia, or a Treatise on Rhetorical Delivery* (1806). With page after page of pictures of men and women correctly posed to convey natural emotions, the "language of the body" is codified as the language of nature in a book that was studiously read by provincials wanting to speak as Englishmen or -women of letters.

Elocution became an established discipline at the same time that an explosion of grammars, dictionaries, and treatises were formalizing and standardizing educated taste and usage. Over four hundred editions of English grammars and some 215 editions of English dictionaries appeared after 1750, with over five times more new dictionaries and grammars appearing after 1750 than had been published in the first half of the century. The spread of print both expanded the audience for English and provided a model for its standardization. The number of books published annually almost quadrupled in the latter half of the century. The sales of newspapers tripled between 1711 and 1753, then doubled again to about fourteen million a year by 1780. Swift's "Proposal for Correcting, Improving, and Ascertaining the English Tongue" (1712) ceased being an avocation for neoclassicists and became the vocation of a whole class of critics, lexicographers, grammarians, elocutionists, and professors of English.

While the centers of English education remained aloof from these popular trends, professorships were founded to teach English literature, composition, and rhetoric in Ireland, Scotland, and America as well as in the academies that Dissenters had established when religious tests were imposed on students and faculty at Oxford and Cambridge upon the Restoration. [*See* Composition, *article on* History of English departments in the United States; *and* Speech.]

Belletristic Rhetorics. The impact of these trends is evident in the belletristic orientation of the most widely read rhetoric published in the period, Hugh Blair's *Lectures on Rhetoric and Belles Lettres* (1789). Blair's *Lectures* went through over one hundred and ten complete and abridged editions to become the standard text in the courses that first made English into an object of formal study in higher education. Blair was formally made Regius Professor of Rhetoric and Belles Lettres at Edinburgh University in 1762. Interest in the subject had been promoted by Henry Home, Lord Kames, who published another influential belletristic text, *The Elements of Criticism,* in the same year that Blair was awarded his royally endowed professorship. Home had persuaded Adam Smith to deliver a public series of lectures on rhetoric and belles lettres in Edinburgh from 1748 to 1751. When Smith and his successor, Robert Watson, were given positions at other Scottish universities, Blair continued the lectures in Edinburgh from 1759 to 1760, and then within the university itself until he was formally awarded a professorship, in part because of his leadership in the Moderate wing of the Scottish church. With the support of gentry such as Kames who saw cultural refinement as social progress, Moderates had suppressed the Presbyterian tradition of electing clergy and reinstituted patronage. In Blair's lectures on rhetoric and belles lettres, and in those that Smith delivered on the subject at Glasgow while professor of logic and then moral philosophy, Scottish students were taught to imitate the taste, usage, and modes of behavior of polite English society, and thereby to distance themselves from the oral traditions and divisive politics of their own society.

The belletristic goal of instilling taste is the pivotal point for the transition from the classical emphasis on the composition of persuasive discourse to the modern emphasis on critical interpretation. Blair's Lectures begin by eulogizing the classical sense of rhetoric that identified *ratio* with *oratio* on the assumption that the ability to deliberate together is essential to citizenship and fundamental to civilized society. Blair then moves on to outline his fundamental concepts—taste, genius, and the sublime sentiments that they make possible. After sketching out the progress of politeness from primitive genius to refined taste, Blair turns to the work of instilling it through the criticism of style as an index to character. Fifteen of the twenty-five lectures of the first volume are devoted to commentary on the finer points of English syntax. The essays of taste and manners of the *Spectator* are analyzed as exemplars of moderate style and character, with Swift also praised as a model worthy of imitation. The second volume of Blair's *Lectures* begins with the eloquence of the pulpit, bar, and assembly, though the only modern texts discussed are sermons. The *Lectures* then survey the traditional parts of the classical oration, the art of delivery, and the means of improving eloquence. The last half of the second volume extends the study of rhetoric in the characteristic belletristic manner to survey genres ranging from history and philosophy to various types of poetry and drama.

Like other "new" rhetoricians, Blair dismissed the classical art of *inventio* because he assumed that having something to say is a matter of natural capacity and thus cannot be taught. While Howell praises this general trend as consistent with the logic of the sciences, such assumptions treat those who are having problems discovering and developing ideas as naturally inarticulate rather than as simply in need of instruction. By characterizing the creative process as a matter of natural genius and concentrating on stylistic proprieties, the pedagogy that Blair helped institutionalize alienated students from the productive resources of discourse. Classical rhetoric had provided students with heuristics (topics, places) to explore what had been said about a matter and assess the status of a debate by determining whether it turned on a question of fact, definition, evaluation, or procedure. The eighteenth-century dismissal of *stasis* theory and the topics was consistent with the modern belief that facts should speak for themselves, and, ironically, it was also consistent with belletrists' Romantic commentaries on the sublime power of untutored genius. [*See* Stasis; *and* Topics.] However, such beliefs mystified the process of producing discourse in a way that was particularly debilitating for the provincial students who comprised much of the primary audience for such rhetorics. The belletristic mixture of primitivism and proprieties worked to silence those who could not speak correctly, while valorizing receding oral traditions according to the values of the dominant culture. The most notorious example is Blair's *Critical Dissertation on Ossian* (1763). Blair gained international fame for his Romantic defense of the cultural authenticity of the ancient Highland bard Ossian, which his protégé James Macpherson had actually fabricated from scraps of Gaelic. Blair did not know the Highland culture or its language, but when the "translations" were brought to him in 1759, he seized upon them as exemplars of the sublime power of the untutored primitive, and his lectures on them established his reputation as a commentator on polite taste.

Like other Scottish teachers of English such as Adam Smith and James Beattie, Blair taught provincials who stood at a distance from the centers of political power, and he turned that political marginalization into a positive benefit by idealizing the man of taste who maintains a critical distance from the factional rhetoric of party politics. This ideal is personified as the "impartial spectator" in Adam Smith's *Theory of Moral Sentiments* (1759), which along with *The Wealth of Nations* (1776) developed out of his teaching as professor of moral philosophy at Glasgow from 1751 to 1763. Smith also continued the lectures on rhetoric and belles lettres that he had begun in Edinburgh. (At his direction, the lecture notes from his course were burned upon his death, and copies of students' notes were not rediscovered until 1958). While Smith's lectures on rhetoric and belles lettres have been claimed as the origin of the "new" rhetoric and of college English studies, his direct influence on rhetoric was largely exercised through the *Lectures* of his popular successor, Hugh Blair, who admitted drawing on his predecessor's use of stylistic criticism to instill character. Smith and other Scottish moral philosophers such as Francis Hutcheson, David Hume, and Thomas Reid influenced the development of

rhetoric in a more indirect way by propounding the philosophy of human nature that shaped the guiding assumptions of epistemologically oriented works on rhetoric.

Epistemological Rhetorics. The turn toward epistemology has long been seen as the most intellectually significant innovation in eighteenth-century rhetoric. George Campbell's *Philosophy of Rhetoric* (1776) was by far the most influential effort to redefine rhetoric according to "the science of human nature," rivaled only by Joseph Priestley's *A Course of Lectures on Oratory and Criticism* (1777). While Priestley began teaching rhetoric at the innovative Dissenting Academy at Warrington in 1762, he is best known as the discoverer of oxygen, propounder of Unitarianism, and Dissenting rhetorician who opposed the British constitutional union of church and state and defended the rights of the American colonies. Campbell was a professor at Aberdeen closely associated with the advocates of commonsense philosophy—Thomas Reid, Alexander Gerard, and James Beattie. Campbell's *Philosophy of Rhetoric* has been described as "perhaps the most comprehensive and original treatment of rhetoric since the classical period" in James L. Golden and Edward P. J. Corbett's very useful anthology, *The Rhetoric of Blair, Campbell and Whately* (New York, 1968, p. 140). Campbell redefined the classical emphasis on purpose as the controlling element in discourse by identifying purposes with individual mental faculties. When the end is to "enlighten," the reason is addressed. The imagination is involved when the aim is to please, the passion when the aim is to move, and the will when the purpose is persuasion. Drawing on Bacon, Locke, and especially Hume, Smith, and Reid, Campbell conceived of communication as mirroring the reception of sensory input and the association of impressions through resemblance, contiguity, and cause and effect, with the will necessary to move the reason to action.

Campbell systematically reinterpreted each member of the trivium (grammar, logic, rhetoric) in terms of the scientific method. According to Howell, Campbell was a major proponent of inductive logic as well as the "new" rhetoric. Repudiating the syllogism as more concerned with linguistic vagaries than advancing knowledge of the world, Campbell represented induction as the natural method of reasoning from empirical inquiries to natural laws. While the epistemological orientation of Campbell's rhetoric is its most noted aspect, the chapters on how rhetors can accomplish their intended purposes in particular situations with specific audiences are incisive restatements of classical doctrines. Unfortunately, they are also among the shortest in the *Philosophy of Rhetoric.* Practicing the introspective method of the armchair empiricist, Campbell remains within his abstract model of the isolated mind and does not examine contemporary examples of judicial, forensic, and religious discourse. While Campbell's theories of rhetoric and logic have received the most attention, he made even more influential contributions to the study of grammar. Again, rivaled only by Priestley, Campbell was a leading eighteenth-century advocate for basing grammar on a systematic description of the conventions of the educated. He rejected speculations about universal grammars and redefined grammar as the study of current, national, and reputable usage—standards for assessing usage that retained their authority into the twentieth century. Most of *The Philosophy of Rhetoric* is devoted to "verbal criticism" concerned with giving "Law to Language" by generalizing from the conventions of the reading public to the principles that can be used to make language into a transparent medium for conveying the "vivacity" of sensory impressions.

The limitations of the epistemological perspective on rhetoric are most evident in how Campbell and his associates defined common sense in psychological terms as a natural faculty rather than as a sociological matter concerned with the shared beliefs of a particular group or era. Founded on the authority of nature, common sense could be invoked to treat any challenge to the status quo as non sense. Campbell's *Philosophy of Rhetoric* has been criticized for helping to institutionalize the commonsense realism that became prevalent in nineteenth-century education in America, and in Europe too, with the reaction against the French Revolution. Priestley, on the other hand, was one of the first to criticize Scottish moral philosophers for representing common sense as a natural faculty. As a Dissenter he did not want to see established conventions given a natural authority, and as an unmitigated empir-

icist he refused to put any phenomenon beyond the realm of scientific study. This debate over common sense underlines the broader limitations of the epistemological turn in eighteenth-century rhetoric. As provincials who had consciously taught themselves English taste and usage, Scottish moral philosophers and rhetoricians had a dialectical awareness of differences in cultural conventions, and the Enlightenment consequently took on a more sociological orientation in Scotland than in England. However, the "science of man" provided a universal foundation and disinterested methodology for containing the awareness of cultural differences that expanded as Britain became an empire and English a world language.

Civic Rhetoric. While the psychological orientation of the "new" rhetoric is its best-known contribution to modern rhetoric, less attention has been paid to how the turn toward epistemology departed from rhetoric's traditional continuities with the civic concerns of moral philosophy. In his *Inquiry into Human Understanding* (1751), Hume defined moral philosophy as "the science of human nature" to distinguish his approach from those who, in treating "man chiefly as born for action," had enlisted the art of "eloquence" to move audiences with scenes of "common life." Hume taught readers to turn inward and apply a "microscope" to the workings of their own minds (Indianapolis, 1955, pp. 15–16, 74). Hume was referring to such moral philosophers as Francis Hutcheson, who had lectured eloquently on practical morality at the University of Glasgow while Smith was a student there. Scottish moral philosophy remained an eclectic discipline ranging across ethics, politics, economics, sociology, psychology, history, and law until the social sciences evolved out of it in the next century. The works of a figure such as Adam Smith on ethics, political economy, rhetoric, and literature are hard for us to understand as part of a unified project because we read them through the disciplinary developments that followed upon them. Students of the time, however, often studied rhetoric and moral philosophy together, with Cicero and Aristotle serving as classical authorities for both subjects. The introspective method of Hume and his successors marks a shift away from this broader focus on the practical affairs of public life, and this shift considerably diminished rhetorical theory's civic engagement with rhetorical practice.

Neoclassical rhetoricians provided civic justifications for rhetorical studies, and Blair and other "new" rhetoricians often reiterated such justifications in their introductions to position rhetoric and belles lettres as liberal arts of value to citizens. Yet the only significant rhetorician to develop a civic philosophy on rhetoric was John Witherspoon. After graduating alongside Blair at Edinburgh in 1739, Witherspoon became a spokesman for the Presbyterians who opposed the reinstitution of patronage. In 1768, he was convinced by Benjamin Rush to become president of Princeton University (founded 1746 in the British colony that became New Jersey). There, he lectured on two of the subjects that had gained prominence in Scottish educational reforms—moral philosophy and rhetoric. James Madison studied with him, and Alexander Hamilton and Thomas Jefferson pursued such studies under other Scottish college graduates. Witherspoon helped popularize Hutcheson's moral philosophy, which provided a practical synthesis of natural rights and civic duties that supported the rights of colonies and opposed slavery. Witherspoon's rhetoric course surveyed the classical art of public discourse, offering practical advice on composition, suggestions on improving taste, and commonsense doctrines opposed to the skepticism of Hume. Witherspoon touched on belletristic and epistemological issues, but he was far more historically significant as a practicing rhetorician than as a rhetorical theorist. While notes from his courses on rhetoric and moral philosophy were published posthumously in his *Works* and then in a separate joint edition in 1810, he had been politically active from his arrival in America. He preached independence, helped set up provincial assemblies to organize resistance, and became the only clergyman to sign America's Declaration of Independence (1776).

Eighteenth-Century Rhetorical Practices. In his lectures at Princeton, Witherspoon paused to wonder why historians of rhetoric had concentrated on "teachers of that art" and largely ignored "its progress and effects" as a practical political art (1990, p. 254). The political rhetoric of the eighteenth century was in fact far more his-

torically important than the works thus far discussed, and those works themselves cannot be adequately understood as rhetorics when they are read only as philosophies of language. The traditional way to develop a more rhetorical stance on the history of rhetoric is to examine the philosophical and educational sources that influenced political orators and writers. The eighteenth century presents rich possibilities for such biographical research and rhetorical analysis of civic discourse. But eighteenth-century rhetorical theory is itself a form of discursive practice that needs to be read rhetorically, rather than simply as part of the history of ideas about rhetoric. The translation of rhetoric into a modern discipline was a highly rhetorical process. That process was integrally involved with the transformation of the public sphere by cheap print literacy, which offered access to groups who had had few opportunities to speak or write in public, and fewer still to theorize about the arts involved in doing so.

The expansion of print created a need to assimilate readers who a generation earlier would not have had been able to purchase books or read cosmopolitan periodicals. In the eighteenth century, print became more than a technology for reproducing texts, it became an economy for the circulation of knowledge. That economy transformed public institutions ranging from provincial colleges to the British post office, which began mailing newspapers free of charge to the provinces in 1787, with some four-and-half million being shipped annually from London by 1790. Just as authorship was expanding to new classes of people, belletrists subordinated production to reception in order to teach provincials how to read with tasteful self-restraint, and rhetoric was thereby reoriented from sites of political conflict to the logic of a well-ordered mind. The "science of man" is usually cited as a philosophy of ideas shared by theorists such as Blair and Campbell, but introspection was more than an idea, it was a rhetorical practice. When readers were invited to perform mental experiments on themselves to assess claims made by Hume and like-minded philosophers and rhetoricians, introspection quickly became introjection as accounts of how a literate person thinks, responds, and reads became internalized as how one ought to think, respond, and read. This process helped formalize and instill a modern individualized *ēthos* as part of the economy of print, as has been discussed in Michel Foucault's *Les mots et les choses* (The Order of Things 1966/1970) and Jurgen Habermas's *Strukturwandel der öffentlichkeit* (The Structural Transformation of the Public Sphere 1962/1989).

While they were studiously ignored in the rhetorical theory of their time, some of the most powerful speeches ever delivered in English were remapping the world on the floor of the British Commons. Eighteenth-century commentators could not find modern models of political eloquence, though they wrote in the era of Edmund Burke, Charles James Fox, William Pitt the Younger, and Richard Sheridan (the son of the elocutionist). Histories such as Oliver's *The Influence of Rhetoric in the Shaping of Great Britain* (1986) follow in a long tradition of characterizing the era of empire as a golden age of oratory. British Parliamentary orators first were canonized in 1852 in *Essays from Select British Eloquence* by Chauncey A. Goodrich, professor of rhetoric at Yale from 1817 to 1839. Goodrich's popular commentary on the civic arts of deliberative and forensic discourse established modes of rhetorical criticism that were only supplanted by the resurgence of research on rhetoric among American scholars of speech a century later. (To further that research, Goodrich's *Essays* was reprinted as the first volume in Southern Illinois University Press's Landmarks in Rhetoric and Public Address series, which has provided almost the only twentieth-century editions of eighteenth-century rhetorics.) Goodrich represented Parliamentary orators as citizens of practical wisdom, with Burke the greatest of British civic orators. As an Irishman of English letters, Burke exemplifies how outsiders can sometimes apprise the workings of a culture better than those raised within it. Coming from the first land to be savaged by the British Empire, Burke had a dialectical perspective on British politics and tastes, as is evident in the way he could mimic an English lord so well that his satire of Lord Bolingbroke in *A Vindication of Natural Society* (1756) was read as arguing for the primitive virtues that he was ridiculing.

Traditional rhetorical criticism has concentrated on how individuals used the rhetorical arts to shape history, rather than on how history itself shaped those arts and so determined what could be said and who could say it. Pivotal periods in the history of rhetoric such as the eighteenth century take on new meaning, particularly when they are read from the margins where one may attend to the historical experiences of groups positioned at the periphery of the dominant culture. Women began writing for the press and claiming the right to speak in public in unprecedented numbers in the eighteenth century. Following upon Margaret Fox's *Women's Speaking Justified, Proved and Allowed by the Scriptures* (1666) and Mary Astell's *A Serious Proposal to the Ladies, Part II* (1697), women argued for more access to education and through it to public life by drawing on Dissenting traditions and prevailing assumptions that women had refined characters suited to polite studies. An influential example of a woman who gained her independence by writing for the press was Mary Wollstonecraft. Before gaining notoriety for her responses to Burke in *A Vindication of the Rights of Men* (1790) and *A Vindication of the Rights of Woman* (1792), Wollstonecraft taught school and wrote essays of self-improvement and conduct manuals such as *Thoughts on the Education of Daughters* (1787). As noted above, when Wollstonecraft published an elocutionary textbook on the art of public speaking, she felt the need to represent herself as a man. As a minor elocutionist and major rhetor, Wollstonecraft is the sort of figure who will become central to our understanding of the history of rhetoric once it is expanded beyond philosophies of rhetoric to examine the rhetorical practices that oppressed groups used to speak against prevailing conventions. [*See* Feminist rhetoric.]

BIBLIOGRAPHY

Bender, John, and David E. Wellbery. "Rhetoricality: On the Modernist Return of Rhetoric." In *The Ends of Rhetoric: History, Theory, and Practice,* edited by John Bender and David E. Wellbery, pp. 3–39. Stanford, Calif., 1990. Bender and Wellbery argue that the Enlightenment brought an end to a classical sense of rhetoric by setting the transparency and neutrality of scientific discourse in opposition to the subjectivity of literature, representing the public in terms of liberal political economy, replacing oratory with print as the model of communication, and making national languages the domain of educated culture.

Blair, Hugh. *Lectures on Rhetoric and Belles Lettres.* 2 vols. Edinburgh, 1783, edited by Harold F. Harding, Carbondale, Ill., 1965. This complete facsimile edition from Southern Illinois University's Landmarks in Rhetoric and Public Address series is out of print, but an abridged edition is currently being prepared for Southern Illinois by Linda Ferreira Buckley and S. Michael Halloran.

Campbell, George. *The Philosophy of Rhetoric.* Edinburgh, 1776: Edited by Lloyd Bitzer, rev. ed. Carbondale, Ill., 1988. Bitzer's introduction insightfully examines Campbell's philosophical sources and historical context. Bitzer's introduction and Vincent Bevilacqua's introduction to his edition of Priestley's *Lectures on Oratory and Criticism* (Carbondale, Ill., 1965) are still useful, though both volumes are out of print.

Conley, Thomas M. *Rhetoric in the European Tradition.* New York, 1990; reprinted Chicago, 1993. Providing a much needed international perspective that includes many less well-known Continental works, Conley moves beyond traditional histories of ideas about rhetoric to examine how rhetorical studies were affected by the rise of national literatures and the educational reforms that made them objects of formal study.

Crowley, Sharon. *The Methodical Memory.* Carbondale, Ill., 1990. Crowley incisively analyzes how eighteenth-century rhetoricians such as Campbell reinterpreted the composing process as the methodical representation of sensory impressions. Crowley maintains that the still tacitly accepted "current-traditional rhetoric is a direct descendant of the work of the British new rhetoricians" (p. 56).

Eighteenth-Century British and Continental Rhetoric and Elocution. Ann Arbor, 1953. These sixteen microfilm reels contain 143 works on rhetoric, enabling scholars to read past the few widely available eighteenth-century rhetorics.

Halloran, S. Michael. "Rhetoric in the American College Curriculum: The Decline of Public Discourse." *Pretext* 3 (1982): pp. 245–269. Halloran's essay examines the transition from civic to belletristic rhetorics after the American Revolution.

Horner, Winifred Bryan, and Kerri Morris Barton. "The Eighteenth Century." In *The Present State of Scholarship in Historical and Contemporary Rhetoric,* edited by Winifred Bryan Horner, pp. 117–151. Revised edition. Columbia, Mo., 1990. Horner and Barton survey the major trends in British rhetoric and provide a still useful bibliography of research on rhetoric in English.

Howell, Wilbur Samuel. *Eighteenth-Century British Logic and Rhetoric.* Princeton, 1971. Currently out of print, Howell's account is the most comprehensive analysis of eighteenth-century developments in rhetoric

and logic in the English-speaking world, though his historiographical assumptions can no longer be sustained with the certainty with which he advanced them.

Kennedy, George A. *Classical Rhetoric and Its Christian and Secular Tradition from Ancient to Modern Times.* Rev. ed. Chapel Hill, N.C., 1999. Kennedy has revised his survey of classical rhetoric's lasting influence to expand his concluding comments on contemporary rhetorical studies. He has also revised his chapter on the eighteenth century to take account of recent scholarship.

Michael, Ian. *The Teaching of English: From the Sixteenth Century to 1870.* Cambridge, U. K., 1987. Michael provides a richly detailed history of the works and trends that introduced English composition, rhetoric, and literature into the British schools.

McIntosh, Carey. *The Evolution of English Prose, 1700–1800, Style, Politeness, and Print Culture.* Cambridge, U.K., 1998. McIntosh relates the development of theories of rhetoric to a detailed analysis of the influence of print on the standardization and gentrification of English syntax.

Miller, Thomas P. *The Formation of College English: Rhetoric and Belles Lettres in the British Cultural Provinces.* Pittsburgh, 1997. This is but one of several recent histories that treat eighteenth-century rhetoricians as the founders of college English studies, with the other most notable being Robert Crawford's *Devolving English Literature* (Oxford, 1992) and Franklin E. Court's *Institutionalizing English Literature: The Culture and Politics of Literary Study, 1750–1900* (Stanford, Calif., 1992).

Moran, Michael G., ed. *Eighteenth-Century British and American Rhetorics and Rhetoricians.* Westport, Conn., 1994. This volume provides short biographies, critical commentaries, and bibliographies for thirty-four figures, including not only some less known British rhetoricians such as John Henley but also three French rhetoricians influential in Britain (Fénelon, Faucheur, and Rollin).

Smith, Adam. *Lectures on Rhetoric and Belles Lettres,* edited by J. C. Bryce. *Glasgow Edition of the Works and Correspondence of Adam Smith.* New York, 1983. This volume maintains the high editorial standards of Smith's *Works,* which were actually published by Oxford University Press. Bryce's introduction is complemented by the more wide-ranging discussion of Smith's social context in John Lothian's introduction to the out-of-print Southern Illinois University edition of Smith's *Lectures* (1963).

Ulman, H. Lewis. *Things, Thoughts, Words and Actions, The Problem of Language in Late Eighteenth-Century British Rhetorical Theory.* Carbondale, Ill., 1994. Ulman examines how contemporary philosophies of epistemology and language influenced Blair, Campbell, and the other major British rhetoricians.

Vico, Giambattista. *On the Study Methods of Our Time.* Indianapolis, 1965. Vico's writings have generated considerable scholarly interest, including a journal, *New Vico Studies,* and such books as Michael Mooney's *Vico in the Tradition of Rhetoric* (Princeton, c.1985) and Brian Vickers's *In Defence of Rhetoric* (Oxford, 1988), which has criticized Vico for sustaining the tropological tradition in rhetoric that has been revitalized by such contemporary theorists as Paul de Man.

Warnick, Barbara. *The Sixth Canon: Belletristic Rhetorical Theory and Its French Antecedent.* Columbia, S.C., 1993. Warnick provides a detailed account of the French sources of the belletristic emphasis on taste in British rhetoricians such as Hugh Blair.

Witherspoon, John Witherspoon. *Selected Writings,* edited by Thomas Miller. Carbondale, Ill., 1990. This volume reprints notes from Witherspoon's courses on rhetoric and moral philosophy, along with examples of his influential sermons and pamphlets. The introduction relates American educational reforms to trends in Scottish rhetoric and moral philosophy.

—THOMAS P. MILLER

ELEGY. *See* Eloquence; *and* Epideictic genre.

ELLIPSIS (Lat. *defectio*), which Puttenham (*The Arte of English Poesie,* 1589) calls "figure of default," is a subtractive metataxeme that deletes parts of sentences or clauses for the sake of economic brevity. It is used in public signs (e.g., No Smoking), military language, advertisements, as well as in poetry: "A sudden blow: the great wings beating still / Above the staggering girl, her thighs caressed / By the dark webs, her nape caught in his bill, / He holds her helpless breast upon his breast" (Yeats, *Leda and the Swan*). Its effect ranges from clearcut brevity to intended obscurity.

[*See also* Figures of speech; *and* Style.]

—ANDREA GRÜN-OESTERREICH

ELOCUTION. *See* Delivery; Eighteenth-century rhetoric; *and* Nineteenth-century rhetoric.

ELOQUENCE. Modern usage applies the concept of eloquence in various ways, at times with an implication of distrust, as if a choice had to be made between art and sincerity. But if we consider eloquence as one of the defining aims of formal oratory, as opposed to the aim of persuasion, then it will refer primarily to the artistic expression of a speech as opposed to its argumentation. [*See* Persuasion.] Artistic expression, however, is something more than mere style, and should not be limited to the embellishments of figures of speech or thought; instead, it may entail the expression of sophisticated thinking in simple language. [*See* Style.] Thus, eloquence may include invention, insofar as it adds depth and interest to themes that arise in the speech. [*See* Invention.] It would quite properly include expansion and digressions, and the commonplaces developed by ancient orators for general use. One preliminary restriction is that eloquence is not generally applied to literary texts, that is, to poetry or fiction, except when they are representing extended or formal speech.

Historical and Critical Outline: Classical Rhetoric. Did a concept of eloquence exist before the Latin word *eloquentia* was coined (first recorded in the second century BCE)? There is no single noun denoting artistic expression in any of the major Greek writers about rhetoric during the intellectual revolution late in the fourth century BCE and the ensuing antagonism between rhetoric and philosophy. Instead, each challenger, from the Sophist Gorgias (c.483–c.376 BCE) through Plato (c.428–c.347 BCE) to Gorgias's long-lived pupil Isocrates (436–338 BCE) and Aristotle (384–322 BCE), speaks with approval or disapproval of the magic or power of *logoi* (that is, speeches, but also arguments, propositions, and even words). [*See* Logos.]

Greek forerunners of "eloquence." Nonetheless the leading Greek thinkers all considered the art of expression from various points of view. As Jacqueline de Romilly comments in *Magic and Rhetoric in Ancient Greece* (Cambridge, Mass., 1975, p. 16), "in [Gorgias's] system the very meaning of the power of speech has been transformed . . . [by making explicit] the link between poetry and rhetoric, a link concerning both their aims and their means." Alongside persuasion, Gorgias stressed in his *Encomium of Helen* the almost incantatory power of *logos* to sway the soul, a form of deception achieved as much through rhythm, parallelism, and antithesis as through argument. This kind of *psychagōgia,* or mind-bending, provoked Plato's anger because Gorgias unashamedly boasted of being able to override the truth; hence Plato's initial denunciation of Gorgias and political rhetoric in the dialogue *Gorgias.* Later, in the *Phaedrus,* Plato touches on the art of expression in Socrates' review (*Phaedrus* 266–267) of early manuals of rhetoric. Yet none of the rhetorical handbooks or rubrics evoked, even Polus's "Artistic Collection of *Logoi,*" in any way resembles eloquence. Instead, Socrates proposes a rhetoric based on analysis of concepts and a new kind of *psychagōgia,* based on psychological selection of arguments to affect and persuade the audience. Only with Isocrates do we have a clear concern with the expression of the orator's thought. Readers will frequently see the word *eloquence* in the Loeb translation of his *On the Exchange* (354–353 BCE), yet Isocrates has no single word to denote the concept, except the all-purpose *logoi,* or a combination like "the power of / over *logoi*"; "using *logoi* beautifully"; or more significantly, "cleverness in using *logoi.*" This corresponds to the modern pejorative use of "eloquent" and "eloquence" to imply a display of art used to conceal or distort the facts. However, it would not be fair to ignore Isocrates' insistence on the need for philosophical content, for the combination of good thinking and good speaking (*On the Exchange* 308) that will recur in the Ciceronian tradition.

We come closer to a composite definition of eloquence in Isocrates' school brochure *Against the Sophists.* When he sets out his own ideals, he professes that he will teach his pupil (1) to speak in a manner worthy of his subject, and (2) to discover in it topics not explored by previous speakers. To these criteria of propriety of style and originality of treatment, he adds another kind of propriety, fitness for the occasion. [*See* Decorum.] But he comes closest to what we might associate with eloquence in promising to teach how "to adorn the speech appropriately with striking thoughts and clothe it in flowing and artistic diction, so that he will speak with more grace and charm than any other man" (*Against the Sophists* 16–17). The chief element missing from this ac-

count is affect, the emotion in the speaker that will produce emotional response in the hearer. [*See* Pathos.]

Of the three canonical genres of rhetoric, judicial or forensic, political or deliberative, and epideictic or ceremonial, eloquence is undoubtedly most necessary and least suspect in epideictic, the genre of funeral eulogy and patriotic or courtly panegyric. [*See* Deliberative genre; Epideictic genre; Forensic genre; *and* Panegyric.] Isocrates' model encomium for the dead ruler Evagoras (374 BCE) opens with a careful argument that prose *logoi* can match the beauty and power of poetry, despite the greater charm of poetic form and freedom of diction and content allowed to poetry (*Evagoras* 5–12). But he goes further in his coda, claiming that a memorial in words, as a portrait of character, is better able to immortalize than statues, mere likenesses of the body, because a speech "adorning the subject in words" (*Evagoras* 73–76) can reach across distance and time and thus be known and imitated by far more people (Isocrates did not deliver his own speeches but wrote them primarily to be read or read aloud). Cicero will make the same claims for both poetry and oratory in his speech for the poet Archias, greatly admired and cited in the Renaissance.

Eloquence as a recognized ideal in and before Cicero. The Latin word *eloquentia* first appears in the second century BCE with the full rhetorical sense of personal skill in speaking. But it may already have been suspect. The anonymous author of the *Rhetorica ad Herennium* (after 86 BCE), avoids eloquence as a goal in his fourth book on style, preferring the more restrained values of elegance and distinction (4.17–18). He uses the word *eloquentia* only in citing the encomiastic commonplace that the achievements of the honorand "exceed the eloquence of all eulogists" (3.6.11).

In contrast, the early and derivative manual *De inventione* of the young Cicero (106–43 BCE), opens with reflections on "fluency in speaking and the pursuit of eloquence." In a kind of cultural reconstruction, he attributes the formation of civil society to the eloquence of a wise man. Similarly, Cicero will later gloss eloquence as "wisdom expressed with fluency" (*Partitiones oratoriae* 79). But although the Isocratean combination of eloquence and wisdom generated civilization, the combination itself points to the separate role of content and form. And because eloquence deals with form, Cicero can both hypothesize that it was discredited when depraved men abused it for the sake of wealth and power, and hymn the benefits conferred by eloquence on the speaker, his friends, and his country, provided it is accompanied by wisdom. The role of art is to enhance eloquence, and rhetoric itself is defined as "eloquence based on the rules of art" (*On Invention* 1.6., as translated by H. M. Hubbell). Yet, in a work that is in fact devoted to argumentation, this concept of eloquence is subordinated to the aim of persuasion and is left too broad for our needs: we must wait for the mature Cicero.

Two of Cicero's mature works define eloquence in the sense of artistic expression: the first and fullest treatment is spread over the three books of *De oratore* (55 BCE), then he returns to eloquence from a different starting point in *Orator* (46 BCE), his discussion of variation, propriety, and rhythmic enrichment of style. Four separate discussions in *De oratore* present cumulative aspects of eloquence: the education and intellectual equipment of the orator (Book 1), the achievement of artistry through imitation and the power of emotion in speaking (Book 2, 89–98 and 185–215), and the inherent and added adornments of a speech (Book 3).

In the preface to the whole work (1.17–19, cf 73), Cicero enumerates the general knowledge necessary if mere fluency of language is not to be ridiculous; besides literary culture, a knowledge of history and exemplary national heroes, of statutes and civil law, he will add the equivalent of moral and political philosophy. Even Antonius, who puts more weight on expressive power and claims that a good orator can borrow any knowledge as and when he needs it, gives the verdict that he had met many good speakers, but did not know any truly eloquent man (1.94).

Antonius's role is to provide a convincing outline of rules for invention, based on the Aristotelian system of "persuasive techniques" (*pisteis*). While factual argument and characterization have little to do with artistic eloquence, emotional power is, as Cicero recognizes, essential to effective speaking: indeed, Cicero does not see the elevated speech as possible without it. Antonius makes his point both through precepts and through personal memories. He demonstrates the effect on generations of Greek speakers of imitating master orators, recalling how his own former pupil Sulpicius benefited when he changed to using Crassus as his model.

On the use of emotional effect, Antonius shows how the orator, just like an actor, must experience the emotions which he wishes to convey and transfer to his audience. It will help him to feel and convey passion if he makes himself imagine the full circumstances he is presenting to provoke answering pity or anger. He illustrates this first from a key moment in the final appeal—his own moving evocation of the ruin of his once heroic client Aquilius. Then, in dialogue with Sulpicius, the two orators illustrate how Sulpicius moved the audience to easy indignation against a defendant accused of causing a riot, but Antonius, in defending him, was able to manipulate and reverse their emotions. He first conciliated them in his opening arguments, then exploited their indignation against the blunders of the defendant's enemy, so that once they were inclined favorably toward his client's actions, he could play on their sympathy and understanding. More than once, Cicero speaks of the crowd as the speaker's instrument upon which he must know how to play.

In the later *Orator,* Cicero illustrates this micromanagement of both negative and positive emotions from a famous speech of the Athenian orator-statesman Demosthenes (384–322 BCE), whom he and contemporary Greek critics saw as the most powerful and versatile of orators because of his command of emotional manipulation. Following both Plato and Aristotle, Cicero's spokesman outlines the major emotions, and the kind of arguments that will generate negative or positive emotions in given audiences. The truly eloquent man will be like the wise elder statesman in Virgil's famous simile of the uprising (*Aeneid* 1.148–153), who can control and calm the hearts of the unruly crowd by his words. Emotive power is as much an essential to artistic eloquence as to practical persuasion. The combined use of indignation, *pathos*, and timely humor, first recognized by Cicero, recur in the sixth book of Quintilian's *Institutio oratoria* between his outline of invention theory and his theory of style.

At the end of Book 2, Cicero's chief spokesman, Crassus, claims that Antonius has covered invention but not "the ornaments of speech and that excellence from which eloquence derived its name." *Eloquentia* and *elocutio,* the standard rhetorical term for expression (style), come from the same verb, to "speak out," or "express fully."

Book 3 of *Orator* offers the most varied and multiple approaches to the aesthetics of speech, call it eloquence, expression, or style, of any rhetorical treatise. These begin with a distinction between the different styles appropriate to oratory and tragic and comic drama, the spoken literary genres, adding the refinement of personal idiom which distinguishes orators and poets among themselves. Shifting approach, Cicero applies the criteria applied by Aristotle's pupil, the philosopher/critic Theophrastus (c.372–c.287 BCE), which require four virtues of a speech: clarity, correct use of language, appropriateness, and ornament. At least three of these criteria concern the expressive aspect of eloquence; but he pauses after covering the first two, as minimal prerequisites, to insist on the comprehensiveness of eloquence, which he describes as "one of the greatest virtues, . . . a power which encompasses the knowledge of things, and explains its thoughts and intentions so effectively that it can sway its listeners whichever way it inclines" (*De oratore* 3.55). Postponing the other two criteria, Cicero introduces an apparent digression. In a revision of the cultural retrospective in *De inventione,* he offers a history of rhetoric and philosophy in which the two arts of right thinking and right speaking were originally one (as taught by Homer's Phoenix in the *Iliad,* 9.439, and echoed by Isocrates), then were harmfully split apart by the denunciation of Socrates, so that philosophers withdrew from the amoral specialization of rhetoric by Sophists and their politician pupils. [*See* Sophists.] Cicero's aim is to reincorporate what he calls philosophy into the equipment of the orator, and enrich rhetoric both morally and aesthetically with ethical and psychological reflections (here they are seen as part of *elocutio,* a means to variety and dignity, not as a source of persuasive argument).

A new approach (3.96f) turns to the diffused idiom that pervades the body of a fine speech, like blood giving health and color; this section calls on other senses to illustrate the need to avoid ex-

cessive sweetness. Variety is needed in sound as in color and smell, to forestall excess and boredom.

Cicero has now demonstrated that expression can be distinctive without the formal embellishment of tropes and figures. After a section on applying analytical methods to both the practical rhetoric of public life and theoretical debate, Cicero's spokesman finally reaches Theophrastus' third and fourth requirements of propriety and ornament, which he discusses in reverse order. He divides adornment into (1) diction and the ornamental choice of individual words from special registers (archaic, poetic, coined), or of tropes such as metaphor and metonymy (3.149–172); (2) the ornamental use of rhythm, especially in sentence cadences (3.173–199); and (3) a summary listing of the obvious figures of speech (types of repetition, or *chiasmus*) and of thought (ways in which a speaker can replace a statement by other syntactical or speech forms—question, demand, wish, or threat 199–204). There is probably no fuller account of how a well-argued speech can be made truly eloquent in its expression. In other passages, and in his defense speech for the poet Archias, Cicero stresses the power of eloquence to make the absent vivid (our "evident" comes from *evidentia,* as "representation" comes from *re-praesentare*): eloquent words can convey a personality more vividly than a painting or statue, and may survive to eternity.

Cicero would return to the issue of expression in a final work, *Orator* (46 BCE), concerned to advocate his personal ideal of eloquence to a new generation that favored a plainer style. It is important to understand the novelty and outline the arguments of this treatise, because it had a great influence on Augustine's prescription of Christian eloquence. In it, Cicero tried to answer the criticism of a new purist group of orators whose war cry was Attic simplicity, and the doubts of his philosophical friend Brutus about the utility of clothing honest argument in fine expression. [*See* Atticist–Asianist controversy.] Brutus was probably unconvinced by the opening argument that there must be a perfect form of eloquence comparable to Platonic forms of the good, but it served Cicero's need to disclaim his recommendations as a mere reflection of his own successful style. Indeed, Cicero's own public eloquence had simplified and become less exuberant after 50 BCE.

Cicero moves from Plato's analogy of philosophy as exercise essential to mental health, arguing that no man can speak richly on important matters without philosophy (*Orator* 15); this richness or fullness (*copia*) of speech is his own ideal, which he maintains, even while acknowledging the need for at least three levels of style, and for modulation of style in response to the audience's mood and expectations (24). [*See* Copia.] This work describes a variety of styles, personal and generic, as used by philosophers, sophistic display speakers, and even historians, who normally wrote to be read, not for public performance: it is perhaps the first time a rhetorical critic has considered the kind of eloquence proper to a written prose genre. Cicero grants the name of *eloquent* only to the man who by his speech can achieve the three purposes of proving his argument, charming his audience, and swaying its emotions (69), and argues for a control of stylistic level determined by appropriateness. But while he conceives eloquence as a skilled blend of all three levels of speech, his ideal remains that of the grand speaker, because he claims only the man capable of the fullest level of speaking can also use the milder more balanced middle style and the austere plain style, which make useful contrast. In effect, two sections of this rather formal treatise present the ingredients he sees as necessary for eloquence; first come portraits of the three levels of style (75–90, 91–96, 97–100), and the kinds of ornament appropriate to each kind of speech, which culminates in his sketch of the "full, abundant, weighty and ornate speaker" commanding a volume and flow of eloquence. The second component is the long justification and survey of rhythm in prose speech (162–233). *Orator* breaks new ground in giving priority to the ears as well as the minds of the audience. Ideals of rhythm will change in the Middle Ages and thereafter, but the aural impact of preferred rhythms will always be a vital component of eloquence, and it is analyzed most carefully in this treatise.

Reactions against and for Cicero in the first century CE. Between the death of Cicero and the renewal of Ciceronianism by Quintilian, three new voices bear significantly on the development of eloquence. The first, however, seems to me purely negative; it was the teaching method called *declamation,* in which pupils were assigned a deliberative or judicial situation and set to compete and outdo each other in the originality and impact of their speeches. [*See* Declamation.] The drive for originality led to increasingly far-fetched and paradoxical argument, and the striving for effect manifested itself chiefly in the coining of drastic and pregnant apothegms or *sententiae.* The excerpts from declamations preserved by the elder Seneca (c.55 BCE–c.39 CE) reflect a mannerism that is the opposite of eloquence, distracting the hearer with abrupt shifts of thought and an indigestible concentration of figured utterance.

More constructive was the reaction of his son, the tragic poet and moralist Seneca (c.4 BCE–65 CE), best illustrated from his criticism of excessive eloquence in the fortieth of his *Moral Letters.* His friend has reported being overwhelmed by the torrential fluency of a Greek moralist. Philosophy is concerned with truth and with healing sick minds, its adornment should be simple and unaffected, so as to sink into the mind: "to soothe men's fears, dispel their delusions, restrain their self-indulgence and condemn their greed, philosophy should set its words down carefully, not hurl them out: it can sometimes soar, but not so as to detract from the speaker's dignity" (40.5, 7–8). The style of the Senecan diatribe, nagging at its worst, is the foundation of protreptic, and will be adopted and readopted by philosophical and religious preaching to come. The letters also contain an influential discussion of imitation practice, advocating that the speaker/writer form his style by reading and assimilating multiple models (*Letter* 84).

Best known of all Seneca's letters for its critical comment is Letter 114, whose point of departure is the assumption that in certain periods eloquence is corrupted, as intellects decline into faults, such as bloated or effeminate diction. It is, he argues, men's lifestyle that rots their verbal style, as Maecenas's poetry reflects his indulgence in luxury, and the prose of Sallust and his followers affects an abrupt and obscure compression. Just as a sickly mind will produce decadent behavior, a healthy mind manifests itself in healthy speech. Ironically, Seneca himself became a prize example of corrupt and corrupting eloquence for Quintilian in the next generation. With the loss of Quintilian's separate treatise "On the Causes For the Corruption of Eloquence" (*Io* 5.12.23, 6. preface 3), his strictures on Seneca in the *Institutio oratoria* (10.1.125–132) become the primary evidence for the reaction in taste.

The third advance in criticism is made in the treatise *On The Sublime* (now dated c.60 CE), by an unidentified author, Longinus, who proposes sublimity as a new goal for eloquence in writing or speech. [*See* Sublime, the.] The (partly damaged) text notes and illustrates five means by which this value can be attained; by speaking on exalted subject matter, by applying emotional power (*pathos*), by the application of figures, by the use of noble arguments, and of elevated and harmonious composition. Though this sophisticated treatise was to have a great effect on European literary values (perhaps more in poetry than in prose), the text was late in discovery and not published until 1554; scholars date its influence from the translation (1674) and critical comments (1694) of Nicolas Boileau-Despréaux (1636–1711), long after the Renaissance.

Quintilian (c.35–c.100 CE), was in his own time more teacher than orator, but upon the rediscovery of his work in the fifteenth century he became a powerful influence on Renaissance ideals of eloquence. Much of his teaching echoed Ciceronian principles. Indeed for Quintilian, Cicero was "the name not of a mere man but of eloquence itself" (10.1.116). At the beginning of his work, Quintilian sets out his expectations of eloquence and the relationship between imagination and emotive power: "a very great part of eloquence depends on the imagination: the speaker's heart must be moved and imagine events and adapt itself to the nature of what it is describing." Later he will introduce the concept of the mental image (*phantasia*, 6.2.31) to explain how the orator may induce in himself the emotions he wishes his listeners to experience.

But although Quintilian echoes Cicero in the traditional definition of eloquence as consisting of all five elements, invention, arrangement, style, memory and delivery (3.3.7), he too reserves *eloquentia* more precisely for excellence of expression. He devotes two whole books to tropes, figures, and rhythm, and another to enriching one's eloquence through imitation of admirable models, as much poetic and literary, as rhetorical. Only a long but late chapter in his final book (12.10) concerns itself with eloquence as personal idiom. Recapitulating his discussion, he offers the conclusion that "eloquence has many manifestations, but every form, provided that it is correct, has a proper use, and the very thing which is usually called style [*genus dicendi*] is not a single thing peculiar to the orator: rather he will use each style as required by the circumstances, not just for any given speech but for any given part of it" (12.10.69). Eloquence, then, depends on the appropriate selection among a variety of styles.

However, in this quasi-evolutionary survey we have passed over two ancient approaches to eloquence that are constantly renewed through the ancient theorists: the first was to stress the importance of delivery, a skill which did not lend itself to verbal illustration, but was reckoned by Demosthenes as the first, if not the sole, requirement for success in speaking, and by all who came after him, including Cicero and Quintilian. [*See* Delivery.]

The second approach was to advocate ideals of eloquence by distinguishing the proper style and deportment of the orator from other rejected manners. Cicero warned the would-be orator to avoid the language of poets: orators must communicate in language and with ideas and values that were already familiar to the audience; similarly, they must avoid the mimicry and gesture of actors, which could be either extravagant or vulgar. Already in Cicero's late years, and through to the age of Quintilian and Tacitus (c.56–c.120 CE), critics were using metaphors of physique, gender, and adornment to describe and proscribe style: younger critics found Cicero's style effeminate and broken backed, or bloated, or mincing and almost too soft for a real man; while Quintilian (12.10.12–14) calls the Attic purists "parched, sapless and bloodless." Other conservatives, such as Seneca the Elder, spoke of the perfumed curls and makeup of modern style.

Tacitus's modernist orator Aper in the *Dialogue on Great Orators*, develops the physiological metaphor in detail: "a speech, like a man's body, is only beautiful when the veins do not protrude and the bones cannot be counted, but good healthy blood fills the limbs and throbs in the muscles, while a ruddy glow and grace covers the sinews" (21). Yet, he wants his orator's eloquence equipped like a rich home with the glitter of gold and jewels, and the orator himself to be glossy with the fine grooming of his language (22, 23). His conservative antagonist Messala contrasts the honest hairshirt of early primitive speech with the curling tongs, the whorish dyed garments, and unmanly dress of modern oratory. Modern speakers do not even assume the deportment of man, but speak in a singsong and prance like stage performers (26).

Quintilian's own metaphorical model is more of a compromise: he wants the orator trained to have the muscle tone and endurance of a soldier, not the hypertrophy of a professional athlete (10.1.33). Although he deprecates the flashy and luxurious, he would encourage "the glamorous, lofty, lavishly equipped man at the top of the profession to control and command (a military image) his superabundant resources of eloquence . . . but his abundance should have a limit, without which nothing is praiseworthy or healthy, his gloss should come from manly grooming, and his inventive power show good judgment (12.10.79–80). All these analogies reflect the tension inherent between the desire to give eloquence full fling and the fear of absurdity and loss of manly dignity through excess.

Historical and Critical Outline: Christian Rhetoric—Augustine's Formulation of Christian Eloquence. The need for eloquence in moral protreptic was recognized by Cicero in his lost dialogue *Hortensius,* and both practiced and preached by the philosopher Seneca, as we have seen. Seneca himself acknowledges both the stylistic and moral influence of the Greek philosophers of the Sextian school and of Fabius Papirianus, whose works are now lost. But an important strand in the evolution of epideictic and protreptic oratory was woven by a quite different kind of Greek eloquence, the epideictic speeches usually called the Second Sophistic, of men from Greece and Greek Asia who displayed their eloquence as ambassadors for their cities, as lecturers to the educated adult public in Greece and at Rome, as authors of eulogies and of diatribes and essays intended for reading. Leading figures were Dio "Chrysostom" of Prusa (c.40–c.110 CE), Favori-

nus of Arles (85–155 CE), Polemon of Laodicea (88–144 CE), Lucian of Samosata in Syria (c.120–after 180 CE), who wrote mostly for readers, and Aelius Aristides (c.120–c.180 CE), the author of "Praises Dedicated to Rome." All these men aimed at a polished and flowery eloquence, whose influence on postclassical rhetoric was limited in impact by their relatively late rediscovery.

In Latin, however, leading Christian apologists trained in Ciceronian rhetoric employed a high level of eloquence in their sermons and treatises: the most important of these are the Africans Tertullian (c.160–c.220 CE) and Lactantius (c.240–c.320 CE). But only with Augustine (Aurelius Augustinus, 354–430 CE), another Roman from Africa, do we have a significant and lasting contribution to the history of eloquence. [*See* Homiletics.] A professional rhetorician and trained admirer of Cicero, Augustine was over thirty when he abandoned secular life as a teacher of rhetoric to devote himself to promoting Christianity. For forty years he educated his fellow Christians through sermons, letters, treatises, and finally a manual of Christian eloquence, "On Christian Teaching" (*De doctrina christiana*) in four books. Although the first three books up to 3.35 were composed around 397, Book 4 was only completed thirty years later. Like Cicero, Augustine begins by insisting that the preacher must know fully and understand what he is to teach, but this corpus is limited to the Holy Scriptures as Word of God. In considering invention, Augustine has to introduce a new hermeneutic principle, distinguishing between words and signs: thus, where the literal meaning of a biblical statement appears immoral or obscure, it is because the words of the text are only signs for something quite different, and reflect Scripture's need to speak differently to different implied audiences—a kind of propriety.

The most influential part of Augustine's treatises was to be the fourth book, in which he moves to consider the form in which the preacher should present the word of God. As a teacher of pagan rhetoric, the young Augustine had been alienated by the linguistic clumsiness of the Vulgate Bible, and its lack of eloquence (*Confessions* 3.5.9), but in his maturity he argues that the Christian speaker must not let the inelegance of the Vulgate blind him to its message, rather, he should use good Christian writers such as the

Apostle Paul or the Old Testament prophet Amos as his models.

He does, however, take over bodily the framework of Cicero's *Orator* and will work with the four Theophrastean virtues of speech, and the three functions of the orator, which determine by propriety the use of each of the three levels of style. Of the four virtues, clarity and appropriateness are obviously essential, and he will define the plain style simply by its merit of clarity. Appropriateness leads to a key distinction between what should be said to a popular audience, and what can be said in books or even conversations: for difficulties and obscurities can be discussed in conversations and explained in books. Here, "the speaker should not consider the eloquence of his teaching but the clarity of it" (4.23 translated by D. W. Robertson).

On the other hand, Christian teaching requires not just understanding, but consent and action: "when what is taught must be put into practice ... the eloquence of the discourse pleases in vain unless what is learned is implemented in action" (4.29, translation modified). As Kennedy puts it, the purpose of Christian eloquence is "to deepen understanding and convert belief into works" (1999, p. 180). However, Augustine is eager to use appropriate ornament in all three levels of style: the preacher will use each style as needed, speaking "in a subdued manner if he teaches, in a moderate manner if he is praising, and in a grand manner if he is moving an adverse mind to conversion" (4.38). He illustrates this dramatically from his own experience, describing how he set out to persuade the people of a Mauretanian city to abandon a ritualized custom of civil slaughter, and employed the grand style "to make them drive this entrenched evil from their hearts." This needed their active consent: so when they applauded him, he did not believe he had achieved anything until he actually made them weep (4.53). For Augustine, the function of eloquence is to persuade: the choice of style is determined by the best means of producing persuasion, and unless the orator persuades, "he has not attained the end of eloquence" (4.55). [*See* Religion.]

Medieval and Renaissance Eloquence. Throughout the Middle Ages, clerics still sought an artificially refined level of diction for oral preaching and controversy as well as for letter writing. The dictamen tradition of letter-writing manuals seems to arise first, starting around the mid-eleventh century with the *Flowers of Rhetoric* (on figures) and *Breviarium* (on rhythm and composition) of Alberic of Monte Cassino. Handbooks of preaching begin to appear in the twelfth century, and become increasingly abundant with the influence of the Franciscan and Dominican preaching orders from the thirteenth to fifteenth century.

Although formal eloquence was still restricted to Latin, Dante used Latin to make his powerful plea for a vernacular eloquence, a highest common denominator of language refined from the many local forms of Italian (*De vulgari eloquentia*, composed between 1304–1307). But his chief focus is on vernacular poetry: Only in the first book does he echo Ciceronian criteria for the superior form of language: that the language should be elevated, chosen for excellence, clearness, completeness, and polish, with power to sway the hearts of men so that the unwilling become willing (1.16,17), and dealing with high and worthy themes (2.1,2). Soon after him, Petrarch (1304–1374) developed his interest in classical eloquence at the Papal court in Avignon, where he found and copied a manuscript of Cicero's, *On Behalf of Archias*, with its praise of poetry, and of his *Letters to Atticus*. Petrarch collected and annotated Cicero, Livy, and St. Augustine, modeling his own Latin prose works on those of Saint Augustine (the *Secretum*, his dialogue of self-examination) and the moral works of Seneca. Petrarch sought eloquence in his prose writings (including the late *Familiar Letters* addressed to Cicero, Seneca, and other classical writers), as well as his epic poem *Africa*. The next generation could be represented by the chancellor of Florence, Coluccio Salutati (1331–1406), in his official correspondence and private sponsorship of the search for classical authors. Under his influence, the full text of Quintilian was discovered in 1416, and the complete texts of Cicero's *De oratore, Brutus*, and *Orator* in 1421: the last three were among the first books to be published in Italy (1465), while the popular drive for rhetorical skill also saw the first publication of *De inventione, Rhetorica ad Herennium*, and Quintilian in 1470.

The fifteenth century in Italy was dominated

by humanism, in which educated clerics functioned alike in church and state, and as both orators and scholars. For example, Leonardo Bruni, chancellor of Florence, published an oration in praise of that city in 1403, and translated Plato's *Gorgias* and *Phaedrus,* with other dialogues, and the speeches of Demosthenes and Aeschines *On the Crown.* Humanistic education was advanced by teachers such as Guarino at Verona (1374–1460) and Vittorino da Feltre (1378–1446) at Mantua, and by the six books of *Latin Elegancies* of the papal secretary Lorenzo Valla (1407–1457), instructing in correct grammar and usage. More than a grammar, Valla's monumental work was revered by others for the same reason he himself praised it: he claimed "the preservation of the Roman language" as a key to maintaining Italy's intellectual domination over Europe. The second half of the century saw a new, more sterile phase in the evolution of formal eloquence, with learned literary disputes over classical imitation as the basis of personal style. Thus, the poet-scholar Politian (1454–1494) famously refused to imitate Cicero, claiming that instead he expressed *himself.* Around 1512, Cardinal Pietro Bembo (1470–1547) and the young GianFrancesco Pico de la Mirandola exchanged fierce letters, the former defending and the latter attacking the faithful imitation of Ciceronian eloquence.

Literal imitation of Cicero, to the point of avoiding any word-form (not just word) not found in Cicero's works, was now being carried to extremes on both sides of the Alps. Hence, Desiderius Erasmus (c.1466–1536), educated at Deventer in the dialectical tradition of the Dutch humanist Rodolphus Agricola (1444–1485), and master of a flexible Latin eloquence based on many authors, mocks the Parisian Christophe de Longueil (1488–1522) as the addict Nosoponus in his dialogue *The Ciceronian.* His own spokesman naturally recommends a discriminating Erasmian eclecticism. Besides Erasmus's model *Colloquies,* his constantly expanded collection of *Adages,* and his manual of letter writing (*De conscribendis epistolis,* 1515), two of Erasmus's many contributions to the history of eloquence demand special attention. In 1511, he composed a handbook for his friend John Colet, founder of Saint Paul's School, London, which was widely used for over a century. This is his *On Two Kinds of Abundance in Word and Reference* (*De duplici copia verborum et rerum.* He argues in his preface that speakers as well as writers of Latin should be exhaustively well read and keep commonplace books; if they need to be concise, the same skills which enable them to amplify and expand their text will enable them to compress it to essentials. [*See* Commonplaces and commonplace books.] The first book shows how to expand a subject in words, through a variety of tropes and figures; the second, perhaps more significantly, how to expand content. Modeling his teaching on what the *Rhetorica ad Herennium* calls "refining" (*expolitio,* 4.54–57), Erasmus recommends achieving richness of subject matter by "assembling, explaining and amplifying arguments through the use of examples, comparisons, similarities and dissimilarities, opposites and other like procedures" (*Collected Works* 24.1.7 p. 301). Latin was still the required vehicle of formal speech, and this manual for schoolboys makes a virtue of variety as a source of fluency.

A very different and long postponed work was Erasmus's *Ecclesiastes: On the Art of Preaching* (1535). Erasmus aimed to provide a manual for those preaching in vernacular languages, and to take into account their need to address an audience that included both peasants and kings; the latter, despite their power, the preacher must somehow serve as father, teacher, and censor. The first book defines the role, echoing Cicero's demanding educational requirements and Augustine's concern with clear communication. The second and third books follow the precepts of the *Rhetorica ad Herennium,* on argument, expression, and performance. The last part of Book 3 and first part of Book 4 deal explicitly with Christian exegesis, the double meaning of tropes, like the body of the church and the major theological concepts to be taught. Erasmus frequently refers to Augustine's sermons and echoes his *De doctrina christiana* in its concern with biblical terms as signs. Erasmus's reaction to excessive and literal Ciceronianism was still Ciceronian in spirit, but a stronger reaction set in with the Jesuit preference for adapting the style of Seneca's diatribe to their own homilies. We might take as a turning point Nicholas Caussin's *Parallels of Sacred and Human Eloquence* (Paris, 1619). As Fumaroli (1980) demonstrates at length, seventeenth-century public eloquence had to steer a course between the would-be austerity of the Augustinian tradition and the secular pagan tastes of court and courtroom. Sacred rhetoric was already being infected by pagan practices in the time of Erasmus, when certain preachers called God "Jupiter Optimus Maximus," but the worldly nature of elite preaching would repeatedly lead to what has aptly been called sacred sophistic, a tendency that could only be fought by the reformist teaching of Philip Melanchthon (1497–1560) in Switzerland, or the preaching of the Jansenistes of Port-Royal, or again, the divines of the English Commonwealth and the new American Colonies.

[*See also* Classical rhetoric; *and overview articles on* Medieval rhetoric *and* Renaissance rhetoric.]

BIBLIOGRAPHY

Chief Original Texts Discussed: Editions with English Translation

Saint Augustine. *On Christian Doctrine / De doctrina christiana*. Translated by D. W. Robertson. Indianapolis, 1958.

[Cicero.] *Rhetorica ad Herennium*. Edited and translated by Harry Caplan. In *Cicero,* vol. 1. Cambridge, Mass., 1949.

Cicero. *De inventione*. Translated by H. M. Hubbell. In *Cicero,* vol. 2. Cambridge, Mass., 1954.

Cicero. *De oratore*. Translated by E. W. Sutton and H. Rackham, vols. 3 and 4. Cambridge, Mass., 1942.

Cicero. *Orator*. Translated by H. M. Hubbell, vol. 5. Cambridge, Mass., 1939.

Erasmus, Desiderius. *Foundations of the Abundant Style. (De copia). Collected Works of Erasmus,* vol. 24. Toronto, 1982.

Erasmus, Desiderius. *The Ciceronian / Ciceronianus. Collected Works of Erasmus,* vol. 28. Toronto, 1986.

Erasmus, Desiderius. *Ecclesiastes: On the Art of Preaching.* See modern studies.

Isocrates. *Antidosis/ On the Exchange, and Against the Sophists*, vol. 2. Edited by George Norlin. Cambridge, Mass., 1929.

Isocrates. *Evagoras*, vol. 3. Edited by George Norlin. Cambridge, Mass., 1945.

Quintilian. *On the Education of the Orator / Institutio oratoria*. Translated by H. E. Butler. 4 vols. London and Cambridge, Mass., 1920.

Seneca. *Moral Letters / Epistulae morales*. Translated by R. M. Gummere. 3 vols. Cambridge, Mass., 1917.

Tacitus. *Dialogus / Dialogue on Distinguished Orators*. Translated by W. Petersen and M. Winterbottom. Cambridge, Mass., 1980.

Modern Studies

Bowersock, G.W., ed. *Approaches to the Second Sophistic.* University Park, Pa., 1974. Five essays on the Greek epideictic orators and lecturers of the second century CE, with bibliography.

Brown, Peter. *Augustine of Hippo: A Biography.* Berkeley, 1969. The best account to date of Augustine's life and work.

Burke, Peter. *The Italian Renaissance: Culture and Society.* Princeton, 1987. Study contextualizing spoken and written eloquence in the world of patronage and visual culture. Revised edition of *Culture and Society in Renaissance Italy, 1440–1520.* London, 1972.

Caplan, Harry. "The Decline of Eloquence at Rome in the First Century A.D." In *Of Eloquence: Studies in Ancient and Medieval Rhetoric.* Edited by Anne North and Helen King. Ithaca, N.Y., 1970.

Chomarat, Jacques. Introduction. In *Erasmus: Ecclesiastes, Erasmi opera omnia,* vol. 5. Amsterdam, 1991. Introduction is in French, edition is in Latin.

Fumaroli, Marc. *L'age d'eloquence.* Geneva, 1980. Exhaustive study of the development of eloquence, especially preaching, from the Renaissance to seventeenth century France.

Gray, Hanna H. "Renaissance Humanism: The Pursuit of Eloquence." *Journal of the History of Ideas* 24 (1963). Reprinted in *Renaissance Essays.* Edited by P.O. Kristeller and Philip P. Weiner, pp. 192–216. New York, 1968.

Kennedy, George. *The Art of Rhetoric in the Roman World, 300 B.C.–A.D. 300.* Princeton, 1972. The fullest history of rhetoric in oratory, literary prose, and poetry at Rome.

Kennedy, George. *Classical Rhetoric and its Christian and Secular Tradition from Ancient to Modern Times.* 2d ed., Chapel Hill, N.C., 1999. Unique continuous survey from Greece and Rome through medieval and Renaissance eloquence to the present day.

Kleinhans, Robert G. "Ecclesiastes sive de ratione concionandi." In *Modern Essays on the works of Erasmus.* Edited by D. L. De Molen, pp. 253–267. New Haven, 1978. See Chomarat (1991) above: critical outline of Erasmus's untranslated manual of preaching.

Kristeller, P. O. *Renaissance Thought; The Classic, Scholastic, and Humanistic Strains.* New York, 1961. Essays on the fusion of pagan and Christian thought in the Italian Renaissance.

Leeman, Anton. *Orationis ratio: The stylistic Theories and Practice of the Roman Orators, Historians and Philosophers.* 2 vols. Amsterdam, 1963. Unlike Kennedy's *Art of Rhetoric* in its focus on stylistics, illustrated by abundant quotation.

Murphy J. J., ed. *Renaissance Eloquence; Studies in the Theory and Practice of Renaissance Rhetoric.* Berkeley,

1983. Useful collection of specialist essays by multiple authors.

O Malley, J. J. *Praise and Blame in Renaissance Rome: Rhetoric, Doctrine and Reform in the Sacred Orators of the Papal Court, 1450–1521.* Durham, N.C., 1988. A vindication of the integrity of high Renaissance preaching.

Siegel, Jerrold. *Rhetoric and Philosophy in Renaissance Humanism: the Union of Eloquence and Wisdom, Petrarch to Valla.* Princeton, 1968. On the Italian revival of Ciceronian rhetorical ideals.

Weiss, Roberto. *The Spread of Italian Humanism.* London, 1964. Survey of the impact on Italian orators and writers of rediscovering classical eloquence.

Vickers, Brian, ed. *Rhetoric Revalued.* Binghampton, N.Y., 1981. Collection of multiauthored papers covering major periods and genres in the history of Rhetoric.

Vickers, Brian. *In Defense of Rhetoric.* Oxford, 1988. A strong personal version of the continuing conflict between rhetoric and philosophy.

— ELAINE FANTHAM

ENALLAGĒ (Lat. *permutatio*), called "Figure of exchange" by Puttenham (*The Arte of English Poesie,* 1589), a figure of syntactic substitution that replaces a grammatical form (person, case, gender, number, tense) by a deviant or ungrammatical one. Of person: "I *takes* my Friday with me" (Defoe, *Robinson Crusoe,* 1719). Of number: "Equality of domestic power / *Breed* scrupulous faction" (Shakespeare, *Antony and Cleopatra,* 1.3.47). In narrative texts, a substitution of the past tense by the present tense (*praesens historicum*) takes place, when the intended effect is a vivid representation (*enargeia*). Not merely a solecism or a grammatical mistake, *enallagē* is employed with a functional intentionality, which gives it the status of a rhetorical figure.

[*See also* Figures of speech; *and* Style.]

— HEINRICH F. PLETT

ENARGEIA. *See* Art; Descriptio; Enallagē; History; Law; *and* Style.

ENTHYMEME. From rhetoric's emergence as an art during the fifth and fourth centuries BCE, its central preoccupation has been persuasion, the process through which human beings are induced by symbols to adhere to certain attitudes and opinions and to decide on particular courses of action. The proper *means* of persuasion has been a matter of inquiry and controversy ever since. The Sophists of Sicily (Corax and Tisias of Syracuse, Gorgias of Leontini) and later of Athens (Gorgias, Protagoras of Abdera, Thrasymachus of Chalcedon, Prodicus of Ceos, and others who lived and taught in Athens during the fifth century) were the first teachers of the art. In their practical instruction, they emphasized appeals to common belief, argument from probability, and the arousal of audience emotion. Plato (c.428–c.347 BCE), the great Athenian philosopher, ostensibly followed the intellectual preferences of his teacher Socrates and rejected both the Sophists' reliance on opinion and the idea that probabilities can yield genuine knowledge about practical matters. Accordingly, he stressed the centrality in a "true art" of rhetoric of rigorous deductive argument grounded in the absolute and unchanging nature of things. Aristotle (384–322 BCE), whose *Rhetoric* is the first systematic treatise on the speaker's art, sought to bridge the gap between these two orientations by bringing the rigor of deductive logic to bear on matters that by their very nature are probabilistic and mutable. The key link in this bridge is his concept of *enthymeme.*

The nature of this concept has long been central—and controversial—in discussions of Aristotle's theory of persuasion, and thus, of his view of rhetoric. Interest in the enthymeme flows not so much from the proportion of his treatise directly addressing the subject as from the fundamental place he gives it in the speaker's art. My present aim is to explain Aristotle's conception of the enthymeme and to illuminate briefly its impact on the theory and practice of argument since the classical era.

"Since we are most strongly convinced," Aristotle writes, "when we suppose anything to have been demonstrated," and since "proof is a sort of demonstration," the principal concern of the speaker's art is with proofs. "Rhetorical demonstration," he observes, "is an enthymeme, which, generally speaking, is the strongest of rhetorical proofs" (*Rhetoric,* section 1355a). Indeed, it is "the body of proof" (1354a). To grasp how Aristotle conceives the enthymeme, consequently, is to understand in great part how he views the nature and function of rhetoric.

Aristotle opens his treatise by stating that "rhetoric is a counterpart (*antistrophos*) to dialectic." The form of reasoning proper to dialectic is the *syllogism,* "an argument which, certain things being laid down, something other than these necessarily comes about through them" (*Topics* 100a). Now, the enthymeme is "a kind of syllogism" (*Rhetoric,* 1355a). Thus, in order to understand the enthymeme—the "rhetorical syllogism"—we must first see how Aristotle conceives the dialectical syllogism. Dialectic is for Aristotle the art of philosophical disputation. It is employed in examining problems of a general nature, basing proofs on opinions "held by everyone, or by the majority, or by the philosophers." It serves to critique propositions and arguments advanced in response to certain kinds of questions or problems, examples of which include the nature of the good, or the proposition that "one ought to do good to one's friends and harm to one's enemies," or the question, "Ought one to obey one's parents or the laws, if they disagree?" Such issues are examined dialectically by having one speaker state a thesis (for instance, that "pleasure is the only good"), followed by a second speaker who tries to refute the thesis. Arguments advanced on either side of the question can be either inductive or syllogistic. In the former instance, they proceed from many similar instances to a general conclusion, while in the latter, reasoning proceeds deductively from premises to a conclusion such that the conclusion follows necessarily from the terms of the premises. The syllogism, accordingly, follows a general structure of Major Premise, Minor Premise, (hence) Conclusion, where the Major Premise is a generally accepted belief or opinion (or is the result of a previous syllogism) and the Minor Premise a specific shared belief or observation about the subject under consideration. An example of a syllogism drawn from the study of ethics might look like this: "It is held by the wise that the good for a human being is something final and valued for itself alone" (Major Premise); "wealth is always valued for something beyond itself, that is, for what it can buy" (Minor Premise); "consequently, wealth cannot be the human good" (Conclusion). [*See* Dialectic; *and* Syllogism.]

Now, as a counterpart to the dialectical syllogism, the enthymeme follows this general structure. It is a form of deductive reasoning, in contrast to the example (*exemplum* or *paradeigma*), which is a rhetorical induction. [*See* Exemplum.] In addition to this formal similarity, both syllogisms and enthymemes are grounded in opinion. Just as "a syllogism is dialectical when drawn from generally accepted opinions," says Aristotle (*Topics* 100b), "so it is necessary for [rhetorical] proofs and speeches to be formed on the basis of common [beliefs]" (*Rhetoric* 1355a). Finally, both syllogisms and enthymemes can derive their premises from probabilities. [*See* Contingency and probability.] Along with these similarities, however, the enthymeme and the dialectical syllogism differ in several important respects.

The first contrast concerns their principal applications and objectives. Dialectical reasoning is typically applied to the critical examination of broad moral questions in an effort to discover propositions that can withstand refutation. Rhetoric, on the other hand, involves discovering the available means of persuasion, means of inducing a readiness to choose one course of action over another. Moreover, "since the persuasive is persuasive to someone," the speaker must form enthymemes from what seems true to the particular audience rather than to "all, or most, or the wisest" people. It is the audience in its particularity to which the rhetor must have recourse in constructing persuasive enthymemes, for these draw their premises from the common beliefs of the specific audience to be persuaded.

A second distinction between the dialectical syllogism and the enthymeme lies in the kinds of conclusions to which they are applied. Whereas the syllogism seeks to demonstrate an answer to general question (e.g., the nature of the good, or whether parents or the laws should be obeyed, if they disagree), the enthymeme—like rhetorical discourse generally—is applied to specific questions (i.e., whether a particular policy would be good or not, or whether a given individual was justified in disobeying the law). Accordingly, the enthymeme always deals with a particular issue, and in this respect is different from the dialectical syllogism.

The nature of the rhetorical audience sheds still more light on how enthymemes function as means of persuasion. Enthymemes are designed to provide proof in speeches to "the multitude," to people who "are unable to take into view a complex argument or to follow a lengthy chain of reasoning" (*Rhetoric* 1357a). The audience, because it is "untrained" in dialectical reasoning, can only follow lines of reasoning that are presented in a compressed form. An enthymematic argument is built on the tacit knowledge and beliefs an audience holds, and these are usually invoked only implicitly in the argument itself. Accordingly, one feature of the enthymeme is that "it is drawn from few premises," and that, "if one of these is known [by the audience], it does not have to be stated, since the hearer supplies it" (1357a). More broadly, enthymematic reasoning leaves unstated whatever premises the audience itself can be counted on to provide. Thus, the enthymeme is a deductive argument in which the audience itself helps construct the proofs by which it is persuaded. [*See* Tacit dimension, the.]

Imagine a public meeting at which an election will be held for the office of city treasurer. A citizen rises to speak: "I support Philopolis, for he is an honorable man and a wealthy one, and a lover of the city." This statement, for all its brevity, represents a rather complicated reasoning process in which most of the argument remains implicit. Such a proof can only work if the audience will provide the missing elements, and thereby both follow the reasoning and find it persuasive. The only explicit support for the barely articulated claim that Philopolis should be elected treasurer comes in the form of three attributions made about Philopolis. What remains unstated are the general propositions linking these attributions to the claim; and these propositions are precisely what the audience, out of its own beliefs, convictions, and opinions, must provide in order to complete the implicit chain of reasoning. If the dialectician were to elaborate the entire argument, he or she would trace three lines of deduction, each resting upon the particular audience's beliefs concerning the nature of honor and the relationship of trustworthiness to financial status and patriotism. All this remains tacit in the enthymematic argument. In order for the argument to be persuasive, the audience must invoke these tacit rationales from within itself. Moreover, it does not do so consciously and systematically; it does not mentally rehearse each of these lines of reasoning. Rather, each system of justification is invoked all at once, perhaps in the form of a

maxim: "The rich have no need to steal." The auditor knows just what the speaker means to suggest; he or she requires nothing more in the way of explanation.

This, then, is the fundamental character and operation of the enthymeme, insofar as we can discern its nature from Aristotle's treatment. Its function, following the general purpose of rhetoric, is to guide decision concerning "things about which we deliberate, but for which we have no systematic rules" (*Rhetoric* 1357a). For Aristotle, rhetorical persuasion generally, and enthymematic argument in particular, deals with practical decisions about legislative, forensic, and epideictic questions. The enthymeme, therefore, constitutes one form of practical reasoning, the process by which human beings reach decisions about what should and should not be done.

The rhetor's principal task, on this account, is to discover or invent enthymemes that will be persuasive to a given audience on a particular legislative, judicial, or epideictic issue. Thus does Aristotle's inventional system employ a system of topics (*topoi*) as the means of discovering premises and lines of reasoning for producing enthymemes that will be appropriate to each of the three types of public discourse.

Though subsequent writers on rhetoric and argumentation have sometimes ignored or misrepresented the concept, the enthymeme has been a persistent thread running through rhetorical doctrines since Aristotle made it the "body of proof," illustrating his continued impact on the development of rhetorical theory. Moreover, it continues to serve a useful heuristic purpose for both speakers and critics of speech. Aristotle's immediate successors, Theophrastus and the Peripatetic school of philosophy, and then the Stoics, appear not to have maintained the idea. The extant fragments of these writers, known to have written rhetorical treatises, reveal instead an interest in the logical subtleties of the syllogism. The influence of the Stoic philosopher Hermagoras (second century BCE) on the later Roman theorists of rhetoric, particularly Cicero and Quintilian, passed on a tendency to confuse the enthymeme and the syllogism. Both of these theorists deal with the enthymeme, but neither embraces a conception that is faithful to Aristotle's, and the subsequent influence of Cicero's early work *De inventione,* on medieval rhetorical doctrines transmitted this infidelity into the Middle Ages. Such early medieval writers as Fortunatianus and Cassiodorus conceive the enthymeme as an incomplete or "imperfect" syllogism, and St. Augustine's application of rhetoric to the art of preaching emphasized the use of the dialectical syllogism as the means of rhetorical demonstration.

The tendency to view the enthymeme as a truncated or broken syllogism persisted in the rhetorical treatises of the Renaissance and the Enlightenment. At the same time, the applicability of formal or syllogistic logic to reasoning about probabilities and moral questions has been challenged. In *The Philosophy of Rhetoric* (1776), for example, George Campbell describes the enthymeme as a deduction in which the "major proposition . . . is suppressed as obvious." He also attacks the syllogistic method of proof as "unnatural and prolix" when employed in the resolution of moral questions. More recently, some critics have challenged the concept of deduction itself as having no connection to the way people actually reason about practical and moral matters. Stephen Toulmin, for instance, devotes much of *The Uses of Argument* (1958) to his contention that the validity standards of formal, analytical argument have little relevance to our everyday reasoning. At the same time, he has sought to rehabilitate an informal mode of inference-making, in which common knowledge provides grounds for reaching conclusions from stated evidence.

The enthymeme continues to be useful as a heuristic tool for both speakers and critics. It directs attention to the beliefs, opinions, and attitudes of the addressed audience as sources of persuasion and as factors to be considered in the analysis and appraisal of rhetorical discourse. For all its antiquity, the enthymeme remains a useful concept in rhetorical theory.

[*See also* Classical rhetoric; *and* Logos.]

BIBLIOGRAPHY

Aristotle. *Nicomachean Ethics.* Translated by H. Rackham. Cambridge, Mass., 1934.
Aristotle. *Politics.* Translated by Benjamin Jowett. In *The Basic Works of Aristotle,* edited by Richard McKeon. New York, 1941.
Aristotle. *"Art" of Rhetoric.* Translated by John Henry Freese. Cambridge, Mass., 1932.
Aristotle. *On Rhetoric.* Translated by George A. Kennedy. Oxford, 1991.
Aristotle. *Topics.* Translated by W. A. Pickard-Cambridge. In *The Basic Works of Aristotle,* edited by Richard McKeon. New York, 1941.
Bitzer, Lloyd F. "Aristotle's Enthymeme Revisited." *Quarterly Journal of Speech* 45 (1959), pp. 399–408.
Conley, Thomas M. "The Enthymeme in Perspective." *Quarterly Journal of Speech* 70 (1984), pp. 168–187.
Cronkhite, Gary. "Enthymeme as Deductive Rhetorical Argument." *Western Speech* 30 (Spring 1966), pp. 129–134.
Gage, John T. *The Shape of Reason.* 2d ed. New York, 1991.
Gage, John T. "Towards a General Theory of the Enthymeme For Advanced Composition." In *Teaching Advanced Composition,* edited by Katherine H. Adams and John L. Adams, pp. 161–178. Portsmouth, N.H., 1991.
Harper, Nancy. "An Analytical Description of Aristotle's Enthymeme." *Central States Speech Journal* 24 (1973), pp. 304–309.
Lanigan, Richard L. "Enthymemes: The Rhetorical Species of Aristotle's Syllogism." *The Southern Speech Communication Journal* 39 (1974), pp. 207–222.
McBurney, James H. "The Place of the Enthymeme in Rhetorical Theory." *Speech Monographs* 3 (1936), pp. 49–74.
Miller, Arthur B., and John D. Bee. "Enthymemes: Body and Soul." *Philosophy and Rhetoric* 5 (1972), pp. 201–214.
Wiley, Earl W. "Enthymeme: The Idiom of Persuasion." *Quarterly Journal of Speech* 42 (1959), pp. 19–24.
—CHRISTOPHER LYLE JOHNSTONE

EPANALĒPSIS (Lat. *geminatio, resumptio*), which Puttenham (*The Arte of English Poesie,* 1589, p. 200) calls "Eccho sound," is the repetition of the beginning at the end, a figure *per adiectionem.* "Rejoice in the Lord alway: *and* again I say, Rejoice" (*Phil.* 4.4). A generic term, *epanalēpsis* encompasses the repetition of single words (*iteratio*) and of whole phrases (*repetitio*). When it comes at the beginning and end of a longer passage, it is termed *inclusio* (Arthur Quinn, *Figures of Speech,* Davis, Calif., 1993, p. 88). Although the sentence or paragraph structure would be potentially complete without it, epanalēpsis is introduced to rouse strong affections like love and hate and to add emphasis to a statement.

[*See also* Figures of speech.]

BIBLIOGRAPHY

Alsted, Johann Heinrich. *Encyclopaedia.* Herborn, 1630. Facsimile edition, 4 vols. Stuttgart, 1989.

— HEINER PETERS

EPANODOS (Lat. *reversio*) is an isomorpheme that repeats one or more words in a reverse way, "What's mine is yours, and what is yours is mine" (Shakespeare, *Measure for Measure* 5.1.537), thus creating a sort of mirror-symmetry, which often has a playful function. The combination of semantic *antithesis* with this reverse symmetry of word order is also called *antimetabolē.* "For hete of cold, for cold of hete, I dye" (Chaucer, *Troilus and Criseyde* 1.420). This may have a surprising, even paradoxical effect: "Fair is foul, and foul is fair" (Shakespeare, *Macbeth* 1.1.11).

[*See also* Antithesis; *and* Figures of speech.]

— ANDREA GRÜN-OESTERREICH

EPENTHESIS (Lat. *interpositio*), called by Thomas Wilson in *The Arte of Rhetoric* (1560) "interlacing in the middest," a metaplasm adding one or more letters to the middle of a word, such as "steaddifast" for "steadfast." A deviation (barbarism) from correct usage, such an "infix" (cf. Heinrich F. Plett, *Systematische Rhetorik,* Munich, 2000), can occur (or intrude) for a number of reasons, for example, when the pronunciation of a word is thereby facilitated ("cham*b*er" from Lat. *camera*) or when the meter requires an additional syllable. Though permitted in the latter case as poetic license, it is not usually favored by linguistic purists and lexicographers.

[*See also* Figures of speech.]

— HEINER PETERS

EPIDEICTIC GENRE. Ancient writers, beginning with Aristotle, identify three genres of rhetorical discourse: symbouleutic, dicanic, and epideictic (cf. e.g., Aristotle *Rhetoric* 1358a36–58b20; *Rhetorica ad Alexandrum* 1421b7; *Rhetorica ad Herennium* 1.2.2; Quintilian *Institutio oratoria* 3.3.14).

According to Aristotle (384–322 BCE), the first two of these genres have the most precisely-defined contexts, purposes, and audiences. Symbouleutic (or "Deliberative") rhetoric generally took place in a public, political assembly, such as the Athenian assembly or council, and sought to persuade its audience, the people of the city-state, to a particular future course of action, while dicanic (or "forensic") rhetoric was written to be delivered in the law courts and sought to convince a jury of the litigant's innocence or guilt regarding a past action (cf. *Rhetoric* 1358b1–20). [*See* Deliberative genre; *and* Forensic genre.] The third genre, epideictic (sometimes called "demonstrative"), however, was without a distinct or fixed setting; it mostly concerned the present, but might also invoke the past and the future (*Rhetoric* 1358b18–20); and this in turn left its audience less clearly defined. Aristotle refers to the recipient of this speech simply and noncomitally as "spectator" (*theōros; Rhetoric* 1358b6), whereas he denotes the audience of symbouleutic speech as the "assemblyman" (*ekklēsiastēs*), and of dicanic speech as the "juryman" (*dikastēs; Rhetoric* 1358b4–6).

The adjective *epideictic* comes from the Greek verb *epideiknumi,* which seems to have a nontechnical sense of "to reveal" or "to tell," and which occurs, for instance, in legal speeches to introduce witness speeches (e.g., the orator Lysias 1.22). But *epideiknumi* has also among its senses "to display" or "to show (off)," and display and performance are original and central to the aim of the genre of epideictic discourse. Following Aristotle, Greek and Roman authors state that epideictic rhetoric involves praise (Gk. *epainos*) or blame (Gk. *psogos*) (*Rhetoric* 1358b12–13, 27–28; *Herennium* 1.2.2, 3.6.10; Cicero *De inventione* 1.5.7; *Laudandi et vituperandi officium,* Quintilian *Institutio oratoria* 3.4.3). Quintilian (c.39–c.100 CE), the Roman rhetorician, later observes that praise and blame are present in every genre, but especially in epideixis (3.4.11). He goes on to note that there are some who offer other names for the discourse of praise and blame—"laudatory" (*laudativum*), "demonstrative" (*demonstrativum,* which most obviously refers to the Greek *epideiknumi*), "encomiastic" (*engkomiatikon*), and "epideictic" (*epideiktikon*) (3.4.12). The orator praises or censures actions, individuals, speeches, and qualities, drawing attention to external circumstances, physical attributes, and character and attributing characteristics that are not present (*Alexandrum* 1425b38 and *Herennium* 3.6.10).

The Greek and Latin rhetorical treatises and handbooks set out the methods of praise and blame in some detail. Epideictic discourse exemplifies rhetoric as a language of transformations—of old to new, of great to lowly, of familiar to unfamiliar, and vice versa (Isocrates 4.8; Plato *Phaedrus* 267a; Pseudo-Plutarch *Life of the Ten Orators* 838f). It involves amplification (*auxēsis* or *amplificatio*) of its subject where praise is concerned, or the diminution of what is notable and the amplification of what is disreputable where blame is concerned (*Alexandrum* 1425b39–40, 1426b13–22). [*See* Amplification.] The fourth-century BCE rhetorician Isocrates confirms this when he writes that people who wish to praise, exaggerate the number of good qualities displayed by their subject, while those who wish to blame, do exactly the opposite (Isocrates 11.4). Topics must be appropriate for praise or blame. Eulogy concerns what is just, lawful, expedient, noble, and easy to accomplish, while censure concerns the opposite qualities (*Alexandrum* 1425b40–26a4; 1426a8–9 with 1421b37–22a23). According to the author of the *Rhetorica ad Alexandrum* (fourth century BCE), to amplify or minimize topics, the orator should show that the subject being portrayed has been responsible for either many good or many bad results; or else he should introduce a previous judgment about his subject to help emphasize his own statement; or set similar things but of different grades—such as men of medium height and short men—side by side to highlight the qualities of the subject; or finally, establish the intentionality of the acts carried out by the subject (1426a32–26b13).

Aristotle, concerned with the psychological dimensions of rhetoric, declares that the audience member must be involved in the speech such that he thinks he himself, or his family, or actions, or some other aspect of his life, is being praised: so the philosopher notes that it is easy for the orator to praise the Athenians to the Athenians but not before the Spartans (*Rhetoric* 1451b28–32). The author of the *Rhetorica ad Herennium* sets out the importance of involving either the orator, the subject, or the audience in his introduction, such that the involvement is more widely distributed (3.6.11).

The epideictic genre formalizes the material to be dealt with by the orator and the order in which this material should be presented. Following Roman rhetoricians, where the praise of men is concerned, one offers a narrative of subject, dealing with the time before he lived, his life, and even the period after his life. The orator treats the subject's fatherland, parentage, and ancestry in order to show that he was noble or that he brought honor to a humble background. He should then deal with any prophecies concerning the subject's future accomplishments, such as the oracle concerning the heroism of Achilles. Where the subject's own life is concerned, the orator should describe his upbringing and education, his character, and his physical attributes, dividing the praise according to each of the subject's virtues—courage, justice, modesty, and so on, and account for his use of these qualities and attributes (*Herennium* 3.7.13–3.8.15; Quintilian 3.7.10–18). Quintilian adds that the orator might also on occasion treat the honors granted to his subject after his life to demonstrate his contribution to his community. Where blame is the aim of the speech, the orator does the exact opposite, showing that the subject has ignoble origins or disappointed noble ones, that his qualities have been neglected or that they are base, and that he has only acted to the detriment of his community.

These treatises describe the form of the epideictic speech on the basis of preexisting examples. The formal structure of the epideictic speech is already apparent in earlier Greek texts such as the *Encomium of Helen* by the fifth-century BCE Sophist Gorgias, ostensibly a defense of its subject but otherwise identified by scholars as an example of epideictic (Buchheit, 1960, pp. 27–38). Gorgias declares at the outset of the work that his subject was preeminent among men and women in birth and descent, and proceeds to relate her extraordinary beginnings from Leda and Tyndareus or Zeus (3–5). The remainder of the speech seeks to absolve Helen from criticism by attributing her departure from Troy to forces beyond her control, physical force, persuasion, or *erōs*. Isocrates' *Evagoras*, the first encomium to be written in prose (9.8–11), begins the eulogy proper with an account of the birth and ancestry of Evagoras (9.12–19), and then moves to his youth and qualities displayed in his youth (9.22–23), only after declaring that he will not treat oracles concerning Evagoras's career. Treatment of Evagoras's virtues (23–24), his accomplishments with emphasis on his moral and intellectual virtues (25–40), his concern to govern humanely (41–64), and his legacy (71–end) follow in turn, suggesting that the speech is a model of epideictic structure.

The style of epideictic rhetoric was distinctive. Gorgias (c.480–c.380 BCE), one of the innovators of epideictic, developed a style conspicuous for its balanced diction, its oppositions, and parallelisms, which was not necessarily confined to his encomiastic writings. [*See* Gorgianic figures.] Isocrates (436–338 BCE) laments that prose writers are deprived of poetic language, namely borrowings, coinages, and metaphors, which adorn their verse, and must instead employ current language and ideas relevant to the material. But the reader should be wary of his protestations, for the rhetorician still insists that he is bound to attempt a prose eulogy of his subject Evagoras (9.10–11). Aristotle declares the epideictic style as one that is most literary (*graphikotatē; Rhetoric* 1414aa18–19). Writing in the Roman period, Quintilian notes that this genre is one that admits of more ornamentation or figurality than others, and especially than dicanic oratory, inasmuch as it is composed to delight its audience (11.1.48).

The Values of Epideictic. The value of a genre that exists to praise and to blame is open to different views, even expressed by the same authors, and this has to do with the fluidity of the genre as one unattached to any particular discursive setting, audience, or indeed, function. Different authors attach the description of "display rhetoric" to different kinds of discourse, and attribute particular functions to it in acccordance with their different agendas, and from these uses of the term, it is possible to offer a sociology of the genre.

On the one hand, epideixis is seen as serving only to provide the audience with pleasure, and therefore as being without any utility. The Athenian historian Thucydides (c.465–c.400 BCE) contrasts his history, which is to stand as an eternal possesion (*ktēma te es aiei*) that has the potential to provide the community with a model for political behavior, with the ephemeral competition pieces produced by others (1.22.4). Later in the *History,* the new politician Cleon offers a criticism of Athens' public speakers, presenting oratory as something of a spectator event where the audience has become accustomed to watching speeches and hearing deeds such that they are now "slaves" of the unconventional (*atopoi*) and despisers of what is customary (3.38.4–5). The Athenians, according to Cleon, now resemble viewers of Sophistic contests won over by the pleasure of what they hear (3.38.7). Later in the Roman period, in Cicero's (106–43 BCE) *De oratore,* Antonius sees the genre as more suited for reading and entertainment than for public life, and associates it with delight (cf. *delectare*) (2.84.340; cf. *Orator* 11.37; 12.38; 12.42; 61.207–8 and Vickers, 1988, p. 57). In the *Orator,* Cicero characterizes epideictic speeches as entertainment pieces for the sake of pleasure (cf. *delectationis causa,* 11.37; *ad voluptatem aurium,* 12.38; 12.42; 61.207–8; also *Brutus* 12.47). Elsewhere, the author of the *Herennium* sees it as a form of speech that has entertainment as its purpose (4.23.32), and Quintilian writes that this genre is suited to please and aims at the audience's pleasure (3.4.6; 8.3.11; 10.1.28).

The nonutility of epideictic discourse may in large part be due to its association with the Sophists of ancient Greece, and to its performance among the social elite, who defined themselves as a leisured class. Cicero writes of the genre that it "belongs to the Sophists" (*proprium sophistarum*), and identifies the earliest authors of speeches of praise and blame as Thrasymachus of Calchedon, Gorgias of Leontini (cf. *Brutus* 12.47), Theodorus of Byzantium, whom Socrates refers to as a craftsman of words (*logodaidalos*) in the *Phaedrus* (266e4–5; cf. Cicero *Orator* 12.39, 13.42). These professional teachers are associated with speeches on paradoxical but useless topics (Pease, 1926). They praise bumblebees or salt, subjects that seem pointless and without purpose when the teacher of rhetoric might otherwise praise a ruler, as Isocrates does in the *Evagoras* or Xenophon in the *Agesilaos* (cf. Isocrates 10.12; Plato *Symposium* 177b1–c3). Elsewhere, in the preface to the *Helen,* Isocrates criticizes individuals who pass time on arguments that offer no benefit and trouble those in their proximity (1). The rhetorician goes on to speak of Protagoras and the Sophists contemporary with him—Gorgias, Zeno, and Melissus are named in the following section—who left behind "troublesome" compositions (2–3). If these sophistic teachers successfully demonstrated anything, it is the ease with which one may produce false speeches (4). Isocrates seems to allude to sophistic discourse and teaching also at *Antidosis* 269, where he refers to "useless" (literally "excessive") verbiage (*perittologia*), and at *Panathenaicus* 1, where he mentions "fiction" (*pseudologia*), which stand in contrast to *logos politikos* (Too, 1995, p. 30). [*See* Sophists.]

Epideictic speech, it would appear, forms the basis of the Sophist's curriculum. Scholars such as Kennedy (1959, pp. 169–170), Buchheit (1960, p. 39), Ober (1989, p. 48), and Cole (1991, p. 81) think that teachers used to give their students a written text, usually of an "epideictic" nature as a model to emulate. Thus, they consider Gorgias's *Helen* and *Palamedes,* Antisthenes' *Ajax* and *Odysseus,* Alcidamas's *Odysseus,* Antiphon's *Tetralogies,* and Isocrates' *Helen, Busiris,* and *Evagoras* as model speeches for students to learn by heart and to imitate when writing their own compositions. Indeed, Thomas Cole (1991, p. 78) argues, for instance, that Gorgias's *Helen,* as an encomium, should be viewed not just as a "toy" (*paignion,* cf. *Helen* 21) but also as an "educational toy," that is, as a teaching text. Cole (1991, p. 81; also see Too, 1995, pp. 164–171) also suggests that the sophistic epideixis might constitute the teacher's *technē,* a word that has among its senses "skill," "art," and "treatise," and furthermore, Cole notes that *technai* are credited to many classical Athenian teachers, among them Antiphon, Lysias, Theramenes, and Isocrates, and he proposes to view Isocrates' *Helen, Plataicus,* and *Archidamus* as examples of a rhetorician's epideictic *technai.*

In sophistic culture, epideixis also has an important role to play in seducing the student to enter into a pedagogical relation with the teacher, by offering a demonstration of the teacher's skill. Its rhetoric serves not so much as a discourse that instructs in virtue and its value (cf. Lysias 2.56), but as the professional teacher's advertisement, or promise, the literal *profession* of intellectual professionalism.

Socrates (469–399 BCE) reports that in his private capacity, Gorgias offered demonstrations (*epideixeis*) of his rhetorical skills and earned money for spending time teaching young men (Plato *Hippias Major* 282b4–9). In other dialogues, Plato (c.429–c.347 BCE) depicts this famous or, alternatively, notorious Sophist as someone always eager, and indeed too eager, to display his wares (*Gorgias* 447a–b). Then, Euthydemus and Dionysodorus, the Sophists of Plato's *Euthydemus,* are described as "advertising themselves" (273e5). In the *Protagoras,* the Sophist from Abdera presents his advertisement (*epangelma*) as a claim to be able to teach political skill, namely the art that makes men good citizens (319a4–7). According to Aristotle's *Rhetoric* (1402a23–25), Protagoras's advertisement consists in the promise of being able to make the weaker argument stronger.

The characterization of epideixis as a useless genre aimed at pleasure may be in large part due to the Sophists themselves, the professional teachers, who by and large come from outside of the city-state to prey on young men for the sake of their own economic advancement and who are regarded as contributing nothing to the community they enter. Socrates makes the point that, if the Sophist is a trader or shopkeeper who extols what he sells, namely the things that nurture the soul, then he also deceives and is after all no different from the trader or shopkeeper who purports to sell the things that nurture the body (*Hippias major* 313c–d). Aristotle speaks of the Sophist as an individual who makes money on the proceeds of an "apparent wisdom" rather than an actual one (*Sophistic Refutations* 165a22). In the *Nicomachean Ethics,* he describes the Sophists as doing none of the things that they say they will, referring to their "exaggerated promises," undoubtedly the substance of their epideictic displays (1164a27–29; also 1180b35, 1181a12; cf. also Plato *Euthydemus* 273d8–9 and 274a3–4).

The Politics of Epideixis. On the other hand, other writers attribute a pedagogical function to epideictic discourse that is quite distinct from its sophistic context, and in doing so, they have significant precedents. Epideixis as a mode of teaching has its origins in encomium prior to the systemization of rhetoric that begins with the Sophists. Pindar's (c.522–c.443 BCE) epinician poetry, which celebrated the victories of athletes and their patrons, is notable for offering a model for the literature of praise as a form of instruction. Typically, embedded within the epinician's structure of praise are mythical or narrative and moralistic teachings, which serve to warn the poem's addressee about the dangers, for example, of pride, ambition, impiety toward the gods, and which overall seek to maintain the victor's community as an orderly society in which each member knows his proper place and duties. The assumption is that the epinician articulates praise and a paradigm for the audience's behavior.

Later, Plato acknowledges that praise and blame are effective for educating the young and the old (cf. *Republic* 492b–c; *Protagoras* 326a; *Laws* 730bc; 801e–2a; 822d–3a; 829c–e; *Gorgias* 483b–c; also Nightingale, 1995, p. 105). Encomia of heroes and of the community's ancestors serve as models for imitation by the young, and this is the function that Isocrates sees for his eulogy of the deceased Cypriot king Evagoras (9.73–77). Aristotle acknowledges a distinct ethical dimension of praise and blame when he declares that the aim of this genre is to praise what is good (*to kalon*) and to blame what is base (*to aischron*) (*Rhetoric* 1358b28); however, Quintilian declares that both the philosopher and Theophrastus (c.372–287 BCE) removed it entirely from the realm of public and political life (3.7.1). Cicero reinforces the ethical program of epideictic speech, observing that it encourages men to virtue and draws them back from vice (*De oratore* 2.9.35), while elsewhere he observes that there can be no form of rhetoric that is more useful for city-states than one in which the orator is engaged in the recognition of virtues and vices, that is epideictic (*De partitione oratoria* 20.69; also 21.70). While affirming that the pleasure of the audience is the goal of epideictic discourse, Quintilian still attests to its usefulness when he affirms that panegyric, an example of the speech of praise and blame, treats what is useful for Greece (3.4.14). [*See* Panegyric.] Indeed, Isocrates' *Panegyricus* had treated the benefits of empire (*archē*) for Athens (4.20–128), and argues that loss of the *archē* is the beginning of the city-state's woes (4.119).

E. Buchner (1958, p. 7) has argued that the *epitaphios* or Funeral Oration is the most epideictic of the rhetorical genres as the commemoration and praise of the war dead; but beyond this, it is the form of epideictic speech that has the most apparent political agenda (Loraux, 1986; Ober, 1989, pp. 47–48). If the audience of the sophistic display is a private one, the audience of the Funeral Oration is the wider public, including citizens, women, and metics, rather than the narrower elite of display rhetoric. The nature of the audience determines that this rhetorical form is a particularly Athenian one, indeed, one where an Athenian praises other Athenians in an explicitly public context. Loraux observes (1986, pp. 42–44) that the Roman *laudatio funebris* or speech of praise at a funeral may borrow from its Greek model, but unlike its Attic counterpart, it is rather a celebration of an individual hero and his family in a private context.

There are six extant *epitaphioi* from the classical Greek period: the twenty-two lines of Gorgias's oration preserved in Dionysius of Halicarnassus; Pericles' Funeral Oration in Thucydides Book 2; Lysias 2; Plato's *Menexenus;* Demosthenes (Oration 6); and Hyperides (Oration 6) (Kennedy, 1963, pp. 154–155). Of these, the most celebrated is the Funeral Oration placed in the mouth of Pericles in Book 2 of Thucydides' *History,* and represented as being delivered at the end of the first year of the war, 431 BCE (2.35–46). The speaker presents the oration as a form of political instruction as he proposes his own role as a civic teacher when he declares that Athens does not require a Homer or any other poet who writes for delight, implying that as the city's appointed encomiast, he displaces society's traditional teachers (2.41.4; cf. Plato *Republic* 606e). Furthermore, he observes that the discourse provides Athens with a lesson (*didaskalia*) regarding the present struggle with Sparta (2.42.1); as the present eulogy of the recent war dead serves as a lesson in the recent past in order to provide instruction on how the Athenians are to deal with the progress of the war. Parents are told to *recall* and to celebrate the honor won by their sons and, if they are not too old, to have more children; sons and brothers are instructed to attempt to rival their deeds; widows are to *remember* female virtue and remain unnoticed (2.44.2–2.45.2).

Part of what the public assembly learns is that Athens itself is the "teacher" of all Greece as a city that serves as a model for other states and is emulously imitated by them (2.37.1 and 2.41.1). Pericles identifies Athens with skill and knowledge, but beyond this, he is also declaring the city-state's hegemonic status, for to be the teacher of Greece is a way of articulating the preeminent status of Athens in terms of military strength and culture. The speech offers an etiology of this power with a historical section that praises the audience's ancestors for their great courage in defending the city-state against its enemies, barbarian and nonbarbarian (2.36.2–4). History is a conventional feature of the *epitaphios,* and Lysias (c.445–380 BCE) offers a much more extended historical narrative in his Funeral Oration, dealing with a number of mythological *topoi* including the Amazons, the Seven against Thebes, and Heracles (2.4–16) and then, with major historical moments that attest to Athens' superiority, such as the victory at Marathon (20–26) and the defeat of Xerxes (27–43). In the Thucydidean oration, Pericles accounts for Athens' power, furthermore, by setting out the education, constitution, and character of the Athenians (2.36.4): education and character are also topics treated at sections 49–50 of Isocrates' *Panegyricus,* a speech often regarded as having affinities with the Funeral Oration (Buchner, 1958, p. 7; Too, 1995, pp. 80, 146–147). It presents the city-state as one in which the laws serve the interests of all (2.37), where cultural and religious institutions entertain the people (2.38), where training and education prepare people adequately for war without wearing them out as at Sparta (2.39). Athens is a city that loves beauty and philosophy (2.40.1) and that admits of *logos,* that is, speech and reason, before action such that calculation (cf. *eklogizesthai*) goes hand in hand with risk taking (e.g., 2.40.2–3).

Conclusion. Much more fluid and open to negotiation than its other counterparts, dicanic and symbouleutic oratory, epideictic is a form of oratory to be performed in private and elite settings (as with the sophistic "displays"), but also on large public occasions, above all, the commemoration of the war dead (as with the Funeral Oration). It is a form of oratory that either has no use because its concern is the pleasure of the audience, or else it performs a significant function as a means of inculcating a civic history and ideology in the masses.

Because it was never tied to a particular site of performance, the epideictic genre came into its own after the decline of the classical city-state.

After the fall of Athens, epideictic became the prominent form of oratory to the extent that it was imposed upon all other forms of discourse—poetry, history, and even philosophy—from the Hellenistic period onward, which sustained a highly rhetorical culture. Strategies of praise were formalized in school exercises known as *progymnasmata,* which become a mainstay of rhetorical education well into the Roman Empire (1956, pp. 268–269, 275–277; Kennedy, 1963, pp. 260–261). In the later imperial period, writers of the Second Sophistic, such as Lucian (117–c.180 CE; e.g., *Encomium of the Fly*), revived the sophistic paradoxical encomium to display their talents, while Christian writers, such as the fourth-century church historian Eusebius (e.g., praise of Paulinus, bishop of Tyre, *Ecclesiastical History* 10.4), also made use of epideictic as they adopted pagan rhetoric for their own ends.

Later, in the Middle Ages and the Renaissance, epideictic rhetoric came to eclipse the other two genres: all literature came to be subsumed under the category of praise and blame (Vickers, 1988, p. 54). In the Renaissance, the discourse of praise and blame made itself felt in different areas of literary culture. In the church, sermons sought to persuade their audiences to assume moral behavior through praise of virtue and censure of immoral activities (Vickers, 1988, p. 291); in drama, epideixis might be found in such passages as Mark Antony's funeral oration in Shakespeare's *Julius Caesar* (1599); in poetry, encomium was conspicuous in such works as Milton's *Ode on the Morning of Christ's Nativity* (1629) or Dryden's *A Song for Saint Cecilia's Day* (1687), and in poems written to praise one's mistress, or in invective, often mock, of such topics as love, while the sophistic mode of paradoxical encomium made a notable resurgence with a work such as Desiderius Erasmus's *The Praise of Folly* (1511), in which Folly offers praise of herself. [*See* Renaissance rhetoric, *article on* Rhetoric in Renaissance language and literature.]

Epideictic rhetoric is evident wherever there is praise or blame, and today it continues to make its presence known in such forms as political propaganda and in advertising, where the virtues of products are sold to audiences.

[*See also* Classical rhetoric; Epideictic genre; *and* Sophists.]

BIBLIOGRAPHY

Buchheit, V. *Untersuchungen zur Theorie des Genos Epideiktikon von Gorgias bis Aristoteles.* Munich, 1960. A standard study of the epideictic genre.

Buchner, E. *Der Panegyrikos des Isokrates. Eine historich-philologische Untersuchung.* Wiesbaden, Germany, 1958.

Burgess, T. C. *Epideictic Literature, Studies in Classical Philology,* vol. 3. Chicago, 1902.

Cole, T. *The Origins of Rhetoric in Ancient Greece.* Baltimore, 1991. A study that argues that "rhetoric" was invented by Plato.

Kennedy, G. "The Earliest Rhetorical Handbooks." *American Journal of Philology* 80 (1959), pp. 169–78.

Kennedy, G. *The Art of Persuasion in Greece.* Princeton, 1963. A standard but now outdated work on Greek rhetoric.

Loraux, N. *The Invention of Athens: The Funeral Oration in the Classical City.* Translated by A. Sheridan. Cambridge, Mass., 1986. A translation of *L' Invention d' Athènes: Histoire de l' oraison funèbre dans la "cité classique,"* a thorough study of funeral epideixis in classical Athens.

Marrou, H. I. *A History of Education in Antiquity,* translated by G. Lamb. New York, 1956.

Nightingale, A. W. *Genres in Dialogue: Plato and the Construction of Philosophy.* Cambridge, U.K., 1995.

Ober, J. *Mass and Elite in Democratic Athens: Rhetoric, Ideology and the Power of the People.* Princeton, 1989. A valuable study of the tensions between popular and elite interests in the politics of classics Athens.

Pease, A. S. "Things without Honour." *Classical Philology* 21 (1926), pp. 27–42.

Russell, D. *Greek Declamation.* Cambridge, U.K., 1983. Excellent survey of declamation in Greek oratory.

Too, Yun Lee. *The Rhetoric of Identity in Isocrates: Text, Power, Pedagogy.* Cambridge, U.K., 1995.

Vickers, B. *In Defence of Rhetoric.* Oxford, 1988. A magisterial defense of rhetoric as a mode of communication from antiquity to the present.

—YUN LEE TOO

EPIPHORA (Lat. *conversio*), which Puttenham (*The Arte of English Poesie,* 1589) calls "counter turn," an isomorpheme that repeats one or more words at the end of successive clauses, sentences, or verses. "When I was *a child,* I spake as *a child,* I understood as *a child,* I thought as *a child:* but when I became a man, I put away childish things" (*1 Cor.* 13.11). The prominent place at the end combined with the repetition strongly emphasizes the isomorpheme, thus focusing the recipient's attention. "I'll have *my bond!* Speak not against *my bond! /* I have sworn an oath that I will have *my bond"* (Shakespeare, *Merchant of Venice* 3.3.4–5).

[*See also* Epistrophē; *and* Figures of speech.]

—ANDREA GRÜN-OESTERREICH

EPISTOLARY RHETORIC. If epistolary rhetoric is defined as explicit instruction in the composition of letters, then it has very little recorded history before the Middle Ages. Among the ancient Latin rhetoricians whose works are preserved, only Julius Victor treated letters, in a brief appendix to his *Ars rhetorica* (fourth century CE), and that work had very limited influence. Ancient letter writers certainly received some kind of training, but if textbooks for that purpose once existed, they have long since been lost. More significant for the history of epistolary rhetoric was the implicit instruction provided by the great letter writers of antiquity. The letters of Seneca the Younger (c.4 BCE–65 CE), Pliny the Younger (c.61–c.113 CE), and above all Cicero (106–43 BCE) were the chief models for Renaissance humanists, whose epistolary rhetoric was defined in conscious opposition to that of the Middle Ages.

Medieval letters were viewed as belonging to formal rhetoric. The medieval art of letter writing (*ars dictaminis*) made this connection explicit by analyzing a letter's structure by analogy with the parts of a Ciceronian oration, by emphasizing its persuasive function within a hierarchical social context, and by prescribing rules for its language and style. Variation from structural and stylistic norms was kept within strict bounds: no premium was placed on originality or individuality, since both sender and recipient defined themselves as members of a social category or class and in terms of their relative ranks (superior, equal, or inferior). Letters often were read aloud in public, and even those that were not were composed as if they might be. A confidential message was more likely to be conveyed orally by the letter's bearer than by the written text, in part to prevent breaches of confidence due to a highly insecure system of transmission. [*See* Ars dictaminis.]

The paradigm shift that distinguishes modern from medieval epistolary rhetoric is in the conception of letters as primarily personal, informal, and private rather than official, formal, and public. This fundamental shift was complicated by other important changes in the form and function of letters and took place gradually, with vestiges of the older paradigm surviving to the present day. For the purposes of this overview, the developments in Western European and American epistolary rhetoric since the Middle Ages may be divided into three major historical stages: (1) the return to classical ideals in Renaissance humanism; (2) the "golden age" of letter writing in the seventeenth and eighteenth centuries; and (3) the age of technology from the nineteenth century to the present.

The first important step away from the medieval conception of the letter as a modified oration was the Renaissance humanists' return to the classical conception of the letter as, in Erasmus's words, a conversation between absent friends. The catalyst for this change was the rediscovery of Cicero's two letter collections, the *Epistolae ad Atticum*, by Petrarch in 1345, and the *Epistolae Familiares*, by Coluccio Salutati in 1392. As the chief models for humanist epistolography, Cicero's letters were invoked in support of a more "conversational" epistolary style purged of the "barbaric" medieval Latin of the *ars dictaminis*. In practice, however, the letter-writing treatises of the humanists retained much of their predecessors' prescriptiveness, substituting Cicero's letters for the model letters composed by medieval teachers while regulating epistolary practice almost as tightly. An influential challenge to the Ciceronian hegemony was *De conscribendis epistolis* (On writing letters; 1522), in which Erasmus argued for a more flexible style and structure determined by the particular correspondents, the subject matter, and the occasion and based on broad reading of classical authors. However, Erasmus too considered letters part of traditional rhetoric, as evidenced by his aligning the first three of his four categories of letters—deliberative, demonstrative, judicial, and familiar or extraordinary—with the three varieties of ancient rhetoric. [*See overview article on* Renaissance rhetoric.]

Many of the earliest practitioners of humanist style, especially in Italy, were professional secretaries and notaries who continued to employ the *ars dictaminis* in their official correspondence and the newer style in their personal correspondence. Once the humanist style became the standard for all types of letters, distinctions between personal and official correspondence became less sharp. As political power became more centralized, for example, letters played an ever more important role in the business of court. Ambitious courtiers exploited the conventions of epistolary rhetoric to construct an attractive self-image and to ingratiate themselves with the powerful through flattery and other forms of courtesy. While such letters might advance specific petitions, many served no other purpose than to create or strengthen social and ideological connections: like letters to members of one's family, their function was to maintain a community of interest.

The Renaissance humanists also resembled the medieval *dictatores* (professional letter writers) in that their letter-writing treatises were intended for a male, Latin-educated elite. Although letter-writing manuals in Italian began to appear as early as the thirteenth century, the great majority of the medieval and humanist treatises were in Latin. Vernacular treatises became more common in the sixteenth century: the first one in English, William Fulwood's *The Enimie of Idlenesse* (1568), was itself translated from the French. However, it was not until the seventeenth century that vernacular letters truly became the norm for the upper as well as the middle and lower strata of society, with important rhetorical consequences across an ever broader spectrum of letter writers.

At the upper end of society, the vernacularization of European letters was accompanied by increased cultivation of the familiar letter, which by the late seventeenth century had become arguably the preeminent literary form. Although such letters continued to be more public than private—Madame de Sévigné wrote the much-admired letters to her daughter in the knowledge that they would be collected and circulated—the stylistic ideals that governed their composition changed in significant ways. Naturalness and simplicity came to be valued over obvious artifice and complexity. The virtues of good conversation, such as variety, ease and clarity of language, liveliness and wit, became the virtues of good letters. Since conversation was itself an art, however, epistolary rhetoric came to be the art of simulating sincerity, artlessness, and spontaneity. To see how artful the artlessness of the seventeenth-century letter writers was, one need look no farther than the immensely popular, often translated and imitated collections of Jean-Louis Guez de Balzac (1597–1654) and Vincent Voiture (1597–1648). The letter as product became less important than the letter as process: correct style and a logical structure gave way to colloquial rhythms and associative leaps. Above all, letter readers prized authenticity. Hence, letter writers strove to counterfeit an authentic voice, one that would produce the effect of conversation overheard.

Letter-writing guides proliferated as never before during the seventeenth and eighteenth centuries. In keeping with the ideals of the familiar letter, these guides relied less on precepts and more on examples that illustrated a range of voices appropriate to diverse persons and diverse circumstances. Collections of such letters were read for enjoyment as much as for edification, and often formed part of more comprehensive instruction in polite conduct and morals. The same double function accounts for the widespread collecting and publishing of actual letters, often without the consent of their authors. On the one hand, such collections offered the voyeuristic pleasure of overhearing unguarded, "authentic" discourse for which letters were prized, while, on the other hand, they provided models of expressive writing, as well as fine sentiments or sound morals.

The fashion for familiar letters also generated more purely entertaining collections, such as those containing fictional letters that purported to be actual letters found by accident. The earliest such collection in English, Nicholas Breton's *A poste with a madde packet of letters* (1602), like others of its kind, is significant for including letters by persons from the lower classes. Even more useful in providing scope for impersonating a variety of voices, most notably those of women, within a wide range of circumstances, were the extremely popular epistolary novels. Such works, like so many of the guides to letter writing, linked epistolary rhetoric with moral instruction: Samuel Richardson's epistolary novels *Pamela* and *Clarissa* share more than their authorship with his letter-writing manual *Letters Written to and for Particular Friends, on the Most Important Occasions* (1741).

In addition to their expressive functions, letters naturally continued to fulfill performative functions, such as the communication of news, the transaction of business, and the consolidation of familial and social networks. To some extent, the performative and expressive functions overlapped, but from the late Renaissance on we find an increasing tendency to separate the business letter from the familiar letter and to treat it in more specialized, generally more mechanical manuals. Collections of formulaic documents for narrowly specified business and legal purposes existed already in the Middle Ages and continue to be published to the present day. With the growth of literacy and the expansion of commerce, the numbers of such works increased dramatically during the Early Modern period. Directed to the working classes and the mercantile bourgeoisie, they provide pragmatic, goal-oriented instruction, often in the form of models that are no more than templates to be copied, with blanks left for names and other particulars. Epistolary rhetoric, understood as a set of formal rules or conventions governing the language and format of letters, has come to be associated almost exclusively with letters belonging to this tradition. Indeed, what is probably the fastest-growing variety of contemporary letter, the direct mail advertisement, is also the variety most governed by formal "rhetorical" rules spelled out in the many guides currently available. Nonetheless, the business letter continues to be viewed as a secondary category, while the personal letter is still considered to be the primary form of the genre.

Since the eighteenth century, the nature and status of the familiar letter have been transformed above all by new technologies. Faster, more dependable postal systems have altered epistolary rhetoric in several key ways, perhaps most importantly by making truly private letters a reality. Speed of transmission and cheaper writing materials and postage have combined to make letters less precious: as more letters are exchanged, both readers and writers tend to devote less time to any given letter and the practice and appreciation of epistolary "art" diminish correspondingly. By providing more efficient means of communicating news of general interest, the mass media have further reduced the extent to which letters are likely to be read by persons other than the addressee. Letters are no longer written with a view to publication, in either the formal or informal sense.

While certain technological innovations have helped to make letters more private, others have allowed them to be less personal. Various means of mechanical reproduction, such as the type-writer, the photocopier, and more recently the word processor, have complicated the status of letters as unique physical objects. Rather than the norm, the handwritten letter is now marked as exceptionally personal. In an era of mass mail-ings, the "personal effect" has become so rhetor-ically powerful that computer technology has been used to counterfeit it. Just as eighteenth-century familiar letters strove to sound like con-versations, modern direct mail advertisements strive to look like personal letters.

Perhaps most significantly, the telephone has ended the letter's monopoly of communication across great distances. Since one can conduct an actual conversation with absent friends by tele-phone, the letter inevitably fulfills other func-tions, such as those more closely bound up with its materiality and permanence. Most interesting of all the new technologies is the Internet, which, like the telephone, eliminates the time lag that has always defined epistolary communication, but which transmits a written text rather than an audible voice, albeit an immaterial text that, even if printed out, bears no physical trace of the sender. With e-mail we seem to have come as close as possible to writing as conversation, while reaching or perhaps exceeding the limits of what can be called a letter.

BIBLIOGRAPHY

Altman, Janet Gurkin. *Epistolarity: Approaches to a Form.* Columbus, Ohio, 1982. An influential study of epis-tolary fiction that attempts to distinguish letters from other forms of discourse (see especially chapter 4, "Epistolary Discourse").

Camargo, Martin. *Ars Dictaminis, Ars Dictandi.* Typolo-gie des sources du moyen âge occidental, 60. Turn-hout, Belgium, 1991. Defines the genre and sketches its history.

Chartier, Roger, Alain Boureau, and Cécile Dauphin. *Correspondence: Models of Letter Writing from the Mid-dle Ages to the Nineteenth Century.* Translated by Chris-topher Woodall. Princeton, 1997. Boureau provides a good survey of the *ars dictaminis,* while Chartier and Dauphin analyze the letter-writing manuals

published in France from the sixteenth through the nineteenth century.

Earle, Rebecca, ed. *Epistolary Selves: Letters and Letter-Writers, 1600–1945.* Aldershot, U.K., 1999. Ten es-says that emphasize the social functions of letters.

Favret, Mary A. *Romantic Correspondence: Women, Politics and the Fiction of Letters.* Cambridge, U.K., 1993. Ar-gues that public and private letters were a focus of ideological and political tensions during the period 1790–1840s.

Hornbeak, Katherine Gee. *The Complete Letter Writer in English, 1568–1800.* Smith College Studies in Mod-ern Languages, vol. 15, nos. 3–4. Northampton, Mass., 1934. An important catalog of the earliest guides to letter writing in English.

Irving, William Henry. *The Providence of Wit in the En-glish Letter Writers.* Durham, N.C., 1955. A lively sur-vey that includes the classical and continental writ-ers whose letters most influenced the English.

Mitchell, Linda, and Carol Poster, eds. *Letter-Writing Manuals from Antiquity to the Present.* Forthcoming. The fullest, most up-to-date survey of the topic. Nineteen essays, plus separate bibliographies for each major historical period.

Murphy, James J., ed. *Renaissance Eloquence: Studies in the Theory and Practice of Renaissance Rhetoric.* Berkeley, 1983. Several of the twenty-three essays are con-cerned with epistolary rhetoric, and the collection as a whole provides a useful rhetorical context within which to situate the theory and practice of letter writing.

Redford, Bruce. *The Converse of the Pen: Acts of Intimacy in the Eighteenth-Century Familiar Letter.* Chicago, 1986. Studies the letters of Lady Mary Wortley Mon-tagu, William Cowper, Thomas Gray, Horace Wal-pole, James Boswell, and Samuel Johnson, empha-sizing their status as conversation and performance.

Robertson, Jean. *The Art of Letter Writing: An Essay on the Handbooks Published in England during the Sixteenth and Seventeenth Centuries.* Liverpool, U.K., 1942. Still the standard survey of the earliest prescriptive guides in English, emphasizing their relationship to the French tradition.

Stewart, Keith. "Towards Defining an Aesthetic for the Familiar Letter in Eighteenth Century England." *Prose Studies* 5 (1982), pp. 179–192. Shows that let-ters were valued for "substance, the sense of char-acter, and the effect of immediacy."

Whigham, Frank. "The Rhetoric of Elizabethan Suitors' Letters." *Proceedings of the Modern Language Associa-tion* 96 (1981), pp. 864–882. An excellent study of courtiers' letters in their sociopolitical context.

Zaczek, Barbara Maria. *Censored Sentiments: Letters and Censorship in Epistolary Novels and Conduct Materials.*

Newark, Del., 1997. Treats the important connections between letters and conduct books.
—MARTIN CAMARGO

EPISTROPHĒ (Gk. also *epiphora;* Lat. *reversio*), called "counter-turne" (*Antistrophē*) by Puttenham in *The Arte of English Poesie* (1589, p. 198), a rarely found term that denotes a figure of morphological equivalence, by which several clauses or sentences end with the same word(s). Its alleged infrequency makes Puttenham quote his own poetry, though the Bible gives us, "When I was a child, I spake as a child, I understood as a child, I thought as a child" (*1 Cor* 13.11). Plett, among others, prefers the term *epiphora,* when in his *Systematische Rhetorik* (Munich, 2000) he discusses figures of equivalence systematized according to position, extension, frequency, and other criteria.

[*See also* Epiphora; *and* Figures of speech.]
—HEINER PETERS

EPIZEUXIS (Lat. *geminatio*) is an isomorpheme consisting in the repetition of a word or phrase without an interpolation of other elements. Words can be repeated at the beginning of a verse or sentence: "*My God, my God,* why hast thou forsaken me?" (*Mt.* 27.46); in the middle: "Come, *stir, stir, stir!* The second cock has crow'd" (Shakespeare, *Romeo and Juliet,* 4.4.3–4); or at the end: "O poor Zabina! O *my queen, my queen!*" (C. Marlowe, *Tamburlaine, Part I,* 5.2.212). In these examples, *epizeuxis* bestows a strong pathetic effect on the speech.

[*See also* Figures of speech; *and* Poetry.]
—ANDREA GRÜN-OESTERREICH

ERISTIC. A derivative of the Greek term *eris,* which means strife, eristic belongs to the agonistic ethic whose goal is victory. As used in classical texts about rhetoric, it designates a manner of argumentation that seeks to win at all cost in debate. Some of the typical techniques of eristic arguers (eristics) include disputation, refutation, and contradiction. Generally, an eristic tries to overwhelm his opponent by drawing him into logical traps, confusing him with logical puzzles and paradoxes, exploiting the ambiguities of language, using fallacious reasoning, and showing that the other's argument leads to absurd consequences. Some of the better-known examples of eristic include the following: when one is telling the truth about lying, he is lying; if you know your father, and do not know the veiled person in front of you, but that person is your father, you both know and do not know the same person; if you have not lost something, you obviously have it—you have not lost horns, therefore you have them. Many eristic practices are illustrated by the characters Euthydemus and Dionysodorus in Plato's (c.428–c.347 BCE) *Euthydemus.*

According to Diogenes Laertius (c. third century CE), the eristics constituted a school of thought whose roots were traceable to Eleatic philosophy, which posits, à la Parmenides, the permanence and unity of being. Generally known in antiquity as the Megarians, this school flourished in the fourth and third centuries BCE. It included such figures as Euclides, Stilpo, Eubulides, and Alexinus.

As a practice, eristic is often likened to athletics or war. In the *Sophistical Refutations,* for example, Aristotle (384–322 BCE) explains eristic analogically:

> Just as cheating in a game and dirty fighting have a certain distinct character, so eristic is dirty fighting in argument. In the former case those who are determined to win stop at nothing, and the same is true of eristic arguers. People who argue in this fashion merely to win, seem to be eristic and contentious. (171b)

Plato employs the vocabulary of war when he has Socrates advise Theaetetus about eristic arguers:

> A mercenary skirmisher in the war of words might lie in wait for you armed with a thousand [trapping] questions. . . . He would . . . put you to confusion, sustaining his attack until your admiration of his inestimable skill betrayed you into his toils, and thereupon, leading you captive and bound, he would hold you to ransom for such a sum as you and he might agree upon. (*Theaetetus* 165d–e)

Each classical author explains eristic in a different way. Aristotle, for example, explains in the *Rhetoric* that the motivation behind eristic is the pleasure derived from victory: "Since victory is pleasant, competitive and eristic amusements must be so too, for victories are often gained in them." In the same passage, he also observes that "the practice of forensic rhetoric and eristic are especially pleasant to those who are familiar with them and able to engage in them successfully" (1371a). For Plato, however, those who engage in eristic do so out of ignorance and misuse of dialectic. Accordingly, he asserts that if someone "finds pleasure in dragging words about and applying them to different things at different times, with the notion that he has discovered something difficult to explain, our present argument asserts that he has taken up seriously matters which are not worth serious attention; for this process is neither clever nor difficult" (*Sophist* 259c). Plato goes on to belittle what eristics do by saying that:

> [T]o show that in some sort of fashion the same is the other and the other the same, and the great small, and the like unlike, and to take pleasure in thus always bringing forward opposites in argument—all that is no true refutation, but is plainly the newborn offspring of some brain that has just begun to lay hold upon the problem of realities. (*Sophist* 259d)

Eristics are often associated with or discussed alongside Sophists, dialecticians, antilogicians, and disputants. The common thread uniting all these groups is their interest in language and argument in the service of proof and refutation. But there are differences as well. What distinguishes eristics from Sophists for Aristotle is not so much their manner of arguing as their purpose—eristics are mainly after victory whereas Sophists are more interested in "publicity and financial gain" (*Sophistical Refutations* 171b).

Plato points out that the line between dialectic and eristic is very thin. [*See* Dialectic.] Even so, dialecticians "apply the proper divisions and distinctions to the subject under consideration" whereas eristics do not. Eristics simply pursue verbal oppositions (*Republic* 454a). Generally, Plato claims that:

> Young men, when they first get a taste of disputation, misuse it as a form of sport, always employing it contentiously, and imitating confuters, confute others. They delight like puppies in pulling about and tearing with words all who approach them. (*Republic* 499b)

More specifically, Plato observes that a dialectical (that is, philosophical) discussion proceeds first by assuming a single form in a thing and then looking for two or more forms of the same thing, all the way to an infinite number. By contrast, an eristic (that is, contentious) discussion moves from the one form to the infinite number without taking into account the intermediate number of forms (*Philebus* 16d–17a). In sum, eristics for Plato concern themselves with quibbling, raising trivial objections, all of which lead to opinion-based strife in courtrooms or in private discussions. By contrast, philosophers endeavor to find the truth at any cost for the sake of knowledge (*Republic* 499a).

Isocrates (436–338 BCE) often differentiates in his rhetorical compositions between "those who dispute subtly about trifling matters" and those who devote themselves to the study of philosophy and rhetoric (*Against the Sophists* 1, *Helen* 1, *To Nicocles* 39, *Letter* 5, 3–4). Like Plato and Aristotle, he condemns eristic practices but his reasoning is different. He regards these practices as being largely useless when it comes to what matters most, practical wisdom in public affairs. His condemnation is generally directed at the teachers of eristic, not their students, who, as young men, are drawn to and are easily impressed by astounding and extraordinary things (*Helen* 6). However, Isocrates detects eristic practices across several classes, which include philosophers, dialecticians, Sophists, antilogicians, and some orators. He also equivocates when he assigns some educational value to eristic, claiming that it helps sharpen the mind in the same way that astronomy and geometry do (*Antidosis* 261–265). His point is that while these studies may be helpful at a younger age, they are no longer suitable for more mature men (*Panathenaicus* 27–28).

[*See also* Classical rhetoric; *and* Sophists.]

BIBLIOGRAPHY

Kerferd, George B. "Dialectic, antilogic and eristic." In *The Sophistic Movement*, pp. 59–67. Cambridge, U.K., 1981. Offers fine discriminations between dialectic, antilogic, and eristic.

Kerferd, G. B. "Gorgias on Nature or That Which Is Not." *Phronesis* 1 (1955–1956), pp. 3–25. Discusses Gorgias's explorations of identity and negation for rhetorical purposes.

Rankin, H. D. "Ouk estin antilegein." In *The Sophists and their Legacy.* Edited by G. B. Kerferd. Wiesbaden, Germany, 1981. Provides a useful discussion of negation and contradiction in the traditions of sophistic and eristic.

Rankin, H. D. *Sophists, Socratics, and Cynics.* Croom Helm, U.K., 1983. Describes the contributions of eristic to the development of logic and offers useful accounts of specific eristic thinkers.

—JOHN POULAKOS

ETHICS. *See* Casuistry; Conviction; Epideictic genre; Ēthos; Judgment; Logos; Medieval rhetoric, *article on* Medieval grammar; Modern rhetoric; Philosophy; *and* Prudence.

ĒTHOPOEIA (Lat. *notatio*) designates a textual unit, in which the individual nature of a given character is imitated through the assignment to that character of specific discourses or speech.

The most elaborated doctrine of this figure comes from the ancient Greek "exercise handbooks" (*progymnasmata*). Apart from the definition of this figure, different types of it can be distinguished in these handbooks, according to different parameters. On the one hand, they distinguish between the invention of discourses attributed to real living characters (*ēthopoeia*), to real dead characters (*eidōlopoeia*), or to unreal characters (*prosōpopoeia*). On the other hand, it is usual to distinguish between moral ēthopoeia, when the character predominates; emotive ēthopoeia, when an emotion predominates; and mixed ēthopoeia, when a mixture of both components occurs.

In the elaboration of these figures, authors always insist on the necessity of keeping at all events the virtue of decorum, that is to say, the appropriateness of the style to the variables of age, sex, social condition, and linguistic origin of the given character. They also insist on the relationship between the contents of the imagined discourse and the concrete circumstances within which it is produced.

[*See also* Classical rhetoric; Decorum; Ēthos; Figures of speech; *and* Prosōpopoeia.]

BIBLIOGRAPHY

Lanham, R. A. *A Handlist of Rhetorical Terms.* Berkeley, 1991.

Lausberg, H. *Handbuch der literarischen Rhetorik.* P. 822; Munich, 1960.

Mayoral, J. A. *Figuras retóricas.* P. 187. Madrid, 1994.

Morier, H. *Dictionnaire de Poétique et de Rhétorique.* Paris, 1981.

—JOSÉ ANTONIO MAYORAL
Translated by A. Ballesteros

ĒTHOS. From its inception, classical rhetoric has grounded persuasion upon a speaker's knowledge of the varieties and complexities of human character. [*See* Classical rhetoric.] This knowledge enables the speaker to project a favorable self-image and to shape arguments in ways that accommodate differing audiences and occasions. Demonstrably, most theories within the history of rhetoric proceed from unique premises concerning the nature of the human psyche (particularly the complex interrelations among the intellect, will, and emotions); in addition, most classically based theories acknowledge the influences of class and culture that subject audiences to a range of typical (and, thereby, predictable and exploitable) motives, values, prejudices, and appeals. In short, most versions of historical rhetoric proceed from a prior "theory" (in modern parlance, "ideology") of "the human," that is, from a set of assumptions, whether explicit or unexamined, regarding human psychology and social relations, yielding in each case a distinctive model of *ēthos*—which we may here define, broadly and tentatively, as "character as it emerges in language." More than the fact that *ēthos* assumes several competing, even contradictory meanings throughout the history of rhetoric, our study is complicated by the fact that models of character, "selfhood," and human psychology have continued to evolve since antiquity; hence an effective Hellenic *ēthos* (such as the Greek orator Lysias creates or the philosopher Aristotle theorizes) differs palpably from the *ēthos* of the Roman orator and statesman Cicero, which differs in turn from Saint Augustine's early Christian *ēthos*, Machiavelli's Renaissance *ēthos*, Campbell's Enlightenment *ēthos*, Burke's modern *ēthos*, Barthes's postmodern *ēthos,* and so on. The following discussion, then, charts the development of *ēthos* as a classical rhetorical concept and its subsequent transmutations, in accordance with changing cultural notions of character or "self-hood."

Ēthos in Lysian, Platonic, and Isocratean Rhetoric. Though realistic character portrayal was long a feature of poetry (witness the Homeric epics), historians of rhetoric credit the speech-writer Lysias (c.445–380 BCE) with developing the techniques of *ēthopoiea*—the delineation of human character by means of speech. [*See* Ētho-poiea.] To the extent that Athenian courts compelled individuals to speak on their own behalf, without benefit of legal advocacy (as would later become Roman practice), individuals who availed themselves of the "artifices" of persuasion sought instruction from a teacher or a handbook (hence the development of "technical" rhetoric); otherwise, they could purchase a speech from a logographer or speechwriter, to then memorize and deliver. Suiting his ghostwriting to reflect the age, status, and personality of each client, Lysias's fame as a logographer rested upon his "skill in constructing means of persuasion from character," as Dionysius of Halicarnassus notes (*Lysias* 19.3–4), making his client's character "appear trustworthy by referring to the circumstances of his life and of his parentage, and often again by describing his past actions and purposes. And when the facts fail to provide him with such material, he creates his own moral tone, making his characters seem by their speech to be trustworthy and honest."

A critic of Lysias and the Sophists, Plato (c.428–c.347 BCE) devoted several dialogues to rhetoric, most notably the *Phaedrus,* in which his mouthpiece, Socrates, questions the morality of *ēthopoiea* and ghostwriting and, indeed, of writing in general. Criticizing Lysias's oration on the subject of love, which the young Phaedrus has memorized and recited, Socrates composes two speeches in response, though prefacing the first with the declaration, "I shall cover my head before I begin; then I can rush through my speech at top speed without looking at you and breaking down for shame" (237a). More than an admission of shame (in that his first speech, in imitation of Lysias, blasphemes the god of love), his act of covering symbolizes the disjunction between a speaker's moral character and a ghostwritten text. As James S. Baumlin observes in "Positioning *Ethos* in Historical and Contemporary Theory"

(1994), Socrates speaks the words but he does not, himself, appear *in* them; thus his speech masks rather than reveals the self and its intentions.

In so doing, Socrates invokes *prosōpopoiea,* a rhetorical figure similar to *ēthopoiea:* it is related etymologically to the Greek *prosōpon,* "visage" or "mask" (from which the Latin *persona* likely derives). [*See* Persona; *and* Prosōpopoeia.] More than an aspect of dramatic costume, the actor's mask provides an instrument of projection, amplifying his voice and enlarging (as well as fixing) his facial expression. Here, though, the cloth covering effaces rather than fixes the speaker's character. Yet Socrates is interrupted "by a familiar divine sight" demanding "atonement for some offense to heaven" (242b); for we find that he has sinned, not simply in blaspheming the god of love, but also in speaking to "deceive a few miserable people and win their applause" (243). Socrates delivers his second speech, then, in praise of love "and no longer veiling my head for shame, but uncovered" (243b), thereby signaling a restoration of the ethical relation between a speaker and his words.

Granted, Plato does not use the term *ēthos* in the rhetorical sense later established by his pupil, Aristotle; by inference, though, one can work toward a Platonic definition. If "right rhetoric," as Plato describes it, seeks to discover and express the truth of the soul, then *ēthos* describes the inner harmony among language, character, and truth: in Platonic fashion, *ēthos* defines the space where language and truth meet and are made incarnate within the individual. A Platonic definition of *ēthos,* then, is premised on the moral and, ultimately, theological inseparability of the speaker-agent from the speech act. Throughout the dialogues, Plato is uncompromising in asserting this equation: truth must be incarnate within the individual, and a person's language must express (or, first, discover) this truth. Conversely, any attempt to separate a person's speech from his actual character serves to deny the incarnational aspect of truth and discourse alike. Thus rhetoric becomes a *psychagōgia* or leading of the soul to truth. As Socrates says to Phaedrus, "If we are to address people scientifically, we shall show them precisely what is the real and true nature of that object on which our discourse is brought to bear. And that object, I take it, is the soul" (270e).

Among other necessary accomplishments, then, the *rhētōr* must be able to "classify the types of discourse and the types of soul, and the various ways in which souls are affected, suggesting the type of speech appropriate to each type of soul, and showing what kind of speech can be relied on to create belief in one soul and disbelief in another, and why" (*Phaedrus* 271b). Indeed, knowledge of the various *eidē psychēs* or "types of soul" stands as the centerpiece of Plato's purified rhetoric. In a later passage (277b–c), Socrates advises the rhetor to "order and arrange . . . discourse" in accordance with "each nature" of the soul, "addressing a variegated soul in a variegated style . . . and a simple soul in a simple style." This vague distinction marks the extent of Plato's explanation of the "types of soul," though quite possibly Socrates's earlier "myth of the chariot" (*Phaedrus* 246b–257a) allegorizes the different souls and their capacities for temperance, modesty, and nobility. Otherwise, Plato leaves it to later authors to codify the different souls and their means of accommodation.

Subsequent theorists responded variously to Plato's assault against the ethics of sophistic rhetoric. In *Antidosis*, Isocrates (436–338 BCE) seeks to guarantee the speaker's moral character through *paideia*, a lifelong training in Greek rhetorical culture. He admits that there is no "art which can implant honesty and justice in depraved natures," but says that nonetheless "an ambition to speak well" can make one "better and worthier" (337). The rhetor will seek out noble models to emulate and "will feel their influence not only in the preparation of a given discourse but in all the actions of his life" (339). Thus "the man who wishes to persuade people will not be negligent as to the matter of character, . . . for who does not know that words carry greater conviction when spoken by men of good repute than when spoken by men who live under a cloud, and that the argument which is made by a man's life is of more weight than that which is furnished by words?" (339). In fact, "the power to speak well," Isocrates asserts, "is taken as the surest index of a sound understanding, and discourse which is true and lawful and just is the outward image of a good and faithful soul" (327).

Though a champion of *paideia*, Isocrates' ideal rhetor falls short of Plato's call for a purified

rhetoric grounded in a "knowledge of the soul." No less pragmatic, Aristotle (384–322 BCE) admits not only the amorality of rhetoric but also the role of appearances in persuasion: Isocrates asserts the speaker's need to be good; Aristotle asserts the sufficiency of seeming. And whereas Plato sought to raise rhetoric up to be a handmaiden of eternal, unchanging truth, Aristotle lowers it to serve in the discovery of probable arguments situated within the realm of changing human, social affairs. Over against Platonic theology, Aristotle outlines a sociology of rhetoric, with particular implications for *ēthos*.

Aristotelian *Ēthos*: Definitions and Etymologies. Organized around the *partes orationis* or sections of a speech, such handbooks as the *Rhetorica ad Alexandrum* and the pseudo-Ciceronian *Rhetorica ad Herennium*, relegate *ēthos* to a speech's exordium (wherein the speaker aims at gaining the audience's goodwill) and, to a lesser degree, to the effects of style; similarly, the handbooks relegate *pathos* or emotional appeal to the rousing peroration. [*See* Arrangement, *article on* Traditional arrangement; Pathos; *and* Style.] In contrast, Aristotle's *Rhetoric* treats *ēthos* as an aspect of invention, thus emphasizing *heurēsis* or the discovery, "in each case," of "the available means of persuasion" (1355b). [*See* Invention.] Within this inventional system, *ēthos* joins *logos* and *pathos* as one of three entechnic *pisteis* or "artistic proofs" (1.2.2). [*See* Logos; *and* Pathos.]

> [There is persuasion] through character whenever the speech is spoken in such a way as to make the speaker worthy of credence; for we believe fair-minded people to a greater extent and more quickly [than we do others] on all subjects in general and completely so in cases where there is not exact knowledge but room for doubt. And this should result from the speech, not from a previous opinion that the speaker is a certain kind of person; for it is not the case, as some of the technical writers propose in their treatment of the art, that fair-mindedness [*epieikeia*] on the part of the speaker makes no contribution to persuasiveness; rather, character is almost, so to speak, the controlling factor in persuading. (1356a)

Following Aristotle's earlier definition of artistic proof (1355b–1356a), the speaker's moral character is to be constructed within (and solely by means of) the speech itself, apart from the speaker's previous reputation or prior acquaintance with the audience; otherwise, as George A. Kennedy notes in *The Art of Rhetoric in the Roman World* (Princeton, 1972), "the authority of the speaker would be analogous to the role of a witness and would thus be *atechnos,* something not created but used" (p. 82).

Compared to Isocrates' assertion that "a man's life is of more weight" than his words (339), Aristotle's rejection of prior reputation offers a striking innovation. How shall we understand this? While modern readers often frown at his moral neutrality and emphasis upon appearances, Aristotle by no means condones shape-shifting or hypocrisy on the speaker's part; here rather, in a unique passage focused on deliberative (as opposed to forensic) oratory, the philosopher outlines the means by which a speaker, *who is presumed to be unknown to an audience,* could give all indications of telling the truth. [*See* Deliberative genre; *and* Forensic genre.] In *Ethos and Pathos from Aristotle to Cicero* (1989), Jakob Wisse offers to explain: since rhetoric "is concerned with things about which certainty cannot, or at least not easily, be attained," an audience "must often rely on its impression of the trustworthiness of the speaker" (p. 247). For this reason, Aristotle "takes as the fundamental aim of *ethos* the audience's conviction that what the speaker is saying is the truth . . . *ethos* may therefore be defined as the element of a speech that presents the speaker as trustworthy" (pp. 32–33).

Having established the importance of the speaker's trustworthiness, Aristotle expands his discussion to include the moral character of the judge in both deliberative and forensic (or judicial) proceedings, thereby acknowledging that specific audiences' predispositions—particularly of friendliness or hostility to given persons or policies—must also be accommodated (2.2–4):

> But since rhetoric is concerned with making a judgment . . . it is necessary not only to look to the argument, that it may be demonstrative and persuasive but also [for the speaker] to construct a view of himself as a certain kind of person and to prepare the judge; for it makes much difference in regard to persuasion . . . that the speaker seem to be a certain kind of person and that his hearers suppose him to be a certain

kind of person and that his hearers suppose him to be disposed in a certain way. . . . (1377b)

While words like *seem, suppose,* and *construct* again suggest the amorality and potential manipulativeness of his system, we must remember that Aristotle is here describing the effects of *ēthos* as an artistic proof and, thus, as an effect arising from within the speech itself, separate from any considerations of the speaker's prior reputation or true moral character.

In a later passage (2.5–7), Aristotle identifies the three qualities of entechnic *ēthos:* "for there are three things we trust other than logical demonstrations. These are practical wisdom [*phronēsis*] and virtue [*aretē*] and good will [*eunoia*]; for speakers make mistakes in what they say or advise through [failure to exhibit] either all or one of these. . . . Therefore, a person seeming to have all these qualities is necessarily persuasive to the hearers" (1378a). [*See* Phronēsis.] In "From Aristotle to Madison Avenue" (1994, pp. 171–190), James L. Kinneavy and Susan C. Warshauer offer the following gloss. Given the "complex interrelation among speaker, hearer, and subject matter" (p. 174)—terms recapitulating the three *pisteis, ēthos, pathos,* and *logos*—Aristotle refers *aretē* specifically to the speaker's moral character (thus denoting the "ethical" component of *ēthos* per se), *eunoia* to his disposition toward the audience (suggesting by this means the convergence of *ēthos* with *pathos*), and *phronēsis* to his "self-assurance and expertise" (thereby displaying the speaker's mastery of *logos*). But while it is the speaker's task to display such qualities, any judgment as to their effectiveness belongs solely with the audience. Thus *aretē*—related etymologically to *ariston,* the "noble" (or, roughly, "aristocratic")—necessarily invokes "a type of *cultural appeal*," as Kinneavy and Warshauer suggest, for the speaker must exhibit qualities that the community, "and not the individual, defines as virtue" (pp. 174–175). This implies a rather conservative approach to rhetorical character, more Isocratean than Platonic in its conformity to societal convention. *Eunoia,* too, requires that speakers "identify with the audience, holding some of their basic aspirations, speaking their language, and if necessary, sharing and affirming their prejudices," for, as Kinneavy and Warshauer note, "members of the audience are persuaded by sentiments resembling their own" (p. 176).

Needing to display qualities convincing to particular audiences, the speaker must have knowledge of various governments, social classes, and ages of life. For it is "most important," Aristotle tells us, "to grasp an understanding of all forms of constitution [*politeia*] and to distinguish the customs and the legal usages and advantages of each" (1365b). And as "the 'end' of democracy is freedom, of oligarchy wealth, of aristocracy things related to education and the traditions of law, of tyranny self-preservation, . . . we should be acquainted with the kinds of character distinctive of each form of constitution; for the character distinctive of each is necessarily more persuasive to each" (1366a). Thus a speaker shapes his own *ēthos* in direct response to the political *ēthē* of each changing audience.

Like Isocrates' account of the speaker's moral character, Aristotle's subsequent discussion (2.12–17) of the different *ēthē* or "kinds of character" offers a partial answer to Plato's call for "a scientific *psychagogia*" (Wisse, p. 37), a rhetoric addressed to the soul of the individual and grounded, thus, in a study of the "types of soul." But whereas the soul assumes a theological significance for Plato, Aristotle's "group psychology" demystifies the soul or psyche, rendering it subject to a range of physiological processes and social/ideological pressures. Reducing the Platonic *eidē psychēs* to a typology of conventional roles, Book 2 of the *Rhetoric* reads much like a cast list of Hellenic dramatis personae—the scheming, parsimonious old man; the brash, boasting youth; the man of anger; the cold coward; the pining lover—each considered "in terms of emotions and habits and age of life and fortune . . . including what sorts of things each type of person chooses and does" (1388b). Finally, a cluster of brief passages pertain to "stylistic ēthos" and *ēthopoiea* as, for example:

> The narration ought to be indicative of character [*ēthikēn*]. This will be so if we know what makes character [*ēthos*]. One way, certainly, is to make deliberate choice [*proairesis*] clear: what the character is on the basis of what sort of deliberate choice [has been made]. . . . Other ethical indications are attributes of each character, for example, that someone walks

away while talking; for this makes his arrogance and his rudeness of character clear. (1417a–b)

Modern scholars have often noted an instability in Aristotle's terminology, which leaves the definition and scope of *ēthos* open to debate. Indeed, one might wish that the Stagyrite had made clearer distinctions among these many effects, reserving the term *ēthos* solely for the artistic proof described early in Book 1. Yet Aristotle's judgment seems correct in observing that character—and not just of the speaker, but of the "judge" in law courts and assemblies, of various audiences, of different communities, and as depicted in narrative—functions variously in discourse. Aristotle interrelates these various functions by establishing their etymological "family resemblances" as *ēthos* (the apparent trustworthiness of a speaker's rhetorically constructed self-image); *ēthos* (moral character as reflected in "custom" or "habit"); *ēthē* (the various character types identifiable with each audience, including the *ēthē* of political states; and *ēthopoiea*, the verbal depiction of character).

Treated as an aspect of rhetoric, Aristotelian *ēthos* presumes that human nature is knowable, reducible to a range of types, and manipulable by discourse. Here, though, we must consider whether classical theory squares with current anthropological understanding of human character and its historical development. For "there is no such thing as human nature independent of culture," as anthropologist Clifford Geertz writes in *The Interpretation of Cultures* (New York, 1973), meaning by culture not simply the "complexes of concrete behavior patterns—customs, usages, traditions, habit clusters" but also, and more significantly, "a set of control mechanisms—plans, recipes, rules, instructions" (p. 51) aimed at governing behavior. Certainly, Aristotle and rhetoricians before him incorporate aspects of their cultures' "rules" and "recipes" into their advice regarding persuasion. Geertz offers an insight, then, into the sociological origins of rhetorical *ēthos*, origins that have been illuminated, in turn, by such etymological studies as Charles Chamberlain's (1984), and Arthur B. Miller's "Aristotle on Habit and Character" (*Speech Monographs* 41, 1974, pp. 309–316). As Chamberlain notes, the earliest Homeric usage refers *ēthos* to the "haunts" or "arena in which people and animals move" (p. 99). Given its original connection with places, "early on it was used of the 'places' where a city was located," and, eventually, "to the peculiar characteristics which citizens of a *polis* acquire as part of their civic heritage" (p. 101). This later usage suggests that, "in reflecting upon both the soul and the state writers felt the need to express some sort of center of belonging" (Chamberlain, p. 101). The *polis,* then, forms that "center of belonging" wherein individuals "are trained in virtuous, habitual conduct," as Miller puts it, and where "a person's character is formed" (p. 311). By such reasoning, "one portrays character best by showing its origin in habit and disposition" (Miller, p. 311). Used often in its plural form to describe effective child rearing, Plato and other writers imply that "the cumulation of individual *ethe* forms a kind of moral ambience which is peculiar to a certain polis and whose most important influence is upon the children of that place" (Chamberlain, p. 102), thus binding *ēthē* to *paideia.* Individual character, then, becomes a reflection not just of individual habit or disposition but of one's cultural education, which (as Aristotle notes in 1.8.1) varies with each political constitution. Such is the range of meanings lurking throughout the Aristotelian terminology. It remains to be seen whether *ēthos* bears the same meanings and effects through later rhetorical tradition.

History of Selfhood: From Greece to Rome. Grounded solely in the effects of discourse and repudiating all prior reputation, Aristotelian *ēthos* "would have been incomprehensible to a Roman steeped in the tradition of the *mos maiorum,* surrounded by a nobility of rank, and influenced by the culture's general assumptions concerning human nature and character" (May 1998, p. 9). Rather, the Roman view, as James M. May (1988) observes, "is succinctly if somewhat obliquely expressed in Cicero's *De oratore:* 'Feelings are won over by a man's dignity [*dignitas*], achievements [*res gestae*], and reputation [*existimatio*]' (2.182). Aristotle's conception of an *ethos* portrayed only through the medium of a speech was, for the Roman orator, neither acceptable nor adequate" (May, p. 9). Personal character, then, exerted a powerful influence upon Roman rhetorical practice. Not only was character presumed to remain constant, thereby determining an individual's

choices and actions; the Romans also assumed that character was "bestowed or inherited by nature," so that an individual could not "suddenly, or at will, change or disguise for any lengthy period his ethos or way of life" (May, p. 6). Further, the Romans believed that "in most cases character remains constant from generation to generation of the same family" (May, p. 6). As anthropologist Marcel Mauss suggests in "A Category of the Human Mind" (*The Category of the Person.* Edited by Michael Carrithers, Steve Collins, and Steve Lukes, Cambridge, U.K., 1985, pp. 1–25), we must take the notion of an "inherited" *ēthos* literally; for, historically, a Roman's persona was bound legally to his family name, and citizenship accorded one the rights of a civil persona that a slave, in contrast, was denied. Following Roman law, "*servus non habet personam.* He does not own his body, nor has he ancestors, name, *cognomen,* or personal belongings" (Mauss, p. 17). Thus, Roman culture leads in the direction of modern personhood: whereas the Greek *ēthos* (expressing "custom" or "habit") emphasizes the influences of culture and education upon self-identity, the Roman *persona* describes a legal concept defining an individual's rights of self-possession. As Martin Hollis suggests in "Of Masks and Men" (*The Category of the Person,* pp. 217–233), it is only "with legal ideas about rights, Christian ideas about the soul, and Cartesian ideas about the ego that our modern, categorial self is born" (p. 223).

Roman *Ēthos*: Cicero and Quintilian. However innovative, Aristotle's system of *pisteis* was soon overshadowed by handbook rhetoric. Thus, after Aristotle's death in 322 BCE, it was not until Cicero's *De oratore* (55 BCE) that *ēthos,* again treated as one of three modes of proof, would be restored to a central place in theory. Cicero (106–43 BCE) is unlikely to have read Aristotle's *Rhetoric* in its entirety (Wisse, pp. 106–107), though he may have had access to a redaction or to other Peripatetic sources. Yet Cicero claims to have written *De oratore* "in Aristotelian fashion" (May, p. 3), as reflected in Antonius's outline of the *officia* or "duties" of the *rhētōr.* For "the art of speaking," Antonius tells us, "relies wholly upon three things: the proof of our allegations, the winning of our hearers' favor, and the rousing of their feelings" (2.115)—recalling the Aristotelian *logos, ēthos,* and *pathos* respectively. Indeed, the three duties, formulated variously as *probare/docere, conciliare/delectare,* and *movere/flectere* and repeated throughout the Ciceronian canon (*De oratore* 2.182, 310, 3.104; *Orator* 69; *Brutus* 185, 276; *De optimo genere* 3) are central to his rhetorical theory. Having pointed to such similarities, though, May concludes that "Cicero's analysis of ethos is not, in its details, particularly Aristotelian" (p. 4). For while having much to say about character and authority, Cicero ignores the Aristotelian notion of a "rational ethos" (Wisse, p. 33) or "ethos of trustworthiness" and, in its place, emphasizes *conciliare* or an "ethos of sympathy." Rather than serve as a projection of truthfulness and trustworthiness, Ciceronian *ēthos* resembles a milder form of *pathos.*

Cicero's major discussion (*De oratore* 2.182–184) warrants particular attention. Describing the role of character in forensic oratory, Antonius notes that:

> [A] potent factor in success, then, is for the characters, principles, conduct and course of life, both of those who are to plead cases and of their clients, to be approved, and conversely those of their opponents condemned; and for the feelings of the tribunal to be won over, as far as possible, to goodwill towards the advocate and the advocate's client as well. . . . (2.182)
>
> Now feelings are won over by a man's merit, achievement or reputable life, qualifications easier to embellish, if only they are real, than to fabricate where nonexistent. But attributes useful in an advocate are a mild tone, a countenance expressive of modesty, gentle language, and the faculty of seeming to be dealing reluctantly and under compulsion with something you are really anxious to prove. (2.182)

The Ciceronian concept is thus "broader and more inclusive than Aristotle's," as May observes; "it is an ethos that deals with the emotions (*affectus*), closely related to pathos but involving the milder feelings," and it is "attentive to and more intricately associated with style" (p. 5). It is also adapted to Roman legal procedure, as it applies to the character of "the advocate and the advocate's client as well" (2.182).

In his discussion of character, as in other aspects of rhetoric, Quintilian (c.35–c.100 CE) develops and makes "more specific the teaching of Cicero" (Kennedy, 1999, p. 505). While following

earlier tradition in equating *pathos* with "the more violent emotions" and *ēthos* with emotions that are "calm and gentle" (6.2.9), his *Institutio oratoria* ultimately grounds *ēthos* in the revelation of moral character, marked "by goodness more than aught else," and whose "chief merit . . . lies in making it seem that all that we say derives directly from the nature of the facts and persons concerned and in the revelation of the character of the orator in such a way that all may recognize it" (6.2.13). Thus, Quintilian's rhetorical ideal, the *vir bonus dicendi peritus* or "good man skilled in speaking," is Isocratean in sentiment: for "ēthos in all its forms requires the speaker to be a man of good character and courtesy" (6.2.18). Finally, the orator must himself feel the emotions he wishes to raise in his audience: "if we wish to give our words the appearance of sincerity, we must assimilate ourselves to the emotions of those who are genuinely so affected, and our eloquence must spring from the same feeling that we desire to produce in the mind of the judge" (6.2.27). For Quintilian, then, as for Cicero, *ēthos* and *pathos* remain thoroughly intertwined.

Saint Augustine and Christian *Ēthos*. Moving out of antiquity, we note the ways that Greco-Roman rhetoric, the Ciceronian system especially, is assimilated by Christianity. Most influential in this assimilation is Saint Augustine (354–430 CE), whose *De doctrina christiana* (427 CE) outlines a classically based synthesis of Scriptural hermeneutics and Christian homiletics. [*See* Hermeneutics; Homiletics; *and* Religion.] His major discussion of *ēthos* (4.59–63) initially follows Cicero regarding the three styles, their uses, and typical effects; yet Augustine refuses to reduce *ēthos* to an aspect of style, asserting that "the life of the speaker has greater weight in determining whether he is obediently heard than any grandness of language" (4.59). Rather, "he should prefer to please more with the things said than with the words used to speak them; nor should he think that anything may be said better than that which is spoken truthfully" (4.61). Augustine addresses matters of *ēthos* throughout, particularly regarding the question of "inspired" language; for "there is a kind of eloquence fitting for men most worthy of the highest authority and clearly inspired by God. Our authors speak with eloquence of this kind, nor does any other kind become them" (4.9). The distinction between an *ēthos* of "good works" and of inspired eloquence creates an apparent tension between competing modes of Christian authority; on the one hand, it is learned and implicitly Ciceronian—in most respects, a baptized version of the Roman *vir bonus*—on the other hand, it is charismatic, erupting in extemporaneous, Spirit-filled speech. Elsewhere (4.32) Augustine observes (*Mt.* 10.19–20): "Take no thought how or what to speak: for it shall be given you in that hour what to speak. For it is not you that speak, but the Spirit of your father that speaketh in you." Passages such as this confound classical notions of *ēthos,* since the "speaker" both is, and is not, the human creature, who serves as a mouthpiece for the Spirit.

From the Middle Ages to the Renaissance: Wilson and Machiavelli. Medieval authors contribute little to the tradition of rhetorical *ēthos,* tending either to affirm the Augustinian position on a speaker's life and "good works" or to follow the classical handbooks (the *Rhetorica ad Herennium* and *De inventione* especially) by relegating ethical appeal to the exordium or to aspects of style. [*See overview article on* Medieval rhetoric.] During the Middle Ages, nonetheless, notions of selfhood and cultural identity continued to evolve; and for this reason, the age remains important to the history of *ēthos.* As Roy F. Baumeister notes in *Identity* (1986), medieval culture "considered the value of the person's life to reside in how well that life approximated" the Christian ideal (p. 30). Medieval self-representations tended to be exemplary, reducible to social rank and occupation; and salvation remained collective, dependent upon one's participation in corporate worship and the Church sacraments, rather than on one's private actions or beliefs. Yet numerous cultural changes led from the medieval "collective self" to modern individualism; of these, most significant was an increase in social mobility, so that rank and status would no longer rest exclusively upon birth. With increased mobility came the understanding that an individual's actions affected one's identity as well as status. Concomitantly, the Protestant Reformation rendered each individual (and not the Catholic Church) responsible for his or her own salvation, which would itself be determined by private choices (including choices of belief) as well as actions. Baumeister

(pp. 35–36) notes additional influences upon the development of modern individualism, including "a heightened awareness of individual development and potentiality," changed attitudes toward death, which suggest "a growing concern over individual fate," and "a new concept of an inner or hidden self, symbolized by concern over sincerity and over discrepancies between appearances and underlying realities"—this last development leading directly to the "Machiavellian rhetoric" of Renaissance humanism. [*See* Humanism.]

Humanist rhetoricians such as Thomas Wilson (c.1525–1581) remain largely faithful to Ciceronian practice, particularly in their emphasis upon *conciliare* or the "ethos of sympathy." Following handbook tradition, Wilson's *Art of Rhetoric* (1560; first published 1553) reserves its major discussion for the exordium or "entrance" (p. 131), as he calls it, advising that "we shall get the good wills of our hearers four manner of ways: either beginning to speak of ourselves; or else of our adversaries, or else of the speaker and company present; or last of all, if we begin of the matter itself" (p. 135). As we might expect, Wilson's discussion of the speaker's personal character is not "artistic" in the Aristotelian sense but rather, in Ciceronian fashion, rests upon one's prior deeds and reputation:

> We shall get favor for our own sakes, if we shall modestly set forth our bound duties and declare our service done without all suspicion of vaunting, either to the commonweal, as in serving either in the wars abroad, or else in bearing some office at home concerning the tranquility of our country, or in helping our friends, kinsfolk, and poor neighbors. . . .
> (p. 135)

Nor should speakers hesitate to flatter the judges, "their worthy doings and . . . just dealing and faithful execution of the law" (p. 136). Wilson offers similarly extensive advice in deprecating an adversary, making "such report of them that the hearers . . . shall hate to hear of them" (p. 135). Here and elsewhere, Wilson adapts Ciceronian precepts to the unique circumstances of the Tudor courts of law.

If Wilson typifies the age's Ciceronianism, a more controversial thinker was Niccolò Machiavelli (1469–1527), whose infamous *Prince* (1513) asserts that men "are ingrateful, fickle, hypocritical, and dissimulating, avoiding perils, avid for gains, all yours as long as you are their benefactor, and . . . offering you their blood, belongings, life, and children when the need is distant, but when it approaches, they revolt" (p. 89). Given this viciousness of human nature, "a prudent lord . . . cannot and must not keep faith when this is to his disadvantage" (p. 91). Far exceeding Aristotle's rhetoric of appearances—indeed, rendering all questions of morality irrelevant—Machiavelli states that "it is not necessary for a prince" to possess such qualities as mercy, loyalty, humaneness, honesty, and Christian faith, though "it is truly necessary that he appear to have them" (p. 92), for "men, in general, judge more with their eyes than with their hands. Everyone sees what you appear to be, few feel what you are, and these few do not dare oppose the opinion of the many who have the majesty of the state to defend them" (p. 92). In such passages, we find the definition par excellence of the Renaissance Machiavel, who exploits the disjunction between the age's recognition of a "hidden self" and the grounding of rhetoric in appearances.

Ēthos from the Eighteenth to the Nineteenth Century. Thus far our discussion has focused on oratory, irrespective of the complications writing introduces to the study of *ēthos*. Yet Michel Foucault describes the relatively recent development of one particular category of selfhood, "the notion of 'author,'" whose "coming into being . . . constitutes the privileged moment of individualization in the history of ideas, knowledge, literature, philosophy, and the sciences" (1979, p. 141). Indeed, questions of copyright, plagiarism, and ownership of texts—in a phrase, questions of authorship—first become intense during the late Renaissance and the eighteenth century, ages not only of increased literacy but also of entrepreneurial capitalism. As Marxists are wont to observe, the development of Cartesian philosophy coincides with the development of capitalism and private ownership. Only at this late stage do texts become objects of private possession; treated as objectifications of self in language, they become, thus, a mode of self-possession. At this same time, the birth of Ro-

manticism represents in many respects the great flowering of Cartesianism in literature. The Romantic poets, it is often said, sought to write *in propria persona*. Never before has literature expressed so forcefully the "cult" of selfhood, experiencing self-presence with such obsessive wonder (Baumlin, 1994, p. xx). Emphasizing the personal fulfillment of each individual's unique potential, Romanticism placed increased value on "work, especially creative expression in art and literature," and on "subjective passion, especially love" (Baumeister, p. 60). In addition, "a vague but important interest in the cultivation of one's inner qualities emerged" (p. 60), such emphases contributing to the age's growing distaste over the "artifices" of neoclassical style, its rejection of rhetorical ornament, and its mistrust of the social "masking" associated with the Early Modern "hidden self." Indeed, as Rosalind J. Gabin notes in "*Ethos* and Ethics" (*Ethical Issues in College Writing*. Edited by Fredric G. Gale, Phillip Sipiora, and James L. Kinneavy, New York, 1999, pp. 107–136), even the notion of audience accommodation, central to classical theory, fades from the age's rhetorical practices, "for audience mattered less, if at all, as the speaker concentrated on transmitting to the listener as closely as possible the stirrings of his or her own heart" (p. 115).

Perhaps the most significant Victorian contribution to modern selfhood is the increased emphasis upon private family life which, by the end of the nineteenth century, "far outweighed the value placed on public life and public affairs" (Baumeister, p. 71); and this split between public and private domains contributed, Baumeister notes, to the modern individual's "fragmentation of consciousness," since modern life now "divides itself between work, in the public domain, and personal and emotional life, which is centered in private life" (p. 72). In consequence, the age's rhetoric textbooks emphasize skills of written self-expression, literary–aesthetic discrimination, and grammatical correctness, in each case valuing clarity of communication over powers of persuasion—all useful, middle-class accomplishments, to be sure, but far removed from the public, civic ideals of Isocrates and Cicero. [*See* Eighteenth-century rhetoric; *and* Nineteenth-century rhetoric.]

Typically, rhetorics of the late eighteenth and

early nineteenth centuries offer truncations of classical theory, as the elocutionary school represented by Thomas Sheridan's *Course of Lectures on Elocution* (1762) and Gilbert Austin's *Chironomia* (1806) focused on pronunciation and delivery, while belletristic rhetoric exemplified by Hugh Blair's *Lectures on Rhetoric and Belles Lettres* (1783) focused on matters of arrangement, style, and the development of literary "taste." [*See* Arrangement, *article on* Traditional arrangement.] In fact, the general removal of invention from most textbooks left the *pisteis*—again, the centerpiece of Aristotelian theory—almost entirely out of consideration. [*See* Invention.] These emphases would continue throughout the "managerial rhetorics" of the late nineteenth and early twentieth centuries, which tended to reduce *ēthos* to literary *persona* or "a skill of stylistic adaptability" (Gabin, 1999, p. 114), at the same time eschewing questions of public morality and the traditional aims of civic discourse. In fact, the truncation of classical rhetoric to instruction in written composition reduced rhetoric's historically public, civic aspirations to mere belletrism.

Rejecting such abridgements, George Campbell (1719–1796) sought a fuller adaption of classical theory. Treating speech as well as writing, his *Philosophy of Rhetoric* (1776) is among the most influential treatises of its age; featuring an extensive discussion of civic *ēthos,* it addresses the unique problems facing the preacher, politician, and barrister. In chapter 8, "Of the Consideration which the Speaker ought to have of the Hearers, as such men in particular," Campbell notes that "the difference between one audience and another is very great, not only in intellectual but in moral accomplishments. That may be clearly intelligible to a House of Commons, which would appear as if spoken in an unknown tongue to a conventicle of enthusiasts" (p. 223). While the major differences among audiences arise from "the different cultivation of the understanding" (p. 223), nonetheless "different habits afterwards contracted, and different occupations in life, give different propensities, and make one incline more to one passion, another to another." And accommodation of each individual's "favorite passion" affords "the intelligent speaker an easier passage to the heart. . . . liberty and independence will ever be prevalent motives with republicans, pomp and splendour with those attached to monarchy" (p. 223). Thus Campbell melds the typically eighteenth-century notion of a "ruling" or "favorite passion" to Aristotle's *ēthē tōn politeōn* or the "characters of states." In chapter 9, "Of the Consideration which the Speaker ought to have of Himself," Campbell discusses the audience's perception of a speaker's character as an effect of "sympathy" (p. 224), by which implicitly Romantic term he means the capacity to raise in one's hearers the same emotions projected within a speaker's discourse—clearly an English Enlightenment version of Ciceronian *conciliare,* the aim of which is to exercise "power over the passions" of one's audience (p. 224).

Twentieth-Century Contexts: Psychology, Ideology, and "The Divided Self." Though bourgeois individualism remains at the ideological center of modern capitalism, the early twentieth century records an increasing sense of social alienation and economic helplessness, culminating in widespread political unrest and, at least temporarily in Russia and elsewhere, in communist revolution. After the worldwide Great Depression, "the traditional ideals of rugged individualism and self-sufficient autonomy became quite literally obsolete," as Baumeister (p. 78) notes. Given the individual's utter dependence upon the larger economy, "it no longer made sense to think of society as a loose collection of individuals who happened to have some common interests; instead, society was like a machine, with the individual cog useless and worthless except when functioning as part of the whole" (p. 78). As Robert Con Davis and David S. Gross observe in "The Ethos of the Subaltern" (1994), recent cultural criticism goes so far as to reject "the Enlightenment view of the great, isolated individual," thereby transforming "the concept of the personal agent into something more akin to the ancient Greek sense of *ethos* as 'habit,' that is, as a pattern of social practice inseparable from social relations" (p. 65). [*See* Criticism.] Indeed, several major influences on modern thought—particularly the political philosophy of Karl Marx (1818–1883), the linguistic theory of Ferdinand de Saussure (1857–1913), and the depth psychology of Sigmund Freud (1856–1939)—have served to decenter and fragment the Cartesian ego consciousness. No longer can the Cartesian *Cogito* or "I" of discourse claim to "speak for itself" and to stand as the self-sufficient origin or point of enunciation; rather, the *Cogito* has become a point *of intersection* of various cultural, linguistic, and psychic forces, each lying largely beyond the individual's conscious control.

Synthesizing Marx, Saussure, and Freud, Mikhail M. Bakhtin (1895–1975) explores the dialectical interplay among psychology, sociology, and language: as he writes in "Discourse in the Novel" (1935), "as a living, socio-ideological concrete thing . . . language, for the individual consciousness, lies on the borderline between oneself and the other," making "the word in language" half one's own and "half someone else's" (p. 293). In *Marxism and the Philosophy of Language* (1929), V. N. Vološinov (likely a pen name for Bakhtin) argues similarly, asserting that *"the reality of the inner psyche is the same reality as that of the sign"*:

> Outside the material of signs there is no psyche. . . . By its very existential nature, the subjective psyche is to be localized somewhere between the organism and the outside world, on the *borderline* separating these two spheres of reality. It is here that an encounter between the organism and the outside world takes place, but the encounter is not a physical one: *the organism and the outside world meet here in the sign.* (p. 26)

Like the "subjective psyche" that it seeks to represent, *ēthos* exists "somewhere between the organism and the outside world," this "somewhere between" being none other than a discourse whose language is in part one's own but in equal part the construction of one's history and culture.

Evidently, a postcapitalist, post-Cartesian *ēthos* must rest upon a different "ideology of the human" than one premised upon a unified ego consciousness whose distinguishing qualities are self-presence and self-possession. We must also observe the assault poststructuralist theory makes against classical notions of *ēthos*. As Aristotle describes it, the "artistic" creation of *ēthos* is quintessentially a linguistic phenomenon, a verbal construction of self-image. Yet his *Rhetoric* describes the role of character in oral discourse and, following classical tradition, subsequent discussions of literary *ēthos* have typically, if naively, assumed a rough equivalency between writing and

speaking. As previously mentioned, we must consider in more detail the ways that writing "textualizes" an author's projected self-image, at the same time distancing writers physically and temporally from their discourse. We often say that a text has "voice," and recent composition textbooks teach students to "find" or fashion the same; indeed, "voice" is often used interchangeably with *ēthos*. [*See* Communication; *and overview article on* Composition.] Yet the Latin *vox* originally meant no more than *verbum* or "word" *in its spoken form*. Etymologically, *vox* is that sound which is a spoken word, though we tend now to identify it with the *speaker* and his or her *manner* of speech (Baumlin, 1994, pp. xxiii–xxiv).

Voice, then, from a Cartesian perspective, describes an activity of consciousness within the human body, making use of the material organs of speech and marking the essential unity of a word with its point of enunciation. To say that a text has "voice" thus resorts to a fundamentally incarnationist metaphor, in which the written text "speaks" as a unified, consistent, self-present consciousness—as if hypostatizing the author's own living speech. From an incarnationist perspective, one might argue that all discourse is oriented toward (or proceeds from) the human body; in this sense, *ēthos* denotes the material, bodily presence "standing before" the texts that it speaks or writes. Articulating such a perspective in *Body Theology* (New York, 1973), theologian Arthur A. Vogel suggests that words are, indeed, "extensions of the body," a sort of "meaning in matter, a location of presence"—literally, an *embodied* presence. For meaning is in words, Vogel claims, "as we are in our bodies, and it is only because we are our bodies that we can 'be' our words—or, as it is usually put, mean what we say" (p. 92).

Historically, Western philosophy has fostered belief in such "phonocentrism," as Jacques Derrida terms it in *Grammatology* (translated by Gayatri Chakravorty Spivak, Baltimore, 1974); equated with the "interior voice" that "one hears upon retreating into oneself," textual meaning is presumed to express the "full and truthful presence of the divine voice to our inner sense" (p. 17). Implicitly theological in character, such phonocentrism continues to sustain our culture's belief in the self-presence of the *Cogito,* in the "copresence of the other and the self" (Derrida, p.

12), and in "intersubjectivity as the intentional phenomenon of the ego" (p. 12). Of course, Derrida makes such observations precisely to set writing against the "fantasy" of authorial self-presence and, in so doing, questions the very possibility of an inscribed or textualized *ēthos* (Baumlin, 1994, pp. xxiii–xxiv). Is writing a faithful record of an author's living speech? Or is it the death of speech and the effacement of voice and self-presence, as poststructuralism claims?

The problem of writing thus returns us, not surprisingly, to the *Phaedrus*, specifically to Socrates' denial that writing incarnates an author's conscious intention and meaning. Written words, Socrates argues, "seem to talk to you as though they were intelligent":

> But if you ask them anything about what they say, from a desire to be instructed, they go on telling you just the same thing forever. And once a thing is put into writing [it] drifts all over the place, getting into the hands not only of those who understand it, but equally of those who have no business with it; it doesn't know how to address the right people, and not address the wrong. And when it is ill-treated and unfairly abused it always needs its parent to come to help, being unable to defend or help itself. (275d–e)

Serving no more than to mimic or ventriloquize an author's living speech, the written text, as a mere "dead letter," lacks not only conscious understanding but also moral responsibility for its effects upon readers. Contemporary poststructuralist theory goes further, reducing the written text to its author's death mask. As Roland Barthes (1915–1980) writes in "Death of the Author," writing "is the destruction of every voice, every origin." It is that obliquity "into which our subject flees, the black-and-white where all identity is lost, beginning with the very identity of the body that writes." By means of writing, thus, "the voice loses its origin" and "the author enters into his own death" (p. 49).

In declaring the loss of "the very identity of the body that writes," Barthes's semiotics offers to refute Vogel's incarnationist theology of language, at the same time pointing to the very real, very rhetorical dilemma facing minorities and "marginalized" writers, whose textualized "death" or "disembodiment" threatens to efface precious differences in color, gender, sexual preference, and cultural voice. In "The World, the Text, and the Critic" (*Critical Theory Since Plato*. Edited by Hazard Adams, Fort Worth, Tex., 1972, pp. 1210–1222), Orientalist and colonialist critic Edward W. Said asserts that the critic (and, one must add, the literary artist and rhetorician) remains responsible "for articulating those voices dominated, displaced, or silenced by the textuality of texts" (p. 1222). In so arguing, Said stands against Derridean deconstruction, countering its implicit antihumanism by denying any essential difference between writing and speech and by maintaining the ethical relation between writers and their texts; for by this means only can written texts remain identified "with living beings in particular historical circumstances," as Hazard Adams notes (*Critical Theory Since Plato*, p. 1210). But Said's valorization of speech over writing "does not ensure the equality of every voice in the text or even the power of every voice to be heard" (Adams, p. 1210): whereas Bakhtin's *heteroglossia* assumes a rough equality among competing cultural voices, Said points to the ways that at least some writing inscribes an author's "self-confirming will to power," thereby sustaining "the unequal relation of colonizer to colonized" (p. 1210).

As Bakhtin argues, all acts of discourse must speak or write themselves against a background of prior voices, many of which claim an inviolate political, intellectual, or religious authority. Before one speaks, in other words, one confronts the already spoken, which can itself assume many guises: a text, an institution, a tradition, a reigning theory or, more insidiously, a particular gender, color, or class. [*See overview article on* African-American rhetoric; Feminist rhetoric; *and* Queer rhetoric.] (The terms have been equated since Aristotle: *to have* "ēthos" is *to be* "an authority.") The issue of authority thus raises additional questions concerning the status of the marginalized or minority speaker: if authority lies in the dominant cultural voice, must such a speaker *impersonate* that voice, in order to be heard? Is such an impersonation a capitulation or an act of empowerment? Does it serve to subvert authority, or does it simply reinscribe and preserve the dominant political culture? As Davis and Gross suggest (1994), a colonialist critic like Said writes of "the ethos of those who speak while positioned at the site of social oppression" (p. 67), and "the difficulty of representing the other is the problem of identifying the concept of *ēthos* in a manner responsive to the critique" of the dominant cultural authority (p. 68).

Aristotle *Rediviva*: Kenneth Burke and (Post-) Modern *Ēthos*. Given this emphasis upon competing cultural voices and the textualizations of self-image, it is not surprising that twentieth-century rhetorical theory has recovered the Aristotelian *pisteis* and, in particular, the notion of *ēthos* as an "artistic proof." [*See* Modern rhetoric.] In this respect, the technologies of mass media have profoundly influenced modern discourse, enabling speakers not only to multiply audiences beyond their own local communities but also to shape (and continually reshape) their self-image in film, videotape, and other media. As a result, the art of "publicity" and public relations has once again made ghostwriting a lucrative industry, with advertising agencies—whose clients include today's celebrities, politicians, and corporations—standing in the place of Lysias and the older Sophists. Recent communication theory has sought quantitative and experimental data to test and corroborate Aristotle's inferences; at the same time, theorists have reappropriated his rhetorical system, transforming the *pisteis* from a heuristic into an interpretive method. Treated thus, Aristotelian *ēthos* provides an instrument of cultural criticism as much as a means of rhetorical invention, teaching its students to analyze, critique, and even resist a speaker's manipulations of self-image.

At the forefront of this reappropriation stands Kenneth Burke (1897–1993), arguably the greatest rhetorician of the twentieth century, whose notions of "identification," "consubstantiality," and "courtship" all serve to (post-)modernize the Aristotelian vocabulary and to reground *ēthos* in the effects of group psychology. [*See* Identification.] As Burke writes in *The Rhetoric of Motives* (1969),

> You persuade a man only insofar as you can talk his language by speech, gesture, tonality, order, image, attitude, idea, *identifying* your ways with his. Persuasion by flattery is but a special case of persuasion in general. But flattery can safely serve as our paradigm if we

systematically widen its meaning, to see behind it the conditions of identification or consubstantiality in general. (p. 55)

In fact, Burke situates his theory of persuasion-as-identification within a social psychology of scapegoating, wherein communal identity is strengthened by the presence and threat, whether real or imaginary, of an ethnic, racial, or religious "other," whose cultural image has been demonized and against whom the community's cooperative efforts and resources can be directed. Implicitly, Burke redescribes Aristotle's *ēthē tōn politeōn* as a rhetorical manipulation of ideologies, cultural stereotypes, and unconscious projections, whereby an idealized racial or ethnic character is defined by its presumed *differences* from potential enemies: such *ēthos* or cultural identity enacts a dangerous dialectic, then, between self and other, the self *needing* the other in order to fashion and defend its idealized self-image. Placed in the hands of a manipulative, charismatic authority, such *ēthos* has proved capable of gaining mass support for acts of political violence, even to the point of genocide.

Clearly indebted to Burke, communication theorist Otis M. Walter (1964) turns similarly to group psychology in explaining the workings of "political ethos." As he writes, the effects of charismatic authority derive from two psychic mechanisms, "first, the desire for a savior or father-figure and second, the frustrations necessitated by one's idealized image" (p. 41). As Walter argues, "the source of ethos is a need, a want, a goal, a lack, a frustration, a weakness, a deficiency, a wish."

> [But], whatever the mechanism by which ethos is actualized, the starting point of ethos is need. *Ethos, therefore, is not a separate mode of persuasion,* coordinate with logic and emotion; *it is, rather, an aspect of motivation. The power of ethos derives not from a mysterious "third force" but from the strengths of one's motives which are responsible for patterning the image of a person.* To an audience with one set of needs, a given speaker will have a certain kind of ethos, but to audiences with other needs, he may have a different kind of image. (p. 41)

As Walter suggests, the projected need that underlies *ēthos* must be not only intense, autonomous, and widespread, but also the sort that "cannot be gratified by one's self. . . . Moreover, the person to whom we accord ethos not only must be one who can gratify a strong need, but one who has some sort of *exclusive ability to gratify the motive or ability to gratify it better than others*" (p. 42). Only by such reasoning, Walter adds, "can one understand the fatal collapse of the German people toward Hitler" (p. 40). A crucial role for contemporary theory, thus, is to develop further our culture's capacities to identify, critique, and resist such mass appeals; indeed, Walter declares our need for "*defenses* against the ethos" (p. 43) of charismatic political authority: "if ethos arises in seemingly hopeless situations where needs are desperate, then one defense must be to *reduce the needs* that pave the road down which the man on horseback rides" (p. 44).

Whereas Burke describes *ēthos* as an implicitly violent practice of self-identification by means of scapegoating (the speaking self defined, once again, in its difference from the threatening other), and Walter as a social pathology to be resisted by all means, still other contemporary theorists have sought to "save" *ēthos*, restoring its positive, ethical uses and minimizing its potential for abuse. For our time is one "of fragmentation and isolation," as S. Michael Halloran observes (1975), a time when *ēthos* can succeed only by the degree to which a speaker "is willing and able to make his world open to the other," thus risking "self and world by a rigorous and open articulation of them in the presence of the other" (pp. 627–628). Rather than maintain the speaker's expertise, power, or superiority over an audience, this final model grounds *ēthos* in the equal, ethical *copresence* of self and other. Describing this rhetoric, Jim W. Corder (1978) writes, poignantly, that

we are "apart from each other," and it may be, as Burke said, that the only thing we have in common is our separateness. Distances open between us. We keep trying to enter their world or bring them to ours. Often we fail, but we keep trying. The trouble is that our speaking-forth—the primary need and issue of any age—is complex, confused, and messy, and often creates as many problems as it solves. Language is our way of composing ourselves. It is our first and last line of defense, and we are vulnerable in each line. (p. 2)

Thus Corder and Halloran affirm the mutual risk facing speakers and audiences alike, as well as the need for developing a commodious discourse, wherein language becomes the means, not just of "composing ourselves," but of making our "world open to the other"—opening a space, as it were, for the copresence of self and other, as "we keep trying to enter their world or bring them into ours." Existentialist in implication, such a model turns *ēthos* into a collaboration, raising the audience up to be an equal participant, valuing ethical self-revelation and communication over persuasion, demystifying the projections of charismatic authority, and valuing the audience's welfare over the speaker's personal advantage.

BIBLIOGRAPHY

Aristotle. *Aristotle on Rhetoric: A Theory of Civic Discourse.* Translated by George A. Kennedy. New York, 1991. The best contemporary translation and commentary of the most important classical text on *ēthos.*

Augustine. *On Christian Doctrine.* Translated by D. W. Robertson, Jr. Indianapolis, 1958.

Bakhtin, Mikhail M. *The Dialogic Imagination: Four Essays.* Edited by Michael Holquist, translated by Caryl Emerson and Michael Holquist. Austin, Tex., 1981.

Barthes, Roland. "The Death of the Author." In *The Rustle of Language.* Translated by Richard Howard, pp. 49–55. New York, 1986. A poststructuralist critique of authorial "self-presence."

Baumeister, Roy F. *Identity: Cultural Change and the Struggle for Self.* Oxford, 1986. A history of the cultural and psychological development of Western selfhood. Though not rhetorical in focus, its historical survey helps explicate the evolving rhetorical concepts of *ēthos.*

Baumlin, James S., and Tita French Baumlin, eds. *Ethos: New Essays in Rhetorical and Critical Theory.* Dallas, Tex., 1994. An essay collection exploring classical, historical, and contemporary theories of *ēthos.*

Baumlin, James S. "Positioning *Ethos* in Historical and Contemporary Theory." In *Ethos: New Essays in Rhetorical and Critical Theory,* edited by James S. Baumlin and Tita French Baumlin, pp. xi–xxxi. Dallas, Tex., 1994.

Burke, Kenneth. *A Rhetoric of Motives.* Berkeley, 1969. First published 1950.

Campbell, George. The Philosophy of Rhetoric. In *The Rhetoric of Blair, Campbell, and Whately.* Edited by James L. Golden and Edward P. J. Corbett, pp. 139–272. Carbondale, Ill., 1990. First published 1776. Includes Campbell's major discussions of *ēthos* and ethical argument.

Carrithers, Michael, Steven Collins, and Steven Lukes, eds. *The Category of the Person: Anthropology, Philosophy, History.* Cambridge, U.K., 1985.

Chamberlain, Charles. "From Haunts to Character: The Meaning of Ethos and Its Relation to Ethics." *Helios* 11 (1984), pp. 97–108. A valuable brief discussion of etymology.

Cicero. *Cicero on Oratory and Orators.* Translated by J. S. Watson. Carbondale, Ill., 1970. Reprint of a serviceable Victorian translation of *De oratore.*

Cope, E. M. *The Rhetoric of Aristotle with a Commentary.* Edited and revised by J. E. Sandys. Dubuque, Iowa, 1966. First published 1877. The seminal discussion of Aristotelian *ēthos,* highly influential upon twentieth-century scholarship.

Corder, Jim W. "Varieties of Ethical Argument." *Freshman English News* 6 (1978), pp. 1–23. Thinking beyond the classical-Aristotelian categories and vocabulary, this seminal essay offers to re-conceptualize modern *ēthos.*

Davis, Robert Con, and David S. Gross. "Gayatri Chakravorty Spivak and the *Ethos* of the Subaltern." In *Ethos: New Essays in Rhetorical and Critical Theory,* edited by James S. Baumlin and Tita French Baumlin, pp. 65–89. Dallas, Tex., 1994.

Dionysius of Halicarnassus. *The Critical Essays.* 2 vols. Translated by Stephen Usher. Cambridge, Mass., 1974–1985.

Foucault, Michel. "What Is an Author?" *Textual Strategies: Perspectives in Post-Structuralist Criticism.* Edited by Josue V. Harari, pp. 141–160. Ithaca, N.Y., 1979. A poststructuralist critique of literary *ēthos.*

Gale, Fredric G., Phillip Sipiora, and James L. Kinneavy, eds. *Ethical Issues in the Teaching of Writing.* New York, 1999. An essay collection exploring *ēthos* and ethical argument in contemporary writing instruction.

Grimaldi, William A., S. J. "The Auditor's Role in Aristotelian Rhetoric." In *Oral and Written Communication: Historical Approaches.* Edited by Richard Leo Enos, pp. 65–81. Newbury Park, Calif., 1990. Diverges from traditional Aristotelian scholarship in asserting that the character of the audience, as well as of the speaker, is "artistically" constructed by means of speech.

Halloran, S. Michael. "On the End of Rhetoric, Classical and Modern." *College English* 35 (1975), pp. 621–631. A seminal discussion of modern/existentialist *ēthos.*

Isocrates. *Isocrates.* Translated by George Norlin. Cambridge, Mass., 1968.

Kennedy, George A. *Classical Rhetoric and Its Christian and Secular Tradition from Ancient to Modern Times.* 2d ed. Chapel Hill, N.C., 1999. A valuable historical survey of rhetoric generally and of the changing definitions of *ēthos.*

Kinneavy, James L., and Susan C. Warshauer. "From Aristotle to Madison Avenue: *Ethos* and the Ethics of Argument." In *Ethos: New Essays in Rhetorical and Critical Theory,* edited by James S. Baumlin and Tita French Baumlin, pp. 171–190. Dallas, Tex., 1994.

Machiavelli, Niccolò. *The Prince.* Translated by Paul Sonnino. Atlantic Highlands, N.J., 1996.

May, James M. *Trials of Character: The Eloquence of Ciceronian Ethos.* Chapel Hill, N.C., 1988. A full discussion of Ciceronian theory and practice.

Plato. *The Collected Dialogues.* Edited by Edith Hamilton and Huntington Cairns. Princeton, 1961. A standard edition of the *Gorgias* and *Phaedrus,* Plato's major dialogues on rhetoric.

Quintilian. *Institutio Oratoria.* Translated H. E. Butler. 4 vols. Cambridge, Mass., 1920–1922.

Solmsen, Friedrich. "The Aristotelian Tradition in Ancient Rhetoric." *American Journal of Philology* 62 (1941), pp. 35–50, 169–190. A seminal discussion of the influences of Aristotelian concepts, the *pisteis* especially, upon subsequent theory.

Vološinov, V. N. *Marxism and the Philosophy of Language.* Translated by Ladislav Matejka and I. R. Titunik. Cambridge, Mass., 1986. First published 1929.

Walter, Otis M. "Toward an Analysis of Ethos." *Pennsylvania Speech Annual* 21 (1964), pp. 37–45. A compelling critique of modern political rhetoric and its manipulations of *ēthos.*

Wilson, Thomas. *The Art of Rhetoric (1560).* Edited by Peter E. Medine. University Park, Pa., 1994.

Wisse, Jakob. *Ethos and Pathos from Aristotle to Cicero.* Amsterdam, 1989. Arguably the most complete and important discussion of the distinctions between Aristotelian and Ciceronian *ēthos.* Wisse includes an exhaustive critical survey of previous classical scholarship.

—JAMES S. BAUMLIN

EULOGY. *See* Epideictic genre; *and* Hybrid genres.

EVIDENCE. *See* Descriptio; *and* Eloquence.

EXEMPLUM, or example, is an ancient and almost ubiquitous rhetorical figure, though less often acknowledged than metaphor, simile, and metonymy. The original Latin term *exemplum* is the source of two modern terms, *example* and *ex-*

emplum. Although in antiquity and the Middle Ages, the Latin *exemplum* seems merely to have been the equivalent and cognate of the English *example,* the vernacular *exemplum,* which dates apparently from nineteenth-century literary criticism, is used to designate narratives with a didactic intention, as typified by such narratives within medieval sermons.

The Greek *paradeigma* (example), is described in Aristotle's *Rhetoric* and *Topics* as one of the two means of persuasion. In the first book of the *Rhetoric,* Aristotle identifies the only two rhetorical means of producing belief as example (*paradeigma*) and *enthymeme* (1356b). [*See* Enthymeme.] Examples are here linked with induction, since they connect particular cases to a general rule. Aristotle's definition should be broadened, however, since *example* has long been used not only to *prove* but also to *clarify* or simply to help the audience remember a general proposition, and these complementary uses may be the major distinction between rhetorical example and dialectical (or logical) induction.

Aristotle divides examples into factual and fictitious, the former relying on historical experience and the latter invented to support the argument. These invented examples in turn are divided into "comparisons" (*parabolē*) and "fables" (*logos*) (*Rhetoric* 1393a–b). Thus, in ancient rhetoric there were three types of example: historical example, parable, and fable, a tripartite arrangement described in detail by Cicero (106–43 BCE), in *De inventione.* In describing narratives in oratory, Cicero notes that one form of narrative conveys the facts of the case at hand, a second is a digression merely to amuse the audience, but the third use, as described by Cicero is "wholly unconnected with public issues, which is recited or written solely for amusement but at the same time provides valuable training." Within this category, Cicero locates history (*historia*), "an account of actual occurrences remote from the recollection of our own age"; argument (*argumentum*), "a fictitious narrative which nevertheless could have occurred"; and fable (*fabula*), "the term applied to a narrative in which the events are not true and have no verisimilitude." Cicero's three narrative types parallel Aristotle's categories of example, since the content of the *parabolē* or

comparison is clearly possible even though it is fictitious, while the fable in both cases is both fictitious and impossible.

Holding together the categories of example, historical-factual and poetic-fictitious, are two major ideas: first, that concrete experience, especially when it is familiar to an audience, is highly significant; and, second, that things (both material objects and events) repeat themselves. Martin Bloomer (1992) shows the power of familiarity in Cicero's preference for Roman examples over foreign ones, though in certain periods such as the Renaissance, ancient or exotic examples are sometimes preferred as more weighty or memorable. The second major idea, a belief in predictable repetition of precedent, leads to the paradox that example often draws on historical material but fragments and decontextualizes it for the purposes of a new context, in effect denying the specificity or uniqueness of historical incidents.

There are conventions for the way examples appear in discourse. Many examples begin with expressions like "for example," or *exempli gratia* (our familiar *e.g.*). These are *explicit examples.* The combination of a general rule (generally given in the present tense) with a specific historical event (generally given in a past tense) is another way example manifests itself in a text. A third convention is the clustering of examples within the text itself. Aristotle himself pointed to conventions of number and location of examples, saying that examples are best used as "a kind of epilogue to the enthymemes," for if examples come first, "they resemble induction," which is not suitable to most rhetorical occasions; but if examples come last, "they resemble evidence, and a witness is in every case likely to induce belief." In this latter configuration, only one is necessary (*The Art of Rhetoric* 1394a).

Aristotle's comment on the order of presentation leads the twentieth-century theorists Perelman and Olbrechts-Tyteca (1969) to distinguish *example* from *illustration.* Arguing that the sequence of presentation of the particular case is not important, they claim that when the example comes first, what Aristotle had viewed as something like induction, is, simply, example; and when examples come last, this is *illustration.* For

Perelman and Olbrechts-Tyteca, the term *example* is most appropriate to describe the appeal to a particular case to establish a generalization when such a generalization is in doubt, whereas the *illustration* clarifies and applies a rule that is not in dispute. Although this refinement of the classical description of example may be useful in some theoretical contexts, there seems to be no reason to exclude illustration from example. In ordinary use of the terms, illustration is a form of example.

In medieval Europe, example flourished in the church not only as a basis for sermons but as the link between preaching and visual arts. Many exemplary stories, from the scriptures or from legend, such as Dives and Lazarus or Potiphar's wife, appear frequently in stained glass windows, sculpture, and manuscript illuminations. [*See overview article on* Medieval rhetoric.] During the Renaissance, classical antiquity provided a large increase in secular examples, used heavily by such authors as Machiavelli and Montaigne, and inspired significant literary works that, instead of taking traditional ecclesiastical or historical stories, made entirely new fictions cast in the form of "exemplary stories" (e.g., Cervantes's *Novellas ejemplares,* 1612). [*See* Renaissance rhetoric, *article on* Rhetoric in Renaissance language and literature.] This use of example is often paradoxical, since the Early Modern world, after being shaken by the discovery of the New World and the Cartesian philosophical challenge to the value of learning from antiquity, often wondered whether the predictable cyclical worldview that had earlier given example its value was still valid. But example is not only based on the idea of repetition; it also, as noted earlier, thrives on the basis of empirical experience. In the sixteenth century and after, religious conflicts, geographic exploration, scientific experimentation, and a surge of memoir writing provided a new range of concrete experience, invigorating example-based discourse, particularly in polemic. Voltaire's *Candide* (1759) is a series of mostly fictitious and satirical examples.

In the nineteenth century, the Romantic emphasis on metaphor and symbol drew attention away from example among theorists of rhetoric. Some major manuals, such as Pierre Fontanier's *Figures autres que tropes* (Paris, 1827), do not mention example. While example now receives a

small amount of attention in theory, it continues to be one of the workhorse rhetorical figures in contexts ranging from political speeches to television journalism.

BIBLIOGRAPHY

Bloomer, W. Martin. *Valerius Maximus and the Rhetoric of the New Nobility.* Chapel Hill, N.C., 1992.
Croce, B. "L'efficacia dell'esempio." In *Etica e Politica,* pp. 119–123. Rome, 1973. First published 1931.
Geremek, B. "L'*Exemplum* et la circulation de la culture au moyen âge." In *Mélanges de l'École Française de Rome,* pp. 153–179. Rome, 1980.
Lyons, J. D. *Exemplum. The Rhetoric of Example in Early Modern France and Italy.* Princeton, 1989.
Perelman, C., and L. Olbrechts-Tyteca. *The New Rhetoric.* Translated by John Wilkinson and Purcell Weaver, pp. 350–410. Notre Dame, Ind., 1969.
Warminski, A. "Reading for Example: 'Sense-Certainty' in Hegel's *Phenomenology of Spirit.*" *Diacritics* 11.2 (Summer 1981), pp. 83–94.

—JOHN D. LYONS

EXHORTATION (intensive form of Lat. *hortari,* to encourage, *Oxford English Dictionary*) might be broadly described as the use of rhetorical means to encourage ongoing moral reformation or, more immediately, to encourage morally significant action on the basis of common experience, conviction, or hope. Exhortation may be dissuasive, being against certain actions, or persuasive, being toward responsibility in positive action. With variation, exhortation is normally marked by an appeal to belief and action congruent with moral principles, social vision, or religious experience already *shared* by speaker and audience. It is, therefore, a call to a moral turning that often bears a conservative dynamic of preservation, perseverance, or return to good conscience. As such, exhortation need not argue over contested convictions or claims. It is more often found in discourse seeking to reinforce and incite rather than deliberate. Therefore, exhortation might be described metaphorically as persuasion aimed toward the heart and hands rather than the head and eyes. It is concerned with arousing a hearer's emotional bond to shared knowledge and identifying that bond with recommended practice.

In ordinary discourse, exhortation is often associated with preaching or the use of a "sermonic" tone. Indeed, the rhetorical tradition has often interpreted preaching as almost exclusively hortatory, but when interpreted from their classical origins to the present, the rich histories of both exhortation and preaching exceed simple equation. This essay explores exhortation by summarizing broadly recurring commonplaces in religious and nonreligious exhortation, discussing related terms from ancient use, and noting the adaptation and transformation of exhortation in early and medieval Christian practice. Though reference is made to both cross-cultural and contemporary practice, the Greco-Roman and Christian origins of exhortation are given particular attention, since this is where we find a vocabulary enabling rhetorical theoretical consideration of the practice.

Recurring Characteristics of Exhortation. While able to use various rhetorical forms, styles, genres, and levels of indirection, hortatory language most often represents direct speech between speaker and hearers and puts this speech in a style congruent with the ordinary speech of those engaged. This may be because exhortation takes a high stake in appeals from *ēthos*, which may be built on the represented authority of a third person, a shared theological, philosophical, or social vision, common experience, or agreed on religious, military, political, or other purpose. [*See* Ēthos.]

Often coming in the conclusion of a discourse, following narration or extended proof, an exhortation rests an appeal to action on the *pathos* of an audience's desire to participate in the shared *ēthos* represented. [*See* Arrangement, *article on* Traditional arrangement; *and* Pathos.] It is for this reason that exhortation is commonly found in the classical epideictic genre (ceremonial, basing arguments regarding character or action on available common feeling), even though epideictic is often constructed in grand style and in descriptive rather than direct address. [*See* Epideictic genre.] A shift from grand to plain style and nonpersonal to direct address in the midst of an epideictic appeal is a common marker for a turn from celebration or condemnation to exhortation. Nevertheless, if shared vision is strong, the credibility of a represented author high, and com-

mendation of certain action the overall purpose of a discourse, then an entire discourse, including parts that do not meet the tests of direct speech, plain style, or moral reference may still be called an "exhortation." Modern papal "exhortations" are examples (e.g., John Paul II, 1995). One can also find examples in narrative, poetic, or even musical forms (e.g., Karega et al., 1989).

With this general emphasis on direct speech, plain style, moral reference, and the *ēthos* of intimacy or shared beliefs, letters have proven an apt form for exhortation. Ancient examples include the letters of Seneca (c.4 BCE–c.65 CE) to Lucilius (Malherbe, 1986, pp. 43–46, 69–71) and the New Testament *Epistles*. However, later rhetorical training emphasized eloquence and style in letter writing in a way less conducive to exhortation (Murphy, 1974, pp. 194–269). The decline of belles-lettres has allowed letters again to become a significant form for exhortation. Martin Luther King, Jr.'s 1963 "Letter From the Birmingham Jail" is a recent example. On the *ēthos* built through an appeal to shared faith and implied moral vision, King is able to use the perceived intimacy and direct speech of a letter to turn extended refutation, argument, and explanation into exhortation.

Wilson (1997) has argued that Greco-Roman exhortation displays three personae. The first is the exhorter, or the "I" of direct speech. The second, or audience, is relatively specific, for hortatory rhetoric rarely addresses a universal, nonspecified, audience. The third reference includes those whose actions or opinions frame the substance of the action that is called for or the community of moral formation that is evoked. In the case of an appeal to an authoritative text, such as a scripture, exemplary stories from the text may be used as examples or the scripture itself may be appealed to as though an authoritative "person" to be emulated or honored. As implied, a third persona may also be represented as a character to honor (e.g., honoring fallen comrades by fighting for victory) or its antithesis. It should also be noted that a *rhētōr* might represent him or herself as both a first and a third persona in exhortation (e.g., *1 Tm.* 1; see Fiore, 1986, pp. 184–190).

A topic characteristic, but not definitive, of exhortation is *example* (Fiore, 1986). [*See* Exemplum.] In *Arte of Rhetorique (1560),* for instance,

Thomas Wilson (c.1525–1581) follows Erasmus (c.1466–1536) in naming seven commonplaces for exhortation: praise for a deed or a person worthy of emulation; the expectation others have of a hearer's good action; assurance of divine aid or certain victory; hope of renown through sacrifice; fear of shame in refusing to sacrifice; desire for eternal reward for good deeds; and the "rehearsal of examples from all ages, and especially of things lately done" (1993, 100). [*See* Commonplaces and commonplace books; *and* Topics.] Examples may buttress each topic on the list even as the use of examples is its own topic. Other figurative techniques common to exhortation include hyperbolē, antithesis, aphorisms, and warnings. [*See* Antithesis; *and* Hyperbolē.]

Classical Variation. Ancient terms related to exhortation include *paraklēsis, paraenesis, protreptic,* and *diatribē. Paraklēsis* gathers into exhortation the notions of beseeching and consolation. This is consistent with ancient practice, for example, because funeral discourse could include an encouragement to mourners to honor the dead through bravery and virtue (*Theological Dictionary of the New Testament,* 5, p. 776). Traces of this form of epideictic exhortation remain in funeral liturgies.

Paraenesis is used interchangeably with *exhortation,* but most often refers to a work that uses exhortation among other pedagogical tools to shape a discipline of moral formation in a school or similar context. *Paraenesis* encourages adherents toward virtue, normally encompassing a broad view of the good and happy life in the form of precepts (principles by which to live) (Malherbe, 1986, pp. 125–126). Clark has shown the way such precepts were used in rhetorical education (1957, pp. 181–188). Precepts were elaborated upon in written exercises (*chreia*) using topics common to Greco-Roman exhortation. One finds in *paraenesis* the practical application of philosophy or theology to children's education or self-control in adults (Malherbe, 1986, pp. 30–33). The former is more characteristic of Greco-Roman *paraenesis* and the latter of early Christian (e.g., *Tit.* 2).

Considering *paraenesis* outside its ancient technique, one can identify analogues though the ages. A twelfth-century example of a *paraenesis* might be Hugh's *Didascalicon* (1128), by which

monastic pedagogy and moral life were shaped through disciplines of reading, meditation, and the interpretation of texts. Contemporary examples might include *Life Together,* Dietrich Bonhoeffer's paraenetic guide for the training of clergy for Germany's anti-Nazi "confessing church" (New York, 1954), or possibly the structured patterns of communal moral training in the American civil rights movement. This paraenetic formation included the liturgical invocations of divine aid and repeated exhortations to nonviolence, communal action, honorable self-sacrifice, and the hope of final victory.

Protreptic and *paraenesis* often merge, but can be distinguished in ancient usage in focus and, to a lesser degree, rhetorical form. *Protreptic* generally cultivates a certain kind of knowledge and its specific virtue (Fiore, 1990, p. 162). Malherbe sees in *protreptic* exhortation to an enterprise or discipline through a demonstration of a hearer's condition of lack and the superiority of the advocated way of life (1986, p. 122). The term is used for exhortations to the philosophical life, such as the *Protrepticus* of Aristotle (384–322 BCE), or the *Exhortation to Philosophy* of Iamblichus (250–330 CE).

The *diatribē* is another form convivial to exhortation (Malherbe, p. 130). It is a lively, dialogic pedagogy. Diatribe is built through heightening contrast and contradiction, rhetorical questioning, exclamation, word plays, antitheses, lists of vices and virtues, lists of hardships (between virtues and vices), and short, open-ended responses to posed problems. The Apostle Paul's Letter to the Romans is a good example of the use of diatribe. Quite apart from its contemporary use as a synonym for invective, the forms that compose diatribe remain active tools for exhortation.

Ancient Jewish exhortation used collections of proverbs, lyric, and stories for moral training, such as *Proverbs* and *Job.* Hebrew writings also contain records of exhortations in direct speech (e.g., *Tb.* 4; *Am.* 5). Traditional liturgical poems, or *piyyutim,* sometimes exhort hearers to the love of the Torah. Moreover, some have argued that the extended narratives of Hebrew apocalyptic literature, such as the Book of Zechariah, and its related Christian expressions, such as The Apocalypse of John or The Shepherd of Hermas, served a particular hortatory purpose during periods of intense social crisis and perceived persecution (Osiek, 1986). [*See* Hebrew rhetoric.] Ancient Vedic literature also contains exhortation, as does the Qur'an. Qur'anic exhortation strongly relies on antitheses of promise and warning (e.g., chapter 35: "The good word is heard by Him and the good deed exalted. But those that plot evil shall be sternly punished."), and displays fewer of the Greco-Roman forms. [*See* Arabic rhetoric.]

Christian Adaptation and Development. Most Greco-Roman forms of exhortation can be found in early Christian literature. Their use, however, is looser and their purposes more urgent. The Gospels contain considerable hortatory rhetoric in the forms of parables (e.g., *Lk.* 10.25–37), rhetorical contrast (e.g., *Mt.* 5.20–48), hyperbolē (*Mt.* 23.24), and the like. Often addressed to Hellenistic audiences, the epistles of Paul and the pastoral epistles are rich in exhortation. Wilson (1997) interprets *Colossians* as a classic paraenetic form, as does Malherbe (1983; see *1 Thes.*). Possible interpretation of apocalyptic literature as hortatory has been mentioned. An example of another early Christian exhortation is Origen's *Exhortation to Martyrdom* (c.235 CE).

Early Christian exhortation shifted the locus of hortatory authority. While classical proofs and stylistics are apparent, they are sublimated to the apodeicticity (reliable proof) of scripture taken up from Jewish devotion. To this is added appeals to divine power and presence as both proof and purpose for commended action (e.g., *1 Cor.* 1.30). Saint Augustine's transformation of rhetorical proof through *caritas* (love in action, with moral implication) is characteristic and influential (Murphy, 1983, pp. 286–292).

Beginning by assuming the synagogue practice of weekly public interpretation of scripture, the Christian sermon was eventually described as almost exclusively exhortation, with each homiletic argument buttressed by scriptural reference and moral "significations" (Murphy, 1983, p. 296). [*See* Homiletics.] Only the question of appropriate topics, forms of proof, balance between protreptic and aprotreptic appeals, and effective style remained at issue—never the status of preaching as exhortation. As late as the nineteenth century, Richard Whately (1787–1863) acknowledges in *Elements of Rhetoric* (7th ed., 1846; 1963) that most "popular" sermons "consist avowedly and almost exclusively of exhortation, strictly so called" (2.2.1). Though he calls for a more didactic style, he does so in order that by a more "oblique" approach those deadened to a "vehement" style might yet be persuaded. Thus, he both reiterates the fundamental purpose of preaching as exhortation and shows the way in which common usage of exhortation was reduced over the centuries to mere vehemence. As shown here, however, the history of the practice is more complex, and also, one hopes, its prospects.

Characteristic of twentieth-century philosophical developments, Kenneth Burke and Emmanuel Levinas have taken exhortation to the phenomenological origin of human consciousness itself (Burke, 1968; Levinas, 1987). Their descriptions of human sociality originating in hortatory negation ("Do not!") before ontological description ("It is . . .") have opened important new avenues of investigation. Exhortation thus exhorts to further study.

BIBLIOGRAPHY

Bonhoeffer, Dietrich. *Life Together.* Translated by John W. Doberstein. New York, 1954. English translation of 1930s paraenetic text for training of clergy for anti-Nazi "confessing church," with an introduction by the translator.

Burke, Kenneth. *Language as Symbolic Action.* Berkeley, 1968. Builds a philosophy of language around hortatory discourse as the "origin" of symbolic action, especially in chapter 7.

Chroust, Anton-Hermann. *Aristotle: Protrepticus: A Reconstruction.* Notre Dame, Ind., 1964. Classic exhortation to the philosophical life, reconstructed from fragments, with an introduction.

Clark, Donald Lemen. *Rhetoric in Greco-Roman Education.* New York, 1957. Helpful source on paraenetic exhortation and the use of rhetoric in the ancient schools.

Fiore, Benjamin, S. J. *The Function of Personal Example in the Socratic and Pastoral Epistles.* Analectica Biblica 105. Rome, 1986. Scholarly treatment of the use of example in Hellenistic and early Christian literature, with extensive discussion of exhortation and detailed bibliography.

Fiore, Benjamin, S. J. "Paranesis and Protreptic." In *The Anchor Bible Dictionary,* vol. 5. Edited by David Noel Freedman, pp. 162–165. New York, 1990. Succinct summary with ample bibliographic references.

Hugh of Saint Victor. *Didascalicon: A Medieval Guide to the Arts.* Translated by Jerome Taylor. New York,

1961. English translation of Latin paraenetic text of 1128, with introduction and notes.

Iamblichus. "The Exhortation to Philosophy." In *The Exhortation to Philosophy: Including the Letters of Iamblichus and Proclus' Commentary on the Chaldean Oracles*. Translated by Thomas Moore Johnson; edited by Stephen Neuville, pp. 21–112. Grand Rapids, Mich., 1988. First published 1907. An example of Hellenistic *protreptic* based on early second-century text.

John Paul II. *Ecclesia in Africa: Post-Synodal Apostolic Exhortation of the Holy Father to the Bishops, Priests and Deacons, Men and Women Religious, and all the Lay Faithful on the Church in Africa and Its Evangelizing Mission Towards the Year 2000*. Nairobi, Kenya, 1995. Example of contemporary extended written religious exhortation.

Karega, Muthoni et al., eds. *The River Without Frogs and Other Stories, Plays and Poems: An Anthology of Kenyan Writing in Exhortation of Child Survival and Development*. Nairobi, Kenya, 1989. An anthology of African poems, short stories, and plays for children under twelve written in response to the 1987 Dakar Plan of Action for the Preservation and Development of the African Child. An example of the use of these literary forms in exhortation.

King, Martin Luther, Jr. "Letter From the Birmingham Jail." In *Testament of Hope: Essential Writings of Martin Luther King, Jr.* Edited by James Melvin Washington, pp. 289–302. San Francisco, Calif., 1986. Recent use of the letter form for public exhortation.

Levinas, Emmanuel. *Collected Philosophical Papers*. Translated by Alphonso Lingis. Dordrecht, The Netherlands, 1987. Representative collection of the author's phenomenological essays on language, ethics, and human sociality. Translated from French. The hortatory origin of human consciousness in the "command of the other" is investigated. See especially, "Freedom and Command," pp. 15–24.

Malherbe, Abraham J. "Exhortation in First Thessalonians." *Novum Testamentum* 25 (1983), pp. 238–256.

Malherbe, Abraham J. *Moral Exhortation, A Greco-Roman Sourcebook*. Philadelphia, 1986. Thoroughly surveys the social setting, rhetorical forms, and conventional topics of Greco-Roman moral exhortation with many helpful excerpted examples.

Murphy, James J. *Rhetoric in the Middle Ages: A History of Rhetorical Theory from Saint Augustine to the Renaissance*. Berkeley, 1974. Contains a most helpful survey of medieval homiletic theory.

Origen. "The Exhortation to Martyrdom." In *Ancient Christian Writers*, no. 19. Edited by Johannes Quasten and Joseph Plumpe, *Prayer. Exhortation to Martyrdom*. Translated and annotated by John J. O'Meara, pp. 141–198. Westminster, Md., 1954. First pub-

lished c.235 CE. Extended work of early Christian exhortation.

Osiek, Carolyn. "The Genre and Function of the Shepherd of Hermas." In *Early Christian Apocalypticism: Genre and Social Setting*. Special issue guest edited by Adela Yarbro Collins. *Semeia* 36 (1986), pp. 113–122. Explores the genre and function of early Christian apocalyptic.

"Paraklesis." In *Theological Dictionary of the New Testament*. Edited by Gerhard Kittel and Gerhard Friedrich; translated by Geoffrey W. Bromiley. 10 vols. Grand Rapids, Mich., 1964–1976. Translated from a German article by Otto Schmitz and Gustav Stählin that examines Hebrew, Greek, Roman, and New Testament contexts.

Petuchowski, Jakob J. *Theology and Poetry: Studies in the Medieval Piyyut*. London, 1978. Analysis and presentation of medieval Jewish liturgical poetry, with certain hortatory use.

Whately, Richard. *Elements of Rhetoric*. Edited by Douglas Ehninger. Carbondale, Ill., 1963. This edition is a facsimile edition of the 1846 seventh edition, with an introduction. Nineteenth-century English rhetoric with interest in homiletics and reference to exhortation as vehemence.

Wilson, Thomas. *The Art of Rhetoric (1560)*. Edited by Peter E. Medine. University Park, Pa., 1993. English Humanist rhetorical theory with explicit discussion of exhortation. New edition with annotations.

Wilson, Walter T. *The Hope of Glory: Education and Exhortation in the Epistle to the Colossians*. Leiden, 1997. A strong resource with detailed argument that the Letter to the Colossians is a Christianized Hellenistic *paraenesis*, including a helpful survey of Greco-Roman exhortation.

—WESLEY D. AVRAM

EXPEDIENCY. Considerations of expediency play a central role in Aristotle's treatment of deliberative rhetoric in ancient Greece. Deliberative rhetoric refers to the art of speaking in front of legislative assemblies about the future promised by the policies being considered. The objective of the deliberative speaker is *sympheron* (the expedient), which means the advantageous: whatever benefits the city-state.

For Aristotle (384–322 BCE) advantage consists of two parts—means and ends. Ends, such as honor, justice, or wealth, are not subject to dispute. Rather, they are ideals predicated on the views of the audience and grounded in ordinary ways of talking. What may be debated would be which ends to call upon in a specific case (whether honor, justice, or wealth, for example). Means are also debated. Which is the best means, the one most likely to achieve the end, achieve it economically, bring with it fewer or less serious disadvantages, and so forth; these questions call for deliberation.

Aristotle's *Rhetoric* enumerates five subject areas addressed in the deliberative genre: finances, war and peace, national defense, imports and exports, and the framing of laws. He urges his students, in preparation for speaking before a legislative assembly, as a matter of expediency, to seek knowledge and to do research on specific subject areas in contemporary and historical contexts.

But how is expediency accomplished? Plato and Aristotle offer different answers to this question. Plato (c.428–c.347 BCE) believed that calculations of the good will improve when a philosopher king is put in charge. In perhaps his most famous dialogue, the *Republic,* his protagonist Socrates argues that the practical task of weighing advantages and disadvantages in making decisions is best left not to a tyrant, one who simply wants power over others, but to a philosopher king. That is the person who, among his fellows, is freest from self-interest and has the purest soul. This implies that, for Plato, expediency is judged in a system favoring rule by one. There is, in such a system, little room left for persuasion. In fact, Plato's *Republic* banishes poets and rhetoricians, so that their ignorant chatter will not divert citizens from or confuse them about the words of the philosopher king.

In contrast, Aristotle holds that calculations of expediency can be improved when the most intelligent and most civic-minded people deliberate. He rejects Plato's philosopher king. In his lectures on *Politics,* Aristotle asks: Who is the best judge of a building? Not the architect, but the people who live in it. Who is the best judge of food? Not the chef, but the people who eat it. He then gets to the key question: Who is the best judge of the laws? Not the legislator, but the citizens who have to live by their decisions.

Aristotle thus rejects rule by a single party, even when it is popular (monarchy) because the philosopher kings are limited and because of the threat of abuse (tyranny) associated with one-per-

son rule. In place of rule by a single party, Aristotle advocates rule by the few (aristocracy), an educated elite having the interests of the entire city-state at heart.

Aristocrats consider the views of the many, representing the poor (the democrats), and the views of the few, interested in wealth (the oligarchs), with an eye to finding a middle ground. Their objective would be solutions that would be just (fair to both sides) and which would command the support of the middle classes of politically active citizens belonging to neither party.

The great Roman rhetorical theorist and educator, Quintilian (35–100 CE) criticized Aristotle's solution. In the midst of the Roman Empire, Quintilian argued that the advantageous (*utilitas*) was liable to ignore the claims of justice. He urged that the principle of honor (*dignitas*) be used to regulate and evaluate deliberations over advantage. Honor was grounded in the social order, and it described the values held by the upper classes, so that the aristocracy Quintilian had in mind judged the advice, arguments, and solutions offered in assembly against the ideals that bound them together.

The practical problems signaled by the different treatments of expediency in Plato, Aristotle, and Quintilian found expression in Thucydides's *History of the Peloponnesian War.* Trained in the art of rhetoric, Thucydides (c.460–c.400 BCE) was a practical man. Elected to high office in Athens, he later became a general in the Athenian army. Because of a military setback, he was banished from Athens and, during his twenty years in exile, wrote his great history.

Thucydides chronicled, among other things, an overreliance on success and a suppression of principle in the Athenian deliberation of advantages. He includes important speeches and debates in his narrative, places them in a larger context, and notes their outcomes. Perhaps the most famous speech was Pericles' *Funeral Oration* (431 BCE). Pericles was the leader of the democratic party in Athens and the author of a strategy for expanding its empire.

In this speech honoring those who died for their country, Pericles praised Athenian principles. He praised its commitment to democracy and proper discussion, by which he meant free, open, and informed public deliberation. So principled was Athens and so just were its policies, he declared, that the cities it dominated had no reason to complain of being governed by a people unfit for their responsibilities.

Pericles purported to speak for the dominated—those who had no reason for complaint. His argument about the advantageous thus expanded beyond Athens to include other peoples and other city-states. A year later, after the Athenians retreated behind their walls and had lost tens of thousands to disease, Pericles (in the *Plague Speech,* 430 BCE), once again had occasion to weigh the advantages of domination. In the midst of this terrible and unexpected reversal in Athenian fortunes, Pericles was forced to admit that imperialism had nothing to do with democracy. The empire, rightly understood, was a tyranny. Then he turned to his critics: Those who were now pointing out the disadvantages of his policies, he claimed, were not engaging in proper discussion. They were fair-weather friends, people fit only to be citizens in city-states dominated by Athens.

This preoccupation with success and retreat from principle—democratic principles in particular—continued in the Mytilenian Debate (427 BCE). Here Cleon, Pericles' successor as leader of the democratic party in Athens, was deliberating over what to do to a city-state that wished to withdraw from the empire. He advised the execution of all adult males and the sale of the women and children into slavery as fit retribution for a city-state rebelling against Athenian rule. The assembly voted to implement his recommendation, but the next day it reversed itself. Cleon responded by declaring that democracy had become an obstacle to governing other people. If Athenians were going to overcome this obstacle and be able to maintain and expand their sphere of influence, citizens would have to observe three rules in fulfilling their civic responsibilities: Do not give in to feelings of pity; avoid being carried away by clever arguments; set aside the claims of decency. Do not, he cautioned, be guilty of these things.

The break with principle in the interest of success was completed in the Melian Dialogue (416–415 BCE). The Athenians were about to invade a city-state, which, although founded by Sparta, had remained neutral during the war. The Meli-

ans sent out ambassadors to plead their case with the Athenian generals. To invade Melos, the ambassadors argued, would be unjust. It was unjust not only from their point of view but on the basis of Athenian standards. The generals dismissed this argument and, in doing so, turned the notion of justice upside down. Justice, they declared, amounted to what the strong can compel of the weak.

After a fierce struggle, the Athenians were victorious. Further, they were able to use their victory as a warning to other city-states. To underscore this warning, they executed every adult male in Melos and sold the women and children into slavery. The Athenians were, by their own lights, successful. History had been just in awarding its victories to the strong and defeats to the weak. But in the long run, such victories eventuated in the destruction of Athens; they did so spiritually, by dissolving the community of ends once at the center of Athenian life; and they did so militarily, causing others to expand their coalition and redouble their efforts to stop Athenian expansion.

Modern understandings of expediency echo yet differ from classical definitions. The notion of deliberation is no longer restricted to public policy and the assembly. It is expanded into interpersonal contexts and personal thinking. This trend from public debate to monological thought and the rise of the individual as a basic unit of action have added an individualistic flavor to the meanings of deliberation and expediency. It has also cast expediency in a negative light (as in "mere expediency" or "opportunistic"), henceforth rendering it undesirable as a criterion of action, whether individual or social. The reasons for this development are worth considering.

Immanuel Kant (1724–1804) proposed a standard for judgment called the "categorical imperative." An action is principled when it holds for anyone else facing a similar situation. This recalls the Golden Rule in Christian tradition—do unto others as you would have them do unto you. It emphasizes the individual as a moral agent. In an age of revolution and civil war, it also affirmed the importance of justice, though it does not translate easily into the practical task of deliberating public policy. The contribution of Kantian idealism to discussions of the expedient "good" was to universalize the value domain of ethics, and to dismiss calculative thinking itself as unworthy of this domain.

The German philosopher Martin Heidegger (1889–1976), writing in the aftermath of World War I, argued for an end in Being. Entering into the here and now while facing the threat of impending death, one encounters authentic existence and discovers that ordinary talk is merely chatter, that ordinary goals are absurd and time consuming, that philosophy and poetry are cultivated in Being. Being declares an end to deliberation in its public and social sense. Expediency is a mark of nonphilosophical reflection and therefore irrelevant. Contemporary French and American literary critics, invoking Heidegger, confront language with Being. They locate the end in transcendent, personal experience (the Sublime). [See Sublime, the.] This experience may be related to deliberation; for example, through negating what is. Here, a moment of saying "No!" to a miserable reality may open onto a world of potential (what could be and ought to be but is not yet). Treated as a terminal experience, however, Being and the Sublime mark the end of practical deliberation and the beginning of appreciation, poetry, and profound silence.

Parallel to the individualistic turn in deliberation in the nineteenth century, there emerged a mass-based understanding of decision making. Increasingly, deliberation was viewed as occurring in private and interpersonal contexts rather than in public assemblies. In this category may be found both British utilitarianism and American pragmatism.

British utilitarians, such as Jeremy Bentham (1748–1832) and John Stuart Mill (1806–1873), promoted political and social reforms, during the rise of industrialism, poverty, and starvation. They argued on the basis of future advantages backed up by a specific principle—the greatest good for the greatest number. Bentham tried to calculate the value of his reforms through the number of people they affected, the amount of pleasure they provided, and the amount of pain they avoided. Mill thought that "pleasure" was too vague (card games and poetry both give pleasure). He included a judgment about the quality of the happiness or pleasure promised in advocating a particular reform or social movement.

American pragmatists tried to break the grip of abstract ideals and European philosophy. They stressed the practical, what William James (1842–1910) called the "cash value" of ideas. In the midst of the Great Depression during the 1930s, John Dewey argued for an imaginative rehearsal of practical alternatives as a way of solving well-defined problems. Although Dewey came from a strong religious background, he felt that in practical matters reliance on sacred texts, world spirits, and prayer led to fuzzy thinking and bad politics. A carefully researched scientific approach to change offered more realistic hope for social and political reform.

Meanwhile in Germany, during the 1920s and 1930s, the Frankfurt school of critical theory struggled against fascism and the growing success of the National Socialist Party (the Nazis). The threat was all too real. They advocated socially conscious research and theorized ways of building oppositional coalitions. The second-generation Frankfurt theorist, Jürgen Habermas, advanced dialogue as a way to move beyond subject-centered rationality (i.e., individualistic thinking), the lure of mass media (where oligarchic interests prevail and social stereotypes are reinforced), and the oppression of bureaucratic institutions (where, recalling Hitler and Stalin, tyranny remained a threat).

Habermas theorizes the possibility for practical deliberation ("communicative action") and coalition building around important social issues. He argues against academic specialization (divorced from the life-world) and professional jargon (dismissive of the life-world) that make practical deliberation in ordinary language all but impossible.

Utilitarianism and pragmatism promoted usefulness and practicality in relation to the needs of the many and measured real, material benefits they might enjoy. In this, they echoed Aristotle's view of expediency using alternative words (practical, useful rather than expedient). Habermas's concern for the pubic sphere marks an anti-individualistic revival of deliberation. [See Politics, articles on Rhetoric and legitimation and Rhetoric and power.] However, these views promote the good, the practical, and the utilitarian among a hypothetical body of deliberative agents—a community in which everyone is a member by virtue of being a human being or, at least, an intelligent human being.

Recalling the earlier discussion of Thucydides, one may ask, "expedient for whom? Practical for whom? Greatest number of what group?" Principles of expediency, utilitarianism, and pragmatism are currently under attack by scholars and critics who pay attention to exclusionary principles in social and public deliberation.

The greatest good for the greatest number could overlook the claims of justice. Bengalis, for example, recalling British imperialism and Mill's position as an executive officer in the East India Company that dominated India, did not make it into the "greatest number." Still, an emphasis on utility and future consequence, and a corresponding deemphasis on precedent and the past, promoted social change in the nineteenth and twentieth centuries in various parts of the world.

In the United States, theorists like W. E. B. Du Bois (1868–1963), sensitive to the exclusion of black people from deliberative processes, saw the problem as not one of means and ends but the fact that the ends assumed and the pleasures experienced by some audiences did not count. [See African-American rhetoric, article on Double-consciousness.] Struggling with the relationship between power and knowledge, French philosopher and political activist Michel Foucault (1972), noted that minorities got talked about but rarely got to talk for themselves in the public space. Audre Lorde, a black poet and social theorist; Edward Said, a Palestinian American and literary theorist; and Trinh T. Ming-Ha, a Vietnamese-American social theorist, have explored exclusionary communication inside reform movements dedicated to overcoming social oppression.

Recalling the disintegration and collapse of the French student movement in 1968, Jean-François Lyotard in his book *The Postmodern Condition* (Minneapolis, 1979) declared war on language itself. Winning the war against ideologically driven clichés, he argued, could lead to new thoughts, new ideas, and more effective personal communication. A postmodern world calls for deliberation freed from the burden of abstract and unpersuasive ideas (like democracy, Marxism, Catholicism, etc.). These "master narratives" no longer bind peoples together. What is worse, they often conceal terrible injustices—whole peoples have been oppressed, even liquidated in the name of some abstract ideal. Language, if it is to speak, must respect difference and the importance of justice among diverse groups, if they are to cooperate in real and effective movements for social and political change.

Theorizing rhetoric and expediency in contemporary life, one confronts an obvious fact. Political struggle too often overlooks the claims of the poor, the immigrants, the minorities, the wives and daughters of the elites, the uneducated, the foreign, the others we are led to ignore, objectify, ridicule, or eliminate. A greater sensitivity to context in relation to deliberation grows out of and is a response to a history of social exclusion, economic oppression, and ethnic, religious, and racial genocide in both modern and postmodern worlds.

[*See also* Classical rhetoric; Deliberative genre; *overview article on* Politics; *and* Utility.]

BIBLIOGRAPHY

Aristotle. *The Politics of Aristotle.* Translated by Ernest Barker. London, 1946. A readable translation with an emphasis, in the appendixes, on the interconnections between rhetoric, ethics, and politics.
Aristotle. *On Rhetoric: A Theory of Civic Discourse.* Translated by George A. Kennedy. New York, 1991. Readable and helpful, it links rhetoric to the study of ethics, poetics, and politics.
Collins, Randall. *The Sociology of Philosophies: A Global Theory of Intellectual Change.* Cambridge, Mass., 1991. A monumental effort to locate philosophers in historical, cultural, and social contexts. Also the "classical" can be seen in various cultures and periods.
Conner, W. Robert. *Thucydides.* Princeton, 1984. A learned and brilliant discussion of the rhetorical strategies employed by the "historian," it also relates the importance of the topic to contemporary politics.
Du Bois, W. E. B. *Color and Democracy: Colonies and Peace.* Millwood, N.Y., 1975. First published 1945. A critical inquiry into democracy, exclusion, and international conflicts that brings Thucydides into the modern world.
Foucault, Michel. *The Archaeology of Knowledge and the Discourse on Language.* Translated by A.M. Sheridan-Smith. New York, 1972. A breakthrough in the connection between language, history, ideology, and power.
Grassi, Ernesto. *Rhetoric as Philosophy.* University Park,

Pa., 1980. A student of Heidegger who, like Herbert Marcuse, Jean-Paul Sartre, and Hannah Arendt, admitted Being into the world and took a decisive and different political turn.

Habermas, Jürgen. *The Structural Transformation of the Public Sphere: An Inquiry into a Category of Bourgeois Society.* Translated by Thomas Burger and Frederick Lawrence. Cambridge, Mass., 1989. First published in German, 1962. An incisive account of the movement from collective to privatized deliberation of public issues.

Held, David. *Introduction to Critical Theory: Horkheimer to Habermas.* Berkeley, 1980. Offers an excellent and readable summary of the work of the Frankfurt school.

Minh-ha, Trinh T. *Woman, Native, Other.* Bloomington, Ind., 1989. A poetical protest against the exclusion of women, women of color, and the importance of cultural differences.

Struever, Nancy S. *The Language of History in the Renaissance: Rhetoric and Historical Consciousness in Florentine Humanism.* Princeton, 1970. An important study that recovers the contribution of the Sophists and the war between rhetoric and philosophy and locates it in the midst of social change and historical conflict.

Said, Edward W. *Culture and Imperialism.* New York, 1993. A study of the way the rhetoric of power produces the illusion of benevolence in imperial settings.

West, Cornel. *The American Evasion of Philosophy: A Genealogy of Pragmatism.* Madison, Wis., 1989. Outlines an "American" approach to philosophy that reintegrates political engagement and public deliberation back into scholarship.

— PHILLIP WANDER

EXPOSITORY RHETORIC AND JOURNALISM. As the main facilitators of public debate and controversy, journalists are involved in every aspect of rhetorical activity. Journalists stand in for the mass audience, recording and relaying information for public debate, a role that makes them among the most informed citizens. Journalists participate in public debate by providing news analysis and editorials. Almost all political rhetoric is communicated through journalism.

While journalists may deny it, they are practitioners of rhetoric on at least three levels. First, all communication has a rhetorical dimension. Everyone who authors a message to produce an effect engages in rhetoric, even when the desired effect is only to inform. Second, journalists employ a writing style ostensibly based on the objectivity of scientific investigation, in which, however, certain rhetorical processes govern the way they select, gather, and communicate news. Third, when journalists author persuasive messages in the form of editorials, columns, or analysis, they participate in the ancient art of public address.

Informative Discourse. Aristotle listed three modes of rhetoric: deliberative, forensic, and epideictic, representing the discourses of politics, law, and ceremony. [*See* Deliberative genre; Epideictic genre; *and* Forensic genre.] In each category, the author of a message tries to persuade an audience to adopt an opinion or a mood. Lloyd Bitzer (1988) suggests that contemporary journalists represent a fourth category of discourse whose aim is not to persuade but to inform. They supply information for others involved in debate, and they record and mediate arguments and reactions between actors in public debate and their audiences. Thus, when professional journalists function in this capacity, they attempt to mediate public discourse without influencing the outcome of public discourse. This mode of rhetoric uses rhetorical strategy to produce an effect—to inform.

Conventions of Objectivity. Most conventions of informative discourse are borrowed from popular views of science. Whereas political rhetoric proceeds from the assumption that argumentation and judgment are required to discover truth, science seems to assume that the accumulation of facts, or data, reveals truth without requiring argumentation. Thus scientific discourse ostensibly focuses not on the persuasive use of facts in argumentation, but rather on the objective production of the facts themselves. [*See* Science.] Similarly, journalists claim to report news objectively. The conventions of objective news reporting limit the reporter to communicating only information that was observed by the reporter or relayed through the reporter from a named source. For example, if a reporter inspects the site of a plane crash, the crash can be reported as fact because of direct observation. If the crash occurs on a restricted air force base, and the reporter interviews a witness, then the reporter is reporting the fact that someone claiming to be a witness gave an account of the crash. In the former case, the reported fact is that the crash occurred; in the latter, the reported fact is that someone claiming to be a witness made certain statements about the incident. The reporter, then, like the scientist, is not arguing a point, but rather objectively relaying seemingly verifiable information.

Thus the ideal of objective news reporting does not argue for agreement, it assumes it. Perelman and Olbrechts-Tyteca (1969) point out that this is an illusion. They contend that facts cannot speak for themselves. Facts become facts only through the consent of an audience. Thus science and journalism falsely appear to be forms of demonstration. Journalism is actually a form of argumentation that Perelman and Olbrechts-Tyteca call expository discourse.

Other conventions of journalism that give the impression of objectivity are third person narration, the omission of overt reporter opinions, and the inverted pyramid writing style. Third person narration and omission of reporter opinion literally leave the reporter out of the story. The effect is that of the information revealing itself without coloration by a human agent. The inverted pyramid is a method of arrangement that organizes information from most to least important. It is mainly used in the ordering of paragraphs, but is sometimes manifest in paragraph and even sentence structure. The inverted pyramid represents the rejection of arrangement as rhetorical strategy. By seemingly negating the strategic influence of context, the reporter is further establishing the illusion that the facts speak for themselves. The overall effect of these conventions of objectivity on reporting is multidimensional for a profession that commodifies information. The information itself appears more credible, and it can be useful to consumers of news who have opposing points of view.

The quasi-scientific turn in the development of journalism began in the late nineteenth century. It was driven in part by the economic incentive to make stories appeal to the broadest range of readers. Whereas previously hundreds of partisan publications appealed to hundreds of small publics, in theory a more profitable penny press newspaper attempted to market news stories to the larger public made up of all the factions of all

political persuasions. Thus developed the modern form of the news story, intended to be read, not spoken, which contained what appeared to be facts and was devoid of political context.

Technology also contributed to the emerging conventions of objective journalism. The telegraph first made it possible for a reporter, called a correspondent, to cover news in one city and send out news stories to several newspapers in other cities. It was advantageous that the story appear to be as objective as possible, since the newspapers receiving the news copy might not be politically homogeneous. Furthermore, the high cost of sending telegraph messages caused journalists to take expository writing to new levels of sparseness. Thus, while apparent objectivity and brevity were already stylistic options for the rhetorician, emerging technology made them almost mandatory for the journalist.

Journalism and Advocacy. While ostensibly objective journalism is the most prominent category of journalistic output since 1900, it is predated by a long history of advocacy in the tradition of public address. Contemporary editorials, columns, analytical essays, and letters to the editor are remnants of the eighteenth- and nineteenth-century period of transition from public address and print. Before the penny press made newspaper publication profitable, newspapers were published mainly to express the partisan political views of publishers. When the public sphere was forming in Great Britain and France, some citizens entered the public debate over the development of democratic systems of government by publishing their views in broadsides and journals.

The content of these publications was not news or even editorials as they appear today, but printed speeches and polemical essays in the form of letters. Both the speeches and the letters were intended to be read aloud in coffee houses and at other public gatherings and to be catalysts for public debate. In Great Britain, these publications included the *Tatler,* the *Guardian,* and the *Spectator.* Hundreds of journals were published in Paris during the French Revolution. Similarly, in the eighteenth and early nineteenth century United States, speeches in the form of letters to the editor were the mainstay of newspaper content because almost every faction of every political party had its own partisan publication. Thus, advocacy journalism has the strongest possible link to the long tradition of public address.

When newspapers became profitable businesses marketing to the broadest possible audience in the late nineteenth century, they began to separate informative rhetoric from polemical rhetoric. Strict reporting of news took on the appearance of discourse rhetoric, and argumentation was restricted to clearly marked editorial and letters to the editor pages. Thus, the newer tradition of informative discourse, based on the principle of objectivity, developed alongside the tradition of argumentation that has its roots in classical Greece and Rome. Both editorials and letters to the editor remain close to the tradition of public address in their use of invention, arrangement, and style. [*See* Arrangement, *article on* Traditional arrangement; Invention; *and* Style.] Most can be read as speeches. Ties to the ancient oral tradition are particularly apparent in those rare instances when editorials and rebuttals are delivered on radio or television.

Columns and reviews are also outside the constraints of informative journalism, yet neither is part of the tradition of public address as reflected in editorial and letter writing. Editorials are marked by resoluteness, whereas the column is often contemplative. The use of invention, arrangement, and style in columns bears a greater resemblance to the rhetorical tradition of letter writing. [*See* Epistolary rhetoric.] Reviews, on the other hand, have always been part of a tradition of literary criticism and philosophy. [*See* Criticism; *and* Philosophy, *article on* Perennial topics and terms.]

Legitimation Crisis. Both Bitzer (1987) and Daniel Hallin (1985) perceive a crisis in journalism generated by its conflicting epistemologies in science and public address. Hallin traces what he calls the news media legitimation crisis in the United States to the 1960s when it became apparent that objective news style was inadequate for reporting values-laden issues like the war in Vietnam and the civil rights movement. For instance, an objective news story might report that twenty-five U.S. troops and three Vietnamese civilians were killed in a battle, or that two hundred protesters marched in downtown Chicago, but it would leave out the essential political discourse on the value of human life as weighed against diplomatic objectives, or the inhuman living con-

ditions of ghettoized urban minorities. This is explored as a context issue by James Carey (1986), who argues that the objectivity standard hides the ideological context of news stories, yet readers require context for understanding. Hallin notes that journalists became aware of this deficiency in informative rhetoric but failed to resolve it because of the strength of their commitment to objectivity. While there was experimentation in what was called the New Journalism, journalists tried to address audience need for context mainly by authoring a kind of objective analysis, which still failed to address ideological context issues and at the same time threatened to compromise the rules of objectivity. Using system theory as a model, Hallin argues that readers and viewers demand context, yet the goal of objectivity rejects context. The unavoidable outcome is legitimation crisis where the profession of journalism fails to meet the requirements of its environment of readers and viewers and simultaneously fails to live up to its goal of objectivity.

In more traditional rhetorical terms, Bitzer notes that each category of rhetoric has a governing virtue: for deliberative rhetoric it is the *expedient;* for forensic rhetoric it is *justice;* and for epideictic rhetoric it is the *honorable.* The governing virtue for journalism, according to Bitzer, is *truth.* Journalists look for truthful facts to assist others in making judgments. Journalists' usefulness to society is dependent on the extent to which others see them as possessing this virtue. According to Bitzer, journalists must safeguard their commitment to truth. If they fail to do this, their identity blurs with those of politicians and entertainers, and they lose public trust. This, again, is the legitimation crisis. If journalists only supply objective facts, they fail to provide context and meaning for their audience. If they provide context and meaning through argumentation, then they become partisan participants in public debate and lose their authority. Put another way, journalists offer one ethical proof based on their scientific process for generating news, and another ethical proof as partisan members of a public debate. [*See* Ēthos.] Logically, the two proofs cancel each other out. If one is objective, one cannot be partisan, and if one is partisan, one cannot be objective.

Journalism and the Public Sphere. Newspaper editorials and news stories are a hybrid of rhetorical conventions that serve the unique demands of public discourse in a mass democracy. The discourse of news takes place in a public forum, it is limited to matters of public interest, and its methods are bound by the prescriptive traditions and proscriptive laws of professional journalism. A journalist selects a topic for a news story because it is of public, not private, interest. Readers expect the story to be researched fairly, typically by interviewing spokespersons on opposite sides of an issue. Next, the story should be written objectively. Last, there may be an expectation that where the story is placed in the newspaper will reflect the importance of the story compared to other news.

Typically when there is no democratic government, the public is not well informed about matters of state. Private citizens have little need of information about the affairs of state if their opinions have no impact on the actions of the state, and they can have little influence on the actions of the state if they are without information regarding affairs of the state. It is through publicity—the publicizing of matters of state—that this discursive cage is broken. Political public debate and democratic institutions began to develop at the end of the feudal period in Western Europe when trade between cities initiated the exchange of public information.

Once the affairs of the state are made public, then citizens may leave the private realm and engage in public debate for the purpose of influencing the actions of the state. The public realm is what Jürgen Habermas calls the public sphere (1989). A limited form of public sphere emerged in ancient Greece and Rome, and a more inclusive public sphere emerged after the Enlightenment, first in England and France and then in America. [See Politics, articles on The personal, technical, and public spheres of argument and Rhetoric and legitimation.] Anyone engaged in public debate over a matter of public interest has entered the realm of the public sphere. It is a defining characteristic of democracy that its laws protect and do not inhibit public access to information about the state. Since almost all modern democracies are mass democracies, publicity requires mass communication. While they usually have no more rights than the average citizen,

journalists have become the proprietors of this publicity process.

It is axiomatic in mass democracies that one must engage mass media to reach a mass audience with a political message. [See Audience, article on Mass audiences.] However, economic and technological constraints make sending messages through mass media like television and radio more difficult than giving a speech or printing and distributing a broadside. Most forms of mass media are institutions governed by economic principles and technical limitations. They are administered by professionals like journalists who have guidelines for the selection and editing of information for public distribution. Thus, the author of a political message must first meet the criteria of mediation processes in order to reach a mass audience. In the twentieth century, journalists were the professionals most responsible for overseeing the collection and distribution of political rhetoric. However, accessing the journalistic mediation process is so complex and prohibitive for the average citizen that a parallel profession, public relations, has developed to assist rhetors in making their messages attractive to journalists.

Communication researchers in the 1960s and 1970s identified a second face of power: agenda-setting (Bachrach and Baratz, 1963; Macombs and Shaw, 1972). [See Politics, article on The third face of power.] In ancient Greece, a citizen wishing to influence a political decision needed to speak to a relatively small number of fellow citizens to influence public consensus. Today, in contrast, a citizen wanting to influence a political decision not only has to have an effective message, but also must have the consent and assistance of those who act as gatekeepers to the technology of mass communication. The exercise of control over what goes in the newspaper or over the airwaves by editors and producers is called agenda setting. It is a higher level exercise of power than creating a public argument because someone with control over the agenda for a channel of mass communication can frame the argument in ways that are helpful or hurtful or eliminate the argument altogether by denying access to the mass audience. Thus, compared to the citizen who authors a political message, someone with control over the agenda of public discussion has greater potential to influence the issues as well as the outcome of public debate.

Summary: The Objectivity Paradox. The significance of informative rhetoric in the twentieth century is due mainly to the proliferation of democratic states, the expansion of their populations, and the extension of voting rights. Self-government is dependent on citizens having equal access to public forums so they can acquire information and participate in civic debate, and almost all modern democracies are mass democracies. It is therefore necessary that citizens in modern mass democracies employ methods of mass communication. The profession of journalism has held the proprietary role in this process. Using print and broadcast technology and applying rhetorical methods modeled after the objectivity standards of science, journalists collect and disseminate information to citizens. In principle, they apply expository rhetoric not to participate in public debate, but to facilitate it. Their purpose is to harvest and disseminate the rhetoric of others.

While no other method of democratically facilitating mass communication has emerged, the inadequacies of the journalistic mediation process have become increasingly apparent. Clearly the unmediated public address model of communication employed in classical democracies cannot serve populations of millions and hundreds of millions of citizens. Mass communication technology is not an impediment for modern democracies, it is a requirement; however, it provides only half of the classical equation for public address. It can send messages from one rhetor to the entire audience, but it cannot afford members of the audience the opportunity to send messages back to the speaker or to one another. Furthermore, the person selecting which messages to send through the channels of mass communication has more power than other citizens, and, arguably, more power than those whose messages are sent.

The methods of expository rhetoric employed by journalists are meant to dissolve these inequalities. Hypothetically, just as the processes for generating deliberative, forensic, or epideictic rhetoric select the best available means of persuasion, the process of informative rhetoric is meant to distill objective facts and discard persuasion. Yet all human communication and all decisions made by journalists are subjective. At best, objectivity serves as a standard employed by journalists to help minimize mediation influence. Thus, informative rhetoric can never produce its intended effect—it can never merely inform. The rhetoric of objective journalism informs, but so does argumentation. Both informative rhetoric and argumentation carry opinions. The difference is only a matter of degree and alleged intent. In the final analysis, the foundation of the modern democratic state rests on a method that is more apparent than real.

BIBLIOGRAPHY

Bachrach, Peter, and Morton S. Baratz. "The Two Faces of Power." *The American Political Science Review* 56 (1963), pp. 947–952.

Bennett, W. Lance. *News: The Politics of Illusion.* 2d ed. New York, 1988. An analysis of how news is made, reported, and consumed.

Bird, S. Elizabeth, and Robert W. Dardenne. "Myth, Chronicle, and Story: Exploring the Narrative Qualities of News." In *Media, Myths, and Narratives: Television and the Press,* pp. 67–86. Newbury Park, Calif., 1988.

Bitzer, Lloyd F. "Political Rhetoric." In *Landmark Essays on Contemporary Rhetoric.* Edited by Thomas B. Farrell, pp. 1–22. Mahwah, N.J., 1998. Bitzer explains the scope and nature of political rhetoric and pays particular attention to the unique role of journalists. Unlike other discussions of journalism and the public sphere, this explication is entirely in the context of traditional rhetoric.

Bitzer, Lloyd F. "Rhetorical Public Communication." *Critical Studies in Mass Communication* 14 (1987), pp. 425–428. Bitzer looks at journalists as rhetorical mediators of public debate.

Broder, David S. *Behind the Front Page: A Candid Look at How the News is Made.* New York, 1987. This text, written by a journalist, provides an anecdotal, inside look at journalism.

Carey, James. "Why and How? The Dark Continent of American Journalism." In *Reading the News.* Edited by Robert Karl Manoff and Michael Schudson, pp. 270–308. Baltimore, 1986.

Entman, Robert M. *Democracy Without Citizens: Media and the Decay of American Politics.* New York, 1989. This study looks at the political outcomes of journalism failing to meet its own objectivity standards.

Fallows, James. *Breaking the News: How the Media Undermine American Democracy.* New York, 1997.

Gans, Herbert J. *Deciding What's News: A Study of CBS*

Evening News, NBC Nightly News, Newsweek and Time. New York, 1980. This is a sociological study of how journalists apply their craft.

Glasser, Theodore L., and James S. Ettema. "When the Facts Don't Speak for Themselves: A Study of the Use of Irony in Daily Journalism." *Critical Studies in Mass Communication* 10 (1993), pp. 322–338.

Goldstein, Tom, ed. *Killing The Messenger: 100 Years of Media Criticism.* New York, 1989.

Habermas, Jürgen. *The Structural Transformation of the Public Sphere: An Inquiry Into a Category of Bourgeois Society.* Translated by Thomas Burger and Frederick Lawrence. Cambridge, Mass., 1989. Habermas reveals journalism as part of an evolving process of political communication.

Hallin, Daniel C. "The American News Media: A Critical Perspective." In *Critical Theory and Public Life.* Edited by J. Forester, pp. 121–146. Cambridge, Mass., 1985. Hallin discusses the relationship between news media rules and legitimacy; this is also one of the first references to a third face of power.

Macombs, Maxwell E., and Donald Shaw. "The Agenda-Setting Function of Mass Media." *Public Opinion Quarterly* 36 (1972), pp. 176–187.

Paletz, David L., and Robert M. Entman. *Media Power Politics.* New York, 1981.

Perelman, Chaim, and L. Olbrechts-Tyteca. *The New Rhetoric: A Treatise on Argumentation.* Translated by John Wilkinson and Pucell Weaver. Notre Dame, Ind., 1969. First published 1958. Perelman and Olbrechts-Tyteca are the first to offer a prominent position to expository discourse as a genre of rhetoric.

Schudson, Michael. *Discovering the News: A Social History of American Newspapers.* New York, 1978.

Tuchman, Gaye. "Objectivity as Strategic Ritual: An Examination of Newsmen's Notions of Objectivity." *American Journal of Sociology* 77 (1972), p. 661.

—THOMAS JESSE ROACH

F–G

FABLE. *See* Arrangement, *article on* Modern arrangement; Exemplum; *and* Invention.

FALLACIES. According to a standard definition that was generally accepted until fairly recently, a fallacy is an argument that seems valid but is not. In the last decades, however, argumentation theorists have made several important objections to this definition: "seems" brings in an undesirable amount of subjectivity and "valid" is misleadingly presented as an absolute and conclusive criterion; the definition ignores that some well-known fallacies are, by certain logical standards, valid arguments; the definition restricts the concept of fallaciousness to patterns of reasoning, whereas a great number of generally recognized fallacies fall outside this scope. These objections explain why a broader definition is nowadays preferred. Currently, fallacies are usually viewed as *deficient moves in argumentative discourse.*

Brief History of the Study of Fallacies. The history of the study of fallacies begins with Aristotle (386–322 BCE), who discusses the fallacies most thoroughly in *De sophisticis elenchis (Sophistical Refutations)*, which refers to the refutations as they were exploited by the Sophists and suggests why fallacies are also called *sophisms*. [*See* Sophists.] Aristotle places fallacies in the context of a dialectic in which one person attacks a thesis and another person defends it. Refuting the thesis is one of the ways of winning the debate. In this perspective, fallacies are false moves employed in the attacker's efforts to refute the defender's thesis. *Sophistical Refutations* deals with those that are only apparent refutations (*paralogisms*), which Aristotle considers typical of the Sophists' way of arguing. In his treatise on dialectic, *The Topics,* he discusses both the correct moves attackers may use to refute the defender's thesis as well as incorrect moves in reasoning, such as *petitio principii* (better known as *begging the question* or *circular*

reasoning). Aristotle's *Prior Analytics* contains additional remarks, and in *Rhetoric*, Aristotle discusses a selection from the fallacies compiled in *Sophistical Refutations,* referring also to the fallacy now known as *post hoc ergo propter hoc* ("after this, therefore on account of this"). [*See* Dialectic.]

In *Sophistical Refutations,* Aristotle distinguishes thirteen different types of incorrect refutations and indicates how these false moves can be parried. He divides the dialectical fallacies into two groups: refutations dependent on language (*in dictione*), and refutations independent of language (*extra dictionem*). The first group consists of six types, all connected with ambiguities and shifts of meaning which, because of its imperfections, may occur in ordinary language (accent, form of expression, combination of words, division of words, equivocation, amphiboly). The second group, which contains fallacies that could also occur if the language were perfect, consists of seven types (*accidens; secundum quid* [later known as hasty generalization], affirming the consequent; noncause as cause; *petitio principii; ignoratio elenchi* or ignorance of refutation; many questions).

Aristotle's standard definition of a fallacy, as seemingly valid reasoning that is really invalid, has remained authoritative for a long time. All the same, later authors often ignored the dialectical context of the definition, and overlooked the differences between a deductively valid argument and Aristotle's view of good reasoning as having a conclusion that not only follows necessarily from the premises of the syllogism, but is also different from, as well as based on, these premises. [*See* Syllogism.] Until the Renaissance, however, most scholars only seemed to repeat Aristotle. Then there were also authors, such as the French dialectician Petrus Ramus (1515–1572), who have dismissed his views or abandoned the study of fallacies altogether.

Although the British philosopher Francis Bacon (1561–1626) considers the study of fallacies to be "excellently handled" by Aristotle, his contention in *The Advancement of Learning* (1605) is that there are more important fallacies, such as errors of thought and "vain opinions" caused by false appearances or *idols*. Among the latter are the idols of the marketplace: "false appearances that are imposed upon words, which are framed and applied according to conceit and capacities of the vulgar sort" (p. 134). The Aristotelian list of fallacies is also the starting point in *Logic or the Art of Thinking* (1662), the "Port-Royal Logic," by the seventeenth-century French scholars Antoine Arnauld and Pierre Nicole, possibly together with Blaise Pascal. These fallacies are in the first place seen as sophisms of scientific method. Second, fallacies found in popular discourse are listed, such as using the force of threats (without yet calling them arguments *ad baculum*), and drawing a general conclusion from an incomplete induction. This division between fallacies associated with scientific subjects and fallacies in public discourse replaces the language-dependent versus language-independent distinction.

The British philosopher John Locke (1632–1704) introduced the *ad* arguments: *ad verecundiam* was, originally, the "argument on shame," because one should not dare to question the authority mentioned in the argument, but it is now used to refer to a fallacy that involves a wrong appeal to authority. The second is *ad ignorantiam*, which originally required the adversary to admit what he alleged as a proof, but is now often used to refer to the fallacy of concluding that a contention is true because the opposite has not been successfully defended. The third is *ad hominem*, which originally made use of the other party's concessions in one's argument, but is now a general term for the fallacy of attacking the other party's person either directly or indirectly by depicting him or her as stupid, bad, or unreliable. [*See* Ad hominem argument.] There are variants: the *abusive* variant indirectly casts suspicion on the opponent's motives; the *circumstantial* variant points out a contradiction in the other party's words or deeds; and the *tu quoque* or "you too!" variant. It is clear from *An Essay Concerning Human Understanding* (1690) that Locke was aware of the intended effect on others of these three kinds of arguments, saw them as frequently oc-

curring, and considered them inferior to the standard set by the argument *ad judicium,* for using proofs drawn from the foundations of knowledge or probability, but did not condemn them as fallacious. In this respect, he differs from the authors of the Port-Royal Logic, who distinguish, for instance, between legitimate and illegitimate uses of authority.

In his *Elements of Logic* (1826), the logician and rhetorician Richard Whately (1787–1863) aims at giving an improved account of the fallacies from a logical point of view. Defining a fallacy in the appendix as "any argument, or apparent argument, which professes to be decisive of the matter at hand, while in reality it is not," he replaces the established definition with a wider one. Next to the class of (syllogistic) logical fallacies (e.g., four terms as a violation of the rule defining a syllogism as a form of reasoning with no more than three terms, and the, semilogical, fallacy of false analogy), Whately distinguishes in his tree of classification a broad class of (valid) nonlogical (or material) fallacies, divided into fallacies that involve a wrongly-assumed premise (*petitio principii*, false premise) and irrelevancies (*ignoratio elenchi*), such as the *ad* fallacies.

Whately has had a great influence on the textbook tradition in both Britain and the United States. Whereas Whately holds that reasoning should conform to the syllogism, the British philosopher John Stuart Mill (1806–1873) propounds in *A System of Logic, Ratiocinative and Inductive* (1843) that only inductive inferences count as reasoning. Although Mill created a category of inductive fallacies, his views on the fallacies have not led to crucial theoretical innovations.

An important characteristic of traditional accounts in later logic textbooks is the shift in the approach to the fallacies, that replaced the Aristotelian dialectical perspective by a monologic perspective. Fallacy theory then deals exclusively with errors in reasoning instead of deceptive maneuvers made by a party who tries to outwit the other party. Because some of the fallacies on Aristotle's list are intrinsically linked with the dialogue situation, one of the consequences of abandoning the context of debate is that the reason a particular fallacy should be regarded as a fallacy may become obscure. An example is "many questions" in Aristotle's category of language-independent fallacies. This fallacy occurs when a question is asked that can only be answered by answering at the same time at least one other question that is "concealed" in the original question. In modern interpretations, the answer to the original question presupposes a particular answer to one or more other questions. In the well-known example, "When did you stop beating your wife?" a person who answers this question as intended thereby not only admits that he no longer beats his wife, but also accepts the presupposition that he has been in the habit of beating his wife. Since "many questions" hinges on the dialogue situation, this fallacy can only be adequately analyzed in a dialectic approach. In the type of debate discussed by Aristotle, the defender is allowed to split up such questions into several questions and to answer them separately. Although it is clear why Aristotle regards "many questions" as a fallacious refutation in the context of debate, it is less clear why exactly he classifies this wrong move in the category of language-independent fallacies. After all, it is precisely the way in which the question is framed that offers the possibility of checkmating one's adversary.

Instead of distinguishing fallacies *in dictione* from fallacies *extra dictionem,* logic textbooks frequently make a distinction between fallacies of ambiguity or clearness and fallacies of relevance (e.g., Copi, 1972). [*See* Ambiguity.] The first are caused by lexical or grammatical ambiguity ("Pleasing students can be trying") or shifts of accent ("Why *did* Adam eat the apple?", "Why did *Adam* eat the apple?"); they correspond more or less with Aristotle's fallacies *in dictione.* Fallacies of *relevance* also include the *ad* fallacies. They are "irrelevant" because they offer no logical justification for the opinion expressed; all the same, they may be rhetorically effective means to persuade an audience. Alongside *secundum quid, accidens,* many questions, *ad hominem, ad verecundiam,* and *ad ignorantiam,* this category includes false analogy, ethical, and pathetic fallacies (parading one's own qualities or playing on the sentiments of the audience); *petitio principii* ("God exists because the Bible says so, and the Bible is God's word"); *ignoratio elenchi* (not addressing the point at issue, but a different opinion); *non sequitur* (the conclusion does not follow from the ar-

gument, although both may be correct); *ad baculum* ("argument of the stick," using force by resorting to threats against an adversary who refuses to accept one's standpoint); *ad misericordiam* ("pity argument," unjustified appeal to compassion); *ad populum* ("argument directed at the people" such as appealing to the audience's prejudices); *ad consequentiam* (casting a specific light on a factual thesis by pointing out its favorable or unfavorable consequences, as in, "God exists, otherwise life would be without hope"); "slippery slope" (carrying to an extreme speculation on unsubstantiated negative consequences of a proposed course); and "straw man" (attributing to the other party a fictitious or distorted standpoint that is easier to deal with). Somewhere between the fallacies of ambiguity and those of relevance, are the fallacies of composition (characteristics of the parts are attributed to the whole to make a standpoint acceptable, as in "We use real butter, cream, and fresh lettuce, so our meals are delicious"); and *division* (the converse: "The Catholic church is a church for poor people, therefore the Catholic church is poor").

Modern Theoretical Approaches to the Fallacies. In *Fallacies,* an influential survey of the history of the study of fallacies, the Australian philosopher Charles Hamblin (London, 1970) observes such a uniformity in contemporary treatments of fallacies in prominent logic textbooks that he speaks of the *standard treatment.* This characterization is based on textbooks by Cohen and Nagel (London, 1934), Black (Englewood Cliffs, N.J., 1946), Oesterlee (Englewood Cliffs, N.J., 1952), Copi (New York, 1953), Schipper and Schuh (London, 1960), and Salmon (Englewood Cliffs, N.J., 1963), but also applies to other textbooks, such as Beardsley (Englewood Cliffs, N.J., 1950), Fernside and Holther (Englewood Cliffs, N.J., 1959), Carney and Scheer (New York, 1964), Rescher (New York, 1964), Kahane (Belmont, Calif., 1969, 1971), Michalos (Englewood Cliffs, N.J., 1970), Gutenplan and Tamny (New York, 1971), and Purtill (New York, 1972). Hamblin's criticisms of the standard treatment are devastating. In his opinion, there is no theory of fallacy at all, in the sense in which there are theories of correct reasoning or inference.

According to Hamblin, the shortcomings of the standard treatment already reveal themselves in the definition of a fallacy as an argument that seems to be valid but is not so. Except for a few formal fallacies, such as "denying the antecedent" and "affirming the consequent" (two cases of treating a sufficient condition as a necessary condition), most fallacies discussed in the standard treatment do not fit this definition; sometimes, because there is no argument (e.g., "many questions"); in other cases, because the argument, in modern interpretations, is not invalid at all (e.g., *petitio principii*); in still other cases, the fallaciousness has not primarily to do with the invalidity of an argument but with the incorrectness of an unexpressed premise (e.g., *ad verecundiam, ad populum, ad hominem*). If an objection is made, it is in the last cases more likely that the criticism pertains to the content than to the form of the argument. A good illustration is Copi's example of the abusive variant of *ad hominem*: "Bacon's philosophy is untrustworthy because he was removed from his chancellorship for dishonesty" (1972, p. 75). The fallaciousness of this argument is caused by the unacceptability of the unexpressed premise ("A swindler cannot have any interesting philosophical ideas") rather than by the invalidity of the argument. More often than not, an *ad hominem* is not even presented as an argument with the form of a premise–conclusion sequence, and can also not be easily reconstructed as such.

Hamblin's criticisms of the standard treatment have led to various kinds of reactions. In textbooks on logic, initially very little effect can be noticed. An extreme reaction is Lambert and Ulrich's, who think that informal fallacies would better be dropped from logic textbooks (1980, pp. 24–28). As exemplified in Hans V. Hansen and Robert C. Pinto's collection of readings, *Fallacies* (University Park, Pa., 1995), Hamblin's book has been a great source of inspiration to argumentation scholars. Post-Hamblin attempts to create a better alternative to the standard treatment may differ considerably in their approaches, objectives, methods, and emphases, but they invariably refer to his criticisms. *Pace* philosophers such as Augustus de Morgan (1806–1871) and Gerald Massey (born 1934), who do not believe that a theory of fallacies is possible, several new theoretical approaches have developed.

Apart from their own, Hansen and Pinto's book shows the active involvement in the study of the fallacies of other contemporary Canadian and American informal logicians, such as J. Anthony Blair, Ralph H. Johnson, Alan Brinton, Trudy Govier, James B. Freeman, and David Hitchcock. They pay special attention to the conditions under which a specific argumentative move should count as a fallacy. The philosophers John Biro and Harvey Siegel's (1992), still embryonic, epistemic approach represents a different view of the fallacies as failed attempts to expand our knowledge. Besides Hamblin's (1970) own contribution to the theory of fallacies, which is cast in the mold of a system of rules called *formal dialectics*, other constructive proposals are made by the American philosopher Maurice Finocchiaro (1987) and the Finnish-American logician Jaakko Hintikka (1987). Finocchiaro opts for a middle course between abstract theoretical considerations and data-oriented empirical observation. Hintikka argues, in a dialectical vein, that the Aristotelian fallacies should not be primarily viewed as wrong inferences, but as interrogative mistakes in question-dialogues.

The most continuous and extensive post-Hamblin contribution to the study of the fallacies is provided by the Canadian logicians and argumentation theorists John Woods and Douglas N. Walton. In a series of coauthored articles and books and several independently authored publications, they substantiate their remedy for the standard treatment: dealing with the various kinds of fallacies by calling on more sophisticated modern logics than just syllogistic, propositional, and predicate logics. The Woods-Walton approach is exhibited in the textbook *Argument: The Logic of the Fallacies* (Toronto, 1982).

As *Fallacies: Selected Papers, 1972–1982* (Berlin, 1989) makes clear, Woods and Walton take the view that the fallacy itself should determine how it may be dealt with theoretically. Common methodological starting points of their approach are that fallacies can be usefully analyzed with the help of the structures and theoretical vocabulary of logical systems, including systems of dialectical logic, and that successful analyses of a great many fallacies will have features that qualify those analyses as *formal* in some sense. They tend to organize the fallacies into grades of formality. First, there are fallacies such as the classical fallacy of "four terms," that are formal in the strict sense: they are analyzable with the help of concepts wholly or partly described with the technical vocabulary or the formal structures of a system of logic or other formal theory ("four terms," for example, with the help of the classical definition of a syllogism). At the second grade of formality, there are fallacies such as the fallacies of ambiguity, which are not formal in the strict sense, but whose commission is partly made explicable by reference to logical forms. At the third grade of formality, there are fallacies such as *petitio principii,* which are formally analyzable in an even weaker sense. In their analyses of fallacies, Woods and Walton draw upon Hamblin's concepts of commitment sets and retraction. Thus, their analysis is not only formally oriented, but also dialectical. Another typical feature of the Woods–Walton approach is that it is pluralistic. History has endowed a great many rather different phenomena with the name of *fallacy.* In Woods and Walton's view, it makes no sense to suppose that they must all be given a common analysis. Their analysis of composition and division, for instance, rests on a theoretical account of the part–whole relation. These fallacies involve incorrect inferences from properties of wholes to properties of parts, and from properties of parts to properties of wholes. Woods and Walton show that neither ordinary set theory nor "mereology" will suffice for a correct analysis of these fallacies (1989, chap. 8). The formal theory of the part–whole relation known as aggregate theory, as developed by Tyler Burge (1977, pp. 97–118), is a more adequate theoretical tool.

A major methodical attempt to create a "formal-dialectical" theoretical framework, partly based on the dialogue logic of the Erlangen School, is undertaken by the Dutch philosophers and logicians Else M. Barth and Erik C. W. Krabbe. They envisage a theory of rational argumentation as a finite set of production rules for rational arguments. Only (and all) arguments that can be generated by these rules are rational arguments, and fallacies can be analyzed as argumentative moves that can *not* be generated by the rules. They provide a description of the sets of rules constituting such systems of formal dialectics in *From Axiom to Dialogue* (Berlin, 1982). Instead of being given ad hoc explanations, as in the standard treat-ment, in formal dialectics the fallacies can be systematically analyzed, which is illustrated in Barth and Martens (1977) with respect to the *argumentum ad hominem.*

The "pragma–dialectical" approach, developed in *Speech Acts in Argumentative Discussions* (Berlin, 1984) and *Argumentation, Communication, and Fallacies* (Hillsdale, N.J., 1992) by the Dutch argumentation theorists Frans H. van Eemeren and Rob Grootendorst, links up with formal dialectics. It starts, however, from the conviction that the single-minded preoccupation with the logical aspects of arguments should be abandoned and that the fallacies can be better understood as wrong moves in the communication process of argumentative discourse. A fallacy is in the pragma–dialectical approach regarded as a hindrance or impediment for the resolution of a disagreement, and the specific nature of a particular fallacy depends on the way in which it interferes with the resolution process.

In the pragma–dialectical theory of argumentation, a critical–rationalist philosophy of reasonableness is given shape in an ideal model of critical discussion that specifies the stages that are to be distinguished analytically in the resolution process and the verbal moves that are constitutive of each of these stages. In all stages of a critical discussion, the protagonist and the antagonist of the standpoint at issue must observe all the rules for the performance of speech acts that are instrumental to resolving the dispute. These rules can be recapitulated in a series of basic principles, each of which expresses a separate standard or norm for critical discussion. Any infringement, whichever party commits it, and at whatever stage in the discussion, is a possible threat to the resolution of a difference of opinion and must therefore be regarded as an incorrect discussion move or "fallacy." The term *fallacy* is thus systematically connected with the rules for critical discussion and defined as a speech act which prejudices or frustrates efforts to resolve a difference of opinion. [*See* Speech acts, utterances as.]

When it comes to the detection of fallacies, the pragma–dialectical analysis starts with interpreting an utterance in a discourse aimed at resolving a difference of opinion as a particular kind of speech act. Then it is determined whether the performance of this speech act agrees with the rules for critical discussion. If the speech act proves to violate any of these rules, it must be determined what kind of norm violation it entails. Only after it has become clear which specific criterion for satisfying a norm pertaining to a particular stage of the resolution process has not been met can it be determined which fallacy has been committed.

Rather than considering the fallacies as belonging to an unstructured list of nominal categories inherited from the past, as in the standard treatment, or considering all fallacies to be violations of one and the same (validity) norm, as in the logicocentric approaches, the pragma–dialectical approach differentiates a functional variety of norms. A comparison shows that fallacies which were traditionally only nominally lumped together are now either shown to have something in common or clearly distinguished, whereas genuinely related fallacies that were separated are brought together. For instance, two variants of *ad populum* are distinguished, the one being a violation of the Relevance Rule that a party may defend its standpoint only by advancing argumentation related to that standpoint, the other being a violation of the Argumentation Scheme Rule that a standpoint may not be regarded as conclusively defended if the defense does not take place by means of a correctly applied appropriate argumentation scheme. This shows that these variants are, in fact, *not* of the same kind. And analyzing one particular variant of *ad verecundiam* and one particular variant of *ad populum* as violations of the same Argumentation Scheme Rule makes clear that, seen from the perspective of resolving a difference of opinion, these variants *are* of the same kind.

The pragma–dialectical approach also enables the analysis of thus far unrecognized and unnamed "new" obstacles to resolving a difference of opinion. Examples are "declaring a standpoint sacrosanct," a violation of the Freedom Rule that parties must not prevent each other from putting forward standpoints or casting doubt on standpoints; "evading or shifting the burden of proof," violations of the Burden of Proof Rule that a party who puts forward a standpoint is obliged to defend that standpoint if asked to; "denying an unexpressed premise," a violation of the Unexpressed Premise Rule that a party may not falsely present something as a premise that has been left

unexpressed, or deny a premise that has been left implicit; and "making an absolute of the success of the defense," a violation of the Closure Rule that a failed defense must result in the protagonist retracting the standpoint and a successful defense in the antagonist retracting the doubt.

Written in a similar theoretical vein, Douglas Walton's *Informal Fallacies* (1987) marks a new stage in his development. To find a solution to the problems involved in analyzing fallacies, Walton now not only makes formal logic subservient to dialectic, but also turns to pragmatics, albeit in a very broad sense. Walton, a highly prolific author, now tends to combine the study of individual fallacies with examining real-life cases and making theoretical observations. In his analyses, he associates fallacies with illicit "dialectical shifts" from one type of dialogue to another. An argument that appears correct may actually be incorrect when it appears after a shift in a type of dialogue where it is no longer appropriate or even obstructive in view of the type of dialogue the participants were originally engaged in. An *ad baculum* involving a veiled threat, for example, can be appropriate in a negotiation dialogue but not in a persuasion dialogue. A systematic treatment of normative models of dialogue, which can serve as guidelines for a critical evaluation of fallacious dialogue shifts, is given in Walton and Krabbe (1995).

[*See also* Argumentation; Argument fields; *and* Logic.]

BIBLIOGRAPHY

Arnauld, Antoine. *The Art of Thinking (Port Royal Logic).* Translated and with an introduction by James Dickoff and Patricia James. New York, 1964. English translation of *La logique, ou l'art de penser,* first published 1662.

Bacon, Francis. *The Advancement of Learning.* Edited by G. W. Kitchen and with an introduction by A. Johnston. London, 1973. First published 1605.

Barth, Else M., and J. L. Martens. "Argumentum *Ad Hominem:* From Chaos to Formal Dialectic. The Method of Dialogue Tableaus as a Tool in the Theory of Fallacy." *Logique et Analyse,* n.s. 20 (1977), pp. 76–96.

Biro, John, and Harvey Siegel. "Normativity, Argumentation and an Epistemic Theory of Fallacies." In *Argumentation Illuminated.* Edited by Frans H. van Eemeren, Rob Grootendorst, J. Anthony Blair, and Charles A. Willard, pp. 85–103. Amsterdam, 1992.

Burge, Tyler. "A Theory of Aggregates." *Nous* 11 (1977), pp. 97–118.

Copi, I. M. *Introduction to Logic.* 4th ed. New York, 1972.

Finocchiaro, Maurice A. "Six Types of Fallaciousness: Toward a Realistic Theory of Logical Criticism." *Argumentation* 1 (1987), pp. 263–282.

Hintikka, Jaakko. "The Fallacy of Fallacies." *Argumentation* 1 (1987), pp. 211–238.

Lambert, K., and W. Ulrich. *The Nature of Argument.* New York, 1980.

Massey, Gerald J. *Understanding Symbolic Logic.* New York, 1970.

Walton, Douglas N. *Informal Fallacies. Towards a Theory of Argument Criticisms.* Pragmatics and Beyond Companion Series, vol. 4. Amsterdam, 1987.

Walton, Douglas N. *Informal Logic. A Handbook for Critical Argumentation.* Cambridge, U.K., 1989.

Walton, Douglas N. *Slippery Slope Arguments.* Oxford, 1992.

Walton, Douglas N. *A Pragmatic Theory of Fallacy.* Tuscaloosa, Ala., 1995.

Walton, Douglas N. *Fallacies Arising from Ambiguity.* Dordrecht, The Netherlands, 1996.

Walton, Douglas N., and Erik C. W. Krabbe. *Commitment in Dialogue. Basic Concepts of Interpersonal Reasoning.* New York, 1995.

—Frans H. van Eemeren

FANTASY THEME ANALYSIS. *See* Rhetorical vision.

FEMINIST RHETORIC encompasses advocacy for women, analyses of patriarchy, a communicative style, the recovery of women's words and history, the extrapolation of theory from women's rhetorical practices, and the development of critical methods adapted to the special conditions that women face as rhetors. It emerged in the nineteenth century as women asserted their right to a voice on moral issues, such as the abolition of slavery, the sale of alcohol, and the treatment of prostitutes. The term *feminist rhetoric* refers to discourse advocating enlarged legal, economic, and political rights for women and to the scholarly recovery of women's history and the development of theory and modes of analysis better suited to women than those developed by and for men in the past.

What is a Feminist? The meaning of the word *feminist* changed in response to women's activism. Formerly a synonym for *feminine,* attacks on women activists created negative connotations such that it came to mean *assertiveness, aggressiveness,* and *immodesty,* qualities at odds with traditional conceptions of womanliness. In other words, as women moved into the public sphere and claimed the right to participate fully in their communities, what had been a neutral term became an epithet used to silence women.

Nancy Cott (*The Grounding of American Feminism,* New Haven, 1987), however, identifies the use of the word *feminism* as arising around 1910, when it was distinguished from *suffragism,* the effort to gain the franchise for women. She identifies feminism as a contested term identified with three core ideas: opposition to sex hierarchy; the assumption that women's condition is socially constructed; and the notion that women perceive themselves as a social group with which they identify. In a history of the second wave, Alice Echols (*Daring to Be Bad: Radical Feminism in America, 1967–1975,* Minneapolis, 1989) identifies four strands of feminism, distinguished by ideology and goals: (1) socialist/Marxist feminism, which was committed to organizing women around the issues of gender and class; (2) liberal or equity feminism, which sought equality in the existing system; (3) radical feminism, which sought to eliminate gender as a basis for distinction; and (4) cultural or social feminism, which emphasized women's differences from men and celebrated women's culture. Accordingly, feminist rhetoric reflects the diversity of feminisms and expresses divergent points of view.

The Origins of Feminist Advocacy. The Origins of Feminist Advocacy. Feminist efforts to improve the conditions of women emerged out of struggles for change unrelated to what came to be known as woman's rights. The norms for proper female behavior, sometimes called the Cult of Domesticity, True Womanhood, or the Woman-Belle Ideal (Barbara Welter, *Dimity Convictions: The American Woman in the Nineteenth Century,* Athens, Ohio, 1976) made public activity by a woman taboo. The ideal woman was seen as naturally pious and domestic, but the contradiction between these qualities emerged when women were energized by moral outrage to work for the abolition of slavery, for temperance, and for aid to prostitutes and were told that, despite their moral authority, such public efforts were unwomanly. A good example is African-American activist Maria W. Miller Stewart, who spoke in Boston in the early 1830s to protest slavery and the treatment of free African Americans in the North. Her final address of 21 September, 1833, was a powerful expression of the religious motive that led her to speak and of the social pressure that forced her to abandon the platform.

Abolitionists such as Sarah Grimké (1792–1873) and her sister Angelina (1805–1979) along with Abby Kelley Foster (1810–1887) came to recognize that they would be able to advocate for slaves only if they also asserted their own rights. The earliest work of feminist theory published in the United States is Sarah Grimké's *Letters on the Equality of the Sexes and the Condition of Woman* (Boston, 1838), which defends the right of women to public advocacy on moral issues. Grimké's letters refuted theological arguments silencing women by arguing that women's advocacy is part of the prophetic tradition of the Bible; she also argued that gender norms were socially constructed and contrary to the teachings of Jesus. She carefully limited her claims to argue for moral, not physical, equality and contended that women who acted publicly for moral causes would become better wives and mothers than those who remained at home.

As Grimké's letters illustrate, rhetoric grows out of prior rhetoric, and the invention of feminist rhetors reflects rhetorical history. Thus, early women's discourse was shaped by the social mythology that proscribed woman's place. Until the modern period, when an organized movement emerged, the denial of education to women and the suppression of women's history prevented later generations of women from building on earlier efforts. In the first wave of feminism, women had to respond to three justifications of woman's subordinate position and limited sphere of activity: the theological argument that God ordained woman's place; the biological argument that anatomy is destiny; and the political/sociological argument that the fundamental unit of society is the family, represented in public by the male head of the household. The watchword was "a woman's place is in the home," a motto that denied women any role in public deliberation.

The most troublesome obstacle to early wom-

en's right to speak was the theological view that woman's role had been ordained by God, which prohibited women from teaching or preaching. Early feminists noted internal contradictions in the Pauline epistles, called attention to female judges, prophets, and leaders in Israel and in the early church, and used the words and actions of Jesus, including the Sermon on the Mount, to assert a single moral standard applicable to both sexes. Disputes over God's plan for women generated a substantial amount of discourse, including *Woman, Church, and State* (Chicago, 1893) by Matilda Joslyn Gage, which was an attack on established churches; *The Woman's Bible* (2 vols., New York, 1892, 1895) edited by Elizabeth Cady Stanton, which provided a hermeneutic analysis of biblical passages treating women; and *Woman in the Pulpit* (Boston, 1888) by conservative Woman's Christian Temperance Union president Frances E. Willard, which defended a woman's right to preach.

Early women also were aided by religious ideas. Protestantism's rejection of the priest as intercessor and its assertion of a "priesthood of believers" was a powerful argument for a woman's spiritual rights. The Society of Friends rejected the concept of original sin and believed that an "inner light" was in everyone. Accordingly, Quakers educated girls as well as boys, treated preaching as a form of prophecy open to women, and allowed women to become "public Friends" who addressed outsiders. Quaker women, such as Sarah and Angelina Grimké, Lucretia Coffin Mott (1793–1880), Susan B. Anthony (1820–1906), and Alice Paul (1885–1977), played major roles in the first wave of U.S. feminism and were active in many reform movements.

Theology continued to be an important barrier in the second wave, illustrated by the works of contemporary feminist theologians. Of special significance are *Beyond God the Father: Toward a Philosophy of Women's Liberation* (Boston, 1973) and *The Church and the Second Sex* (New York, 1975) by Mary Daly and *Sexism and God-talk: Toward a Feminist Theology* (Boston, 1983) by Rosemary Radford Ruether. In her earlier book, Daly summed up the link between sexism and religion by saying, "[I]f God is male, then the male is God" (p. 19).

In the nineteenth century, beliefs about biology, often inaccurate, also were used to justify women's exclusion from the public realm. Of particular note is the use of biological characteristics as the basis for claims about women's mental and political capacities. If females were educated, it was believed that their ovaries and wombs could not develop properly because blood needed for their development would be diverted to the brain. Moreover, because females generally were smaller than males, their brains were assumed to be smaller, hence, too small to undertake public deliberation. Their supposedly smaller nerves were thought too delicate and fragile to withstand the rigors of the marketplace, law courts, or legislature. The most famous work in this vein was *Sex in Education; or, A Fair Chance for the Girls* (Boston, 1873) by Edward Clarke, a former professor at Harvard Medical School. His book provoked a storm of protest; *A Reply to Dr. E. H. Clarke's "Sex in Education"* (Boston, 1874) was a collection of responses edited and introduced by Julia Ward Howe (1819–1910).

In more recent times, biological and psychological studies have been used to argue that women's traditional roles are "natural." Prior to the beginnings of the second wave, Ruth Herschberger published *Adam's Rib* (New York, 1948), a pointedly humorous critique of the primate experiments at the Yerkes laboratories that were used to demonstrate that traditional gender roles were part of primate biology. Others, such as Ruth Bleier (*Science and Gender: A Critique of Biology and Its Theories on Women*, New York, 1984), have attacked similar conclusions based on primate research, clinical psychology, and sociobiology. A trenchant classic of the second wave was Naomi Weisstein's *Kinder, Küche, Kirche as Scientific Law: Psychology Constructs the Female* (Boston, 1968).

Another rationale for silencing women was the claim that the family, not the individual, was the fundamental social and political unit publicly represented by its male head. As political theorist Susan Miller Okin points out in *Women in Western Political Thought* (Princeton, 1979), although liberalism is associated with individualism, English philosopher John Stuart Mill (1806–1873) was the first to argue that the rights of individual women might not be well represented by the family. In *The Disorder of Women: Democracy, Feminism, and Political Theory* (Stanford, 1989), po-

litical theorist Carole Pateman demonstrates that the political theories of John Locke (1632–1704) and Jean-Jacques Rousseau (1712–1778) presumed the natural inferiority of women and their subjugation to men. Laws treating women, particularly wives, differently than men were the targets of early woman's rights advocates as well as of more recent feminist activists.

Struggling for Credibility. Once women found a voice, the struggle for credibility began. Gender plays a powerful role in rhetorical action and a *rhētōr's ēthos*. Qualities traditionally valued in rhetoric—assertiveness, leadership, rational argumentation, debating skills, and expertise—are associated with masculinity. Similarly, economic issues, military matters, legislating, and foreign relations, the common topics of deliberation, are thought of as the purview of men. In other words, those who engage in public discourse are expected to display qualities traditionally associated with masculinity and to discuss issues traditionally identified with men. [*See* Ēthos.]

Gender affects persuasion because the speaker's character or *ēthos* influences the ways ideas are received. The rhetor's *ēthos* depends on community *ēthos* or the extent to which the individual mirrors the values of the community. To be credible, a woman must exemplify the community's norms of femininity, but as a rhetor, she must embody qualities usually coded as masculine. In other words, as Susan Jarratt wrote in a special issue of *Rhetoric Society Quarterly,* any public performance by a woman, except as an actress or prostitute, is a form of cross-dressing (Winter 1992, p. 2). The experiences of nineteenth-century African-American women are vivid illustrations of the dual barriers of sex and race to a speaker's credibility. As Carla Peterson demonstrates in *"Doers of the Word": African-American Women Speakers and Writers in the North (1830–1880)* (New York, 1995), such women were often viewed as performers or actresses, rather than as advocates, and in some cases, they were accused of being men. [*See overview article on* African-American rhetoric.]

As Sarah Grimké's letters and Jarratt's comment suggest, the social construction and performance of gender have been key issues for feminists. In *Gender Trouble: Feminism and the Subversion of Identity* (New York, 1990) and *Bodies*

That Matter: On the Discursive Limits of "Sex" (New York, 1993), Judith Butler argues that gender is a performance, an illusion maintained discursively by words, actions, and gestures. She makes a distinction between one's sex, the arrangement of one's genitals, and gender, the cultural meanings of masculinity or femininity embodied in performance. This behavior is culturally disciplined through approval or censure. The woman who wishes to be credible is constrained to embody cultural norms. In other words, when a woman speaks, she is expected to enact gender norms signaling her femininity and to enact rhetorical norms coded as masculine.

The women who began speaking in the nineteenth century in the United States devised many creative strategies to overcome this apparent dilemma. Angelina Grimké, for example, adopted public personae that made it difficult for audiences to reject her. In addressing the Massachusetts state legislature on 21 February, 1838, she compared herself to Queen Esther, who risked her life violating powerful taboos against women's public action in order to save her people. Addressing abolitionists of mixed sex and ethnicity in Pennsylvania Hall, Philadelphia, on 16 May, 1838, she spoke as a prophet, emulating female models in the Old and New Testaments; as a Southerner who knew slavery intimately; and as a woman who urged women to do what was possible for them—petition legislators.

Some inventional strategies were common. Many women advocates quoted male authorities to avoid claiming expertise for themselves. Most addressed audiences as sisters or as supplicants. Many developed arguments inductively based on personal experience, a form of womanly expertise, to give audiences the illusion that they were drawing the conclusions rather than being led by a woman. The appearance of debating was avoided, although opposing views were refuted indirectly with debunking examples or humorously revealed inconsistencies. As a group, these inventional choices constitute a strategic "feminine style" adapted to hostile or hesitant audiences, which simultaneously enacted cultural norms for femininity while meeting rhetorical expectations.

The struggle for the right to speak abated as the nineteenth century ended, but the struggle to be credible continued. Although suffrage advocacy had continued for more than sixty years, only persistent militancy begun in the 1910s, primarily by the National Woman's Party led by Alice Paul, moved woman suffrage to the top of the national agenda. Marches, demonstrations, picketing the White House, and burning President Wilson's paeans to a democracy that did not include women, accompanied by a women's press corps to attract media attention, demonstrated women's intense commitment to enfranchisement and kept the issue before the public and Congress. This led to passage of the Nineteenth Amendment in 1920, which stated that the right of citizens to vote shall not be denied on account of sex.

The struggle for credibility is dramatically illustrated by the speaking careers of African Americans. Ida B. Wells (1862–1931) spearheaded the campaign against lynching in the 1890s, but it was only when she traveled to England to present her case that she attracted the attention of white U.S. audiences. Mary Church Terrell (1863–1954) spoke throughout the country protesting against lynching, segregation, sharecropping, and the convict-lease system, but she was denied access to such major journals of opinion as *McClure's* when she attempted to refute the claims of Southerners who defended lynching.

Natural Rights versus Sexual Difference. Conflict between norms of femininity and feminist aims influenced the grounds from which activists argued. Some based their arguments on natural rights; others based their advocacy on sexual difference, still others combined them, despite obvious inconsistencies. Arguments grounded in natural rights assumed women's legal and political equality based on personhood and, in their pure form, did not recognize biological differences. Those who argued from sexual difference claimed that women's distinctive qualities would benefit the public sphere and giving women legal and economic rights would enable them to be better wives and mothers. Some advocates sought legal and political equality but argued that women would have a positive influence on public affairs. Some called for economic recognition of the social value of maternity and child rearing, while others argued that only after equality of opportunity could natural sexual differences be ascertained. Some claimed special insight from women's biology; for example, that women were natural pacifists unwilling to risk the lives of sons they had borne and nurtured.

These differing assumptions persist because of differing views of the importance of socialization and biology. Some blame socialization for women's disadvantaged position. Others hold systematic patterns of discrimination—the patriarchy—responsible. Still others adopt a "pro-woman line," arguing that women's choices, however constricting, reflect rational assessments of the options available to them.

Patriarchy and Consciousness-Raising. Earlier advocates laid the foundation for a kind of discourse that in the modern period can be identified as feminist both in content and style. In content, feminist rhetoric drew its premises from a radical analysis of patriarchy, which identified the "man-made world" as one built on the oppression of women. The most sophisticated analysis of the dynamics of patriarchal thinking is found in *Man's World, Woman's Place: A Study in Social Mythology* (New York, 1971) by Elizabeth Janeway. In *Feminism Unmodified: Discourses on Life and Law* (Cambridge, Mass., 1987), Catharine MacKinnon dramatized the insidious character of patriarchy by claiming that women's lot is worse than that of slaves because it was never assumed that slavery was created for the slaves' pleasure and enjoyment. Addressing the link between sexual identity and patriarchy ("Compulsory Heterosexuality and Lesbian Existence," *Signs* 5, 1980, pp. 631–660), Adrienne Rich described heterosexism as an institution dedicated to the oppression of women. In other words, feminists have called attention to a power struggle between men and women in which the economic, political, and social systems maintain female inferiority and dependency.

Those oppressive systems, feminists argued, are sustained by policies of exclusion ("the glass ceiling"), by resistant attitudes to sharing parenting and housework, and by social norms that define wives as personal body servants for their husbands and children, norms enforced through sexual harassment and sexual assault, which are reinforced in popular culture and eroticized in the rhetoric of pornography. The feminism of the 1960s rudely disclosed the ways in which patriarchy benefited males and disadvantaged fe-

males. At its most extreme, feminist rhetoric pointed to the victims of the war between the sexes—to survivors of rape and incest and wives and girlfriends battered and murdered by their husbands and "lovers." Feminist scholars also explored the history of patriarchy and identified the emotional and economic grounds for male resistance to change.

Feminist rhetoric also incorporates a communicative style known as consciousness-raising, which emerged in the small women's liberation groups of the more radical wing of 1960s feminism, but typified much of the public discourse through which feminist ideas were disseminated. In small groups, consciousness-raising was a process through which women shared personal experiences in order to distinguish what was idiosyncratic or personal from what was systemic. Participants learned that what they had believed to be individual difficulties were common problems, a product not of character, personality, or ability, but of their status as women. Hence, the well-known slogan "The personal is political," which referred to this process and rejected individual therapy as a solution to women's problems.

As a method of discovering social truths, consciousness-raising is only partly personal and experiential. Distinguishing the personal from the systemic requires research and critical analysis. It also requires a relatively homogeneous, leaderless group in which all participate. Thus, as a style of learning, consciousness-raising is experiential, participatory, and, hence, emotional and egalitarian. Analysis proceeds inductively, moving from individual experiences through criticism and testing toward generalizations that identify the conditions that systems impose on women.

Although it began as a small-group process, consciousness-raising can be a rhetorical style strategically adapted to addressing women as audiences. In such cases, feminists use their own experiences or those of others as a prime source of evidence; they structure arguments inductively to develop conclusions out of many instances; they use questions to prompt the audience participation, and they address women as peers, not as authorities. Virginia Woolf's much-praised feminist classic, *A Room of One's Own* (London, 1929; New York, 1957), is a prime example of this style in writing. In *Virginia Woolf and the Languages of Pa-*

triarchy (Bloomington, Ind., 1987), English professor Jane Marcus argued that in *A Room of One's Own* Woolf deconstructed the lecture, a form that for her was an instance of the discourse of male domination. Instead, she enacted the lecture as a conversation among equals, among women. Readers are not told the truth as Woolf sees it but instead are invited to participate in the process of asking questions and searching for answers. Marcus described the text as a "trio-logue" between the woman writer, the women students in her audience, and women readers.

The socialization most women experience is one reason that women find this style congenial. Women's traditional tasks illustrate craft learning, a lore developed through trial and error, usually supervised by a mentor. Parenting, satisfying the competing demands of spouse and children, and performing most household tasks, cannot be learned from books; one learns their contingencies through trial and error. Consciousness-raising style mimics the participatory, experience-based, inductive processes of craft learning, substituting research into and comparison with the experiences of other women for mentoring. Accordingly, although not the exclusive purview of women, this is a style of communicating with which many women as rhetors and as audiences feel comfortable.

In some instances, the assumption underlying consciousness-raising—that truth emerges out of women's lived experience—became an integral element in feminist analysis, a feminist epistemology. In *Women's Ways of Knowing: The Development of Self, Voice, and Mind* (New York, 1986), Mary Belenky et al. argued that women's ways of learning are distinctive. Their work built on research by Carol Gilligan on the ethical choices of adolescent girls in *In a Different Voice: Psychological Theory and Women's Development* (Cambridge, Mass., 1982). Gilligan claimed that women's moral development followed a path different from that described by Lawrence Kohlberg as applying to all, based on research done with males. Gilligan's studies suggested that whereas males are more likely to value autonomy, females are more likely to value connections with others, to communicate care and responsiveness, and to preserve relationships. From one perspective, Gilligan's work esteemed the principles underlying

adolescent girls' moral choices; from another perspective, her work was an example of essentializing women, of predicating their value systems on their biology.

Echoing the thinking of the group headed by Belenky, some contemporary feminists, including such French feminists as Hélène Cixous and Luce Irigaray, see feminism as a way of knowing. Catharine MacKinnon and Andrea Dworkin, for example, call attention to the ways in which pornography silences women, and Dworkin speaks and writes in ways that privilege the voices of women who experience pornography's effects.

Neither the analysis of patriarchy nor consciousness-raising as a small-group process, a style of discourse, or a source of knowledge are the creations of contemporary feminism. Scattered analyses of patriarchy emerged in the earlier movement. Similarly, consciousness-raising mimics the "testimony" of some religious practices and appeared in some revolutionary guerrilla movements. Contemporary feminists, however, have produced more systematic analyses of patriarchy than their predecessors, and they have used consciousness-raising as a way of radicalizing women and of discovering truths about their condition.

In 1955, eight women formed a group that became the Daughters of Bilitis, and in 1956, they began publishing *The Ladder,* a magazine for lesbians. As the second wave began, lesbians were significant voices; one of the most articulate was Rita Mae Brown, whose *Rubyfruit Jungle* (Plainfield, Vt., 1973) is a feminist classic. *Freedom to Differ: The Shaping of the Gay and Lesbian Struggle for Civil Rights* (New York, 1998) by Diane H. Miller is a sophisticated study of the rhetoric of gay and lesbian activists in their struggle against discrimination. [*See* Queer rhetoric.]

Feminists also have addressed the ways in which feminist ideas are shaped by media systems dominated by men. In *Prime-Time Feminism: Television, Media Culture, and the Women's Movement since 1970* (Philadelphia, 1996), Bonnie Dow analyzed the interaction between feminism and popular culture, particularly in the prime-time programs that focused on the lives of women, from the debut in 1970 of *The Mary Tyler Moore Show* to the introduction of *Doctor Quinn, Medicine Woman* in 1993. In *Backlash: The Unde-*

clared War Against American Women (New York, 1991), Susan Faludi argued that the practices of the news and entertainment media worked against the efforts of feminists. In *Feminism and Its Fictions: The Consciousness-Raising Novel and the Women's Liberation Movement* (Philadelphia, 1998), however, Lisa Hogeland argued that the women's and feminist fiction of the 1970s was dominated by the consciousness-raising novel, which enabled a wider circulation of ideas related to the women's liberation movement. In *Decoding Abortion Rhetoric: Communicating Social Change* (Urbana, Ill., 1990), Celeste Condit traced the stages in the development and interaction of pro- and antiabortion rhetoric and the treatment of these arguments in popular culture, law, and public discourse between 1960 and 1985. All of these, among many others that continue to appear, examine the relationships between feminist ideas and the various media of public and popular culture.

Feminist Rhetorical Theory. One important outcome of the second wave of feminism has been scholarship that attempts to recover the voices of women of the past. The earliest were efforts to reclaim women's speeches, illustrated by *Outspoken Women* (Dubuque, Iowa, 1984), edited by Judith Anderson; *We Shall Be Heard* (Dubuque, Iowa, 1983), edited by Patricia Scileppi Kennedy and Gloria Hartmann O'Shields; and *Man Cannot Speak for Her* (vol. 2, Westport, Conn., 1989), edited by Karlyn Kohrs Campbell. The works of early African-American women have been collected by Shirley Wilson Logan, Marilyn Washington, and others.

Another development has been efforts to recuperate the rhetorical theory implicit in the practices of women of the past. The earliest sustained effort in that direction was *Rereading the Sophists: Classical Rhetoric Refigured* (Carbondale, Ill., 1991) by Susan Jarratt, who argued that the first Sophists should be given a more prominent place in the study of rhetoric. [*See* Sophists.] Moreover, rereading sophistic works offered a new lens for viewing contemporary social issues, including feminist writing. Jarratt argued that the philosophical framework of binaries and hierarchies developed by Plato and Aristotle provided a conceptual ground for centuries of excluding both Sophists and feminists. By contrast, the sophistic notions of contingency, practice, and the rejection of essence are congenial to feminist ways of reading. [*See* Classical rhetoric; *and* Contingency and probability.]

Several collections have rescued the theory and practice of women from the classical period to the present. *Reclaiming Rhetorica: Women in the Rhetorical Tradition* (Pittsburgh, 1995), edited by Andrea Lunsford, treats the fifth-century Greeks Aspasia and Diotima, the fifteenth-century Englishwoman Margery Kempe and her French contemporary Christine de Pizan, the seventeenth-century English woman Mary Astell, the eighteenth-century Englishwoman Mary Wollstonecraft, the nineteenth-century Americans Margaret Fuller, Sojourner Truth, and Ida B. Wells, and such modern theorists as Susanne K. Langer and Julia Kristeva. [*See* Eighteenth-century rhetoric.] *Political Rhetoric, Power, and Renaissance Women* (Albany, N.Y., 1995), edited by Carole Levin and Patricia A. Sullivan, analyzes the rhetorical strategies of Christine de Pizan (1365–c.1429), Elizabeth I of England, and Anne Askew (1521–1546), among others. Similarly, *The Changing Tradition: Women in the History of Rhetoric* (Calgary, Alberta, 1999), edited by Christine Mason Sutherland and Rebecca Sutcliffe, addresses feminist issues beginning with the works of Plato and ending with such contemporary writers as Donna Haraway.

Two single-authored books merit special mention. *Rhetoric Retold: Regendering the Tradition from Antiquity through the Renaissance* (Carbondale, Ill., 1997) by Cheryl Glenn provides general rhetorical context and then focuses on key figures in the classical, medieval, and Renaissance periods, particularly in England. The analyses are insightful; the treatments of *The Book of Margery Kempe* (c.1373–c.1440; transcribed c.1432–1436), perhaps the first autobiography by a woman, and the *Examinations* of Anne Askew (1546) are particularly astute. What emerges is a sense of the ways in which feminism has permitted critics to approach texts in fresh ways in order to recognize the originality and sophistication of women whose works do not follow traditional formats or fall into traditional genres.

Anglo-American Feminist Challenges to the Rhetorical Traditions (Carbondale, Ill., 1996) by Krista Ratcliffe represents an effort to extract from the discursive practices of women the rhetorical theory that is implicit in them. In the introductory chapter, Ratcliffe describes four kinds of feminist challenges to the rhetorical traditions: (1) recovering, the discovery of lost or marginalized rhetorical theories, such as Margaret Askew Fell's *Women's Speaking Justified* (London, 1666); (2) rereading, or reinterpreting canonical and recovered rhetorical theories, illustrated by Susan Jarratt's work on the Sophists; (3) extrapolating, or rereading texts not obviously rhetorical as theories of rhetoric, for example, reading Christine de Pisan's *Treasure of the City of Ladies* as an etiquette manual and a rhetorical treatise; and (4) conceptualizing, or writing new theories of rhetoric. Ratcliffe combines these in her efforts to extrapolate rhetorical theories from the works of Virginia Woolf, Mary Daly, and Adrienne Rich. Because she uses the five arts (invention, arrangement, style, delivery, and memory) as the template for describing theory, the results are limited, but her book initiates efforts that other feminist theorists would do well to follow.

Feminist rhetorical theory also has an essentialist form, which first emerged in an essay in *Communication Monographs* 62 (1955, pp. 2–18) entitled "Beyond Persuasion: A Proposal for an Invitational Rhetoric" by Cindy Griffin and Sonja Foss. The essay holds that persuasive efforts are coercive and that the corrective is an invitational rhetoric grounded in the feminist principles of equality, immanent value, and self-determination. That view is elaborated in *Feminist Rhetorical Theories* (Thousand Oaks, Calif., 1999), edited by Karen Foss, Sonja Foss, and Cindy Griffin, a collection of works by women.

Feminist rhetoric is advocacy for women, analysis of patriarchy, a style of communicating, the recovery of women's voices, the extrapolation of theory from women's practice, and the development of critical methods responsive to the special conditions that women face as *rhētors*.

BIBLIOGRAPHY

Beauvoir, Simone de. *Le deuxième sexe.* Paris, 1949; *The Second Sex.* Translated by H. M. Parshley. New York, 1953. The first modern analysis of the dynamics of patriarchy.

Black, Naomi. *Social Feminism.* Ithaca, N.Y., 1989. An extended treatment of domestic or cultural feminism.

Campbell, Karlyn Kohrs. "The Discursive Performance of Femininity: Hating Hillary." *Rhetoric and Public Affairs* 1 (1998), pp. 1–20. A study of the conflicting demands that women face as public speakers, applied to the First Lady Hillary Rodham Clinton.

Campbell, Karlyn Kohrs. *Man Cannot Speak for Her: A Critical Study of Early Feminist Rhetoric.* Westport, Conn., 1989. An analysis of the rhetoric of the first wave treated as a social movement that begins as a struggle for woman's rights and becomes a movement for woman suffrage.

Cooper, Anna Julia. *The Voice of Anna Julia Cooper.* Edited by Charles Lemert and Esme Bahn. Lanham, Md., 1998. A collection of texts by an extraordinary African-American woman.

Daly, Mary. *Gyn/Ecology: The Metaethics of Radical Feminism.* Boston, 1978. Investigates global patriarchy using such practices as suttee, foot-binding, genital mutilation, witch burnings, and U.S. gynecological practices.

Davis, Angela Y. *Women, Race, and Class.* New York, 1981. A critique of white racism in the first wave and of the use of rape to justify the lynching of black men.

Deem, Melissa. "From Bobbitt to SCUM: Re-memberment, Scatological Rhetorics, and Feminist Strategies in the Contemporary United States." *Public Culture* 8 (Spring 1996), pp. 511–537. Uses the SCUM Manifesto to analyze the Lorena Bobbitt case.

Dworkin, Andrea. *Pornography: Men Possessing Women.* New York, 1981. A radical analysis of pornography as part of women's oppression.

Giddings, Paula. *When and Where I Enter: The Impact of Black Women on Race and Sex in America.* New York, 1984. The best single-volume history of African-American women's activism.

hooks, bell. *Ain't I a Woman: Black Women and Feminism.* Boston, 1981. An early and important exploration of the extent to which feminism meets the needs of African-American women.

Jamieson, Kathleen Hall. *Beyond the Double Bind: Women and Leadership.* New York, 1995. This book takes issue with some of the claims made by Susan Faludi and addresses the problems faced by women in politics.

Jarratt, Susan C., ed. "Feminist Rereadings in the History of Rhetoric." Special issue. *Rhetoric Society Quarterly* 22 (Winter 1992). Essays reexamining the tradition from a feminist perspective.

Lerner, Gerda. *The Grimké Sisters from South Carolina: Pioneers for Woman's Rights and Abolition.* New York, 1971. A historical biography of two key figures in the history of women's rhetoric.

Logan, Shirley Wilson. *"We Are Coming": The Persuasive Discourse of Nineteenth-Century Black Women.* Carbondale, Ill., 1999. An analysis of African-American women's discourse with some additional texts in an appendix.

Logan, Shirley Wilson, ed. *With Pen and Voice: A Critical Anthology of Nineteenth-Century African-American Women.* Carbondale, Ill., 1995. Includes texts by Maria Miller Stewart, Sojourner Truth, Frances Ellen Watkins Harper, Anna Julia Haywood Cooper, Ida B. Wells, Fannie Barrier Williams, and Victoria Earle Matthews.

Russett, Cynthia Eagle. *Sexual Science: The Victorian Construction of Womanhood.* Cambridge, Mass., 1989. Examines the scientific literature of the nineteenth and early twentieth centuries concerning the differences between men and women.

Smith-Rosenberg, Carroll. *Disorderly Conduct: Visions of Gender in Victorian America.* New York, 1985. Essays on the dramatic changes in male–female relations, family structure, social custom, and sexual behavior in the United States in response to immigration, industrialization, and urbanization.

Morgan, Robin. *Sisterhood is Powerful: An Anthology of Writings from the Women's Liberation Movement.* New York, 1970. A collection of works reflecting the diverse voices of the beginnings of the second wave.

Sterling, Dorothy. *Ahead of Her Time: Abby Kelley and the Politics of Anti-Slavery.* New York, 1991. The life story of an early activist and the obstacles she faced.

Stewart, Maria Miller. *Maria W. Stewart, America's First Black Woman Political Writer: Essays and Speeches.* Edited and introduced by Marilyn Richardson. Bloomington, Ind., 1987. The volume includes all of her speeches with an introduction that provides historical and biographical background.

—KARLYN KOHRS CAMPBELL

FIGURES OF SPEECH are the smallest structural units of rhetorical stylistics (*elocutio*). [*See* Style.] As such they have been constitutive elements in all kinds of texts from antiquity to the present: in the Homeric epics and the Bible, in medieval chronicles and romances, in Cicero's orations and John Donne's sermons, in religious pamphlets of the Reformation and the Counter-Reformation, in libels and speeches of the French Revolution, in fascist and communist propaganda, in all kinds of persuasive and poetical communication.

The Classical System: Its Origin and Tradition. The Greek sophist Gorgias of Leontini (c.483–c.376 BCE) was the first to deliberately use figures of speech in his writings, above all figures of phonological, morphological, and syntactic equivalence such as *homoeoteleuton, asyndeton,* alliteration, assonance, *paronomasia, epanalēpsis,* and *isocolon,* which later became known as Gorgianic figures. [*See* Gorgianic figures.] With the rise of rhetorical treatises, the figures of speech began to assume a systematic character, which was, however, quite heterogeneous depending on their respective origin and purpose. As a consequence the figures of speech increased in number and were located in systematic arrangements of ever-growing complexity. Whatever their descent, they were based on the fundamental distinction of tropes (Gk. *tropoi*) and schemes (Gk. *schēmata,* Lat. *figurae*). Most rhetorical works in the Greco-Roman tradition maintain the same dichotomy, for instance Henry Peacham's treatise *The Garden of Eloquence* (1593): "Figures of the Grecians are called Tropes and Schemates and of the Latines, figures, exornations, lights, colours and ornaments" (11). According to Quintilian (*Institutio oratoria,* first century CE, 9.1.4–5), "the name of trope (*tropos*) is applied to the transference of expressions from their natural and principal signification to another, with a view to the embellishment of style" (*a naturali et principali significatione translatus ad aliam ornandae orationis gratia*); "a *figure,* on the other hand, is the term employed when we give our language a conformation other than the obvious and ordinary" (*conformatio quaedam orationis remota a communi et primum se offerente ratione*). Among the tropes are usually numbered such stylistic categories as metaphor, *catachrēsis,* metonymy, synecdochē, hyperbolē, irony, allegory and *periphrasis* (cf. the pseudo-Ciceronian *Rhetorica ad Herennium,* first century BCE), and Quintilian's *Institutio oratoria*). In many classical treatises (cf. Martin, part 3, 1974, chap. 2), the schemes or *figurae* are in their turn subdivided into "figures of thought" (*schēmata dianoias, figurae sententiae*) and "figures of word (diction)" (*schēmata lexeōs, figurae elocutionis*); the former including, among others, antithesis, apostrophē, *descriptio, ēthopoeia, hysteron prōteron, praeteritio, prosōpopoeia* and simile, the latter comprising, among others, *anadiplōsis, anaphora, anastrophē, antistrophē,* asyndeton, ellipsis, *enallagē, epanadiplōsis, epiphora, epizeuxis, gradatio, hyperbaton,* isocolon, paronomasia, *polyptōton, polysyndeton, syllepsis,* and *zeugma.* The medieval *Poetriae novae* propagated two kinds of rhetorical exornation: *ornatus facilis* and *ornatus difficilis,* the one lacking and the other employing more complicated stylistic categories such as tropes and figures of thought.

A daring attempt at establishing a logically correct elocutionary system was undertaken by the French theorist Petrus Ramus (1515–1572), who subjected all the figures of speech to a consistent binary classification leading from a more general to a less general category. Thus, starting from the dichotomy of tropes and figures (schemes), he continued to subdivide the tropes into metonymy and metaphor and the figures (schemes) into figures of word and figures of sentence, and so on with further stemmatic subcategorizations. In the English Renaissance, Abraham Fraunce, an ardent admirer of Petrus Ramus, follows the same binary practice in his *Arcadian Rhetorike* (1588; cf. the table in Sonnino 1968, p. 246).

An idiosyncratic division of the figures is offered in Puttenham's Book 3 ("Of Ornament"; 1589). Its axiomatic foundation is the effect on the hearer, which is differentiated according to the appeal on ear, on conceit, or both on ear and conceit. Thus, three classes of figures are established: *auricular* figures ("apperteining to single words"); the classical *figurae verborum:* enallagē, asyndeton, polysyndeton, *hendiadys,* and others; *sensable* figures ("because they alter and affect the minde by alteration of sence"), the traditional tropes: metaphor, catachrēsis, metonymy, synecdochē, allegory, periphrasis, and others; and *sententious* figures "otherwise called Rhetoricall" ("such as do most beautifie language with eloquence and sententiousness"): anaphora, epizeuxis, *antitheton,* and others. Moreover, Puttenham is the first Renaissance theoretician to attempt a translation of the Greco-Latin terminology of the figures of speech into the vernacular. Some specimens of his terminological anglicizing are: "*Allegoria,* or the Figure of false (faire) semblant" or "the Courtier;" "*Auxesis,* or the Auancer;" "*Apostrophe,* or the turn tale;" "*Parenthesis* or the Insertour;" "*Metaphora,* or the Figure of transporte;" "*Metonimia,* or the Misnamer;" "*Ironia,* or the Dry mock;" "*Erotema,* or the Questioner;" "*Histeron proteron,* or the Preposterous;" "*Hiperbole,* or the Ouer reacher, otherwise called the loud lyer;" and "*Paradoxon,* or the Wondrer."

Yet, in spite of such attempts at a terminolog-ical and systematic reformation of the figures of speech, the classical model, though with minor variations, remained substantially intact and was propagated by most handbooks of rhetoric through Lausberg's handbook (1960). However, what was abandoned in the course of the nineteenth century was the traditionally strict distinction between tropes and figures/schemes (Sharon-Zisser, 1993). It gave way to the overall terms "figures du discours" (Fontanier), "figures of speech" (Quinn), "rhetorical figures" (Mayoral), "figures de style" (Suhamy, Bacry), or simply "figures" (Genette), which were used by these figurists in their book titles.

From the nineteenth century onward, the habit became popular of compiling alphabetical catalogs and "handlists" of the figures of speech as well as of the other rhetorical terms (Lanham, 1968) serving the purpose of providing brief information for the praxis of textual analysis. It was only with the rise of modern linguistics and stylistics in the twentieth century that rhetoricians ventured to modernize the traditional system of figures, for instance, Todorov in his "Essai de classification" (1967) with its terminologically ambiguous distinction between *anomalies* and *figures,* and the Groupe Mu (Liège) in *Rhétorique Générale* (Dubois, 1970) with their creation of several innovative categorial groups of figures, for instance metasememes and metalogisms, of which the former are identical with the traditional tropes and the latter related to the so-called figures of thought.

Modernizing the Classical System. A practical modern model that takes account of most traditional figures of speech has a bipartite structure with two basic components: rhetorical *langue* (Saussure) or *competence* (Chomsky) and rhetorical *parole* or *performance.* As for the elementary structural unit of this model, the figure of speech, the following basic assumptions seem warranted:

From the perspective of rhetorical *competence,* a figure of speech is subject to a threefold semiosis, which, following Charles W. Morris's tripartite semiotic concept of the (semio-)syntactic (relation: sign-sign), the pragmatic (relation: sender/recipient-sign), and the (semio-)semantic (relation: sign-referent) dimensions, results in three classes of figures: (a) (semio-)syntactic figures, (b) pragmatic figures, and (c) (semio-)semantic figures. In their totality, it is claimed, these figures represent a tripartite secondary grammar (of rhetoricity) that is superimposed upon a primary grammar (of textual grammaticality).

Each figure of speech participates in the transformational procedure of deviation. This has to be defined differently for each semiotic dimension. Consider, for instance, the class of (semio-)syntactic figures, whose specific deviation consists of an alteration of the "normal" sequence (combination) of the language signs. The latter represents the linguistic *degré zéro* and is formulated in the shape of a text grammar describing the primary norm of the standard language. As compared to this type of primary grammar, figures of speech are systematized within the framework of a secondary grammar which is not a random collection of linguistic aberrations but constitutes a norm of its own, the norm of a virtual rhetoricity.

A *(semio-)syntactic model of figures* is composed of two basic linguistic dimensions: (1) linguistic operations (first axis) and (2) linguistic levels (second axis) (Table 1). The linguistic operations consist of two types of rules, the first violating and the other enforcing the primary norm. The fig-

ures produced by the former rules are also known as rhetorical licences, anomalies, metaboles, or simply deviations (antigrammatical forms), the figures generated by the latter rules are known as equivalences, isotopes, or simply repetitions (syngrammatical forms). The rule-violating operations consist of additions, deletions, substitutions, and permutations of language units corresponding roughly to Quintilian's (1.5.38) "fourfold method" (*quadripartita ratio*) of *adiectio, detractio, immutatio,* and *transmutatio;* the rule-enforcing operations mainly affect their repetition. Subordinate operations concerning similarity, frequency, and distribution can be added. Moreover, there exist the linguistic levels of phonology, morphology, syntax, semantics, graphemics, textuality, and intertextuality. As in the case of the linguistic operations, these admit of further differentiations and subclassifications.

The (semio-)syntactic model of figures outlined so far now works in such a way that the linguistic operations are applied to the linguistic levels and thus generate a large body of categories. In a series of transformational acts, the primary linguistic norm is changed into a secondary one; that is, from grammaticality into rhetoricity.

Figures of speech. TABLE 1. *A (Semio-)Syntactic Model of Rhetorical Figures*

I. linguistic operations / II. linguistic levels	rule-violating				rule-enforcing
	1. addition	2. deletion	3. substitution	4. permutation	5. equivalence
1. phonological					
2. morphological					
3. syntactic					
4. textological					
5. semantic					
6. graphemic					
7. intertextual					

Figures of speech. TABLE 2. *Basic Categories of a (Semio-)Syntactic Model*

I. linguistic operations / II. linguistic levels	rule-violating	rule-enforcing
	metaboles	isotopes
1. phonological	metaphonemes	isophonemes
2. morphological	metamorphemes	isomorphemes
3. syntactic	metataxemes	isotaxemes
4. semantic	metasememes	isosememes
5. graphemic	metagraphemes	isographemes
6. textological	metatextemes	isotextemes
7. intertextual	meta-intertextemes	iso-intertextemes

All conceivable figures of the (semio-)syntactic class can be generated in this way. The heuristic purpose of this model is the better fulfilled, the more the linguistic operations and levels are sub-divided. Thus, the (semio-)syntactic model grows in complexity and completeness on a clearly defined axiomatic basis.

A terminological standardization of the complex system of linguistic operations and levels in the (semio-)syntactic model of figures can be attained in the following way: In analogy to the term *metabole,* the linguistic units generated by the rule-violating operations are termed *metaphonemes, metamorphemes, metataxemes, metasememes, metagraphemes, metatextemes,* and *meta-intertextemes,* according to their linguistic levels. Correspondingly, the figures produced by the rule-enforcing operations are named—in an extension of the term *isotope*—*isophonemes, isomorphemes, isotaxemes, isosememes,* and so on. Thus, the phonological figures are subcategorized as *metaphonemes* and *isophonemes,* the morphological figures likewise as *metamorphemes* and *isomorphemes,* and so on (Table 2).

By means of this generative model, the number of figures of speech can be increased to a degree that surpasses any historical precedent. In order to avoid a categorical and terminological inflation, it is prerequisite to put a greater emphasis on the procedural factors (linguistic operations and levels) that constitute a figure of speech rather than on the individual figure as such. A few traditional figures may illustrate this. Thus, alliteration can be classified as a consonantal phonological figure of equivalence or an isophoneme of identical consonants in the initial position of a word. Furthermore, the parenthesis is a deviant syntactic figure of addition or an additive metataxeme in the middle of a sentence. Metaphor and metonymy in this (semio-)syntactic matrix represent subclasses of *metasememes,* the first being constituted by the semantic substitution of similarities, the second by the semantic substitution of contiguities. The anagram (ex.: <ARMY> – <MARY> [George Herbert]) is a permutative *metagrapheme* consisting of the transposition (*metathesis*) of the letters of a meaningful word resulting in another meaningful word that is related to the first in a symbolic way. A textological figure of deviation or, in other terms, an additive metatexteme is the digression. On the basis of the same (semio-)syntactic model of figures, allegory and periphrasis can be defined as substitutional semantic metatextemes, the first as a textological metaphor, or, in terms of the classical tradition, as a continued metaphor (Quintilian's *continua metaphora,* or Puttenham's "a long and perpetuall Metaphore"), the second as a textological metonymy. The intertextual figures can be regarded as an extension of the classical system of figures, and hence as a source of categorical innovations, of which an illustrative specimen is the citation—generated by the substitution of a "proper" text segment (*proprium*) by an "improper" text segment (*improprium*) taken from a pre-text (Plett, 1991).

The class of (semio-)syntactic figures is supplemented by the classes of *pragmatic* and *(semio-) semantic figures.* These claim pseudocommunication and pseudoreferentiality as the axiomatic bases of their respective secondary grammars. The pragmatic figures are constituted as pseudospeech acts: for instance, the *interrogatio* (Gk. *erōtēma*) as pseudoquestion ("rhetorical question"), the *concessio* as pseudoconcession, and so on. Irony may be subsumed under all three semiotic categorizations of the figures.

As stated in the section on "Modernizing the Classical System," the model of rhetorical *langue/ competence* has to be supplemented by one of *parole/performance* in order to meet the exigencies of practical communication. Not every deviant language utterance can, however, be described as a rhetorical figure that contributes to an act of persuasive communication. Deviances such as an alliteration, an epizeuxis, an ellipsis, or a parenthesis may also be indicative of linguistic deficiencies (e.g., with aphasics) or occur in colloquial speech. The distinctive feature of expressly rhetorical communication is persuasion, which is characterized by the use of *ēthos* or *pathos* covering the entire range of the emotions. Henry Peacham (1593) describes the effect of rhetorical figures in enthusiastic comparisons: "I say they are as stars to giue light, as cordials to comfort, as harmony to delight, as pitiful spectacles to moue sorrovvfull passions, and as orient colours to beautifie reason" (9). In works of literature, the functions of the figures of speech are determined by the concept of literariness or poeticity underlying them. If the poetical telos is defined as self-referential or autotelic, the figures of speech do not pursue the function of persuading recipients but to engender aesthetic delight or, in Kant's terminology, *interesseloses Wohlgefallen* ("disinterested pleasure"). [*See* Ēthos; Pathos; *and* Poetry.]

The Intermediality of the Figures. Though created for the sake of linguistic artistry, the use of figures of speech was not restricted to verbal discourse, but by analogy extended to supply instruments for the production and analysis of pictorial and musical works of art. The idea underlying these transformations is that the figures of speech basically constitute semiotic categories of an intermedial character. Renaissance art treatises (e.g., by Leon Battista Alberti) and artworks (e.g., by Leonardo da Vinci) make use of the figures as categories of theoretical analysis or practical invention. [*See* Art.] By analogy, the same holds true for musical theory and the practice of music. From the Age of Claudio Monteverdi through the Age of Johann Sebastian Bach, theoreticians and composers interpreted the classical figures of speech as descriptive of musical structures as well. [*See* Music.] In modern times, the intermedial character of the figures of speech has largely been neglected or has been replaced by semiotic categories. Attempts at reintroducing the figures as categories for the analysis of iconic texts were undertaken by Barthes (1964), Bonsiepe (1968), and later, on a broader semiorhetorical basis, by the Groupe Mu from Liège (Edeline, 1992).

[*See also* Linguistics.]

BIBLIOGRAPHY

Arbusow, Leonid. *Colores Rhetorici.* 2d ed. Göttingen, 1963. A useful representation of the medieval categories of rhetoric, above all, the figures of speech, with many illustrations from medieval texts.

Bacry, Patrick. *Les figures de style et autres procédés stylistiques.* Paris, 1993.

Barthes, Roland. "La rhétorique de l'image." *Communications* 4 (1964), pp. 40–51.

Bonsiepe, Gui. "Visuell/verbale Rhetorik." *Format* 4.5 (1968), pp. 11–18.

Chomsky, Noam. *Aspects of the Theory of Syntax.* Cambridge, Mass., 1965.

Rhetorica ad C. Herennium. Edited with an English translation by Harry Caplan. Cambridge, Mass., 1954.

Fontanier, Pierre. *Les figures du discours (1821–1830),* edited by Gérard Genette. Paris, 1977.

Genette, Gérard. *Figures.* 3 vols. Translated by A. Sheridan. New York, 1982. English translation of a selection of essays published in French in several volumes under the title *Figures,* the first in 1966.

Dubois, Jacques, et al. *Rhétorique Générale.* Paris, 1970. In spite of its title, a figurative rhetoric, an approach toward a redefinition, and a new systematization of the figures of speech in the light of modern linguistics.

Edeline, Francis, et al. *Traité du signe visuel: Pour une rhétorique de l'image.* Paris, 1992.

Lanham, Richard. *A Handlist of Rhetorical Terms.* Berkeley, 1968.

Lausberg, Heinrich. *Handbuch der literarischen Rhetorik: Eine Grundlegung der Literaturwissenschaft.* 2 vols., 3d ed. Stuttgart, 1990. English translation by Matthew T. Bliss, Annemiek Jansen, and David E. Orton. *Handbook of Literary Rhetoric: A Foundation for Literary Study,* edited by David E. Orton and R. Dean Anderson. Leiden, 1998. The standard work of a systematic representation of classical rhetoric, with numerous citations of Greek and Latin definitions of rhetorical categories and extensive illustrations by literary texts from classical sources.

Martin, Josef. *Antike Rhetorik: Technik und Methode.* Munich, 1974.

Mayoral, José Antonio. *Figuras Retóricas.* Madrid, 1993. A modern Spanish classification of the figures.

Morris, Charles W. *Writings on the General Theory of Signs.* The Hague, 1971.

Peacham, Henry. *The Garden of Eloquence* (1593), edited with a historical introduction and commentary by B.-M. Koll. Frankfurt, 1996. An important English Renaissance figurative rhetoric in the classical tradition.

Plett, Heinrich F. *Systematische Rhetorik.* Munich, 2000. A modern system of the figures of speech on a semiotic and linguistic basis.

Plett, Heinrich F. "Intertextualities." In *Intertextuality,* edited by H. F. Plett, pp. 3–29. New York, 1991.

Puttenham, George. *The Arte of English Poesie* (1589), edited by Gladys Doidge Willcock and Alice Walker. Cambridge, U.K., 1936. Reprint, 1970. Book 3; "Of Ornament," contains an idiosyncratic concept of the figures whose classical terminology is partly anglicized.

Quinn, Arthur. *Figures of Speech.* Davis, Calif., 1993.

Quintilian. *Institutio oratoria.* Translated by H. E. Butler, 4 vols. Cambridge, Mass., 1966.

Saussure, Ferdinand De. *Cours de Linguistique Générale.* Edited by C. Bally and A. Sechehaye. Paris, 1916.

Sharon-Zisser, Shirley. "A Distinction No Longer in Use: Evolutionary Discourse and the Disappearance of the Trope/Figure Binarism." *Rhetorica* 11.3 (1993), pp. 321–342.

Sonnino, Lee A. *A Handbook to Sixteenth-Century Rhetoric.* London, 1968.

Suhamy, Henri. *Les figures de style.* Paris, 1970.

Taylor, Warren. *Tudor Figures of Speech.* Whitewater, Wis., 1972.

Todorov, Tzvetan. "Essai de classification." In T. Todorov. *Littérature et signification,* pp. 107–114. Paris, 1967.

—HEINRICH F. PLETT

FORENSIC GENRE. In forensic, or legal, rhetoric, the speaker addresses a jury or judge selected to adjudicate issues surrounding a past event. Through pro and con argumentation by prosecution and defense (forensic rhetorical theory has historically examined criminal trials), advocates engaged in an inventional process grounded in *stasis* theory to craft arguments from probability drawing upon circumstantial evidence. Advocates who articulated the moral merit of their arguments also promoted the achievement of justice, the ultimate goal of forensic rhetoric. While the forensic practitioner's objective is to win the case, posttrial publication of courtroom orations has served multiple purposes, including teaching, as well as attempts to exert political influence, enact character, and provide aesthetic pleasure to later audiences.

The classical conception of forensic rhetoric, perhaps born of necessity from litigation in the ancient Greek world, reflected the rhetorical nature of that highly oral society. The Romans, and Cicero in particular, maintained the Greek synthesis of rhetoric and law as they refined the forensic genre. With the decline of the Roman republic, forensic rhetoric was eviscerated in both practice and theory. The Renaissance restored consideration of forensic rhetoric, particularly in written form, with a return to the classical character of legal oratory under the common-law systems of Great Britain and later the United States. Professionalization, university education, and codification in the nineteenth century again severed law from rhetoric in ways reminiscent of the earlier division between logic and rhetoric propounded by Peter Ramus (1515–1572). The rise of argumentation and narrative theory in the latter stages of the twentieth century reinvigorated the conception of forensic rhetoric as integral to the law.

The classical forensic genre established the art of rhetoric's instrumental nature as theory and practice intertwined to meet practical exigencies. Greek tradition held that the art was invented out of the need to resolve legal disputes. Syracuse had overthrown its tyrannical government around 467 BCE. As a result, land titles became uncertain and those disputing ownership found themselves in court. Aristotle and Cicero maintained that Corax and Tisias, two advocates and teachers in Syracuse, Sicily, initiated the formal development of the genre in response to the land crisis. While historical accounts differ, it does appear that the Syracusans wrote some of the first handbooks, or instruction manuals, on the forensic genre. These texts presented fundamental points on legal oratory, including consideration of the parts of an oration and of types of argument from probability, in which an advocate asserts that his interpretation of circumstantial evidence is more likely to be true. The reverse probability argument became a key feature of the forensic genre. The archetype draws upon the supposed teaching of Corax and Tisias, in which a hypothetical fight between a weak man and a strong one is employed to show how each litigant would argue the improbability that he initiated the bout. Antiphon (c.480–411 BCE), a later forensic practitioner and theorist, wrote the *Tetralogies,* a set of fictive speeches designed to demonstrate how to craft forensic speeches of prosecution and defense. Among them is "On the Murder of Herodes," which offers excellent examples of fact and probability arguments. [*See* Classical rhetoric.]

Greek forensic rhetoric reflected fundamental features of the Greek legal system. Under Greek law, parties represented themselves in a single, time-regulated speech (one rebuttal could be offered in a private lawsuit). Antiphon observed that jurors were "forced to reach a verdict on the basis of nothing else than the speeches of the plaintiff and defendant. . . . [their] vote [would] necessarily be cast on the basis of likelihood rather than clear knowledge" (Antiphon, 6.18). No procedural rules limited the types of arguments an individual offered, and no rule of precedent applied in Greek courts. Litigants instructed juries on relevant law. In the first half of the fifth century BCE, jurisdiction of legal matters shifted from magistrates to citizen juries ranging

in size from 201 to 501 members; they returned a verdict without group deliberation. The later Hellenistic legal system replaced the large juries of the Athenian democracy with one or more judges. This reformation encouraged litigants to present legally technical speeches during which the judges were invited to interrupt and interrogate the speakers.

Beyond the requirement of self-representation that elevated the need for Greeks to study forensic rhetoric, Athenians found that private prosecutions and lawsuits for political as well as legal reasons increased the number and the significance of trials. Demosthenes (384–322 BCE) and others gained political stature in part through the reputations they acquired as forensic orators. Often praised as the greatest Greek orator, Demosthenes defended himself in his masterful "On the Crown" (330), which interwove argumentative brilliance and aesthetic appeal in an early example of forensic rhetoric's political significance.

The Sophists contributed to the Greek forensic genre in their belief that courtroom arguments should be both legally and rhetorically effective, a synthesis of the legal and the rhetorical that continues to resonate in the use of the term *forensic*. Critics of rhetoric, such as Plato (c.428–c.347 BCE), saw an ethical ambivalence in these features of rhetorical theory that, especially when associated with abuses within legal advocacy, led to a condemnation of the entire art as deceptive and manipulative, an objection that some continue to express. Plato, in disparaging rhetoric in *Gorgias*, focused upon probability argument within the forensic genre as proof that the art favored persuasion to belief over the teaching of truth. Identification of issues and analysis through two-sided argumentation and debate, forensic rhetoric's paradigmatic protocol, raised additional ethical concerns. [*See* Sophists.]

Despite these charges, a group emerged to assist Greek litigants who had to appear personally in court. These logographers, or speechwriters, would craft a forensic speech for a litigant's delivery before the jury. Their skill rested in part in writing a speech that reflected the speaker's *ēthos*, or character, and his rhetorical abilities, for a litigant would wish to sound as though he were uttering his own thoughts; otherwise, the jury might believe the litigant insincere. Some logographers presaged modern legal practice by offering legal advice, particularly on specialized legal matters such as inheritance. Numerous Greek rhetoricians, including Lysias (c.445–after 380 BCE) and Isocrates (436–338 BCE), engaged in logography, often publishing their speeches as a means of advertising their skills. Isocrates' *Antidosis,* for example, set forth an imaginary trial in which Isocrates was forced to defend himself against charges that he failed to provide financial support for a military ship.

Aristotle (384–322 BCE) solidified forensic rhetoric's status as a legitimate, ethical *technē* in his *Rhetoric,* as established in part in his consideration of *logos, pathos,* and *ēthos.* Although Aristotle maintained that the litigant should confine himself to rational proof of what happened, especially as juries often allowed passions to influence verdicts, *pathos* appeals were an appropriate means of inducing the proper frame of mind within the jury to render a decision. As each Greek litigant had to represent himself, it is apparent why *ēthos* appeals invoking one's character were critically important in the forensic genre. [*See* Ēthos; Logos; *and* Pathos.]

Five chapters of Book 1 of Aristotle's *Rhetoric,* one of the most significant discussions of legal rhetoric, set forth the premises applicable to this genre. Aristotle analyzed pleasure (the motivation of criminals), the types of law (written, customary, and universal), the types of people who commit wrongdoing and those they often wrong. Universal laws, which are those principles that every person understood to be valid, were linked to appeals to equity, which covered situations that written law did not satisfactorily address.

Rhetorical argument, Aristotle continued, consisted of two forms of proof. Inartistic proofs, which did not call upon the advocate's inventional skills, included reliance upon laws, witnesses, contracts, torture, and oaths. Aristotle focused instead upon *logos* and the legal advocate's skill in crafting artistic proofs—enthymemes, examples, and signs. Consistent with the forensic genre's emphasis upon argument from probability, Aristotle emphasized enthymemes, which were arguments whose premises might be drawn from special or common topics. [*See* Enthymeme.] Argument from interpretation, in which the facts are not disputed but causation or re-

sponsibility is at issue, is the other major rhetorical form under the forensic genre.

Greek rhetorician Hermagoras of Temnos (second century BCE) is credited with formulating *stasis* theory, an early version of which may be found in Aristotle's *Rhetoric* (3.17–18) and other Greek sources. *Stasis* theory's focus upon issue identification and argument construction guided legal advocates. The prosecutor's accusation and defendant's argument of denial established the points of disagreement, which concerned either rational or legal matters. Through engaging in a pro and con analytical process, the legal advocate would work through the arguments specific to each of the *stasis* questions of conjecture, definition, quality, and process. Hermagoras also set forth four general questions specifically pertaining to legal matters. The first involved the interpretation of law, which essentially asked whether the law's literal meaning or the framer's intent should prevail. Second, the advocate might generate arguments that focused upon the fact that the applicable laws were contrary. Next, ambiguity in the law might give rise to arguments. If no precise law covered the act, then the advocates might offer present contentions regarding this void.

The *Rhetorica ad Herennium,* which may be said to mark the birth of Latin rhetoric around 84–90 BCE, amplified consideration of *stasis* theory. Book 2 examined forensic rhetoric, explaining how to apply invention to each type of issue. In this way, the *Rhetorica ad Herennium's* treatment of forensic rhetoric was closely akin to that of Cicero's *De Inventione,* thus explaining in part the now-questioned attribution of this text to Cicero (106–43 BCE). Antonius's "Defense of Norbanus" (c.95 BCE) is an exemplar of an advocate's invocation of *stasis* theory and *ēthos* in a Roman trial. In essence, the Roman view of forensic rhetoric maintained the Greek emphasis upon argument from probability.

The Roman forensic speech consisted of six parts. The introduction, or *exordium,* sought to win the jury's goodwill. Next, the advocate related the events in dispute in the *narratio.* The *partitio* or *divisio* explained the points upon which the two sides agreed and disagreed; the advocate might also set forth the disputed issues. In the *confirmatio,* the prosecutor would set forth the proof of his charges, invoking *loci,* or topics, to enhance the probability of his arguments. The defendant would then offer rebuttal arguments in the *confutatio.* Finally, the advocates ended their speeches in the *peroratio,* which might summarize the argument, attack the opponent, and address the jury's sympathy, anger, or other emotions. The *divisio* was the section in which the advocate set forth the points upon which the two sides agreed, stated the issues remaining to be resolved, and previewed what would be said on each issue.

Legal and political innovations under the Roman republic cultivated notable transformations in the forensic genre. In perhaps the most significant change for forensic oratory, third persons, often an influential citizen, or *patronus,* would represent litigants. Especially in the later republican period, the practice of legal assistance by a forensic *patronus* elevated the Roman emphasis upon *ēthos* as a form of proof. By the first century BCE, another type of Roman legal expert, the *advocatus,* offered technical legal advice in much the same manner as had Greek logographers.

Marcus Tullius Cicero (106–43 BCE), a leading figure of the Roman Republic, gained power and prestige through his prowess as a forensic orator. His forensic speeches, including his prosecution of Verres in 70 BCE (the first two speeches are landmark legal orations) and his "Pro Sexto Roscio Amerino" (80 BCE; Cicero's invocation of *ēthos* is especially noteworthy) sustain his reputation for crafting prudential arguments grounded in *ēthos,* justice, and equity. Cicero supplemented his theoretical works on rhetoric with publication of forensic orations revised after the trial or, as in the case of his "Pro Milone" (52 BCE) and the latter speeches of *In C. Verrem,* never delivered. These written works served as pedagogical exemplars for students of forensic oratory and also promoted the virtues of decorum and prudence as ethically appropriate to legal and political life. [*See* Decorum; *and* Prudence.] While the emotive and extralogical appeals of these orations invited criticism of Cicero as a purely instrumental orator who broke from his own theories regarding forensic rhetoric, contemporary reconsideration of his legal orations has illustrated their rhetorical and ethical complexity.

In his corpus on forensic rhetoric, Cicero articulated a set of characteristics he deemed essential in the forensic orator (Enos, 1988). Natural ability, an apprenticeship relation with a mentor, imitation of exemplary forensic speakers, and a liberal education were considered prerequisites of forensic eloquence. A reputation for ethical probity enabled the forensic orator to invoke a *vir bonus* ("good man") image to enhance his argument. Dialectical analysis helped to determine the probable truth in a specific case. [*See* Dialectic.] Rejecting rigid adherence to rhetorical precepts, Cicero held that the case specificity of legal disputes required that advocates exercise prudential judgment to determine the situationally appropriate arguments.

With the rise of the Roman Empire, opportunities to engage in Ciceronian forensic rhetoric largely dissipated. Students of Quintilian (c.35–c.100 CE) and other rhetoric instructors were largely limited to declamatory exercises. [*See* Declamation.] In this period, the Second Sophistic (c.50–400 CE), schools concentrated upon two types of declamation—the *suasoria* and the *controversia*—with the latter focused upon legal questions. [*See* Controversia and suasoria.] *Controversia* had changed from Cicero's time. As Lucius Annaeus Seneca (c.55 BCE–c.39 CE) explained, the Augustan *controversia* was no longer realistic because students offered sententious, melodramatic speeches on improbable legal disputes (Clarke, 1953). Quintilian, in his *Institutio oratoria,* noted that despite the transformation in its practice and study, forensic rhetoric remained an instrumental art that could determine the resolution of a private lawsuit, a form of public rhetoric still exercised in Imperial Rome.

Italian humanists within the universities, particularly in Bologna, resuscitated the classical art of forensic rhetoric in the late Middle Ages and Quattrocento. Cicero's *De inventione,* as well as the *Rhetorica ad Herennium,* were central to this revival, which was built on the earlier efforts of Isidore of Seville (c.560–636), Alcuin (c.732–804), and others to recover the Ciceronian precepts on forensic rhetoric and utilize them in promoting legal studies. These rhetorical scholars adapted the classical forensic tradition (with its singular emphasis upon oral advocacy) to written works, establishing the *ars dictaminis* (the art of letter writing) and, more directly, the *ars notaria* (the art of drafting legal documents). [*See* Ars dictaminis.] One example is the *Ars Notaria* (1226–33) of Rainerius of Perugia, which offered instruction on preparing contracts, covenants, judgments, and wills.

Oral forensic advocacy in the classical tradition returned to prominence under English common law. Legal education in England's Inns of Court and Scotland's Faculty of Advocates taught forensic rhetoric through an apprenticeship approach that immersed students in observation of actual practice. Renaissance students could augment their study of forensic rhetoric through reading Thomas Wilson's *The Rule of Reason* (1551) and *The Arte of Rhetorique* (1553), both of which considered the manner in which legal advocates might discover arguments. Wilson drew upon Quintilian and the *Rhetorica ad Herennium,* translating their concepts into English for ease of study for law students and others. Sixteenth-century England revitalized the classical interrelationship among law, rhetoric, and literature (Schoeck, 1983). *Divisio* was a core element of the forensic genre during this period as lawyers honed their skills in forensic rhetoric through practice, observation, and, as is becoming increasingly evident, through instruction in treatises and legal manuals such as Abraham Fraunce's *Ramistic Lawiers Logike* (1588).

The emphasis upon classical forensic rhetoric and the high regard for oral persuasion explains why the late eighteenth century and early nineteenth century saw many renowned courtroom advocates in England and America. These speakers, who like Cicero often secured political power through their forensic successes, included Thomas Erskine (1750–1823), John Philpot Curran (1750–1817), John Quincy Adams (1767–1848), William Wirt (1772–1834), and Daniel Webster (1782–1852). Erskine, often called England's greatest forensic orator, won initial recognition through his defense of Captain Baillee (November 1778). Curran, an Irish lawyer, won renown for his defense of Wolfe Tone and other participants in the 1798 insurrection. Adams, who served as the Boylston Professor of Rhetoric and Oratory at Harvard University (1806–1809) before becoming the sixth president of the United States (1825–1829), lectured on forensic rhetoric. In these lectures, he noted a fundamental change in forensic rhetoric

pertaining to *stasis* theory. Under the Anglo-American legal system, an advocate was well advised to consider two types of issues: questions of law and questions of fact. Questions of law pertained to technical matters of law and were addressed to the judge. Questions of fact, Adams explained, remained within the jury's purview. In addition to teaching forensic rhetoric, John Quincy Adams was a powerful forensic advocate, demonstrating his ability as a defense attorney for slaves who seized control of the schooner *Amistad* (November 1839–January 1840). William Wirt also established a reputation as a brilliant forensic rhetor in his prosecution of Aaron Burr (August–September 1807) and in arguments before the United States Supreme Court. In one of many examples of his forensic skill at both the trial and appellate levels, Daniel Webster offered an eloquent prosecution of the Knapps in the White case (July–November 1830).

As the nineteenth century progressed, however, professionalization of the American bar and the growth of law firms undermined the classical conceptions of oral forensic rhetoric that these advocates practiced. This evolution, together with the emergence of law schools, fostered specialization within the law. Most American lawyers no longer appeared in court, and those who did were increasingly educated in a Socratic manner that developed legal scientists no longer schooled in oral advocacy and other key elements of classical forensic rhetoric. University-based legal education, in its departure from the apprenticeship model followed for centuries, insulated students from study of forensic advocacy before judge and jury. The emergence of Langdellian legal science, introduced by Dean Christopher Columbus Langdell (1826–1906) at Harvard Law School in the 1870s, completed a break with classical understandings of forensic rhetoric that would prevail within United States law schools for a century or more. His transformation of legal education promoted study of judicial opinions as the source of immutable, objectively derived legal principles at the expense of classical understandings of forensic rhetoric as the practice of prudential oral persuasion before an immediate audience.

In addition, codification engendered substantial changes in the Anglo-American common-law tradition that altered the forensic genre. Throughout the centuries, of course, laypeople had complained of the law's technical nature and the resultant inaccessibility of the law to all but those trained in its specialized language and procedures. The influence of the Napoleonic Code and the civil law's preference for statutory rather than common law increased as the nineteenth century progressed, especially when the United States embraced codification through the efforts of David Dudley Field (1805–1894) and others. Legal arguments increasingly invoked statutory provisions rather than customary principles and maxims.

Codification, university legal education, and professionalization effected the transformation of forensic oratory that in classical times was accessible to all, into a technical field of argument that limited advocates' use of *pathos* and *ēthos.* Reflecting this limitation upon the classical model, rules of professional conduct in the United States propagated by the American Bar Association and others explicitly ban key features of the classical practice of forensic rhetoric, including arguments "calculated to inflame the passions or prejudices of the jury," as well as advocates' expression of personal belief, diversion of the jury's duty to decide the case solely upon the evidence, and injection of issues beyond guilt or innocence. In sum, the field of forensic rhetoric, and oral legal argument in particular, was substantially constrained and removed beyond the ken of the common audience.

While twentieth-century rhetorical scholars recognized the central role that forensic rhetoric played in the classical tradition, this dissociation of law and rhetoric and the complexity of legal rules of evidence dissuaded the discipline from critically examining contemporary forensic oratory. Only those practitioners of forensic rhetoric, including Clarence Darrow (1857–1938) and William Jennings Bryan (1860–1925), who maintained adherence to legal oratory as classically conceived, won critical and popular acclaim. In addition to his famous battle with Bryan in the Scopes trial (July 1925), Darrow successfully defended accused murderers Nathan Leopold, Jr. and Richard Loeb (1924) in a moving, twelve-hour plea for mitigation. His ability in this case and others to craft a broadly principled argument

grounded in history, his adept invocation of moving emotional appeals and of his *ēthos,* and his disdain of legal technicalities suggest the classical orientation of Darrow's forensic skill.

Darrow's audience-centered approach to forensic rhetoric can be seen in the care he took in *voir dire,* the process of jury selection in which the advocate poses a series of questions to prospective jurors to determine potential biases and their amenability to the lawyer's case. In forensic rhetoric alone, and particularly in the United States with its liberal *voir dire* rules, does a speaker have the opportunity to choose the audience for an argument. Perceived abuses in the *voir dire* process, including attempts to craft a favorable audience rather than a neutral one, have prompted some common-law jurisdictions to restrict this process.

The advent of informal logic and narrative theory in the latter half of the twentieth century furthered the ongoing reunification of rhetoric and law. Chaim Perelman and Lucie Olbrechts-Tyteca examined the interplay of rhetoric and justice in their *La Nouvelle Rhétorique: Traité de l'Argumentation* (Paris, 1958). Rejecting the formalist faith in objective and universal truth that pervaded the law, they asserted that legal rhetoric encouraged a logic that incorporated communal values. [*See* Conviction.] Other scholars adopting this perspective critiqued the technical rules of law, including those regarding burdens of proof, legal presumptions, and the admissibility of evidence, as they distinguished technical, rule-bound law and casuistry. Casuistry, in which verdicts are based upon case-specific considerations, invites prudential examination of situational elements as well as practical deliberation along Ciceronian lines. [*See* Casuistry.]

The shift from formalism was augmented in the emergence of storytelling theory, captured in James Boyd White's claim that the "narrative is the archetypal legal and rhetorical form, as it is the archetypal form of human thought in ordinary life as well" (1985, p. 175). Building upon the narrative theory of Seymour Chatman and others, contemporary legal scholarship in the 1980s promoted storytelling theory as the primary critical lens through which contemporary forensic oratory might best be analyzed. Rhetorical scholars Lance Bennett, Martha Feldman, and others found that forensic advocates offered juries competing stories that framed the trial evidence in a believable manner and that offered implicit normative standards for deliberation. Other academic critics of formalist forensic rhetoric advanced the practice of storytelling as a means of promoting oppositional rhetoric within the legal arena, in part because storytelling offers a perspective that subverts the rational world paradigm of formalist legal philosophy.

The conclusion that narrative techniques and elements of the classical forensic genre facilitate oral advocacy has not been lost upon lawyers. They herald storytelling as a persuasive method for crafting forensic rhetoric, particularly as it permits subtle *pathos* and *ēthos* appeals. At the same time, storytelling only partially mended the rift between rhetoric and law in ways that implicitly reflect the conventional division between philosophy (content) and rhetoric (form). The inventional process of crafting knowledge through analysis of the law and facts, which is part of the Ciceronian conception of forensic rhetoric, is little discussed in the storytelling literature. Together with the argumentation scholarship identified above, however, contemporary narrative theory fosters reappreciation of the intimate connection between rhetoric and law.

Further, the contemporary law and literature movement promoted the use of interpretive methods grounded in literature as a means of engaging the law. This approach, its supporters maintained, encourages readers to discard positivist assumptions regarding meaning and authorial intent that have predominated the practice of law since Langdell's time. Scholarly differences existed between law *in* literature and law *as* literature. The latter, while focused upon the advocate's efforts to persuade an immediate audience, utilizes tools of literary criticism to interpret and construe *written* forensic rhetoric that comprises much of modern legal practice. Consistent with the law *as* narrative movement, contemporary rhetorical critics have expanded the genre's scope to include judicial rhetoric, primarily the written judicial opinion stating the court's decision. Under the principle of *stare decisis* (precedent), written judicial opinions are binding legal authority, which elevates the significance of this form of forensic

rhetoric and has invited critical use of hermeneutic methods to analyze this segment of the genre. [*See* Criticism; *and* Hermeneutics.]

[*See also* Invention; Law; *and* Stasis.]

BIBLIOGRAPHY

Adams, John Quincy. *Lectures on Rhetoric and Oratory.* 2 vols. New York, 1962. Highlights the transition to modern legal practice and its rhetorical implications.

Antiphon, *The Speeches.* Translated and edited by Michael Gagarin. Cambridge, U.K., 1997. English translation of speeches first published c.425–422 BCE. An excellent introductory section on early Greek forensic rhetoric.

Bennett, W. Lance, and Martha S. Feldman. *Reconstructing Reality in the Courtroom: Justice and Judgment in American Culture.* New Brunswick, N.J., 1981. A seminal text on legal storytelling theory.

Clarke, M. L. *Rhetoric at Rome.* London, 1953. Offers helpful background on Roman rhetorical practices.

Conley, Thomas M. *Rhetoric in the European Tradition.* New York, 1990.

Enos, Richard Leo. *Greek Rhetoric before Aristotle.* Prospect Heights, Ill., 1993. Survey of rhetorical tradition often focuses upon forensic rhetoric.

Enos, Richard Leo. *The Literate Mode of Cicero's Legal Rhetoric.* Carbondale, Ill., 1988. A careful analysis of a primary classical authority on forensic rhetoric.

Friedman, Lawrence M. *A History of American Law.* 2d ed. New York, 1985. A comprehensive examination of transformations in law and legal practice, the text observes how these changes impacted forensic eloquence.

Gagarin, Michael. "Probability and persuasion. Plato and early Greek rhetoric." In *Persuasion: Greek Rhetoric in Action,* edited by Ian Worthington, pp. 46–68. London, 1994. Insightful account of the centrality of argument from probability in forensic rhetoric.

Gaskins, Richard. *Burdens of Proof in Modern Discourse.* New Haven, 1992. An analysis of contemporary argumentation with clear relevance to forensic rhetoric.

Kennedy, George A. *Comparative Rhetoric.* Oxford, 1998. Remarks upon the limited evidence available regarding non-Western forensic rhetoric.

Kennedy, George A. *A New History of Classical Rhetoric.* Princeton, 1994. Helpful overview highlights the role of forensic rhetoric in the discipline's development.

Levinson, Sanford, and Steven Mailloux. *Interpreting Law and Literature.* Evanston, Ill., 1988.

Michigan Law Review. *Legal Storytelling,* vol. 87, pp. 2073–2494. Ann Arbor, Mich., 1989. This special collection of essays offers a variety of perspectives on legal storytelling, its possibilities, and its problems.

Murphy, James J., ed. *Medieval Eloquence: Studies in the Theory and Practice of Medieval Rhetoric.* Berkeley, 1978.

Murphy, James J. *Rhetoric in the Middle Ages: A History of Rhetorical Theory from Saint Augustine to the Renaissance.* Berkeley, 1974. Especially helpful in understanding the development of written modes of forensic rhetoric.

Perelman, Chaim, and Lucie Olbrechts-Tyteca. *The New Rhetoric: A Treatise on Argumentation.* Notre Dame, Ind., 1969, first published 1938. Promotes a philosophical analysis of rhetoric and justice and their enactment in forensic argumentation.

Schoeck, Richard J. "Lawyers and Rhetoric in Sixteenth-Century England." In *Renaissance Eloquence,* edited by James J. Murphy, pp. 274–291. Berkeley, 1983.

White, James Boyd. *Heracles' Bow: Essays on the Rhetoric and Poetics of the Law.* Madison, Wis., 1985. White's essays invite reflection upon the relationship between law and language.

White, James Boyd. *Justice as Translation: An Essay in Cultural and Legal Criticism.* Chicago, 1990.

—TERENCE S. MORROW

FORMALISM. *See* Criticism; *and* Renaissance rhetoric, *article on* Rhetoric in Renaissance language and literature.

FORMULARY RHETORIC. *See* Ars dictaminis; Imitation; *and overview article on* Renaissance rhetoric.

FUNERAL ORATION. *See* Epideictic genre.

GAY AND LESBIAN LIBERATION. *See* Queer rhetoric.

GENERATIVE - TRANSFORMATIONAL GRAMMAR. *See* Linguistics.

GENRES. *See* Deliberative genre; Epideictic genre; Forensic genre; *and* Hybrid genres.

GORGIANIC FIGURES. Already by the early fourth century BCE, the name of the Sicilian orator Gorgias had become an adjective for extravagant prose. In Xenophon's *Symposium,* Socrates seeks leave to use a "Gorgianic expression"

(*e Gorgieiois rhēmasin*) and suggests that the servants at the banquet "besprinkle" (*epipsakazōsin*) the guests. The word is rare and poetic, and is startling when it appears in ordinary conversation. When Gorgias of Leontini had arrived in Athens in 427 as an ambassador, he had likewise dazzled the city with his rhetorical display, the stylistic details of which have come to be called "Gorgianic figures" (Dionysius of Halicarnassus, hereafter D. H., *On Demosthenes* 5, 25; for the story of the embassy, see D. H. *On Lysias* 3; Diodorus Siculus 12.53.4). Some time after his embassy, Gorgias settled in Athens to teach his method: the application of figures (*schēmata*) to prose, or language without meter, to render it nonetheless *rhythmic* and *poetic,* two adjectives often used by ancient commentators to describe Gorgias's style (e.g., Aristotle *Rhetoric* 3.1.9; 3.3.4; 3.7.11; on Gorgias's teaching method, see Aristotle *On Sophistical Refutations* 183b–184a).

Gorgias is credited with the invention of six figures in particular: (1) *antithesis,* or the juxtaposition of clauses or phrases containing contrasting thought or subject matter (D. H. *On Thucydides* 24; Cicero *Orator* 175); (2) *paronomasia,* or wordplay, often with parallel phrases or clauses containing assonances and punning syllables at corresponding positions within the phrase (D. H. *On Thucydides* 24); (3) *anadiplōsis,* or the simple repetition of words (*Suidas, s.v.* "Gorgias"); (4) *parēchēsis,* or the repetition of sounds in neighboring words; alliteration is its most recognizable form (*Suidas, s.v.* "Gorgias"); (5) *homoeoteleuton,* a specific form of parechesis, where the repetition of sounds occurs at the ends of successive words or clauses to produce rhyme (Cicero *Orator* 175); and (6) *parisōsis* and *isocola,* or forms of parallelism wherein clauses or phrases have the same number of syllables; the term *parisōsis* is used when the clauses are parallel in sound as well as in length (Cicero *Orator* 175; D. H. *On Thucydides* 24). [*See* Alliteration; Anadiplōsis; Antithesis; Isocolon; *and* Paronomasia.]

It should be noted that all six figures use repetition and contrast and therefore can be used simultaneously. The first sentences of Gorgias's funeral speech provide a good example:

What did these men lack (*apēn*), which men must have (*dei proseinai*)?

What did they have (*prosēn*) which one
should not have (*ou dei proseinai*)?
May I say what I crave but crave what is
right, now avoiding god's revenge,
Now escaping human envy.

(fr. 6, H. Diels and W. Kranz.
Die Fragmente der Vorsokratiker. Berlin, 1951)

Gorgias begins with antithesis (lack/have), which
also provides wordplay in the Greek, since *apeinai*
is contrasted to *proseinai,* and repetition ("these
men"/"men"). Then the first sentence is reversed
in the second with another antithesis—instead of
asking what the dead soldiers lack, Gorgias asks
what they have—and the wordplay continues
with the repetition of *dei* and *proseinai* (the latter
appearing in different forms). Then follow two
clauses with rhyme or homoeoteleuton (May I
say what I crave but crave what is right . . . ; *eipein
dunaimēn ha/boulomai, bouloimēn d' ha dei*) as well
as antithesis, anadiplōsis, and parēchēsis; and finally, the third sentence concludes with an almost perfect isocolon that once again employs
antithesis. In the Greek of the last two clauses,
first nine syllables and then ten (in the English,
seven and then eight) are used to set divine
against human, revenge or nemesis against envy,
and "avoiding" against "escaping" or "fleeing."

Gorgias is also credited with—or accused of,
depending on the commentator's critical outlook—having encouraged frequent use of high-
flown metaphors, allegories, apostrophes, epithets,
newly coined, non-Greek words, and compound
words, and for having taught people to answer
seriousness with jokes and jokes with seriousness
(Aristotle *Rhetoric* 3.3.4; 3.7.11; 3.18.7; Longinus,
On the Sublime 3.12; Suidas *s.v.* Gorgias). Cicero
called all of these "fripperies" (*festivitatibus, Orator* 176), and criticized Gorgias for their immod-
erate use. Dionysius of Halicarnassus, a first-century BCE literary critic and historian, argued that
Gorgias wrote many of his speeches in a quite vulgar, inflated style, using language that was sometimes "not far removed from dithyrambic verse"
(*On Lysias* 3); moreover, he thought these techniques puerile (*On Isaeus* 19) and trashy (*On Demosthenes* 25).

Yet all these critics also praise Gorgias for having turned the attention of fifth-century BCE
Greeks to prose, and for having developed some
of its techniques; it is always antithesis and *pari-*

sōsis, techniques of thought as well as speech, for
which they were especially grateful (D. H. *On Demosthenes* 4–5, 25; Demetrius *On Style* 15, 29; Cicero *Orator* 164–165). As we have seen, Gorgias
developed his techniques in the early years of the
development of Greek prose and felt a kinship
with the poets (*Helen*); syntactical structures allowed him to prove this kinship. According to
Demetrius, Gorgias's periods and phrases succeeded each other with no less regularity than
the hexameters in Homer (*On Style*). And Cicero
wrote, "If [words] have similar case-endings, or
if clauses are equally balanced, or if contrary
ideas are opposed, the sentence becomes rhythmical by its very nature, even if no rhythm is
intended. It is said that Gorgias was the first to
strive for this sort of symmetry" (*Orator* 164–
165; cf. 166–167).

Gorgias's influence on literary criticism derives precisely from his opinion that all language
was, like poetry, figural; the only difference between poetry and other genres is the reliance of
the former on meter (*Helen*). As Jacqueline de
Romilly has pointed out, Gorgias was sure of the
power of figural language; he argues in his *Defense
of Helen* that Helen must be forgiven for going to
Troy since she was forced to do so, either by the
gods, by Paris, by *erōs*, or by persuasion. Language
can aspire to divine power or to power like magic;
it wields an irresistible force. In the twentieth century, Paul de Man revived a Gorgianic notion of
the figural to remind literary critics and theorists
that all language employs figures in order to produce representations of reality. It is impossible for
language-using beings to think or act outside
these figured representations and in some realm
of true apprehension. In this regard, language's
force is indeed irresistible. Dionysius of Halicarnassus preferred orators like Lysias to Gorgias, because he believed Lysias wrote a pure, lucid Attic
Greek. He approved of his lack of poetic ornamentation and his use of words that "fit the true
nature (*prophuēs*) of the subjects he discussed"
(*On Lysias* 2–3). Gorgias's poetic devices, in contrast, constantly remind the reader that words figure and represent reality and so also always make
it; they do not transparently reflect whatever exists beyond language.

[*See also* Classical rhetoric; *and* Figures of
speech.]

BIBLIOGRAPHY

Blass, F. *Attische Beredsamkeit.* Hildesheim, 1962. First published 1887.

Burgess, T. C. *Epideictic Literature.* Chicago, 1902.

de Man, Paul. *Allegories of Reading: Figural Language in Rousseau, Nietzsche, Rilke, and Proust.* New Haven, 1979.

de Man, Paul. "Literature and Language: A Commentary." In *Blindness and Insight.* Minneapolis, 1996. First published 1971.

de Romilly, J. *Magic and Rhetoric in Ancient Greece.* Cambridge, Mass., 1975.

de Romilly, J. *The Great Sophists in Periclean Athens.* Translated by J. Lloyd. Oxford, 1992.

Denniston, J. D. *Greek Prose Style.* Oxford, 1952.

MacDowell, D. M., ed. and trans. *Gorgias, Encomium of Helen.* Bristol, U.K., 1982.

—DANIELLE S. ALLEN

GRADATIO (Gk. *climax;* Lat. also *incrementum*), called the "Marching figure" by Puttenham (*The Arte of English Poesie,* p. 208), 1589, a patterned repetition of morphemes in a text augmenting its quantity and semantic content in a step-by-step order. It can be regarded as a continued *anadiplōsis* extending over more than two syntactic units. "Abraham begat Isaac; and Isaac begat Jacob; and Jacob begat Judah . . ." (*Mt.* 1.2) is a climactic genealogy culminating in Jesus. Its artificiality makes it a difficult figure, as Quintilian (*Institutio oratoria* 9.3.54) points out; this is especially so when it is combined with other rhetorical devices, as in George Herbert's seventeenth-century poem with the programmatic title "A Wreath."

[*See also* Anadiplōsis; *and* Figures of speech.]

—HEINER PETERS

GRAMMAR. *See* Linguistics; Medieval rhetoric, *article on* Medieval grammar; Modern rhetoric; Religion; *and* Trivium.

GREEK RHETORIC. *See* Classical rhetoric.

H

HEBREW RHETORIC developed from an already ancient preclassical rhetorical tradition that dates to the beginning of recorded history. Sumerian scribal schools, called "tablet houses," produced a literate class now known to have preserved a rich legacy of rhetorical discourse in this early society (c.3000 BCE). The Sumerians wrote poetry having repetition, parallelism, epithet, and similes, the latter occurring with some frequency, as one might expect from a people given to analogical thinking. Cuneiform texts of the third and second millennia show that this tradition survived in Old Babylonia, Assyria, and Ugarit. A rhetorical tradition doubtless developed in Egypt during the same period, where scribal schools are known to have existed from the early third millenium, and where poetry was also written, but about this tradition little is known.

Israel's oldest literature, to judge from its earliest lyric poems (*Ex.* 15; *Jgs.* 5), are finished works of fine art. A simplified twenty-two- to thirty-letter alphabet, introduced at Ugarit two to three centuries before Israel's thirteenth-century BCE entry into Canaan, created still more possibilities for oral and written discourse, as words began replacing older cuneiform signs. Ancient Hebrew rhetoric survives largely in the Hebrew Bible (Old Testament), from which it may be concluded that during the eighth to sixth centuries BCE, it had already experienced its "golden age," a full three centuries and more before the art achieved classical expression by Aristotle in Greece and by Cicero, Quintilian, and others at Rome.

Hebrew poetry existed from the earliest times, this fact having been recognized in the major medieval codices of the Hebrew Bible (tenth–eleventh centuries CE), and in the older Dead Sea Scrolls (c. second century BCE–first century CE), where portions of text are written in block form (*Ex.* 15; *Jgs.* 5; *Dt.* 32; *Ps(s).; Prv.;* and *Jb.*). The recognition in modern times that Hebrew poetry is characterized largely by parallelism derives from Bishop Robert Lowth, who demonstrated this in Lecture 19 of his now-famous *De sacra poesi Hebraeorum* (Oxford, 1753), given at Oxford beginning in 1741. Lowth also showed that large portions of prophetic discourse were in fact poetry, not prose, as previously thought (Lecture 18). Lowth based his parallelism doctrine on a sixteenth-century essay by Rabbi Azariah de Rossi of Ferrara, who discussed Hebrew rhythm in his larger work, *Me'or 'enayim.* The recognition of parallelism in Hebrew poetry, but more along rhetorical lines, appeared also in the early eighteenth-century work of Christian Schoettgen, *Horae Hebraicae et Talmudicae I* (Leipzig, 1733), where the phenomenon was called *exergasia* (Lat. *expolitio*). Hebrew poetry, in addition, has stanza formation, as can be seen from the existence of acrostics and refrains.

Hebrew rhetorical tradition produced neither theoretical work the likes of Aristotle's *Rhetoric* (340–325 BCE) nor handbooks such as the *Rhetorica ad Herennium* (c.86–82 BC) or Quintilian's *Institutes* (c.90 CE). Nevertheless, in the Bible are figures performing the same functions as in classical rhetoric, also modes of argumentation known and classified by the later Greek and Roman authors. On occasion, one will meet up with figures and argumentative strategies that appear to be uniquely Hebraic, or possibly Semitic, in that they are not cited in Aristotle or any of the classical rhetorical handbooks. Yet some turn up in modern discourse. [*See* Classical rhetoric.]

The importance of repetition in Hebrew rhetoric can hardly be overstated. Repetitions express the superlative ("holy, holy, holy" in *Is.* 6.3), provide emphasis (*epanalēpsis*), give structure to psalms, prophetic oracles, and other compositions, and terminate debate. In the Bible's *locus classicus* on divine revelation (*Ex.* 3.12–15), repetition assumes a debate–closure function. There, God promises a hesitant Moses regarding the trek out of Egypt, "I will be with you" (12). But Moses demurs, wanting to know God's name. God then responds, "I will be what I will be" (14), which terminates the debate, but does furnish Moses and Israel with a name for future generations: "I will be," modified to "He will be" = Yahweh (15). This *idem per idem* tautology, as it is called, occurs in Arabic and in modern discourse, but is not mentioned in the classical rhetorical handbooks.

The Bible's rhetorical prose *par excellence* is in Deuteronomy, also less prominently in Kings and portions of Jeremiah, where an array of figures embellish, provide structure, and effect closure in legal, historical, biographical, and sermonic discourse. Deuteronomy is characterized by stereotyped phrases and an abundance of accumulation (*accumulatio*), where nouns and verbs heap up in twos, threes, and fours, and longer phrases balance rhythmically in parallelism (4.28: "and there you will serve gods of wood and stone, the work of men's hands, that neither see, nor hear, nor eat, nor smell"). The core of *Deuteronomy* (chapters 1–28) makes extensive use of the *inclusio*, which gives emphasis to parenetic admonitions, restores focus, and brings about closure:

These are the *statutes and ordinances* which *you shall be careful to do* in the land. . . .
(Dt. 12.1).

Every word that I command you, *you shall be careful to do;* you shall not add to it or take from it
(Dt. 12.32)

For you are a people holy to Yahweh your God
(Dt. 14.2)

For you are a people holy to Yahweh your God
(Dt. 14.21)

The preachers of *Deuteronomy* were probably Levitical priests, some of whom were trained scribes and went by the name *scribe* (*2 Chr.* 34.13). But the real *rhētors* in ancient Israel were the prophets, who reflect the same rhetorical tradition as other literates in society, suggesting that they must have received training in letters and the arts before venturing forth as heralds of the divine word. Isaiah, Jeremiah, and Ezekiel may well have attended a Jerusalem school where writing and rhetorical skills were taught. In Jeremiah's time (622 BCE), this school would have been headed by Shaphan, the scribe, and at-

tached to the temple as in neighboring societies (*2 Kgs.* 22.8–10).

Prophets embellish their oracles and other public discourse with an array of rhetorical figures, such as metaphor, simile, comparison, euphemism, epithet, *chiasmus, asyndeton,* alliteration, rhetorical question, *hyperbolē, paronomasia,* and irony. Amos is the prophet of the rhetorical question; Hosea, the framer of oracles with broken bicolons, also the prophet of extraordinary *pathos;* Isaiah, the master of verbal irony; and Ezekiel, the prophet of the extended metaphor. [*See* Pathos.] But the prophet with greatest rhetorical skill is unquestionably Jeremiah, who can hold rank with the best of the Greek and Roman rhetors, anticipating them as he does in style, structure, and modes of argumentation.

Hebrew rhetoric does not employ reason (*logos*) to the extent that Greek rhetoric does. [*See* Logos.] For Aristotle, logic was everything, the true aim of rhetoric being to prove your point, or seem to prove it. However, if the prophet's message is set over against the controlling message of *Deuteronomy,* where the latter is assumed by the prophet, but left unexpressed, a great enthymeme emerges [*See* Enthymeme.]:

[Deuteronomy: An Israel in violation of the covenant will be punished]

The prophets: Israel has violated the covenant

Israel will therefore be punished.

Hebrew rhetoric appeals only occasionally to the emotions (*pathos*), as, for example, in the preaching of *Hosea* (11.1–4, 8–9) and *Jeremiah* (3.19–20; 31.15–20). *Ēthos* appeals are similarly rare, seen occasionally in Jeremiah's confessions to Yahweh (*Jer.* 8.6; 12.3; 18.20), but not usual in public discourse. [*See* Ēthos.] The place of *ēthos* is taken largely by authority, which is the dominant element in Hebrew rhetoric, and the driving force in almost all prophetic preaching. Yet in Jeremiah, there is an observable break away from authority preaching; that is, oracles become open-ended, and the audience is thereby made a partner with the prophet in discerning the import of the divine word (3.1–5; 5.1–8).

Jeremiah makes extensive use of repetition,

not simply as a stylistic device, but to structure his oracles. Examples abound of *anaphora* and *epiphora*, the former enriched often by onomatopoeia. A fivefold repetition of "sword" (50.35–38) simulates the repeated stabbing of victims, where, at the end, is a climactic paronomasia with the similar-sounding "drought." On a happier note, the threefold "again" (31.4–5) simulates the resumption of city life in a resettled Zion. A change in rhythm is another way of creating onomatopoeia, for example, in Jeremiah's chaos vision (4.23–26), where decreasing colon length simulates a cessation of life in the entire created order. Jeremiah also repeats verbal roots in succession (11.18): "Yahweh made me know, and I knew."

Repeated words and phrases—otherwise synonyms or fixed word pairs—structure stanzas as well as entire poems. Jeremiah constructs elaborate word schemes, often with inversion (*chiasmus*). Key word *chiasms* (2.5–9; 5.1–8; 51:34–45), are similar to those in *Lamentations* (1–2). Reflecting the homiletical prose of Deuteronomy, Jeremiah makes liberal use of the *inclusio* in both prose (7.3–7, 8–11, 12–14) and poetic (3.1–5; 20.7–10) oracles, also in his defense before the court (26.12–15):

> *Yahweh sent me* to prophesy against this
>   house and against this city
> —*all the things* that you have heard . . . (26.12)
>
> . . . for in truth *Yahweh sent me* to you to
>   speak in your ears
> *all these things* (26.15)

The *inclusio* frames oracles by the prophetess Huldah (*2 Kgs.* 22.16–20) and by Jeremiah's adversary, Hananiah (*Jer.* 28.2–4). This figure is present in Akkadian poetry, in classical poetry, where it is called "ring composition," and in modern poetry (e.g., the poems of Carl Sandburg).

Jeremiah's discourse, like that in *Deuteronomy,* is replete with *accumulatio* (in poetry: 1.10, 12.7; in prose: 7.5–6, 33–34). It also contains *asyndeton* (in poetry: 4.5, 5.1; in prose: 7.9), which classical authors used to heap up praise or blame. The string of six infinitive absolutes in the Temple oracle (7.9) assigns blame. Jeremiah uses this figure to enliven a judgment on the nations (25.27) and underscore the joy in announcing Israel's salvation (31.7).

The expansion of Hellenism in the fourth century BCE, followed by Rome's entry into the eastern Mediterranean in the first century BCE, brought an infusion of Greco-Roman rhetoric into postexilic Jewish intellectual life. We see now a use of the "sortie" (Gk. *climax;* Lat. *gradatio*) in Jewish writings (Pirqe Aboth 1.1, 4.2; *Wis.; Sol.* 6.17–19), which is a catalog of statements, each picking up a key word from the statement preceding, leading finally to a climax. The sortie is used often by Paul in the New Testament (*Rom.* 5.3–5: "More than that we rejoice in our *sufferings,* knowing that *suffering* produces *endurance,* and *endurance* produces *character,* and *character* produces *hope,* and *hope* does not disappoint us"; see also *Romans* (8.29–30, 10.14–15). The locust parade of Joel (1.4), "what the *cutting locust* left, the *swarming locust* has eaten; what the *swarming locust* left, the *hopping locust* has eaten; and what the *hopping locust* left, the *destroying locust,* has eaten," is not really a sortie, but a chain created in the interest of expressing totality, which is another defining characteristic of the older Hebrew rhetoric.

Jewish apocryphal and pseudepigraphal works, supplemented by the sectarian documents found at Khirbet Qumran (Dead Sea Scrolls), all provide valuable insights into Hebrew rhetorical tradition as it developed during the so-called Intertestamental period. Rhetorical discourse from the prototannaitic and tannaitic periods (c.100 BCE to 200 CE) survives in the Mishnah and Talmud, the latter completed c.500 CE in Babylon. Here Hellenistic philosophy and rhetoric are seen to have influenced rabbinic methods of interpretation, particularly the hermeneutical rules developed by the great Pharisee Hillel (c.30 BCE). [*See Hermeneutics.*] We should also not overlook the New Testament as an important first century CE document of Hebrew rhetoric, even though it survives (and was probably written from the beginning) in Greek, not Hebrew or Aramaic. It teems with figures, structures, and modes of argumentation derived from ancient Hebrew rhetoric. In the early Middle Ages, and again in modern times, Jewish rhetoric has been influenced by contemporary philosophical thought, and has combined it in each case with its own rich tradition of rhetoric rooted in preclassical antiquity.

[*See also* Comparative rhetoric; *and* Figures of speech.]

BIBLIOGRAPHY

Daube, David. "Rabbinic Methods of Interpretation and Hellenistic Rhetoric." *Hebrew Union College Annual* 22 (1949), pp. 239–264. Reprinted in *Understanding the Talmud,* edited by Alan D. Corré, pp. 275–89. New York, 1975.

Fischel, Henry A. "The Uses of Sorties (*Climax, Gradatio*) in the Tannaitic period." *Hebrew Union College Annual* 44 (1973), pp. 119–151.

Herder, Johann Gottfried von. *The Spirit of Hebrew Poetry,* 2 vols. Translated by James Marsh. Burlington, Va., 1833. English translation of *Vom Geist der Ebräischen Poesie,* 2 vols. first published in 1782–1783. A classic work on the inner spirit of ancient Hebrew poetry.

Kramer, Samuel Noah. "The Sumerian School: A Pre-Greek System of Education." In *Studies Presented to David Moore Robinson,* vol. 1, edited by George E. Mylonas, pp. 238–245. Saint Louis, 1951.

Kramer, Samuel Noah. "Sumerian Similes: A Panoramic View of Some of Man's Oldest Literary Images." *Journal of the American Oriental Society* 89 (1969), pp. 1–10.

Kramer, Samuel Noah. *The Sacred Marriage Rite.* Bloomington, Ind., 1969. See especially, chapter 2: "The Poetry of Sumer: Repetition, Parallelism, Epithet, Simile."

Lund, Nils W. "The Presence of Chiasmus in the Old Testament." *American Journal of Semitic Languages and Literatures* 46 (1930), pp. 104–126.

Lund, Nils W. *Chiasmus in the New Testament.* Chapel Hill, N.C., 1942. Reprinted: Peabody, Mass., 1992. The primary text for chiasmus in large panels in both the Old and New Testaments.

Lundbom, Jack R. "God's Use of the *Idem per Idem* to Terminate Debate." *Harvard Theological Review* 71 (1978), pp. 193–201. Discusses the two important Old Testament passages on divine revelation in Exodus (3.12–15, 33.18–23).

Lundbom, Jack R. "Poetic Structure and Prophetic Rhetoric in Hosea." *Vetus Testamentum* 29 (1979), pp. 300–308. The broken bicolon is shown here to be a structural and closure device in Hosea's preaching.

Lundbom, Jack R. "Jeremiah and the Break-Away from Authority Preaching." *Svensk Exegetisk Årsbok* 56 (1991), pp. 7–28. Qualifies the widely-held view that Hebrew (also early Christian) discourse is based solely on authority.

Lundbom, Jack R. "Jeremiah (Prophet)." In *The Anchor Bible Dictionary,* vol. 3, edited by David Noel Freedman et al., pp. 684–698. Includes section on "Rhetoric and Preaching."

Lundbom, Jack R. "The Inclusio and Other Framing Devices in Deuteronomy I–XXVIII." *Vetus Testamentum* 46 (1996), pp. 296–315. The *inclusio* is shown here to be the controlling structure in the homiletical discourse of *Deuteronomy* 1–28.

Lundbom, Jack R. *Jeremiah: A Study in Ancient Hebrew Rhetoric.* Second enlarged edition. Winona Lake, Ind., 1997, first published in 1975. Contains an introductory essay, "Rhetorical Criticism: History, Method and Use in the Book of Jeremiah" (pp. xix–xliii); also an English translation of Christian Schoettgens's *Exergasia Sacra* in an Appendix (pp. 155–163).

Lundbom, Jack R. *Jeremiah 1–20.* Anchor Bible 21A. New York, 1999. Introduction contains sections on the modern method of rhetorical criticism (pp. 68–85), rhetoric and composition in the book of *Jeremiah* (pp. 85–92), and rhetoric and preaching of the prophet (pp. 121–139).

Muilenburg, James. "A Study in Hebrew Rhetoric: Repetition and Style." *Vetus Testamentum Supplement* 1 (1953), pp. 97–111. Reprinted in Thomas Best, *Hearing and Speaking the Word,* pp. 193–207. Chico, Calif., 1984.

Muilenburg, James. "Form Criticism and Beyond." *Journal of Biblical Literature* 88 (1969), pp. 1–18. Reprinted in Thomas Best, *Hearing and Speaking the Word,* pp. 27–44. Chico, Calif., 1984. The first essay to define Old Testament rhetorical criticism as a method.

—Jack R. Lundbom

HENDIADYS, which literally means "one [expressed] by two"—called by Puttenham (*The Arte of English Poesie,* 1589, p. 177) "Figure of Twinnes"—a descriptive rather than strictly technical term for a form of semantic equivalence. The elements of a compound notion are coordinated instead of subordinated. Thus, a tune is "nice and easy" for the performer who likes it nicely easy. *Hendiadys* amplifies and emphasizes several aspects of a notion. When Shakespeare's Hamlet talks about the "chief good and market of [man's] time," this is glossed over as "profit" (4.4.54). Semantic equivalences are often enhanced, as Heinrich F. Plett in his *Systematische Rhetorik* (Munich, 2000) points out, by phonological equivalences, as in "bag and baggage."

[*See also* Figures of speech.]

—Heiner Peters

HERMENEUTICS refers to the essential capacity of human beings to understand and give expression to the world in meaningful ways. The term also refers to the study of the methodological principles and rules that govern acts of interpretive understanding and the compositions they produce (from texts and works of art to the intersubjective domains of meaning that inform and guide the interpersonal dynamics of a given culture). This second understanding of hermeneutics presupposes its first and more existential function. One cannot study a composition unless it already exists in some form. As the anthropologist Clifford Geertz (*The Interpretation of Cultures*, New York, 1973) notes, "A good interpretation of anything—a poem, a person, a history, a ritual, an institution, a society—takes us into the heart of that of which it is the interpretation" (p. 19).

To speak of the "heart" of some matter is to refer to its essential or most vital part(s), that which enables it *to be what it is*. A hermeneutical investigation of a given composition, in other words, is directed toward getting at the "truth" of the composition. The oldest and perhaps best-known application of hermeneutics—biblical interpretation or the exegesis of Scripture—provides a classic example of what this task entails.

Biblical Hermeneutics. The "simple" truth in question is that of God's Word, which—as in the King James Bible—was uttered "in the beginning" when God "created the heaven and the earth" (*Gn.* 1.1). With the tradition of Jewish mysticism—Kabbalah—which originated in the late twelfth century, one is taught, however, that the common translation of the first line of *Genesis* is, in fact, a mistranslation, for the actual words in Hebrew can be read another way: "With a beginning, [It] created God (*Elohim*), the heavens and the earth." The "truth" of God is more than the story that unfolds throughout the Old and New Testaments. "His is the Word, ours the paraphrase," writes Rabbi Abraham Joshua Heschel (*God in Search of Man*, New York, 1955, p. 160). And with this Word—the source from out of which the potential to begin was first created—we are given something that can be understood (paraphrased) symbolically as "God," but whose truth transcends, as an ongoing process, even the richest and most reverent meaning of this word. *Infinity* is the term commonly associated with the

"meaning" of this process. For the Kabbalist, however, the process, referred to as *Ein Sof,* is not restricted by infinity; rather It created it. Commenting on the hermeneutical problem involved here, Rabbi David Cooper (*God Is a Verb,* New York, 1997) remarks: "Indeed, we have suddenly run out of words because the idea of 'trans-infinite' is a logical absurdity. What can go beyond infinity? . . . . This is *Ein Sof*" (p. 67).

With this example of biblical hermeneutics, one sees how the activity of interpretative understanding may also be conceived as a matter of "translating," "explaining," and "asserting" or "saying." These specific functions of hermeneutical analysis have their etymological roots in the Greek verb *hermēneuein* ("to interpret") and the noun *hermēneia* ("interpretation"). In ancient Greek mythology, it is the wing-footed messenger god, Hermes, who is credited with the initial enactment of these functions, whereby the words of the gods are communicated in a form that human intelligence can comprehend. Commenting on this "Hermes process," Richard Palmer (*Hermeneutics,* Evanston, Ill., 1969), further clarifies the nature of hermeneutics when he notes that with this process "something foreign, strange, separated in time, space, or experience is made familiar, present, comprehensible; something requiring representation, explanation, or translation is somehow 'brought to understanding'—is 'interpreted'" (p. 14).

Especially in the case of biblical hermeneutics, one receives instruction in how the process of interpretation is made possible by the human capacity for awe, which is the cardinal attitude stressed in the Old Testament; and with this particular way of experiencing the world a person is *drawn toward* the "heart" of some matter of concern. Awe is evoked not in moments of calculation but rather in moments of *being open to and in rapport with* the truth of what one is witnessing. In a moment of awe, one's relationship to the world is that of respecting beings by letting them be what they are. The moment is "holy," for now the manner in which one experiences the presence of things is most like the "saying" that first acknowledged life and called it into being: "And God said, Let there be light . . ." (*Gn.* 1.3). In moments of awe, things "speak" in mysterious ways. The experience is humbling. It is a time of wonder, of finding oneself in a place for acquiring wisdom. According to Rabbi Heschel: "There is . . . only one way to wisdom: awe. Forfeit your sense of awe, let your conceit diminish your ability to revere, and the universe becomes a market place for you. The loss of awe is the great block to insight" (p. 78). Caught up in wonder and awe, we are in "the state of being asked," the state where one is addressed and acknowledged ("Where art thou?" *Gn.* 3.8–9), where one is thereby given the opportunity to respond and be accountable ("God . . . said unto him, Abraham: and he said, Behold, here I am" *Gn.* 22.1), and where one's capacity for moral feeling is called forth and directed ("And now . . . what doth the Lord thy God require of thee, but to fear thy Lord thy God, to walk in all his ways, and to love Him, and to serve the Lord thy God with all thy heart . . ." (*Dt.* 10.12).

Biblical hermeneutics stresses the moral quality of what it is doing as it translates, explains, and expresses the awesome and wonderous nature of the Word. As just noted, this quality of interpretive understanding is related to the "heart," which is a "gift": "I will give them a heart to know Me, that I am the Lord" (*Jr.* 24.7). In the Old Testament, the use of the term *heart* is generally associated by rabbinic scholars with moral consciousness or "conscience" and the emotions such as fear, guilt, joy, and love that oftentimes come with it. In returning God's favor of acknowledgment, we ought to be, at the very least, conscientious as we try to "know together" (Gk. *sun-eidēsis;* Lat. *conscientia*) with God and others all that is right, true, good, and just. In the New Testament, this heartfelt way of knowing is emphasized by the Apostle Paul (*1 Cor.* 8–10) when discussing how people with whom we disagree should still be treated with tolerance and patience as ways to reform.

Notice then that with biblical hermeneutics, the interpretive challenge of getting to the "heart of the matter" is essentially a "matter of the heart" (or conscience)—that gift of moral consciousness that enables us to remain open to, such that we can judge fairly, the goodness of all that stands before us. Made as it is by a creature who is mortal, however, such judgment is not infallible; its paraphrase may be utterly mistaken because of cultural and psychological influences

("The heart is deceitful above all things, and desperately wicked: who can know it?" *Jr.* 17.9). The gift that enables us to be awestruck by all that we may witness is ever in need of instruction. In both Judaism and Christianity, this educational task gives rise to the hermeneutical enterprise of casuistry, which is specifically concerned with *casus conscientiae* or "cases of conscience." [*See* Casuistry.] In their extensive treatment of the topic (*The Abuse of Casuistry,* Berkeley, 1988), Albert Jonsen and Stephen Toulmin note that the goal of casuistry is to register descriptions of moral behavior in which moral precepts and the details of action are looked at together in order to determine how a person, concerned to act rightly, should make a judgment of conscience in a specific kind of situation. Casuistry thus exhibits genealogical links to the Aristotelian tradition of practical reasoning (*phronēsis*). [*See* Phronēsis.] Hence, in any of its cases of conscience one expects to see "'rhetorical' analyses whose powers of persuasion [depend] not merely on their intrinsic content but also on the circumstances in which they [are] put forward: for example, on being advanced by 'people of good judgment' (*phronimoi*), and on finding 'reasonable and understanding hearers'" (p. 257).

Hermeneutics and Rhetoric. The paraphrase of the Word (as seen in the parables of the New Testament, for example) admits the practice of rhetoric into the hermeneutical process. In his discussion of the relationship between these two "arts," the philologist and founder of modern hermeneutic theory, Friedrich Schleiermacher (1768–1834) (*Hermeneutics: The Handwritten Manuscripts,* Missoula, Mont., 1997, p. 97), points out that hermeneutics "at once depends upon and presupposes composition," whether spoken or written. Schleiermacher associates the composition of a text with the art of presentation (rhetoric), an art that enables the author to explicate his or her subject matter so that it may be understood by others. Hence, Schleiermacher maintains that "hermeneutics and rhetoric are intimately related in that every act of understanding is the reverse side of an act of speaking [or writing], and one must grasp the thinking that underlies a given statement" (p. 97).

The hermeneutical task being emphasized here defines a fundamental goal of Schleiermacher's theory of interpretive understanding. In order to gain the fullest access to the intended meaning in a given text, the reader must attempt to reconstruct and reexperience the distinctive mental processes that were at work in its composition. Schleiermacher points to the author's particular style as a major source of evidence for comprehending these processes: "Thoughts and language are intertwined, and an author's distinctive way of treating the subject is manifested by his organization of his material and by his use of language" (pp. 148–149). An appreciation of the rhetorical competence that informs the text is therefore needed by the interpreter.

Adhering to Scheiermacher's take on the relationship between hermeneutics and rhetoric, one might wonder whether there was rhetorical competence at work when "With a beginning, [It] created God, the heavens and the earth." If so, then anyone who attempts a paraphrase of Its Word should be seen as a type of rhetorical critic. With Schleiermacher, however, one must be careful in advancing this ambiguous claim. Rhetorical criticism is naturally an effort in rhetorical competence: the critic is involved in the process of crafting a composition that is intended to be persuasive but which is also devoted to cultivating judgment and practical wisdom in others. In contrast, Schleiermacher maintains that hermeneutics, which he sought to elevate to the art of a scholarly discipline, is basically a philosophical endeavor; it "deals only with the art of understanding, not with the [interpreter's] presentation of what has been understood" (p. 96). Yet, as Kurt Mueller-Vollmer (*The Hermeneutics Reader,* New York, 1990) notes, the problem here is that by excluding from its agenda the element of presentation, hermeneutics cannot fulfill the task that Schleiermacher envisions. "For the art of the philologist consists largely in generally accepted procedures, assumptions, verbal strategies, an institutionalized body of knowledge and the tacit agreement on standards for hermeneutic competence. The presentation of one's understanding is an integral part of the art in question" (p. 12). Indeed, the art of understanding, dedicated as it is to advancing the hermeneutic competence of those interested in being part of its scholarly enterprise, must itself employ the practice of rhetoric to disclose clearly and to justify any truth claim regarding the authorial intentions of a given text. "Convincing and persuading," writes Hans-Georg Gadamer (*Philosophical Hermeneutics* [*PH*], Berkeley, 1976), "are obviously as much the aim and measure of understanding and interpretation as they are the aim and measure of the art of oration and persuasion" (p. 24).

In its relation with the art of understanding, rhetorical competence must be acknowledged as something more than an object of study, something more than a passageway of stylistic signposts directing the reader back to the subjective confines of an author's thought. Of course, rhetorical competence can include a concern with the author's subjective thought; but Schleiermacher's exclusive focus on this goes against the grain of the rhetorical intentionality that is at work in the text and that, as aimed by the author, is *directed toward* the other as hearer, reader, and audience. In short, the rhetorical competence that informs a text leads hermeneutics in the direction it must go to reach out to and engage others so that its declared understanding of a particular subject matter can be shared, agreed with, or disputed. This is how hermeneutics achieves practical significance: by returning, with the help of rhetoric, from the workings of the mind to the everyday world of situated, practical concerns.

Audience Reception and Response. The whole enterprise of hermeneutics—from the interpretive understanding that is needed to compose and present a work of art to the interpretive understanding that is needed to compose and present a critical response to the work—is a rhetorical process of meaning formation that would be impossible without the active participation of audiences. Hans Robert Jauss (*Toward an Aesthetic of Reception,* Minneapolis, 1982) emphasizes this point when he notes that:

> In the triangle of author, work, and public, the last is no passive part, no chain of mere reactions, but rather itself an energy formative of history. . . . For it is only through the process of its mediation that the work enters into the changing horizon-of-experience of a continuity in which the perpetual inversion occurs from simple reception to critical understanding, from passive to active reception, from recognized aesthetic norms to a new production that surpasses them. (p. 19)

Implied in Jauss's assessment here—especially as it emphasizes the hermeneutic phenomenon of "perpetual inversion"—is a requirement of interpretive and rhetorical competence on the part of those audience members who are attempting to form a critical understanding of a work of art. According to Barbara Herrnstein Smith (*On the Margins of Discourse*, Chicago, 1978), such competence provides a way for works "to endure as something other than vivid historical artifacts" in that it enables one to comprehend how works "serve as metaphors and parables of an independent future"—that is, how they "continue to have meanings independent of the particular context that occasioned their composition, which will inevitably include meanings that the author did not intend and could not have intended to convey" (p. 151). Furthermore, the competence being emphasized here would be at work whenever an audience was engaged in the critical task of determining whether or not a new production had surpassed recognized and accepted norms and, in turn, whether or not the aesthetic and sociopolitical implications of the new production warranted any respect and allegiance. [*See* Reception theory.]

The specific factor in the hermeneutical and rhetorical process of meaning formation that keeps a work alive is that of the hearer, reader, and audience. With the lessons of biblical hermeneutics in mind, one might think of the interaction here as having something of a "spiritual" nature. Seeking the life-giving gift of acknowledgment, the author's work calls out "Where art thou?" and awaits a response ("Here I am!") from those who are interested and competent enough to keep the conversation going about the meaning and significance of the pertinent issue(s) at hand. A work without a receptive audience is a work whose truth remains mute.

Abraham Lincoln's Gettysburg Address (1863) provides a classic example of this point. With this address, delivered as it was within a situation fraught with social, political, and economic problems and filled with immense heartbreak over the loss of life, Lincoln initially emerged as rhetorical "failure" in the pragmatic and immediate sense. In the long run, however, we have come to know better: with this masterpiece of rhetorical competence that, according to Gary Wills (*Lincoln at Gettysburg*, New York, 1992) "remade America" as it set forth a "revolution" in thought and speech, we witness a work of art whose distinctive and appropriate use of grammer, syntax, signs, tempo, topics, figures, tropes, emotion, narrative, and argument itself creates a dwelling place or character (*ēthos*), of eulogized time and space, an opening in the midst of immense suffering where there is still hope to be found as we acknowledge the devotion and courage not of individuals dressed in blue or gray but, as Lincoln tells us, of those "brave men, living and dead, who struggled here" and who would have us realize "that the nation shall, under God, have a new birth of freedom, and that government of the people, by the people, and for the people, shall not perish from the earth." The form and content of Lincoln's Address are inextricably bound together in a rhetorical disclosure of conscience that calls for assistance in building a common *ēthos*—dwelling place, character, ethic—for the nation. [*See* Ēthos.] The Gettysburg Address is rationally designed and arranged so to have us acknowledge and "know together" (*conscientia*) something of the truth of being-with-and-for others, of feeling at home in their company, and of treating them in a just and moral way. In short, and in hermeneutical terms, to dwell with Lincoln at Gettysburg is to learn how important it is to have a heart that is open to the world and, hence, to the experience of wonder and awe that shows itself in acts of commitment, courage, and sacrifice. Further, might it be said that with such an interpretive reading of the Gettysburg Address, one is getting at the heart of its being, its truth, its genuine meaning and significance? This might also explain why the Address has become a "rhetorical touchstone": in speaking as it does about a time and place wherein wounded humanity begged for relief and wherein such relief called for the medicaments of a variety of healing emotions and virtues that are known to make human beings feel and do "good," the Address offers a "fitting response" to a situation of crisis (war and its many horrible consequences). Perhaps the Gettysburg Address remains alive today because its hermeneutical–rhetorical–moral message is essential to the well-being of a public who, in being able to understand its teachings and rejoice in putting them into practice, continues to be receptive to the message's appeal and, hence, to its meaning and significance.

Meaning, Significance, and the Hermeneutical Situation. In speaking about the hermeneutical and rhetorical relationship that exists between the author's work and present and forthcoming audiences, I have continued to employ the phrase "meaning and significance" as a way of explaining how it is that the work's truth is able to endure over time. In *Validity in Interpretation* (*VI*, New Haven, 1967) and *The Aims of Interpretation* (*AI*, Chicago, 1978), E. D. Hirsch, Jr., makes much of the difference between those two major terms. "*Meaning,*" writes Hirsch, "is that which is represented by a text; it is what the author meant by his use of a particular sign sequence. . . . *Significance,* on the other hand, names a relationship between that meaning and a person, or a conception, or a situation, or indeed anything imaginable" (*VI*, p. 8). Only by keeping this distinction in mind, argues Hirsch, can one hope to offer a "valid" interpretation of a given text. "Validity requires a norm—a meaning that is stable and determinate no matter how broad its range of implication and application. A stable and determinate meaning requires an author's determining will . . . All valid interpretation of every sort is founded on the re-cognition of what an author meant" (*VI*, p. 126). Or to put it another way: "If an interpreter did not conceive a text's meaning to be *there* as an occasion for contemplation or application, he would have nothing to think or talk about. Its thereness, its self-identity from one moment to the next allows it to be contemplated. Thus, while meaning is a principle of stability in an interpretation, significance embraces a principle of change" (*AI*, p. 80).

What was said above about the meaning and significance of Lincoln's Gettysburg Address is consistent with Hirsch's directives. Rhetorical critics generally agree that this short but robust and revolutionary Address was intended to be a call of conscience directed toward the uniting of the nation and encouraging its moral integrity and growth. The "obviousness" of this meaning required temporal distance from a blood-soaked and haunting battlefield in order to rise above the blinding prejudices of the day such that Lincoln's "determining will" could be properly identified. Lincoln addressed a particular situation with a

rhetorical strategy that accommodated cultural differences and directed people to think about humankind in more universal terms. He spoke not only to the actual consciousness of his immediate audience but also to the potential consciousness of forthcoming generations who, with continuing experience and education, could develop the practical wisdom and interpretive competence that is needed to prevent, or at least heal, the horrible wounds of war. Hence, the applicability (significance) of the meaning of Lincoln's Address: it continues to *speak* and thus to have something to *say* to people who have yet to overcome completely their violent tendencies but who nevertheless have the hermeneutical, rhetorical, and moral capacities to understand and develop a feeling for the importance of cultivating unity and peace.

Although the Gettysburg Address is a text that can help illustrate Hirsch's take on the relationship between meaning, significance, and the validity of interpretation, I suspect that he nevertheless would object to the way I phrased the last point. For, according to Hirsch, "It is natural to speak *not of what a text says*, but of what an author means, and this more natural locution is the more accurate one" (*VI*, p. 244; emphasis added). This claim reflects Hirsch's opposition to the program of philosophical hermeneutics that is rooted in the works of such twentieth-century philosophers as Martin Heidegger, Hans-Georg Gadamer, and Paul Ricoeur. This program advocates a theory of meaning that is not confined to the intentions of an author and that stresses how any act of interpretive understanding unfolds within a "hermeneutical situation" where texts do, in fact, "speak" to those who are willing to remain open to what these texts have "to say."

Unlike Hirsch, whose appreciation of hermeneutics reflects the philologist's methodological interest in "validity," Heidegger (*Being and Time* [*BT*], New York, 1962) emphasizes the term's more primordial and existential association with the essential capacity of human beings to understand and give expression to the world in meaningful ways. Heidegger's ontological assessment of this event of interpretive understanding unfolds as an answer to a question: what is the meaning, the truth, of Being? For Heidegger, Being refers not merely to a thing but rather to the *coming to presence* of that which is. Being is more of a verb ("to be") than it is a noun (a name for things: for example, that thing called a "book"); it is active, not static. For something "to be" means for it to be revealed, disclosed, made manifest—time and again. This is Being's "way," that which must be thought through as much as possible so as to come to a genuine understanding of its meaning and truth, of how the world presents itself to human consciousness, with its capacity for interpretive understanding.

Heidegger's philosophy, from beginning to end, unfolds as a hermeneutic discourse on Being. He initiates his project by offering a phenomenology of human existence. Phenomenology is a way of thinking devoted to interpreting, analyzing, and describing how the immediate content of experience actually presents itself. It seeks to disclose with "demonstrative precision" the "appearing" or "presencing" of some phenomenon, "to let that which shows itself [*phainesthai*] be seen from itself in the very way in which it shows itself from itself" (p. 58). Phenomenology, in other words, attempts to generate a discourse that is especially attuned to the way in which some phenomenon happens to how it reveals or manifests itself within the temporal horizon of human understanding. The discourse of phenomenology assumes the task of disclosing a phenomenon's own disclosure, *its* being and truth. It may thus be said that phenomenology is a truth-telling activity; for as Heidegger points out in his discussion of the matter, truth happens first and foremost as a disclosing of the world, as a revealing or uncovering of the "givenness" of something that is perceived to be (pp. 256–273).

What Heidegger is referring to here is not "the truth" that may be disclosed in some verbal judgment ("The sky is blue"), in some epistemic correspondence of some reified proposition with some equally reified state of affairs. The truth of such a disclosure presupposes a more original happening of truth, a more original instance of disclosing: the actual presencing of that which shows itself and thus gives itself for thought and understanding. This is the truth (of Being) that Heidegger is after; his phenomenology is directed toward a hermeneutic assessment of how this primordial showing and giving take place. Heidegger comes to describe this task as requiring one to

"listen" to the "call of Being." Moreover, he tells us that in order to do this "[t]he point is not to listen to a series of propositions, but rather to follow the movement of showing" (*On Time and Being*, New York, 1972, p. 2). This may sound a bit strange. How is it that this "showing" "calls"?

Hermeneutic phenomenology goes about telling the truth by "letting-something-be-seen" with its discourse. Heidegger (*On the Way to Language*, New York, 1971) identifies such a disclosing or evocative use of discourse with what he defines as the "essential being of language" (*logos*): its "saying" power, its capacity to "speak" by pointing to and showing us something (pp. 122–124). "Language speaks," insists Heidegger, and it does so especially in those discourses that warrant praise for being revelatory and perhaps even awe-inspiring because of the way in which they call forth and disclose their subject matter, thereby enabling us to better our understanding and appreciation of what is being talked about. So, for example, in order to understand and appreciate what Lincoln is trying to tell us with his Gettysburg Address (a most evocative discourse, to be sure), we must listen not only to him (which of course we can no longer do) but also to the power of his language as it displays a capacity for making manifest certain matters of importance, for saying something to us by showing us what this something is thought to be. If the Gettysburg Address is to speak to us in a truthful manner, this, at the very least, is what it must do: through an act of saying, of showing, it must give us something to understand. Heidegger reminds us that the "oldest word" for "saying" is *logos*: "Saying which, in showing, lets beings appear in their 'it is'" (p. 155; *BT*, p. 56). The saying power of language is what enables any discourse to give expression to things that call for attention. Heidegger further reminds us that the word for "saying" is also the word for Being (*logos*). Indeed, Being is constantly disclosing and showing itself in how things are, in the presencing of all that lies before us, in the circumstances of life that call for thought. The truth of Being is a saying, a showing, a phenomenon that gives itself for understanding. This is what Heidegger is referring to when he speaks of the "call of Being": that primordial "saying" whose showing is thought provoking. And this is why Heidegger tells us that if we are to "listen" attentively to this call, we must "follow the movement of showing" so as to let whatever concerns us speak for itself. [*See* Logos.]

Heidegger hears and answers the call differently than Hirsch does, who, as noted above, restricts hermeneutics to the issue of validity: determining the original and stable verbal meaning intended by an author. For Heidegger, however, the "hermeneutical situation" that is present whenever one tries to uncover such willed meaning is more complex than acknowledged by defenders of objectivity and validity. As it emerges and takes form in the world of everyday concerns, meaning is not something that is simply willed and intended by some author; rather, any speech act operates in an already established realm of intersubjective understanding that speaks of what things are according to the established points of view and prejudices that are operating at the time and that constitute the tradition of the author's culture. Moreover, as Ricoeur (*Interpretation Theory,* Fort Worth, Tex., 1976) points out, with any speech act there emerges a dialectical process that is already at work within a tradition and that refers to the meaning or truth of something that may yet have to be articulated and comprehended by the majority of the culture's members. This dialectic is borne in the ways in which "[d]iscourse refers back to its speaker at the same time it refers to the world. This correlation is not fortuitous, since it is ultimately the speaker who refers to the world in speaking. Discourse in action and in use refers backwards and forwards, to a speaker and a world" (p. 22). Ricoeur thus argues that the meaning of a text is not simply "behind" the text but rather, and more importantly, "in front of it." Meaning "is not something hidden, but something disclosed" as an author makes use of tradition and his or her own creative abilities to "project a world." Hermeneutics "has less than ever to do with the author and situation. It seeks to grasp the world-propositions opened up by the reference of the text. To understand a text is to follow its movement [its saying and showing] from sense to reference: from what it says, to what it talks about" (pp. 87–88). Texts speak and thereby show us a world. The ongoing debate over whether the Constitution of the United States supports a woman's right to abortion, for example, is based in part on how legal scholars interpret the way this text speaks of a world wherein such matters as "freedom of choice" and "privacy" are deemed essential to humankind.

With his emphasis on the intention of an author, Hirsch fails to account for this process of world disclosure. Hence, although his theory is instructive in alerting us to how, for example, the Gettysburg Address is steeped in the hermeneutic and rhetorical capacities of its author, his theory marginalizes the fact that Lincoln offers only an interpretation of a world whose "true" meaning may still lie beyond what Lincoln was able to put into words. Although I have suggested above that the acknowledged significance of the Address lends support to how wise Lincoln was with his interpretation of the meaning of the world in question, the fact still remains that without this world the issue of what Lincoln meant with his Address would not arise. Of course, an author's intended meaning gives critics something to think and write about, but this meaning is only one factor in a hermeneutical situation whose enduring nature is dependent on the receptivity of potential interpreters who, with additional time and experience, may be able to correct and extend an author's assessment of the meaning of a world that, for whatever reason, continues to warrant attention with all that it has to say. Hirsch contends that this understanding of the hermeneutical situation exposes interpretation theory to the problem of relativism since it collapses the distinction between meaning and significance by insisting that the meaning of some matter can evolve and thus change over time. But such relativism, one should realize, would not merely be a game of throwing the truth up for grabs. On the contrary, the project of philosophical hermeneutics at issue here is dedicated to getting to the heart and thus to the truth of some matter. With time and changing circumstances, this truth may disclose itself to people who are better prepared to receive, understand, and express it in a rhetorically competent manner such that others, too, can put its meaning to good use. The project of philosophical hermeneutics, in other words, is more aligned with what was described earlier as the rhetorical enterprise of casuistry than with the "anything goes" attitude of relativism.

Rhetorical Competence and Ideology. Hence, we return once again to the relationship that exists between hermeneutics and rhetoric— a relationship wherein, according to Gadamer (*PH*), rhetoric is not primarily a theory of forms, speeches, and persuasion, but instead is the "practical mastery" or knowhow that people have for making known to others that which is understood (p. 20). Or to put it in more Heideggerian terms, rhetoric serves as a basis for "the everydayness of Being with one another," or what Heidegger also designates as "publicness" (*BT*, pp. 149–168). Although Heidegger associated this realm of common sense and common praxis with the breeding ground for the evils of conformism, he also was inspired by Aristotle (384–322 BCE) to see it as providing the necessary background for coming to terms with who we are first and foremost as social beings and for determining whether or not our extant ways of seeing, interpreting, and becoming involved with things and with others might be changed "for the better." Hence, like Aristotle, Heidegger (*Sein und Zeit,* Tübingen, 1979) admits that rhetoric can play a valuable role in rousing the emotionally attuned interests of people and guiding them "in a right and just manner" (*"in der rechten Weise,"* p. 139; cf. *BT*, p. 178). This is how rhetoric helps to promote civic engagement and civic virtue and how it thereby lends itself to the task of enriching the moral character of a people's communal existence by encouraging collaborative deliberation about contested matters. Gadamer (*Truth and Method,* New York, 1991) describes this rhetorical process as defining a "hermeneutical conversation" that is directed toward the understanding of the truth of some matter and thus wherein the people "conversing are far less the leaders of it than the led" (p. 383). Rhetoric is not simply an art given over to manipulation, deception, and selfish motivation; although as is all too often seen in the ideological realm of politics, for example, it certainly can be made to serve such purposes. It was rhetoric, after all, with grammar, which first set forth interpretive protocols; hermeneutics by contrast puts these means to more general ends.

In what is perhaps the most influential critique of the project of philosophical hermeneutics, Jürgen Habermas makes much of the ways in which this project, especially as it is defined by Heidegger and Gadamer, fails to provide a precise methodology for critiquing those interpretations that inform the rhetoric of a given ideology and that dogmatically assert a world-view without satisfying what Habermas (*Moral Consciousness and Communicative Action,* Cambridge, Mass., 1990) identifies as the "validity conditions" of "the ideal community of communication" wherein the "competence" of "communicative rationality" can thrive. These conditions include: (1) choosing a comprehensible expression; (2) intending to communicate a true proposition; (3) expressing intentions truthfully; and (4) choosing an appropriate expression with respect to the dialogical situation at hand. As demonstrated by Thomas B. Farrell (*Norms of Rhetorical Culture,* New Haven, 1993), Habermas's critical theory can certainly serve the interests of rhetoricians who would expose the ideological element of authority that inhibits collaborative deliberation in a given rhetorical situation. Moreover, with Farrell one also learns that Habermas's theory fails to appreciate certain "positive" functions of rhetoric— for example, its use of emotion to move people toward the truth—that make possible such deliberation and that, as I have further demonstrated elsewhere (*The Call of Conscience: Heidegger and Levinas, Rhetoric and the Euthanasia Debate,* Columbia, S.C., 2001), are fundamentally related to the ontological, hermeneutical, and moral structure of human being.

Hermeneutics and rhetoric form a symbiotic relationship with each other. The relationship defines the process of interpretive understanding and meaning formation that lies at the heart of our temporal existence. We live lives that are open to the future and its questioning call: Where art thou? The history of the relationship of hermeneutics and rhetoric reads as a constant reminder of how important it is to respond to this call in a caring and competent manner.

[*See also* Commonplaces and commonplace books; Criticism; Law; *and* Religion.]

BIBLIOGRAPHY

Aristotle. *De interpretatione (Peri hermēneias; On Interpretation)* Translated by J. L. Ackrill. In *The Complete Works of Aristotle,* vol. 1. The Revised Oxford Translation, edited by J. Barnes, pp. 25–38. Princeton,

1984. Concerned principally with the consequences of interpretation for an understanding of the claims of "assertions" or "propositions."

Bruns, Gerald L. *Hermeneutics: Ancient and Modern.* New Haven, 1992. Belongs in the "canon" of creative presentations on the nature and purpose of hermeneutics.

Cooper, David A. *God is a Verb: Kabbalah and the Practice of Mystical Judaism.* New York, 1997. An exceptionally lucid discussion of the hermeneutic precepts associated with the thought and practice of Kabbalah.

Dilthey, Wilhelm. "The Development of Hermeneutics." In *Selected Writings.* Translated and edited by H. P. Rickman, pp. 247–263. Cambridge, U.K., 1976. Sets forth the thesis that understanding human beings and society is more like interpreting a text than acquiring knowledge of the physical world by using the methods of physics or chemistry.

Eden, Kathy. *Hermeneutics and the Rhetorical Tradition: Chapters in the Ancient Legacy and Its Humanist Reception.* New Haven, 1997. Study of the convergence of rhetorical theory and hermeneutics.

Fish, Stanley. *Is There a Text In This Class: The Authority of Interpretive Communities.* Cambridge, Mass., 1980. Argues for a "model of persuasion" to explain how critical activity is constitutive of its object.

Holub, Robert C. *Reception Theory: A Critical Introduction.* New York, 1984. A concise discussion of major reception theorists.

Hyde, Michael J., and Craig R. Smith. "Hermeneutics and Rhetoric: A Seen but Unobserved Relationship." *Quarterly Journal of Speech* 65 (1979), pp. 347–363. The first essay by American rhetoricians to detail the ways in which hermeneutic phenomenology provides ontological directives for rhetorical theory and criticism.

Jonas, Hans. "Heidegger and Theology." In *The Phenomenon of Life: Toward A Philosophical Biology,* pp. 235–261. Chicago, 1966. A classic critique of Heidegger's influence on theological thought.

Jost, Walter, and Michael J. Hyde, eds. *Rhetoric and Hermeneutics in Our Time: A Reader.* New Haven, 1997. A collection of twenty essays by leading scholars who explore the ways in which the disciplines of rhetoric and hermeneutics inform each other and influence a wide variety of intellectual fields.

Kennedy, George A. *New Testament Interpretation through Rhetorical Criticism.* Chapel Hill, N.C., 1984. An exceptionally clear exposition of how rhetorical criticism can complement other critical methods commonly used to interpret the New Testament.

Ricoeur, Paul. *The Conflict of Interpretations: Essays in Hermeneutics.* Edited by D. Ihde. Evanston, Ill., 1974. Twenty-two essays that relate the author's theory of hermeneutics to structuralism, psychoanalysis, phenomenology, and various religious topics.

Robinson, James M., and John B. Cobb, Jr., eds. *The New Hermeneutic,* vol. 2. New York, 1964. A collection of eight essays that critically assess the promise of philosophical hermeneutics for advancing the "science" of interpreting Scripture.

Schrag, Calvin O. *Communicative Praxis and the Space of Subjectivity.* Bloomington, Ind., 1986. An award-winning philosophical study of communication practices that eventually leads to a ground-breaking assessment of the relationship between hermeneutics, rhetoric, and ethics.

Smith, P. Christopher. *The Hermeneutics of Original Argument: Demonstration, Dialectic, Rhetoric.* Evanston, Ill., 1998. The first comprehensive study and critical assessment of Heidegger's reading of Aristotle's *Rhetoric.*

—MICHAEL J. HYDE

HEURISTICS. *See* Topics.

HISTORY. It is impossible to discuss *history* without first establishing some terms of reference, since the word is at least as slippery as *rhetoric* itself. In one of its senses, history means "events that have happened in the past"; in another of its senses, it is equivalent to "historical writing" (for which *historiography* is often a synonym). This overlap of meaning constitutes a helpful reminder that very often we know of events only because they have been written down. However real an event was at the time when it occurred, the past is an abstraction: witnesses may carry with them mental images of a past event, but they cannot transmit them to others except in some reified form; in earlier epochs, this form was writing, to which today can be added film and the like. Thus, one of the cardinal events of history is what happened to Julius Caesar on 15 March 44 BCE; but we know of this event (in the sense that we can know anything at all about the past) only because written statements about it have been handed down to us; and, unless we are dealing with (say) a medieval chronicle that restricts itself to utterances such as "famine this year," almost all written statements are rhetorical constructs.

For example, the statement "Julius Caesar died

on 15 March" is true but positively misleading. The statement "Caesar was killed on 15 March" is more true, but it is still not the whole truth: to anyone who does not know the story already, Caesar might have been killed by a runaway wagon. The latter statement can be clarified by the addition of the phrase "by Brutus and Cassius," but this too is inadequate: Brutus and Cassius might have encountered Caesar on the field of battle and killed him there. If we substitute "was murdered," the possibility of a battlefield encounter is immediately excluded, since we do not normally talk of a military engagement in terms of murder. At the same time, however, "murdered" undeniably colors the statement, and if we turn the sentence around ("Brutus and Cassius murdered Julius Caesar on 15 March"), the coloring is greater still, since active verbs are more vivid than passive. In these last two versions, the reader's sympathy seems to be enlisted for the victim, whereas, if we substitute "the tyrannicides" for "Brutus and Cassius," the situation is reversed: these days we have no sympathy for tyrants. Moreover, if we substitute "the Ides of March" for "15 March," other resonances are activated for the modern reader who is familiar with Shakespeare's play. Thus, not only is it very difficult to separate an event from its statement, but even apparently straightforward statements raise issues that come under the heading of "rhetoric."

A second terminological problem is that, when "history" is used as an equivalent of "historical writing," it is used indifferently of the texts both of classical historians (such as Herodotus, who wrote in Greek in the fifth century BCE, or Tacitus, who wrote in Latin in the second century CE), and of modern historians (such as Sir Ronald Syme, 1903–1989, the twentieth century's greatest historian of ancient Rome, or James M. McPherson, historian of the American Civil War and prize-winning author of *Battle Cry of Freedom*, Oxford, 1988). Such usage, no doubt aided by the similarity of "history" to the ancient Greek *historia* (from which it is indeed derived), encourages a presumption that there is an identity of meaning between modern "history" and classical "history," and that from classical times to the modern era, there stretches a continuous tradition of writing whose nature ("historical") is familiar and recognizable.

This presumption is rarely subjected to hard questioning by modern historians of the classical world, who, if they were to entertain seriously the possibility that the texts of Herodotus and Tacitus are fundamentally different from those that they write themselves, would begin to jeopardize the very evidence on which their own constructions depend. If a nonhistorian questions the presumption, he or she is said to be guilty of "a misconception of the nature of history" (M. Crawford, *The Roman Republic*, 2d ed., London, 1992), a phrase founded precisely on the supposed immutability of the genre. Modern historians who study aspects of the modern era are in a rather different position. On the one hand, most of them inevitably lack both the textual knowledge and technical expertise that are necessary for a personal inquiry into the nature of classical historical writing. But, even if they possessed this knowledge and expertise, they would very rarely have the degree of interest that such an enquiry presupposes: historians of the American Civil War are by definition, and quite properly, interested in the American Civil War; they neither have nor see any reason to question the orthodoxy repeated in successive handbooks of historiography, almost all of which begin by referring to the Greek etymology of "history" and by situating the origins of the modern genre in ancient Greece. In this respect, such modern historians have a passive belief in the immutability of history. On the other hand, it is usual for those same modern historians also to hold the active belief that in the early nineteenth century, the writing of history underwent a profound change, associated above all with Leopold von Ranke (1795–1886), and that pre-Rankean practitioners have little in common with their more "scientific" successors. Thus the word *history* will mean not only different things to different categories of scholars but also different things to the same category of scholars at (as it were) different moments.

Ranke's work facilitated, if it did not actually set off, the familiar debate as to whether history is a science or an art, each view famously championed by successive holders of the Regius Chair of Modern History at Cambridge, respectively J. B. Bury (1861–1927) and G. M. Trevelyan (1876–1962). In either case, however, the type of history under discussion was narrative history, which has dominated modern historiography until very recent times and was virtually the only kind of history known to the ancient world. According to Cicero, the celebrated Roman orator and statesman (106–43 BCE), the "father of history" was Herodotus (*De legibus,* On the Laws 1.5). Herodotus's work is long and discursive, building up gradually to the wars between Greece and Persia, which began in 490 BCE and are his main theme. Modern readers will be struck in particular by the amount of direct speech, such as that between Persian chiefs (7.8–18): how could Herodotus possibly transmit, apparently verbatim, conversations and discussions held at considerable length, in a foreign language, and in the closed confines of a foreign court? This does not look like "history" in our sense at all. The fact is, however, that Herodotus derived his manner of writing from the model of Homeric epic poetry. Half of the *Iliad* and two-thirds of the *Odyssey* are taken up with direct speech, which not only exhibits rhetorical refinement in itself but enjoys a subtle and complex relationship with the narrative in which it is embedded. Hence, one way in which Herodotus's work is rhetorical is that it contains a high proportion of direct speech.

Given Herodotus's position as the father of history, his practice helped to establish speech as a canonical element in classical historiography. The proportion of speech to narrative varies between historians, and naturally, between different books of the same historian. For example, in the case of the Roman historian Sallust (c.86–c.35 BCE) a quarter of his monograph *The War with Catiline* is taken up with direct speech, half as much again as his subsequent *Jugurthine War.* Sallust was one of those criticized for their speeches by the slightly later Roman historian Pompeius Trogus, although the precise grounds of his criticism (see Justin 38.3.11) are disputed. The Greek historian Polybius (c.200–118 BCE), who described the rise of Roman imperialism in a work of many volumes, criticized other historians for inventing speeches while practicing similar invention himself (e.g., 12.25a–25b and 36.1). Diodorus Siculus, a Greek historian who was roughly contemporary with Sallust, complained about the number and length of the speeches that some historians inserted into their works, saying that they cause too great an interruption of the narrative

(20.1.1–2.3). The classic example of a speechifying historian is Dionysius of Halicarnassus, who wrote in Greek and published the first book of his *Roman Antiquities* in 7 BCE. Dionysius was also a literary critic, and in his essay *On Thucydides* (18. 34–48), he makes it quite clear that such speeches were understood by their readers to be compositions by the historians themselves (see also Quintilian 10.1.101). When Jane Austen has the heroine of *Northanger Abbey* remark that "The speeches that are put into the heroes' mouths . . . must be invention," she not only recognizes the convention for what it is but attests to its enduring into at least the late eighteenth century.

Arnaldo Momigliano, one of the greatest and most learned historians of historical writing, acknowledged cheerfully that he "never worried if a historian chose to write in epic style or to introduce speeches into his account." Momigliano must mean that in his opinion direct speech is easily isolated and has no further implications beyond itself; and that, even if the relationship constructed by Herodotus between speech and narrative is as subtly integrated as it is in Homer, it is the "factual" narrative that determines the fictive speech. But how factual is the "factual" narrative?

The first historical work in which the word *historia* occurs is that of Herodotus, where its meaning varies from context to context: either "enquiry" or "information," or, perhaps, "(narrative) history." The first of these, a common meaning of the word in contemporary authors, is the most frequent (though the overall figures are small); and indeed, Herodotus's work is generally thought to be based on the autopsy and travels to which he makes regular reference. Yet a minority of recent scholars, building on doubts that were first expressed in antiquity and which then resurfaced in the nineteenth century, have argued that Herodotus's claims are not borne out—or are even disproved—by modern evidence; rather, they are simply literary strategies of a traditional type. If these arguments are correct (and they are fiercely disputed by more traditionalist scholars), it seems unsatisfactory to conclude that Herodotus intended to practice large-scale deception upon his readers, claiming to represent as historically true matters that he knew were not true at all. More plausible is the view that an "historical" text in the Greek world twenty-five hundred years ago was different from what "history" is today, and that there is an essential affinity between Herodotus's narrative and his invented speeches. If that is the case, it is perhaps not surprising that the most recent critics have started to apply the term *rhetorical* to Herodotus's work as a whole.

Herodotus's immediate successor was Thucydides, author of a contemporary account of the Peloponnesian War (431–404 BCE) between Athens and Sparta, whose modern reputation as the greatest of the classical historians is due partly to the magisterial assurance of his account and partly to his having included, in the preface to his work, the so-called chapter on method (1.22). In this famous chapter, perhaps the most discussed passage in the whole of Greek literature, Thucydides explains the compositional background to the speeches and events which his work contains. It is interesting that he deals with speeches (1.22.1) before events (1.22.2–3): this is no doubt a reflection of Athenian democratic practice, according to which every citizen had the right to address his fellow citizens in the assembly (*ekklēsia*) on matters of public policy and concern. As an Athenian himself, Thucydides was brought up to appreciate that discussion preceded action and that there was a close link between the enunciation of a policy and its implementation. Certainly his work exhibits a large number of formal speeches; sometimes the speeches are paired, one answering another as would happen in the *ekklēsia* or some similar forum; and always there is a highly complex relationship constructed between the speeches and the narrative. The question that has preoccupied scholars is whether, or to what extent, the speeches in Thucydides' work correspond to speeches that were actually delivered. Although the author appears to have provided the answer to this question in his preface, he has so expressed himself that his words have been interpreted to refer either to verbatim transcription or to almost total invention or to various combinations of both.

Thucydides' treatment of events is likewise problematic. Modern scholars have been impressed by the way in which in his preface he refers to autopsy, the questioning of eyewitnesses, the difficulties of the investigative process, and

the issues of bias and memory. But these seeming anticipations of "scientific" historiography sit uneasily in a preface that otherwise uses a range of standard rhetorical devices to "prove" the relative insignificance of all previous history (including the Trojan and Persian Wars), and to magnify the importance of the author's own subject, the Peloponnesian War, which he presents almost exclusively in terms of its unprecedented disasters and sufferings (1.23.1–3). A focus upon disaster and suffering is usually associated by scholars with various (now fragmentary) historians of the fourth and third centuries BCE who were criticized by Polybius and who have sometimes been said to represent a particular type of historiography misleadingly called "tragic history"; but Thucydides' preface makes it clear not only that this focus existed long before their time but also that it is another of the legacies that historiography inherited from the poetry of Homer.

Thucydides concludes his chapter on method by expressing the hope that he will have satisfied readers looking for "clarity" or "clearness" (1.22.4 *to saphes*). Almost all scholars interpret this term as a synonym for "the truth," although a very few have argued that Thucydides is referring to the narrative "vividness" for which he was praised by later authors. Essential elements of the linguistic creation of vividness (*enargeia*) are "turning the reader into a spectator" and bringing events "before the reader's eyes." In *How to Write History*, the only essay of its kind to have survived from antiquity, the second-century CE writer Lucian says that the ideal work of history is that which makes its reader think that "he is actually seeing what is being described" (p. 51). Plutarch (c.50–120 CE), the Greek biographer and philosopher, said of Thucydides that "in his writing he is constantly striving for this vividness [*enargeia*], wanting to turn his readers into spectators, as it were, and to reproduce in their minds the feelings of shock and disorientation which were experienced by those who actually viewed the events" (*Moralia* 347A).

A celebrated example of Thucydidean *enargeia* is his description of the battle in Syracuse harbor (7.70–1), but to say that he "turns the reader into a spectator" of the battle is of course a mere *façon de parler*. The Sophists, who were contemporary with Thucydides, insisted among other things that language is incapable of communicating reality. [*See* Sophists.] Thus Gorgias, a leading Sophist, maintained that "what a man speaks is speech . . . no[t] an object" (Aristotle, *On Melissus, Xenophanes and Gorgias* 980b1). An insistence on the limitations of the referential capacity of language is one of the hallmarks by which numerous intellectuals in the second half of the twentieth century may be distinguished (Roland Barthes is a classic example); but it has a lengthy pedigree and was recognized by the ancients themselves. Thus Diodorus wrote as follows in the late first century BCE (20.43.7):

> In this respect one might criticize history too, seeing that, whereas in life many different acts are performed at the same moment, those writing them up find it necessary to interrupt their narrative and to apportion a plurality of times to simultaneous performances contrary to nature, with the result that, whereas the truth of actions encapsulates the event, their writing-up, deprived as it is of a similar capacity, does indeed represent occurrences but falls far short of their true disposition.

Hence, while historians in antiquity were encouraged to turn their readers into spectators of the past, they were aware at the same time that their medium of language cannot properly reflect or recreate the past—a consideration that gives an additional twist to the point with which we began, namely that a past event cannot be transmitted except in a verbalized form.

Classical historians were nevertheless in no way inhibited from vivid description, and those who were best able to turn their readers into spectators were those who could visualize events for themselves. "Visualization" (*phantasia*) was long a formal part of rhetorical training and may be illustrated by the *suasoria*, which was used as an educational device for young men at Rome. [*See* Controversia and suasoria.] In this type of speech, a development from Greek predecessors, one was required to speak on a set theme in a given historical situation, urging a character from history that he should, or should not, embark on a particular course of action. As we know from Quintilian, who professed rhetoric at Rome in the first century CE, one such theme was whether Julius Caesar should attack Britain. Discussing the kinds

of question that might occur in a *suasoria*, Quintilian continues (7.4.2):

> [F]or example, if Caesar is deliberating whether to attack Britain, one must bring into consideration what the nature of the Ocean is, whether Britain is an island (for that was unknown at the time), what its area is, and what number of troops is required for the invasion.

A young man about to debate this theme would have to visualize himself in Gaul in the middle of the first century BCE in the presence of the great conqueror, whom he would exhort in one direction or another.

Now the requirement to visualize oneself in a historical situation seems very close to the principle formulated by R. G. Collingwood, who, in the words of W. H. Dray, believed that "historical understanding requires a re-enactment of past experience or a re-thinking of past thought." Collingwood is a particularly interesting scholar in that he was not only an archaeologist-historian and author of *Roman Britain* (rev. ed., Oxford, 1932) but also a philosopher of history and author of the celebrated *The Idea of History* (Oxford, 1946). In yet a third book, *Roman Britain and the English Settlements* (2d ed., Oxford, 1937), he provides a practical example of his ideas of re-enactment:

> Caesar was on the horns of a dilemma. So long as Gaul was restless, Britain, a refuge and reservoir of disaffection within a few hours' sail, was an added danger: for the sake of Gaulish security, therefore, Britain must be made harmless. But so long as the restlessness of Gaul was acute a campaign across the Channel was hazardous: it was an incitement to revolt in Gaul while the Roman armies were overseas. Either way there was a risk. . . . The question which risk to take could be decided only in the light of an estimate of possible gains; that is, in the light of an answer to the question what a British campaign might hope to achieve. (pp. 32–33)

Here Collingwood has set before himself the very issue that we know was debated by young men at Rome: since his use of "free indirect discourse" (as it is now called) suggests that he has put himself in Caesar's position, his practice strongly resembles that close relative of the *suasoria* that is known as *prosōpopoeia,* whereby a speaker would impersonate an historical figure. [*See* Prosōpopoeia.]

It has been said that Collingwood regarded Giambattista Vico (1668–1744) as the founder of the theory of history. Vico was professor of rhetoric at the university of Naples for more than forty years, during which time he produced his most famous work, *New Science* (first published 1725); and Collingwood seems to have seen in Vico some kind of forerunner of himself, attributing to him the view that "the historian can reconstruct in his own mind the process by which these things [such as law] have been created by men in the past." On the other hand, there appears to be no evidence that Collingwood was, or believed himself to be, influenced by classical rhetoric; and the seeming resemblance between Quintilian's debater and the modern historian serves only to underline the difference between ancient and modern.

It is clear from the context that Collingwood was genuinely concerned to understand, in the way he considered best, the circumstances of Caesar's invasion of Britain, which he saw exclusively in terms of political and military risk. The first topic of Quintilian's debater, on the other hand, would be "the nature of the Ocean." The Ocean was the great sea or river that in ancient thought encircled the known world and of which the North Sea and English Channel were supposed to be a part. It was a quasi-mythical subject, inviting the graphic description of sea monsters, wild storms, and voyaging into the unknown where the world ends. These were the kinds of thing to be elaborated by Quintilian's debater; and, though the debater is not himself a historian, Quintilian's statement elsewhere that impersonation (*prosōpopoeia*) "is of the greatest use to future poets and writers of history" (3.8.49) is highly revealing: unlike Collingwood, the classical historian would put himself in Caesar's position by transferring to historiography the methods and techniques he had learned in the schools of rhetoric. Collingwood's is a genuine inquiry for the truth; but rhetoric "does not pose questions of truth," as Momigliano in an essay on historicism pointed out; "[a]bove all, rhetoric does not entail techniques for the research of truth" (*Essays in Ancient and Modern Historiography,* Oxford, 1977). Quin-

tilian's debater would simply search for what was required to be said in the situation given to him, the implied theory being that this was somehow already "there," though latent; indeed the situation itself might be utterly counterfactual, in that one could be obliged to argue toward a decision that in reality had never been reached or acted upon (such as Caesar's not having invaded Britain). These distinctions between ancient and modern may be clarified by a famous passage of Cicero.

In his dialogue *De oratore,* which appeared in 55 BCE but is set some decades earlier in 91 BCE, Cicero depicts a small group of distinguished orators and politicians in conversation with one another. It is generally accepted that one of these speakers, M. Antonius, is in some sense the mouthpiece of Cicero himself; and, when the conversation turns to the writing of history, Antonius speaks as follows (2.63–64):

> [T]he actual superstructure consists of content [*rebus*] and style [*verbis*]. It is in the nature of content [*rerum*], on the one hand, that you require a chronological order of events and topographical descriptions; and also that you need—since in the treatment of important and memorable achievements the reader expects (i) intentions, (ii) the events themselves, and (iii) consequences—in the case of (i) to indicate whether you approve of the intentions, of (ii) to reveal not only what was said or done but also in what manner, and of (iii) to explain all the reasons, whether they be of chance or intelligence or impetuousness, and also to give not only the achievements of any famous protagonist but also his life and character. The nature of style [*verborum*] and type of discourse, on the other hand, require amplitude and mobility, with a slow and regular fluency and without any of the roughness and prickliness associated with the law-courts.

Surely this is one of the most important passages in any discussion of classical historiography, although its meaning and significance have become matters of controversy. According to the traditional view, Cicero in the main section of the passage is not expressly advocating a type of historical exposition different from that commonly employed by modern political historians; it is a usual corollary of this view that any "rhetorical"

element is confined to Cicero's concluding remarks on style, which, perhaps surprisingly in the
light of the relative space devoted to each topic,
is quite often said to be Cicero's primary concern.
A very different interpretation of the passage,
however, is suggested by the context from which
the passage has been extracted.

Antonius has remarked, just previously (2.62),
that writing history is a task for an orator but that
he cannot find a separate treatment of the subject
set down in the rules of rhetoric. It is to supply
this deficiency that he formulates the rules quoted
above, after which he concludes (2.64) by repeating the point with which he began: namely, that
these rules are numerous and important but they
are nowhere to be found in books entitled *Art of
Rhetoric*. If, then, history is to be written by an
orator and Antonius has supplied rules for the
writing of history that one might have expected
to find in rhetorical handbooks, it seems to follow
that these rules are rhetorical rules and hence that
the whole of the extracted passage is to be seen
in rhetorical terms.

Using a building metaphor ("superstructure"),
Antonius begins by dividing the writing of history into content and style. This division has
been taken over directly from rhetorical theory
and practice: "every speech consists of content
and style," says Quintilian (8 preface 6). Likewise
each of the matters listed under "content" corresponds to those with which an orator was expected to deal in the narrative section (*narratio*)
of a forensic speech: a good example is the "chronological order of events," discussed in identical
terminology in Cicero's work of rhetorical theory
entitled *De inventione* (1.29). In other words, Cicero has simply transferred to historiography the
various rules and requirements that conventionally applied to an oratorical *narratio*. It is scarcely
surprising that Lucian, in his *How to Write History*,
should say that "the body of a work of history is
simply an extended *narratio*" (p. 55).

Moreover Quintilian, having said that "every
speech consists of content and style," proceeds
immediately to add that "with reference to content we must study invention" (8 preface 6). Invention, one of the five techniques in which
speakers were expected to be expert, was defined
by Cicero as "the devising of matter true or lifelike which will make a case appear convincing"

(*De inventione* 1.9); and what is convincing is
"that which for the most part happens or which
does not strain credibility or which contains
within itself an approximation to either of these,
whether it be true or false" (*De inventione* 1.46).
[*See* Invention.] Now, since invention determines
content (as we have just seen confirmed by the
fact that the "chronological order of events" is
discussed in Cicero's *De inventione*), and since the
constituent elements of content have been transferred from an oratorical *narratio* to historiography (as we have also just seen), the implications
of this transference for historical writing are very
considerable: any element of content, such as the
"chronological order of events," may but need
not be true; the minimum requirement was that
it should be lifelike and convincing.

When Cicero, at the end of the quoted extract,
moves from content to style, he advises the writer
of history to use a different type of style from that
usually adopted in the law courts. [*See* Style.] The
phrases "amplitude and mobility" and "a slow
and regular fluency" suggest that he means the
Herodotean style, since these are the terms in
which Herodotus's writing is conventionally described. The choice of style, like the choice of individual words, was an important part of rhetoric,
and historians sought particular resonances by
choosing one style rather than another. Sallust a
few years later would disregard Cicero's advice in
this respect, preferring instead to imitate the
brevity and inconcinnity of Thucydides and
thereby to imbue his own works with the spirit
of disillusionment by which Thucydides' history
is characterized. Early in the second century CE,
Sallust in his turn would be imitated by Tacitus,
whose difficult and awkward style in the *Annals*
perfectly complements his jaundiced view of Roman imperial history.

Thus, style is not a synonym for rhetoric, as it
is often represented to be, but is a part of rhetoric;
and rhetoric, if the passage of Cicero is any guide,
is not, like this or that choice of style, an option
to be taken up or laid down by the historian at
will: rhetoric is a precondition of historical writing in the classical world, and everything that
constitutes the content of a historical work will
be driven by rhetoric and permeated by rhetoric.
This may be confirmed by the fact that in another
of his works, Cicero links historiography and pan-

egyric as examples of epideictic or "display" oratory, and says that closest to epideictic oratory is "historiography, in which the narrative is elaborate and regions or battles are regularly described" (*Orator* 37, 66). [*See* Epideictic genre; *and* Panegyric.] Here the great man is offering an alternative perspective to that of forensic oratory (with which epideictic had much in common), but the alternative is no less rhetorical.

Rhetorical historiography persisted throughout later antiquity and the Middle Ages. "To ask why medieval writers claimed that what appears to us obviously invented material was true is another reminder of the incommensurability of our cultures," as Ruth Morse has pointed out; "[b]ooks which now seem to belong to the category fiction once belonged to the category history." But in the later decades of the twentieth century it also came to be argued that even nineteenth-century history is also profoundly rhetorical in nature. The argument is associated above all with the American scholar Hayden White, whose hypothesis, as summarized by Lionel Gossman, is that "history is a linguistic and rhetorical artifact constrained by a genre rule specifying reference to conventionally agreed upon historical facts." In *Metahistory: the Historical Imagination in Nineteenth-Century Europe* (Baltimore, 1973), the first and most well known of a series of books, White considered the work of four major historians: Jules Michelet (1798–1874), historian of France and the French Revolution; Leopold von Ranke (1795–1886), whom we have already encountered as the founding father of modern historiography; Alexis de Tocqueville (1805–1859), the historian of America; and Jakob Burckhardt (1818–1897), the historian of Renaissance Italy. Each of these, in White's view, "emplotted" his work according to the "mode" of one or other nonhistorical genre: "Michelet cast all of his histories in the Romantic mode, Ranke cast his in the Comic mode, Tocqueville used the Tragic mode, and Burckhardt used Satire." White summed up his general position three years later in an essay entitled "The Fictions of Factual Representation" (reprinted in *Tropics of Discourse: Essays in Cultural Criticism*, Baltimore, 1978):

> Although historians and writers of fiction may be interested in different kinds of events, both

the forms of their respective discourses and their aims in writing are often the same. In addition, in my view, the techniques or strategies that they use in the composition of their discourses can be shown to be substantially the same, however different they may appear on a purely surface, or dictional, level of their texts.

Such a narrowing of the gap between historiography and realistic fiction not unnaturally provoked a swift reaction from historians, and an entire supplementary volume of the periodical *History and Theory* was devoted to White's work (vol. 19, "Metahistory: Six Critiques," 1980).

One historian to react was the redoubtable Momigliano, to whom reference has already been made more than once, and whose extraordinary learning allowed him to survey the whole sweep of historical writing from its very earliest days to the most recent. In two papers belonging to the years 1981 and 1982, he attempted to refute Hayden White by using two principal tactics that seem mutually exclusive. On the one hand, he denied that rhetoric played any role at all in historiography: "The historian works on evidence. Rhetoric is not his business." On the other hand, he argued that White's hypotheses were not nearly so novel as some supposed: "rhetoric has long been for the historian an effective (never essential) device to be used with caution." This latter statement alludes to a small group of historians who were said in antiquity to have been influenced by the Greek rhetorician Isocrates (436–338 BCE) and who used to be described by modern scholars as representatives of "Isocratean" or "rhetorical" historiography. By alluding to this small group, Momigliano is able to create the initial impression that "rhetorical historiography" was a relatively minor and self-contained phenomenon that sprang up well after the principal features of historiography proper had been established by Herodotus and Thucydides. Of course, so important a figure as Cicero said much later that historiography "is a task which is singularly well suited to an orator" (*De legibus* 1.5): this statement implies that "rhetorical historiography" was neither minor nor self-contained, but Momigliano is able to cope with this (to him) unwelcome implication because he sees rhetoric as no more than a "device" or series of "devices" that the historian can either use "with caution" or choose not to use at all. For Hayden White, however, rhetoric is intrinsic to narrative and hence also to historical writing.

Although White's position thus seems very similar to that put forward by Cicero in the extract from his *De oratore* quoted earlier, there is an important distinction between them. That there is no difference between history and fiction seems not to be an inevitable consequence of White's arguments; on the contrary, as White himself remarks, "The events reported in a novel can be invented in a way that they cannot be (or are not supposed to be) in a history." If we take as example the French Revolution, Ann Rigney notes that at least seven prominent histories thereof had been published by midway through the nineteenth century: "So many histories, so many French Revolutions— each one claiming to represent the French Revolution itself." Such differences arise because the individual historians have selected and treated events differently, and it was Hayden White's concern to shift attention away from the (then conventional) emphasis on events to the selection and treatment of events by historians. But the fact that literary analysis of this kind is applied to histories in the same way as to novels does not of course mean that one believes histories to be no different at all from novels.

The events of the French Revolution allow considerable scope for difference because they are so numerous; but, if we move forward to the twentieth century, the events surrounding the Bolshevik Revolution are even more numerous: the more recent the history, the more numerous the events (because of the increased availability of evidence). Hence E. H. Carr (1892–1982), author of the classic *What is History?* (London, 1961), devoted three of the fourteen volumes of his *History of Soviet Russia* (London, 1950–1978) to the Bolshevik Revolution, but ignored, in the words of R. J. Evans, "the military conflict of the civil war, the brutal suppression, murder, torture, and imprisonment in the Gulag Archipelago, of opposition by the Cheka, Lenin's secret police, and all the other aspects of the subject that involved what one might call defeated alternatives to the Bolshevik vision of the future." One scholar has maintained that "an open-minded and judicious handling of the evidence" is one of the "great strengths" of Carr's history; but it is more plausible to conclude that Carr suppressed evidence and omitted events that did not conform to the pro-Soviet view he was anxious to promote. Clearly it would be possible to admit such evidence and to select such events, leading to an entirely different history of the decade in question. Somewhat analogously, Tacitus's disillusioned account of the reign of the emperor Tiberius (14–37 CE) in Books 1–6 of his *Annals* is entirely different from that provided by the contemporary historian Velleius Paterculus.

Though written roughly a century later, Tacitus's account of Tiberius is many times longer than that of Velleius, and it is generally assumed by traditionalist scholars that he relied upon primary sources for his narrative of what was the relatively recent past. Conversely, the Roman historian Livy (59 BCE–17 CE), who began his history of Rome before the foundation of the city (the traditional date of which is 753 BCE) and took five volumes (almost four hundred pages in the standard Oxford edition) to reach the year 390 BCE, was in quite a different position: how could he possibly have written so much about a period buried centuries in the past and lacking any modern method for storing and retrieving information? Many scholars believe that much of Livy's narrative cannot be "true" in any genuinely historical sense, but rather, illustrates the kind of lifelike and convincing invention discussed by Cicero in his *De oratore*. It is perhaps significant that Dionysius of Halicarnassus, a contemporary of Livy, took more than seven times as long to describe the first eighty years of Rome's history: presumably the difference resides not in the availability of evidence but in the application of rhetorical invention. Since it is difficult to distinguish the lifelike or convincing from the true unless there is some external evidence, and since there is relatively little external evidence in the case of early Roman history, we cannot know the extent or precise areas of Livy's invention; but that much of what he wrote in his early narrative resembles (in our terms) a historical novel seems likely enough. The difference between ancient and modern, however, is that classical historians took for granted the validity of a fictional element which, as Hayden White himself has made clear, a modern historian would not countenance.

It would be mistaken to conclude from the validity of this fictional element that classical historians were somehow less serious about history and the writing of history than are their modern counterparts. No one who devoted the whole of his working life to producing 142 volumes, as did Livy, could be described as anything other than serious about his project. But seriousness can take many forms. E. H. Carr was at least as serious-minded as Livy, but we have seen that he eschewed entirely that objectivity for which all historians are supposed to aim. Absolute objectivity is of course no more than an ideal, since all writers of history will have their own point of view; but the eighteenth-century German theologian J. M. Chladenius drew a reasonable distinction between "point of view," from which no one is immune, and outright "bias," which historians ought to avoid. Classical historians showed themselves particularly sensitive on this issue, disclaiming in their prefaces any suggestion of prejudice or bias with reference to the characters of history whom they treated in their works. Such sensitivity was natural for practitioners of a genre so thoroughly inseparable from rhetoric, which, as was maintained by the fifth-century BCE Sophist Protagoras, had the capability of making "the weaker cause the stronger."

History, as the twentieth century has shown only too well, can be placed at the service of any cause, however ignoble; but this simply attests to the fact that the past and the manner of its recording are recognized by many societies as being of fundamental importance. In his *De oratore* (2.36), Cicero described history as "the witness to time, the light on reality, the life of memory, the mistress of life, the messenger of antiquity"—adding "whose voice but the orator's entrusts history to immortality?"

[*See also* Classical rhetoric.]

BIBLIOGRAPHY

Canary, Robert H., and Henry Kozicki, eds. *The Writing of History: Literary Form and Historical Understanding.* Madison, Wis., 1978. Essays on historiography, narrative form, and the nature of representation.

Carr, E. H. *What is History?* London, 1961. Classic book that helped to trigger the modern interest in the writing of history.

Dray, William H. *History as Re-Enactment: R. G. Colling-wood's Idea of History.* Oxford, 1995. An explication of Collingwood's work on re-enactment and the historical imagination.

Elton, G. R. *The Practice of History.* Sydney, 1967. Classic riposte to Carr.

Evans, Richard J. *In Defence of History.* London, 1997. Excellent and up-to-date discussion with wonderful bibliography.

Ginzburg, Carlo. *History, Rhetoric, and Proof.* Hanover, N.H., 1999. Chapters on Aristotle, Lorenzo Valla, and Jesuit historiography.

Gossman, Lionel. *Between History and Literature.* Cambridge, Mass., 1990. An important collection of essays on the relationship between historiography and literary criticism, with a focus on the Romantic historians.

Grafton, Anthony. *The Footnote: a Curious History.* Cambridge, Mass., 1997. Contains much of interest on the history of historiography and the "culture of erudition."

Herodotus and the Invention of History, guest edited by Deborah Boedeker. *Arethusa* 20. 1–2. (1987). Special issue on the Greek historian Herodotus's status as the "father of history."

Hornblower, Simon, ed. *Greek Historiography.* Oxford, 1994. Valuable introductory essay by the editor. An attempt to outline new procedures for historiography.

LaCapra, Dominick. "Rhetoric and History." In *History and Criticism,* pp. 15–44. Ithaca, N.Y., 1985.

Laird, Andrew. "Fictions of Authority: Discourse and Epistemology in Historical Narrative." In *Powers of Expression, Expressions of Power,* pp. 116–152. Oxford, 1999.

Momigliano, Arnaldo. "The Rhetoric of History and the History of Rhetoric: On Hayden White's Tropes" [1981] and "Considerations On History in an Age of Ideologies" [1982], in *Settimo Contributo alla Storia degli Studi Classici e del Mondo Antico,* pp. 49–59, 253–269. Rome, 1984. Responses to Hayden White's work on the rhetorical basis of historiography.

Morse, Ruth. *Truth and Convention in the Middle Ages: Rhetoric, Representation, and Reality.* Cambridge, U.K., 1991. An exploration of the role of rhetorical invention in medieval historiography.

Rebenich, Stefan. "Historical Prose." In *Handbook of Classical Rhetoric in the Hellenistic Period 330 B.C.– A.D. 400.* Edited by Stanley E. Porter, pp. 265–337. Leiden, 1997. Dull but heavily annotated.

Rigney, Ann. *The Rhetoric of Historical Representation: Three Narrative Histories of the French Revolution.* Cambridge, U.K., 1990. The introduction provides a most helpful survey of modern debate.

White, Hayden. *The Content of the Form: Narrative Dis-

course and Historical Representation. Baltimore, 1990. First published 1987. Eight essays on the nature of history as narrative.

White, Hayden. *Figural Realism: Studies in the Mimesis Effect.* Baltimore, 1999. Essays on the treatment of history in recent literary critical discourse.

Wiseman, T. P. *Clio's Cosmetics.* Leicester, 1979. Brilliant and radical appraisal of early Roman historiography.

Woodman, A. J. *Rhetoric in Classical Historiography.* London, 1988. A study of the rhetorical aspects of the works of Thucydides, Cicero, Sallust, Livy, and Tacitus.

—A. J. WOODMAN

HOMILETICS is the art of preaching; its history is perhaps best understood as shifting conceptions of a homiletic triad that consists of the scriptural text, the preacher, and the preacher's audience. Each conception depends on distinct yet recurring beliefs about human nature, the intelligibility of scripture, the function of the institutional church, and the accessibility of God and divine truths. Thus, homiletics as a rhetorical art influences and is influenced by psychological, hermeneutical, ecclesiastical, and theological doctrines that reemerge, in differing combinations and with differing emphases, throughout the Christian tradition.

Although the homiletic triad recalls other triads from the Greco-Roman rhetorical tradition (especially Aristotle's *logos, ēthos,* and *pathos*), the most distinctive element of Christian preaching—the discussion of a scriptural text—has its origin in the rabbinical sermons delivered in synagogues. The term *homiletics* comes from the Greek noun *homilia* or "conversation" (*sermo* in Latin). It designates the relatively straightforward and informal oral interpretation of a scriptural text and stands in contradistinction to a *logos* (*oratio* in Latin), which denotes a more self-consciously rhetorical composition modeled on secular forms such as the encomium, invective, and apology. Origen (c.185–254 CE), a Neoplatonic theologian, and John Chrysostom (c.347–407 CE), the patron saint of preachers, are usually credited with elevating the *homilia* to a higher level of rhetorical sophistication. Origen identified nonliteral (moral, allegorical, theological) levels of meaning in Holy Scripture, which allowed him to make the dead letter of scripture

speak to the lived spiritual experiences of his listeners. Chrysostom composed eloquent expository homilies on Old and New Testament texts that employ a more grammatical and historical method of scriptural interpretation and, like his numerous topical sermons, vividly depict the religious and social conflicts facing early Christian communities.

De doctrina christiana (On Christian Learning; completed in 427 CE) by Augustine (354–430 CE) has been called the first and most important Christian rhetorical treatise because it adapts, some say distorts, Ciceronian rhetorical principles for homiletic purposes. In its first three books, Augustine discusses rules for discovering the meaning of scripture and posits the rule of *caritas,* charity or love (for Augustine, the double love of God and neighbor) as the ultimate criterion for judging the validity of an interpretation. In its final book, he defends the Christian use of classical rhetoric, calling it a potent weapon against the enemies of the nascent church. Echoing Cicero, he writes that the preacher's three duties are to teach, delight, and move; and that these three duties correspond to the three traditional levels of style: the simple teaches, the middle delights, and the grand moves.

The period between the late fifth and the twelfth century is noted for the codification of existing homiletic techniques rather than the invention of new ones. In the Eastern Church, homilies and panegyric discourses by Chrysostom, Gregory of Nazianzus (c.330–389 CE), and other Greek Fathers were copied down, imitated, and incorporated into the liturgical calendar. In the Western Church, the same period witnessed the prolific production of homiletic aids—such as *homilaria* (collections of printed sermons by famous preachers to be read aloud at the pulpit), postils, concordances, gatherings of *exempla*— meant to aid inexperienced or incompetent preachers. These materials helped to canonize the sermons and rhetorical strategies of the Church Fathers. [*See* Exemplum; *and* Panegyric.]

The first major innovation in the sermon form and the handling of its scriptural text arose with the medieval *ars praedicandi,* which theorized the "thematic" (or "university" or "modern") sermon as a method of treating any scriptural text or religious topic: the preacher reads a short scriptural passage (the "theme"), divides it into members (specific words, images, or subjects, usually in groups of three), and makes further subdivisions, which are in turn elaborated upon using citations and *exempla* from scripture, saints' lives, and even pagan literature. Unlike the "ancient" sermon, which offered a running, oral, scriptural commentary, the thematic sermon highlighted the preacher's skill (or lack thereof) in invention and arrangement; it also betrayed the influence of Aristotle's newly rediscovered writings on logic (although many *artes praedicandi* incorporated terms from the Ciceronian *partes orationis*). A later sermon form, influenced by Ramist dialectic and popularized by the puritan William Perkins's *The Arte of Prophesying* (Lat. 1592, Engl. 1607), divided the sermon into the explication of a scriptural text, the statement of doctrinal points, and the application of these points to the "manners" of the audience; these parts were frequently subdivided further. This schematic text–doctrine–application structure encouraged outlining and allowed preachers to avoid the twin perils of reading aloud a previously written sermon and of preaching *ex tempore;* the same structure helped listeners to remember and reconstruct the sermon. [*See overview article on* Medieval rhetoric.]

Later homileticians influenced by the Renaissance and the Reformation complained that such sermons relied too heavily on ingenious scholastic subtleties, crumbled the sacred text into mere dictionary forms and innumerable divisions, and (especially with the thematic sermon) encouraged the use of profane *exempla* to elaborate the written Word of God. Treatises by Desiderius Erasmus, Philip Melanchthon, and numerous Catholic rhetoricians in the sixteenth century, by Bartholomew Keckermann, Gerardus Vossius, and François Fénelon in the seventeenth, Hugh Blair, George Campbell, and Richard Whately in the eighteenth, and Charles Broadus in the nineteenth all modified the standards of contemporaneous rhetorical theory to include sermons, in structure and style if not in substance and with strictures of varying severity for sticking to the scriptural text at hand. Homiletics increasingly became a species of rhetoric, preaching became pulpit oratory, and sermons became moral discourses. Less bound to classical rhetorical models,

zealous fundamentalist and twentieth-century homileticians adapted various inductive, narrative-based sermon strategies derived, respectively, from biblical models (jeremiad, parable, Pauline exhortation, revelation), and theories of mass communication.

Opponents of the historical affiliation of rhetoric and homiletics note that, at several points in the New Testament, the preacher is figured as a herald (*kēryx*) who proclaims God's message (*kērygma*) free of rhetorical embellishment and cultural accommodation. This figure has inspired various orthodox movements to distinguish, sometimes vehemently, between the preacher as God's herald and the preacher as (to use other biblical metaphors) ambassador, steward, or shepherd who prudently accommodates and applies divine truths to a fallen audience's intellectual and spiritual capacity. Because many Church Fathers were celebrated orators, they took pains to distinguish the Christian preacher from the pagan orator more in terms of his motives than his methods. Chrysostom, for example, who before taking orders studied rhetoric under the notoriously pagan Sophist Libanius (314–393 CE), decried those preachers who sought the admiring applause of their listeners as would an ambitious declaimer. If the preacher uses the art of rhetoric, he must hide it. Chrysostom and other Greek Fathers also developed the doctrine of divine accommodation that provided a key theological justification of the preacher's rhetorical artistry: just as Jesus Christ, the divine *logos,* became flesh (1.14) and took human form for the benefit of humankind, so too could Christian orators (like Saint Paul before them) imitate this divine accommodation and prudently adapt God's Word to suit their fallen listeners in various rhetorical situations. While justifying the preacher's rhetorical methods, the Church Fathers also note that the example of the preacher's moral behavior while away from the pulpit often has a greater persuasive force than his verbal eloquence. To this view, Augustine adds that a bad man may compose and deliver a doctrinally-sound sermon and that the same sermon can later be recited to better effect by a good man. This latter statement anticipates the possible charge (a version of the Donatist heresy) that the efficacy of Christian preaching is located in the preacher's holiness rather than in God's grace or in the working of the Spirit.

The splintering of the church following the Reformation brought into question the source of a preacher's authority: must he be appointed (and presumably trained) by an established church, elected by the congregation he is to serve, or impelled by Spirit and witnessed by the testimony of his conscience? In order to mediate between possible disparities between a preacher's ecclesiastical and spiritual authority, Christian rhetoricians adopted the classical principle that only the moved speaker is able to move an audience (cf. Quintilian, *Institutio oratoria,* first century CE, 6.2.5–7) while adding the Holy Spirit to the equation: only the preacher whose heart is inflamed by the Spirit is able to inflame the hearts of his listeners. The authority given to the speaker's *ēthos*—his personality, sense of calling, previous spiritual experiences—in later generations licensed the preaching to groups traditionally occluded from the pulpits of mainstream churches (e.g., women and African Americans) and allowed them to champion social reform in their sermons. In the nineteenth century, the character and presence of the preacher were emphasized—as in Phillips Brooks's (1835–1893) definition of preaching as "truth through personality"—and this emphasis created figures as different as the solemn Victorian pulpit orator and charismatic American tent revivalist. This same emphasis also prompted neo-orthodox countermovements, such as the one led by the Swiss theologian Karl Barth (1886–1968). He denounced the idea that the preacher's primary task was to reveal, convey, or adapt divine truths to fit a particular rhetorical situation; the preacher must obey, rather than clarify or apply, the Word of God. In preaching, the preacher does not bring us to Jesus, He comes to us. Homiletics does not belong with the art of rhetoric, but rather with biblical studies and church dogmatics. [*See* Ēthos.]

The audience in homiletic theory is usually distinguished from those of two ancillary ministries: missionary preaching aimed at persuading individuals hostile to or ignorant of the Christian faith; and *catēchēsis* aimed at explaining core doctrinal beliefs. But faith can lapse and doctrines can be misunderstood or forgotten, so the audi-

ence that is implied in most homiletic theory (both converted and indoctrinated) requires admonition, consolation, and exhortation to proper conduct and to strong faith. The audience can also be thought of as either a congregation of believers or as discrete individuals. As a congregation, it forms a kind of microcosm of humanity, possessing members with diverse strengths and weaknesses. The widely-disseminated treatise entitled *Pastoral Care* by Gregory the Great (c.540–604 CE), for example, catalogs methods for admonishing three dozen opposing character types (men and women, the humble and the proud, even those who should preach but do not and those who should not preach but do). In this context, preaching targets the conduct and the beliefs of individual members in the hope of edifying and maintaining the integrity of the worldly church. Preaching takes its place alongside other rites of public worship—the liturgy and the sacraments—and becomes a mark of the true church on earth.

But preaching has always had as its ultimate objective the cure of souls; it is the mantra of preachers that "faith comes from what is heard, and what is heard comes by the preaching of Christ" (*Rm.* 10.17, RSV). Sermons address the so-called inner man. Preachers need and in their sermons help to form (pessimistically) inveterate sinners struggling toward heaven or (optimistically) unperfected saints sojourning on earth. Usually the goal is to elicit some sort of nonrational response, to stir the heart instead of or in addition to the head. Augustine observes that a tear in a listener's eye is a sign of a persuasive sermon (centuries later, Alan of Lille, c.1128–1202, would agree, but add that nothing dries so quickly as a tear); post-Reformation homileticians stressed the individual's affective response to the Word preached and elaborated techniques for prompting it; preachers in the Age of Reason targeted the emotions and the imagination as a mechanism for goading the apprehending mind into action; eighteenth-century revivalists employed theatrical tactics (as explicated by the elocutionary movement), and modern evangelists use the strategies of mass communication in order to inspire awakenings, conversions, and rebirths. But preaching poses the additional challenge of discerning the true source of this emotional response: comfort at hearing the Gospel and terror at hearing the Law can be claimed as evidence either of spiritual regeneration or of spiritual lethargy, depending on how one views the process or event of salvation. Ultimately, homiletics, like other rhetorical arts, requires the management of doubt, especially doubt about the burning question: "What shall I do to be saved?"

[*See also* Hermeneutics; *and* Religion.]

BIBLIOGRAPHY

Barth, Karl. *Homiletics.* Translated by Geoffrey W. Bromiley and Donald E. Daniels. Louisville, Ky., 1991. Succinct, polemical statement of neo-orthodox attack on rhetorical homiletics with brief survey of earlier German theorists.

Buttrick, David. *Homiletic: Moves and Structures.* Philadelphia, 1987. Influential modern treatment with extensive bibliography.

Fant, C. E., Jr. and W. M. Pinson, Jr. *20 Centuries of Great Preaching: An Encyclopedia of Preaching.* 13 vols. Waco, Tex., 1971.

Hirst, Russel. "*Ethos* and the Conservative Tradition in Nineteenth-Century American Protestant Homiletics." In *Ethos: New Essays in Rhetorical and Critical Theory,* edited by James S. Baumlin and Tita French Baumlin, pp. 293–318. Dallas, Tex., 1994.

Kennedy, George A. *Classical Rhetoric and its Christian and Secular Tradition from Ancient to Modern Times.* 2d ed., revised and expanded. Chapel Hill, N.C., 1999.

Lischer, Richard, ed. *Theories of Preaching: Selected Readings in the Homiletical Tradition.* Durham, N.C., 1987. Useful anthology weighted toward nineteenth- and twentieth-century examples.

Murphy, James J. *Rhetoric in the Middle Ages: A History of Rhetorical Theory from Saint Augustine to the Renaissance.* Berkeley, 1974. The best survey of the medieval *ars dictaminis.*

Osborn, Ronald E. *Folly of God: The Rise of Christian Preaching,* vol. 1, *A History of Christian Preaching,* Saint Louis, 1999. Surveys the Greco-Roman rhetorical tradition and preaching through the third century CE.

Resner, André, Jr. *Preacher and Cross: Person and Message in Theology and Rhetoric.* Grand Rapids, Mich., 1999. Focuses on *ēthos* in patristic and twentieth-century homiletics.

Shuger, Debora K. *Sacred Rhetoric: The Christian Grand Style in the English Renaissance.* Princeton, 1988. Contains an extensive discussion of Neo-Latin Christian rhetorical theory and its sources.

Spencer, H. Leith. *English Preaching in the Late Middle Ages.* Oxford, 1993. Contains a lucid discussion of the distinction between "thematic" and "ancient" sermons.

—GREGORY KNEIDEL

HUMANISM. Humanism is one of the most characteristic traits of the European Renaissance, to a greater or lesser extent affecting all aspects of the culture of that period, which extends approximately from 1300 to 1600 CE.

Although in current discourse the term *humanism* often denotes an emphasis on human values in general, Renaissance humanism is, in the wake of most nineteenth- and twentieth-century historians, to be understood as that particular concern with the study and imitation of classical antiquity, which is typical of the period and finds its expression in scholarship, education, and in many other areas, including the arts and sciences. During the fourteenth and early fifteenth centuries, humanism was centered in Italy. It spread to the rest of Europe, apart from a few earlier episodes, only during the fifteenth century and especially the sixteenth century. Whereas early Italian humanism had its own medieval antecedents, eastern and northern manifestations of humanism are much indebted to Italian influences but assumed in each country some individual traits that reflected, at least in part, the medieval traditions of the particular country, which differed in turn from those of other countries, including Italy.

The modern term *humanism,* current since the early nineteenth century, is derived from the term *umanista,* and was coined in the late fifteenth century to designate a teacher and student of the "humanities" or *studia humanitatis.* The Latin word *humanitas,* in English *humanity,* is semantically related to Greek *paideia,* education, and *philanthrōpia,* love of mankind. As such, the word is indicative of an attitude of mind that attaches prime importance to man, the development of his faculties, and respect for human values at large, especially benevolence, kindness, and sympathy, opposed as these latter notions are to the bestial and, if less conspicuously so in classical Greek and Roman writers, to the divine. The term *humanitas* first occurred in 85 BCE in the pseudo-Ciceronian *Rhetorica ad Herennium,* in the sense suggested and in an even wider application, associating it, for instance, with a "liberal education." The word *humanity* was used with great frequency by the Roman orator, philosopher, and statesman Cicero (106–43 BCE) himself (e.g., *Pro Archia* 1.1–3.4), whereas after him, a Roman author like Aulus Gellius (c.123–c.165 CE) conceived of it in narrower terms of benignity and clemency (*Noctes Atticae* 13.17). In between, there was a rich unfolding of the concept of "humanity" in classical Latin literature that resurfaced with Italian humanists in the fourteenth century and by the middle of the fifteenth century it came to stand for a well-defined cycle of studies, known as *studia humanitatis.*

According to contemporary definitions, the *studia humanitatis,* that is, the "humanities," included the fields of grammar, rhetoric, poetry, history, and moral philosophy. Unlike the "liberal arts" (*artes liberales*) of the earlier Middle Ages, the humanities, indebted though they were to the medieval trivium, did not include logic or the subjects of the former *quadrivium* (arithmetic, geometry, astronomy, and music). The humanists on the whole also steered clear of, or were even opposed to, the chief subjects of instruction at the universities during the later Middle Ages and throughout the Renaissance, such as theology, jurisprudence, medicine, and the philosophical disciplines other than ethics. Thus, humanism had its proper domain in the humanities, language and literature being their core, whereas all other areas of learning followed their own, still largely medieval, trajectory. Nonetheless, all these areas, though not belonging to the territory of the humanists, came to be strongly influenced by humanism in the course of time. [*See* Trivium.]

The scholarly interests of the humanists centered upon the search, throughout Europe, for old manuscripts of the Latin and Greek classics. Once a Latin or Greek classical text was found, it was edited with annotations and commentaries. Since even among humanist scholars a knowledge of Greek was never as widespread as a knowledge of Latin, the task of translation had next to be performed, first from Greek into Latin and later from Latin into the various European vernaculars. Related to this activity was the teaching or cultivation of Latin, for the purpose of mastering it as a written and spoken language, especially in the

manner and style of Cicero, the avowed linguistic model of the humanists. All this, to be sure, could still be subsumed under the "trivial" art of grammar, whereas a further and more exalted activity was to be seen in rhetoric, the second of the humanities but in many ways the key to them all. Limited not only to the theory and practice of prose composition, or to the method of finding plausible or probable arguments, or to the ways and means of persuasion, rhetoric was claimed by most humanists to aid, through the pursuit of eloquence (*eloquentia*), in the acquisition of wisdom (*sapientia*), an ideal envisioned by Cicero in his *De oratore* when depicting the orator as the perfect humanist (1.64, 71; 3.92). The Roman rhetorician Quintilian (c.35–c.100 CE), Cicero's one rival as the chief teacher of classical rhetoric—who, in his *Institutio oratoria* (c.90 CE), became the most comprehensive authority on classical art, both during the Renaissance and today—likewise conceived of the orator as the perfect or truly universal man (1.pr.9; 2.15.1). [*See* Classical rhetoric.]

Traditionally and technically, rhetoric in its classical period distinguished five stages of composition: *inventio,* the discovering of material; *dispositio,* its structuring and arrangement; *elocutio,* its formulation in language; *memoria* and *pronuntiatio,* its memorizing and appropriate delivery. Furthermore, there were three kinds of oration or, by extension, literary work (hence, the fusion of rhetoric and poetics in the Renaissance): the judicial or forensic type; the deliberative type; and the demonstrative or epideictic type. Each type of speech or literary genre had a style appropriate to itself, the choice of which was governed by the principle of decorum. Yet, what thus appeared as an elaborate and coherent system tended to get fragmented into its constituent parts during the Middle Ages, and that, above all, to meet contemporary needs. In other words, the study of what in antiquity had been the art of public speaking, was by the twelfth century in Italy narrowed down to the *ars dictaminis,* the art of letter writing; and its practitioners, the *dictatores,* applied their mainly stylistic skills to the business of their feudal patrons and the legal profession. [*See* Ars dictaminis.] Therefore, it was incumbent on the Renaissance—while remaining indebted to *dictamen* for one of its major genres, letter writing—

to reintegrate the ancient system of rhetoric, a task performed first by the recovery of the surviving classical Latin texts on oratory, epistolography, and rhetoric, later to be followed by the recovery of the Greek rhetorical tradition. In addition, the humanists devoted themselves all the more enthusiastically to this task because they loved the arts of language. For to the humanists, it is the gift of language that distinguishes human beings from animals. This is a fundamental point in Renaissance treatises on "the dignity of man," the most famous of which is the posthumously-published *Oration* (1486) by the Italian humanist and philosopher Giovanni Pico della Mirandola (1463–1494). Based on the universality of his knowledge, the dignity of man, if we are to believe Pico and his fellow humanists, further enabled him to freely choose his place in the hierarchy of the world and thus to lead many forms of life, from the lowest to the highest. Small wonder, then, that a great variety of professional activities were opened up to the humanists during the Renaissance.

In keeping with their strong interest in the *studia humanitatis,* the humanists were best known in their role as educators, for they indeed played an important part as theorists, teachers, and tutors in reforming secondary education, first in Italy and then in the rest of Europe. At the heart of their instruction was the careful study of classical Latin, its vocabulary and grammar, metrics and prose style, and to a lesser extent, of classical Greek, plus the attentive reading and interpretation of the major ancient Latin and Greek writers, in both prose and verse. The schools of the two humanists Guarino da Verona (1374–1460) in Ferrara and Vittorino da Feltre (1378–1446) in Mantua, organized along these pedagogic lines, attracted students from all over Europe, and their curriculum and methods served as models for both the Protestant reformers and the Jesuits. Similarly, in the curriculum of the universities, although still dominated by medieval Scholasticism with its emphasis on theology and philosophy (i.e., logic), grammar was taught as an elementary subject, while rhetoric and poetry, involving the reading of the canonical classical authors, began to gain ground at Italian universities from the early fourteenth century on, so that a century later, the chairs of Latin and Greek oratory and poetry, often denominated as chairs of "the humanities," greatly increased in number and prestige.

Another professional activity frequently practiced by the humanists as masters of prose composition was that of acting as chancellors or secretaries. Popes, cardinals, and bishops as well as emperors, kings, princes, and republics needed them in this capacity, while in turn many churchmen, princes, or patricians of the time were humanists in their own right, serving as patrons to their former teachers or the cause of humanism at large. Yet another form of employment for a growing number of humanist scholars was the book trade, allied as this activity was to work as copyists or calligraphers, not only for princes or patrician patrons but also for professional booksellers such as the Florentine Vespasiano da Bisticci (1421–1498). The texts of these humanist scribes were written in one of two new styles of handwriting that were both different from the earlier "Gothic" script: the Roman script and the humanist cursive, destined to become the model for the italic type, are still with us today. The technique of printing was invented about 1440 by Johannes Gutenberg of Mainz (c.1397–1468), but it did not reach Italy, for example, before 1465. Many of the early printed books contain both classical Latin texts and writings of contemporary humanists, and they were usually printed in the same (modern) roman and italic characters to be found in the humanist manuscript books of the period that immediately preceded it. The humanists soon got involved with the printing presses, preeminently as advisers and editors at such leading international centers of publishing and book trading as Venice, Lyons, and Basel.

The humanists, given their love of language in the guise of rhetoric, most frequently cultivated the literary genres of the oration and the letter, both of which were closely connected with the humanists' professional activities as chancellors and secretaries, while at the same time including the private or personal, even subjective, dimensions. Although the skill of the humanists as orators and practicing rhetoricians found its most direct expression in their (mainly epideictic) speeches and (official as well as private) letters, it also shaped the form, if not the content, of all their other prose compositions, including their historical and philosophical writings, as well as their contributions to poetical theory and literary criticism. But more than anything else, it was their own Latin poetry that bore witness to a pervasive rhetoricization of Renaissance culture.

The Historical Development of Humanism. The origins of Renaissance humanism have traditionally been traced to the work and writings of the Italian scholar and poet Petrarch (Francesco Petrarca, 1304–1374), but more recently, research has singled out a group of "prehumanists" or "protohumanists" active in Northern and Central Italy during the late thirteenth and early fourteenth centuries. Among these, Albertino Mussato (1261–1329), a lawyer and politician of Padua, and Giovanni del Virgilio (died after 1327), an early professor of rhetoric and poetry at the University of Bologna, stand out for their contributions to Neo-Latin literature. Still, to all intents and purposes, pride of place must be accorded to Petrarch for the real beginning of Italian humanism. He attained international fame during his own lifetime, and was in a position to raise the prestige of humanistic studies and to promote their diffusion throughout Italy and the rest of Europe.

Italy. Petrarch virtually inaugurated the Renaissance revival of classical rhetoric in 1333, when he discovered Cicero's oration *Pro Archia,* later to be followed by Quintilian's *Institutio oratoria* in 1350. The discovery of the latter work did not, however, give him the immeasurable joy he experienced from a text by Cicero, his favorite classical author. Petrarch conducted a dialogue with Cicero throughout his entire career as a humanist writer. His vast literary output included Latin poetry (culminating in his epic poem *Africa,* 1342)—which earned him the title of "poet laureate" in 1341—plus a series of treatises, and a very large number of private letters. Humanist concerns are most directly addressed in his invective on ignorance, *De sui ipsius et multorum ignorantia* (1367), in which he offers a defense of poetry, eloquence, and ethics, the very subjects of the humanities, against the claims of Scholastic philosophy and speculative science. His scholarly leanings found their clearest expression in two earlier Latin treatises on solitude and leisure, *De vita solitaria* (1356) and *De otio religiosorum* (1357), where, in regard to the traditional opposition between *vita activa* and *vita contemplativa,* he speaks up for the ideal of a contemplative life. The peak of Petrarch's literary achievement might perhaps be seen in another treatise written in his maturity, which deals with the remedies for both kinds of fortune, that is, good and ill, entitled *De remediis utriusque fortunae* (1366), and which, by discussing the virtues and vices on the basis of Stoic doctrines, provides consolation in either case. Yet undoubtedly Petrarch is best known today for his vernacular poetry and above all for the great cycle of sonnets, the *Canzoniere* (1470), in which he celebrates his love for a presumably fictitious lady named Laura, leading to the literary fashion for composing sonnets that spread throughout Europe during the Renaissance and beyond.

Next in order of chronology and importance comes Lorenzo Valla (1407–1457) who, in true humanist manner, developed a philological approach to classical, literary, scriptural, and historical scholarship. This approach, enabled him to challenge the claims of the papacy to temporal power, and expose the alleged grant by the Emperor Constantine to Pope Sylvester I as a forgery, in his *De falso credita et ementita Constantini donatione declamatio* (1440). His philosophical interests are apparent in his writing on pleasure, *De voluptate* (1431), or on freedom of the will, *De libero arbitrio* (1435–1443). In both treatises, he took to task Stoic, Epicurean, and Christian conceptions of the true good. Valla gives further proof of his originality in the *Dialecticae disputationes* (from the 1430s onward), in which he attacks Aristotelian and Scholastic logic in the interest of clarity and simplicity, even going so far as to subordinate philosophy to rhetoric, reformulating principles of dialectic on the basis of rhetoric. And to the latter discipline should be added his concern for grammar, to wit, his *Elegantiae linguae latinae* (1471), intended to restore the classical purity of Latin in grammar, phraseology, and style before its corruption by the (medieval) barbarians. An important contribution to humanist philology, the *Elegantiae* became a major influence on subsequent humanists, most notably those involved in education.

Having earlier noted the medieval dismemberment of the classical art of rhetoric and the Renaissance need for reintegrating this system, we find the task performed in the fifteenth century by the émigré Byzantine humanist George of Trebizond (Trapezuntius; 1396–1486) in his *Five Books on Rhetoric,* the *Rhetoricorum libri V* (published at Venice in 1433–1434), the one and only great Quattrocento work on rhetoric to rival Quintilian's from antiquity. In restoring rhetoric to its full five classical arts, George synthesized not only the classical Latin tradition of rhetoric as represented above all by Cicero and Quintilian, but also the Greek tradition as exemplified by the rhetorical writings of the philosopher Aristotle (384–322 BCE) or the orator and Sophist Hermogenes of Tarsos (second century CE). It was to the latter's work that George owed his complex system of stylistic categories, far better suited for textual analysis than the former simple Latin division of high, low, and middle styles. But no less innovative was George's section on invention, which paved the way for his *Introduction to Dialectic,* the *Isagoge dialectica* (c.1440), the first humanist manual of logic, teaching as it does the methods of rhetorical argumentation along revised Aristotelian lines.

With George of Trebizond, we witness yet one more instance of the Greek impact on the Renaissance that started back in the 1390s when the Byzantine humanist Manuel Chrysoloras (c.1353–1415) introduced the study of Greek to Florence. Further, George's massive synthesis of the rhetorical tradition helped advance the art of speech and composition and extended it into practically all fields of knowledge. Take, for example, the Italian humanist, art theorist, and architect Leon Battista Alberti (1404–1472), whose treatise on painting, *De pictura* (1435), or *Della pittura* in its Italian version (1436), and his work on architecture, *De re aedificatoria* (1452), were thoroughly informed by the terminology of rhetoric. Similiar observations could be made with regard to the theory and practice of music during the period of Renaissance humanism. In short, more than one major text yielded to the period's ubiquitous rhetoricization, as evidenced by Julius Caesar Scaliger (1484–1558), the Italian–French humanist, whose equally voluminous seven books on poetics, *Poetices libri VII* (1561), offer the ultimate fusion of all forms of knowledge about literature in nearly one thousand pages, and once more in rhetorical terms.

France. Rivaling Italy, France herself could also boast outstanding scholars, poets, and rhetoricians of humanist persuasion during the fifteenth and especially sixteenth centuries. The philosopher and theologian Jacques Lefèvre d'Étaples (c.1455–1536) and the philologist and legal writer Guillaume Budé (1467–1540) are of particular note. D'Étaples was known mainly for his French translation of the Bible (1530), Budé for a variety of works, including commentaries on the *Pandects* (1508), the bulkiest part of the great codification of Roman law undertaken in the sixth century; a treatise on coins, *De asse* (1515), its title being taken from the *as,* a copper coin of the earlier Roman Republic; and further, a reflection on his philological ideal, *De philologia* (1532). What is more, in 1530 he successfully persuaded King Francis I to establish Regius professorships in Greek, Hebrew, Latin, and mathematics, which formed the institutional nucleus of what was later to become the Collège de France. In the sphere of rhetoric and poetry, French humanists, while conceiving of rhetoric as the crown of both grammar and dialectic, tended well into the sixteenth century to distinguish between a first (*première*) and a second (*seconde*) rhetoric. The first was reserved for everyday Latin prose or oratory, the second for vernacular versification, that is, metrics, as was above all borne out by the respective theoretical manuals of a group of poets labeled the *Rhétoriqueurs.* Yet, opposed to them was a somewhat later and far more prestigious school of poetry, the so-called *Pléiade,* whose foremost representatives, namely Pierre de Ronsard (1524–1585) and Joachim du Bellay (c.1522–1560), tried to acclimatize classical and Italian models of poetry in France by way of "imitation" and "emulation," their manifesto being Du Bellay's *Deffence et Illustration de la Langue Françoyse* (1549). Nevertheless, this work itself harks back to arguments propagating the rights of the vernacular as used in Italy only a few years before in the context of the *Questione della lingua* (e.g., by P. Bembo or S. Speroni). And as for rhetoric proper, finally, it was changed almost beyond recognition by the controversial French philosopher and educational reformer Petrus Ramus (Pierre de La Ramée, 1515–1572) who, obsessed as he was with method in his *Dialectique* (1543), for instance, reduced rhetoric to a sort of universal topical logic, everywhere trying to simplify and to come down to essentials.

But this and his other manuals became immensely influential, particularly in Protestant countries, after his murder in the Saint Bartholomew's Day Massacre (1572).

Spain and Portugal. When it came to Spain and Portugal, humanism was no less implicated in religious politics. In Spain, strengthened as it was by a national monarchy in the kingdom of Castile and the ubiquitous Inquisition in matters ecclesiastical, humanism from the start became part of a political agenda. Thus, Alfonso de Cartagena (1384–1456), bishop of Burgos and close to the royal court, propagated the new educational ideals of humanism with a view to pitting the Roman Stoic philosopher Seneca (4 BCE–65 CE), born at Corduba in Spain, against Roman poets such as Virgil (70–19 BCE) and Ovid (43 BCE–17 CE), in order thereby to create an indigenous counterbalance to the cultural dominance of Italy. Similar patriotic motives underlay the work of the Spanish humanist and biblical scholar Elio Antonio de Nebrija (1441–1522), professor at Salamanca and later at Alcalá, most notably in his capital grammar of the Castilian tongue, the *Arte de la gramática castellana* (1492), where he gave the hoary "language question" an obvious imperialistic twist. By contrast, the greatest Spanish humanist, Juan Luis Vives (1492–1540), was far more cosmopolitan in outlook. Of Jewish descent and afraid of the Inquisition, he worked mainly abroad, especially in Flanders and England, writing extensively on problems of moral philosophy, psychology, social theory, and educational reform. And to the latter sphere belongs his comprehensive treatise, *De disciplinis* (1531), consisting of his search into the causes of cultural degeneration—Scholasticism, of course—as well as into the transmission of knowledge (*De causis corruptarum artium* and *De tradendis disciplinis*), in this context also reviewing the history of rhetoric, alongside other disciplines, in a highly critical spirit.

But there were other voices, and not only in Spain but in Portugal, too, tied together culturally and religiously as the two countries were. To begin with, we find personal contacts between humanists and princes that worked both ways—Alfonso de Cartagena, for example, was also close to the Portuguese court—or there were quite a few Spanish Jesuits active in Portugal, writing

practical and theoretical manuals in a genre known as the "art of preaching" (*ars concionandi*). Yet, proudly independent of Spain, if not of classical antiquity, seeing that Virgil's *Aeneid* (composed 30–19 BCE) served as his model, was Portugal's humanistic national poet Luís de Camões (c.1524–1580), when in his epic *Os Lusíadas* (1572) he sang the praises of the seafaring Portuguese, descended from the legendary ancestor Lusus (hence the poem's title).

The Netherlands. Politics apart, the very career of Vives testified to the international character of Renaissance humanism once again. Having been both a student and tutor at Louvain between 1517 and 1523, he was thus associated with the famous College of the Three Languages, the *Collegium Trilingue,* a stronghold for the study of Latin, Greek, and Hebrew, founded in 1517. Accordingly, he belonged to the same European network of humanists as, for instance, the Frisian scholar Rudolph Agricola (1444–1485) who, either on account of or in spite of his long stay in Italy, developed a peculiarly Northern approach to oratory in his three highly influential books *On Dialectical Invention* (*De inventione dialectica;* 1479, but printed only in 1515, and then frequently afterward until 1657), in which he focused on the first part of rhetorical art, namely, the *inventio* of the so-called dialectical *topoi,* that is, the *loci communes* (commonplaces), as being the theoretically possible points of view that allow any author to treat an argument in an orderly and persuasive fashion. To find these *loci* is the task of logic, to arrange them properly that of rhetoric. Rhetoricizing logic in this manner, Agricola not only looked back to Valla but also forward to Ramus, and at the same time, provided an adaptation of Italian humanism that suited the North.

If Agricola was the first northern humanist, then Desiderius Erasmus of Rotterdam (c.1446–1536) was the greatest. His European reputation rested on a great number of widely-read publications, including textbooks and teachers' manuals, plus editions of Christian as well as pagan classical writers. His *Adagia* (1500, with many additions in later versions) is not only a treasure house of style but also of classical proverbial wisdom, still to be enjoyed today, as is his satire the *Praise of Folly, Moriae encomium* (1511, with thirty-six Latin editions up to 1536, the year of his death), really a mock *encomium* full of multiple ironies. In the field of rhetoric, the outstanding contributions of Erasmus are his treatise on letter writing, *De conscribendis epistolis* (1498 and 1522), the most successful of many sixteenth-century manuals on this topic, and above all, his immensely influential textbook on *copia*, that is, abundance, *De duplici copia verborum ac rerum* (1512, and throughout the sixteenth century, at least one hundred and fifty editions). This work teaches the precepts of amplification, that is, the ways to a rich and varied style, as a result mediating between stylistic and argumentative devices in the manner of Agricola or Melanchthon. After Erasmus, only the Flemish humanist Justus Lipsius (1547–1606) was to exert a comparable European influence in initiating the Neo-Stoic movement through his book on constancy in adversity, *De constantia* (1584).

Germany. With Philip Melanchthon (1497–1560), though, we are in the midst of German humanism already. Its somewhat isolated precursor was the "itinerant" scholar Peter Luder (c.1415–1472), who held forth on the *studia humanitatis* in a lecture delivered at Heidelberg in 1456. But it was later, thanks to imperial patronage or the foundation of new universities, that the movement was able to gather momentum in Germany. There was, for example, the Sienese humanist Aeneas Silvius Piccolomini (1405–1464), who became Pope Pius II, attached as he was to the Habsburg court, or the famous German humanist Conradus Celtis (1459–1508), who was not only crowned "poet laureate" by Emperor Frederick III in 1487 but, a decade later, also appointed to the chair of rhetoric and poetry at the University of Vienna, founded in 1365. After Vienna, there were quite a few universities established between 1365 and 1502, the relevant date for Wittenberg, the cradle of the German Reformation. Melanchthon, the "*praeceptor Germaniae*" (teacher of Germany), lectured there on Greek from 1518 onward, supported his friend Martin Luther (1483–1546) during the Reformation, and embarked on a lifelong program of educational reform, which bore upon rhetoric, too. Between 1519 and 1532, he published three textbooks on the art, from *De rhetorica*, through *Institutiones rhetoricae*, to *Elementa rhetorices*, which, in taking up and elaborating on positions of Agricola as well as of Eras-

mus, emphasized the topics of invention, the *loci communes,* important as they were, not least for the interpretation of wordly as well as sacred texts. In his pedagogic endeavors, Melanchthon was seconded, so to speak, by the Strasbourg humanist and educator Johannss Sturm (1507–1589), who on account of his methodologically-oriented contributions to both dialectic and rhetoric, clearly was the most important classicizing authority on the latter art in Northern Europe during the sixteenth century.

England. Despite her peripheral position in Western Europe, England also joined the mainstream of Renaissance humanism, albeit belatedly and with an important difference. Wherever possible, English writers stressed the value of an active life over the contemplative ideal of the Middle Ages or the aesthetic conception of man that was to be found in Italy. A comparison between Baldassare Castiglione's (1478–1529) *Il Cortegiano* (1528), translated into English by Thomas Hoby as *The Courtier* in 1561, with Sir Thomas Elyot's (c.1490–1546) *The Governor* (1531) can easily exemplify this opposition. Still, the first generation of Tudor humanists, the "Oxford Reformers" William Grocyn (1446–1519), Thomas Linacre (c.1460–1524), and John Colet (1467–1519), owed practically everything to their firsthand contact with Italian humanism—especially true in the case of Colet, the founder of Saint Paul's School—and to their friendship with Erasmus, who visited England several times. Above all, Erasmus and the leading representative of the second generation, Sir Thomas More (1478–1535), were kindred spirits. More than anyone else, More bears witness to Tudor humanism's involvement in the active life both by his death and by his *Utopia* (1516). This work addressed contemporary symptoms of crisis in society and economics, thereby—notwithstanding the fact that it looked back to Plato's (c.428–c.347 BCE) *Republic*—giving rise to an entirely new genre of literature. The ways in which oratory may be helpful in the pursuit of eloquence, patriotism, and piety in a Tudor context, were then pointed out by, among others, Thomas Wilson (c.1525–1581) in *The Arte of Rhetorique* (1553). This work was, in itself, however, already a product of the third generation of English humanists who were more insular and patriotic in outlook—see especially

Roger Ascham's (1515–1568) Italophobic *Schole-master* (1570)—than their cosmopolitan predecessors. What is more, when authors like Richard Sherry (c.1506–c.1555) in his Erasmian *Treatise of Schemes and Tropes* (1550), Henry Peacham (c.1546–1634) in *The Garden of Eloquence* (1577), or George Puttenham (c.1529–1590) in *The Arte of English Poesie* (1589) concentrated almost exclusively on elocution and the figures of speech, they perhaps give proof of the fact that under Tudor absolutism, rhetoric's function could no longer be political, unless in disguise (Puttenham), but mainly ornamental and literary.

Eastern and Northern Europe. Not unexpectedly, in eastern and northern Europe the reception of humanism followed historical patterns similar to those discussed already. Therefore, points of entry into the various countries concerned are again the courts of princes, both secular and ecclesiastical, as well as newly-established universities, normally in towns with printing presses. As to worldly courts, that of the Hungarian king Matthias Corvinus (1458–1490) deserves particular mention, and not only for its famous Italian emigrants but also for the king's library, the "Corviniana," acclaimed as the richest humanist collection in eastern Europe of the time. János Vitéz (c.1408–1472), archbishop of Esztergom, primate of Hungary and Croatia and founder of Pozsony University (1467), may stand for the humanist interests (i.e., letter writing) of an eminent churchman. Long before that date, however, the Universities of Prague (1348) and Cracow (1364) were founded, soon to develop into academic centers for the study of the humanities not only for Bohemia and Poland but, like the even older universities of Italy, for all of Europe. There is a sense in which Renaissance humanism is the golden period of intellectual exchange throughout Europe, allowing scholars to move freely over the entire continent. Thus, Petrarch is a guest of Charles IV, emperor and king of Bohemia, at Prague in 1356, whereas more than a century later, eastern humanists finally came into their own as poets and scholars and gained international reputations for themselves. Special attention should be paid to Janus Pannonius (1424–1472) of Hungary, one of the most important Neo-Latin poets of the Renaissance; Matthias Flacius Illyricus (1520–1575) of Croatia, promi-

nently involved as he was in the German Reformation; and his countryman Francesco Patrizi (1529–1597), hailing from the Adriatic island of Cherso and teaching Platonic philosophy at Ferrara and Rome. In turn, proximity to Italy certainly accounts for Dubrovnik (Ragusa) being the foremost city of Croat Renaissance literature, both in Latin and in the vernacular.

Geographical proximity further played a role when it came to transferring humanism from the south to the far north, namely from Germany to Scandinavia, which is tantamount to saying that northern humanism can neither be separated from Luther's Reformation nor from Melanchthon's educational reorientation with regard to Latin grammar or rhetorical method. That the latter could also be used—or rather misused—for political purposes may be mentioned, by way of conclusion, instances being, after the collapse of the Scandinavian Union in 1523, Swedish historiography of the sixteenth century (e.g., the brothers Johannes and Olaus Magnus) as well as anti-Danish propaganda from the Vasa court under king Erik XIV (1533–1577), the "rhetorician on the Swedish throne."

2. The Afterlife of Humanism. While reverting to the past of classical antiquity, Renaissance humanism in many cases paved the way for modern times. In addition to the examples adduced already, one may here further point to the Florentine *Camerata* (sodality), which, in mistakenly assuming a combination of words and song for Greek drama, unwittingly provided the theoretical basis for a new kind of art, the modern opera. Yet one more instance of this process may be seen in the *Essais* (1580, 1588) of the French humanist Michel de Montaigne (1533–1592), who, familiar though he was with Greek philosophy, uttered his thoughts in a new, that is, open and subjective genre of writing. In spite of such fruitful interactions between the old and the new, however, the heyday of humanism did not last. The decline of the movement set in through the rise of the natural sciences around the beginning of the seventeenth century, more exactly, through the replacement of humanism's "culture of memory" by a "logic of discovery" usually associated with the English philosopher Francis Bacon (1561–1626). Even so, humanism did not lose its prestige for good.

It is a fact that what is well and truly past for science can never entirely be so for the humanities. And this conviction is the basis for humanist revivals that take place from time to time, such as during the historically-minded nineteenth century, when the very term, *Humanismus,* was coined (in 1808) by the German educator F. I. Niethammer (1766–1848) and Jakob Burckhardt (1818–1897) recreated the Renaissance in his authoritative *Civilization of the Renaissance in Italy* (1860). Further attempts at resuscitation followed in the twentieth century: for example, by the classical scholar Werner Jaeger (1888–1961), who turned to the ancient Greeks and their ideal of *paideia;* and, by not excluding appropriations of the term on the part of postwar philosophy—be they in the name of existentialism, as with Jean-Paul Sartre (1905–1980) in his *L'existentialisme est un humanisme* (1946) or in the interest of ontology, as with Martin Heidegger's (1889–1976) rejoinder in a *Letter on Humanism* (1947). So, for better or worse, the term is bound to stay with us in order to enrich the discourse of the humanities with all its connotations.

Whether the same can be said for rhetoric, humanism's former key subject, remains to be seen. Having been relegated to a place inferior to logic in Bacon's *Advancement of Learning* (1605), rhetoric less than two hundred years later almost suffered its death blow at the hands of the German philosopher Immanuel Kant (1724–1804), who condemned it outright in paragraph 53 of his *Critique of Judgement* (1790). After that, the discipline went through a number of historical ups and downs, the worst being the Romantic period with its belief in original expression. In the twentieth century, while rhetoric and philosophy were kept distinct once more, there began to be a sort of rehabilitation of the ancient "craft of speech," albeit mainly in academic circles. And for their benefit, the Romance scholar Heinrich Lausberg (1912–1992) magisterially reconstructed the entire classical system of the art in his *Handbook of Literary Rhetoric* (1960). Whatever the future course of rhetoric, one humanist insistence will be clear in view of this great synthetic achievement: there is no thought without language, but there should never be language without thought.

[*See also* Eighteenth-century rhetoric; Modern rhetoric; *and overview article on* Renaissance rhetoric.]

BIBLIOGRAPHY

Bolgar, R. R. *The Classical Heritage and Its Beneficiaries.* Cambridge, U.K., 1954; reprinted 1977.

Buck, August. *Humanismus: Seine europäische Entwicklung in Dokumenten und Darstellungen.* Freiburg and Munich, 1987.

Burckhardt, Jacob. *The Civilization of the Renaissance in Italy.* Translated by S. G. C. Middlemore; edited by Benjamin Nelson and Charles Trinkhaus. 2 vols. New York, 1958. English translation of *Die Kultur der Renaissance in Italien,* first published 1860.

Burke, Peter. *The European Renaissance: Centres and Peripheries.* Oxford, 1998.

Caspari, Fritz. *Humanism and the Social Order in Tudor England.* Chicago, 1954; reprinted New York, 1968.

Curtius, Ernst Robert. *European Literature and the Latin Middle Ages.* Translated by Willard R. Trask. New York, 1953. English translation of *Europäische Literatur und lateinisches Mittelalter,* first published 1948.

Davies, Tony. *Humanism. The New Critical Idiom.* London, 1997.

Hale, John. *The Civilization of Europe in the Renaissance.* A Touchstone Book. New York, 1995; first published 1993.

Howald, Ernst. *Humanismus und Europäertum.* Zurich and Stuttgart, 1957.

Kraye, Jill, ed. *The Cambridge Companion to Renaissance Humanism.* Cambridge, U.K., 1996; reprinted 1997.

Kristeller, Paul Oskar. *Renaissance Thought and Its Sources.* Edited by Michael Mooney. New York, 1979.

Lausberg, Heinrich. *Handbook of Literary Rhetoric: A Foundation for Literary Study.* Translated by Matthew T. Bliss, Annemiek Jansen, David E. Orton; edited by David E. Orton and R. Dean Anderson. Leiden, 1998. English translation of *Handbuch der literarischen Rhetorik,* first published 1960.

Moss, Ann. *Printed Commonplace Books and the Structuring of Renaissance Thought.* Oxford, 1996.

Mout, Nicolette, ed. *Die Kultur des Humanismus: Reden, Briefe, Traktate, Gespräche von Petrarca bis Kepler.* Munich, 1998.

Nauert, Charles G., Jr. *Humanism and the Culture of Renaissance Europe.* Cambridge, U.K., 1995; reprinted 1998.

Plett, Heinrich F., ed. *Renaissance-Rhetorik, Renaissance Rhetoric.* Berlin, 1993.

Plett, Heinrich F., ed. *Renaissance-Poetik, Renaissance Poetics.* Berlin, 1994.

Plett, Heinrich F. *English Renaissance Rhetoric and Poetics: A Systematic Bibliography of Primary and Secondary Sources.* Leiden, 1995.

Rabil, Albert, Jr., ed. *Renaissance Humanism: Foundations, Forms, and Legacy.* 3 vols. Philadelphia, 1988.

Schirmer, Walter F. *Der englische Frühhumanismus: Ein Beitrag zur englischen Literaturgeschichte des 15. Jahrhunderts.* 2d ed. Tübingen, 1963.

Schmitt, Charles B., general ed. *The Cambridge History of Renaissance Philosophy.* Cambridge, U.K., 1988; reprinted 1990.

Ueding, Gert, ed. *Historisches Wörterbuch der Rhetorik,* vol. 1–. Tübingen, 1992–.

Vickers, Brian. *In Defence of Rhetoric.* Oxford, 1988; reprinted 1997.

Weiss, R. *Humanism in England during the Fifteenth Century.* 3d ed. Oxford, 1967.

—CLAUS UHLIG

HUMOR is elusive, for many of the reasons that rhetoric is elusive. The nature of both is culturally dependent, and their effectiveness is linked to place, time, and occasion. "Dying is easy," the actor George Burns (1896–1996) once remarked, "comedy is hard." There is, moreover, no other art except comedy where laughter and its uses belong. Writings on humor in the rhetorical tradition suggest a twofold rationale for its inclusion: humor is an audience pleaser, and as such, has long been considered an important communicative strategy; at the same time, humor is unstable and perverse, resisting rules and abstractions while favoring the evanescent and situational.

In the Western tradition, the strategic uses of humor were first described by the Sophists in the fifth century BCE. Aristotle, echoing the Sophist Gorgias's teaching, acknowledged that provoking laughter can be a valuable tactic in controversy (*Rhetoric* 1419b), but he declined to discuss the subject at length, claiming that he had already done so under a (now lost) section on comedy in his *Poetics.* From antiquity, the most influential discussion of humor in rhetoric appears in Cicero's *De oratore* (c.55 BCE, 2.53.217–290), where it occurs, significantly, in a debate about the relative importance of practice as opposed to theory. Cicero's speakers agree that humor can be rhetorically efficacious, and although it may not be precisely definable the subject can apparently be divided, subdivided, and abundantly exemplified. The question of whether it can be taught remains open. Later Quintilian too classified and exemplified humor while remaining theoretically irresolute, in *Institutio oratoria* (first century CE, 6.3). The Ciceronian pattern is repeated in Castiglione's popular *Il Cortegiano* (The Courtier, 1528, 2.43–89): again, the question of humor's teachability produces a loose classification of types and page after page of examples. Decorum becomes the governing and most teachable principle repeated by early writers: humor won't work unless it is appropriate to the audience, speaker, and occasion and unless it is relevant to the point of the speech. [*See* Classical rhetoric; *and* Decorum.]

This deference to decorum, along with slight theorizing, continues in modern public speaking textbooks as well as in the compendia of jokes and witticisms published from time to time as "treasuries" for the public speaker. On the Internet, lists of speechwriters often provide links to data banks of gags and quips or to subsidiary services such as individualized consultation by humor specialists. The ongoing pedagogical principle is clear: humor can create a community through stimulating a uniform response, it can reflect well on the character of the speaker, and it can serve to emphasize or make memorable features of the speaker's argument, so long as its use is decorous.

But any posited rules of humor are unstable: most can be countered by social and political changes—even decorousness can be flaunted to humorous effect—and the fit between joke and circumstance often requires some deft, individualized tailoring. In short, humor is and always has been a risky enterprise.

There is thus a second reason for its inclusion within the art of rhetoric, one that extends beyond the strategic use of humor and into the unique nature of rhetoric itself among the humane disciplines. From the time of Galen (second century CE), the word *humor* signified a person's emotional disposition, resulting from the predominance of certain bodily fluids. Through the centuries, both physicality and immediacy adhered to the concept, as did spontaneity, at least apparent spontaneity. The "humorous," according to Samuel Johnson's dictionary (1755), is "without any rule but the present whim." Even that latter insight can be stood on its head and used to advantage, as it was, for example, by Adlai Stevenson when he employed the hoariest of all public speaking clichés to comment whimsically on his failed presidential campaign in 1952: "A funny thing happened on my way to the White House."

From the Renaissance to the present, philosophers and scientists have made serious efforts to set forth theories of humor and explore the laughable, to learn not only what makes people laugh but also why they laugh at all. Hobbes's *Leviathan* (1651), Kant's *Kritik der Urtheilskraft* (Critique of Judgment, 1790), Darwin's *Expression of Emotions* (1872), Bergson's *Le Rire* (Laughter, 1900), and Freud's *Der Witz* (1905) may come immediately to mind. But to the rhetorician, *that* people laugh is the idea to be exploited, and any serious effort to grasp the protean nature of humor is oxymoronic from the outset, like trying to capture rhetoric itself within the covers of an encyclopedia.

Something of that point is made by Erasmus's persona in his scandalous *Moriae encomium* (The Praise of Folly, 1511). Although "Folly" mentions favorably Democritus (fifth century BCE), the "laughing philosopher" for whom the goal of life lay in maintaining cheerfulness, she finds closer kinship with the rhetoricians, for they alone recognize the unruly impulses of humor and prize its sharp use in deflating philosophical (i.e., theological) pomposity. It is surely no accident that the first English versions of traditional rhetoric and logic exemplify "Folly's" praise. Thomas Wilson's *Arte of Rhetorique* (1553) follows the Ciceronian pattern of discussing humor, stressing the importance of decorum while providing a theory that is all but swamped by jokes and witticisms. Humor's perversity had infiltrated Wilson's earlier work on logic (1551)—as when, for example, he defines a proposition as something uttered without any ambiguity but exemplifies it with the famous Cretan paradox "Every man is a liar." Modern logicians who caution against communicative ritual and formalism continue to revitalize the spirit of humor in that otherwise desiccated subject. The modern rhetorician Richard Lanham (*The Motives of Eloquence*, 1976) has observed that there are two kinds of writers in the Western world, *homo rhetoricus* and *homo seriosus*. Humor is unmistakably their dividing line. [*See overview article on* Renaissance rhetoric.]

In sum, the twofold rationale for the ongoing inclusion of humor serves to reveal the nature of rhetoric itself. As the ancients taught, humor can be efficacious in communication. But its efficaciousness is usually quotidian and only variably predictable. Its ribaldry as well as its chanciness necessarily run counter to settled rules.

[*See also* Pathos.]

BIBLIOGRAPHY

Apte, Mahadev L. *Humor and Laughter: An Anthropological Approach.* Ithaca, N.Y., 1985. What's funny depends on where you are and who you are, your culture and ethnicity, age, sex, and even your sense of well-being.

Bateson, Gregory. *Steps to an Ecology of Mind: Collected Essays in Anthropology, Psychiatry, Evolution, and Epistemology.* New York, 1972. Bateson is a logician for whom "change" and "humor" are necessary ingredients of communication.

Grant, Mary A. *The Ancient Rhetorical Theories of the Laughable: The Greek Rhetoricians and Cicero.* In *University of Wisconsin Studies in Language and Literature,* No. 21. Madison, Wis., 1924. An aging dissertation that continues to reward study (e.g., oratory may be considered among the comic genres, p. 145).

Gray, Frances. *Women and Laughter.* Charlottesville, Va., 1994. Gray advances the argument that women must clarify their relation to humor, in view of the subject's political dimensions.

Huizinga, Johan. *Homo Ludens: A Study of the Play Element in Culture.* London, 1949. First published Haarlem, 1938. Huizinga argues for the significance of the nomenclature "man the player."

Monro, D. H. *Argument of Laughter.* Melbourne, 1951. A comprehensive review of major theories, ending in a synthesizing view that humor always contains an element of the inappropriate.

Prochnow, Herbert V., and Herbert V. Prochnow, Jr. *The Public Speaker's Treasure Chest: A Compendium of Source Material to Make Your Speech Sparkle.* 4th ed. New York, 1986.

Sprague, Jo, and Douglas Stuart. *The Speaker's Handbook.* 3d ed. Fort Worth, Tex., 1992. A standard textbook approach to the use of humor in public speaking.

Online Resources

Executive Speaker. *http://www.executive-speaker.com.* Maintained by The Executive Speaker®. Offers speech and speech-writing resources, including links to humor consultants.

Jester. *http://shadow.ieor.berkeley.edu/humor.* Maintained by Alpha Lab at UC Berkeley, under the direction of

Professor Ken Goldberg. Tailors jokes to the user's own sense of humor.

—THOMAS O. SLOANE

HYBRID GENRES. *Genre* is a word borrowed from the French to signify a distinct species, form, type, or kind. The act of isolating genres implies that significantly similar characteristics inhere in works of the same type regardless of author and period of production. A genre of rhetoric contains elements that share characteristics distinguishing them from elements of other rhetorical genres.

For centuries, the discipline of rhetoric anchored itself in the generic distinctions of Aristotle (384–322 BCE), who classified rhetoric as deliberative, forensic, and epideictic. Aristotle's view was that genre is defined by the kind of audience that makes a certain sort of decision on a distinctive issue, developed through recurring lines of argument, characterized by a typical style, and employing certain strategies that are particularly apt for these circumstances. Genres are not only dynamic responses to circumstances but also a potential fusion of elements that may be energized or actualized as a strategic response to a situation. Karlyn Kohrs Campbell and Kathleen Hall Jamieson (1978) defined genres as dynamic fusions of substance, style, and situational elements and as constellations that are strategic responses to the demands of the situation and purposes of rhetoric.

Hybrid genres can be a fusion of elements of existing genres arising from unprecedented rhetorical situations, or they can be the product of antecedent genres. "Rhetorical hybrid" is a metaphor intended to emphasize the productive but transitory character of these new combinations of rhetorical acts. Hybrids are important to understanding the coherence of complex rhetorical forms. Stable or constant rhetorical situations over time will encourage generic standardization of forms. Variance or change in rhetorical situations will encourage generic modification. To the extent that exigencies, media, audience expectations, and the natural context remain constant, a rhetorical situation may be viewed as unchanging. Alteration in any of these variables will encourage generic modification.

Because speech acts are governed both by the rhetorician and by the situation, complex combinations will bring about new kinds of discourse. A literary genre, for example, will maintain a standardized form only so long as it is capable of carrying the intended meaning of authors. When authors are unable to express their vision within the prescribed generic confines, those authors will either create a flawed work or will alter the stock genre to fit their needs. Unable to express his symbolic vision within the confines of the narrative novel, Flaubert expanded the options of future novelists by writing *Madame Bovary.*

Rhetorical critics, in their analysis of great speeches, have come to recognize that the elements of forensic, epideictic, and deliberative genres identified by Aristotle overlap and combine in practice. Harold Zyskind (1950) details the complex intertwining of epideictic and deliberative elements in Abraham Lincoln's Gettysburg Address. Michael Leff and Gerald Mohrmann (1974) identified in Lincoln's address at Cooper Union a fusion of deliberative and epideictic elements into a form they labeled the campaign oration. This fusion produced a new kind of genre.

Another hybrid—the deliberative eulogy—fuses the elements of the ceremonial address, which Aristotle called epideictic, and the legislative form, which he called deliberative. In her analysis of the eulogies by members of Congress in honor of Robert Kennedy, Jamieson (1982) identified rhetorical moments when the situation warranted generic modification and a shift to rhetorical hybrids. Eulogies are required to mark the death of another person. Even if speakers have never heard or read a eulogy, they will, if they are not insensitive to the situation, deliver eulogistic rhetoric. The situation demands it and audiences expect it. In Western culture, a eulogy will acknowledge the death, transform the relationship between the living and the dead from present to past tense, ease the mourners' terror at confronting their own mortality, console them by arguing that the deceased lives on, and encourage unity within the community. The eulogies of Robert Kennedy met those criteria.

These eulogies went further, however, and in the process created a hybrid genre. Those members who were supporters of Kennedy and his legislative actions also called for handgun control—a call appropriate to deliberative discourse. The situation at issue was that of the assassination of an active legislator by a man with a gun. In this context, the eulogies prompted demands for gun control as a means of memorializing RFK. If Kennedy had opposed such legislation, these calls would have been inappropriate. Because the deliberative subform risks dividing the community that the eulogy must reknit, there is little likelihood that calls for action would be controversial or that they would contradict the presumed wishes of the deceased. Kennedy, however, was a proponent of handgun legislation. Colleagues who supported Kennedy's proposals while he lived were comfortable using the situation to call for their enactment as a memorial. Colleagues who did not share Kennedy's legislative proposals did not include a deliberative section in their eulogies but instead memorialized his integrity and character.

Rhetorical fusions, then, are rule governed. In the eulogies of Kennedy delivered in Congress, the eulogistic requirements predominated and deliberative appeals we subordinate. Deliberative elements fuse to form organic wholes when they are consistent with and contribute to the goals of the eulogy. In observing these eulogies, one can draw three conclusions. First, in eulogistic settings, one generic form predominates. Second, hybrids are called forth by complex situations and purposes and, as such, are transitory and situation bound. Identification of different generic elements and occasionally of whole genres within such acts allows the critic to understand how such acts work and to predict their appearance.

Eulogistic hybrids, such as the one occasioned by Robert Kennedy's death, occur infrequently and under variable circumstances. As a result, they have not altered the expectations audiences bring to eulogistic occasions or rites of investiture. There are times, however, when a fusion occurs with some regularity and creates formal expectations in knowledgeable audiences. The fusion of some hybrids is sustained by a recurrent situation, such as presidential inaugurals, which combine constant epideictic elements with varying deliberative elements. Lincoln's first inaugural masterfully blended these two genres. He called for the unifying of the nation while reaffirming core communal values; these were epideictic elements. And he asked the audience to consider whether or not secession was the appropriate solution to the problem of sectional disputes; these were deliberative elements. Successful inaugurals will establish unity after a divisive campaign, rehearse traditional values, and reassure the citizenry that the newly-elected president is not a tyrant but a person who needs the help of God, the people, and Congress in order to govern. At the same time, they outline the philosophy or tone of the administration and set its agenda.

The fusion of other hybrids is sustained by an institution such as the papacy, illustrated by encyclicals that fuse the elements of the apostolic letter with those of the Roman imperial decree. The papal encyclical is a didactic letter. In an encyclical, the pope, speaking as Christ's visible representative on earth, addresses his intended audience on matters of serious moral concern. The content, intent, and form of the papal encyclical betray its apostolic ancestry. The imprint of early epistles is particularly evident in the salutations and concluding exhortations of the contemporary encyclicals. The apostolic epistles and papal encyclicals situate themselves to their audiences in a dichotomous fashion as either fraternal or paternal. Finally, the contemporary encyclicals' use of classical Latin, an authoritative tone, and use of protocols echo the epistles. When rhetoricians are confronted with unprecedented situations, often they perceive the situation through antecedent genres. This perception facilitates the emergence of hybrid genres.

Genres should not be viewed as static forms but as evolving phenomena. The notion of hybrid genres frees rhetoric from a concern that genres are fixed and unchanging. Rhetoricians perpetually modify genres. These modifications, as a result of new institutional structures or situations, give rise to rhetorical hybrids, oftentimes arising out of antecedent genres. Some scholars have proposed that rhetorical criticism would be advanced by constructing hierarchies or exhaustive taxonomies of genres. By their very nature, rhetorical hybrids, formed out of variable generic elements, will be difficult to place in such a hierarchy. Moreover, they may confound efforts to construct exhaustive generic taxonomies as new situations and generic combinations develop.

Generic analysis enables us to appreciate the idiosyncratic as well as the recurrent, and to recognize the appropriate response to a complex situation. It enables a critic to describe the special characteristics of an address. It further allows the critic to recognize when conflicting demands from the audience, the institution, or the rhetorician will arise, and the circumstances under which elements from different genres are demanded. Genre analysis provides the critic with the ability to parse the rhetorical constraints governing their successful combination.

A generic critic recognizes the combination of recurrent elements that forms a hybrid. At the same time, such a critic can perceive the unique fusion that is a response to the idiosyncratic needs of a particular situation, institution, and rhetorician. The rhetorical hybrid represents a fusion of elements that, however transitory, stands as a potential kind of response to situations that future rhetoricians perceive in similar ways. Without a generic perspective, a critic would be less likely to perceive the recurrent elements as recurrent or the variable elements as an extension of the recurrent core of the eulogy or the presidential speech. Without the concept of the rhetorical hybrid, the critic would be less likely to capture the dynamic nature of rhetorical invention operating within the constraints of the situation. [*See* Invention.]

[*See also* Deliberative genre; Epideictic genre; *and* Forensic genre.]

BIBLIOGRAPHY

Campbell, Karlyn Kohrs, and Kathleen Hall Jamieson. "Form and Genre in Rhetorical Criticism: An Introduction." In *Form and Genre: Shaping Rhetorical Action,* edited by Karlyn Kohrs Campbell and Kathleen Hall Jamieson, pp. 18–25. Falls Church, Va. 1978.
Jamieson, Kathleen Hall. "Antecedent Genre as Rhetorical Constraint." *Quarterly Journal of Speech* 61 (1975), pp. 406–415.
Jamieson, Kathleen Hall. "Generic Constraints and the Rhetorical Situation." *Philosophy and Rhetoric* 6 (1973), pp. 162–170.
Jamieson, Kathleen Hall. "Rhetorical Hybrids: Fusions of Generic Elements." *Quarterly Journal of Speech* 68 (1982), pp. 146–157.
Leff, Michael C., and Gerald P. Mohrmann. "Lincoln at Cooper Union: A Rhetorical Analysis of the Text." *Quarterly Journal of Speech* 60 (1974), pp. 346–358.
Zyskind, Harold. "A Rhetorical Analysis of the Gettysburg Address." *Journal of General Education* 4 (April 1950), pp. 202–212.
—KATHLEEN HALL JAMIESON AND
JENNIFER STROMER-GALLEY

HYPALLAGĒ. The term designates the particular device that consists of an exchange within a statement between (1) the epithets assigned to specific nouns, or (2) activities associated with certain words or their complements. For example, note (1) the following pairs of mythological deities and their respective epithets, then (2) an exchange applied to the activities associated with them, devices that recur in classical and Western poetry:

1. chaste Diana / lustful Venus → lustful Diana / chaste Venus
2. Diana the hunter / Thetys the fisher → Diana the fisher / Thetys the hunter

[*See also* Figures of speech.]

BIBLIOGRAPHY

Lanham, R. A. *A Handlist of Rhetorical Terms.* Berkeley, 1991.
Lausberg, H. *Handbuch der literarischen Rhetorik.* Pp. 565–566. Munich, 1960.
Mayoral, J. A. *Figuras retóricas.* Pp. 247–248. Madrid, 1994.
Morier, H. *Dictionnaire de poétique et de rhétorique.* Paris, 1981.
—JOSÉ ANTONIO MAYORAL
Translated by A. Ballesteros

HYPERBATON (Lat. *transgressio*), a transposition called by Puttenham (*The Arte of English Poesie*, 1589, p. 168) "The Trespasser," which is a deviation from correct word order. It inserts extraneous material between syntactic elements not normally separated. For Puttenham, it can be a generic term for phrases "wrought by disorder." *Hyperbaton* is indicative of the speaker's affective involvement in trying to formulate developing ideas. Thus, Desdemona's skin is whiter than snow, but what Shakespeare's Othello says is, "that whiter skin of hers than snow" (5.2.4).

Viewed as splitting correlated elements (*tmēsis*) and adding new aspects (*parenthesis*), hyperbaton is a difficult ornament, since it potentially lends itself to obscurity.

[*See also* Figures of speech.]

— HEINER PETERS

HYPERBOLĒ (Lat. *superlatio, veri superiectio*), a semantic figure of exaggeration or overstatement that exceeds the truth and reality of things. It is mostly a kind of metaphor or allegory that raises the referential object beyond probability, as in Richard Crashaw's "Heavens thy fair eyes be, / Heavens of ever-falling stars" (*The Weeper,* 1652), where the microcosm of the human eyes is metaphorically identified with the planetary macrocosm. Of Puttenham's two English translations of *hyperbolē,* "the loud liar" and "the overreacher," the first finds its literary impersonation in the *miles gloriosus,* a soldierly braggart of Roman and Renaissance comedy, of whom a prominent representative is Shakespeare's Falstaff. "The overreacher" is impersonated, as Harry Levin's monograph of the same title (1954) demonstrates, in Christopher Marlowe's titanic Renaissance heroes, such as Tamburlaine (1590) with his hyperbolic oration: "I hold the Fates bound fast in iron chains, / And with my hand turn Fortune's wheel about." In these verses, as is proper for a work of literature, the *hyperbolē* appears as a mythological metaphor. Excessive *hyperbolē* is criticized as rhetorical bombast, for example, in Shakespeare's *Love's Labour's Lost* (5.2.407): "Three-pil'd hyperboles, spruce affectation, / Figures pedanticall." In everyday communication, this figure often assumes the forms of a numerical overstatement, a comparative, a superlative, an upgrading adjective, or an exaggerating constituent of a nominal compound ("mega-city"). Advertising slogans make ample use of hyperbolic language.

[*See also* Figures of speech; *and* Style.]

— HEINRICH F. PLETT

HYPERTEXT is a form of text made up of individual blocks of text and the links that join them together. Rather than being continuous and uninterrupted like most print texts, hypertext is comprised of independent text blocks (*lexias*) connected to other text blocks, documents, or hypermedia (photographs, graphics, videos). Early versions of hypertext were designed to be stored on main frame computers, disks, or CD-ROMs; more current versions take the form of Hypertext Markup Language (HTML), a standard language used in World Wide Web documents. As a markup language, HTML uses special codes to format text and to define links with other documents located in Internet environments.

Hypertext displaces many features of print text. For example, a print text has a beginning, middle, and end, whereas hypertext is differently organized. With the exception of a few print texts that are broken into lexias (e.g., Wittgenstein's *Philosophical Investigations*, 1953), most texts can be approached and experienced by readers via an identifiable point of entry and a demarcated series of events or ideas that are usually chonologically or logically sequenced. Hypertext, however, functions like a matrix of independent and cross-referenced discourses that the reader can enter more or less at random.

Hypertext thus calls into question the standard forms of organization linked to writing and print, and it relies on new patterns of organization and new forms of reading. Since Aristotle's *Poetics* (fourth century BCE), Western audiences and readers have expected linear sequencing of events, a certain unity of the whole, and patterns that unfold as the text progresses. Hypertext exhibits multivoicedness, discontinuity, and the blending of media and modes. It operates more as performance than as exegesis or story. Some forms of interactive hypertext take shape only in response to the reader's action, disclosing their contents or stories as a result of the reader's probing and curiosity. It may not be too far-fetched to imagine future stories and various rhetorical forms as coconstructed by author(s) and reader(s) of hypertext.

This possibility suggests the second feature of print text that is displaced in hypertext—the unitary text. Hypertext decreases the hierarchical separation between the text and its annotation or apparatus (footnotes, marginalia, commentary). Readers of hypertext can often select a link that will take them directly to a reference citation, digressive remark, separate explanatory lexia, or other text block that supports the initial text. They are then free to return to the original text or to follow the selected link into new textual pathways that take them further from the text where they started.

As George P. Landow (1997) has observed, then, digital text is "always open, borderless, unfinished and unfinishable, capable of infinite extension." To the extent that the pathways between lexias can be followed so variously and unpredictably, hypertext becomes malleable and unstable. This phenomenon is intensified by the technological environment in which it is situated. In the hypertext environment of the World Wide Web, for example, various linked texts on dispersed sites can disappear when the sites on which they are stored are removed from the Internet. Furthermore, many texts posted to the Internet are constantly being revised and changed. Although books can be misplaced, destroyed, or lost, they have comparatively more endurance and shelf life than many texts stored as hypertext that depend on a networked environment and constantly changing technology for their preservation.

The flexibility of hypertext structure (organization of content) has benefits and disadvantages. On one hand, it allows readers greater freedom to structure their reading experience according to their proclivities and interests. On the other hand, it lends itself to reader disorientation. Theorists who discuss the experience of reading hypertext often speak in terms of navigating or voyaging through hypertext documents, and it is easy to lose one's way. One may be uncertain about where one wants to go or how to get there. One may not know the boundaries or configuration of the textual space and thus become lost in a maze of juxtaposed lexias.

A third aspect of the print text that is displaced in hypertext has to do with the text author. Whereas in print text, the author is usually viewed as the point of origin or anchor for ideas, in hypertext, authorship function is decentered. In the hypermedia environment of the World Wide Web, for example, many sites are posted by collaborators and groups of writers; others are anonymous. Hypertext lends itself to texts that are an assemblage of text blocks and images borrowed from other sites and brought together through pastiche or through links. In light of such practices, intellectual property and copyright are put at risk, and the process of determining the credibility of a text by considering the credibility of its author is jeopardized.

Hypertext also affects the writing function. The hypertext environment does not lend itself to long, complex texts because readers are disposed to read quickly and to require textual markers to keep their bearings. Much hypertext writing therefore calls upon writers to break up the text, write short paragraphs, and insert headers, images, and links to keep the reader's attention. Writers must also create pathways that link lexias so that readers can understand their structure.

There are various ways of organizing hypertext, but they differ from organization in print text. A hypertext document may take the form of a central hub surrounded by links, an initial thread that branches into unfolding paths, a cluster of ideas, or some other pattern. In all cases, writers must map concepts so that readers can understand how they are related to each other. Navigational devices such as site maps, links to a "home" or starting point, or frames take the place in hypertext of the thesis statement, preview, and summary found in print texts.

The emergence of hypertext and new media calls for a new kind of media literacy. Hypertext authors must know how to organize and display hypertext documents so as to promote reader comprehension. They must also stay abreast of new markup languages, changes in design practices, adjustments in copyright law, and new critical and theoretical approaches to visual argument. Their readers must know how to navigate through hypertext, how to manipulate it, and how to critically judge its content. These requirements for hypertext literacy will continue to develop and change until hypertext itself is supplanted by new media forms such as Internet-based digital video and audio.

[*See also* Arrangement, *article on* Modern arrangement.]

BIBLIOGRAPHY

Landow, George P., ed. *Hyper/Text/Theory*. Baltimore, 1994. This collection of eleven essays by various authors explores the theoretical and critical implications of hypertext for narrative, literacy, rhetoric, and other aspects of writing and reading. The essays are thoughtful and suggestive. Their commentary and predictions are no less interesting in light of the fact that most were written prior to 1994 and can now be evaluated in light of the advent and growth of the World Wide Web.

Landow, George P. *Hypertext 2.0.* Baltimore, 1997. As the definitive work on hypertext to date, this book describes the development, nature, and applications of hypertext, primarily in the period just prior to its use on the World Wide Web. Applying the critical theories of Deleuze and Guattari, Derrida, Barthes, Lyotard, and others, Landow explains how the phenomenon of hypertext changes how we write, read, think, and experience literature. One can only wish that Landow's update in this book of his earlier *Hypertext* had provided a more thorough account of how the advent of the World Wide Web has affected our conceptions of hypertext and how it operates.

Ong, Walter J. *Orality and Literacy: The Technologizing of the Word.* London, 1982. Ong's work compares primary orality, manuscript communication, print communication, and secondary orality via electronic media. He believes that these various modes of communication have profound effects on human consciousness and on how people relate to themselves and each other. Ong's focus is on describing the characteristics of each of these modes and their ef-

fects on society. One weakness of this book is a tendency to view print texts as comparatively uninfluenced by and unresponsive to other texts.

—BARBARA WARNICK

HYSTERON PRŌTERON (Gk. also *hysterologia;* Lat. *praeposteratio*), called by Puttenham (*The Arte of English Poesie,* 1589, p. 170) "the cart before the horse," is the reversal of a causal or (chrono-)logical sequence as distinguished from a grammatical one. [*See* Anastrophē.] It is classified as a semantic deviation, occasionally bordering on the absurd. Thus, in Shakespeare's *Antony and Cleopatra,* Cleopatra's flagship is reported to "fly and turn its rudder" (3.10.3). Though strategies of disorder are sometimes censured as "deformities" (Puttenham, p. 171), *Hysteron prōteron* finds its recommended equivalent on the textual level in the narrative or dramatic *in-medias-res* approach (Horace, *Ars Poetica,* first century BCE, l. 148), where what is of greatest psychological interest is presented at the outset.

[*See also* Figures of speech.]

—HEINER PETERS

I–J

ICONOGRAPHY. The striking thesis, advanced by Marshall McLuhan and by Walter J. Ong, of a paradigm shift in Western European culture from an oral to a visual epistemology might be taken to suggest that traditional rhetoric had been innately hostile to visualization. Such an inference would be mistaken. The classical art of memory, in which the *rhētōr* commits ideas to memory by associating them with vivid images placed in a series of background settings, remained vital throughout the Middle Ages and in the Renaissance took on a new emphasis from occult philosophy. [*See* Memory.] From the beginning, then, visual imagery was integral to the rhetorical process and the visual representation of the discipline itself a natural development. Possibly the earliest such representation was a *synecdochē* that Cicero (*De finibus* 2.6) attributed to Zeno of Elea (fifth century BCE), the legendary inventor of dialectic. [*See* Dialectic.] Contrasting the expansive and the compressed styles of the two arts, Zeno said that rhetoric is an open palm and dialectic a closed fist. Later, an enduring metaphor attached to the Athenian orator Demosthenes (384–322 BCE)—the force of whose delivery commonly was likened to a thunderbolt.

Classical mythology supplied the first embodiment of rhetoric in the figure of Hermes, the messenger of the gods, whom the Romans identified with Mercurius (Mercury). One of the twelve Olympians, Hermes is marked in the fables as a quick-witted, amoral, good-natured deity. While still an infant, he stole his brother's cattle; and, when caught, mollified Apollo by inventing a lyre and singing Apollo's praises. The siblings parallel the close connection of rhetoric and poetry; Hermes' early career as thief can suggest commonplace invention; his moral neutrality and pragmatism resemble those of argumentation *in utramque partem*. [*See* Invention.] The ancients paid tribute to the amorous feats of Hermes with the herms—stone pillars with a bust of the god on top and a phallus on the front—commonly used as milestones. Sexual prowess became a metaphor for the creative potency of language that Renaissance writers—among them Pietro Aretino (1492–1556), François Rabelais (c.1494–1553), and Michel de Montaigne (1533–1592)—exploited.

The attributes that Hermes received from his father Zeus (Lat. Jove or Jupiter) when he became herald made him the most unmistakable of the gods: his herald's staff, the caduceus, usually represented as winged and entwined with two serpents; the petasus, his round, winged, often pointed hat; and his golden, winged sandals. Related characteristics or qualities in other myths, as well, sometimes caused them to be assimilated to the iconography of rhetoric. The conviction that rhetoric requires the union of eloquence with wisdom (Cicero, *De inventione* 1.1–2), for example, drew attention to the goddess of wisdom, Pallas Athena (Lat. Minerva), whose armor, helmet, and shield could be reassigned to the figure of rhetoric. Since the purpose of any *rhētōr* is to "move" his audience, the story of animals, birds, and trees literally swayed by the power of Orpheus's song (Ovid, *Metamorphoses* 10) could, even better than Hermes' epideictic song to Apollo, symbolize the affective strength and harmony of eloquent speech. [*See* Epideictic genre.] Similarly, the story of Amphion's lyre moving stones to construct the walls of Thebes could figure not only persuasion but arrangement. [*See* Arrangement, *article on* Traditional arrangement.] The two strategies of representation—either by direct recourse to classical myth or through personification by attributes, whether borrowed from mythical deities or derived from rhetorical practice—from the beginning were closely intertwined and would remain so.

Medieval and Renaissance Personifications. *The Marriage of Philology and Mercury* (c.410–439 CE), by the Roman African Martianus Capella, who may have been a lawyer or proconsul, incongruously mingles abstractions, gods of various kinds, and ancient worthies, wrestling them all into personification allegory. Mercury (Eloquence) proposes marriage to Philology (Learning), a course approved by an assembly of gods who decree that the bride should become an immortal. Suffering a bout of premarital queasiness, Philology is induced to vomit a great quantity of books, which some young women collect. After the wedding, these women are presented one by one as handmaidens to grace the new household; Philology's bridal gift is the Seven Liberal Arts, each of whom makes a speech explaining herself. Rhetoric (Book 5) is statuesque, beautiful, and self-confident. She wears a robe ornamented with rhetorical figures and a jeweled belt that displays the "colors" of eloquence. Minervalike, she is armed, flourishing the weapons with which she defends herself or wounds her enemies; above her helmet is a crown. Behind Rhetoric follows a train of orators, headed by Demosthenes and Cicero. When she speaks, she honors Cicero for both theory and practice and delivers a full and decidedly Ciceronian exposition of her art. Martianus's personifications of the Seven Liberal Arts and their attributes became canonical for the Middle Ages. They recur frequently in Latin poetry and were familiar to the devout from the façades of half-a-dozen cathedrals. The image of Rhetoric was durable enough to last, with occasional modification, into the Renaissance and well beyond.

The fifteenth-century image of "Rhetorica" in the Liberal Arts sequence of the so-called Tarot Cards of Mantegna (which were neither Tarot cards, nor by Mantegna) virtually illustrates Martianus's concept. (*See* Figure 1.) The tall, sober, young woman, wearing a jewelled breastplate and crowned helmet, is a commanding figure. In her right hand, she holds upright a sword; with her left she modestly drapes the hem of her robe. No doubt perplexed by the design problem, the artist has omitted the specification that the robe should be embellished with rhetorical figures. Instead, he provides Rhetoric with two attendants; on each side a putto blows mightily on a trumpet. This may substitute for Martianus's visually difficult prescription that the clash of Rhetoric's weapons evokes the thunder of Jupiter himself. More likely, however, the artist borrows a familiar

attribute from Fame to suggest rhetoric's power to immortalize both speaker and subject. In either case, the anonymous artist follows Martianus in the attempt to personify Cicero's ideal union of wisdom and eloquence.

An altogether different representational strategy, and order of artistic achievement, may be seen with Antonio Pollaiuolo's *Tomb of Pope Sixtus IV* (Rome, 1493). Pollaiuolo created a free-standing, bronze monument, suggesting a sarcophagus; on the top center lies a recumbent effigy of the pope, with relief images of the virtues surrounding his pallet. On the chamfered sides of the tomb are ten fields with reclining female figures of the arts and sciences. The serene and smiling, nude figure of "Rhetorica," with drapery across her thighs, leans casually on her left forearm. In that hand and across her left shoulder, she holds a rustic staff that branches into clusters of oak leaves. Her outstretched right hand touches an open book, across which is inscribed (in Latin): "With clear and strong speech according to circumstances I take to all disciplines. I speak suitably to persuade or dissuade." The sentences are drawn from the *Rhetorica ad Herennium,* then still attributed to Cicero, possibly through the intermediary of Quintilian. The design and style of this and the other bronze reliefs are distinctly modern, evoking a sense of movement and vivacity, and truly Renaissance in the return to classical form, adapting the pose from the figure of Tellus on a Hadrianic coin. Nonetheless, while Pollaiuolo has avoided the clutter of overt attributes, he has transformed, rather than dismissed, them. The oak stave, gracefully alluding to the pope's family name (Rovere, "oak"), culminates with intertwined branches in a pattern that echoes the entwined serpents of Mercury's *caduceus;* and, if Rhetorica's right hand were turned about, the positioning of her fingers on the book would be revealed as the familiar open-palm gesture, the synecdoche for her art.

Pollaiuolo's elegant solution might well have served as a model for the next century; but only rarely was the direction to which he pointed, simplicity and naturalness of representation, explored. The Italian vernacular writer, Pietro Aretino, cultivated the role of a demonstrative orator, dispensing praise or blame. In half-length portraits painted by Sebastiano del Piombo and by

Iconography. FIGURE 1. *"Rhetorica" from the "Tarot Cards of Mantegna" (before 1467).* [Photo courtesy of M. Knoedler & Co., New York.]

Titian, Aretino adopted the pose of an orator. The author portraits in his books, by which he made his face famous, only afforded scope for a bust, ruling out the oratorical stance. Instead, a number of the woodcuts depict him open-mouthed in the simplest possible image of eloquence—a man speaking. These naturalistic projections of Aretino as an eloquent speaker, without recourse to gods or attributes, were the exception, however, not the rule.

Medals, *Imprese*, and Emblems. At the time Pollaiuolo was completing the *Tomb of Sixtus IV,* already a number of converging factors gave new energy to the Martianus tradition by focusing intensely upon the symbolic attributes. Pisanello (Antonio Pisano, c.1395–c.1455), responding to the example of imperial Roman coins, in the 1530s and 1540s created the portrait medal. Medals never were used for money, but followed the coin format of a portrait obverse and a symbolic reverse. The portrait showed the subject's body; the reverse, often obscurely or riddlingly, some inner quality, his "soul." Medals, in turn, fed a taste for the *impresa* or personal device, usually consisting of an abstract image with a motto. The French invasion of Italy in 1494 introduced a new fashion, the hat badge, another medium for displaying one's personal device. The rediscovery of the *Hieroglyphica* of Horapollo (manuscript recovery 1419; printed 1505), a pictorial dictionary of symbols, lent the authority of ancient wisdom to these modern fashions. The result often was to diminish the role of personification, instead concentrating on attributes and investing them with deep symbolic resonance.

Clemente da Urbino's medal of Federigo da Montefeltro (1422–1482), the celebrated prince of Urbino and *condottiere,* will illustrate the process. Although Federigo never lost a battle, causing his services to be much sought after, and never allowed war to touch his own state, his humanist credentials were equally impressive. He had been a pupil of Vittorino da Feltre (1378–1446), whose Ciceronian lessons he embraced. Throughout his life, Federigo delighted in Latin; and, when responding to the petitions of his citizens, would deliver his judgments in that language. Clemente's medal reverse depicts an eagle balancing on its wings a complex set of attributes:

those of war (cuirass, sword, and shield) to the left; those of peace (olive branch and whisk broom) on the right; in the center, a cannon ball. Above are three stars, Jupiter between Mars and Venus. Edgar Wind has read this as a symbol of *discordia concors,* the balance between Mars and Venus under Jupiter, who is represented by his attributes, the eagle that is his messenger and the thunderbolt evoked by the cannon ball. Clemente's medal is dated 1468, however, which adds a further significance. In that year, Federigo built a palace to serve as his court, the administrative center of his duchy, and a site for his literary and artistic interests—effectively, a monument to civic humanism. Federigo's favorite rooms were devoted to the library in which he amassed the largest private collection of manuscripts in Italy. It seems likely that the medal was commissioned in relation to this project. The cannon ball, thus, punningly epitomizes the balance in Federigo's life; it alludes both to his military prowess (which financed the palace) and to humanist eloquence (Jupiter's thunder being one of Rhetoric's attributes in Martianus). Not only eloquent himself, through his patronage Federigo created the palace as a treasury of eloquence. [*See* Eloquence.]

In contrast, less occult reverse designs sometimes used Mercury to represent eloquence. The medal of Lorenzo de Giovanni Tornabuoni (1466–1497), for example, has a reverse (without motto) of Mercury, wearing the winged sandals and petasus, and carrying the caduceus in the crook of his right arm. At his left hip is a sheathed sword; both his right hand, by his side, and his left, thrust outward, offer the open-palm gesture. The unclassical sword assimilates Minerva's wisdom to Tornabuoni; and the entire image reduces the god to a one-dimensional figure of eloquence, indistinguishable from his attributes. A half-century later, another anonymous medallist honored Pierio Valeriano Bolzanio (1475–1558), author of the symbolic lexicon *Hieroglyphica* (1556), with a different Mercury. (*See* Figure 2.) The reverse features the god, nude except for winged hat and sandals, with caduceus in his right hand, leaning insouciantly against a broken obelisk inscribed with hieroglyphics. Paralleling the obelisk is the inscription *Instaurator* ("follower" or "preserver").

Iconography. FIGURE 2. *"Mercury" on Reverse of Medal of Valeriano (1475–1558).* [Photograph copyright Board of Trustees, National Gallery of Art, Washington, D.C.]

Valeriano is credited with recovering the lost tradition of hieroglyphics (the broken column) and Mercury's proprietorial hand on the column implicitly asserts, as does his classical nudity, that true eloquence will be found in the Egyptian pictograms, an ancient tradition of wisdom now accessible once again through Valeriano's scholarship.

Pisanello's earlier medals were conceived without a reverse inscription, except for the artist's signature; the last ones have a Latin motto related to the image. Succeeding medallists usually followed the latter format, from which evolved the notion of the *impresa* as combination of symbolic image and motto. The next step was taken by Andrea Alciato (1492–1550), the distinguished Milanese legal scholar, whose *Emblematum liber* (1531) inspired a host of imitations and itself achieved over one hundred and fifty editions by the end of the eighteenth century. The emblem adds a third term—title, image, and a moralizing, epigrammatic verse—the whole to be understood as a rhetorical set. Alciato's Emblem 119 will exemplify the concept. The title or motto asserts that fortune is the companion of excellence; the picture presents a caduceus framed by two cornucopia and crowned by Mercury's winged hat.

The verse explains that abundance (*copia*) blesses men who are powerful in mind and skillful speakers. The Ciceronian ideal of wisdom and eloquence, therefore, promises the reward of good fortune and prosperity; but the multiple emphasis on eloquence—both caduceus and winged hat, plus the unavoidable play on *copia* as facility in rhetorical invention—implies that rhetorical skill is a blessing in itself. [*See* Copia.]

Whereas the *impresa* was meant to be understood only by the initiate, the emblem, with the explicit moral, was a didactic medium. By the 1550s, however, books of imprese were being published in response to the emblem vogue; and, thereafter, the distinction between the two blurred. The study of ancient coins, which helped generate medals and *imprese,* also influenced emblems. The Hungarian humanist Johannes Sambucus (1531–1583) published his *Emblemata* (1564) with an appendix illustrating a selection of classical coins. One of these, a coin of Marcus Aurelius, reappears two decades later in the first English emblem book, Geoffrey Whitney's *A Choice of Emblems* (1586). The coin reverse of Orpheus charming the beasts with his lyre becomes the emblem of "Orphei Musica." The verse explains that the power is not simply a natural gift: "besides his skill, hee learned was, and wise: / And coulde with sweetness of his tonge, all sortes of men suffice." Orphic music symbolizes rhetorical efficacy.

Ripa's *Iconologia.* The increasingly available resources of the illustrated book, whether by woodcut or engraving, were a boon not only to numismatics and emblematics. The preface to Vicenzo Cartari's *Imagini de gli dei de gli antichi* ("Images of the ancient gods," 1556) claims that Cartari provides the first descriptions of their statues, making the book particularly valuable to artists and poets. This feature was enhanced by the eighty-five illustrations added to the 1571 edition. A similar concern motivated Cesare Ripa's *Iconologia* (1593; illustrated, 1603), a handbook explaining how to represent virtues, vices, passions, temperaments, qualities, and the like. The title page asserts that the book will be a necessity for orators, preachers, poets, artists, and devisors of emblems and *imprese.* Ripa (1560–c.1623) knew whereof he spoke. Seven Italian editions were published in his lifetime; after his death, editors continued to expand the allegories until they numbered over a thousand; and the original Italian was translated into half-a-dozen other modern languages.

Ripa's method is to describe the allegorical figure embodying the specified concept, explain the type and colors of the clothing and the symbolic attributes, then to justify the description by the authorities he has consulted. The 1603 edition offers two versions of Rhetoric and six descriptions of Eloquence. The brief figure of "Rettorica" simply is a woman exemplifying Zeno's *synecdochē:* her right arm outstretched, hand with the palm open; her left arm folded, the hand clenched in a fist. The more elaborate image gives us a beautiful lady with a ruddy complexion, richly dressed, her head nobly attired, showing herself pleasingly. In her right hand, she holds a scepter and in the left a book; on the hem of her dress are the words "ornatus persuasio." The scepter is a sign that she rules the affections; the book shows that her art is perfected by study, not a gift of nature; the words confirm the office of rhetoric, to instruct others to speak pleasingly and persuasively.

Two descriptions of "Eloquenza" present myths, Orpheus and Amphion; the remaining four are female personifications. In the longest, she is symbolized by a beautiful young woman, because the ancients depicted Mercury as young, pleasing, and beardless. Eloquence wears a golden crown over a helmet, a breastplate, and sword over a purple dress; her arms are bare; in her right hand she holds a staff and in her left a thunderbolt. The bare arms signify the delicacy of her words, whereas the armor indicates the foundation of reason and knowledge without which eloquence is weak and helpless. The thunderbolt, deriving from Demosthenes' epithet, alludes to the sublime force of eloquence. The crown of gold and the purple dress are clear signs of Eloquence's dominion over the spirits of humans, a point Ripa confirms by quoting Plato on oratory as the queen of arts.

Ripa's influence was lasting. An eighteenth-century English architect, George Richardson (c.1736–c.1817), who specialized in the decoration of London apartments in neoclassical style, undertook an extensively illustrated translation of Ripa (*Iconology,* 1779). The engravings of Rhetoric and Eloquence (pl. 34) give us ladies in Gainsborough-like poses, decorously swathed in classical robes. Richardson's translation simplifies and refines Ripa: "The power of persuasion is the act of speaking not merely with propriety, but with art and elegance" ("Rhetorick"). But the specifications recognizably are Ripa's. Through such intermediaries as Ripa, Martianus Capella's Rhetoric had a very long career.

Renaissance Syncretism: Hermathena; and Hercules, Eloquent and Silent. Thus far, for the most part, we have traced iconographic traditions that were widely employed and would have been generally understood. The veneration of classical antiquity, however, sometimes endowed obscure images and puzzling phrases with profound meaning, even the status of religious mysteries. A philosophical context for such speculations emerged from the neoplatonic circle of Marsilio Ficino (1443–1499), who translated all of Plato into Latin. Ficino's own commentaries on Plato amount to a discursive mythography in which the individual fables have changeable, rather than static, meanings. Neoplatonic theories of myth and symbolic images account for the excitement aroused by Egyptian hieroglyphics and provide an intellectual foundation for theories of the *impresa.* Manifestations of such syncretism were the cultivation of hybrid gods and, alternatively, the paradoxical attribution of opposite qualities to a single god.

"Hermathena" actually has a classical pedigree, if a minor one. Cicero's letters record his search for an appropriate herm to ornament his lecture hall and his delight in obtaining a Hermathena, since the qualities of both gods were singularly appropriate to his academy (*Ad Atticum* 1.1 and 1.4). We owe the sixteenth-century currency of this composite to Achille Bocchi (1488–1562), a Bolognese academic, who chose that image as the *impresa* of his own academy and included it in his *Symbolicarum Quaestionum* (1555). A sense of this emblem book's oddity can be suggested by Bocchi's image for the art of rhetoric (no. 137): Bellerophon taming the Chimera. Rhetoric is not, as one might expect, Bellerophon but the monster, whose tripartite body (lion, goat, serpent) corresponds to the three functions of rhetoric (moving, pleasing, teaching), which need to be governed by heavenly truth (Bellerophon). By contrast, Bocchi's Hermathena emblem (no. 102) is a masterpiece of lucidity in symbolizing the Ciceronian union of wisdom and eloquence. Represented as herms placed on the corner of a building, Hermes (with *caduceus* and winged hat) and Athena (armed with spear) link arms as they look toward each other. Between them stands Eros atop a monster that he reins with one hand; with the other he points to Athena. Three mottoes tell us that this is how monsters are tamed; this is the guide to perfecting oneself and the one divinity that perfects happiness. Hermathena gained a fair degree of currency, appearing in Cartari and in several subsequent emblem books, the last being Francis Tolson's *Hermathenae, or Moral Emblems* (c.1740).

Classical tradition had attributed strength of mind, as well as body, to Hercules; and occasionally he was linked with Mercury. Lucian of Samosata (second century CE) contributed a description of the Celtic god Ogmius, whom he identified with Hercules, as an old man in a lion skin and armed with bow and club; from his mouth issue fine chains that connect to the ears of his audience. The translation by Erasmus (1512) made the "Gallic Hercules" accessible in the sixteenth century; Alciato popularized it with an emblem (no. 181: "Eloquence surpasses strength"; *see* Figure 3); Bocchi's emblem (no. 43) interpreted the chains as the wisdom directing eloquence. The "Gallic Hercules" later was adopted as a device for Henri IV (r. 1589–1610), appearing on medals and used for royal entries. The image took a last, bizarre twist with the personification of "Rhetorica" in Christophoro Giarda's *Icones Symbolicae* (1626). The tall, crowned, young woman wears a richly figured dress and mantle; she holds a *caduceus* in her right hand and her left outstretched in the familiar, open gesture. At her right side, a pot of fire stands for the thunderbolt of Demosthenes. In the left foreground, a rather jolly, three-headed monster—Bocchi's chimera revived—is bound by the fine chains that emanate from Rhetorica's mouth, a condition which may account for her lugubrious expression. E. H. Gombrich has argued, plausibly, that Giarda conceived the symbolic images as direct representations of Platonic Ideas; but the personification of rhetoric also seems an embodiment of eclectic and incoherent source reading.

Less incongruous and far more subtle is an imagistic sequence expressing the identity of eloquence in silence. On several occasions, Cicero had remarked on the eloquent effect of silence (see, e.g., *Ad Atticum* 13.42 and *In Catalinum* 1.8.20). In the Renaissance, Ficino's Latin translation of the *Corpus Hermeticum* (1564), the supposedly ancient, Egyptian religious treatises, contributed to an association of their putative author, "Hermes Trismegistus," with the Greek god of eloquence, Hermes. The Greeks already had misunderstood the gesture of the child-god Harpocrates, touching a finger to his lips, as a symbol of silence; this became conflated with the Pythagorean injunction to silence, as it is in Alciato (no. 11: "Silence"). Bocchi's Emblem 64 ("Worship God in Silence") shows a nude Hermes, identified by his winged hat, holding a seven-branched candelabrum and making the gesture of silence. A circle of light overhead represents the divine illumination he seeks. In another emblem (no. 143), Hermes stands in fire, making the silence gesture, as the Holy Spirit descends; the motto tells us that the divine lover suffers and conquers in silence. Bocchi's mystically silent Hermes acts as psychopomp, guiding spirits to transcendence. In 1609, George Chapman, a lonely, Platonic mystagogue among English poets, imagined that "Herculean silence bore/His craggie Club; which up, aloft, he held;/With which, and his forefingers charme he stild/All sounds in ayre" allowing the poet to hear the music of the spheres and the heavenly choir (*The Teares of Peace*, lines 1105–1111). Chapman's remarkable image merges Herculean eloquence with Hermetic silence, a typological adaptation that carries syncretism to a new level.

The span from approximately 1475 to 1650 was the grand period for the expression of abstract ideas in the form of symbolic images. Whether conceived in the open, emblematic mode or the occult line of the impresa, whether executed as woodcut, sculpture, poem, or ceiling painting, the iconography of eloquence never was more imaginatively devised. As well as imaging a predominantly Ciceronian theory of rhetoric, the

Eloquentia fortitudine præftantior.
EMBLEMA CLXXXI.

Iconography. FIGURE 3. *"Gallic Hercules" by Alciato (1492–1550), from* Emblemata *(Padua, 1621).* [Photo courtesy of R. Waddington.]

iconography itself is a visual form of rhetoric, both mnemonic and trope.

BIBLIOGRAPHY

Andreas Alciatus: Index Emblematicus. Edited by Peter M. Daly with Virginia W. Callahan and Simon Cuttler. 2 vols. Toronto, 1985. Translation of the emblem book, from both Latin and vernacular language editions, with elaborate indices.

Bar, Virginie, and Dominique Breme. *Dictionnaire iconologique: Les allegories et les symboles de Cesare Ripa et Jean Baudoin.* 2 vols. Dijon, France, 1999.

Cunnally, John. *Images of the Illustrious: The Numismatic Presence in the Renaissance.* Princeton, 1999. Discusses the illustrated books on ancient coins and their influence.

Curtius, Ernst Robert. *European Literature and the Latin Middle Ages.* Translated by Willard R. Trask. Bollingen Series no. 36. New York, 1953. English translation of *Europäische Literatur und lateinisches Mittelatter,* New York, 1948. Invaluable study of rhetorical topics.

Davidson, Jane Reid. *The Oxford Guide to Classical Mythology in the Arts, 1370–1990s.* New York, 1993.

Ettlinger, L. D. "Pollaiuolo's Tomb of Pope Sixtus IV." *Journal of the Warburg and Courtauld Institutes* 16 (1953), pp. 239–274.

Gombrich, E. H. *Symbolic Images: Studies in the Art of the Renaissance.* London, 1972. See "Introduction: Aims and Limits of Iconology" (pp. 1–25), and *"Icones Symbolicae:* Philosophies of Symbolism and their Bearing on Art" (pp. 123–195).

Gordon, D. J. *The Renaissance Imagination.* Edited by Stephen Orgel. Berkeley, 1975. See "Ripa's Fate" (pp. 51–74).

Hall, James. *Dictionary of Subjects and Symbols in Art.* New York, 1974.

Martianus Capella and the Seven Liberal Arts. No. 84 of the Records of Civilization: Sources and Studies; vol. 1, *The Quadrivium of Martianus Capella,* by William Harris Stahl. New York, 1971; vol. 2, *The Marriage of Philology and Mercury.* Translated by William Harris Stahl and Richard Johnson with E. C. Burge. New York, 1977.

Okayama, Yassu. *The Ripa Index: Personifications and Their Attributes in Five Editions of the Iconologia.* Doornspijk, The Netherlands, 1992.

Tervarent, Guy de. *Attributs et symboles dans l'art profane: Dictionnaire d'un langage perdu (1450–1600).* 2d ed. Geneva, 1997.

Vivanti, Corrado. "Henry IV, the Gallic Hercules." *Journal of the Warburg and Courtauld Institutes* 30 (1967), pp. 176–197.

Waddington, Raymond B. "The Iconography of Silence and Chapman's Hercules." *Journal of the Warburg and Courtauld Institutes* 33 (1970), pp. 248–263.

Waddington, Raymond B. "Myth." In *Encyclopedia of the Renaissance,* vol. 4, edited by Paul F. Grendler, pp. 268–273. New York, 1999.

Watson, Elizabeth See. *Achille Bocchi and the Emblem Book as Symbolic Form.* Cambridge, U.K., 1993.

Wind, Edgar. *Pagan Mysteries in the Renaissance.* 2d ed., rev. and enl. New York, 1968. Seminal study of the intellectual contexts of Renaissance iconography.

—RAYMOND B. WADDINGTON

IDENTIFICATION is the central theme in the rhetoric of symbolic action that was articulated by Kenneth Burke (1897–1993). Sigmund Freud's (1856–1939) views on identification and Karl Marx's (1818–1883) concern with alienation inspired Burke to consider how individuals use symbols to manage human relations. In contrast with rhetorics that preceded his, Burke's explored the symbolic actions of courtship, estrangement or alienation, identity, and consubstantiation. Each one of these allowed him to restate his central theme.

Burke employed a nonaxiomatic, sociological approach to rhetoric as opposed to what he characterized as earlier rhetoricians' commitment to a button-pushing explicit design of arguments. The earlier propositional rhetorics were devoted to the test of statements about reality (epistemology). In contrast, Burke's identification operates on a battleground of merger and division, a rhetorical tug of war between "us" and "them," allowing him to add depth and definition to the central theme of the new rhetoric; namely, a concern with issues of collaboration and mediation rather than with instrumental persuasion and ratiocination.

Burke's view of rhetoric focused explicitly on the powerful attraction of words, their ability to foster courtship through identification. Words serve as terministic screens that filter what people see and shape how they act toward one another and all of reality. It is language that enlivens thought and lifts humans beyond sheer experience. He argued that people use words as a means for acting together rather than as an instrument for conveying truth from one mind to another. He thus moved beyond a view of rhetoric as the contest of propositions of fact, to explain how people engage in the wrangle of courtship by which they foster mergers and divisions through symbols that allow them to share intersubjective knowledge.

Years before it influenced his views on rhetoric, identification enriched Burke's poetics. This seminal analysis appeared in his article "On Re and Dis," published in *The Dial* in 1925. He reasoned that artistic appeal occurs "in the 'margin of overlap' between the writer's experiences and the reader's" (p. 168). A poem bridges individual experiences by focusing attention on similarities of experience and shared knowledge. A poem does not merely convey feeling but gives the reader the opportunity to identify with the author as they share feelings in a cathartic release. Burke called this poetic experience "the dancing of an attitude."

Extending this notion to support his theory of rhetoric, Burke reasoned that identification allows people to share views they need in order to collaborate with as well as compete against one another. He observed that people use rhetoric to think of themselves as similar to or dissimilar from one another as they live in cooperative competition. They act in concert and associate with those with whom they identify and dissociate themselves from others. They may act against, scapegoat, even symbolically kill those with whom they do not identify. Thus, rhetoric is a contest of identifies and loyalties, the courtship of coming together and separating. For Burke, this external struggle of association and dissociation leads to and compensates for feelings of estrangement or alienation.

For Burke as for Freud, identification is an antidote to those feelings of alienation that were so crucial to Marxian analysis. To some extent, each person is unique and separate from other individuals and therefore naturally feels estranged. Alienation results from the realization that the meaning that an individual and certain institutions share can privilege those institutions and some people, but at the expense of other institutions and individuals. Through identification, people can share experience—that "margin of overlap"—and reduce their feelings of alienation, or look for and even create new identifications.

Such appeals give individuals a sense of how they identify with one another, as well as the opportunity to see their identity reflected in society. Making that point in *The Philosophy of Literary Form,* Burke reasoned:

> By "identification" I have in mind this sort of thing: one's material and mental ways of placing oneself as a person in the groups and movements; one's ways of sharing vicariously in the role of leader or spokesman; formation and change of allegiance; the rituals of suicide, parricide, and prolicide, the vesting and divesting of insignia, the modes of initiation and purification, that are involved in the response to allegiance and change of allegiance, the part necessarily played by groups in the expectancies of the individual . . . clothes, uniforms, and the psychological equivalents; one's ways of seeing one's reflection in the social mirror. (p. 227)

Identification is potent because estrangement frustrates human relations. The rhetorical situation reduces to this dynamic, as Burke explained in *A Rhetoric of Motives* (*RM*): "Identification is affirmed with earnestness precisely because there is division. Identification is compensatory to division. If men [people] were not apart from one another, there would be no need for the rhetorician to proclaim their unity" (p. 22). The potency of identification allowed Burke to formulate a robust rhetoric based on *"the use of language as a symbolic means of inducing cooperation in beings that by nature respond to symbols"* (*RM*, p. 43; italics Burke's). As Burke reasoned, "A is not identical with his colleague, B. But insofar as their interests are joined, A is *identified* with B. Or he may identify himself with B even when their interests are not joined, if he assumes that they are, or is persuaded to believe so" (*RM*, p. 20). Because of estrangement, people yearn to belong to one another and to institutions. "'Belonging' in this sense is rhetoric" (*RM*, p. 28). People "belong" to one another through identification. For this reason, "rhetorical language is inducement to action (or to attitude, attitude being an incipient act)" (*RM*, p. 42).

Through identification, people develop various collective identities with which they govern themselves and form human relations. For Burke, rhetoric entails appeals for identification in "the region of the Scramble, of insult and injury, bickering, squabbling, malice, and the lie, cloaked malice and the subsidized lie" (*RM*, p. 19). Rhetorical theory gives insights into "the Scramble, the Wrangle of the Market Place, the flurries and flare-ups of the Human Barnyard, the Give and Take, the wavering line of pressure and counterpressure, the Logomachy, the onus of ownership, the Wars of nerves, the War" (*RM*, p. 23). These conflicts, endemic to the struggle of human relations, can be revealed by a rhetorical analysis that isolates those threads of concurrence and conflict that account for the mergers and divisions that shape society. The rhetorical situation is a battleground whereby people appeal to "us" at the expense of polarizing against "them." [*See* Rhetorical situation.] As well as bringing people together, rhetoric can thus actually magnify feelings of estrangement. Moreover, identification is central to Burke's explanation of how the ruler influences the ruled (as the ruled influences the ruler) by applying the principle of the state as a "margin of overlap" to bridge the estrangements of region, class, party, and position. The courtship of the classes applies identification to create and reduce division. Likewise, the divorce of classes is the clash of identifications, another concept Burke derived from the writings of Marx.

Identification, finally, is the bridging of interests through consubstantiation. "In pure identification there would be no strife. Likewise, there would be no strife in absolute separateness, since opponents can join battle only through a mediatory ground that makes their communication possible, thus providing the first condition necessary for their interchange of blows" (*RM*, p. 25). Substance is the basis for sharing, the "margin of overlap" between individuals. By sharing substance, people become consubstantial—one of many—so that they think and act together. As Burke observed, "A doctrine of *consubstantiality,* either explicit or implicit, may be necessary to any way of life. For substance, in the old philosophies, was an *act;* and a way of life is an *acting-together,* men [people] have common sensations, concepts, images, ideas, attitudes that make them consubstantial" (*RM*, p. 21).

How does substance give potency to rhetoric? Burke answered, "In being identified with B, A is 'substantially one' with a person other than himself. Yet at the same time he remains unique, an individual locus of motives. Thus he is both joined and separate, at once a distinct substance and consubstantial with another" (*RM*, p. 21). The dialectic of individualism and collectivism—alienation and merger—is a tension with which humans struggle. To overcome or compensate for differences, they engage in the symbolic action of consubstantiation.

Identification blended with Burke's interest in transcendence. To identify, people must transcend their individualism and seek a higher identification that can join them in the dancing of an attitude. Transcendence can reduce estrangements that occur at individual or unique levels of experience. For instance, men identify with men because of shared knowledge unique to their gender, as women identify with women. By appeals for identification they can find a transcendent level needed to build symbolic bridges that reduce alienation. One such merger is marriage. Other identifications can employ abstract terms that bridge differences—such as those provided by biology (human), geography (American), religion (Catholics), education (college), and so forth. Higher level identifications can become causes such as shared commitment to environmentalism, a shared knowledge that marks collective affiliation. Burke reasoned that people are separated from reality by tools (language, symbols, words) of their own making. They seek transcendence to overcome individuality and separation. They struggle toward perfection as a motive for identifications of an ever higher and more pure nature.

With his rhetoric of identification, Burke could embrace and transcend other approaches to rhetoric. The purpose of rhetoric is persuasion, although it can take many forms. [*See* Persuasion.] By extrapolation, he reasoned that all approaches to persuasion entail identification. If rhetors stress form and style of presentation, they can persuade those who identify with those forms and styles. If rhetors build their appeals on propositions of fact, those who identify with that process and that fact yield to their persuasiveness. If manipulation and deceit are the trade of a rhetor, those who identify with those strategies and are benefited by them are persuaded. Each of these cases features the contest of opposites that calls for interested parties to make choices, the heart of identification, between "us" and "them."

Rhetoric, in sum, works its symbolic magic through identification. It can bring people together by emphasizing the "margin of overlap" between the rhetor's and the audience's experiences, and even lead to consubstantiation. If people find that old identifications are unacceptable, they can be persuaded, and even persuade themselves, to abandon them and adopt new ones.

[*See also* Perspective by incongruity; *and* Secular piety.]

BIBLIOGRAPHY

Burke, Kenneth. "The Rhetorical Situation." In *Communication: Ethical and Moral Issues,* edited by Lee Thayer, pp. 263–275. New York, 1973.

Burke, Kenneth. *A Grammar of Motives.* Berkeley, 1969. First published 1945.

Burke, Kenneth. *A Rhetoric of Motives.* Berkeley, 1969. First published 1950.

Burke, Kenneth. "Definition of Man." *Hudson Review* 16 (1963–1964), pp. 491–514.

Burke, Kenneth. *The Philosophy of Literary Form: Studies in Symbolic Action.* 3d ed. Berkeley, 1973. First published 1941.

Burke, Kenneth. "The New Criticism." *American Scholar* 20 (1954), pp. 86–104.

Heath, Robert L. *Realism and Relativism: A Perspective on Kenneth Burke.* Macon, Ga., 1986.

Rueckert, William H. *Kenneth Burke and the Drama of Human Relations.* 2d ed. Berkeley, 1982.

—ROBERT L. HEATH

IDEOGRAPH. As a technical term in rhetorical theory, an ideograph is a figure of thought, often a one-term summary of an aspect of a people's historical ideology; for example, a clear case is the English word *Liberty*. It has an ordinary use, as in the sentence "I am not at liberty to divulge that information." Most English speakers, however, utter the word with a gesture at the long history of intense arguments and struggles to achieve rights and freedoms within a political state. Some may think of the struggle against Fascism, the raising of the American flag at Iwo Jima, for instance; or dynamiting the Nazi stadium at Nuremberg. Others may think of "Our Founding Fathers," or of Temperance advocates and Suffragists. Countless other historical incidents are available in the history of Liberalism: the four hundred years separating us from the first usage of Liberty in its ideographic sense, in the slogan "Religion! Liberty! Property!" used by the Roundhead coalition in the Puritan Revolution of the seventeenth century. Importantly, whether referring to a few or to all specific instances of conflict involving Liberty, the term becomes a figurative, often one-term summary, a *synecdochē* of all the arguments, narratives, deep emotions, fearful commitments, and dangerous actions that resulted in the political structuration of the English-speaking world.

The working ideograph is also a clear case of the floating signifier in semiotic theory. At issue is the way specific ideographs retain meaning even in situations where they appear to have no meaning at all. At its birth, and in all subsequent conflict situations, an ideograph is the "top-down" usage of social theorists or the "bottom-up" usage of street-fighting politicians. The People are at war with one another (or enaged in symbolic warfare), and ideographs become ways to distinguish and to justify all the sides that are involved in the conflict. Narratives and arguments at this stage promote detailed distinctions among the various senses of Equality, for instance. All the fragments of the political culture, all classes, all races, all religions, all gender-related differences are dispersed into fleeting coalitions so that necessary Actions can be portrayed as "either this which will destroy us, or that which will save us." At this stage, each contested ideograph has a concrete meaning articulated in the discourse that creates and exploits the issues that divide society. This is neither the correct meaning, nor the preferred meaning, nor the rational meaning, but it is a meaning, one concrete and relatively stable meaning derived from the necessity of polarizing into warring camps.

As the conflict winds down, one "side" or another prevailing, but with a "disgruntled minority" of "losers," ideographs change in their function and in their meaning. Ideographs are abstracted in several senses. First, it is most important to draw apparent "losers" back into the dominant Myth that "We are all One." That is, ideographs expressed at a higher level of generality will include all cultural fractions previously excluded within the "winning side's" discourse. A clear case of this shift in usage is the formulary topic in all presidential inauguration speeches that "the election is over now, and we must all pull together for the good of the country." That which originally, and rightly, polarized the nation in an election now must be reconceived for the good of the nation. When successful, this reorientation minimizes the risk that defeated minorities will stay "in the streets," thus creating instability and the inescapable corollary of instability, a diminution of productivity and profits.

Close on the heels of unity-promoting schemes is the gradual falling apart of the so-called "winning" coalition. Any Democratic Party victory in a United States election is a clear example, as the party itself is a coalition of easily-distinguishable fragments. The move here is also to abstract the meaning of ideographs, but this time the meanings are uncontested. The unity of Race fragments within the Democratic Party is historically an "election only" coalition, as whites and Blacks return immediately to their European-American and African-American communities and cultures. Each accomplishes the move by agreeing that Racism, for instance, is a big enough term to provide for "unity in division." Members of the coalition may believe that "Racism is an unsolved problem" and that "Racism is a problem almost resolved after a long gradualism" without threatening the coalition. The ideograph at this level of abstraction has lost almost all of its street-level meaning, its power to promote decisive action.

On the highest level of abstraction, ideographs are completely emptied and left to "float" in political discourse until they are needed again to justify in-the-streets Action. Among the bottom-up street-level users, ideographs become pure figures, in the sense of added ornaments to discourses of celebration (*encomia*). [*See* Epideictic genre.] We encounter them in schoolbooks offering children narratives of "great heroes" such as Nathan Hale, who purportedly said, "I only regret that I have but one life to give for my country." We find floating ideographs in Fourth of July orations, in political anthems such as *The Star-Spangled Banner,* and in cultural rituals such as the Super Bowl. But most of all, we find them in the discourse of politicians without vision or passion, who sprinkle them liberally in the most mundane of discourses.

Among the top-down street-level users, ideographs become figures of thought, topics that theorists use to discuss the possible ideal sense of pure Liberty, Justice, Equality, and so forth. The term *pure* here means consideration without memory of street-level usages, and with little sense of political history. Eminent philosopher John Rawls, for instance, wrote the impressive, impeccably-reasoned book *A Theory of Justice* (1971). As an exercise in the history of philosophy, the book forgets both that "justice is as justice does" and that intellectual history is no substitute for political history when it comes to explaining how rights and freedoms emerged and are maintained in the English-speaking world.

When not functioning as quasi-rational justification for extreme political action in the streets, ideographs "float up" the ladder of abstraction. When politics intensify to the point where basic values are in question, ideographs are "pulled down" the ladder of abstraction and given a very concrete meaning. Each time an ideograph is pulled down, it expands in meaning to include yet another example of its application.

In addition to vertical structurations, ideographs also exhibit horizontal structuration at all levels of abstraction. When pulled down as weaponry for political street fighting, in other words, Liberty may be defined in relationship to Religion, Equality, Property, and dozens of other ideographs. Vertical meanings give Liberty some stability, in its historical precedents, while horizontal meanings give it vitality, in its structural nuances. Liberty thus seems to be on everyone's side. Arguments in the 1970s about so-called "open housing," for instance, pitted Liberty–Equality links against Liberty–Property links. One side argued, in effect, "Liberty gives me the Right to sell my house to whomever I please," while the other side argued "Liberty gives me the Right to live in whatever house I can afford." The conflict resolved in agreement that when they clash as they define Liberty, Equality should take precedence over Property. Most Constitutional and revolutionary political arguments are characterized by conflicts of this sort, struggles for the power to define ideographs in a concrete case, either absolutely or in their structural relationships.

Over time, ideographs become rhetorical determinants embedded in political discourse. This is not the same determinism that suggests that there are historical forces, genetic forces, or spiritual forces driving humanity inevitably along a predictable course. Rather, it is a determinism derived from a discursive economy of proofs and evidence. Like the game of chess, the game of political argumentation is played within a closed system. Constitutions, Laws, and Cultural memories establish a set of expectations about what can be said, what should be said, in political conflicts. These expectations are boundaries, fences, rules that leave political advocates to decide what contested ideographs may mean in their current invocation. Although frequently-used ideographs, such as Equality or Liberty for instance, have been invoked in countless political crises, the number of acceptable usages is far smaller. The ideograph's usage in losing causes, for instance, is unacceptable after the loss, and all meanings that can be shown to be anachronistic (such as the Constitutional mandate to count slaves as three-fifths of a person) are unacceptable. Other meanings may be off the point of the ideograph's proposed usage in current political arguments. When political advocates think ahead far enough to see how their argument is likely to play out, they discover that what they can say is "determined," not by invisible forces, but by the anticipated moves of opponents and by the range of meanings acceptable to audiences. Usages of Liberty determine outcomes in political conflict when advocates run out of evidence, out of instances and examples that prove their version of its meaning.

Because they are rhetorical determinants, ideographs are not revolution friendly. They support political, social, and cultural stability by constituting the lines outside of which politicians rarely color. Suppose that Jane Doe seeks to isolate acceptable meanings for Law and Order, each with excellent historical precedents. Jane first arranges distinguishable meanings on a dialectical continuum, between poles designated (political) Right and (political) Left. Hundreds of possible meanings for Law and Order are scattered outside the Right pole and the Left pole, abandoned as "unacceptable" for any number of reasons. Suppose that forty "acceptable" meanings remain in the continuum, not so much placed there for positive reasons, but rather left as a residue of culling the unacceptable. Since these meanings are a residue, the fact that one need not herself subscribe to any particular meaning becomes an important principle. The forty are instead meanings one agrees to tolerate. Jane has thus supplied the illusion of free choice of meanings for Law and Order in a political competition. She may choose meanings between the poles, inventing elegant and intricate arguments to make her case. She may even be herself a Law and Order "agnostic," so to speak (which is to say that she need not subscribe to any of the alternatives, but only tolerate them all). However, she may not go outside the pole to the Right, say to Syndicalism, or outside the pole to the Left, say to Communism, in search of what Law and Order may mean.

Ironically, political advocates promoting revolutionary change are obliged to attack the very set of ideographs that the People of a State use to Identify themselves politically. The decision to work with meanings inside the boundary conditions of political argument is, in most cases, a surrender to the prevailing system, an agreement to be co-opted in thinking about "changing direction." Trying to work with meanings outside the boundary conditions is frustrating because the advocate has no audience, at least no audience with enough cohesion and power to be useful. Further, each step beyond the pale of the acceptable puts the politician in bad company, linked with radicals and communists beyond one pole, racists and fascists beyond the other.

Gender Equality offers a clear case. From the publication of John Knox's *First Blast of the Trumpet Against the Monstrous Regiment of Women* (1558) to the waves of feminist thinking in Europe and the Americas in the 1970s, "the enemy" of progressive thinking has always been a deep cultural prejudice against the possibility that women could be Equal. [*See* Feminist rhetoric.] At every turn, politicians had to step outside the boundary conditions to invent new understandings; but the most important task was creating audiences and preparing them to hear new meanings. So-called consciousness-raising group interactions created an audience for feminist political arguments beyond the pale of the acceptable. Such groups have been of little significance as a powerful political force in and of themselves. Their power is symbolic; they provide an alternative moment of identification for women who stay within the realm of the acceptable in their everyday lives. To keep the attention of the groups that empower their arguments, politicians must draw their new, originally-unacceptable meanings back toward "the system." This, of course, brings us back to the problem of co-optation. Have advocates of revolutionary change been successful because they have moved society and culture to expand the boundaries of Equality's acceptable meanings? Or have advocates of revolutionary change "sold out" by making new meanings of Equality seem little different, eminently more tolerable, than they were before?

[*See also* Identification; Invention; *overview article on* Politics; *and* Rhetorical vision.]

BIBLIOGRAPHY

Arendt, Hannah. *Between Past and Future,* New York, 1968.

Brown, William R. "Ideology as Communication Process," *Quarterly Journal of Speech* 64 (1978), pp. 123–140. An important investigation of the role of ideology in modern conceptions of communication.

Burke, Kenneth. *A Rhetoric of Motives.* Berkeley, 1969. First published 1950. Together with Burke's *Grammar,* contributes to an understanding of relationships among terms, situations, and motives.

Charland, Maurice. "Constitutive Rhetoric: 'The Case of the *Peuple Quebecois.'*" *Quarterly Journal of Speech* 73 (1987), pp. 133–150. Offers a rich reading of the inventional component of ideographic rhetoric.

Collingwood, R. G. *The Idea of History.* Oxford, 1972.

Suggests that the Content or ultimate subject matter of history should consist of explaining such recurrent usages ("ideographs") as "freedom" and "progress."

Condit, Celeste M. *Decoding Abortion Rhetoric: Communicating Social Change.* Urbana, 1990.

Condit, Celeste M., and J. L. Lucaites. *Crafting Equality: America's Anglo-African Word.* Chicago, 1993.

Condit, Celeste M. *The Meanings of the Gene: Public Debates about Human Heredity.* Madison, Wis., 1999.

Cuklanz, Lisa M. *Rape on Trial: How the Mass Media Construct Legal Reform and Social Change.* Philadelphia, 1996. In this work and her most recent one (*Rape on Prime Time: Television, Masculinity, and Sexual Violence* Philadelphia, 2000), "Terminism" is the featured theoretical/explanatory term, "ideograph" an occasionally-mentioned reference.

Foucault, Michel. *The Archeology of Knowledge.* Translated by A. M. S. Smith. New York, 1972.

McGee, Michael C. "In Search of the 'People': a Rhetorical Alternative." *The Quarterly Journal of Speech* 61 (1975), pp. 235–249.

McGee, Michael C. "The 'Ideograph': A Link Between Rhetoric and Social Theory." *The Quarterly Journal of Speech* 66 (1980), pp. 1–16.

McGee, Michael C., and John Nelson. "Narrative Reason in Public Argument." *Journal of Communication* 35 (1985), pp. 139–155.

Rawls, John. *A Theory of Justice.* Cambridge, Mass., 1971.
—MICHAEL CALVIN MCGEE

IMITATION (Gk. *mimēsis;* Lat. *imitatio;* German *Nachahmung*) has different meanings with rhetorical significance, depending on the object, the purpose, the means, and the agent of imitation. This article discusses imitation as practiced in rhetorical schools, with some remarks on other uses of the term.

Imitation of Models of Speech and Writing in Antiquity. Before the introduction of writing, speech skills were learned, and still are to some extent and in some places, by listening to effective older speakers, imitating their methods and styles, and profiting from the reaction of audiences and the advice of mentors. The most common application of *mimēsis/imitatio* in rhetoric has, however, been to the teaching of oral and written composition by study of approved written models of invention, arrangement, and style, followed by exercises in which students imitate the models. This was apparently the method of

the Greek Sophists in the fifth century BCE, who composed and published model speeches that could then be imitated; surviving examples include Gorgias's *Defense of Palamedes* and *Encomium of Helen,* as well as the *Tetralogies* once attributed to Antiphon. In Plato's *Phaedrus,* young Phaedrus has secured a written copy of a speech by Lysias arguing that the attentions of a non-lover should be preferred to those of a lover. As the dialogue opens he is studying this, probably with the intention of imitating it, and, somewhat reluctantly, he reads it to Socrates, who criticizes it, imitates it with better arrangement of the material, and then argues the other side of the case. [*See* Classical rhetoric.]

Imitation was a major feature of the school that Isocrates directed in Athens from about 390 to his death in 338 BCE. As described in his orations, *Against the Sophists, Antidosis,* and *Panathenaicus,* he composed speeches on issues of the age, which he polished, read to his students, and eventually published. The students' chief occupation seems to have been writing speeches or essays on subjects suggested by Isocrates, imitating his thought and style (*Against the Sophists* 16–18). The subjects, Isocrates insists (e.g., *Antidosis* 274–278), must be "great and beautiful and humane," and by focusing on such things he claims a student will "feel their influence not only in regard to the speech at hand but also in other actions, so that speaking and thinking well will come to be an attribute of those who are philosophically and ambitiously disposed." Imitation is thus regarded as both morally and aesthetically edifying. "Philosophy," that is, "love of wisdom," is Isocrates' preferred term for what was taught in his school, and imitation, not dialectic, was the method of attaining it.

Rhetorical schools became common in cities of the eastern Mediterranean region beginning in the late fourth century BCE when Greek culture was spread by the conquests of Alexander the Great. By the second century BCE, some Romans were beginning to study rhetoric. In these schools, students practiced exercises in written composition (*progymnasmata*) and in declamation; probably models for imitation were furnished by teachers. Between the fourth and the first centuries BCE, linguistic and rhetorical standards deviated widely in some areas. This was the time of the highly artifical rhetorical style known as Asianism, and also the development of the *Koinē*, the simplified "common" Greek of everyday communication. [*See* Atticist–Asianist controversy.] In the late first century BCE, a reaction occurred among Greek teachers, rejecting the excesses of Asianism and demanding the use in formal speech and writing of Attic Greek, the dialect of Athens as found in writings of the fourth century, especially speeches of the so-called "Attic Orators."

An account of this reform is found in the critical treatises and epistles of Dionysius of Halicarnassus, who was teaching in Rome shortly after 30 BCE. Imitation of Attic models by students was crucial to this effort, and among Dionysius's works is a treatise *Peri Mimēseōs* (*On Imitation*), preserved only in part (Greek text and French translation by G. Aujac in the "Collection Budé" edition of Denys d'Halicarnasse, *Opuscules rhetorique,* vol 5, Paris, 1992, 26–40). Dionysius defined *mimēsis* as "an activity making a model of the example by means of inspection." With it should be combined *zēlos,* "emulation," "an activity of the soul when stirred by admiration of what seems to be beautiful." In the best preserved part of the work, Dionysius surveys Greek poetry and prose literature, suggesting what models to study and what qualities in their writings should be imitated. About the same time, the Roman poet Horace (65–8 BCE) urged study of Greek exemplars in his *Art of Poetry* and imitation of life and morals (lines 268–269 and 317–318). His comparison of poetry to painting (*ut pictura poēsis,* line 361) became an important concept in neoclassical conceptions of the imitative arts. There is some additional Greek discussion of imitation in chapters on pedagogy (13–17) in Aelius Theon's *Progymnasmata,* and in the treatise *On Sublimity* traditionally attributed to Longinus. Imitation, that author says (ch. 13), can lead to emulation and inspiration.

The best description of how imitation was understood and practiced in classical rhetorical schools is found in Book 10, chapter 2, of Quintilian's *Institutio oratoria,* published in 95 CE. It is, Quintilian says (10.2.2), "a rule of all life that we wish to copy what we approve in others." Imitation, however, is not sufficient. What progress would ever be made if no one did more than imitate another (10.2.7)? There is need of emulation, an attempt to go beyond what has been done. We must consider whom to imitate (Quintilian had provided a reading list in the previous chapter) and what to imitate in each model. Imitators are apt to exaggerate the faults of authors they seek to copy (10.2.15). Students must consult their powers, for some things will be beyond one's ability (10.2.19). We should imitate models in the genre in which we are writing (e.g., orators not poets in oratory). It is best not to concentrate exclusively on one model, not even on Demosthenes or Cicero. Do not imitate only the words of the model, but imitate also the treatment of the subject (10.2.27). By means of imitation, one can make good one's own deficiencies and cut down one's own redundancies (10.2.28).

Imitation of Classical Models in the Renaissance. Imitation of models of language and literature was little discussed in the Middle Ages, though imitation of moral exemplars was taught; a famous example is *Imitatio Christi* by Thomas à Kempis (c.1380–1471). Literary imitation became fundamental, however, to the practice of Italian humanists of the Renaissance, paralleling imitations of classical art and architecture in the same period. As scholars acquired a reading knowledge of Greek and rediscovered Latin works, including long unknown works of Cicero, they came to regard medieval Latin as barbarous and saw the best antidote to it in imitation of the language and style of classical Latin writers. Imitation of classical literary genres, for example, Greek epideictic oratory and the Platonic or Ciceronian dialogue forms, was also practiced. [*See* Humanism; *and overview article on* Renaissance rhetoric.]

The main question current in humanist circles in the fifteenth and early sixteenth centuries was *what* classical Latin should be the standard model: should it be that of Cicero or writings by Sallust, Livy, Seneca, Tacitus, or others as well? About 1440, Lorenzo Valla (1407–1457), a papal secretary who lectured on rhetoric in Rome, recommended a flexible Ciceronianism in *De elegantiis linguae latinae.* Later in the century, Paoli Cortesi argued for strict Ciceronian Latin in exchanges of letters with the more eclectic Politianus (Angelo

Ambrogini, 1454–1494), and in 1512 Gianfranco Pico della Mirandola took up the moderate cause in an epistulary debate with the Ciceronian Pietro Bembo. Bembo (1470–1547) sought to use no Latin word that could not be found in Cicero. Mario Nizzoli's *Lexicon Ciceronianum* (1535) provided a useful tool for such composition. In 1528, however, Erasmus had published his *Ciceronianus,* a plea for a flexible Latin style, drawing vocabulary from a variety of Latin authors. Despite the negative reactions of J. C. Scaliger and others, Erasmus's work had wide influence. Theological discussions seemed to require the continued use of some medieval Latin terms, and new scientific discoveries sometimes necessitated the coining of new Latin words. The anti-Ciceronians then found a new defender in Justus Lipsius (1547–1606), who preferred the epigrammatic style of Seneca and the pregnant brevity of Tacitus. Cicero was labeled an Asianist, as he had been by some of his contemporaries; less accurately, Seneca and Tacitus came to be regarded as Atticists. The earliest discussion of imitation as an educational method in English is probably that found in Roger Ascham's *Scholemaster* (1570). Imitation long continued a pedagogic practice, although brought into question in the quarrel of "Ancients and Moderns" that erupted in France and England in the late seventeenth and early eighteenth centuries.

Plato and Aristotle on Mimesis. Greek *mimēsis* is derived from *mimos,* "mime," and literally refers to dramatic enactments of comic, satiric, or tragic incidents by actors wearing masks. The word *mimēsis,* as discussed in Greek philosophy and criticism, is often translated *representation* rather than *imitation.* In Book 3 of Plato's *Republic* (392d), Socrates makes a formal distinction between third-person narrative descriptions (*diēgēsis*), pure imitation (*mimēsis*), as in drama where the entire text is spoken by actors, and a mixed form, combining narrative with speeches attributed to characters, as in the Homeric epics. Socrates criticizes the mimetic forms as tending to corrupt performers whose roles may involve expression of passions or wicked deeds, and he bars such poetry from his ideal state. In Book 10 (595a–608b), he returns to the subject and extends his criticism beyond dramatic imitation to include all poetry and all visual art, on the ground that the arts are only poor, "third-hand" imitations of true reality existing in the realm of "ideas." Plato's conception of metaphysical mimesis was further developed in later dialogues, *The Sophist* and *Timaeus,* and by Neoplatonist philosophers.

Aristotle did not accept Plato's theory of the visible world as an imitation of the realm of abstract ideas or forms, and his use of *mimēsis* is closer to its original dramatic meaning. In the first chapter of *Poetics,* he states that the poetic genres are all imitations, differing in means, object, and manner of imitating. In chapter 4, he attributes the origins of poetry to the fact that imitation is a natural human activity and is pleasurable. And in chapter 6 (1449b24–28), he defines tragedy as "an imitation (*mimēsis*) of an action"; that is, the poet creates a plot by imitating the incidents of a myth such as the story of Oedipus.

Imitation in Modern Criticism. The *Poetics* was little known until the mid-sixteenth century in Italy, and even then not well understood. Imitation of literary models or imitation of nature and life, as Horace had urged, remained the dominant concept in critical writings of the period. Imitation of nature became the standard view of neoclassical critics in the seventeenth and eighteenth centuries, authoritatively stated for French by Boileau in *Art poétique* (1674), for English by Dryden in his *Essay of Dramatic Poesy* (1668), and for German by Johann Christop Gottschied in *An Essay in Critical Poetics* (1731). Lessing's *Lacoön* of 1766 reformulated Horace's *ut pictura poēsis* by defining imitation of nature as the domain of painting, and imitation of life and action as that of poetry. Imitation as a source of art was rejected by Sir William Jones in his *Essay on the Arts Commonly Called Imitative* in 1772, and by Romantic poets and critics of the late eighteenth and early nineteenth centuries, who gave priority in composition to genius, inspiration, and spontaneity. In the twentieth century, however, the concept found favor with some critics interested in realism in literature, drama, and the arts. A well-known instance is the book entitled *Mimesis: Representations of Reality in Western Literature* by Eric Auerbach (English translation by Willard Trask, Princeton, 1953).

[*See also* Copia; Criticism; *and* Poetry.]

BIBLIOGRAPHY

Note: bibliography on *mimēsis*/imitation in literature and literary criticism is very extensive; bibliography on imitation as a pedagogical technique is sparse.

Abrams, M. H. *The Mirror and the Lamp: Romantic Theory and the Critical Tradition.* Oxford, 1953. Chapter 2, "Imitation and the Mirror," reviews classical and neoclassical theories of literary imitation.

Conte, Gian Biagio. *The Rhetoric of Imitation: Genre and Poetic Memory in Virgil and Other Latin Poets,* ed. by Charles Segal. Ithaca, N.Y., 1986. Discusses imitation of Greek and earlier Latin poets by classical Latin writers.

Else, G. F. "'Imitation' in the Fifth Century." *Classical Philology* 53 (1958), pp. 73–90. The background for *mimēsis* as discussed by Plato and Aristotle.

Else, G. F., and H. R. Elam. "Imitation." In *The New Princeton Encyclopedia of Poetry and Poetics,* edited by Alex Preminger and T. V. E. Brogan, pp. 575–579. Princeton, 1993. In addition to a survey of early uses, includes (pp. 578–579) a brief account of imitation as a concept in poststructuralist literary theory; bibliography.

Fantham, Elaine. "Imitation and Evolution: The Discussion of Rhetorical Imitation in Cicero." *Classical Philology* 73 (1978), pp. 1–16.

Greene, Thomas M. *The Light in Troy: Imitation and Discovery in Renaissance Poetry.* New Haven, 1982.

Kennedy, George A., ed. *The Cambridge History of Literary Criticism,* vol. 1. Cambridge, U.K., 1989. Numerous discussions of imitation in different senses in Greek and Latin writers; consult the index under "Mimesis."

McLaughlin, Martin L. *Literary Imitation in the Italian Renaissance: The Theory and Practice of Literary Imitation in Italy from Dante to Bembo.* Oxford, 1995.

Mitchell, W. J. T. "Representation." In *Critical Terms for Literary Study,* edited by Frank Lentricchia and Thomas McLaughlin. Chicago, 1990.

Nisbet, H. B., and Claude Rawson, eds. *The Cambridge History of Literary Criticism,* vol. 4, Cambridge, U.K., 1997. See especially pp. 531–538, 681–699, and 730–741 for discussion of *mimēsis*/imitation in eighteenth-century criticism.

Peterson, W. *M. Fabi Quintiliani, Institutionis Oratoriae Liber Decimus.* Oxford, 1891. The Latin text of Book 10 of Quintilian's work, with an extensive commentary in English. There is also a school edition with a briefer introduction and commentary, Oxford, 1967.

Quintilianus, M. Fabius. *Institutio oratoria.* Translated by H. E. Butler. 4 vols. Cambridge, Mass., 1922. Translation of Book 10, chapter 2, in vol. 4, pp. 75–91. Revised translation in preparation by D. A. Russell.

Russell, D. A. *Criticism in Antiquity.* Berkeley, 1981. See especially chapter 7, "Mimesis."

Twining, Thomas. "Dissertation on Poetry as an Imitative Art," appended to his edition of *Aristotle's Theory of Poetry.* London, 1789. Reprinted in *Aristotle's Poetics and English Literature,* edited by Elder Olson, pp. 42–75. Chicago, 1965.

Verdenius, W. J. *Mimesis: Plato's Doctrine of Artistic Imitation and Its Meaning to Us.* Leiden, 1962.

West, D. A., and A. J. Woodman, eds. *Creative Imitation and Latin Literature.* Cambridge, U.K., 1979.

—GEORGE A. KENNEDY

INDIAN RHETORIC. The expression *Indian rhetoric* has two signifiers, both of which are equally evasive. First, "India," which is as large and varied as Europe, is not one but many, and "living in India means living simultaneously in several cultures and times" (Sheik, 1989). The formation of the nation, which occurred fairly recently, is a product of the colonial historiography that brought about a "knitted unit" for purely administrative purposes; at the psychological level, "India" is the creation of anti-colonial hostility, which brought various regional, linguistic, and ethnic groups with their separate histories and ideologies under one umbrella called "India." It is therefore almost impossible to define or describe anything as "Indian"; at best one can call "Indianness" a network of "'modules' as in computer technology where each one, though self-contained, performs a particular function" (Krishnaswamy, 1998).

The second component of the term *Indian rhetoric* highlights the notion that the Greco-Roman-Western perspective of rhetoric is very different from that of any tradition in the Indian subcontinent. It is obvious that any community using language will develop its own art and techniques for empowering certain linguistic expressions to bring forth desired effects in the hearer/reader. A theory of rhetoric as a significant subject matter or a distinct discipline, however, is not the same in all linguistic communities; hence, the same yardstick often cannot be used precisely to measure the "art of eloquence" or the "science of persuasion" found in different languages and cultures. Even within the Greco-Roman-Western tradition, the distinction between poetry and rhetoric, logic and rhetoric, philosophy and rhetoric, or stylistics and rhetoric is sometimes blurred, even though rhetoric itself was considered an important component of the trivium: grammar, logic, and rhetoric. [*See* Trivium.]

In the Sanskritic traditions of India, the Vedas and the Upaniṣads (c.2000 BCE) demonstrate the effective use of diction, intonation, and music. In addition, the two ancient epics of the subcontinent, the *Rāmāyaṇa* and the *Mahābhārata* (dating to the pre-Buddhist period) contain several instances that illustrate an art of persuasion, not only through what is spoken and how, but through what remains unspoken. A classic example of *deliberative* oratory in the epics is that of Kṛṣṇa's (Krishna's) exhortation to Arjuna in the *Mahābhārata*, with the famous discourse known as the *Bhagavadgītā*. [*See* Deliberative genre.]

In his *Nāṭyaśāstra*, an important treatise on theater, dance, poetry, and music, Bharata (c.500 BCE) discusses in detail the features of *kāvya* (literature of which poetry and drama are two manifestations). These include *vacika-abhinaya* (linguistic representation), *vāga-abhinaya* (diction), *bhāṣā-abhidānam* (modes of address and intonation), and *vṛtti-vikalpaḥ* (diversity of styles).

Inspired by Bharata, many scholars developed various concepts that form an organic whole of what may be called "the art of giving effectiveness to truth." Among these are Pāṇini (c.500 BCE), Patañjali (c.150 BCE), Bhartṛhari (c.500 CE), Bhāmaha (c.550 CE), Daṇḍin (c.700 CE), Vāmana (c.800 CE), Ānandavardhana (c.900 CE), his commentator, Abhinavagupta (c.1000 CE), Kuntaka (c. tenth-eleventh century CE), Bhoja (eleventh century CE), and Jagannātha and Appayya Dīkṣita (both seventeenth century CE).

Some of the major concepts that they developed are: *lakṣaṇa* (the natural grace in one's linguistic expressions); *alaṅkāra* (embellishment and the use of figurative language); *rīti* or *mārga* (style); *vakrokti* (obliquity, creative deviation); *anumāna* (inference); *aucitya* (propriety, decorum); *dhvani* (suggestiveness and the power to evoke *rasa*, the dominant aesthetic); *rasa* (relish, delight, mood, or the art-emotion, resulting from the interplay between the work of art and the spectator or reader); *bhāva* (conditions producing an emotion); and *anubhāva* (the overt expression exhibiting an emotion).

Of these concepts, the one most widely used in Sanskrit poetics and aesthetics is *alaṅkāra*, which in a broad sense means "making a thing fit by imparting a power to it for bringing forth the desired effect." Bhāmaha, Daṇḍin, Vāmana, and Bhoja equated it with "beauty": In Vāmana's words, *saundaryam alaṅkāraḥ*, that is, "Beauty is *alaṅkāra*." The concept of *alaṅkāra* is based on the theory of meaning propounded by *vaiyākaraṇa*s (grammarians), *Mīmāṃsaka*s (exegetists), *Naiyāyika*s (logicians), and other philosophers. In its narrow sense, *alaṅkāra* refers to "figure of speech," "adornment," "costume," "make-up," and so forth. In the name of *alaṅkāraśāstra*, the *alaṅkārika*s, who were literary critics or aestheticians (and incorrectly labeled "rhetoricians" by some writers), have listed more than one hundred twenty-five *alaṅkāra*s. The classification of figurative-types was borrowed from Sanskrit and continues to be used in several languages of the subcontinent.

In addition, the concept of style (Sanskrit: *rīti* or *mārga*) and its specific qualities (*guṇa*s) has been studied in great detail by Sanskrit aestheticians such as Bhāmaha, Daṇḍin, Vāmana, Kuntaka, Bhoja, and Jagannātha. Kuntaka mentions three kinds *sukumāra* (a delicate style with spontaneous beauty), *vichitrā* (a studied and difficult style full of natural obliquity of expression), and *madhyama* (a style with the beauty of the first and the obliquity of the second). The *alaṅkāra*s contribute to the enrichment of meaning (*arthaguṇa*s) and sound (*śabda-guṇa*s) in *rīti*.

Daṇḍin and Vāmana list ten important qualities of style, as follows.

a) *ojas* (energy or brilliance with compactness of syllabic structure, expressed through significant adjectives and sentences, and using one for many and many for one as appropriate)
b) *prasāda* (lucidity, clarity, and precision of expression)
c) *śleṣa* (well-knit constructions skillfully employing many levels of meaning)
d) *samatā* (uniformity in the manner of expression)
e) *samādhi* (symmetry; regular alteration of tautness that brings about a balance in sound and meaning)

f) *mādhurya* (sweetness in the refinement of expression)

g) *saukumārya* (delicacy or tenderness by avoiding hard-sounds and harsh words, and by using euphemistic expressions)

h) *udāratā* (extraordinariness or liveliness with graded use of alliteration and rhyming structures)

i) *arthavyakti* (explicitness or directness by avoiding obscure words, punning, and so forth)

j) *kānti* (glow or luminosity through elegant turns of expression)

These features of discourse, which concern rhythm, diction, imagery, vision, attitude, mood, and thought, are relevant not only to poetic language but to the art of persuasion as well.

It must be stated that the Indic literature has not distinguished sharply between prose and verse, or between literary prose and non-literary prose. The verse form and sometimes a poetic-prose form (called *sūtra* in Sanskrit) were used in subjects such as grammar, medicine, and astronomy. On the other hand, the Pāli works relating to the Buddha's life and teachings, as well as the compositions on Jainism in the various Prakrits are in prose, which came to be used for expository and commentarial works. As early as the fifth century CE, stone inscriptions and copper plates demonstrate the use of prose in the earliest formulations of Indic vernacular languages. Modern prose in the Western sense (journalistic writing, scientific writing, biography, history, travelogue, and so forth) became established only during the nineteenth century under European influence and specifically through the use of the printing press. Because there was no need in the ancient past to maintain a distinction between poetics and rhetoric, some scholars (e.g., Zvelebil) even today consider *alaṅkaraśāstra*, which is only a branch of *kāvyaśāstra* (theory of literature), rhetoric.

In the southern part of the subcontinent, the *Tolkāppiyam* (c.500 BCE) written in Tamil (a Dravidian language), describes the major aspects of Tamil language, literature, culture, and social conventions. The third chapter of the work is divided into nine subsections that describe and discuss the following: the conduct of private life (*akattiṇaiyial*), of public life (*puṛattiṇaiyial*), of courting and the conventions of love life (*kaḷaviyal*), and of marriage and the conventions of family life (*karpiyal*). Next, it includes treatises on meaning (*poruḷiyal*), on emotions (*meippāṭṭiyal*), on metaphor (*uvamaiyial*), on prosody (*ceyyuḷiyal*), and on the conventions of use and usage (*marapiyal*). The *Tolkāppiyam* offers a sophisticated theory of discourse in which social and ecological forces, the landscape, flora and fauna, the seasons of the year, and the time of the day are considered as participants in the act of communication. Three different commentaries composed during the twelfth and thirteenth centuries give elaborate arguments and illustrations from Sangam literature to explain the principles outlined in the ancient work. Although it discusses metaphor in detail, the *Tolkāppiyam* does not use the term *alaṅkāra,* or *aṇi* (in Tamil). Later, when the notion of five-fold grammar (in Tamil, *aintilakkaṇam*) was formulated, *aṇi* was placed as the fifth branch, the other four being *eluttu* (phonology and orthography), *col* (morphology, syntax, and etymology), *poruḷ* (semantics), and *yāppu* (prosody and poetics). The *Vīracōliyam* (eleventh century) is the only treatise to discuss all five parts in detail.

Islam also had considerable impact on the development of style and rhetoric in the subcontinent. In the early years of Muslim rule (thirteenth and fourteenth centuries), Persian replaced Sanskrit as the language for royal, legal, and administrative purposes. Paradoxically, as Islamic rule waned, Indic literature showed an increased use of the Perso-Arabic vocabulary, concepts, and ornate style.

Many factors contributed to the rapid expansion of functional prose even in the modern Indian languages, among them Western travelers, Christian missionaries, European cultural influences, British colonial rule that derived power from the written word, the emergence of science and technology, and the use of English in administration, education, and the media. Along with the expansion of prose, India was introduced to the notion of "rhetoric," which by then had been reduced to "written composition" in the Western educational system. [*See* Eighteenth-century rhetoric.] In spite of the rich oral tradition that exists in most parts of the subcontinent even today, the power of the written word increased with the impact of colonialism; as a result, in India's colonial educational system, rhetoric has become synonymous with prose composition.

Nonetheless, the older traditions of poetic-rhetoric are still preserved in most of the modern Indian languages in the following forms: (a) folk-drama, such as *yakṣagāna* in Kannada and Telugu, *terukkūttu* in Tamil, *jātra* in Bengali, *tamāśa* in Marathi, and Moghul *tamāsa* in Oriya; (b) religious discourses, such as *harikathā;* (c) folksongs, ballads, and festival songs; and (d) other *kathā* traditions. The rhetorical features found in these traditions are worthy of attention, study, and interpretation if we are to construct a theory of Indian rhetoric in the Western sense.

[*See also* Comparative rhetoric.]

BIBLIOGRAPHY

Ānandavardhana. *Dhvanyāloka*. Edited with an introduction, English translation, and notes by K. Krishnamoorthy. Hubli-Dharwar, India, 1975.

Bharata. *Nāṭyaśāstra*. 2 vols. Edited with translation by Manomohan Ghosh. Calcutta, India, 1967.

Chari, V. K. *Sanskrit Criticism*. Delhi, 1973.

George, K. M., ed. *Comparative Indian Literature*. 2 vols. Chennai, India, 1985.

Krishnamoorthy, K. *Indian Literary Theories–A Reappraisal*. New Delhi, India, 1985.

Krishnaswamy, N. *The Politics of Indians' English*. Delhi, 1998.

Kuntaka. *The Vakrokti-Jivita of Kuntaka*. Edited and translated by K. Krishnamoorthy. Hubli-Dharwar, India, 1977.

Kushwaha, M. S., ed. *Indian Poetics and Western Thought*. Lucknow, India, 1988. Sixteen essays by Indian scholars on various aspects of Indian poetics.

Motilal, B. K. *Epistemology, Logic and Grammar*. The Hague, 1979.

Raghavan, V. *Studies on Some Concepts of the Alaṃkāra Śāstra*. Chennai, India, 1973.

Raja, K. Kunjunni. *Indian Theories of Meaning*. Chennai, India, 1963.

Sethuraman, V. S., ed. *Indian Aesthetics–An Introduction*. Chennai, India, 1992.

Sheik, Gulam Mohammed. "Among Several Cultures and Times." In *Contemporary India*, edited by Carla M. Border. Delhi, 1989.

Tolkāppiyam: The Earliest Extant Tamil Grammar–Text in Tamil and Roman Scripts with a Critical Commentary in English. Translated by P. S. Subrahmanya Sastri. Chennai, India, 1949.

Zvelebil, Kamil V. *Lexicon of Tamil Literature*. Leiden, 1995.

—N. KRISHNASWAMY

INDUCTION. *See* Exemplum.

INFERENCE involves the reflective human activity of drawing more or less reliable conclusions from some available evidence. There is a broad sense of this term that could include all intellectual and practical intelligence—from reading, to higher math, to turning quickly in the direction of a skid to regain control of a vehicle. In this broad construal, any conscious or even intuitive cognitive connection could be considered an inference. For the even broader, less differentiated, terrain of the rhetorical, such an enlarged construal of inference poses something of a conceptual problem. Consequently, this article begins with assumptions that allow us to specify more precisely the relationship of inference to rhetoric in theory and practice.

Theoretically, it is worth asking whether there is a meaningful difference between inference-based theories of rhetoric and those theories that are not inference based. In practical terms, it is relevant to ask whether there might be something akin to *rhetorical* inference. If both of these questions may be answered in the affirmative (and they might), then it may be possible to specify certain criteria for what counts as *sound* rhetorical inference. Still, it is best to turn first to the assumptions.

First, like many a term and concept in this volume, *inference* is not an honorific term in its own right but rather a term admitting to variations in performative quality. Unlike a term such as *validity*, for something to be called an *inference* does not yet speak to its successful performance. One might make a bad inference, a sloppy inference, an unfounded inference, just as one may make a correct, sound, or proper inference. Once we have identified or characterized a thought-constituted connection as inference, we are at the beginning of a process of appraisal, rather than at the end. This appraisal process is ongoing, of course, and surely not limited to purely technical matters. From art criticism to political controversy, to family discipline, to sports officiating, inference has the dubious distinction of usually being open both to notice and to critique.

A second assumption to be made about inference is one that many students of rhetoric and logic might wish to contest. This is because the assumption is part of a controversy as old as the history of rhetoric itself. While the origins and roots of the capacity for inferring are deep and mysterious (as with *logos* itself, for that matter), inference is assumed to be a higher-order human skill that may be cultivated and improved. This assumption is over and against the position that one is either blessed or not with sophistication in this capacity by the vicissitudes of nature. In practice, these assumptions work together, since there would not be much point in appraising the quality of inference were we to rule out the possibility of its improvement.

Although there is an indisputable connection between inference and rhetoric, given its provenance of suasory matters, there are emphatic differences between theories of rhetoric that are inference based, and those that are not. It is worth noting that the earliest practical manifestations of rhetoric were as a sort of mythopoetic monologue. In the self-interested pronouncements of Gorgias (c.483–c.376 BCE), among others, rhetoric is construed as a sort of irresistible force that literally overwhelms its audiences.

So understood, the very point of rhetoric is either to cancel out or short-circuit inference, so that only a single preferred reaction is possible. In rhetorical theory, the legacy of this noninferential tradition may be found in hermeneutic conceptions of rhetoric as the prerational and primordial foundation of other cultural norms and values (Grassi, 1980). It also may be found in visions of rhetoric that give primacy to qualities of eloquence, style, and figuration, as in the movements of sophistic and belletristic rhetoric. There are practical implications, as well, which will be noted at this essay's conclusion.

But for rhetoric as pedagogy and as theory, it has been the inference-based conception that has dominated our historical understanding. This conception, it is generally believed, originated with Plato's still-forceful challenge to the Sophists to defend the rigor and coherence of their educational practices. Such a task would seem to be impossible if rhetoric only appealed through the niceties of style to the reactions and prejudices of its audience: Plato (c.428–c.347 BCE) knew this, of course. And so it is possible to read his call for rigor and method as a demand for an inference-based conception of rhetoric.

It was Aristotle (384–322 BCE) who came the furthest in fulfilling this demand. In his foundational treatment, rhetoric is the logocentric counterpart to that other universal method, Plato's own preferred dialectic. [*See* Dialectic.] Together with dialectic, rhetoric investigates and deliberates uncertain matters so as to reason and decide the best available conclusions. But unlike dialectic, rhetoric yields practical choices and actions, rather than general "truths." It also works in concert with audiences, as partners in inference, rather than singular interlocutors. Perhaps most importantly, rhetoric's most coherent overarching form is the universal mode of inference known as the enthymeme. [*See* Enthymeme.] This version of rhetorical inference deploys commonly-accepted conventions and modes of proof before an audience in the best position to decide and act. Understood in this way, rhetoric became an essential feature of civic life *rationally* understood.

Since Aristotle, however, there have been many understandings of civic life, not all of them rationally based. Moreover, the manifestations of human psychology and cognition have made reason, at best, only an occasional arbiter of human projects. Grandiose expectations for the emancipatory potential of reason, as during the Renaissance and the Enlightenment, have yielded to equally extreme denunciations of reason as having exhausted itself, devolved into technique, or otherwise betrayed its humanist origins.

This is not the place to critique the credibility of these epochal pronouncements, just as it would be unfair to saddle nonrational visions of rhetoric with late modernity's own nonrational adventurism. Perhaps a more prudent position is to suggest that there are many forms of reason, that quality of practical inference is not an all or nothing affair, but, like rhetorical practice itself, a matter of difference and degree. Rhetorical theories as diverse as those of Chaim Perelman (1969), Stephen Toulmin (1964), and Kenneth Burke (1969) have all featured elements of inference in their equally diverse understandings of rhetorical practice. So it would seem premature, at best, to regard inference-based conceptions of rhetoric as having depleted their potential.

As for the characteristics of rhetorical inference, these would include subjects that are practical and issue based, contexts that are public and audience specific, lines of reasoning that are topical and probabilistic, rather than analytic and distributive. The hope of an inference-based rhetoric has always been to draw the most plausible conclusions about public conduct in an uncertain world. In so doing, it also enhances and encourages the serious deliberation of contested issues by engaged and informed audiences.

[*See also* Logic; *and* Logos.]

BIBLIOGRAPHY

Aristotle. *On Rhetoric: A Theory of Civic Discourse.* Translated by George A. Kennedy. New York, 1991. The most comprehensive and readable translation of this classic text.

Bitzer, Lloyd F. "Aristotle's Enthymeme Revisited." *Quarterly Journal of Speech* 45 (1959), pp. 399–408. A landmark reinterpretation of Aristotle's prototype for rhetorical inference.

Burke, Kenneth. *A Rhetoric of Motives.* Berkeley, 1969. First published 1950. The great literary theorist and critic's principal contribution to the "new rhetoric" of the twentieth century.

Farrell, Thomas. *Norms of Rhetorical Culture.* New Haven, 1993.

Grassi, Ernesto. *Rhetoric as Philosophy: The Humanist Tradition.* University Park, Pa., 1980. A strong proponent of the "non-inferential" rendering of rhetoric.

Havelock, Eric A. *Preface to Plato.* Cambridge, Mass., 1963. A fascinating, albeit speculative account of rhetoric's origins from mythopoetic discourse.

Perelman, Chaim, and L. Olbrechts-Tyteca. *The New Rhetoric: A Treatise on Argumentation.* Translated by J. Wilkinson and P. Weaver. Notre Dame, Ind., 1969.

Plato. *Gorgias.* Translated by W. C. Helmbold. New York, 1956. Socrates' famous dismantling of sophistic rhetoric.

Steinberger, Peter J. *The Concept of Political Judgment.* Chicago, 1993.

Toulmin, Stephen. *The Uses of Argument.* Cambridge, U.K., 1964.

—THOMAS B. FARRELL

INTERPRETATION. *See* Hermeneutics; *and* Law.

IN UTRAMQUE PARTEM. *See* Classical rhetoric; Law; *and* Persuasion.

INVENTION is one of the most prominent terms in the rhetorical vocabulary. Some rhetorics make rhetoric primarily a matter of invention; others disparage invention in the interests of truth. Rhetorics of invention may draw upon all the arts and sciences for their materials, as in the architectonic rhetoric of Cicero, or they may take their materials from the sphere of public opinion, as in the disciplinary rhetoric of Aristotle. Similarly, rhetorics of truth may draw upon truths that transcend the rhetorical situation, as in the dialectical rhetoric of Plato, or they may use the truths that are immanent in the rhetorical situation, as in the scientific rhetoric of Nausiphanes. We must examine each of these possibilities. It should be noted at the outset that, while English distinguishes between *invention,* which brings into existence something new, and *discovery,* which finds what is already there, both Latin and Greek use the same word, *inventio* or *heurein,* for both.

Invention in Cicero. Invention in Cicero (106–43 BCE) is illustrated not only by his orations, but by all of his writings. Invention itself is discussed briefly in *De partitione oratoria* (2.5–3.8), and *Orator* (13.44–15.49), and the topics, or places, used in invention are presented systematically in the *Topica.* Cicero's two full-scale discussions of the subject are in the youthful work called *De inventione* and in Book 2 of the late work *De oratore.* Characteristic features of Cicero's thought and style that are nascent in the early work appear fully developed in the later one. *De inventione* begins with Cicero's basic conviction that eloquence and wisdom must be united, but it seems to have no effect on his treatment of invention, which is more or less that of a standard textbook. *De oratore* has the form of a dialogue rather than a treatise, and the principal speaker in Book 2 pokes fun at the textbook approach but does not repudiate it. Thought is throughout treated as relative to individuals rather than as separable from them, so that education is not the teaching of a discipline but an interaction of teacher and student. The importance of wisdom for invention appears in Cicero's assertion, made at the beginning of Book 2 and illustrated by its principal speakers, that no one can ever flourish and excel in eloquence without learning not only the art of speaking, but the whole of wisdom (2.1). The many particular places (*loci*) used for invention in the early work are replaced by relatively few heads (*capita*), but their use requires experience (*usus*). The relevance of experience to invention is reflected in the dramatic reality of the dialogue, which is that of actual historical persons who illustrate what they say about rhetoric with actual historical occurrences. The rhetorical method of debate, which in the earlier work takes the form of representative arguments on both sides of a case, is here extended to rhetoric itself, which is seen to involve an interplay of differing views. Finally, more difficult for us to appreciate, the style of the later work exhibits the perfection that made Cicero for later ages the model of Latin prose.

The merits of *De oratore,* however, were not those needed for introductory instruction, and it was *De inventione* that became the most influential of all accounts of rhetorical invention and probably the most influential textbook of any kind in the history of Western education. Its content can be briefly summarized.

Invention is the first and principal part of rhetoric, for the other four parts work upon what invention has invented. Invention (*inventio*) is the excogitation or thinking up of things either true or similar to the true that render the cause probable; arrangement (*dispositio*) is the distribution in order of the things invented; expression (*elocutio*) is the fitting of suitable words to the invention; memory (*memoria*) is the firm grasp by the mind of the things and words; delivery (*pronuntiatio* or *actio*) is the management of voice and body in accordance with the dignity of the things and words.

This division, like all of *De inventione,* is directly applicable to the process of making of a speech. One must first invent what is persuasive, then arrange in order what has been invented, then express what has been ordered in suitable words, then memorize what has been expressed, and, finally, deliver what has been memorized. [*See* Arrangement, *article on* Traditional arrangement; Delivery; Memory; *and* Style.] *De inventione* in its two books treats the first phase only. Inven-

tion itself has a preliminary phase, which is not yet the excogitation of things that render one's cause probable, but rather the determination of what that cause is. The dispute may concern a fact, or, if there is agreement as to the fact, the name to be given to the fact, or, if there is agreement as to the fact and the name, the genus or quality of the fact named, or if there is agreement as to fact, name, and quality, the correctness of the legal proceeding itself. These are the four *constitutiones* or issues (*stases*) from which the case arises: the issue may be one of fact, or of definition, or of the genus or quality of a thing, or of the legal proceeding, which last is called the translative issue. [*See* Stasis.]

Once the issue is discovered, the next question to be answered is whether the case is simple or complex, and if complex, whether it is so because it involves several questions or a comparison. The next question is whether the case depends on reasoning or on a written document, and if on a written document, whether the case arises because it seems that the intent is at variance with the letter, or because of a conflict of laws, or because of an ambiguity, or because of an inference from what is written to what is unwritten, or because of the meaning of a word, as in the definitional issue. Finally, it is necessary to discover the *quaestio,* or question in dispute, the *ratio,* or reason which gives rise to the dispute with respect to the question, the *judicatio,* or point to be decided, and the *firmamentum,* or fundamental argument for the defense.

After all these points have been discovered, one can proceed to invent the separate parts of the speech: exordium, narration, partition, confirmation, refutation, and conclusion. All these are treated in the first book of *De inventione.* The second book gives a systematic treatment of the invention of arguments for confirmation and refutation. Cicero's method, at once instructive and entertaining, is to present an example of each type of case and to indicate the kinds of arguments that can be advanced on each side. Each argument has its place (*locus*), and Cicero defines a place as the seat of an argument. The place is the basic device by which invention is made a matter of art. "Just as the finding (*inventio*) of things that are hidden is easy when the place is pointed out and marked, so, if we wish to track down some argument, we ought to know the places" (*Topica* 1.7). Universals in mathematics and the exact sciences determine the particulars that fall under them, but places, the rhetorical universals, only suggest the particulars that fall under them. Places thus have a kind of generative potentiality, not a potentiality that can be realized through a specified procedure, but one that requires excogitation by the inventor.

In sum, the principal devices used in this most practical art of invention are divisions, places, and examples. The art takes the form of places ordered by successive divisions and provided with examples. Lists of places can be called inventories, and in this context the accent can properly be placed on the second syllable.

Invention in Aristotle's *Rhetoric*. Cicero begins *De inventione* by recommending the union of eloquence and wisdom; Aristotle (384–322 BCE), on the other hand, begins his *Rhetoric* by separating off rhetoric from wisdom and the other arts and sciences: "Rhetoric is the counterpart of dialectic, for both are concerned with such things as come, more or less, within the general ken of all men and belong to no definite science" (1.1.1854a1). Both dialectic and rhetoric take their premises from what people say or think, and if they go into a subject to the extent of hitting upon its principles, they pass over into the science of that subject. Dialectic is limited to valid arguments, whereas rhetoric uses whatever means it can to produce an effect on the mind of the hearer, that is, to persuade. [*See* Dialectic.] It is defined by Aristotle (1.2.1355b26) as "the power of perceiving (*theōrein*) in each case the possible persuasive." Persuasions (*pisteis*) are either atechnical, outside the art, such as witnesses, tortures, contracts, and the like, or entechnical, within the art. The former have only to be used; the latter must be invented (*heurein*). The same words, *heurein* and *theōrein,* are used in the sciences to mean the discovery and contemplation of the truth; here they mean the invention and awareness of the persuasive.

Persuasion is conceived by Aristotle in a way that makes his work on rhetoric of unsurpassed interest for the study of invention. The person who is to be persuaded is for Aristotle self-determining or autarchic. Persuasion does not work by bypassing this self-determination, treating the hearer like a puppet subject to external manipulation, but rather by accepting this self-determination and working through it. The premises are his premises, the argument is his argument, the conclusion is his conclusion. And since the speech, if effective, persuades him of something new, a belief he did not hold before or not in the same way, the whole process is one in which the mind of the hearer invents itself. Just as the universal good is for Aristotle mind thinking itself, so the good of rhetoric, persuasion, is mind inventing itself.

The study of persuasion in rhetoric is not, however, a matter of investigating what is actually going on in the mind of a hearer. This depends on other factors besides the rhetor. The persuasion that is the work of the rhetor is to be found in the speech itself. A speech can be persuasive whether anyone is actually persuaded or not, just as a tragedy can be moving whether anyone is actually moved or not.

We have then invention in the sense of the process by which the speech is invented and also in the sense of the process of invention within the speech. Invention in the second sense, so far as it is successful, must conform to the ways in which the mind works in invention. Consider, for example, the invention of enthymemes. [*See* Enthymeme.] Invention in the first sense would involve selecting a topic of enthymeme and filling it with definite content. One could thus invent many different kinds of enthymemes, but the process of invention would be similar in all cases. Yet if we recognize the enthymeme as itself inventive, a process by which the mind moves from what is given to something new, then there are as many forms of invention as there are topics of enthymeme.

Rhetoric is an art, and, as an art, formulates causes on the basis of experience. The parts of rhetoric are for Aristotle not determined by the sequential phases in the making of a speech, but by the different causes of persuasion. (For the four senses of "cause," see *Metaphysics* Δ.2.1013a24.) Invention on this view is not a separate part of rhetoric, but the speech in all its aspects is an invented whole. We now consider the causes of persuasion conceived as the invention by the rhetor of the mind of the audience inventing itself.

The materials of invention: Notions (eidē).

Aristotle distinguishes three kinds of rhetoric, and this distinction has become a commonplace of the rhetorical tradition. Deliberative rhetoric is exhortation or dehortation, its end is the advantageous or harmful, and it relates primarily to the future. Forensic rhetoric is accusation or defense, its end is the just or unjust, and it relates primarily to the past. Epideictic rhetoric is praise or blame, its end is the noble or the base, and it relates primarily to the present. Thus deliberative rhetoric invents the future, forensic rhetoric invents the past, and epideictic rhetoric invents the present. [*See* Deliberative genre; Epideictic genre; *and* Forensic genre.]

THE INVENTION OF THE FUTURE: DELIBERATIVE RHETORIC. Deliberative rhetoric makes use of four sorts of materials in its invention of the future. The deliberative *rhētōr* needs to know something about the subjects of public deliberation, which are mainly ways and means, war and peace, national defense, imports and exports, and legislation. To know the truth about these matters belongs to the science of politics, and rhetoric is here continuous with politics. It remains distinct from politics, however, since it deals with political matters not as they are in truth but as they enter into public discourse and public opinion.

The *rhētōr* needs to know not only the particular matters about which we deliberate, but also, at the opposite extreme, the ideal end to which people look in choice and avoidance. This is happiness and its parts, and here the difference between the scientific treatment of happiness in the *Ethics* and its treatment in the *Rhetoric* is immediately evident. The *Rhetoric* offers four definitions of happiness, which would be three too many in ethics, for how would one know which to choose; but four definitions provide a wider scope for invention.

The *rhētōr* needs to know not only the political facts and ultimate ends, but also the advantageous, which is a means but also a proximate end and a good. Anything that is thought to be good can serve as a basis for a deliberative argument, and so the *rhētōr* needs to know all the kinds of things that are thought to be good. If the good is a disputed one, he must be able to argue for or against it, and if two things are both thought to be good, he must be able to argue that either is the greater good. As we move into the region of disputed goods and things that possess some degree of goodness, arguments for opposite conclusions are not difficult to construct and the invention of the deliberative *rhētōr* has its widest scope.

Finally, what is most important and effective for being able to persuade and to deliberate well is to understand the different constitutions—democracy, oligarchy, aristocracy, and monarchy—and to distinguish the character, institutions, and interests of each. This will enable the rhetor to speak as the voice of the community and lead the citizens to adopt his recommendations, whatever they may be, as their own.

No beliefs are fixed and unalterable by nature, and in this sense the rhetorical world is a wholly inventable world; but the world cannot be invented all at once or *ex nihilo*. Persuasion of the new requires some ground or basis from which it can proceed, and this can only be supplied by beliefs already held. Innovation is thus inseparable from tradition. The problem for the *rhētōr* is to use beliefs already held as a ground for arriving at new beliefs. The premises that can be used to change beliefs are of two kinds. There are first the premises proper to each genus of rhetoric, such as those we are here considering, premises concerning the advantageous, the noble, and the just. These Aristotle calls *eidē*. Second, there are the premises common to all genera alike. These Aristotle calls *topoi*, topics (1.2.3158a31). In the sciences, *eidē* means "the species or forms of things"; the analogue in rhetoric is the basic forms of opinion, what might be translated as "views," "conceptions," "notions," "ideas." I shall use *notions* as the technical term. Aristotle refers to topics not only as "topics" but also as "common notions" (1.9.3168a26). Nearly all of the translators of the *Rhetoric* into English read Cicero (*De inv.* 2.15) back into Aristotle by translating *eidē* as "special topics" and *topoi* as "common topics," even though the first phrase is oxymoronic and the second redundant and neither is ever used by Aristotle. This translation tends to obscure the difference between invention in Cicero, which uses topics to speak about materials from the other arts and sciences, and invention in Aristotle, which uses notions already belonging to the rhetorical domain.

THE INVENTION OF THE PRESENT: EPIDEICTIC

RHETORIC. Epideictic rhetoric invents the present in the sense that the present occasion is made what it is by the epideictic *rhētōr*. It may, like Lincoln's Gettysburg Address, speak about past, present, and future, but it does so by way of heightening the significance of the present. Epideictic rhetoric is praise, what is praised is the noble, and the noble is found in its exemplary form in man, and first of all in his excellences or virtues. Although it is individual men who are praised, the communal context of rhetoric is still evident, for the virtues are not defined, as they are in ethics, in relation to the individual, but as powers of benefiting others. Not only is virtue noble, as well as what produces it and the signs and works that come from it, but also what is done for unselfish ends, and superiority to others, and whatever can be identified with what is esteemed by the audience. These notions provide the materials from which to invent the noble as an object of praise. In praising noble individuals, the community honors those to whom it is indebted and celebrates its own values in their highest realization. It thus invents itself in its nobility, as in Pericles' Funeral Oration.

THE INVENTION OF THE PAST: FORENSIC RHETORIC. To say that forensic rhetoric invents the past sounds paradoxical because the past is wholly determinate and in no respect inventable. The past as it is in truth cannot be invented, yet the past as it is in opinion is inventable. But the past must be invented precisely as something wholly determinate and uninventable. The particular past that is the primary concern of accusation and defense is injustice, since all human communities depend for their existence on punishing those who voluntarily violate their norms, and injustice is voluntary injury contrary to the law.

The notions proper to forensic rhetoric provide the materials from which to invent a past unjust act as determinate. The notions extend from the universal causal determination of all things to the formal determination of the particular act as unjust. To determine the act as unjust, one must first be able to determine it as voluntary. The seven possible causes of all acts are, in Aristotle's account, chance, nature, compulsion, habit, reasoning, spirit, and desire, and of these the last four are voluntary. Once an act has been determined as voluntary, it is further determined by its

motive. The motive for voluntary acts is some advantage or pleasure. In order to determine the voluntary act as unjust, we must determine the elements from which the injustice emerges. These are to be found in the state of mind of the doer, in possible victims, and in wrongs for which the doer is likely to escape punishment. The action, finally, must be given determinate form in its injustice and the degree of its injustice. This involves showing that it is contrary to some law, and laws are either those of a particular community, written or unwritten, or the universal law of nature. Written laws cannot fully determine what is just and unjust, and equity is justice that goes beyond the written law. Still further factors determine the degree of injustice, as the injustice of an act is greater when the agent is more unjust. The prosecutor of an unjust act thus invents it as fully determinate in its cause, motive, circumstances, and injustice.

THE SELF-SUFFICIENCY OF THE INVENTABLE WORLD: THE ATECHNICAL MEANS OF PERSUASION. A fourth kind of material from which the arguments of the speech are constructed is the atechnical means of persuasion, laws, witnesses, contracts, tortures, and oaths. They are proper to forensic rhetoric, although also used by the other kinds. They test the self-sufficiency of the inventable world, for to the extent that it is governed by elements that are not invented, it is a dependent world and not autarchic. Although the atechnical means are not invented by the rhetor, it is not difficult to find notions that make their use a matter of invention. For example, if the written law is against us, we can appeal to the universal law as more just, as in Antigone, or to equity.

The motivation of invention: Character (ēthos) and emotion (pathos). Rhetoric is for the sake of decisions, decisions are made by judges, and judges are influenced by more than arguments. The *rhētōr* must therefore be able to invent the motivation that will lead to the decision he is advocating. The three sources of persuasion, speaker, audience, and speech, all provide possibilities for the invention of motivation. [*See* Ēthos; Logos; *and* Pathos.]

THE CHARACTER OF THE SPEAKER. The character of the speaker is persuasive, Aristotle says, because we believe good men more fully and more readily no matter what the subject, and especially when the subject does not admit of exact knowledge but is a matter of doubt. Speakers are persuasive apart from arguments if they are thought to possess good sense (*phronēsis*), good character (*aretē*), and good will (*eunoia*). [*See* Phronēsis.] The persuasive speaker must therefore invent himself in his speech as possessing all three of these characteristics, whether he really has them or not. The speaker's invention of himself is the first step in inventing motivation, for if the audience does not think him trustworthy they will not be inclined to believe, or even listen to, what he has to say.

THE EMOTIONS OF THE AUDIENCE. Persuasion apart from argument is effected through the audience when the speech arouses emotions in the audience that affect its judgments. Emotions are unique among the means of persuasion because they are not opinions about the real, but the reality itself. It is somewhat as in dreams, in which the dreamwork distorts the way things appear, but cannot distort the emotions, which are always real and appropriate to the underlying thought. And because the emotions are real, they have propulsive force. The speaker invents the emotion in the sense of bringing it into existence, and the emotion is inventive in the sense of bringing what is thought by the audience into conformity with its demands. It thus differs from the emotional catharsis effected by poetic works. The emotions aroused by poetic works are enjoyed for their own sake and do not aim at anything beyond themselves.

THE CHARACTER OF THE SPEECH. Trust in the speaker results in a general inclination to believe whatever he says. Emotions are a powerful motivating factor tending to move us in a more particular direction. It is our character, however, that gives definite form to the things that we do. Character is not easily changed, and there can be no question of inventing the character of the audience. To give definite form to the inclinations of the emotions the *rhētōr* must adapt his speech to the character of the audience. The audience is then more ready to accept as their own whatever the speech asserts. The speech seems to be speaking their language, to be speaking for them, to be their own. Character is distinguished according to emotions, habits, ages, and fortunes.

DECISION (KRISIS). Decisions, unlike choices in the practical sciences, which result from inquiry into how an end may be attained, require alternatives and a judge who decides between them. In political rhetoric, the judges must decide in accordance with the constitution, and the speech must therefore be given a character appropriate to the constitution. This completes the motivational factors, which all work together build up the motivation for the decision.

The form of invention. We come now to invention itself, the various ways in which the mind moves from the familiar and accepted to the new. These are neither wholly logical nor wholly illogical.

TOPICS (TOPOI) OR COMMON NOTIONS (KOINAI EIDĒ). Notions about the advantageous, the noble, and the just each provide premises proper to one kind of rhetoric. The whole treatment of motivation is common to the three kinds, but deals with particular sources of motivation, and therefore precedes the treatment of topics or common notions. The common notions concern things in their possibility, their existence, either past or future, and their magnitude. The topics of possibility and existence infer the possibility or existence of one thing from the possibility or existence of another. The inference is immediate, without the mediation of a connecting term. If there is thunder, there has been lightning, if there is lightning there has been or will be thunder. This kind of inference is at the level of experience. It is found in some animals, such as Pavlov's dogs, and for the philosopher David Hume (1711–1776) it is the basis for all experimental reasoning concerning "matter of fact and existence." There is a sense in which the inventiveness of the mind is shown in making any connection at all between things at this level, but the inventiveness is more evident in cases where the connection is less firmly established by custom. For example, if one of two like things is possible, so is the other, or if a man was able to do a thing and wished to do it, he did it. [*See* Inference.]

Mathematics and rhetoric meet in the topic of magnitude, and here we encounter a remarkable contrast. Mathematics is the inferential science *par excellence*, yet rhetoric does not treat magnitude along with the other common notions as providing inferential forms, but among the notions or premises of deliberative rhetoric. Aristotle there begins from the abstract mathematical definition, "One thing exceeds another if it is as great plus something more," which provides the reason for concrete propositions such as, "Better the happiness of all than that of one or a few." But the mind does not think the concrete proposition as inferred from the abstract one, nor as embodying any inference at all. No mathematical proofs are suitable to a rhetorical work: the proposition is either too obvious to require proof, or too recondite for rhetoric. Notions of the greater and less serve as premises for invention but not as forms of invention.

COMMON PERSUASIONS (KOINAI PISTEIS). There are two genera of persuasive arguments, the example or paradigm (*paradigma*) and the enthymeme (*enthymēma*), corresponding respectively to induction and syllogism in dialectic. [*See* Exemplum; *and* Syllogism.]

The paradigm has three species, the relating of things that have actually happened, comparison (*parabolē*), as in the Socratic dialogues, and fables (*logoi,* in one of its senses). In all three, the universal on which the argument depends is present in the paradigm, although it is not actually stated, as it would be in dialectical induction. The mind of the audience again makes an inventive leap, guided by the universal present in the paradigm, to the new particular.

The relating of things that have happened is the counterpart of scientific induction, since it depends on finding facts belonging to the same subject genus as the facts under discussion. The use of comparisons is the counterpart of dialectical induction, since it makes use of analogies to other genera that are accepted by the hearer but would be out of place in the sciences. The fable, finally, would be out of place in the sciences, since its story is not true of any subject genus, and also out of place in dialectic, since no one even believes its story to be true. It is a form of argument peculiar to rhetoric, and of the three species of paradigm it is the one which is most the invention of the speaker.

The fable is a story that is an argument. Literary authors also invent stories, and it is at this point that the content of rhetoric approximates most closely to that of poetic works. [*See* Criticism; *and* Poetry.] Since antiquity, fables have in fact been collected not as resources for the rhetor but as poetic works to be enjoyed for their own sake. But when rhetorical fables are made into poetic works, the argument is subordinated to poetic ends and loses its inventiveness. The simple prose of the rhetorical fable is usually elaborated and given metrical form, which makes it more enjoyable in itself but distracts the reader from it as an argument. The moral of the rhetorical fable, which concerns a particular case, is generalized to suit the requirements of poetry, and the motivation for decision is lost. Finally, the characteristics of the fable that suit it to a popular audience, such as speaking animals, need to be presented in a way that makes them palatable to an educated audience, as La Fontaine (1621–1695) presents his fables from his own sophisticated and entertaining point of view, with the result that the hearer becomes a spectator of the fable and no longer engages in inventing the decision.

With the maxim and enthymeme we reach the explicit universal. Maxims function inferentially as starting points for inferences to any of the unlimited particulars that fall under them.

Enthymemes are syllogisms adapted to a popular audience. Their premises are probabilities, signs, or necessary signs, and their conclusions are mainly probable rather than necessary. They do not draw conclusions from remote premises or include all the steps of the inference, for otherwise the argument would be unclear because of its length or would waste words by stating what is manifest. Just as in dialectic one can distinguish between real and apparent syllogisms, so in rhetoric one can distinguish between real and apparent enthymemes, but nothing is made of the distinction. We are dealing here with the way in which the mind moves in reaching a novel conclusion, whether formally valid or not. Its inferences are not fully formulated, its conclusions are probable rather than necessary, and they may even depend on logical fallacies. [*See* Inference; *and* Tacit dimension, the.]

The invention of enthymemes requires first of all a knowledge of the facts that belong to the subject, as many facts as possible and as close to the subject as possible, close to the subject in the sense of belonging to that subject and not to others. These facts must be sought out by the *rhētōr;*

they are not part of the general art. What is needed in each case is a selection of all the facts that pertain to that case, the facts of the case. The first way of selecting them is by topics, topics not in the technical sense previously defined, but in the more familiar sense of headings under which a number of items can be grouped. All the notions and motivational factors are grouped by topics in this sense. The selection of facts can make use of these same topics. For example, the facts about the Athenians that pertain to their waging war can be grouped together, and similarly the facts for which the Athenians could be praised, and the facts for which they could be blamed, and so on; and the same for each subject, whether the Athenians or the Lacedaemonians, a man or a god, or an abstraction such as justice. Thus the *rhētōr* will have selections of facts relating to many different subjects and cases. If he does not have the facts relating to the case at hand he will need to search them out. Then, when he comes to invent his enthymemes, he will have at hand whatever facts are useful or necessary. If, for example, the speech is to be a eulogy of Achilles, he will have at hand the selection of facts about Achilles for which Achilles can be praised. He will also have at hand all the notions of the noble. He can then construct enthymemes that use the facts about Achilles to connect Achilles with the notions of the noble.

TOPICS (TOPOI) OR ELEMENTS (STOICHEIA) OF ENTHYMEMES. The justly celebrated chapter 23 of Book 2 is the heart of Aristotle's *Rhetoric* and of invention. Aristotle here takes up the whole subject of rhetorical inference in a new way. The inferential connections thus far considered are grounded in immediate experience or in logical forms corresponding to induction and syllogism. Yet the mind has in addition its own ways of making connections, and chapter 23 identifies the elements of enthymemes in the sense of the different kinds of middle terms by which the mind tends to make connections. A name, for example, is an element that may serve to connect the bearer of the name with its meaning, as one might say of Stalin, "O steel in heart as thou art steel in name." At a deep level, the mind tends to identify a thing with its name and therefore to accept the meaning of the name as a property of the thing. It is above all in these topics that one

sees the inventiveness of the mind, the multiple ways in which it can use connecting links to move from the given to the novel.

Aristotle lists a total of thirty-eight topics of enthymemes: twenty-eight topics of real enthymemes and ten of apparent enthymemes. In their general form, they are empty, and their power and significance become clear only as one sees what can be done with them. One indication of their power is that Aristotle in four cases notes that the single topic is the basis for a whole art of rhetoric. The topic of the consequence uses the consequences of actions to exhort or dissuade and to accuse or defend and to praise or blame. This corresponds to a form of what we call pragmatism. Since it most often happens that the same thing is followed by both good and bad consequences, this element can be used on either side of a question. This topic together with the common notions is, Aristotle says, the art of Callippus. Again, one of the topics of apparent enthymemes is to take what is true of a thing in a particular sense as true without qualification. In dialectic, this takes the form of arguing that what is not is, because it is what is not, or that the unknown is known, because it is known to be unknown. In rhetoric, it is used to make the improbable appear probable, as, for example, if a weak man is accused of assaulting and battering a strong man, this is not probable, while if a strong man is accused of assaulting and battering a weak man, this also is not probable just because it was bound to appear probable. The art of Corax, Aristotle says, is composed of this topic.

SOLUTION (LYSIS). The final component of the inferential forms that constitute the thought of the speech is the solution of refutations. (Our translators again read Cicero [*De inventione* 1.42] back into Aristotle by translating *lysis* as "refutation.") The difference between the solution of refutations in dialectic and rhetoric illustrates the difference between the two arts. In dialectic, a solution exposes false reasoning by making clear the fallacy on which the falsity depends. In rhetoric, there is no examination of the opposing argument, and the solution simply rebuts the conclusion by a counterargument or an objection.

When refutations are solved by rebuttal rather than by exposing a fallacy, the hearer is not distracted from the argument of the speech by having to examine an argument moving in a different direction. And even though no fallacy is exposed, it seems nevertheless that something must be wrong with the opposing argument. Also, the argument of the solution provides fresh support for the other arguments of the speech. The solution is thus a way of using opposing arguments, so far as possible, to one's own advantage. The tendency of the mind that is at work here is the tendency to avoid inconsistencies or cognitive dissonance. A solution in rhetoric, whether or not it is a refutation, enables the mind to dismiss opposing views or arguments that are perceived as inconsistent with its own. When the opposing arguments are solved and the arguments of the speaker are left in possession of the field, the thought or inferential component of the speech is completed, just as the actional component is completed in the decision.

The finality of invention: Style (lexis) and arrangement (taxis). All of the invention thus far considered finds its full actualization or finality in style and arrangement. This finality is found first of all in the final phase of the process of invention, which is delivery.

FINALITY OF THE PROCESS OF INVENTION: DELIVERY (HYPOKRISIS). Aristotle says at the beginning of Book 3 that it is not enough to know what to say, one must also know how to say it. The latter is the concern of style, which in this broad sense includes delivery. Following the natural order, and this is where Cicero's genetic sequence finds a place in Aristotle, we proceed from the things from which the persuasive is derived, to setting them out in style, to delivery. Delivery is not only the final phase of the making of a speech, however; as a matter of art it also has a history of its own which, Aristotle finds, has barely begun. The art of delivery was first developed by actors and rhapsodes, and in the *Poetics,* knowledge of delivery is conceived as belonging to the architectonic art of elocution (1456b8–19), which is used by actors, rhapsodes, *rhētors,* and everyone who speaks. With respect to rhetorical delivery, however, Aristotle says only that no art has yet been composed with respect to it, that it concerns the volume, harmony, and rhythm of the voice, that it has great power because of the imperfection of the hearer, and that it depends on natural gifts and is more atechnical.

FINALITY OF INVENTION ITSELF: STYLE. The finality of invention in the sense of that which fully actualizes what invention is, is the setting out of all the preceding inventions in language. In poetics, the plot has a life of its own, so to speak, and language gives it a habitation, whereas the inventions of rhetoric come to life only in language. This is why *lexis* in the *Poetics* is appropriately translated as "diction," but in the *Rhetoric,* as "style." It is also why for Aristotle there is no general art of style or expression: expression in different arts has generically different functions, and the analysis of expression is therefore relative to the art. But if rhetoric is the preeminent art of effective expression, it may be conceived as the art of effective expression in general. Thus George Campbell begins his *Philosophy of Rhetoric* (1776) by defining eloquence as "That art or talent by which the discourse is adapted to its end," and in this he is followed by Hugh Blair (1783). For analogous reasons, rhetoric may be conceived as the architectonic art of elocution just mentioned. We thus have today a somewhat confusing situation in which three different arts, the art of persuasion, the art of expression, and the art of elocution, are all called by the same name, rhetoric.

A first aspect of style concerns the selection of words. Every word is either standard, strange, metaphorical, ornamental, coined, extended, contracted, or altered (*Poetics* 1457b1). The virtue of style is clarity, and clarity is achieved by standard words. The *rhētor* seeks not only clarity, however, but also the distinction (*to xenikon*) that is admired by, and pleasing to, the audience. This is achieved by nonstandard words, but their use tends toward poetry and the artificiality that is not persuasive. Consequently, the *rhētor* must as a rule limit himself to standard and familiar words and metaphorical words, together with epithets and similes, which are not kinds of words but are treated here because epithets involve selecting words that are honorific or pejorative, and similes, like metaphors, talk about one set of things by means of another.

Style to be effective must be suited to the situation. The *archē* of style, its beginning and foundation, is to speak Greek, or whatever language the audience understands. To this beginning, various determinants can be added. The language may be expanded to make it impressive, or contracted to make it concise. It may express emotion and character and be proportionate to the things being discussed. Finally, it may be opportune in the sense of appropriate to a particular point within the speech itself. The progression here is from the common language to the language suited to the momentary situation.

The form of style should be neither metrical nor without rhythm. Meter is suited to poetry but is too contrived for rhetoric. Still, some kind of periodicity and closure is desirable, and this is found in the paean and in the periodic style. The possibilities of the period are realized in antithesis and similarities of beginning and ending.

The culmination of style is found in lively and esteemed sayings. Their invention requires natural talent or long practice, but it is possible to enumerate their sources. Their sources in thought are the metaphors, similes, style, and enthymemes by which we learn something rapidly. Their sources in style are antitheses, metaphors, and the setting of things before our eyes, or vividness. Aristotle proceeds to identify within these the sources of greatest liveliness and esteem, so that the progression is from thought and style in general toward the highest achievements of style. Proportional metaphors are the most esteemed, and vividness is best achieved by representing things by words that signify activity or functioning. Metaphors should be drawn from what is akin but not obvious, and their liveliness is increased if the hearer is surprised, for then it becomes more clear that he has learned something. The more concise and antithetical the expression, the more it is esteemed, and liveliness is increased by personal relevance and by what is rightly said. The more sources of the lively and esteemed the saying possesses, the more lively and esteemed it will be.

The style of the speech is thus in its components both familiar and strange, in its relation to the case at hand both common and unique, in its forms both recurrent and novel, and in its functioning both known and unknown. This joining of tradition and innovation corresponds to the nature of invention itself.

FINALITY OF THE MEDIUM OF INVENTION. Invention is actualized in style, but different media require different styles. This topic, which Aristotle treats briefly, requires a more extensive treatment in modern rhetoric, in which many different media are used. Aristotle is concerned principally with the difference between the written and the spoken language, between speeches written to be read and speeches to be delivered in public debate. Speeches written to be read may appear weak in public debate, and speeches that are effective in public debate may appear simpleminded when read. Frequent repetitions and asyndeta are, for example, effective in public debate but not in written speeches.

FINALITY OF THE INVENTED WHOLE: ARRANGEMENT. The finality of rhetorical invention is found, finally, in the speech itself as an invented whole composed of parts. The parts are conceived functionally. Only two are essential: the proposal (*prothesis*) and the persuasion (*pistis*). To these may be added an introduction and an epilogue. Other parts that may be functional are narration, self-presentation, interrogations, and humor. Refutation is included in persuasion. Each part has a function, but it may function differently in different kinds of wholes, that is, in the different kinds of rhetoric. This finality of invention is realized when all the parts function well relative to the whole of which they are a part.

We see that Aristotle, locating rhetorical invention within the domain of public opinion, distinguishes at every point the inventions of rhetoric from the truths of science. The *heurein, theōrein, eidē,* and demonstrations of rhetoric are not the *heurein, theōrein, eidē,* and demonstrations of the theoretical sciences. The happiness and virtue and decisions of rhetoric are not the happiness and virtue and choices of ethics. The way the facts of politics are used in rhetoric is not the way they are used in political science. [*See* Politics.] The treatment of magnitude in rhetoric is not the treatment of magnitude in mathematics. The emotions and fables and style of rhetoric are not the emotions and fables and style of poetics. Similarly, the inductions, syllogisms, and solutions of rhetoric are not the inductions, syllogisms, and solutions of dialectic. Invention in rhetoric reigns supreme, but it is for an educated audience held in check on all sides by the truths of the sciences and the formal validity of dialectic. All this is in contrast to the rhetoric of Cicero, for whom the audience is instructed, delighted, and moved by hearing the truths of the sciences presented in the inventions of the best kind of orator (*De optimo genere oratorum* 1.3)

We now turn to the rhetorics of truth, which can here be treated rather briefly just because they are primarily concerned with truth rather than invention.

Truth and Invention in Plato's *Phaedrus*. Philosophy for Plato (c.429–c.347 BCE) is not a doctrine but a method, dialectic. It is expressed not in treatises but in dialogues, each of which takes its principles from the interlocutors. If the arguments are sound and the truth is one, all the dialogues in their dependence on their own principles will be consistent with one another, but they do not form parts of a single doctrine and their principles and conclusions may differ (Walter Watson, "Dogma, Skepticism, and Dialogue," in *The Third Way: New Directions in Platonic Studies,* ed. Francisco J. Gonzalez, Boston, 1995, pp. 189–210). There is thus no Platonic doctrine with respect to rhetoric, although we have examples of deliberative rhetoric in the *Phaedrus,* epideictic rhetoric in the *Symposium,* and judicial rhetoric in the *Apology,* and the degradation of rhetoric when separated from dialectic is demonstrated in the *Gorgias.* We shall consider truth and invention in the *Phaedrus.*

Rhetoric is defined in the *Phaedrus* as the art of verbal psychagogy, or leading of souls by means of words (261a). Souls are led not by a connection of two terms through a middle, as in enthymemes, but by a likeness between two terms. To know whether the likeness is genuine requires a knowledge of the truth. "He who knows the truth always knows how to discover (*heuriskein*) likenesses most excellently" (273d). Dialectical rhetoric depends on the truth, but in the absence of knowledge rhetorical rhetoric becomes a matter of invention. "Shall we not bring before us the most excellent Evenus of Paros who first invented (*heuren*) 'covert allusion' and 'indirect praise'?" (267a).

Socrates in the *Phaedrus* gives two speeches on love, one favoring the nonlover, the other the lover. He illustrates the knowledge of likenesses by the two divisions of madness, one in each speech, that lead to two different definitions of love. Neither the madness of human love nor the madness of divine love are Socrates' inventions.

Both are real, though ideal realities, and their persuasiveness depends upon their truth. The collections and divisions by which they are discovered are the work of dialectic as here practiced and defined, and indeed the whole dialogue is structured dialectically by successive divisions into left and right, or rhetorical and dialectical, halves. Rhetoric and dialectic are here joined in a single organism.

Socrates accepts what the rhetorical textbooks say about style and arrangement as a necessary prerequisite to the art of rhetoric, but as insufficient, because to know these things is not to know the conditions of their use. This requires a knowledge of the soul and its various forms, and how they act and are acted upon, so that discourse can be suited to the soul to which it is addressed, and this again requires dialectic. For Aristotle, rhetoric invents a speech that has the hearer's own character and thought; the rhetoric of the *Phaedrus* uses dialectic to present the soul of the hearer with the likeness of an ideal which the soul discovers as its own. The human psychagogy of rhetoric is thus a likeness of the divine psychagogy of love. Rhetoric for both Aristotle and the *Phaedrus* generates novelty, but in the one case it is by the soul's invention of its own opinions, in the other by the soul's discovery of its true ideal.

Truth in the Rhetoric of Nausiphanes. In rhetoric, as in other fields, our perception of Greek achievements is skewed by the lack of complete works from the Democritean tradition. Epicurus (341–270 BCE) wrote a work *On Rhetoric* in which, according to Diogenes Laertius (10. 13), he thought fit to require nothing beyond clearness. Similarly, almost twenty centuries later, John Locke, in a well-known and eloquent passage, asserts that the inventions of rhetoric are impediments to the truth:

> But yet if we would speak of things as they are, we must allow that all the art of rhetoric, besides order and clearness, all the artificial and figurative applications of words eloquence hath invented, are for nothing else but to insinuate wrong ideas, move the passions, and thereby mislead the judgment, and so indeed are perfect cheats; and therefore, however laudable, or allowable oratory may render them in harangues and popular addresses, they are

certainly, in all discourses that pretend to inform, or instruct, wholly to be avoided; and where truth and knowledge are concerned, cannot but be thought a great fault, either of the language or person that makes use of them. (*An Essay Concerning Human Understanding*, 1690, 3.10.34)

Nausiphanes of Teos, a fourth-century BCE Democritean, develops the positive side of this view, the persuasive potentialities of the truth. Our knowledge of Nausiphanes is derived almost entirely from the criticism of his views on rhetoric by Philodemus, a first-century BCE Epicurean criticism, which itself is preserved only in badly damaged papyri. The fragments that relate to Nausiphanes have been selected and edited by Hermann Diels and Walther Kranz in *Die Fragmente der Vorsokratiker* (7th ed., Berlin, 1954). In what follows, I refer to the fragments in Diels-Kranz by the page numbers of Book 6 of Philodemus's *Rhetoric* as edited by Siegfried Sudhaus (Leipzig, 1896).

Nausiphanes is said to have claimed that the physicist (*physikos*) and wise man will be able to persuade his hearers (p. 1). The physicist has the rhetorical habit (*hexis*) even if he never exercises it by reason of not entering into public affairs (p. 48). The wise man will, however, prefer to engage in rhetoric and politics (p. 5). What in the opinions and memories of the many is honorable and worthy of notice depends upon political skills (*politikai deinōtētes*) rather than vainly vaunted virtues and nobilities (p. 33). Reasoning about the things to come from the things that are evident and now in existence is always useful, and the most able leaders, whether in democracies or monarchies or any other constitution, always at some time use this mode of reasoning (p. 38). The cause of persuasive power comes not from histories but from the knowledge of things, so that the physicist might persuade any *ethnos* in a way similar to his own (p. 19). What is persuasive is knowledge, from whence comes the advantageous (p. 9). The *rhētors* know what the many wish for and will not regret by reason of having deliberated advantageously (p. 16). Only the physicist, by knowing and saying what nature wishes and arguing with a view to this, will be able to persuade (p. 10). The argument of the wise man and the argument of the political speaker

differ almost only in form (*schēma*), so that in their thoughts those who know the truth according to nature do not differ from political speakers, but only in the form of their arguments and those things prepared in relation to no argument (p. 36). One must also admire the talk of the physiologue (*physiologos*), for it has been perfectly composed for a pleasant journey of the company, and is by metaphors carried over best to the unknown matter, and has come to be not from empty artifice and rule but from the nature of things and according to usage (p. 27).

The effective *rhētōr* and the scientist here have the same knowledge. By knowing what is truly advantageous and knowing how to make this clear to his hearers, the scientist-*rhētōr* is able to persuade them, because what is truly advantageous is what they truly want. The Democritean tradition is often a sort of mirror image of the Platonic, and we see this here, for both Plato and Nausiphanes make rhetoric a matter of knowing what is truly desirable and what is not, and knowing how to make this clear to the audience by likenesses or metaphors. To know what is truly desirable is in the one case to know the ideal realities that transcend the given situation, in the other the physical realities that are immanent in it.

Rhetorical Invention and Scientific Discovery. We have examined the treatment of invention in four exemplary rhetorics. The four kinds of rhetoric they represent can usually be found in any historical period, but their particular forms and relative prominence vary from one period to another. The modern period has been marked by the development of science and technology and includes a development of scientific rhetorics that makes them more prominent than in earlier periods. We see also an interest in furthering the process of scientific discovery, and we shall conclude by examining the relevance of rhetorical invention to scientific discovery. There is first the possibility of adapting the devices of rhetorical invention to scientific discovery, of which Francis Bacon (1561–1626) provides the classic example. [*See* Science.]

Bacon divides the intellectual art of inquiry or invention into two parts, the invention of arts and sciences and the invention of speech and arguments. His new art of inventing arts and sciences uses all the basic devices of Cicero's *De inventione*. In *The Advancement of Learning* (1605), he uses the method of division to map out the intellectual globe, and the basic divisions concern the way in which knowledge is generated, just as those in Cicero concern the way in which a speech is generated. Bacon distinguishes general from special topics, and receives the latter as things of great use, for by their use new special topics are discovered and the art of discovery advances. Bacon planned to provide an example of inquiry and invention according to his method in every kind of subject, and the second book of the *New Organon* (1620) provides one such example in the investigation of the form of heat. The arguments pro and con in Cicero become in the investigation of things the instances of presence and absence. And just as *De inventione* specifies just how to go about inventing, so Bacon's adaptation of its methods to the investigation of things goes far to level men's wits and leaves but little to individual excellence.

Bacon preserves the distinction between the invention of speech and arguments and the invention of arts and sciences, even though both use similar rhetorical devices. There is also the more radical possibility of uniting them by conceiving science as rhetoric. Rhetoric is concerned with matters about which there is some doubt and which are subject to debate. Debates occur in the sciences, and the truths of science are subject to change over time. If the truths of science are conceived simply as what the scientific community is persuaded of at any particular time, then science becomes a matter of rhetoric, and the world is wholly inventable. This is the world of the Skeptical or sophistic tradition. It is succinctly characterized by the well-known opening sentence of Protagoras's *Truth:* " Man is the measure of all things, of the things that are, that they are, and of the things that are not, that they are not." It is as the inventor of all things that man determines their existence.

If one does not share Protagoras's view of truth as invention, one may still find a more modest role for invention in science. Einstein views the fundamental concepts and principles of physics not as abstractions from its subject matter but as free inventions of the mind (Albert Einstein, "On the Method of Theoretical Physics," in *Ideas and Opinions*, New York, 1954, p. 272; "Physics and Reality," *ibid.*, pp. 292–295). This free invention, however, is subject to a double constraint: the goal of science is, first, so far as possible, the complete conceptual grasp and connection of the entire manifold of sense-experience, and, second, the achievement of this goal with the use of a minimum of primary concepts and relations; that is, with the greatest possible logical simplicity of the foundations. Thus the freedom of the inventor does not extend very far: it is not the freedom of a storyteller, but rather the freedom of a man who is set a well-designed word puzzle. He is free to propose any word as the solution, but there is only one which actually solves the puzzle in all its parts.

If one finds sense-experience and logical simplicity insufficient to account for decisions among competing scientific inventions, rhetorical persuasion may be called upon to fill the gap. Thomas Kuhn in *The Structure of Scientific Revolutions* (Chicago, 1962) stresses the variation of scientific paradigms over time, and distinguishes normal science, which is puzzle-solving within a paradigm, from the innovation that invents a new paradigm. Kuhn extends the rhetorical concept of paradigm from speech making to science. The instructor in rhetoric, according to Isocrates (436–338 BCE), "must in himself furnish such a paradigm (*paradigma*) that those formed by him and able to imitate him will from the outset show in their speaking more grace and elegance than others" (*Against the Sophists* 18). Those who share the same paradigm will be similar in what they do: "All who have been under a true and intelligent guide will be found to have a power of speech so similar that it is evident to everyone that they have shared the same education" (*Antidosis* 206). Instead of a group of speakers following the paradigm of their instructor, we have in Kuhn a group of scientists following the paradigm of an innovative scientist.

The persuasion that leads scientists to adopt a new paradigm gives rise to a new branch of rhetoric. "To discover how scientific revolutions are effected," Kuhn says, "we shall . . . have to examine not only the impact of nature and of logic, but also the techniques of persuasive argumentation effective within the quite special groups that constitute the community of scientists" (p. 93). How is conversion to a new paradigm induced and how resisted? "What sort of answer to that question may we expect? Just because it is asked about techniques of persuasion, or about argument and counterargument in a situation in which there can be no proof, our question is a new one, demanding a sort of study that has not previously been undertaken" (p. 151).

These accounts, which argue for science as rhetoric or as employing rhetorical devices and involving invention and persuasion, suggest the possibility of a single art that would unite rhetorical invention and scientific discovery. Richard McKeon, in a number of articles published between 1964 and 1975, has proposed such an art as the new rhetoric suited to our times. McKeon's philosophy is a not a doctrine but the power of inventing many different doctrines, just as rhetoric itself is not a speech but the power of inventing many different speeches, and his various articles on rhetoric are not parts of a single doctrine but various ways of conceiving the new rhetoric and its components. In "The Uses of Rhetoric in a Technological Age: Architectonic Productive Arts" (*Rhetoric: Essays in Invention and Discovery,* ed. Mark Backman, Woodbridge, Conn., 1987, pp. 1–24) McKeon proposes rhetoric as an architectonic productive art suitable to a technological age.

Just as rhetoric uses accepted beliefs to produce new beliefs, so McKeon examines the whole history of his subject as a guide for his innovations. McKeon finds in the history of the West two periods in which rhetoric used the devices of amplification and schematization to make itself an architectonic productive art. In the Roman Republic, rhetoric was such an art with a practical orientation, as we see in Cicero, and in the Renaissance it was such an art with a productive orientation. McKeon argues that in our times we are in need of such an art with a theoretic orientation.

McKeon uses Cicero to invent a form and content for this new art. Cicero's four kinds of *constitutiones, stases,* or issues suggest the necessary component arts of the new rhetoric. To treat the issue of fact, we need an art of creating the data of existence; such an art would make use of places not only for invention in language but also for discovery in existence. Thus discoveries made in a book or work of art should provide places by which to perceive creatively what might otherwise not be experienced in the existent world we constitute. To treat the definitional issue, we need an art of defining or judging facts; such an art would begin from hypotheses as to what the fact is and would interpret both texts and existence. To treat the qualitative issue, we need an art of connecting the fact with its qualities or characteristics; such an art would trace themes as they move in variations from field to field and would establish connections in both discourse and the world. Finally, we need an art of objectifying and systematizing data, facts, and relations; such an art would posit theses to form, and explore the operations of, compositions of things, constitutions of communities, and constructs of communications. In other articles, McKeon treats these four arts as, respectively, new forms of rhetoric, grammar, logic, and dialectic, but since rhetoric is here architectonic, they are all brought together under the aegis of rhetoric.

Arts require fields in which to operate, and for these McKeon turns to Cicero's three kinds of rhetoric and to dialectic. In a technological age, we do not find subject matters ready-made, nor do we encounter problems distributed precisely in fields. We rather make subject matters to fit the examination and resolution of problems. In practical inquiries, for example, the problem is not how to devise means to achieve accepted ends, but rather the calculation of uses and applications that might be made of the vastly increased available means in order to devise new ends. The field of the new demonstrative or epideictic rhetoric should provide the grounds for going beyond the bounds of what is already known and the fields of that knowledge. The field of the new judicial rhetoric includes all recorded literature and the facts as well as the records of experience. The field of the new deliberative rhetoric is all arts and methods. The field of the new dialectic is systematic organization both as a system of communication for a universal audience, mankind, and as a system of operation of an ongoing development and inquiry. In sum, just as Bacon's great instauration was a reinvention of Cicero's *De inventione* as an art of discovery to further the rebirth of learning, so McKeon's article is a reinvention of the same work as a universal art of invention and discovery appropriate to the needs of our technological age.

Of the four component arts and fields of the new rhetoric, it is the art and field of creativity that now exist most conspicuously. Creativity has become an academic specialty with its conferences, journals, and burgeoning literature. A recent bibliography of the literature runs to three volumes (*The Creative Research Handbook*, ed. Mark A. Runco, Cresskill, N.J., 1997). McKeon's conception of a new rhetoric provides a possible intellectual context and structure for the investigation of creativity. But whatever the fortunes of the new architectonic rhetoric, new technologies of communication ensure that there will be no lack of opportunity for innovations by disciplinary, dialectical, and scientific rhetorics even in an age of architectonic rhetorics.

[*See also* Classical rhetoric; Commonplaces and commonplace books; Perspective by incongruity; *and* Topics.]

BIBLIOGRAPHY

Architectonic Rhetorics

Kuhn, Thomas S. "The Essential Tension: Tradition and Innovation in Scientific Research." In *Scientific Creativity: Its Recognition and Development,* edited by Calvin W. Taylor and Frank Barron, pp. 341–354. New York, 1963. Innovation inseparable from tradition: "The productive scientist must be a traditionalist who enjoys playing intricate games by pre-established rules in order to be a successful innovator who discovers new games and new pieces with which to play them" (p. 352).

McKeon, Richard. "The Liberating Arts and the Humanizing Arts in Education." In *Humanistic Education and Western Civilization: Essays for Robert M Hutchins,* edited by Arthur A. Cohen, pp. 159–181. New York, 1964. "The art of differentiating viewpoints and of translating them for communication is the art by which *tradition* is related to *innovation* in the many frameworks in which novelty is encountered and treated" (p. 179).

McKeon, Richard. "The Future of the Liberal Arts." In *Current Issues in Higher Education,* edited by G. Kerry Smith, pp. 36–44. Washington, D.C., 1964. "A new rhetoric is developing as a liberal art to provide the discipline for investigating the structure of facts and the interrelations of facts" (p. 39).

McKeon, Richard. "Arts of Invention and Arts of Memory." *Critical Inquiry* 1 (1975), pp. 723–739. "This analysis and history of places . . . has exhibited them in their multiplicity and interaction revivifying the past and preparing a novel future" (p. 739).

Zyskind, Harold. "A Case Study in Philosophic Rhetoric: Theodore Roosevelt." *Philosophy and Rhetoric* 1 (1968), pp. 228–254. Shows concretely how rhetoric, which can argue either side of any issue, can itself provide a basis for forceful leadership, and how philosophy, science, history, and politics can all be brought within its domain.

Zyskind, Harold. "Some Philosophic Strands in Popular Rhetoric." *Perspectives in Education, Religion, and the Arts,* vol. 3 of *Contemporary Philosophic Thought: The International Philosophy Year Conferences at Brockport,* pp. 373–395. Albany, N.Y., 1970. Popular rhetoric embodies principles, methods, and a subject matter that permit it to usurp the functions of philosophy.

Disciplinary Rhetorics

Perelman, Chaim, and Lucie Olbrechts-Tyteca. *The New Rhetoric: A Treatise on Argumentation.* Translated by John Wilkinson and Purcell Weaver. Notre Dame, Ind., 1969. English translation of *La Nouvelle Rhetorique: Traité de l'Argumentation,* first published 1958. A comprehensive study of arguments that secure adherence without being formally compelling. Extensive bibliography.

Dialectical Rhetorics

Burke, Kenneth. *A Rhetoric of Motives.* New York, 1950. Psychagogy by identification, ranging through the whole of Western culture and culminating in examples of identification with an ultimate order.

Scientific Rhetorics

Berger, Peter L., and Thomas Luckmann. *The Social Construction of Reality: A Treatise on the Sociology of Knowledge.* New York, 1967. The reality of everyday life is both the paramount reality and a social construction. Scientific rhetoric in its architectonic form. Derives from the work of Edmund Husserl and Alfred Schutz.

Hovland, Carl I., Irving L. Janis, and Harold H. Kelley. *Communication and Persuasion: Psychological Studies of Opinion Change.* New Haven, 1953. A scientific rhetoric in which correspondences to the nonscientific rhetorics are evident.

Rosnow, Ralph L., and Edward J. Robinson, eds. *Experiments in Persuasion.* New York, 1967. A collection of research papers on opinion change exhibiting the remarkable scope and detail of modern scientific rhetoric.

Creativity and Rhetoric

Bergson, Henri. *The Two Sources of Morality and Religion.* Translated by R. Ashley Audra and Cloudesley Brereton. New York, 1935; paperback edition, 1954. English translation of *Les deux sources de la morale et de la religion,* first published 1932. The creative power of *pathos:* "That a new emotion is the source of the great creations of art, of science and of civilization in general there seems to no doubt" (p. 43).

Ghiselin, Brewster, ed. *The Creative Process: A Symposium.* Berkeley, 1952. A very useful collection of statements by thirty-eight well-known creative individuals, past and present, from many different fields, all describing their own creative processes. Problem: find in each case the rhetorical device(s) at work, if any.

Gordon, William J. J. *Synectics: The Development of Creative Capacity.* New York, 1968. An account of creative problem-solving in small groups, the result of research over a period of more than fifteen years. Personal, direct, symbolic, and fantasy analogies comparable to Aristotle's *paradigmata.* Bibliography.

Kubie, Lawrence S. *Neurotic Distortion of the Creative Process.* New York, 1961. The preconscious as the enthymemic faculty: "A type of mental function, which we call technically 'the preconscious system,' is the essential implement of all creative activity; and . . . unless preconscious processes can flow freely there can be no true creativity" (p. 137). Preconscious processes are subject to distortion and obstruction by the rigidities of conscious processes on the one hand and of unconscious processes on the other.

Sternberg, Robert J., ed. *The Nature of Creativity: Contemporary Psychological Perspectives.* Cambridge, U.K., 1988. Assembles various fruitful approaches to creativity with a view to establishing a unified research field.

Wallace, Doris B., and Howard E. Gruber. *Creative People at Work: Twelve Cognitive Case Studies.* New York, 1989. The primacy of the particular: each creative person is unique, and must be understood in his or her uniqueness.

Weber, Max. "The Types of Authority and Imperative Co-ordination." *The Theory of Social and Economic Organization.* Translated by A. M. Henderson and Talcott Parsons, pp. 324–423. New York, 1947; paperback edition, 1964. English translation of *Wirtschaft und Gesellschaft,* Part I; first published 1922. The creative power of *ēthos:* charismatic authority, as contrasted with traditional and rational authority, is a specifically revolutionary force.

—WALTER WATSON

IRONY. Irony's general characteristic is to make something understood by expressing its opposite. We can therefore isolate three separate ways of applying this rhetorical form. Irony can refer to (1) individual figures of speech (*ironia verbi*); (2) particular ways of interpreting life (*ironia vitae*); and (3) existence in its entirety (*ironia entis*). The three dimensions of irony—trope, figure, and universal paradigm—can be understood as rhetorical, existential, and ontological.

The General Structure of Irony. Irony presents an intellectually demanding phenomenon of communication (e.g., as opposed to metaphorical speech), where the dialogical relation is a constitutive element, requiring the addressee to follow a double negation. The original intention is refuted by expressing the opposite, which is then refuted again by the simultaneously sent signals of irony. Accordingly, irony conveys meaning by indirect reference rather than by direct statement. Irony plays with the possibilities of extreme otherness of speech, of life, or of existence as such. The full range of irony is only intelligible through an awareness of the problematic relationship between the expressed and the intended, between character and statement, and between essence and appearance. Linguistic irony, for example, might represent reality as an illusion, or an illusion as reality. Kenneth Burke remarks that irony is one of the four "master tropes," which preconfigured mankind's conceptual worldview. Irony represents the typical shape of the liberal, enlightened intellect, in contrast to the metaphor, the metonymy, or the *synecdochē,* expressed in the naive consciousness of mythological worldviews.

Irony as Trope. As defined by Quintilian in his *Institutio oratoria* (first century CE), irony in its function of rhetorical trope expresses the opposite of what is being said: "*in utroque enim contrarium ei, quod dicitur, intelligendum est*" (9.2.44). Irony is therefore an indirect idiomatic expression in which meaning is substituted by its semantic opposite. An ironic phrase expresses its meaning through an opposite; for instance, to give someone a rebuke by praising, or to praise by censure. Therefore, irony presents an extreme form of tropelike substitution, which stands in contrast to tropes operating on the principle of similarities such as metaphor and allegory. As opposed to a lie, however, the indirectness of the phrase reveals itself through signals of irony. According to rhetorical tradition, two basic forms of irony can be distinguished: dissimulative and simulative irony. Dissimulation describes the negative act of concealing the truly intended (to pretend as if not), whereas simulation describes the positive act of presenting the "untrue" (acting as if). The concept of dissimulating irony had particular influence on Socratic irony in philosophy and the educational ideals of the Renaissance nobility.

Irony as a Rhetorical Figure. Irony as a rhetorical figure does not refer exclusively to ironic speech, but rather, for example, to the specific lifestyle of a person or to the fashion in which a case is being tried in court. Socrates could be considered the prototype of the ironist. His entire life appears to be shaped by irony, according to Quintilian. Socrates pretended to be ignorant, and in awe of the apparently wise. Socratic irony constitutes a turning point toward a philosophical appreciation of irony, based upon the recognition of its revelatory potentials. Socratic dialogue uses ironic disguise as a conversational technique, which serves a philosophical self-recognition and plays an important role in Socrates' maieutic. Extending beyond conversational technique, Socrates' philosophical irony plays a recurring role, which characterizes his life and mental state. As a result, Socrates' character, whose entire life (*Symposium* 216e) is described as a continuous play of ironical disguise, becomes a new philosophical ideal of existence. Socrates introduced the ironical style of conduct into the urbane art of living, which should, according to this ideal, determine the mentality and lifestyle of the philosophically educated.

Irony as a Universal Paradigm. During nineteenth-century Romanticism, irony was viewed as a universal paradigm. According to the F. W. J. Schelling (1775–1854), nature itself was to be understood as an expression of divine irony and disguise. In his work *Athenäum* (1798–1800), the Romantic theorist Friedrich von Schlegel (1772–1829) develops a philosophy of infinite irony. Herein irony announces itself as a clear consciousness of lasting alertness and of infinite chaos. Schlegel's universal irony rejects the conciliatory quality of Hegel's dialectic and rules out any stagnation through a final synthesis. Romantic irony elevates the interlude of permanently changing and opposing viewpoints to the actual creative principle of life and the universe. In art, the concept of universal irony leads to the notion of a progressive universal poetry, a struggle for a process of infinitely creative poetic vision and productivity. Above that, progressive universal poetry should mold life into an incompletable cycle of permanent self-creation and self-destruction. This infinite chain of irony becomes the medium of universal education. Schlegel thereby extends the humanist ideal of *homo universalis,* which demands urbaneness, liberality, and tolerance toward others. Still, the Romantics' view of infinite irony also reveals a tendency to an exaggerated self-criticism, to epistemological skepticism, and to ethical relativism.

Postmodern Concepts of Irony. The idea of infinite irony gains relevance in postmodern and neoliberal ironical writing, but not always with awareness of its roots in Romantic thought. Postmodern irony, inspired by Nietzsche (1844–1900), removes figurative infinite irony from its context of synthetic thinking in conventional reasoning, while preserving its pattern. Like Schlegel's ironic theory, postmodern irony revokes the binary model of the rhetorical trope, that is, the fixed opposition of inside and outside, of the intended and the stated, of authentic and inauthentic. According to Paul de Man, this creates the impression of infinite possibilities of combinations where all opposites can be interchanged and substituted deliberately. Thereby, as Derrida (1976) points out, infinite irony is being modified into a concept of infinite reversibility, in which all semantic categories can be deconstructed, dissolving the determinacy of their own sense.

Philosopher Richard Rorty formulated the positive utopia of a liberal society, where a universal irony should prevail, in order to transcend the negativity of a deconstructionist concept of irony. This neoliberal concept of irony attempts to revive the essential themes of early Romanticism—such as infinite irony, artistic individuality, liberalism, and universal education—on the basis of a language-analytical philosophy. For Rorty, the true Romantic ideal is the self-creation of the human being through its vocabulary. Yet in language-analytical analogy to Schlegel's ideal of self-creation and self-destruction, Rorty's ethic demands an unceasing awareness of the limitation and frailty of the self-creating and self-created vocabularies or language games that we use to define the world and ourselves. Helmut Willke is now applying this concept of irony, which Rorty exclusively related to the individual's sphere and interaction, to public institutions of today's liberal society: irony, as a collective virtue, should bring into agreement what rational logic of the polycentric society cannot. These postmodern theoretical approaches to irony document—each in its own way—the imminent presence of the Romantic ideal of irony. Toward the end of the twentieth century, infinite irony remained a basic, though problematic, figure reflecting modern subjectivity. The apparent potentials of speech, thought, and existence in our pluralist society manifest themselves through infinite irony.

[*See also* Contingency and probability; Figures of speech; *and* Style.]

BIBLIOGRAPHY

Alford, S. E. *Irony and the Logic of Romantic Imagination.* Bern, Switz., 1984.
Booth, Wayne C. *A Rhetoric of Irony.* Chicago, 1974.
Burke, Kenneth. "Four Master Tropes." In *A Grammar of Motives,* pp. 503–517. Berkeley, 1969.
Derrida, Jacques. *Éperons: les styles de Nietzsche.* Venice, 1976.
Knox, Dilwyn. *Ironia: Medieval and Renaissance Ideas on Irony.* Leiden, 1989.
Knox, Norman. *The Word Irony and Its Context, 1500–1755.* Durham, 1961.
de Man, Paul. "The Rhetoric of Temporality." In *Blindness and Insight: Essays in the Rhetoric of Contemporary Criticism,* pp. 187–228. New York, 1971.
Müller, Wolfgang F. "Ironie, Lüge, Simulation und Dissimulation und verwandte Termini." In *Zur Terminology der Literaturwissenschaften,* edited by C. Wagenknecht, pp. 189–208. Würzburg, 1986.
Plett, Heinrich F. *Einführung in die rhetorische Textanalyse.* Hamburg, 1991.
Rorty, Richard. *Contingency, irony, and solidarity.* Cambridge, U.K., 1989.
Swaeringen, C. J. *Rhetoric and Irony: Western Literacy and Western Lies.* New York, 1991.
White, Hayden. *Metahistory: The Historical Imagination in Nineteenth-Century Europe.* Baltimore, 1973.
Willke, Helmut. *Ironie des Staates: Grundlinien einer Staatstheorie polyzentrischer Gesellschaft.* Frankfurt a.M., 1992.

—PETER L. OESTERREICH
Translated by Andreas Quintus

IRREPARABLE, THE. A type of argument offered in deliberative contexts, the irreparable is

a claim that certain courses of action irretrievably damage the social fabric, that therefore they should be excluded from consideration. The Greek historian Thucydides (died c.401 BCE) cites an early use of this type of argument. When the island of Melos (a colony of Sparta) refused to surrender to Athenian forces during the Peloponnesian War, the Athenians warned its leaders: "Reflect again that it is for your country that you are consulting, that you have not more than one, and that upon this one deliberation depends its prosperity or ruin." When the Melians still refused, the Athenian army pressed its siege, putting to death all men of military age and taking Melos for its own.

Recent rhetorical scholarship traces the basis for the argument from the irreparable to the problem of human judgment addressed by Greek dialectical reasoning and oratory. Chaim Perelman and Lucie Olbrechts-Tyteca, authors of *The New Rhetoric: A Treatise on Argumentation* (1969; first published 1958), maintain that the irreparable is associated with a particular category of the "commonplaces" of argument, what they term *loci communes* of the "preferable." These are premises of a general nature used by a speaker to intensify an audience's adherence to a value or to the desirability of a course of action. The problem facing such a speaker, Perelman and Olbrechts-Tyteca contend, is similar to the issue Aristotle treated under the heading of "accident" in Book 3 of the *Topics*. There the dialectical problem is how to judge which one of two things is better or more worthy of choice. Aristotle was concerned with things that are "closely related"; on these occasions, he claimed, we are likely to discuss which of the two we ought to prefer, because we do not at first detect any advantage of one over the other. "In such cases," he proposed, "if we can show a single advantage, or more than one, our judgment will record our assent that whichever side happens to have the advantage is the more desirable" (3.116a). Although Aristotle did not, himself, identify the topic of the irreparable, much of Book 3 proceeds to identify the common topics (*koinoi topoi*) by which such a judgment of advantage can be made.

In a similar manner, Perelman and Olbrechts-Tyteca describe the *topic* of the irreparable as a kind of warrant or principle that assists the speaker in discovering arguments that enhance the value of an object. They stress the irreparable is a commonplace related to the preferable only to the extent that the object to which it refers is already valued, whether we fear or prize it. For example, in her 1991 study of technological and environmental "risk communication," Katherine E. Rowan notes that perceptions of the severity of the risk may be heightened by emphasizing that the damage may also be irreparable. The topic or place of the irreparable thus becomes pertinent to our deliberation when its object (what is "damaged" or lost) is associated with certain commonplaces that establish its value.

The authors of *The New Rhetoric* propose that two commonplaces appear especially to be linked to the appeal of the irreparable. These are the *topics* of the "unique" and the "precarious," attributes of a broader family of what the authors term *topics* of quality. (Considered under aspects of length or duration, the irreparable, Perelman and Olbrechts-Tyteca explain, may also be connected to *topics* of quantity, "the infinity of time which will elapse after the irreparable [act] has been done or established, the certitude that the effects, whether or not they were wanted, will continue indefinitely" (p. 92). Still, it is mainly in its association with the various *topics* of quality that the irreparable finds its distinct appeal.

To be irreparable, Perelman and Olbrechts-Tyteca insist, an object must be unique, exceptional, or rare. It is one, they state, that cannot be replaced or reproduced, and it "acquires a value by the very fact of being considered under this aspect" (p. 92). Claims of uniqueness, such as the warning to the Melians to reflect on their country ("you have not more than one"), take on intensity, precisely because of this contingency; the subject of such claims (one's country, life, and so on) is unique, exceptional, and therefore irreplaceable. The unique, Perelman and Olbrechts-Tyteca note, is thus associated with the irreparable when its singular quality is contrasted with the fungible, with what is common or easily replaceable in human experience.

A singular or unique object, such as one's life or country, acquires value when its very existence is seen as precarious, fragile, or threatened. The effect of argumentation that is drawn from the *topic* of the precarious, Perelman and Olbrechts-Tyteca suggest, can be quite powerful. As illustration, they cite the peroration of the French cleric Saint Vincent de Paul (1581–1660), appealing to pious women to support the orphans under his care. "If you continue to give them your charitable care, they will live; but I tell you before God, they will all be dead tomorrow if you forsake them" (p. 91). The precarious object, Perelman and Olbrechts-Tyteca point out, is therefore linked to judgment by means of another *topic* of quality, identified by Aristotle in the *Topics* as "timeliness": everything is more desirable at the season when it is of greater consequence (3.2.117a).

Though Perelman and Olbrechts-Tyteca do not, themselves, link a *locus* of "timeliness" with the irreparable, it is precisely this feature that other rhetorical scholars have found interesting. J. Robert Cox argues that in its evocation of the timely, as a forewarning and an opportunity to reflect before it is "too late," the irreparable has implications for a theory of judgment or practical decision making. In "The Die Is Cast: Topical and Ontological Dimensions of the *Locus* of the Irreparable" (1982), Cox proposes that the irreparable is available to ground judgment either in a norm of prudence or in the urgency that may be required to save something that is both rare and in jeopardy. Such a dialectic of prudence and urgency, he says, invites several considerations for deliberation: (1) an expanded time frame for weighing consequences; (2) heightened information seeking; (3) a minimum condition rule; and (4) a warrant for extraordinary action.

First, because the irreparable act lasts an "infinity of time," Cox states that deliberation invoking this *topic* invites an expanded time frame in defining what are the relevant (potential) outcomes of a decision. Consideration of long-term, cumulative effects, which cannot be altered once they are set in motion, elevate the saliency of a norm of prudence, whereas incremental (and remediable) steps presumably lessen the need for prudential conduct. Under such circumstances, we would also expect heightened information seeking about alternative, possible consequences of our judgments. Cox notes this is often the situation confronting the physician who must decide whether to end medical procedures that serve only to prolong the life of a terminally ill, comatose patient. He notes the reflection of one physician at a large U.S. hospital: "In some cases we don't have enough information. If we don't know what the patient's life was like, we have to be supportive because not being supportive is irrevocable."

Decisions involving the risk of severe and irreversible consequences may also invite a third strategy for judgment, what Cox terms a minimum condition rule. Such a rule posits a threshold criterion. To be considered further, "a course of action whose consequences turn out to be 'unacceptable' must be remediable." This, he says, is the jurist William Blackstone's dictum, in his *Commentaries on the Laws of England* (1765–1769), that it is better that ten guilty defendants should go free than one innocent person be falsely convicted. This precautionary principle, Cox contends, is drawn from a fundamental presumption of society, the wish to preserve future choice. Thus it is that environmental advocates, he says, are able to discover a particularly credible form of argument: "Preserving land and water resources today still allows for development at some future time. Uncontrolled development now leaves few options for the future." Strategically, the invocation of such a minimum condition rule, he contends, allows decision makers to subsume other, conflicting values under the "remediable" alternative, that is, in those choices left open for the future.

Finally, the argument from the irreparable, Cox states, may, in unusual circumstances, serve as a warrant for what he calls extraordinary actions. A person may feel justified, he observes, in going to extreme ends to forestall the loss of what is rare or unique, since otherwise it will be lost forever. He also argues that one may find a justification for urgency in knowingly choosing an irrevocable course when, in doing so, one is trying to salvage what (else) may still be reparable. Cox terms recourse to the latter use of the *topic* of the irreparable, the "Rubicon ploy." The reference is to the historian Gaius Suetonius's account of Julius Caesar's deliberation ("as he stood, in two minds") with his forces poised to challenge the Roman Senate and Pompey's armies. Caesar had joined his advance guard at the Rubicon, which formed the frontier between Gaul and Italy. Aware of how critical was his decision, he coun-

seled his staff, "We may still draw back [now]; but, once across that little bridge, we shall have to fight it out." In invoking what is imputed to be an irrevocable action (as Caesar does), one alleges that any further choice will have been removed. The decision to go forward would presumably be irreversible: "*Iacta est alea,*" Suetonius records Caesar as saying: "the die is cast." Such a strategy, rhetorically, is an appeal for deliberateness, a plea to follow through a decision.

More recent rhetorical treatments of the irreparable have urged a somewhat different interpretation of this topic. Although Cox emphasizes the function of the irreparable as a warrant for caution (or urgency) in the face of the catastrophic consequences of human choice, at least one other scholar begins with the irreparable as a given or an imputed state.

In his study of "apocalyptic rhetoric," rhetorical theorist Stephen O'Leary argues that the irreparable may function as a tragic mode of interpretation of events, such as the forewarning of crisis or the end of the world. He explains, "the tragic apocalyptic vision looks forward to catastrophe as a given, and situates human choice within a cosmological narrative, in which the conclusion is not affected by the individual's decision." Within such a narrative, religious proselytizers invoke this irreparable moment—the apocalypse or Judgment Day—as a *topos* of Time, positing a date or temporal horizon beyond which humans no longer have an ability to choose at all.

O'Leary looks particularly at the doctrine of the "secret rapture," a radical (and irremediable) moment in time in which adherents to the doctrine believe that select individuals are spared the end of the world. By positing a "floating 'locus of the irreparable,' a temporal threshold that will cut the audience off from the chance to avoid the persecutions of the Last Days," the rapture, he suggests, functions as a strong incentive for the conversion of unbelievers. Although the "Last Days" are inescapably forecast, O'Leary continues as well to identify the irreparable as *a premise for deliberation.* An individual's fate, he suggests, is still contingent on human choice in much of apocalyptic rhetoric. The old American hymn "The Great Day," he notes, expresses this juxtaposition of tragic fatalism with individual choice: "I've a long time heard that there will be a judgment. . . . Sinner, where will you stand in that day?"

In its development as a *topic* of the "preferable" in Perelman and Olbrechts-Tyteca's *The New Rhetoric* to O'Leary's tragic mode of interpretation, the irreparable says much about the ways a culture views its own future. It invites inspection, Cox suggests, of what audiences count as "good reasons" for the acceptance of an irrevocable loss, as well as the sense a culture has generally of its own efficacy. Speakers who believe they can successfully exhort or dissuade audiences to act with prudence or to intervene to forestall the loss of what is precious, presume an ability to deliberate about the contingent, the impetus for the rhetorical act itself.

[*See also* Commonplaces and commonplace books; Contingency and probability; Deliberative genre; *and* Topics.]

BIBLIOGRAPHY

Aristotle. *Topica and De Sophisticis Elenchis.* Translated by W. A. Pickard-Cambridge. In *The Works of Aristotle,* edited by W. A. Ross. Oxford, 1928. See especially the discussion of the commonplaces of "accident" in Book 3, 116a–119a.
Cox, J. Robert. "The Die Is Cast: Topical and Ontological Dimensions of the *Locus* of the Irreparable." *The Quarterly Journal of Speech* 68 (1982), pp. 227–239.
Farrell, Thomas B., and G. Thomas Goodnight. "Accidental Rhetoric: The Root Metaphors of Three Mile Island." *Communication Monographs* 48 (1981), pp. 271–300. Argues that the limits of technical discourse are severe and perhaps irreparable and urges reflection on the critical dilemmas that speakers face in a technological era.
O'Leary, Stephen D. "A Dramatistic Theory of Apocalyptic Rhetoric." *The Quarterly Journal of Speech* 79 (1993), pp. 385–426.
Perelman, Chaim, and L. Olbrechts-Tyteca. *The New Rhetoric: A Treatise on Argumentation.* Translated by John Wilkinson and Purcell Weaver. Notre Dame, Ind., 1969. English translation of *La Nouvelle Rhétorique: Traité de l'Argumentation,* first published 1958. Groundbreaking discussion of the irreparable as a general premise useful in accenting a value or hierarchy of values in argument.
Rowan, Katherine E. "Goals, Obstacles, and Strategies in Risk Communication: A Problem-Solving Approach to Improving Communication about Risks." *Journal of Applied Communication Research* 19 (1991), pp. 300–329. Good discussion of the irreparable as a strategy in communication involving decisions about risk.

—J. ROBERT COX

ISOCOLON. The Greek term *isocolon* (Lat. *compar*), whose literal meaning is "equality of members," designates a group of discursive phenomena that have at their foundation (1) the symmetrical construction of the syntagmatic constituents of sentence structures, and (2) the distribution of those in equivalent positions in the progression of discourse, whether in verse or in prose; that is, parallel constructions, discursive sections that correspond in meaning, length, or rhythm. These "plurimembrations" usually occupy the final segment or "closure" either of a stanzaic unit in poetic discourse or of a period in prose discourse.

[*See also* Figures of speech; Gorgianic figures; *and* Poetry.]

BIBLIOGRAPHY

Lanham, R. A. *A Handlist of Rhetorical Terms.* Berkeley, 1991.
Lausberg, H. *Handbuch der literarischen Rhetorik.* P. 719. Munich, 1960.
Mayoral, J. A. *Figuras retóricas.* Pp. 161–165. Madrid, 1994.

—JOSÉ ANTONIO MAYORAL
Translated by A. Ballesteros

JOURNALISM. *See* Expository rhetoric and journalism.

JUDGMENT. Aristotle (384–322 BCE) asserts, at 1377b, pages 21–22 of the *Rhetoric* in the Kennedy translation (New York, 1991), that "rhetoric is concerned with making a judgment." One reading of this would be that it is a merely functional description: audiences for rhetoric decide that an accused party is guilty or innocent or that a proposed policy is expedient or inexpedient. On this view, Aristotle's statement is consistent with Plato's (c.428–c.347 BCE) assertion in *Gorgias* that rhetoric effects persuasion. William M. A. Grimaldi (*Studies in the Philosophy of Aristotle's Rhetoric,* Wiesbaden, Germany, 1972) rejects such an equation between Aristotle's and Plato's views, since the latter sees persuasion as typified by coercion, shoddy reasoning, and crass emotional appeals. Instead, he argues that Aristotle believed that good rhetoric places before audiences all the means necessary for sound decision making: it approaches subjects open to deliberation "with the intention of presenting the matter in such a way as to make accessible to the other the possibility of reasonable judgment" (p. 3).

This still leaves a degree of ambiguity regarding Aristotle's meaning, however. Edwin Black (*Rhetorical Criticism,* Madison, Wis., 1978) notes that judgment is the translation of *krisis.* Black argues that judgment is a term with varied meanings in English and, further, that previous commentary has left it unclear which of these meanings best captures Aristotle's. Black identifies six meanings that might be relevant to Aristotle's use of *krisis* in the *Rhetoric,* arguing further that those may be consolidated into three: "judgment as a faculty, judgment as a process, and judgment as an object" (p. 95). After examining a wide array of Aristotle's uses of *krisis,* he concludes that Aristotle's statement that judgment is the object of rhetoric refers to a process of judging. He further supports this conclusion by looking at passages in which *krisis* is used as an alternative, or in contrast, to *doxa* (opinion) and *pistis* (belief). Aristotle's view of rhetoric is contrasted with that of Plato, who saw *doxa* as the end of rhetoric and *pistis* as the state of mind it sought to produce. "Whatever else rhetoric meant to Aristotle, it was a faculty that realized its end in the act of judgment" (p. 108). Black distinguishes the process of coming to a judgment from that of coming to a belief, insisting that the former requires systematic, formalized procedures whereas the latter can occur through a wide array of unsystematic means. On this basis, Black rejects the Aristotelian conception of rhetoric as too narrowly rationalistic and rigid, noting that there are (and presumably were in Aristotle's time) many instances in which rhetoric is used to produce something other than judgment, instances in which its end is to "inculcate new convictions by obliterating an audience's capacity for making judgments" (p. 109).

Ronald Beiner's examination of political judgment would suggest that Black's characterization of judgment as a highly systematized, determinative process owes more to Kant (1724–1804) than to Aristotle. Beiner argues that Aristotle conceived of rhetoric as closely tied both to particular situations and to the beliefs and desires of the audience. The process of judgment set in motion by rhetoric is typified not by a formalistic vision of judgment, as described by Kant, in which universal principles and procedures subsume particulars, but by *phronēsis,* in which practical wisdom is engaged in a reflexive movement between the general and the particular. [*See* Phronēsis; *and* Practical wisdom.] In contrast to the formal conception of judgment that Black attributes to Aristotle, Beiner notes that Aristotle understood judgment as a means of mediating between the general, substantive beliefs and values of a community and the demands of particular situations. Judgment was a component of *phronēsis,* which was judgment put into action. In contrast to *sophia* (theoretical wisdom), which sought to overcome common opinion (*doxa*), *phronēsis* is rooted in common opinion and is the means by which people oriented themselves in the public world. As a medium in which judgment is formed, rhetoric not only expresses a sense of community, but also is a means by which a community determines its ends. As Beiner reads Aristotle, judgment is not opposed to belief, because beliefs are integral materials from which judgments are formed.

Thomas B. Farrell develops this reading more fully. Farrell rereads the *Rhetoric* in light of its place in the larger Aristotelian corpus, especially the treatises on ethics and on politics, and in relation to contemporary social and political theory. He argues that Aristotle's thinking on both rhetoric and ethics displayed a predilection for building toward rather than from the general. A Platonic rhetoric would move from a knowledge of universal, transcendent Truths toward certain conclusions about what should be done in a given case, employing rhetorical techniques to steer the actions and beliefs of the many who are incapable of arriving at such knowledge on their own. Kant rejects rhetoric because of his belief that moral judgments move subsumptively from universal, transcendental premises to conclusions about what action is right in the given case. In neither instance are the reasoning, feelings, and values of audiences taken seriously as an agency for proper choice. Aristotelian rhetoric, on the contrary, starts from the premise that rhetoric deals with contingent, probable matters that do not admit of certainty. Thus, it must engage the beliefs, values, and attitudes of interested audiences to the end of forming sound judgments. Central to Farrell's reading of Aristotle is the contention that the audience is the decisive rhetorical agency, the efficient cause of public character and of judgment. [*See overview article on* Audience.]

Farrell, following Grimaldi, views rhetoric as a practice with a reflective dimension. Where its most severe critics have attacked rhetoric as a knack, a technique for manipulating auditors by appealing to prejudice, self-interest, and passion, Aristotle presents his rhetoric as both a technical practice and a *dynamis* (potential), a reflective body of knowledge. Farrell argues that Aristotle's justification of rhetoric, in Book 1, functions as an argument for a cogent relationship between rhetoric as technique and rhetoric's ideal of enacting good judgment. First, Aristotle argues that, since truth and justice naturally prevail over their opposites, actual instances in which they do not prevail can only be attributed to failures of rhetorical technique. Next, he echoes Plato's assertion that knowledge of the true and the right are not always sufficient to persuade an audience. But, from this, he concludes that we must make use of *doxa,* the common opinion of a community, in constructing our rhetorical appeals. Third, he appropriates the *dissoi logoi* of Protagoras, the practice of arguing both sides of any question. Farrell argues that this is significant because Aristotle suggests that it is only through such exercises in perspective taking that we can see the facts clearly. Finally, Aristotle argues that rational speech is integral to being human and, thus, inability to defend ourselves through its use is shameful. While it is true that rhetoric can be used unjustly, he argues that this is true of all good things, save virtue. For Farrell, this points to the ethical significance of rhetorical practice: while it may be used unethically, it also admits of ethical usage and is therefore a valuable resource for civic life.

Rhetoric, then, is seen as an ethically significant practice that seeks to engage audiences as agencies of sound judgment. Ideally, it engages audiences in a manner that engenders reflection on their life world, not only making use of the materials of common opinion, but also reconfiguring and transforming them in their application to particular moments of choice. Moreover, it has the potential of addressing what is best in them in such a way that they become better than they are. Farrell sees rhetoric as connected to judgment in at least two ways. First, the proper practice of rhetoric, by calling for imaginative engagement with the beliefs and values of interested others, helps to cultivate the master virtue of *phronēsis* in the *rhētōr*. Second, in actual engagement with others as rhetorical audience, rhetorical practice can cultivate deliberative insight in audiences and, therefore, enhance civic life. [*See* Deliberative genre.] Moreover, in enthymematic reasoning, *rhētōr* and audience together construct proofs, thereby translating judgment into *praxis* and enacting the master political virtue of *phronēsis*. [*See* Enthymeme.] For Farrell, judgment is both a rhetorical process and a human faculty, capable of cultivation and improvement.

In recent years, a number of critical studies have investigated the relationship between rhetoric and judgment. Studies such as those by Browne (1993) and by Jasinski (1992) suggest that rhetorical practice both enacts the judgment of the rhetor and models political judgment for audiences. That is, not only do such texts manifest the application of the *rhētōr*'s judgment to a particular case, they exteriorize the judgment of the rhetor, offering his or her exercise of the faculty as a possible model for audience members. The critical studies also suggest that rhetorical practice negotiates the tension between enduring principles of political judgment and the flux of concrete political conditions, providing stability amid change. The need to rely on common opinion anchors rhetorical practice in relatively stable systems of belief and value and promotes reliance on relatively stable political vocabularies of ideographs. [*See* Ideograph.] At the same time, Farrell and others argue that the inventional capabilities of *rhētors* and the shifting demands of particular contexts also promote refinement, revision, and reconfiguration of rhetorical materials and, with them, the common opinion that shapes public life.

This last point raises an issue that concerns

much postmodern writing about rhetoric and judgment: is the judgment enacted and cultivated by rhetorical practice necessarily circumscribed by the perspectives and values of the powerful? Martha Cooper ("Decentering Judgment" in *Judgment Calls,* edited by John M. Sloop and James P. McDaniel, Boulder, 1998) writes that from a postmodern perspective, "At best, the values and first principles serving as grounds for judgment appear to be partial. . . . At worst, such grounds for judgment seem only canonized preferences that secure the interests of those who occupy positions of power" (p. 64). Cooper notes that many postmodern perspectives make emancipation rather than judgment the *telos* of rhetoric, but this does not eliminate the problem of judgment. Emancipation requires critique to guide it, and "critique requires some prior ground for judgment" (p. 64). Cooper rejects a move to *phronēsis,* arguing that the classical tradition takes for granted its own grounds for judgment.

Maurice Charland ("Property and Propriety" in *Judgment Calls*) shares some of Cooper's reservations about the viability of the classical tradition, but suggests that it has utility within certain types of contexts. He argues that a central problem raised by postmodern perspectives is that of incommensurability of discursive frames or language games. The rhetorical tradition delineated by Beiner, Farrell, and others participates in the language game of republicanism. Within this frame, incommensurable perspectives are domesticated by submitting disputes to a judging instance and a recognized judging agent. He sketches the limits of this language game by elaborating on Lyotard's distinction between *litige* and *differend*. The former refers to disputes that take place within the horizon of a shared language game; the latter refers to disputes "in which the wrong one party claims to have suffered cannot be expressed in the language of the court and judge, of the judging instance" (Charland, p. 222). Charland also acknowledges the significance of incommensurability as a problem for rhetorical judgment, but he notes that the language game of republicanism has proven quite serviceable as a means of reaching judgment in existing republican cultures.

[*See also* Contingency and probability.]

BIBLIOGRAPHY

Arendt, Hannah. *Lectures on Kant's Political Philosophy.* Edited and with an interpretive essay by Ronald Beiner. Chicago, 1982. An innovative rereading of Kant's *Critique of Judgment* as his true thinking about political judgment, written by one of the foremost contemporary political philosophers. It is especially noteworthy because of the centrality Arendt attributed to rhetoric as the cornerstone of political life. Beiner's fine interpretive essay introduces some of the important themes developed in his *Political Judgment.*

Beiner, Ronald. *Political Judgment.* Chicago, 1983. Beiner explores the concept of political judgment via an exploration of the influence of Aristotle and Kant on the thinking of Hannah Arendt, Hans-Georg Gadamer, and Jürgen Habermas.

Browne, Stephen H., and Michael C. Leff. "Political Judgment and Rhetorical Argument: Edmund Burke's Paradigm." In *Argument and Social Practice: Proceedings of the Fourth SCA/AFA Conference On Argumentation,* edited by J. Robert Cox, Malcolm O. Sillars, and Gregg B. Walker, pp. 193–210. Annandale, Va., 1985. A critical analysis of the rhetoric of Edmund Burke.

Browne, Stephen H. *Edmund Burke and the Discourse of Virtue.* Tuscaloosa, Ala., 1993. An important study not only of the parliamentary rhetoric of Burke, but of the vision of political judgment presented and enacted in his speeches.

Farrell, Thomas B. *Norms of Rhetorical Culture.* New Haven, 1993. Perhaps the most significant recent rereading of Aristotle's *Rhetoric,* this book envisions rhetoric as a practice that aims at and cultivates individual and collective judgment.

Jasinski, James. "Rhetoric and Judgment in the Constitutional Ratification Debate of 1787–1788: An Exploration in the Relationship between Theory and Critical practice." *Quarterly Journal of Speech,* 78 (1992), pp. 197–218. Building on a detailed case study, Jasinski develops a typology that clarifies significant tensions regarding the space required for judgment; that is, the need for both critical and temporal distance from the particulars that one is judging.

—MARK A. POLLOCK

K–L

KAIROS is variously described in relation to a temporality and to a way of acting: it is the opportune moment. Be that as it may, it is an elusive word, appearing, disappearing, and reappearing in the history of rhetoric in a variety of complex ways. *Kairos* has been personified, referred to, made use of, and stressed by artists, orators, Sophists, rhetoricians, and philosophers for more than twenty-five centuries. Although *kairos* underlies theoretical discussions on rhetoric from the fifth to the fourth century BCE, it is not a definitive term, such as *enthymeme* in Aristotle's *Rhetoric*. Following Rostagni (1922), who describes the history of rhetoric as a history of dependence upon Aristotle, Kinneavy (1986) shows that *kairos* has been a neglected concept in the contemporary study of classical rhetoric, especially in the United States (pp. 79–80). Toward the end of the twentieth century, *kairos* began to play a prominent role in the rethinking of rhetorical theory and came to be used as a key term in describing practices that were moving away from an Aristotelian tradition of rhetoric and toward an Isocratean one. Although both recognize time with respect to speech, differences exist, especially in the field of application. In the Aristotelian strand, *kairos* is absorbed in part of a comprehensive system of rhetoric and emerges through moderation, the appropriate, and the good. In the Isocreatean strand, *kairos* is put in the foreground as "knowing" (that is, itself subject to contingency), by which the *rhētōr* works to bring what people think and believe closer to the demands of a situation. Below, the meanings of *kairos* and their relevance to the study of contemporary rhetoric are examined.

Both ancient and modern authors affirm that *kairos* is difficult to define. Dionysius of Halicarnassus, first-century historian of rhetoric, reports Lysias, the fifth-century BCE Sophist and orator, asking, "How are we to define what is called *kairos*?" (*Critical Essays*. Translated by Stephen Usher,

1979, pp. 1–9). He also notes in "On Literary Composition" that no *rhētōr* or philosopher has succeeded in defining *kairos*, "not even Gorgias of Leontini" (*Critical Essays*. Translated by Stephen Usher, 1985, pp. 2–43). In S. H. Butcher's *Harvard Lectures on Greek Subjects* (London, 1904), he states that *kairos* is a Greek word "with no single or precise equivalent in any other language" (pp. 118–119). It is translated in English as "the right time," "due season," "occasion," "opportune," "appropriate," "suitable," "the fitting," "the propitious moment," "arising circumstances," and "opportunity." Besides numerous translations, *kairos* has undergone several transformations in meaning. For example, in tracing the career of *kairos* through eighteen centuries, Cook (1965, p. 862) notes the change from a masculine sexual identity to a feminine one during the third and fourth centuries BCE as *kairos* becomes the goddess *Occasio*. *Kairos* is also a proper noun. Detienne and Vernant (1978, p. 202) explain that it is the name of a horse in the chariot team of Adrastus. The proper noun *Kairos* also refers to the statue *Opportunity* by the Greek sculptor Lysippus (c.360–c.320 BCE). According to Gardner (1987, p. 411), the statue of *Kairos* has been the subject of "many epigrams and rhetorical descriptions" from the fourth century BCE onward.

The origin and etymology of *kairos* is uncertain. This uncertainty has produced a variety of interpretations about the relation of *kairos* to rhetoric. This relation may be discerned provisionally along three lines of thought: first, *kairos* calls for decisive action; second, it refers to the right moment to speak; third, it expresses what is appropriate. Its embodiment as an athlete seems to represent *kairos* as swift, decisive action. Lysippus features *Kairos* as a fit young man pressing ahead with winged feet. And yet, the athlete seems poised at rest. The head of the statue shows a lock of hair on the front and bald behind. This figure is, as de G. Verrall (1890, p. 129) translates

Pausanias, time "possessed by action, seized, and utilized by human energy." Viewed from the perspective of the athletic figure, *Kairos* figures rhetoric as "man and time" coming together.

Chariot races and foot races indicate that the rhetor must seize opportunities in order to master a situation. Although Homer never uses the word *kairos,* the idea is in the episode of the Games in Book 23 of the *Illiad.* As Detienne and Vernant (1978) explain, Antilochus wins the race because he finds "a way and an opportunity" when the path narrows "of slipping in front" of his opponent "without letting the moment pass" (p. 15). It is not enough to have the swiftness of horses: "one must know how to spur them on to decisive action" (p. 16). In the fifth century BCE, the poet Pindar portrays *kairos* with respect to female life. Danaos arranges the swiftest possible marriage for his fifty daughters in the form of a foot race. Before midday overtakes them unwed, the daughters seize *kairos,* the opportune moment for marriage (*Pythia* 9.114).

In the rhetorical discourse of ancient Athens, the decisive moment is characterized by deliberation and has a positive orientation. [*See* Deliberative genre.] Yet this same concept may be neutral or negative, especially when it is linked to emotion. The rhetor or orator seizes upon an opportunity that coincides with the temporal needs of the situation. Demosthenes, the Athenian orator and statesman, in "On the Treaty with Alexander," urges a course of action because "justice and opportunity and expediency all concur." He asks, "Will you actually wait for some other season to claim your liberties and the liberties of all Greeks?" (*Demosthenes.* Translated by J. H. Vince et al., 1926, p. 3). Similarly, Isocrates' *Panegyricus* depicts *kairos* as an opportunity presenting itself for the taking. To miss an opportunity is to throw away a chance and, therefore, neglect the present situation (160.2). Aristotle directs the significance of *kairos* and opportunity through rhetoric's relation to the emotions. Those who have been wronged or think they have been wronged are always on the watch for seizing an opportunity, always on the lookout for a chance to get even (*Rhetoric* 1382b.11).

In contemporary discussions of the Sophists and rhetoric, particularly in the United States, Germany, and France, theorists and critics turn to

kairos as a site for renewing a sense of the present and timely action. The force of acting in the "now" is the inverse of Walter Benjamin's definition of a catastrophe: "to have missed the opportunity" (1983–1984, p. 23). Similarly, in his *Sophistical Rhetoric in Classical Greece* (Columbia, S.C., 1995), J. Poulakos focuses on *kairos* as a guide to speech and action. Unless ideas are voiced "at the precise moment they are called upon, they miss their chance to satisfy situationally shared voids with a particular audience" (p. 39). Thus, *kairos* is not only what presses the rhetor forward to speak but also what constitutes the value of speech.

Second, *kairos* is figured temporally and tied to a Pythagorean conception of the universe modeled on the number seven, the number of Opportunity (Aristotle, *Metaphysics* 985b.30; 990a.20; 1078b.20). According to Rostagni (1922) and Untersteiner (1954), this worldview converges in Gorgias, the fifth-century BCE rhetorician who possibly wrote a treatise entitled *On the Right Moment in Time.* As a master word, *kairos* is both the context and the guide for the right time. In contemporary rhetoric, Consigny describes *kairos* as the "realm" and the "tool" of speech. Metaphorically, the weaver of fate images *kairos* as the right time. In *The Origins of European Thought* (New York, 1973), R. Onians explains the analogy between weaving and *kairos.* At the opening in the warp are the threads "representing length of time." The opening lasts "only a limited time" for the path of the woof thread to pass (pp. 346–347). This "opening" in weaving characterizes "time" as a window of opportunity in rhetorical deliberation.

E. White's *Kaironomia: On the Will to Invent* (Ithaca, N.Y., 1987) presents weaving as a region having no fixity but with openings or apertures in time *from* which to speak. As the guide or tool used in invention, *kairos* recognizes that the persuasive force of speech "must be renewed at every occasion and cannot become, therefore, a routine accomplishment" (p. 15). De Certeau renders *kairos* the tactic of the "*bricoleur,*" the one who puts language to new use (pp. xix–xx). The *bricoleur* is like the Sophists employing *kairos* at the right time and like the *rhētōr*-horse *Kairos* always on the watch for opportunities offered by the particular situation. *Kairos* bears upon the practice of speaking in terms of what to say, the warp, and when to say it, the woof. The metaphor of weaving reveals a unique relation between speech and *kairos*. Rhetoric makes demands on the occasion and yet is bound to "present necessities" (see *Rhetoric* 1365a.20; *Topics* 117a.26–117b.2). *Kairos* stresses what Wichelns (1925, p. 212) described as rhetoric's "bondage to the occasion and the audience," a characteristic that distinguishes rhetoric from poetry.

This use of *kairos* as the right time not only duplicates the meaning of rhetoric itself but also designates a technique of rhetoric. Conceptually, *kairos* insists upon the situational aspect of speech, the right time to present a point of view. Recognizing "present necessities," the *rhētōr* turns the argument just in the nick of time (compare Demosthenes, *Exordia* 18.1.12; Aristotle, *Rhetoric* 1415b.12). Finding the right time to present a point of view has been depicted as the ground upon which the Sophist proposed to speak on any subject (see Philostrates' *Lives of the Sophists*). Poulakos (1997) stresses that the Sophists' ability to speak extemporaneously coincides with the temporal demands of the situation as they unfold, *kairos*. Bitzer (1968) depicts the speaking situation from within a set of circumstances that are independent of the *rhētōr*'s perception of them but yet bind the *rhētōr*'s words.

An appeal to *kairos* (as the right, fitting, or critical time as opposed to time in general) enables the *rhētōr* to put off a discussion, a detail, or a story and, thus functions as a strategy. A prominent use of *kairos* being bound to the right moment concerns the continuance of speech. In his *Archhidamus*, Isocrates defers to *kairos* when justifying the acquisition of land. The occasion or the time does not permit him to go into legendary history and to explain the titles to the land (24.2). In *To Philip*, Isocrates obliges *kairos* and says it would be unseasonable, "unkairoslike," to tell how the Atheninas helped Heracles win his immortality (33.7). Presumably, Isocrates' observance of *kairos* seems to solve a problem of exposition: what to say and when to say it. The expression "enough has been said for the moment" designates this technical use of *kairos* (see Aristotle, *Rhetoric* 1366b.24).

Over different historical periods, the virtue of style and contrasting arguments have come to represent *kairos*. The virtue of style is attributed to *kairos* as "the present occasion." *Kairos* as style denotes what is "appropriate." The force of the appropriate concerns "good taste," which in turn yields to ethical considerations to be observed as "due measure." For example, in "On Literary Composition," Dionysius of Halicarnassus says "good taste" does not exceed due measure by beginning or ending with the same words too often (12.43).

Kairos is a critical component in argument. Following Diogenes Laertius's account in his *Lives of the Philosophers* (9.52) and H. Gomperz's *Sophistik und Rhetorik* (Berlin, 1912), Robinson finds *kairos* preserved in the doctrine of the *dissoi logoi*, contrasting arguments. This doctrine attributes the origin of *kairos* to Protagoras, the fifth-century BCE Sophist, who maintained that there are two sides to every question in rhetorical deliberation. Attentive to *kairos*, the *rhētōr* delivers the appropriate choice in the face of changing positions or relative truths. Sound judgment appears to be predicated upon what is fitting (see Demosthenes, "On the Crown" 178.7). The circumstances of time, for example, give a praiseworthy character to particular actions (see Aristotle, *Rhetoric* 1368a.13; 1381a.13; 1385a.21). In other words, what is appropriate is not fixed but recognized as a situational interpretation.

Centered in contrasting arguments, *kairos* as decisive action, the right time, and as the appropriate alludes to an aspect of the probable. The ambiguity surrounding the meaning and etymology of *kairos* not only fosters debate on the idea of rhetoric but also promises to invent new directions in the study and teaching of rhetoric.

[*See also* Classical rhetoric; Decorum; Occasion; *and* Rhetorical situation.]

BIBLIOGRAPHY

Barrett, W.S., ed. *Euripides' Hippolytos.* Oxford, 1964. Offers the range of meaning of *kairos* in the fifth century BCE.

Baumlin, James S. "Decorum, Kairos and the 'New Rhetoric'." *Pre/Text* 5 (1984), pp. 171–183.

Benjamin, Walter. "N [Theories of Knowledge, Theory of Progress]." Translated by Leigh Hafrey and Richard Sieburth. *The Philosophical Forum* 15 (1983–1984), pp. 1–40.

Biesecker, Barbara. "Rethinking the Rhetorical Situation

from within the Thematic of *Différence*." *Philosophy and Rhetoric* 22 (1989), pp. 110–130.

Bitzer, Lloyd. "The Rhetorical Situation." *Philosophy and Rhetoric* 1 (1968), pp. 1–14. See also Vatz; Consigny; and Biesecker.

Cahn, Michael. "Reading Rhetoric Rhetorically: Isocrates and the Marketing of Insight." *Rhetorica* 7.2 (1989), pp. 121–144. Explains why Isocrates' indebtedness to *kairos* could not produce a theory of rhetoric. Compare Takis Poulakos. *Speaking for the Polis: Isocrates' Rhetorical Education*. Columbia, S.C., 1997.

Certeau, Michel de. *The Practice of Everyday Life*. Translated by Steven F. Rendall. Berkeley, 1984.

Consigny, Scott. "Rhetoric and Its Situations." *Philosophy and Rhetoric* 7 (1974), pp. 175–188.

Cook, Arthur Bernard. *Zeus: A Study in Ancient Religion*. vol. 2, *Zeus: God of the Dark Sky*. New York, 1965. Traces the career of *kairos* (through Chronos and Bios) for eighteen centuries. Appendix A (pp. 859–868) provides iconography and sculptures of *Kairos*. The author accepts the view that the statue of *Kairos* held a razor. Interpretation of the allegory of the razor is based on a relation between the Greek verb *Kaíro* ("cut, shave, cleavage") and *kairos*. Barrett, however, claims the etymological connection between *kairós* and *kaíro* is uncertain.

Detiene, Marcel, and Jean-Pierre Vernant. *Cunning Intelligence in Greek Culture and Society*. Translated by Janet Lloyd. Atlantic Highlands, N.J., 1978. Excellent discussion of *kairos* with respect to *mētis*, a domain of human intelligence which incorporates multiple and flexible intellectual operations.

Gardner, Ernest Arthur. *A Handbook of Greek Sculpture*. London, 1897. Gives physical description of Lysippus's statue of *Kairos* or *Opportunity*.

Kennedy, George A. *The Art of Persuasion in Greece*. Princeton, 1963. Includes a definition of *kairos* in relation to early Greek rhetoric and expands the discussion in *A New History of Classical Rhetoric*. Princeton, 1994.

Kerferd, G. B. *The Sophistic Movement*. Cambridge, U.K., 1981. Discusses *kairos* through Gorgias's ethics and aesthetics. Connects the sophistical notion to modern advertising techniques.

Kinneavy, James L. "Kairos: A Neglected Concept in Classical Rhetoric." In *Rhetoric and Praxis*. Edited by Jean Dietz Moss, pp. 79–105. Washington, D.C., 1986. Landmark essay in outlining a "*kairos*-based" writing program. The ideas behind this program are developed in Stephen P. Witte, Neil Nakadate, and Roger D. Cherry, eds. *A Rhetoric of Doing: Essays on Written Discourse in Honor of James L. Kinneavy*. Carbondale, Ill., 1992; and James Kinneavy and Cath-

erine Eskin. "Kairos in Aristotle's Rhetoric." *Written Communication* 11 (1994), pp. 131–142.

Kittel, Gerhard, ed., and Geoffrey W. Bromiley, trans. and ed. *Theological Dictionary of the New Testament*, vol. 3. Grand Rapids, Mich., 1965. Provides research on the linguistic development of *kairos* to indicate three major nonbiblical uses: spatially, *kairos* is used as a point in time; materially, as moderation; and temporally, as the decisive moment. Also includes research on the biblical use of *kairos*.

Robinson, T. M. *Contrasting Arguments: An Edition of the Dissoi Logoi*. New York, 1979. Explores *kairos* through Protagoras and disputes the Pythogorean–Gorgian doctrine of *kairos*.

Rostagni, Augusto. "Un Nuovo Capitolo Nella Storia della Retorica e della Sofistica." Translated by Phillip Sipiora. *Studi Italiani di Filogia Classica* 2 (1922), pp. 148–201. English translation published in James S. Baumlin and Phillip Sipiora. *Kairos in Translation*. New York, forthcoming.

Sullivan, Dale L. "Kairos and the Rhetoric of Belief." *Quarterly Journal of Speech* 78 (1992), pp. 317–332. Argues that New Testament rhetoric has more in common with sophistic rhetoric than the rhetoric of Aristotle.

Trédé, Monique. *Kairos: L'À-Propos et L'Occasion*. 1992. Traces the word and the concept of *kairos* from Homer to the end of the fourth century BCE. Includes chapters on the meaning of *kairos* in relation to medicine, politics, and oratory. In the chapter concerning oratory (pp. 247–294), the author reexamines the contested relationship between rhetoric and *kairos* through generic distinctions.

Untersteiner, Mario. *The Sophists*. Translated by Kathleen Freeman. New York, 1954. Credits Gorgias with a generalized theory of *kairos*. Compare E. Dupréel's *Les Sophists*. Neuchâtel, 1948.

Vatz, Richard. "The Myth of the Rhetorical Situation." *Philosophy and Rhetoric* 6 (1973), pp. 155–160.

Verrall, Margaret de G. *Mythology and Monuments of Ancient Athens: Being a Translation of a Portion of the "Attica" of Pausanias*. London, 1890. Discusses *kairos* in the context of the god Hermes, seizing a lucky moment in a wrestling contest. Includes an introductory essay and archaeological commentary by Jane E. Harrison.

Wichelns, Herbert A. "The Literary Criticism of Oratory." *Studies in Rhetoric and Public Speaking in Honor of James Albert Winans*. New York, 1925. Landmark essay credited with implicitly distinguishing rhetoric from "literature" on the basis of *kairos*.

Online Resources

Crane, Gregory R., ed. *The Perseus Project*. http://www.perseus.tufts.edu Searches for words in several Greek and Latin texts. Able to display frequency and can illustrate, for example, *kairos* growing exponentially in usage from the eighth to the fourth century BCE.

Kairos: A Journal for Teachers of Writing in Webbed Environments. http://english.ttu.edu/kairos. Explains the meaning of *kairos* with hypertext links to the following: The modern rebirth of *kairos* (situation, theory, technology); Historical connections; Etymology; Metaphor and analogy; The rhetorical situation; *Kairos* as tool, *kairos* as realm; and Technological connections.

Rhetoric and Composition. http://english-www.hss.cmu.edu/rhetoric/ Provides scholarly and pedagogical resources, including a link to a hypertext and plain text of Aristotle's *Rhetoric*.

—JANE SUTTON

LAW. A fragment collected in the seventh-century CE compilation of Roman laws, the *Digest*, records that any citizen who "appeared on the stage to act or recite" was subject to the penalty of *infamia*, meaning loss of citizenship or civil death (Watson, ed., Philadelphia, 1987, 3.2.1). While there are numerous instances of later laws banning particular plays or genres of theater, the extremity and violence of the classical Roman prohibition is unique. The reasons for this censorship are complex, specific, and disputed, but a principal and incontestable cause of the ban lay in the proximity of theater and law. The staging of the drama of social life, the enunciation of the discourses of the fates, and the determination of innocence and guilt were to take place in the space and language of law. Theater, and in particular Athenian tragedy, threatened to constitute a rival representation of the origins and laws of civic life.

Theater and law shared a common basis in myth and, arguably, also a comparable symbolic function in the staging of truth or enactment of the real. The proximity of theater and law, in other words, was the source of their antagonism: both addressed the violence of fate and the passage of life toward death; both operated by means of fictions and within the formal constraints of staging or demonstrating their narrative; both instituted the subject as an actor—a persona or mask—within the institutions of the intimate and commercial public spheres. Law, in short, was bound by its architecture, language, forms of representation, costume, and training to a history

of proximity to and rivalry with theater. It is a competition or sympathy that is fundamental to an understanding of the relation of law to rhetoric. Legal rhetoric, what in the Baroque period was fondly termed *theatrum veritatis et iustitiae* (the theater of justice and truth), is the discipline that studies the social communication, both the language and the theatricality of law. Its object is explicitly the study of verbal action, of the force and effect of law. It is a study of legal performances, of the enactment of law through argumentative persuasion, and through the written justifications of statute, doctrine, and judgment.

Whether addressing the *agōn* of trial or the rules of composition and interpretation of written laws, the determinative context of legal rhetoric historically has been that of casuistry, that of the decision of cases and the resolution of conflicts, whether real or imagined. To the extent that forensic rhetoric encodes and formalizes the affective and performative dimensions of legal practice, to the extent that it acknowledges and elaborates the constructed and emotive character of legal language—the drama of trial and the figuration of juristic texts—it too has been the object of the hostility of jurists. This essay will trace the history of proximity as well as of conflict between the two disciplines and will pay particular attention to the antinomic or combative character of law's staging of a truth that ironically was defined scholastically as a wisdom without desire (Aristotle, *Politics* 3.11.4). [*See* Casuistry.]

Rhetorics of Origin and Recovery. In both theocratic and secular forms, the rhetoric of Western law has always been heavily invested in the discourse of origins. The art of law was explicitly defined as knowledge of things divine and human (*rerum divinarum humanarumque scientia*) and the origin or source of law has habitually reflected that hierarchical and distant point of derivation across the boundary that demarcates the human and the divine. Law had to stage the transmission of juristic authority from a source prior to or other than its human representatives, a point of origin in the scriptures, in the breast of the Emperor, in the will of the people, in time beyond memory, in custom and use, or in one maxim "the tacit and illiterate consensus of men." The legitimacy of law, in other words, depended upon its being traced to a point of origin so old or so extreme that its authority could not be challenged. Law preceded and exceeded its human inscriptions, it was a will or power, *vis* or *potestas,* that temporal rule could only mimic, shadow, and approximate.

Granted that the Western legal tradition defined law by reference to a divine or arcane source beyond the reaches of history or "imperite" (unlearned) knowledges, there is an obvious and broadly theatrical significance to the tendency to attribute a legal origin to rhetoric. If law was classically depicted as a mute magistrate, a voiceless or sleeping natural form, a second nature, then, to borrow from Quintilian (first century CE), laws could have no effect unless sustained by pleaders. Rhetoric was the art that would give speech to an innate or hidden rule. It was rhetoric that would stage and perform the solemn ritual of discovery and interpretation of what was explicitly a spiritual or ghostly will. It is not, in other words, an accident that tradition relays that rhetoric was born in the context of law, nor is it surprising that the narrative of the origin of laws is told in terms of the rhetorical forms of their first inscriptions or sites of enunciation as commandments, codes, dooms, or constitutions.

The paradox of legal rhetoric is that the historical and continuing concentration upon the form of law, upon law as writing or law as charismatic oral tradition and judgment, has been a concentration upon the source and authority of law and not upon the fundamentally rhetorical character of legality. Thus the earliest narrative of the foundation of rhetoric attributes the origin of the discipline to the teaching and practice of Corax and Tisias of Syracuse. Their practice is said to have developed out of the need to tutor those who wished to claim back land after the overthrow of the mid-fifth-century BCE tyrants of Sicily. Technical rhetoric, in this narrative, emerged simultaneously with the transition from tyranny, to what would later be termed the *rule of law.* Advocacy emerged at the same time as adversarial procedures and so, to borrow from Nietzsche's lexicon, there was something republican about a rhetoric of law: it served to support a certain freedom in the causes of action. Whatever the political connotations of this narrative of origin, its juristic significance lies in the central role that rhetoric is accorded in the emergence of law.

Rhetoric gave meaning to rights and a voice to laws. Rhetoric was the medium through which the drama of law was staged and played out. [*See* Classical rhetoric.]

Another narrative of the origins of rhetoric acknowledges a long prehistory of legal and political oratory in Homeric and subsequent oral traditions but locates the birth of the discipline of rhetoric in the writings of Plato (c.428–c.347 BCE) and Aristotle (384–322 BCE). Again, the origin of rhetoric was bound to the practice of law. Where Plato criticizes rhetoric for valuing persuasion or semblance over truth, the example that he uses is that of the style of argument in court. The legal orator, subject to the constraints of the adversarial process, imbued with self-interest, and terrorized by the surveillance of judges, develops a "tense and bitter shrewdness; he knows how to flatter his master and earn his good graces, but his mind is narrow and crooked. An apprenticeship in slavery has dwarfed and twisted his growth and robbed him of his free spirit . . ." (*Theaetetus* 173a–b). The complaint that Plato lays before the legal orator is one that is repeated in a different form in the *Laws*. If the deficiency of the legal orator was that of trying to please an audience, that of playing to the gallery, the criticism of such melodrama was predicated upon the need to distinguish legal rule from theatocracy or theatrical rule. The judge should not decide cases so as to please the spectators any more than the orator should confuse the character of representation with flattery or distraction of the jury: "To tell the plain truth, the judge takes his seat not to learn from the audience, but to teach them" (*Laws* 659b). It is important to note, however, that while it is evident that for Plato law should govern judgment, rather than some theatrical principle of persuasion drawn from comedy, tragedy, or burlesque, Plato conceives of just legal rule as itself a theater of truth obedient to the essentially poetic or musical norms of a higher order of persuasion. Thus "the true lawgiver will persuade" so as to instruct or lead or bend the will of the auditor, the subject of laws.

For Aristotle, as was so often the case, it was the more confined or legalistic version of the argument against rhetoric that is presented in his synthetic account of the origin and purpose of the discipline. Aristotle too, on the first page of the *Rhetoric,* defines rhetoric as the art of proof—the study of enthymemes, of syllogisms based on probabilities—in the context of legal trial (1354a). [*See* Enthymeme.] Rhetoric teaches the discipline of speaking before a judge and is in consequence an art that is inseparable from law. For Aristotle, at least in Book 1 of the *Rhetoric,* argumentation should uncover the facts of the case and hence rhetoric is closely related to dialectic, the study of the logic of probable arguments, which governed the ethical use of language and the proper application of law. [*See* Dialectic.] By contrast, "the exciting of prejudice, of anger and such like emotions of the soul, has nothing to do with the fact, but has regard to the judge" (1354a).

The originary proximity of rhetoric to law is in each of the above accounts an uneasy and potentially unequal one. The concern of rhetoric with the form of social communication, its attention to the affective and performative dimensions of legal argument, set it in many respects in opposition to the Platonic and early scholastic conception of a logic or truth of law that could somehow escape the artifice of words. The subsequent history of rhetoric's relation to law, the fluctuating trends of decline and revival, were marked more than anything else by the uncertain epistemic status of rhetoric. It was deemed dangerous or it was denounced as irrelevant just as often as it was recognized as being intrinsic to a profession of law that was explicitly a study of the meaning of words and, depending upon viewpoint, an art of arguing (dialectic) or of chattering (*ars bablativa*). The great irony of the history of legal rhetoric is that while all of the major reforms of the Western legal tradition were in a broad sense rhetorical interventions into the study and practice of law, rhetoric also always seemed to suffer a correlative disparagement or denunciation.

The eleventh-century reception of Roman law in the West, which inaugurated the discipline of law within the universities, was explicitly a recovery of a language, of a system of communication and its texts, and the art of the medieval jurist was that of glossing, of defining, collating, and cohering a corpus of fragments and words. [*See overview article on* Medieval rhetoric.] The glossator studied the meaning of words, the names and signs of law, and the standard treatises on *De verborum significatione* would be prefaced by an exposition of the figures and rules of rhetoric. When humanism swept through the legal academy in the fifteenth century, its goal was precisely to recover the original words of the law, what Budé called the spirit of true *latinitas,* from sophistic overlay and corrupt rhetoric. [*See overview article on* Renaissance rhetoric.] Law needed to be reformed because its rhetoric had failed, because it had come to misuse words and misunderstand the techniques of appropriate argument. When the Ramist reforms of the sixteenth century were applied to law, it was again the rhetorical art of argument, the rules of dialectical disputation, together with an understanding of the argumentative force of sentential figures (rhetorical schemes), which were the source of legal renewal.

In a more contemporary context, the principal twentieth-century revival of rhetoric was the work of a Belgian jurist, Chaim Perelman and his collaborator Lucie Olbrechts-Tyteca (also a lawyer), and was explicitly concerned to use rhetoric not only to reform the infelicities of legal style but the justice of argument and the ethics of law. In addition to Perelman's explicit revival of an Aristotelian rhetoric of law, the other most notable contemporary movements for reform of law, legal realism, critical legal studies, feminist jurisprudence, and critical race theory have all been informed by and addressed to the rhetorical dimensions of legal governance. The social drama of the application or practice of law, the purposive character of interpretation, the indeterminacy of language and of judgment, the color and the gender of legal words, of the fictions and other stagings of law, are alike intrinsically rhetorical topics lodged in the interstices of the law's empire of argument. [*See* Modern rhetoric.]

The ambivalence of the relation between the disciplines of rhetoric and law, what might be termed the antagonistic dependence of law upon rhetoric, reflects a practical constraint. At the level of professional practice, the lawyer has been defined historically as an advocate. Whether appearing in court or negotiating privately, the lawyer was tied to a client, or classically a friend, and represented that person's interests against circumstance, adversaries, or the blandishments of time. The adversarial character of practice, and particularly the zero-sum game of the trial, had a significant impact upon the style and self-representation of the profession. At its most extreme, legal action resulted in the violence of imprisonment, fines, confiscation of property, prohibition, and even death. The lawyer's rhetoric was designed in part to hide the stakes of legal action and specifically the human causes of the infliction of sanctions. At one level, this meant that the successful advocate needed to blame the law rather than his or her own rhetorical failings for the sanction or pain to which the client was subjected. In medieval French courts, to take an extreme example, advocates would wear metal helmets to protect them from irate clients. In other and less violent traditions, the helmet was replaced by the coif, and then the *perruque,* or wig, along with the rites and "hotchpot" or painted words of the professional drama of legal rule.

A second way of formulating the constraint upon the recognition and acknowledgement of the rhetoric of law is doctrinal. In the rhetorical forum of law, the advocate was placed in an agonistic position, and while necessarily relying upon the techniques of rhetoric was also tied to a more profound or ritualized staging of the authority and authenticity of law. Legal argument had to take place by reference to law. It had to have a sacramental aura and a didactic quality that would remove it from mere social use to the domain of doctrine or truth. The theater of law demanded that advocacy and even more particularly judgment appear in the form of the discovery or necessary logic of law rather than that of a rhetoric, if the latter was to be understood in a popular sense as passion or persuasion. The rhetorical function of law was here that of solemnizing the social discourse of authority, that of establishing the conditions of persuasion under which the truth of doctrine, and so the legitimacy of law-applying acts, could be referred to a source exterior to those who were professionally responsible for imposing their interpretations of legal texts upon litigants, clients, students, or colleagues.

Passionate Conviction. The first and most accessible meaning of legal rhetoric is that of advocacy. Each of the narratives of origin alluded to above treated rhetoric as the art of composing speeches for presentation in court. While it should be acknowledged that other cultures have often forbidden advocacy or limited the role of

adversarial proceedings, the figure of the forensic orator has dominated the Western model of legal rhetoric and the adversary process has been the principal form of representation and communication of the rule of law. It has both enshrined and marginalized the role of rhetoric in law by reference to an exemplary and agonistic function that represents but a small part of the lawyer's work.

The earliest practice of law, both in Greece and in Rome, was synonymous with legal oratory. The rhetor was a specialist in the forms of representation or argument before a jury or law court, and according to the available evidence would play the role of tutor or friend to the party on trial. Within the Greek tradition, the earliest type of legal rhetorician was the "logographer," someone who would write the speech that the client would orate at trial. In the later tradition, the forensic rhetorician would not only compose speeches but would also act as *synergos,* as someone who spoke with the litigants and eventually would speak for them. The advocate as a vicarious voice, as representative of a friend or client, developed most distinctively within the Roman tradition. The link between patronage, friendship, and advocacy was marked linguistically by the early use of the terms *amicus* and *patronus* to refer to the legal orator, though by the time of Cicero (106–43 BCE) *advocatus, causidius,* and *togatus* added further connotations of specialization, adversary process, and social distinction. [See Oratory.]

By the time of Cicero, the Roman advocate stood at the pinnacle of the legal profession, and where the jurist, the *iurisconsultus,* or scholar of law merely knew the written and unwritten laws, the advocate put them into practice and so in a very real sense made them. The skill of the legal orator was thus much broader than that of simply knowing the law, and indeed the jurist was for this reason frequently viewed as little more than a failed advocate. In Cicero's definition, the forensic orator needed a knowledge of history, philosophy, geography, politics, and law. The orator strove for an eloquence that would protect the innocent and defend their friends. It was a goal that exceeded the confines of any single discipline and required both scholarly erudition and a practical appreciation of the emotions. It is important, however, also to stress that the art of legal eloquence was far more than simply a functional one. The eloquence of the legal orator was for Cicero an embodiment of virtue, and sought to express a distinctively social *ēthos* and ethics. In pleading successfully, the orator would foster the distinctly Roman values of urbanity and equity rather than simply success or failure. This larger political context and ethical purpose to legal argument found its strongest expression in the definition of the "great lawyer" as a priest of the law, as *lux a tenebris* ("light in our darkness"), someone whose house was "the oracular seat of the whole community" (*De oratore* 1.45.201).

While the role of the advocate was primarily that of defending or prosecuting legal causes of action, the adversarial function has to be understood in its broader rhetorical and cultural context. The advocate was a friend and sought to serve his friends, and while legal knowledge was important to pleading, the advocate as an orator was someone whose eloquence was gauged also to serve the community and the cause of justice. Rhetoric was tied to equity in the sense of the ethical development and political fairness of legal judgment, and in those respects rhetoric was also always at risk of conflict with strict law or the claim to a specialist and inflexible application of legal rules. In more technical terms, the legal orator was a specialist in invention and narration, in finding arguments from all the disciplines, and in relating that pluralistic learning to the narration of the facts or application of the law. [*See* Invention.] Forensic rhetoric in its Ciceronian guise was an art that avoided specialization and promoted a sense of legal virtue that valued friendship and recognized the importance of a culture of argument and persuasion to the affective life or growth of the law. The legal orator was in this sense a poet as well as a lawyer, a friend as well as a functionary, a diplomat as well as a decision maker.

The professions of advocate and lawyer were fused by the time of the later Roman Empire, and in the process the erudition and urbanity as well as the affectivity and poetics of the orator's role tended to be subordinated to the demands of specialization and the specific procedures of adversary trial. To borrow from Aristotle and Cicero, it was the metaphor of military engagement and of the orator as soldier that increasingly came to dominate the tradition. The advocate was essentially an expert in proof and would arm his exposition of the facts of the case with a combative rhetoric of their truth. What is important to the status and fate of the discipline of legal rhetoric is that proof was conceived as an agonistic and theatrical craft. Concerned less with a knowledge of law than with persuasion of judge or jury as to the particulars of the case, the advocate used rhetoric as a tool in the staging of the facts of the case. In this more specialized form, the advocate used rhetoric to put passion in the service of proof. [*See* Pathos.]

The theatrical or performative role of legal rhetoric remained essential to eloquence, but the scope of the orator's concerns and his self-conception of the role of oratory were greatly diminished. [*See* Eloquence.] As the *Dialogue of Orators* (c.101 CE) traditionally attributed to Tacitus, famously puts it, if the sovereign makes the law and the judge decides its meaning, then there is little need of skillful argumentation. The orator, therefore, will stage the facts of the case and will use metaphor, and particularly the mimetic figures of icon (*eikōn*) and of *enargeia* or vivid image, to demonstrate and instruct the judges as to the facts and so persuade them to action. The figure of *enargeia* is defined as a movement that brings the object represented before the eyes of the listener. In other words, it stages the proof through persuasive evocation of the facts, through images or *phantasmata* that allow the auditor to imagine and so understand the particulars of the case pleaded.

In addition to demonstrating in as theatrical or visual a form as possible the facts of his client's case, the legal orator would also attack alternative versions or interpretations of those facts. Where the rhetorical schools had taught narration, praise, and vituperation, the later tradition taught argument through apprenticeship in court or through the mock agon of moots and bolts. In either case, legal argument tended to emphasize figures of antagonism, of confession, and of dismissal as well as of antithesis and rebuttal. The staging of a trial for the medieval and early modern tradition was explicitly a verbal combat, a linguistic form of ordeal or duel, and the advocate was in these contexts the champion of his client. Borrowing from the schools of declamation and their *controversiae,* the Renaissance legal orator would go to war for his client, he would fight with words. [*See* Controversia and suasoria.] In one popular description, advocates were soldiers of the law and were explicitly trained in arguments as to "contraries," against orthodoxy and common sense. Their rhetorical style was comparably combative with figures of altercation such as those of antithesis, augmentation, exclamation, as also of mocking and dismissal, looming large in their argument.

The negative connotations of rhetoric in law owe much to the corrupt or at least diminished role of forensic rhetoric in those eras of the legal tradition, from which the contemporary should not be excluded, when law has taken priority over equity, precedence over eloquence, and dogmatics over a concern with the performance of rules. The notion of rhetoric as a noisome weed, of eloquence as "the nursling of indiscipline," and of advocacy as an art of chattering, as the railing of pettifoggers, declaimers, and ranters, belongs to those epochs of legal rule in which lawyers have misunderstood the relation of oratory to ethics and of theater to legality. Preferring to understand law in terms of a science or truth that exceeds the realms of contingency, dogmatics loses all sense of appropriateness or of the merely probable status of the relationships to which legal argument and its enthymemes were best directed. Written law in particular was the subject of a "restrained rhetoric" and was treated historically by lawyers more in terms of truth than of Aristotelian verisimilitude.

Writing Law. The adversarial role and animadversions of the advocate have frequently set the tone of discussions of legal rhetoric and the image of the ordeal of trial has correspondingly detracted from the less vivid yet more constant role of rhetoric as the technical art of composition and interpretation of legal documents. In this latter and historically more significant or at least expansive sense, rhetoric is the theory of inscription and of *interpretatio scripti,* that of writing and interpreting law. Again, its role has been a critical one but it has also been a boring and intricate one, hidden from public view and in general lacking any obvious ethical purpose. Here it is the figure of the lawyer as notary rather than

the rhetor or advocate who is hated for the rigidity, prolixity, and barbarisms (*cacozēlia*) of written law.

For most of the Western legal tradition, the oral arts of disputation have existed in uneasy relation to a prior and written law. Conceived as written reason, the various historical codes, commandments, instruments, and constitutions existed in written form and derived much of their power or mystique from the sacred status of writing in eras where literacy was limited to clerics and the upper classes. While some, most famously Lycurgus, lawgiver and king of ancient Sparta, believed that writing served only to encourage forgetfulness of laws that ideally should be inscribed invisibly in the heart, the symbolic function of the written sign was that of signaling permanence, generality, and visibility. The writing of law, whether in the form of an edict, a contract, a doom, or a code, turned the transitivity and ephemerality of speech into the intransitive, sepulchral, and sacred form of the written sign. Even unwritten (uncodified) law was from early in the tradition to be found in books, in *coutumiers,* mirrors, plea rolls, and cases, or not at all.

Legal writing has generally had an exorbitant status: legislation and the other textual *corpora* of law have had a foundational and at times sacred status in which written law was written reason, and any inconsistencies or contradictions within legal scripture were attributed to failures of interpretation rather than error of law. As Sir Edward Coke (1552–1634) would put it, men could err but law could not: *in hominis vitium et non professionis* (*The Reports,* 1611, London, 1777, 5.4.c.b.b.). The records of law promulgated an incontestable truth, one which the lawyer might expound or extol, collate or implement, but could not criticize or divagate from. It was this classically motivated and essentially theological reverence for the writings of law that the rhetoricians criticized and the revival of rhetoric has generally been gauged to reform. When the humanist Lorenzo Valla (1407–1457), for example, said that the lawyers knew nothing of eloquence, he meant that the glossatorial tradition was ignorant of Latin grammar and of the philological skills necessary to the reconstruction of a dead language and its long dead laws.

The legal rhetorician as a critic of legal method

is, however, a complex and ambivalent figure. Cicero and Quintilian, in particular, addressed the central role of the interpretation of writing, of laws, wills, and contracts, in terms of disputes arising out of written reason by virtue of ambiguity, conflict of laws, or disputed analogies. Writing was to be interpreted rhetorically in the same manner as other forms of meaning, and the student was therefore trained to dispute the writing *in utramque partem,* by looking at the arguments for and against the position advocated. The written law or document was a site of controversy and was to be treated most generally in terms of the conflict between word (*scriptum*) and intention (*voluntas*), a conflict resolved by looking to the whole text as well as to the "other writings, acts, words, disposition and in fact [the] whole life" of the author (*De inventione* 2.40.117).

The later tradition, and most particularly the glossatorial method that developed around the twelfth-century reception of Roman and Canon law, generated a new position and status for legal writing. Trained in the techniques and knowledges of a law formulated in a foreign language and substantively relevant to a society that had fallen some six centuries earlier, the lawyer perforce became an advocate—an ideologue—of the written law. The rhetoric of written reason (*ratio scripta*) within the domain of influence of Roman law was profoundly polemical in its defense and promulgation of the written law. The text of the law took priority over all earlier sources of law and explicitly prohibited any later commentaries or emendations of the very words themselves (*ipsissima verba*) of written reason. In the context of such a tradition, one which emerged around the recovery of a long lost and rapidly sanctified code of an earlier and greater law, the role of the legal rhetorician or interpreter of the laws became that of systematizing, collating, and cohering, parsing and praising the text. The first article of legal faith was that the text contained all the law and by explicit principle the text was incapable of error, incompleteness, or contradiction.

In a style that has survived into the modern legal era, the lawyer was trained to treat the written words of the law as belonging within the space of truth. Written law had a status greater than that of other writings and the professional expertise of the lawyer in such a context was that of knowing and applying the words of an archaic law formulated in a foreign or "inkpot" tongue. Two features of this apologetic approach to law are of particular significance. The first is that method and, in the language of Ramism, the logic of law, displaced the explicit study of rhetoric from law to literature. By the end of the Renaissance, in the wake of the printing press and the rules of method developed by the Ramists, rhetoric explicitly connoted neither proof nor argument, but rather the study of style and elocution. Rhetoric was here seen to address questions of poesie and the "exornations" of language; its object and method was that of ornament, fiction, and aesthetic pleasure, rather than the serious and prosaic business of law. If rhetoric retained an explicit place in the legal curriculum of early modern tradition, it was that of the practice of argument taught by way of apprenticeship, through moots and bolts. In this pragmatic and restricted sense, rhetoric was not an aspect of law and had no place in the prosaic and printed domain of legal texts.

The second feature of the restrained or unacknowledged relation of rhetoric to written law is that of the polemical status of the denial of the rhetorical quality of legal regulation and judgment. In one sense, outside of the agon of trial and the obviously rhetorical role of the advocate, the postreception lawyer was archetypically a notary, *doctor artis notariae,* a scrivener who set down the disposition of property, goods, or will in writing. The lawyer was a man of records and of instruments, he tabled fines, enrolled pleas, recorded arguments (and later judgments), and in general held custody of the antique scriptural remains of both local and national law. The image of the lawyer as scrivener or notary was neither glamorous, nor, in the main, was it popular. Expert in a legal language which, even when translated into the vernacular, diverged markedly from popular use and retained many of its Latin and French terms, the lawyer was constantly subject to scholarly criticism and popular attack.

Whatever the specific causes of legal apologetics, and historically they have varied greatly according to religious, political, and technological contexts, the dogmatic rhetoric of a truth or necessary logic of written law has borrowed significantly from theological dogmatics. The lawyer as notary was classically someone who professed a faith in the scriptural instruments of law (*de fide instrumentorum*). The single most important principle of early modern legal method was the reformist one of the text alone (*sola scriptura*). It staged the authority and meaning of legal writing in terms of the denial of the rhetoric of law. Borrowing from the religious model of defense of the faith, the lawyer increasingly adopted the "antirrhetical" style of the apology. The figure of *antirrhēsis* refers to words or discourses against iconoclasts, heretics, women, and foreigners. In its legal variants, though theology and jurisprudence should not be thought of historically as separate disciplines, antirrhesis connoted both a discourse of denunciation directed at those who would deny the logic, system, or authority of legal writing, and a discourse against mere words or any signs that stand in the way of an extralinguistic truth.

Within the dogmatic conception of law, the language of law was the transparent vehicle of a truth that preceded and survived its merely temporal inscriptions. Law was a written record of an authority and intention, a logic or will that ultimately escaped the inessential domain of appearances, of images, and words. Put differently, what has characterized the dogmatic tradition of written law, from the *Corpus Iuris* to the Napoleonic Code, from *Magna Carta* to the American Constitution is the belief in a will, meaning, or intent that exists outside and authorizes the words of the law. In its classical formulation, "to know the law is not to know the text of the law but its force and power" (*Digest* 1.3.17). For Sir Edward Coke, similarly, it is not the words of the law but the truth that deserves to be loved: *in lectione non verba sed veritas est amanda* (*The Reports,* 1611, 3.2.c.7.b). In the face of such a theological principle of an exterior or extralinguistic truth, lawyers too adopted the religious dogma that signs, words, and images were potentially an obstacle to apprehension of an invisible object of faith. Rhetoric, as the study of the theatrical force, the figuration or affect of the text, was in this sense idolatrous. Just as worship of the image confused sense and reference, study of the signs of law was deemed to conflate form with content, power with textuality, and wisdom with desire.

Legal Semiotics and the Poetics of Law. In an era that is increasingly dominated by visual media of communication and by virtual information networks, it is appropriate to recollect that legal rhetoric has always been concerned with much more than the language of law. Rhetoric was historically an expansive discipline, and even where its concern was with the technical composition of legal speeches, it analyzed language as a sign. Even when addressed quite strictly to the figures of diction, rhetorical analysis was gauged to apprehending the force and effect of language use. The classification of figures and tropes reflected their argumentative context and role, their significance as well as their sense. [*See* Figures of speech.] It is for this reason that the curricular tradition paid attention also to the architecture, portraiture, and other heraldic insignia (*symbola heroica*) of law, to dress and deportment, to elocution, manual rhetoric and gesture, as also to the physical condition and mental attitude of the legal orator. [*See* Delivery.] There is a sense in which rhetoric has always recognized that it needed to train the body (both *corpus* and *imago*) to perform the work of law. [*See* Ēthos.]

To understand legal rhetoric as a part of the semiotics of law, that is, as a subspecies of a general study of the signs by means of which law is communicated, would not necessarily have surprised the authors of earlier rhetorical handbooks. Their concern with vivid speech, with images conveyed by words, with the aesthetic force of argument, was always bound to an appreciation of audience, context, and juristic tradition that exceeded any simple analysis of the form of words. The historical concern of legal rhetoric with appearances, with the schematic logic of argument as also with the flowers of speech, with semiotics as well as aesthetics, has been integral to the contemporary revival of interest in the discipline and to attempts to revise and apply it to the modern media of legal communication.

A critical rhetoric of law, or in a more adventurous coinage a rhetoric that "plays" the law, is precisely one that attends to "the other scene" of legal communication and specifically to the plastic supports, medial relays, textual and visual effects of legal rule. In that law's cultural presence is increasingly a question of media staging or filmic representation, and its archives virtual positivities in a political drama of governance, rhetoric is forced to return to the study of a more expansive domain of the social theater of legal rule. For all that Plato descried the inappropriate or unethical use of rhetoric in the implementation of law, he also understood the polity ideally to be "a dramatization of a noble and perfect life" (*Laws* 817b). The true lawgiver was the man of poetic gifts whose speech was imbued with rhythm, melody, and rhyme. The Ciceronian tradition similarly ennobled the legal orator whose *ēthos* was that of loyalty and of never failing his friends. It is to the Renaissance lawyer and poet George Puttenham, however, that the finest synthesis of Plato's alternative vision of the good orator belongs. For Puttenham, the chief virtue of the poet-lawyer was that of someone who spoke by means of images or the figures of speech directly to the soul. What in contemporary terms would be viewed as a radical lawyer, was an orator who understood a rhythm or poetic of rule that bridged the unbridgeable gap between justice and law, poetry and prose. The legal orator in this description was a critic capable of appreciating the age-old phantasmata of the soul. Such was not the "phantasticall man" of whom traditional lawyers complained, but rather "*euphantasiste*, and of this sort of phantasie are all good Poets . . . all Legislators, Polititiens & Counsellours" (*The Arte of English Poesie*, 1589, p. 19).

It remains to say that whether conceived in terms of semiotics, criticism, or poetics, the rhetoric of law, in its judicial and professional guises, has remained overwhelmingly a Western rhetoric, a white oratory, a masculine linguistic usage. The rhetorical study of the appearances, of the forms and figures of legal discourse, of the force and theater of law, has been subversive of this apologetic and antirrhetical doctrinal tradition of legal studies. Rhetoric has been the tool of a variety of critical analyses of law and has increasingly become an interdisciplinary study of the signs of law, of the iconic or exemplary images through which law gains its most powerful or political forms of social presence. Critical legal studies, feminist jurisprudence, critical race theory, and the law and literature movement are all informed by rhetoric and attempt to analyze the law through a political reading of the social narrative contained in the discourse of law and manifested in the figures that govern legal texts. As a literary politics or criticism of law, rhetoric allows

at the least for an exposition of the constructed character of legal rule and for attention to the images through which law is communicated to its nonspecialist audiences. The authority of law, in other words, is (and arguably, through differing technologies, always has been) more a question of verbal and visual images, of a theater of sovereignty and of great trials, than it is exclusively a question of an esoteric logic of any specifically legal form of argument.

The critical impulse that informs contemporary uses of rhetoric in the analysis of law suggests two principal avenues of future development. The first and more directly political dimension of an expanded rhetoric of law returns it to the opening concern of this essay, that of the relation of law to theater. Attention to the dramatic staging of law focuses legal studies upon the social force, the performative violence, and the trauma of legality. A rhetorical legal studies in this form offers a critical point of entry into the relation of law to the enactment and violence of social identities. It provides the tools to analyze the images through which law inhabits and constitutes the dominant social narratives of community and belonging through the drama of justice, and the figures of reparation and retribution. To the extent that the cultural identity that law enacts fails to incorporate minority cultures or nonconformist identities, rhetoric can provide the means of a more ethical practice of law, one that is appropriate to the plural audiences of a multicultural and increasingly global community.

The other dimension to the revival of the rhetorical study of law can be addressed best by reference to the history of juristic antagonism toward the flowers or ornaments of rhetorical practice. To read the history of rhetoric through the lens of law, through what, by way analogy with the *querelle des femmes*, could be termed the *querelle des lois*, is to accede to the notion that rhetoric has a lesser epistemic status and social value than the adversarial model of law. It is well and perhaps also prescient to recollect that the Ciceronian conception of legal rhetoric linked it closely to poetics, as also to the dialogue of friendship, and to the uses of fiction in the enactment of equity. Later traditions of rhetoric and of local law revived this poetic *ēthos* both in the literary form of amatory law, women's courts, and judgments of love, as well as in the local jurisdiction of lovedays (*dies amoris*) and amicable settlements. In one eleventh-century Anglo-Norman code, it was explicitly legislated that "agreement prevails over law and love conquers judgment" (*Leges Henrici Primi* c.49.a.). In brief, the adversarial model of law and the agonistic form of legal practice is not the only genre or jurisdiction of laws. Rhetoric supplies a ready history of alternative jurisdictions, modes, and fictions of law. Rhetoric suggests an ethics of law that looks to the appropriateness of legal practice, not simply to the case but to the community and audience, procedure and justice that any given law implies.

[*See also* Forensic genre.]

BIBLIOGRAPHY

Cover, Robert. "Violence and the Word." *Yale Law Journal* 95 (1986), pp. 1601–1640. Classic essay that begins with the oft quoted words "Legal interpretation takes place in a field of pain and death."

Crook, J. A. *Legal Advocacy in the Roman World*. London, 1995. An excellent and innovative account of legal rhetoric in Rome from the second century BCE to the fifth century CE.

Douzinas, Costas, and Lynda Nead, eds. *Law and the Image. The Authority of Art and the Aesthetics of Law*. Chicago, 1998. A significant edited collection of essays on the visual culture of law.

Dupont, Florence. "La scène juridique." *Communications* 26 (1977), pp. 62–77. An erudite account and interpretation of the two-century-long prohibition of theater in Rome.

Eden, Kathy. *Poetic and Legal Fictions in the Aristotelian Tradition*. Princeton, 1986. A highly persuasive study of the formal links between theater, poetics, and law.

Eden, Kathy. *Hermeneutics and the Rhetorical Tradition: Chapters in the Ancient Legacy and Its Humanist Reception*. New Haven, 1997.

Fraunce, Abraham. *The Lawiers Logike, Exemplifying the Praecepts of Logike By the Practice of the Common Lawe*. London, 1588. The first and exemplary application of Ramism to the study of law.

Goodrich, Peter. *Oedipus Lex. Psychoanalysis, History, Law*. Berkeley, 1996.

Goodrich, Peter. "Law in the Courts of Love: Andreas Capellanus and the Judgments of Love" *Stanford Law Review* 48 (1996), pp. 633–675.

Goodrich, Peter. "Epistolary Justice: The Love Letter as Law." *Yale Journal of Law and Humanities* 9 (1997), pp. 245–295.

Hutson, Lorna, and Victoria Kahn, eds. *Rhetoric and Law in Early Modern Europe*. New Haven, 2000.

Kahn, Victoria. "Rhetoric and the Law." *Diacritics* 19 (Summer 1989), pp. 21–34.

Kelley, Donald. *Foundations of Modern Historical Scholarship. Language, Law and History in the French Renaissance*. New York, 1970.

Legendre, Pierre. *Law and the Unconscious. A Legendre Reader*. Edited and translated by Peter Goodrich. London, 1997. Essays on the mythological, theatrical, and ritual functions of law.

Lysyk, Stephanie. "Loving the Censor: Legendre, Censorship, and the Theatre of the Basoche." *Cardozo Studies in Law and Literature* 1 (1999), pp. 113–133.

Maclean, Ian. *Interpretation and Meaning in the Renaissance: The Case of Law*. Cambridge, U.K., 1992. An excellent and exhaustive account of Renaissance jurisprudence and specifically of legal theories of meaning.

Mellinkoff, David. *The Language of the Law*. Boston, 1956.

Perelman, Chaim, and Lucie Olbrechts-Tyteca. *The New Rhetoric: A Treatise on Argumentation*. Notre Dame, Ind., 1969; first published 1958.

Perelman, Chaim. *Logique Juridique, Nouvelle Rhetorique*. Paris, 1976. Unfortunately as yet untranslated, this work explicitly applies the New Rhetoric both to jurisprudence and to the analysis of legal judgment.

Sarat, Austin, and Thomas Kearns, eds. *The Rhetoric of Law*. Ann Arbor, 1994.

Weisberg, Richard. *Poethics, and Other Strategies of Law and Literature*. New York, 1996.

White, James Boyd. *Heracles' Bow: Essays on the Rhetoric and Poetics of Law*. Madison, Wis., 1985. Exemplary humanistic studies of the rhetorical culture of law, and of the importance of rhetoric to the building of legal community.

—PETER GOODRICH

LESBIAN AND GAY LIBERATION. *See* Queer rhetoric.

LETTERS. *See* Ars dictaminis; Epistolary rhetoric; *and overview article on* Medieval rhetoric.

LINGUISTICS. Linguistics is the scientific study of language, and language can be briefly defined as a kind of creative communicative interaction that uses a system of grammatical rules and a lexicon. Linguistic description today takes into account virtually all conceivable aspects, functions, and dimensions of language.

The theoretical development of linguistics in

the twentieth century was shaped by three towering figures: the Swiss linguist Ferdinand de Saussure (1857–1913), the father of linguistic structuralism; the American linguist Noam Chomsky, (1928–), the founder of generative grammar; and the Austrian philosopher Ludwig Wittgenstein (1889–1951), whose indirect influence on the development of functional and pragmatic approaches in linguistics has been enormous. Both Saussure's and Chomsky's contributions were crucial to the development of the high standard of methodological sophistication in contemporary linguistics. Their theoretical claims also made linguistic theory widely known and influential in other disciplines like philosophy, literary criticism, anthropology, psychology, sociology and, last but not least, rhetoric. However, their theoretical approach was also criticized and challenged by the more functional and communication-oriented frameworks inspired by Wittgenstein, which, especially during the last decades of the twentieth century, led to a fruitful interaction between linguistics and rhetoric in the study of texts, style, speech acts, and argumentation.

Branches. The field of linguistics can be divided into branches and subbranches according to the levels and dimensions of language under scrutiny, and according to the prevailing methods and overlapping interests of linguists and scholars from other disciplines.

Ferdinand de Saussure introduced a major distinction concerning two basic dimensions of language into modern linguistics. He distinguished diachronic and synchronic linguistics, the former referring to the study of language change across historical periods (also called historical linguistics), the latter to the study of the state of language(s) during a particular period. When linguistics is mainly concerned with general principles for the study of all languages and basic properties of language, it is called general or theoretical linguistics. When linguistics concentrates on the description of particular languages or one specific language system, it is called descriptive linguistics. In the twentieth century, linguistics has been mainly concerned with empirical description. This was also a reaction against the prevailing normative tendency in traditional grammar. There is, however, a growing awareness of the importance of a reconciliation of empirical and normative approaches and a critical discussion of linguistic norms and their ideological implications. This has led to the rise of critical linguistics (more particularly, critical discourse analysis and feminist linguistics).

When linguistic methods are applied to other subjects or are used for the solution of problems connected with language, especially foreign language teaching, the term *applied linguistics* is used. *Contrastive linguistics* is the term used when linguistic studies focus on the differences among languages. The description of common properties of languages (within or across language families) or of linguistic properties occurring in all languages (so-called language universals) is the main concern of typological linguistics. The development of artificial languages, like Esperanto, designed for international communication, is studied within interlinguistics.

The term *structural linguistics* is used for those European and American schools and traditions of the first half of the twentieth century, which focused on the abstract language system and tended to neglect the actual use of language in communication. In the last decades of the twentieth century, linguistic pragmatics was established as a flourishing and rapidly expanding branch of linguistics, studying the use of language both in everyday communication and in various social institutions.

From the 1950s onward, linguistic methods have been applied to neighboring disciplines (and vice versa), a development that led to a host of overlapping new disciplines, such as anthropological linguistics, clinical linguistics, computational linguistics, ecolinguistics, ethnolinguistics, mathematical linguistics, neurolinguistics, psycholinguistics, and sociolinguistics, to list but a few.

Frameworks. Taken in a broad sense, linguistics as the scientific study of language has a very long history, starting with the work of philosophers and grammarians in ancient China, India, and Greece more than two thousand years ago. The merits of this ancient tradition and its continuation in medieval and early modern times should not be underestimated. However, in a more narrow sense, linguistics as a modern academic discipline was developed in Europe and the United States only much later, in the nineteenth and twentieth centuries.

The main achievement of nineteenth-century linguistics was the establishment of reliable and precise methods for the historical and comparative (diachronic) description of languages and the identification of common characteristics of language families. So far as methodology is concerned, linguistics in the twentieth century could be characterized by the development of rigorous methods for the description of the state of language(s) at a given point in time; the use of modern technology for data collection; the development of experimental methods and computer-based data analysis; and, finally, the implementation of formal languages for the explicit presentation of linguistic structures.

Historical linguistics. The nineteenth century was dominated by the success of historical linguistics. The history of the Indo-European languages in particular was described in detail. The Indo-Europeanists were strongly influenced by theoretical concepts of the contemporary natural sciences. They tried to establish linguistic "sound laws" without exceptions, comparable to the laws of nature studied in the hard sciences. Moreover, some of them tried to apply Darwin's theory of evolution to the historical development of languages, postulating a highly problematic analogy between languages and biological species. However, the German linguist Hermann Paul, the most distinguished representative of the "neogrammarians" (the leading school of historical linguistics in the nineteenth century), criticized the concept of exceptionless sound laws. Still, much in the spirit of the linguistic mainstream of his time, he claimed that only a historical description could be called a scientific description of language. However, a small minority of linguists were ahead of their time and anticipated a number of theoretical concepts that were only taken up and developed into full-fledged theories in the twentieth century. Among them, the German linguist Wilhelm von Humboldt (1767–1835) especially deserves to be mentioned. He was interested not only in the diachronic, but also in the synchronic description of languages. He tried to deal with all languages of the world, was active in the development of a typological characterization of languages, and explored the influence of language on thought and worldview.

Structuralism. The biography of the Swiss linguist Ferdinand de Saussure connects the nineteenth and twentieth centuries both at a personal and at a theoretical level. He was familiar with the concepts of the neogrammarians and made groundbreaking contributions to historical linguistics. Toward the end of his life, he delivered several courses on general linguistics, which were published posthumously as the famous *Cours de linguistique générale* (Paris, 1916) by Charles Bally and Albert Sechehaye. Although research on the manuscripts underlying this edition has shown that Bally and Sechehaye had partially modified Saussure's position, today most linguists agree that they did not distort his thoughts to such a degree that the main ideas developed in the *Cours* would no longer be attributable to Saussure himself.

Saussure distinguished the diachronic and synchronic description of language(s): in diachronic linguistics, language change is described across historical periods; in synchronic linguistics, the state of language(s) at a certain period is described. He differed from the mainstream of historical linguistics in the nineteenth century in stressing that the synchronic description is the main goal of linguistics. Moreover, influenced by the French sociologist Emile Durkheim (1858–1917), Saussure emphasized the collective aspect of language, that is, the priority of the socially binding system of a language (*langue*) over the individual use of language in speech (*parole*). According to Saussure, separating language from speech amounts to separating the social from the individual sphere and the essential aspect of language from the accidental aspect.

In this view, language as a social system (*langue*) is beyond the control of individual speakers, while speech (*parole*) is an individual activity that is performed intentionally. Saussure restricted linguistic description mainly to the sound system, morphological structures, and the lexicon of a language, because he believed that the virtually infinite variability of sentences would make them a part of *parole* (speech) rather than language proper (*langue*).

Seen from a rhetorical perspective, this emphasis on the abstract language system (*langue*) to the disadvantage of the study of the spoken word has had deplorable effects. For many years, various schools of structural linguistics concentrated on the abstract structures of language systems rather than on the strategic use of language in different speech genres.

Saussure also developed a semiotic model of the linguistic sign, distinguishing the signifying sounds (*signifiant*) from the signified concept (*signifié*). Saussure stressed the fact that sounds do not represent objects in extralinguistic reality, but concepts that are part of the minds of the speakers. According to Saussure, the relationship between sounds and meaning is arbitrary, for more or less the same concept can be signified by differing sounds in different languages. For example, the concept of "tree" is signified by *tree* [tɹiː] in English, *Baum* [baom] in German, *arbor* ['arbor] in Latin, *dendron* in Ancient Greek (*see* Figure 1).

Even onomatopoetic words are no exception to this principle of arbitrariness, argues Saussure, because, apart from their very low frequency, they, too, differ from one language to another. Words for animal sounds support his claim: for example, the cock's *cock-a-doodle-doo* in English, *cocorico* in French, *kikeriki* in German, and *kukorékolás* in Hungarian.

Saussure's most important and most fruitful theoretical contribution to modern linguistics was his insight that linguistic units cannot be described in isolation. Sounds, words, phrases, and sentences are always part of a (sub-) system of a language. In this system, they have a certain value, which very often differs from one language to the other. Two examples help illustrate the point:

1. In sound systems of different languages, the same phonetically distinguishable sounds can have different values. For example, the nonaspirated and aspirated voiceless plosives [t] and [tʰ] are merely phonetic variants in English and German, but the same pairs of sounds are used to distinguish words in many other languages; for example, Ancient Greek and Mandarin Chinese: The Greek verbs *teinō* ("to stretch") versus *theinō* ("to hit") are distinguished solely by [t] and [tʰ]; likewise, the Chinese verb *tuì* [tʰuì] ("to give back") and the Chinese adjective *duì* [tuì] ("right") are solely distinguished by [t] and [tʰ].

Saussure's suggestions greatly contributed to the development of phonology, a systematic description of the functionally relevant sound units (cf. "Phonetics and Phonology" below).

2. The lexical systems of languages also differ as to the value of specific lexical items. Thus, for example, French *mouton* (which can mean sheep or mutton) has a different value in the lexical system of French than its correspondent items in English, *sheep* and *mutton*: the French word covers a broader zone of meaning than its two English counterparts. Similarly, English *sky* and *heaven* have a more specialized meaning than German *Himmel,* which covers both the meteorological meaning of *sky* and the religious meaning of *heaven.* English *you* or Latin *tu* correspond to both French *tu* and *vous* (or German *du* and *Sie*), as the English and Latin systems of personal pronouns do not distinguish formal and informal modes of address.

Saussure's observations influenced the theory of lexical fields, which was first developed by the German linguists Jost Trier and Leo Weisgerber and refined as a part of structural semantics by the Romanian linguist Eugenio Coseriu (cf. "Semantics" below).

A final, important distinction Saussure introduced into modern linguistics was the division of all structural relations in language into two classes: syntagmatic and paradigmatic relationships. The former concerns the linear dimension of language, that is, all relations combining sounds, syllables, words, phrases, clauses, and sentences to form ever increasing linear chains of

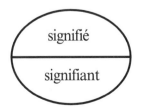 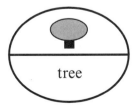 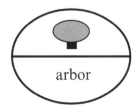

Linguistics. FIGURE 1. *Semiotic Model of a Linguistic Sign*

units *X, Y,* and *Z.* The latter deals with the paradigms of those linguistic units *Z* which, at a given point in the linear sequence, can be used alternatively (*X* or *Y* or *Z*).

Luckily, even Saussure's enormous impact on linguistic structuralism did not completely prevent the treatment of functional and rhetorical aspects of language within the structuralist traditions. In the Geneva school of structuralism, for example, Charles Bally extensively treated stylistic phenomena in French. It was one of the founders of the Prague school of structuralism, Wilem Mathesius, who introduced the systematic study of the distribution of old ("given," "thematic," "topical") and new ("rhematic," "focused") information in sentences, the so-called functional sentence perspective (cf. "Pragmatics" and "Synthesis" below).

American structuralism, however, was not so directly influenced by Saussure. Furthermore, the interest in Indian languages, which very often were only accessible to empirical investigation through oral tradition, and the study of various speech genres of Native American cultures led to contributions that are highly relevant from a rhetorical point of view. In this context, the work of the American linguists Franz Boas, Edward Sapir, and his student Benjamin Lee Whorf must be mentioned. Their studies centered on the relationship between culture, thought, and language. Whorf especially became known to a broader public through his widely discussed claim that language largely determines our thought and worldview (the so-called Sapir–Whorf hypothesis or linguistic relativity principle).

Furthermore, there were pioneers who as early as the 1940s and 1950s tried to lay the foundations for a linguistic study of the text. Louis Hjelmslev, for example, the main representative of the Copenhagen school of structuralism; the American linguists Zellig Harris and Kenneth Pike, the founder of tagmemics, yet another framework within American structuralism; and the Romanian linguist Eugenio Coseriu were the leading figures.

Selected developments in linguistic structuralism, which are particularly relevant from a rhetorical point of view, will now be presented in greater detail. The Russian linguist Roman Jakobson (1896–1982), the most eminent member of the Prague school, favored a functional view of language, describing language as a means of communication (cf. his *Selected Writings,* 2 vols, The Hague, 1962, 1971). Jakobson extended the organon model (ancient Greek *organon* = "tool") developed by the German psychologist Karl Bühler, another important member of the Prague school, in his book *Sprachtheorie* (Jena, 1934). Bühler assumes three basic functions of language in communication, namely, the representational, the expressive, and the directive (*see* Figure 2).

Jakobson added three further functions. These functions mirror six factors involved in every communicative message: the expression of the speaker/writer's emotions (emotive function); the triggering of the hearer/reader's reactions (conative function); the reference to objects and states of affairs (referential function); the maintenance of contact through the acoustic or visual channel used for transmission of the message (phatic function); the special attention paid to the formulation of the message, that is, the focus on the message itself (poetic function); and the self-referential use of the sign system (metalingual function).

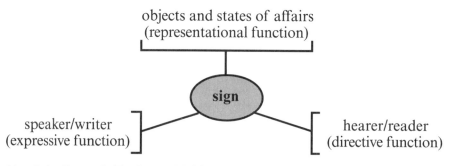

Linguistics. Figure 2. *The Organon Model*

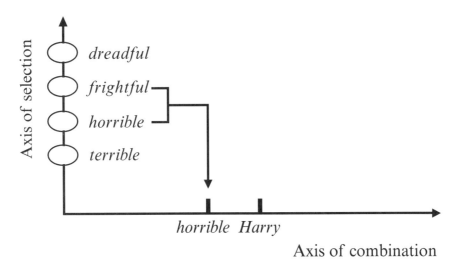

Linguistics. FIGURE 3. *A Basic Strategy of Poetic Language: The Principle of Equivalence*

Jakobson is fully aware of the fact that in actual communication, these functions mostly occur in a mixed form. For example, in advertisements or slogans in election campaigns, where the conative, persuasive function clearly dominates, at the same time usually great care is taken to formulate the message in an appealing and often highly elaborate form, which is also typical of the poetic function.

Moreover, taking up Saussure's distinction between paradigmatic and syntagmatic relations, Jakobson uses the terms *selection* and *combination* to describe a basic strategy of poetic language, namely, the principle of equivalence. In his own words, "The poetic function projects the principle of equivalence from the axis of selection into the axis of combination." Thus, in poetic texts the author selects such words from a paradigm of semantically similar or identical items, which in their syntagmatic combination form figures of speech. For example, to characterize a person called *Harry,* the speaker/writer chooses *horrible* from a paradigm of possible adjectives (instead of the semantically similar adjectives *dreadful, terrible, frightful,* etc.) because he or she wants to form the alliterating noun phrase *horrible Harry* (*see* Figure 3).

Furthermore, Jakobson used the dichotomy of selection and combination to classify all tropes as instances of two basic classes: tropes of similarity (metaphor) and tropes of contiguity (metonymy).

This way, he connects metaphor with the paradigmatic relationship of semantic similarity and metonymy with the syntagmatic relationship of causal or spatial or temporal contiguity. Moreover, he extends this distinction to the realm of nonverbal arts like painting and cinema and also tries to characterize speech disorders and literary traditions of art by their preference for one of the two basic tropes. Although this classification can be criticized as a kind of reductionism, it is an interesting contribution to the question of how to classify tropes and other figures of speech, which has kept rhetoricians busy since antiquity (cf. "Pragmatics").

Jakobson also criticized Saussure's principle of arbitrariness. Although there is no doubt that this principle does explain many facts concerning the sound–meaning correlation in natural languages, Jakobson plausibly demonstrated the copresence of an opposite principle, the iconic principle, following the ideas of the American philosopher and founder of modern semiotics, Charles Sanders Peirce (1839–1914). The iconic principle explains the following tendency in natural languages: certain sounds, rhythms, morphological structures, and syntactic constructions seem to correspond in a more direct way to extralinguistic objects than others. This tendency does not refute the principle of arbitrariness, but restricts the universality of its application.

The examples below serve to illustrate the iconic principle. Psycholinguistic experiments show that people regularly associate sounds in artificial words like *maluma* and *takete* with certain visual objects (*see* Figure 4).

The results of the experiments overwhelmingly showed that round lines and curves are associated with *maluma*, zigzag lines and sharp edges with *takete*. To a certain extent, this correlation of sound and meaning also seems to be present in nonartificial expressions taken from natural languages. Vowels like [e, ɛ, i, ɪ] often occur in expressions associated with light (cf. English *glitter, glimmer, gleam, light, lightning, fire, shine,* etc.), vowels like [ɑ, o, u] are often associated with darkness (cf. English *dark, gloomy, somber, smoke, smog, dust,* etc.). There are similar examples in other languages: compare words like German *Licht* [lɪçt] ("light"), *Blitz* [blɪts] ("lightning"), and French *lumière* [ly'mjɛːʁ] ("light"), *éclair* [e'klɛːʁ] ("lightning") and German *dunkel* ['dʊŋkəl] ("dark"), *Dunst* [dʊnst] ("smoke"), and French *sombre* ['sõːmbʁə], *ombre* ['õːmbʁə], ("shadow"). Of course, there are many counterexamples like English *night,* German *finster* ['fɪnstər] ("dark") or French *jour* [ʒuːʁ] ("day"), but these do not refute the claim that iconic tendencies can indeed be found in natural languages.

Moreover, quite often the morphology of natural languages shows iconic tendencies, like the correlation of shorter singular forms and longer plural forms (cf. English *boy* vs. *boys* or German *Junge* vs. *Jungen* or Latin *puer* vs. *pueri*). Similarly, the comparative and the superlative of adjectives usually have increasingly longer forms than the positive: compare English *big—bigger—biggest* and German *groß—größer—am größten* or French *grand—plus grand—le plus grand.* In syntax, the relative position of subordinate clause and main clause often mirrors the causal or temporal order of events. There is a universal tendency in all languages for conditional clauses or causal clauses to precede and final clauses to follow their main clause.

Jakobson's insights recall classical rhetorical concepts: iconic phenomena have been dealt with in the doctrine of *style* (e.g., *onomatopoeia*) and composition (*dispositio*), where the temporal order of events can be mirrored by the word order (*ordo naturalis*). Moreover, poets and rhetoricians have always used the iconic principle to choose and combine sounds, syllables, words, and metrical feet in a way that maximizes the iconic effect.

Another great linguist of the twentieth century, the Romanian Eugenio Coseriu (1921–), refined linguistic structuralism and successfully tried to overcome its theoretical weaknesses. Inspired especially by Wilhelm von Humboldt, he reestablished the importance of individual linguistic creativity, which indeed is far from being less important than the collectively shared language system. Individual language use is not wholly determined by the abstract system, but

Linguistics. Figure 4. *The Iconic Principle*

only presupposes it as a mutually shared technique for communication. When speaking and writing, we reproduce, but also creatively modify and extend the system of our language in a never ending process. At the heart of this process is the creation of new metaphors, metonymies, synecdoches, and other figures of speech.

As mentioned above, Saussure claims that the discourse of individual language users (*parole*) is situated at the periphery of language proper (*langue*). Seen from this perspective, language change is merely the unintended side-effect of individual speech, which thus damages the structural harmony of the synchronic system. However, Coseriu makes clear that the very essence of language is manifested in the dialogue: "la esencia del lenguaje se da en el dialogo" (*Sincronia, diacronia e historia,* Montevideo, Uruguay, 1958). In addition, according to Coseriu, there is no fundamental opposition between the language system and language change. Because the system is always dynamically realized through its reproduction and (partial) modification in dialogue, linguistic change is no failure or accident, but always follows systematic ways of using language in an innovative way.

This does not mean that Coseriu would deny the truth behind Saussure's insight that there are indeed collectively valid norms of a language. These norms reinforce traditional usage and restrict the full range of options for individual speakers/writers, at least if they are not willing to deviate from common usage and to face the sanctions sometimes connected with these deviations. Coseriu, therefore, tries to distinguish between two different aspects within Saussure's *langue* and replaces the dichotomy of *langue* and *parole* by a trichotomy of system, norm, and discourse.

The norm is the set of all traditional realizations of the system, the fixation of the possibilities offered by the linguistic system: the correct pronunciation of words according to the accepted standard, all dead or frozen metaphors, the most frequently used sentence patterns, the stock of derivations or compounds available at a given point in time. For example, in English you can regularly derive semantic opposites of adjectives with the help of the prefix *un-*; for example, *just/unjust, happy/unhappy, certain/uncertain, pleas-*

ant/unpleasant. However, the norm blocks the application of this quite general rule in the case of adjectives like *sad* or *small: unsad, unsmall* would be possible derivations according to the system, but are not acceptable according to the present norm of English. Similarly, French adverbs can regularly be derived from adjectives by adding the suffix *-ment,* for example *facile* (easy) and *facilement* (easily), *heureux* (lucky), and *heureusement* (luckily). But according to the standard norm, the derivation is blocked in the case of *possible* (*possiblement*).

The system is the sum of all linguistic techniques underlying the norm, which always remains open for creative and original applications of this technique, even beyond the traditional usage: all new forms, words, constructions, and metaphors (e.g., *virus, mouse, hacker, software, hardware, Internet, cyberspace, floppy disk, chat corner*) coined in the past few decades in connection with the needs of computer technology make this point clear.

Discourse is the level of language use, where the system is in particular contexts and situations. This can be done according to the system and the norm of a language or by creative innovations, for example, figures of speech, which (partially) transgress the norm and realize new ways of expression according to the system or even change the system itself.

Generative grammar. Generative grammar has been shaped primarily by the work of Noam Chomsky. The starting point of the "generative enterprise" was 1957, when Chomsky published his book *Syntactic Structures.* In the sixties, he wrote *Aspects of the Theory of Syntax* (Cambridge, Mass., 1965), where the Standard Theory was developed (also based on contributions by Jerrold J. Katz and Paul Postal). Over the years, many modifications of the Standard Theory have been suggested, among them Chomsky's own model of Government and Binding or, alternatively, Principles and Parameters (based on Chomsky's book *Lectures on Government and Binding,* Dordrecht, The Netherlands, 1981). Besides, a number of theoretical alternatives have been suggested by students and colleagues of Chomsky (e.g., James McCawley, George Lakoff, Charles Fillmore, Joan Bresnan, and many others), for example, Generative Semantics, Case Grammar, Lexical Functional Grammar, Generalized Phrase Structure Grammar, some of which are only distantly related to the generative mainstream (e.g., D. Perlmutter's Relational Grammar). Together with other approaches like Montague Grammar—developed by the American logician Richard Montague, who claimed that natural languages and formal languages do not differ in principle—most varieties of generative grammar belong to the formal as opposed to the functional paradigm, which describes language primarily as a means of communication (cf. "Pragmatics" below).

The Chomskyan revolution in linguistics has to be understood in relation to its historical context; namely, American structuralism. Its leading figure was Leonard Bloomfield (1887–1949), whose theoretical background was empiricism and behaviorism. Bloomfield claimed that useful generalizations in linguistics could only be inductive generalizations. Moreover, he argued that linguists should always base their description on a corpus of spoken or written utterances of a language. Bloomfield's behavioristic background also explains his skepticism about the possibility of a scientific description of meaning. In contrast to the sounds and the form of words and syntactic structures, the meaning of utterances is not directly observable. Chomsky's teacher, Zellig Harris, was even more radical than Bloomfield in excluding the study of meaning from linguistics. In his early work, Chomsky followed this attitude toward semantics and at least in this respect still adhered to American structuralism.

In most other respects, however, Chomsky radically challenged the premises of Bloomfieldian linguistics. First, he reintroduced mentalism into linguistic methodology, assuming that language ultimately is an organ, an innate mental capacity that grows in the mind. Against behaviorists, who assume that children mainly learn their mother language by imitating the linguistic behavior of their parents and older siblings, Chomsky argues that the poverty of stimulus, that is, the occurrence of interrupted or otherwise incorrect utterances, would make it impossible for children to learn their mother language via imitation. Therefore, he assumes a genetically given language acquisition device. This device guarantees that children can learn any language in a remarkably short period of time.

Furthermore, Chomsky makes the methodological distinction between competence and performance. In his *Aspects,* Chomsky claims that "linguistics is concerned primarily with an ideal native speaker" and the competence that enables him or her to produce and understand an infinite set of sentences, including new sentences that never have been expressed before. In this context, Chomsky quotes Wilhelm von Humboldt's famous dictum that to speak a language means to "make infinite use of finite means." A generative grammar, therefore, never can start from a—necessarily finite—corpus of utterances.

The term *generative* does not mean that a generative grammar is a production model of language. Rather, a generative grammar is any linguistic model that assigns explicit structural descriptions to the grammatical sentences of a language. One of Chomsky's major theoretical achievements was the introduction into linguistics of descriptive tools taken from logic and mathematics, to make possible this explicit description of all grammatical sentences of languages. The formal apparatus used by Chomsky includes elements of formal logic, set theory, and algebraic systems. Beginning with axiomatic starting points, explicit production rules enumerate all grammatical sentences of a language. Recursive mechanisms guarantee that the same rules can operate again and again. Therefore, there is no limit to the length of grammatical sentences the grammar can generate. Furthermore, although practical applications have never been Chomsky's main concern, the formalized model of generative grammar has been implemented in computer programs for such practical purposes as machine translation.

In later stages of the development of generative grammar, the descriptive ideal of a formal grammar recursively enumerating all grammatical sentences of a language (descriptive adequacy) has become less important than the ideal of reconstructing the "internal language" of a native speaker and the reconstruction of universal grammar as a part of the language acquisition device (explanatory adequacy). When studying the linguistic competence of a native speaker, Chomsky maintains a modular view of the human mind, where the language capacity is independent of other cognitive abilities. Likewise, he as-

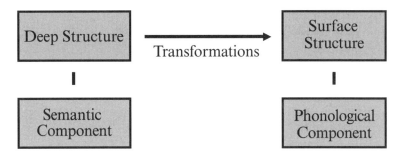

Linguistics. FIGURE 5. *Chomsky's Standard Theory, Distinguishing between Deep Structure and Surface Structure*

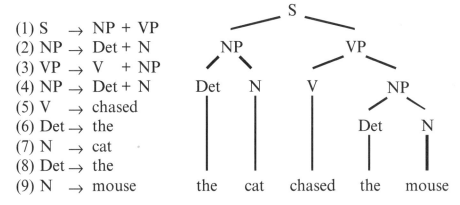

(1) S   → NP + VP
(2) NP → Det + N
(3) VP → V   + NP
(4) NP → Det + N
(5) V   → chased
(6) Det → the
(7) N   → cat
(8) Det → the
(9) N   → mouse

Linguistics. FIGURE 6. *Syntactic Structure of a Sentence, as Represented by a Phrase Marker.* Abbreviations: S = sentence; NP = noun phrase; VP = verbal phrase; N = noun; V = verb; Det = determiner.

sumes that syntax can be studied as an autonomous module that has to be separated from semantic or pragmatic aspects of the linguistic competence.

In his Standard Theory, Chomsky makes a fundamental distinction between surface structure and deep structure. Surface structure consists of structures that are more or less directly observable in written or spoken utterances of a language and necessarily contains language-specific elements. Deep structure is an abstract level of description that is assumed to be universal. Moreover, sentences that are ambiguous in their surface form (cf. Chomsky's examples, *Flying planes can be dangerous* or *the shooting of the hunters*) are assigned unambiguous deep structures, and synonymous sentences with differing surface structures (cf. *John gave Bill the book* and *John gave the book to Bill*) are assigned one and the same deep struc-

ture. Thus, deep structure is assumed to represent the meaning of sentences unequivocally. Therefore, in Standard Theory the semantic component of the grammar is attached to deep structure, whereas the phonological component is connected with surface structure (*see* Figure 5).

The sentences in deep structure are generated by a set of rules that produce phrase structures. Phrase structure rules have the general format "*X → Y*" ("rewrite constituent *X* as *Y*"). They start from the symbol *S* (= sentence) and recursively enumerate all parts of the sentence. The syntactic structure of a sentence can also be represented by a so-called phrase marker, a tree graph with a root, branches, and nodes. With these rules, the sentence *The cat chased the mouse* can be described as illustrated in Figure 6.

Deep structure is mediated with surface structure via a series of syntactic operations, called transformations, which map syntactic structures (phrase markers) onto other syntactic structures (phrase markers).

Transformations are classified according to the type of operational change they bring about in a given phrase marker. Four general types can be distinguished: (1) deletion (e.g., *Sincerity is admired by John ⇒ Sincerity is admired*); (2) adjunction (the addition of a constituent to the right or left of some other constituent); (3) substitution (a combination of deletion and adjunction, e.g., *I want that he should construct the machine ⇒ I want him to construct the machine*); (4) permutation (a combination of substitutions resulting in a change of word order, e.g., *Yesterday, he came home ⇒ He came home yesterday*). (*See* Figure 7.)

These classes of transformations closely resemble the so-called quadripertita ratio (1) *detractio* = deletion; (2) *adiectio* = addition; (3) *immutatio* = substitution; (4) *permutatio* = permutation) of ancient rhetoric. The Roman rhetorician Quintilian (first century CE) introduced this fourfold classification of all figures of speech according to the possible changes that their realization causes in words, phrases, and sentences (e.g., ellipsis, parenthesis, *hyperbaton,* metaphor). Moreover, in the phonological component of Standard Theory, an underlying abstract phonological representation of words and sentences is mapped onto their actual phonetic realization via phonological rules,

which again come close to the four basic operations mentioned above. In classical rhetoric, the corresponding figures of speech include *aphaeresis* (deletion), *prosthesis* (addition), *paronomasia* (substitution), and *metathesis* (permutation). [*See* Figures of speech.]

In the 1970s and 1980s, Chomsky revised and extended the Standard Theory considerably. In his Extended Standard Theory or Principles and Parameters (*PP*) Model, the phrase structure rules are replaced by *X*-Bar Syntax, an attempt to arrive at a truly universal format for constituent structure. *X*-Bar Syntax assumes more intermediate levels of division. Intermediate levels are specified with the help of bars or superscripts (e.g., X^0, X^1, X^2, X^3 . . .). To date, there is no consensus as to the exact number of intermediate levels. Every phrase has a head and every head of the next level of division belongs to the same lexical or functional category, a fact that is captured by the following general rule: $X^n \rightarrow \ldots X^{n-1} \ldots$ Phrases that cannot be further expanded are called maximal projections (X^{max}, e.g., noun phrase). Phrases can contain a specifier (one level below X^{max}), complements (one level above X^0). X^0-elements are lexical categories like noun (*N*), verb (*V*), or functional categories like inflection (= grammatical categories like agreement or tense) and complementizer. Finally, there are optional elements called adjuncts (e.g., modifiers). The phrase mark-

Deletion:

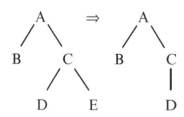

Substitution:

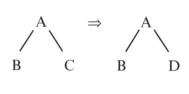

Adjunction:

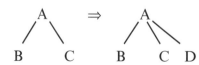

Permutation:

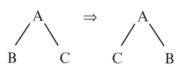

Linguistics. FIGURE 7. *Four General Types of Transformation*

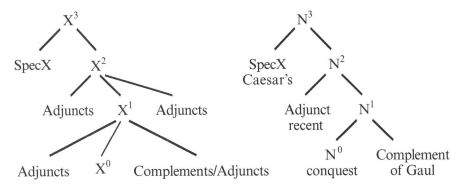

Linguistics. FIGURE 8. *X*-Bar Syntax

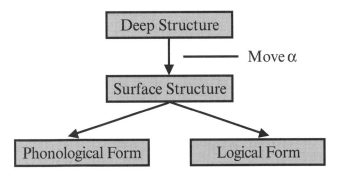

Linguistics. FIGURE 9. *Semantic Interpretation Using Chomsky's Principles and Parameters Model*

ers in Figure 8 illustrate the general format of *X*-Bar Syntax with an example, the noun phrase *Caesar's recent conquest of Gaul.*

The emphasis on universal grammar and explanatory adequacy led to a rigorous reduction of the transformational component, as it is more plausible to assume that the language acquisition device is equipped with only a few innate categories. The only basic type of transformation assumed is Move α, that is, free movement of constituents of some type α. Movement is constrained in its application by universal conditions of movement rules, for example, the subjacency condition, which blocks the movement of a constituent across two constituent borders ("barriers") like *NP* and *S*. Compare the following grammatical and ungrammatical (*) sentences:

> *The fact that* [S [NP *a critical review of his latest book* NP] *has just appeared* S] *is very worrying.*
> *The fact that* [S [NP *a critical review* _____ NP]

has just appeared of his latest book S] *is very worrying.*

> **The fact that* [S [NP *a critical review* _____ NP] *has just appeared* S] *is very worrying of his latest book.*

This reduction of the transformational component also led to a reevaluation of surface structure, which plays a more eminent role in PP than in Standard Theory. In PP, the component of semantic interpretation (logical form) starts from a modified and enriched surface (*see* Figure 9).

PP tries to formulate universal principles that are fixed via language-specific parameters. For example, PP assumes the following universal principle: every sentence has a subject. Even in the case of languages without an overt subject at the surface structure, an abstract subject pronoun ("pro") is postulated in deep structure, and the "pro drop" parameter distinguishes languages where the pronominal subject also appears at the surface structure (e.g., English, French, German, Dutch) from languages that (optionally) drop the pronominal subject at the surface structure (e.g., Latin, Italian, Spanish, Turkish): compare *It is raining/Il pleut/Es regnet/Het regent* and *Pluit/Piove/ Llueve/(Yağmur) yağiyor.*

In his recent minimalist program, Chomsky has continued his striving for explanatory adequacy. He, therefore, dropped both deep structure and surface structure as independent levels of linguistic description, thus arriving at a still more parsimonious theoretical apparatus. Lexical elements are directly taken from the lexicon and concatenated by transformational operations (Merge and Move), which are subject to general conditions of economy. At any point of the derivation, phrase markers can be directed to the phonological component via the operation Spell Out, which marks the beginning of phonological operations on the phrase marker (*see* Figure 10).

Pragmatics. From the late sixties onward, empirical problems and theoretical weaknesses of generative grammar caused a number of critical reactions, including the rise of sociolinguistics and ethnolinguistics, (e.g., the British sociologist Basil Bernstein and American linguists Dell Hymes, John Gumperz, and William Labov). Against the structuralist and generative idealizations and abstractions prevailing for many years, the processes of speech production and reception and the diversity of language use (that is, Saussure's *parole* and Chomsky's *performance*) increasingly began to attract the attention of linguists. This movement toward the study of communicative competence originated what is now called linguistic pragmatics, conversation analysis, text linguistics, or discourse analysis. Seen from a rhe-

torical perspective, these approaches are perhaps the most attractive linguistic theories developed in the twentieth century.

Philosophers Ludwig Wittgenstein, J. L. Austin (1911–1960), and John Searle emphasized the importance of ordinary language as an object of study. In his seminal book *Philosophical Investigations* (2d ed., Oxford, 1958), Wittgenstein systematically compared language to games of different types. Accordingly, he claimed that a language game is played according to rules for the use of linguistic expressions. The meaning of a word is defined as its use in a language. A language game always consists both of verbal and nonverbal activities. It is part of a complex activity, or, ultimately, a form of life. Austin and Searle continued this line of thought and tried to formulate explicit rules for the performance of speech acts. Moreover, they distinguished elementary communicative acts that are the building blocks of speech acts, like the utterance act (= the act of uttering linguistic expressions), the propositional act (= the act of referring to propositions, that is, semantic representations of true or false states of affairs), and the illocutionary act (the act of conveying the illocution, that is, the communicative role of a speech act, for example, statement, question, request, promise; cf. "Semantics" below). Direct realizations of speech acts with the help of corresponding sentence types (e.g., the realization of requests via imperative sentences like *Pass me the salt!*) were distinguished from indirect speech acts (e.g., the realization of requests via interrogative sentences like *Could you pass me the salt?*).

In linguistics, speech act theory was taken as a theoretical background both for the detailed de-

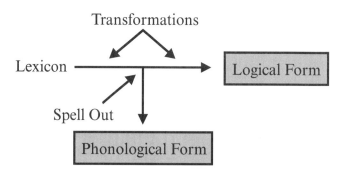

Linguistics. Figure 10. *Phonological Operations on the Phrase Marker*

scription of individual speech acts and their combination in spoken and written discourse (e.g., speech act sequences like question-answer or reproach-justification). Earlier typologies of speech acts were elaborated and the cross-linguistic realization of speech acts was taken on the agenda of linguistic research. Complex speech acts (or "discourse acts") such as "to describe" or "to interview" were distinguished from elementary speech acts such as "to state" or "to ask."

These developments in linguistic pragmatics have their predecessors in classical rhetoric. Indirect requests, reproaches, or statements are often treated as rhetorical questions. Speech act sequences are frequently described in ancient rhetoric within *stasis* theory; for example, reactions to reproaches, like justifications or excuses, closely correspond to categories in the *status qualitatis*—*remotio criminis, purgatio,* or *deprecatio.* [*See* Stasis.] Rhetorical school exercises (*progymnasmata*) dealt with complex speech acts such as describing or arguing. The main difference between these approaches and modern speech act theory lies in the fact that ancient rhetoric presented these sequences of speech acts as a kind of recipe or blueprint for the rhetorical practice, whereas linguistic pragmatics tries to deal with speech acts empirically.

This does not mean, however, that there are no recent approaches combining empirical and normative perspectives. In their book *Speech Acts in Argumentative Discussions* (1984), the Dutch linguists Frans H. Van Eemeren and Rob Grootendorst combined speech act theory and dialogue logic to develop Pragmadialectics, a framework that is designed to describe the speech acts occurring in argumentative discussions and also to provide a set of explicit normative rules for rational discussions.

A more descriptively oriented framework was developed by the French linguists Oswald Ducrot and Julien Anscombre, who adopted the ideas of the Russian linguist and literary theorist Mikhail Bakhtin (1895–1975) and combined them with a revival of Aristotelian topics. With Bakhtin, they assume that verbal utterances are inherently polyphonic, that is, they convey different opinions or "voices": the person actually uttering a speech act (*sujet parlant*) has to be distinguished from the responsible source of the utterance (*locuteur*) and

from the voice of the character (*énonciateur*) in a reported utterance that presents a perspective on the points of view referred to by the locutor. In their book *L'argumentation dans la langue* (Brussels, 1983), Anscombre and Ducrot described argumentative particles and the argumentative laws or *topoi* underlying their use. Later, they extended their approach to a general theory of meaning, which claims that the meaning of all linguistic expressions consists of a bundle of *topoi* allowing certain inferences to be drawn. [*See* Topics.] Therefore, language is seen as inherently argumentative.

At approximately the same time that speech act theory was developed, a parallel and partially overlapping linguistic movement extended the focus of linguistic analysis from the sentence level to the text or discourse level. Such linguists as the Dutch Teun Van Dijk, the Austrian Wolfgang Dressler, the Hungarian Janos Petöfi, the German Harald Weinrich, to name but a few, convincingly argued that (1) texts cannot be reduced to lists of single sentences; (2) sentences are connected within a text by a number of syntactic and semantic devices; (3) texts have global structures that underlie certain text genres such as narratives, discussions, or interviews (cf. "Text Grammar").

The linguistic study of discourse was strongly influenced by contributions from philosophy and sociology. In a highly influential paper on conversational logic, the British-American philosopher H. Paul Grice established a cooperative principle ("Make your conversational contribution such as is required, at the stage at which it occurs, by the accepted purpose or direction of the talk exchange in which you are engaged") with adjacent conversational maxims that echo Kant's categories of Quantity, Quality, Relation, and Manner (e.g., "Make your contribution as informative as is required" or "Do not say what you believe to be false" or "Be relevant" or "Be perspicuous"). Apparent violations of these maxims trigger conversational implicatures (cf. "Semantics" below). In their book *Relevance* (Oxford, 1986), the linguists Dan Sperber and Deirdre Wilson have tried to reduce the conversational maxims to one basic principle, namely, the principle of relevance, and have developed a theory of communication based on this principle.

American sociologists Harold Garfinkel, Harvey Sacks, Emanuel Schegloff, and Gail Jefferson, among others, have laid the foundations for an empirical analysis of everyday conversation. Their theoretical background is philosophical phenomenology (as developed by the German philosopher Edmund Husserl and the Austrian-American sociologist Alfred Schütz), which Garfinkel used to elaborate ethnomethodology, a framework for the study of rational and structured routines underlying everyday communication. Using authentic data like taped phone calls or private conversations, they established rules for the system of turn taking in everyday dialogues, described the mechanisms for opening and closing conversations, and also dealt with topic organization and repair mechanisms.

Another recent development within discourse analysis deals with politeness. Politeness phenomena were systematically described as a kind of interpersonal rhetoric by the British linguist Geoffrey Leech in his book *Principles of Pragmatics* (1983). Moreover, in their highly influential book *Politeness* (1987), the American anthropologist Penelope Brown and the British linguist Stephen Levinson developed the most comprehensive theory of politeness to date, including a detailed typology of politeness strategies, which contains many figures of speech from the rhetorical tradition. Leech, Brown, and Levinson started from Grice's framework, seeing politeness as a conscious deviation from maximal informativeness, which triggers various conversational implicatures. These implicatures have the function of protecting and enhancing the positive self-image or face of the interlocutors and of hedging potentially face-threatening acts via indirect ways of expression.

The development of text linguistics and discourse also contributed to the refinement of rhetorical concepts like the classical distinction between tropes, figures of diction, and figures of thought. In the seventies, a group of Belgian linguists and literary criticists (cf. Jacques Dubois et al., *Rhétorique générale,* Paris, 1970) defined all figures of speech as deviations from a kind of neutral "zero variety" of language and classified them according to the levels of language and the operations used for producing them. In his book *Textwissenschaft und Textanalyse* (Heidelberg, 1975), the German linguist and rhetorician Heinrich F.

Plett elaborated this approach, distinguishing deviation in the narrow sense (rule-violating deviation, e.g., figures of speech like *prosthesis,* tautology, ellipsis, *metathesis,* metaphor, irony) from rule-strengthening deviation (e.g., figures of speech like alliteration, anaphora, parallelism, synonymy). He cross-classified all rule-violating figures of speech according to the level of language (phonology, morphology, syntax, semantics, graphemics) and the operations involved (addition, subtraction, permutation, immutation). Although the definition of figures of speech as deviations can be criticized from a point of view that characterizes language as a creative activity and, hence, as inherently figurative, the standards of explicitness, demarcation, and consistency in these typologies are considerably higher than in traditional approaches.

The developments within linguistic pragmatics and discourse analysis sketched above encouraged several linguists to construct alternatives to structuralist and generative models. These functional frameworks include M. A. K. Halliday's Systemic Functional Grammar, Simon C. Dik's Functional Grammar, Konrad Ehlich's Functional Pragmatic Grammar, and W. A. Foley and R. D. Van Valin's Role and Reference Grammar. Further models could be classified as functional approaches in a broad sense: W. U. Dressler's Natural Phonology, Natural Morphology, and Natural Text Linguistics; W. Maierthaler's Natural Syntax; Eugenio Coseriu's Functional Syntax; Richard A. Hudson's Word Grammar; Igor A. Mel'cuk's Meaning-Text Model; and Ronald Langacker's Cognitive Grammar.

The main difference between functional and formal models does not involve the use (or renouncing the use) of an explicit formal metalanguage. On the contrary, many of the functional models just mentioned have been formalized and implemented for computer applications. Differing from approaches belonging to the formal paradigm, they share the assumption that syntax is not autonomous in relation to semantics or pragmatics and that linguistic form is determined by the communicative function of a linguistic unit.

Functional approaches have also been integrated into a framework called Critical Discourse Analysis, which has been designed for a critical analysis of the relation between power, ideology, and discourse by scholars like the English linguist Norman Fairclough, the Austrian Ruth Wodak, or the Dutch Teun A. Van Dijk. Some of Chomsky's political writings (e.g., Edward Herman and Noam Chomsky, *Manufacturing Consent. The Political Economy of the Mass Media,* New York, 1988) could also be included here, although Chomsky himself does not consider them as linguistic studies. A critical perspective concerning ethnocentric or anthropocentric views of the physical and social world is also typical for ecolinguistics, where concepts of ecology and linguistics are integrated in studies about the complex relationship between human behavior, nature, and language.

Levels and Structures of Language. According to the levels of language, the following subbranches of linguistics can be distinguished: the study of the production, transmission, and reception of sounds (phonetics); the description of minimal distinctive sound units (phonemes) and the sound patterns of specific languages (phonology); the study of the (minimal) meaningful units of grammar and vocabulary (morphology, lexicology); the study of the formal structure and the meaning of phrases and sentences (syntax); the study of texts and discourse (text grammar); and the overall study of meaning at various levels (semantics).

Phonetics and phonology. The phonetic description of language is concerned with the articulation, acoustic transmission, and reception of speech sounds. Modern phonetics has been advanced considerably by the development of a universally applicable system of phonetic transcription, the International Phonetic Alphabet (IPA). The IPA is based on the Latin alphabet, but uses many additional characters and diacritics. By these means, the sometimes enormous discrepancies between systems of writing and actual pronunciation can be bridged.

Most sounds occurring in all languages are produced by various manipulations of the pulmonic airstream as it passes through the speech organs: the larynx with the glottis and the vocal chords, the pharynx, the oral cavity with the tongue, the uvula, the velum, the palate, the alveoli, the teeth and the lips, and the nasal cavity. These manipulations result in the production of tones and noises. All sounds that are produced with vibrating vocal chords are voiced (e.g., [b,

d]), the rest are unvoiced (e.g., [p, t]). All sounds with a bifurcation of the airstream, which thus passes both through the oral and the nasal cavity, are nasal (e.g., nasal vowels like [õ, ã] or nasal consonants like [m, n]), those with the airstream passing only through the oral cavity are nonnasal. When the speech organs produce a full stop of the airstream, they are called plosives (e.g., [p, t]). If they produce a narrow passage, the resulting noises are called fricatives (e.g., [f, v]). Vowels (e.g [a, e]) are produced without such stops or passages of friction. Combinations of two vowels are called diphthongs (e.g., [aɪ, ɔɪ]). Some vowel-like consonants are called approximants (e.g., [ɹ, ɻ, l, j]).

Phonology is the study of the phonemes, which can be defined as the minimal distinctive sound units of a language. Their main function is to distinguish words that have different meanings and differ only in one sound, for example (British) English *bright* [bɹaɪt], and *bride* [bɹaɪd]. If the words differ only phonetically, but do not express different meanings, we are not dealing with phonemes, but with phonetic variants or allophones: compare the (British English) alveolar approximant in [bɹaɪt] with the retroflexive R-sound in (American English) [bɻaɪt].

While every language has an infinite number of allophones, the number of phonemes varies from about a dozen (e.g., in some Austronesian languages) to more than one hundred phonemes (e.g., in some Caucasian languages). Most languages, including English and French, have about twenty to forty phonemes.

Besides phonetic segments like vowels and consonants, the phonology of natural languages also contains accent and pitch as suprasegmental or prosodic units. Like segmental phonemes, accent can distinguish words: compare the noun *insert* ['ɪnsɜːt] and the verb *insert* [ɪn'sɜːt]. In tone languages like Chinese, pitch is used to distinguish words. For example, Mandarin Chinese has four different pitch levels/contours. Therefore, the Chinese segment [ma] can mean mother (1. tone: high), hemp (2. tone: rising), horse (3. tone: falling and rising), or scold (4. tone: falling). Finally, intonation can be used for distinguishing sentences with different meanings. In many languages, a rising intonation at the end of sentences is used to mark them as interrogative sentences.

In structuralist phonology, phonemes were first conceived of as the minimal units of linguistic analysis. Later developments led to their being analyzed as bundles of distinctive features like [consonantal], [nasal], [bilabial]. Roman Jakobson suggested a universal inventory of these features as a basis for describing all phonemes occurring in the languages of the world.

Generative phonology, as developed by Noam Chomsky and Morris Halle (*Sound Patterns of English*, New York, 1968) dismissed the phoneme as theoretical concept. Instead of phonemes, generative phonology uses a presumably universal set of distinctive features and tries to develop a system of phonological rules for deriving the actual phonetic articulation of a language from an underlying abstract phonological representation. The general format of phonological rules is $A \rightarrow B / X\_Y$ (read: phonological feature A is replaced by feature B if it occurs between X and Y). Later developments in phonology tried to overcome weaknesses of early generative phonology, such as the abstractness of the underlying phonological presentation, and concentrated on prosodic properties of syllables (cf. frameworks like Metrical Phonology, Autosegmental Phonology, or Natural Phonology).

Morphology. Morphology deals with morphemes, which are the minimal meaningful linguistic units. They can be divided into free (e.g., *tree*) and bound (e.g., *-s* in *tree-s*) morphemes. Words can be defined as minimal free forms (e.g., *tree, big, love*). Furthermore, morphemes can be divided into lexical morphemes (or lexemes) like English *hunt-* in *hunt-ed* and grammatical morphemes (cf. *-ed*). Typologically, languages can be classified as (1) inflexional or fusional languages (e.g., Latin, Russian, Navajo), where lexical and grammatical morphemes tend to fuse and where a great deal of phonetic variants of morphemes (allomorphs) exist; (2) agglutinative languages (e.g., Turkish, Hungarian, or Japanese), where lexical and grammatical morphemes tend to be clearly separated and only a few allomorphs exist; and (3) isolating languages (e.g., Chinese, Thai, Vietnamese, and, in most respects, also English), where few grammatical morphemes exist and grammatical relations are indicated by word order.

The number of lexemes is considerably higher than the number of grammatical morphemes (ranging from five to eight thousand in indigenous languages like the Papuan languages of New Guinea, three hundred to five hundred thousand in languages like English, French, Russian, Chinese, or Arabic, not including the lexemes used in languages for special purposes). Lexemes are listed in dictionaries and encyclopedias. In inflexional or agglutinative languages, their meaning is carried by the word stem; for example, Latin *lauda-* in *lauda-bat* (he or she praised) or Russian *pomn-* in *pomn-it* (he or she remembers). Lexical morphemes carry manifold meanings (cf. "Semantics" below).

The number of grammatical morphemes ranges from a few dozen in isolating languages to several hundred in inflexional languages. Grammatical morphemes carry meanings like past tense (e.g., *-ed* in *hunt-ed*). They are either suffixed to the stem (e.g., in many Indo-European languages) or prefixed to the stem (e.g., in Bantu languages like Swahili the prefix *–na-* indicates present tense: *ni-na-soma,* literally *I-Present-read,* that is *I am reading*) or infixed within the stem (e.g., in Native American languages like Lakota: [i'tʃu] *to take,* [-wa-] *I,* [i'watʃu], *I take*).

Political changes in a society, technological inventions, and also grammatical necessities constitute an urgent need for new words. Therefore, all languages have devices for coining new words. The main processes of word formation are composition and derivation. Composition combines two or more lexical morphemes (e.g., *back* and *ground* yield *background*). Derivation uses two or more affixes (prefixes or suffixes) for deriving new words (cf. *compute → computer → computation → computational*).

While structuralist morphology emphasized the description of differences between the morphological paradigms of languages, generative morphology tries to describe universal morphological patterns with principles taken over from syntax (e.g., *X*-bar principles, cf. "Generative Grammar"). As with phonology, further alternative frameworks emerged, for example, Natural Morphology, which emphasizes the distinction between marked and natural morphological processes and structures: the latter are more widespread, are earlier acquired by children, and are relatively more resistant to historical change or corruption caused by language disorders.

Syntax. The combination of morphemes or words to form constructions like phrases (word groups), clauses, or sentences is dealt with by syntax. For sentence grammars (e.g., most variants of structuralist and generative grammar), linguistic description ends at the sentence level. However, text linguistics and many functional frameworks include a text grammar.

For centuries, many linguists have tried hard to provide a satisfying definition of sentence. This involves many complex problems, for example, the distinction between complete and elliptic syntactic units (e.g., brief answers to questions like: A: *When does Paul come home?* B: *At five o'clock*), one-word utterances (e.g., *Yes, No, Thanks*), and the distinction between meaningful and odd, poetic or absurd sentences (cf. Chomsky's much-quoted example, *Colourless green ideas sleep furiously*). Following Bloomfield (1933), we can define the sentence as an independent linguistic unit, which is not embedded into a larger syntactic unit by virtue of any grammatical construction and add the important qualification that every sentence is used to express an illocution, that is, a communicative role (e.g., statement, question, request, promise, etc.).

From the point of view of text linguistics, however, this definition has to be relaxed because sentences are integrated into text structures with the help of grammatical constructions in a broader sense (cf. "Text Grammar"). Phrases are combinations of free morphemes (words), which are embedded into a larger syntactic unit by virtue of grammatical constructions.

Syntax has to deal with the form and the meaning (cf. "Semantics" below) of sentences, which can be described as to their (1) constituency, (2) dependency, (3) functional, and (4) transformational structure, and contemporary syntactic theories differ considerably so far as their view of these is concerned. Some approaches combine a treatment of constituents with a transformational component (e.g., Chomsky's generative grammar), others deny the necessity of a transformational component (e.g., Halliday's systemic functional grammar or Dik's functional grammar), all adherents of dependency grammar assume the necessity of a component of grammar that describes dependency structures, while some of them deny the necessity of a transformational component.

Here, however, a more pluralistic view will be adopted because all these approaches capture important properties of grammatical structures while none covers all of them.

From antiquity onward, sentences have been divided into constituents (e.g., clauses, phrases). But only in recent syntactic theory has a comprehensive set of syntactic tests been developed. These tests are designed to make our intuitions about syntactic structures, which are sometimes pretty vague, more precise and transparent. Here is an example: if our task is to determine whether *buy the book* should be assumed as a specific constituent (namely, a verb phrase) of the sentence *Mary will buy the book,* we can try the following tests: (1) insertion, (2) coordination, (3) deletion, (4) substitution. Insertion is not freely possible within constituents, hence the dubious grammaticality of *Mary will buy tomorrow the book.* Constituents can be coordinated: *Mary will buy the book and sell the car.* Constituents can be deleted given an appropriate context, for example, answers to questions: Speaker A: *Who will buy the book?* Speaker B: *Mary will.* Constituents can be substituted with a pronoun: *I will buy a book, and so will Mary.* But even these tests cannot "decide" definitively between competing divisions of constituents because tests can be applied in different ways (e.g., alternative coordinations like *Mary will buy a book and work hard*) and do not apply in the same way in different languages (e.g., the German counterpart of *Mary will buy tomorrow the book* is perfectly grammatical: *Maria wird das Buch morgen kaufen*).

Dependency grammar in its modern sense was first developed by the French linguist Lucien Tesnière (*Éléments de syntaxe structurale,* Paris, 1958). It was elaborated by linguists like the Germans Gerhard Helbig, Hans Jürgen Heringer, and Christian Lehmann, the Russian Igor Mel'cuk, and the British Richard Hudson. Dependency grammar is a framework where the sentence structure is conceived of as a hierarchy of governing and dependent elements. These are represented with stemmas or dependency trees (*see* Figure 11).

The head of a syntactic unit (e.g., a noun phrase) can be defined as the element which controls the external relations of the constituents of the unit (e.g., the noun *book* within a noun phrase like *the interesting book*). The predicate is

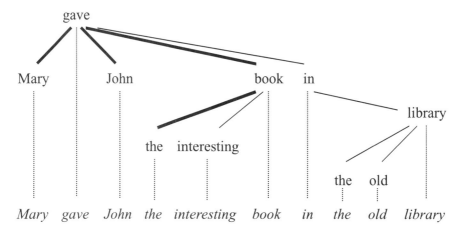

Linguistics. FIGURE 11. *Dependency Tree*. Bold lines indicate obligatory elements; uninterrupted lines show optional elements like the modifier *interesting* and the adjunct *in the old library*.

assigned the highest place in the syntactic hierarchy. The subject, the objects, and the subject/object complement are treated as arguments that are required by the valency of the predicate. Most dependency grammarians assume one place (X *sleeps*), two place (X *sees* Y), and three place (X *gives* Y Z) predicates. In contrast to traditional linguistics, but also to generative grammar, dependency grammar treats the subject as an argument that does not differ from other arguments in terms of syntactic hierarchy. Adjuncts (also called satellites) and modifiers are not required by the valency and can be freely added or deleted.

In functional grammar, the functions of constituents are the basic elements of linguistic description. More specifically, in Dik's Functional Grammar, semantic, syntactic, and pragmatic functions are treated in separate components of the overall grammatical model. Within the semantic structures, which are assumed to underlie the clauses and sentences of a language, predicates (e.g., *give*) open up predicate frames that require a set of terms (arguments) having semantic functions, for example, Agent (the entity controlling an action), Recipient (the entity into whose possession something is transferred), and Goal (the entity affected or effected by some agent) in the sentence: *Mary*$_{Ag}$ *gave John*$_{Rec}$ *the book*$_{Go}$. Predicates and arguments together designate some state of affairs. Syntactic functions like Subject underline a certain perspective from which

the state of affairs is seen. Active and passive constructions are used for assigning the subject function according to the prevailing perspective; for example, an Agent, a Recipient, or a Goal perspective:

> *Mary*$_{AgSubj}$ *gave John*$_{Rec}$ *the book*$_{Go}$.
> *John*$_{RecSubj}$ *was given the book*$_{Go}$ *by Mary*$_{Ag}$.
> *The book*$_{GoSubj}$ *was given by Mary*$_{Ag}$ *to John*$_{Rec}$.

Pragmatic functions specify the informational status of the constituents. More specifically, *topic* is the pragmatic function assigned to terms designating the things we talk about, which at the same time is often, but not always, old or contextually given information. *Focus* is the pragmatic function assigned to constituents designating the most important or salient parts of what we say about the topical things. Focus elements either provide new information or replace old information. In many languages, focus elements carry emphatic accent or are marked by particles, special constructions, or a special constituent order. For example, if somebody asks whether it was Jane who gave the book to John, the answer could be:

> *No, Mary*$_{Foc}$ *gave John the book.*
> *No, it was Mary*$_{Foc}$ *who gave John the book.*

Over the years, transformations have played different roles in components of generative grammar (cf. "Generative Grammar" for a more detailed presentation). From a rhetorical perspective, they can be conceived of as stylistic operations that can be used to transform syntactic structures of a certain type (phrases, sentences) into other structures having slightly different aesthetic or persuasive functions. Active sentences, for example, can be transformed into passive sentences lacking an agent constituent if the persuasive goal of the speaker/writer is the concealment or backgrounding of the agent (compare *The police killed some demonstrators* with *Some demonstrators were killed*).

Text grammar. Sentences are usually not simply listed in a well-formed text. Grammatical means for creating a well-formed text aim at the cohesion of a text, semantic means try to establish the coherence of a text. A text or discourse can be defined as a cohesive and coherent message, which is formulated in such a way that it adequately fulfills its communicative purpose in a given communicative context. Many phenomena of text grammar have been studied already by classical rhetoric as means of composition or as figures of speech (e.g., *anaphora*, parallelism, *gradatio*). A short list follows of syntactic and semantic phenomena relevant for the cohesion, coherence, and adequacy of a text:

- Anaphoric and cataphoric expressions: repetition of lexical units at the beginning or the end of phrases, clauses or sentences; chains of synonyms, hyponyms, or antonyms (cf. following section on semantics); personal and demonstrative pronouns pointing backward and foreward; ellipsis of contextually given elements).
- Sentence connectives (also called disjuncts or discourse markers) like *and, but, both . . . and, on the one hand . . . on the other hand, furthermore.*
- Grammatical means for distinguishing given or background information (topic, theme) and new or foreground information (comment, focus, theme). This includes means for introducing a new topic at the beginning of a text, which then becomes the discourse topic, a paragraph topic, or a sentence topic.
- The distribution of tenses within a text, which can be used to structure passages of a complex narrative; for example, to foreground and background certain events.

- Lexical, syntactic, and intonational means for starting, maintaining, or closing a conversation (greeting formulas, particles, idioms etc.).
- Rules for turn taking in conversations (e.g., self-selection and other-selection, repair and correction phenomena) and conventionalized speech act sequences (e.g., question-answer, offer-acceptance, argument-counterargument).

Semantics. The semantics of linguistic units like morphemes, words, phrases, clauses, sentences, and texts cannot be described in isolation because the respective units are parts of semantic networks at all levels of description. To begin at the lowest level, lexical morphemes (lexemes) are parts of lexical fields. Lexical fields can be defined as a set of lexemes that together constitute a division of a semantic continuum (e.g., temperature) into smaller sections (e.g., *hot, warm, tepid/lukewarm, cool, cold, freezing*). The meaning of the lexemes can be conceived of as a bundle of semantic features (or semes, represented within square brackets). The lexemes in a field share some general semantic properties, for example, the features [member of the family], [human being] in the case of the lexical field "family members," but differ from each other according to some more specific features, for example, [brother of the mother or the father] versus [sister of the mother or the father] in the case of the English lexemes *uncle* and *aunt* and the corresponding French (*oncle, tante*) or German (*Onkel, Tante*) lexemes. Lexical fields often differ from one language to the other. For example, the lexical field "family members" in Latin distinguishes [brother of the mother] *avunculus* from [brother of the father] *patruus* (the same holds for languages like Arabic and Turkish).

Within a lexical field, lexemes are connected via semantic relations like synonymy, polysemy/homonymy, antonymy, hyponymy. Synonymy in the strict sense would mean that two or more lexemes are semantically fully equivalent and can be exchanged in all contexts in which they occur. This, however, is hardly ever the case because even lexemes that are closely related in semantic terms differ as to stylistic or grammatical properties. For example, English synonyms like (1) *eye doctor* and *oculist* or (2) *urinate* and *piss* or (3) *pretty* and *handsome* differ because they either (1) belong to a more technical or more common section of the vocabulary; (2) represent a more refined or a more vulgar speech style; or (3) cannot be collocated with nouns like *man, woman, boy, girl* in exactly the same way. Polysemy and homonymy are cases of ambiguity, where one form expresses two or more meanings. In the case of polysemy, the different senses can be described as context-specific variants of a more general meaning. The English noun *wing,* for example, at a general level is [a part stretching out at the side]. More specifically, it can be the wing of a bird, building, or army. In the case of homonymy, a word has two completely different meanings that cannot be reduced to one more general meaning (e.g., the English noun *pupil,* which conveys either the meaning [a person who is learning] or [a circular opening in the center of the eye]).

Antonymy is a semantic relation between lexemes that have the same semantic properties, but differ in one pair of opposite semantic features: for example, the English nouns *man* and *woman* share the features [human being] and [adult], but differ in the opposite features [male] versus [female]. The same holds for adjectives like *long* and *short,* verbs like *buy* and *sell,* and adverbs like *left* and *right.* Hyponymy is the semantic relation connecting lexemes with a more general meaning, which have fewer semantic features, and lexemes with a more specific meaning, which have additional semantic features. Two examples illustrate the point well: the English nouns *man,* which contains the features [human being], [male], [adult], and *bachelor,* with the additional feature [unmarried]; or the verbs *follow* and *chase:* the first verb contains the features [activity], [movement], [adjusted to the changes in position of some entity *X*]; the latter has the additional features [at high speed], [with the intention to catch *X*].

At the phrase level, semantics has to deal with the semantic distribution of lexical units. Predicates require that their arguments have appropriate semantic features. Accordingly, they differ as to their semantic valency or selection restrictions. Verbs like *eat,* for example, require human beings or animals as their subjects, which at the same time must be able to fulfill the semantic role of the agent (e.g., *The boy ate the hamburger* or *Cats eat mice*). However, exceptions occur whenever

new metaphors are created or dead metaphors (and other figures of speech like metonymy) are integrated into the lexicon of a language (cf. *Rust eats iron*). Semantic valency is language-specific. Thus, the English verbs *eat* and *drink* can describe the respective activities of both human beings and animals, whereas the German verbs *essen* and *trinken* are normally asserted of people and *fressen/saufen* are used for animals—at least, in default cases.

At the sentence level, several layers of meaning have to be distinguished: the core meaning of sentences consists of an illocution or communicative purpose and most of the time also a proposition, that is, a representation of a (true or false) state of affairs. For example, the sentence *I will visit you tomorrow at 5 PM,* if intended as a promise, expresses the commitment of the speaker to come to the hearer's place next day, together with the expectation that this news is welcomed by the hearer. Moreover, it expresses the proposition that at a certain point in time in the future, a certain state of affairs will be true, namely, the arrival of the speaker at the hearer's place.

Beside their core meaning, sentences convey implications (or, alternatively, entailments) and presuppositions, which belong to the implicit meaning of sentences, but can be inferred automatically from what has been said or written explicitly. Normally, implications and presuppositions cannot be denied without committing the basic logical mistake of self-contradiction. For example, you cannot utter the sentence *I will visit you tomorrow at 5 PM* and at the same time deny its implication *I will come to your place at a certain point of time in the future* without contradicting yourself. Implications differ from presuppositions insofar as they are canceled under negation whereas presuppositions remain constant under negation. For example, *I will visit you tomorrow at 5 PM* entails *I will go to the hearer's place.* But the negated sentence *I will not visit you tomorrow at 5 PM* does not entail *I will go to the hearer's place.* However, both the affirmative and the negative version presuppose *I exist and you exist,* that is, the existence of both the speaker and the hearer.

A last layer of sentence meaning concerns conversational implicatures (e.g., allusions, irony, *hyperbolē,* understatement). These are peripheral parts of the implicit meaning of sentences that are defeasible, that is, they can usually be canceled without contradiction. The speaker can use the sentence *I will visit you tomorrow at 5 PM* conversationally implying that he or she expects to be served something, for example, a cup of tea and cookies. If the hearer complains about having to prepare tea and cookies, the speaker could reply *I only said that I wanted to visit you, I did not say that you have to prepare anything.*

At the text level, the meaning of the individual sentences is embedded into global semantic structures of texts (macrostructures): the general theme or meaning of a text is a highly condensed summary of the meaning of the paragraphs and chapters of written texts or the turns and stages of dialogues. Similarly, these paragraphs or turns can be conceived of as a summary or condensation of the specific meanings of single sentences. Moreover, texts of different types or genres have a characteristic structure (superstructures): narrative texts usually contain a plot with a setting, one or more episodes with a complication, a solution, and an evaluation of the plot. Argumentative texts contain an opening stage where a conflict of opinions arises, a confrontation stage with an explication of the contrasting points of view, an argumentation stage with pro and contra arguments, and, finally, a concluding stage. [*See* Arrangement, *article on* Traditional arrangement.] These concepts take up and generalize attempts in classical rhetoric to classify the standard parts of a (forensic) speech: introduction, narration, argumentation, closing statements.

One of the most difficult problems of linguistic semantics is the distinction of language-specific meaning and reference; that is, the relation between linguistic units and the objects and entities of the extralinguistic world. Reference theory describes different types of reference; for example, reference to individuals or specific sets of individuals or nonspecific sets of individuals: compare names like *Napoleon* or noun phrases with definite or indefinite articles like *a man, the man,* or *the man over there* and generic reference in sentences expressing commonsense statements like *Tigers are dangerous.*

Some twentieth-century linguists and philosophers like Bertrand Russell, Willard Van Orman Quine, and Saul Kripke maintain that linguistic description can and should get rid of the notori-

ously vague concept of meaning and replace it by reference. The English philosopher Hilary Putnam argued that what is called the linguistic meaning of expressions referring to natural substances like *water* is nothing else than a collection of stereotypes of lay speakers (e.g., colorless, transparent, tasteless, thirst-quenching liquid), which is always open to historical change and falsification. The only stable element is reference as described by science (e.g., H_2O).

Ludwig Wittgenstein and other philosophers have claimed that a description of meaning should describe the rules for the use of linguistic utterances in some contexts. A use theory of meaning is a challenge both for structural semantics and for reference theory, because it questions not only the existence of abstract meanings out of context but also the concept of a reference to extralinguistic objects independent of rules of usage of different social groups. Similarly, text linguists claimed that there is no abstract word or sentence meaning out of context and that the text level is the only level where meaning can be described in a way that makes sense.

The theoretical assumptions of both structural semantics and reference theory have also been challenged by recent developments in cognitive psychology leading to the prototype theory of meaning. Experiments by the American psychologist Eleanor Rosch have shown that native speakers differ in their speed of recognition and categorization of images showing various members of a category. This cannot be explained by theoretical approaches trying to provide neat definitions of meaning or reference, which list necessary and sufficient conditions of category membership. First, there are representatives of categories that are experienced as more prototypical than others (e.g., a robin is categorized as a more typical bird than an ostrich or a penguin). Second, the borderlines between categories are not so clear-cut as neat definitions would suggest. There are fuzzy borderlines between prototypical and peripheral members of categories designated by expressions like *cup, mug,* or *bowl.*

Prototype theory is in line with other trends in contemporary semantics and discourse analysis that adopt a cognitive perspective. To explain the impressive speed of the production and interpretation of spoken discourse, the existence of mental models (or, alternatively, frames, scripts, plans, schemas) has been assumed. These models organize linguistic and encyclopedic knowledge and thus provide patterns for the production and comprehension of discourse, which make it much easier to encode or decode complex information. Similarly, it has been assumed that knowledge about global structures of discourse, for example, superstructures of texts like narratives, discussions, or interviews, further the production and comprehension of discourse. Moreover, psycholinguistic experiments have shown that stylistic patterns (e.g., figures of speech) enhance our ability to recall even minute formal details of discourse structure, such as the phonological or morphological shape of constituents, although we normally store only the semantic content of a text in long-term memory (cf. Willem Levelt, *Speaking. From Intention to Articulation,* Cambridge, Mass., 1989; Teun A. Van Dijk and Walter Kintsch, *Strategies of Discourse Comprehension,* New York, 1983). [*See* Memory.]

Recently, the important cognitive role of metaphor (and other figures of speech like metonymy) has been highlighted by the American linguist George Lakoff and the American philosopher Mark Johnson, who wrote the highly influential book *Metaphors We Live By* (Chicago, 1980). [*See* Metaphor.] Inspired by philosophers such as I. A. Richards, Max Black, and Paul Ricoeur, they have shown that metaphor is not merely an ornament or an aesthetic device, but is cognitively basic and shapes our cognition and view of reality. Moreover, metaphors form networks that portray abstract concepts like "argument" or emotions like "love" or "anger" on the basis of our everyday bodily experiences; for example, fights (e.g., *Her arguments gained ground, He shot down their ideas*), boiling liquids in containers (e.g., *You make my blood boil*), fire (e.g., *She was doing a slow burn*).

Cognitive approaches also deal with the complex problem of modelling processes of human thinking like representing complex states of affairs or drawing inferences. Practical outcomes of these studies are models of artificial intelligence, which can be implemented as computer programs (e.g., expert systems or simulations of human communication).

Many of the problems of semantics mentioned above call for a more comprehensive view from which language is described. If pragmatics is not so much conceived of as a further component of linguistic description, but rather as a general cognitive, social, and cultural perspective on linguistic phenomena in relation to their usage, as suggested by the Belgian linguist Jef Verschueren in his book *Understanding Pragmatics* (London, 1999), linguistic pragmatics could solve at least some of the problems of semantic description mentioned above.

[*See also* Comparative rhetoric; *and* Speech acts, utterances as.]

BIBLIOGRAPHY

Austin, John L. *How to Do Things with Words.* Oxford, 1962. A classic treatise on speech act theory. Austin claims that speaking is a kind of action that expresses different communicative roles ("illocutions").

Bakhtin, Mikhail. *The Dialogic Imagination.* Austin, Tex., 1981. Edited by Michael Holquist; translated by Caryl Emerson and Michael Holquist. First published in Russian, 1975. A long time before the introduction of pragmatics and discourse analysis into linguistics, Bakhtin claimed that language is inherently dialogic.

Beaugrande, Alain de, and Wolfgang U. Dressler. *Introduction to Text Linguistics.* London, 1981. An introduction into discourse analysis that stresses the cognitive perspective; that is, the mental processes and models underlying the production and interpretation of written and spoken texts.

Bloomfield, Leonard. *Language.* New York, 1933. One of the best general introductions to linguistics ever written. Bloomfield introduced high standards of explicitness and provided many classical definitions of linguistic units like *word, phrase, sentence.* However, his strong attachment to behaviorism and the resulting antimentalism today is outdated and only historically interesting.

Bright, William, ed. *International Encyclopedia of Linguistics.* 4 vols. Oxford, 1992. This encyclopedia contains a comprehensive treatment of the basic concepts of linguistics and also provides overviews on the structure and history of most languages of the world.

Brown, Penelope, and Stephen Levinson. *Politeness.* Cambridge, U.K., 1987. The most comprehensive theory of politeness, based on empirical data from a variety of genetically unrelated languages and widely discussed ever since its publication. The most important criticism concerns the fact that politeness is mainly seen as a means for protecting the "face" of speakers/hearers from "face-threatening acts."

Chomsky, Noam. *The Minimalist Program.* Cambridge, Mass., 1995. A recent revision of generative grammar that seeks to simplify the model, thus trying to retain only the minimal apparatus that is necessary for explaining the innate language acquisition device.

Crystal, David. *Cambridge Encyclopedia of Linguistics.* Cambridge, U.K., 1987. A clear and comprehensive overview dealing with all relevant aspects of language and its use in communication.

Dik, Simon C. *The Theory of Functional Grammar.* 2 vols. Edited by Kees Hengeveld. Berlin, 1997. One of the most elaborate functional approaches in contemporary linguistics, which unites formal rigor with an application to a wide range of languages; the text level, however, so far has received less attention than the sentence level.

Eemeren, Frans H. van, and Rob Grootendorst. *Speech Acts in Argumentative Discussions.* Dordrecht, The Netherlands, 1984. A systematic overview of the speech acts typically occurring in argumentative discussions and at the same time a normative attempt to formulate explicit rules for the rational resolution of conflicts of opinions.

Grice, H. Paul. "The Logic of Conversation." In *Speech Acts.* Edited by P. Cole and J. L. Morgan, pp. 41–58. Chicago, 1975. A classic paper on the implicit layers of meaning of utterances, which is based on the assumption of a cooperative principle and a set of maxims triggering conversational implicatures.

Halliday, M. A. K. *An Introduction to Functional Grammar.* 2d rev. ed. London, 1994. One of the most comprehensive functional approaches in contemporary linguistics, with a special emphasis on the description of the text level and an application to the critical analysis of ideological aspects of texts.

Lakoff, George. *Women, Fire and Dangerous Things.* Chicago, 1987. A reconstruction of the important cognitive functions of metaphor, metonymy, and other figures of speech with the help of concepts like mental models and prototype theory.

Leech, Geoffrey. *Principles of Pragmatics.* London, 1983. An introduction to pragmatics containing an important chapter on politeness, which is characterized as an "interpersonal rhetoric."

Sapir, Edward. *Selected Writings.* Edited by David G. Mandelbaum. Berkeley, 1968. Sapir greatly contributed to the description of Native American languages and, in several papers of this collection, described the close interrelations between language, culture, and thought.

Searle, John. *Speech Acts.* Cambridge, U.K., 1969. In this highly influential book, Searle further develops Austin's ideas on speech act theory and formulates explicit rules for the performance of speech acts, without, however, basing his analysis on authentic empirical data and neglecting the discourse level.

Whorf, Benjamin L. *Language, Thought and Reality.* Edited by John B. Carroll. Cambridge, Mass., 1956. A collection of papers containing Whorf's widely discussed and highly controversial hypothesis that genetically unrelated languages with very different structures express incommensurable worldviews ("linguistic relativity principle").

Online Resources

"The Human-Languages Page." *http://www.june29.com/HLP/* This Web site is maintained by its creator Tyler Chamber and contains more than eighteen hundred resources covering about one hundred languages.

"Ethnologue. Languages of the World." 13th ed. Edited by Barbara F. Grimes. 1996. *http://www.sil.org/ethnologue/ethnologue.html.* The Ethnologue contains short descriptions, maps, and language family trees of more than six thousand languages and is also available on CD-ROM.

"The Linguist List." Eastern Michigan University/Wayne State University. *http://www.emich.edu/~linguist/* This Web site offers comprehensive information about linguistics: academic institutions, conferences, publications, languages, and computer support.

"Language, Linguistics, Speech." Haskins Laboratories. *http://www.haskins.yale.edu/haskins/MISC/DEST/language.html.* A collection of links to institutions dealing with acoustic phonetics, speech analysis, synthesis, and computational linguistics.

"Noam Chomsky Home page." MIT Linguistics Faculty. *http://web.mit.edu/linguistics/www/chomsky.home.html.* The home page of the founder of generative grammar. Noam Chomsky is one of the most distinguished twentieth-century linguists.

—MANFRED KIENPOINTNER

LITERARY CRITICISM. *See* Classical rhetoric; Criticism; Imitation; *and* Renaissance rhetoric, *article on* Rhetoric in Renaissance language and literature.

LITOTĒS (Lat. *diminutio, extenuatio*), or "the Moderatour" (Puttenham, *The Arte of English Poesie*, 1589, p. 184), is a metasememe that substitutes what is meant by denying its semantic opposite. The effect is a contextually appropriate understatement. "We are not amused," from a monarch means strong disapproval. *Litotēs* can downplay the pride taken in an achievement when a speaker makes sure that his or her audience is "not unaware" of the speaker's considerable merits, yet it need not take precisely this syntactic form. There seems to be, as can be inferred from the discussion of Dubois et al. (*Rhétorique Générale,* Paris, 1970), a kind of psychological *litotēs*; for example, a lady's hairstyle described as "owing little to nature" signals that the hairstyle is "highly indebted to her hairdresser's art."

[*See also* Figures of speech; *and* Style.]

— HEINER PETERS

LOGIC has been studied and taught as a separate discipline since at least the time of Aristotle (384–322 BCE), and logic manuals were available in the ancient Greek and Indian worlds. It was one of the subjects (along with grammar and rhetoric) taught as the *trivium* in medieval European universities, and it has been taught in Chinese and Tibetan Buddhist monasteries and other sites of formalized debate. It is so valued as a medium for philosophical analysis that it is required of philosophy students in many colleges today, and it is so esteemed as a critical thinking tool that many nonphilosophy students are required to take it. [*See* Trivium.]

The classroom (or study) is a setting that plays an important role in logic because examples can be devised there that manifest certain logical relations or properties:

Either Jones is ill or Smith is away.
Smith is not away.
So, Jones is ill.

This example is typical of logic illustrations in that no one is being quoted and no invitation is being given to imagine anyone to be quoted.

What logicians say about this example seems puzzling. Most questionable, perhaps, is the idea that merely by writing out a set of sentences (and using a conclusion indicator "so"), an "inference" or "argument" is generated. Also questionable is that it passes logical muster without any consideration of when it might actually be made. In fact, the logical correctness or *validity* of the so-called argument is unrelated to the content or subject matter, but is dependent entirely on its form:

Either *p* or *q;*
not *q.*
So, *p.*

That a premise of an argument with this form may be true or false (or unwarranted) is a nonlogical matter (unless it is a logical tautology or a contradiction). What is logical is the relationship between premises and conclusion, and the relationship of validity is so strong that it guarantees that the argument will never be refuted by the construction of another argument of the same form with true premises and a false conclusion. [*See* Syllogism.]

Also puzzling is the consensus that what *p* or *q* represents admits of truth or falsity, even though there is disagreement over whether what is true or false is a sentence, statement, or proposition. It is puzzling because any question, for example, about whether it really is true that either Jones is away or Smith is ill, would have to be based on the misconception that someone or something is being quoted.

Moreover, although it is easy to imagine a context for the example where there is something to be true or false, it is much more difficult to imagine that an inference is being given, let alone one that is valid. Suppose that a group of friends have a basketball team, but have trouble getting everyone to City League games. "Are we going to have enough players for the game?" David asks. "I doubt it." Fred replies. "It is the same story every game. Either Jones is ill or Smith is away." He is expressing frustration about getting Smith and Jones to the same game, not offering assurance that the problem is going to continue. So, even if others share his frustration and so concede that what he is saying is true, nevertheless when David says, "Smith is not away. I just saw him a few blocks from here," Fred is not going to respond by saying, "Well, then, Jones must be ill," unless he is making a cynical joke.

These puzzles about the consensus concerning the logic of the example can be explained away by considering what may be referred to as the "rhetoric" of the example. The rhetoric of the person who is being quoted cannot be considered, because no one is being quoted. Nevertheless, by acknowledging that the example is being devised for the logic classroom, we can consider what is to be done with the example, namely, that certain operations are to be performed in connection with it on the blackboard or on paper. Each premise or the conclusion turns out to be an instruction on how to operate with certain classroom contingencies or possibilities; for example, the first premise rules out the possibility when making determinations, for example, about validity or implication, of neither Jones being ill nor Smith being away.

Given this understanding of the rhetoric of the so-called inference, it is easy to see how it could be logically correct independent of its subject matter. The explanation is that it does not really have a subject matter, that the references to the whereabouts of Jones and Smith really are references to classroom contingencies, where all that matters is that it be possible to identify the same contingencies when they appear in the course of the inference or implication. This understanding also makes clear that what the letters p and q represent are not true or false, but are assigned truth values or acquire them under an assignment to a *schēma* or *schēmata*, when determining, for example, whether two *schēmata* are equivalent or whether one implies the other. What seemed puzzling—namely, how there is anything to be true or false in connection with what is devised to serve as an illustration or exercise—no longer is puzzling once it is realized that we are talking only about assignments of truth values.

A rhetorical analysis of the subject matter also helps to explain, what seems paradoxical, that each of the following is considered valid:

Not p. So, if p then q.
q. So, if p then q.

Any hint of paradox can be dispelled by making explicit the fact that each such "inference" is understood to apply to the classroom contingencies marked by p and q. Given that the contingency p does not obtain, or that q does obtain, it is impossible for p to obtain and q not to obtain. That is all there is to the claim that each of these argument forms is valid.

Categorical Logic was introduced by Aristotle before the systematic treatment by the Stoics of Propositional Logic, which deals with an inference like the one we have been discussing. The variables in Categorical Logic represent collections of things, categories, or classes. They may also represent individuals. For example,

All S is P.
x is not P.
So, x is not S.

S and P represent classes, whereas x stands for a certain individual. That an inference is of this valid form depends on a certain understanding of a problem like the following:

All people who own houses pay a house tax.
Boima does not pay a house tax.
Does he own a house?

The answer, that Boima does not own a house, follows from the premises of the problem because of the validity of the argument form cited above, where S represents "houseowners"; P represents "house taxpayers" and x represents "Boima."

Many unschooled Liberian subjects whose responses to the problem are reported by Scribner answered differently. For example:

Boima does own a house.
But he is exempted from paying a house tax because he is a tax collector.

The subject who gave this answer did not realize that to solve the problem he did not need to think about how taxes are actually collected, or that for purposes of answering the question the information given in the statement of the problem rules out the possibility that someone is a member of the class *houseowner* but is not of a member of the class *housetaxpayer*. Outside of the context in which the problem is being posed, a stamp collection, for example, would not be referred to as a "class," "category," or "set." But, so far as the solution of the logic problem is concerned, it does not matter which of these words are used because the collection in question is to be understood as a mathematician would understand it.

Andrea Nye (1990) is one of the few who analyzes the rhetoric of logicians. She motivates her analysis by explaining how distracting she found it as a student to come upon the example: "Either Jones is ill or Smith is away" in Willard V. Quine's text (1982). "Was Jones often ill?" she wanted to ask. "Not ill today for once? And why? And Smith so often gone. Where?" However, her focus is on what their choice of examples and expressive language reveal about the underlying longings and desires of male philosopher-logicians, like Plato,

Aristotle, the Stoics, or Gottlob Frege, and not on the rhetoric of the logic that they do develop.

Rather than be concerned about that rhetoric, logic, especially in the twentieth century, developed in response to problems or questions internal to the subject. Certain logical forms were studied, and methods of proof and disproof were developed. The discovery of these methods prompted logicians to ask whether the methods are sufficient to show that any valid form is valid or to determine whether or not it is valid. Aristotle's methods, for example, turn out to be sufficient for his purposes, but only because he confined his attention to a limited number of forms. The Stoics, by contrast, were unable to study all of the possible argument forms that interested them because they lacked the conceptual apparatus to enable them to ask what the possible argument forms are that their methods should be able to show as valid (or not valid). When the concept of a truth function, whose values are determined by the values of its components, was introduced, it became possible to answer this question. This led to the development of other mathematical techniques, such as those involving the use of truth tables, which made it feasible to answer decisively questions about validity, implication, and other logical relations and properties.

The mathematization of logic came to dominate twentieth-century developments. The authority of this approach was reinforced by some of its results, even when they concerned what could not be proven. One of these is a discovery about the First-Order Predicate Calculus, which incorporates Propositional Logic into Categorical Logic, and extends the latter by including relations, as well as universal and existential quantifiers, in a variety of combinations. The discovery is that even though there are methods of proof for validity of *schēmata* in the First-Order Calculus that are complete, in that everything valid can be shown to be valid, and sound, in that nothing invalid can be shown to be valid, nevertheless no such method could decisively determine whether or not any schema in the Calculus is valid.

An especial focus of the mathematization of logic has been the development of the concept of a formal system as a medium for revealing the logic of a mathematical system. The guiding principle behind this project is that every step in a proof requires explicit authorization: a theorem is what can be produced from certain initial formulas or axioms by means of transformation rules. However, Kurt Gödel (1906–1978) discovered that no such system, suitably defined, could be designed for Elementary Number Theory that would be complete if it was consistent, a proof that was so imaginative and ingenious, a result so unexpected, that the authority of mathematical logic was reinforced rather than undermined.

Although the questions internal to logic are of interest and important in their own right, some explanation is needed for why many logicians have neglected or ignored questions about the rhetoric of their subject matter. Part of the explanation has to do with the separation of logic from rhetoric. These disciplines had a common origin in some societies where debating and public speaking were important practices. Logic began to detach itself from rhetoric when philosophers started to give arguments, and where the arguments themselves came to be discussed and criticized. The ancient Chinese philosophers, for example, did not place the same emphasis on argument as did the ancient Greeks, and logic, as a discipline in its own right, did not take hold there. This may have been because philosophers like the later Mohists, who had a sufficient interest in argument to formulate logical principles and to catalog (as did Xunzi, a Confucian) the fallacies that are the hazards of philosophical disputation, were not treated as important in Chinese culture. [*See* Chinese rhetoric.] However, logic did take hold where argument was treated as interesting in its own right, in ancient Greece and India, in the medieval European and Arab world, and in the Western world from the Renaissance until today. [*See* Argumentation.]

Another factor in the separation of logic from rhetoric was the Platonic attack on the teaching of rhetoric in the *Gorgias* on the grounds that the merits of an argument have nothing to do with whether it commands the adherence of its audience. This attack still seems effective to logicians because of their view that the logical merit of an argument is a function only of whether the premises provide adequate support for the conclusion (or whether another argument of the same form is obviously unacceptable). However, rhetorical considerations are of critical importance when it comes to determining what is being argued or how responsive it is to what is at issue in the argument. Moreover, what is being argued only becomes clear(er) in the course of a series of dialectical exchanges. [*See* Dialectic.] So, the separation of logic from rhetoric is encouraged by a certain conception of argument that seems to lead to the neglect of considerations that are important when it comes to the critical reading or interpretation of an argument.

Another factor in the development of logic and its separation from rhetoric is the reliance on mathematics as a model for reasoning and argument. The ideal of certainty was one consequence of the reliance on this model. Another was the presumption of neutrality by the logician. Ironically, Plato's most characteristic way of arguing, the method of *division,* required an interlocutor who would identify to which of two categories, for example, the rhetorician belongs, in order to show, as Socrates purports to show in the *Sophist,* that the rhetorician hooks young people for profit. Although Aristotle treated the syllogistic and rhetoric as part of the same science of reasoning, nevertheless he was also responsible for making possible a sharp distinction between them. This is because, with his concept of *demonstration* or *proof* that Aristotle applied to the syllogistic, the services of the interlocutor no longer prove necessary, which means that logicians are freed from participation in the dialectic whose arguments they are critically examining. Logicians need only to determine what follows from certain premises: the inferences that they study are like geometric demonstrations in that who is making them or to whom they are made is considered irrelevant.

Philosophical debate seems especially amenable to treatment by logic, when the claims of philosophers are treated as moves in a game the object of which is to catch one of the debaters in a contradiction or in any of a host of other missteps. However, when it is acknowledged that philosophers say what they do in response to what other philosophers have said, or when it is questioned whether or when the claims made in setting up or solving a philosophical problem

would actually be made, then, as Henry W. Johnstone (1953) has argued, there should be resistance to the treatment of the argument as a contextless sequence of premises and conclusion.

Most logicians believe that logic is not limited in its application either to the artificial constructs of the classroom or to philosophical discourse. This is because they think that any reasoning or rhetoric is to be counted as a case where an argument is being given only if certain conditions are satisfied: one is that a position is being taken by the arguer, a position that can be formulated as a declarative sentence, that is, the conclusion; the other is that that position be given support by the arguer, support that also can be formulated as one or more declarative sentences, that is, as the premises. Typically, the argument, when reformulated as a premises–conclusion sequence, is an enthymeme, and it is incumbent on the argument paraphraser to supply its missing premises (or conclusion), a notoriously difficult task. [*See* Enthymeme.]

The requirement that reasoning or rhetoric be reconstructed as a premises–conclusion sequence also has the effect of deflecting attention from rhetorical considerations. Not only are paraphrasers substituting their voices for that of the *rhētōr,* but even if the *rhētōr*'s words are somehow retained, the argument ceases to have a rhetorical context. Logic assumes that if any features of that context are relevant to the determination of what is being argued then they can be included in the rephrasal of the argument. However, no matter how much is packed into this rephrasal, the fact is that the net result is not to be understood as requiring either a *rhētōr* or an audience.

The open-endedness of logic is one of its strengths, but it has also led logicians to continue to ignore rhetoric. Logic is open-ended in the sense that it does not presume to have adequately captured the logic of all kinds of discourse. Moreover, it is emboldened by its apparent success in developing, for example, *modal logic,* which deals with the logical relationships involving claims of necessity and possibility. Aristotle was the first to theorize about this logic, concerning which considerable progress has been made in recent years because of the use of the concept of *possible worlds.* The fact that logic seems to be constantly discovering ways of applying itself to hitherto un-charted realms of discourse has encouraged logi-cians to think that there is no need to look be-yond the methods and values of logic.

Another reason for the neglect of rhetoric by logic is that many of the criticisms that logic has taken seriously have not required it to do so. Most of these criticisms are directed against the pref-erence for a formal model for the appraisal of the support provided by the premises for the conclu-sion. Logicians have long recognized the exis-tence of inductive inference or argument, but they have struggled to explicate its logic because of their preference for the formal model. Infer-ences based on sampling are thought to be in-ductive. However, as Nielsen (1967) has pointed out, the pains taken in drawing the sample, es-pecially when they involve a physical process like stirring, shaking, or selecting from different sites, seem to be a function of what is known about how what we are sampling for is distributed in the population from which the sample is being drawn. Consequently, the mathematics, for ex-ample, of probability or decision theory, does not seem to be sufficient to account for the role played by different sampling techniques. Another diffi-culty with the way logicians have talked about in-duction is that in order for sampling to seem pro-totypical of it, everything learned from experience must be thought of as a form of sampling. This includes not only a claim about the properties, for example, of a lemon or tomato, but also a claim that something is a lemon or tomato. This view—that sampling is behind everything learned from experience—is responsible for the problem of induction, the problem of how any projection from past experience to the future can be justified without relying on experience, and therefore beg-ging the question.

Another criticism that logic has taken seri-ously is that there are many predicates where the boundary between where they apply and where they do not apply cannot be exactly drawn. This has led to the development of *fuzzy logic,* as well as part of the motivation for the development of *many-valued logics,* (i.e., systems that recognize that certain claims are neither true nor false). Al-though various claims have been made by Kosko (1993) and others about the value of fuzzy logic, especially when applied to computer program-ming, the problem with it is that it discusses ap-plications of a predicate without any concern for the rhetorical circumstances in which those ap-plications would actually be made.

The criticism that logic is not concerned with how people actually reason has been taken up by researchers in cognitive psychology whose focus is on how we are programmed to reason. These psychologists design experiments to explain why subjects tend to give the wrong answers to certain logic problems involving, for example, negation, or the conditional, or probability. However, be-cause they are not sufficiently attentive to the rhetoric of their own examples, these psycholo-gists obtain results that seem to reflect as much on their own failure to explain how they want these problems to be understood as they do either on the limitations of the subjects' powers of rea-soning or on the heuristics or biases that may be doing the thinking for these subjects (and every-one else).

Many criticisms of formal logic are loosely as-sociated with the so-called *informal logic* move-ment, which constitutes itself by insisting that there are approaches to the critical appraisal of an argument that are not based on a formal model. One of these criticisms is that the premises–con-clusion model is too crude to accommodate the fact that arguments in different fields or with very different subject matter depend on quite different kinds of warrants. This criticism was pressed by Stephen Toulmin (1958), who was concerned with avoiding the infinite regress that arises when a request for the justification of an inference from premises to conclusion requires the authorization of a more general principle which, in turn, re-quires justification from still another principle, and so on. Toulmin's way of blocking this regress was to distinguish between the data an arguer re-lies upon, the warrants that provide the authori-zation for passing from that data to the claim or position she is taking, and the backing for those warrants. However, not only is the concept of a warrant difficult to apply in practice, but that ap-plication has limited value unless it is accompa-nied by a heightened sensitivity to rhetorical considerations.

Another recent innovation in logic, the con-cept of a *convergent* (Thomas, 1986) argument, is based on the recognition of the limitations of the

LOGIC ◆ 455

premises–conclusion sequence model for the reconstruction of a given argument. An argument may have subarguments; support for a conclusion may be the cumulative effect of several premises operating independently of one another. To handle convergence, diagramming techniques have been developed. However, after it has been diagrammed, the argument is to be understood and evaluated as though it has no rhetorical context, so diagramming seems to inherit many of the problems of the premises–conclusion sequence model.

Many informal logicians have adopted an approach that does seem to be a response to the need to acknowledge a rhetorical dimension to argumentation. This dialogical approach, which was initiated by C. A. Hamblin's (1970) writings on fallacy, is a hybrid of logic and rhetoric, and has adherents in both fields. The approach acknowledges that argumentation does not occur in a rhetorical vacuum, but should be understood as a series of dialectical responses that take a question-and-answer form. The question–answers model is an obvious improvement over an approach that treats argument as lacking a rhetorical context. However, in order to provide a theory for what constitutes a good or bad move in a dialectical exchange, dialogicians conceive of such an exchange as a game, and so try to identify the rules that the participants need to observe in order to play the game properly or well. Moreover, the samples of question-and-answer dialectic are devised by the dialogician or quoted with inadequate details of the rhetorical context, and this contributes to the impression that dialogicians are retaining some of the unfortunate assumptions of the formal approach while trying to improve on it.

These developments—however earnest they are in trying to bridge the gap between actual rhetoric and the artificial settings in which logic is generated—are problemmatic because they fail to acknowledge the rhetorical dimension of argumentation and discourse. If a theory is needed, any adequate theory of argumentation should address the question addressed by logic, namely, what it is that makes an argument something that should command the adherence of an audience. Although it has yet to happen, perhaps a logic that is sensitive to rhetoric can be developed.

[*See also* Contingency and probability; *and* Inference.]

BIBLIOGRAPHY

Bochenski, I. M. *A History of Formal Logic.* Notre Dame, Ind., 1961. A source book that includes a section on Indian logic.

Garrett, Mary M. "Chinese Buddhist Religious Disputation." *Argumentation* 11 (1997), pp. 195–209. A discussion of the strategies Buddhists employed to cope with the threat to the tenets of their religion that were opened up by their regular participation in public debate.

Giere, Ronald N. *Understanding Scientific Reasoning.* New York, 1984. The best introductory textbook in providing a reliable account of the logic of scientific thinking.

Govier, Trudy. *Problems in Argument Analysis and Evaluation.* Dordrecht, The Netherlands, 1987. A thoughtful argument for the consideration of arguments that seem hard to categorize as either deductive or inductive.

Graham, A. C. *Disputers of the Tao.* La Salle, Ill., 1989. A chronological survey of the thinking of ancient Chinese philosophers that includes sections on logic, by the scholar who has done the most to establish the texts of the Later Mohist logicians.

Hamblin, C. A. *Fallacies.* London, 1970. A work whose critical discussion of the treatment of the subject led him and others to emphasize the importance of considering argument in the context of a formalized debate or dialogue.

Heijenoort, Jan van, ed. *From Frege to Gödel: A Source Book in Mathematical Logic 1879–1931.* Cambridge, Mass., 1967. Includes many of the most important essays or proofs from this period of mathematical logic.

Hughes, G. E., and M. J. Creswell. *A New Introduction to Modal Logic.* London, 1996. A good textbook in modal logic.

Johnstone, Henry W., Jr. "Argumentation and Formal Logic in Philosophy." *Argumentation* 3 (1953), pp. 5–15. Examines how the use of formal logical techniques leads to the neglect of the "intertextuality" of philosophical arguments.

Kneale, William, and Martha Kneale. *The Development of Logic.* New York, 1984. A critical discussion of the major developments in the history of logic from the perspective of how they anticipate Fregean and post-Fregean concepts and discoveries.

Kosko, Bart. *Fuzzy Thinking.* New York, 1993. A lively brief for fuzzy logic that also includes some of the history of the subject.

Kripke, Saul. *Naming and Necessity*. Cambridge, Mass., 1980. An attempt at applying modal concepts to such philosophical problems as universals and mind-body dualism.

Manktelow, Ken, and David Over. *Inference and Understanding*. London, 1990. An excellent survey of the results and controversies in the cognitive psychology of reasoning.

Matilal, Bimal Krishna. *The Character of Logic in India*. Albany, N.Y., 1998. A discussion of the philosophical issues raised by Indian logic, whose development is presented chronologically.

Nielsen, H. A. *Methods of Natural Science; an Introduction*. Englewood Cliffs, N.J., 1967. A short and thoughtful text that argues effectively that formal techniques are inadequate to capture what is involved in sampling correctly.

Nye, Andrea. *Words of Power*. New York, 1990. A beautifully written attempt at exposing the longings and desire for power and control of certain key figures in the history of logic by a consideration of their choice of examples and expressive language.

Quine, W. V. *Methods of Logic*. 4th ed. Cambridge, Mass., 1982. A text that is distinctive because of its emphasis on algorithmic methods for determining implications and because it is written by one of the most influential contemporary philosophers.

Scribner, Sylvia. "Modes of thinking and ways of speaking: Culture and logic reconsidered." In *Mind and Social Practice*, pp. 125–144. Cambridge, U.K., 1997. A discussion of research on the effects of illiteracy on reasoning power by someone who is less willing than earlier researchers to conclude that illiteracy makes people less logical.

Thomas, Stephen N. *Practical Reasoning in Natural Language*. 3d ed. Englewood Cliffs, N.J., 1986. A text that pioneered in the utilization of diagramming techniques for analyzing "convergent" arguments.

Toulmin, Stephen. *The Uses of Argument*. Cambridge, U.K., 1958. A critique of such formal logical concepts as "validity" and "deduction" that has been influential on rhetoricians, and which played a role in the development of the informal logic movement.

—DON S. LEVI

LOGOS.

For as long as rhetoric has been a formal object of study, *logos* has been one of its central terms. It has always referred to the verbal structure of arguments—to words, the connections among them, and their power to persuade. It has never been a simple term.

Word and Argument in Antiquity. The earliest rhetoricians saw themselves as teachers of *logos*—specifically *orthos logos*, effective or right speech, which could be taught through *logōn technē*, the productive art of speaking. The Greek word *logos* had the primary sense of language or discourse, or the use of words generally. *Logos* could also refer to reasoning—and an older sense of *logos* as numbering or giving an account perhaps survived in those meanings. Finally, *logos* could refer to situations in the world about which one might want to reason. All these meanings were specified, amplified, and contested in the disputes among the rhetoricians and philosophers of antiquity; they continued to shape the meaning of *logos* as a technical term within rhetorical theory. [*See* Classical rhetoric.]

Fifth-century Greek rhetoricians: The Sophists. Protagoras (c.485–c.410), first of the Sophists, said at least two things about *logos:* that two opposing *logoi* existed for every subject, and that he could instruct students so that they would be able to make the weaker *logos* stronger. Later commentators, including Plato and Aristotle, took these aphorisms to mean that Protagoras was an unscrupulous teacher of deceptive speech. But Protagoras may have used the idea of two *logoi* to demarcate a discrete realm of language and discourse, within which objects have more than one meaning. The notion of strengthening the weaker *logos* may refer to the rhetorician's power to find support for ideas that are not yet popular or accepted. Both aphorisms must be read within the context of Protagoras's assertion that the deployment of *logoi* is a skill that can be taught. [*See* Sophists.]

Similar issues arise in an anonymous fourth-century BCE treatise influenced by Protagoras, the *Dissoi logoi,* which argues that the same things can be both good and bad, seemly and disgraceful, just and unjust, true and false, and wise and foolish. Arguments can even be advanced about whether or not these contradictories can be true of the same thing. The text ends by asserting that a speaker skilled in argument will be able to find something worthwhile to say on any public topic that faces the city—such a speaker would have the skill of *orthōs legein,* or right speech.

Both in the surviving fragments of Protagoras and in the *Dissoi logoi, logos* refers to a discursive domain within which propositions can be discovered and asserted. The study of *logos* secures an understanding of possible relations among propositions, a freedom from commonsense assumptions. A later Sophist, Gorgias (c.483–c.376 BCE) explored these themes in two major texts, *The Encomium on Helen* and *On the Nonexistent.* In *On the Nonexistent,* Gorgias argued that nothing exists, that if things exist they are unknowable to us, and that even if they were apprehended, they could not be communicated. Gorgias's defense for his final proposition asserted, "for that by which we reveal is *logos,* but *logos* is not substances and existing things" (Sprague, 1972, p. 84). Here as in Protagoras, *logos* is a term of art for the discursive domain that bears on external reality but is not identical to it.

However, *logos* was seen as immensely powerful within the world of experiences and objects. In the *Encomium on Helen,* Gorgias defended Helen of Troy: she was helpless, he argued, against *logos,* the power of persuasive speech. *Logos* acts on the soul just as a drug acts on the body; like a drug, *logos* is powerful for both benefit and harm (Sprague, 1972, pp. 12–14). For this reason, Gorgias names *logos* as *dynastēs,* or lord, master, and ruler, full of arbitrary power.

Fourth-century Greeks: Plato, Aristotle, Isocrates. It was exactly this power of rhetoric that aroused Plato's mistrust, and very many of his dialogues (for example, the *Ion,* the *Phaedrus,* the *Euthydemus,* the *Laches,* the *Gorgias,* and *The Sophist*) criticize the Sophists. Plato (c.428–c.347 BCE) disputed their claims as instructors of youth, as experts in *logos,* as producers of properly directed persuasive speech. In particular, Plato attempted to stabilize the domain of *logos* by annexing it to a particularly philosophical mode of inquiry. In the early dialogue *Protagoras,* for example, Socrates constrains Protagoras to admit that every term has but one opposite, and to concede that opposites are stable, necessarily attached to specific actions and agents rather than dangerously floating in their own domain (334).

In the *Gorgias,* Plato undertook a wholesale revision of the concept of *logos.* Instead of locating *logos* in the domain of public discourse, Plato transposed it to the private world of philosophic conversation. Further, Plato displaced *logos* from the agonistic discourses of the law court and assembly to the private conversations of philoso-

phers. The participants in such dialogue are seen, not as antagonists engaged in a contest, but as servants of the truth, seeking a demonstration "for the discussion [*logos*], to have it proceed in such a way as to make the thing we're talking about most clear to us" (453C2–4). Finally, Plato refuses to concede that rhetoric can be a productive art, or *technē,* considering it a mere knack or skill precisely because it lacks *logos,* the ability to account for itself (465a). Only philosophy can offer access to stable meanings; only philosophy can account for its own power to represent the world.

Contemporary theorists have seen the argument about *logos* in the *Gorgias* as a reactionary attempt to deprive the city of rhetoric as a tool for democratic self-governance (Bruno Latour, "Socrates' and Callicles' Settlement—or, The Invention of the Impossible Body Politic," *Configurations* 52, 1997, pp. 189–240); as a proposal for a deeply ethical and original rhetoric (James Kasteley, *Rethinking the Rhetorical Tradition: From Plato to Postmodernism,* New Haven, 1997); or as an attempt to build the educational prestige of philosophy at rhetoric's expense. However Plato's intervention is read, his treatment of *logos* consistently removes it from the domain of both rhetorical theory and public rhetorical practice. Disjoined from the ethical and political practices of *orthōs logein,* rhetoric was to become a storehouse of persuasive techniques subject to the ethical and epistemological mandate of some other science.

Aristotle (384–322 BCE) addressed Plato's critique of rhetoric systematically. His *Rhetoric,* a compilation of lectures given over some forty years (c.367–323), has been massively influential in the history of rhetorical theory. The *Rhetoric* offers a systematic theory of *logos* as an element of rhetoric. First, Aristotle establishes the sense in which rhetoric is a *technē,* a productive practice that can give an account of itself. Rhetoric deals with finding the available means of persuasion on any topic: in practice, rhetoric takes up topics related to public issues, including what has already happened (forensics), what should be done (deliberation), and what is to be valued (the epideictic). [*See* Deliberative genre; Epideictic genre; *and* Forensic genre.] Although these matters are not open to certain knowledge, they are open to rational dispute; although all the elements of such discourse cannot be predicted, the way of finding means of persuasion in a given situation can be taught. For Aristotle, then, rhetoric is neither a knack, a debased art, nor a mode of access to an unchanging truth. It is oriented toward production rather than contemplation, and toward particular exigencies rather than eternal forms.

But Aristotle was also prepared to give the account of persuasion that Gorgias had been (in Plato's dialogue) unable to supply. He divides rhetoric into elements, and orders and describes the relations among them. He demonstrates what the multitude of discursive forms have in common and what is distinct to particular genres, practices, and individual performances. All these materials are presented pedagogically, and study of them is expected to help students to speak better, to understand what is at stake in a given situation, and to respond critically and productively to the discourses of others.

The *Rhetoric,* despite having been transcribed over an extended period, proceeds systematically. The first book discusses the definition of rhetoric, the kinds of speeches, and the kinds of governments that the rhetor might need to persuade, particularly on ceremonial or forensic occasions. The second book considers means of persuasion oriented to the speaker or the emotions of the audience, and then turns to enthymemes and examples. [*See* Enthymeme; *and* Exemplum.] The third and last book discusses language and the arrangement of the main divisions of a speech. [*See* Arrangement, *article on* Traditional arrangement; *and* Style.] Aristotle's *Rhetoric,* therefore, can be seen as an attempt to include the materials developed in the tradition of handbook or technical rhetoric, and to incorporate the elements of philosophic rhetoric that had interested the Sophists, replying to the criticisms of Plato. Contemporary rhetoricians have understood and evaluated this project in different ways. William Grimaldi, in his magisterial *Aristotle's Rhetoric: A Commentary* (New York; 1980), sees the *Rhetoric* as founding a theoretical and analytic discipline; Janet Atwill, in *Rhetoric Reclaimed: Aristotle and the Liberal Arts Tradition* (Ithaca, N.Y., 1998), sees it as establishing a specifically productive art, nonfoundationalist and radically democratic. Either reading, however, establishes the first of the major interventions of the *Rhetoric* in relation to lo-

gos: the *Rhetoric* asserts a *logos* of rhetoric, a way of establishing it as a *technē.*

Besides establishing rhetoric as a discipline oriented to *logos,* Aristotle's *Rhetoric* also redefines *logos* within rhetoric, as one of three means of persuasion. *Logos* is therefore placed in relation to the other means of persuasion, *ēthos* and *pathos.* [*See* Ēthos; *and* Pathos.] In the first book of the *Rhetoric,* explaining the kinds of proof that are invented by the rhetorician's art, the artistic or entechnic proofs, Aristotle defines three kinds of entechnic proofs (the Greek word is *pisteis,* means of persuasion). He says that "some are in the character [*ēthos*], and some in disposing the listener in some way [*pathos*], and some in the argument [*logos*] itself, by showing or seeming to show something" (1356a). *Logos* did not denote for Aristotle as it did for the Sophists an independent realm of discourse, within which propositions relate to one another discursively. Nor did it represent, as it did for Plato, a domain of certain knowledge that cannot be approached through rhetorical performance. In Aristotle's *Rhetoric, logos* is an element of persuasion, which is discovered or worked up, an artistic means of influencing an audience—persuasion based on "truth or apparent truth." *Logos* as entechnic proof is intimately connected to the status of rhetoric as knowledge: it establishes rhetoric as a discipline that is related to philosophy and to politics, but distinct from them both. Like dialectic, it is concerned with methods; unlike dialectic but like politics, rhetoric concerns arguments that are persuasive in courtrooms or deliberative bodies. [*See* Dialectic; Law; *and* Politics.] Therefore, in the place of syllogisms and inductions, rhetoric employs the enthymeme and the example, both of which Aristotle discusses at length in Book 1. [*See* Syllogism.]

Just as contemporary critics have debated what Aristotle might have meant by calling rhetoric an "art," they have debated what it means to see *logos* as a means of persuasion. Traditionally, *logos* was associated with Aristotle's system for inventing means of proof, the topics, or places for finding arguments. [*See* Topics.] The expansion, development, and refinement of lists of topics occupied rhetoricians from antiquity through the Early Modern period: explicitly or implicitly, they connected the topics to *logos,* considering "logical proof" as a means of persuasion distinct from proofs referring to character or emotion. In fact, after Aristotle, theorists were much more likely to speak of topics or enthymemes than to discuss *logos* itself. Sometimes, arguments were characterized by their predominant appeal, so that *logos* characterized a certain genre of persuasion, superior in some way to persuasion motivated by *ēthos* or *pathos*. William Grimaldi's persuasive commentary on the *Rhetoric* (New York, 1980–1988) suggests that all three means of proof were seen as rational: rational judgments motivate both our opinions of speakers and our emotions. "Logical proof," for Grimaldi, simply refers to proofs based on a given state of affairs, on what was the case. Unlike such inartistic proofs as physical evidence, logical proofs had to be invented, or "artistically" produced; unlike appeals to *ēthos* or to *pathos*, they operated primarily through the hearers' judgment about the issue under debate. Most speeches use all three means of proof; enthymemes and examples can support any of them, and topics can suggest enthymemes for them all. The three means of persuasion are present, in different proportions, in all speeches that attempt to persuade. And although Aristotle insists repeatedly that it is easier to persuade audiences of things that are true or just than of things that are false or unjust—so much so that it is blameworthy when the worse case prevails—for him, *logos* did not guarantee truth, but only plausibility. *Logos* does not denote what is eternally or certainly the case, but only what is true or can be made to seem true to a given audience.

Whether or not *ēthos* and *pathos* can generate enthymemes, it is certain that *logos* does, and the common topics are the ways in which enthymemes are developed. Aristotle is careful, in the first book of the *Rhetoric*, to distinguish enthymeme and example from their dialectical counterparts, syllogism and induction. Enthymemes in particular are said to be the "body" of persuasion (1.1.4), and so properly the concern of the rhetorician's art. Aristotle defines an enthymeme as "a sort of syllogism" (1.1.11), or as a rhetorical syllogism, not different in its kind from the syllogism of dialectics, a statement that has been glossed in many ways. Roman rhetoricians saw the enthymeme as a shortened syllogism with a single term suppressed. There is some support for

this definition in Book 2 of the *Rhetoric*, where Aristotle says that in enthymemes, "the conclusion should not be drawn from far back, nor is it necessary to include everything" (2.22.1). Most modern commentators, however, do not see the enthymeme as abbreviated, truncated, or otherwise compromised. Instead, contemporary readings emphasize Aristotle's statement that the enthymeme deals with conclusions drawn "not only from what is necessarily valid, but also from what is true for the most part" (2.22.3). Just as Aristotle defines rhetoric as the counterpart of dialectic, dealing with issues that need to be decided on the basis of probability rather than certainty, he defines the enthymeme as a way of reasoning closely about probable rather than certain matters.

Aristotle's final step in developing the concept of *logos* in the *Rhetoric* is the elaboration of a system of topics suited to the development of logical proofs. Aristotle offers a great many topics for the development of arguments based on the facts of the case and their connections. Since the word *topos* meant "place," the topics were seen as sites where such arguments could be found: they are general ideas like "the greater and the less," or "cause and consequence," which can suggest lines of investigation and argument. The topics resemble the image orators would use as an aid to memory, that of an elaborate house in which the central points of a speech would be placed, so that the orator could walk through the rooms to collect points as the speech progressed. As the "house of memory" aided delivery, the topics aided invention by guiding the selection of enthymemes: Aristotle gives twenty-eight common topics for enthymemes—issues or ideas that can generate arguments on any subject. The rhetor can consider such questions as the opposite of the proposition at hand, or issues of greater and less, the passage of time, and definition. The elements of a proposition can be varied—verbs can be turned to nouns, and the proposition tested in that form. Aristotle also discusses topics that generate false enthymemes so that the speaker can refute them, and offers strategies for "undoing" the opponent's enthymemes. Earlier in the *Rhetoric*, Aristotle had listed special topics that are useful in generating proofs for each of the three major species of rhetoric. Logical proof in deliberative discourse, for example, turns on the usual issues of political dispute: war and peace, imports and exports, and making laws. Logical proof in forensic, or courtroom, rhetoric, can turn on the reasons for wrongdoing, the persons who do or suffer wrong, or questions about justice and injustice.

The special topics for various rhetorical exigencies (1.4–15), and the common topics for all issues that might require demonstration (2.22–25), were enormously durable and influential. Later writers often combined the treatment of the topics in the *Rhetoric* with material presented in Aristotle's more philosophical discussion in his *Topics*. The twenty-eight common topics of the *Rhetoric,* variously augmented, appear in Cicero and Quintilian; other Roman rhetoricians commented on them, and they were the subject of a number of Arabic treatises. [*See* Arabic rhetoric.] Through these sources, the topics entered medieval and early modern rhetorical treatises, so closely identified with logical proof that both the alternate means of logical proof (examples, maxims) and the distinction among logical topics and those related to *ēthos* and *pathos* (goodness and happiness, anger and its incitements) were assimilated into the topical system.

An alternate approach to the discovery of truth based on the facts of the case and their connection was elaborated by the Greek rhetorician Hermagoras. His theory of *stasis* is a development of Aristotle's discussion of the special topics of forensic oratory. [*See* Stasis.] None of Hermagoras's works has survived, but quotations of his texts by later rhetoricians indicate that *stasis* theory categorized possible issues for legal disputation, and considered the possible sources of support and refutation for those issues. *Stasis* theory was popularized in the *Rhetorica ad Herennium* (c.80 BCE), one of the few rhetorical treatises of antiquity continuously available through the medieval period. Its prestige was only enhanced by its enduring and mistaken assignment to Cicero.

Roman Rhetoric: Cicero and Quintilian. Cicero (106–43 BCE) was by far the most influential theorist of the topics for Roman, medieval, and early modern rhetoricians. He took up the topics in his very early work *De inventione* (c.87 BCE), possibly drawing on the same source as the nearly contemporaneous *Rhetorica ad Herennium. De inventione* discusses both the topics and *stasis* theory as means of invention. [*See* Invention.] Here, the topics are issues associated with legal cases, and therefore common in forensic oratory. If a case turned on a question of fact, for example, the orator ought to recall what he knew about the case, and review these facts using questions very close to those specified in Aristotle's *Rhetoric*. The orator might consider the consequences of changing the facts of the case, or their order in time, or the agents by whom they were performed. He would reflect on signs and their relative significance. During such attentive study, "the topics (*loci*) mentioned above which are stored up will come forth of their own accord; then sometimes from one, sometimes from a combination of topics definite arguments will be produced, part of which will be classed as probable and part as irrefutable" (2.13.45). Cicero also discusses "common topics" in *De inventione*; these are not limited to general forms of argument, but include maxims on which there is general agreement, useful for confirming propositions. Cicero offers numerous common topics that address quite specialized situations. We learn, for example, the common topics to be used against someone who proposes a change of procedure (2.20.61), and many topics for generating arguments in disputes about documents (2.40.116).

In *De oratore* (55 BCE), Cicero offers the topics as an aid to flagging or untalented invention. Rather than prompting thought, the topics offered the orator ready access to common beliefs, ideas so readily accepted that they needed no argumentative support. Once the status of the case had been determined, the topics could serve as a lexicon of argument: "just as, whenever we have some word to write, we need not search out its component letters by hard thinking, so, whenever we have some case to argue, our right course is not to fall back upon proofs laid away for that particular type of cases, but to have in readiness sundry commonplaces [*sed habere certos locos*] which will instantly present themselves for setting forth the case, as the letters do for writing the word" (2.30.130). [*See* Commonplaces and commonplace books.] Cicero goes on to explain that the commonplaces are specific to the literal place in which they are uttered: they require familiarity with a city's customs, history, and values, which will suggest certain images, themes, and lines of argument.

Contemporary scholars have identified many such *topoi* in Cicero's orations: figures such as the captured city, the superiority of the country to the city or of Europe to Asia, or of the north to the south, of the waywardness of youth, or the military achievements of the accused. Such figures could migrate from oratorical performance to oratorical theory; speakers could also draw on examples of these *topoi* from philosophers and historians (Ann Vasaly, *Representations: Images of the World in Ciceronian Oratory*, Berkeley, 1993). These Ciceronian "common topics" or *loci communi* are the remote ancestors of the "commonplaces," the received ideas, including quotations, maxims, and stories, that played a critical role in the production of amplitude (*copia*) for Renaissance rhetoricians; from the time of Cicero, they served as points of exchange among the various means of proof and genres of discourse.

Later, Cicero wrote the short treatise *Topica* (44 BCE); the discussion of the topics in this text repeats the list given in *De oratore* (2.162–73). Again, the topics are a convenience to the orator. "It is easy to find things that are hidden, if the hiding place is pointed out and marked; similarly if we want to track down some argument we ought to know the places or topics: for that is the name given by Aristotle to the regions [*sedes*] as it were, from which arguments are drawn" (1.7). The listed topics include some from Aristotle's *Topics,* some from the list in the *Rhetoric,* and some collected from common practice, illustrated with examples drawn from legal disputes—appropriately enough, since *Topica* is presented as a letter to a lawyer. Enthymemes are presented as a special kind of topic that can draw conclusions from contradictory statements.

Quintilian's (c.35–c.100 CE) treatment of the topics acknowledged their origin in Aristotle. Quintilian counseled that, in certain circumstances, orators may need to make up topics of their own; the topics are also seen as ways of undermining such "inartistic proofs" as physical evidence, documents, oaths, or testimony given under torture (*Institutio oratoria* 5.4–6). Many of

the topics associated with such refutations are emotional or ethical: the orator will consider whether a timid witness can be intimidated, or will argue for the credibility of his client's oath of innocence by pointing to his blameless life. Among the artistic proofs, Quintilian includes indications, arguments, and examples, *"aut signis aut argumentis aut exemplis"* (5.9.1). He defines arguments, or enthymemes, as propositions given with reasons and arguments drawn from incompatible propositions. Quintilian mentions that the enthymeme can be called an incomplete syllogism (5.10.1–3), but holds that the enthymeme is most properly defined as a proof of a definite proposition that includes at least three parts (5.10.5).

For Quintilian, the "places of argument" are distinct from the commonplaces: he compares them to spots where fishermen might find a particular kind of fish. Quintilian's list of topics is long, filling most of Book 5: he draws from all of Cicero's sources; from the sections of Aristotle's *Rhetoric* that offer *loci* for all the means of proof, including ethical and emotional proofs as well as those based on *logos;* and from Cicero's theory or practice, court precedents, and other handbooks. While Quintilian repeatedly insists that these lists are only a guide to practice, and that a good rhetor must find and refute arguments in the public world of the court, the system of commonplaces and places of argument is deeply pedagogical in its orientation. Both commonplaces and places of argument allow a student to organize the experience of hearing and analyzing speeches and to access that experience easily during later classroom exercises or in the combat of judicial oratory.

Logos *in late antiquity: Augustine and Boethius.* The tasks of orators and the means available to them change dramatically according to the range of public discussions that a culture fosters. During the Roman empire and after the widespread adoption of Christianity, the terms of Greek and Latin rhetoric, especially *logos,* underwent a wholesale translation. The first words of the gospel of John, "In the beginning was the Word" (*Jn.* 1.1) in the Greek New Testament, invoke *logos.* The central term in sophistic rhetoric, the term that Plato had appropriated for philosophy and that Aristotle had refunctioned as a means of invention, thereby became a pivotal term in Christian theology, expressing the relation between Christ and the Father. [*See overview article on* Medieval rhetoric.]

For Augustine (354–430 CE), writing at the end of the fourth century of the common era, the words of John's gospel collocated directly with the teachings of neoplatonism. Augustine admitted in the *Confessions* that he learned about the primacy of *logos* from Neoplatonic writing, and that it was "some time later that I learnt, in relation to the words, 'The Word was made flesh,' how Catholic truth is to be distinguished from the false opinion of Photinus" (7.19.23). Augustine's conversion to Catholicism was also quite specifically a rejection of his profession as a rhetorician, which, as a Christian, he was legally prohibited from practicing. Augustine resented this prohibition, but was also relieved to "quietly . . . retire from my post as a salesman of words in the market of rhetoric" (9.2.2). As a bishop, however, Augustine took up the task of framing a Christian rhetoric, using the scriptures as a model. In *De doctrina christiana*, Augustine outlines a rhetoric based on the Ciceronian "offices" of teaching, pleasing, and persuading. These aims are to be accomplished through stylistic ornament, astute appeals to emotion, and the exemplary life of the orator. The Christian orator would find logical proofs in scripture, or by prayer that God would "place a good speech in his mouth" (5.30). Both *De doctrina christiana* and the *Confessions* deploy all the power of *logos* to argue for its subordination to other means of persuasion, other ways of accessing truth. [*See* Religion.]

Boethius (480–524 CE) took up exactly the questions of demonstration, persuasion, and logical appeal that Augustine would have taught as a Latin rhetor; his development of these issues was critical for medieval rhetoric and logic. Boethius wrote two texts on the topics: *In Ciceronis topica* and *De topicis differentiis*. *De topicis differentiis*, the longer and more serious work, draws on both Aristotle's *Topics* and Cicero. Its first three books deal with dialectical topics, understood as unstated principles that connect the parts of an enthymeme. For Boethius, enthymemes were truncated or abbreviated syllogisms that depended on unstated terms, or topics: topics, therefore,

were general rules for connecting propositions. *Differentiae* are broad categories of topics, ways of organizing and grouping their infinite number. In the final book of *De topicis*, Boethius considers rhetoric as a discipline or faculty oriented to persuasion or to speaking well; his rhetorical topics are organized lines of inquiry into judicial issues related to persons and to acts. Boethius's topics are almost entirely Ciceronian, although they are more general than those in *De oratore*. They are completely detached from any consideration of the means of proof, questions of audience or purpose, or of a logical proof distinct from *ēthos* and *pathos*.

Summary: Logos *in Greek and Latin antiquity.* During the millennium that separated the Sophists from Boethius, *logos* had been put to a variety of rhetorical uses, from the most relentlessly technical to the most sublime. Four general questions or issues emerge in relation to this term: that of the relation of the discursive world to experience; that of the effect of persuasion on the listener; that of the disciplinary status of rhetoric; and that of the relation between rhetorical production and other kinds of reflective thought.

Logos, for the Sophists, invoked the discursive world as an autonomous realm, subject to its own laws, a world where the same object could be either good or bad. This autonomy, shocking for Plato, is contained within Aristotle's *topoi*: the discursive world of Aristotle's *Rhetoric* can be mapped, and that map is assumed to correspond to the world of experience. The notion of a discursive map was, of course, immensely powerful and capable of endless elaboration; by specifying a relationship between the world of *logos* and the world of experience, it stabilized the Sophists' fluidity of discursive relationships.

Not only were such relationships fluid; they were also acknowledged to be powerful. While the Sophists celebrated such power, Plato warned against its dangers. Again, Aristotle's codification of the logical proof can be seen as an attempt to stabilize the threatening possibilities of the discursive world: while rhetoric is understood to work on the emotions and to build trust (*pathos* and *ēthos*), it is also expected to persuade through a correspondence between the arguments presented by the orator and the accepted facts of common life or the accepted ideals of a community. While *logos* invoked, for the fifth-century Greek rhetorician, an ungovernable force, the "logical appeal" of Roman rhetoric was simply a technique for inserting a given speech into the fabric of what was already credible.

Since Plato, critics have argued that because rhetoric was so radically limited by times and places, it was no discipline at all, so that the exigent situation of rhetorical practice offered no reliable access to *logos*. And indeed, in Cicero and Quintilian, temporal exigency is offered as a reason why the orator should have recourse to lines of argument that cost no thought. In such situations, the topics become devices for quickly accessing received ideas rather than means of reflecting on a changing situation in order to say something new about it. But these very devices insured the success of rhetoric as a pedagogical subject. *Logos,* as the autonomous world of discourse or the consistency of arguments, had been central to the educational project of the Sophists, and the goal of *orthos logos,* however defined or disputed, has perennially been associated with rhetorical education. The logical appeals and the associated apparatus of the topics offer a model for the production of arguments that is eminently teachable and immediately productive. Whether the production of arguments was seen as a way of forming the student as a citizen or as a rehearsal for later speaking and writing, *logos* earned rhetoric its place in the trivium. [*See* Trivium.] Along with grammar and logic, rhetoric was seen as a necessary element in basic education.

The Fortunes of *Logos*: From the Middle Ages to the Enlightenment. The handful of Roman rhetorical texts available in the Middle Ages included a variety of treatments of logical proof: works of Cicero, especially *De inventione* and *De oratore,* the *Rhetorica ad Herennium,* and selections from Quintilian. In addition, Aristotle's *Topics* and his *Sophistical Refutations* were widely used as textbooks for scholastic disputation. The fourth book of Boethius's *De topicis differentiis* was very commonly presented in university lectures on rhetoric; it offered medieval scholars access to the basic apparatus of the topics detached from the specific speech situations of courtroom and deliberative rhetoric. Aristotle's *Rhetoric,* however, was generally regarded as part of his political and eth-

ical theory, and does not seem to have been studied as a rhetoric text. Logic flourished as a separate branch of philosophy, making liberal use of the Aristotelean *Topics.* [*See* Eighteenth-century rhetoric; *and overview article on* Renaissance rhetoric.]

Late medieval and early Humanist scholars saw themselves as reconstructing a whole art of speech. Reorienting rhetoric toward persuasion, they refunctioned the topics as elements of proof rather than as logical figures. For John of Salisbury in the *Metalogicon* (1159), for example, reason (*ratio*) was demonstrated both in formal disputation and in other kinds of verbal performance. The *Metalogicon* is a defense of reason and the training of reason, especially through the arts of the trivium. Logic, the invention of reasons, could be taught through an examination of the Aristotelian topics, supplemented with other Aristotelian works, especially the *Sophistical Refutations.* The *Refutations* were recommended not only as a guide for unmasking Sophistry, but also as a guide to producing Sophistry—which John of Salisbury held to be especially useful to students who, not being wise, must labor to appear so. In the *Metalogicon,* the very apparatus of logic became a gateway admitting the ungovernable *logos* of the Sophists; Sophistry can either be a "handmaid of truth and wisdom" or an "adulteress who betrays her lovers" (*The Metalogicon of John of Salisbury,* translated by Daniel McGarry, Berkeley, 1955, pp. 236–237).

Later Humanists, such as George of Trebizond (1395–c.1472) and Lorenzo Valla (1407–1457), augmented the topical apparatus transmitted through Boethius with a commitment to a civilizing discursive mission for rhetoric. Given the Humanist emphasis on purity of style and elaboration of figures, these early modern rhetorics seldom focused on argument and logical means of proof. The tendency of rhetorical theorists to concentrate on stylistic matters was confirmed by the writings of Rudolphus Agricola (1444–1485) and Peter Ramus (1515–1572), widely read university lecturers who considered invention and judgment (Arrangement) to be parts of dialectic rather than rhetoric.

With the Enlightenment, rhetoric was dismissed by philosophers like John Locke as an "art of deceit and error" (*Essay Concerning Human*

Understanding, 1690), even as it flourished as a school subject and general pedagogical enterprise. George Campbell (1719–1796), for example, adapted Humean psychology in his *Philosophy of Rhetoric* (1776). He argued that rhetoric was proper to moral rather than scientific reasoning, and that persuasion therefore depended more on appeals to the senses, imagination, and fancy than on the rigor of syllogisms. During the eighteenth and nineteenth centuries, the forms of argument received serious attention from philosophers and were discussed within the emerging natural sciences; the outlines of the modern division of intellectual labor among academic disciplines began to emerge. With that differentiation, the history of *logos* also differentiates: *logos* means quite different things in philosophy, literature and aesthetics, and rhetoric.

Modernity: *Logos* Divided. The establishment of modernity is marked by the development of the sciences, the specialization of knowledge in academic disciplines, the revolutionary transformation of customary political forms, and the construction of subjectivity as a particular mode of knowledge. Under these circumstances, the central issues related to *logos* are contested. The nature of logical persuasion, the power of verbal argument, the relation between persuasion and rationality, and the disciplinary status of rhetoric are discussed in disciplines indifferent or hostile to rhetoric, often by scholars unaware of each other's work. In modernity, even the fiction of a connected history of *logos* must be dropped in favor of an investigation of how the relationships among *logos,* argument, rhetoric, and language have been understood in the nineteenth and twentieth centuries. [*See* Contingency and probability; *and* Modern rhetoric.]

Logos *and argument.* While the survival of rhetoric as a school subject insured that argument would always be taught in some form, if only as a list of logical fallacies to be avoided, the development of modern philosophical theories of argument has encouraged a reexamination of both the Aristotelean means of persuasion and the Enlightenment critique of rhetorical proof. The theorists most influential in this process have been Stephen Toulmin, a philosopher (1922–), and the coauthors Chaim Perelman (1912–1984) and Lucie Olbrechts-Tyteca (1900–1987), a philosopher

and a social scientist. Toulmin's *The Uses of Argument* and Perelman and Olbrechts-Tyteca's *The New Rhetoric: A Treatise on Argumentation,* both published in 1958, theorize the elements of responsible persuasion, as distinguished from formal, logical demonstration. Toulmin addressed general conditions of argument and proof; he did not deal with special topics or evaluate particular figures of argument, leaving this work to specialists in particular fields. Although Toulmin's early discussions of rhetoric were both thin and hostile, the notion of probability is central to both his theory of argument and Aristotle's *Rhetoric.* Many contemporary rhetorical scholars have made use of Toulmin's theories of "argument fields," or logical types of argument, and of claims as disputable statements based on data, warranted by rules of inference, and backed by assurances that establish the relation among these elements.

Perelman and Olbrechts-Tyteca developed a category of practical reasoning, distinct from formal logic; they saw *logos* as working through both the extended speech of the orator and the movement of philosophical conversation (*The Realm of Rhetoric,* Notre Dame, Ind., 1978). Perelman and Olbrechts-Tyteca's rhetoric reconstructed the ways that arguments about values are formed. These arguments, they found, turned on the classical topics—in fact, those discussed in Aristotle's *Topics.* Reacting against the refunctioning of the *topoi* as commonplaces, Perelman and Olbrechts-Tyteca instead called them "an indispensable arsenal on which a person wishing to persuade another will have to draw, whether he likes it or not" (p. 84). Perelman and Olbrechts-Tyteca saw the topics as methodologically neutral, bundles of concepts organized in the general categories of quantity, quality, order, existence, essence, and the value of the person. In *The New Rhetoric,* the *topoi* are indeed very general rules for establishing hierarchies of value: it is better to have more of a good thing; it is better to have things that are of better quality, and so forth. Many scholars have disputed the claim that these common topics are universal: the topic of the value of the person, particularly, seems deeply embedded in the historical and ideological situation of the writers.

Such studies of naturally occurring arguments were important in laying the groundwork for an extremely productive research program in the rhetoric of inquiry, which examines the specific conditions for the construction of successful arguments in academic disciplines and public policy; a representative collection of such studies can be found in J. S. Nelson, A. Megill, and D. McCloskey, *The Rhetoric of the Human Sciences: Language and Argument in Scholarship and Public Affairs* (Madison, Wis., 1987). In the rhetoric of inquiry, discussions of logic are closely connected to analyses of metaphor, narration, identification, and the other devices for establishing *ēthos* and *pathos.*

Logos *without Rhetoric.* One of the most important contemporary theorists of rationality is Jürgen Habermas, whose theory of communicative rationality grounds universal (but not foundational) norms of rationality on the assumptions that participants in communication necessarily make. These include assumptions about the correspondence between what the parties are saying and states of affairs in the world, about the sincerity with which participants are approaching communication, and about the appropriateness of the relations they establish with one another. Each of these assumptions can become an issue in discourse; each corresponds to a particular form of rationality, a particular logic of proof, demonstration, and utterance. Habermas makes no substantial claim about how communication produces viable descriptions of the world and plans for acting in it; he argues only that communication would be impossible if its participants did not expect it to do so. That assumption, like the assumptions of sincerity and appropriateness, operates counterfactually: participants in communication attend to such assumptions only when a clear violation of them forces such costly reflection.

Habermas has, throughout his long career, alternated theoretical expositions of issues of rationality with sustained investigations of the social conditions of communication. His first published work, *Structural Transformation of the Public Sphere* (1962), was an investigation of the public sphere as a site for deliberation, created in the Enlightenment but endangered by the growth of mass media, which has "refeudalized" public culture into a domain of spectacle. In *Between Facts and Norms* (1996), Habermas argues that de-

liberation and rational discourse are precariously situated in contemporary society between the untheorizable, customary, lifeworld and the "steering media" of money and bureaucratic power: both these domains resist discourse and communication. Habermas sees political organizations, governmental systems, and legal institutions as ways of organizing communication between lifeworld and system, of opening the structures of bureaucratic organizations and corporations to rational argument and public debate. The far-reaching implications for rhetoricians have only recently been explored by Thomas Farrell, in *Norms of Rhetorical Culture* (New Haven, 1993) and Susan Wells in *Sweet Reason: Rhetoric and the Discourses of Modernity* (Chicago, 1996).

Logos *without Rhetoric, Rhetoric without* **logos.** Rhetoric and literary criticism, fused in Ramus's reduction of rhetoric to style and delivery, developed as separate academic disciplines in the late nineteenth and early twentieth centuries. But for literary criticism, *logos* and its related terms continued to be important. It can be argued, in fact, that the construction of a prose canon of literary texts, exemplars of clarity, brevity, and sincerity, was an attempt to induct students into a world of order, moderation, clarity, and conventional argument, a world in which the logical means of proof were unproblematic (Kathryn Flannery, *The Emperor's New Clothes: Literature, Literacy, and the Ideology of Style,* Pittsburgh, 1995).

Conversely, many important modern literary critics from Northrup Frye (1912–1991) to Harold Bloom (1930–) and Paul de Man (1919–1983) have often defined an imaginative or linguistically playful discursive domain as one disjoined from *logos* or argument. Frye, in his late work *Words with Power* (San Diego, 1990), analyzed discourse as a relation between imaginative *mythos* and authoritative *logos;* this relation can be organized in a variety of modes, from poetry, in which *mythos* dominates and persuasion is not propositional, to scientific texts, dominated by *logos* and compelling belief. An early ally of Frye's, Harold Bloom, dissociated imagination from *logos* altogether in his study *Yeats* (New York, 1970). For deconstructionist critic Paul de Man, in "Semiology and Rhetoric," rhetoric itself was denominated as the source of the experience of indeterminacy organized most particularly in trope and ornament (in *Textual Strategies,* edited by Josue Harari, Ithaca, N.Y., 1979).

***Argument against* Logos.** In searching for alternatives to a narrowly defined *logos,* these literary critics inherited a philosophic tradition critical of conventional notions of reason, a position most forcibly stated in the work of Friedrich Nietzsche (1844–1900). In his early lectures on rhetoric, Nietzsche raised the issue of the relation between verbal expression and truth that had been central to rhetorical theory since Protagoras, writing, "What is truth? A mobile army of metaphors, metonyms, anthropomorphisms, in short, a sum of human relations which were poetically and rhetorically heightened, transferred, and adorned, and after long use seem solid, canonical, and binding to a nation" ("On Truth and Lying in an Extra-Moral Sense," 1873, in *Friedrich Nietzsche on Rhetoric and Language,* edited by Sander Gilman, Carole Blair, and David Parent, p. 250. New York, 1989). Since Nietzsche considered rhetoric to be the production of such figures and tropes, he identified truth with rhetoric, which heightens human relations, making them comprehensible and present to us, but also constructing a frozen hierarchy of received ideas.

The sense of *logos* as both powerful—even violent—and statically frozen was investigated by contemporary French deconstructionist critic Jacques Derrida in *Dissemination* (Chicago, 1981). Discussing Plato's critique of writing and rhetoric in the *Phaedrus,* Derrida used the language of Jacques Lacan's psychoanalytic theory to associate *logos* in the form of writing with the father, or more precisely with the absence of the father. If the speaking subject fathers his speech, then the writing subject is an absent father to his own words. For Derrida, *logos* is so deeply implicated in the presence of the Good (or the father, the sun, or economic capital) that it cannot be directly apprehended (pp. 75–84). Later, in *Dissemination,* Derrida invoked the sophistic understanding of *logos* as unstable, powerful speech as a prefiguration of Plato's ambivalence toward *logos* (pp. 113–116). In Derrida, as in Nietzsche, the senses of *logos* connected to critical reflection, to discourses open to responsive arguments, or to the constraints of probability are submerged. Rather, *logos* evokes the desire for a fully present, living word—exactly the desire that Derrida places at the heart of Western metaphysics, exactly the desire that deconstruction is invoked to exorcize.

Both Jacques Lacan's (1901–1981) understanding of the Word as associated with the father and the Nietzschean critique of *logos* have been analyzed critically by French feminist theorists, including Catherine Clément and Hélène Cixous. In *The Newly-Born Woman* (1986), cowritten with Clément, Cixous argued that the distinction between *logos* and writing is analogous to that between male and female. Later, in *Coming to Writing,* Cixous compared a woman searching for a way to write to Red Riding Hood wandering in the forest, drawn into a fatal duel with *mythos,* which ends when "Logos opens its great maw, and swallows us whole" (*"Coming to Writing" and Other Essays,* Cambridge, Mass., 1991, p. 15). Within American feminism, the place of received forms of argument, the logical appeal, and agonistic contest have all been investigated, both by compositionists and by feminist historians of rhetoric such as Susan Jarratt. [*See* Feminist rhetoric.]

Language, Rhetoric, and Argument. If treatments of *logos* in rhetoric have alternated between calibrations of the unstable and autonomous power of discourse and attempts to understand argument as a system of logical forms and topics, then Kenneth Burke (1897–1993) is the modern theorist who has most successfully worked both sides of this quite treacherous street. In his *Book of Moments* (1955), Burke offered a "Dialectician's Hymn," later reprinted in *Language as Symbolic Action: Essays on Life, Literature, and Method* (Berkeley, 1966, p. 55). This anthem invokes *logos* as "the "Vast Almighty Title in Whose name we conjure" and asks that "we give true voice to the statements of Thy creatures," speaking for them with accuracy and willingness to "correct our utterances in the light of [their] rejoinders." Just as the "Dialectician's Hymn" playfully suggests an impossible meeting of Gorgias and Habermas, Burke's critical work has attended to the persuasive force of all discourses (including literary discourse), seen as expressions of the human capacity for symbol making. Burke characteristically supports his theories with close analyses of arguments and texts, disclosing surprising relations between language and society. And for Burke, society is always considered as a domain of competition and contest, of rhetorical agon. Burke characterized the topics of Aristotle's *Rhetoric* as "epitomized *situations*" (*Language as Symbolic Action*, p. 297), conserving their function as a set of mnemonic devices, but opening them to reflection and criticism. Burke's comprehensive theory was addressed to specific instances of symbolic action, to symbolic action itself, and finally to theories of symbolic action; he named that theory, at different times, "logogogy" and "dramatism," and continually reexamined the role of agency within it. [*See* Identification.]

Logos *and the Public Sphere.* Contemporary rhetorical theory examines problems that have perennially been connected to *logos:* creating frameworks for deliberation on uncertain matters, constructing agreement among disputants, and restoring a public sphere. In investigations of the relation between the discursive world and the social, rhetorics based on *logos* offer the possibility of deliberating on uncertain matters; in recognizing the power of *logos* to change the dispositions of disputing parties, such rhetorics have examined how agreements are forged. By marking out a domain of rhetorical production, and placing that domain in a practical relation to philosophical reflection and aesthetic production, these rhetorics establish conceptual preconditions for the reconstruction of a public sphere and a disciplinary project for rhetoric.

However, rhetorics that emphasize *logos* cannot by themselves reconstruct a public sphere, or even analyze productively all the contemporary forms of political persuasion. For such rhetorics, the material practices of language are abstracted, and virtually invisible; the persuasive force of figures of sound and gesture, or of claims of membership, are discounted. Since public discourse is necessarily staged in a material space, and since contemporary public discourse has a strong disposition to experiment with the materiality of language, contemporary rhetoric will need to address these practices with additional theoretical tools. Perhaps such tools may be found in theories of ideology and performativity proposed by Slavoj Žižek (1989) and Judith Butler (1993), theories that sketch out an alternate understanding of symbolic agency for a society in which all such notions have become deeply problematic.

[*See also* Argumentation; Argument fields; Contingency and probability; Logic; *and* Persuasion.]

BIBLIOGRAPHY

Aristotle. *On Rhetoric: A Theory of Civic Discourse.* Translated by George Kennedy. New York, 1991.

Augustine. *On Christian Doctrine.* Translated by D. W. Robertson. Indianapolis, 1958. Translation of *De doctrina christiana.*

Augustine. *The Confessions.* Translated by Henry Chadwick. New York, 1991.

Biesecker, Barbara. *Addressing Postmodernity: Kenneth Burke, Rhetoric, and a Theory of Social Change.* Tuscaloosa, Ala., 1997. Reexamines Burke in the context of postmodernism; includes critical analysis of Habermas.

Boethius. *Boethius's De topicis differentiis.* Translated by Eleonore Stump. Ithaca, N.Y., 1978. Stump's introduction and essays set in order the tangled history of the topics.

Burke, Kenneth. *A Grammar of Motives.* Berkeley, 1969. First published 1945.

Burke, Kenneth. *A Rhetoric of Motives.* Berkeley, 1962. First published 1950.

Butler, Judith. *Bodies that Matter: On the Discursive Limits of "Sex."* London, 1993.

Cixous, Hélène, and Catherine Clément. *The Newly Born Woman.* Translated by Betsy Wing. Milwaukee, 1986. Translation of *La Jeune née.* Paris, 1975.

Dearin, Ray. *The New Rhetoric of Chaim Perelman: Statement and Response.* Lanham, Md., 1989. Important collection of essays, including Perelman's rejoinder.

Garver, Eugene. *Aristotle's Rhetoric: An Art of Character.* Chicago, 1994. Philosophic treatment of the *Rhetoric.*

Habermas, Jürgen. *The Structural Transformation of the Public Sphere.* Translated by Thomas Berger with Frederick Lawrence. Cambridge, Mass., 1989. First published 1962.

Habermas, Jürgen. *Between Facts and Norms: Contributions to a Discourse Theory of Law and Democracy.* Translated by William Rehg. Cambridge, Mass., 1996.

Jarratt, Susan. *Rereading the Sophists: Classical Rhetoric Refigured.* Carbondale, Ill., 1991. Feminist reading of the Sophists.

Kennedy, George. *Classical Rhetoric and Its Christian and Secular Tradition from Ancient to Modern Times.* Chapel Hill, N.C., 1980. Still the standard narrative history of ancient rhetoric; very full treatment of invention.

Leff, Michael. "The Logician's Rhetoric: Boethius' *De differentiis topicis,* Book IV." In *Medieval Eloquence: Stud-*

ies in the Theory and Practice of Medieval Rhetoric. Edited by James Murphy, pp. 3–24. Berkeley, 1978. Excellent account of logical proofs in the Middle Ages.

Neel, Jasper. *Aristotle's Voice: Rhetoric, Theory, and Writing in America.* Carbondale, Ill., 1994. Critical discussion of Aristotle.

Plato. *Plato on Rhetoric and Language: Four Key Dialogues.* Edited by Jean Nienkamp. Mahwah, N.J., 1999. Translations of *Ion, Protagoras, Gorgias,* and *Phaedrus.*

Poulakos, John. *Sophistical Rhetoric in Classical Greece.* Columbia, S.C., 1995. Analysis of the Sophists emphasizes the importance of competition and spectacle in ancient Greek culture.

Rorty, Amélie Oksenberg. *Essays on Aristotle's Rhetoric.* Berkeley, 1996. Comprehensive collection of essays examining Aristotle's *Rhetoric* as philosophy.

Schiappa, Edward. *Protagoras and Logos: A Study in Greek Philosophy and Rhetoric.* Columbia, S.C., 1991. Full discussions of all the Protagorean fragments.

Sprague, Rosamond Kent, ed. *The Older Sophists.* Columbia, S.C., 1972. Translations of Protagoras, Gorgias, the *Dissoi logoi* and other sophistic texts. Out of print, but widely available in libraries.

Wardy, Robert. *The Birth of Rhetoric: Gorgias, Plato, and Their Successors.* London, 1996. Discussion of *logos* in Gorgias, Plato, and Aristotle.

Žižek, Slavoj. *The Sublime Object of Ideology.* London, 1989.

—SUSAN WELLS

M–N

MASS AUDIENCES. *See* Audience, *article on* Mass audiences.

MASTER TROPES, FOUR. *See* Irony; Metaphor; Metonymy; *and* Synecdochē.

MEANING. *See* Hermeneutics; Reception theory; *and* Religion.

MEDIEVAL RHETORIC. [*This entry comprises two articles. The first article surveys medieval rhetoric from two broad perspectives: the transmission and reception of ancient sources, and the major medieval genres of rhetorical precept, poetics, letter writing, and preaching. The second article studies the medieval treatments of grammar, including the ways in which these treatises took part in the moral, religious, philological, and sexual debates raging around the issue of correct language usage in Latin and in the vernacular.*]

An overview

Perhaps in no period since antiquity has rhetoric had such a broad impact on intellectual formation and practical, institutional production as in the Middle Ages. Rhetoric in the Middle Ages can be studied as a history of practices as recorded in textual precepts, as a conservation of classical culture, as an academic discipline and part of the history of ideas, as an element of literary history, as part of social and pedagogical history, and as an ever-present undercurrent in hermeneutics and literary theory. This essay will survey medieval rhetoric from two broad perspectives: the transmission and reception of ancient sources, and the major medieval genres of rhetorical precept, poetics, letter writing, and preaching.

Classical and Late Classical Textual Sources and Traditions. Medieval rhetoric in the Latin West began with a number of classical and late-classical texts that remained fundamental to the study, theory, and practice of rhetoric until the Early Modern period. [*See* Classical rhetoric.] The texts that were used for systematic treatments of rhetorical theory were Cicero's *De inventione*, the Pseudo-Ciceronian *Rhetorica ad Herennium* (both first century BCE), and Book 4 of Boethius's *De topicis differentiis* (early sixth century CE). These texts in the "Ciceronian" tradition, which lay out the internal structures of argumentation in terms that are closely related to dialectical study, were the most basic components of the rhetorical curriculum throughout the Middle Ages. [*See* Dialectic.] Alongside Ciceronian theory, there was a strong tradition of grammatical teaching, focusing on written composition, style, and arrangement. [*See* Arrangement, *article on* Traditional arrangement; *overview article on* Composition; *and* Style.] For this, the key classical references remained Horace's *Ars poetica* (first century BCE) and the *Barbarismus* of Donatus (Part 3 of his *Ars grammatica* or *Ars maior*, fourth century CE), along with Book 4 of the *Ad Herennium* (like the later *Barbarismus*, a schematic survey of figures and tropes). The texts of Horace and Donatus were standard features of elementary as well as more advanced instruction in literary composition and poetics in the medieval schools. Finally, there was a Christian theological tradition of late antiquity that combined semiotics and scriptural hermeneutics with an evangelical ministry of preaching. [*See* Hermeneutics.] This tradition is given its definitive preceptive expression in Augustine's *De doctrina christiana* (c. fourth to fifth century CE) which combines teaching on how to interpret scriptural meaning (Books 1–3) with teaching on how to deliver an effective public message regarding the meaning of scripture (Book 4). [*See* Religion.]

It was Cicero's youthful, schematic (and incomplete) treatise *De inventione*, and not any one of his mature and synthetic theoretical works (or the even fuller account in Quintilian's *Institutio oratoria*) that became the shaping influence on so much medieval rhetorical teaching. This in itself tells us much about the interests and institutional character of medieval rhetoric, especially when we consider the great variety and intellectual depth of medieval treatments of this Ciceronian inheritance. Both the *De inventione* and the *Ad Herennium* proved to be excellent, coherent teaching texts. Between them they conveyed complete and concise information about the parts of rhetoric, topical invention, status theory (the issues upon which the case rests), attributes of the person and the act, the parts of a speech, the genres of rhetoric, and stylistic ornamentation. [*See* Stasis; *and* Topics.] The *De inventione* in particular was a perfect vehicle for Late Antique commentators and compilers of rhetorical lore, including Marius Victorinus (fourth century), Martianus Capella (fifth century), and Boethius himself, whose own influential treatment of rhetoric in Book 4 of his *De topicis differentiis* offered a dialectician's approach to Ciceronian inventional doctrine. Boethius differentiates rhetoric from dialectic in terms of rhetoric's particularity and dialectic's generality, rhetoric's use of the hypothesis (particular case), and dialectic's use of the thesis (general question). We owe to the Late Antique Latin commentators the survival into the Middle Ages of classical (Ciceronian) rhetorical doctrine, and for these commentators and teachers rhetoric was more an intellectual discipline, allied closely with the terms and system of dialectic, than a practical art of oratory. Oratory, as Cicero had known and defined it, had declined steadily during the years of the empire under political conditions that did not encourage the forensic and judicial oratory of earlier periods. But rhetorical teaching survived through late antiquity and into the Middle Ages because of its intellectual and cultural prestige, and in the course of its survival it took on other forms and found many other purposes. [*See* Oratory.]

Rhetoric was studied continuously as an essential element of the trivium, one of the *artes sermocinales* or arts of language, along with grammar and dialectic. [*See* Trivium.] Isidore, Bishop of Seville (seventh century) devotes a book of his encyclopedia of knowledge, the *Etymologiae*, to

rhetoric (basing his treatment on Cicero and Late Antique summaries of Ciceronian texts); Alcuin (eighth century) records his efforts to teach the art of rhetoric to Charlemagne; and from the early Middle Ages onward, a clearly Ciceronian rhetorical theory is routinely featured in the curricula of monasteries in northern and southern Europe. The monasteries also contributed a great deal to the conservation and transmission of rhetorical texts. There is an unbroken tradition of academic commentary on the *De inventione* (called the "old rhetoric," *rhetorica vetus*) culminating in the work of the twelfth-century cathedral schools in France and Germany, where rhetoric was studied as a close partner of dialectic, and where the *De inventione* was read alongside of Cicero's *Topica* and other related texts on dialectical topics. Commentaries on the *Ad Herennium* (*rhetorica nova*) also begin to appear in the eleventh and twelfth centuries in these northern European schools, with new attention directed to the stylistic teaching in Book 4.

In the thirteenth century, rhetoric was incorporated into study at the emergent universities, in northern Europe at Paris and Oxford (and not long afterward at other sites such as Orléans), and in southern Europe especially at Bologna, Pavia, and Ravenna. The earliest statutes of Paris and Oxford (1215 and 1268, respectively) are famously obscure about the actual place of rhetoric in the curriculum, although the Paris statutes mention limited lecturing on Book 4 of Boethius's *De topicis differentiis*. In the arts faculties at Paris and Oxford, logic was the dominant subject, and rhetoric probably assumed the role that it had taken in the earlier cathedral schools, as another dimension of dialectical study. In the Italian universities, however, the early emphasis on the study of law and on preparation for careers in civic and church bureaucracies gave the Ciceronian textual tradition much more centrality, not specifically for the teaching of oratory, but rather for the models of topical invention (in which so much Roman legal theory is also embedded) and for the precepts about style, structure, and form, concerns leading to the *ars dictaminis* (discussed below). It was first in Italy that the Ciceronian tradition found its way into the vernacular, with Brunetto Latini's *Rettorica*, a free translation of the *De inventione* (composed c.1260, while Brunetto was in exile in France). His purpose in this translation was to open a conduit between academic learning and an educated civic culture.

Aristotle's *Rhetoric* was translated into Latin from Greek by William Moerbeke about 1270 (a translation and commentary based on an Arabic version of Aristotle's text had circulated earlier). The new Latin translation of the *Rhetoric* seems to have had an immediate impact at Paris, where it was commented on by several masters between the late thirteenth and the mid-fourteenth centuries, and where copies of the text itself were distributed by the university stationers. But Aristotle's text found no official place in a university curriculum until the 1431 Oxford statutes, where it is mentioned along with Boethius's *De topicis differentiis* Book 4 and the *Ad Herennium:* these statutes may reflect teaching practices that were ongoing and long established by the fifteenth century. If indeed Aristotle's *Rhetoric* was being taught at Oxford and Paris, it would likely have been read in relation to the texts of Aristotle's *Organon* (the logic texts of the Aristotelian canon), which, by the late thirteenth century, formed the backbone of the curriculum in the arts faculties. Aristotle's definition of rhetoric as the "antistrophe" of dialectic, an art of discourse that draws its techniques from the same pool as dialectic, offered a newfound theoretical justification for what had been the actual institutional place of rhetoric as a counterpart of dialectical study in the urban schools of the twelfth and thirteenth centuries.

Horace's *Ars poetica* has as long and unbroken a tradition of study and commentary as the Ciceronian rhetorical texts, but in both practical and theoretical terms it had a very different place in the curriculum. The *Ars poetica* is a text about writing, literary style, stylistic decorum, and finding one's subject matter through imitation of existing literary sources. It is not necessarily an easy text to understand, but it is not theoretically dense, and it presents a self-contained system of prescriptive poetics. Since the first century CE (at least on the evidence of Quintilian's *Institutio oratoria* 1–2), some of the more elementary principles of rhetoric were taught side by side with the principles of literary composition that were handled by grammarians,

and a text like Horace's *Ars poetica* could be made useful to the study of either discipline. As the teaching of rhetoric, especially at more elementary levels, became increasingly text-based, the stylistic principles that had earlier been studied as part of the art of grammar could be just as well taught under the aegis of rhetoric. Thus, Horace's *Ars poetica* could be joined, in common pedagogical purpose, with Donatus's *Barbarismus,* a grammatical text discussing figures, tropes, and their correct and incorrect usage, and as well with Book 4 of the *Ad Herennium,* the section of this rhetorical text dealing also with figures, tropes, and stylistic ornamentation. It could also be joined with newer grammatical textbooks that restated ancient doctrine.

But the uses to which Horace's *Ars poetica* were put were decidedly prescriptive, aiming at what has been called the "future text": Horace's text filled a need for a certain kind of rhetorical instruction. There were extensive commentaries written on the *Ars poetica* during late antiquity, which often accompanied the text in medieval manuscripts, and during the twelfth and thirteenth centuries, many new commentaries were written to explain the text. The commentaries pay special attention to Horace's treatment of imitation, variation on one's sources, translation, arrangement, and stylistic consistency. [*See* Imitation.] This suggests that the *Ars poetica* would have been valuable in elementary teaching of students who were just acquiring their own Latinity and who were embarking on literary (i.e., compositional) exercises of imitation, abbreviation and amplification, character study, and stylistic augmentation. [*See* Amplification.] But these compositional teachings also carried beyond the elementary classroom into a general poetic theory. Because the *Ars poetica* was a cornerstone of schooling, it was also one of the classical texts most familiar to active medieval poets, including vernacular poets such as Jean de Meun and Chaucer, who could avail themselves of Horatian precepts about translation as a legitimate form of imitation and "invention" of subject matter. Horace offers a famous ethical justification for poetry as both instructive and pleasurable, themes which resonate with the Ciceronian rhetorical doctrine that the orator's task is to prove, please, and persuade. Medieval reception of Horace reflects this double legacy of ethics and rhetoric, as these audience-oriented principles could be invoked to defend the utility of poetic fiction. The powerful influence of Horace's text also lies behind one of the key medieval preceptive rhetorical genres, the *ars poetriae* (discussed below).

Augustine's treatise *De doctrina christiana* deserves to be considered the first Christian rhetoric. This text sets into motion a theological tradition of rhetoric which takes the form not only of preaching, but of scriptural interpretation, semiotics (theory of signs and symbols within and beyond language), and spiritual disciplines of reading and meditation. Before his conversion, Augustine had been a professional rhetorician, both as teacher and orator. But in *De doctrina christiana* (written between 396 and 427 CE), Augustine explicitly reacts against the classical (Ciceronian) rhetorical inheritance. The work is systematic, but it does not reproduce a Ciceronian system of invention, arrangement, style, memory, and delivery. [*See* Delivery; Invention; *and* Memory.] Rather, it incorporates some of these elements into a new system, which is divided into two parts: the "means of discovering (*modus inveniendi*) what is to be understood" (Books 1–3), and the "means of setting forth (*modus proferendi*) that which has been understood" (Book 4). The "means of discovering" represents his treatment of invention; the "means of setting forth" presents a composite treatment of arrangement, style, and delivery, either in speech or writing. In its totality, *De doctrina christiana* is a guide to fulfilling a new evangelical ministry, which involves not only preaching, but correct and responsible interpretations of scripture. In Books 1 to 3, Augustine treats discovery (invention) in terms of techniques of scriptural exegesis: these include philology and grammar; a knowledge of the difference between literal and figurative language; and most importantly, a semiotic theory (grounded in philosophical and theological principles) that distinguishes between signs (words and other symbols) and things (truths and realities, especially spiritual realities) to which signs must refer. It is in laying down this semiotic theory, the distinction between linguistic signs and truths, that Augustine reintroduces, now in Christian theological terms, the old Platonic distrust of rhetoric as manipulation of language detached from truth. In the Augustinian model of rhetoric, invention is a process of interpreting a text, the Bible, in which all truths have already been revealed. The notion that truth is fixed, that the subject matter (the truth of salvation) has already been revealed, and that this subject matter will always be the same in any Christian discourse, underwrites Augustine's theory of delivery, the "means of setting forth that which has been understood." In Book 4 of *De doctrina christiana*, Augustine sets out a theory of levels of style, which appropriates some of Cicero's discussion in *Orator* (21–29) of the low, middle, and high styles. But Augustine ties level of style to the spiritual needs of the audience, rather than, as in Cicero, to the relative dignity of different subject matters; if for the pagan orator there can be elevated or base subject matters, for the Christian orator the subject matter is always the revealed truth of salvation, which can be treated across a spectrum of stylistic registers, rendering the humblest style lofty in its effects.

Augustine's rhetoric cuts directly into classical rhetorical theory, appropriating and revaluating its most essential elements. [*See* Religion.] The effects of this over the next one thousand years almost defy summary because of its virtually universal impact on Christian thought about discourse. The most obvious example of the effect of Augustine's rhetoric is the art of preaching, which will be discussed below. Other forms that this effect took can be noted here. Augustine's treatment of the levels of style is taken up by the monastic writer Rabanus Maurus (c.780–856) in his compendium on clerical training, *De institutione clericorum*, in which his account of rhetoric is based on Augustine's *De doctrina christiana*. Rabanus quotes directly and at length from Augustine's text, including those sections where Augustine is quoting whole sections of Cicero's *Orator* on levels of style and the offices of rhetoric (to prove/teach, please, and persuade). Thus Rabanus in turn becomes a conduit for the transmission of Ciceronian precepts on style; apart from those sections quoted in Augustine and then Rabanus, Cicero's *Orator* and its important doctrines were almost unknown in the Middle Ages (the complete text was rediscovered in the fifteenth century). The Ciceronian–Augustinian doctrine of the levels of style had a significant influence on medieval prose composition, offering a theoretical underpinning for the use of an impassioned high style; for example, the sublime, rhythmic style of the twelfth-century Cistercian monk Bernard of Clairvaux in his sermons on the Song of Songs, or the ecstatic, musical prose of the fourteenth-century English mystic Richard Rolle, who wrote in both Latin and English. But it also gave a justification for the plain or restrained (middle) style that characterizes such monumental prose achievements as the Wycliffite translation of the Bible into Middle English (c.1395).

One other form of the Augustinian influence is the combination of the grammatical tradition of descriptive poetics (i.e., the lists of figures and tropes in the *Barbarismus* of Donatus) with a theological rhetoric based in textuality. This is well exemplified in the work of the Venerable Bede (c.673–735), who wrote a textbook called *De schematibus et tropis* (Concerning figures and tropes) for the pupils of the monastic school at Jarrow in the north of England. Bede argues that the scriptural text is the original source of teaching about eloquence, and that all the figures and tropes treated in classical pagan rhetoric were first used in Holy Scripture. In substituting scripture for pagan authors, Bede imitates the pedagogy of the Church Fathers, including Augustine. Moreover, his treatment of scriptural eloquence introduces many hermeneutical principles that echo Augustine's concerns. Bede's treatment of scriptural rhetoric is part grammatical teaching and part exegetical program, showing how rhetorical theory is converted to the purposes of textual interpretation.

Indeed, Augustine had captured the textual and textually interpretive character of Late Antique Jewish and Christian culture, and had articulated this exegetical imperative in rhetorical terms: invention, the key intellectual process of rhetoric, was converted to the discovery and hermeneutical penetration of truths contained in writing. One could argue that if the master genre of Roman antiquity was the forensic oration, the master genre of medieval culture was exegesis. [See Forensic genre.] To interpret correctly was seen as challenging and carried a tremendous burden of personal responsibility, as Augustine recognized. Thus, the intellectual tools provided by the system of rhetorical invention could be most valuable to the new purpose of finding and

giving expression to the hidden, obscure, or ambiguous meanings contained in Holy Scripture and other textual authorities. We see the influence of this "hermeneutical rhetoric" in such signature productions as the monastic meditation, in which reading a text, and ruminating on a passage or an image, eventuated in an act of composition grounded in recognizably rhetorical techniques of topical invention and locational memory (see Mary Carruthers, *The Craft of Thought,* Cambridge, U.K., 1998).

Yet despite the clear and continuing importance of classical rhetorical theory and precept during the Middle Ages, medieval writers and thinkers often expressed ambivalence about the compatibility of pagan rhetoric with their own Christian outlook. Saint Jerome (c.347–c.420 CE) famously records (in *Ep.* 22) his own struggles to give up his affection for pagan learning and especially pagan rhetoric: "What communion has light with darkness? . . . What has Horace to do with the Psalter, Virgil with the Gospels, and Cicero with Paul?" In the same letter, he describes a dream in which he saw himself before the seat of judgment in heaven; asked to state his condition he said that he was a Christian, to which the Judge replied: "Thou liest: thou art a Ciceronian, not a Christian." And Augustine, with similar vehemence, turned his back on his earlier vocation as a teacher of rhetoric, denouncing it as the "selling of words" in the marketplace (*Confessions* 9.5). Early Christianity differentiated itself sharply from its contemporary pagan culture in various ways, including by renouncing pagan rhetoric, in which "truth" was more or less contingent on style, presentation, and legal or persuasive purpose. Of course, Christianity never actually rejected pagan rhetorical teaching; but at many junctures Christian theorists injected comparisons between merely human eloquence, in which meaning can be always subject to tropological distortion, and the stable and divinely "authored" eloquence of Scripture, in which truth is unitary and meanings—however complex—are not contradictory. Bede makes such claims in his *De schematibus et tropis;* so does Thomas Aquinas (1225–1274) in his *Summa theologiae* 1.1.9–10; and more controversially, this distinction between human eloquence and divinely sanctioned Scriptural language is the basis of the literalist hermeneutics of such heterodox theologians as John Wyclif (c.1324–1384).

The Major Genres of Medieval Rhetoric: Poetics, Letter Writing, Preaching. With the transmission, reception, and study of the ancient rhetorical traditions in the Middle Ages, new literary and institutional uses of rhetoric evolved, and the practice of rhetoric began to be organized into distinct genres, each with its own textual forms and traditions. The three major genres of "preceptive" rhetoric (i.e., a rhetoric that teaches a system for producing texts rather than simply describing existing texts), poetics, letter writing, and preaching, are interconnected in their use of common sources, and to some degree also in the pedagogical and institutional functions they serve. But they also developed along very different lines, and in many respects in different cultural spheres.

Ciceronian rhetoric and the Horatian-grammatical system of poetics meet in the medieval tradition of the *artes poetriae* (arts of poetry), compositional textbooks written in Latin for the Latin-based school curricula. [*See* Poetry.] These *artes* were products of grammatical teaching, but they were rhetorical in their aims. They were written during a relatively short period, between 1175 and 1280, in northern France, England, and Germany. The texts, in the order of their appearance, are Matthew of Vendôme's *Ars versificatoria* (Art of versifying; c.1175); Geoffrey of Vinsauf's *Poetria nova* and *Documentum de modo et arte dictandi et versificandi* (Instruction in the method and art of prose and verse writing; both written between 1208 and 1213); Gervase of Melkley's *Ars poetica* (c.1215); John of Garland's *Parisiana poetria de arte prosaica, metrica, et rithmica* (Paris poetics of the art of prose, meter, and rhythm; after 1229); Eberhard the German's *Laborintus* (meaning roughly "that which contains difficulty or hardship"; before 1280).

The arts of Matthew of Vendôme, Geoffrey of Vinsauf, and John of Garland make use of recognizably Ciceronian elements and vocabulary, discussing arrangement, style, and to varying degrees of explicitness, invention. Gervase of Melkley and Eberhard the German are more concerned with style, tropes, and versification, making their works closer to the grammatical tradition. The treatment of invention in the treatises by Mat-

thew, Geoffrey, and John is really directed to finding one's own matter in inherited literary materials. In Matthew and Geoffrey especially, the discussions of invention are encased in discussions of how to amplify or abbreviate one's given matter; that is, in terms reminiscent of Horace, how to present traditional matter in a way that is fresh and varied. This may reflect two conditions, one practical and one intellectual. First, this may suggest that these treatises were used in the same circumstances in which Horace's *Ars poetica* was used, to teach students who were engaged in imitation of literary models. But second, and more broadly, this also reflects the orientation of medieval poetic theory, which privileged inherited materials that carried the authority of written tradition.

The contents of Geoffrey's *Poetria nova* (meant to be a "new" *Poetics* in contrast to the "old" *Ars poetica* of Horace) can be summarized here to illustrate the nature of these Latin arts of poetry. The *Poetria nova* begins with general observations about planning a poem and finding what one will say, with an emphasis on prudent restraint and imagining the whole work in one's mind, which includes planning how verbal style will clothe the work, how the poem will begin, how thought or theme (*sententia*) will be balanced, and ensuring a positive effect on the audience. After this short introduction (the only place where a notion that corresponds to invention is treated separately), Geoffrey moves into a section on arrangement, in which he considers natural and artificial orders. In relation to the topic of arrangement, he introduces a long and important discussion of amplification and abbreviation, taking up the various figures that can be used to swell out or cinch in a discourse. He illustrates his precepts on amplification and abbreviation with a number of poems; for example, a lament on the death of King Richard I (the Lion-Hearted), which demonstrates the use of apostrophe (this particular poem was memorable enough for Chaucer to allude to it in the *Nun's Priest's Tale*). [*See* Apostrophē.] There follow the long central sections on tropes, figures of diction, figures of thought, grammatical conversion (turning nouns and adjectives into their declensions, verbs into participles, etc., all for the purpose of achieving stylistic variation), and stylistic decorum; again in these sections, the various devices are often illustrated with poems composed for these purposes. Two short sections at the end describe memory (based on *Ad Herennium* 3), and recitation (corresponding to delivery). While invention in the strict sense of finding one's material is only considered briefly at the beginning of the work, inventional techniques are actually distributed throughout, as topics of circumstance, place, character, attribute, and the like pervade the discussions of arrangement and style.

The *Poetria nova* achieved particular success as a school text. It survives in over two hundred manuscripts across Western and Eastern Europe, some of them as late as the end of the fifteenth century. It was often bound or copied in collections containing Latin poetry and other rhetorical treatises and exercises. It acquired its own commentaries early in its circulation, and in most of its later manuscripts (and many of its early ones as well) it is accompanied by a marginal commentary or interlinear glosses; there are at least twelve distinct commentaries on the text that survive. The *Poetria nova* was equipped with almost all of the exegetical trappings that an authoritative text could receive. Its success lay in its comprehensiveness, its form (a verse text about verse writing, illustrating its precepts with verse compositions written to the illustrative purpose), and its almost perfect synthesis of Ciceronian precepts of style and structure, Horatian teaching on narrative arrangement and stylistic decorum, and grammatical teaching on verbal ornament. It was used in elementary (preuniversity) teaching, taught in conjunction with other grammatical or classical rhetorical texts. But it was also used at some universities, as collections associated with certain university centers suggest (Woods, 1991). Thus it may have been used to supplement or even replace the teaching contained in the *Ad Herennium*. While not all the other *artes poetriae* were so successful, the popularity of the *Poetria nova* attests to the pedagogical and intellectual importance of this distinctive medieval genre.

The *ars dictaminis* (art of letter writing) is a most distinctive medieval preceptive genre, an original technical invention in response to the needs of the bureaucracies that arose especially with the emergence of new urban cultures during and after the twelfth century. [*See* Ars dictaminis.]

The *ars dictaminis* has some ancient precedents: there are theoretical precepts for letter writing from the period of the later Roman Empire; and there are ancient examples of epistolary art that gave shape to the literary genre, including the letters of Cicero, the Pauline epistles, and the letters of Saint Jerome. However, the medieval *dictatores* (teachers of letter writing and prose composition), beginning in the early twelfth century, produced a genre of such technical specificity that it far surpasses what was offered by ancient literary or theoretical sources.

The evolution of the *ars dictaminis* is very much influenced by geography. The first stage of this preceptive movement is firmly sited in Italy. The earliest surviving rhetorical texts to deal with an art of letter writing are two treatises composed before 1100 by Alberic of Montecassino (an ancient Benedictine monastery in central Italy). Neither of these treatises sets forth a full-fledged theory of letter writing. It was the following generation of Italian writers that gave a complete and formal expression to this doctrine. With these writers, the center of dictaminal teaching activity shifts to the important northern city of Bologna, with as many as eight *dictatores* producing significant treatises during the first half of the twelfth century.

Among the Bolognese *dictatores*, the art soon reached a standardized format for producing a five-part letter: salutation, securing good will (*captatio benevolentiae*), narration, petition, and conclusion. This format is clearly descended from the Ciceronian system of the parts of an oration. It may be surprising how quickly these preceptive manuals narrowed their scope, often dispensing with any reference to classical rhetorical theory. But the historical milieu of the Bolognese *dictatores* helps to explain this. The dictaminal art evolved in conjunction with the study of law at the University of Bologna, as a practical response to the needs of those being trained as lawyers, judges, and other lesser professionals, such as notaries and clerks, in the ecclesiastical and civic bureaucracies. For such pragmatic interests, the new dictaminal art could, for some, replace study of traditional rhetoric.

A summary of one important theoretical treatise from the middle of the twelfth century can indicate the nature of dictaminal teaching during this period. The anonymous treatise *Rationes dictandi* (Principles of letter writing), composed in 1135, would offer the student a concise introduction. It begins with definitions of terms ("written composition," "metrical," "rhythmic," "prose," "approved and basic format [of a letter]"); it also defines an epistle and its parts. The body of the treatise then discusses each of the five parts of a standard letter, with special weight given to the salutation (giving twenty examples that stress hierarchies of rank and other social, familial, and class hierarchies). There follow some observations about how the parts of a letter can be rearranged to suit different circumstances; and finally some remarks on syntax and grammatical variation.

In the early thirteenth century, a French dictaminal tradition emerged, imported from Italy, but inflected by the disciplinary character of the French institutional centers where it was taught, notably Tours and Orléans. In these French locales, dictamen was taught by grammar masters, rather than, as at Bologna, in conjunction with law. The French *dictatores* tended to position *dictamen* closer to traditional conceptions of grammatical and rhetorical doctrine. It is not surprising, therefore, that John of Garland, whose *Parisiana poetria* has already been mentioned above in the context of the grammatical *artes poetriae,* includes a section on dictamen in his treatise.

The French schools, which were sending their own trainees to careers in the papal court in Italy, also exported their influence back to a second generation of Bolognese *dictatores,* who adopted some of the features of French teaching while also reacting against it. These later generations of Italians favored a plainer style suited to the practical needs of their students. The most important figures of the "second" Bolognese school, Guido Faba (1190–1240), Bene da Firenze (fl. 1220s), and Boncompagno da Signa (1165–1240), cemented a distinctively Italian conception of dictamen as a quasi-autonomous branch or form of rhetoric. The Bolognese theoretical propensities are also manifested in the model letters or *formulae* that they incorporate in their treatises, according to a practice that had become standard in the *ars dictaminis.* Quentin Skinner (*The Foundations of Modern Political Thought,* vol. 1, Cam-

bridge, U.K., 1978) notes that the model letters incorporated in thirteenth-century Bolognese dictaminal treatises were the crucial medium through which rhetorical study first truly entered into vital intercourse with the public and political affairs of the Italian city republics: the model letters were often of contemporary topical interest (so as to be relevant to student careers), and quickly became "vehicles for offering advice about the problems of city life" (p. 30).

Dictamen spread through Western Europe to Germany and Iberia. But some of its most interesting late manifestations were in England. At Oxford University, as Martin Camargo has shown (*Medieval Rhetorics of Prose Composition,* Binghamton, N.Y., 1995), in lower schools affiliated with the university, a number of grammar masters used dictamen to teach "remedial" Latinity (such as would be required for further study at the advanced university level), and prose composition, and, with dictamen as the foundation of study, offered courses in "business education," of which one component was the *ars notaria.* That Oxford University, not otherwise known for its curricular attention to rhetoric, should have supported a thriving extramural industry of "business studies" based on dictaminal teaching, is testimony to the social, economic, and political importance of this art.

As a formal preceptive genre, the medieval art of preaching (*ars praedicandi*) has virtually no precedent in classical rhetoric. [*See* Homiletics.] Rather, it appears that rhetorical doctrine was pressed into service to address the needs of an explosion of new preaching practices that occurred during the first quarter of the thirteenth century. Of course, preaching is as old as Christianity itself, and as a distinctively oral practice (in contrast to verse writing and letter writing) it would seem to be closest in spirit to ancient oratory. Moreover, Augustine's *De doctrina christiana,* and many other texts had provided various forms of guidance about preaching. Augustine's text is the most important ancient source, and thus a link with Roman rhetorical precept. But the *De doctrina christiana* also declines to set forth a systematic technique for constructing a sermon. The nuts-and-bolts question of how to put a sermon together did not find expression until there was a need for a newly expanding class of preachers to preach *on a regular basis* to many different kinds of audiences. This need came into being with the Fourth Lateran Council of 1215, which decreed compulsory annual confession for all Christians. Among the responses to the decree was a new industry of confessional and penitential texts and teachings. The two major preaching orders, the Dominicans and the Franciscans, were also established (1216 and 1223, respectively), adding a new, mobile population of licensed preachers to the traditional ranks of bishops, priests, and monks. In response to the call of Lateran IV for an increased and routinized care of souls, was a flowering of preaching theory and practical aids for preachers: collections of *exempla* and other homiletic materials; alphabetical lists and concordances to organize scripture and related texts for quick reference; sermon collections; and preceptive sermon manuals, *artes praedicandi*. [*See* Exemplum.] As James J. Murphy observes, for twelve centuries the Church had been concerned with *what* to preach, not *how* to preach it (1974, p. 282). The new social and institutional pressures of the thirteenth century changed that equation radically.

Before the thirteenth century, there had been some notable attempts to treat preaching in its largest terms: Gregory the Great's *Cura pastoralis* (sixth century); Rabanus Maurus's *De institutione clericorum* (ninth century), mentioned above for its transmission of Augustinian and Ciceronion doctrines; and an influential treatise (*Summa de arte praedicandi*) by the Parisian Cistercian and teacher Alan of Lille. Alan's treatise is interesting for the way it integrates broad and humane advice about the preacher's character and his emotional appeals, along with invention, arrangement, and style. But of the forty-eight sections of the treatise, only the preface and first section deal preceptively with preaching. The remaining chapters offer examples of *what* is to be preached, exemplifying a system of scriptural exposition through the exegetical and logical principle of division and the accumulation of authorities. In exegetical terms, Alan's treatise may be seen as an important development and application of the ideas initiated by Augustine's *De doctrina christiana*.

From the thirteenth century onward, we have vastly more evidence for the range of preaching practices. Sermons can be divided roughly into three types: a straightforward, simple exposition of scripture; the methods of exposition and division associated with the learned style of university sermons; and popular (especially vernacular) preaching by means of anecdote, fable, saint's legend, miracle story, and moralized *exempla*. The formal manuals of preaching overwhelmingly represent the second style, the university (also called the "thematic") sermon. There are more than three hundred extant arts of preaching dating from the early thirteenth century to the Reformation. This preceptive literature reflects two major influences. With their attention to the parts of an oration, to rhetorical coloration, to means of persuasion, and to the character of the preacher and the effects on an audience, the *artes praedicandi* seem clearly to descend from Ciceronian rhetoric. But with their attention to division of subject (or "theme") as a device of analysis, the *artes* seem also to be indebted to the scholastic methods of university arts and theology faculties. Many authors of these treatises were themselves preachers to university communities, and the sermons preached at universities (especially at Paris) came to represent a standard form.

The form of sermons outlined most typically by *artes praedicandi* consists of six parts: (1) theme: a quotation from scripture (from the day's liturgical readings), followed by a prayer; (2) protheme, which is the exordium for the theme (this could consist of a quotation from another part of scripture that had corresponding relevance to the first quotation); (3) antetheme: the introduction of the theme, a restatement that sets forth the purpose of the sermon; (4) division of the theme, into three or further multiples of three, with authorities cited to "prove" each division; this was both a part of the sermon and the key exegetical and inventional activity upon which the sermon depended; (5) subdivision of the theme; (6) amplification or dilation (or "distinction") of each of the divisions and subdivisions.

These elements are clearly present in an early thirteenth-century treatise, the *Summa de arte praedicandi* by Thomas of Salisbury. The main topic headings of Thomas's *Summa* provide a strong sense of the rhetorical as well as hermeneutical character of its contents: preaching, on prothemes or prologues; on preaching and invention and its part; on narration; on the art of varying narrations and parabolas (figurative speech); on artistic narration by means of persons; on persuasion by the similitude of things; on division in preaching; on three falsehoods (concerning preaching); on persuasion; on the art of remembering; on the art of distributing; on the style of the art; on delivery of the art (these last four closely follow the Ciceronian parts of rhetoric). Scripture is the material of invention (a notion that can be traced back to Augustine), but the techniques for invention are modes of topical analysis drawn from the *Rhetorica ad Herennium* and other late classical sources.

The genre of the *ars praedicandi* reaches the zenith of elaboration in the fourteenth century, with such comprehensive treatises as the Englishman Robert of .Basevorn's *Forma praedicandi,* composed probably c.1322. In fifty sections, Robert lays out a remarkably complete prescription for composing a thematic ("university") sermon. Beginning with the institutional question of who should preach (under what office or license), he gives a brief history of preaching and then turns to precept. He divides the six parts of a sermon into fifteen "ornaments," which are themselves subdivided and analyzed, and copiously illustrated with examples. The last section deals with practical advice about such topics as voice, gesture, and timely humor, suggesting the meeting point between the preceptive art and the material environment of speaker, audience, and speech. [*See* Homiletics.]

[*See also* Commonplaces and commonplace books.]

BIBLIOGRAPHY

Augustine. *De doctrina christiana.* Edited by W. M. Green. Vienna, 1963; *On Christian Doctrine,* translated by D. W. Robertson. Indianapolis, 1958.

Bagni, Paolo. *La costituzione della poesia nelle artes del XII–XIII secolo.* Bologna, Italy, 1968.

Boethius. *De topicis differentiis.* Translated by Eleonore Stump. Ithaca, N.Y., 1978.

Briscoe, Marianne G., and Barbara H. Jaye. *Artes Praedicandi and Artes Orandi.* Turnhout, Belgium, 1992. Comprehensive survey and study of arts of preaching.

Camargo, Martin. *Ars Dictaminis, Ars Dictandi.* Turnhout, Belgium, 1991. Recent and definitive study of dictamen; contains all important references to primary texts and secondary literature.

Cameron, Averil. *Christianity and the Rhetoric of Empire: The Development of Christian Discourse.* Berkeley, 1991. An important and highly readable account of early Christianity's crafting of a populist, plain rhetoric.

Caplan, Harry. *Of Eloquence: Studies in Ancient and Medieval Rhetoric.* Ithaca, N.Y., 1970. These are Caplan's collected essays (from 1927 to 1944); they are foundational and very readable essays on various subjects, especially preaching.

Carruthers, Mary. *The Book of Memory: A Study of Memory in Medieval Culture.* Cambridge, U.K., 1990. This treats the theory as well as practice of the *ars memoria.*

Charland, T. M., ed. *Artes praedicandi: Contribution à l'histoire de la rhétoriaue au moyen âge.* Paris, 1936. One of the principal modern editions of the arts of preaching.

(Pseudo-) Cicero. *Rhetorica ad Herennium.* Edited and translated by Harry Caplan. Cambridge, Mass., 1954.

Cicero. *De inventione.* Edited and translated by H. M. Hubbell. Cambridge, Mass., 1949.

Clanchy, M. T. *From Memory to Written Record: England 1066–1307.* Oxford, 1993. First published 1979. This study of literacy and the importance of documents has great relevance to the teaching of rhetoric in the later Middle Ages.

Copeland, Rita. *Rhetoric, Hermeneutics, and Translation in the Middle Ages.* Cambridge, U.K., 1991.

Enders, Jody. *Rhetoric and the Origins of Medieval Drama.* Ithaca, N.Y., 1992.

Faral, E., ed. *Les arts poétiques du XIIe et du XIIIE siècle.* Paris, 1924. This is the principal edition of the Latin arts of poetry.

Kelly, Douglas. *The Arts of Poetry and Prose.* Turnhout, Belgium, 1991. Recent and authoritative study of the *artes poetriae;* see for further bibliography of primary and secondary sources, and for references to translations of Latin texts.

Kennedy, George A. *Classical Rhetoric and Its Christian and Secular Tradition from Ancient to Modern Times.* Chapel Hill, N.C., 1980. A broad historical survey, containing excellent chapters on late classical and medieval rhetoric (both Latin and Byzantine traditions).

Lawler, Traugott, ed. and trans. *The Parisiana poetria of John of Garland.* New Haven, 1974. A particularly helpful edition of one of the arts of poetry, equipped with a facing page translation and many useful notes.

McKeon, Richard. "Rhetoric in the Middle Ages." *Speculum* 17 (1942), pp. 1–32. Reprinted in R. S. Crane, ed., *Critics and Criticism,* pp. 117–45. Chicago, 1952. Along with Murphy (1974; see below), McKeon's essay is the major contribution to the study of this field. Its approach is through intellectual history.

Miller, Joseph M., Michael H. Prosser, and Thomas W.

Benson, eds. and trans. *Readings in Medieval Rhetoric.* Bloomington, Ind., 1973. Translations of and short commentaries on a wide selection of medieval rhetorical texts from the fifth to the fifteenth centuries.

Murphy, James. J., ed. *Three Medieval Rhetorical Arts.* Berkeley, 1971. Translations of Geoffrey of Vinsauf's *Poetria nova,* Anonymous of Bologna's *Rationes dictandi,* and Robert of Basevorn's *Forma praedicandi.*

Murphy, James J. *Rhetoric in the Middle Ages: A History of Rhetorical Theory from Saint Augustine to the Renaissance.* Berkeley, 1974. The foundational survey of medieval rhetoric, the most comprehensive monograph in any language.

Murphy, James J., ed. *Medieval Eloquence: Studies in the Theory and Practice of Medieval Rhetoric.* Berkeley, 1978. An unsurpassed collection of essays on historical, theoretical, and literary issues.

Vickers, Brian, ed. *Rhetoric Revalued.* Binghamton, N.Y., 1982. Includes informative chapters on various aspects of medieval rhetoric.

Ward, John O. *Ciceronian Rhetoric in Treatise, Scholion, and Commentary.* Turnhout, Belgium, 1995. A definitive account of how Ciceronian rhetoric was studied and used in medieval universities and schools.

Woods, Marjorie C., ed. and trans. *An Early Commentary on the Poetria nova of Geoffrey of Vinsauf.* New York, 1985. Important treatment of the pedagogical circulation of this art of poetry.

Woods, Marjorie C. "A Medieval Rhetoric Goes to School—And to the University." *Rhetorica* 9 (1991), pp. 55–65.

— RITA COPELAND

Medieval grammar

In the Middle Ages, the world of learning became schematized as the seven liberal arts, divided into the trivium (grammar, rhetoric, and dialectic, the last of which was often treated as being identical with logic) and quadrivium (arithmetic, geometry, astronomy, and music). [*See* Dialectic; *and* Trivium.] The first grouping was designated as the arts of discourse (Lat. *artes verbales, artes sermocinales, artes logicae*), since all three of its constituents were concerned with words and verbal analysis and were studied to attain skills in formulating and evaluating discourse, spoken as well as written, in Latin.

Although the balance of power among grammar, rhetoric, and logic underwent constant recalibrations between late antiquity and the Renaissance, grammar remained for more than a millennium the foundation of all study in the liberal arts. The ultimate aim was mastery of Latin, which although not the original tongue of any book in the Bible still had status alongside Hebrew and Greek as one of three sacred languages.

As the special status of Latin suggests, the linguistic situation that prevailed in medieval Europe differed strongly from the norm nowadays throughout the West. Medieval Latin coexisted alongside the many mother tongues, but modern scholars have characterized it, in contrast, as a "father tongue"—not a dead language but rather a school-taught foreign language that no one spoke from infancy but that everyone with formal education was expected to deploy in both speech and writing. It served in the Christian church not only as a scriptural and liturgical language but also as the normal means of communication, and it was used in many other contexts as well.

Instruction in Latin grammar was a rite of passage that was restricted almost entirely to boys and mainly to the upper strata of society. It is with good cause that the spoken languages were designated by terms, such as *vulgar tongue, vernacular,* and *mother tongue,* that emphasize their associations with socially subordinate groups, such as common people (Lat. *vulgus*), servants or slaves (Lat. *vernacula*), and women. Such groups seldom had any access to Latin or to grammar, both of which they often held in great awe. In popular views, many of the magical qualities that surrounded literacy and book learning in general became attached to grammar in particular, a progression that can be detected most easily as fossilized in the Scots-English derivative of grammar, *glamor.*

Grammatical instruction usually began with repetition of the Latin text of the *Book of Psalms,* to familiarize young children with the alphabet and the rudiments of reading and writing. Then the basics of Latin grammar were conveyed through the *Ars minor,* a grammar treatise by the fourth-century schoolmaster Donatus. A question-and-answer dialogue that surveys the eight parts of speech, the *Ars minor* was the bedrock of the medieval grammar school. It prompted many commentaries and its author's name (shortened to *donat* and similar forms) became a byword for grammar itself in a number of spoken languages.

The aspects of grammar that the *Ars minor* embodied were only the most elementary of the conceptions that people had of grammar. More complex approaches to grammatical analysis could be found in the eighteen-book *Institutiones grammaticae* of the late Latin grammarian Priscian (fifth–sixth century CE), which covers orthography and the parts of speech in the sixteen books of the so-called *Priscianus maior* and syntax in the final two of the *Priscianus minor*. This treatise, especially the *Priscianus minor,* was conventionally studied to cap higher education in the foundational art and for this reason Priscian became as emblematic of more advanced grammar as Donatus was of basic grammar.

For much of the Middle Ages in Western Europe, the study of grammar was restricted almost entirely to Latin. The identification was so strong that the word *Latin* and its cognates were sometimes synonyms for language itself. By a similar process, *grammatica* and its derivatives were taken to refer above all to Latin grammar. In the first section of the *De vulgari eloquentia* (probably composed 1303–1305), when Dante (1265–1321) differentiates between the vernacular languages that people acquire from infancy and the literary forms of Latin, which must be studied in order to be learned, he relates that the Romans called the latter language *grammatica*. Treatises on the grammar of vernacular languages are exceedingly rare in comparison with Latin grammars, and it is telling that the earliest extant grammar in a vernacular is the grammar of Latin that Ælfric (c.955–c.1010) wrote in Old English, with extensive reliance on Donatus and Priscian.

Especially from the fifth century through the tenth, Christianity spread the study and use of Latin among peoples who had not belonged to the Roman Empire and had never made the transition from their own native languages to spoken Latin. This encounter necessitated changes in the teaching of Latin. Some grammar treatises were Christianized by replacing examples from the pagan classics with ones drawn from the Scriptures, while others were modified to make the workings of Latin more comprehensible to non-Romance speakers.

As a father tongue, Latin was closely implicated in the patriarchy of the Church. Throughout the Middle Ages, Latin was the official ecclesiastical language. As such, it played a leading role in forming a powerful and privileged class of men, the clergy. What the sword and jousting were to a knight in the making, the book (or manuscript codex) and beatings with the rod were to the aspiring cleric. This pairing of discipline and punishment in an all-male environment was a staple of life for boys during the seven years or so (roughly from age seven to fourteen) that were devoted to the acquisition of Latin through grammar. The reality behind the idioms "to teach someone a lesson" and "school of hard knocks" would have been immediately understandable to anyone who had attended grammar school in the Middle Ages.

Although Latin was not alive in the same sense as a mother tongue, pupils were not taught simply to read it as a dead language. *Lessons, lections,* and *lectures* are all connected etymologically with reading, but the reading was not always based on perusing folios of a real book. Sometimes the costliness of manuscripts meant that only the schoolmaster would have had a copy of the text being parsed, while the boys would have been expected to write it on wax tablets and study daily portions, consult a manuscript shared by the group, or simply learn it by repetition as the words were read aloud. On other occasions, the master would have delivered instruction without having before him an actual book, although the presence of its content or even its words could have been felt or implied. In the Middle Ages, more than in most eras, authority resided in authors, but the words and thoughts of the authors were internalized as much through hearing and saying aloud as through pen and parchment.

Grammatica as understood in the Latin Middle Ages encompassed much more than a prescriptive system of rules about morphology, syntax, and the like. It entailed more even than "the skill of speaking and writing correctly," as it was sometimes defined. In its more advanced stages, it embraced all of literature and much of what would now be styled "literary criticism" "hermeneutics," and "imitation," since grammar involved the close reading and exposition of authors, often using glosses and commentary, as well as the mastery of principles and techniques through the composition of set pieces in prose and poetry. Although in the late fifth century, Martianus Capella (whose *Marriage of Mercury and Philology* was one of the most important encyclopedias to purvey grammatical doctrine) took matters to an extreme by declaring that "man is a grammatical animal," grammar gained ethical and theological dimensions that made the grammatical man almost as moral a character as Quintilian's (c.35–100 CE) definition of the rhetor as "a good man who knows how to speak." On a humble but culturally pervasive level, grammar was linked throughout the Middle Ages to moral philosophy on the grounds that the reading of most literature in school was justified by subsuming it under the heading of "ethics."

Even apart from the fact that until the twelfth century most students would have learned grammar and rhetoric (as well as any of the other arts they studied) from one and the same schoolmaster, grammar overlapped with rhetoric in a number of areas, foremost of which was style and especially figurative language. [*See* Figures of speech; *and* Style.] Donatus's *Ars maior,* more comprehensive than its lesser sibling, the *Ars minor,* was valued above all for its third book, which examines grammatical errors and figurative language. This book, entitled *Barbarismus,* addresses errors in diction (barbarism), in syntax (solecism), and in style. In addition, it deals with departures from normal style dictated by meter (metaplasm). Finally, it presents figures of speech and tropes. The influence of this book by Donatus was extensive. For example, the earliest formal rhetoric in a vernacular language is the section of the *Enchiridion* (c.1011) by Byrhtferth of Ramsey (c.960–1012) that translates into Old English Bede's Latin treatise on schemes and tropes, which was itself based on the *Barbarismus.* Elsewhere in the Old Germanic world, the third of four grammatical treatises composed in Old Icelandic between the mid-twelfth and the mid-fourteenth century (written c.1250 by Olaf Thortharson) comprises two sections, one of which is devoted entirely to figures of speech and reflects the same interest in figurative language.

The third book of the *Ars maior* could be seen as trespassing on the territory of rhetoric, which was often regarded in the Middle Ages as being concerned first and foremost with verbal embellishment. Figurative language held a central importance in medieval thinking about language.

For one thing, many texts, not solely classics written by pagan authors, were perused with the assumption that they had significances hidden and yet also signaled by the adornments of the style. They were interpreted as having a level or levels that figured meanings not apparent on the surface. For another, it was accepted that for talking about God normal human language was insufficient and that figurative language was indispensable. [*See* Allegory.]

In the twelfth century and later, the overlaps of grammar and rhetoric where style was at issue meant that treatises on the art of poetry were subsumed now under grammar, now under rhetoric. The connections between style as the implement (the *stilus*) wielded in the physical act of writing, style as a characteristic of the person producing the writing, and style as a quality of the resultant document, were at least as intricate as they are today. Complicating matters further, new textbooks that were created as sequels to Donatus were composed in Latin verse, such as the *Graecismus* of Eberhard of Béthune (died c.1212) and the *Doctrinale puerorum* (1199) of Alexander of Villa-Dei (c.1170–c.1250). These developments indicate the fineness of the line that demarcated grammar (traditionally understood as the art of correct reading and writing) and rhetoric (the art of persuasive writing and speaking). Accordingly, it is not surprising that twentieth-century philologists such as Ernst Robert Curtius (1886–1956) and Erich Auerbach (1892–1957) drew their evidence for medieval stylistics from texts that would have been studied both grammatically and rhetorically, often without an explicit change in method of analysis from one to the other.

Beyond the increasing interpenetrations between grammar and rhetoric, medieval grammar had a more forceful intellectual impact from the late eleventh century on, owing to its integration into branches of logic and philosophy in those reaches of thought that could be called *terminist logic, linguistic theory,* and *epistemology.* The interchanges between grammar and logic, although often nearly a rivalry, were profound in both directions. Priscian furnished questions, terminology, and techniques to scholars who were caught up in the fever of logic. In a rediscovery of a relationship that had proven itself stimulating already in the ninth century, Priscian came to be taught often from the late eleventh century on-ward in conjunction not so much with the ca-nonical classical authors of the school curriculum as with the modes of analysis favored in logic and often directed to philosophical ends (especially in confronting the problem of the universals). The most extensive philosophical approaches to Pris-cian emerge after Aristotelian logic had been ab-sorbed into the trivium, in Martin of Dacia (died 1304), Boethius of Dacia (died before 1284), and other late thirteenth-century grammarians. Des-ignated variously as speculative grammarians, nominalist grammarians, or *modistae,* these think-ers devoted their attentions to the very nature of language in "modes of signifying"—how what is expressed in language corresponds to what exists in reality and what we know of that reality. Be-cause their grammar looked at how language mir-rors the physical and metaphysical, it was called speculative, from the Latin word for mirror (*speculum*).

Wherever the Latin language infiltrated in the Middle Ages, there grammar arrived too. An es-sential prerequisite to even the simplest reading and writing in Latin, grammar was also a constit-uent of all the most serious thought about lan-guage—and *in* language. For this reason any at-tempt to treat medieval rhetoric in isolation from medieval grammar, or vice versa, would fail, and it would have seemed a bizarre endeavor to those who had received their formation in the trivium.

BIBLIOGRAPHY

Gehl, Paul F. *A Moral Art. Grammar, Society, and Culture in Trecento Florence.* Ithaca, N.Y., 1993. This study, based on careful analysis of many manuscript sources, shows how even in fourteenth-century Florence, masters of elementary grammar continued to restrict the curriculum to moral texts that for centuries had been used to promote Christian values.

Hunt, R. W. *Collected Papers on the History of Grammar in the Middle Ages.* Edited by G. L. Bursill-Hall. Amster-dam Studies in the Theory and History of Linguistic Science, series 3; Studies in the History of Linguistics, vol. 5. Amsterdam, 1980. These classic studies helped achieve recognition of the broad significance that changes in linguistic theory held in the intellectual climate of the twelfth century.

Huntsman, Jeffrey F. "Grammar." In *The Seven Liberal Arts in the Middle Ages.* Edited by David E. Wagner, pp. 58–95. Bloomington, Ind., 1983. This essay pres-ents a clear and interesting overview of the nature, basic texts, and workings of grammar in the Middle Ages.

Irvine, Martin. *The Making of Textual Culture. "Gram-matica" and Literary Theory 350–1100.* Cambridge, U.K., 1994.

Law, Vivien. *Grammar and Grammarians in the Early Mid-dle Ages.* London, 1997. Law traces the adaptations that treatises for grammar teaching from the third century through the sixth underwent as Latin was taught to Celtic and Germanic peoples in the early Middle Ages and follows the rediscovery of Aris-totle's works on logic and their incorporation into new theories on the relationship between language and thought.

Minnis, A. J., and A. B. Scott, with the assistance of Da-vid Wallace. *Medieval Literary Theory and Criticism c.1100–c.1375. The Commentary-Tradition.* Oxford, 1988. This anthology of texts in translation surveys medieval commentaries. These commentaries, many of which would have been staples of grammatical training, contain insights into topics such as the un-derstanding of history and fiction, the ethics of lit-erature, the nature of authority and authorship, and literary genres and styles.

Ziolkowski, Jan. *Alan of Lille's Grammar of Sex. The Mean-ing of Grammar to a Twelfth-Century Intellectual.* Spe-culum Anniversary Monographs, vol. 10. Cambridge, Mass., 1985. Although devoted generally to one au-thor's use of grammatical terms as metaphors for sex-ual acts, this book includes an overview of the roles that grammar played in twelfth-century intellectual life, including philosophical and theological contro-versies.

—JAN ZIOLKOWSKI

MEMORY. "Our whole discipline," declares Quintilian, the first-century CE teacher of rheto-ric, "relies on memory" (11.2.1). This is an ex-traordinary claim—that the whole edifice of rhetoric developed by Greek and Roman theorists rested on the ability to remember. It is also far from unique in the history of rhetoric. Quintilian was, if anything, one of the more skeptical writers on the powers of memory, but even he made them central to the orator's arsenal. A rhetorician in the Roman courts had to master his speech so carefully that he could respond to interruptions, change direction, omit sections that had become superfluous, and improvise on new topics that suddenly became important. He also needed to have at his fingertips the variegated body of Roman law and to recall as they were advanced each of the arguments of his opponents. All these very different tasks—reciting a well-learned speech, grasping the elements of somebody else's argument, organizing new statements as they were read or spoken, recalling the specifics of a tortuous system of laws, responding fluently to unexpected questions, objections, or turns in a discussion—were grouped under the single part of oratory called memory. With so many tasks to fulfill, nothing could fully compensate an orator for an inadequate memory; it was, as some writers called it, "the treasure house of eloquence." Ancient orators and statesmen are credited with astonishing feats of memory. There are credible accounts that Hortensius, Cicero's elder rival, could recall at will not only all his own words during a case, but also everything his adversaries had said. Seneca the Elder (c.55 BCE–c.39 CE) claimed that he could repeat two thousand names in the order they were dictated, or two hundred separate verses chosen individually by his pupils backward or forward. But even the unlikely reports that the Persian emperor Cyrus knew every man in his army by name, or that the Athenian statesman Themistocles (who, when he was told about the art of memory, supposedly answered that he had more need of an art of forgetting) knew the name of every Athenian citizen, reveal in what high regard memory was held.

The study of memory encompasses not just ideas of memory at a particular historical moment, but entire regimes of memory, ways of privileging certain types of knowledge, certain values, certain ideas, beliefs, symbols—in short, an entire cultural ethnography coalesces around the apparently innocuous ability to remember the past. Memory serves as the locus of personal history and individual identity. For the Platonic philosopher, the dim memory of the forms embedded in the soul offered the only accurate measure for the use of reason; for the Roman orator, memory was the first of his rhetorical tools and the one that gave him access to all the others; it was what allowed the medieval scholar to recall and compare thousands of Biblical verses and commentaries; in the Renaissance, it promised a way of mastering the information explosion that came with new worlds across the sea and in the sky. Perhaps because of the vagueness of its role in

rhetoric, the arts of memory have a particularly rich history as the subject of speculation and fantasy.

Two principal images of how the memory functions appear not only in the ancient rhetoricians and poets, but up to the time of Descartes and even into our own. The first is the idea of memory as a kind of internal writing in the soul or heart; the second is memory as a kind of storage space containing whatever is remembered. Both are at least as old as Plato, who calls them up one after the other in his late dialogue *Theaetetus,* first comparing the memory to a slab of wax in which perceptions and thoughts impress a mark that can be reviewed later (194c–195b), and then revising his first metaphor to suggest that the mind contains memories like an aviary contains birds, so that we can possess a memory and yet still need to hunt for it—and sometimes lay hands on the wrong one (197e–199e). The idea of memory as a form of writing is Biblical as well: the *Proverbs* writer enjoins the reader to take his words and "Write them on the tablet of your heart" (*Prv.* 3.3). Both images are still current—we speak of *writing* a file onto our hard drive or asking how much *space* is left on a floppy disk.

Memory is labeled as one of the parts of rhetoric by Roman and later writers, but discussions of it are complicated because, uniquely among the parts of rhetoric, it is also a mental faculty, like imagination and reason. It is thus never entirely clear to what extent a rhetorician merely benefits from having a strong memory, as he might from having a good voice, or if memory has a specific function in the construction of a speech, like, for instance, invention or arrangement. Certainly, memory, along with the other less codified part of rhetoric, delivery, is often given short shrift in rhetorical treatises. In general, Roman writers on rhetoric (and, according to them, their Hellenistic predecessors) avoided deciding whether memory was a natural ability or a learned skill by dividing it into two kinds. There was what was called the *natural memory,* which was simply an individual's aptitude for recalling things. This natural memory could be supplemented by the techniques of *artificial memory,* a set of practices that enabled their user to remember more clearly, more completely, more systematically, or simply *more* than his natural memory would allow. Over time, as the needs of its practitioners changed from delivering speeches in court to organizing their readings, the practices of artificial memory also developed and changed. An association of memory with the arrangement of space and imagery, though, remains remarkably consistent from its earliest discussions until Descartes in the seventeenth century.

After Descartes, memory as a part of rhetoric fell into disregard, and in the eighteenth and nineteenth centuries it existed on the fringe of rhetorical theory, enduring in guides to elocution and recitation. Nowadays, mnemonics is principally taught as part of foreign language study and in self-help books. But its eclipse in the field of rhetoric has certainly not meant that it has declined in significance. The nature of memory, its relation to symbolic expression, and its unmatched rhetorical force as authentic knowledge, continue to be in the forefront of contemporary cultural concerns. From debates about the reality of "recovered memories" to the possibility of reviving cultural memories to oppose dominant history among African-American writers, what and how we remember, why and how we put those memories of the past into words in the present, are crucially defining issues for a startling number of cultures, including our own.

Memory before Rhetoric. From its origins in Homer and Hesiod, Greek literature was concerned with memory and recollection. The principal topic of early epic poetry was the preservation of memory, whether of the origins of the universe or the reputations and histories of the great heroes of the past like Achilles or Odysseus. In the *Iliad*, Achilles passes time in his tent by singing of "the fames of men" (9.524), recalling the deeds of the heroes who have gone before him. Hesiod begins *Theogony,* his ninth century BCE poem on the origins of the gods, with praise of those who gave him the ability to recite poetry—the Muses, the daughters of Memory. Memory is here something external to the poet, a fleeting power that may forsake him in midverse. The Muses' heritage suggests both how central the idea of remembering was to early poetry and how important the ability to remember was to the early poet. Epic poems like the *Iliad* or *Theogony* were not originally written down but were performed from memory, although they were not

memorized verbatim. Rather, the poet learned an artificial diction that could be stitched together to recount both conventional and novel stories and composed his work anew in each performance. A poet might well have faced every performance with anxiety about his ability to recall all the details of his story, and in fact these poems attest to this concern. The ability to recall also has as much to do with the physical endurance to recite thousands of verses as it does with the mental effort of producing them. Homer begins his long catalog of the heroic commanders of the Trojans and the Greeks with a prayer to the Muses first to grant him "a voice never to be broken, and a heart of bronze within me" (*Iliad* 2.490), only then turning to what may seem the more proper concern of memory, to "remember . . . all those who came beneath Ilion" (2.492). For Homer and Hesiod, memory was both the first source of their poetic powers and the guarantor of their accuracy. The poems themselves were technologies of memory that could preserve for the world "the fames of men" that otherwise were doomed to fade with their deaths.

Although Roman theoreticians of rhetoric remark that many Greek writers treated the art of memory, none of their works survive. Plato (c.428–c.347 BCE) and Aristotle (384–322 BCE), however, although they do not consider memory from the perspective of rhetoric, define its workings in ways that are deeply influential in the later development of mnemotechnics. Plato's philosophy is deeply connected to memory through the doctrine of *anamnēsis,* the recollection of knowledge of the time before their incarnation that every soul preserves more or less imperfectly. The ability to remember is more than merely instrumental, as it is in Homer or Hesiod; anamnesis underlies any capacity we have to grasp what is true and good in the world, for without at least some dim memory of what we are looking for, it is impossible that we could ever find it, or know it when we did, as Plato demonstrates in *Meno* and recalls synoptically in *Phaedo.* Plato addresses memory as it relates more directly to rhetoric in *Phaedrus.* In that dialogue, Socrates encounters young Phaedrus, who has just come from meeting the renowned Athenian orator Lysias and is carrying a scroll of one of his speeches to a private place to read and memorize. Socrates criticizes

Lysias's speech (a paradoxical argument that a young man should take as his lover a man who does not sincerely love him) on several grounds— it is improperly organized, its argument is immoral, and finally its conclusion is untrue—and proposes several better alternatives, but he ends his discussion and the dialogue by questioning Phaedrus about the effect of recording the speech in *writing*. According to Plato's Socrates, writing simulates memory like a well-executed painting resembles its model; also like a painting, writing is helpless to respond to any questions that its reader may put to it. It cannot explain itself, but must repeat, interminably, what it has already said. Furthermore, because writing circulates from person to person, its originator has no control over whom his words reach or how they may take or mistake them. The very form Phaedrus has chosen, Socrates tells him, is bad, because learning Lysias's speech from a written text will force Phaedrus to rely on external marks rather than on the memory that is written within his soul. What seems to be a device to preserve memory, argues Socrates, in fact will end up devaluing and destroying it. Plato is not unaware of the irony of writing against writing on behalf of memory; the discussion in *Theaetetus,* where Plato presents the metaphors of memory as writing and as container, is read by one of the interlocutors from a book, since he has forgotten the details of the conversation as it was first told to him. Replacing Hesiod's external Muse with an inner writing, *Phaedrus* broaches a suspicion that becomes increasingly significant in later writings on memory and mnemonics—that what is held in the memory is more intimate, accurate, or otherwise privileged than what is stored outside the mind in writing. This suspicion provides the motivation for some of the excesses of early modern mnemonics, in which elaborate systems were devised to organize the whole realm of human learning in memorable form.

Aristotle, although he writes extensively on memory as a mental faculty, never squarely addresses the art of memory in his treatise *Rhetoric.* But Aristotle's psychological theory of memory (anticipated in *On the Soul* 427b–429a and developed in *On Memory and Reminiscence*) was tremendously influential in the development of a specifically rhetorical mnemotechnics for two reasons.

First, Aristotle stressed, much more than Plato did, the importance of the visual image in memory—past events were stored in the memory like images impressed in a wax tablet (*On Memory* 450a–451a). In *Phaedrus,* Plato had used the metaphor of memory as a painting in order to point out the problems with writing, which was a much more practical, although errant, mimic of memory. For Aristotle, though, memory did not just metaphorically resemble a visual image, it actually required images to function. Second, Aristotle tried to explain how one memory calls up another by specifying certain laws of association that recollection tended to follow (*On Memory,* 451b–452b). Experiences can remind us of other experiences on the basis of similarity, contrast, or contiguity; any of these relations indifferently can cause us to recall something, although the more frequently we make a particular connection, the more readily it will spring to mind again. Together, Aristotle's theory of the memory image and his laws of association provided a theoretical basis for an artificial memory that depended on places and on images to organize and secure recollection.

The Architectural Memory of Rome. The art of memory in its most distinctive form is first described in the anonymous *Ad Herennium,* a rhetorical treatise composed c.86–82 BCE and later attributed to the young Cicero. This work presents the ancient art of memory in its most complete form (3.16.28–3.24.40), perhaps because it is an elementary text; more advanced works mention the art as something already familiar. The author of *Ad Herennium* begins by distinguishing natural from artificial memory; a strong natural memory works much like an artificial memory, but strong or weak, any memory can be improved by means of some simple steps (the author also admits that there are some who dismiss the possibility of a teachable art of memory). In preparing the artificial memory for use, a large space, such as a house or a portico, is first constructed in the mind; it is from this imaginary structure that later writers give the name *architectural memory* to this form of the art. The structure is in turn subdivided into a series of rooms or spaces, with every fifth or tenth marked to enable the user to recognize their positions and keep them in order. The author warns that the places of memory must be chosen carefully, for they remain permanently in the memory, like the wax tablet that remains when the letters written in it are erased. In the course of stocking the memory, these spaces were filled with symbols or images that triggered particular memories. In using the architectural system, one moved from place to place in the imaginary structure in whatever order one wished, mentally reviewing the images in any order and recalling what they represented.

The author's precautions in *Ad Herennium* to the budding memory artist suggest how fully virtual he imagines the memory to be. Memory spaces should be of moderate size and well lit, since that aids in the perception of the images they contain. They should not be too far away from the user, lest distance obscure the images; thought, the author tells us, is like sight (3.19.32). Most crucially, to be easily remembered, the images must be "extraordinary": brightly dressed, violently active, or smeared with paint or blood, so that they produce a strong emotional effect on their deviser (3.22.35). But although the images are treated as if they were literally visual, they are not simply mental copies of what one has seen; if they were, there would be no advantage to the artificial memory over the natural memory. Although the author does not say it outright, these striking images must always be deciphered before they can be understood, since in the interests of brevity, one image must often stand for several concepts. To condense the memory images so that one image embraces a whole concept, the practitioner is advised to use puns and idiosyncratic associations. The images in the system described in *Ad Herennium* are not naturalistic, but representational, and thus need to be decoded like hieroglyphs, not viewed like photographs. One example given in *Ad Herennium*, for instance, is the undeniably startling image of a man holding the testicles (*testiculos*) of a ram; this is meant to recall, through a pun, the presence of witnesses (*testes*) at a trial (3.20.33). The architectural system of memory thus neatly conflates the psychological image of Aristotelian memory and the metaphor of internal writing offered by Plato, for a practitioner must both *see* the images and *read* them.

The *Ad Herennium* author acknowledges that many of his Greek predecessors included lists of images that corresponded to individual words, but points out that it is impossible to come up with images for all the words that exist, and hardly easier to remember such a set of random images than to remember the words themselves (3.23.38). Furthermore, many images that appear vivid and memorable to one person are uninteresting to another. This seemingly offhand observation significantly differentiates artificial memory from similar symbolic systems. The images of memory are symbolic, but they are not part of a shared set of symbols; instead, they are close to a private language, idiosyncratic and unsystematic. Because they are not simply mimetic, memory images must be created by their user rather than learned from a teacher or a book. Creating one's own memory images further anchored personal identity in the faculty of memory; it required that one combine private fantasies, perceptual stimuli, and intense feeling in a mental experience that was simultaneously physical, sensual, and emotional. While the images were stored in abstract, formal spaces, the process by which memories were gathered, assembled, and brought to bear on the present was understood as itself a form of experience. Remembering was holistic, linking intellect and feeling, past and present, and early accounts of trained memories sometimes include physical postures and affects that to us appear pathological. Finally, artificial memory blurs the differences between shared and individual experience. It was imagined as spatial, and thus, as something that existed independent of individuals, but since memory artists were encouraged to develop their own privately relevant images and places, it was equally dependent on the accidental and idiosyncratic connections established between images and the things they represented by the individual memory artist. The work of memory included both "objective" elements (things "out there," upon which the memory artist stumbled) and "subjective" ones (recreations of experiences within the memory artist and subject to his control).

The author of *Ad Herennium* also distinguishes two kinds of artificial memory: memory for words and memory for things, the first suitable for memorizing a text exactly as it is written, the second used to recall the outlines of an argument or a set of issues. They work identically through images and places, although memory for words is more exacting. It is also, for that reason, less practical, and the author recommends it merely as a kind of mental exercise so that the artificial memory for things will seem easier. In general, Roman writers were more interested in using the techniques of artificial memory to recall things rather than words, probably because their needs were much more geared to public oratory. Long before *Ad Herennium,* the moral voice of republican Roman values, Cato, had advised, "Grasp the things; the words will follow." But the idea of a practical memory for words returns when exact memory of authoritative texts became a greater concern than it was for an orator. Medieval monastics, who were concerned with remembering the exact words of the Bible, paid more attention to techniques for verbatim memorization. *Margarita philosophica* (1503), a one-volume encyclopedia of the liberal arts, includes a list of images that can be used to represent the individual letters in words, so that theoretically texts can be remembered *verbatim,* although one wonders if it would really be easier to remember the stacks of images required to spell out the words letter by letter than the sentence itself (3.1.23).

Both Cicero in *De oratore,* a dialogue on the practice of rhetoric written when Cicero had all but retired from public life (c.55 BCE), and Quintilian (11.2.11–16) recount a story of the origins of the art of memory. *Ad Herennium* offers a better technical explanation of the art, but the origin story hints at memory's ideological significance to Roman culture. According to the story, the art of memory was first discovered by Simonides, a Greek poet of the fifth century BCE. Simonides had been hired by a nobleman to perform a song in his honor at a banquet. As was customary in poems of this kind, Simonides included a digression on the divine twins, Castor and Pollux. When the song was over, though, his host told him that since Simonides had given him only half a poem, he would pay only half Simonides' price, and Simonides could go to Castor and Pollux for the rest. Shortly afterwards, a slave came in to tell Simonides that two young men were outside asking for him. When Simonides went out to the street, he found nobody there, but as he turned to go back inside the house, the roof of the banquet hall suddenly collapsed, killing

everybody inside. The bodies were so mangled that they could not be recognized, but Simonides discovered that he could recall where each guest had been sitting and so could identify the bodies for burial. This led him to realize that the memory could be aided by an orderly arrangement of images and to develop the techniques later described in *Ad Herennium.*

Quintilian is probably right in dismissing the story as fictional, but although it may not be historically true, it suggests something of the true significance of memory. Simonides was famous as a composer of epitaphs and thus, like Homer, had the task of memorializing both virtuous and shameful deeds. He is therefore an appropriate inventor for an art of memory. The story is also emblematic of the link between memory and death that the art of memory seems always to skirt; memory becomes increasingly significant in the face of death and oblivion, and the salvation it offers is not the same as life, but the comfort of being—here, literally—aptly laid to rest. Simonides' memory is presented as the double payment of a debt to mortality: his life is spared because he recalled the fame of Castor and Pollux, and his ability to remember is given back to the families of the dead as fulfillment of another obligation, in thanks for his own life. Finally, in contrast, the prosaic technicalities of the account in *Ad Herennium,* the story of Simonides is itself an example that memorably demonstrates the art that *Ad Herennium* only describes.

This etiology of the art of memory also suggests how personal memory, as opposed to an officially sanctioned history, could function in a rhetorical context. When Cicero and Quintilian remember the story of Simonides, they emphasize different details that give it a varying suasive force. Cicero foregrounds the issue of the poet's payment and the difficulty of being in a situation where, neither fully guest nor employee, Simonides is subject to the highhanded whims of the nobleman for his fee. Like all Roman, and Greek, orators, Cicero was legally barred from accepting any payment for speaking on behalf of a client in court; although there were many professional rhetoricians in both Athens and Rome, their fees had to be disguised as something besides business transactions. Cicero thus offers the Greek poet, an intellectual professional, as a model for the Roman orator. For his part, Quintilian dutifully reports that although Simonides successfully identified the bodies, there is in Quintilian's time no consensus about the identity of Simonides' host (11.2.14–15). His name has slipped from memory. Quintilian's point is that the art of memory has important limitations. Both retellings do much more than simply recall the past; they make it active again in their own arguments, even revive it for their own ends. In the medieval art of memory, it is this affective reconstruction of the past in the present that will link the art of memory, surprisingly, to ethical behavior.

The Grid Memory of the Middle Ages. Quintilian points out that memory for things is useful for lists but is less apt to be useful for recalling speeches, and his advice on memorization is a practical alternative to more difficult versions. Learn a long speech in parts rather than trying it whole; annotate sections that are especially difficult; use the same tablets on which you wrote the speech to commit it to memory; murmur the words aloud as you read to engage more senses (11.2.27–29, 32–34). Quintilian is clearly thinking of learning the words of an already-composed text rather than of recalling a complex of ideas or points that are not committed to writing, and so his dismissal of the memory for words as needlessly arcane has less to do with the usefulness of remembering something word for word than with the practicality of the art of memory for it. In the slow transition from the culture of the Roman forum to that of medieval monasteries and schools, the art of memory went through a gradual change in emphasis, focusing more and more on memory as a way to have passages of the texts of the Bible and the Church Fathers at the tip of one's tongue. Augustine's *Confessions* (c.397–400 CE) provides a good example of this function of memory. A classically trained teacher of rhetoric himself, Augustine discusses his own memory in a manner that suggests a knowledge of the architectural memory as described by Cicero; he describes his memory as "like a great field or a spacious palace, a storehouse for countless images" (10.8). But Augustine's text is also a constant dialogue between the self of his memory and that of his present self, carried out in the words of the Bible that have become so much a part of his identity that they emerge in his most intimate

moments of self-examination. These Biblical interpolations appear on every page of Augustine's text, equally his own words and those shared by all Christians. Instead of a private language in a public space, Augustine's memory presents the reverse—an incorporation through memory of another's language. [*See overview article on* Medieval rhetoric; *and* Religion.]

With this shift in emphasis, the art of memory also underwent a subtle but significant change of technique from the architectural mnemonic to what Mary Carruthers (1990) calls the "grid memory." This form of mnemotechnic seems to have been considered more elementary than the architectural memory; it was, for instance, taught to schoolboys, while the architectural mnemonic was reserved for more advanced students. Hugh of St. Victor, a clerical educator of twelfth-century Paris, explains the grid memory in "Three Chief Memory-Fixes for History" (*De tribus maximis circumstantiis gestorum*). Hugh tells his young readers (the work is addressed to "children") that to commit something to memory, one must first mentally construct a number line and practice moving quickly to each of the numbers in any order. With the number line secure, a reader then associates the opening phrase of each Psalm with a number. Rather than condensing a verbal concept by representing it as an image, Hugh reduces it to a few words that can be easily recalled. When each Psalm is linked mentally to its number, the reader can provide a similar number line, at right angles, as it were, to the first, and memorize each Psalm by its verses, associating them with the numbers of the second line. The result is a mental grid by which one can recite any Psalm in any order by recalling its number and its verse numbers.

While it seems to have yielded impressive results—even the most unlearned monks were expected to know the Psalms well enough to recite them freely—the grid memory at first looks disappointingly ordinary compared to the weird spaces and images of the architectural memory. But when Hugh repeats Quintilian's advice to memorize always from the same surface (significantly, Quintilian, thinking of an orator composing his own speech, specifies the tablet that the user wrote on; Hugh, in a monastic library, simply says to use the same copy), it is clear that Hugh retains a sense of physical space and image in memory. But whereas the primary existence of spaces and images in architectural memory is mental—that is, they are created first in the rememberer's mind—in the grid memory, they are laid out on the plane of the page, which sometimes was even drawn to resemble the façade of a building. Rather than moving in his mind through an imaginary architectural space, the user of the grid memory recalled the prior motion of his eyes across the page, *reading* in what Dante, in *The Divine Comedy,* called "the book of memory" rather than *wandering* through what were for Augustine its "cloisters" and "palaces." In fact, although their relative prevalence may have varied, probably neither the grid system nor the architectural system was ever used to the exclusion of the other, in the Middle Ages or the classical period—Albertus Magnus (c.1200–1280 CE), for example, Thomas Aquinas's teacher, uses *Ad Herennium* as the basis for his discussion of memory. The grid memory presupposes learning something from a written text, and so is more useful in a society that values this kind of retentive knowledge, while the architectural memory is itself an organizational tool. Medieval texts produced for study in the twelfth century and after frequently take account of the grid system of memory. As early as the ninth century, one finds tables of numbers arranged in (drawings of architectural) columns in Bibles and other texts. The practice of illuminating initial letters and placing striking or comical pictures in the margins of even very weighty texts made individual pages memorable, whether for rapid reference to the actual text or for securing the contents of a page in the mind with a memorable image as its index. The practice of digesting long texts into short segments, such as Biblical books into verses or a single scholastic problem into individual questions, first mentioned by Quintilian, is also connected to the practice of grid memory.

While in practice the architectural memory was losing ground to the grid, it was also finding an afterlife in fiction. Allegories like the French *Romance of the Rose,* a long narrative poem of the thirteenth century, or Dante's *Divine Comedy* in the fourteenth century drew on the traditions of the architectural memory to create ordered spaces filled with memorable images and characters.

Such texts served to record everything from moral lessons to scientific truths in a way that, like the brightly illuminated illustrations that adorned the margins of manuscripts, lent itself to recollection. Some works of literature also took the space of memory as a theme, most notably in Geoffrey Chaucer's *House of Fame,* a work that precedes *The Canterbury Tales* (c.1390s). In it, Chaucer recounts a dream in which he is lifted into a literal space of memory, the House of Fame, filled with voices and pictures from history, some accurately depicted, some garbled by the clamor around them (the *Ad Herennium* writer warns that situating a memory space in a well-traveled locale will present problems), some drowned out altogether. Chaucer had earlier translated part of *The Romance of the Rose* into English; in his own dream vision, he takes memory itself as a topic of exploration, and logically sets his dream into the form of an artificial memory structure.

In texts like Chaucer's or even Hugh's, memory remained dynamic rather than static, a way of applying knowledge to present circumstances as much as preserving it unchanged. As with Cicero's and Quintilian's memories of Simonides, acts of memory in the Middle Ages are often explicitly rhetorical—texts represent characters recalling words or events aptly or incompetently and they produce similar effects in their readers. Conforming to the emphasis on personal experience and idiosyncrasy in *Ad Herennium,* aptness is something different from strict fidelity; it demands the production of the proper emotion or feeling that would move the rememberer to do the right thing. The constant hum of the Gospel that inhabits Augustine's personal confession is a good example of how memory was understood to inform the present. Because memory could conserve moral teachings so that they were literally ever-present to the mind of the rememberer, it was in particular associated with the ethical virtue of prudence, or foresight, the ability to apply one's learning to the specific and mutable situation in which one found oneself. It was this association that allowed for the apparently nonsensical but common formula in medieval times of *remembering* events at which one was not present, such as the Crucifixion, or that had not yet occurred, such as the judgment of one's soul. When humanist writers of the fifteenth century secularized these moral ideals and applied the lessons of prudence to nonreligious texts, this connection between memory and ethics remained almost entirely unchanged. But the uses of memory were changing again.

"Real" Memories of the Renaissance. The art of memory paradoxically flourished during the fifteenth, sixteenth, and seventeenth centuries as it grew less necessary for practical rhetoric. Guides to memory proliferated, but also grew increasingly dogmatic or esoteric, as if their authors were rehearsing something of which they understood the theory but had not experienced the practice. Humanist scholarship placed a premium on reviving originals at the level of the word and even of the letter. The flexibility and rhetoricity of memory were ill-suited to this precise reproduction, and actual material remainders of the past like written documents, old coins, ancient inscriptions were held to be its more faithful witnesses. While memory was dismissed as error-prone, it was also often seen as excessively rigid, merely repeating itself (in an ironic echo of Socrates' fears about writing) without developing, regardless of context. In his *Book of Memorable Things,* the fourteenth-century Italian humanist Petrarch recounts the story of a friend whose memory was so exceptional that in conversation he could correct Petrarch's recollection of the words of their earlier talks. But Petrarch's point seems to be that this prodigious memory is actually an impediment; it means that his friend can never really discuss anything, because he remains fixated on his past, forever correcting the present to correspond to it. [*See* Humanism; *and overview article on* Renaissance rhetoric.]

Two related memory practices emerged and developed rapidly in Renaissance Europe—Lullism and Ramism. Neither is explicitly a memory art, but they draw on the two major traditions developed in the memory arts, of memory as a kind of writing and as an ordering of space. Directly contravening the traditions of earlier memory arts, though, both Lullism and Ramism were "logical" systems in that they sought to eliminate the idiosyncratic elements that had irreducibly individuated each trained memory and replace them with predictable universals. Lullism was invented by Raimond Lull, a thirteenth-century Catalan merchant, to bring Christianity to Jews and Muslims who were unconvinced by arguments relying on the Bible or the Church Fathers. A finite number of elements were combined according to a fixed set of rules; when all possible combinations were exhausted, Lull argued, the truth was revealed. Renaissance Lullist works kept Lull's combinatory structure but added more elements, so that "true" statements could be produced in fields like medicine, jurisprudence, and the liberal arts as well as theology. Francis Bacon, seventeenth-century theorist of science and Chancellor of England, rejected Lullism as a way to speak well on topics one knew nothing about (*Advancement of Learning,* 2.17.14), but that did not prevent its wide acceptance. The mathematician Leibniz's algebraic combinatory system derived in part from Lull's art.

Where Lullism was an art of synthesis—setting things together—the fundamental operation of Ramism, the teachings of the French logician Pierre Ramus that flooded Europe in the sixteenth century, was division and analysis. Ramus taught that rhetoric, and in fact every field of learning, could be correctly understood only when it was simplified into subordinated series of binaries. In practice, this meant recasting every discipline into a system of forking branches (not coincidentally, the French form of Ramus's name, *Ramée,* means branch) that divided and subdivided its topic into ever finer categories. Ramist texts often featured pages of printed Ramist trees demonstrating the proper division of their subject; because they eliminated the sensual and provocative images of the older arts of memory, they were much favored by Protestant writers. Although Ramus himself excluded memory from rhetoric, arguing that correct arrangement of matter could replace it, his diagrams were easily assimilated to the places and images of the grid memory.

The standardization practiced by Lullists and Ramists differs from the arts of memory as a possible extension of their practices rather than a complete rejection of them. What these newer techniques share is the desire to collect and preserve not just a particular speech or written text, but knowledge itself as a whole. As memory became less practically important to rhetoric—there was little demand for impromptu speaking and learning no longer required mastery of authoritative texts—it was increasingly justified as an art for managing what was felt to be the vertiginous growth of knowledge. One of the most famous of such attempts was that of the sixteenth-century rhetorician Giulio Camillo, who described in his *L'Idea del Teatro* a memory space in the form of an amphitheater that allowed its user, visualizing himself standing at the center of the stage, to organize and command all humanly available knowledge in ranks of images placed in the seats. Camillo's vast claims for his memory art shade into the language of hermeticism. According to contemporary eyewitnesses, though, the *Teatro* was probably much less mystical. Under the images was concealed a very literal storehouse of texts, tabulated and indexed for easy reference. Camillo's artificial memory was not what we would call memory at all, but an elaborate filing system that imitated the working of a trained memory and made it available to any user.

Perhaps the most striking change in this period was that, like Camillo's, the spaces of memory did not remain imaginary. These heretofore imagined spaces were realized in actual rooms filled with odd or precious objects through which a user could now physically instead of mentally walk. For the person who could afford to build a space but not to fill it with marvelous objects, there was the alternative of decorating it with painted mottoes or sayings on the walls, thus producing an architectural book that not only lay open to the reader's gaze but also opened to admit him in actuality. Since these rooms were in effect realizations of memory palaces, to enter one was almost literally to step into the mind of its maker and share his thought. Michel de Montaigne (1533–1592) composed his *Essais* in a circular library surrounded by the same aphorisms that appear in his writings painted on the walls and beams. But although memory had always been imagined as a space, actually to build a space of memory introduced unexpected contradictions as energy of the ideal collided with the reality of inertia. In 1570, Francesco I de' Medici, the duke of Florence, commissioned the construction of a room that would organize his collection of artwork and natural curiosities into a display of universal knowledge. After two unsuccessful plans, his architect discovered that he had "to accommodate the stories to the places and not the places to the stories, because the narratives can

change but the rooms and walls cannot." In the world of bricks and mortar, the freedom of memory to take its own shape was curbed.

The mechanization of memory continued in the work of René Descartes (1596–1650), for whom memory was a corporeal phenomenon physically lodged in the tissues of the brain, glands, and even limbs. Such memory was not, for Descartes, part of what was essentially human; he grants it, for instance, to his thought-experiment of a soulless man-machine. Descartes's truly human memory was spiritual, and thus divorced from the spaces or images, real or imagined, of the memory arts. More significantly, Descartes has lost faith in memory. It is one of the deceptions of consciousness that he must strip away as he seeks a secure foundation for knowledge in his *Discourses*. Descartes's separation of memory from what had so long served as its props marked the end of another period in the arts of memory. Lengthy and involved treatises continued to be written, published, and translated from Latin into modern languages, but more and more memory was itself a subject of study rather than a rhetorical instrument for understanding the world.

Memory after Rhetoric. Memory crystallized as an object of investigation in the nineteenth century with the so-called "sciences of memory"—medical discourses that tried to quantify and regularize its workings. Near the turn of the twentieth century, memory was given two startling new interpretations in the atomistic philosophy of Friedrich Nietzsche (1844–1900) and in the psychoanalytic writings of Sigmund Freud (1856–1939). For Nietzsche, memory posed a threat to the ability to live and function in the present. Freud proposed that memory was in the final analysis a thing distinct from experience and consciousness alike. Today, the memory of places and images continues to exist in terms that Cicero or Hugh of St. Victor would recognize. Psychologists write papers analyzing the effects of bizarre imagery on memory, or debating whether too many memory places can confuse rather than aid recollection. But its role has changed again, and most modern mnemonists are in the position predicted by Francis Bacon, who complained that the art of memory was impressive without being useful, a rope-dancer's tricks rather than a practical skill (*De augmentis*, 6.280–82). The memory feats on which Seneca and Hortensius prided themselves, and to which Quintilian credited the discipline of rhetoric, have become party games or psychological quirks.

BIBLIOGRAPHY

Primary Sources

While the ancient sources on memory are well-documented, medieval and early modern sources are much harder to come by; only a few have been reprinted in the twentieth century and many of these are still untranslated. Consult the bibliography by Berns and Neuber for further resources.

Augustine, Aurelius Augustinus. *Confessions.* Translated by R. S. Pine-Coffin. Harmondsworth, 1961. English translation of *Confessiones* (c.397–398 CE). See especially 10. s. 8–28, an extended meditation not only on the trained memory but on the significance of memory in the formation of identity and ethical development.

[Cicero.] *De ratione dicendi. (Rhetorica ad Herennium) (On the system of speaking/Rhetoric for Herennius).* Translated by Harry Caplan. Loeb Classical Library. Cambridge, Mass., 1964. Latin and English on facing pages. Text originally written c.86–82 BCE. Caplan's notes and introduction are a thorough introduction to Roman oratory in general; his translation in the memory section is at times somewhat free and must be used with some caution.

Hugh of Saint Victor. "The Three Chief Memory-Fixes for History" [*De tribus maximis circumstantiis gestorum*]. In Mary Carruthers, *The Book of Memory,* Appendix A, pp. 261–266. A brief and dense introduction to the grid memory. Carruthers includes translations of this and two other medieval texts in her superb book.

Chaucer, Geoffrey. *Love Visions: the Book of the Duchess; the House of Fame; the Parliament of Birds; the Legend of Good Women.* Translated, introduced, and annotated by Brian Stone. Harmondsworth, 1983. Chaucer's works are also widely available in Middle English.

Camillo, Giulio. *L'idea del teatro e altri scritti di retorica.* Turin, 1990. The works of Camillo edited for modern readers. As yet, Camillo remains untranslated into English.

de Montaigne, Michel. *The Complete Essays.* Translated by Donald Frame. Stanford, Calif., 1957. Translation and compilation of three editions of the *Essais,* Books 1 and 2 published 1580; Book 3 in 1588. See essay 3.3 for Montaigne's description of his library.

Plato. *Phaedrus and Letters VII and VIII.* Translated and introduced by Walter Hamilton. Harmondsworth, 1973. Readily available and accurate translation of Plato's dialogue on memory and rhetoric.

Collected Sources and Bibliography

Berns, Jörg Jochen, and Wolfgang Neuber, eds. *Das enzyklopädische Gedächtnis der Frühen Neuzeit: Enzyklopädie- und Lexikonartikel zur Mnemonik* (The Encyclopedic Memory of Early Modernity: Encyclopedia and Lexicon Articles on Mnemonics). Frühe Neuzeit, vol. 43. Tübingen, 1998. An excellent source of several hard-to-find early modern texts on memory; however, translated only into German.

Berns, Jörg Jochen, and Wolfgang Neuber. "Ars Memorativa: Eine Forschungs-bibliographie zu den Quellenschriften der Gedächtniskunst von den antiken Anfängen bis um 1700" (The Art of Memory: A Research Bibliography for Original Sources from the Ancient Origins until 1700). *Frühneuzeit-Info* 3 (1992), pp. 65–87. A helpful list of early sources on the art of memory, in German but easily usable by English speakers.

Secondary Sources

Much of the recent work on the art of memory has been in Italian and German.

General and Introductory Studies

Caplan, Harry. "Memoria: Treasure-House of Eloquence." In *Of Eloquence: Studies in Ancient and Medieval Rhetoric.* Edited and introduced by Anne King and Helen North, pp. 196–246. Ithaca, N.Y., 1970. Caplan's sweeping and learned survey includes many memorable observations and cites copious examples of references to memory as a part of rhetoric.

Carruthers, Mary. *The Book of Memory: A Study of Memory in Medieval Culture.* Cambridge, U.K., 1990. Together with Yates, an invaluable resource on the study of the arts of memory. Carruthers's work is more narrowly focused than Yates's and has the advantage of elucidating much that her predecessor's density leaves obscure. Carruthers also includes translations of three medieval memory texts in appendices.

Yates, Frances. *The Art of Memory.* Chicago, 1966. Yates's magisterial work remains the necessary starting point for any study of memory. Its analyses of the history of the art of memory from Greece to the eighteenth century are brilliant and rapid, sometimes to the point of obscurity. Yates is also perhaps too inclined to detect elements of magic in the works she surveys; nonetheless, this is an indispensable book.

Specialized Studies of Author or Periods

Bolzoni, Lina. *La stanza della memoria: modelli letterari e iconografici nell'età della stampa* (The space of memory: Literary and iconographic models in the age of print). Turin, 1995. A convenient collection by one of the leading scholars of the early modern art of memory, unfortunately only available in Italian.

Eco, Umberto. "An *Ars Oblivionalis?* Forget It!" *PMLA* 103.3 (1988), pp. 254–261. Translated by Marilyn

Migiel. A semicomic consideration of the potential uses for and possibility of devising an art of forgetting.

Engel, William E. *Mapping Mortality: The Persistence of Memory and Melancholy in Early Modern England.* Amherst, Mass., 1995. Considers a variety of mnemonic practices and applications in sixteenth- and seventeenth-century England and France. Chapter 1 describes and interprets a number of realized memory spaces, and the chapter on Montaigne's library is also helpful in understanding the physical construction of memory spaces.

Farrell, Joseph. "The Phenomenology of Memory in Roman Culture." *The Classical Journal* 92.4 (1997), pp. 373–383. Convincingly and suggestively examines what the artificial memory might have meant (rather than simply how it was defined) to its Roman practitioners.

Hacking, Ian. *Rewriting the Soul: Multiple Personality and the Sciences of Memory.* Princeton, 1995. This account of the significance of the diagnosis of multiple personality also reviews the growth of the nineteenth-century "sciences of memory" and the importance of memory as an idea in the late twentieth century.

Johnson, Mark D. *The Spiritual Logic of Ramon Lull.* Oxford, 1987. A brief and clear introduction to Lull's art. For the developments of Lull in the Renaissance, consult Yates.

Krell, David Farrell. *Of Memory, Reminiscence, and Writing/On the Verge.* Bloomington, Ind., 1990. A highly selective, primarily philosophical review and deconstruction of theories of memory from Plato to Derrida by a scholar of Heidegger. Always interesting, not always related clearly to rhetoric.

Luriia, A. R. *The Mind of a Mnemonist: A Little Book about a Vast Memory.* Translated from Russian by Lynn Solotaroff; new foreword by Jerome S. Bruner. Cambridge, Mass., 1987. In other editions, the author's name is spelled "Luria." A popular psychological account of a man so gifted or burdened with memory that he could literally recall a string of nonsense syllables for decades, using a variation of the architectural mnemonic that he discovered on his own.

Ong, Walter. *Ramus, Method, and the Decay of Dialogue: From the Art of Discourse to the Art of Reason.* Cambridge, Mass., 1958. An exhaustive treatment of Ramus's influence and a dazzlingly argued account of the cultural turning-point from the dynamics of learning based on oral and manuscript sources to one based on print.

Spence, Jonathan D. *The Memory Palace of Matteo Ricci.* Harmondsworth, 1984. A historical account of a sixteenth-century Jesuit missionary and practitioner of the art of memory in China. Spence's book is both a fascinating story of Ricci's use of his trained memory and an equally interesting experiment in writing modern academic history through the lens of the art of memory.

—William N. West

METAPHOR. A metaphor (Lat. *translatio*) is a metasememe that is constituted by a substitution of similarities. If it is regarded as a semantic master trope comprising all possible relations of similarity, then hyperbolē, irony, and allegory may also be considered as signifying a metaphoric relationship (Plett, 2000, p. 183). [*See* Allegory; Hyperbolē; *and* Irony.]

The classical tradition described metaphor in syntactic as well as in semantic terms. Following Aristotle (384–322 BCE), who had emphasized the kinship between metaphor and simile in his *Rhetoric* (3.3.3), Roman authors such as Quintilian (*Institutio oratoria,* first century CE, 8.6.8) and Cicero (*De oratore,* 55 BCE 3.39.157) define metaphor syntactically as an elliptic form of simile (*brevior similitudo*). Semantic criteria are used when metaphor is described as a form of translation. In chapter 21 of his *Poetics,* Aristotle lists the following four types of a metaphorical transference: (1) from genus to species; (2) from species to genus; (3) between species; and (4) by analogy. Whereas, according to a modern understanding, the first two types would be regarded as instances of metonymy, the third and fourth are examples of a metaphorical relationship. As an example of analogy, Aristotle cites the expression "the evening of a man's life," which implies the idea that the phases of a personal lifetime are proportionate to those of a day. [*See* Metonymy; *and* Simile.]

Taking into account the semantic features that are affected by metaphorical substitutions, the following classes may be distinguished (Plett 2000, 183 ff.): they include the substitution of (1) concrete for abstract or abstract for concrete, (2) animate for inanimate or inanimate for animate, (3) nonvisual for visual or visual for nonvisual, (4) positive for negative or negative for positive, and (5) large for small or small for large. Possible realizations include substitutions (1) of concrete for abstract: "the *Slough* of Despond" (Bunyan, *Pilgrim's Progress*); (2) of animate for inanimate: "Earth *fills her lap* with pleasures of her own"

(Wordsworth, *Intimations of Immortality*); (3) of nonvisual for visual: "Some books are to be *tasted*, others to be *swallowed*" (Bacon, *Of Studies*); (4) of positive for negative: "Brutus is an *honourable* man" (Shakespeare, *Julius Caesar*); and (5) of small for large: "To have *squeezed* the universe *into a ball*" (Eliot, *Prufrock*). It is interesting to note that (4) coincides with irony in that it represents the dissimulatory speech act of "blame by praise" (Plett, 2000, p. 186).

Uses of metaphor have been restricted with respect to the stylistic ideals of *latinitas, perspicuitas, ornatus,* and *aptum.* According to the *Rhetorica ad Herennium* (c.84 BCE), metaphors are recommendable if they are used: (1) to create a "vivid mental picture," (2) for the sake of brevity, (3) to avoid obscenity, (4) for the sake of magnifying, (5) minifying, or (6) embellishment (4.34). Mixed metaphors, which result from a combination of lexemes belonging to disparate semantic fields, are generally considered as instances of a bad style (e.g., "The bitter cup of misfortune hovers in the air"). Stylistic restrictions, however, do not apply to all fields of discourse in the same way. Thus, Aristotle states in *Rhetoric* (3.3.4) that metaphors should not be "far-fetched," but he also concedes that the standards in poetry are different from those in the other arts.

Regarding grammatical structure, five classes of metaphor have been distinguished (Brooke-Rose, 1970): (1) the simple replacement; (2) the pointing formula in which the proper term is also expressed ("The apparition of these *faces* in the crowd; *petals* on a wet black *bough*"; Pound, *Metro*); (3) the copula ("Life . . . *is a tale* told by an idiot," Shakespeare, *Macbeth*); (4) the link with "to make" ("The experience of war had *made* him *a nervous wreck*"); and (5) the genitive link ("the *crown* of creation").

The following instances may be regarded as special cases of metaphorical usage: (1) the necessary metaphor, or *catachrēsis,* which compensates for the absence of a *nomen proprium* in a given language ("the *foot* of a hill," "the *neck* of a guitar"), and (2) the dead metaphor, which has become a part of the lexicon and is no longer recognized as a trope ("He was *killing* [wasting] time"). [*See* Catachrēsis.]

Twentieth-Century Theories. In discussing metaphor in his *Philosophy of Rhetoric* (New York,

1936), I. A. Richards introduced the term *tenor* to denote the subject referred to, and *vehicle* to denote the lexeme employed. Although these terms have become widely adopted, the relationship between the two categories has remained a matter of debate. Max Black (1962) distinguishes between traditional theories of substitution and comparison on the one hand and interaction theories on the other. In the latter, the meaning of a metaphor is understood as a resultant of the interaction of tenor and vehicle (Richards, 1936, p. 93). Accordingly, a metaphorical expression cannot be retranslated into a literal one without risking a loss of meaning. Writing in the tradition of Richards and Black, Paul Ricoeur describes metaphor as an "impertinent predication" that includes the contrastive semantic elements "is like" and "is not" (1977). According to Ricoeur, it is the tension between these two poles that constitutes the "truth" of a metaphor.

In his influential article, "Two Aspects of Language and Two Types of Aphasic Disturbances" (1971), Roman Jakobson describes metaphor and metonymy as two basic linguistic categories. Referring to Ferdinand de Saussure's distinction between a paradigmatic and a syntagmatic level of language, Jakobson associates metaphor with the principle of selection and metonymy with the principle of combination. Whereas the former implies a relationship of similarity, the latter is associated with contiguity. In the field of literature, poetry is characterized as being dominated by the metaphorical, realistic prose by the metonymic principle (pp. 91–92).

Speech act theory has emphasized the pragmatic functions of metaphorical expressions. Metaphors are regarded as indirect speech acts that a hearer has to interpret in the light of his knowledge of a given context of situation (Searle, 1993, pp. 90–95). An analytical tool for interpreting metaphorical speech acts is provided by H. Paul Grice's concept of "conversational implicatures" (1975). [*See* Speech acts, utterances as.]

Philosophical approaches to metaphor have mainly focused on questions of epistemology and modes of thinking. Hans Blumenberg (1960) concentrates on the importance of metaphorical concepts in the course of European intellectual history. More than a rhetorical device, metaphor is seen as a mode of perception, the different traces of which are discernible in the history of philosophical thought. Similarly, Kenneth Burke, in *A Grammar of Motives* (1969), proposes a system of "Four Master Tropes" that are regarded as modes of thought rather than linguistic procedures. Metaphor, being one of these tropes, is defined in terms of perspective: it represents "a device for seeing something in terms of something else" (p. 503).

Modern philosophies of metaphor have been influenced considerably by the German philosopher Friedrich Nietzsche (1844–1900) who, in his essay "On Truth and Lie in an Extramoral Sense" (1873), described metaphor as an indispensable factor in man's understanding of the world. According to Nietzsche, the process of naming is itself metaphorical, because it involves two kinds of transference: one from a nerve stimulus into an image, and one from an image into a sound. As a result, man possesses "nothing but metaphors for things." In the light of Nietzsche's understanding of metaphor as a ubiquitous phenomenon, recent discussions have focused on the question of whether a nonmetaphorical level of language can be assumed at all (MacCormac, 1985, pp. 53–78).

Cognitivist theories have focused on the role of metaphor in everyday experience. Again, metaphor is understood as a mode of thought rather than as a linguistic device (Lakoff and Johnson, 1980). Conceptual metaphors, which structure man's understanding of reality, may surface in a variety of linguistic expressions. Even if language users may be unaware of a conceptual metaphor like "Time is money," they will reveal it in a number of ready-made expressions (e.g., "to spend one's time"). "Mapping" is a concept that is central to the cognitivist approach. An expression like "See how far we've come!" is taken to indicate an underlying conceptual metaphor "Love is a journey." The metaphorical process consists of a mapping from the source domain "journey" to the target domain "love" (Lakoff, 1990, pp. 47–51).

Finally, recent discussions have focused on the function of metaphor in science, an area that has often been regarded as nonmetaphorical. Aiming at a one-to-one relationship between *res* and *verba*, early modern scientists and philosophers tended to regard metaphorical language as a su-

perfluity that diverted man's attention from the "facts of nature." Critical attitudes toward metaphor can be found in the writings of such philosophers as Thomas Hobbes (1588–1679) and John Locke (1632–1704). Despite intensive strivings for a nonmetaphorical language, metaphors in the history of science and philosophy abound. Instances are provided by the "*tree* of Porphyry" (*arbor Porphyriana*), the "*book* of nature," and by Charles Darwin's notion of "natural *selection*." It seems appropriate, however, to distinguish between the different functions that metaphors may serve in different communicative situations. The metaphorical "genetic code," which describes a biological process in terms of information theory, for instance, is a *catachrēsis*. It is a heuristic tool, because it allows for analogical extensions in expressions like genetic "message," "transcription," or "translation" (Halloran and Bradford, 1984, p. 188). Didactic discourse, on the other hand, employs illustrative metaphors in the interests of perspicuity.

[*See also* Figures of speech; Style; *and* Tacit dimension, the.]

BIBLIOGRAPHY

Black, Max. *Models and Metaphors*. Ithaca, N.Y., 1962.

Blumenberg, Hans. *Paradigmen zu einer Metaphorologie*. Bonn, Germany, 1960.

Brooke-Rose, Christine. *A Grammar of Metaphor*. London, 1970.

Grice, H. Paul. "Logic and Conversation." In *Syntax and Semantics,* edited by Peter Cole and Jerry L. Morgan, vol. 3, pp. 41–58. New York, 1975.

Halloran, S. Michael, and Annette N. Bradford. "Figures of Speech in the Rhetoric of Science and Technology." In *Essays on Classical and Modern Discourse,* edited by Robert J. Connors et al., pp. 179–192. Carbondale, Ill., 1984.

Haverkamp, Anselm, ed. *Theorie der Metapher.* 2d ed. Darmstadt, 1996.

Jakobson, Roman. "Two Aspects of Language and Two Types of Aphasic Disturbances." In *Fundamentals of Language,* 2d ed., by Roman Jakobson and Morris Halle, pp. 67–96. The Hague, 1971.

Lakoff, George. "The Invariance Hypothesis: Is Abstract Reason Based on Image-Schemas?" *Cognitive Linguistics* 1 (1990), pp. 39–74.

Lakoff, George, and Mark Johnson. *Metaphors We Live By.* Chicago, 1980.

MacCormac, Earl R. *A Cognitive Theory of Metaphor.* Cambridge, Mass., 1985.

Nietzsche, Friedrich. "Über Wahrheit und Lüge im auss-
    ermoralischen Sinne" (1873). In *Der Streit um die Me-*
    tapher: Poetologische Texte von Nietzsche bis Handke.
    Mit kommentierenden Studien, edited by Klaus Müller-
    Richter and Arturo Larcati, pp. 31–39. Darmstadt,
    1988.
Plett, Heinrich F. *Systematische Rhetorik.* Munich, 2000.
Ricœur, Paul. *The Rule of Metaphor: Multi-Disciplinary*
    Studies of the Creation of Meaning in Language. Trans-
    lated by Robert Czerny et al. Toronto, 1977. English
    translation of *La métaphore vive,* first published 1975.
Searle, John R. "Metaphor." *Metaphor and Thought,* ed-
    ited by Andrew Ortony, 2d ed., pp. 83–111. Cam-
    bridge, U.K., 1993.

—RICHARD NATE

METONYMY. Metonymy (Lat. *denominatio*) is
a metasememe that is constituted by a substitution of contiguities. Contiguity can be defined in
terms of a causal, a local, or a temporal relationship. If contiguity is taken as a distinguishing criterion, metonymy may be said to comprise also
antonomasia, which signifies the substitution of
an appellative noun and a proper name, and *synecdochē,* which involves a relationship of part for
whole, or *pars pro toto* (Plett, 2000, pp. 191–192).
[*See* Synecdochē.]

Traditional descriptions of metonymy have varied. Whereas Cicero deals with it as a subclass of
metaphor (*De oratore,* 55 BCE, 3.42.167–169),
Quintilian introduces it as a separate category in
his *Institutio oratoria* (first century CE) and lists five
subclasses (8.6.23–28). He declares, however, that
"to follow out these points is a task involving too
much detail." The author of the *Rhetorica ad Herennium* (c.84 BCE) lists seven types, and also gives
a qualifying remark: "It is harder to distinguish all
these metonymies in teaching the principle than
to find them when searching for them, for the use
of this kind is abundant not only amongst the poets and orators but also in everyday speech" (4.32).

Among others, the following subcategories of
metonymic relations have been discussed: the
substitution (1) of author for work ("He knows his
Shakespeare [Shakespeare's works]"); (2) of producer for product ("He drives a *Ford*"); (3) of effect
for cause ("Death *is* [i.e., makes] *pale*"), (4) of container for a thing contained ("He drank a *cup* [of
tea]"); (5) of garment for person ("The *bluecoats*
[soldiers] were advancing"); (6) of location

for person ("The *White House* [the president] has
announced the end of the peace negotiations");
(7) of location for institution ("He would write no
more for *Tin Pan Alley* [the music publishing
houses there]"); and (8) of part for the whole
("They found some helping *hands* [i.e., people]").

Aiming at a more systematic description, the
following substitutions have been distinguished
(Plett, 2000, pp. 192–196): (1) of the general for
the particular and vice versa; (2) of the cause for
an effect and vice versa; (3) of the substance for
an accident and vice versa; and (4) of the container for the things contained and vice versa. Being of a more general nature, these classes allow
for a reduction of the categories given above.
Thus, the substitutions of "author for work" and
"producer for product" may be regarded as instances of a causal relationship (2); the substitutions of "garment for person" and "location for
person" may be subsumed in the relationship
"container and contained" (4).

Twentieth-Century Theories of Metonymy.
Although the classical tradition tended to neglect
metonymy in favor of metaphor, the concept of
metonymy has been subject to several revisions
in recent decades. In an influential article, "Two
Aspects of Language and Two Types of Aphasic
Disturbances" (1971), Roman Jakobson (1896–
1982) helped revive an interest in the concept by
describing it in terms of structural linguistics. Metonymy is regarded as a fundamental linguistic
category, which is connected to the principle of
combination and represents the counterpart of
metaphor that is connected to the principle of
selection. Jakobson identified two types of apha-
sia, one of which can be explained as a "selection
deficiency" or "similarity disorder," and the other
as a "contexture deficiency" or "contiguity disorder" (1971, pp. 77–78). The distinction between metaphorical and metonymic processes is
regarded as being "of primal significance and
consequence for all verbal behaviour and for human behaviour in general" (1971, p. 93). Jakobson suggests that the distinction between the
"metaphoric and metonymic poles" of language
can provide a general mechanism of analysis with
a wide range of applications. The established dichotomy is thought to be relevant for the description of linguistic entities (paradigmatic vs. syntagmatic levels); logical relations (similarity vs.

contiguity), linguistic operations (selection vs. combination); and different forms of language disturbance (selection deficiency vs. contexture deficiency). The established dichotomy is also relevant, however, for the classification of dream representations (symbolism vs. displacement); forms of magic (imitative vs. contagious); art forms (drama vs. film); literary genres (poetry vs. prose); film techniques (montage vs. close-up); periods in the history of art (Surrealism vs. Cubism); and cultural history in general (Romanticism and Symbolism vs. Realism) (pp. 90–96). [*See* Metaphor.]

Jakobson's evaluation of metonymy and metaphor as constituting the distinguishing features of literary genres has attracted the interest of literary critics and historians. Whereas poems are found to be marked by relationships of similarity, prose literature is often characterized by a predominance of relationships of contiguity. Poetry is thus apt to illustrate Jakobson's definition of the poetic function as directing a reader's attention to language itself, while realistic prose "tends to disguise itself as nonliterature" (Lodge, 1977, p. 93). Following Jakobson's suggestions, specific periods of cultural history have been characterized with respect to their preference for poetry or prose. Whereas Romantic and Symbolist authors would have recourse to metaphorical strategies, the age of Realism was marked by a predominance of metonymic strategies. Protagonists of realistic novels, for instance, tend to be representatives of a social class; the conflicts in which they are involved metonymically reflect general tensions within a society. The "metaphoric and metonymic poles" have also been used as analytical tools in the investigation of particular periods of literary history; for example, the development of Renaissance poetry (Hedley, 1988).

As Jakobson points out, an "oscillation" between the metaphoric and the metonymic poles is also evident in "sign systems other than language" (1971, p. 92). The art of the cinema appears to be marked by a predominance of *pars pro toto* representations. Although the technique of montage can be described as metaphoric, the shot and the scene, which constitute the basic units of a film, are metonymic (Lodge, 1977, p. 84). Further instances of metonymic representations are the close-up, the slow-motion sequence, and the

high- or low-angle shot, all representing a departure from a real-life experience of events and scenes (Lodge, 1977, p. 84). A metonymic effect can be achieved by a series of shots that are juxtaposed in such a way that the viewer feels obliged to attribute a causal relationship to them if the sequence of pictures is to be meaningful. Thus, a turkey and a face presented in a sequence might suggest the idea of hunger (Lodge, 1977, pp. 84–85). Finally, one may point to the technique of suspense in crime movies where a moving shadow may metonymically indicate a murderer or a camera pan may reflect the nervousness of the protagonist.

Jakobson's structuralist interpretation of Sigmund Freud's concepts of "condensation" and "displacement" as being metaphorical and metonymic types of dream representation was further developed by the French psychoanalyst Jacques Lacan (1901–1981). Starting from the assumption that the unconscious is structured like a language, Lacan described the Freudian types of dream representation as instances of a "rhetoric of the unconscious" (1977). On the other hand, Jakobson's analyses have also met with criticism. Maria Ruegg (1979), for example, observes that the explanations of cultural and psychological phenomena that are derived from Jakobson's principles are often so general that they border on being "virtually meaningless" (pp. 143–144).

An interpretation that conceives of metonymy as a mode of thought rather than a linguistic operation has been proposed by Kenneth Burke (*A Grammar of Motives*, Berkeley, 1969). In his classification of "Four Master Tropes," which points back to a similar scheme by the Italian philosopher Giambattista Vico (1668–1744), metaphor is associated with "perspective," metonymy with "reduction," *synecdochē* with "representation," and irony with "dialectic" (1969, p. 503). [*See* Irony.] Metonymy is defined as an "archaicizing device" that aims "to convey some incorporeal or intangible state in terms of the corporeal or tangible" (p. 506). An example is the substitution of "heart" for "emotion." Like Jakobson's scheme, Burke's system exceeds the limits of traditional *elocutio* in that it involves a perspective of cultural criticism. Metonomic relations, for instance, are viewed as being typical not only of poetic realism but also of scientific realism, as well as the philosophical materialism from which it has sprung (1969, p. 507).

In Hayden White's *Tropics of Discourse* (1978), Burke's "Master Tropes" are applied to the realm of historical analysis. On the grounds that a respective predominance of metaphorical, metonymic, synecdochical, and ironic principles could be responsible for the existence of different schools of historiography, the works of historiographers are classified with respect to their reliance on one of the "four master tropes."

Cognitivist theorists have dealt with metonymy under a new methodological premise. In accordance with an early suggestion made by Nicolas Ruwet (1975), the emphasis is on the common quality of metaphor and metonymy as a means of structuring man's perception of reality rather than on the semantic differences that may exist between these categories. According to George Lakoff and Mark Johnson, metaphors and metonymies are parts of the "ordinary, everyday way we think and act as well as talk" (1980, p. 37). Within this theoretical framework, an underlying conceptual metonymy like "The face for the person" may be proposed, which reflects an everyday experience and is responsible for a variety of metonymic expressions (e.g., "There are some new faces in the crowd"). At the same time, it points to a specific domain of culture. Whereas in passport pictures the metonymy "face for the person" is current, in sports it may be the physical stature ("There are some strong bodies on our team"), and in scholarly circles, the head as the signifier of intellectual capacities ("There are some good heads in the department") (Croft, 1993). Metonymic expressions may also serve an economical function by directing the listener's attention to a certain target domain (e.g., "The appendicitis in room 102 has called for a glass of water").

[*See also* Figures of speech; *and* Style.]

BIBLIOGRAPHY

Croft, William. "The Role of Domains in the Interpretation of Metaphors and Metonymies." *Cognitive Linguistics* 4 (1993), pp. 335–370.

Hedley, Jane. *Power in Verse: Metaphor and Metonymy in the Renaissance Lyric.* London, 1988.

Jakobson, Roman. "Two Aspects of Language and Two Types of Aphasic Disturbances." *Fundamentals of Language,* by Roman Jakobson and Morris Halle, 2d ed., pp. 67–96. The Hague, 1971.

Lacan, Jacques. "The Agency of the Letter in the Unconscious, or Reason since Freud." *Ecrits: A Selection.* Translated by Alan Sheridan. New York, 1977. English translation of "L'instance de la lettre dans l'inconscient, ou la raison depuis Freud," first published 1966.

Lakoff, George, and Mark Johnson. *Metaphors We Live By.* Chicago, 1980.

Lausberg, Heinrich. *Handbook of Literary Rhetoric: A Foundation for Literary Study.* Translated by Matthew C. Bliss, Annemiek Jansen, David E. Orton; edited by David E. Orton and R. Dean Anderson. Leiden, 1998. English translation of *Handbuch der literarischen Rhetorik,* first published 1960.

Lodge, David. *The Modes of Modern Writing: Metaphor, Metonymy, and the Typology of Modern Literature.* London, 1977.

Plett, Heinrich F. *Systematische Rhetorik: Konzepte und Analysen.* Munich, 2000.

Ruegg, Maria. "Metaphor and Metonymy: The Logic of Structuralist Rhetoric." *Glyph* 6 (1979), pp. 141–157.

Ruwet, Nicolas. "Synecdoques et Métonymies." *Poetique* 6 (1975), pp. 371–388.

White, Hayden. *Tropics of Discourse: Essays in Cultural Criticism.* Baltimore, 1978.

—RICHARD NATE

MIMĒSIS. *See* Imitation.

MODERN RHETORIC. Modern Western rhetoric is a twentieth-century phenomenon with roots in the nineteenth century. It emerged out of intellectual developments in linguistics, philosophy, and literary theory, and out of the redefinition and reinvigoration of the classical tradition. It became part of the pedagogy in departments of English, composition, rhetoric, and speech communication. A series of interrelated shifts in focus distinguishes modern rhetoric from earlier theorizing and pedagogy: a shift from argument to language as the basis of influence; from the invention of the speaker to the interpretations of the consumer of discourse; from historical and biographical studies of speakers and speeches to close readings of texts; from explication of a single text to critiques of bodies of discourse; and from a conception of rhetoric as orally delivered speeches to a reconception of rhetoric as symbolic action, indeed, as symbolic action through which as humans we construct the worlds in which we live. The result was an enlarged idea of rhetoric and of the means through which influence emerges. These shifts also fostered a flowering of rhetorical criticism of all forms of discourse from novels and poetry and plays to speeches and nonverbal, visual symbols and rituals.

Like all subsequent theorizing and practice, modern rhetoric grew out of and in response to the classical tradition that began with the ancient Sophists in the sixth century BCE and was contested and elaborated in the works of Plato, Aristotle, Cicero, Quintilian, and Augustine. It also was influenced by later theorizing that attempted to incorporate developments in science, particularly the writings of Francis Bacon (1561–1626), as well as the works of such nineteenth-century British theorists as Hugh Blair (1718–1800), George Campbell (1719–1796), and Richard Whately (1787–1863), who revived and revised the classical tradition.

The Impact of Language Studies. What became modern rhetoric was presaged in the works of German philosopher Friedrich Nietzsche (1844–1900), a philologist who was intimately acquainted with the classical tradition. In his "Lecture Notes," he wrote that the specific differences between the ancients and moderns constituted the site for the remarkable change in the understanding of what rhetoric is. Nietzsche laid the foundation for a conception of rhetoric grounded in language through which humans socially construct their reality; the "lie" that becomes the "truth" that permits social interaction ("On Truth and Lie in an Extramoral Sense," 1873). He asked, "What then is truth?" and answered: "A movable host of metaphors, metonymies, and anthropomorphisms." In his work, truth became an artistic and social construction effected through language, and his writings initiated a view of rhetoric as truth-creating or as hermeneutic, that is, as a process by which humans interpret themselves and their world in and through symbols. Although Nietzsche pioneered these ideas, the pathbreaking character of his work was recognized only in retrospect. [*See* Metaphor.]

Studies of language in the twentieth century generated findings that led to the growth of modern rhetoric. Perhaps the most influential figure was the Swiss linguist Ferdinand de Saussure (1857–1913; *Cours de linguistique générale*, Lausanne, 1916), whose work laid the foundation for structuralist approaches to language and semiotics, especially in the works of such later theorists and critics as Roland Barthes (*Eléments de sémiologie*, Paris, 1965) and Umberto Eco (*A Theory of Semiotics*, Bloomington, Ind., 1976). Saussure distinguished *la langue,* a linguistic system that provides rules for usage, and *la parole,* actual utterances or people's use of language, practices from which the rules of a linguistic system must be inferred. Saussure understood language to be a system constituted by conventions, rules, and their internal relations. His work was influential internationally in shaping structuralist views of language as a system and of social practice as fundamental to its workings. [*See* Linguistics.]

U.S. pragmatists took up the study of language. Charles Sanders Peirce (1839–1914) saw logic, in its general sense, as semiotic, and treated pragmatism purely as a theory of meaning. He argued that signs can never have fixed meanings, and he distinguished three types of signs: the icon, which resembles its object; the index, which rests on an associative relationship; and the symbol, whose meaning depends on social or cultural conventions. His catalog of signs emphasized that interpretation is a human activity mediated by culture and interaction. Peirce also transformed the medieval trivium of grammar, logic, and rhetoric and described what he called a "speculative rhetoric" that focused on language as the mediator among subject, reality, and community. Developing the ideas of Peirce and of George Herbert Mead in *Mind, Self, and Society* (Chicago, 1934), Charles Morris in *Foundations of the Theory of Signs* (Chicago, 1940) and in *Signs, Language, and Behavior* (New York, 1946) presented what he thought of as a comprehensive science of signs. Morris set forth a model of the universe of discourse that distinguished among literary, persuasive, scientific, and systemic discourse in terms of their end or purpose, central criterion of evaluation, language characteristics, source, typical forms, character of claims, and relevant theory. Morris emphasized Mead's position that a symbol capable of communicative use arises only within cooperative social action in which behavior aimed at a common goal makes shared meaning necessary, noting that Mead included forms of conflict in cooperative acts. Thus, Morris treated rhetoric as part of semiotics.

Literary theorists C. K. Ogden (1889–1957) and I. A. Richards (1893–1979) built on the work of Saussure and Peirce in *The Meaning of Meaning: A Study of the Influence of Language upon Thought and of the Science of Symbolism* (New York, 1923), a book that attempted to address the difficulties raised by the influence of language upon thought. That, in turn, laid the foundation for *Principles of Literary Criticism* (New York, 1925), in which Richards attempted to provide the same critical foundation for the emotive function of language as had been attempted earlier by Ogden and Richards for the symbolic function. In *Principles of Literary Criticism,* Richards claimed that criticism is an effort to discriminate between our experiences of literary works and to evaluate those experiences, reflecting his psychological approach to literary study, which foreshadowed what is now called reader response criticism. That approach was enlarged and applied in *Practical Criticism: A Study of Literary Judgment* (New York, 1929), which analyzed the results of an experiment asking students to respond to unidentified poems and distinguished four kinds of meaning based on sense, feeling, tone, and intention.

Richards turned his attention directly to rhetoric in *The Philosophy of Rhetoric* (New York, 1936), in which he proposed a new role for rhetoric as the study of meaning, specifically, as "a study of misunderstanding and its remedies." Accordingly, he described rhetoric as "a philosophic discipline aiming at mastery of the fundamental laws of the use of language, not just a set of dodges that will be found to work sometimes" (p. 7), a perspective that greatly enlarged the purview of rhetoric. In particular, he attacked what he called the "Proper Meaning Superstition," the widely held belief that a word has a single meaning independent of and controlling its usage. His work recognized the shifts in emphasis that were occurring; for example, he commented that whereas older notions of rhetoric treated ambiguity as a fault to be eliminated or contained, newer understandings of rhetoric treat ambiguity as inevitable and as indispensable to the discourse of poetry and religion. [*See* Ambiguity.] He

emphasized the interanimation of language, the ways in which terms affect each other's meaning. He recognized metaphor as an ever-present principle of language, and his analysis of metaphor as the interanimation of two terms, and his development of the concepts of *tenor* (the principal subject, e.g., "My love") and *vehicle* (the second or metaphorical term, e.g., "is a red rose") as the means by which the workings of a metaphor may be understood, have had enduring influence.

Richards's perspective was psychological and strategic; by contrast, the work of Richard Weaver emphasized the ethical dimensions of language use. For Weaver, "language is sermonic," meaning that all uses of language must be seen as persuasive, rhetorical, and infused with ethical values (*The Ethics of Rhetoric,* Chicago, 1953). Although dedicated to the view that there are eternal principles that ought to be the bases for sound and ethical argument, Weaver reinterpreted the classical tradition in ways that emphasized the importance of rhetoric and the centrality of language, as illustrated in his allegorical reading of Plato's *Phaedrus.* [*See* Classical rhetoric.] In his interpretation of that dialogue, he treats the three speeches as instances of the ways in which language might work its wiles. It might fail to move us, as represented by Lysias's speech urging the case of the nonlover, an illustration of scientific or technical communication. It might move us toward evil, as represented by the obsessed lover of Socrates' first speech, a kind of discourse that takes the form of advertising and propaganda. Or it might move us toward the good, as represented by the lover of Socrates' second speech, which enacts an ideal, noble rhetoric. Based on that dialogue and other Platonic works, Weaver argued that dialectic is exhausted in the processes of definition, analysis, and synthesis and must be followed by rhetoric, the figurative language in which truth is expressed analogically in the *mythoi* of the dialogues. This reading of the dialogue gave rhetoric a central and vital role in making truth effective, a view that echoed Francis Bacon's conception of rhetoric as linking reason and imagination to enable the will to make ethical choices (*The Advancement of Learning,* London, 1605). Weaver's stance also can be interpreted as assigning the truth functions of invention entirely to dialectic or philosophy, reviving the Platonic and later Ramistic division that reduced rhetoric to ornamentation.

The Impact of Philosophical Studies. Philosophers, particularly in philosophical studies of language, also contributed to the development of modern rhetoric. The work of Austrian philosopher Ludwig Wittgenstein (1889–1951) was particularly influential. In the posthumously published *Philosophical Investigations* (London, 1953), he developed a theory that posited meaning as a product of language usage within different language games whose rules are shaped by social practice, a theory that denied essentialistic views of language (that terms have a single, fixed meaning). This theory also rejected the idea that a language of perfect clarity and accuracy could be devised, which had been the aim of logical positivists, such as German philosopher Gottlob Frege (1848–1925) and British philosopher and mathematician Bertrand Russell (1872–1970). [*See* Philosophy.]

The development of ordinary language philosophy increased interest in the pragmatic uses of language. Of particular import was *How to Do Things with Words* (Cambridge, U.K., 1962) by John L. Austin, which introduced the concepts of speech acts. Austin differentiated the locution, a grammatical entity; the illocution, an utterance to perform a function, or "In saying *x*, I did *y*," best illustrated by the special class called performatives, such as "I bet" or "I promise"; and the perlocution, or "By saying *x*, an effect or uptake was produced." These ideas were analyzed and elaborated in *Speech Acts: An Essay in the Philosophy of Language* (London, 1969) by John R. Searle, which was followed by his *Expression and Meaning: Studies in the Theory of Speech Acts* (London, 1979). [*See* Speech acts, utterances as.]

European phenomenologists also were interested in language and meaning. In 1960, Maurice Merleau-Ponty published *Signes* (Paris), translated by Richard McCleary (Evanston, Ill., 1964). Merleau-Ponty explored the inseparable relation between the intentions of a constituting consciousness, which is the origin of the meaning of our experience, and the external, constitutive meaning structures to which they are connected. The problem of meaning is how we constitute it and simultaneously find that it is always already constituted by meanings we have not bestowed on it.

The problem posed for science, as he saw it, was the relationship between the judging subject and objective things because consciousness is always perspectival. In other words, phenomenology suggested that all meaning was rhetorical.

Of particular significance for an enlarged conception of rhetoric was the work of U.S. philosopher Susanne K. Langer. First in *Philosophy in a New Key: A Study in the Symbolism of Reason, Rite, and Art* (Cambridge, Mass., 1942) and later in *Feeling and Form: A Theory of Art* (New York, 1953), Langer argued that language does not copy facts; rather, facts are transformed when turned into propositions, which have discursive form. Many items do not fit grammatical or discursive patterns; however, these include images or *fantasies* (her term) whose symbolic character is demonstrated by our willingness to use them as metaphors; for example, fire as a symbol of passion, a rose as a symbol of beauty, an onrushing locomotive as a symbol of danger. Unlike languages, artworks such as paintings have no elements with fixed meanings (no vocabulary or grammar as such); they are nondiscursive symbols with a kind of semantic Langer calls "presentational symbolism," whose elements are understood only through the meaning of the whole, that is, through their relations within the total structure. Thus, Langer developed a theory of the artwork as symbol; however, the distinction between the discursive qualities of language and the presentational symbolism of art is breached by metaphor, an element of language that also has presentational characteristics. Langer's work illustrates how philosophical studies of language led to an enlarged view of rhetoric and to greater understanding of the ways in which nonlinguistic symbols become part of what is broadly understood as rhetoric. Later cultural studies theorists, like Stuart Hall, would study the ways that humans make meaning of nonlinguistic symbols.

U.S. philosopher and humanist Richard McKeon also contributed to an enlarged conception of rhetoric. In *Thought, Action, and Passion* (Chicago, 1954) and in *Rhetoric: Essays in Invention and Discovery* (Woodbridge, Conn., 1987), he treated rhetoric as central to the philosophical and cultural revolutions that began in the early decades of the twentieth century. He saw rhetoric as an "architectonic" art that provides the issues and instrumentalities that lead to creative investigations into new areas. McKeon held that modern rhetoric could be broadened from the narrower emphasis on persuasion to include all elements of existence and to provide commonplaces or topics for discovery of the unknown in all fields.

Because linguists and philosophers saw language as central to understanding meaning and interpretation, and as the medium through which social conventions and cultural knowledge were created, rhetoric came to be seen as a more important area of study than had formerly been the case.

The Impact of Literary Theory. These developments in linguistic theory and philosophy greatly enlarged how rhetoric was understood and linked processes of communication and influence to qualities present in all language usage. Developments in literary theory were of equal importance in fashioning what became modern rhetoric. In particular, for literary theorists rhetoric increasingly came to be seen as all of the strategic resources available to people in adapting all kinds of discourse, including literary works, to achieve their ends with audiences.

Theorizing about modern rhetoric differs from theorizing in earlier periods because of the close relationship between criticism and theory. Criticism as we now understand it was absent from the theorizing of the earliest writers. Textual analysis appears only briefly in Book 4 of *De doctrina christiana* (426 or 427 CE) in which Augustine dissects biblical passages in order to demonstrate that the biblical prophets, the author of the Pauline epistles, and the leaders of the church also used the rhetorical techniques associated with the pagan Greco-Roman tradition. Four centuries earlier, for example, Philo had provided a schema for analysis (see *Philon Rhetor,* Berkeley, 1984). In contrast, much of modern rhetorical theory emanated out of intellectual ferment related to what criticism should be and do. [*See* Criticism.]

A key development in literary theory was the emergence of what came to be called New Criticism, named from John Crowe Ransom's *The New Criticism* (1941, Norfolk, Conn.). Many literary theorists contributed to its development. New Criticism derived in part from the ideas of I. A. Richards, from the critical essays of T. S. Eliot, and from the works of such theorists and critics as

Cleanth Brooks and Robert Penn Warren, whose textbook *Understanding Poetry* (New York, 1938) did much to establish New Criticism in the pedagogy of U.S. colleges. In their composition textbook *Modern Rhetoric* (New York, 1949), Brooks and Warren placed language at the very center of the life of thought and of feeling both for individuals and for individuals as members of society. They distinguished between grammar and rhetoric in a metaphor adapted to undergraduates: They described the "grammar" of football as the rules and conventions governing the conduct of the game, including its scoring, and its "rhetoric" as the knowledge of strategy and maneuver that leads to effective play and winning. To play by the rules would not necessarily be to play effectively, but effective play would have to conform to the rules of the game. That strategic conception of rhetoric harks back to the *Philosophy of Rhetoric* (1776), in which George Campbell defined rhetoric as "[t]hat art or talent by which discourse is adapted to its end."

The New Critics differed from one another in many ways, but all held that a literary work should be treated as an object in itself, as an autonomous entity existing for its own sake. This view echoes ideas found in chapter 7 of *On the Sublime* (first century BCE), which claims that sublimity exists in such works as please all well-read, intelligent readers in all times. [*See* Sublime, the.] Accordingly, the New Critics warned readers against the intentional fallacy, the error of interpreting a work by reference to the design or plan of the author in producing it. Instead, they contended that the meaning and value of a work reside in the actual text. They also warned against the affective fallacy, the error of evaluating a work by its effects, especially its emotional effects, on the audience. Their distinctive procedure or method was explication or close reading, a detailed and subtle analysis of the component elements within a work. In *Explication as Criticism* (New York, 1963), W. K. Wimsatt claimed that "explication *is* criticism; it *is* the evaluative account of the poem" (p. ix). This statement summed up the strategic perspective of the New Critics.

When described as explication, close analysis of texts could seem to be a cold and impersonal approach to discourse. In a letter to the poet Stephen Spender in May 1935, T. S. Eliot vividly described the personal commitment such criticism entailed, requiring that critics surrender themselves to authors: "[Y]ou have to give yourself up, and then recover yourself, and the third moment is having something to say, before you have wholly forgotten both surrender and recovery. Of course the self recovered is never the same as the self before it was given" (*Selected Prose of T. S. Eliot,* New York, 1975, p. 13). Critics like Eliot understood criticism to be an intense engagement between the critic and the text out of which explication became possible.

The principles developed and illustrated by the New Critics constituted a revolution in literary study. In place of the philological and historical–biographical approach to literary study that had its roots in nineteenth-century German universities, the New Critics insisted on the aesthetic value of the text itself, which they thought was more important than the biographical background of its author or the influence of the historical milieu in which it was produced. The ferment created by these new ideas would affect many areas of study, including studies of historical fiction and nonfiction and analyses of public speeches and other forms of public discourse. New Criticism also influenced literary and rhetorical theory.

Criticism based on close readings of texts diminished distinctions between genres. New Critics approached all texts as rhetorical works insofar as they were strategic efforts to achieve particular ends, whether that end was to create an experience or to influence policy decisions. In *The Rhetoric of Fiction* (Chicago, 1961), Wayne C. Booth argued that all literature is discourse addressed to a reader, and that critics should examine the techniques, all of the rhetorical resources, available to authors who attempt to persuade readers to accept the fictional worlds they have created. In the third edition of *A Glossary of Literary Terms* (New York, 1971), M. H. Abrams labeled this development *rhetorical criticism,* and its practice was illustrated and presented to students in works such as John Ciardi's *How Does a Poem Mean?* (Boston, 1959).

As the boundaries of older genres were eroded, literary critics offered new conceptions of literary genres. In *Anatomy of Criticism* (Princeton, 1957),

Northrop Frye offered a unified, coherent view of literature that incorporated an altered conception of genres, which stressed their interrelationships. Like Booth and others, Frye emphasized analysis of literary works, but his system encompassed works of prose, including speeches and other forms of public discourse. For example, he linked the rhetoric of comedy to the rhetoric of jurisprudence. As he developed an elaborate theory of interrelated genres, he commented, "The basis of generic criticism in any case is rhetorical, in the sense that the genre is determined by the conditions established between the poet and his public" (p. 247). When rhetoric is understood as adaptation based on purpose and audience, its scope is enlarged, and its role becomes central to all discursive production.

The Impact of Kenneth Burke. The single most important influence on the development of modern rhetoric was the theory and criticism of Kenneth Burke (1897–1993), whose interdisciplinary approach affected scholarship in many fields, including sociology, literary theory, journalism, composition, and speech communication.

Burke's work had such widespread impact because it was comprehensive. It offered an alternative way of understanding how language worked to influence people, it offered an enlarged conception of rhetoric that could encompass the varied forms of discourse that emerged in the twentieth century, and it offered a human ontology that explained persuasion as a result of the interaction between humans and language. Burke called his approach dramatism, which he described as a technique for analyzing thought and language as modes of action rather than as the means for conveying information. His theory was accompanied by brilliant examples of criticism that were models for how this approach to discourse could be used. Of particular note are the essays "The Rhetoric of Hitler's 'Battle'" and "Antony in Behalf of the Play," which appeared in *The Philosophy of Literary Form* (Baton Rouge, La., 1941).

From Burke's dramatistic perspective, all discourse is a symbolic drama that can be analyzed and understood through the relationships among the terms of his pentad—"scene," "act," "agent," "agency," and "purpose"—all of which he claimed were implicated in any developed statement of motive, although he privileged the scene–act, scene–agent, and act–agent relationships or ratios. The result was a form of criticism that focused on what discourse did, what symbolic functions it performed, rather than on its accuracy or truth. The critic's job was to explicate the ways that a rhetor construed the world in and through language, to interpret what kind of symbolic work that construal performed, and the ways that it might invite others to see the world in similar terms. Burke held that "where there is meaning, there is persuasion, and where there is persuasion, there is rhetoric," a view of influence that enlarged the sphere of rhetoric to include any and all symbolic acts. Accordingly, he treated literary works as equipment for living (*Counter-Statement*, New York, 1931) and scientific works as infused with the motives of their creators. For Burke, as for Nietzsche, language (or symbols) is rhetoric.

Burke's theory was appealing to rhetorical critics in part because he presented it as an addition to, not a substitute for, the standard lore, and because it offered an ontology that encompassed alternative views of humans as rational, social, and political that undergirded traditional theory. That ontology emerged clearly only late in his work, first in the opening section of *The Rhetoric of Religion: Studies in Logology* (Boston, 1961) and then explicitly in "Definition of Man," the opening essay in *Literature as Symbolic Action* (Berkeley, 1966). Burke described humans as symbol-using and -misusing creatures, whose biology was infused with and transformed by linguistic motives arising out of the naming, abstracting, and negating capacities of language. From Burke's perspective, humans' experience of the world is shaped by their terministic screens or vocabularies (language's capacity to name reflects, selects, and deflects reality); they are goaded by a spirit of hierarchy and "rotten with perfection" (animated and driven by the ladders of abstraction inherent in terminologies); and transformed by the negative, which exists only in language and is epitomized by the hortatory "thou shalt not." For Burke, motives are distinctly linguistic products, a position he developed and illustrated in all his works, but particularly in *A Grammar of Motives* (New York, 1945) and *A Rhetoric of Motives* (New York, 1950).

Burke's emphasis on symbolic action and the importance of language shifted the locus of rhetorical influence from arguments to symbols as the means of evoking shared meaning. What he called the "new rhetoric" focused on the linguistic resources of identification, the processes by which symbols invite and implicate others in cooperative enterprises; in contrast, the "old rhetoric" emphasized persuasion or conscious, intentional efforts to influence others. He spoke of rhetoric as being at work where literary and sociological concerns overlap, positing a "consubstantiality" among humans that is based on common experience, and identifying language or symbols as the mediating element through which that common experience becomes shared meaning, out of which emerge a sense of community and a willingness to act together. [*See* Identification.]

Burke's influence was so great because his work integrated theory and criticism and presented a unified approach to all discourse. His work incorporated the developments in linguistics, philosophy, and literary theory and built on the classical traditions of rhetorical study, and, in that sense, his work was the culmination of the various intellectual processes described earlier.

The Emergence of Speech Communication. Speech communication departments in the United States came into existence early in the twentieth century in order to rectify what some scholars saw as the tendency of literary scholars to overlook the significance of the role of public discourse—oratory and public address—in society. Speech communication scholars taught public speaking and produced studies of public speakers that emphasized historical and biographical material, following in the traditions of literary scholars. The ferment in literary theory over what criticism should be and do influenced the scholarship and practices of those whose primary interest was orally delivered speeches. For the most part, studies of public addresses during the first half of the twentieth century were biographical studies of speakers and historical studies of the influence of history on discourse. Examples include the essays found in the three volumes of *A History and Criticism of American Public Address* (New York, 1943, 1955) edited by W. N. Brigance and Marie Hochmuth and in *American Public Address: Studies in Honor of A. Craig Baird* (Columbia, Mo., 1961) edited by Loren Reid, as well as Robert Oliver's *History of Public Speaking in America* (Boston, 1965). These works tended to follow the approach taken earlier by Chauncey Goodrich in *Select British Eloquence; Embracing the Best Speeches Entire, of the Most Eminent Orators of Great Britain for the Last Two Centuries; with Sketches of Their Lives, an Estimate of Their Genius, and Notes, Critical and Explanatory* (New York, 1852). The theory underlying this approach to criticism was set forth in detail by Lester Thonssen and A. Craig Baird in *Speech Criticism* (New York, 1948) and described by Marie Hochmuth in "The Criticism of Rhetoric," which introduced volume 3 of *A History and Criticism of American Public Address* (1955). In the face of the coercive anticommunist rhetoric of Senator Joseph McCarthy and the House Un-American Activities Committee, such scholars as Karl Wallace in "The Substance of Rhetoric: Good Reasons" in the *Quarterly Journal of Speech* 49 (October 1963, pp. 239–249) and Thomas Nilsen in "The Interpretive Function of the Critic" in *Western Speech* 21 (Spring 1957, pp. 70–76) argued that rhetoric remained an honorable art that was relevant to the world and capable of ethical judgments.

Even works such as *Pioneer Women Orators: Rhetoric in the Ante-Bellum Reform Movement* by Lillian O'Connor (New York, 1954), which broke new ground in focusing attention on the U.S. women who first resisted the prohibition against women speaking, followed the traditional pattern in emphasizing historical background and biographical information and limiting analysis to an application of the most basic precepts of Greco-Roman rhetoric. This traditional approach to public discourse persisted in Barnet Baskerville's *The People's Voice: The Orator in American Society* (Lexington, Ky., 1979). [*See* Speech.]

Critical Ferment and the Classical Tradition. Although some voices had been raised earlier, the crisis over what public address criticism should be and do came to fruition with the publication of Edwin Black's *Rhetorical Criticism: A Study in Method* (New York, 1965). Black's work reflected the insights of the New Critics, and his critique of traditional modes of studying public discourse, which he called neo-Aristotelian, echoed Wimsatt's critique in *The Verbal Icon: Studies in the Meaning of Poetry* (New York, 1954), of the University of Chicago scholars Richard McKeon

and R. S. Crane. Black's book was a watershed in the history of public address criticism. Based on an analysis of the essays in the three volumes of *A History and Criticism of American Public Address,* Black characterized neo-Aristotelian criticism as a formulaic application of the three genres (deliberative, forensic, and ceremonial) and three modes of proof (*ēthos, pathos,* and *logos*) originally described by Aristotle, and of the five arts elaborated by Cicero (invention, arrangement, style, delivery, memory). He also argued that neo-Aristotelians evaluated speeches exclusively in terms of their effects on an immediate audience. Accordingly, he claimed that critics who adopted this approach were hobbled. They could not explicate the enduring power of a text to speak through time to many audiences, nor could they consider a work as part of a cultural conversation or apply critical insights developed subsequent to the period in which the discourse appeared. He made that point particularly telling with an insightful critique of John Chapman's 1912 "Coatesville Address," delivered before perhaps three people, without any immediate noticeable effects, but a speech that remains powerful and moving for modern readers. His analysis was a model of close reading of a text informed by an understanding of the symbolic function of the morality play as a genre.

Black proposed an alternative frame of reference grounded in modern understandings of language. His alternative was based on what he called the "rhetorical transaction," which included three interrelated constituents: situations, strategies, and effects. He argued that these were part of an indivisible process, based on an assumption underlying any system of rhetorical criticism, "that there will be a correspondence among the intentions of a communicator, the characteristics of his discourse, and the reactions of his auditors to that discourse" (p. 16). To deny that assumption, he argued, is to deny the possibility of communication. Accordingly, a scale measuring any one of these elements would reflect the others because underlying language use are the presumptions that certain strategies are suited to certain situations and symbolic functions, and that certain strategies produce certain effects. He identified two genres that he called exhortation and argumentation, which represented points at which discourses congregate on the scale of effects. The result of his theorizing was an intensified interest in generic analysis as a mode of criticism of public discourse, as demonstrated by Karlyn Kohrs Campbell and Kathleen Hall Jamieson's *Form and Genre: Shaping Rhetorical Action* (Falls Church, Va., 1978).

The impact of Black's work was enhanced by the timing of its publication. It appeared in a milieu of social movement protest and at a time when the writings of Kenneth Burke were promoting alternative approaches to rhetorical criticism.

The 1960s were a time of protest. Beginning in the 1950s, civil rights protests had developed new energy in bus boycotts, freedom rides, and sit-ins, accompanied by the eloquence of Martin Luther King, Jr., the powerful arguments and appeals of Malcolm X, the confrontational style of Stokely Carmichael, and the evocative narratives of Eldridge Cleaver, forms of rhetoric that could not easily be accommodated by traditional modes of criticism. [*See overview article on* African-American rhetoric.] The antiwar rhetoric of the Yippies and of the teach-ins against the Vietnam War, the demonstrations and speeches of members of Vietnam Veterans Against the War, and the confrontations at the 1968 Democratic National Convention in Chicago and in the trial of the Chicago Eight that followed, cried out for criticism that was attuned to their distinctive character. At the same time, the second wave of feminism emerged, and its distinctive organization and consciousness-raising techniques prompted new critical approaches adapted to its rhetoric, all of which were legitimated by the powerful critique Black had made of the traditional critical system that had dominated criticism of public discourse, which tended to dismiss or condemn these new forms of rhetoric. At this point a number of critiques appeared that analyzed the rhetoric of black protest, the second wave of feminism, the antiwar screeds of the Yippies, and the confrontational rhetoric of the student antiwar protest. All these were significant departures from traditional modes of criticism. Many of them were generic studies that focused on the symbolic functions of certain kinds of discourse and demonstrated the riches of criticism based on close readings of texts and informed by theorizing with roots outside the clas-

sical tradition. The influence of Burke and the search for alternative critical theory were reflected in Ernest G. Bormann's *The Force of Fantasy: Restoring the American Dream* (Carbondale, Ill., 1985), which explained historical movements between 1620 and 1860 as the result of dramatic scenarios that attracted large communities to accept the interpretations of reality that these narratives presented. [*See* Rhetorical vision.]

Critical ferment and attacks on traditional theory prompted rereadings and reinterpretations of the original works of the early Greek and Roman theorists, including those of the much-maligned Greek Sophists. The revival of sophistic approaches to rhetoric began with Robert L. Scott's influential essay, "On Viewing Rhetoric as Epistemic," published in the *Central States Speech Journal* 18 (February 1967, pp. 9–17). Scott argued that the only view of truth consistent with rhetoric as a mode of inquiry or way of knowing is one that views truth, not as fixed and final, but as created moment by moment in the circumstances in which humans find themselves and with which they must cope. Similarly, such scholars as Edward Schiappa in *Protagoras and Logos: A Study in Greek Philosophy and Rhetoric* (Columbia, S.C., 1991) and John Poulakos in *Sophistical Rhetoric in Classical Greece* (Columbia, S.C., 1995) returned to original texts in order to explicate the sophistic understanding of rhetoric and to demonstrate its continued salience. In *Rereading the Sophists: Classical Rhetoric Refigured* (Carbondale, Ill., 1991) Susan Jarratt reinterpreted the writings of the Sophists to emphasize their delight in the play of language, their emphasis on contingency, and the importance of their teachings for democracy. She also showed that sophistic theories of rhetoric have much in common with contemporary feminist theory, particularly in linking theory and political action. An expanded history of the contest between logic and rhetoric is found in *Logic and Rhetoric in England, 1500–1700* (Princeton, 1956) by Wilbur Samuel Howell. That was followed by Howell's *Eighteenth-Century British Logic and Rhetoric* (Princeton, 1971), which continued the story begun in the earlier volume. [*See* Classical rhetoric; *and* Sophists.]

Classicist George A. Kennedy also contributed to the development of modern rhetoric. His trilogy, *The Art of Persuasion in Greece* (Princeton,

1963), *The Art of Rhetoric in the Roman World, 300 B.C.–A.D. 300* (Princeton, 1972), and *Greek Rhetoric under Christian Emperors* (Princeton, 1983), traced the history of rhetoric as it appeared in theoretical treatises and speeches from its earliest beginnings through 1300 CE At the beginning of the second volume, Kennedy acknowledged the enlarged conception of rhetoric that informed his work, pointing out that, defined narrowly, rhetoric is the art of persuasion as practiced by orators and described by theorists and teachers of speech. Echoing the enlarged conception of rhetoric as strategic adaptation, he noted that it may be extended to include the art of all who aim to influence others, and then applied to what he called "secondary rhetoric: critical or aesthetic theory" (p. 3). In *The Beginnings of Rhetorical Theory in Classical Greece* (New Haven, 1999), Edward Schiappa scrutinized classical texts to demonstrate that Plato was the first to use the term *rhetoric* to describe a discipline taught by the Sophists, a discipline which challenged received notions of the origins of the conflict between rhetoric and philosophy. In *Rhetoric in the European Tradition* (New York, 1990), Thomas Conley surveyed rhetorical history in order to show the preeminence of Ciceronian influence. In *Aristotle, Rhetoric: A Commentary* (2 vols., New York, 1980, 1988) William Grimaldi returned to the primary texts to produce detailed commentaries on the first two books of Aristotle's *Art of Rhetoric*. Contemporary translations of Aristotle's *Art of Rhetoric* by George Kennedy (New York, 1991) and by H. C. Lawson-Tancred (London, 1991) prompted reexamination of Aristotelian theory, including Eugene Garver's provocative *Aristotle's Rhetoric: An Art of Character* (Chicago, 1994). Thomas O. Sloane's critical study, *Donne, Milton, and the End of Humanist Rhetoric* (Berkeley, 1985), explored the humanist conception of rhetoric as exemplified in the seventeenth century by the poetry of John Donne and linked it to the *controversiae* of Roman pedagogy and the conception of rhetoric as "proving opposites" in Aristotle's *Art of Rhetoric*.

The classical tradition in argumentation was reinvigorated by the works of philosophers. In England, philosopher Stephen E. Toulmin published *The Uses of Argument* (Cambridge, U.K., 1958), and in France, philosophers and legal scholars Chaim Perelman and Lucie Olbrechts-Tyteca published *Traité de l'argumentation: La nouvelle rhétorique* (Paris, 1958), translated as *The New Rhetoric: A Treatise on Argumentation* (Notre Dame, Ind., 1969). These works were studies of practical reasoning, and they stimulated work on argument fields, and on the role of prudence and decorum in public deliberation. Toulmin's book was a philosophical defense of practical reasoning, against the view that only analytical reasoning could be valid. *The New Rhetoric* was a revival of dialectical reasoning as a substitute for the formal logic characteristic of mathematical reasoning. Both were efforts to breathe new life into the kinds of deliberation celebrated by Greco-Roman theorists for use in making moral and ethical decisions. As Toulmin notes elsewhere (*American Scholar,* Summer 1988, pp. 337–352), seventeenth-century philosophers banished the oral, the particular, the local, and the timely in order to privilege arguments that did not rest on human perception. Formal logic replaced rhetoric. The works of these philosophers have been the focus of an effort to reclaim practical reasoning.

The links between modern and postmodern approaches to rhetoric are most evident in the work of feminist theorists and critics. Feminist rereadings of early texts recovered traditions that support feminist theories, illustrated by Susan Jarratt's 1991 book on the Sophists (see above). They also recovered the voices of women of the past. In *Rhetoric Retold* (Carbondale, Ill., 1997), Cheryl Glenn charts women's inscriptions on and contributions to rhetorical theory, beginning with Sappho and continuing with the Greek Aspasia and Diotima, the Roman Hortensia, and the English women Julian of Norwich, Margery Kempe, and Anne Askew, among others. *Sappho is Burning* by Page duBois (Chicago, 1995) presents this early Greek poet as a disruptive figure whose fragmentary writings need to be reread in light of contemporary developments in gender studies and cultural criticism. The final chapter is an important addition to the Atticist–Asianist controversy that privileged the more severe, plain Attic style. [*See* Atticist–Asianist controversy.] In *The Allegory of Female Authority: Christine de Pizan's "Cité des dames"* (Ithaca, N.Y., 1991), Maureen Quilligan illuminated the pathbreaking character of the writings of the fifteenth-century French writer Christine de Pizan, who was probably the first true female "author," that is, one who spoke in her own voice and who is now recognized as an early rhetorical theorist. [*See* Feminist rhetoric.]

In other words, the impulse toward close textual reading that characterizes modern rhetoric was applied to primary texts in order to reconsider the meaning and implications of works produced in earlier periods. Feminist re-readings incorporated insights from cultural and gender studies, suggesting ways in which modern and postmodern rhetorics can inform each other.

As it emerged in the middle of the twentieth century, modern rhetoric had certain distinctive characteristics. It greatly enlarged the scope of rhetoric, and it emphasized the role of language or symbols in the processes by which influence occurs. It fostered close readings of all kinds of discourse, making little or no distinction between literary and rhetorical works. It replaced philological, biographical, and historical approaches to analysis of discourse with explication of texts, and it encouraged the development of critical modes suited to protest rhetoric and the discourses of groups and movements. The scholarship it promoted revived, reexamined, and reinterpreted the classical tradition.

BIBLIOGRAPHY

Conley, Thomas M. *Philon Rhetor, a Study of Rhetoric and Exegesis: Protocol of the Forty-seventh Colloquy.* Berkeley, 1984. A study of one of the earliest theorists to present a schema for analyzing texts.

Hernadi, Paul. *Beyond Genre: New Directions in Literary Classification.* Ithaca, N.Y., 1972. An attempt to survey the history of approaches to genre.

Lakoff, George, and Mark Johnson. *Metaphors We Live By.* Chicago, 1980. Metaphors are much more common than we think because they exemplify deep needs both individual and cultural.

Langer, Susanne K. *Mind: An Essay on Human Feeling.* 3 vols. Baltimore, 1967, 1972, 1982. For this author, feeling is the starting point of a philosophy of mind because feeling stands at the midpoint between the lowliest organic activities and the rise of the mind. Langer traces the roots of science and art to a common ground in the special nature of human feeling. This is her masterwork, the culmination of her earlier studies.

Nietzsche, Friedrich W. *Friedrich Nietzsche on Rhetoric and Language.* Edited and translated by Sander L. Gilman, Carole Blair, and David J. Parent. New York, 1989. A collection of works that focus on matters of special significance for rhetorical studies.

Peirce, Charles S. *The Collected Papers of Charles Sander Peirce,* vols. 1–6, edited by Charles Hartshorne and Paul Weiss. Cambridge, Mass., 1931–1935; vols. 7–8, edited by Arthur Burks. Cambridge, Mass., 1958. The complete works of one of the most significant contributors to semiotics and pragmatism.

Rueckert, William H. *Kenneth Burke and the Drama of Human Relations.* Minneapolis, 1963. A study of Burke's writings that provides an account of the development of his thought with special emphasis on his literary theory and critical practice and how these help to explain his conception of dramatism.

Sloane, Thomas O. *On the Contrary: The Protocol of Traditional Rhetoric.* Washington, D.C., 1997. This book closely examines three works: Cicero's *De oratore* (55 BCE), Erasmus's *De copia* (1534), and Thomas Wilson's *Discourse on Usury* (1572) in order to reveal the contrarianism at the heart of rhetorical invention, in which all sides of a question must be given a fair hearing. Ideally, such rhetoric goes beyond antagonism to prompt a process through which readers give birth to ideas in their own heads, a process Socrates called *maieutic* or midwifery, which the author believes is the core of rhetorical thinking.

Sullivan, Sister Thérèse. *De doctrina christiana, liber qvartvs; A Commentary.* Washington, D.C., 1930. This commentary on Augustine's treatment of rhetoric in book 4 of *On Christian Doctrine* emphasizes the influence of Cicero on his thinking.

Thomas, Douglas. *Reading Nietzsche Rhetorically.* New York, 1999. This book explores the ways in which Nietzsche's work resists and disrupts the Platonic philosophical tradition and emphasizes the importance of examining Nietzsche's style as a means to understanding his thought.

Wheelwright, Philip. *Metaphor and Reality.* Bloomington, Ind., 1962. Contrasts scientific and literary usage and presents language as an instrument of imagination and vision.

Wichelns, Herbert A. "The Literary Criticism of Oratory." In *Studies in Rhetoric and Public Speaking in Honor of James Albert Winans,* edited by A. M. Drummond, pp. 181–211. New York, 1925. The foundational essay arguing for a distinctive kind of criticism suited to analysis of public address.

Wimsatt, William K., Jr., and Cleanth Brooks. *Literary Criticism: A Short History.* New York, 1957. A survey of ideas about verbal art and its elucidation and criticism that argues for the continuity and intelligibility of literary history from Aristotle's *Poetics* to the mid-twentieth century.

—KARLYN KOHRS CAMPBELL

MORPHOLOGY. *See* Casuistry; *and* Linguistics.

MUSIC. Since music alone, without text, has always communicated a message, even in antiquity it was regarded as an art related to language. Especially in its function of holding humans to moral behavior and fear of God (Pseudo-Plutarch, *Peri mousikēs* [On music], 26), the conviction that music could represent emotions as well as elicit them is mirrored in the idea that it could produce effects as language could. Today, it is still the intention of composers to convey meaning or to "speak" to the emotions through their work.

Music as "Language." The relationship of music and language is based on a joining of constitutive elements (their "vocabulary") as well as on their articulated performance. In this regard, language and music are based on an "idea," a "thought" (Neidhardt, 1724) or a "theme" or "subject." The understanding of the vocabulary and of the general thinking was thus above all possible, when through "cultural unity" (Eco, 1972, pp. 74–75) a similar receptivity was present. Such a capacity for receiving was based on "musical rhetoric" from the Renaissance to the mid-nineteenth century when humanism proffered a basis of symbolism, the after-effects of which are still developing today.

Levels of Musical Rhetoric. We can credit the most systematic view of the total structure to the German musicologist Johann Nicolaus Forkel, 1788, pp. 36–68). He clearly set "musical rhetoric" apart from "musical grammar," from the "composing of individual thoughts out of pitches and chords (and) out of single notes, then multiple musical words into a sentence." The union of whole thoughts were for him on the other hand "musical rhetoric," which includes music as well as language, and which possesses the following system: "1) Musical periodicity. 2) Styles of writing. 3) Genres of music. 4) The ordering of musical thoughts, alongside the theory of figures. 5) The recitation or the declamation of the mu-

sical works." The "theory of the figures," according to Forkel, comprises the complete "aids for expression," be they intended "to produce a sensation," or intended "for the understanding" or are to be used "for the imagination" (that is, as "musical paintings"). [*See* Figures of speech.]

Grammar and rhetoric. Musical Grammar is comprised of keys, harmony, prosody ("*Rhythmopoeia*"), acoustics, "theory of the division of sounds," and the "theory of signs (semeiography)" (Forkel, 1788). By the Middle Ages, metric and modal theory were seen from the viewpoint of grammar. The German cantor and theorist Joachim Burmeister (1606, pp. 17ff.) referred to the combining of consonants and chords as "Syntax." Johannes Lippius (1610) allocated grammar to simple speech, whereas he assigned the rhetoric of ornate speech to the affective domain. William Tansur's tract *A Compleat Melody: or, The Harmony of Sion* (London, 1734) soon reappeared as *A New Musical Grammar* (London, 1746), and in 1806 in London, John Wall Callcott's theory of music was characterized as *A Musical Grammar*. On the other hand, Friedrich August Kanne (1820) held in esteem "the bare grammarian," who as "the bare schoolmaster" regarded grammar as "the skeleton of music."

Periods, form, and views of types. The smallest, usually four-beat unit of musical "conversation" was the "sentence"; the cadences were understood as periods or commas by Johannes Galliculus (1520). Johannes Lippius (1612) then laid down the dictum that has been adopted by numerous authors: "*Item velut Oratio Commatis, Colis et Periodis debitis, ita Cantilena Harmonica pro natura Textus compta distinguitur Pausis minoribus et majoribus, atque Clausulis. . . .*" (In the same way, just as a speech is punctuated by the necessary phrases, clauses, and complete sentences, so too a harmonic song is punctuated by minor and major pauses and clauses in accordance with the arrangement of the text.)

The theory "of the cutting off and the cutting into musical speech" was also important for the "speaking" (lingually articulated) production of the speech of music (Mattheson, 1739, pp. 180–195). Simultaneously, the "rhetorical view" of music had an impact on the construction of forms and types. The sonata was considered "musical conversation, or the aping of human conversation" (Schubart, 1806, p. 360); the main form of a sonata as a "drama" about a (single) theme (also, in the sense of its content, building to a climax in accordance with the theory of drama [Reicha, 1826, p. 298]); a fugue had, as a symphony does, to express the "feeling of a fore-gathered crowd of people"; a "concert" was characterized as a "passionate conversation of the soloist with the accompanying orchestra" (Koch, 1802, cols. 610 and 354).

Word–tone relationship and semantics. Special artistic tricks were employed in music to indicate content, above all "figures," which Johannes Tinctoris (1477; 1975, p. 140) saw as "liberties" (primarily dissonances). The figures were first systematically represented by Joachim Burmeister (1599; and 1601, p. 4). In the course of the century, over one hundred musical–rhetorical figures were named (Krones, 1997): to be understood as "imitative" semantifying of the emotional or rational as well as of the pictorial.

Declamation and recitation. In his time, Zarlino saw the "accento Rhetorico" as the highest virtue of the performer and placed it above the "accento Grammatico," which paid no attention to the total sense (1588, p. 325). In the eighteenth century, the instrumentalists were also required to articulate "as with words" as well as to insert artistically "musical punctuation" (Türk, 1789, p. 340). Even Carl Czerny (1791–1857) in his *Pianoforte-Schule* (1842) compared the note values with syllables and spoke of "musical declamation." [*See* Declamation.] The performance elements that were specially marked by rhetoric included the "speaking pause," which is documented, among others, in the works of Beethoven, whose "artistic speech at the pianoforte" Anton Schindler emphatically reports (1860, p. 237).

The recognition of all symbolically lingual means, especially of the figures, is necessary for the interpreters, since they all "must make musical thoughts sensible to the ear, according to their true content and affect, whether sung or played (Bach, 1753, p. 117). For the figures bring close to us the "whole meaning" (Walther, 1955, p. 158).

The Composition Theory of Musical Rhetoric. The "artes dicendi" were taught in the Latin schools according to the principles of rules (*praecepta*), example (*exemplum*), and imitation (*im-*

itatio), and music was taught in the same way (for example, the various styles of "musical" speech along with levels of rhetoric as well as the *virtutes elocutionis*). A student's encounter with musical rhetoric took place after an instruction in the techniques of the musical setting (of *Musica poetica*), in other words, after the study of musical grammar. Here the student became acquainted with "the means by which he could form a composition more artistically and express a text musically" (Ruhnke, 1955, p. 132).

Steps in the study of musical rhetoric. The fully worked out pattern has five or six steps and comprises *inventio, dispositio, elocutio* (*elaboratio*), *decoratio, memoria,* as well as *executio* (or *actio* or *pronuntiatio*); besides this, there are short forms known as *inventio-dispositio-elocutio* or *inventio-elaboratio-executio*. A further systematization resulted via the combining of *inventio* and *dispositio* (parts that plan the content of a speech), with the category of *res* as well as through the removal of *elocutio* (carrying out of the *res*) as a category of *verba*. In the eighteenth and nineteenth centuries, the designations *inventio, dispositio,* and *elaboratio* were replaced by the concepts "arrangement," "carrying out," and "elaboration" (Koch, 1802, col. 146–148), but the rhetorical view remained basically the same.

INVENTIO. In music the "topic" formed a "storehouse," in which one found thoughts at certain "places" (*loci*). These *loci topici* are based on Quintilian's *loci communes* or *loci argumentorum* and result in a "rather slick assistance for invention" (Mattheson, 1739, p. 123). The principle of *inventio* is first addressed by the Swiss humanist Heinrich Glarean (1488–1563) in his *Dodecachordon* (Twelve Strings; Basel, 1547) and was developed into a richly inclusive theory on how composers can access useful ideas. For example, Johann Kuhnau (1660–1722), the German composer and "Thomaskantor" in Leipzig before J. S. Bach, suggested in 1709 in "Texte zur Leipziger Kirchen-Musik" that in the case of setting Bible texts, in the absence of *inventio*, the composer should reach for *Versiones* in the three "holy languages" Latin, Greek, and Hebrew, a technique that had previously been used by Heinrich Schütz. Johann David Heinichen (1728, pp. 30–60) showed with the example of "a few shallow texts" how even here an acceptable setting could be found through

Antecedentia, Concomitantia, and *Consequentia Textus.* Mattheson presented in his *Capellmeister* (pp. 123–132) the most inclusive theory of the learnability of *inventio;* he enumerated fifteen "sources of invention" (for example, *locus notationis, locus descriptionis*). His emphasis of an *"inventio ex abrupto, inopinato, quasi ex enthusiasmo musico"* (*inventio* derived from abrupt, unexpected, even ecstatic music) does, however, point to the natural gift of the *ingenium.* J. S. Bach saw his "inventions" as "not only providing guidance to good inventions, but also, of course, following through with the same."

The *dispositio* is considered analogous to rhetoric. Gallus Dressler (1563) saw the sections *exordium, medium,* and *finis* as parts of "musical speech." [*See* Arrangement, *article on* Traditional arrangement.] Joachim Burmeister (1601, p. L4[rv]) referred to the rhetorical *dispositio* of a motet by Orlando di Lasso (1532–1594). In an example for constructing a fugue, Angelo Berardi (1689, p. 179) gave an example of a *dispositio* that connected elements of logic and rhetoric, and Mattheson brought together his view of *dispositio* (p. 235) in the following way: It must "observe precisely those six items, which are prescribed for an orator, namely the introduction, narration, proposition, the confirmation, the refutation, and the conclusion. *Exordium, narratio, propositio, confirmatio, confutatio,* and *peroratio.*" In the *exordium,* "the whole intent is indicated"; the *narratio* is a "report" that hints at "the meaning and properties of the forthcoming speech"; the *propositio* "contains briefly the content or purpose of the tone-oration"; the *confutatio* "is a resolution of the objections"; the *confirmatio* is "an artistic confirmation of the oration"; and the *peroratio* is "the exit or closing of our 'klangrede' " (tone-oration). An analysis of J. S. Bach's third Brandenburg Concerto shows that the composer proceeded exactly in this way (Budde, 1997, pp. 69–83).

The *elaboratio* (*elocutio*) proceeded with the help of all the means of compositional technique (including the figures) and was among other things responsible for the ornamentation (*ornatus*) of the "musical oratory." [*See* Gorgianic figures.] Correspondingly, it was designated by Mattheson (p. 235) with *decoratio* as "elaboration and decoration [of the melodies]." In musical literature, learning (*memoria*) is not a subject in regard

to spoken rhetoric, however it is given consideration. Finally, the realization of the music (*pronuntiatio, actio, executio*) had to obey the laws of rhetoric to a high degree; the affectively influenced singing was considered nonetheless as a bridge between song and speech. [*See* Delivery; *and* Memory.]

Virtutes elocutionis: Tropes, musical–rhetorical figures. *Tropes* result rhetorically in changes in meaning through the use of metaphors. Since musical elements hardly possess distinct lexical meaning, there can be no tropes in music in the strictest sense of the word. Nonetheless, Sethus Calvisius (1611, p. 35) compares the application of tropes and figures of speech with the use of various intervals, chords, phrases, and fugues in music, and also Francis Bacon (1627, p. 38) speaks of "certain Figures, or Tropes," "almost agreeing with the Figures of Rhetorike." However, the authors do not differentiate between these *artes dicendi.*

MUSICAL-RHETORICAL FIGURES. Whereas, according to Quintilian, figures are defined as departing from the general kind of speaking, they are interpreted, according to Burmeister, as "tractus musicus," which differentiates itself from the simple manner of composition (1601, p. 12R). According to Athanasius Kircher (1650, p. 366), musical figures render this service: "*idem, quod colores, tropi, atque varij modi dicendi in Rhetorica.*" (The same thing, which colors, tropes, and various ways of speaking do in Rhetoric.) [*See* Color.] When there was a departure from the laws of counterpoint, it was important to justify this on the grounds of content. Burmeister (1601, p. Dd1v) says this departure can be worked out by ornamentation *ornatus,* and in this case, the *poeticum decorum* of musical speech. Such figures, which represented content only as exceptions, were regarded as *figurae principales* or *figurae fundamentales,* because according to Christoph Bernhard (c.1670) they belong to the polyphonic "old style" (i.e., to fundamental composition). On the other side there were the figures that primarily carried meaning: passions, content, pictures, feelings, the *figurae minus principales.* They were later called *figurae superficiales* and were at home in the *stylus luxurians,* the *stylus modernus* (the *monody* of the early and middle seventeenth century), and especially concerned dealing with dissonance. The "meaning" resulted via the degree and manner of the departure from the "law," through "similarity" of that which was represented to the musical content; through etymological hints (through the names of the figure, for instance *kyklōsis*); through analogies between extermal and internal "givens" (e.g., "lofty matters"—"good matters"); or through obvious emotionality. Many figures provided decorative as well as content-related clarifications and served the *delectare* (to please) along with the *movere* (to move). Therefore, Burmeister made no attempt to classify them, but rather sorted the figures according to their phenomenology into harmonic, melodic, and melodic-harmonic *ornamenta*.

Phrases, voice management, or technique of setting belong to the *figurae principales* or *fundamentales*. Johannes Nucius (1613) puts them into this order: "fuga" (also considered as *mimēsis*, imitation), "commissura" (transition; also *symblēma* or *transitus*), and "repetitio" (repetition). Joachim Thuringus (1624) names here the "syncopatio" (later also "ligatura"), others bring in various forms of the fugue, among them the *hypallagē* (counterfugue with a return of the theme). [*See* Hypallagē.] It appears with Henry Peacham the Younger (*The Compleat Gentleman*, London, 1622) as "antistrophe" ("a revert"). Matheson (pp. 367–368) as well as even Luigi Antonio Sabbatini (1802, p. 46) see the fugue completely as a dialogue or discussion. Also in France, theorists (Mersenne, 1627; de La Voye-Mignot, 1656) give forms of the fugue a high value in their description of musical rhetoric.

The definitions and meanings of *figurae minus principales* show a great similarity with the various authors of the sixteenth through nineteenth centuries. *Melodic figures* represented for the moment a picturesque sketch (in the sense of the superior figure of "hypotypōsis"), also in a figurative sense. Thus the *anabasis* (Lat. *ascensus*) represents an ascent (also "good" or joyful), the *katabasis* (Lat. *descensus*) represents a descent (or "bad"); the melodic turning motion of the *kyklōsis* (Lat. *circulatio*) something like "turning," circling, but also "embrace," "round," or beautiful." The quick run of the *tirata* stands for "to fling" or "lightning" among others; the small note values of the *fuga alio nempe sensu* clearly show literally "flight," "a hurry," "run," but also "fleeting."

Other melodic figures imitate a speech intonation like the *ekphōnēsis* (Lat. *exclamatio*), a symbolized exclamation by means of a large interval (usually upward), whereby consonantal intervals "paint" something positive, and dissonant ones paint something negative, or the *interrogatio* (question; an upward movement at the end of a phrase). The *passus duriusculus* (chromatic step[s], especially as a particularly painful "case of chromatic quarter notes," or as an "on-the-knees pleading" ascent) appears to simulate weeping speech.

Melodic repetition figures are *epizeuxis* (repetitions primarily at the beginning of a phrase), *replica* (a fugal repetition of a theme), *palillogia* (immediate repetition of the same melody), *epanalēpsis* (repetition of an opening thought at the end of a period: formation of a frame), and *anadiplōsis* (repetition of the ending tones of a phrase [motive] at the beginning of the next section). A varied repetition is the *traductio* (Henry Peacham the Elder, *The Garden of Eloquence*, 2d ed., London, 1593); one with a new, special, and emphatic ingredient (Scheibe, 1745, p. 691) is the *paronomasia* ("giving a nickname"); a descent of the melody under its "natural" momentum was called "hypobolē," and an excess was called "hyperbolē." The "climax" or *gradatio*, the repetition of a phrase on another, especially a higher step, was also called *hyperbaton* by Scheibe (p. 688). [*See* Anadiplōsis; Epanalēpsis; Epizeuxis; Gradatio; Hyperbaton; Hyperbolē; *and* Paronomasia.]

Melodic as well as harmonic figures are *pathopoeia* ("excitement of passions" or pain through tones that are strange to the harmony or the key of the tones) and *parrhēsia* ("freedom of speech"; a chromatic diagonal). [*See* Pathopoeia.] With the latter, it is important that they sound in consonant chords, "not causing an unpleasant sound" (Walther, 1732), which in their practical application led to ambivalent (both positive and negative) occurrences or emotions.

Harmonic figures employ the "givens" of the techniques of setting or contrapuntal techniques for clarification of text. "Pictorial" or demonstrative signposts contain *noēma* ("thought," a clarifying chordally homophonic movement); *analēpsis* (immediate repetition of a noēma); *anaplocē* ("choral" repetition); and *mimēsis* (redoubling of a noēma on another step)—these four possess a "pictorial" or demonstratively indicative character. The latter, "mimēsis," is later also a synonym for the *imitatio* and is therefore a fugue. Also "antithesis" ("contrast" in the texture), *synoeciōsis* (contrapositum; according to John Hoskyns, a "music made of cunning discords"), *polyptōton* ("duplication"; repetition of a theme in various voices), and *auxēsis* (ascending "growth" of harmony or rising of the melody several times) possess an indicative character without speaking to special emotional situations, while the *multiplicatio* (recurring impinging of a dissonant note) clearly contains emotion. [*See* Antithesis; *and* Auxēsis.]

This obtains also for the "fauxbourdon" (parallel sixth chords), which in the first instance symbolizes "falsity" ("faux") and the sinful, the *pleonasmus,* an enrichment of the cadence through syncopation and forward motion, and the *catachrēsis* ("misuse"), an "extraordinary and hard method" (Walther, 1732) of a dissonance-continuation; special "contents" are represented here by the diminished seventh chord (doubt), the deceptive conclusion (also *inganno*; indication of deception), or the neapolitan sixth chord (representation of death or the death wish). [*See* Catachrēsis.] Harmonic figures are, in the end, all fugues.

Burmeister names *melodic–harmonic figures* as *congeries* (*synathroismos*), a heaping up of third-fifth and third-sixth tones (achieved by means of a syncopated upper voice), and a new "fauxbourdon" (*simul procedentia*), *anaphora* (a repetition especially in an ostinato-style bass voice for the representation of passions), as well as the *fuga imaginaria* (canon). [*See* Anaphora; *and* Congeries.]

The *rest figures* are represented through silence or pauses. Important are *suspiratio* (*stenasmos*; a "sigh," which through small pause values expresses groaning, sighing, or yearning and can even tear words apart); *tmēsis* (multiple "laceration" of a movement through rests); *aposiōpēsis* (a general pause symbolizing "remaining mute," "death," or "nothing"); *apocopē*, "cutting off" a voice in the fugue, but also the shortening of final notes "in such words, which appear to require it" (Walther, 1732); *abruptio*, "tearing off" of a movement or also the premature end of a melody line before the final resolution through use of the cadence. [*See* Apocopē; *and* Aposiōpēsis.]

Historical Overview. The combining of music and language meant the highest step of human artistic expression for Greek antiquity (c.800 BCE to 200 CE); so the poet-singer appears (for example in Homer) as a godlike artist (as *theios*, "the divine"). In tragedy, the chorus takes on the function of the narrator and commentator as well as admonisher who has been installed by the gods, also in view of the conviction that music not only represents emotions, but also (according to Aristotle) brings about "effects" (for example "purifying" effects). Thus, music became a specialized "language" and was even expected to fulfill duties of state as didactic duties.

Knowledge of music as well as of the musical qualities of speech were also highly desirable for the Roman rhetoricians, in order to increase the effectiveness of their oratory, which was underscored by Cicero (*De oratore,* 53 BCE, 3.44.173) and Quintilian (*Institutio oratoria,* first century CE, 1.10.9–33), among others. Quintilian also emphasized the ethical function of music for the education of a *vir bonus,* and its similarity to speech (in form, sound, recitation, gesture, and rhythm), and its emotional effect (9.4.9).

Middle Ages and Renaissance. Music was also regarded as "speech" in the Middle Ages, with the functions of providing information (giving "meanings") and "producing an effect" (and impressions). Boethius (480–524) contributed to this view by acting as a middleman in summarizing the contents of Greek and Latin books of antiquity, which were then read by musicians, and the innate devotional nature of church songs; Isidor of Seville (c.560–636) emphasized it (*Etymologiae sive origines,* c.630), as did Jacobus Leodiensis (c.1330), and the Franco-Flemish composer and music theorist Johannes Tinctoris (c.1470; 1978, pp. 159–177), who listed twenty "effectus" of music.

There was already a conscious *explicatio textus* in Gregorian chant as well as in early polyphony. In the Notre Dame repertoire (c.1200), one can discover elements of musical rhetoric; the mode was consciously picked according to the content of the text and the emotions it expressed, and rhetorical–dynamic ideas infuse the formation of the music (Reckow, 1986). The explication of texts became even more distinct in the fourteenth century, when humanism was beginning to be an influence, as well as in the fifteenth and sixteenth centuries. It peaked when Italian composer and theorist Franchinus Gaffurius (1451–1522) maintained (1496) that music must be fully and completely congruent with both text and sense: "*Studeat insuper cantilenae compositor cantus suavitate cantilenae verbis congruere*" (The composer should also strive to make the song pleasantly correspond to the words of the song). This is because of the composer's intended effect of the music, which is still obligated to follow ethical standards, as Agrippa von Nettesheim emphasized (1532). Gioseffo Zarlino's *Institutioni harmoniche* (Venice, 1558) postulates then that music results in *oratione*, and discusses the effects of music.

Simultaneously, with deepened explication of the text, consciousness focused on the artistic means that had replaced rhetoric. Marchettus of Padua compared (c.1325) the *colores ad pulchritudinem consonantiarum* (colors relating to the beauty of consonances) in music with the *colores rhetorici ad pulchritudinem sententiarum* (rhetorical colors relating to the beauty of sentences) in grammar and understands them as a means of text expression, which would be allowed to use "false" idioms. This was over and above the fact that, according to Jacobus Leodiensis, they are *varietas* and are to follow emotion. Finally, they represent means for the *ornatus* of "musical speech," which are dependent on the text, as Heinrich Eger von Kalkar also maintains (c.1380, rpt. 1952): *Ornatus etiam habet musica proprios sicut rhetorica* (Music, like rhetoric, has its proper ornaments). Gobelinus Person allows a *cantus irregularis* as *color rhetoricus* in 1417 in his *Tractatus musicae scientiae* (see Müller, 1907), and finally Johannes Tinctoris, in his *Liber de arte contrapuncti* (1477), borrows from Quintilian the term *figura* for such liberties.

In Italy, Nicola Vicentino emphasizes (1555) the substantive similarity of music and speech, and Zarlino promotes the emotional unity of text, composition, and musical performance (*Institutoni harmoniche*, 1558, pp. 339–341). In England, Henry Peacham the Younger (*Compleat Gentleman*, 1622, p. 96) speaks of music as the "sister to Poetrie" and asks "hath not Musicke her figures, the same which Rhetorique?" (p. 103), and in France, even a collection (c.1650) of lute

compositions by Denis Gaultier (1603–1672) is called *La Rhetorique des dieux*. Aspects of the theory of figures became likewise important early on, until Burmeister produced his compilation of composition and figure theory.

The strengthened bond of music to text led to numerous freely declamatory compositions. On the other hand, composers busied themselves with the rhythmic imitation of prosody. In Germany, at the end of the fifteenth century, there was choral singing between acts during Latin school dramas, and Petrus Tritonius (c.1465–c.1525) set Horatian odes to music homophonically ("metrically") (*Melopoiae*, Augsburg, 1507), in that "rhythmically" he used long beats and short beats in the ratio of 2:1. In France, Claude Goudimel published (1555) *Horatii Flacci poetae Lyrici odae omnes quotquot carminum generibus differunt ad rhythmos musicos redactae*; a second line led within the framework of the "Académie de Poésie et de Musique" to "vers mesurés." In Italy there was partly improvised "declamatory" music as well as sonnets or *terza rima*, into which any relevant text could be fitted ("Modo de cantar sonetti" or "Modus dicendi capitula"). In the humanistic circle of the Florentine "Camerata," there arose the "spoken song" of monody (piece sung by a single voice) of opera.

Whereas music in the Middle Ages in the framework of the *septem artes liberales* was a fixed component of the four *artes mathematicae* brought together by the Quadrivium, from the late fifteenth century onward, under the influence of humanism, the viewpoint that music belonged by dint of its relationship with poesy and rhetoric to the *artes dicendi* continued to make headway— music belonged to the "spoken arts" (grammar, logic, and rhetoric), thus in the system of the Trivium. [*See* Humanism; *and* Trivium.]

The High Flowering (1599–1821). Since the end of the sixteenth century, the *artes dicendi* have represented the main disciplines, especially of the Protestant grammar schools of Germany; however, they were also cultivated in similar form in Elizabethan England and in the Catholic south. Against this background, the "tried and true teaching system of rhetoric" (Forchert, 1985–1986, p. 10) also maintained itself in the area of music. English writers (above all, poets) typically busied themselves primarily with general representations of the relationship of music and rhetoric, and in France, this connection also took on high value. In Italy, fundamental written tracts are lacking, but a few authors again placed the fugue under the rhetorical viewpoint. The theoretical bond of "seconda prattica" (second practice, a style of composition in which the text reigns) and the theory of figures takes place in any case not with Italian authors, but rather with Christoph Bernhard (1648). "To couple Words and Notes lovingly together" (Campion, c.1613), is an assertion common to all writings on the subject, as is the view "[t]hat music is very precisely bound together with the art of poetry and the art of rhetoric" (Scheibe, 1745, p. 654).

The theory of figures was also of importance in the compositional thinking of high-ranking "practitioners." In 1696, Johann Kuhnau in the foreword to his collection *Frische Clavier-Früchte* censured some older masters because of their attempts "under the guise of reason to hide the bad and natural blending of consonances and dissonances, as it were, under their oratorical figures." According to his foreword to *Fortsetzung des Harmonischen Gottesdienstes* (1731), Georg Philipp Telemann strove "to make the enunciation understandable and to apply the rhetorical figures in such a way, that the emotional impulses that reside in the poetry might be awakened." Johann Abraham Birnbaum (Scheibe, 1745, p. 997) praises J. S. Bach's art of musical rhetoric: "he knows so perfectly the parts and advantages which the development of a musical piece has in common with the orator's art that one not only listens to him with a feeling of pleasant satiety when he guides his careful conversation toward the similarity and agreement of both, but one is also astounded at the skillful utilization of same in his works."

By the middle of the eighteenth century, both the instrumental schools and the interpreters are in agreement that music should be performed above all "speakingly" or "singably." Thus, C. P. E. Bach is of the opinion (1753, pp. 121–122) that the performers must learn to "think while singing" in order to be able to properly perform the music. Johann Joachim Quantz (1752, pp. 100–111) compares musical execution with "the delivery of an orator," and D. G. Türk (1789, pp. 343–347) similarly compares "an entire musical piece rightly with an oration." Indeed also in aesthetic writings, musical rhetoric remained present in a general way until 1788, when Forkel delineated the system in its totality (1788). In France, the same thing obtained; here it was seen from the viewpoint of the aesthetic of imitation, that music would need a dictionary because of its rich vocabulary (Jean-Jacques Rousseau, "Essai sur l'origine des langues où il est parlé de la mélodie et de l'imitation musicale," *Works*, vol. 16, Geneva, 1782, p. 265). Moreover, its effect (as the language of feeling) on the human psyche would be enormous (Chabanon, 1779).

In the nineteenth century, Ernst Theodor Amadeus Hoffmann, in his critical review of Beethoven's Fifth Symphony, spoke of a "climax" that intensified what was happening. He developed a semantic interpretation that was extracted from elements (mostly "figures") that carry meaning. An especially important "rhetorical" informant is then the Prague cantor and teacher Jan Jakub Ryba, who in his *First and General Principles of the Whole Art of Music* (in Czech; Prague, 1817), enumerates thirty-one figures that in an interesting manner combine traditional rhetorical figures with "musical painting." Finally, also with Friedrich August Kanne (1818), the "old" aesthetic of imitation holds pace beside the "new" aesthetic of feeling, and forms an enormous compendium of the means of explicating text and content on the basis of and in the further development of musical rhetoric (Krones, 1988).

Continuing effects into the present. The conviction that music is a language also remained in the nineteenth and twentieth centuries in regard to semantic implications allied with that idea. Georg Wilhelm Friedrich Hegel (1965, section 273) considered "the interjections" as "a point of departure of music"; for him, sound as an interjection was already external to art—the cry of pain, sighing, and laughing were already the immediate living expression of the condition of the soul and of feelings; likewise for Arthur Schopenhauer, music is "a completely universal language, which clearly goes even beyond the observable world" (1819; 1859, 3d ed.).

Carl Czerny also documents the survival of rhetoric in music in the third part of his *Vollständige theoretisch-practische Pianoforte-Schule* (Complete theoretical-practical Pianoforte-School, Vienna, 1842), which especially places the level of performance within rhetorical premises. Composers whose work relates to the aesthetic of feeling or expression have long recognized the symbolic language of rhetorical figures: Franz Liszt, Richard Wagner, Anton Bruckner, Johannes Brahms, Hugo Wolf, but also Hector Berlioz, who was "rhetorically" instructed by Anton Reicha (Krones, 1993). Liszt even designated music as the "twin sister of language" and spoke of "gestures of musical grammar, logic, syntax and rhetoric."

Especially the three proponents of the Viennese school, Arnold Schönberg, Alban Berg, and Anton Webern were convinced of the linguistic characteristics of music. Webern even says in his 1933 lecture series *Der Weg zur neuen Musik* (The path to new music, Vienna, 1960, p. 17) that music has developed "as a result of the need to express thoughts which cannot be expressed in any other way but by sounds. In this sense music is a language." Additionally, many of the resources of composers' symbolic language spring from a musical-rhetorical well (Krones, 1992).

A similar situation obtains for many contemporary composers, who write an emphatically "speaking" music. Titles like "Shouts," "Voices," or "Adventure" document this, just like the reproduction of the act of speaking; for example, the musical work "Glossolalie" (Speaking in Tongues) by Dieter Schnebel, 1961. The Viennese composer Robert Schollum worked quite consciously with musical-rhetorical figures. The most recent developments show that growing numbers of composers reach back to the periodicity of movements, recitative declamation, and oratorical gesture as well as to the store of traditional symbolism, which in many areas are based on musical-rhetorical figures, or at least have common roots with them.

[*See also* Art.]

Bibliography

Bach, C. P. E. *Versuch über die wahre Art, das Clavier zu spielen 1* (Treatise on the True Manner of Piano Playing 1), vol. 1. Berlin, 1753.

Bacon, Francis. *Sylva Sylvarum*. London, 1627.

Berardi, Angelo. *Miscellanea musicale*. Bologna, Italy, 1689.

Bernhard, Christoph. "Tractatus compositionis augmentatus." In *Die Kompositionslehre Heinrich Schützens in der Fassung Seines Schülers Christoph Bernhard* (The Composition Theory of Heinrich Schütz in the Version of his pupil Christoph Bernhard), edited by J. Müller-Blattau, 2d ed. Kassel, 1963. First published 1926, written c.1648.

Bernhard, Christoph. "Ausführlicher Bericht vom Gebrauche der Con- und Dissonantien" (Exhaustive Report on the Use of Consonance and Dissonance). In *Die Kompositionslehre Heinrich Schützens in der Fassung Seines Schülers Christoph Bernhard* (The Composition Theory of Heinrich Schütz in the Version of his Pupil Christoph Bernhard), edited by J. Müller-Blattau, 2d ed. Kassel, 1963. First published 1926, article written c.1670.

Budde, Elmar. "Musikalische Form und rhetorische dispositio" (Musical Form and Rhetorical Dispositio). In *Alte Musik und Musikpädagogik* (Ancient Music and Music Pedagogy), edited by Hartmut Krones. Vienna, 1997.

Burmeister, Joachim. *Hypomnematum musicae poeticae*. Rostock, Germany, 1599.

Burmeister, Joachim. *Musica autoschediastikē*. Rostock, Germany, 1601.

Burmeister, Joachim. *Musica poetica*. Rostock, Germany, 1606.

Calvisius, Sethus. *Exercitatio musica tertia*. Leipzig, Germany, 1611.

Campion, Thomas. Foreword to *The First Book of Ayres*. London, c.1613.

Chabanon, Michel-Paul-Guy de. *Observation sur la musique et principalement sur la métaphysique de l'art*. Paris, 1779.

Dressler, Gallus. *Praecepta musicae poeticae*. Edited by B. Engelke. Magdeburg, Germany, 1914–1915. First published 1563.

Eco, Umberto. *Einführung in die Semiotik* (Introduction to Semiotic). Munich, 1972.

Forchert, Arno. "Musik und Rhetorik im Barock" (Music and Rhetoric in the Baroque). In *Schütz-Jahrbuch* (1985–1986).

Forkel, Johann Nicolaus. *Allgemeine Geschichte der Musik* (General History of Music), vol. 1. Leipzig, Germany, 1788.

Gaffurius, Franchinus. *Practica Musicae*. Milan, Italy, 1496.

Galliculus, Johannes. *Isagoge de compositione Cantus*. Leipzig, Germany, 1520.

Hegel, Georg Wilhelm Friedrich. *Ästhetik 2*. Edited by Friedrich Bassenge. Berlin, 1965.

Heinichen, Johann David. *Der General-Bass in der Komposition*. Dresden, Germany, 1728.

Hoskyns, John. *Direcciones for Speech and Style*. Unpublished ms. c.1599.

Isidor of Seville. *Etymologiae sive origines*. c.630.

Kalkar, Heinrich Eger von. "Cantuagium." In *Beiträge zur rheinischen Musikgeschichte* (Contributions to Music History of the Rhineland), edited by Hüschen, vol. 2. Cologne, 1952. First published c.1380.

Kanne, Friedrich August. "Über die musikalische Mahlerey" (Concerning musical tone-painting). In *Allgemeine musikalische Zeitung, mit besonderer Rücksicht auf den österreichischen Kaiserstaat* (1818).

Kanne, Friedrich August. "Über die Bildung des Tonsetzers." In *Allgemeine musikalische Zeitung, mit besonderer Rücksicht auf den österreichischen Kaiserstaat* 4 (1820).

Kircher, Athanasius. *Musurgia universalis*, vol. 1. Rome, 1650.

Koch, Heinrich Christoph. *Musikalisches Lexikon* (Music Dictionary). Frankfurt a.M., 1802.

Krones, Hartmut. "Rhetorik und rhetorische Symbolik in der Musik um 1800" (Rhetoric and rhetorical symbolism in music around 1800). In *Musiktheorie* 3 (1988), pp. 117–140.

Krones, Hartmut. "'Wiener' Symbolik? Zu musiksemantischen Traditionen in den beiden Wiener Schulen" ("Viennese" symbolism? Concerning music-semantic traditions in both Viennese Schools). In *Beethoven und die Zweite Wiener Schule* (Beethoven and the second Viennese school), edited by Otto Kolleritsch. Vienna, 1992.

Krones, Hartmut. "Das Fortwirken symbolhafter Traditionen im frühen Vokalschaffen Franz Liszts" (The continuing effects of symbolic traditions in Franz Liszt's early production of vocal music). In *Liszt-Studien* 4 (1993).

Krones, Hartmut. "Musik und Rhetorik" (Music and Rhetoric). In *Musik in Geschichte und Gegenwart*, vol. 6, 2d ed. Kassel, 1997.

Kuhnau, Johann. *Frische Clavier-Früchte* (Fresh Fruits for the Piano). Leipzig, Germany, 1696.

Kuhnau, Johann. "Texte zur Leipziger Kirchen-Musik" (Texts for Leipzig Church Music). In *Monatshefte für Musikgeschichte*. Edited by B. F. Richter, 1902. First published 1709.

La Voye-Mignot, de. *Traité de musique*. Paris, 1656.

Leodiensis, Jacobus. "Speculum musicae," [c.1330]. Manuscript. In *Corpus scriptorum de musica*, edited by Roger Bragard, vol. 3/1–7. Rome, 1955–1973.

Lippius, Johannes. *Disputatio musica tertia*. Wittenberg, 1610.

Lippius, Johannes. *Synopsis musicae novae*. Strasbourg, 1612.

Marchettus of Padua. "Pomerium." In *Corpus scriptorum de musica*, edited by G. Reaney, vol. vi. Rome, 1961. First published c.1325.

Mattheson, Johann. *Der vollkommene Capellmeister* (The Compleat Music Master). Hamburg, 1739.

Mersenne, Marin. *Traité de l'Harmonie Universelle*. Paris, 1627.

Müller, H. "Der 'tractatus musicae scientiae' des Gobelinus Person (1358–1421)." In *Kirchenmusikalisches Jahrbuch* 20 (1907).

Neidhardt, Johann Georg. *Sectio canonis harmonici*. Königsberg, 1724.

Nettesheim, Agrippa von. *De vanitate et incertitudinae scientiarum*. Cologne, 1532.

Nucius, Johannes. *Musices poeticae*. Neisse, 1613.

Quantz, Johann Joachim. *Versuch einer Anweisung, die Flöte traversière zu spielen* (Attempt at instruction to play the transverse flute). Berlin, 1752.

Reckow, Fritz. "Processus und Structura: Concerning Tradition of Types and Understanding of Form in the Middle Ages." In *Musiktheorie* 1 (1986), pp. 5–29.

Reicha, Anton. *Traité de haute Composition musicale*. Vol. 2. Paris, 1826.

Ruhnke, Martin. *Joachim Burmeister*. Kassel, 1955.

Sabbatini, Luigi Antonio. *Trattato sopra le fughe musicali*. Venice, Italy, 1802.

Scheibe, Johann Adolph. *Critischer Musicus*. Leipzig, Germany, 1745.

Schindler, Anton. *Biographie von Ludwig van Beethoven*. 3d ed. Münster, 1860.

Schopenhauer, Arthur. *Die Welt als Wille und Vorstellung* (The World as Will and Representation), chap. 3, sect. 52. Frankfurt a.M., 1859. First published 1819.

Schubart, Christian Friedrich Daniel. *Ideen zu einer Ästhetik der Tonkunst* (Ideas About an Aesthetic of Musical Composition). Vienna, 1806. First published 1784.

Telemann, Georg Philipp. *Fortsetzung des Harmonischen Gottesdienstes* (Continuation of the Harmonious Church Service). Hamburg, 1731.

Thuringus, Joachim. *Opusculum bipartitum*. Berlin, 1624.

Tinctoris, Johannes. "Complexus effectuum musices." In *Opera theoretica II*, edited by A. Seay, pp. 159–177. Neuhausen, 1978. Written c.1470.

Tinctoris, Johannes. *Liber de arte contrapuncti*. Edited by A. Seay. Rome, 1975. Written 1477.

Türk, D. G. *Klavierschule* (Piano School). Leipzig, Germany, 1789.

Vicentino, Nicola. *L'antica musica ridotta alla moderna prattica*. Rome, 1555.

Walther, J. G. *Praecepta der musicalischen Composition* (Precepts of Musical Composition). Edited by P. Benary. Leipzig, Germany, 1955. First published 1708.

Walther, J. G. *Musicalisches Lexikon*. Leipzig, Germany, 1732.

Zarlino, Gioseffo. *Sopplimenti musicali*. Venice, Italy, 1588.

—H. KRONES

Translated by Frank Sitchler

NARRATIVE. *See* African-American rhetoric, *article on* Abolitionist rhetoric; Arrangement, *article on* Modern arrangement; Color; Forensic genre; *and* Politics, *article on* Constitutive rhetoric.

NINETEENTH-CENTURY RHETORIC.

The discipline of nineteenth-century American rhetoric—the focus of this article, although many of the enumerated characteristics pertain to nineteenth-century European rhetoric as well—was founded on the ideological belief that the development of rhetorical expertise conferred critical intelligence and moral character and the pedagogical assumption that any individual willing to learn the principles of form could become an eloquent speaker and writer. [*See* Arrangement, *article on* Traditional arrangement; Invention; *and* Style.] The dominion of rhetoric in this period was absolute in the nineteenth-century American college where the study of rhetoric was considered a prerequisite course of study in the liberal arts, and equally powerful in the public sphere where the powers of oratory and eloquent composition were regarded as indispensable to the acquisition of economic and personal fortune. What is particularly remarkable about the nineteenth-century discipline of rhetoric is that it exerted its cultural influence on the academy and the public throughout the century. The skills of oratory, elocution, prose composition, critical analysis, and letter writing all fell under the dominion of the nineteenth-century tradition, which was promoted within the academy and the public sphere by treatises and lecturers articulating guidelines for all forms of communication.

Nineteenth-century rhetoric, both academic and public, promoted the understanding of rhetoric as an intellectual habit of mind that prepared any speaker or writer to argue and inform no matter the audience or occasion. Nineteenth-century rhetoric manuals, written for the scholar as well as the "private learner" studying rhetoric in the parlor, offered to the ever greater numbers of Americans seeking entrance to public and professional life an opportunity for self-improvement and influence in daily life, which proved an enduring invitation in the decades before and after the Civil War.

Nineteenth-century rhetoricians consistently defined rhetoric as an art that exerted its force in all types of communicative occasions both oral and written. Continuing the extension of the sphere of rhetoric beyond public speaking to the arts of writing is one of the major achievements of nineteenth-century rhetoric. Because the study of rhetoric was constructed as an opportunity that any literate American could take up, and because rhetorical skills were defined as universally applicable to all communicative occasions, the discipline of rhetoric defined itself as both accessible and indispensable. In an historical period in which progress and expansion were prized, nineteenth-century rhetoric promised access and utility, a promise that mitigated against the traditional elitism of rhetorical education but preserved the status of rhetorical eloquence as the distinctive skill of the cultivated citizen.

Adaptation. The foundation of nineteenth-century rhetorical theory drew upon a fusion of classical rhetorical principles and the epistemological orientation of the New Rhetoric, as defined in the influential eighteenth-century treatises of George Campbell and Hugh Blair (and later Richard Whately), who reconciled traditional rhetorical theory and post-Enlightenment theories of the mind and language. The theoretical foundation that preserved a classical commitment to universally applicable rules of invention, arrangement, and style, and a post-Enlightenment view of the mind assumed that the mental and emotional responses of the rhetorician's audience were knowable, predictable, and able to be addressed by a wide range of textual choices. Nineteenth-century rhetoricians successfully capitalized on both the neoclassical components and the epistemological rationales of the New Rhetoric to craft a theory that explained in formulaic terms the principles of how to compose effective discourse for all occasions. Like their eighteenth-century colleagues, nineteenth-century rhetoricians reiterated the classical view that the key to effective rhetoric was the adaptation of basic rules of form and style to the requirements of audiences and contexts. [*See* Eighteenth-century rhetoric.]

The principle of adaptation was promoted by influential nineteenth-century rhetoricians throughout the century. Samuel Newman and John Franklin Genung, whose treatises collectively represent the orientation of American rhetorical theory before and after the Civil Way, recast the classical wisdom that the powers of eloquence were available to anyone who could master rhetorical form and come to understand how audiences responded and why. The definition of rhetoric Samuel Newman offers in his influential antebellum treatise, *A Practical System of Rhetoric* (1834), the "power of producing and applying our knowledge as occasion demands" (p. 26), is reiterated in other treatises circulating in the early decades of the century such as Increase Cooke's *The American Orator* (1814) and Alexander Jamieson's *A Grammar of Rhetoric and Polite Literature* (1837). Similarly, Genung, whose series of treatises *The Practical Elements of Rhetoric* (1886), *Handbook of Rhetorical Analysis* (1888), and *Working Principles of Rhetoric* (1893) dominated rhetoric scholarship between 1880 and 1900, stresses the principle of adaptation as the most basic rhetorical process and acknowledges the traditional status of that assumption [*See* Decorum; *and* Occasion.]:

This idea of adaptation is the best modern representative of the original aim of the art. Having at first to deal only with hearers, rhetoric began as the art of oratory, that is, of convincing and persuading by speech. Now, however, as the art of printing has greatly broadened its field of action, rhetoric must address itself to readers as well, and must therefore include more forms of composition and more comprehensive objects, while still the initial character of the art survives, in the general aim of so presenting thought that it shall have power over men, which aim is most satisfactory defined in the term *adaptation*. (*Practical Elements*, p. 1)

Genung reveals in his definition of "adaptation" the challenge that nineteenth-century rhetoricians met so well: the articulation of a theory of rhetoric for an era in which the modes of rhetoric could no longer be contained in the traditional genres of deliberative, forensic, and epideictic. "Adaptation" was the primary theoretical response of nineteenth-century rhetoricians to the task of translating the fundamental insights of previous traditions to the practical discursive demands of a culture in which rhetorical sites had burgeoned beyond the rationalization of traditional definitions of major rhetorical occasions.

A. S. Hill, whose widely circulated treatise *Principles of Rhetoric* (1878) rivaled the popularity of Genung's *Practical Elements* in the postbellum academy, updates conventional classical wisdom about the importance of adjusting to audience and occasion, and stresses that the art of rhetoric is based on flexible principles and rules that can be defined and variously applied:

Rhetoric, being the art of communication by language, implies the presence . . . of at least two persons, the speaker or writer, and the person spoken or written to. Aristotle makes the very essence of Rhetoric to lie in the distinct recognition of a hearer. Hence its rules are not absolute, like those of logic, but relative to the character and circumstances of the person or persons addressed . . . for the ways of communicating truth are many. (pp. v–vi)

The kind of explicit attention Hill gives to articulating the principle of adaptation of purpose and form to audience and occasion is a standard feature of nineteenth-century rhetoric treatises in both the postbellum and antebellum periods, as well as in more specialized treatments of particular rhetorical modes such as preaching and letter writing. [*See* Epistolary rhetoric; *and* Homiletics.] The hegemony of theoretical opinion within the nineteenth-century tradition regarding the principle of adaptation becomes clear when we note that Newman, Hill, and Genung are among the principal architects of nineteenth-century rhetorical theory after the Civil War, and that Cooke, Newman, and Jamieson's texts were widely read rhetoric manuals in America in the early decades of the century.

The prominence of the principle of adaptation as a distinctive theoretical feature of nineteenth-century rhetoric is corroborated by the promotion of this view of the rhetorical process in nineteenth-century homiletic treatises and letter-writing manuals, which claimed their theoretical authority from the discipline of rhetoric and its ancient authority. In *A Treatise on the Preparation and Delivery of Sermons* (1870), John A. Broadus points out the importance of the principle of adaptation in his discussion of the "application" of instructional materials to various audiences. Broadus advises the preacher to apply illustrative or developmental material to the interests of the "classes" of listeners being addressed and to remember that without this consideration of how to adapt purpose to audience, the sermon will be ineffective. Although Broadus and other homileticians typically refer to this strategy as "application," the theoretical commitment to the principle of adaptation is unmistakable (pp. 230–231). Similarly, in popular letter-writing treatises such as *Martine's Sensible Letter-Writer* (1866), hopeful correspondents are advised that the fundamental principle of the art of letter writing is to remember that "style should be determined, in some measure, by the nature of the subject, but in a still greater degree by the relative positions of the writer and the person addressed" (p. 15). The fact that the principle of adaptation was articulated in popular rhetoric manuals like *Martine's Sensible Letter-Writer,* which enjoyed wide circulation in the 1860s and 1870s, indicates how widely influential this principle was across the nineteenth-century tradition as a whole. In the estimation of any particular rhetorical tradition, the relationship between the theoretical orientation of the academic or elite discipline and its public sector counterparts provides insight into how influential particular rhetorical presumptions were in any given era. The consistency of opinion supporting the principle of adaptation in both the academic and popular spheres, both before and after the Civil War, indicates how successfully the nineteenth-century tradition adhered to the classical wisdom regarding decorum in the management of subject, audience, and occasion.

Finding its way even into the self-help literature of the late nineteenth century, the principle of adaptation was explained to the "private learner" in materials designed to educate Americans in rhetoric at home or in the "parlor." For example, in *The Universal Self-Instructor: An Epitome of Forms and General Reference Manual* (1882), the reader is offered instruction in oratory, elocution, prose composition, and letter writing. The extensive pedagogical sweep of this "parlor curriculum" in rhetoric indicates how important rhetorical skills were to nineteenth-century Americans and how inclusive the scope of rhetorical practice was considered to be. Figuring prominently in *The Universal Self-Educator's* treatment of argumentative style is the principle of adapting the rhetorical text to audience and occasion:

What is a proper argumentative style will always depend upon the character of the class of readers or hearers whom it is attempted to persuade. In making a political speech, or any other oration before a popular audience, a florid and highly ornamental style may be used to advantage. In a composition to be read before a cultivated audience, however, the expression should be pruned of all luxuriances and redundancies. (p. 15)

The theoretical recapitulation of the principle of adaptation in a representative text of the nineteenth-century encyclopedia tradition, like *The Universal Self-Educator,* indicates the consistency with which nineteenth-century pedagogies reinscribed a basic classical rhetorical principle, and reveals the extensive influence of academic rhetorical theory on the theoretical configurations of popular manuals. Nineteenth-century students of rhetoric, both in the classroom and in the parlor, were presented with a uniformly neoclassical interpretation of the rhetorician's fundamental task: to adapt subject and text to audience and occasion. Promotion of the principle of adaptation allowed academic and popular rhetorical pedagogy to define rhetoric in terms implying that although a fundamental grasp of the principles of form and style had to be secured before one could become a successful speaker or writer, that mastery would prove infinitely versatile.

Epistemology. The articulation of the classical principle of adaptation in the nineteenth-century tradition is complimented in both academic and popular manuals by a theoretical emphasis on the importance of understanding human nature or the "mental" disposition of audiences and readers. Supplementing classical advice regarding adaptation with a distinctly epistemological turn, nineteenth-century rhetorical theorists followed the lead of New Rhetoricians Campbell and Blair in equating a knowledge of human nature with understanding the faculties of the mind and the ways in which intellectual and emotional responses are affected by rhetorical choices. Powerfully influenced by Campbell's often quoted formulation that the aim of rhetoric is "to enlighten the understanding, to please the imagination, to move the passions or to influence the will," nineteenth-century rhetoricians represent rhetoric as an art that depends upon an understanding, as John Bascom (*Philosophy of Rhetoric*, 1866) puts it, of "how the mind expresses itself according to its own laws" (p. 13). A theoretical commitment to a philosophical understanding of what is often defined in nineteenth-century treatises as "the whole nature" of the reader or hearer, expanded the principle of adaptation beyond the traditional goal of adapting text to audience and occasion to include a mandatory understanding on the part of the writer or speaker of how the rhetorical devices of persuasion, argumentation, description, and narrative appealed to the mind. Newman, who is highly dependent on Blair's interpretation of how rhetorical elements interact with the mental faculties, explains in *A Practical System of Rhetoric* that an epistemological rationale must govern adaptation of inventional strategies. Newman reiterates both Campbell's and Blair's assumption that the aims of rhetoric and the function of particular canons are linked directly to the the governing intentions of all discourse: to enlighten the understanding, please the imagination, move the passion, or influence the will:

> Writings are distinguished from each other as didactic, persuasive, argumentative, descriptive and narrative. These distinctions have reference to the object, which the writer has primarily and principally in mind. Didactic writing, as the name implies, is used in conveying instruction. . . . When it is designed to influence the will, the composition becomes of the persuasive kind. . . . Another kind of composition, and one which is found united with most others, is the argumentative. Under this head, are included the various forms of argument, the statement of proofs, the assigning of causes, and generally, those writings, which are addressed to the reasoning faculties of the mind. (p. 28)

Reinforced by Campbell's and Blair's refusal to separate the faculties of the mind from the kinds of rhetorical techniques most suited to affect them, Newman reiterates the New Rhetorical tenet that epistemological aims and generic strategies should be considered simultaneously when the speaker or writer makes inventional, depositional, or stylistic choices. In Newman's treatise,

as well as in influential academic texts that appeared after the Civil War, such as Henry N. Day's *Elements of the Art of Rhetoric* (1866) and Genung's *Practical Elements of Rhetoric,* the principle of adaptation is clearly augmented beyond a consideration of audience and occasion to include a strategic sensitivity to how the understanding, the will, the passions, and the imagination are influenced by discourse. Day and Genung advise the speaker and writer to adapt the aim and style of discourse to how the reading or listening mind will respond. For example, Day explains that listeners will not change their minds unless they are first provided with new information, and that a new perception must be put in place before feelings can be affected. Persuasion is not possible, Day argues, unless the will is changed, and the will cannot be changed without an engagement of feeling, and an engagement of feeling depends on being shown the object or issue in a new way: "persuasion properly follows the other three processes, as in order to a change of will, the feelings are generally to be aroused, the judgement convinced, and the understanding informed" (p. 43). Genung's account of the ways in which rhetoric conforms to the "laws of sound thinking" in *The Working Principles of Rhetoric* (1900) indicates the firm hold that the epistemological view of adaptation retained in rhetorical theory at the century's close:

> From the consideration of these human powers and capacities, with the countless limitations that culture, occupation, and original character impose upon them, it will easily be seen how broad is the field of rhetorical adaptation, and how comprehensive must be the art that masters and applies its resources. (p. 4)

Genung's definition of "rhetorical adaptation" as the fundamental challenge of the art of rhetoric indicates the longevity of the epistemological interpretation of this principle within the nineteenth-century tradition. The epistemological interpretation of adaptation also influenced popular rhetoric manuals that interpret in slightly more rudimentary terms the importance of the speaker's or writer's understanding of human nature. In *Hill's Manual of Social and Business Forms* (1883), an extremely successful popular text that went through fifty editions between 1883 and 1911, the reader is advised in the chapter on "The Public Speaker" that "[I]n public speaking, one of the great secrets of success is a knowledge of human nature. To acquire this, the speaker should carefully study men—the passions and impulses that influence mankind—their mental characteristics, and know them as they are" (p. 60). While the authors of *Hill's Manual* do not provide a detailed account of the "passions and impulses" and "mental characteristics" a reader would expect to find in a full-length rhetorical treatise of the period, the parlor reader receives essentially the same general advice: the intellectual and emotional responses of audiences and readers must be taken into account when considering how to persuade and by what means. The stress on "mental" capacities in *Hill's Manual* makes this advice distinctly epistemological in orientation, and not simply an enlivened version of Aristotle's traditional advice to consider the effectiveness of the pathetic appeal. [*See* Pathos.]

Delivery/Elocution. The conventionality of the epistemological interpretation of the principle of adaptation in nineteenth-century theory is also evident in the advice offered to prospective speakers in elocution manuals of the period, which typically address the relationship between techniques of *delivery* and the effective stimulation of the mental processes of the audience. In Henry Mandeville's *The Elements of Reading and Oratory* (1845), a widely reprinted and cited elocution manual between 1845 and 1890, the speaker is advised repeatedly to consider the responses of the mind:

> I need scarcely say that the judicious management of force is a distinct and important addition to that variety which renders good reading and speaking so singularly attractive to all classes of hearers . . . the students must be governed in their delivery by the relative importance of the thought, or the nature of the sentiment or passion expressed. . . . Force is under the control of the will; and is measured and regulated by the judgement.
> (pp. 61–62)

In this advice on the use of "force," Mandeville's acknowledgement of the dynamic relationship between the faculties of the "will" and the "judgement" is typical of the theoretical orientation of nineteenth-century approaches to delivery. A "natural" relationship was stressed between the mental responses of the audience and techniques of delivery such as the properties of the voice (articulation, inflection, accent, emphasis, pause, time, and pitch), and the properties of action or gesture (stance, hand and arm gestures, position of the feet and limbs, and expressions of the face and eyes). In *Practical Elocution* (1886), J. W. Shoemaker prefaces his treatment of these issues with an explanation of how delivery interacts with the mental faculties in which he advises his reader that one of the "essentials" that every speaker should keep in mind is "adaptation":

> The listener, hearing and being familiar with the words, obtains an intellectual knowledge of the thought expressed. He is *impressed* with the words only to the degree that he is *interested* in the thought. . . . The same sentiment may be spoken so that it shall not only express the idea indicated, but that it shall *impress* that idea upon the mind and heart. (Shoemaker's emphasis, 113; vii)

Shoemaker's explanation focuses on the function of the understanding, the passions, the imagination, and the will, and the interdependence of these faculties in securing the listener's attention. The epistemological weight of this account, of how the listening mind reacts to delivery, closely parallels definitions of how the faculties of the mind are interrelated in responses to argument typically included in general rhetoric treatises (e.g., Day). This theoretical parallel draws attention to how extensively the epistemological rationale permeated all manifestations of nineteenth-century theory.

Arrangement. While insisting that rhetorical composition and practice depended on the strategic assessment of subject, audience, and occasion, as well as an understanding of the mental characteristics of the listening and reading mind, nineteenth-century theorists also claim that an understanding of arrangement, style, and the invention of material will prepare any speaker or writer for the complexity of adaptation. Following the lead of Campbell and Blair in preserving a theoretical attention to the canons of arrangement, style, and invention, nineteenth-century rhetoricians contextualized the discussion of these canons with a consistent focus on the principle of adaptation. Although neoclassical principles are preserved in the theoretical core of treatments of the canons, nineteenth-century rhetoricians instructed speakers and writers to give priority to how the arrangement of discourse and stylistic choices would enhance the intellectual and emotional response of the audience. Blair's neociceronian scheme provided the model for antebellum treatments of arrangement, which defined a traditional six-part arrangement sequence of introduction, division, statement or narration, the argument, the pathetic appeal, and the peroration or conclusion. The six-part definition of arrangement dominated discussions of arrangement until after the Civil War, when theorists such as Day and A. S. Hill popularized a simpler four-unit division that collapsed the function of the introduction and division into one and included the pathetic appeal in the conclusion. The four-part arrangement scheme of introduction, statement, main discourse or argument, and conclusion proved a more versatile model for arrangement for nineteenth-century theorists striving to bring all forms of oral and written discourse under the heading of the rhetorical arts, and by the 1880s, treatments of the four-part arrangement scheme were standard in influential treatises such as Genung's *Practical Rhetoric* and A. S. Hill's *Principles of Rhetoric*.

Like Blair, whose neoclassical discussion of arrangement is predisposed by a strong epistemological interest in how the "imagination" can be engaged by structural choices, nineteenth-century rhetoricians maintain the traditional integrity of the classical canon of arrangement, but they also treat organizational strategies as opportunities for engaging all mental faculties in particular ways. David J. Hill, whose treatises *Elements of Rhetoric* (1878) and *The Science of Rhetoric* (1877) are two of the most distinctly epistemologically oriented treatises of the postbellum period, illustrates in his discussion of arrangement how nineteenth-century theorists tended to reread classical precepts with a predisposition toward foregrounding the cognitive processes:

> 1) There should be an Introduction. This . . . is usually required to bring the discussion into connection with the occasion. 2) There must be a discussion. By this is meant that we cannot establish anything in the mind of another

> without using facts, illustrations, or arguments to assist us. 3) There must be a conclusion. When we invite others to accompany our thoughts, we are under an obligation to conduct them to some new state of mind. . . . We should always have some definite state of mind in view to which everything should tend. (pp. 16–17)

The combination of classical and epistemological elements of theory illustrated in D. J. Hill's discussion of adjusting arrangement to motivate whatever "state of mind" is desired in writing and speaking, becomes more pronounced after midcentury. Theorists in earlier decades, such as Newman, Jamieson, and Henry Coppee (*Elements of Rhetoric*, 1859), reinscribe Blair's primary epistemological interest in how rhetoric moves the imagination and the passions. Later treatises, such as Hill's, Day's *Elements*, Genung's *Practical Rhetoric*, and A. S. Hill's *Principles of Rhetoric* provide more detailed explanations of the relationship between the canons and all the mental faculties.

The greater theoretical range of the epistemological point of view in treatises after 1850, is illustrated in treatments of arrangement in popular rhetoric manuals of the latter decades of the nineteenth-century, in which advice on composition closely imitates that defined in the academic tradition. In a representative treatment of arrangement in the handbook, *The New Select Speaker* (1902), the chapter on "Composition and Letter Writing" outlines an abbreviated arrangement model of three parts: "the Introduction," the body or Discussion, and "the Conclusion" (pp. 22–23). Although not an academic treatment of the epistemological impact of arrangement, the discussion of arrangement in *The New Select Speaker* offers readers a working understanding of the relationship between arrangement and the mental faculties of listeners and readers as this analysis of the function of the introduction illustrates:

> The Introduction. This should be brief, its object being merely to introduce the subject. Much depends on this part of the composition. The reader's mind is not engaged with the consideration of the facts. . . . make the introduction striking enough in itself to awaken the interest and hold the attention of your reader. (p. 23)

The emphasis placed here on "awakening the interest" (engaging the understanding), and "holding the attention" (engaging the imagination), indicates that the epistemological interpretation of arrangement by academic rhetoricians had successfully shaped the substance of popular rhetoric pedagogies, and that the theoretical emphasis on relating rhetorical technique to inducing mental reactions had achieved conventional status by the end of the century.

Style. Like discussions of arrangement, nineteenth-century treatments of the canon of style are founded on the recasting of classical advice in combination with guidelines for achieving stylistic influence over the faculties. In their discussions of style, nineteenth-century theorists make frequent reference to classical advice and follow the example of the "ancients" in illustrating preferred stylistic techniques with model examples. Within nineteenth-century rhetorical theory, style is defined primarily in terms of how diction, sentence structure and arrangement, and the use of the figures contribute to the speaker's or writer's intention to move the understanding, the imagination, the passions, and the will in particular ways. Nineteenth-century rhetoricians are influenced not only by Blair's and Campbell's definitions of style, but also by Richard Whately's treatment of the rhetorical aims of style in *Elements of Rhetoric* (1828), a treatise that, like Campbell's and Blair's treatises, enjoyed wide circulation and imitation in America in the first half of the nineteenth century. Whately's use of the term *energy,* for that quality of style that engages the imagination and fixes the audience's attention, proved more popular in nineteenth-century theories of style than Campbell's term *vivacity* for the same epistemological effect. Whately's triad of perspicuity, energy, and elegance was widely adopted as a framework for discussing style, although nineteenth-century theorists tended to also include Blair's definition of "beauty" as a quality of style that engages the highest intellectual and emotional sensibilities. Collectively, nineteenth-century treatments of style stress the importance of (1) purity or grammatical correctness in diction and sentence structure; (2) the importance of perspicuity or the clear presentation of thought in diction, sentence structure, sentence arrangement, and the use of paragraph transitions; (3)

the creation of force (energy, strength) in expression through usage, sentence structure, sentence arrangement, and the use of the figures; (4) the expression of elegance or beauty in style through diction, arrangement, and the use of the figures; and (5) the general rule that purity, perspicuity, force, and elegance were the central attributes of an effective style in all forms of discourse.

The emphasis in nineteenth-century treatments of style on the general applicability of the rules of style to "all communication" is summed up by A. S. Hill, who observes that "[T]he efficiency of all communication by language must depend on three things: 1) the choice of those words that are best adapted to convey to the persons addressed the meaning intended; 2) the use of as many words as are needed to convey the meaning, but no more; 3) the arrangement of words, sentences, and paragraphs in the order most likely to communicate the meaning" (p. 74). Hill's condensed summary of the importance of stylistic choices is often cited in popular rhetoric manuals in which the qualities of purity, perspicuity, force, and elegance are treated as qualities that result from choices about "words." The author of Gaskell's *Compendium of Forms: Social, Educational, Legal, and Commercial* (1880), a widely reprinted parlor manual between 1880 and 1900, similarly observes: "All the errors in the use of language can be embraced under four heads: Too many words; too few words; improper word order or expression, and improper arrangement of words" (p. 72). The theoretical predisposition that influences this treatment of "words" is a dominant assumption of nineteenth-century treatments of style that affects popular and academic rhetoric alike: intelligibility, liveliness of ideas, and intensity of emotional impressions are rhetorical effects directly associated with stylistic choices.

Genres. The epistemological orientation of nineteenth-century theory so obvious in treatments of the canons of arrangement and style was also immensely influential on treatments of the major divisions of rhetorical genres. The staunch belletristic commitment of nineteenth-century theory, to regard all oral and written genres as arts of rhetoric, results from the reassertion of the liberal view of the scope of rhetoric promoted by the New Rhetoricians. Blair defines a wide field for the rhetorical arts by treating the species of oratory, prose composition (essay writing, historical writing, etc.), poetry, and fiction as the major genres of rhetoric. Campbell treats oratory as well, but tends to discuss oratory and prose genres in terms of the kind of compositions that would affect the faculties of the mind. Whately imitates Campbell's treatment of the divisions of rhetoric by grouping types of rhetoric under particular epistemological aims rather than defining an inclusive list of major genres. Nineteenth-century theorists combine the Blair and Campbell–Whately approaches to defining the genre of rhetoric by reinscribing Blair's general belletristic perspective that all forms of discourse are rhetorical with the Campbell–Whately framework for categorizing modes of rhetoric by epistemological aim. As the century unfolds, nineteenth-century rhetoric continues to define an ever-broadening range of rhetorical forms by moving steadily toward an "aims" rather than "divisions" model of discussing rhetorical practice. This move to associate types of prose and speaking with particular epistemological aims, such as appealing to the understanding or the imagination, modified the discrete generic system of Blair's belletristic model by regrouping such genres as historical and essay writing under "aims" headings like "Explanation" or "Argument." This shift in the treatment of the divisions of rhetoric to an epistemological aims format allowed nineteenth-century rhetoricians the flexibility to offer rationales for rhetorical practice that exceeded even Blair's wide belletristic field. By 1880, Blair's generic list of the "species" of rhetoric: oratory, historical writing, philosophical writing, epistolary writing, fiction, and poetry had been replaced by the "four kinds of composition": description, narration, exposition, and argument.

Nineteenth-century theorists considered oratory to be a type of argumentation, or appeal to the will, and treated oratory both as an epistemological intention and as a species of discourse. Strongly influenced by Blair's and Campbell's approach to oratory, nineteenth-century rhetoricians such as Newman, Day, Genung, and A. S. Hill preserved a classical perspective on oratory by defining the major types of oratory as judicial, deliberative, and sacred; however, treatments of the conduct of these types of oratory is governed by an interest in what kinds of arguments and evidence are best suited to engaging the understanding, the will, and the other faculties. This interest in the epistemological aims of oratory encourages nineteenth-century theorists to formally define a fourth type of oratory, "popular oratory." Popular oratory is defined in postbellum treatises as a type of oratory designed to move "the will of the people," as in campaign speeches, after-dinner speeches, lectures to lyceums, and college addresses. The creation of this new division of oratory indicates the prominence that public lecturers and platform speakers had achieved by the latter half of the century, and the proliferation in nineteenth-century society of communal occasions during which platform speaking was a central activity. The extention of the domain of oratory also points to an ongoing regard in American life for oratory as a political and cultural force.

Invention. Nineteenth-century theorists treat oratory as a composition that must achieve the same engagement with the will as any prose form of argument. From the point of view of nineteenth-century theory, the phrase "kinds of composition" is intended quite straightforwardly to mean "ways of writing" not genres of writing. Nineteenth-century theorists use these headings to discriminate among aims or intentions that speakers or writers might have and to stress the kinds of developmental choices that a writer or speaker must make in order to engage the appropriate faculties. As A. S. Hill makes clear in his definition of the "general principles that apply in varying degrees to all kinds of composition," description, narration, exposition, and argument (which includes oratory) are not modes but inventional processes:

> The purpose of description is to bring before the mind of the reader persons or things as they appear to the writer. The purpose of narration is to tell a story. . . . [to move from beginning to end and hold the reader's attention]. . . . The purpose of exposition is to make the matter in hand more definite. The purpose of argument is to influence opinion or action, or both. (pp. 246, 281)

Because nineteenth-century theorists stress the processes by which particular faculties can be engaged rather than the conduct of discrete genres, the canon of invention is subsumed under discussions of how the major aims of exposition, narration, description, and argument are to be achieved. While nineteenth-century theory recapitulates a generally classical notion of the canon of invention as "finding, sifting, and ordering the material of discourse" (Genung, *Practical Elements*, p. 217), invention is defined primarily as a process of adaptation of material along epistemological lines. Campbell's treatment of the relationship between invention and appeals to the mind had a substantial influence on nineteenth-century treatments of invention and the divisions of rhetoric. Nineteenth-century theory reiterates Campbell's argument that invention is a process of learning how to adapt rhetorical materials in such a way that the mental activities are engaged in the proper sequence. From Campbell's epistemological point of view, the invention or "composition" of materials for different texts is primarily directed not by generic expectations but by assessments of what rhetorical techniques will influence the reader's or listener's mental processes. For example, Campbell explains that "describing" an object is an attempt to engage the imagination of the audience and can only be achieved by the use of rhetorical techniques that exhibit to the imagination "'a lively and beautiful representation of the object" (p. 21). The "lively" representation is the aim of description and can be achieved by various means in many different kinds of texts.

Nineteenth-century rhetoricians understood Campbell's stance on the epistemological aim of invention as implying that the analysis of the development of rhetorical materials and the modes of rhetoric are inseparable issues. They urge speakers and writers to think of exposition, narration, description, and argument as intentions: the aim of exposition is to explain to the faculty of the understanding; narration strives to tell a story that engages the understanding and the imagination at the same time; description aims to present a scene, event, or person in vivid terms that engage the imagination and the passions; and argumentation seeks to present evidence to the understanding so convincingly and to move the passions so forcefully that the will is moved to action. Like Campbell, nineteenth-century rhetoricians point only secondarily to types of discourse that illustrate these processes at work.

Genung's analysis of "Invention Dealing with Observed Objects: Description" captures the tendency of the nineteenth-century theorist to discuss invention, textual features, and affective response as mutually reinforcing considerations:

> Description is the portrayal of concrete objects, material or spiritual, by means of language. Observe in this definition, first that description is portrayal. It is much more, therefore, than the mere enumeration of the parts and qualities of an object. [T]his is only the unsifted material for description, not the description itself. Description is such a treatment of an object, as a whole and in its parts, as produces a unified and consistent picture of it, aiding the reader to reproduce it in imagination with something of the vividness with which the writer originally perceived it. (p. 327)

A theoretical construction of "description" as a "portrayal" that aims to engage the reader's imagination through strategies of vivid depiction allows Genung to stress description as an inventional process which applies to particular varieties of writing and speaking. Advocating an intentional definition of description rather than a generic one, Genung is not limited in the range of model texts he can cite as "descriptive" in aim, and he lists several: Ruskin's description of the continent of Europe; Henry James's description of Chartres Cathedral; Victor Hugo's description of the Battle of Waterloo; and a description of Queen Elizabeth in nineteenth-century historian J. R. Green's *History of the English People* (pp. 330–331).

Genung's references to varied applications of description make the point to his reader that descriptive invention applies to an inexhaustible list of possible occasions and varieties of text. Genung's discussion of description is typical of how he treats exposition, narration, and argument. It is representative of treatments of invention and the genres in other widely used rhetoric manuals published in the decades after the Civil War, such as the treatises of A. S. Hill and the texts of John S. Hart (*A Manual of Composition and Rhetoric*, 1870) and Alexander Bain (*English Composition and Rhetoric*, 1866). The theoretical emphasis in these rhetorics echoes Genung's treatment of the kinds of composition as inventional processes rather than generic types, and generally serves to strengthen the cultural status of rhetoric in the latter half of the century as a rational art of unlimited application. It is this view of rhetoric as an inventional art energized by the universality of human beings' "natural" intellectual habits and practical communicative tasks, and unfettered by the imposition of a finite list of rhetorical occasions and genres that contextualizes how rhetoric is perceived at the close of the century.

BIBLIOGRAPHY

Brigance, William Norwood, and Marie Hochmuth, eds. *A History and Criticism of American Public Address*. 3 vols. New York, 1960. Notable for its essays on prominent nineteenth-century speakers but tends to overlook women orators, except Doris G. Yoakum, "Women's Introduction to the American Platform," pp. 153–192.

Campell, Karlyn Kohrs, ed. *Man Cannot Speak for Her*. 2 vols. New York, 1989. Essential revisionist collection featuring major women orators of the nineteenth century overlooked in twentieth-century accounts of the "golden age" of American oratory, including Lucretia Coffin Mott, Sojourner Truth, Elizabeth Cady Stanton, Susan B. Anthony, Frances Willard, Ida B. Wells, and Mary Church Terrell.

Clark, Gregory, and S. Michael Halloran, eds. *Oratorical Culture in America*. Carbondale, Ill., 1994. A useful collection of essays addressing the range and status of oral arts of rhetoric in pre-1900 America.

Guthrie, Warren. "The Development of Rhetorical Theory in America, 1635–1850." *Speech Monographs* 13 (1946), pp. 14–22; 14 (1947), pp. 28–54; 15 (1948), pp. 61–71; 16 (1949), pp. 98–113; 18 (1951), pp. 17–30. Pioneering set of articles particularly helpful in tracing the status of oratory. Regrettably, Guthrie neglects the prose arts.

Horner, Winifred Bryan Horner. *Nineteenth-Century Scottish Rhetoric: The American Connection*. Carbondale, Ill., 1993. Essential background on the theoretical and pedagogical links in the early nineteenth-century between American and Scottish rhetorical theory.

Hubert, Henry A. *Harmonious Perfection: The Development of English Studies in Nineteenth-Century Anglo-Canadian Colleges*. East Lansing, Mich., 1994. A helpful treatment of nineteenth-century rhetorical theory in Canada and its debt to the same Scottish and English traditions that also influenced the foundations of rhetorical theory in nineteenth-century America.

Johnson, Nan. *Nineteenth-Century Rhetoric in North America*. A survey of the foundations of nineteenth-century academic rhetoric, theoretical adaptations, and the nineteenth-century rhetorical arts. Carbondale, Ill., 1991.

Johnson, Nan. "Quintilian and the Nineteenth-Century Rhetorical Tradition." *Composition in Context; Essays in Honor of Donald C. Stewart*. Edited by W. Ross Winterowd and Vincent Gillespie, pp. 3–16. Carbondale, Ill., 1994. A close look at the nineteenth-century debt to Quintilian.

Logan, Shirley Wilson. *We Are Coming: The Persuasive Discourse of Nineteenth-Century Women*. Carbondale, Ill., 1999. Groundbreaking survey of the oratorical careers of African-American reformists in the nineteenth century.

Miller, Thomas P. *The Formation of College English: Rhetoric and Belles Lettres in the British Cultural Provinces*. Pittsburg, 1997. Useful background for understanding the rise of the Anglo-American model of English studies in which rhetoric played a central role.

O'Connor, Lillian. *Pioneer Women Orators*. New York, 1954. A thorough treatment of antebellum women speakers.

Rosner, Mary. "Reflections on Cicero in Nineteenth-Century England and America." *Rhetorica* 4 (1989), pp. 153–182. A close look at theoretical debt to Ciceronian rhetoric and sources. Useful for its Anglo-American perspective.

Secor, Marie J. "The Legacy of Nineteenth-Century Style Theory." *Rhetoric Society Quarterly* 12 (1981), pp. 76–94. One of the most useful summaries of the nineteenth-American canon of style as it was applied to prose.

Wallace, Karl R. *History of Speech Education in America: Background Studies*. New York, 1954. Informative range of studies on major speakers, schools of oratory and elocution, theoretical trends, and a helpful chapter on women speakers.

—NAN JOHNSON

NOMOS-PHYSIS DEBATE. *See* Sophists.

O

OCCASION. We have become accustomed to thinking of all communicative situations as rhetorical. Aristotle (384–322 BCE) himself opines (*Rhetoric* 2.18) that rhetoric is at play even in a conversation involving only two people. This very modern-sounding notion may obscure the fact that ancient Greek theorists had very strong ideas about the occasionality of rhetoric that were profoundly rooted in their cultural institutions. The latter are especially reflected in Aristotle's three "kinds" (*eidē*) of oratory: deliberative (*symbouleutikon*), judicial (*dikanikon*), and epideictic (*epideiktikon*). [*See* Deliberate genre; Epideictic genre; *and* Forensic genre.] Each of these was appropriate to a specific type of situation/occasion in Athenian society: deliberative, based on arguments of advantage and disadvantage, for speeches in the civic assembly, where the goal was to move the audience to a course of action in the future; judicial, based on arguments of justice and injustice, for speeches in the law courts, where the goal was to induce a jury to render a judgment about events in the past; and epideictic, based on arguments of praise or blame, for ceremonial occasions where the goal was to move an audience to a certain disposition in the present. Clearly, then, although Aristotle does not say so himself, each of these kinds of oratory was elicited by, and suited to, a different sort of (civic) occasion.

While the Greek concept of appropriate occasion (*kairos*) looms large in any discussion of rhetorical occasion, its semantic field is actually broader than is sometimes acknowledged. As with many abstract concepts, it was also hypostatized as a divinity: the second-century CE geographer Pausanias (5.14.9) mentions an altar to Kairos at Olympia, and reports a tradition naming this god as the youngest son of Zeus. The sculptor Lysippus (fl. mid-fourth century BCE) depicted Kairos as a youth holding a razor (no doubt an emblem of his divine attributes), with his hair long in front and short in back. For the poets from Hesiod to Pindar (eighth to fifth centuries BCE), *kairos* has the sense of "accurate choice and prudent restraint, the sense of what suits the circumstances, tact, discretion," or even "due measure" (Fränkel, 1973, pp. 447, 498). For the Pythagoreans, it manifested the *harmonia* that "reduces the opposite qualities in the universe to a unity" (Untersteiner, 1954, p. 82). Such conceptual dyads were fundamental to Greek thought; one may cite as examples the cosmological "love" and "strife" (*philotēs* and *neikos*) of Empedocles, the "opposing arguments" (*antikeimenoi logoi*) of Protagoras, and the "stronger" and "weaker" arguments (*kreitton* and *hēttōn logos*) mentioned by Protagoras and Aristophanes. As conflict is one of the great creators of occasion, it may be that the Pythagorean connection of *kairos* with strife or contention underscored its relevance to agonistic rhetoric.

In the work of the Sophists Gorgias, Prodicus, and Antiphon (Pindar's younger contemporaries), as in the Hippocratic writings, *kairos* also manifests a sense of time, specifically "point in time" (as opposed to *chronos,* "sequential time"; cf. Lat. *occasio* and *tempus* respectively, although the latter is sometimes also used in the sense of *kairos*). In its temporal sense, rhetorical *kairos* represents the "opportune moment" for a point to be made. Because our primary sources for the older Sophists survive only in the most exiguous fragments, we cannot establish the exact nature of their teaching on *kairos*. But Gorgias, whom ancient tradition names as a disciple of Empedocles, and who was probably influenced by Pythagorean thought, clearly considered *kairos* an important topic; he is said to have written specifically on it (Diels-Kranz, *Die Fragmente der Vorsokratiker,* 1952, 82 B 13). This tradition reinforces Gorgias's reputation (attested, for example, in Plato's *Gorgias*) as a skilled practitioner of extemporaneous oratory. Possibly as early as the Sophists, but certainly by the Hellenistic period, *kairos* came to be associated with the notion of *to pre-pon,* that which is "fitting" (Lat. *aptum, decorum, decens*): the orator must fit his speech, not only to himself and the audience, but to the time and place of the event (see Cicero's *Orator* 71), which are all aspects of occasion. [*See* Decorum.]

The sophistic treatise known as *Dissoi logoi* or *Dialexeis,* which apparently dates from the beginning of the fourth century BCE, enunciates a temporal kairotic ideal (2.20) as a general guide for human conduct. Alcidamas, a student of Gorgias, writes of rhetorical *kairos* primarily in its temporal sense. By contrast, his contemporary Isocrates (436–338 BCE), a student of both Gorgias and Prodicus, conceived of *kairos* in oratory as proper proportion and "conformity with initially decided subject matter and presentation" (O'Sullivan, 1992, p. 93). Doubtless this reflects his work as a logographer rather than a deliverer of oral/extemporaneous discourses. Both Alcidamas and Isocrates emphasize the differences between written and oral, signaling that these two modes of discourse reflect different types of occasion, thus making disparate demands upon the *rhētōr.* For oral discourse, above all in improvisatory situations, *kairos* will certainly have a temporal sense: an instantaneous awareness of, and reaction to, what the moment requires, lends power to communication. No writer can account in advance for every such need, so "occasion" for written texts must refer to the situation initially eliciting the writing, whereas *kairos* itself will pertain more to the harmonious and appropriate fashioning of a suitable text.

Depending on one's worldview and pedagogical philosophy, one may conceptualize *kairos* either as something prescriptive, which is intended to narrow the *rhētōr*'s focus according to what is *prepon,* or as an adaptive and open-ended principle that views "the production of meaning in language as a process of continuous adjustment to and creation of the present occasion" (White, 1987, p. 14). In other words, a rigid notion of *prepon* will prescribe certain proprieties, according to categorical assessments of what formulae a given rhetorical occasion demands; for example, one should be sober and serious, rather than festive or flippant, in a funeral oration. A radical approach to *kairos,* however, suggests that, since each occasion is composed of so many factors as to make prescription effectively impossible, the skilled *rhētōr* should be able to react in the moment itself, deciding what strategies best suit that particular situation. The latter position is usually presented as the sophistic doctrine of *kairos.* Ironically, though they are not typically aligned with the sophistic tradition, both Plato's Socrates and Aristotle espouse this radical sort of kairotic skill: Socrates, in stipulating that the *rhētōr* should understand the minds (*psychai*) of his audience, and fit his discourse sensitively to them (*Phaedrus* 271); and Aristotle, in defining rhetoric as "the ability [*dynamis*] of discerning the available means of persuasion in each situation" (*Rhetoric* 1.2.1).

A more prescriptive approach was delineated by theorists of *stasis* (the Greek term; cf. Lat. *status, constitutio*), a system developed by later rhetoricians such as Hermagoras and Hermogenes, and fully inculcated into Roman theory by writers such as the author of the *Rhetorica ad Herennium,* Cicero, and Quintilian. [*See* Stasis.] *Stasis* theory was very widely applied, especially in judicial oratory. The word *stasis,* coming from the verb *stand,* means, literally, "stance" or "position," and, by extension, the (rhetorical) position adopted in discourse. In political contexts, it may have the further sense of "faction" or even "discord," which harks back to the agonistic aspect of occasionality. The purpose of *stasis* theory was to determine the question at issue, and to tailor the discourse to that. Thus, if one (or one's client) had not committed the crime of which he was accused, one could argue this by *stasis* of *fact.* If the case was one of homicide, in which the accused was indeed involved, one could argue (by *stasis* of *definition*) that the death occurred as a matter of manslaughter and not of premeditated murder. If the murder was in fact premeditated, but there were extenuating circumstances (e.g., that the victim was a tyrant), one could argue (by *stasis* of *quality*) that the act was justified. Failing all else, one might argue (by *stasis* of *transference*) that the court was not competent to hear the case. *Stasis* theory, then, is a highly prescriptive occasion-based system, allowing nonetheless for some flexibility of approach. Cicero (106–43 BCE), for example, in his orations, often explicitly delineates the *stasis* he is (or is not) using, but sometimes he will make as if to argue more than one *stasis* simultaneously.

Of the five canons of Quintilianic rhetoric (first century CE)—invention, arrangement, style, memory, and delivery—all are in some respect occasion-sensitive. [*See* Arrangement; *article on* Traditional arrangement; Delivery; Invention; Memory; *and* Style.] Invention, the "finding" of argument, will of course be especially so. *Stasis* theory was the most popular inventional strategy in the Roman period. But Aristotle's inventional system—the arguments based on the *rhētōr's* perceived good character (*ēthos*), the arousal of the audience's emotion (*pathos*), and logical inference (*logos*)—is quintessentially a matter of occasion as well, for knowing which of these arguments to use in a given situation will likely be crucial to one's rhetorical success. [*See* Ēthos; Logos; *and* Pathos.] Arrangement, the ordering of the parts of the discourse, was probably at the heart of the sophistic system of rhetorical training (Solmsen, 1941); in such case, one would expect it to have been taught along with a theory of *kairos*. Style is to form what invention is to content, and as such is critical to the effective presentation of ideas; here as much as anywhere, the doctrine of *prepon* will have been brought into play. Memory and delivery pertain to the discursive event *per se*. One can only memorize orations for occasions that have been scheduled in advance, whereas kairotic skill may equip one to address rhetorical situations as they arise. Delivery, whether of memorized or extemporized discourse, is crucial for the *rhētōr's* adaptation to the occasion; in a sense, it is the most occasion-oriented of the five canons.

In postclassical times, the most important discussions of rhetorical occasion have centered on what Lloyd Bitzer famously termed "the rhetorical situation." [*See* Rhetorical situation.] Bitzer contends that this is comprised of an *exigence,* an *audience,* and certain *constraints.* He defines the rhetorical situation as "a complex of persons, events, objects, and relations presenting an actual or potential exigence which can be . . . removed if discourse . . . can so constrain human decision or action as to bring about the . . . modification of the exigence" (1968, p. 6) and, later, "a factual condition plus a relation to some interest" (1980, p. 28). The exigence itself is "an imperfection marked by urgency . . . a defect, an obstacle, something waiting to be done, a thing which is other than it should be" (1968, p. 6). The audi-

ence is distinguished from "mere hearers and readers" by their capacities "of being influenced by discourse and of being mediators of change" (1968, p. 8). Constraints are such things as "persons, events, objects, and relations" that "have the power to constrain decision and action needed to modify the exigence" (1968, p. 8). Bitzer's influential model has elicited multifarious responses, including emulation, modification, and rejection (cf., among many others, Pomeroy, 1972; Burke, 1973; Vatz, 1973; Consigny, 1974; Patton, 1979; Garret and Xiao, 1993). The nature of rhetorical exigence (from both essentialist and constructivist perspectives) and of the audience have been especially at issue in these discussions.

Occasion has a long history in poetry as well, and is closely tied to matters of genre. [*See* Poetry.] Here again, we may consult the ancient Greek tradition, in which specific occasions required specific types of verse: for example, hymns for divine worship; *epithalamia* in honor of weddings; *thrēnoi* (dirges) for funeral lamentation; *epinikia* (victory songs) to celebrate winners in athletic contests like the Olympics; odes and encomiums solemnizing various other occasions. Attic drama, which developed in connection with annual religious festivals, was occasional in a more complex way. What unites all these genres is a public or social aspect to their presentation (Miner et al., 1993; Dolan, 2000).

Occasional verse is a pervasive, possibly global phenomenon; one finds it in the Islamic as well as in several Asian traditions. In some cultures, a poet (such as England's poet laureate) may be officially designated to produce such verse. The increasing informality of much modern culture, together with the ascendancy of the private voice over the public where poetic composition is concerned, has relegated occasional verse to a very minor role in our culture; on the whole, Westerners now seem disinclined to solemnize formal occasions with the special composition of verse.

[*See also* Classical rhetoric; Kairos; *and* Sophists.]

BIBLIOGRAPHY

Bitzer, Lloyd F. "The Rhetorical Situation." *Philosophy and Rhetoric* 1 (1968), pp. 1–14. A landmark essay, essentially positivistic in its approach, that set the terms for much subsequent discussion.

Bitzer, Lloyd F. "Functional Communication: A Situational Perspective." In *Rhetoric in Transition: Studies in the Nature and Use of Rhetoric,* edited by Eugene E. White, pp. 21–38. University Park, Pa., 1980. Bitzer's own revisitation of the issues after numerous other scholars had weighed in.

Burke, Kenneth. "The Rhetorical Situation." In *Communication: Ethical and Moral Issues,* edited by Lee Thayer, pp. 263–275. New York, 1973. A very different approach to matters previously addressed by Bitzer.

Consigny, Scott. "Rhetoric and Its Situations." *Philosophy and Rhetoric* 7 (1974), pp. 175–186. An attempt to resolve the Bitzer/Vatz conflict by proposing rhetoric as an "art of topics."

Dolan, John. *Poetic Occasion from Milton to Wordsworth.* New York, 2000. A most readable account of the notion of poetic occasion.

Fränkel, Hermann. *Early Greek Poetry and Philosophy.* Translated by Moses Hadas and James Willis. New York, 1973. One of the best single-volume surveys of classical Greek literature.

Garret, Mary, and Xiaosui Xiao. "The Rhetorical Situation Revisited." *Rhetoric Society Quarterly* 23 (1993), pp. 30–40. A useful overview of the terrain, plus a number of new contributions to the discussion.

Kennedy, George A. *The Art of Persuasion in Greece.* Princeton, 1968. One of the fundamental reference works on ancient Greek rhetoric, with several useful pages on *kairos.*

Kinneavy, James L. "*Kairos:* A Neglected Concept in Classical Rhetoric." In *Rhetoric and Praxis,* edited by Jean Dietz Moss, pp. 79–105. Washington, D.C., 1986. A learned and detailed treatment of the subject.

Miner, Earl, A. J. M. Smith, and T. V. F. Brogan. "Occasional Verse." In *The New Princeton Encyclopedia of Poetry and Poetics,* edited by Alex Preminger and T. V. F. Brogan, p. 851. Princeton, 1993. The article is a succinct, useful treatment of the subject.

O'Sullivan, Neil. *Alcidamas, Aristophanes and the Beginnings of Greek Stylistic Theory.* Stuttgart, 1992. Deeply learned yet highly readable; breaks important new ground in the history of classical rhetoric.

Patton, John H. "Causation and Creativity in Rhetorical Situations." *Quarterly Journal of Speech* 65 (1979), pp. 36–55. Builds on Bitzer (1968).

Pomeroy, R. "Fitness of Response in Bitzer's Concept of Rhetorical Discourse." *Georgia Speech Communication Journal* 4 (1972), pp. 42–71. Builds on Bitzer (1968).

Poulakos, John. *Sophistical Rhetoric in Classical Greece.* Columbia, Mo., 1995. An important recent treatment of the topic.

Solmsen, Friedrich. "The Aristotelian Tradition in Ancient Rhetoric." *American Journal of Philology* 62 (1941), pp. 32–50, 169–190. One of the most significant twentieth-century articles on classical rhetoric.

Untersteiner, Mario. *The Sophists.* Translated by Kathleen Freeman. New York, 1954. Still a fund of useful information and provocative conjectures.

Vatz, Richard E. "The Myth of the Rhetorical Situation." *Philosophy and Rhetoric* 6 (1973), pp. 154–161. A head-on rebuttal of Bitzer (1968).

White, Eric Charles. *Kaironomia: On the Will-to-Invent.* Ithaca, N.Y., 1987. A thought-provoking assessment of rhetorical invention, with an interesting treatment of *kairos.*

—JOHN T. KIRBY

ORALITY AND LITERACY. The concept of orality stems from ethnographic descriptions of oral poetry in particular and of oral traditions in general. A foundational work is *The Singer of Tales,* by Albert B. Lord (2000), which documents the pioneering research of Milman Parry on oral traditions in the former Yugoslavia, from 1933 to 1935 (Parry, 1971). Parry died in 1935, at the beginning of his academic career, before he could publish the results of his research on living oral traditions; his own publications are limited almost entirely to his earlier research, which was based on the textual evidence of Homeric poetry. As a professor of ancient Greek, Parry had been seeking new answers to the so-called Homeric question, which centered on the historical circumstances that led to the composition of the Homeric *Iliad* and *Odyssey.* Basically, the question came down to this: were the Homeric poems composed with or without the aid of writing? Parry's project, the comparing of Homeric poetry with the living oral traditions of South Slavic heroic poetry, led him to conclude that the Homeric texts were indeed the products of oral composition. Parry's student Albert Lord conducted his own fieldwork in the former Yugoslavia after Parry's death (especially between 1950 and 1951), and *The Singer of Tales* represents the legacy of their combined efforts.

The cumulative work of Parry and Lord is generally considered to be the single most successful solution to the Homeric question, though debate among classicists continues concerning the historical contingencies of Homeric composition. The ultimate success of Parry and Lord, however, can best be measured by tracking the applicability of their methods to a wide range of literatures and preliteratures beyond the original focus on ancient Greek literature. In the case of preliteratures, Lord's *Singer of Tales* has become a foundational work for the ethnographic study of oral traditions in their many varieties, and the range of living oral traditions is worldwide: Scottish ballads, folkpreaching in the American South, Xhosa praise poetry, and the list can be extended to hundreds of other examples (bibliography in Foley 1985; the journal *Oral Tradition,* edited by John M. Foley since 1986, gives an idea of the vast range: see the representative entries in the bibliography below).

In the case of literatures, the application of the Parry–Lord method to ancient Greek traditions was extended by Lord to medieval traditions in Old English and Old French, and it has been further extended by other scholars to Old Norse, Middle English, Middle High German, Irish, Welsh, and other medieval European traditions. Even further, the Parry–Lord method has been applied to a vast variety of non-European literatures, including classical Arabic and Persian, Indic, and Chinese traditions (again, see the representative entries in the bibliography below). In effect, then, the methodology of Parry and Lord has transcended the Homeric question. Their work has led to an essential idea that goes far beyond the historical context of Homeric poetry or of any other tradition. That idea, as formulated by Parry and Lord, is that oral traditions formed the basis of literary traditions.

This is not to say that such thinking was without precedent. In fact, it did evolve ultimately from debate among classicists focusing on the Homeric question. Prototypical versions of the idea can be found in the Homeric theorizing of François Hédelin, Abbé d'Aubignac (*Conjectures académiques ou dissertation sur l'Iliade,* already as of 1664; posthumous publication 1715), Thomas Blackwell (*An Enquiry into the Life and Writings of Homer,* 1735), Giambattista Vico (*Principi di una scienza nuova,* 1744), and Robert Wood (*Essay on the Original Genius and Writings of Homer,* private publication 1767; posthumous edition 1769). The evolving idea reached a decisive phase in the work of two of history's most influential editors of Homer, Jean Baptiste Gaspard d'Ansse de Villoison (*Prolegomena* to his edition of the codex

"Venetus A" of the *Iliad,* 1788) and Friedrich August Wolf (*Prolegomena,* 1795, to his editions of the *Iliad,* 1804, and *Odyssey,* 1807). Both of these classicists posited a prehistory of oral poetry in the evolution of the Homeric *Iliad* and *Odyssey.* The notion of such a preliterate phase in the history of ancient Greek epic is also at work in the 1802 *Iliad* commentary of another major figure in the classics, Christian Gottlob Heyne. The impact of such notions encouraged a romantic view of oral poetry, as exemplified most prominently by Johann Gottfried Herder, who compared the preliterate phases of Homeric poetry with Germanic folk traditions (*Homer, ein Günstling der Zeit,* 1795). Romantic views of oral poetry led to the creation of literary folkloristic syntheses like Elias Lönnrot's *Kalevala* (1849; first ed. 1835), based on genuine Finnish oral traditions. The romantic literary appropriation of oral traditions could easily lead to abuses: some such literary productions were of dubious ethnographic value, as in the case of James Macpherson's recreations of Scottish highlands folklore in *The Complete Works of Ossian* (1765).

Given all these precedents, we may well ask why Parry and Lord are primarily credited with the definitive formulation of the general idea that oral traditions formed the basis of literary traditions. The answer is straightforward: Parry and Lord were the first to perfect a systematic way of comparing the internal evidence of living oral traditions, as observed in their fieldwork, with the internal evidence of literary traditions. It is primarily their methodology that we see reflected in the ongoing academic usage of such terms as *orality* and *oral theory.* (On the pitfalls of using the term *oral theory,* see Nagy, 1996, pp. 19–20).

The systematic comparatism of Parry and Lord required rigorous empiricism in analyzing the internal evidence of the living oral traditions—in their case, the South Slavic evidence—which was to be compared with the textual evidence of Homer. To be sure, there have also been other models of internal analysis: an outstanding example is the ethnographic research of Matija Murko on the epics of South Slavic Muslim peoples in the regions of Bosnia and Hercegovina (1913; see especially Lord, 2000, pp. 280–281n1). Another distinguished forerunner was Wilhelm Radloff, who investigated the Kara Kirghiz oral poetic traditions of Central Asia (1887; see Lord, 2000, p. 281n4). Such projects, however, were primarily descriptive, not comparative. In the case of Central Asian epics, for example, the systematic application of comparative methodology, as evident in the work of Karl Reichl (2000), is founded directly on the work of Parry and Lord.

What primarily distinguishes Parry and Lord from their predecessors, then, is their development of a systematic comparative approach to the study of oral traditions. The point of departure for their comparative work, which happened to be primarily the Muslim epic traditions of the former Yugoslavia, gave them an opportunity to test the living interactions of oral and literary traditions. They observed that the prestige of writing as a technology, and of the culture of literacy that it fostered, tended to destabilize the culture of oral traditions—in the historical context that they were studying. What they observed, however, was strictly a point of comparison with other possible test cases, not some kind of universalizing formulation (Mitchell and Nagy, 2000, p. xiii; *pace* Finnegan, 1976). For example, Lord himself makes it clear in his later work that there exist many cultures where literary traditions do not cause the destabilization of oral traditions and can even coexist with them (Lord, 1991; see also especially Lord, 1986b). In general, the textualization or *Verschriftung* of any given oral tradition needs to be distinguished from *Verschriftlichung*, that is, from the evolution of any given culture of literacy, any given *Schriftlichkeit* (Oesterreicher, 1993).

For Parry and Lord, the opposition of literacy and "orality"—of *Schriftlichkeit* and *Mündlichkeit*—is a cultural variable, not a universal. Moreover, their fieldwork experiments led them to think of literacy and "orality" as *cognitive* variables as well (Mitchell and Nagy, 2000, p. xiv). Moreover, just as "orality" defies universalization, so does literacy. The mechanics and even the concepts of reading and writing vary from culture to culture (Nagy, 1998; cf. Svenbro, 1993). A striking case in point is the cultural variability of such phenomena as *scriptio continua* and "silent reading" (Nagy, 2000; Gavrilov, 1997).

For Parry and Lord, the histories of literary and oral traditions, of literatures and preliteratures, were interrelated. To underline his observation that the mechanics and esthetics of oral and literary traditions are historically linked, Lord would even speak of "oral literature" (Lord, 1995, especially chapter 8). Further, Lord developed the comparative study of oral and literary traditions into a new branch of comparative literature (Guillén, 1993, pp. 173–179). It is no accident that Lord's *Singer of Tales* was originally published in a comparative literature monograph series, and that the author of the Preface of 1960 was Harry Levin, who at the time figured as the *doyen* of the new field of comparative literature—and who had actually taken part in Lord's thesis defense (Mitchell and Nagy, 2000, p. xvii).

Despite this stance of Parry and Lord, it has been claimed—many times and in many ways—that the Parry–Lord theory is founded on a hard-and-fast distinction between orality and literacy. These claims stem from unfamiliarity with the ethnographic dimension of Parry's and Lord's work, and, more generally, from ignorance about the observable mechanics and esthetics of oral traditions. Such unfamiliarity fuels prejudices, as reflected in the criticism directed at Lord for even attempting to undertake a comparison of South Slavic oral traditions with the literary traditions represented by the high cultures of the classical and medieval civilizations of Western Europe. The implicit presupposition, that oral traditions are inferior to the esthetic standards of Western literature, is tied to romanticized notions about distinctions between literacy and orality. As Mitchell and Nagy have recently argued (2000, p. xiv):

> Much of this kind of criticism, as Lord documents in his later books (1991a, 1995), has been shaped also by an overall ignorance of the historical facts concerning literacy and its cultural implications in the Balkans. Beside this additional obstacle, there is yet another closely related one: many Western scholars romanticize literacy itself as if it were some kind of uniform and even universal phenomenon—exempt from the historical contingencies of cultural and even cognitive variations. Such romanticism, combined with an ignorance of the ideological implications of literacy in the South Slavic world, have led to a variety of deadly prejudices against any and all kinds of oral traditions. In some cases, these prejudices have gone hand in hand with a resolute

blindness to the potential ideological agenda of literacy in its historical contexts.

Thus, the danger of Romanticism is two-sided: much as some humanists of the nineteenth century romanticized oral tradition as if it were some kind of universal phenomenon in and of itself, humanists today may be tempted to romanticize literacy as the key to "literature," often equated with "high" culture (on empirical approaches to distinctions between "high" and "low" culture, as occasionally formalized in distinctions between oral and written traditions; see Bausinger, 1980). Yet, the only universal distinction between oral and literary traditions is the historical anteriority of the first to the second. Beyond this obvious observation, it is pointless to insist on any universalizing definitions for the "oral" of "oral tradition." *Oral tradition* and *oral poetry* are terms that depend on the concepts of "written tradition" and "written poetry." In cultures that do not depend on the technology of writing, the concept of orality is meaningless (Lord, 1995, p. 105n26). From the standpoint of comparative ethnography, "Written is not something that is not oral; rather it is something in addition to being oral, and that additional something varies from society to society" (Nagy, 1990, p. 8). The absence of this technology has nothing to do with whether there can or cannot be poetics or rhetoric. Poetics and rhetoric exist without writing.

A common misconception about oral traditions is that they are marked by a lack of organization, cohesiveness, or unity. The problem here, again, is a general unfamiliarity with the ethnographic evidence from living oral traditions, which can be used to document a wide variety of poetics and rhetoric (see especially Lord, 1995). The verbal art or *Kunstsprache* of oral traditions can reach levels of virtuosity that are indirectly or sometimes even directly comparable to what is admired in the classics of script and print cultures. In some cultural contexts, the *Kunstsprache* of oral traditions can be even more precise than that of counterparts in literary traditions, because the genres of oral poetics and rhetoric tend to be more regularly observed (Smith, 1974; Ben-Amos, 1976; Slatkin, 1987). In the history of literature, genres can become irregular through a striving for individual greatness: if we follow the perspec-

tive of Benedetto Croce (1902), a literary work is great because it defies genres, because it is sui generis.

By contrast, the forms of genres in oral traditions are sustained by the forms of everyday speech in everyday life. Thus the *Kunstsprache* of oral tradition allows its participants to "connect," even in modern times (Martin, 1993, p. 227):

> Modern hearers of a traditional epic in cultures where the song making survives are observed to comment appreciatively on the smallest verbal changes, not in the way a three-year-old demands the exact words of a bedtime text, but with a full knowledge of the dozens of ways the teller could have spun out a line at a given point in the narrative. In a living oral tradition, people are exposed to verbal art constantly, not just on specific entertainment occasions, which can happen every night in certain seasons. When they work, eat, drink, and do other social small-group activities, myth, song, and saying are always woven into their talk. Consequently, it is not inaccurate to describe them as bilingual, fluent in their natural language but also in the *Kunstsprache* of their local verbal art forms.

[*See also* Law; *and* Speech acts, utterances as.]

BIBLIOGRAPHY

Bakker, E. J. *Poetry in Speech. Orality and Homeric Discourse.* Ithaca, N.Y., 1997. An empirical study of syntactical patterns typical of oral traditions and even of "everyday" speech, as preserved in the text of the Homeric poems.

Bauman, R. *Verbal Art as Performance.* Prospect Heights, Ill., 1977. A sophisticated analysis of various types and degrees of interaction between performance and composition as combined aspects of oral traditions.

Bausinger, H. *Formen der "Volkspoesie."* 2d ed. Berlin, 1980. A historical study of culturally and ideologically determined distinctions between "high art" and "low art," as associated respectively with literary and oral traditions.

Ben-Amos, D. "Analytical Categories and Ethnic Genres." *Folklore Genres.* Edited by D. Ben-Amos, pp. 215–242. Austin, 1976. A wide-ranging survey of variations in the forms and functions of genres in oral traditions.

Blackburn, S. H., P. J. Claus, J. B. Flueckiger, and S. S. Wadley, eds. *Oral Epics in India.* Berkeley, 1989. Ethnographic approaches to oral traditions as analyzed in their historical contexts, with special attention to the mechanics of diffusion (and the changes related to the widening or narrowing of the radius of diffusion). A striking example of the potential coextensiveness of oral and written traditions: oral traditions can aetiologize themselves in terms of written traditions (p. 32n25).

Croce, B. *Estetica.* 2d ed. Bari, 1902. A foundational meditation on creative tensions between great works of literature and the genres to which they are supposed to belong.

Davidson, O. M. *Comparative Literature and Classical Persian Poetry.* Bibliotheca Iranica, Intellectual Traditions Series, no. 4. Costa Mesa, Calif., 1999. Explores the intellectual history of expanding the methodology of comparative literature by including the study of oral poetics, especially with reference to classical literary forms that stem ultimately from oral traditions.

Finnegan, R. "What is Oral Literature Anyway? Comments in the Light of Some African and Other Comparative Material." In *Oral–Formulaic Theory: A Folklore Casebook.* Edited by J. M. Foley, pp. 243–282. New York, 1990. First published 1976. Disputes any universalizing distinction between "orality" and literacy, claiming that Parry and Lord had sought to establish such a distinction. An underlying assumption in the book: that the concept of "oral" can be equated with anything that is *performed.* Both the claim and the assumption are disputed by Lord, 1995.

Foley, J. M. *Oral-Formulaic Theory and Research: An Introduction and Annotated Bibliography.* New York, 1985. The editor's Introduction offers a general survey of a wide range of oral traditions throughout the world, with extensive bibliography of ongoing research applying the methods of Parry, Lord, and others.

Gavrilov, A. K. 1997. "Techniques of Reading in Classical Antiquity." *Classical Quarterly* 47 (1997), pp. 56–73. Investigates the cultural and cognitive variables of "silent reading" and reading out loud; concludes that a mutually exclusive dichotomy is untenable.

Goody, J., and I. Watt. "The Consequences of Literacy." In *Literacy in Traditional Societies.* Edited by J. Goody, pp. 27–68. Cambridge, U.K., 1968. Argues that literacy produces measurable differences in cognitive capacity; the argument is weakened by a lack of descriptive specificity in considering the forms of oral traditions in any given historical context.

Guillén, C. *Entre lo uno y lo diverso. Introducción a la literatura comparada.* Barcelona, 1985.

Guillén, C. *The Challenge of Comparative Literature.* Harvard Studies in Comparative Literature, no. 42. Cambridge, Mass., 1993. Situates the study of oral traditions within the academic discipline of comparative literature.

Johnson, J. W. "Yes, Virginia, There Is an Epic in Africa." *Research in African Literatures* 11 (1980), pp. 308–326. A spirited polemic concerning the application of universalizing criteria in describing the genres of oral traditions.

Lord, A. B. "Perspectives on Recent Work on the Oral Traditional Formula." In *Oral–Formulaic Theory: A Folklore Casebook.* Edited by J. M. Foley, pp. 379–405. New York, 1990. First published 1986a. Continuation of the bibliographical survey in Lord, 1974. Another vital supplement.

Lord, A. B. "The Merging of Two Worlds: Oral and Written Poetry as Carriers of Ancient Values." In *Oral Tradition in Literature: Interpretation in Context.* Edited by J. M. Foley, pp. 19–64. Columbia, Mo., 1986b. A seminal study of historical coextensiveness between the poetry performed in the coffee houses, as observed by Parry and Lord, and the poetry of the court poets in the "good old days" of Ottoman rule.

Lord, A. B. "Perspectives on Recent Work on Oral Literature." In *Oral–Formulaic Theory: A Folklore Casebook.* Edited by J. M. Foley. New York, 1990. First published 1974. A bibliographical essay surveying the ongoing research on oral traditions throughout the world. A vital supplement to the abbreviated bibliography given here.

Lord, A. B. *Epic Singers and Oral Tradition.* Ithaca, N.Y., 1991a. Explores oral "lyric" as well as "epic." In-depth reassessments of debates over "orality" and literacy.

Lord, A. B. "Homer's Originality: Oral Dictated Texts." In *Epic Singers and Oral Tradition.* Ithaca, N.Y., 1991b. First published 1953. It was rewritten, with minimal changes, for the present work, pp. 38–48 (with an "Addendum 1990" at pp. 47–48). An engaging attempt to reconcile the transmitted text of the Homeric poems, as a historical given, with empirical observations about the process of composition-in-performance as found in living oral traditions.

Lord, A. B. *The Singer Resumes the Tale.* Edited by M. L. Lord. Ithaca, N.Y., 1995. A posthumous publication, originally intended as a direct continuation of *Singer of Tales.* Sustained rebuttal of critics who insist on the inferiority of "orality" to literacy.

Lord, A. B. *The Singer of Tales.* 2d ed. Harvard Studies in Comparative Literature, no. 24. Cambridge, Mass., 2000. First published 1960. With a new Introduction by S. Mitchell and G. Nagy. This book remains the most definitive introduction to the pioneering research of Parry and Lord. The first part documents their findings in the course of their ethnographic research on the living oral traditions that they recorded in the former Yugoslavia; the second part applies these findings as points of comparison with the textual evidence of ancient Greek and medieval European epic.

Martin, R. P. *The Language of Heroes: Speech and Performance in the Iliad.* Ithaca, N.Y., 1989. A case study of oral poetic sub-genres embedded within the "super-genre" of epic, with special attention to applications of "speech-act" theory.

Martin, R. P. "Telemachus and the Last Hero Song." *Colby Quarterly* 29 (1993), pp. 222–240. A critical reassessment of epic as the essential genre of "heroic" poetry.

Mitchell, S., and G. Nagy. "Introduction." In *The Singer of Tales,* by A. B. Lord, pp. vii–xxix. Cambridge, Mass., 2000. Offers historical background on the evolution of Lord's work and on its connections to the earlier work of Parry. Summarizes the impact of Parry's and Lord's combined legacy on such fields as classics, comparative literature, and folklore studies.

Nagy, G. *Pindar's Homer: The Lyric Possession of an Epic Past.* Rev. ed. Baltimore, 1994. First published 1990. Examines the interactions of theme/formula/meter in both "epic" and "lyric" traditions, with special reference to the historical context of archaic Greece.

Nagy, G. *Homeric Questions.* Austin, 1996. Addresses ten basic "misreadings" of Parry and Lord; provides explanatory models for the historical contingencies of transition from oral to written traditions.

Nagy, G. 1998. "Homer as 'Text' and the Poetics of Cross-Reference." In *Script Oralia,* edited by C. Ehler and U. Schaefer, vol. 95, *Verschriftung und Verschriftlichung: Aspekte des Medienwechsels in verschiedenen Kulturen und Epochen,* pp. 78–87. Tübingen, 1998.

Nagy, G. "Reading Greek Poetry Aloud: Evidence from the Bacchylides Papyri." *Quaderni Urbinati di Cultura Classica* 64 (2000), pp. 7–28. Examines phenomena of literacy that defy universalization, such as the practice of *scriptio continua* in archaic, classical, and post-classical Greek, to be contrasted with the practice of leaving spaces for word-boundaries, as in the traditions of writing Hebrew.

Nagy, J. F. "Orality in Medieval Irish Narrative." *Oral Tradition* 1 (1986), pp. 272–301. A detailed survey of evidence provided by the contents and the conventions of the narratives themselves.

Niditch, S. *Oral World and Written Word: Ancient Israelite Literature.* Library of Ancient Israel. Louisville, Ky., 1996. A lively confrontation of scripture, as the ultimate written word, with the rhetoric of the spoken word.

Oesterreicher, W. "*Verschriftung* und *Verschriftlichung* im Kontext medialer und konzeptioneller Schriftlichkeit." In *Schriftlichkeit im frühen Mittelalter.* Edited by U. Schaefer, pp. 267–292. Tübingen, 1993. Shows that the historical circumstances of transformations from nonliterate to literate societies are notable for their diversity.

Okpewho, I. *The Epic in Africa: Toward a Poetics of the Oral Performance.* New York, 1979. A sound ethnographic *and* literary survey, leading to a critical reassessment of epic as a genre.

Opland, J. "Xhosa: The Structure of Xhosa Eulogy and the Relation of Eulogy to Epic." In *Traditions of Heroic and Epic Poetry,* edited by J. B. Hainsworth and A. T. Hatto, vol. 2, *Characteristics and Techniques.* pp. 121–143. London, 1989. This study describes a distinct genre, the praise poetry of the Xhosa, and then proceeds to compare it with the ancient Greek genre of epic. By recognizing praise poetry as distinct from epic, this work avoids the imposition of external models on the internal evidence of the oral tradition being examined.

Parry, M. *The Making of Homeric Verse: The Collected Papers of Milman Parry.* Edited by A. Parry. Oxford, 1971. The first part contains Parry's work on the Homeric texts, before he undertook his fieldwork research in the former Yugoslavia. The second part combines his experience in fieldwork with his expertise in the organization of Homeric poetry.

Radloff, W. *Proben der Volksliteratur der nördlichen türkischen Stämme,* vol. 5, *Der Dialekt der Kara-Kirgisen.* Saint Petersburg, 1885. A distinguished prototype of research in the "field," with a focus on the oral traditions of Central Asia.

Reichl, K. *Singing the Past: Turkic and Medieval Poetry.* Ithaca, N.Y., 2000. Continues where Radloff left off, a century later. Centers on typological parallels to the oral traditions studied by Parry and Lord.

Slatkin, L. M. "Genre and Generation in the *Odyssey.*" *METIS: Revue d'Anthropologie du Monde Grec Ancien* 1 (1987), pp. 259–268. Views genres in oral traditions as neatly complementary to each other, diachronically as well as synchronically.

Smith, P. "Des genres et des hommes." *Poétique* 19 (1974), pp. 294–312. Acute synchronic perspectives on the complementarity of genres in oral traditions.

Svenbro, J. *Phrasikleia: Anthropologie de la lecture en Grèce ancienne.* Paris, 1988.

Svenbro, J. *Phrasikleia: An Anthropology of Reading in Ancient Greece.* Rev. ed. Translation by J. Lloyd. Ithaca, N.Y., 1993. Disputes universalist definitions of reading as a cognitive activity. Examines the mentality of equating the activity of reading out loud with the act of lending one's voice to the letters being processed by one's eyes.

Toelken, J. B. "An Oral Canon for the Child Ballads: Construction and Application." *Journal of the Folklore Institute* 5 (1967), pp. 75–101. Vigorous application of comparative ethnographic evidence to the text of a collection shaped by Child's text-bound criteria.

Zumthor, P. *La Poésie de la Voix dans la civilisation médiévale.* Paris, 1984. Uses the textual evidence of medieval literature to highlight the dynamics of oral traditions as revealed by the variability or *mouvance* inherent in the textual transmission.

Zwettler, M. J. *The Oral Tradition of Classical Arabic Poetry.* Columbus, Ohio, 1978. Studies the rich documentation of variant readings in the textual history of Arabic poetry as a reflex of variations in oral poetry.

—GREGORY NAGY

ORATORY. Although in a formal sense we might associate the practice of oratory in ancient Greece with the development of the art of rhetoric in the fifth century BCE, it in fact goes back much further. In the two earliest extant Greek texts, Homer's *Iliad* and *Odyssey,* we find debate and oratory employed on a variety of occasions where speakers address public audiences at some length. In the world depicted in Homer, men win renown not only for their prowess on the battlefield, but also for the wisdom and persuasiveness of their advice in political assemblies and councils. Two Homeric figures are most closely associated with oratorical ability. The first is Nestor, a wise elder statesman, characterized as "Nestor the fair-spoken . . . the lucid speaker of Pylos, from whose lips the stream of words ran sweeter than honey" (*Iliad* 1.247–249, Lattimore translation). If Nestor unambiguously characterizes the positive aspects of sound political advice expressed through clear, honest, and forceful persuasive speech, the character of Odysseus embodies the broader potential of the spoken word. Odysseus is also renowned for his ability to persuade, advise, and contrive strategies, but in his case this ability is closely connected to deceit, trickery, and lies. As Athena affectionately chides him when she reveals herself in Book 13 of the *Odyssey,* "You wretch, so devious, never weary of tricks, then you would not even in your own country give over your ways of deceiving and your thievish tales. They are near to your very nature. But come, let us talk no more of this, for you and I both know sharp practice, since you are by far the best of all mortal men for counsel and stories, and I among all the divinities for wit and sharpness"

(*Odyssey* 293–299, Lattimore translation New York, 1975).

The preeminence of these two characters in Homer's pantheon of heroes represents the two faces of Greek oratory in the later world of the classical *polis.* Great speakers may be praised for the persuasiveness of their wise council or damned as treacherous deceivers, self-interested demagogues who lead the public astray. While Odysseus's abilities earn him unreserved renown in the quasi-anarchic heroic culture depicted by Homer, in the world of the classical *polis* the recognition of the destructive potential of such "sharp practice" leads the tragedians to use the figure of Odysseus to embody the unscrupulous and amoral orator/politician, as in Sophocles' play, *Philoctetes.* To understand why oratory occupies such a central yet ambiguous place in the culture of the *polis,* we must step back and consider the nature of classical political and legal institutions.

The Institutional Context. In his discussion of the nature of the peculiarly Greek conception of political community conveyed by the word *polis,* Aristotle (384–322 BCE) considers the question of size. If a political community is too small, it cannot be a *polis* because it would not be self-sufficient. On the other hand, if the population is too large, he argues, it would be a nation (*ethnos*) rather than a *polis* because, among other things, no mortal would have a voice loud enough to address the assembled population (*Politics* 1326b1–8). For Aristotle, and here he is representative of Greek (and especially Athenian) thinking, a *polis* is a political community that governs itself through the medium of reasoned speech (*logos*). [*See* Logos.] It is this capacity that distinguishes human beings from animals (*Politics* 1253a8–19). The citizen of a *polis,* for Aristotle, is one who uses this capacity "to rule and be ruled," that is, to participate in the political and judicial institutions of his city (*Politics* 1274b32–1275b22). What all of this implies, of course, is that oratory is at the very core of the life of the *polis,* and most forcefully so in democratic ones. (Aristotle concedes that his definition of citizenship best fits cities with some form of democracy.) In Athens, the Greek *polis* about which we know by far the most, political and judicial decisions were not made behind closed doors but in public. The vehicle by which those decisions were made was oratory and debate. This points up another crucial feature of Greek oratory, which is that it generally operated in a competitive context. Ancient Greek society may be classified as agonistic because almost all arenas of political and cultural life were imbued with a strong spirit of competition. Given the participatory nature of citizenship and self-governance described above, this meant that all citizens could, in principle, hope to compete for prestige and renown in a variety of public settings. Mastery of the spoken word was vital to success for anyone with such ambitions.

It is difficult for those accustomed to thinking of public life in modern terms to appreciate the importance of oratory in the largely oral culture of a society like democratic Athens. A brief consideration of the nature of Athenian political institutions in the period of the "radical democracy," from the midfifth to the late fourth centuries, will help to explain why this is the case. The two most important institutions in Athens were the Assembly and the law courts. The former was open to any citizen who wished to attend. Any citizen (except those who had been penalized with the loss of legal rights; women, however, were not considered citizens) could address the Assembly or propose a measure for its consideration. Proposals were debated and decisions made by a vote of those attending. To enter into debate required addressing a mass audience of perhaps six thousand citizens gathered in an outdoor amphitheater. The speaker had to be capable of projecting his voice to an audience this large; nor were the Athenians tolerant of poor speakers. One would also have to be prepared to speak above the boos, catcalls, or mutterings of those who opposed one's point of view. As numerous critics of the Athenian Assembly inform us, the audience (at least in their view) was particularly likely to follow the advice of those who were skilled and forceful speakers. As one might expect, training in how best to persuade such audiences was valued by young men bent on political careers. Indeed, those who vied for leadership roles in the management of the affairs of the *polis*, whom we would call "politicians," were referred to by the Greeks as *rhētors*, that is, orators, those who engage in rhetoric. Oratory was, from this perspective, indistinguishable from political activity. The prestige of political leadership was not bestowed by the nomination of political parties, but by the ability of one's speeches consistently to persuade the Assembly that one had the best advice to give.

The law courts were no less dominated by oratory. Like the pursuit of political leadership, a lawsuit was also seen as a contest, or competition. Lawsuits are thus frequently described in Greek by the word *agōn*, meaning a competitive struggle. Litigation, which will be discussed in more detail below, consisted of little more than two opposing speeches. First the judges heard an opening speech by the plaintiff and then a speech in response by the defendant. After the two speeches, the judges voted immediately, without discussing the case among themselves. The participants were all ordinary citizens. Litigants were required to speak for themselves. There were no attorneys, though one could engage the services of a speechwriter (*logographos*). One would still have to deliver the lengthy oration oneself to the mass audience of 201 or 501 lay judges. Being a defendant would have meant that one could not simply read a prepared text because one would have to adapt one's argument to what the plaintiff had alleged. Thus, even ordinary citizens with no aspirations for political power might find themselves, in this highly litigious society, confronted with the necessity of delivering a formal oration to a large audience. There were no professional judges or jurists in Athens. Judges for a particular case were selected by lot from a panel of six thousand citizens over thirty years of age who had volunteered to serve (for which, after a point, they received a small sum in payment). Because the judges had no special training of any kind, they were, in a sense, largely like the audience of the Assembly, representing the *dēmos*, the people of Athens (more accurately, adult males of citizen status). For reasons that will be elaborated upon later, one can see how the political struggles of the Assembly could intrude upon the judicial realm. Athenian orators thus had to be equally ready to operate in either institutional setting.

Development of the Oratorical Tradition in Fifth-Century Athens. Tradition has it that the formal study of rhetoric was introduced to Athens in the last three decades of the fifth century BCE. The figure conventionally associated with this development was the Sophist Gorgias, who visited Athens in 427 BCE. [*See* Sophists.] There is little doubt that Gorgias's oratory made a vivid impression on the Athenians. Gorgias was famous for his adaptation of poetic devices to public speaking and the highly mannered style evident in his few extant works like the *Encomium of Helen*. Plato's dialogue *Gorgias,* whatever the accuracy of its portrayal of the historical Gorgias, doubtless captures the way in which would-be teachers of oratory (like Polus in the *Gorgias*) or aspiring young politicians (like Callicles) would flock to hear the oratorical displays of such famous figures. They would also seek instruction, for which they were prepared to pay well. The nature and shortcomings of the kind of education offered by famous orators is perhaps most famously depicted in Plato's dialogue *Phaedrus,* though it must be remembered that Plato (c.428–c.347 BCE) was by no means a disinterested observer. Phaedrus is there depicted as memorizing and repeatedly declaiming a display oration he has heard performed by Lysias, the noted late-fifth-century speechwriter and orator. Plato criticizes the uncritical imitation and rote learning, which he views as characterizing contemporary oratorical training. Does all this mean, however, that the Athenian oratorical tradition begins with this introduction of formal training in the art of rhetoric? Clearly, as the introductory section on oratory in Homer already implied, it does not. Although our knowledge of earlier periods is very incomplete, at the very least, the career of Pericles demonstrates that great oratory was already valued and practiced in Athens as the foundation of political leadership well before Gorgias's visit and the introduction of formal rhetorical training. The career of the well-known Athenian orator, politician, and speechwriter Antiphon also begins more than a decade before Gorgias's visit.

In his history, *The Peloponnesian War,* Thucydides (died c.401 BCE) depicts an Athens where political oratory is highly developed and is, moreover, the central vehicle for political deliberation. Pericles looms large in the early part of Thucydides' history, until his death some two years after the war began in 431 BCE. Despite the near certainty that the speeches, which are the main instrument of his analysis, were largely written by Thucydides rather than the speakers he depicts as delivering them, we can nonetheless be quite confident that these debates mirror the political and oratorical culture of the period. [*See* History.]

Thucydides describes Pericles in words that reflect the Greek conception of political excellence (*aretē*) as being most highly embodied in an individual who is preeminent both as a speaker of words and a doer of deeds. (The antithesis of word and deed is fundamental in Greek political thought, and many other contexts, from Homer onward.) He introduces the first of Pericles' three speeches with the following comment: "Among the speakers was Pericles, the son of Xanthippus, the leading man of his time among the Athenians and the most powerful in both action and debate" (1.139, Rex Warner translation, Harmandsworth, 1954). Through his intelligence, integrity, and powerful oratory, Pericles so dominated the politics of his period that, "In what was nominally a democracy, power was really in the hand of a first citizen" (2.65). Thus, Pericles was able to prevail so consistently in debate that during his lifetime, the policies of the Athenian Assembly became virtually identical with the political vision of its foremost speaker. This must in part explain why the speeches of other Thucydidean speakers are always paired with an opponent in debate, whereas Pericles' orations stand alone. What was the secret of Pericles' success as an orator? As depicted by Thucydides, Pericles' political oratory is a model of political deliberation as rational calculation. In his two major policy speeches in Books 1 and 2, Pericles lays out for his audience the different factors that must be taken into account, weighs the advantages and disadvantages, analyzes the various contingencies and possible countermoves by Athens' enemies, and explains why his own suggested course of action will best serve Athens' interests. Thus, one central feature of Pericles' oratory is its reliance on rational argument. Another feature, however, adds to the persuasive force of his arguments, and that is his character. [*See* Ēthos.] Thucydides comments that because of his known integrity, Pericles could lead without arousing suspicion that he did so from self-interested motives. This enabled him to speak bluntly and honestly to the Assembly so as to prod them into following (in his view) the wisest course in moments of crisis. Pericles himself uses this argument from his character when the Athenians have begun to realize that considerable hardship will follow his policy of going to war with Sparta, at least in the short run: "So far as I am concerned, if you are angry with me you are angry with one who has, I think, at least as much ability as anyone else to see what needs to be done and to explain what he sees, one who loves his city and who is above being influenced by money" (2.60).

Viewed in this light, in the figure of Pericles, Thucydides may be regarded as constructing an ideal of antidemagogic oratory. The essential elements are honesty in expressing one's opinion, presentation of a rational calculation of policy from a long-term perspective, and a character of absolute integrity so as lend one's arguments greater persuasive force. Thucydides' ideal sets the stage for the contrast with those leaders who emerged after Pericles' death. The Athenians followed Pericles, because "he never sought power from any wrong motive . . . [and] was under no necessity of flattering them." His successors, on the other hand, "who were more on a level with each other and each of whom aimed at occupying first place, adopted methods of demagogy which resulted in their losing control over the actual conduct of affairs" (2.65). Thucydides' portrayal of post-Periclean politics depicts a process of political deliberation where orators in their quest for influence increasingly adopt a style at odds with the antidemagogic ideal. This new oratorical style, personified most clearly by Thucydides in the person of Cleon, relies on attacking the character and motives of one's opponent and arousing the emotions of the audience.

In his famous account of the Mytilenean Debate, Thucydides captures the political dilemmas brought about by this new state of affairs by juxtaposing two speeches out of the many that were made as the Athenian Assembly struggled with its decision. At issue is not just the fate of a city (Mytilene, on the island of Lesbos) that has surrendered to the Athenians, but also the very character of public discourse at Athens. For Thucydides, and many other Athenian thinkers, this meant no less than that the political fate of the Athenian democracy (and its empire) were at stake in this contest over the nature and proper role of oratory as a medium for political decision making.

The city of Mytilene had, under the influence of an oligarchic faction, revolted against Athens. After a protracted siege, the city surrendered and the Athenian Assembly, "in their *angry* mood," took the decision to put not only the oligarchs, but also the entire male population to death, and to sell the women and children into slavery. Thucydides tells us virtually nothing about the speeches that led to this decision. Instead, he focuses upon the debate that took place the next day, "when there was a *sudden change of feeling* and people began to think how cruel and unprecedented their decision was. . . ." (3.36, my emphasis). This debate to a significant degree centers on the larger issue of whether arousing anger and other emotions or rational calculation of Athenian interests should serve as the proper mode of persuasion employed in political oratory. [*See* Pathos.] It is no coincidence then that Thucydides describes Cleon, who speaks for the destruction of Mytilene as follows: "He was remarkable among the Athenians for the violence of his character and at this time he exercised far the greatest influence over the people" (3.36). Indeed, Cleon's speech serves as a Thucydidean portrait of the essence of demagogic oratory.

Much ink has been spilled in commentary on the Mytilenean Debate. For our purposes, however, three points are of central importance in Cleon's speech. First, he attacks the very notion of oratorical debates as the right way for a democratic *polis* to govern itself: "Personally I have had occasion often enough already to observe that a democracy is incapable of governing others, and I am all the more convinced of this when I see how you are changing your mind about the Mytileneans." Second, he attacks the character of his opponents by arguing that anyone who urged the Athenians to use debates to think carefully about whether their policy is wise, must be doing so from highly suspect or criminal motives. Thus, he claims, his opponents, who urge full debate, are "intellectuals" who in trying to show off their abilities "very often bring ruin on their country" and who "must have been bribed to put together some elaborate speech with which [they] will try to lead you off the right track" (3.38). Third, the right way for the Athenian Assembly to reach decisions is to stop wasting their time listening to clever speeches and to act quickly before their anger has cooled (2.38). The proper role of the orator, as exemplified by the central thrust of Cleon's speech, is to use his words to arouse the anger of the audience and to encourage them to act on it.

To Cleon's fiery invective, Thucydides juxtaposes, through the person of an otherwise unknown figure named Diodotus, the antidemagogic model of oratorical debate as the only possible vehicle for rational calculation of policy and wise governance. His opening words deserve to be quoted at length:

> I do not blame those who have proposed a new debate on the subject of Mytilene, and I do not share the view . . . that it is a bad thing to have frequent deliberations on matters of importance. Haste and anger are, to my mind, the two greatest obstacles to wise counsel. . . . And anyone who maintains that words cannot be a guide to action must either be fool or one with some personal interest at stake; he is a fool if he imagines that it is possible to deal with the uncertainties of the future by any other medium. . . . The good citizen, instead of trying to terrify the opposition, ought to prove his case in fair argument. . . . (3.42)

Thucydides presents the reader with a series of orators and leaders (from Athens, Sparta, and Syracuse) who embody this ideal of oratory. In this regard, he is starkly at variance with oratory's most vehement ancient critic, Plato, who, in his dialogue *Gorgias,* condemned even men like Pericles and Themistocles as mere panderers to the mob.

While Plato believes (even in his most charitable opinion, as articulated in *Phaedrus*) that at best oratory can hope to be a useful handmaiden to philosophy, Thucydides' view is quite different and offers us an important insight into the way oratory was regarded by its most famous Greek practitioners, the Athenians. Thucydides is well aware of the harmful effects that oratory can have on the political process. Indeed, in the Mytilenean Debate, his account of civil war in Corcyra, and in many other passages, he presents with devastating clarity what harm can ensue when public discourse becomes debased by self-seeking leaders under the pressure of war or national crises. But at the same time, as he has Diodotus argue, he is well aware that a self-governing political community (unlike a tyranny) has no other choice but to employ persuasive discourse because the *logos* (word, speech, argument, discourse, reason) is the only medium by which human beings can wisely govern a well-ordered political community. In this regard, he is very close to the views of Aristotle mentioned above. He is also expressing the dominant cultural understanding of oratory in Athenian society. The tirades of Plato should not blind us to the fact that Athenians were well aware of the dangers of oratory. These dangers are explored in Athenian comedy, tragedy, historiography, and the speeches of the orators themselves. This awareness is also manifested in the tendency of the Athenians to prosecute and harshly punish orators who, rightly or wrongly, they felt had led them astray. But they also realized that true democracy and oratory were inseparable. Indeed, as Diodotus puts it, deliberative issues facing a political community "cannot be dealt with by any other medium." [*See* Deliberative genre.]

Thucydides offers us a view, *his* view, of how oratory developed in the late fifth century from its use by Pericles as the means of steering the *dēmos* (the people) on a wise course, to its contested identity as a new generation of orators emerged after the death of Pericles. In a way, his *History* may be read as a catalog of the possibilities for oratory under crisis conditions when states confront their most difficult decisions. Many of these conditions still prevailed in the fourth century, the golden age of Attic oratory, and the tensions and ambivalence they produced remained a powerful presence. Part of Thucydides' view of oratory is clearly that the greatest practitioner of the art in his lifetime was Pericles. While in later classical antiquity, orators like Cicero (106–43 BCE) would single out Demosthenes (384–322 BCE) as Athens' greatest speaker, it is also probably the case that today the single best-known Greek oration is not from one of the Ten Attic Orators. (This canon, though established later, played a large role in determining which orators' works survived. The Ten are Antiphon, Andocides, Isocrates, Lysias, Isaeus, Demosthenes, Aeschines, Lycurgus, Hyperides, and Dinarchus.) The best-known oration is, in contrast, the Periclean Funeral Oration in Book 2 (35–46) of Thucydides. This work is neither a political nor a forensic speech, but rather falls into the third class of oratory, epideictic or display oratory: speeches delivered in contests or to commemorate great public occasions. [*See* Epideictic genre.] This Funeral Oration (leaving aside the vexing issue of to what extent it represents Pericles' own words) vividly demonstrated the power of great oratory to transcend its own limitations and the occasion on which it is delivered. It offers a vision of Athens' identity as a political community that expresses the ideals of Athenian democracy and Athens' cultural mission with a force great enough to have inspired later ages to model themselves on an imagined construction of the Periclean Age. The contrast between these ideals and the realities of Athenian behavior under the pressures of war and other disasters is brought out in the ensuing description of the Plague (2.47–54) as well as in the famous Melian Dialogue in Book 5.

While Pericles had a natural genius for oratory, as exemplified in the Funeral Oration and his other speeches, teachers of oratory claimed to be able to train those less gifted to be effective speakers and leaders. This kind of instruction served to professionalize and standardize oratory, to encourage the belief that anyone can become an orator, not just those rare, naturally talented, great speakers like Pericles. Here lies the beginning of a debate that would be continued by rhetoricians for centuries (as in Cicero's *De oratore* and *Brutus*) about the role of training as opposed to talent, and whether the truly great orator, as opposed to the merely competent, can be produced by such education. In Athens, the availability of formal training and the circulation of rhetorical handbooks served to broaden access to oratory, at least to those who could pay. This is a limited, but doubtless far wider group than the natural and social elite to which Pericles belonged. Indeed, part of the criticism of demagogy was that it enabled "lower" strata to compete successfully for political influence. Oratorical training offered possibilities for social mobility and power in opening the path of leadership to ambitious young men who could master its techniques. Nonetheless, with some very important exceptions, most political leaders came from the wealthier strata because they had both the means to pay teachers and the leisure to pursue a political career. In turning to oratory in the fourth century, we will examine how oratory functioned in the competition of this elite in the context of Athenian politics and litigation.

The Fourth Century: Oratory Comes of Age. Our understanding of fourth-century Athens is largely shaped by oratory. While the historians (Herodotus and Thucydides) and the dramatists (Aeschylus, Sophocles, Euripides, Aristophanes) are the mirrors of fifth-century Athens, to a very significant degree, we see fourth-century Athenian society and politics through the eyes of the orators, especially Demosthenes, Aeschines, Isocrates, and Isaeus. Philosophy is the other major intellectual tradition of the fourth century that survives. [*See* Philosophy, *article on* Rhetoric and philosophy.] Working out the proper relationship between rhetoric and philosophy was one of the great intellectual projects of the fourth century, from the hostility of Plato to the attempts of Isocrates (436–338 BCE) and Aristotle (384–322 BCE) to describe a framework of complementarity. While Plato's school of philosophy, the Academy (and later the school of his pupil, Aristotle) represented one pole of Athenian higher education, Isocrates' training of ambitious young men (who could pay his notoriously high tuition) in oratory and the other skills required for political leadership, represented the other. Although the corpus of works by Isocrates includes numerous "orations," he himself, perhaps due to a weak voice but also doubtless to other reasons as well, was not a practicing orator. In his early career, he wrote forensic speeches for pay, but then in the fourth century he turned his activities toward educating orator-politicians and writing texts on a variety of political subjects, which took the form of speeches, but were only published in written form. [*See* Forensic genre.] Perhaps Isocrates' best-known contribution to oratory is his attempt to demonstrate that moral virtue and effective persuasion in the political arena were compatible, a proposition strongly denied by Plato. Judging by the surviving fourth-century orations, it cannot be said, however, that Isocrates' educational ideal had a significant impact upon rhetorical practice.

If Pericles is the figure who largely defines the politics of his age, it is Demosthenes who occupies a similar position in fourth-century Athens. The very significant differences between them tell us much about some of the shifts in Athenian political culture in general and in oratory in particular. Unlike Pericles, whose activities were squarely focused in the political and military realms, Demosthenes first made his reputation as a professional orator and speechwriter. Pericles enjoyed not only great wealth, but also aristocratic birth, the combination of which, together with his natural talents, preordained him for a leadership role in the society of his day. Demosthenes, however, whose family was by no means poor, struggled first to make his reputation in the law courts. He did this both through protracted interfamilial litigation concerning his inheritance as well as through writing speeches for clients who sought his services. After almost a decade of having established a reputation through such activity, he entered public life in 351 with his first political oration. Though in the latter part of his career he concentrated his activities on politics, he continued to operate in the courts because in his day they had become an adjunct arena for political struggle. Before examining this phenomenon, we should first consider the state of fourth-century forensic oratory.

Demosthenes was clearly a master of courtroom oratory. Apart from his command of style and rhetorical technique, one also finds in some of his speeches perhaps the best exposition of legal issues anywhere in the fourth-century oratorical canon. Having said this, however, it is also true that in much of his forensic oratory the driving persuasive force is conveyed through invective and emotional appeals (*pathos*). Demosthenes constructs these appeals with consummate skill and great intensity. Indeed, he was famed in antiquity for the intensity and earnestness of both his forensic and deliberative orations. In orations of great length and complexity, he is able to marshal a mass of facts, arguments, tangential narratives, and allegations, while maintaining both a high emotional pitch and a persuasive focus on a central point, which he unrelentingly hammers home again and again. In doing so, no accusation against his opponent is too low and no emotional appeal too sentimental to be included in his repertoire. For example, in a lawsuit he brought against a very prominent, influential, and wealthy Athenian named Meidias, he goes far beyond the acts legally in question to paint his opponent in the blackest terms. Having cata-

loged the countless evil acts that Meidias has inflicted on other Athenians, he raises the question of Meidias's birth, suggesting that he is actually of foreign origin and, hence not even really a citizen:

> And who of you does not know the mysterious story of his birth—quite like a melodrama? . . . The real mother who bore him was the most sensible of mortals; his reputed mother who adopted him was the silliest woman in the world. Do you ask why? The one sold him as soon as he was born; the other purchased him when she might have got a better bargain at the same price. And yet, though he has become the possessor of privileges to which he has no claim [i.e., Athenian citizenship] . . . , his true native barbarism and hatred of the gods drive him on by force. (*Ag. Meidias* 149–150, translated by J. H. Vince)

Demosthenes is equally artful in manipulating the emotions of his audience. In this oration, he skillfully arouses and maintains fear and anger in the judges who, he suggests, are likely to become the next victims of this lawless, brutal bully whose wealth makes him think he is above the law. He enhances these emotional appeals to fear and anger by also creating pity for those that Meidias has already victimized. In one of the most brilliantly constructed pathetic appeals in the oratorical corpus, he presents to his audience a man Strato, who has lost his civic rights (which includes the right to speak in court or the Assembly) through Meidias's machinations:

> Call Strato, the victim of this persecution, for no doubt he will be able to stand up in court. This man, Athenians, is a poor man, perhaps, but certainly not a bad man. He was once a citizen and served . . . in all the military campaigns; he has done nothing wrong, yet now there he stands silent, stripped not only of all our common privileges, but also of the right to speak or protest; he is not even allowed to tell you whether he has suffered justly or unjustly. All this he has endured . . . from the wealth and pride of Meidias, because he himself is poor and friendless and just one of the multitude. (*Ag. Meidias* 95–96, translated by J. H. Vince)

Although such techniques were widely employed in Athenian legal oratory, some practitioners were more moderate in their style and es-chewed the extravagant muckraking one finds in Demosthenes or his rival, Aeschines. The presentation of the case in many of Lysias's orations is often more factually based and emotionally sober. This is even more pronounced in Isaeus, a specialist in inheritance cases, whose orations are characterized by rational argument analyzing the facts and weighing the probabilities. Of course, Isaeus and Lysias both employ ethical and pathetic appeals, but the balance and tone are usually very different. What accounts for this difference in oratorical styles?

There is a significant contrast between Demosthenes' forensic oratory and many of the speeches he delivered in deliberative settings. Unlike Lysias and Isaeus, Demosthenes was involved in competition for political leadership at Athens. In litigating before the democratic courts, Demosthenes and his rivals placed their public selves, their character, and their political identities at stake because they knew that in such cases the decision of the judges would be largely based upon the evaluation of the lives and respective standing of the opponents and not upon the legal issue that brought them into court. He thus had little choice but to adopt tactics like character assassination for, as we will see below, this was the way the game of political rivalry was played.

The admiration Demosthenes has aroused among modern commentators arises largely from his anti-Macedonian policies as expressed through his political oratory. Demosthenes built his political identity largely through his attempt to rally Athens to the dangers to its independence he saw in the growing power of Macedon under Philip. In two series of orations, known as the *Philippics* and the *Olynthiacs,* he turns all of his skill and intensity to this purpose. These orations are largely based on analysis of various political and military issues and calculation of which policy will best serve Athenian interests. Whereas Pericles succeeded in persuading the Athenians to follow his policies, Demosthenes never managed to achieve such a position of preeminent and almost undisputed influence. There are doubtless many reasons why Demosthenes' oratory often failed consistently to persuade the Athenians to adopt his policies. One of them may be that he was unable to establish an *ēthos* of unquestioned integrity, which Thucydides saw as the bedrock of Pericles' success as an orator and leader. Demosthenes' activity as a speechwriter and his litigiousness may have been one factor in undermining his character, for both activities were suspect in fourth-century Athenian political culture. He was also, late in his career, convicted of having accepted a bribe. But another ground may have had to do with the nature of political rivalry in fourth-century Athens.

In Demosthenes' time, the Athenian courts were a secondary arena where the competition for preeminence was played out among the Athenian elite. Demosthenes was engaged through most of his career in long-term feuds in which the rival opponents sought to use the courts as a weapon in their struggles. The forensic oratory of the period is full of various rhetorical *topoi* (topics) relating to the role of personal enmity in the litigation. [*See* Topics.] Demosthenes' prosecution of Meidias, discussed above, is one example of such feuding behavior. An even more famous one is Demosthenes' rivalry with the orator Aeschines. Their bitter struggle for ascendancy was played out before the Assembly, where they were on opposites sides regarding Macedon, and also before the courts. This led orators to accuse one another of sycophancy (vexatious litigation for personal or financial gain), a category of behavior harshly condemned in Athenian political culture.

Attacks through litigation might be direct or indirect. Aeschines, for example, successfully prosecuted one of Demosthenes' associates in the case commemorated in his oration *Against Timarchus,* where he masterfully uses invective and emotional appeals to arouse the disgust of the audience toward his opponent. This prosecution served to postpone Demosthenes' own prosecution of Aeschines in relation to his behavior on an embassy to Philip. They also confronted each other directly, as in Demosthenes' *On the False Embassy* and Aeschines' *On the Embassy,* or, more famously, in the pair of opposing orations, *Against Ctesiphon* (Aeschines) and *On the Crown* (Demosthenes). In this latter oration, Demosthenes defends his entire political career, but also attacks the character of Aeschines with every means at his disposal. This oration has been considered by some critics to be not only Demosthenes' best, but also one of the greatest in the entire oratorical tradition. It is perhaps ironic that Demosthenes' most famous oration should be one in which unrestrained personal invective and emotional ploys play such a prominent role. The success of such tactics, as well as how much was at stake in such oratorical contests, is indicated by the fact that Aeschines was humiliated by his failed prosecution and left Athens to avoid paying a large fine because he had not received one-fifth of the votes. Demosthenes had triumphed.

Because Demosthenes participated actively in a political culture in which orators repeatedly dragged their opponents before popular courts in litigation in which character assassination was the principal tool, it is not surprising that he was not able to raise himself above his rivals through unquestioned personal integrity in the manner of Pericles. Resorting to the courts as a mechanism for the *dēmos* to mediate conflicts over political rivalry may have contributed to the stability of fourth-century Athenian democracy, but it surely left the reputation of most of the participants scarred in the process. Great orators dominated the politics of fourth-century Athens and they practiced their art with consummate technical skill. They did not ultimately succeed, however, in transcending the ambivalence about oratory that had stubbornly accompanied its rise to one of the central forms of cultural expression in the classical Greek world.

Such, at least, were the foundations of the oratorical traditions that extended from ancient Greece through Republican Rome, through the rise of Humanism in Renaissance Europe (when "oratory" was considered to encompass poetry as well), and that arguably ended with the great orators of the English-speaking world in the eighteenth and nineteenth centuries and the rise of modern technology in the twentieth. [*See* Public speaking.]

[*See also* Classical rhetoric; *and* Law.]

BIBLIOGRAPHY

All of the orations of the major Athenian orators can be most easily consulted in English translation in the Loeb Library editions of the individual orators, with Greek on the facing page. French translations of all the major figures can be found in the Bude editions, also with accompanying Greek text. There are also various English collections of Greek orations, such as R. Connor's *Greek Orations* (Ann Arbor, 1966).

Blass, F. *Die attische Beredsamkeit.* 2d ed. Leipzig, Germany, 1887–1898. The classic nineteenth-century German commentary on Athenian oratory. Still unsurpassed in its scope as a reference work.

Cohen, D. *Law, Violence, and Community in Classical Athens.* Cambridge, U.K., 1995. This book examines the role of rhetoric and oratory in Athenian litigation and politics, offering a new interpretation of litigation and its connection to the mediation of rivalry and conflict in democratic Athens.

Connor, W. R. *The New Politicians of Fifth Century Athens.* Princeton, 1971. A seminal account of fifth-century Athenian politics and, hence, an important work on the political oratory of the period.

Dover, K. *Lysias and the Corpus Lysiacum.* Berkeley, 1968. The standard work on Lysias and his corpus of orations by one of the greatest classical scholars of our time.

Finley, M. I. "Athenian Demagogues." *Past and Present* 21 (1962), pp. 3–24. A seminal article on demagogy and its meaning and role in Athenian politics.

Guthrie, W. *The Sophists.* Cambridge, U.K., 1971. A standard reference work on the intellectual background of the sophistic movement, including its connection to oratory. It covers important figures in the development of Greek rhetoric, such as Gorgias.

Hansen, M. H. *The Athenian Assembly in the Age of Demosthenes.* New York, 1987; and *The Athenian Democracy in the Age of Demosthenes.* Oxford, 1991. Two important reference works on the workings of the Athenian Assembly and the practice of democracy in the age of the orators.

Harris, E. *Aeschines and Athenian Politics.* New York, 1995. The most recent full-scale study of the orator Aeschines, his rivalry with Demosthenes, and his important role in fourth-century Athenian politics.

Jaeger, W. *Demosthenes: The Origin and Growth of His Policy.* Berkeley, 1938; and *Paideia: The Ideals of Greek Culture.* 3 vols. New York, 1939–1944. The first of these books examines the politics of Demosthenes, principally as seen through his oratory. The second, a classic work on Greek ideals of education, contains important discussions of figures like Isocrates in their intellectual context.

Jebb, R. C. *The Attic Orators from Antiphon to Isaeos.* 2 vols. London, 1875–1876. Like Blass (above), Jebb's work is still valuable as a reference work.

Kennedy, G. *The Art of Persuasion in Greece.* Princeton, 1963. A useful overview of the entire Greek rhetorical tradition, with lengthy treatments of the oratory of Demosthenes and Aeschines.

Loraux, N. *The Invention of Athens: The Funeral Oration*

in the Classical City. Cambridge, Mass., 1986. A highly original analysis of the funeral oration, and particularly Pericles' funeral oration, as a means for shaping civic identity.

Ober, J. Mass and Elite in Democratic Athens. Princeton, 1989. The best and most important modern treatment of the role of political oratory in Athenian democracy.

Schaefer, A. Demosthenes und seine Zeit. 3 vols. Leipzig, Germany, 1856–1858. The classic comprehensive study of Demosthenes, with discussions of all the orations.

Sinclair, R. Democracy and Participation in Athens. Cambridge, U.K., 1988. An important contribution to the literature on Athenian democracy. Several chapters are relevant for an understanding of the context and practice of political oratory as well as the nature and response of the citizen audience.

Thomas, R. Oral Tradition and Written Record in Classical Athens. Cambridge, U.K., 1989. An excellent account of the way in which the oral tradition continued to play a vital role in Athens long after the introduction of writing.

Worthington, I. A Historical Commentary on Dinarchus: Rhetoric and Conspiracy in Fourth-Century Athens. Ann Arbor, 1991. A book-length treatment of the oratory of the late-fourth-century politician Dinarchus.

Wyse, W. The Speeches of Isaeus. Cambridge, U.K., 1904. Still the standard commentary on the orations of Isaeus, a major figure in the development of legal rhetoric and one of the most important Athenian logographers.

— DAVID COHEN

OXYMŌRON is a metasememe that consists of a collocation of two and more logically contradictory lexemes or sememes bound together by a hypersememe as a common semantic denominator, such as "weight" in the constituents "heavy" and "light" of the oxymōron "heavy lightness" (Shakespeare, Romeo and Juliet, 1.1.178). Oxymōra can be realized in the following syntactic constructions: (1) adjective (or participle) plus noun: "living death" (Milton, Samson Agonistes, 1671, v.100); (2) adjective (or participle) plus adjective (or participle) plus noun: "Eternity, thou pleasing, dreadful thought" (Addison, Cato, 1713, 5.1); verb plus adverb: "Festina lente" ("make haste slowly" [proverb]); (3) adjective plus "be" plus adjective: "Fair is foul and foul is fair" (Shakespeare, Macbeth, 1.1.11)—embedded in the figurative morphosyntactic construction of a chiasmus [See Chiasmus.] Types (1) and (2) are illustrated by O. Henry's description of New York in his story The Duel (1910): "It has the poorest millionaires, the littlest great men, the haughtiest beggars, the plainest beauties, the lowest skyscrapers, the dolefullest pleasures of any town I ever saw." Oxymōra are constituents of Petrarchan love casuistry, as in Romeo's congeries of the contradictory features of love: "O anything of nothing first create! / O heavy lightness, serious vanity, / Misshapen chaos of well-seeming forms!" (Shakespeare, Romeo and Juliet, 1.1.175–177). [See Congeries.] Oxymōra regularly occur in mannerist poetry and poetics (e.g., discordia concors) or in Christian theology (e.g., "felix culpa"). The oxymōron may be regarded as a subcategory of the paradox, which encompasses a broader spectrum of logical, linguistic, and communicative incompatibilities.

[See also Figures of speech; and Paradox.]

BIBLIOGRAPHY

Evans, Robert O. The Osier Cage: Rhetorical Devices in "Romeo and Juliet." Lexington, Ky., 1966. In chapter 2, the author asserts that the oxymōron is the key to the structure of the play.

— HEINRICH F. PLETT

P

PANEGYRIC. The term *panegyric* derives from the ancient Greek expression for a speech delivered at a public festival (*panēgyrikos logos*), such as the *Panegyricus* of the Greek orator Isocrates, written for the Olympic Games of 380 BCE, in which he praises Athens and urges the unification of the Greek city-states. At Rome, the festival context continued to mark the meaning of the term well into the principate (e.g., Dionysius of Halicarnassus *Lysias* 3.7,16.2–3): the first-century CE Roman rhetorician Quintilian identifies panegyric as a subset of epideictic and observes that it is advisory in form (3.4.14), and yet concerned with ornament and audience pleasure (*Institutio oratoria* 2.10.11, 3.8.7). [*See* Epideictic genre.] Hermogenes (second century CE) is more general, effectively equating the term with epideictic by applying it to the work of historians, poets, and even Plato, on stylistic criteria (*On Types of Style,* 387.5–388.2). More specific use of the term in titles such as the late first century BCE *Panegyricus Messallae* (Tibullus 3.7) or the *Panegyric* of Pliny (see below) reflect the usage of a later period.

In contrast to epideictic, as Quintilian remarks, Roman speeches of praise (*laus, laudatio*)—such as the funeral orations of the republican period (*laudationes funebres*) and encomia delivered in the senate or the law court—had a pragmatic function; only the narrow field of *laudationes* of gods and past heroes was limited to display (Quintilian 3.7.1–4; c.f. Cicero, *De oratore* 2.341). Tradition has it that the first *laudatio funebris* was delivered at the state funeral of the consul L. Junius Brutus (Dionysius of Halicarnassus, *Roman Antiquities* 5.17.2; Plutarch, *Publicola* 9.6–7.; cf. Polybius 6.53.1–2). Unlike examples of the genre from classical Athens praising fallen soldiers and the city for which they fought (cf. Pericles in Thucydides 2.34–46 and Plato *Menexenus*), the Roman funeral oration focused on a single (historic) individual, rehearsing his lineage and services to the state. Isocrates' prose work *Ev-agoras* (365 BCE), written in praise of the recently deceased king of Salamis, and Xenophon's *Agesilaus* (360 BCE) provide the earliest Greek precedent for this, and Cicero wrote such a praise of Cato Uticensis after his suicide. However, it is Cicero's *Pro lege Manilia* of 66 BCE, urging the grant of special powers to Pompey, and his speeches to Julius Caesar (*Pro Marcello, Pro Ligario,* and *Pro Rege Deiotaro,* 46–45 BCE, all seeking favor for contemporaries via flattering addresses) to which later panegyrists looked as models.

We have one surviving collection of panegyric speeches from late antiquity, the *Twelve Latin Panegyrics* (*XII Panegyrici Latini*). With one exception, this contains the work of Gallo-Roman orators and teachers of rhetoric writing in the Tetrarchic and Constantinian periods of the late third and fourth centuries CE. The speeches are addressed to Roman emperors ranging from Maximian (Mamertinus's panegyric of 289) to Theodosius (Pacatus Drepanus, in 389). At the head of the collection, but dating to 100 CE, is the so-called *Panegyric* of the Roman senator Pliny the Younger, actually a speech of thanks (*gratiarum actio*) to the emperor Trajan, delivered upon the occasion of Pliny's induction as suffect consul. Such thanksgivings, instituted under Augustus, brought together the combination of speaker, ruler, and elite audience that are characteristic of late imperial panegyric and its descendents. Other prose panegyrics preserved among the works of individual authors include, in Latin, those of Ausonius and Symmachus, and, in Greek, those of Themistius, Libanius, Eusebius, and the second-century Greek rhetorician, Aelius Aristides, who combined praise of famous cities with that of the Roman emperor.

Two third-century handbooks are devoted to the subject of imperial panegyric: the *Technē peri tōn panēgyrikōn* of pseudo-Dionysius of Halicarnassus and a two-part treatise *Peri epideiktikōn* ascribed to Menander Rhetor. These works offered guidelines for panegyric speeches delivered to emperors and dignitaries on such occasions as imperial birthdays, coronations, ceremonial entries into cities (*adventus*), and marriages. Under "address to the emperor" (*basilikos logos,* 368.3–377.30), Menander includes such topics as the addressee's native land, family, birth, education, and his accomplishments in war and peace (cf. *Rhetorica ad Herennium* 3.10–15; Quintilian 3.7.10–19). Adherence to several or more of the four (or more) virtues of temperance, wisdom, courage, and justice was also praised. The late antique panegyrics of the late third century and beyond show a combination of influences: the theoretical prescriptions of Menander and pseudo-Dionysius; Greco-Roman writing on epideictic since the *Rhetorica ad Alexandrum* and Aristotle's *Rhetoric;* literary borrowings from Roman epic; consideration of the political context and the particular accomplishments of the emperor-addressee; and corroboration of imperial propaganda elsewhere reproduced in coinage and visual art. Many of these panegyrics were delivered under Christian emperors; here, the traditional comparisons to Jupiter and pagan heroes continue, but we see also approximations of the emperor to saints or bishops, or, less frequently, a focus on Christian qualities such as humility. The guidelines for pagan panegyric were followed in eulogies of saints, although hostility to the genre is voiced by Augustine (*Confessions,* c.400 6.6), Lactantius (*Divine Institutes,* 303–313, 1.15.3), and others.

Already in Pliny, a favorite device was comparison of the current addressee with a recent predecessor, to the latter's detriment, of course; with this went elaborations on the theme of restoration and frequent protestations of the speaker's frankness (*parrhēsia, libertas*) and sincerity. Pliny elaborately flatters Trajan and condemns earlier praise of Domitian as ambiguous lies, remarking on his own good faith (*Panegyric* 3.4, 3.1); the fourth-century philosopher Themistius claims that only a philosopher can offer truly meaningful praise (e.g., *Orationes* 1.1a, 3c–d), but proceeds to flatter Jovian, Valens, and Theodosius in turn. In the middle of the first century BCE, Cicero had commented already of the *laudatio funebris* that it was a source of falsehood (*Brutus* 62), and much later, Isidore of Seville (c.570–636 CE), following Lactantius, would call pagan panegyric an evil de-

scended from the Greeks, good only for stirring up clouds of lies (*Origins* 6.8.7). Similar criticisms were made, and similar defenses offered, after interest in panegyric revived following Giovanni Aurispa's discovery of the codex containing the *XII Panegyrici Latini* in 1433. Erasmus claimed of his *Panegyricus* of 1504 to Philip, Duke of Burgundy "that by having the image of virtue put before them, bad princes might be made better, the good encouraged, the ignorant instructed, [and] the mistaken set right" (*Epistula* 176, *The Epistles of Erasmus,* translated by F. M. Nichols, London, 1901). But the old suspicions were voiced as well: Thomas Blount defined panegyric in his *Glossographia* of 1656 as "A licentious kind of speaking or oration, in the praise and commendation of Kings, or other great persons, wherein some falsities are joyned with many flatteries." And in fact panegyrists strove for a double goal, working to popularize imperial policy while hoping to restrain the abuses of power.

In both antiquity and Elizabethan and Stuart England, imperial panegyric could be in verse; several of Statius's *Silvae* (first century CE) are addressed to Domitian or incorporate his praises (e.g., 1.1, 1.6, 4.1, 4.3), and Claudian's epic panegyrics, written between 395 and 404, celebrate the deeds of Honorius and the Gothic wars. The first English usage of panegyric for verse eulogy heads Samuel Daniel's poem on the Stuart succession in 1603. Other famous verse panegyrics of the sixteenth and seventeenth centuries include Thomas More's *Carmen Gratulatorium* to Henry VIII (1509) and Dryden's *Panegyrick on the Coronation* to Charles II (1661). Outside the West, the most famous example of the genre in verse is provided by the highly stylized Arabic or Persian ode or *qasida*, which originated in the pre-Islamic period. Mutanabbi (915–965) was the master practitioner of this genre, which ended with a panegyric section (*madih*) in praise of the caliph or a patron, and which, like panegyric in general, functioned as a tool for the legitimization of those it praised.

[*See also* Classical rhetoric.]

BIBLIOGRAPHY

Primary Sources in Translation

Nixon, C. E. V., and B. S. Rodgers. *In Praise of Later Roman Emperors: The Panegyrici Latini*. Berkeley, 1994. An edition and translation of the *XII Panegyrici Latini* with historical commentary.

Russell, D. A., and N. G. Wilson. *Menander Rhetor.* Oxford, 1981. A commentary, edition, and translation of the two-part, late third-century handbook *Peri epideiktikōn.*

Secondary Literature

Braund, Susanna Morton. "Praise and Protreptic in Early Imperial Panegyric: Cicero, Seneca, Pliny." In *The Propaganda of Power: The Role of Panegyric in Late Antiquity.* Edited by Mary Whitby, pp. 53–76. Leiden, 1998. A study of the protreptic elements and contexts of Cicero's Caesarian speeches, Seneca's *De Clementia,* and Pliny's *Panegyricus.*

Garrison, James D. *Dryden and the Tradition of Panegyric.* Berkeley, 1975. An examination of seventeenth-century panegyric, in particular the poetry of Dryden, in relation to the panegyric tradition.

MacCormack, Sabine. "Latin Prose Panegyrics." In *Empire and Aftermath. Silver Latin,* vol. 2. Edited by T. A. Dorey, pp. 143–205. London, 1975. A seminal article on Latin panegyric in late antiquity.

MacCormack, Sabine. *Art and Ceremony in Late Antiquity.* Berkeley, 1981. A study of the ceremonial contexts and contents of late antique panegyric and its relation to the visual arts.

Mause, Michael. *Die Darstellung des Kaisers in der lateinischen Panegyrik.* Stuttgart, 1994. A study of the elements of the portrayal of the emperor in Latin prose and verse panegyric.

Nixon, C. E. V. "The Use of the Past by the Gallic Panegyrists." In *Reading the Past in Late Antiquity.* Edited by G. W. Clarke, Brian Croke, Alanna Nobbs, and Raoul Mortky, pp. 1–36. Rushcutters Bay, Australia, 1990. A study of the references to the legendary, republican, and imperial past of Rome in the Gallic Panegyrists.

Pernot, Laurent. *La rhétorique de l'éloge dans le monde gréco-romain.* Paris, 1993. A methodical treatment of the history, theory, topics, and style of Greco-Roman eulogy, with emphasis on the Second Sophistic.

Russell, Donald. "The Panegyrists and their Teachers." In *The Propaganda of Power: The Role of Panegyric in Late Antiquity.* Edited by Mary Whitby, pp. 17–50. Leiden, 1998. A good summary of the position of imperial panegyric within the epideictic tradition.

Stetkevych, S. P. "Umayyad Panegyric and the Poetics of Islamic Hegemony: Al-Akhtal's 'Kaffa al-Qatinu.'" *Journal of Arab Literature* 28 (1997), pp. 89–122. A discussion of the political function and meaning of a panegyric *qasida* of the seventh-century CE Arab poet Al-Akhtal.

Whitby, Mary, ed. *The Propaganda of Power: The Role of Panegyric in Late Antiquity.* Leiden, 1998. A collection of essays on imperial panegyrists, with sections devoted to theory and practice, the Roman background, and pagan and Christian panegyric.
—SHADI BARTSCH

PARADIGM. *See* Exemplum.

PARADOX, meaning "contrary to *doxa* or received opinion," is a rhetorical term both of invention and of style. As a category of invention, it denotes a specific *causa* named *causa turpis* (*paradoxon schēma*) or, according to Thomas Wilson (c.1525–1581), a "filthy matter," which he defines in *The Arte of Rhetorique* (1553): "Then do we hold and defende a filthy matter, when either wee speake our conscience in an evill matter, or els withstande an upright truthe" (pp. 25–26). In contrast to the other two *genera causarum,* the *causa honesta* (*endoxon schēma*) and the *causa dubia* (*amphidoxon schēma*), which confirm a public opinion or leave an opinion in a dubious ambiguity, the orator in a paradoxical cause is faced with the difficult task of arguing *"praeter opinionem hominum"* (Quintilian, first century CE), *"contra opinionem bonam"* (Augustine, c.427 CE), and *"contra expectationem auditoris"* (Rufinianus, fourth century CE). John Bullokar (*The English Expositor,* 1616) mentions as a specific case in question, "as if one affirme that the earth doth mooue round, and the heauens stand still." A spectacular literary testimony of the Renaissance is provided by Alexandre Pont-Amérys in *Paradoxe apologétique, où il est fidèlement demonstré que la femme est la plus parfaicte que l'homme en toute action de vertu* (1596). In Shakespeare's *Othello,* it is Iago who, by seducing his master, pursues a *causa turpis* ("filthy matter"), because Desdemona is regarded as the paragon of marital fidelity. The paradoxical rhetoric of inversion is above all an exercise of mannerist *ingegno/ingenio* (metaphysical wit); thus Baltasar Gracián dedicates a specific chapter (Discurso 22) to the *"agudeza paradoja"* in his *Agudeza y arte de ingenio* (1642). It is used in the literary genre *paradoxa encomia,* in which negative or trifling issues regarded as blameworthy are praised, as Erasmus's *Encomium Moriae* (Praise of Folly, 1511), Synesius's Praise of Baldness (fourth century CE), Lucian's Praise of the Fly, or even the

Praise of Nothing (second century CE). During the Renaissance, paradoxes were collected in commonplace books, as for example in Ortensio Lando's famous *Paradossi* (1543) or in Ralph Venning's theological *Orthodox Paradoxes* (1647). A voluminous compendium of dozens of paradoxical encomia entitled *Amphitheatrum sapientiae Socraticae joco-seriae* (Hanover, 1619) was compiled by Caspar Dornavius.

As a figure of speech the paradox is anglicized as "the Wondrer" (Puttenham, *The Arte of English Poesie*, 1589). It can be realized by various other figures, above all the *oxymōron*, with which it is often identified. [*See* Oxymōron.] As a general mannerism of style, the term *paradox* was changed to "paradoxisme" by Pierre Fontanier (1821–1830). Oscar Wilde, for his conversational brilliance in using this figure "pour épater le bourgeois," was nicknamed "Prince of Paradox." The paradox has played an important role in philosophy (e.g., Cicero's *Paradoxa Stoicorum*, first century BCE) and in Christian theology, but in everyday communication it is mostly used for expressing astonishment or disbelief at something unusual or unexpected.

[*See also* Figures of speech.]

BIBLIOGRAPHY

Colie, Rosalie L. *Paradoxia Epidemica: The Renaissance Tradition of Paradox*. Princeton, 1966. Reprint, Hamden, Conn., 1976.
Geyer, Paul, and Roland Hagenbüchle, eds. *Das Paradox*. Tübingen, 1992.
Malloch, A. E. "The Techniques and Function of the Renaissance Paradox." *Studies in Philology* 53 (1956), pp. 191–203.
Margolin, Jean-Claude. "Le paradoxe, est-il une figure de rhétorique?" *Nouvelle revue du seizième siècle* 6 (1988), pp. 4–14.
Miller, Henry Knight. "The Paradoxical Encomium with Special Reference to Its Vogue in England, 1600–1800." *Modern Philology* 53 (1956), pp. 145–178.
Plett, Heinrich F. "Das Paradoxon als rhetorische Kategorie." In *Das Paradox*, edited by Paul Geyer and Roland Hagenbüchle, pp. 89–104. Tübingen, 1982.
—HEINRICH F. PLETT

PARALLELISM. The term *parallelism* has been coined in relatively recent times, and it does not belong to the traditional terminology of rhetoric. It usually designates a group of discursive phenomena, both of a formal and semantic nature, known since ancient times under the Greek terms *parison* and *parisōsis*. Their application corresponds to the general artifice whereby discourse is segmented into equivalent and therefore comparable members.

From a formal linguistic perspective, the foundation of those phenomena lies in (1) the construction of the syntagmatic constituents of sentence structures with elements formally equivalent, and (2) the segmentation and distribution of those elements in positions also equivalent in the space of a complete text or of certain segments of it.

For example, consider the following formulation. Given the sequences A and A', formed by the elements a, b (A) and a', b' (A'), elements categorially and functionally equivalent, their distribution in the chain of discourse might correspond to this scheme:

Sequences: A /*/ A'
Elements: a b /*/ a' b'.

This scheme can be seen in the last line of the following fragment from Quevedo:

Arderán tu victoria y tus despojos;
Y ansí, fuego el Amor nos dará eterno:
A ti en mi corazón, a mí en tus ojos.

(Your victory and your spoils will burn; / And thus, Love will give us eternal fire: / To you in my heart, to me in your eyes),

in which the sequences:

A: a ti en mi corazón /*/ A': a mí en tus ojos

are formed by the elements:

a: a ti, a': a mí
b: en mi corazón, b': en tus ojos.

These elements are equivalent from a categorial, functional, and distributional perspective.

As can be inferred from the precedent scheme and example, the constitution and order of succession of the elements in the second sequence (A') repeat faithfully the constitution and distributional order fixed in the elements of the first sequence (A).

Usually, the equivalent lexical elements from

a formal point of view—categorial, functional, and distributional—establish at the same time an equivalence of meaning, either through synonymy (synonymic parallelism) or through antonymy (antithetic parallelism).

The parallelistic scheme may be used in a very diverse way in the organization of a text or of certain segments of it. The example mentioned above can be extended to the constitution of an entire text. Such is the case of the "parallelistic poems" of some traditions, such as biblical poetry, or medieval Galician–Portuguese poetry.

[See also Figures of speech; Gorgianic figures; and Isocolon.]

BIBLIOGRAPHY

Lanham, R. A. A Handlist of Rhetorical Terms. Berkeley, 1991.
Lausberg, H. Handbuch der literarischen Rhetorik. Pp. 719, 722, 736. Munich, 1960.
Mayoral, J. A. Figuras retóricas. Pp. 168–172. Madrid, 1994.

—JOSÉ ANTONIO MAYORAL
Translated by A. Ballesteros

PARENTHESIS (Lat. *interpositio*) is defined in Fontanier's traditional treatise *Les figures du discours* (1821–1830) as *une insertion d'un sens complet et isolé au milieu d'un autre dont il interrompt la suite, avec ou sans rapport au sujet* ("an insertion of a complete and isolated sense in the context of another sense for which it interrupts its flow, with or without relation to its subject"). Translated in a modern concept, it means an additive metataxeme or an insertion of an independent syntactic unit *P* in the linguistic continuum of a sentence *S*, which is thus disrupted. The quality of this disrupture is determined by (1) the specific semantic cohesion of *P* and *S*; (2) the extension of *P*; and (3) the kind of syntactic unit that is severed by *P*. If there exists no close semantic cohesion between *P* and *S*, if the extension of *P* is large, and if *P* severs two closely connected syntactic constituents such as adjective (article) and noun, the disrupture is probably violent. A parenthesis is usually marked by graphic signs (hyphens, brackets, parentheses, italics) in a written or printed discourse. While according to classical treatises this figure is used for amplifying a text, a modern

pragmatic view perceives in it an instrument for a broad range of functions; for example, for establishing two levels of communication, one of essential and another of supplementary information, one of discourse and another of metadiscourse. [See Amplification.] A parenthesis can give an utterance "an additional nuance of meaning and tinge of emotional coloring" (I. R. Gal' Perin, *Stylistics*, 2d ed., Moscow, 1977).

[See also Figures of speech.]

—HEINRICH F. PLETT

PARONOMASIA (Lat. *annominatio*) is a kind of wordplay. Wordplays in general can be described by specific relations of words within the triad of sound structure (phonology), spelling (graphemics), and meaning (semantics). Starting from this premise, a typology of six wordplays can be set up:

Homophonic wordplay, whose features are homophonic (identical sound structure), metagraphic (different spelling), and metasemic (different meaning); for example, "sole"—"soul";

Homographic wordplay, whose features: are homographic, metaphonic, and metasemic; for example, "wind" [wind]—[waind];

Homosemic (synonymic) wordplay, whose features are homosemic, metaphonic, and metagraphic; for example, "big"—"great"; "my old lord of the castle"—"Sir John Oldcastle" (Shakespeare);

Metagraphic wordplay, whose features are homophonic, homosemic, and metagraphic; for example, <light>—<lite>; French: <gauche>—<gôche>, German: <Telephon>—<Telefon> (before the spelling-reform in 1999);

Homonymic wordplay, whose features are homophonic, homographic, and metasemic; for example, English "to lie" (i.e., to be prostrate)—"to lie" (i.e., to tell an untruth); German "Schein" (i.e., light)—"Schein" (i.e., semblance); and

Metaphonic wordplay, whose features are homosemic, homographic, and metaphonic; for example, the two kinds of pronunciation of the name of the poet John *Donne*.

Paronomasia, according to the pseudo-Ciceronian *Rhetorica ad Herennium* (first century BCE, 4.21.29), is "the figure in which by means of a modification of sound or change of letters (*com-*

mutatione vocum aut litterarum) a close resemblance to a given verb or noun is produced so that similar words (*similia verba*) express dissimilar things (*res dissimiles*)." In a similar vein, the famous nineteenth-century figurist Pierre Fontanier in his *Les figures du discours* (1821–1830) gives the following definition: "La *Paronomase,* qu'on appelle aussi *Paronomasie* ou *Prosonomasie,* réunit dans la même phrase des mots dont le son est à-peu-près le même, mais le sens tout-à-fait différent" (347). English Renaissance rhetoricians classify *paronomasia* as a "figure of diction" (Butler, 1598), "a sententious figure" (Puttenham, *The Arte of English Poesie,* 1589) and "a figure of varying" (Hoskins, c.1599–1600). Puttenham (1589) prefers the term *prosonomasia* and defines it as "a figure by which ye play with a couple of words or names much resembling, and because the one seemes to answere th'other by manner of illusion, and doth, as it were, nick him, I call him the *Nicknamer.*" He illustrates this figure in the following way: "As *Tiberius* the Emperour, because he was a great drinker of wine, they called him *Caldius Biberius Mero,* in steade of *Claudius Tiberius Nero.*"

According to the typology of wordplays outlined above, paronomasia is either a homoeophonic or a homoeographic wordplay and hence represents a deviation from homophonic and homographic wordplay; for its characteristic constituents are not identical but similar sounds or letters. This similarity is attained by applying the fourfold paradigm of transformations : (1) *addition;* English "If a swallow cannot make a *summer,* it can bring on a *summary* fall" (G. W. Carryl, *Red Riding Hood*); (2) *deletion:* German "strauch*eln*" (stumble)—"Strauch" (bush) (H. v. Kleist); (3) *permutation:* Latin "Roma"—"amor"; (4) *substitution:* Italian "trad*u*ttore"—"trad*i*tore"; French "Vouloir c'est *p*ouvoir" (proverb).

In many cases, the effect of paronomasia is one of a pseudo-etymological relationship of its members, for instance, in this example taken from Shakespeare's (*As You Like It* 3.3.7–9): "I am here with thee and thy goats, as the most capricious poet, honest Ovid, was among the Goths." The fool Touchstone, who thinks of himself as a witty person as compared to the rural maid Audrey and the rustic population among whom she lives, thus implicitly likens himself to the sophisticated Roman poet Ovid, who was banished to the territory of the Goths. He also draws a paronomastic parallel between a filthy species of animals and the Germanic tribe, which traditionally had a reputation for being uncivilized.

[*See also* Figures of speech; *and* Style.]

BIBLIOGRAPHY

Brown, J. "Eight Types of Pun." *Proceedings of Modern Language Association,* 71 (1956), pp. 14–26.
Butler, Charles. *Rhetoricae Líbri Duo.* Oxford, 1598.
Hoskins, John. *Directions For Speech and Style,* edited by Hoyt H. Hudson. Princeton, 1935.
Mahood, M. *Shakespeare's Wordplay.* London, 1979.
Plett, Heinrich F. *Systematische Rhetorik.* Munich, 2000.
Redfern, Walter. *Puns.* Oxford, 1984.
Stingelin, Martin. "'Au quai?'—'Okay' Zur stilistischen Leistung des Wortspiels (ein Forschungsbericht)." In *Rhetorica Movet: Studies in Historical and Modern Rhetoric in Honour of Heinrich F. Plett,* edited by Peter L. Oesterreich and Thomas O. Sloane, pp. 447–469. Leiden, 1999. A critical review of modern studies of the wordplay, together with an outline of its stylistic functions.

—HEINRICH F. PLETT

PATHOPOEIA (Lat. *imaginatio*), meaning "imagination" (Sherry, Peacham), is a pragmatic figure designed to arouse passions either by being moved oneself or by presenting a moving argument to the audience. According to Henry Peacham's *Garden of Eloquence* (1593), this figure is suitable for arousing passions that were specified by his predecessor Richard Sherry in *A Treatise of Schemes and Tropes* (1555) as fear, anger, madness, hatred, and "like other perturbations of mind." According to Peacham, examples of *pathopoeia* are common in tragedies. Such can be found in the pathetic speeches of the female protagonists in Shakespeare's tragic history play *Richard III.* (1593).

[*See also* Figures of speech; *and* Pathos.]

—HEINRICH F. PLETT

PATHOS. The concern for *pathos* is one of the most distinctive aspects of a rhetorical approach to language, and of all aspects it has occasioned the greatest amount of controversy. The term itself is allied with the Greek verb *paskhein,* to undergo, experience, suffer, or, more generally, to be in a state or condition, and the Greek noun *pathos* preserves this range of meaning. In Greek rhetoric, the term referred variously to the state or condition of the human soul, usually as a result of what the soul has experienced, and by extension to the kind of language that can induce such states. The great currency of the term derives from Aristotle's *Rhetoric,* in which he identifies *pathos* as one of the three principal sources for rhetorical proofs, along with *ēthos* and *logos.* [*See* Ēthos; *and* Logos.] But the concern for *pathos* (by whatever name) long predates Aristotle, and the precise understanding of the term after Aristotle changes with time and culture. For some rhetors, the term conveys little more than the sense that an auditor's state of mind can cloud or supersede his rational capacities for making decisions. For others, the term invites a thorough analysis of the human soul and its broader relations to language and perception.

With the resurgence of interest in rhetoric during the twentieth century, there emerged something of a consensus in American pedagogical circles about the nature of *pathos,* particularly as deemed relevant to the teaching of composition. [*See* Composition.] This consensus is an amalgam of ideas, often incommensurate with one another, and drawn from different ages and writers. In outline, *pathos* is an appeal based on *passion* or *emotion* (the two words are drawn from the Greek and Roman traditions, respectively, and often are used interchangeably). Of the three appeals of *logos, ēthos,* and *pathos,* it is the latter that impels an audience to act. Emotions range from mild to intense; some, such as well-being, are gentle attitudes and outlooks, while others, such as sudden fury, are so intense that they overwhelm rational thought. Images are particularly effective in arousing emotions, whether those images are visual and direct as sensations, or cognitive and indirect as memory or imagination, and part of a rhetor's task is to associate the subject with such images. All of the constituent parts of this contemporary consensus have appeared at different times in the history of rhetoric, but never together at one time in a given author or age, and while it is misleading to read all of it back into the theory or practice of earlier times, this compendious view of *pathos* is useful for contemporary analyses of contemporary persuasion. [*See* Persuasion.]

Early Greek. As early as Homer's *Iliad,* there are attempts to use language to awaken emotions in the listener, although little formal theory can be adduced from these attempts. King Priam, for example, tearfully begs Achilles to return the slain body of his son Hector (Book 24). Achilles does relent, but he had already decided that this was the right thing to do. Thus in Homer, there is the suggestion that emotional appeals may finally impel action, but *pathos* may not be the reason why judgments are changed. A suggestion contrary to Homer's is supplied by the fifth-century historian Thucydides, concerning the fate of the Mitylenians who had rebelled against Athens. At first, the vengeful Athenians voted to execute all the Mitylenians, but by the next day, passions had cooled enough to reverse the vote. The rational arguments for either case were closely matched, so much that on reconsideration, a significant group of voters could go either way, and emotion tipped the balance. The two emotions (anger and mildness) were mutually exclusive, and they entailed judgments that were likewise mutually exclusive. [*See* Oratory.]

Both of these views of *pathos*—as ancillary and as constitutive—would emerge again in later rhetorical theories, but early systematic investigations of *pathos* focused almost exclusively on pleasure and pain, and so laid the foundations for understanding *pathos* in physiological and psychological theories for the next two millennia. Heraclitus (c.575–641 BCE) viewed various emotions in bodily terms using a fourfold balance of dry and wet, hot and cold, and he located pleasure or pain in the contrast of those balances. Anaxagoras (c.500–c.428 BCE) thought of pain as the body's response to any stimulus, since a stimulus is simply the body's contact with something unlike itself, especially if the contact is intense, and pleasure is defined as a negation or cessation of pain. Democritus (c.460–c.370 BCE) reversed the emphasis and found pleasure positive, as a moderation of extremes either in the body or in the emotions, and his view was later expanded by Epicureans. To the earlier fourfold balance, Hippocrates (c.460–c.377 BCE) added the idea of a "pneuma" or vital spirit, which united body and soul, coursing through both in a hydraulic manner, and partaking in a larger pneuma that permeates the world. Constrictions in the flow of pneuma are disorders and manifest themselves as emotions. The notion of the pneuma would be vastly elaborated by later Stoics, and in one form or another would influence writers from Plato to Descartes and beyond.

One of the few who tried to think about the place of *pathos* in rhetoric is the rhetor Thrasymachus of Chalcedon (c.460 BCE), who had a reputation for giving tearful and moving speeches, for arousing and dispelling anger, and who wrote an entire treatise on *Appeals to Pity*. He also wrote a handbook on rhetoric with model openings and closings for students to memorize and emulate, and is one of the earliest to suggest that emotional appeals have most power in the beginnings and ends of speeches. Gorgias of Leontini (c.483–c.376 BCE) introduces a theory of *pathos* into his playful *Encomium of Helen,* arguing that Helen was not responsible for the carnage of the Trojan War, because the persuasive words of Paris stirred her emotions, seized her soul, and ravished her against her will. Speeches can be like drugs (*pharmaka*)—a notion that will be repeated until the twentieth century—seizing the body for good or ill, causing distress, delight, fear, or boldness, leaving the hearer bereft of defenses, and the effect of emotion upon Helen was like another rape (*Helen* 8–14; in Sprague, 1972, pp. 50–54). For both Thrasymachus and Gorgias, the rhetor is in control, and the auditor is passive. The rhetor makes rational choices about how and when to arouse or dampen emotions, about how and when to administer drugs, to auditors who have no control over their responses.

Plato. Plato (c.428–c.347 BCE) had little use for Thrasymachus or Gorgias. In his dialogues *Thrasymachus* (see *Republic* 1) and *Gorgias,* he presents both men as capable technicians whose theories lead directly to tyranny. These and other Platonic dialogues have often been read as condemnations of rhetoric, but in both the *Republic* and the *Laws,* Plato is perfectly content to have persuasion and compulsion in his ideal world. The question instead turns on who has the moral authority and philosophical understanding to persuade and compel. In a series of dialogues (rarely consistent with one another), Plato explores ways to coordinate active ethical understanding with automatic bodily responses for a larger understanding of *pathos.* Socrates argues in the *Protagoras* that the good is pleasant, that evil is painful, and that the emotion of fear or terror is the expectation of evil. Thus the coward finds pleasure in flight because he misunderstands where true evil lies (*Protagoras* 358). Compare this with Gorgias's explanation of cowardice in the *Encomium of Helen;* the physical sight of attacking soldiers enters a person's eyes and travels downward in the body, and so makes the feet move in flight. Gorgias's terrified coward has no more cognition than does his enraptured Helen.

Nearly all of Plato's notions about pleasure, pain, and *pathos* are qualified in other dialogues—notably *Gorgias, Philebus,* and *Timaeus*—that explore relations between cognition and varieties of bodily and mental cravings. In his later dialogues, Plato discriminates three parts of the human soul: the *nous,* in the head where reason and spirit prevail; the *thumos,* in the breast where spirited passions rule; and the *epithumētikos,* below the diaphragm where bodily appetites have sway (*Timaeus* 69; *Republic* 435b–441a, 604d–605c). Plato's tripartite division of the soul will reappear in subsequent approaches to *pathos* for the next two thousand years.

In the *Phaedrus,* Plato offers several different catalogs of emotions: who feels them, toward whom, under what circumstances, and the kind of actions that can be expected consequent upon them. He offers these catalogs in the course of delivering three different speeches, the first intended to be understood as flawed both technically and morally, the second technically correct but morally flawed, and the third correct both technically and morally. The first speech, which Plato facetiously attributes to the contemporary rhetor Lysias, is a nearly random collection of argumentative topics about love and desire, about those who do or do not experience them, and how they act. The speech starts, for example, by observing that when the emotion of love exhausts itself, the lover will repent of earlier generosities to the beloved, whereas a nonlover in an intimate relationship has no such irrational fits of generosity, and thus there are no costs to be regretted at the end of the relationship; therefore the nonlover is to be preferred to the lover (*Phaedrus* 231). The logical leap at the end is a playful, even outrageous joke, but the numerous observations he offers about the lover and nonlover are often very pointed, and this entire speech demonstrates how emotions can be used as premises for rhetorical arguments.

The second speech repeats many of the same pathetic topics as before, but this time Socrates shows how they can be presented in a relentlessly logical progression, beginning with a philosophical definition of the emotion of love. But the definition is faulty by design, since Plato bases it on two principles he has already condemned elsewhere—the appetitive desire of *epithumia,* and the fallible human opinion of *doxa* (*Phaedrus* 237). Socrates' third speech instead describes the soul allegorically in terms of a winged chariot with two horses, the appetitive desire of *epithumia* yoked to the spirited passion of *thumos,* one wanting to pull down toward the base earth, the other up and away. The charioteer who struggles to control both, for a harmonious journey that needs the power of both, is not human *doxa,* but the divine reason of *nous* (*Phaedrus* 246). The dialogue ends with a return to a favorite comparison in Plato for pathetic appeals, between the knowledge that constitutes the art of medicine, and the mechanical administration of drugs. Thrasymachus and others are guilty of the latter, while the task before rhetoricians is to gain better knowledge of the kinds of souls and the kinds of emotions which appeal to those souls through speech.

Despite some early Greek efforts to understand *pathos* in theoretical terms, the prevailing approach was practical, as the references to Thrasymachus demonstrate. Similar injunctions can be found in the *Rhetorica ad Alexandrum* (now attributed to Anaximenes) for arousing the judge's anger, particularly in the closing, where also are found goodwill, pity, love, benevolence, hatred, and envy. Despite such technical advice, in practice nearly all of the rhetors, from the elegant Demosthenes to the scurrilous Dinarchus, felt free to use *pathos* anywhere in their speeches. Less technical uses of *pathos* abound in speeches, but one of the most notorious was by the accomplished rhetor Hyperides (390–322 BCE), who was

defending Phryne, a votive of Aphrodite and a famous courtesan. She had been accused of a capital crime, and when Hyperides saw that he was on the verge of losing his case, he brought Phryne into the middle of the court and ripped open her clothing. The judges supposedly were so moved by the sight of her nude body that they took pity on her and convinced themselves that their religion forbade them to harm a beautiful servant of the goddess (*Athenaeus* 13.590E). Only slightly less dramatic are Plato's reports of defendants pleading to the jury with floods of tears, or parading their infant children in the courtroom (*Apology* 34).

Aristotle. Aristotle of Stagira (384–322 BCE) provides the most complete analysis of *pathos* in the Greek world. In the *De anima* (On the Soul), he looks at *pathos* as a particular part of the general psychology that unites body and mind. In the *Nichomachean Ethics,* he considers its broad place in the larger concern for happiness. And in the *Rhetoric,* he considers it very strictly in terms of public argumentation in the three realms of forensic, deliberative, and epideictic discourse. [*See* Deliberative genre; Epideictic genre; *and* Forensic genre.] There is thus no need to address all emotions, but only those that bear upon his conception of public argumentation. He begins the treatise by criticizing other writers on rhetoric for having focused on *pathos* to the exclusion of other aspects of the discipline. He does not criticize them for addressing *pathos* itself, since he actually agrees with much of what has been said before, and in the final section of Book 3, he concurs that *pathos* should be employed in the closing, but only as a recapitulation of the *pathos* developed throughout the speech. His criticism instead addresses the failure to examine how *pathos* coordinates with *ēthos* and *logos,* and particularly the failure to discuss what he terms *enthymemes.* [*See* Enthymeme.] Aristotle's use of this last term is all but unique, and sharply differing views about what it means persist to the present day, but the competing understandings all acknowledge to some degree that *pathos* both coordinates with the enthymeme and is constituent of it.

Aristotle discusses *pathos* in the *Rhetoric* in two related ways, and the notion of pleasure and pain is central to both. He postulates that pleasure is a sudden and perceptible movement of the soul as it returns to its natural state, while pain is the opposite (*Rhetoric* 1.11). Considered as a motivation for wrongdoing, *pathos* is Aristotle's term for those pleasant or painful cravings and tempers that lead men to act in particular ways (*Rhetoric* 1.10–12). Considered as a motivation for judgment, *pathos* is his term for those pleasant or painful dispositions that lead men to change their minds (*Rhetoric* 2.2–12). [*See* Judgment.]

In forensic rhetoric, men are held accountable for deeds they have chosen to do, either through premeditated reason or *pathos* (1369a18). Of the latter, the deeds can be done in the heat of the moment (*thumos* or *orgē*) or done out of desire (*epithumia*), and while these cravings do not involve any premeditation, they do depend upon belief: first, that what has been perceived is indeed a lack; and second, that the means proposed to satisfy that lack will indeed do so. A person may think he is hungry when he is not, or think a certain food will satisfy a hunger when it will not, and so crave that food. Physical and mental cravings alike are all based on beliefs, which a person can embrace by hearing what other people say (1370a27), or by accepting an appearance (*phantasia*) that may be of the moment, or in memory, or in hope and prospect. These cravings exist only in situations, and Aristotle lists many social settings, mostly presented in terms of contraries. It is, for example, pleasant to do the same things often, as in sports, or with familiar friends; but change is also pleasant in itself, since sameness is boring. Aristotle here creates a storehouse of topics in *pathos,* which can be used as premises on either side of an issue, and which he announces as his intention for exploring *pathos* in forensic rhetoric (1368b1–5). [*See* Topics.] Thus *pathos* is intrinsic to Aristotle's enthymeme, and even his discussion of criminal activities is conducted in terms of enthymemes: men do wrong because they think they will go unpunished or undetected, or because they do not care.

In Book 2 of the *Rhetoric,* Aristotle discusses *pathos* as a motive for judgment, since people judge differently depending upon whether they feel pain or pleasure. He delineates sixteen *pathē* as sets of contrasting pairs, but points out that the forensic cravings can also serve as motives for changing an opinion (1378a1–5), and in fact he discusses anger in both sections. Here again, *pathos* is based on unreflective beliefs about what would bring pleasure or pain, so that a *phantasia* will cause an immediate response. Anger, for example, is a pain caused by what appears to be a personal slight or insult. This focus on pleasure and pain, appearance and belief, determines how the individual *pathē* are paired with their contraries. Based on the criterion of pleasure and pain, the opposite of anger is mildness, since mildness is an absence or lessening of the pain of anger, and the movement from a greater to a lesser level of pain is defined as a pleasure. The progression among the *pathē* reflects these physiological and psychological distinctions:

1a. anger	pain at the appearance of undeserved slight to oneself
1b. mildness	absence of the pain of anger
2a. friendliness	pleasure at the appearance of procuring benefits for another
2b. hatred	absence of the pleasure of friendliness
3a. fear	pain at the appearance of imminent evil to oneself
3b. confidence	absence of the pain of fear
4a. shame	pain at the appearance of dishonor
4b. shamelessness	absence of the pain of shame
5a. gratitude	pleasure at the appearance of favors received
5b. ingratitude	absence of the pleasure of gratitude
6a. pity	pain at the appearance of another person's undeserved bad fortune
6b. indignation	pain at the appearance of another person's undeserved good fortune
7a. [satisfaction]	pleasure at the appearance of another person's deserved bad fortune
7b. envy	pain at the appearance of another person's deserved good fortune

| 8a. rivalry | pain at our lack of rewards to which we and peers aspire |
| 8b. disdain | absence of the pain of rivalry |

The insistence on oppositions creates some inexact pairings, and envy is paired with an unnamed emotion (1388a24–29), but the format aids in constructing enthymemes on both sides of a question. The pairs are mutually exclusive, so that one emotion will drive out its contrary, and they are interconnected, so that one emotion can give rise to another, as anger can lead to hatred.

Here *pathos* is again analyzed in terms of specific social situations, with long catalogs of the occasions and persons that give rise to each emotion, and again for the same stated purpose of providing premises (*protaseis;* 1378a27) for enthymemes on opposing sides. Individual *phantasia* cause pleasure or pain because of prior beliefs about these occasions and persons. In the case of anger, "undeserved slight to oneself" entails unreflective beliefs about what constitutes a slight, what it means to be undeserved, and the relations between oneself and the slighting person. As a result, *pathos* provides the *rhētōr* with an enormous store of argumentative topics for affecting judgments. Suppose in a judicial case a man has been assaulted, and guilt turns on the question of criminal motive. The injured party claims there was a prior slight to the defendant, who then became angry, and the pain of anger called for the sweet pleasure of revenge, and revenge led to assault. The defendant counters that the prior slight was no slight at all, since the offending party had already apologized and made it clear that the apparent slight was really an accident; apology accepted, no slight, no anger, no revenge, no assault, and no guilt.

Since the individual *pathē* are founded upon belief, it is possible to change the grounds for a belief, and so move the audience from one emotion to another. One of the slights that lead to anger is disdain, being held worthless by a friend, beneficiary, dependent, or by someone who has been well treated. In Thucydides' story of the revolt of Mitylene, one *rhētōr* argued that the Mitylenians had disdained the Athenians' friendship; another countered that there was no disdain, but only the mistaken hope for independence. For Aristotle, the task of the *rhētōr* is to initiate a reflection on the unreflective elements that constitute an underlying belief. If some of them can be changed, the audience may shift from one emotion to another, and so their entire judgment about the circumstances may change.

Allied with *pathos* as a means of inducing conviction is the subject of *ēthos,* and Aristotle's views here were largely misunderstood by subsequent writers. In Book 2, he specifies that *ēthos* rests upon the display of three qualities: good sense, virtue, and goodwill toward the audience. The last of these is addressed explicitly in terms of *pathos* (1378a18), since it depends on the rhetor's ability to show the audience how to feel pleasure or alleviate pain. Pain is the more acute sensation, since it is a movement of the soul away from its natural state, while pleasure is the attenuation of pain. Later writers would ally the painful movements in a general way with violent or strong passions, and the desire to attenuate those pains with gentle emotions, thus blurring distinctions between *pathos* and *ēthos.* Aristotle's larger philosophical contexts for understanding *pathos* were lost soon after his death, and without them his surviving pronouncements on *pathos* took on the appearance of cynical manipulation.

Rome and Cicero. The similarities between *pathos* in Athenian and Roman rhetoric do not run deep, although theatrical aspects of emotional appeal are found in both traditions. The corrupt official Servius Galba hoisted a young orphan onto his shoulders in a bid for pity; and the advocate for the former consul and general Manius Aquilius, who wore mourning clothes to his own trial, ripped open the old man's garment to show the scars he bore from a lifetime of battles fought for Rome (Cicero, *De oratore* 1.53; 2.47). By the imperial era, so formulaic was the use of orphans, squalid clothing, blood-stained swords, and bone fragments, that some efforts went awry. One child was found to be crying because his teacher was pinching him; another crying child was dismissed with the remark "Give him a piece of bread to shut him up." In another case, two servants were supposed to bring in a wax effigy of the dead man at the pathetic climax of the speech, but they had no idea what a climax was, and instead kept walking in and out with the effigy, so that the only tears were those of laughter (Quintilian, *Institutio oratoria* 6.1.40 sq.).

Pathetic extravagance was encouraged by the Roman taste for theatrical displays of all sorts, and even the distinctive Roman genre of funeral oratory had its roots in processions of effigies, portraits, symbols, and mourners. Early Latin discourse shows a love of flamboyant stylistic techniques and manipulations of language, and even Cato the Censor, who exiled the professional rhetoricians from Rome, shaped his own writings with repetitions of sound and patterns of thought intended to intensify the ideas conveyed. Thus, the twin notions of stylistic delight and pathetic intensification were built into Roman oratory, even before the importation of Hellenistic theories of style, and the matter-of-fact discussion of tropes and figures in the anonymous *Rhetorica ad Herennium* (now ascribed to an unknown "Cornificius") show that by the first century BCE it was already commonplace to think of linguistic manipulation in terms of pathetic impact. [*See* Figures of speech; *and* Style.]

Despite the Roman affinity for *pathos,* there is relatively little theoretical writing on the subject in the early centuries, and the handbooks from the schools are largely formulaic. The *Ad Herennium* specifies that the *rhētōr* should use both openings and closings to seek pity for his disabilities, need, loneliness, and misfortune; and second, to heap contempt and hatred upon his opponent (1.v.8). Hatred can be generated in ten ways, such as demonstrating that the deed was particularly heinous, or intentionally directed against social superiors, or against the gods, or particularly indefensible coming from this person, or claiming that other criminals are looking at this trial to see how much they can get away with. The topics for pity are equally mechanical and specify the many ways in which misfortunes can be viewed (2.xxx.48–50). Many of these prescriptions sound like classroom assignments for schoolboys, much like the *progymnasmata,* which prepared students for rhetorical studies, but examples of nearly all these techniques can be found in oratory from the period.

Not until Marcus Tullius Cicero (106–43 BCE), one of Rome's foremost politicians and rhetoricians, do the Romans have anything like a theory of *pathos,* but even so, his approach is more practical than systematic. *Pathos* emerges in his mature treatise *De oratore* as something that happens to an audience. The *rhētōr* decides at the outset whether his cause even merits a pathetic appeal, then analyzes the emotional predispositions of the judges—a task made easier by the protracted legal proceedings at Rome—and either amplifies existing emotions or seeks to generate emotions where none exist.

Cicero's emotions are "disturbances of the soul" (*animi perturbationes*), and in order to realize the full power and science of rhetoric, which are found in *pathos* rather than *ēthos* or *logos,* the *rhētōr* needs to understand all such movements of the soul (*omnes animorum motus; De oratore* 1.17). The emotions Cicero actually discusses, however, are restricted to the antithetical pairs of hatred and esteem, malice and goodwill, fear and hope, desire and aversion, joy and sorrow, compassion and punitiveness (2.185 sq.), and this list is changed yet again when he discusses individual emotions—love, hate, wrath, malice and envy, compassion, hope, joy, fear, and vexation (2.206–211). Scholars from the Renaissance to the present have struggled to bring these two lists of emotions into alignment with the lists in Aristotle, but with little success, since Cicero neither shows interest in the pleasures or pains that underpin Aristotle's *pathē,* nor views the emotions as natural and inherent psychological states. What Aristotle and Cicero share is an understanding that emotions are based on beliefs, and that the *rhētōr* can change those underlying beliefs. Love, for example, is gained by demonstrating that the defendant's action was done for the benefit of the audience, and not for his own. Conversely, dwelling upon an opponent's action that was ruinous or unprofitable to the audience breeds hatred. Such dwelling is likely to be accomplished by amplification and devices of language more than by reason alone. [*See* Amplification.]

Cicero's *rhētōr* first must feel the emotion he wants the audience to feel, and Cicero justifies this on grounds of practice, ethics, and theater. From a practical point of view, it is unreasonable to expect the audience to experience an emotion that not even the *rhētōr* can feel. It is possible to feign such emotion, but it is easier actually to feel it, especially since the speech first will seize the *rhētōr* before it seizes the audience, and many a *rhētōr* is carried away with his own words (2.191). From an ethical point of view, the failure to display personal emotion can be a self-indictment of moral chicanery, since the *rhētōr* obviously is arguing for a cause in which he does not believe (*Brutus* 278). Even if the *rhētōr* is pleading on behalf of an unworthy client, it is still morally imperative to display emotion to show that he is loyal to his friends, and noble to the stranger he defends. This last leads into bravura performance, since the *rhētōr*'s own *pathos* and theatricality will be judged right along with (and often in place of) the merits of the case at hand (*De oratore* 2.192), and Cicero underscores oratorical performance by drawing several direct comparisons with pathetic actors and poets. [*See* Pathopoeia.]

There is a reciprocity in *De oratore* between theatrical *pathos* and *ēthos*. The *pathos,* which the audience is supposed to feel, is validated by the perceptions that a trustworthy *rhētōr* feels it first, but at the same time, the trustworthiness of the *rhētōr* is established by the perception that he is capable of feeling *pathos*. The distinction between *pathos* and *ēthos* blurs in other ways as well. In *De oratore*, Cicero presents the three duties of a *rhētōr* as *docere, conciliare, movere*—to instruct the audience, gain their goodwill, and arouse their emotions—but *conciliare* in the Roman context is secured by a preemptive use of *pathos*. When he later writes the rhetorical treatise *Orator,* he revises this formulation to *probare, delectare, flectere*—to prove to the audience, delight them, and victoriously sweep them away—but *delectare* in this context means charming or seducing a sophisticated and jaded Roman audience by arousing the full range of their interests, from voyeuristic curiosity to aesthetic satisfaction (xxi.69). In both formulations, it is difficult to separate out theatrical *pathos* from *ēthos,* and while scholars from the early Middle Ages to the present have struggled to align Cicero's three duties with Aristotelian *logos, ēthos,* and *pathos,* Cicero was probably not thinking in Aristotelian terms at all. Even more striking is the shift in Cicero's two formulations between *movere* and *flectere,* between moving the emotions and moving the entire person.

Within a century, any distinction between *pathos* and *ēthos* all but disappears. The educator Marcus Fabius Quintilianus (Quintilian; c.35–c.100 CE) divides all emotions into just two types, using the Greek term *pathos* to describe violent perturbations of the soul, and the Greek *ēthos* for gentle emotions that secure goodwill (*Institutio oratoria* 6.2.8–11). Most of Cicero's earlier ideas about *pathos* are elaborated at length by Quintilian, but he adds a psychological process to explain how a *rhētōr* can make himself feel an emotion. The body is capable of receiving a *phantasia,* or "vision" that vividly impresses itself upon the imagination, and the *rhētōr* can call upon such visions to generate the clarity of details that will make him, and others, feel they are in the presence of the original event. Quintilian claimed he himself had been so successful with *phantasia* that he had wept and turned pale while speaking (6.2.29–36). This is not Aristotle's concept of *phantasia,* but it is similar to Cicero's understanding of it as a vision that strikes the body from outside, and Cicero attributes it to the Stoic philosophers (*Academica* 1.xi.40).

The Roman vocabulary of *pathos* was the vocabulary of Stoic philosophy, and that vocabulary betrays a way of thinking about *pathos* that runs through Roman society. Stoicism, as Cicero understands it, eliminates the split between the rational and irrational by positing a *logos* that unifies all nature, and by positing a human intellect sufficient to comprehend that *logos*. Reasoning that accords with that *logos* accords with nature itself, but mistakes can happen, and mistaken opinions that are contrary to nature and right reason are called *pathē*. These *pathē* differ from healthy mental dispositions in that they throw the soul into violent motion that interferes with judgment, and thus the Stoic sage tries to diminish *pathē* in his own life, to be apathetic. Whatever the attractions of Stoicism as a personal philosophy, both Cicero and Quintilian strongly rejected it as a basis for understanding or employing *pathos* in public oratory, and both thought that Stoic *rhētōrs* were unbearably tedious. But both accept the Stoic way of discussing *pathos*—it is a violent disturbance of the soul that throws its judgments off balance. Cicero in his later rhetorical treatises uses the same vocabulary that he attributes to the Stoics in his *Tusculan Disputations,* that is, *pathos* is a disorder (*perturbatio*) of the soul, even a disease (*morbus*), but always a movement (*commotio* and *motus*) of the soul away from right reason and contrary to nature, and a longing (*appetitus*) that is too violent (4.8 sq.). In private life, a person would do well to control such disturbances; but in public life, a *rhētōr* will do even better to induce those same disturbances in others.

Medieval to Renaissance. The Christian theologian Aurelius Augustinus (354–430 CE) changed the nature of the discussion by blending *pathos* with volition. In *The City of God,* Augustine accepts that emotions are perturbations of the soul contrary to nature, but Christ and Saint Paul felt emotions, so emotions cannot all be bad. But some are evil, and since evil is incarnate, the emotions cannot be founded upon reason or the body. Augustine instead posits a different view of the faculties of the soul as memory, intelligence, and the will (*voluntas*), and in them he locates the powers of mind, knowledge, and love (*amor*). All emotions thus become subjective experiences of acts of the will, and love becomes the center of human experience. *Pathos* ceases to be a matter of the rational or the irrational, but rather a matter of the direction of volition and object of love (chap. 14).

Augustine had started his professional life as a professor of rhetoric, so his changes to the Ciceronian idea of *pathos* are both informed and significant. In Book 4 of *On Christian Doctrine,* he appropriates Cicero's later formulation of *docere, delectare, flectere* and includes a teleological progression for *pathos* that "deflects" a listener from one mode of life to another. To each of the three oratorical duties he assigns one of Cicero's styles of low, middle, and grand, but where Cicero discriminated among these styles according to whether the particular cause was worthy of a particular style, Augustine discriminates the styles according to the function of each. The low style teaches (*docere*) in an analytical manner nearly devoid of *pathos;* the middle style delights (*delectare*) and so draws the audience to love the good; while the grand style uses all linguistic resources to redirect the will. For Cicero, all three duties and all three styles were needed for persuasion, but for Augustine, all of them are pointed at *flectere* itself. The audience might very well be convinced of what it should do, but only *pathos* would compel them to act upon that knowledge (4.27).

Augustine thus returns to a view of *pathos* that looks very similar to that of the earliest Greeks— that is, reason and volition are separate—but through an altogether different process. This raises again the specter that distressed Plato, the idea of a power over humans that is effectively independent of reason. Augustine forestalls this problem with the first three books of *On Christian Doctrine,* which are devoted to what a Christian should teach, and which again approximates Plato's own response: the power of rhetoric should be wielded only by the wise. *Pathos* is the end of doctrine for Augustine, but doctrine finally controls rhetorical *pathos.* His solution depended upon a commitment to the link between morality and *pathos,* and variations on this solution would prove attractive until the seventeenth century, when the commitment weakened, leading to a modern severing of reason and *pathos.*

During much of the late medieval period, the rhetorical treatises that were most relevant to *pathos*—by Plato, Aristotle, Cicero, and Quintilian— were all lost. What survived was the anonymous *Rhetorica ad Herennium* and Cicero's early *De inventione,* but with the medieval loss of scope for political and judicial oratory, the advice there on *pathos* could only seem mechanical or irrelevant. With the gradual rediscovery of the missing treatises, attempts were made to reconstruct classical ideas about *pathos* in the context of Christian understandings. The Dominican theologian Giles of Rome (Aegidius Romanus, or Egidio Colonna, c.1245–1316) tries in his *Expositio super tribus libris rhetoricorum* to explicate the *pathē* from Aristotle's *Rhetoric* using a theory of emotions developed by his Dominican confrere Thomas Aquinas (1225–1274) in the *Summa theologica.* Thomas discriminates among several kinds of emotions, and identifies *passio animalis* as a movement of the soul that disturbs the body. Once again the tripartite view of the soul is adopted, but this time the intellective appetite regards universal good, while the sensitive appetite regards particular goods and evils. Once again the sensitive emotions are divided into the concupiscible and the irascible, but this time the former are emotions of pursuit and avoidance, and the latter are emotions of resistance and overcoming. Thus Thomas proposes eleven emotions, with the absolute nature of concupiscence taking precedence over the circumstantial nature of irascibility:

Category	Good	Evil
Concupiscible:	love	hate
	desire	repugnance
	joy	sadness
Irascible:	hope	fear
	despair	daring
	—	anger

A comparison with Aristotle's list of sixteen *pathē* shows that these are very different approaches to *pathos;* anger, for example, has no companion emotion in Thomas, and has moved from first consideration to last. Not only do the two writers have different emotions and different pairings, but their generating philosophies are different. Despite these difficulties, Giles of Rome still was able to use Thomas in making the *pathē* in Aristotle's *Rhetoric* coordinate with Christian theology, and his *Expositio* was still being used three hundred years later.

The Venetian humanist Daniele Barbaro (1513–1570), later the patriarch of Aquileia, tries to be more flexible at reconciling Aristotelian and Thomist *pathos* in his *Commentarii* (1544) on the *Rhetoric.* He follows the order of Aristotle's *pathē,* but to do so he reverses the order of Thomas's categories and ignores Thomas's rationale for them, in favor of an altogether different rhetorical synthesis. Barbaro includes, for example, emotions of hope and despair, which are based on good, and emotions of fear and daring, of anger and mildness, based on evil. This distinction is more Aquinas than Aristotle, since hope and despair are not *pathē* for Aristotle, but rather are discriminants he uses for discussing the *pathē.* So also, Barbaro attempts to find an Aristotelian middle between fear and daring, but instead winds up with a discrimination between honorable fear and dishonorable fear. Dishonorable fear accords with what Aristotle calls shame, but honorable fear has no real counterpart in Aristotle and accords poorly with Aristotelian *phobos.* But for Barbaro, honorable fear is a fear of getting things wrong, or of letting wrong triumph over right, or letting falsehood triumph over truth, and thus it is at the heart of the entire rhetorical enterprise; it is the motive for engaging in rhetoric at all. After exploring all the motions of the soul in the *Rhetoric,* Barbaro concludes by urging the rhetors of his day to eschew those *motus animi* devoted to evil and cultivate those devoted to good, in a sense turning Thomas's theological solution to account in civil affairs. This view of *pathos* is far removed from Aristotle's view in the *Rhetoric,* but thoroughly in keeping with the aims of Barbaro's earlier *Dialogo della Eloquenza* (1557), to form a true and perfect gentleman who has the eloquence and wisdom to govern the city-state, to move the souls of the people, and to serve as a sacred rhetor, an illustrious gentleman, and a true Christian.

Renaissance. In some respects, the Renaissance recovery of classical materials actually complicated the efforts to understand *pathos* in rhetoric. Commentators had problems distinguishing among Platonic, Peripatetic, and Stoic notions, between Hellenistic notions and late Roman notions, all made more difficult by assuming that Greek rhetoric was consonant with Roman rhetoric.

The Paduan professor Antonio Riccoboni (1541–1599) tried to sift these confusions in his *Paraphrasis* (1588) of Aristotle's *Rhetoric.* The *pathē,* he noted, had been translated into Latin as *perturbationes animi,* as "disordered movements of the soul." He attributes the translation to the Stoic union of body and soul, with the result that distinctions of bodily agitations must perforce be distinctions of the soul, and he argues that this late Stoic tradition of *pathos* is incompatible with Aristotelian *pathos.* His own solution conflates Aristotle's *De anima* with the *Nicomachean Ethics* to delineate a threefold reciprocity in the human soul; there is a faculty by which men are able to be moved, there are *affectus* that serve as immediate instruments for that faculty, and there are dispositions acquired by repeated use of those instrumental *affectus.* This *pathos* functions within a tripartite division of the universe. There is a physical world that embraces everything, a mental world that can conceive anything in the physical world, and a world of speech in which the entirety of the mental world can be represented. It is rhetoric that governs, moderates, and ornaments this world of speech, and rhetoric that manifests reason that is shared with God. Rhetoric finally is a tool given by a Christian God, the better to know God's universe and bring the soul into closer communion with God. A similar position is elaborated by the Protestant theologian

John Rainolds (1549–1607), who lectured on Aristotle's *Rhetoric* at Oxford during the 1570s. For Rainolds, the *pathē* are natural commotions of the soul, impelled by the senses, and implanted by God for the purpose of seeking good and fleeing evil, even if Aristotle did not fully comprehend this. Turning away from a strict consideration of Aristotle, he declares that eloquence has two parts, "the first belongs to life, the second to the tongue," the latter learned from Cicero, the former from Christ.

Pedagogical approaches to *pathos* proceeded alongside scholarly approaches. The Dutch humanists Rudolfus Agricola (Roelof Huysman; 1444–1485) completed his *De inventione dialecticae* around 1479, published posthumously in 1515, the same year that Giles's *Expositio* was finally published. Agricola establishes that many of the topical procedures useful for dialectic also work for *pathos*. In Book 3, he defines *affectus* as a kind of paroxysm of the soul (*impetus quidam animi*) that drives a person to desire or reject something much more strongly than that person would do in a tranquil state of mind, and while he refers his readers to Aristotle's *pathē* in the *Rhetoric*, his several discussions about vehement and gentle emotions show that his thinking is more indebted to late Latin traditions. His *pathos* is based on a kind of social decorum, in which an auditor's judgment about what happens is matched with a judgment about the person to whom it happens. Thus ill-fortune leads to different emotions depending upon whether it seems merited or unmerited. Agricola emphasizes three pathetic procedures based on decorum. First, certain kinds of language have an affinity for certain kinds of emotion, not simply in terms of meaning, but also in tone and in the shapes and patterns of language treated in *elocutio*. Second, emotion can be explored by describing people who are in the throes of emotion, especially if there is a mimetic correspondence between the narration and the emotion. Third, dialectical topics can be used to explore emotion in terms of what happened, to whom it happened, and the deservedness of either. In all three procedures, the techniques of amplification can be used to dwell upon an emotion, magnify it, diminish it, or dismiss it.

Agricola's three procedures would be important for Renaissance rhetoric and for vernacular practices in poetry, narrative, letter writing, and sermons. The enormous circulation of Agricola's treatise made his ideas current throughout Europe, and examples of his influence are many. Thomas Wilson (c.1525–1581), the future Elizabethan secretary of state, provides an English version of Agricola's formulation: "Affections therefore (called Passions) are none other thing, but a stirring or forsing of the minde, either to desire, or els to detest and loth any thing, more vehemently then by nature we are commonly wont to doe" (*The Arte of Rhetorique* 1553, 130), and he demonstrates how a *rhētōr* can amplify an emotion by working through a series of circumstantial topics:

i.   What is done.
ij.   By whom.
iij. Against whom.
iiij. Vpon what mind.
v.   At what time.
vj.   In what place.
vij. After what sorte.
viij. How much he would haue done.

Governing Wilson's overall approach to rhetorical *pathos* is the prevailing view already seen in Augustine's earlier reshaping of Cicero: "Three thinges are required of an Orator. To teach. To delight. And to perswade." Whatever else happens with teaching and delighting, persuasion itself is nearly synonymous with *pathos*.

The belief that topical invention was common to both rhetoric and dialectic could unite the two disciplines, but it could also separate them, as happens with some of the curricular realignments of the French educator Pierre de la Ramée (Petrus Ramus, 1515–1572), who tried to reduce duplication in the two by assigning the topics to dialectic and leaving rhetoric with just *style*, memory, and delivery. The effect was to isolate *style* from invention, so that its impact was more pathetic than cognitive. The concentration upon *style* for *pathos* can be seen in other works of the period, such as the brief compendium *De arte rhetorica* (1557) compiled by the Jesuit Cypriano Soarez (1524–1593). Soarez blended Aristotle, Cicero, and Quintilian by taking the most accessible parts of each author and ignoring differences, but finally he is less interested in argumentation than in the style (*elocutio*) that can induce faith (*fides*) by moving souls (*motu animorum*), and his school text was studied by many thousands of students in Jesuit schools and colleges.

It was still possible to explain the physiological processes behind these pathetic motions of the soul by adapting the inherited Aristotelian model of physical motions of *phantasia* operating between the intellective and sensitive faculties, but the German educator Philipp Melanchthon (1497–1560) provided a newer model in his several treatises on rhetoric, dialectic, and psychology. Acoustic and visual sense impressions are converted into physical wave patterns within the nerves and travel to the brain, where they are combined with perceptions of language, memories of particular experiences, and universal understandings implanted by God. These new wave patterns then travel to the heart, the seat of the soul where God has implanted love of good and hatred of evil. These new waves beat against the heart, causing it to swell or contract as it senses injury or welfare, and so pour a *spiritus* into the blood vessels leading to the muscles. Thus the physical motions of the external world translate into physical motions within the person, and emotions are manifested as movement. Melanchthon uses a theologically determined physiology to comprehend and govern *pathos*, but *pathos* still dominates in rhetoric, and he specifies in his *Elementa rhetorices* (1539) that the task of rhetoric is to use distinctive language to move souls powerfully and set them in motion (*permovere atque impellere animos*).

Later Centuries. The trend toward placing *pathos* at the center of rhetoric intensified across Europe during the seventeenth century, and on both sides of the confessional divide. The learned Jesuit professor Nicolas Caussin (1583–1651) wrote a huge treatise on *De eloquentia sacra et humana* (1617) in which he discusses the emotions at greater length than his fellow Jesuit Soarez had earlier devoted to the entirety of rhetoric. On the Protestant side, Bartholomaeus Keckermann (1573–1609), a German professor of rhetoric in Prussia, places emotion and volition at the center of his massive *Systema rhetoricae* (1606) and defines the goal of rhetoric as forcing the heart "to do anything" (*compulsio, cordis ad aliquid agendum*, 11). Traditional rhetorical subjects of invention, disposition, and amplification are relevant primarily

as they enable *pathos,* and the major part of Book 1 is an exploration of *elocutio* for the purposes of *pathos*. In Book 2, Keckermann discusses the traditional *genera dicendi,* but he prefers to discriminate among various kinds of oratory according to their emotions and intensities, ranging from *delectatio* to *motus cordis,* reminiscent of late Roman views of *ēthos* and *pathos*. What might appear as crass manipulation of the emotions for "any purpose" is sharply attenuated by his pairing the *Systema rhetoricae* with his companion treatise *Systema ethicae,* which makes it clear that only the good emotions can lead to a good life. Keckermann's theological commitments keep *pathos* under control, but it was possible for contemporaries to read his ethical and rhetorical treatises in isolation from one another. So also, the series of rhetorical treatises by the Dutch Calvinist professor Gerhardus Johannes Vossius (Gerrit Jansz Vos; 1577–1649) were intended to work within a Calvinist theology, but were usually read without that theology. His *Rhetorices contractae* (1621), which is largely a reworking of Aristotelian rhetoric for contemporary purposes, reorders Aristotle's *pathē* to reflect their role in different kinds of oratory, and develops techniques of invention for each kind that will stress the appeals of *pathos* (*de figuris pertinentibus ad argumenta "pathētika"*).

This concentration on *pathos* extends to the Ukraine and Russia. [*See* Slavic rhetoric.] Feofan Prokopovič, the reader in rhetoric at Kiev and later archbishop of Novgorod (1681–1736), devotes an entire book of his *De arte rhetorica libri decem* (1706, manuscript) to the emotions, and ties it closely to the book on *elocutio*. In his attempt to synthesize nearly all previous writers on emotion, Prokopovič redistributes Aristotle's *pathē* between Quintilian's *ēthos* and *pathos,* and delineates how different tropes and figures achieve effects appropriate to each affect. He explores the traditional rhetorical genres, but all along he is aiming at a baroque union of emotion and figuration in Book 9 on sacred oratory.

God guarantees the link between *pathos* and reasoned argument in these writers, but that link is sharply attenuated in the work of Bernard Lamy (1640–1715), a French ecclesiast of the Congregation of the Oratory. In his *De l'Art de Parler* (1675), he loosely follows the ideas of the French philosopher René Descartes (1596–1650), both on "method" and on the physiology of the passions, with the result that *pathos* and reason are all but isolated from one another. Lamy revised his work continually throughout his life, but it was his earlier publication that was translated into English as *The Art of Speaking* (1676) and had most impact on subsequent English thinking.

Lamy's *rhētōr* knows the truth by virtue of Cartesian method, but while Descartes himself came to realize that many human affairs are not susceptible to his method, Lamy is less troubled, and his *rhētōr* is capable of knowing the truth. The problem lies in conveying that truth to audiences who have not followed Cartesian method—either through inattention, laziness, stubbornness, or self-interest—which makes them ignore truths that are clear and distinct. *Pathos* responds to these inadequacies in the audience, and Lamy relies upon a model of the mind reminiscent of Melanchthon's, but without the intellective intervention enabled by God. Thoughts are patterns (*desseins*) in the mind of the *rhētōr*, and are vocalized in the patterns of language as vibrations. But words as linguistic patterns are finally insufficient for the full range of mental patterns a *rhētōr* may wish to communicate, and rarely sufficient to convey the *rhētōr*'s "sentiments" about his own thoughts. The numerous tropes and figures of rhetoric are valuable here, because they can generate many more designs than can the standard lexicon itself. Thus the vibrations in the soul of the *rhētōr* can be reproduced in the auditor with the help of tropes and figures to convey patterns.

The brain itself is a pliable material, so that deep designs can be physically inscribed if a stimulus is powerful and sudden. Violence is part of the rhetorical encounter, and Lamy's true *adversaire* is not the opposing *rhētōr,* but the audience itself; indeed, the *rhētōr* must *imiter un soldat qui combat son ennemi.* The violence of this active assault induces a movement in the soul of the auditor, something like amazement, shock, and wonder (*l'admiration*), and this is an emotion. At the discretion of the *rhētōr,* this "admiration" is then transformed into feelings of either esteem or contempt. Having excited these emotions, the *rhētōr* can then lead the auditor "wheresoever he chooses" (*du coté oú l'on veut les conduire*).

There is no need here for reason or any other active response on the part of the auditor. In Lamy, belief in the inevitability of rational method replaces direct reliance upon God to secure the link between reason and *pathos.* The long-term effect is to deny a place for reason in rhetoric—reasoning is done elsewhere—and reduce the scope of rhetoric to *pathos* alone. In his final revisions of 1699, Lamy tries to forestall a complete divorce between reason and *pathos* by returning to earlier approaches. He postulates an auditor's inherent inclinations toward the good, so that *pathos* will only succeed when it appeals to those inclinations, but it is not clear that this qualification accords with the rest of his account, and the history of rhetoric in later centuries testifies to the impact of his original formulation. Cartesian method to secure the truth did not survive into those later centuries, but Lamy's formulation of *pathos*—as a power to impose what a *rhētōr* believes to be the truth—most certainly did.

With the effective divorce between argument and *pathos* following Descartes, rhetoric itself undergoes some redefinition. Argumentation is assigned to other varieties of discourse, while rhetoric, and more properly "persuasion," becomes the appeal to the passions or to the will, so that the auditor will embrace or act upon the argumentation of other discourses. Typical is the work of George Campbell (1719–1796), a professor of divinity in Aberdeen, who sharply separates argument from *pathos* in his *Philosophy of Rhetoric* (1776). The *rhētōr* must excite some emotion, and he must demonstrate that the action he proposes will satisfy that emotion, but the emotion need not arise directly from the matter at hand, and for the less discerning, there need be no connection at all. For the more discerning, the *rhētōr* needs to draw upon sensation and imagination to transfer emotions from other circumstances to the present situation, and Campbell delineates several associational techniques: probability, plausibility, importance, proximity of time, connection of place, personal relation to the *rhētōr,* and personal self-interest (1.7). Argument does not need *pathos* to make its point, but it must add *pathos* if the point is to have any effect.

The distance between Aristotle's thinking and that of the eighteenth century can be seen in the discriminations Campbell makes among the kinds of *pathos*. Some passions are naturally inert and deject an auditor's mind too much to effect action; these include sorrow, fear, shame, and humility. Others elevate the soul and stimulate to action; these include hope, patriotism, ambition, emulation, and anger. And some fall ambiguously in the middle, such as joy, love, esteem, and compassion. Aristotle, by contrast, viewed nearly all of these as *pathē* that provided resources for enthymematic premises and means by which to change judgments, and Aristotle did not view any of them in terms of elevation or dejection of the soul. The opening paragraphs in Aristotle caution against solitary address to the passions, while the opening paragraphs in Campbell delineate the passions worthy of solitary address. In succeeding centuries, the disciplinary lines only hardened, with argument moving toward positivist formal logic, and *pathos* moving even farther away, to the point where rhetoric is popularly conceived as linguistic manipulation and emotional pandering. [*See* Nineteenth-century rhetoric.] The seventeenth-century effort to find certainty in the midst of conflicting emotional uncertainties has led, in the long term, to the emotional imposition of seeming certainties.

Twentieth Century. In the aftermath of two world wars, writers in a number of fields concluded that formal argument is insufficient for the informal world of human conflict, and that human concerns cannot be reduced to the constraints required by formal logic. The result is a resurgence of interest in the theoretical aspects of *pathos* as a means to manage uncertainty. These reconsiderations are part of larger philosophical movements, and to some extent reawaken the nondogmatic aspects of rhetoric in its earliest centuries. After World War I, the American literary critic I. A. Richards (1893–1979) expands the scope of rhetoric as a communicative rather than simply persuasive enterprise, holding that conflict arises from misunderstanding, and misunderstanding from misplaced expectations. In *The Philosophy of Rhetoric* (1936), he focuses less on emotion and more on sensibilities and dispositions, employing a psychology of *pathos* in which a sensory impression is recorded in the brain as an attitudinal and associational complex (an *engram*) of the context in which the impression was experienced. A *rhētōr*'s reference to any aspect of

that *engram* recalls all of it in its entirety, and he can order various stimuli to trigger mental responses in the audience. But Richard's real interest is in interpretation, and it is the audience who must set aside the expectations formed of their own experiences, in order to understand the rhetor's intended meaning. [*See* Hermeneutics.] This hermeneutic approach to *pathos* is greatly expanded by the German philosopher Hans-Georg Gadamer, who argues in *Wahrheit und Methode, Ergänzungen* (1983) that every text is a response to some question. Both the question and the response are shaped by a unique combination of sensibilities, and without an understanding of the *pathos* of the originating question, the meaning of the response cannot be determined with precision. While recoveries of original meaning may prove elusive, new audiences are free to pose their own questions to received texts, and so generate responses unanticipated by the rhetor.

In the wake of the moral catastrophe of World War II, Chaim Perelman, a philosopher of jurisprudence in Belgium, and Lucie Olbrechts-Tyteca, examined how legislators, jurists, and politicians actually argue about questions of value, and concluded that, despite claims to the contrary, logical arguments in such realms are never devoid of *pathos*. In their *Traité de l'argumentation* (1958; *The New Rhetoric*, 1969), they explore the ways in which states of mind shared by audiences and rhetors alike determine the acceptability of premises for argument, the acceptability of modes of reasoning by which to conduct argument, and the acceptability of patterns of language to convey the sense of engagement that imbues human ideas and conflicts. In their view, Cartesian method effectively eliminated particular human audiences by positing a "universal audience" that exists exclusively in terms of the logical system being pursued. Argument can only deal effectively with human affairs by recovering the attitudinal particularities of the concerned individuals who constitute a particular audience, and in their analysis, those who argue in public instinctively know this.

Beyond the fields of persuasion and interpretation, contemporary metaphysics increasingly focuses upon rhetorical *pathos*. The philosopher Michel Meyer argues in *Le Philosophe et les passions* (1991) that *pathos* presents in sharp relief the problematic relations among the self, the other, and the material world, and the ways in which those relations instantiate (or perhaps fend off) underlying existential questions. Where formal logic has been criticized for the tautology of only being able to conclude its premises, so also there is a logic of the emotions, in which one can only see, and hence conclude, what one wants to see from the beginning. Despite these underlying problematics, modern *rhētors* must mobilize the resources of the emotions and formal logic alike, along with all their other resources.

The long history of *pathos* is one of legacies. Words remain, and statements are carried forward, but the cultural practices and philosophical tides which lifted them have receded and left them stranded on alien shores, to be picked up and used in other philosophies and practices, and so preserve the illusion of continuity with older meanings. On one level, Aristotle's initial formulation that "the listeners are led into a *pathos* by the *logos*" (*Rhetoric* 1356a14) could be repeated safely by all writers on rhetoric. On another level, that famous formulation of *pathos* makes sense only in Aristotle's own terms, and subsequent writers can only make sense of it in theirs.

[*See also* Classical rhetoric; Eighteenth-century rhetoric; *overview article on* Medieval rhetoric; *overview article on* Renaissance rhetoric; *and* Religion.]

BIBLIOGRAPHY

Carr, Thomas M., Jr. *Descartes and the Resilience of Rhetoric: Varieties of Cartesian Rhetorical Theory.* Carbondale, Ill., 1990.

Colish, Marcia L. *The Stoic Tradition From Antiquity to the Early Middle Ages.* 2 vols. Studies in the History of Christian Thought, vols. 34–35. Leiden, 1985.

Conley, Thomas M. *Rhetoric in the European Tradition.* New York and London, 1990.

Conley, Thomas M. "Παθή and Πίστεις (*Pathe* and *Pisteis*): Aristotle "Rhetoric". 2.2–11." *Hermes-Zeitschrift für klassische Philologie* 110 (1982), pp. 300–315.

Cooper, John M. *Reason and Emotion: Essays on Ancient Moral Psychology and Ethical Theory.* Princeton, 1999.

Dahan, Gilbert, and Irène Rosier-Catach, eds. *La "Rhétorique" d'Aristote: traditions et commentaires, de l'antiquité au XVIIe siècle.* Tradition de la pensée classique. Paris, 1998.

Desmouliez, André. *Cicéron et son Goût: Essai sur une définition d'une esthétique romaine à la fin de la Répub-*
lique. Revue D'Études Latines, vol. 150. Brussels, 1976.

Dobson, J. F. *The Greek Orators.* London, 1918.

Dockhorn, Klaus. *Macht und Wirkung der Rhetorik.* Bad Homburg, Germany, 1968.

Fortenbaugh, William W. *Aristotle on Emotion: A Contribution to Philosophical Psychology, Rhetoric, Poetics, Politics, and Ethics.* New York, 1975.

Fortenbaugh, William W., and David C. Mirhady, eds. *Peripatetic Rhetoric after Aristotle.* Rutgers University Studies in Classical Humanities, vol. 6. New Brunswick, N.J., 1994.

Fortenbaugh, William W., and Peter Steinmetz, eds. *Cicero's Knowledge of the Peripatos.* Rutgers University Studies in Classical Humanities, vol. 4. New Brunswick, N.J., 1989.

Gardiner, H. M., Ruth Clark Metcalf, and John G. Beebe-Center. *Feeling and Emotion: A History of Theories.* New York, 1937.

Green, Lawrence D. *John Rainolds's Oxford Lectures on Aristotle's "Rhetoric."* Newark, Del., London, 1986.

Gross, Alan G., and Arthur E. Walzer, eds. *Rereading Aristotle's "Rhetoric".* Carbondale, Ill., 2000.

Kenny, Anthony. *Action, Emotion, and Will.* Studies in Philosophical Psychology. London, 1963.

Kenny, Anthony. *Aquinas on Mind.* Topics in Medieval Philosophy. London, 1993.

Leeman, A. D. *Orationis Ratio: The Stylistic Theories and Practice of the Roman Orators, Historians, and Philosophers.* 2 vols. Amsterdam, 1963.

Mack, Peter. *Renaissance Argument: Valla and Agricola in the Traditions of Rhetoric and Dialectic.* Studies in Intellectual History, vol. 43. Leiden, 1993.

Meyer, Michel, ed. *Histoire de la rhétorique de Grecs à nos jours.* By Michel Meyer, Manuel Maria Carrilho, and Benoît Timmermans. Paris, 1999.

Michel, Alain. *Rhétorique et philosophie chez Cicéron: essai sur les fondements philosophiques de l'art de persuader.* Paris, 1960.

Plett, Heinrich F. *Rhetorik der Affekte: Englische Wirkungsästhetik im Zeitalter der Renaissance.* Studien zur Englischen Philologie, Neue Folge, vol. 18. Tübingen, 1975.

Prestel, Peter. *Die Rezeption der ciceronischen Rhetorik durch Augustinus in "De doctrina Christiana."* Studien zur klassischen Philologie, vol. 69. Frankfurt A.M. 1992.

Rorty, Amélie Oksenberg, ed. *Essays on Aristotle's "Rhetoric."* Philosophical Traditions, vol. 6. Berkeley, 1996.

Shuger, Debora K. *Sacred Rhetoric: the Christian Grand Style in the English Renaissance.* Princeton, 1988.

Sprague, Rosamond Kent, ed. *The Older Sophists.* Columbia, S.C., 1972. This is a complete translation by several hands of the fragments in "Die Fragmente Der

Vorsokratiker," edited by Diels-Kranz, with new editions of "Antiphon" and of "Euthydemus."

Wisse, Jakob. *Ethos and Pathos From Aristotle to Cicero.* Amsterdam, 1989.

—LAWRENCE D. GREEN

PERIPHRASIS. The Greek term *periphrasis* (Lat. *circumitio, circumloquium*), whose literal meaning is "roundabout of words," designates a discursive phenomenon that substitutes a word, in a given context, by a textual unit that is semantically equivalent. Authors usually assign a double function to the use of this figure, especially in poetry: (1) amplifying and ornamenting the discourse, and (2) emphasizing the nature of certain attributes. The possibilities of this figure, as is usually acknowledged, are practically unlimited, given that almost every word can be substituted in discourse by several words that convey its corresponding definition.

Some generalized forms of periphrasis in the classical and Western poetic traditions include the designations of the deities of classical mythology by their attributes: "The son of Latona" (Apollo), "The boy archer" (Cupid), "The field of Amphitrite" (the sea), "Memnon's mother" (Aurora), "Alcides' tree" (poplar), "Venus's flower" (myrtle), and many others.

[*See also* Figures of speech; Hypallagē; *and* Style.]

BIBLIOGRAPHY

Lanham, R. A. *A Handlist of Rhetorical Terms.* Berkeley, 1991.

Lausberg, H. *Handbuch der literarischen Rhetorik.* Pp. 589–598. Munich, 1960.

Mayoral, J. A. *Figuras retóricas.* Pp. 199–201. Madrid, 1994.

Morier, H. *Dictionnaire de poétique et de rhétorique.* Paris, 1981.

Plett, H. F. *Systematische Rhetorik.* Munich, 2000.

—JOSÉ ANTONIO MAYORAL
Translated by A. Ballesteros

PERSONA. When authors or orators use the word *I* in their work, do they refer to some essential element of their actual selves? Or do they create a character—fictional or autobiographical—for the particular persuasive purposes of their

rhetorical context? Or is the speaking "I" always a role negotiated in each context between author and audience? These are the concerns that surround the concept of *persona* in rhetorical study.

"The concept of *persona*" is a phrase to be used with caution, however. The concept of a speaker's or writer's character as something constructed along various degrees of fictionality has long been part of the study of rhetoric, but there is wide variation in the actual terms used to refer to this concept. Within classical rhetoric, the main term for designating the speaker's character was Aristotle's *ēthos*. [*See* Ēthos.] Contemporary rhetoricians are more likely to use the terms *voice, role,* or *identity* (especially if identity is accompanied by a secondary term, as in *constructed identity, socially situated identity,* or *negotiated identity*). In rhetorical studies, the term *persona* is used rarely enough that it is not even indexed in some of the major overviews of rhetorical history, such as those by George Kennedy (1980) or Cheryl Glenn (1997); it appears most often in the work of contemporary literary critics and poets. Accordingly, *persona* is treated here as the wider concept of the degree of construction in the writer–speaker's character, with less attention to the specific semantic relationships surrounding a given author's choice of terms.

Put simply, the concept of *persona* encourages rhetoricians to think of the "I" created in a speech or writing as something constructed by the speaker or writer. What is in question is the degree of this construction. At one extreme, 1970s rhetorician Ken Macrorie (*Uptaught,* New York, 1970) advocates that writers seek a voice in their writing that allows them most direct expression of their selves—in which case, the construction is less fiction than expression. At the other extreme, University of Chicago scholar Wayne Booth (1983) argues that the "implied author" of a text is never the same as the actual flesh-and-blood author, and always should be treated as a constructed character. Somewhere in the middle would lie classical rhetoric's concept of *ēthos*. For Aristotle (384–322 BCE), the speaker's character is something crafted for the purposes of persuasion from the possibilities available in a given situation, not strictly constructed but certainly selected from the real attributes of the speaker. The concept of *persona* asks the student of rhetoric to engage with the issue of the creation of the speaker–writer's character somewhere along this continuum of construction.

In general terms, rhetoricians across the ages explore three main aspects of the construction of character:

1. The rhetorical construction of character—following Aristotle, the construction of an appropriate speaking voice for the current purpose
2. Persona as a literary device—the explicit creation of a speaking voice distinct from the author's self, for an aesthetic or persuasive purpose
3. The problem of the origin of a speaker's *persona*—the exploration of the social systems surrounding the author–speaker that delimit the range of choices available for the construction and reception of character.

The Rhetorical Construction of Character. In both classical and contemporary practice, one major way of treating the construction of character, especially in pedagogical contexts, is to focus attention on the speaker–writer's choices in best crafting self-presentation for the persuasive circumstance. In classical rhetoric, the term *ēthos* usually marks this way of treating character. In contemporary rhetoric, the term *role* is also used for this purpose.

In classical rhetoric, this way of treating character owes much to Aristotle's *Rhetoric* (367 and 322 BCE), which urges speakers to explore possibilities for the construction of their self-presentation. [*See* Classical rhetoric.] Aristotle suggests speakers should search the specific situation for ways to promote three aspects of their *ēthos: phronēsis* (practical wisdom), *aretē* (good moral character), and *eunoia* (goodwill toward the audience). [*See* Phronēsis.] If the audience can be guided to see the speaker as exhibiting these three character traits, the audience is more likely to be persuaded (*Rhetoric* 2.5–7). Later, Roman rhetoricians both altered and continued these ideas. One difference between Greek and Roman practice was the role of the *patronus*. Where Greeks were expected to speak on their own behalf in legal and political matters, a Roman *patronus* often spoke for others. In the early republic, the *patronus* was a patrician with defined responsibility for certain citizens or freedmen who did not know Roman procedures,

lending his authority and sponsorship to legal representation. By the late republic, a *patronus* was anyone who pleaded a case for someone else. *Persona* management for the *patronus* was as important as that of the represented client. In Roman schools, a focus on the construction of character continued, for both roles of client and *patronus*. The schools assigned exercises in which students argued positions in hypothetical court cases or delivered orations recommending courses of action to historical figures, always with due attention to the construction of character. [*See* Declamation.]

In contemporary rhetoric, this focus on the rhetorical construction of character continues, though the concept of role in modern sociology is as often the source as is classical rhetoric's *ēthos*. Many rhetoricians look especially to sociologist Erving Goffman's work (1963, 1959). For Goffman, in any given day, the same individual takes on a range of different social roles, each with its own criteria for performance and definition of self. A student in a university first-year writing class, for example, may also be a computer help line operator, a lover in a new budding relationship, a single parent of a preschool child, and an active member of a political party. Each of these roles requires a different kind of rhetorical expression (the discourse appropriate to preschool parenting, for instance, would be inappropriate in constructing a position paper for writing class). Each of these roles may define the individual's self according to different criteria (is one nurturing and firm enough in parenting; intellectual, logical, and coherent enough in essay writing?). Many contemporary composition teachers draw on such vocabulary when presenting the task of constructing an appropriate writer's role.

Persona as a Literary Device. A second major focus on the character of the speaker–writer emphasizes the creation of a new persona, mask, or character through which the author speaks. According to some historians, this emphasis on *persona* captures the oldest uses of the term, including the Greek (and occasionally Roman) practice of using masks in drama. (One meaning of *persona* in Latin is "theatrical mask," as with the Greek form of the word, *prosōpon*.) Adopting a character to create a rhetorical display was commonplace throughout the classical world. For example, Plato's dialogue *Phaedrus* (c.370 BCE), which ends with a philosophic definition of good and bad rhetoric, begins with a series of three speeches (two composed by Socrates) from an imagined older lover to a younger beloved. Throughout the Greek and Roman periods, exercises for students of rhetoric often involved speaking in the voice of an historical or imagined personage. In the Middle Ages and Renaissance, authors would often write their philosophic texts, not as their own pronouncements but as the words of some entity, such as Folly as first-person speaker in *The Praise of Folly* (1511) by Desiderius Erasmus (c.1466–1536). This tradition existed alongside the conceptualized rhetorical tradition and its emphasis on *ēthos*.

In contemporary times, focusing on *persona* as a literary device has proved especially important for practicing poets and literary critics. Since George Wright's *The Poet in the Poem: The Personae of Eliot, Yeats, and Pound* (Berkeley, 1960), practicing poets have argued over the difference between the poet and the speaker of a poem. Wright's argument was that the poem's speaker always was someone different from the actual author, a persona created for the purposes of expressing a particular emotion, view, and moment in time. His argument did not go unchallenged, and the nature of the gaps between poet, poem's speaker, and *persona* remain hotly debated.

For literary criticism, the major text on this issue remains Wayne Booth's *Rhetoric of Fiction,* which introduced the terms *implied author* and *unreliable narrator.* For Booth, the speaking "I" in a work of fiction can never be equated with the author, but instead can be thought of as an "implied author"—a character created by writers, even when intending to represent themselves, which is always like other characters a feature of the text. Booth's insight made possible generations of exploration of the narrators' character, especially when narrators could be shown to be unreliable in their treatment of other characters or events.

Obviously, *persona* as a literary device is used very frequently in rhetorical practice. While it has accumulated a solid range of exploration in poetry and literary criticism, it is surprisingly underconceptualized in rhetoric itself.

The Problem of the Origin of a Speaker's

Persona. A third main trend in rhetorical treatments of character focuses on the problem of origin. This trend examines the forces that create the possibilities out of which a speaker can form character. Rather than see character as an inalienable trait of the individual, rhetoricians probe the social and linguistic systems that ascribe to individuals certain elements of character and the potential meanings of those elements. Current theory equates this trend primarily with postmodern thought and "social construction" views of rhetoric, but this trend also has classical antecedents, one of which is the use of dramatic masks.

According to many scholars, in pre-Socratic Greek religious rituals, one assumed some of the god's character by wearing a mask of the god. While it is easy to make too much of such excursions into religious prehistory, the idea of character as something almost magical, which exists outside the self, appears to be connected to the earliest uses of masks and may find expression in contemporary rhetoric's writing about voice.

A more direct antecedent exists in sophistic rhetoric, the practice and teaching of rhetoricians in the Greek city-states prior to rhetoric's systematization by Aristotle. It is difficult to be sure what the Sophists thought, given the scarcity of their texts, the negative characterization of them in Plato's dialogues, and the practical or ceremonial nature of most of the texts that do exist. Even so, many scholars assert that the Sophists emphasized the training of *aretē* (moral character) as the purpose for rhetorical instruction, and argued that such character (and indeed all knowledge) was a function of human conventions and human understanding (since ultimate truth was unknowable outside of human conventional systems). Gorgias (c.483–376 BCE) is the rhetorician most associated with this position. [*See* Sophists.]

Contemporary rhetoricians are currently rereading the Sophists, motivated partly by contemporary concerns with the social construction of self. Since the 1980s, much rhetorical scholarship has focused on the ways in which one's social position and background delimit the shaping of one's "identity" or "voice," because of the social systems that already assign meaning to race, class, gender, and academic experience. As many scholars have shown, one's sense of self—and the way one represents and enacts oneself in speaking and writing—are partly a function of one's social location. In developing an identity (and the speaking and writing practices through which to enact it), each individual both must rely on and at the same time manage these elements of social location. At present, significant studies of the rhetoric, dilemmas, and construction of particular situated identities proliferate, and continue to uncover new insights into this aspect of character. An especially thorough example and introduction to these issues remains Shirley Brice Heath's *Ways With Words* (1983).

As this brief survey suggests, the concept of *persona* (or character, voice, identity) remains vital to an understanding of rhetoric. Each of the three main trends identified here has been practiced, taught, and theorized to different degrees throughout rhetoric's history, and gives every indication of receiving continued attention in the future.

BIBLIOGRAPHY

Aristotle. *The Rhetoric and Poetics of Aristotle.* Translated by W. Rhys Roberts. New York, 1984. First published 1954.

Booth, Wayne. *The Rhetoric of Fiction.* Chicago, 1983. First published 1961.

Cherry, Roger. "Ethos versus Persona: Self-Representation in Written Discourse." *Written Communication* 5.3 (1988); pp. 251–276. Useful idea of *ēthos* and *persona* forming a continuum of rhetorical possibilities.

Elbow, Peter, ed. *Landmark Essays on Voice.* Davis, Calif., 1994. A collection of most of the important essays on voice between 1970 and 1990.

Elliot, Robert. *The Literary Persona.* Chicago, 1982. Thorough historical survey of the term *persona* and an interesting application to Jonathan Swift.

Glenn, Cheryl. *Rhetoric Retold: Regendering the Tradition from Antiquity through the Renaissance.* Carbondale, Ill., 1997. Consideration of the presence and absence of women in the rhetorical tradition.

Goffman, Irving. *The Presentation of Self in Everyday Life.* Garden City, N.Y., 1959.

Goffman, Irving. *Stigma: Notes on the Management of Spoiled Identity.* Englewood Cliffs, N.J., 1963.

Heath, Shirley Brice. *Ways with Words: Language, Life, and Work in Communities and Classrooms.* Cambridge, U.K., 1983. Detailed analysis of the social origin of language character in two communities.

Holland, Norman. *The I.* New Haven, 1985. The idea of "identity theme and variation" is usefully applied to the reading and writing of literature.

Jarrett, Susan. *Rereading the Sophists: Classical Rhetoric Refigured.* Carbondale, Ill., 1991. Modern reclamation of sophistic rhetoric.

Kennedy, George. *Classical Rhetoric and Its Christian and Secular Tradition from Ancient to Modern Times.* Chapel Hill, N.C., 1980.

Kooser, Ted. "On Lying for the Sake of Making Poems." *Prairie Schooner* 72.1 (1998), pp. 5–8. A consideration of the morality of the fictionalized *persona* in poetry.
—ROBERT E. BROOKE

PERSONIFICATION. *See* Poetry; *and* Prosōpopoeia.

PERSPECTIVE BY INCONGRUITY. "Perspective by Incongruity" is Kenneth Burke's central critical method in his works of the 1930s, particularly *Permanence and Change* (1935) and *Attitudes toward History* (1937). Perspective by incongruity is an inventional device in the critic's rhetorical arsenal. In *Attitudes toward History*, Burke defines it as "[a] method for gauging situations by verbal 'atom cracking.' That is, a word belongs by custom to a certain category—and by rational planning you wrench it loose and metaphorically apply it to a different category" (p. 308). In *Philosophy of Literary Form* (1941), he refers to it as "a rational prodding or coaching of language so as to see around the corner of everyday usage" (p. 400). It is not, Burke insists, a tool of critical virtuosity, but a way of bringing us closer to the simple truth.

Burke's primary example of perspective by incongruity is Thorstein Veblen's concept of "trained incapacity," which refers to the way in which one's very abilities can function as blindnesses. Another example is T. S. Eliot's characterization of the increased emphasis on sports in U.S. universities as a case of "decadent athleticism" (*Permanence and Change*, pp. 90–91). Students of rhetoric will recognize these as examples of *oxymōron.* [*See* Oxymōron.] Burke also identifies visual analogues to perspective by incongruity in medieval gargoyles (with their juxtaposition of human and animal) and in the image of the "grotesque" (*Permanence and Change*, p. 112).

It may be useful to see perspective by incongruity as part of a Modernist aesthetic of wrenching the viewer or reader out his or her customary habits of perception (on *Burke as Modernist,* see Selzer, 1996). Modernist painters such as Picasso pictured how an object might look if seen simultaneously from two quite different perspectives. The Soviet film director Eisenstein developed montage as a cinematic technique for producing meaning through the juxtaposition of images. Bertolt Brecht's notion of "defamilarization" as a product of his epic theater seems quite similar to Burke's perspective by incongruity, in that both attempt to disrupt "normal" patterns of experience in order to get closer to the simple truth (Brecht, 1964). The Russian Formalists' discussion of *ostranenie,* or "making strange," has a family resemblance to Burke's concept (Erlich, 1980, pp. 176–178). It is unclear whether Burke read the work of Georges Sorel, the French anarchosyndicalist author best known for *Reflections on Violence* (Translated by T. E. Hulme. Glencoe, Ill., 1950), but Sorel's method of "diremption" sounds exactly like Burke's perspective by incongruity. As H. Stuart Hughes (1958) summarizes the concept, it consists "in willfully wrenching out certain aspects of reality from the context that enveloped them and examining them independently of one another. To juxtapose a number of mutually incompatible statements . . . meant to illuminate aspects of reality that might otherwise have passed unobserved" (p. 92).

Stanley Edgar Hyman (1947) writes that the key metaphor of Kenneth Burke's *Permanence and Change* is "Man as Artist," a metaphor that leads Burke to treat social problems in terms of poetic, rhetorical, and critical techniques. Since social problems have increasingly been framed as matters of "science," Burke's metaphor represents a search for a new "perspective" (Hyman, p. 329). Burke developed the term while reading Friedrich Nietzsche on the will to power. He also observed perspective by incongruity in the work of Oswald Spengler's philosophy of history (Hyman, pp. 330–331). Spengler established corresponding periods in different cultural cycles, enabling him to speak of "Arabian Puritanism," or the "Mozartian" elements in Phidias (*Permanence and Change,* p. 89). A later example of perspective by incongruity in literary history is Harold Bloom's notion of "apophrades," or "the return of the dead," in which a strong poet appears to be imitated by his or her ancestors (Bloom, 1975, pp. 100–103).

Burke also links the term to the pun and to metaphor. Perspective by incongruity is a "methodology of the pun," in that it links hitherto unlinked words by rational (rather than tonal, as in the pun proper) criteria (*Attitudes toward History,* p. 309). [*See* Paronomasia.] A metaphor, which Burke later defines as a device for bringing out the "thisness of a that or thatness of a this" also reveals hitherto unsuspected connectives (Burke, *A Grammar of Motives,* p. 503). [*See* Metaphor.] The connections among pun, metaphor, and perspective by incongruity themselves illustrate the results of Burke's critical perspective. Previous rhetorical and literary theory had regarded figures of speech as mere ornaments. Burke, on the contrary, wrenches the figures of metaphor and pun out of this established perspective and treats them as cognitive devices. He contends that whole schools of scientific research are "hardly more than the patient repetition, in all its ramifications, of a fertile metaphor" (*Permanence and Change,* p. 95). The seemingly incongruous juxtaposition of scientist/rhetorician allows a principled critique of the pretensions of science. Further, by juxtaposing scientist/theologian, Burke develops a fascinating image of the scientific ideal of a neutral vocabulary as similar to Christ's dislike of vindictive judgment. In fact, science is "evangelistic" in its efforts to overturn previous perspectives (*Permanence and Change,* p. 80).

In addition to criticizing the trained incapacity of modern science, Burke also uses perspective by incongruity to undermine the notion, later to become canonical in the work of the New Critics, that art and literature are "autonomous" entities, requiring analysis on their own terms without being contaminated by history and politics. Perspective by incongruity enables the critic to establish "modes of convertability between economic, religious, and esthetic vocabularies" (*Attitudes toward History,* pp. 313–314). In a fascinating analysis, Burke refers to Marx's concept of class consciousness as a "gargoyle" that realigns our categories of allegiance. Members of a race or notion move from being allies to seeing themselves as class enemies. Members of different races or nations who were previously enemies now can see themselves as members of an international working class (*Permanence and Change,* pp. 112–113).

Burke also identifies the methods of psycho-analysis with perspective by incongruity. He first compares neurosis to religious observance, contending that the "patient, with pious devotion, had erected a consistent network of appropriatenesses around the altar of his wretchedness." But the psychoanalyst, in contrast, brings a professional, detached point of view to the patient's "pieties of intense personal devoltion, awe, and silence." The psychoanalyst engages the patient in a process of "conversion downwards," identifying the patient's misery as the product of repressed sexual desire (*Permanence and Change*, pp. 125–129).

Perspective by incongruity, then, is a kind of summary term for the important themes of Burke's work in the 1930s: the criticism of science and art for art's sake, the development of a cognitive view of rhetoric and metaphor, the attempt to unify the work of Marx and Freud, and the importance of economic and class analysis of religious and esthetic vocabularies. Blankenship, Murphy, and Rosenwasser (1974) contend that perspective by incongruity is the method of Burke's early work, but that it disappears after it has "birthed" the central metaphor of Burke's later work, dramatism.

Recent works by Case, Dow, Hoban, Levasseur, and Miller and Quashie illustrate the continuing usefulness of perspective by incongruity as a resource for critical invention. Following Selzer's lead, we need further research into the connections between perspective by incongruity and other aspects of the radical Modernism of the 1920s, notably the common interest in the bewildering experience of urban life and in the break with traditional notions of perspective and linear narrative in the arts and literature. A still-neglected topic for rhetorical critics is visual rhetoric; the similarity between the notion of montage and Burke's concept may be a fruitful starting point. Finally, Burke has so influenced the way most scholars now look at rhetoric and language that we may forget that his most audacious perspective of incongruity was once the idea of "symbolic action." Burke's revelation in the 1930s that human beings act through symbols and that all human symbol use has a rhetorical dimension, ran counter to orthodoxies in philosophy, literature, and the social sciences. To-day we speak of "the rhetoric of economics" or "the rhetoric of science," expressions that were (and are still to many) oxymoronic to experts in those fields. The expansion of rhetorical studies itself is perhaps the greatest legacy of Burke's concept of perspective by incongruity.

[*See also* Invention.]

BIBLIOGRAPHY

Blankenship, Jane, Edward Murphy, and Marie Rosenwasser. "Pivotal Terms in the Early Works of Kenneth Burke." *Philosophy and Rhetoric* 7 (1974), pp. 1–24. Discusses perspective by incongruity in relation to other key terms such as *orientation, motive, symbolic action,* and *form.*

Bloom, Harold. *A Map of Misreading.* New York, 1975. Bloom expands Burke's "four master tropes" into six "revisionary ratios" that can be found as poets wrestle with their "precursors."

Brecht, Bertolt. *Brecht on Theater: The Development of an Aesthetic.* Edited by John Willett. New York, 1964. Brecht discusses the role of estrangement or the alienation effect in his "epic theater."

Burke, Kenneth. *Attitudes toward History.* Berkeley, 1984. First published 1937. Defines perspective by incongruity as part of his dictionary of pivotal terms.

Burke, Kenneth. *A Grammar of Motives.* Berkeley, 1969. First published 1945. Perspective by incongruity disappears as a core concept, but clearly survives in Burke's interest in dialectic and transformation.

Burke, Kenneth. *Permanence and Change: An Anatomy of Purpose.* Berkeley, 1984. First published 1935. The primary source for Burke's concept of perspective by incongruity.

Burke, Kenneth. *Perspectives by Incongruity.* Edited by Stanley Edgar Hyman and Barbara Karmiller. Bloomington, Ind., 1964. A useful anthology of Burke's critical writings.

Burke, Kenneth. *The Philosophy of Literary Form.* Berkeley, 1969. First published 1941. A transitional work; emphasis on perspective shifts to an emphasis on "rebirth."

Case, Peter. "Remember Re-engineering: The Rhetorical Appeal of a Managerial Salvation Device." *Journal of Management Studies* 36 (1999), pp. 419–441. Uses Burke's concept to identify and demystify "sacred" appeals in the rhetoric of business process reengineering, an influential theory of management.

Dow, Bonnie J. "AIDS, Perspective by Incongruity, and Gay Identity in Larry Kramer's '1,112 and Counting'." *Communication Studies* 45 (1994), pp. 225–240. Uses Burke's concept to explain the rhetorical strategy of gay activist Larry Kramer.

Erlich, Victor. *Russian Formalism: History/Doctrine*. The Hague, 1980. Discusses "ostranenie," or the "making-strange" function of art and literature (pp. 176–178).

Gusfield, Joseph R. "Introduction." In *Kenneth Burke On Symbols and Society*, pp. 1–49. Chicago, 1989. A sociologist's introduction to Burke's theory; useful anthology of Burke's key writings.

Hoban, James L., Jr. "Solzhenitsyn on Detente: A Study of Perspective by Incongruity." *Southern Speech Communication Journal* 42 (1977), pp. 163–177.

Hughes, H. Stuart. *Consciousness and Society: The Reorientation of European Social Thought 1890–1930*. New York, 1958. Not about Burke, but contains useful discussions of Sorel, Spengler, and other figures who influenced Modernist thinkers and artists of the 1920s.

Hyman, Stanley Edgar. *The Armed Vision: A Study in the Methods of Modern Literary Criticism*. New York, 1955. Chapter 10, "Kenneth Burke and the Criticism of Symbolic Action," is still one of the best general introductions to Kenneth Burke.

Lentricchia, Frank. *Criticism and Social Change*. Chicago, 1983. The best case for the continuing political importance of Kenneth Burke's work of the 1930s.

Levasseur, David G. "Edifying Arguments and Perspective by Incongruity: The Perplexing Argumentation Method of Kenneth Burke." *Argumentation and Advocacy* 29 (1993), pp. 195–203. Compares perspective by incongruity to Richard Rorty's notion of "edifying discourse," and proposes a Burkeian alternative to traditional ways of linking evidence and claims in argumentation theory.

Miller, Keith D., and Kevin Quashie. "Slave Mutiny as Argument, Argument as Fiction, Fiction as America: The Case of Frederick Douglass's 'The Heroic Slave.'" *Southern Communication Journal* 63 (1998), pp. 199–207. Uses Burke's concept to interpret Frederick Douglass's strategies in both his oratorical and fictional works. Links Burke's concept to structuralist methods in Claude Lévi-Strauss and Fredric Jameson.

Selzer, Jack. *Kenneth Burke in Greenwich Village: Conversing with the Moderns, 1915–1931*. Madison, Wis., 1996.

—JAMES ARNT AUNE

PERSUASION has been one of the great continuing mysteries of rhetoric and related disciplines. Somehow, discourse has the capacity to move hearts and minds, to transform people and situations, in remarkably powerful ways. From the beginnings of rhetorical study, identifying underlying principles of persuasion has been a focus of attention. The flowering of the social sciences in the twentieth century quite naturally included attention to persuasion, one of two defining ends of rhetoric. [*See* Eloquence.] What follows is a road map to social–scientific work concerning persuasive communication. Such work represents the application of social–scientific methods to enduring questions of rhetoric—how people direct and shape belief, achieve consensus, move others to action. Sometimes this research confirms intuitions of long standing, and sometimes it yields remarkably counterintuitive findings.

However, persuasion research is not unified within any single disciplinary or conceptual framework. Research has been conducted in a number of academic fields, with few efforts after integration or connection. Nearly all the social sciences (including psychology, communication, sociology, political science, and anthropology) and related applied endeavors in which social–scientific questions and methods appear (such as advertising, marketing, and public health) contain relevant research. An appropriate overview thus will acknowledge the different guises under which persuasion-relevant research has appeared.

Background. In one way or another, persuasion involves influencing the audience's mental state, commonly as a precursor to action. Although a number of mental states may be the focus of a persuader's attention, social–scientific persuasion research has given pride of place to attitude, understood as the general evaluation of an object, such as a policy, proposal, product, or person. Hence, much of the relevant social–scientific work concerns attitude change, because such change represents an exemplary case of rhetorical success.

This research is predominantly experimental work, in which persuasive effectiveness is assessed under systematically controlled conditions. In the simplest research design, experimental participants are randomly assigned to hear one of two versions of a given message, where the versions differ only with respect to the property of research interest; for example, the two messages might vary in the source to which the message is attributed or in the order in which arguments are presented. If the two versions differ dependably in the attitude change evoked, that difference is presumably attributable only to the property that was experimentally varied. However, a given variable may have different effects in different messages; a particular message variation might substantially enhance persuasion in one case but have little effect in another. Hence dependable generalizations about persuasive effects require evidence derived from multiple messages, either within a single study or across many studies.

Theory. Three general kinds of theories have informed social–scientific work on persuasion: theories of attitude, theories of voluntary action, and theories of persuasion proper. The first two, though not directly concerned with persuasion, have nevertheless proved influential in shaping understandings of persuasion processes.

Attitude theories. Because persuasion research has focused especially on attitude change as a paradigm of persuasion, theories of the nature and structure of attitude have been important sources of insight into persuasion. A straightforward example is given by "expectancy-value" models of attitude. Broadly expressed, these models describe the underlying bases of attitude as consisting of beliefs about the attitude object, such as beliefs about properties of the object. Each belief has some associated evaluation, representing the perceived desirability of the attribute, and each belief is held with some degree of certainty or strength, indicating the perceived likelihood that the object has the attribute. Across beliefs, these two facets of belief (the "value" of each attribute and the "expectancy" of its association with the object) are seen to combine to yield the person's overall assessment of, or attitude toward, the object.

This image of underlying attitude structure immediately suggests a number of alternative possible strategies for attitude change. One possibility is to attempt to add some new belief (of appropriate valence) about the object; a second is to try to change the evaluation of some existing belief; a third is to try to change the strength with which some existing belief is held. Naturally, different persuasion situations will require different approaches. In one circumstance, a persuader might conclude that the audience evaluates the outcomes of the persuader's advocated policy just as the advocate wishes, but needs to be convinced that the proposed policy will actually produce those outcomes; in another circumstance, the audience may already agree about the policy's attributes, but disagree about the evaluation of those properties. It will be noticed that this way of thinking can be seen as a particular realization of the familiar rhetorical idea that successful persuasion requires adapting one's discourse to the audience's state of mind.

Functional approaches to attitude exemplify a second set of attitude theories useful to students of persuasion. These approaches suggest that attitudes can serve various psychological functions, such as defending the person's self-image, organizing information about the attitude object, and expressing the person's values. A number of different schemes have been put forward that identify and elaborate these various functions, but there is no consensus yet on any one detailed analysis. However, one broad distinction embodied in nearly all functional attitude classifications is that between symbolic and instrumental (utilitarian) functions. Attitudes focused on symbolic associations of an object—the values it expresses, the moral beliefs it symbolizes—serve symbolic functions; attitudes focused on the intrinsic properties of the object—appraising the object in terms of intrinsic attributes or consequences—serve instrumental functions. For instance, a person's favorable attitude toward a given automobile might serve mainly instrumental functions and so be based on beliefs about gas mileage, luggage capacity, and so on, or mainly symbolic ones, and so be based on beliefs about what sort of personal identity is projected by driving this car or how driving the car makes one feel.

Approached from this perspective, the key to successful persuasion is the matching of the persuasive appeal to the attitude's functional basis, and hence this approach offers another realization of the general idea that rhetorical effectiveness requires audience adaptation. If a negative attitude toward a neighborhood facility for persons with AIDS is based on a symbolic association of AIDS and homosexuality, then changing that attitude might involve providing information that heterosexuals are also susceptible to AIDS. But if that negative attitude is based on instrumental concerns about contagiousness, then presumably a different persuasive approach will be required: indeed, in such a circumstance, emphasizing heterosexual susceptibility to AIDS would presumably backfire. In a number of studies of consumer advertising, instrumentally oriented appeals (emphasizing intrinsic product qualities) have been found more persuasive than symbolically oriented appeals (emphasizing image-based considerations) when the audience's attitudes have an instrumental basis; by contrast, with attitudes that have a symbolic basis, symbolically oriented appeals have been found more persuasive than instrumentally oriented appeals.

Individual personality differences play a role in shaping the function a given attitude serves. Some persons ("high self-monitors") are generally more concerned than others ("low self-monitors") about the image they project, and hence their attitudes are more likely to have symbolic bases. The nature of the attitude object also constrains the kind of function served. Some objects, such as air conditioners, easily accommodate only an instrumental function, others (such as class rings) only a symbolic function. But some objects, such as automobiles, easily permit multiple attitude functions, and hence persuasion concerning such objects needs to be especially attentive to the underlying functional basis of the audience's attitudes. Different appeals will be wanted for persons whose automobile attitudes are based on beliefs about gas mileage and frequency-of-repair records than for persons whose attitudes are based on beliefs about the image projected by driving a given car.

Voluntary action theories. A second relevant group of theories is also not directly concerned with persuasion but rather aims at identifying factors that appear to influence voluntary action. This kind of theory offers insight into persuasion indirectly, because the factors influencing behavior provide natural foci for persuasive efforts. A leading example is Fishbein and Ajzen's (1975) "theory of reasoned action," which suggests that a person's behavioral intentions are influenced jointly by attitudinal considerations (the person's attitude toward the action in question) and by normative ones (the person's "subjective norm," that is, the person's assessment of whether sig-

nificant others desire performance of the behavior). These two factors can vary in their impact on intention; attitudinal considerations may weigh more heavily than normative ones in some circumstances, but less heavily in others.

For a persuader, the theory of reasoned action can be used to identify useful foci for persuasive efforts. For example, if adolescent tobacco use is influenced more heavily by normative than by attitudinal factors, then interventions designed to discourage such behavior should presumably give special attention to addressing those normative factors. Moreover, because the theory also provides an account of the determinants of these attitudinal and normative factors, that is, an account of what underlies each of these, it can supply even further direction to persuaders.

A good deal of research evidence has indicated the usefulness of the theory of reasoned action, to the point where it has become the standard against which potential competitors are compared. Broadly put, the question is whether some additional general factor beyond attitude and subjective norm can be identified that dependably improves the prediction of behavioral intention. Among a number of suggestions, the one with the most research support is that represented by Ajzen's "theory of planned behavior," which recommends additionally considering the person's perceived control over the behavior, that is, whether the person thinks it is easy or difficult to perform the action. The potential merit of this addition can be seen by considering behaviors such as exercise: persons might think that exercising is desirable (positive attitude) and that significant others think they should exercise (positive subjective norm), but believe themselves incapable of performing the behavior because expensive specialized equipment is needed but not owned, the gym is far away, exercise can't be fit into one's schedule, and so forth. Plainly, in such a circumstance, reiterating the advantages of exercise is unlikely to be a successful avenue to persuasion; instead, the perceived obstacles to performance of the behavior will need to be addressed.

These voluntary action theories thus can be seen as identifying general possible points of resistance to a persuader's views—and hence as identifying general possible targets for persuasive efforts (attitude, subjective norm, perceived behavioral control). In a sense, these targets parallel the "stock issues" familiar to students of *stasis* theory, as these identify possible points at issue in a dispute. [*See* Stasis.]

Persuasion theories. The third relevant kind of theory aims at providing an account of persuasion itself. Of these, the most prominent and successful have been "dual-process" models of persuasion, exemplified by Petty and Cacioppo's elaboration likelihood model (ELM). The ELM suggests that there are two broad "routes to persuasion"; which one is activated depends on the degree of elaboration, or issue-relevant thinking, in which the receiver engages. One is the central route, in which the outcomes of persuasive efforts are the result of the receiver's thoughtful consideration of issue-relevant material, such as the message's arguments. [*See* Logos.] The other is the peripheral route, in which persuasive outcomes arise from less thoughtful processes such as the receiver's invocation of some heuristic (a simplifying decision rule); for example, instead of carefully considering the arguments and evidence, a receiver might reach a conclusion based on the communicator's credibility, the communicator's likeability, or the reactions of other audience members to the message. [*See* Ēthos.] These two prototypical forms of persuasion actually represent the ends of an elaboration continuum; at intermediate levels of elaboration, both central-route and peripheral-route processes may be at work.

The degree of elaboration in which a receiver engages is a function of a variety of factors. Some of these factors influence elaboration motivation, such as the receiver's degree of involvement with the message topic, that is, the personal relevance of the topic to the receiver. Others influence elaboration ability, such as the receiver's preexisting knowledge of the topic or the degree to which the persuasion setting permits undivided attention to the message.

As elaboration and, correspondingly, the kinds of persuasion processes involved varies, different factors will play a role in determining persuasive outcomes. Under conditions of high elaboration, for example, one key factor influencing the success of persuasive messages appears to be the evaluative direction of the receiver's thoughts, whether the receiver's issue-relevant thoughts are generally favorable or unfavorable to the position advocated. This in turn is influenced by, among other things, the quality of the message's arguments (their cogency, strength, importance). When elaboration is high, receivers carefully scrutinize the message's arguments, and hence the quality of those arguments becomes an important determinant of persuasive success. But under conditions of low elaboration, variations in argument quality make less difference to persuasive outcomes, and peripheral considerations—such as the receiver's liking of the communicator, or the reactions of other audience members to the advocacy—play larger roles.

One especially attractive aspect of such dual-process models is that they offer the prospect of reconciling apparently inconsistent research findings. For example, experiments examining the effects of accompanying persuasive messages with a distracting stimulus or task have found that distraction can either enhance or reduce persuasive effectiveness. From the perspective of the ELM, just such variation is to be expected, however. Because distraction interferes with elaboration, it will impair persuasive success in circumstances in which the receiver would otherwise have had predominantly favorable thoughts about the advocated view. Distraction will enhance success, however, if the circumstance is one in which predominantly unfavorable thoughts would have occurred. In a number of areas, dual-process models such as the ELM have proved quite helpful in illuminating complex research results; such models represent an important step forward in the social–scientific understanding of persuasion processes.

But dual-process-model research has been strangely inattentive to the particulars of argument quality. Experimental argument quality variations have been created by varying an amalgam of not carefully conceptualized message features, including the importance of the outcomes of the advocated action or view (e.g., strong arguments discussing important rather than trivial consequences) and the quality of the evidence provided (e.g., strong arguments invoking opinions of disinterested rather than self-interested parties). It will plainly take some time to identify the various components of argument quality, tease out their separate and joint contributions, and clarify the mechanisms by which such properties produce the observed effects.

Variable-Oriented Research. Although some persuasion research is guided by the sorts of theories just discussed, a good deal of persuasion inquiry might more appropriately be described as not motivated by any specific theoretical framework, instead being aimed at illuminating the roles that various particular variables play in persuasion. This work can usefully be organized by whether the variable under investigation is a characteristic of the source, the message, or the receiver.

Source characteristics. Two attributes of communicators have been especially prominent in persuasion research: credibility and liking. Credibility, the perceived believability of a communicator, is based on the conjunction of perceived competence (expertise, knowledgeability) and perceived trustworthiness (honesty, sincerity). These perceptions are influenced by knowledge of the communicator's background and circumstance: for example, training and experience, and whether the communicator is self-interested in a way that might induce bias. They can also be affected by aspects of the message or its delivery: for example, nonfluencies in delivery can diminish perceptions of competence. Credibility, thus conceived, is not quite identical to Aristotle's conception of *ēthos,* but plainly there is an underlying common recognition of the role that aspects of character can play in persuasion. [*See* Credibility.]

As one might expect, higher-credibility communicators, those perceived as more competent and trustworthy, are commonly more persuasive than lower-credibility sources, but this generalization needs to be tempered in two ways. First, the impact that credibility has on persuasive outcomes varies depending on such matters as the audience's involvement with the issue (as suggested by the ELM); credibility variations make less difference as the personal relevance of the issue to the audience increases. Second, lower-credibility communicators have been observed to be more persuasive than high-credibility sources in circumstances in which the advocated view is one toward which the audience is initially at least somewhat favorable; it appears that hearing a lower-credibility source advocate one's own viewpoint encourages (covert) compensatory arguing

in the audience (something not encouraged when an apparently expert source is defending one's view), which leads to greater persuasion.

Unsurprisingly, better-liked communicators are commonly more persuasive than their less well-liked counterparts. But, as with credibility, this effect weakens as audience involvement increases. Moreover, several studies have reported effects in which disliked communicators proved more persuasive than liked communicators. This counterintuitive effect is not yet well understood, but appears to arise only when the receiver has chosen to listen to the message; it may be that when receivers have chosen to listen to a communicator who turns out to be unlikable, they search for some reason for having done so—and finding merit in the advocated view might provide such justification.

Other communicator characteristics appear to play roles in persuasion primarily through their influence on credibility and liking. For example, similarities between source and audience, or more precisely, the audience's perception of similarities between source and audience, seem to affect persuasive outcomes only indirectly, by influencing perceived credibility and liking, which then have more direct, if complicated effects on persuasion. The same appears to be true for other communicator characteristics, such as ethnicity or physical attractiveness.

Message characteristics. A large number of different message variations have been studied for their possible contributions to persuasive effects. Three examples can serve to illustrate the nature of this research: studies of message sidedness variations, fear appeals, and conclusion explicitness.

First, considerable attention has been given to the persuasive effects of different means of handling opposing arguments. Broadly, a persuader might either ignore such arguments (what is termed a "one-sided" message) or discuss them (a "two-sided" message); if opposing arguments are discussed, a persuader either might try to undermine those opposing considerations (a refutational two-sided message) or might simply mention some opposing arguments (a nonrefutational two-sided message). A two-sided message, as understood here, thus differs from the "two-sided argumentation" associated with *dissoi logoi* or *in*

ultramque partem. There has often been speculation that the choice among these alternatives
should depend on such factors as whether the audience is already inclined to favor the advocated
view, or whether the audience is familiar with
possible counterarguments; in fact, none of these
factors plays a significant role in influencing the
relative effectiveness of message sidedness variations. Broadly speaking, one-sided messages are
less persuasive than refutational two-sided messages, and do not differ significantly from nonrefutational two-sided messages; thus persuaders
would generally be best advised to attempt
straightforward refutation of possible objections.
However, the advantage that refutational two-
sided messages have over nonrefutational two-
sided messages, when each is compared against a
one-sided message, is diminished when the messages are consumer advertisements; it may be that
the initial skepticism with which consumer advertising is commonly met creates a circumstance
in which nonrefutational acknowledgement of
counterarguments can enhance the advertisement's credibility and hence its persuasiveness.

Fear appeals have been another long-standing
focus of research interest in persuasion. A fear appeal is a message designed to arouse a sense of
threat in the audience, in the hope of motivating
acceptance of the communication's recommended
course of action, which is aimed at alleviating or
avoiding fear. For example, a message might describe the terrible consequences of skin cancer,
and then recommend various sun-protection actions such as using sunscreen or wearing a hat as
means of avoiding these outcomes. In this research area, the message variation of interest is
the intensity or explicitness of the fear-arousing
material; a message might have relatively mild or
relatively strong fear-arousing material, and the
question is what effects such variations have on
fear arousal and persuasive effectiveness. The research evidence makes it clear that it is not easy
for communicators to manipulate fear levels
through messages; for instance, more intense
message material does not always arouse more
fear. However, messages that do arouse greater
fear are likely to be more persuasive than messages that arouse less fear. This effect is contrary
to long-standing beliefs about the impact on persuasion of fear arousal. A common expectation

has been that the impact of aroused fear on persuasion would take the form of an inverted U-
shaped curve, with the greatest persuasion occurring at intermediate levels of aroused fear. But the
evidence to date is inconsistent with such sup-
positions. Students of rhetoric will recognize fear
appeals as one species of emotional appeal. [*See*
Pathos.] Other emotional appeals, such as appeals
to pity or guilt, have received less research attention than have fear appeals.

A third example of message-variable research
is provided by studies of variations in the explicitness with which the message's overall conclusion is put forward. The specific experimental
contrast of interest compares messages in which
the conclusion is stated explicitly and ones in
which it is left implicit, that is, where the audience is left to infer the message's conclusion. It
has widely been thought that the relative persuasiveness of these two message forms will depend
on the audience's ability and willingness to reason to the desired conclusion. Specifically, the expectation has been that with receivers who cannot draw the desired conclusion themselves,
because of intellectual ability, or will not do so
because of holding opposing views, explicit-con-
clusion messages will be more persuasive, but
otherwise implicit-conclusion messages are to be
preferred since such messages will invite the audience's active participation, in an enthymematic
fashion. But the research evidence in hand indicates that in fact messages with explicit conclusions are generally more persuasive than those
that leave the conclusion implicit, regardless of
the audience's initial opinion or intellectual ability. [*See* Enthymeme; *and* Tacit dimension, the.]

This provides only a sampling of the message
features that have been studied in persuasion research. Many other aspects of message organization (e.g., alternative ways of ordering argumentative materials) and content (e.g., the use of
altruistic appeals, rhetorical questions, or figurative language) have also been investigated. Visual aspects of persuasive messages, however,
have received relatively little systematic research
attention. In some ways this is unsurprising; our
vocabularies for describing verbal variation are
rather better articulated than corresponding vocabularies for imagery in persuasive messages
(not to mention vocabularies for describing the

interplay of visual and verbal materials). Still, the prominence of visual images in persuasive messages makes it likely that this will be an increasingly significant focus for research.

Receiver characteristics. Receiver personality traits appear to play rather complicated roles in persuasion. Many personality characteristics can either enhance or inhibit persuasion, depending on the circumstance. For example, as mentioned above in the discussion of functional attitude theories, receivers may differ in self-monitoring (the degree to which they are sensitive to the image they project), with this then predisposing receivers to vary in the degree to which symbolic or instrumental functions are served by their attitudes. Thus a high self-monitoring receiver might be either easier or more difficult to persuade than a low self-monitoring receiver, depending on whether the message's persuasive appeal matched the receiver's underlying symbolic attitude function. Studies of such phenomena (the effects of variation in receiver attributes such as self-monitoring, intelligence, self-esteem, age, and so forth) can be seen as reflecting a continuation of the rhetorical tradition's preoccupation with analyzing the roles that particular audiences' characteristics play in persuasion.

One especially significant area of research concerns how receivers can be made resistant to persuasion, for example, how voters inclined to vote for a given candidate can be made resistant to counterpersuasion by opponents, or how adolescents can be made resistant to offers of drugs. What persuades a person may be different from what makes a person resistant to counterpersuasion, and hence several lines of research have been undertaken concerning distinctive aspects of resistance-to-persuasion phenomena.

The most useful general conception of persuasion resistance relies on an analogy with disease inoculation: by exposing receivers to refutations of weak versions of opposing arguments, receivers can be made resistant to subsequent attacks. For example, in political campaign contexts, such inoculation treatments have been found to reduce the effectiveness of subsequent negative advertising. Additionally, there have been a number of studies of how best to teach children to resist social pressures to use tobacco, alcohol, or illegal drugs. One approach focuses on direct social pressures in the form of offers of such substances, and teaches children skills for refusing such offers, commonly through a combination of modeling (seeing others perform refusals) and practice (role-playing exercises in which the child refuses an offer). A second approach attempts to defuse the indirect social pressure arising from children's normative misperceptions, for example, overestimation of how many of their peers use such substances. The evidence to date gives little reason to think that refusal-skill training prevents subsequent substance abuse, but normative interventions appear more promising.

Application. Interest in persuasion, and hence in conducting persuasion-related research, naturally arises in a number of arenas of practical activity, such as consumer advertising; political communication (e.g., election campaign messages); legal communication, such as witness testimony or attorney argumentation; and health communication, including mass media campaigns aimed at disease prevention, communications concerning biological or environmental risks, and messages communicating product warning information.

Some of the persuasion-related research in these domains represents applications of more general ideas such as those previously discussed. For example, a large number of studies have examined the usefulness of the theory of reasoned action or the theory of planned behavior for understanding various health-related behaviors: exercising, participating in health screening programs such as mammography, taking protective action against skin cancers arising from sun exposure, engaging in breast or testicle self-examination, and so on. Similarly, researchers have investigated the differences between symbolic and instrumental functions of attitudes toward persons with AIDS, the credibility that various sources of drug information have for adolescents, the effectiveness of fear appeals in encouraging seatbelt use, and so on.

Additionally, however, one can find domain-specific research, that is, research focused on questions or variables of distinctive interest in a particular area of application. For example, studies of consumer advertising have examined how one's attitude toward an advertisement (one's evaluation of the ad, as distinct from one's evaluation of the object being advertised) influences advertising effectiveness; better-liked ads are, unsurprisingly, generally more persuasive, but this effect weakens as the audience becomes more familiar with the product being advertised. Similarly, research on political campaign persuasion has given special attention to the effects of negative political advertising; such advertising has often been presumed to be especially effective, but the available empirical evidence suggests that negative political advertising is typically unsuccessful and may even be damaging to the sponsoring candidate.

Within such domain-specific research, one development of special interest for students of persuasion has been the articulation of various "stage" models of health-related behavior, exemplified by the "transtheoretical" model of health behavior, so named because putatively it integrates a number of different theoretical perspectives. The transtheoretical model (sometimes called the "stages-of-change" model) identifies a number of distinct stages in a person's adoption of a given health-related behavior such as engaging in an exercise program. In the precontemplation stage, a person is not even thinking about undertaking an exercise program anytime soon; in the contemplation stage, the person is at least seriously thinking about doing so; a person in the preparation stage is ready to change and may have undertaken planning or other preparatory action (such as signing up for a health club); in the action stage, the person has undertaken the exercise program; finally, a person who has continued to engage in exercise for some time is said to be in the maintenance stage.

From a persuader's perspective, stage models are appealing because of their potential usefulness in suggesting how best to tailor persuasive efforts to a particular audience. For example, for persons in the precontemplation stage, the persuader's challenge will be to get the audience thinking about the target behavior (i.e., moving the audience from precontemplation to contemplation). By contrast, for persons in the preparation stage, the persuader will presumably want to help the audience translate their plans and intentions into actions. These stage models thus offer yet another way of thinking about audience analysis and adaptation.

One especially intriguing finding from transtheoretical-based research concerns "decisional balance," the perceived importance of the advantages and the disadvantages of a given action. Studies of diverse health-related actions (including using sunscreen, undergoing mammography screening, reducing dietary fat, and exercising) have found that as persons move from precontemplation to action, the perceived importance of the action's advantages increases, and the perceived importance of the disadvantages decreases. This much is unsurprising, but the research evidence indicates that these two changes are not symmetrical: the increase in the perceived importance of the advantages is substantially larger than the decrease in the perceived importance of the disadvantages. At face value, this suggests that the adoption of such behaviors may be less a matter of the person's deciding that the disadvantages are insignificant than it is a matter of deciding that the advantages make the action worthwhile; correspondingly, in encouraging movement from precontemplation to action, persuaders may wish to give less attention to undermining potential disadvantages than to increasing the perceived importance of the action's advantages.

Only recently has much research evidence begun to accumulate concerning stage models of health behavior, and a number of thorny conceptual and methodological questions remain unsettled. It is not yet clear, for example, whether the transtheoretical model's typology of stages will prove to be the most generally useful one; more generally, researchers appear not yet to have considered carefully exactly what sorts of evidence will be needed to assess the various claims implicit in stage models. Still, stage models plainly offer the prospect of continuing contributions to our understanding of persuasion processes.

Integration. One question that naturally arises is why there has not been more aggressive integration of the variable-analytic and applied-research findings within the various theoretical frameworks. One reason is simply the span of academic fields in which persuasion-relevant research is to be found. Traditional discipline-centered training models do not always encourage researchers to look abroad for relevant work, and only recently has there been much concerted effort at retrieving and organizing the scattered research literature. Moreover, extant theoretical frameworks have not attempted to speak to the broad range of relevant issues. For example, although emotional and visual aspects of persuasion are plainly important, theoretical models to date have not been designed to accommodate easily, much less focus on, such facets. One may hope that future frameworks are more expansive, both in the sense of being open to taking up a broader range of concerns and in the sense of being ready to engage relevant work across disciplinary boundaries.

At the same time, the development of larger frameworks will encounter a natural and inevitable tension in social–scientific persuasion work—a tension familiar in rhetorical studies—between general frameworks and case- or context-specific treatments. This can be clearly illustrated by considering the question of whether to add this or that particular factor to the theory of reasoned action or the theory of planned behavior, so as to enhance the prediction of intention. It is possible that adding some given factor improves the prediction of intention for one specific behavior, but does not prove generally useful across a variety of behavioral domains, and so would not be an appropriate addition to the general model. That is to say, there is some trade-off between having a parsimonious and widely applicable general account and having a maximally satisfactory account of some particular circumstance. As helpful as general images of persuasion can be, then, it will almost certainly remain the case that individual circumstances require correspondingly individualized treatment. But this will be no surprise to the student of rhetoric.

[See also overview article on Audience; Conviction; Identification; and Judgment.]

BIBLIOGRAPHY

Ajzen, Icek. "The Theory of Planned Behavior." *Organizational Behavior and Human Decision Processes* 50 (1991), pp. 179–211.

Conner, Mark, and Paul Norman, eds. *Predicting Health Behaviour*. Buckingham, U.K., 1996. Chapters provide critical analysis of the application of various models (e.g., the theory of planned behavior) to the explanation of health-related behavior.

Eagly, Alice H., and Shelly Chaiken. *The Psychology of Attitudes*. Fort Worth, Tex., 1993. An excellent comprehensive treatment of the research literature on attitudes.

Fishbein, Martin, and Icek Ajzen. *Belief, Attitude, Intention, and Behavior: An Introduction to Theory and Research*. Reading, Mass., 1975. Organized by the theory of reasoned action.

Jackson, Sally. *Message Effects Research*. New York, 1992. A careful discussion of methodological issues arising in persuasion research.

Maibach, Edward, and Roxanne Louiselle Parrott, eds. *Designing Health Messages: Approaches from Communication Theory and Public Health Practice*. Thousand Oaks, Calif., 1995. Chapters illustrate a variety of theory-based approaches to the design of persuasive messages on health topics.

Messaris, Paul. *Visual Persuasion: The Role of Images in Advertising*. Thousand Oaks, Calif., 1997. Thoughtful treatment of a long-neglected aspect of persuasion.

O'Keefe, Daniel J. *Persuasion: Theory and Research*. Newbury Park, Calif., 1990. A broad survey of theory and research; a new edition is planned.

Petty, Richard E., and John T. Cacioppo. *Communication and Persuasion: Central and Peripheral Routes to Attitude Change*. New York, 1986. Detailed presentation of the elaboration likelihood model.

Pfau, Michael, and Henry C. Kenski. *Attack Politics: Strategy and Defense*. New York, 1990. Reports two field studies of inoculation treatments against negative political advertising.

Prochaska, James O., and Carlo C. DiClemente. *The Transtheoretical Approach: Crossing the Traditional Boundaries of Therapy*. Homewood, Ill., 1984.

Weinstein, Neil D., Alexander J. Rothman, and Stephen R. Sutton. "Stage Theories of Health Behavior: Conceptual and Methodological Issues." *Health Psychology* 17 (1998), pp. 290–299.

—DANIEL J. O'KEEFE

PHILOSOPHY. [*This entry comprises two articles. The first article deals with the ancient, continuing, and often antagonistic relation of rhetoric and philosophy, with particular attention to Plato and Aristotle. The second article describes perennial topics and terms of philosophy, with their contested differences from and implications for rhetoric.*]

Rhetoric and philosophy

On the face of it, philosophy and rhetoric, two large disciplines within the humanities, having different goals and using different methods, should be able to coexist happily. Indeed, in their first recorded appearance, in ancient Greece in the mid-fifth century BCE, philosophy and rhetoric were taught together by the Sophists, who also taught literature, history, ethics, and much else. [*See* Sophists.] The Sophists were itinerant teachers from all over Greece, who gave instruction on request, for a fee. (Isocrates, one of the most influential members of this class, broke with tradition by settling in Athens and opening his own school in 393 BCE, in direct competition with Plato's Academy.) The success enjoyed by the Sophists proves that their teaching answered a growing need in Greek communities for general education, especially training in public speaking. Participation in democracy, for those properly qualified (free Greek adult males only; women, foreigners, and slaves were excluded) took place on a face-to-face basis. In the political arena, as in the law courts, individuals had the right to speak in their own person, and to take part in the collective vote on which the outcome of all democratic processes depended. The Sophists gave instruction in the two main categories of speechmaking, deliberative and forensic, and also practiced the third kind, the epideictic (or "display" speech), which often celebrated virtue. [*See* Deliberative genre; Epideictic genre; *and* Forensic genre.] Although only fragments of their work survive, it seems that they taught the rudiments of organizing a speech, dividing it into clearly marked sections, using the appropriate rhetorical figures and tropes, and appealing to the listeners' emotions as an integral part of the persuasive process (Gagarin and Woodruff, 1995). The word *sophist* originally had no pejorative connotations, and was still being used in the fourth century BCE to designate both orators and philosophers.

The original harmony between rhetoric and philosophy was shattered by Plato (c.428–c.347 BCE), whose diatribes gave the word *sophist* the negative meaning that it still has today. Plato's hostility sprang from several sources. First, believing that government is a science requiring expert knowledge, he was a notorious opponent of democracy, which he judged to be unsystematic and open to abuse. The philosopher Socrates, whom Plato idolized and used as the key speaker in many of his dialogues, was put to death in Athens in 399 BCE, on the charge of introducing

strange gods and corrupting the youth. In Plato's eyes, Socrates' execution was one more proof that democratic systems were powerless to defend themselves against internal corruption or tyranny. Second, Plato was opposed to the Sophists' introduction of a broad education in ethical, social, and political matters. To him, their knowledge was superficial and amateurish, especially compared to the rigorous procedures of dialectic. [*See* Dialectic.] Plato wished to elevate his notion of philosophy into the premier educational position, and to downgrade or even abolish all rival methods. Third, Plato's concept of education was based on a dichotomy of the soul into rational and irrational elements, the latter represented by the emotions. The role of the educator, he believed, was to foster reason and suppress the bodily or emotional instincts, which in their pursuit of pleasure made human beings behave like animals. In the *Republic,* a dialogue discussing the best education for the "guardians" who will be trained to rule the state, Plato argued that tragedy, like other forms of poetry, should be expelled from the state since it freely represents human emotions and could have a deleterious effect on the guardians' morale.

It is ironic in several respects that Plato should have attacked rhetoric and poetry. His own writing is full of quotations from Homer and other Greek poets, whom he must have known intimately. His dialogues are fictional conversations that brilliantly exploit literary effects, such as setting, mood, dramatic reversal, and also make marvellous use of myths, both traditional ones, which Plato reinterprets, and others that he invented himself. The most outstanding imaginative writer among all philosophers, he was also a highly accomplished rhetorician, the speeches within his dialogues displaying his skills in every form of oratory, using arguments of the greatest complexity and an astonishing variety of language, adapted to speaker, context, and purpose, including parodies of his opponents' style.

Yet these unsurpassed literary and rhetorical skills were directed against literature and rhetoric, and on behalf of his form of philosophy. A further irony is that, because of the accidental fortunes of written texts, much of the Sophists' writings have perished, so that we depend on Plato for most of our knowledge of rhetoric in his time and in the preceding century. However, Plato's portrayal of rhetoric is unredeemably hostile, one whole dialogue—*Gorgias*—being directed against political rhetoric as taught by the Sophists and as practiced in Athens. Another dialogue, *Phaedrus,* was directed against the speechwriter Lysias and the rhetoric of the courtroom. Plato attacked the Sophists' activities in politics and philosophy in two further dialogues, *Protagoras* and *Sophist,* while in *Theaetetus* he set the orator and the philosopher against each other. In his last dialogue, the *Laws,* Plato allowed rhetoric a limited role in society, but only in the form of propaganda, including deliberate deception of the people and manipulation of election processes. Here, as in other late works, Plato approved of the state using both coercion and persuasion to regulate its inhabitants, processes that other thinkers would regard as mutually exclusive. (Neither tyrants nor totalitarian states need to persuade their citizens.) Of all his writings attempting to downgrade rhetoric and elevate philosophy, the two most influential works have been *Gorgias* and *Phaedrus,* which deserve separate discussion.

Many readers (especially philosophers) treat a Platonic dialogue either as if it were the record of an actual conversation, which took place at a specified place, often using historical protagonists, or an idealized one, which could have taken place, and in which the protagonists would probably have spoken in the way in which Plato represents them. In fact, in order to achieve his polemical goals, Plato was completely unscrupulous in using every means at his disposal. In both dialogues, Socrates, the master-speaker, dominates the proceedings. Plato makes him engage with the other interlocutors, but always in ways congenial to his system, and deeply unsuited to theirs. Plato's Socrates defines the terms of the discussion, asks the questions that will reveal the weak points of his opponents' case and strengthen his own, and enjoys an unfair advantage in many other ways. Having created the other characters, Plato makes them speak or behave in a way calculated to damage their own cases, as representatives of rhetorical instruction or democracy (as in *Gorgias*), or characterizes them by a piece of writing produced by himself, which is held to be

typical of the faults of speechwriters as a whole (as in *Phaedrus*).

Both dialogues derive great polemical power by using what might be called a polarizing or exclusive dichotomy, one pole of which is accepted, the other disvalued. The argumentative structure of *Gorgias* is built around such dichotomies, all used to discredit democratic politics and rhetoric. According to Plato's Socrates, the goal of a statesman should be to eradicate the citizens' base desires, "persuading and forcing them towards what will make them better," not to "serve and minister to their pleasures" (517b–521a; translated by Irwin). The leaders of Athens, having failed in the first course of action, are judged to be guilty of having "flattered" the people by telling them what they want to hear, rather than what would be best for them, thus indulging their appetites. In order to make this charge, as the best commentaries on this dialogue have shown (E. R. Dodds, Terence Irwin), Plato seriously distorted Athenian history, and he violated all conventions of argument by reducing the statesman's activity to those two poles, either education or corruption. We can object that the statesman's role is not necessarily to educate the citizens, or (if we accept Plato's premises) that education might be a gradual process, not a once-and-for-all success or failure; also, that no balanced discussion can take place if the issue is formulated in such extreme terms, "if not education then corruption." But no one in the dialogue is allowed to make such objections, nor to protest at the other dichotomies that Socrates drives home: that in popular assemblies rhetoric produces "conviction without knowing," that is, a conviction not resulting from learning (*mathēsis*), but from persuasion alone, based on *doxa,* opinion (454b–455a); that rhetoric has no rational principle or *logos,* and hence no status as a *technē,* a systematic discipline based on science or knowledge (*epistēmē*). It is merely an *empeiria,* a "certain knack" discovered by trial and error, that produces "gratification and pleasure" (462c). Rhetoric is more violently denounced as a vicious form of flattery, *kolakeia,* a morally shameful, opportunistic pandering to the taste of the masses (463a–c), and is decisively relegated to the category of spurious activities. Plato's Socrates defines four genuine crafts, two addressing the body, gymnastics and medicine, two addressing the mind, legislation and justice, to which correspond the four spurious crafts: cosmetics and cookery for the body, sophistic and rhetoric for the mind (464a–465b).

These exclusive dichotomies, favoring philosophy and discrediting rhetoric, are not reached by rational investigation but imposed on the discussion by Socrates. Worse still for rhetoric, the three other speakers in the discussion—Gorgias, Polus, and Callicles—whom one might expect to defend the rationality of persuasion, or its legitimacy within a democratic state, are either overpowered by Socrates' negative reasoning or display behavior that shows democracy in the worst possible light. Gorgias, the distinguished elder Sophist, having agreed to the systematic cross-examination of dialectic, is asked to define rhetoric. He does so in such an inept manner that Socrates can make him assent to a number of fatal positions: that rhetoric produces persuasion in us in the same manner as other arts, such as figure painting or arithmetic do; that the orator can speak persuasively "before a crowd" by appearing to know more about the subject than the expert; and that rhetoric can be misused for evil purposes (449a–461b). The second interlocutor, Polus, a younger and inexperienced teacher of rhetoric, is made to accept all the dichotomies unfavorable to rhetoric, and then, in his own person, gives a shockingly amoral account of rhetoric as an unqualified good. It is a powerful art, which grants rhetors (orators, here democratic politicians), the power, "like tyrants," to "kill whoever they want to, and to expropriate and expel from the cities whoever they think fit" (466a). All three of Socrates' interlocutors are made to invoke the persuasive power traditionally claimed for rhetoric, but not as manifested in the open discussions on which democracy was based. Socrates alleges that the rhetor's power is always misused, to maximize the satisfaction of his own desires, for supremacy or pleasure. By the end of a painful cross-examination, Polus has been unable to prevent Socrates bracketing the orator with the tyrant, as a man who "does the greatest injustices . . . and manages not to be corrected or punished" (478b–479a). Callicles, the third speaker, a wealthy, upper-class Athenian who represents an antidemocratic attitude with which Plato fundamentally sympa-

thized, is made to argue that personal desires should be allowed free rein, despite justice and moral laws (482b–484a), a perversion of the true nature of virtue and happiness that Socrates routs with great conviction (487a–501a). The dialogue resolves into a demonstration by Socrates of the superiority of the philosopher's life over that of the politician-orator, and ends with a mythical "Vision of Judgement," which enforces another exclusive dichotomy. In it, souls are examined after death, and those guilty of having indulged their desires are sent to Tartarus (hell), while those who have "lived in piety and truth" go to the Isles of the Blessed (523a–527a). Philosophers are destined for the upper realm, politicians and rhetors for the lower.

Myths, and hierarchical rankings, are used to a similar purpose in *Phaedrus*. In this dialogue, Socrates is confronted by just one other speaker, the young man Phaedrus, an enthusiastic but utterly naïve admirer of the professional speechwriter (or *logographos*) Lysias (c.444–after 380 BCE). The dialogue includes three speeches: the first, attributed to Lysias, is read aloud by Phaedrus from a copy that he happens to have with him; the second and third, superior in every way as rhetoric or philosophy, are improvised by Socrates on the spot. The speech attributed to Lysias is in a crabbed and pedantic style, lacking an introduction, developing its argument in an obsessively concentrated form (230e–234c). It is quite unlike the surviving speeches (twenty-three complete, twelve incomplete) of the historical Lysias, which ancient and modern critics have singled out as showing clarity in the proem, conciseness in the narrative, and above all *charis* or gracefulness (Dionysius of Halicarnassus; Stephen Usher). The suspicion that Plato has written an uncharacteristically bad speech for Lysias is strengthened when, in the conversation on speechwriting that forms the second part of the dialogue (257c–279c), the deficiencies of his speech are said to be typical of the *logographos* as a class, and therefore of rhetoric.

The subject matter of Lysias's speech is an invitation to love based on the paradoxical premise that "favors should be granted to a man who is not in love rather than to one who is" (227c). Socrates, unimpressed by this performance, claims that he could deliver a better speech on the same premise, and does so, following the custom that Plato will later lay down as obligatory by starting with a definition and a division of the subject (237c–d). His speech is lucid, well organized, and compact (237a–241d), qualities earlier denied to Lysias. But having completed it, Socrates feels himself suddenly rebuked by his *daimōn* for having offended the god Eros with this cynical attitude toward love (242b–c), and makes amends by delivering a speech more than three times longer than the first two (244a–257b). This speech, with the famous allegory of the human soul in terms of a charioteer driving two horses, one noble and good, symbolizing the reason, the other "unruly . . . shameful," representing the passions (246–254), includes another elevation of philosophy at the expense of rhetoric. In Plato's allegory, the immortal soul is "perfectly winged" and associates with Zeus, but those souls doomed to return to earth are arranged in a hierarchy according to the nearness with which they approached knowledge of the truth. In the first place comes the philosopher, second is the law-abiding king, third the politician, fourth the physician, fifth the seer, sixth the poet, seventh the craftsman or farmer, eighth "the sophist or demagogue," ninth and last, the tyrant.

Plato's hostility to rhetoric in the *Phaedrus* is unabated from the *Gorgias*, and takes similar forms. Socrates subjects to cross-examination both Lysias's speech and Phaedrus, the susceptible young man who is notionally the spokesman for rhetoric but whom Socrates' withering sarcasm soon turns into an opponent of speechwriting. In the course of these exchanges, Plato accuses rhetoricians of such faults as repeating themselves (265a); of not being able to organize a speech properly (264a–c); of using the tropes and figures without any concern for function (266c–e); of giving probabilities precedence over truth, and of making small things seem large, and vice versa (267a–b); of being clever at arousing the feelings "in large numbers of people all at once" (267c–d); and excelling "at both devising and refuting calumnies" (267d). Socrates had earlier attacked political oratory, describing it as corrupt and corrupting, pandering to the politicians' vanity (257c–258c). The *rhētōr*, once again, is said to persuade his audience with the appearance of knowledge, having no access to "the truth

about just or good things" (259e–260a, 272d–273a). Plato's account, where it can be checked against the surviving written record, or what is known of actual practices in the law court or political arena (Gagarin and Woodruff, 1995; Yunis, 1996; Cole, 1991), turns out to be a grotesque travesty of the truth, just as in *Gorgias*. A different dynamic technique is used here to intensify the attack, through the sudden conversion of Phaedrus to a bitter critic endorsing every charge against rhetoric.

But this dialogue includes an element not found in *Gorgias,* what seems to be a serious suggestion by Plato as to how rhetoric might be reformed so as to become more philosophical. The inferiority of rhetoric to dialectic, expressed so many times throughout the Platonic corpus, appears to be overcome here by the recommendation that rhetoric should cast off its status as a mere knack (*empeiria*) and adopt a "scientific" goal, namely the knowledge of the human soul. The orator should classify "the kinds of speeches and of the soul, and the ways in which these are affected," and then assign "the forms of speeches" corresponding to each (270b–272b). If he can do this, rhetoric may begin to approach the ideal state of dialectic, which plants in a fitting soul "words accompanied by knowledge," bringing immortality and happiness (276a–277c). Some commentators accept these as constructive proposals, but a little reflection shows them to be wholly impractical. The orator addressing a jury composed of five hundred Athenian citizens, or a political assembly of up to two thousand, may know a great deal about the individual types of soul, but there is no way in which he can devise a speech that will simultaneously satisfy all the souls present while he speaks. Nor is it helpful to advise him to address the *kairos,* or opportune moment for each soul, since this will vary enormously; indeed he cannot even choose the time of day at which he must speak. [*See* Kairos.] Any attempt to put this program into practice must instantly fail, and can only seem impossibly cumbersome compared to the privileged position of dialectic, in which a teacher like Socrates, through the practice of a spoken, not written art, can lead a single pupil in the path of knowledge, love, and immortality. [*See* Oratory.]

However, Plato's recommendations are misplaced, for he has omitted all consideration of a key element in Athenian oratory, whether legal or political. The speaker addresses an audience in connection with subjects familiar to them all, and affecting most of them. The jury in a court case hears both sides present their account of the issue, and forms its opinion, well knowing that the process involves considerations of justice from which all benefit. The citizens being advised to undertake or desist from a war, to increase taxation, or to change their legislation concerning foreigners, are well aware of the issues involved, and of what effect a vote either way will have for them, collectively or individually. In both arenas, orators have to address an element totally suppressed by Plato, namely the *res* or subject matter, which will in turn affect the *verba* or substance of the speech. Consideration of the hearers' souls as a collective unit is certainly possible, but any attempt to affect them individually can only fail. In this sense, Plato's recognition of only one legitimate goal for the orator, that of instruction, is irrelevant, for the audience in a democracy needs to hear a well-reasoned argument for one course of action rather than another, not a systematic exposition of virtue. Plato's attempt to remake rhetoric in the image of dialectic ignores all the specifics governing the speech situation in open democratic debate.

By the same token, the annals of Athenian politics and oratory contain many examples of speakers who did not flatter the people, but gave them advice truly designed for their health, advice often ignored during the imperialistic phase of Athens, and bitterly criticized by tragedians and politicians alike. Plato's unquestioned assumptions about the corrupt nature of democracy and public speech render much of his attack on rhetoric a failure by the canons of philosophy, which ought to provide "a rational investigation of the presuppositions that underlie conceptions of being, knowledge, and conduct." Although undeniably effective, it is also a failure by the canons of rhetoric, which guarantees speakers on both sides of a debate a fair hearing.

Plato's hostility to rhetoric brought several Greek writers to its defense. The most important was his own pupil Aristotle, whose *Rhetoric*, a collection of lecture notes from two or more courses held over a thirty-year period (c.363–333 BCE),

presents a reasoned reply to Plato on several issues. Where Plato placed rhetoric at the bottom of a hierarchy dominated by dialectic, Aristotle's text, as we have it, baldly begins: "Rhetoric is the counterpart of Dialectic. Both alike are concerned with such things as come within the general ken of all men and belong to no definite science" (1354a1–3). Against Plato, Aristotle affirms the status of rhetoric as a *technē* (having, therefore, *epistēmē*), since ordinary people use both dialectic and rhetoric, to discuss statements and to defend themselves, either at random or through practice. This shows that the subject "can be handled systematically, for it is possible to inquire the reason why some speakers succeed through practice and others spontaneously; and . . . such an inquiry is the function of an art" (1354a4–11). Aristotle answers other accusations made by Plato in *Gorgias*, that rhetoric is useless, or useful only for immoral ends (1355a21–b3). He affirms rhetoric to be useful in the law courts, because truth and justice "have a natural tendency to prevail over their opposites," so that if judges reach the wrong decision the art of rhetoric is not to blame, but the speakers who have not used it properly. Rhetoric is useful also when addressing less specialist audiences; practicing speaking on both sides of an issue is not an immoral practice but one that helps us to "see clearly what the facts are," and it is quite legitimate to use "rational speech" to defend oneself if attacked. As for the accusation "that one who uses such power of speech unjustly might do great harm," Aristotle replies, "*that* is a charge which may be made in common against all good things except virtue, and above all against the things that are most useful, as strength, health, wealth, generalship," all of which convey great benefits, or great injuries if misused (1355b3–7).

Aristotle's rehabilitation of rhetoric clearly reveals the animus affecting Plato's assumptions about public speech in a democratic community, and the unfair arguments used to express them. Where Socrates had convinced Gorgias that rhetoric shared with many arts the role of persuasion through words, Aristotle replies that persuasion "is not a function of any other art." Individual arts can "instruct or persuade" about their own particular subject matter, but rhetoric is "the faculty of observing in any given case the available means of persuasion," on almost any subject

(1355b26–35). This implies that the orator has legitimate access to the knowledge accumulated in other disciplines, a possibility that Plato ridiculed. Where Plato's approach was exclusive, privileging dialectic, and dismissing rhetoric, Aristotle refuses to oppose rhetoric to philosophy, indeed he integrates it into the whole circle of human sciences. Rhetoric is linked with logic, for *logos,* one of the three modes of persuasion that Aristotle defines, is the "proof" provided by the words of the speech itself (1356a4–5, 18–21), which also uses forms of proof borrowed from dialectic, induction, and the enthymeme (1354a15; 1355a4–18; 1356a37–1357b35). The orator's other two resources, *ēthos* and *pathos,* depend on his knowledge of "human character and goodness in their various forms," and of the emotions. [*See* Ēthos; Logos; *and* Pathos.] So Aristotle judges that "rhetoric is an offshoot of dialectic and also of ethical studies," which in turn "may fairly be called political" (1356a26–30). The link here is to Aristotle's own *Politics,* where the fundamental definition of man as a political animal is strengthened by observing that "man is the only animal who has the gift of speech." Other animals can make noises, but "the power of speech is intended to set forth the expedient and inexpedient, and therefore likewise the just and the unjust," since man alone "has any sense of good and evil, of just and unjust, and the like" (1253a3–17)—these form the topics of the three forms of oratory (see below). *Pathos,* finally, demands a knowledge of human emotions, so Aristotle supplies a brief treatise on psychology (1378b–1388b31).

Aristotle places rhetoric and dialectic below scientific reasoning, since they deal with probable arguments, not with universal or necessary principles, but his treatise was important in rehabilitating rhetoric as an indispensable activity within democracy. Where Plato had described the Athenian citizens as an irrational mob, flattered and corrupted by political speakers, Aristotle retorted with an influential categorization of the main types of speech into "three divisions, determined by the three classes of listeners to speeches. For of the three elements in speechmaking— speaker, subject, and person addressed—it is the last one, the hearer, that determines the speech's end and object" (1358a36–8). Purged of all hostility, Aristotle sees the audience as the key element in speechmaking, being "either a judge, with a decision to make about things past or future, or an observer." As a "judge," making up the jury in a law court, the audience decides about things that have already happened, in terms of the just and the unjust (judicial, or forensic, oratory); as member of a political assembly it decides what must be done, in terms of the expedient and inexpedient (deliberative oratory); and as an "observer" or onlooker listening to a display speech on ceremonial occasions (epideictic oratory), the audience is not expected to reach a decision but its moral judgment will certainly be exercised, for such speeches discuss virtue and vice (1358b1–28).

While legitimizing oratory at every level of democratic society, Aristotle enlarges his triple definition to link rhetoric more firmly with other disciplines. Unlike Plato's image of a demagogue using rhetoric's persuasive force to aggrandize his own power or pleasures, Aristotle's political speaker is expected not only to know about national defense, law and legislation, and other basic issues affecting the *polis;* he must also show that he is concerned with the hearers' welfare, since he is urging them to take or avoid a course of action which will affect their happiness. This fundamental point leads Aristotle to "ascertain what is in general the nature of happiness," for which he offers four definitions and then discusses its constituent parts, in terms of external and internal values (1359a30–1366c22). While not as rigorous a discussion as in Aristotle's philosophical works on ethics, it certainly justifies his claim for rhetoric as an "offshoot . . . of ethical studies." Since the epideictic orator praises virtue and censures vice, Aristotle surveys these topics also, defining virtue as "a faculty of providing and preserving good things; or a faculty of conferring many benefits," and illustrates the forms virtue takes (1366c36–b6). The forensic speaker, too, is sent back to first principles, to study the nature of wrongdoing, law, and criminal psychology (1368b2–1369a6). In this way, responding to Plato's attack on rhetoric, Aristotle rehabilitated it as an art having a rightful place within the humanities, linked to philosophy, both in dialectics and ethics, and having fundamental connections with psychology, politics, and jurisprudence.

Other Greek writers defended rhetoric against Plato. The Sophist Isocrates (436–338 BCE), a contemporary and rival of Plato, did so in several works, but indirectly, never mentioning Plato by name. A later Sophist, Aelius Aristides (117–180 CE), did so explicitly, addressing three orations *To Plato: In Defence of Oratory.* But none of Plato's critics matched Aristotle's comprehensive treatment of speech in its complete individual and social dimension.

The confrontation between Plato and Aristotle defined for all time the terms in which the relation between philosophy and rhetoric would be discussed. Later periods invariably return to one or more of the positions taken up there, but never in such fullness of detail.

Roman writers on rhetoric were familiar with Plato's *Gorgias, Phaedrus,* and *Republic,* although they had only indirect knowledge of Aristotle's *Rhetoric,* which was lost for some time. In his *De oratore,* Marcus Tullius Cicero (106–43 BCE), the outstanding figure in practical oratory, both legal and political, and an influential author of rhetoric books, took issue with the Socrates of the *Gorgias* for having destroyed the unity of philosophy and rhetoric practiced by the Sophists. Socrates, he complained, "separated the science of wise thinking from that of elegant speaking, though in reality they are closely linked together," so making an "absurd and unprofitable and reprehensible severance between the tongue [*lingua*] and the brain [*cor*], leading to our having one set of professors to teach us to think and another to speak" (3.16.59–60). Cicero's remedy for this separation is to urge the orator to take up philosophy, "the creator and mother, as it were, of all the reputable arts" (1.3.9), and to study ethics, dialectic, and "the entire field of practical philosophy" (3.20.76). Cicero, who had studied in Athens at the Middle Academy, practiced what he preached, for his rhetorical works are closely related to the treatises in which he popularized Greek philosophy: *De officiis* (On Duties, largely derived from Panaetius), *De finibus bonorum et malorum* (About Good and Evil Ends), and the *Tusculanarum quaestionum libri quinque.* In his *Institutio oratoria,* Quintilian endorsed Cicero's recommendation that the orator should have a wide knowledge of philosophy, especially ethics, "the better part of philosophy" (1 Pr. 10–17; 12.2.5.15).

Unfortunately, both writers urged rhetoric to take up an aggressive attitude toward philosophy and recapture its own territory, an unproductive approach to this question.

During the Middle Ages, rhetoric, like other disciplines, suffered from the fragmentation that affected both the surviving texts and knowledge of their original function, and from the enormous social and political changes that had taken place in Western society. Power decisions now depended on monarchical rule, not on free debate in democratic assemblies, and legal procedures were quite different. Rhetoric suffered further from the rise of logic and theology to the supreme status among the humanities. In Thomas Aquinas's hierarchy of the arts, poetry and rhetoric occupy the lowest position. Finally, rhetoric was fragmented into pragmatic and utilitarian disciplines, each taught separately, for distinct clienteles: the *ars dictaminis* (the art of letter writing), *ars poetria,* and *ars praedicandi* (the art of preaching) [*See* Ars dictaminis.] No area was left for general discussion of the relation between philosophy and rhetoric, and surviving treatises were little more than collections of devices having no coherent function.

When Renaissance scholars recovered and reedited the classic texts, rhetoric was restored to its role in society and the *vita activa,* once again drawing on philosophy, especially ethics (Garin, 1965). The huge differences between modern and ancient societies still persisted, political and legal systems lacking the central agency of free speech, so that rhetoric took on more importance in education, as helping to form intellectual and moral abilities, and in literature. Where the Middle Ages had placed logic above and against rhetoric, the Renaissance united the two arts, and indeed even imposed rhetorical goals and methods onto dialectic. Medieval philosophical genres, such as the *disputatio,* gave way to newer forms, the dialogue, letter, and essay. Some pioneering figures, such as Lorenzo Valla in his *De vero falsoque bono,* or *De voluptate* (1431–1433), revived the aggressive attitudes of Cicero and Quintilian, calling for rhetoric to attack philosophy and reclaim its proper territory. But most later humanists (those who pursued the *studia humanitatis,* which included *grammatica, rhetorica, poetica, historia,* and *philosophia moralis*), naturally saw rhetoric and philosophy as complementary, each nourishing the other in a new version of the unity practiced by the Sophists. Such attitudes were still being expressed by Francis Bacon in 1605, who described rhetoric as "a science excellent, and excellently well laboured. For although in true value it is inferior to wisdom ... with people it is the more mighty, [for] it is eloquence that prevaileth in an active life." Like Aristotle, Bacon set rhetoric below philosophical inquiry, but he placed it firmly in the circle of the sciences, emphasizing its links with ethics, politics, and psychology.

In the seventeenth century, however, when the full tradition of Greek rhetoric had been restored, the Platonic fissure between the two disciplines reappeared. Thomas Hobbes (1588–1679), whose proficiency in Greek allowed him to prepare a digest of Aristotle's *Rhetoric* and a translation of Thucydides, nonetheless regarded rhetoric with suspicion, and in his early philosophical works (*The Elements* and *De cive*) emulated Plato's *Republic* in wishing rhetoric to be banished from civil society (Skinner, 1996). In his philosophical masterpiece *Leviathan* (1651), rhetoric was given a more positive role in society and in the human sciences, but Hobbes still echoed Plato by attacking orators who can "represent to others, that which is Good, in the likeness of Evill," or vice versa, "and augment, or diminish the apparent greatness of Good and Evil" (Chap. 17); and by describing orators as seducing political assemblies with their passionate eloquence, in order to advance their own interests (Chaps. 19, 25). Similarly, John Locke (1632–1704), in his *Essay Concerning Human Understanding* (1690), took over Plato's dichotomies, opposing the "real knowledge" and "truth" brought by philosophy to the "deception" practiced by rhetoric, which uses eloquence to "insinuate wrong Ideas, move the Passions, and thereby mislead the Judgement" (3.10). Immanuel Kant, further, in his *Critique of Judgement* (1790), followed Plato in using binary categories to privilege one discipline and dismiss another. But now poetry is elevated, rhetoric downgraded as meriting no respect whatever. Yet the philosophers of the Scottish Enlightenment—Adam Smith, George Campbell, Hugh Blair, and Henry Home, Lord Kames—united rhetorical, ethical, and aesthetic discussions without qualms.

In modern times, quarrels between rhetoric and philosophy seem rather unreal. The two disciplines no longer compete against each other for a superior or exclusive position within the humanities, and neither discipline harbors aggressive intentions. They can coexist, in domains that overlap at several points. Philosophy over the last century has developed in many different directions, but in two areas at least, speech-act theory and pragmatics (which in turn overlaps with linguistics), Aristotle's triad of speaker, speech utterance, and audience has been revived. Contemporary philosophers of language view communication as a two-way process, in which speaker and hearer collaborate in establishing meaning and significance. The role of metaphor, both as a heuristic tool and as an indispensable element in communication, has been given serious recognition by several philosophers. Much interesting work has been done on the unspoken assumptions that govern all human communication, the operation of such intangible but vital elements as trust, politeness, and relevance. [*See* Communication; Linguistics; Metaphor; *and* Speech acts, utterances as.]

One of the most influential modern reformulations of rhetorical theory, *The New Rhetoric: A Treatise on Argumentation* (1969), by Chaim Perelman and Lucie Olbrechts-Tyteca, distinguishes proof (the domain of formal logic) from argumentation (the domain of rhetoric), the difference being that argumentation is always addressed to an audience, seeking their agreement. Like Aristotle, the authors see the speaker adapting to his or her audience, considering what is best for them, and legitimately using the whole range of intellectual and affective devices (the topics; rhetorical figures and tropes) in the service of persuasion. [*See* Figures of speech; *and* Topics.] Perelman and his associate set the consensual basis of argumentation over and against the absolutism of Plato, and deliver a penetrating analysis of what they call "philosophical pairs," such as appearance/reality, opinion/knowledge, drawing special attention to Plato's use of them in *Phaedrus* (chap. 4, pp. 411–442). As they point out, in such dichotomies Term I is identified with negative values, Term II with positives, a polemical judgment that is simply embodied in the formulation, never arrived at by rational argument. In their conclusion, they reiterate the danger that such unargued formulas represent to the discourse of philosophy: "we combat uncompromising and irreducible philosophical oppositions presented by all kinds of absolutism," especially in the "dualisms of . . . knowledge and opinion, of irrefutable self-evidence and deceptive will, . . . of a reality binding on everybody and values that are purely individual" (p. 510). If it is true that each of us is either a Platonist or an Aristotelian, then on the relationship between rhetoric and philosophy all the evidence seems to weigh against Plato's exclusive promotion of his form of dialectic, demonizing rhetoric and free speech in democratic communities, and on the side of Aristotle, ready to use them both, in a spirit of complementarity.

[*See also* Classical rhetoric; *and* Prudence.]

BIBLIOGRAPHY

Aristides. *To Plato: In Defense of Oratory,* vol. 1, *Panathenaicus: Rhetoric.* Translated and edited by C. A. Behr. London, 1973.

Aristotle. *Rhetoric.* Translated by W. R. Roberts; edited by Jonathan Barnes. *The Complete Works of Aristotle: The Revised Oxford Translation.* 2 vols. Princeton, 1984.

Bacon, Francis. *Works.* Edited by Brian Vickers. Oxford, 1996.

Cicero, M. T. *De oratore.* Translated by E. W. Sutton and H. Rackham. 2 vols. London, 1942.

Cole, Thomas. *The Origins of Rhetoric in Ancient Greece.* Baltimore, 1991. Fresh reevaluation of the emergence of rhetoric as a formal discipline in the work of Plato and Aristotle, but underestimates the Sophists' contribution.

Dionysius of Halicarnassus. *On the Ancient Orators.* Translated by S. Usher. *The Critical Essays.* 2 vols. London, 1985. First published 1974. See also substantial excerpts translated by D. A. Russell; edited by D. A. Russell and M. Winterbottom. *Ancient Literary Criticism,* Oxford, 1972.

Gagarin, Michael, and Paul Woodruff, eds. *Early Greek Political Thought from Homer to the Sophists.* Cambridge, U.K., 1995. Excellent new translations, with notes, of the key documents in Greek political theory, which is, by definition, rhetorical. Includes all surviving fragments of the Sophists' writings.

Garin, Eugenio. *Italian Humanism. Philosophy and Civic Life in the Renaissance.* Translated by P. Munz. Oxford, 1965.

Hobbes, Thomas. *Leviathan.* Edited by Richard Tuck. Cambridge, U.K., 1991.

Locke, John. *An Essay Concerning Human Understanding.* Edited by P. H. Nidditch. Oxford, 1975.

Perelman, Chaim, and Lucie Olbrechts-Tyteca. *The New Rhetoric: A Treatise on Argumentation.* Translated by J. Wilkinson and P. Weaver. Notre Dame, Ind., 1969. Undistinguished translation of a major work, originally published as *La Nouvelle Rhétorique: Traité de l'Argumentation,* Paris, 1958.

Plato. *Gorgias. A Revised Text.* Introduction and Commentary by E. R. Dodds. Oxford, 1959. Major edition, extremely good on the politics.

Plato. *Gorgias.* Translated with notes by Terence Irwin. Oxford, 1979. Excellent translation, with penetrating commentary.

Plato. *Phaedrus.* Translation and commentary by C. J. Rowe. Warminster, U.K., 1986. Careful translation, cautious commentary.

Skinner, Quentin. *Reason and Rhetoric in the Philosophy of Hobbes.* Cambridge, U.K., 1996. Thorough study of the ambivalence toward rhetoric found throughout Hobbes's philosophical writings.

Usher, Stephen. *Greek Oratory: Tradition and Originality.* Oxford, 1999. Comprehensive treatment of all extant Greek orations, with valuable commentary on the social and legal contexts, and on innovations in rhetorical form and argument.

Vickers, Brian. *In Defence of Rhetoric.* 3rd rev. ed. Oxford, 1997. Includes full discussion of "Plato's Attack on Rhetoric" (pp. 83–147), and "Territorial Disputes: Philosophy versus Rhetoric" (pp. 148–213).

Yunis, Harvey. *Taming Democracy: Models of Political Rhetoric in Classical Athens.* Ithaca, N.Y., 1996. Lucid account of Athenian civic rhetoric from Thucydides to Demosthenes.

—Brian Vickers

Perennial topics and terms

Philosophy is the rational investigation of the presuppositions that underlie conceptions of being, knowledge, and conduct. Its method centers on the interrogation of statements or propositions about issues arising from these conceptions; its aim is to identify, illuminate, and critique the fundamental truths and principles that are implicit in such statements. It emerged in ancient Greece at a time when intellectual, political, and artistic innovations took place that would shape Western civilization ever after.

One such innovation, of course, was rhetoric, the art of the speaker. Philosophy and rhetoric are siblings, conceived and born a little more than a century apart, the offspring of *logos,* reasoned speech (a masculine noun) and the *agora,* marketplace (a feminine noun). The marriage of *logos* and *agora* was made possible by the social, political, and intellectual conditions of the archaic period in Greece (c.750–479 BCE). It is the writings of Thales of Miletus in the first quarter of the sixth century BCE that first gave form to the body of ideas we know as philosophy (although it came to be known as *philosophia* perhaps a half-century later when Pythagoras first used the term to describe "love of wisdom"). Likewise, the genesis of rhetoric can be ascertained with some confidence. While Plato appears to have coined the term *rhētorikē* early in the fourth century BCE, the speaker's art was taught in Sicily as early as the 460s. In order to understand the nature of philosophy and its long and sometimes contentious relationship with rhetoric, we must first have some sense of the origins and early development of this field of study. Then we can examine briefly its principal preoccupations and points of discord with its younger counterpart.

During the archaic period (c.750–479 BCE), in towns and cities throughout the Aegean world, conditions led to the emergence of new political systems, new ways of studying and understanding the world, and new uses of speech and language. This period, indeed, is the incubator of ideas, arts, and intellectual endeavors that flourished—especially in Athens—during the classical period (479–323 BCE). The archaic period followed the decline and disappearance of the rich Mycenaean civilization of the late Bronze Age (c.1500–1050 BCE) and the subsequent Greek "Dark Age" (c.1050–750 BCE). The Mycenaean civilization, named for the great citadel-palace of Mycenae located in the northeastern Peloponnesus, was noted for its fine work in gold and ceramics, its fortified palaces and efficient road system, its hierarchical social–political–economic structure, its practice of warfare, and its use of a written script to record details about taxation and property. Following the decline and disappearance of this civilization during the last two centuries of the second millennium, the Greek world was reduced to small towns, villages, and hamlets generally separated by mountains or sea. Such settlements were peopled by subsistence-level farmers, herdsmen, and fishermen and ruled by a local warrior-chieftain or "king" (*basileus*). Along with the decay of the Mycenaean infrastructure and the consequent decline in communication

among these settlements, during the Dark Age the quality of pottery declined, the use of writing fell into disuse, and the culture became village- rather than city-based. But this period is also known for the emergence of a tradition of oral poetry. It was a time when traveling minstrels or bards known as *rhapsōdes* went from settlement to settlement, where they sang or chanted in rhythmic patterns the elaborate tales of long-dead warriors and heroes, of a great war between the Achaeans and Trojans over the abduction of a Spartan queen, of the contests and jealousies of divine beings who took particular interest in human events, and of a world in which all that took place was the work of such beings.

Starting in the eighth century, this picture began to change, as a new age emerged from the post-Mycenaean darkness. This new age, the archaic era, saw the development of circumstances and conditions that made possible the appearance of new ways of thinking about how the world works and of new procedures of governance. The invention of the phonetic alphabet during the eighth century BCE, the advent of colonization by Greeks throughout the Mediterranean world, and the subsequent expansion of trade and travel by Greeks, were among the most important of these circumstances. However, perhaps most influential was the emergence throughout the Greek world of a new form of political association—the sovereign, democratic *polis* or city-state. These self-governing communities consisted of one city, usually with a citadel (*acropolis* or "high city") and marketplace (*agora*), surrounded by countryside with its villages and farms. Citizens lived in the countryside or in the city itself, but the government of the *polis* was centered in the city. While such communities varied in terms of the forms of government they embraced, ranging from tyranny to oligarchy, to aristocracy, to democracy, in general, the *polis* arose as an antimonarchic state. Government was carried on chiefly by three institutions: the assembly, the council, and the magistracies, all derived from earlier times. Although the political power of the individual citizen varied according to the form of constitution, there was a general democratization of political processes, so that citizens could gather in an assembly to debate issues of war and peace, legislation, and other civic matters. Especially in Athens, this movement toward democracy reached an apex around the end of the sixth century BCE, when constitutional reforms instituted by Cleisthenes significantly broadened the scope of political participation to include all male citizens over the age of eighteen, regardless of wealth or class. In any event, the rise throughout the Greek world of public discussion about social, political, and intellectual topics fostered a climate in which new ideas could be introduced, debated, and criticized.

These were the principal factors that brought reasoned speech and rational inquiry (the masculine *logos*) into "the place where people gather together" (the feminine *agora,* the assembly/ marketplace). Philosophy represented a quest for a naturalistic, rational explanation for the events and processes of experience, in contrast to mythological explanations. The task of rhetoric, the art of the speaker, is to represent the possible, the probable, and the certain as compellingly as possible to those who must make judgments about laws and policies, guilt and innocence.

The Pre-Socratics. The central topics and terms of philosophy emerged during its formative period in the early sixth century BCE. Aristotle attributed to Thales of Miletus, whose works are no longer in existance, the view that the world and everything in it originated as water and ultimately will return to water. Thales' student and fellow Milesian, Anaximander (c.610–547 BCE), was the first Greek thinker to propose a rational account of the origin and destiny of the world. He said that the source of all things was some "unbounded nature, from which come into being all the heavens and the worlds in them," and in which all "existing things" are destroyed "according to necessity" and under the "assessment of Time." Thus, through temporal cycles must the universe ebb and flow in a perfectly ordered cosmos.

Subsequent pre-Socratic thinkers such as Anaximenes (fl. c.545 BCE), Pythagoras (c.580–c.500 BCE), Heraclitus (c.540–c.480 BCE), Parmenides (born c.515 BCE), Empedocles (c.490–430 BCE), and Anaxagoras (c.500–c.428 BCE) further elaborated the lines of speculation that were initiated by Thales and Anaximander. Whether the "basic stuff" of which the universe is made is water, air, fire, earth, number, or being, and whether natural changes are directed by justice and time, or by a process of condensation and rarefaction, or by a divine *logos,* or by the influence of love and strife, or by the operation of mind, these earliest Greek thinkers were asking the first truly philosophical questions: What is the nature of reality? What are the basic laws by which the universe functions? How can human beings come to understand reality and its governing laws? Can we rely on the senses for knowledge of the world? Is there some rational power in the human mind through which the evidence of the senses can be interpreted? What is the relationship between reality and language? Such questions have been pursued by philosophers ever since, and they have given rise to such specific philosophical fields as metaphysics (dealing with questions about the general structure of reality); ontology (involving questions about the specific nature of reality or "being"); epistemology (for questions about the nature of knowledge and coming-to-know); and semiotics (for questions concerning the nature and functions of language).

The Sophists. The second half of the fifth century BCE, the Golden Age of classical Athens, is noteworthy for the development of some new directions in philosophical investigation as well as for the emergence of rhetoric. With the institutionalizing of democratic procedures in the legislative assembly and law courts at the beginning of the century, there was increased demand among Athenian citizens for training in the arts of citizenship. These arts included most particularly a kind of practical and political wisdom, taught under the rubric of "virtue" (*aretē*), and skill in persuasive speaking, taught as the *logōn technē* or art of speech. In response to the demand for instruction in these arts, there appeared in Athens and elsewhere an assortment of itinerant teachers of civic virtue and effective speaking. These professional educators, Sophists (*sophists,* from *sophos,* wise), came to Athens from all parts of the Greek world. Although not all of the fifth-century Sophists considered themselves to be philosophers, several of them raised issues and pursued lines of investigation that contributed significantly to the early development of philosophy. The general philosophical importance of the Sophists lies first in their move away from "natural philosophy" in favor of an interest in politics, ethics, and other "humanistic" topics; and second, in questions they raised about the nature of reality, knowledge, and the substance of speech. [*See* Sophists.]

The earliest and greatest of these Sophists—Protagoras of Abdera (c.490–420 BCE) and Gorgias of Leontini (c.485–380 BCE)—were also known as philosophers who held views regarding the existence of the gods, the nature of knowledge, and the relationship between reality, knowledge, and language. Indeed, their views called into question some of the ontological, epistemological, and semiotic theories of their pre-Socratic predecessors and contemporaries. Protagoras visited Athens several times around the middle of the fifth century and was friends with Pericles, the great Athenian statesman. He was asked to draw up the laws for a colony at Thurii, and he wrote at least two works, *On the Gods* and *On Truth*. Protagoras was known for his religious agnosticism ("Concerning the gods, I cannot know either that they exist or that they do not exist") and for his epistemological relativism and extreme subjectivism. "Of all things," he is held to have said, "the human being is the measure, of things that are, that they are, and of things that are not, that they are not." This has been taken to mean that there is no reality behind and independent of appearances, no difference between appearing and being. Consequently, each of us is the judge of his or her own impressions: what *seems* true for a person *is* true for that person, and thus truth and knowledge are relative to the individual. This view of truth and knowledge, which can be described as "radical subjectivism," introduced problems in epistemology that have occupied philosophical inquiry ever since.

Protagoras was in the forefront of a humanistic reaction against the natural philosophers whose contradictory opinions were bringing them into disrepute among practical men. Like other Sophists, he was acquainted with their theories, and like the other Sophists he turned away from such theorizing to teach the one thing that really mattered: how to take care of one's own affairs and the business of the state.

This highly practical orientation, rooted as it was in epistemological relativism, generated an opportunistic approach to persuasive speech. Protagoras's views implied that if a speaker could make a particular idea appear to an audience as true it would, for that audience, actually *be* true. The emphasis in persuasion, then, was on making the possible seem probable, and thus on making a weak argument seem to be stronger than it was. A major point of contention between philosophy and rhetoric has its origins in this approach, and it has persisted into our own time: the relationship between *truth* and *appearance* and thus between *knowledge* and *opinion*. This conflict, which involves both ontological and epistemological issues, is central to questions about the proper aims of persuasive speech and the responsibilities attendant on its use.

Gorgias—a thinker, statesman, and teacher, and an eloquent speaker—came to Athens in 427 BCE from his native Leontini, in Sicily. His written works included manuals of rhetorical instruction and a treatise entitled *On Nature or the Nonexistent*. He also authored and performed a number of model speeches, of which the *Encomium of Helen* and *Defense of Palamedes* survive. Gorgias's principal philosophical contribution lies in his "three theses," which were presented and defended in his work, *On Nature or the Nonexistent*. Though we possess only later paraphrases of this treatise, it seems clear that Gorgias set out to prove three things: (1) nothing exists; (2) even if anything does exist it cannot be known by a human being; and (3) even if it were knowable, this knowledge cannot be communicated to anyone else.

Scholars disagree over whether this argument was intended as a parody of pre-Socratic reasoning, or as a serious contribution to philosophy (both are probably true). In any event, Gorgias's argument raises important ontological, epistemological, semiotic, and ethical questions. In asserting that "nothing exists," he challenges the idea that there is a fixed, stable reality or being that lurks behind appearances. Further, in saying that, even if such a reality did exist, human beings couldn't know it as such, Gorgias problematizes *all* knowledge. For if we can't know "reality," what can we know and what does it mean "to know"? Finally, in contending that, even if we possess "knowledge," it cannot be communicated to others, Gorgias severs the connection between language and reality that had been proposed by the pre-Socratic thinkers Heraclitus and Parmenides (born c.515 BCE). Heraclitus had written that "speaking truly" meant uttering the cosmic *logos* in virtue of which "all things are one." "True speech," then, is a disclosure or expression of the plan or principle according to which all things come to pass. A generation later, Parmenides wrote a long poem demonstrating, through a rigorous adherence to rules of logical implication, that because "not-being," by definition, cannot exist and, therefore, since "being" *must* exist (since "being" cannot not-be), there is only "being." Furthermore, since, in order for there to be more than one being or thing, individual existences must be separated by not-being, and since not-being cannot exist, there is only one being. What follows from this is that our experience of multiplicity and diversity in the world is an illusion. It was this argument in particular that Gorgias appears to have had in mind when he wrote his treatise, his aim being to turn Parmenides' logic on its head and to show that it can just as easily be used to prove the opposite of what Parmenides concluded. If this is so, then language has no inherent connection to the world of being, and must work only with appearances. As with Protagoras, Gorgias's teachings raised important philosophical issues, and these issues were particularly relevant to the nature and practice of rhetoric.

A principal result of these Sophists' interest in the practical aspects of life, in preference to the theoretical speculations undertaken by the pre-Socratic thinkers, was that philosophical inquiry was directed toward humanistic in addition to naturalistic concerns. Interest in the human condition and in political and practical problems opened the door on a range of questions, which may generally be grouped under the broad heading of "moral philosophy." When a community deliberates over proposed laws and policies, it invokes ideas of the good, the beneficial, and the advantageous. What is *truly* good for human beings, however? In what do true benefit and advantage lie, for an individual or for a community? Moreover, how does one go about investigating such questions? How can we acquire moral knowledge? Shall we turn to myth and tradition alone for answers? Do moral truths arise from the nature of things, or are they merely matters of convention? Such questions turn on both ontological and epistemological issues, and they indicate the substance and direction of the activities of

Socrates, who might truly be called the "father" of moral philosophy.

Socrates. Socrates (c.470–399 BCE) was an Athenian whose adult life coincided almost exactly with the Golden Age. Although he left no writings, we learn about his life and thought from how he is portrayed in Plato's dialogues, the plays of Aristophanes, and the works of Xenophon, all of whom knew him. Early in his life, he seems to have been interested in the speculations of the natural philosophers. However, like the Sophists, he found their conflicting theories ultimately unsatisfying. Consequently, also like the Sophists, he turned his inquiry to the right conduct of life. This he carried on through the familiar Socratic method of cross-examining people with whom he came into contact.

Puzzled by the Delphic Oracle's statement that there was no man wiser than himself, Socrates set about interrogating those in the city—Athenians and foreigners alike—who were reputed to be wise, seeking to discover what the Oracle might have meant. His conversations with prominent Athenian poets and politicians and with such famed teachers as Protagoras, Gorgias, and Thrasymachus attracted a diverse circle of friends and admirers wishing to learn from him. In pursuing his mission, Socrates seems to have angered enough of his fellow-citizens that they later tried and executed him on a charge of "corrupting the youth" of the city.

Among Socrates' principal contributions to philosophy are the subjects into which he inquired and the method of inquiry he used. Most scholars accept the idea that he had no set of positive doctrines to teach. Yet his influence on subsequent philosophical thought was profound. Even more than the Sophists did, Socrates advanced the examination of moral and ethical topics. Judging from Plato's dialogues and other sources, he seems to have been interested in a wide range of questions: What is the nature of virtue? Can it be taught? What is justice? What is the good, for individuals and for states? What is beauty? What is love? What is honor? What is the nature of the human soul? Is the soul immortal? Questions like these eventually gave rise to such areas of philosophical inquiry as ethics, political philosophy, aesthetics, psychology, and metaphysics. In addition to the topics he examined,

Socrates bequeathed to philosophy a method of inquiry that survives into our own time: the critical examination of ideas through a systematic investigation of the logical implications of the meanings of terms. When he asked his various interlocutors to define what they meant by such words as *virtue, justice,* and so on, Socrates hoped to clarify such matters through pursuit of "true definitions" for these terms. In such definitions, he believed, we can find the true ideas represented by the words we use; and in the apprehension of these ideas may lie true knowledge. In any case, Socrates thought that virtuous action is founded on this knowledge. To pursue the good in conduct it is enough to understand what the good truly is. The search for virtue, then, was fundamentally a search for true knowledge.

It is unclear from our historical evidence how fully Socrates had developed his own thinking about such matters or how close he came to obtaining the knowledge he sought. Certainly his recurring acknowledgment of his own ignorance ("All I know is that I know nothing," he is reported to have said) suggests that he fell short of the latter. Perhaps his most important contribution to the development of Greek philosophy lies not in any particular doctrine or theory, but rather in the general spirit of inquiry that animated his life's work and that defines what we might term the *philosophic attitude.* Socrates seems to have taken seriously the injunction engraved on Apollo's temple at Delphi to "know thyself." He is represented by Plato as saying at his trial, as he sought to give an account of his life and ways, that "the unexamined life is not a proper life for a human being." It seems clear, in any case, that his own life was devoted to rigorous self-examination. It is also clear that he lived a highly principled life and that he faced death with courage and equanimity. Furthermore, he pointed to a philosophical position that in some ways opposed the teachings of the first Sophists, even if he did not hold or articulate that position himself. Against their skepticism, relativism, and subjectivism he seems to have believed in the possibility of objectively existing moral realities that are universal and fixed, and in the idea that humans could apprehend them. However close Socrates may have come to grasping these truths for himself, his greatest student, Plato, took up the task left unfinished by his martyred teacher and produced the first body of genuinely philosophical literature in the Western world.

Plato. Plato (c.428–c.347 BCE) was one of the young men who were drawn to Socrates' personality and who were inspired by his devotion to the critical examination of ideas. He was scarcely twenty when Socrates entered his sixth and last decade of life, and he may have been present at Socrates' death. Plato embraced what he saw as the heart of Socrates' life and teaching: he sought the universal, immutable realities that underlie appearances and that constitute the knowledge we can employ in our decisions about how to live. Plato thus set himself up in direct opposition to the relativism and subjectivism of the Sophists, arguing that there *are* objective, universal, fixed realities that lie behind appearances, that these realities *can* be known by human beings, and that, if known, they *can* be communicated to others. Plato was particularly troubled by the ethical implications of sophistic relativism, and he strongly criticized sophistic approaches to persuasion and rhetoric.

Plato was not particularly interested in what the material world is made of nor in the laws that govern natural processes, as the pre-Socratic thinkers had been. Rather, as with Socrates and the Sophists, he pursued ontological, ethical, epistemological, and political questions: What are the ultimate realities behind appearances? What is the nature of virtue? Of justice? Of the good? What is knowledge? How is it acquired? What is the character of the ideal state? In pursuing such questions, he sought fixed, immutable moral realities: the essences of the good, of justice, of beauty. These ideal essences or forms, moreover, were for Plato the *most* real of existences, while particular empirical embodiments of these essences were imperfect approximations of them. The forms exist in a purely intellectual realm, a realm of pure ideas, and they can be known through human intellection or reasoning rather than through the senses. Plato's theories, consequently, gave rise to the metaphysical position known as idealism, which opposed the realism of those, like the Sophists, who held that the senses are the only source of knowledge.

The aim of philosophical inquiry, for Plato, was to apprehend the ideal forms of things. These could be expressed in language as true definitions of the terms used to represent them. For Plato as for Socrates, then, inquiry consisted in the rigorously logical examination of definitions. Accordingly, Plato's dialogues, where his philosophical reasoning and convictions are presented in the form of conversations between Socrates and various other characters, portray this method of investigation.

Plato's views concerning the proper relationship between philosophy and rhetoric are expressed most fully in his dialogue, *Phaedrus*, where he has Socrates explain the requirements for a "true art" of speaking. These include knowing how to define one's subject and how to divide it into logical parts. Further, one must know the nature of the human soul and discover the kind of speech that matches each type of soul. However, the first and most important requirement is that a speaker must "know the truth about every single subject on which he speaks or writes; that is to say, he must be able to isolate it in definition" (277b). Thus, "if he doesn't give enough attention to philosophy, he will never become a competent speaker on any subject" (261a). In this requirement lies the germ of Plato's dispute with sophistic teachings about rhetoric, and in this lies a central problem in the continuing relationship between philosophy and rhetoric: What is the connection between truth, knowledge, and persuasive speech?

Aristotle. Among the key issues informing the theory of rhetoric advanced by Plato's most brilliant student, Aristotle (384–322 BCE), is just this question about the connection between truth, knowledge, and persuasive speech. It is no exaggeration to refer to Aristotle as the most singularly influential philosopher in the history of Western civilization. It may be an overstatement to say, as some have, that all philosophy since the fourth century BCE is but a footnote to Aristotle; however, the impact of his thought on the intellectual history of the West is unrivaled. Endowed with an extraordinary intelligence and a driving curiosity, he was heir to Socrates' spirit of inquiry and was trained at Plato's school (the Academy) to apply the rigorous analytical technique that we can trace back to Parmenides (born c.515 BCE). As a result of these natural gifts and of his philosophical training, Aristotle undertook over his ca-

reer a program of research that yielded the most comprehensive and original corpus of philosophical writings ever produced by a single author. The works connected with his name included early popular works, mostly in dialogue form, and now lost; collections of materials for scientific treatises, also lost; and a body of philosophical and scientific treatises that have come down to us. In these latter works, Aristotle identifies spheres of intellectual inquiry that have directed philosophical activity ever since. Moreover, his philosophy contains the first statement of many of the technical distinctions, the definitions, and the terminology on which later science and philosophy have been based.

His *Organon*, a collection of logical treatises, included such titles as *Categories, On Interpretation, Prior Analytics, Posterior Analytics, Topics*, and *On Sophistical Refutations*. These works are concerned with two major subjects: the technique and the principles of logical demonstration. Regarding the first, and without underestimating the importance of Socratic questioning or of Plato's dialectic, we may attribute to Aristotle the invention of the syllogism, the form of deductive argument and of "scientific" demonstration. This form of reasoning is the foundation of the Western conception of rationality or reason, and it has defined the method of philosophical investigation and proof into our own era.

A second body of treatises can be subsumed generally under the heading of "natural philosophy," a realm of inquiry initiated by the Ionians. In works such as the *Physics, On the Heavens, On Generation and Corruption, On the Soul, On Memory and Reminiscence, The History of Animals, On the Parts of Animals*, and *On the Generation of Animals*, Aristotle laid down the questions and conceptual categories that would ultimately be applied to such sciences as physics, astronomy, psychology, biology, and zoology.

In the area of moral and political philosophy, Aristotle wrote treatises on political theory (the *Politics*), ethical theory (the *Nicomachean Ethics*), drama (the *Poetics*), and the speaker's art (the *Rhetoric*). These works deal with practical rather than with theoretical sciences and are concerned with the principles that underlie the activities of making or doing something, rather than with such activities as contemplating or defining. The practical sciences, according to Aristotle, do not admit the same degree of precision or certainty as do the theoretic sciences because their subject matters are variable and context-bound, and because they involve habits, choices, and other aspects of human agency.

The supreme area of philosophic investigation is what Aristotle termed *first philosophy, wisdom,* or *theology.* It was placed by one of Aristotle's earliest editors after the *Physics,* and so he entitled it the *Metaphysics* (*meta,* "along with," "behind," or "after"). Thus came into existence, at any rate, what is perhaps the most abstract and the most original form of philosophic investigation. Inasmuch as Aristotle's analytical method led him to seek ultimate premises or first principles in all the sciences, both natural and moral, philosophical activity aimed finally at the discovery for each science of the first principles (*archai*) from which derive the phenomena with which it is properly concerned. Thus the science of ethics seeks first principles for rendering moral judgments about practical actions, politics seeks the principles that underlie judgments concerning the public good, physics seeks the principles of motion and change, and so on. The examination of first principles that cannot be proved in any special science will require a proper technique and a separate science. This task is given by Aristotle to first philosophy, so that metaphysics can be described as inquiry into first principles. However, insofar as it considers matters that do not come under the purview of a particular science like ethics, politics, or physics, metaphysics seeks the first principles of things as *things,* not as this or that *kind* of thing. In the end, this inquiry led Aristotle in the same direction that had been pointed out by Parmenides: What does it mean "to be?" Thus, for Aristotle, metaphysics can also be understood as the science of being *as* being.

Aristotle distinguished between two classes of first principles: those that are universal and necessary, and those that are particular and contingent, or dependent on circumstances. The highest form of human knowledge—what Aristotle terms *sophia* or speculative wisdom—consists in apprehending the former and in knowing all that follows from them. It deals with "scientific truth," which can be demonstrated with logical certainty. Thus, scientific knowledge, which is a product of the activity of the "speculative intellect," is itself certain. However, Aristotle also posited a second kind of wisdom—*phronēsis* or practical wisdom—that involves knowing the first principles of things that are contingent and variable, and being able to grasp the particular, practical truths that follow from these principles. Because the principles behind these truths are variable, our knowledge of the things that follow from them admits only of probability. The realm of changeable, situational truths is the realm of the "practical intellect." It is also the realm, for Aristotle, of rhetoric. [*See* Phronēsis.]

This overview of Aristotle's thought illuminates his response to the dilemma posed by the conflict between Plato and the Sophists. By positing two realms of being, two orders of truth, and two kinds of knowledge, Aristotle was able to accommodate the Sophists' ontological and epistemological challenges while maintaining a commitment to the Platonic search for universal, immutable truths. Undoubtedly, his response would satisfy neither Plato or the Sophists, but it has served as grounding for the view that rhetoric and philosophy share an interest in ontological, epistemological, moral, and semiotic questions.

Philosophy and Rhetoric. Insofar as philosophy has been associated with the search for permanence behind the flux of experience—as it was for the pre-Socratic thinkers, Socrates, Plato, Aristotle, and many of the philosophical schools their writings or teachings have engendered—it has been concerned with questions of a very different sort from those that typically occupy the rhetorician. However, when the philosopher turns his or her attention to the sphere of contingent reality, appearances, choice, conduct, probable knowledge, and the practical uses of language, the concerns of philosophy and rhetoric converge. Rhetoric has been rooted for most theorists in the recognition that, in the sphere of action and choice, humans are immersed in a world of appearance, change, and opinion. There have been rhetorical theorists—Saint Augustine in the fourth century CE and Richard Weaver in the twentieth come immediately to mind—who have embraced a Platonic rather than an Aristotelian conception of rhetoric and its relationship to the realm of the absolute and universal. Generally, however, rhetoric has been linked to the problem of how humans can make intelligent decisions about conduct in a world of uncertainty and change.

The relationship between rhetoric and philosophy, therefore, continues to focus on issues and terms that emerged during the early development of these two disciplines. Questions about the nature of reality have pitted realists, materialists, idealists, objectivists, subjectivists, relativists, and others against one another. Each of these metaphysical–ontological stances, moreover, has implications for ethics. Thus, for example, we find ethical objectivists and universalists (who believe that moral principles and standards are objectively real, and that they transcend cultural and social differences) contending with ethical subjectivists and relativists (who hold that moral principles are wholly personal or that they are socially constructed, grounded in social consensus rather than in the "nature of things"). Similarly, epistemological theories and questions have been advanced by those who embrace reason as the path to knowledge (rationalists), those who view the senses as the source of knowledge (empiricists or positivists), and those who doubt that knowledge of any sort is even possible (skeptics). In the area of semiotics and language theory, some adhere to a correspondence view of language, where words represent things that are objectively real, while others adopt a constructionist position, where reality is *created* through language. Thus arise disputes concerning the nature of meaning itself, and numerous theories of meaning have emerged in philosophy since the time of the ancient Greeks.

Philosophy and rhetoric have often been at odds with one another. To be sure, there have been those who view philosophy as a fundamentally practical science, and who consequently have taught that rhetoric in a sense completes the philosophical enterprise. Aristotle's contemporary, Isocrates (436–338 BCE), for example, advocated and implemented an educational regimen for the aspiring citizen-orator that emphasized the study of history, politics, and ethics as well as training in rhetoric. He termed such study *philosophy*. Similarly, the Roman statesman and philosopher Cicero (106–43 BCE) maintained that in the "perfect orator" wisdom and eloquence would be united, and with that goal in mind he elaborated an educational program for the orator-statesman

that emphasized study under the rubric of philosophy of the liberal arts. At the same time, however, we find a long tradition of distrust or even outright hostility toward rhetoric on the part of philosophers. Starting with Plato and echoed by philosophers ever since, suspicions about rhetoric have centered on its lack of a proper subject matter, its reliance on opinion rather than knowledge, its interest in probability rather than certainty, and its association with the nonrational dimensions of the human mind and human behavior rather than with the rational paradigm that philosophers have derived from Aristotle's logical treatises. Of course, Aristotle himself is partly to blame for the disparagement of rhetoric by philosophers. He wrote that, as a faculty of discovering in any given case the available means of persuasion, rhetoric had no proper subject matter; he held that it treats matters about which opinions may differ; he situated it squarely in the realm of the probable and uncertain; he included in the means of persuasion not only logical argument, but also appeals to human emotions.

On these very grounds, philosophers have questioned the legitimacy of rhetoric as an art and a discipline and have, at times, relegated it to an inferior status, as being concerned not with substance, but merely with the expression of thought. In any event, such issues and terms as have been examined here continue both to confound and to guide those who seek to illuminate the relationship between philosophy and rhetoric, which have been intertwined from the outset. At times quarreling, at times cooperating, these two disciplines will, it seems, always have much to say to one another.

[*See also* Contingency and probability; *and* Prudence.]

BIBLIOGRAPHY

Cherwitz, Richard A., ed. *Rhetoric and Philosophy.* Hillsdale, N.J., 1990. An excellent collection of essays exploring the implications for rhetoric of various philosophical orientations.

Cicero. *De oratore.* Translated by E. W. Sutton and H. Rackham. 2 vols. Cambridge, Mass., 1959–1960.

Cole, Thomas. *The Origins of Rhetoric in Ancient Greece.* Baltimore, 1991.

Guthrie, W. K. C. *A History of Greek Philosophy.* 6 vols. Cambridge, U.K., 1962–1981.

Hamilton, Edith, and Huntington Cairns, eds. *The Col-

lected Dialogues of Plato. New York, 1961. See particularly *Gorgias* and *Phaedrus* for Plato's views concerning the relationship between philosophy and rhetoric.

Havelock, Eric A. *Preface to Plato.* Cambridge, Mass., 1963.

McKeon, Richard, ed. *The Basic Works of Aristotle.* New York, 1941. Of particular interest concerning philosophy are the *Metaphysics* and the *Prior* and *Posterior Analytics.* Both the *Ethics* and the *Rhetoric* have implications for the relationship between philosophy and rhetoric.

Saint Augustine. *On Christian Doctrine.* Translated by D. W. Robertson, Jr. New York, 1958.

Schiappa, Edward. *Protagoras and Logos.* Columbia, S.C., 1991.

Snell, Bruno. *The Discovery of the Mind in Greek Philosophy and Literature.* New York, 1982.

Vernant, Jean-Pierre. *The Origins of Greek Thought.* Ithaca, N.Y., 1982.

Vickers, Brian, ed. *Rhetoric Revalued.* Binghamton, N.Y., 1982. This collection of essays includes several that deal usefully with the relationship between rhetoric and philosophy.

Weaver, Richard. *The Ethics of Rhetoric.* Chicago, 1965.

—CHRISTOPHER LYLE JOHNSTONE

PHONETICS. *See* Linguistics.

PHONOLOGY. *See* Linguistics.

PHRONĒSIS. If rhetoric embodies the junction between thought and speech, *phronēsis,* in its most expansive context, combines elements of wisdom, knowledge, virtue, and decorum or propriety. Wisdom searches for the true or the right; knowledge investigates what is accepted learning in a particular field; virtue explores moral goodness; and decorum or propriety focuses on what is appropriate within the framework of a particular time and place. While these four elements make up *phronēsis,* the general emphasis over the centuries has been on "practical wisdom" supplemented by one, two, or three of the other qualities. But because rhetoric seeks to persuade, it frequently uses symbols, metaphors, or other devices that rouse the emotions, thus making *phronēsis* that much more difficult to categorize or pigeonhole.

For example, in Book 12 of the *Odyssey,* Odysseus, upon advice from Circe, the sorceress, has himself tied to the mast of his ship so he can safely hear the song of the Sirens. The rest of his men put wax in their ears. Circe *knows* that the song of the sirens causes men to jump to their deaths; her *wisdom* provides a practical way for Odysseus to hear the song; her *moral* qualities protect the lives of Odysseus and his men; and her action to save lives is *appropriate* to her power. While this example works in a fairly straightforward manner to reveal the four elements of *phronēsis,* the conflicting passions regarding Odysseus's city-state of Ithaca among her Greek neighbors might have produced very different effects upon those responding to this tale.

Perhaps Greek philosophers prior to the fourth century BCE first dealt with *phronēsis.* At least, the concept does not seem to have originated with Plato (c.428–347 BCE). He did, nevertheless, give it an apparently more polished form. In *The Republic,* he scrutinizes the lives of three different kinds of men that he places in hierarchical order from first to last: the philosopher-kings, the artisans, and the soldiers. Their lives have different purposes; the end purpose of the philosopher-king is wisdom. But a kind of speculative or contemplative wisdom is not sufficient. The pursuit of wisdom is to attain what Plato called the Ideal or Form of the Good, for which he uses the metaphorical symbol of the sun. In explaining his world of ideals versus his world of phenomena, Plato makes extensive use of many different language devices. Indeed, because no one can see these ideal forms, their essence can only be deduced from comparisons or contrasts using figures of speech.

Saint Augustine of Hippo (354–430 CE), says Plato devised a system of wisdom consisting of an active and a contemplative part, the active part having to do with the conduct of life, such as the regulation of morals, and the contemplative part, which investigates the causes of nature and pure truth. Augustine further maintains that Plato's Socrates serves as a perfect model for practical wisdom (*The City of God* 8.4).

Aristotle (384–322 BCE) also makes a formal distinction between speculative and practical wisdom, which he calls political wisdom. A former pupil of Plato, as Plato had been of Socrates, he too believed in both the ideal and the phenomenal. But he believed they inhabited the same world and were not separate but contained in the same entities. That view in turn influenced his view of practical wisdom. He viewed self-realization as the goal of human life. Human reason (a combination of wisdom and knowledge) was the chief means of attaining the goal. Reason led him to believe in a life balanced on a continuum between excessive indulgence on one end and excessive self-denial on the other. His literary style was not nearly so metaphor-driven as Plato's, and he was much more empirical in his methods than was his teacher.

Phronēsis also has been employed extensively within a theological framework, which sees both wisdom and knowledge as gifts from God given to those with insight and withheld from those without it, to their pain and agony. Sophocles puts these words in the mouth of Choragos about Creon, who has lost his son, his wife, and his niece, Antigone:

> Human beings can only be happy when they learn their place is under the authority of the gods. There is no wisdom that does not acknowledge this rule. The proud and defiant are always destroyed. And the old learn that with age comes wisdom. (*Antigone* 441 BCE)

By contrast, King Solomon of Israel (tenth century BCE) asked God for the wisdom of an understanding mind to govern the people as well as a mind capable of distinguishing between good and evil (*1 Kgs.* 3.9). God granted Solomon not only the knowledge and the wisdom to rule his people but also, as a reward for asking for wisdom, added a long life, riches, possessions, and honor (*2 Chr.* 1.7–13).

The apocryphal *Book of Solomon* affirms that wisdom is a gift from God; indeed, Solomon's only contribution was to know whose gift it was to give. He concludes by saying, "Wisdom is an associate of God in his works" (8.4) for it teaches self-control, prudence, justice, and courage (7). Interestingly enough, these are the same four characteristics that Plato lists as the four cardinal virtues. In *Laws*, Book 1, Plato discusses virtue (perhaps of the philosopher-king since *The Republic* tells us that wisdom is his province) by placing wisdom as the chief virtue. Next is temperance, and from their union with courage comes justice. Courage is fourth in the scale of

virtue. The authors of *Psalms* and *Proverbs,* King David and his son King Solomon, both give the Old Testament's meaning of wisdom. "Fear of the Lord is the beginning of wisdom" (*Ps(s)*. 111.10 and *Prv.* 1.7), to which is added "knowledge of the Holy One is insight" (*Prv.* 9.10).

In the New Testament, Saint Paul calls Jesus Christ both the power (knowledge) and the wisdom of God (*1 Cor.* 1.24). Moreover, modern rhetorical scholar James Kinneavy argues effectively that a large part of what the New Testament calls faith is found in the old Greek rhetorical notion of persuasion, or *pistis*. He argues that *pistis* meant in Greek both faith and persuasion in that region at the time the New Testament was coming into being. Kinneavy's conclusion that there are rhetorical elements deeply embedded in the concept of faith as it is expressed in the New Testament, opens up a wholly new manner of examining methods of persuasion within that document.

Thus, in its theological settings, *phronēsis* requires a combination of all four of its aspects. Wisdom, knowledge, and virtue are the spheres of the gods, and the proper decorum requires human beings to submit to their higher authority and receive these qualities as their gifts to bestow. In the thirteenth century, Saint Thomas Aquinas summed up these principles: he asserted that sacred doctrines derive their principles directly from divine knowledge, through which all human knowledge is received and arranged (*Summa theologica* 1.1.6). Both the goodness and the propriety of the Judeo-Christian God, if not the ancient Greek gods of Sophocles, are their raison d'etre. The persuasive techniques consist, for the most part, of an appeal to a higher authority that is by definition not subject to verifiable cross-examination. The emotional reaction to such an appeal varies according to the individual or corporate state belief system of those responding.

Since the thirteenth century, the concept of *phronēsis* has flourished but has become the subject of debate over its definition and its essence or properties. But the debate increasingly centers on the role of persuasion. Eighteenth-century rationalist George Campbell saw truth as the purpose of rhetoric. But its means was persuasion, the purpose of which was to stir human resolve to principled action (*The Philosophy of Rhetoric,* 1776). Campbell also argued there is no persuasion without moving the passions. His contemporary Hugh Blair agreed, contending that the purpose of eloquence in rhetoric was to persuade to action, and that in order to accomplish persuasion, the passions need to be roused, but not, he implies, to the point of losing one's power of reasoning (*Lectures on Rhetoric and Belles Lettres*, 1783). [*See* Pathos.] In the twentieth century, Kenneth Burke acknowledged that persuasion can be as crass as advertising or propaganda, as careful as courtship or proper etiquette, or an argument phrased solely for delight. More recently, Jacques Derrida reminds us that all language is metaphorical because there is no other way to express literary ideas than by using metaphorical figures of speech. He defines metaphor not as a comparison of two objects but rather as a comparison of the names of two objects. Then, in his deconstructionist manner, he concludes that there can be no philosophy and by extension no rhetoric or *phronēsis* because metaphor is simply too impoverished a way of apprehending reality.

This essay posited at the beginning that *phronēsis* combines elements of practical wisdom, knowledge, virtue, and decorum, but that these elements are influenced by persuasion, metaphor, and the emotional reactions of the hearers-readers to the rhetorical choices of the speakers-writers. When seen chronologically, the study of *phronēsis* reveals that, while our predecessors always recognized the possibility of using rhetoric to manipulate their audiences by inflaming their passions and robbing them of their reason, this is actually where wisdom and virtue merge. That manipulative possibility has become so much stronger in the twentieth century, as Burke implies, that the study of persuasion can degenerate to the point of becoming completely dissociated from wisdom and virtue and rely more on knowledge, with no moral compass with which to guide it. Finally, says Derrida, a *phronēsis*-based art of rhetoric completely disappears.

[*See also* Casuistry; Decorum; Ēthos; *and* Prudence.]

BIBLIOGRAPHY

Bateson, Gregory. *Steps to an Ecology of the Mind.* New York, 1972. An engaging study that claims mere rationality unaided by art, religion, or the like is dangerous to human life.

Burke, Kenneth. *The Rhetoric of Motives.* New York, 1950.

Derrida, Jacques. *Margins of Philosophy.* Translated with additional notes by Alan Bass. Chicago, 1991. An excellent deconstructionist view of rhetoric.

Garver, Eugene. *Aristotle's Rhetoric: An Art of Character.* Chicago, 1994. The best book of the decade on the subject.

Kinneavy, James. *Greek Rhetorical Origins of Christian Faith: An Inquiry.* New York, 1987. A revolutionary look at persuasion as faith.

Tompkins, Jane P., ed. *Reader-Response Criticism.* Baltimore, 1980. A fascinating look at reader-response criticism from formalism to poststructuralism
—ROBERT A. GAINES

PLACES. *See* Topics.

PLEONASM is a metasememe that consists of a collocation of two and more similar lexemes or sememes, effecting a semantic redundancy. As a stylistic fault (e.g., in "small dwarf," "tall giant," "young boy"), it presents a tautology, a superfluity. As a rhetorical figure, however, it gives an utterance an additional semantic dimension, as in Hamlet's dictum about his father: "He was a man, take him for all in all, I shall not look upon his like again" (Shakespeare, *Hamlet*, 1.2.186–187), where "man" contains the semantic markers (+*human*) and (+*male*) contained in "father" and "he," but according to the context it has the specific meaning "ideal man."

[*See also* Figures of speech.]
—HEINRICH F. PLETT

POETICS. *See* Criticism; Imitation; Law; *overview article on* Medieval rhetoric; Poetry; *and* Renaissance rhetoric, *article on* Rhetoric in Renaissance language and literature.

POETRY. From its first formulation until the present, rhetoric has studied poetry and has had an enormous impact on reading and writing poetry and on poetic theory. The relationship between the rhetoric of the Western classical tradition and poetry has changed greatly over the more than two-and-a-half millenia that separate us from Homer. The principal, constant features underlying this change have been: on the side of rhetoric, its capacity to be adapted to different circumstances and applications, and its central place in institutions of higher education in most of the centuries from 400 BCE to 1900 CE; on the side of poetry, its use of the principles and figures of rhetoric and, especially since the Romantic period, its wish for freedom from rhetoric. Poets and their audiences have usually been formed by a rhetorical approach to the study of language, which poets have had to use and have wanted to transcend.

Contrasts and Connections. One of the factors assisting rhetoric and poetry to make use of each other is that they belong to different levels in any categorization of reality. Poetry, like oratory, is a primary category of objects created by human activity, in this case verbal artifacts obeying certain laws that vary with time and place; rhetoric, like poetics, is a second order category comprising books that discuss the making of such verbal artifacts. (Of course, this separation is not entirely clean, since it is the second order books that codify the laws established by the community of poets.) Whereas rhetoric and poetics, like oratory and poetry, are to some extent defined in opposition to each other and are therefore restricted from overlapping, rhetoric can incorporate examples from poetry and poetry can employ techniques derived from rhetoric.

Rhetoric is less scientific than it seems, consisting more of a large number of particular precepts than of a sequence of deductions from basic axioms. (Rhetoric has principles but they are malleable and can conflict with each other.) This means that poets can make use of particular ideas or figures from rhetoric without committing themselves to the whole system. At the same time, rhetoric owes both its individual precepts and its larger principles to observation of uses of language, with poetic examples of fundamental importance among these. Many rhetorical figures are based on repetition (of sounds, words, and structures, in different positions within the sentence), which is one of the fundamental properties of poetry. Conversely, both rhythm and rhyme, the constitutive features of many forms of poetry, are among the figures of rhetoric.

Poetry is subject to more discipline than rhetoric, but it is less systematic; successful poetic fragments are common. Rhetoric is limited in its immediate goal (training someone to persuade a particular audience to a stated action or decision) where the aims of poems are extremely varied (without excluding persuasion) and often transcendent. Rhetoric is intentionally commonplace in the topics and arguments it recommends, those which are most likely to move or persuade an audience; poetry can embrace subjects that are unique and difficult of access. Officially, rhetoric is concerned with the production of orations, the most prestigious form of prose composition in the ancient world; in practice, its observations transfer easily to other forms of prose and to poetry.

Rhetoric recommends itself to the poet because, in comparison to grammar and logic, which poets also need to master, rhetoric takes an impressively broad view of the nature of language. Rhetoric understands that language involves, among many other things, a speaker's self-presentation, understanding of an audience, patterns of sound, pleasure, and emotion, as well as syntax and argument. Poets need rhetoric because as "perhaps the most careful analysis of any expressive medium ever undertaken" (E. H. Gombrich, *Art and Illusion,* Princeton, 1960, p. 374), its description of the resources, patterns, and effects of language demonstrates and explains the tools of their trade. Rhetoric needs examples from poetry because poetry is the most intensely crafted and strongly emotional form of language and must therefore provide the basis for many of rhetoric's precepts. Quintilian (c.35–c.100 CE) cites examples from Virgil more often than from any other writer apart from Cicero.

In the ancient world, rhetoric was linked to poetry through the educational system. Elementary schools in the Hellenistic period taught music, gymnastics, and grammar, which meant the study of Homer. Those pupils who proceeded to more advanced education studied rhetoric. In Roman education too, the study of poetry, especially epic poetry, preceded rhetorical education. Understandably, the speeches in the epics were quarried by rhetoric textbooks for examples of arguments, style, and figures.

Poetry using Rhetoric. Although Homer wrote before rhetoric was formally established, and although examples of figures and tropes from Homer dominate Greek rhetoric textbooks, most later poets received their training in the advanced use of language from the study of rhetoric, and therefore found it natural to think about writing in the terms which rhetoric provides.

It seems obvious, for example, that the minute analysis of the effects of particular figures of speech that we find in many rhetoric manuals, and in rhetorical commentaries on poetic texts, could be helpful to poets in the exercise of their craft. At the very least, the naming of figures makes writers more self-conscious about the ways in which they use the patterns and resources of language. For this reason, discussions of the figures are often absorbed into manuals for writing poetry.

Rhetoric also encourages analysis of the structure of speeches and poems. Since poems do not usually conform to the bare four-part structure of the classical oration, rhetoricians and commentators are obliged to analyze the functioning of different types of structure peculiar to individual poems, as Dante did in the *Vita Nuova* (c.1292), commenting on the divisions of a number of his youthful poems, or as Rudolphus Agricola did in *De inventione dialectica* (1479), analyzing the different shapes of Virgil's *Aeneid*, Ovid's *Metamorphoses*, and Lucretius's *De rerum natura*.

Since rhetoric is concerned with the effect on an audience of a particular form of expression, it encourages the study of genres of poetry, which connect a particular type of subject and occasion with prescriptions about structure, style, and meter. Adaptations of rhetoric manuals into manuals of letter writing and poetry often consist largely of a series of recipes for particular genres (perhaps combined with discussion of poetic meter and the figures of speech). The awareness of an audience, which is one of the defining characteristics of rhetoric, also encourages poets to think about issues of voice and address, both in verse-drama and in dramatic monologue.

The introductory sonnet to Sir Philip Sidney's sequence, *Astrophil and Stella* (c.1582), explores the problem of writing sincere and affecting poetry in figures and in terms derived from rhetoric.

> Loving in truth, and faine in verse my love
>   to show,
> That the deare She might take some pleasure
>   of my paine:

> Pleasure might cause her reade, reading
>   might make her know,
> Knowledge might pitie winne, and pitie
>   grace obtaine,
> I sought fit words to paint the blackest face
>   of woe,
> Studying inventions fine, her wits to
>   entertaine:
> Oft turning others' leaves, to see if thence
>   would flow
> Some fresh and fruitfull showers upon my
>   sunne-burn'd braine.
> But words came halting forth, wanting
>   Invention's stay,
> Invention, Nature's child, fled step-dame
>   Studie's blowes
> And others' feete still seem'd but strangers in
>   my way.
> Thus great with child to speake, and
>   helplesse in my throwes,
> Biting my trewand pen, beating my selfe for
>   spite,
> "Foole", said my Muse to me, "looke in thy
>   heart and write."

After announcing the subject of his poem in line one, Sidney's second to fourth lines are an excellent example of the figure of climax (Lat. *gradatio*), and included as such in Abraham Fraunce's *Arcadian Rhetorike* (London, 1588, sig. C8r).

In describing his struggle to find suitable material, Sidney employs the technical terminology of rhetoric. When Astrophil writes that he has been "studying inventions fine, her wits to entertaine" (line 6), his readers are expected to distinguish a range of meanings of invention. *Inventio* is primarily the part of rhetoric that teaches the orator how to find subject matter suitable for persuading an audience. [*See* Invention.] But here, Sidney is referring to the inventions of others ("oft turning others' leaves"), that is to say either their completed poems or the outline schemes for their works. It is significant that the term can apply both to the plan and to the completed work. In line nine ("But words came halting forth, wanting Invention's stay"), invention is the structure that sustains, and the impulse that propels, the outpouring of his style. In line ten ("Invention, nature's child, fled step-dame Studie's blowes"), it is the equivalent of poetic inspiration, not to be coerced by labor. In his *Apology for Poetry* (c.1579), Sidney expresses the view that the plan, the *fore-*

conceit, is artistically the most significant part of the work (ed. G. Shepherd, Manchester, 1973, p. 101), thus endorsing the Renaissance view that the most important aspect of composition is *inventio.*

Finally, Sidney makes the body of the sonnet an oblique introduction to its concluding line, itself a conventional statement of an anticonventional attitude, a reworking of the traditional rhetorical precept on the need to avoid the appearance of art. His poem flaunts the rhetorical skills its concluding line pretends to eschew. By simultaneously using and playing with the teachings of rhetoric, Sidney illustrates both his rhetorical education and the poetic potential of rhetoric.

Poets often employ the figures of rhetoric most obviously when writing poems concerned with public issues, where persuasion and emotional manipulation are at the forefront of their concerns. Oliver Goldsmith wrote "The Deserted Village" (1770) to condemn the system of enclosures, through which peasants were deprived of their traditional grazing rights and even their cottages so that landowners could create large country estates.

> But times are altered; trade's unfeeling train
> Usurp the land and dispossess the swain;
> Along the lawn, where scattered hamlets
>   rose,
> Unwieldy wealth and cumbrous pomp
>   repose;
> And every want to opulence allied,
> And every pang that folly pays to pride.
> Those gentle hours that plenty bade to
>   bloom,
> Those calm desires that asked but little room,
> Those healthful sports that graced the
>   peaceful scene,
> Lived in each look, and brightened all the
>   green;
> These far departing seek a kinder shore,
> And rural mirth and manners are no more.
>
>   (lines 63–74)

Goldsmith uses *anaphora, isocolon,* and *zeugma* to establish a parallelism between phrases and thereby to amplify both the wasteful luxury of the rich (in the first half of the extract) and the small, healthy virtues that are driven from the land (in the second half). These balanced phrases produce an effect of grave deliberation against

which the strong condemnatory words (*unfeeling, usurp, dispossess*) have a stronger effect. He employs both personification (trade, hours, desires, sports) and enumeration of detail to assist in the amplification.

W. B. Yeats makes extensive use of figures of balance and parallelism in his public funeral elegy for Robert Gregory, "An Irish Airman Foresees his Death" (1919).

> Nor law, nor duty bade me fight,
> Nor public men, nor cheering crowds,
> A lonely impulse of delight
> Drove to this tumult in the clouds;
> I balanced all, brought all to mind,
> The years to come seemed waste of breath,
> A waste of breath the years behind
> In balance with this life, this death. (lines 9–16)

Yeats builds up to his climax with *praeteritio* matched with anaphora and zeugma in lines nine and ten. Lines fourteen and fifteen present a large *chiasmus.* His overt emphasis on balance and deliberation serves to set off and comprehend the nihilism and the almost aesthetic choice of a violent death ("a lonely impulse of delight"). The grave effect of the alternating rhymes serve to remind us that, from the point of view of rhetoric, rhyme too is a figure (*homoeoteleuton*).

Alongside their function in giving weightiness to the speaker of a poem, figures of balance and parallelism can be used for effects of extreme emotion, as they are in Allen Ginsberg's "Howl" (1956), whose three sections are constructed through a series of anaphora ("who . . ."; "Moloch!"; "I'm with you in Rockland," respectively) and in the Flint Castle scene of William Shakespeare's *Richard II* (c.1595).

> What must the king do now? Must he
>   submit?
> The king shall do it. Must he be depos'd?
> The king shall be contented. Must he lose
> The name of king? a God's name, let it go,
> I'll give my jewels for a set of beads;
> My gorgeous palace for an hermitage;
> My gay apparel for an almsman's gown;
> My figur'd goblets for a dish of wood;
> My sceptre for a palmer's walking staff;
> My subjects for a pair of carved saints,
> And my large kingdom for a little grave,
> A little little grave, an obscure grave,
> Or I'll be buried in the king's highway,

Some way of common trade, where subjects'
  feet
May hourly trample on their sovereign's
  head.   (3.3.143–157)

Richard's speech opens with *subiectio* or *hypophora* (asking a question and answering it himself), moves to an extended series of isocola based on anaphora and antithesis ("My gorgeous palace for an hermitage"), and culminates in *epizeuxis* ("little little"), double *traductio* (repeating a word with new signification) on "little" and "grave," and *topographia* (describing a locale), imagining the subjects' feet walking on his head, as an image of his feeling of helpless victimization. The elaborate formality of the phrasing and the degree of patterning makes the speech more emotional, especially in the voice of a great actor.

Patterning and metaphor are astonishingly combined in one of Shakespeare's most celebrated sonnets (first published 1609).

That time of year thou mayst in me behold,
When yellow leaves, or none, or few, do
  hang
Upon those boughs which shake against the
  cold,
Bare ruined choirs, where late the sweet birds
  sang.
In me thou seest the twilight of such day,
As after sunset fadeth in the west,
Which by and by black night doth take
  away,
Death's second self, that seals up all in rest.
In me thou seest the glowing of such fire,
That on the ashes of his youth doth lie,
As the death-bed whereon it must expire,
Consumed by that which it was nourished
  by.
This thou perceiv'st, which makes thy love
  more strong,
To love that well which thou must leave ere
  long.   (Sonnet 73)

Using a series of similar markers that resemble anaphora ("thou mayst in me behold" [1], "In me thou seest" [5, 9], "This thou perceiv'st" [13]), the poem presents three images of the poet's age followed by a conclusion to be drawn by the beloved, imagined as a listener and viewer. Each image is a *chronographia* (a description of a time), but the lengths of time diminish progressively. In the first quatrain, the speaker is compared to the mo-

ment in autumn between the yellowing and the fall of the leaves, represented through the metaphor of the ruined choir of the church and through personification of the boughs shivering against the cold. In the second, as twilight giving way to night, personified as death's accomplice, with *antanaclasis* on "rest" (sleep and death compared). Finally, as the last ashes of the fire fading, or rather choked by ashes, represented, in a sort of reciprocal metaphor, as the youth of the fire. As the fire is choked by its ashes, we infer so the life of the dying man is destroyed (or taken over?) by (the memory of?) the youth that formerly nourished it. From a relatively simple equivalence of time-slices, the reader is drawn into a mind-wrenchingly complex meditation on the relation between age, youth, and memory. In a surprisingly confident and optimistic conclusion, the young man addressed is presumed to react to this spectacle with an increase in his love brought about by the knowledge of the proximity of inevitable parting. Figures of rhetoric assist the poet to mark the overall structure of the poem and to maintain the interrelated lines of thought. Rather than amplifying the emotion, the figures enable the thought of the poem, but the thought of the poem embodies a degree of patterned comparison beyond the imagining of any manual of rhetoric. While rhetoric is thus mainly a starting point for the poet, there is another way in which poetry completes the potential of rhetoric with a form of organization beyond rhetorical labeling.

The poetic examples analyzed above demonstrate the range of figures that poets have used in different ways. This should not conceal the fact that the figures are extremely heterogeneous in their origins and that poets may treat some figures as verbal patterns and others (for Shelley, metaphor; for Baudelaire also analogy) as the bearers of fundamental truths about language and existence. The last great long poem of the twentieth century, Geoffrey Hill's *The Triumph of Love* (1998), in its concern with "sad and angry consolation," with praise and vituperation, with *epanalēpsis*, parenthesis, irony, and *copia*, at key moments exploits and explores the terminology and preoccupations of rhetoric. [*See* Copia.]

The figures are always the most visible manifestation of rhetoric in any text and they (especially metaphor) may also have been the most important part of rhetoric for poetry, but other elements of rhetoric are also useful to poets. Writers of lyric poetry, for example, must give attention to the presentation of the speaker of a particular poem. Rhetorical textbooks (particularly Aristotle's *Rhetoric*) consider the methods of constructing a favorable persona (*ēthos*). [*See* Ēthos.] Exercises employed in rhetorical education (for example the *progymnasmata*) include character description and the composition of a speech for a historical or mythological figure. Ovid's *Heroides* (c.1 BCE) are mature versions of this school exercise. Similarly, Pope's *Eloisa to Abelard* (1717) seems to be an exercise in *prosōpopeia* in imitation of Ovid, though it might be stretching the point to describe Robert Browning's dramatic monologues (1855, 1863) in the same way. [*See* Persona.]

Poets have used ideas about *inventio* and *dispositio* derived from classical rhetoric, but since processes of invention and arrangement are not apparent on the surface of the text, their traces are harder to find than those of the figures of speech. [*See* Arrangement, *article on* Traditional arrangement.] In his admirable study *The Enduring Monument* (Chapel Hill, N.C., 1962), O. B. Hardison has shown how the topics of epideictic rhetoric influenced the Renaissance understanding of classical epic and the shape of such Renaissance epic poems as the first two books of Spenser's *Faerie Queene* (pp. 33–34, 71–84). [*See* Epideictic genre.] He argued that the three-part epitaph (praise, lament, consolation) derives its content from the topics of praise, figures of exclamation, and commonplaces of consolation (pp. 113–122). He shows that this form and these topics underlie epitaphs by Jonson and Ronsard and the organization of the subsections of Donne's *Anniversaries* (pp. 124–131, 142–145, 176–186). Aron Kibédi Varga (1970) has discovered arguments and structures derived from the three classical genres of rhetoric in French lyric poems from the sixteenth to the nineteenth century and in the speeches from French classical tragedies.

In many educational programs, training in rhetoric is closely allied to imitation of texts by famous authors. Although exercises in imitation (for example imitation of letters by Cicero) often precede training in rhetoric, once rhetoric and later dialectic are introduced, they provide the framework for imitation. Renaissance English grammar school students, for example, were instructed to analyze the form, subject matter, arguments, figures, and diction of their original in order first to vary some of these elements within the framework of the author's original, and later to compose on a different subject an imitation of the form and style of the model. Although in many schools this exercise would have been restricted to prose, pupils were presented with issues concerning imitation in the poetry they read. The most famous example of poetic imitation was Virgil's imitation of Homer in the *Aeneid* (30–19 BCE). Renaissance school editions of the *Aeneid* frequently note parallels to Homer even when they are intended for pupils who are not studying Greek. Ramus's commentaries (Paris, 1555) on Virgil's *Eclogues* (42–37 BCE), arguably the most studied of all classical poems, are studded with quotations from Virgil's originals by Theocritus (c.310–250 BCE) and his school. This was soon extended to other poems and authors. Since much of the poetic production of the sixteenth to eighteenth centuries took the form of imitations of classical originals (Spenser's imitations of Virgil's *Eclogues* in his *Shepherd's Calendar*, 1579); Marlowe's imitations of Ovid; Marvell's "Horatian Ode"; Pope's imitations of Horace; Johnson's imitations of Juvenal; to mention only English authors), we should not neglect the place of rhetoric in imitation. [*See* Imitation.]

A major theme of classical rhetoric, which formed a part of medieval treatises on poetics and became the subject of separate manuals in the sixteenth century, is amplification. As described by Quintilian, or by Erasmus in *De copia* (1512), amplification gathers together a group of techniques for verbal variation and for the invention of additional material suitable for making a person or subject seem more important or immediate to an audience, thereby to make an argument about them more persuasive or more moving. These techniques were envisaged as a method of rewriting (one might almost say supercharging) an earlier version. Poets could use them both for redrafting their own work and for varying and translating existing poems by other authors. Much of Geoffrey de Vinsauf's *Poetria nova* (c.1210) is concerned with amplification and abbreviation in order to refocus the interest of an existing poem or narrative (as one might do in retelling one of the Arthurian legends, for example). Geoffrey Chaucer acknowledges his use of these processes in adapting his original (he does not admit that it is Boccaccio) in *Troilus and Criseyde* (c.1385), at the same time revealing his rhetorician's awareness of the role of the reader in constructing meaning. In retelling to the best of his ability his author's "sentence" (which here probably means the substance of the story as well as the author's meaning), he may have added a few words, out of reverence to love. His readers must do what they wish with his additions.

> For myne wordes, heere and every part,
> I speke hem alle under correccioun
> Of yow that felyng han in loves art,
> And putte it al in youre discrecioun
> To encrease or maken dymynucioun
> Of my langage, and that I yow biseche.
>
> (4.1331–36)

In this extract, increase and diminution are the processes of amplification and abbreviation, normally the province of the poet but here explicitly extended to his readers. Robert O. Payne's classic study, *The Key of Remembrance* (New Haven, 1963), analyzes Chaucer's amplification and abbreviation of his sources, but one could easily imagine the same approach being fruitfully applied in source-based studies of other authors. Equally, much of the detailed description and comparison in later poets could be considered as uses of amplification. [*See* Amplification.]

Verbal techniques of amplification are inevitably linked to the question of diction. Rhetorical treatises recognize different levels of diction in relation to subject matter, although the classical manuals (as in other aspects of rhetoric) oversimplify the issue by allowing only three types of style (high, middle, and low). The plain, or low, style favored by some seventeenth-century poets, as well as by Wordsworth and his followers in the nineteenth century, is as much part of rhetoric as the theory of ornament. Later Greek rhetorics, such as Hermogenes' (born 161 CE) *On Types of Style,* make more distinctions. As well as discussing the types of vocabulary, sentence structure, and figures to be employed in the different levels of style, rhetoric manuals also consider the use and abuse of unusual types of vocabulary such as new coinages, archaic words, dialect words, and words borrowed from foreign languages. Poets have always been sensitive to the necessity and use of unusual words in their art, and many of their writings about poetry are concerned with this matter, which although it strictly belongs to grammar, usually finds a place in manuals of rhetoric.

Other important features of rhetorical education that find their way into poetry include maxims and proverbs, exemplary narratives, commonplaces, and letters. Late antique rhetoricians, such as Menander Rhetor have proved useful to classical scholars seeking to understand the content and disposition of lyric poems since J. C. Scaliger's *Poetices libri septem* (1561).

These examples show the range of uses that poets of many different ages have made of the teachings of rhetoric. This ubiquity of practice stands in strong contrast to changing attitudes to rhetoric in theories about poetry.

Theories of Poetry Opposed to Rhetoric. From the time of Homer and Hesiod, poets have claimed to write under divine instruction. Inspiration, which sets the poet apart from other types of writer, is seen as the necessary condition for the writing of great poetry. It is the poet's task to cultivate sources of inspiration (hence the invocations to the Muses and the gods, which are among the conventions of epic poetry), and to attend carefully to what they tell him or her. In some cases, inspiration is held to provide the subject matter of poetry, in others the actual words the poet employs. Some of the names used to describe poets, such as Latin *vates,* prophet, emphasize this view of poetry. Plato (c.428–c.347 BCE) treats the poet's claim to receive divine inspiration with some irony in *Ion,* where he regards it as the corollary of the poet's incompetence in rational fields of knowledge, but in his later works, such as *Symposium* and *Phaedrus,* he appears to support this claim by relating a myth told him by a priestess or by calling for inspiration before embarking on a metaphoric description of his own. In its strongest form, this theory insists that each successful poem must be inspired individually, and hence that certain poets have only received full inspiration once in their careers. In a weaker form, it can be assimilated to rhetoric's emphasis on *ingenium,* the natural talent that art requires in order to make speakers competent, and which a great orator must have in abundance. It is also the case that religious rhetorics (Erasmus's preaching manual *Ecclesiastes,* 1535, for example) treat divine inspiration as more important than all aspects of human rhetorical technique.

Theorists of poetry writing under the influence of neo-Platonism argued that the poet was greater than other writers and artists because of the capability of going beyond imitation in order to create something new.

> The Lawyer sayth what men have determined. The Historian what men have done. The Grammarian speaketh onely of rules of speech; and the Rethorician and Logitian, considering what in Nature will soonest prove and perswade, thereon give artificial rules, which still are compassed within the circle of a question, according to the proposed matter. . . . Onely the Poet, disdayning to be tied to any such subjection, lifted up with the vigour of his own invention, dooth growe in effect another nature, in making things either better then Nature bringeth forth, or, quite a newe, formes such as never were in Nature. . . .
>
> Nature never set forth the earth in so rich a tapestry as divers poets have done, neither with pleasant rivers, fruitful trees, sweet smelling flowers, nor whatsoever els may make the too much loved earth more lovely. Her world is brazen, the poets only deliver a golden. (Sidney, *Apology for Poetry,* p. 100)

Sidney made his arresting claim in order to persuade an audience that poetry was a better form of moral education than philosophy or history. He elaborated it according to rhetorical notions of amplification, and it sits comfortably within a book filled with precepts for good writing derived from rhetoric. Nevertheless it goes beyond anything that even the most ardent rhetorician would claim for his art. Cicero asserts that rhetoric is indispensable to the growth of human society and civilization, but not that it can create a world from nothing.

Romantic poets, notably Wordsworth in his Preface to the second edition (1802) of *Lyrical Ballads,* attacked the influence of rhetoric on the language of poetry. Wordsworth's sublime notion of poetry and his intention of depicting incidents from common life (colored, to be sure, by the imagination) in the "language really used by men," encouraged him to avoid "transitory and accidental ornaments." "There will be found in these volumes little of what is usually called poetic diction," and only a very sparing use of personification. His aim of employing ordinary language "has necessarily cut me off from a large portion of phrases and figures of speech which . . . have long been regarded as the common inheritance of poets." Wordsworth puts the emphasis on contemplating and recreating feelings that arise from common experiences, in order to express them in the most naturally occurring words and sentence structures rather than on following stylistic models of any kind. Although at first sight, Wordsworth's strictures in the "Preface" might seem capable of being met within the rhetoric of the plain style, the *Essays on Epitaphs* (1810) make it clear that he feared that rhetoric's facility in providing words for the poet might lead to a dangerous detachment from thought and feeling, the necessary foundation of poetry.

Theories of Poetry Compatible with Rhetoric. In his *Poetics,* Aristotle (384–322 BCE) set out to provide a rational account of the composition of tragic poetry by dividing it into parts. Since tragedy is a representation in language of people performing certain types of actions, its aims being to elicit pity and fear from the audience, Aristotle provides for each of these aspects criteria of excellence that are helpful to both authors and viewers of tragedies. His book is not constructed (as rhetoric handbooks are) as a series of procedures designed to produce a tragedy, but under each of his categories, he makes observations about preferred plots, types of character, and forms of language to be followed by someone composing a tragedy. Although he does not openly confront the question of inspiration, the implication of his approach is that by employing reason, talent, and skill a person can write excellent tragedies without needing to depend on the gods. Many of Aristotle's detailed observations about language and emotion are very close to passages on the same subject in his *Rhetoric.*

Horace's (65–8 BCE) *Art of Poetry* emphasizes the craftsmanlike approach. While talent is required for writing good poetry, it is also essential to attend to subject matter, organization, verse form, and diction. Horace gives much advice on all these topics, though he takes care to avoid appearing systematic in the manner of rhetoric handbooks. His practical approach to writing and revising poetry does not prevent him from employing invocations and references to the Muses in his own poems. His comments on the importance of using the common vocabulary of one's age coincide exactly with the views of the rhetorical tradition, perhaps because Quintilian elaborated Horace's remarks in his *Institutio oratoria* (c.95 CE). The importance of careful, craftsman-like consideration of vocabulary and syntax, of correction and rewriting in search of clear and harmonious expression are equally evident in Pope's *Essay on Criticism* (1709) and in T. S. Eliot's "The Function of Criticism" (1923). Neither of these works could be called a rhetoric but both recommend that poets should take the same care of the forms of language as rhetoric expects of the orator.

On the Sublime (first century CE), attributed to Longinus, may be compared with Aristotle's *Poetics* for its theorizing based on analysis of existing examples and with Horace for its craftsman-like approach to poetry. It moves a step closer to rhetoric because it is organized as a list of instructions for generating the sublime. Hermogenes in his *On Types of Style* later developed this type of work within the Greek rhetorical tradition. [*See* Sublime, the.]

One of the three important genres of rhetoric manuals from the Middle Ages is an *Art of Poetry,* which was used as a grammar school and university textbook and which combined instruction on poetic form with advice on amplification, style, and figures of speech. Sixteenth- and seventeenth-century Ramist rhetoric textbooks incorporate the rules of meter within the figures of diction, while George Puttenham's *Arte of English Poesie* (1589) adds a book on the tropes and figures to discussions of the nature of poetry, the principal genres, and poetic forms. These instances are merely extensions of the similarity of outlook between rhetoric textbooks and practical poetic manuals. Although seventeenth- and eighteenth-century composition textbooks concentrate almost exclusively on prose, eighteenth-century theories of poetry are closely aligned with the rhetorical approach to composition. In his *Salon*

of 1859, Baudelaire wrote of the rules of rhetoric and prosody as laws of spiritual being, which assist the poet's imagination to become more original.

Rhetoric and the Reading and Criticism of Poetry. Although rhetoric has played a decisive role in the education of many poets, it has been even more influential in training readers. Renaissance schoolboys were taught to analyze poetry in terms of such rhetorical categories as genres, occasions, structures, arguments, moral teaching, figures of speech, and unusual words. [*See* Hermeneutics.]

Although eighteenth-century schoolmasters taught their pupils to write prose, nevertheless the principles of the chief rhetorical effects aimed for in, for example, Blair's *Lectures on Rhetoric and Belles Lettres* (1783), were largely derived from and illustrated in the reading of poetry, especially the psalms, Virgil, and Homer.

In the twentieth century, as reading of modern poetry has largely become restricted to university graduates, professors of English have introduced models of reading that have had considerable influence on the relatively small audience for poetry. Many of the formalist critics of the early midcentury, notably I. A. Richards (1893–1979), were essentially rhetorical in their approach to the analysis of poetry. Where William Empson (1906–1984) focused on the intricate simultaneous uses of particular words, Donald Davie (1922–1992) concentrated on questions of diction and sentence structure, and Cleanth Brooks (1906–1994) directed attention to the overarching form of the individual literary artifact. In *Blindness and Insight,* Paul de Man (1919–1983) used figures of rhetoric to analyze the approaches that made possible the discoveries of modern critics, which also contradicted their assumptions. Where these approaches can be seen as variations on the different levels of linguistic analysis proposed by rhetoric, the newer generation of critics can be thought of as privileging issues of situation, political purpose, and cultural impact, which are equally part of rhetoric's broad agenda. Even the critical turn away from poetry to mass and visual media, and politics can be understood as a reassertion, within changed circumstances, of the public role of rhetoric.

Whatever concerns one might have about the future audience for poetry (when poets' systems of reference can seem increasingly hermetic), and even about the future of poetry itself (in an age in which great publishers are canceling their poetry lists), rhetoric will continue to provide poets and their successors with the means of reflecting about their medium, their audience, and their purposes. Poetry, for its part, completes and transcends the process of inquiry into the nature and effects of language inaugurated by rhetoric.

[*See also* Criticism; Law; Renaissance rhetoric, *article on* Rederijkers; *and* Style.]

BIBLIOGRAPHY

Abrams, M. H. *The Mirror and the Lamp.* New York, 1953. Fundamental account of romantic poetic theory.

Auerbach, Erich. *Scenes from the Drama of European Literature.* Minneapolis, 1984. Figures in Dante, Pascal, and Baudelaire.

Bonnefoy, Yves, and Odile Boularde. *Poésie et rhétorique.* Paris, 1997.

Curtius, E. R. *European Literature and the Latin Middle Ages.* Translated by W. R. Trask. Princeton, 1953. Fundamental study of the relation between rhetoric, education, and medieval Latin and vernacular poetry.

Edwards, Michael. *Le livre des répétitions.* Paris, 2000.

Eliot, T. S. *Selected Essays.* London, 1951.

Empson, William. *Seven Types of Ambiguity.* London, 1930; reprinted Harmondsworth, U.K., 1973.

France, Peter. *Racine's Rhetoric.* Oxford, 1965.

Ginsberg, Allen. *Collected Poems 1947–1980.* Harmondsworth, U.K.,1987.

Hill, Geoffrey. *The Triumph of Love.* Boston, 1998.

Kibédi Varga, A. *Rhétorique et littérature.* Paris, 1970.

Lanham, R. A. *The Motives of Eloquence: Literary Rhetoric in the Renaissance.* New Haven, 1976.

Man, Paul de. *Blindness and Insight: Essays on the Rhetoric of Contemporary Criticism.* 2d ed. Minneapolis, 1983.

Richards, I. A. *Principles of Literary Criticism.* London, 1924.

Russell, D. A. *Criticism in Antiquity.* London, 1981. Reasoned survey of the major classical writings on literature and rhetoric.

Sloane, T. O., and R. B. Waddington, eds. *The Rhetoric of Renaissance Poetry.* Berkeley, 1974.

Sonnino, Lee A. *A Handbook to Sixteenth Century Rhetoric.* London, 1968. Compilation of sixteenth-century English accounts of the figures of speech.

Stone, P. W. K. *The Art of Poetry 1750–1820.* New York, 1967. Useful contrast of eighteenth-century and romantic English views of poetry.

Vickers, Brian. *Classical Rhetoric in English Poetry.* London, 1970. Useful survey of the uses of the figures of rhetoric in (mainly) Renaissance English poetry.

Vickers, Brian. *In Defence of Rhetoric.* Oxford, 1988. Revises the key chapters of the above and adds later examples.

Wordsworth, William. *Literary Criticism,* edited by W. J. B. Owen. London, 1974.

Yeats, W. B. *Collected Poems.* London, 1950.

—PETER MACK

POLITICS. [*This entry comprises seven articles.*
    An overview
    Constitutive rhetoric
    Critical rhetoric
    Rhetoric and legitimation
    Rhetoric and power
    The third face of power
    The personal, technical, and public
       spheres of argument
The first article provides an overview on rhetoric and the public sphere, the distinguishing mark of which is the separability of domains of citizenship from the traditional taken-for-granted realm of acculturation assumed in traditional rhetoric. The second article discusses constitutive rhetoric in terms of identity formation and collectivization, and in terms of the rhetorical theories of Burke, Charland, Althusser, Derrida, and White. Critical rhetoric, explored in the third article, acknowledges the role of reason, discusses the two forms of critical analysis that comprise the practice of critical rhetoric, and surveys eight principles of critical practice. The discussion on rhetoric and legitimation, the fourth article, confronts these two contested ideas, covers Weber's three "ideal types" of political legitimacy, and briefly presents theories of modern thinkers Rawls, Habermas, and Lyotard. The fifth article, on rhetoric and power, considers issues related to the impact of expanded power on civic discourse. The sixth article discusses the use of third-face-of-power strategies in the twentieth century. The last article discusses the three broad spheres of argument that are recognized in a pluralistic society.]

An overview

The Western tradition has joined politics with rhetoric since its earliest recorded times. The fate of the Acheans and Trojans in the *Iliad* and *Odyssey* of Homer is influenced as much by deliberation among the gods and the guile of Odysseus as by their armed conflict. Hebrew scriptures record exchanges between Yahweh and the Israelites, as well as between mere mortals, who deliberate the ways of God and humanity. The ancient Athenian political accomplishment of a participatory democracy, in theory and practice, rested on the bond between politics and rhetoric. Aristotle (384–322 BCE) formalized this bond in *On Rhetoric,* when he placed rhetoric under the ethical branch of politics.

The ancient union of politics with rhetoric is distinctive for its emphasis on the former as a practical art. Whereas the modern science of politics often focuses on the structural, economic, and legal features of institutional relations associated with power, the rhetorical concern of politics historically has been with the ongoing negotiation over how we shall act and interact. Although that negotiation always involves questions of power, it is also concerned with enabling practical judgment.

Western democracies situate judgment with citizens. A democracy's citizens, in principle, possess ultimate political power through participation in deliberative processes and by exercising their right to vote. Yet democratic politics has never had an easy acceptance of its inherently rhetorical character. Democracies have always been beset by a fundamental tension between the participatory rights of all citizens, regardless of their education, station, or means, and fear among an educated, wealthy, and well-positioned elite that the majority are too ignorant and too easily swayed by the emotional appeals of demagogues to make sound decisions. This tension is expressed well by the ancient adage: the people reign, the elite rule.

Tension between the people and the elite in ancient Athens was managed best by a strong leader, such as Solon early on (c.594 BCE) or Pericles (c.440 BCE), who understood that competing interests could produce powerful and destabilizing factions capable of imposing their will on the minority. Such leaders were as aware in their political context as James Madison (1751–1836) was in his of the need for compromise to maintain order and preserve political freedom for all citizens. The difference between Pericles' Athens and Madison's America, on the other hand, is significant for understanding the evolving role of rhe-

torically constituted politics within the context of democracy's own changing character.

Ancient Athens practiced a politics based on the ideal of civic virtue, which was manifested as a public performance of noble words and deeds. Civic virtue constructed individual identity through citizenship, and Athenian culture emphasized a citizen's public persona as the ground for that individual's meaning. This understanding was italicized by the inscription on Athens's ancient city wall: "The man with no public business has no business," and by the Greek word for the person who was mute on public affairs: *idiot.*

As a model of social organization, civic virtue invaded the private realm; as a political norm, it organized a person's meaning, leaving no buffer between political and social life (Taylor, 1995). It was a model of accomplishment assembled by the state. An individual's virtue was not a personal trait but a public quality that had to conform to the ideals and standards inscribed in the laws and customs of the *dēmos,* or the people as a whole (De Colanges, 1956). The politics of civic virtue emphasized public good by subjugating the private self to the public realm. Excellence (*aretē*) was a quality of publicness that reflected the *dēmos*'s understanding of moral virtue as a public rather than a private attribute. The citizen realized civic virtue by active and continual participation in public political affairs. Civic virtue projected a moral vision of personal choice and action regulated by the sovereign authority of the political community, not by the sovereign or the individual actor. This vision was performed through conformity of the actor's particular will to the community's will. The community's political authority referred not to the obvious fact that it was the source of morality but that the community existed as morality (Seligman, 1995, pp. 202–204). [*See* Oratory.]

The Western tradition of politics continues to embrace as part of its heritage the model of civic life portrayed by civic virtue. However, the change from a participatory to a representative democracy has brought significant changes in the way rhetoric constructs politics. In liberal democratic societies, citizens no longer have a direct voice in the decision-making process and the individual no longer acquires identity through public performances under the sovereign authority of the political community. The power of civic virtue that made the *vita activa* the organizing paradigm of existence began to erode as Rome's centralized power went into decline and the alternative institution of the Christian church began its rise. The church was independent of the state; its dogma taught followers to organize their individual lives around a set of moral principles and ideals rather than political ones. Its paradigm was the *vita contemplativa* (Arendt, 1958), in which a person sought detachment from earthly possessions and power to establish an inner communion with God. Christians were members of two societies, one temporal, the other spiritual, neither subjugated to the other, each constituted by its own rhetorical character.

Equally, with the rise of the monarchy during the Middle Ages and early Renaissance, political power gravitated to court only to encounter new challenges. The powers of feudal lords, who had firmly established property rights, constrained monarchs in their efforts at nation building, as did the church. When monarchs attempted to counter this preexisting social force by granting autonomy to towns, they found the burghers who led them to be both feisty in their independence and too wealthy to be ignored. For some time, monarchs had found it necessary, periodically, to convene the body of estates—assemblies of the clergy, nobility, and burghers who were considered to represent the great collective interests of the nation—to raise resources for governing and waging war. Soon monarchs found themselves vulnerable to the uncertainties of the estates themselves (Hall, 1995).

The rise of the Christian church and of the body of estates eroded the rhetorical understanding of politics forged in the Athenian democracy and projected in its model of civic virtue. Both the church and the estates provided a sense of social identity apart from citizenship. They provided a mode of social organization in which their members could engage in discourse unregulated by the state. This changed locus of identity was formally developed in the political writings of Enlightenment thinkers such as Locke (1632–1704 CE), Montesquieu (1689–1755), and Rousseau (1712–1778). They maintained that humankind formed a community of sorts constituted under natural law and in existence prior to soci-

ety, which was itself prior to the government. Their formulations replaced the link between society and its political organization with the idea of civil society as a third arena, independent of the church and the state. Civil society was multidimensional, with a political dimension that consisted of the network of associations whose members sought to regulate themselves through discursive exchanges that balanced conflict and consensus in ways consistent with a valuation of difference. Enlightenment thinkers associated this arena with the rise of an autonomous public integrated with the state through expressions of its own opinion.

The Enlightenment concept of *publicness* represented a new understanding of politics that went beyond what was objectively present and open to everyone's inspection. It designated a concern that involved the common interest of all citizens. These common concerns, moreover, were explored in new, discursive spaces—newspapers, personal exchanges in coffee houses and salons, political clubs—that extended beyond the court and assembly. With the exception of salons, which frequently were organized by women of high standing, these were gendered spaces open to all males, or at least to those who were literate. These were arenas of open deliberation in which current issues were discussed and, ideally, resolved to the extent that a tendency of shared opinion emerged. This discourse gave rise to a new idea of public opinion as a prevailing opinion dispersed among those who were actively engaged by an issue. It introduced the radical idea that such opinion formed outside the channels and public spaces of the official political structure. Public opinion was purported to be society's opinion; its channels and spaces were those of civil society.

Public opinion expressed society's identity apart from the state and represented a shift in how society engaged in politics. The network of associations that comprised civil society and in which public opinion formed called for a mode of rhetoric different from that practiced in Greek and Roman antiquity. The discursive spaces of government were no longer the only domain in which social will could be articulated and executed. New spaces, populated by difference and relations of mutual dependency, were organized as a lattice of self-regulating rhetorical domains that advanced social coordination. Collectively they forged a public sphere in which a public could form its own opinion, could challenge the state's primacy in setting social purpose, and might expect its shared understanding to bear weight on what the state did.

A second change accompanied the transition from civic virtue to civil society. Classical rhetoric was wedded to politics as a productive art. Its concern was to prepare students to practice political persuasion. With the advent of the scientific revolution, European thought dismissed rhetoric as dangerous, since it invoked a logic of probabilities and engaged emotions in forming decisions (Howell, 1996). Science gained methodological authority because it claimed to be rigorous, objective, systematic, and consistent, and to follow prescribed protocols in gathering data and drawing inferences. It provided a windowpane on reality. In response, thinkers like Giambattista Vico, in the eighteenth century, and Friedrich Nietzsche, in the nineteenth, challenged the authority of scientific reasoning by positing that the human world was composed differently from the realities of nature. The human world of politics, they thought, could not be extricated from rhetoric because politics was constructed through language. This counterargument shifted the fundamental question of rhetoric from a dominant concern with producing persuasive appeals to one of how rhetorical practices were embedded in all language use and, therefore, were constitutive of the human world. This shift has broadened and deepened our understanding of politics as a rhetorical construction (e.g., see Cloud, 1998; Darsey, 1997; Wells, 1996).

Since the end of World War II, the prevailing political problem confronting complex societies and the international community has been to establish effective political meaning among political actors who lack ideological common ground. Sometimes these differences are so profound that the active participants cannot even meaningfully describe shared difficulties to partners with whom they are at odds. The union of rhetoric with politics lies at the center of this problem. The civil society frame highlights society's continuous engagement in negotiation over how we shall act and interact as it occurs in preinstitutional as well as institutional forums. These may be vernacular or formal exchanges and transpire in civic groups and organizations or the counterpublic spheres of social movements, campaigns, protests, and identity enclaves equally as in the official public spheres of political parties and the state.

These differences accentuate the conflict-riven relations of competing interests. But the search by political actors in multiple arenas for shared interests and common judgments on them ultimately stresses codependency and the need for collaboration. The civil society frame models politics as the ability to establish rhetorically salient meaning in multiple public spheres and construes political power as a function of successful "border crossings" (Hauser, 1999). This frame's linguistic turn challenges the dominant realist paradigm of political relations as an exclusively strategic calculus intended to secure advantage (Hariman, 1995). A rhetorically-based theory of this sort—a postrealist theory—grounds politics in what Vico called *ingenium*, an invention of language that takes form in a given case (Grassi, 1980). But this is a volatile politics destabilized by postrealism's own metatheory of rhetorical deconstruction and reconstruction.

The civil society's heavy reliance on the transformational possibilities of rhetorical invention reverses the architectonic relationship Aristotle asserted between politics and rhetoric. It emphasizes rhetoric's productive powers as the architectonic or master art for a political practice that brings divergent perspectives into a collaborative union of common action (Mailloux, 1989; McKeon, 1971). It explains postrealism's transcendent tendency toward fusing the theory of conduct with the debate by which a course of conduct is invented (Beer and Hariman, 1995). It also reminds us that whether the political public sphere is colonized by the state and power elites, as Jürgen Habermas (1962) depicts in his rendition of late capitalism, or remains open to the possibility of its own self-regulation, it is itself subject to the rhetorical possibilities and performances it can sustain (Farrell, 1993; Hauser, 1999).

BIBLIOGRAPHY

Arendt, Hannah. *The Human Condition.* Chicago, 1958.
Aristotle. *Aristotle, On Rhetoric.* Translated by George A. Kennedy. New York, 1991.

Beer, Francis A., and Robert Hariman. "Strategic Intelligence and Discursive Realities." In *Post-Realism: The Rhetorical Turn in International Relations,* edited by Francis A. Beer and Robert Hariman, pp. 387–414. East Lansing, Mich., 1995.

Cloud, Dana. *Control and Consolation in American Culture and Politics: Rhetoric and Therapy.* Thousand Oaks, Calif., 1998.

Darsey, James. *The Prophetic Tradition and Radical Rhetoric in America.* New York, 1997.

De Coulanges, Numa Denis Fustel. *The Ancient City.* Translated by William Small. New York, 1956. First published 1873.

Farrell, Thomas B. *Norms of Rhetorical Culture.* New Haven, 1993.

Grassi, Ernesto. *Rhetoric as Philosophy: The Humanist Tradition.* University Park, Pa., 1980.

Habermas, Jürgen. *The Structural Transformation of the Public Sphere.* Translated by Thomas Burger with the assistance of Frederick Lawrence. Cambridge, Mass., 1989. First published 1962.

Hall, John A. "In Search of a Civil Society." In *Civil Society: Theory, History, Comparison,* edited by John A. Hall, pp. 1–31. Cambridge, U.K., 1995.

Hariman, Robert. *Political Style: The Artistry of Power.* Chicago, 1995.

Hauser, Gerard A. *Vernacular Voices: The Rhetoric of Publics and Public Spheres.* Columbia, S.C., 1999.

Howell, Wilber Samuel. "Renaissance Rhetoric and Modern Rhetoric: A Study in Change." In *The Rhetorical Idiom,* edited by Donald C. Bryant, pp. 53–70. Ithaca, N.Y., 1966.

Mailloux, Steven. *Rhetorical Power.* Ithaca, N.Y., 1989.

McKeon, Richard. "The Uses of Rhetoric in a Technological Age: Architectonic Productive Arts." In *The Prospect of Rhetoric,* edited by Lloyd F. Bitzer and Edwin Black, pp. 44–63. Englewood Cliffs, N.J., 1971.

Seligman, Adam. "Animadversions upon Civil Society and Civic Virtue in the Last Decade of the Twentieth Century." In *Civil Society: Theory, History, Comparison,* edited by John A. Hall, pp. 200–223. Cambridge, U.K., 1995.

Taylor, Charles. *Philosophical Arguments.* Cambridge, Mass., 1995.

Wells, Susan. *Sweet Reason: Rhetoric and the Discourses of Modernity.* Chicago, 1996.

— GERARD A. HAUSER

Constitutive rhetoric

Constructing and providing its addressed audience with an identity, constitutive rhetoric is fundamental to collectivization and to the emergence of nations. It can be understood both as a genre of discourse and as a theory for understanding rhetorical processes. As a genre, constitutive rhetoric simultaneously presumes and asserts a fundamental collective identity for its audience, offers a narrative that demonstrates that identity, and issues a call to act to affirm that identity. This genre warrants action in the name of that common identity and the principles for which it stands. Constitutive rhetoric is appropriate to foundings, what Hannah Arendt called "founding moments," but also to social movements and nationalist political campaigns. It arises as a means to collectivization, usually in the face of a threat that is itself presented as alien or other.

As a theory, constitutive rhetoric accounts for the process of identity formation that this genre depends upon, where audiences are called upon to materialize through their actions an identity ascribed to them. Political oratory and rhetorical theory usually take the identity of the audience to be given, and as a consequence, rhetoric is usually understood to produce persuasion. The persuasion model dominates rhetorical theory and is fundamental to Aristotle's (384–322 BCE) writing on the subject. He considered rhetorical practice to be the art of crafting speech to persuade an audience that is called upon to render a judgment regarding a contingent question. Aristotle's *Rhetoric* is a guide to invention that stresses the need to offer proofs that exploit the typical presumptions, values, character, and affective dispositions of a given audience. In doing so, Aristotle does not consider the role of rhetoric in producing the very identity and character of an audience.

The constitutive model, in contrast, can be traced to the Sophists, who had an appreciation of paradox and recognized the constitutive power of utterances. [*See* Sophists.] Their view emphasized the contingent and conventional nature of knowledge and thus recognized discourse as productive of the very categories by which the world, and indeed the self, are understood. This view of rhetoric is well exemplified in the oratory of Gorgias (c.483–c.376 BCE), a Sophist and contemporary of Socrates. The power of Gorgias's oratory is said to have been based in its capacity to enthral an audience, not addressing their reasoning faculty, but poetically transforming their very experience of being. Kenneth Burke (1897–1993) is heir to this line of thought when he argues that rhetorical discourse produces *identification* or *consubstantiality.* [*See* Identification.] For Burke, rhetorical discourse can rearrange the meaning of terms, so that one thing becomes more or less like another, or members of an audience are brought to share a common identity with each other or a speaker. Inspired by Freud and Marx, Burke viewed discourse as structuring motives "behind the back" of reason. Burke's foregrounding of identification renders possible a rhetorical account of conversion experiences that cannot be explained in terms of Aristotle's conception of persuasion. Consequently, identity itself can be seen as rhetorically produced rather than a given that is prior to persuasion and upon which persuasion depends.

Within contemporary rhetorical theory, Maurice Charland (1987) developed a theory of constitutive rhetoric through a synthesis of post-structuralism and Kenneth Burke's contemporary rewriting of rhetorical theory. Central to Charland's analysis is Louis Althusser's ideological theory of "interpellation," a structuralist approach to narrative, and Burke's concept of identification. Rhetoric's subject is not only posited through the formal pragmatics of narrative structure and its mode of address, but also given meaning though the ideological effect of identification with its *diēgēsis.* Hailing occurs in the moment of address of a rhetorical narrative that "always already" presumes the existence of that which its account both depends upon and validates, the identity of its addressee as an historical protagonist. Constitutive rhetoric constructs political subjects through effects of identification that (1) provide a collective identity for an addressed audience; (2) construct the audience as a subject in history; and (3) demand that subjects act in accordance with their identity as enacted in history.

From the perspective of a rhetorical critic, a constitutive understanding of rhetoric is not necessarily antithetical to a persuasive one. Rather, constitutive rhetoric is logically (if not also temporally) prior to persuasive rhetoric. Before audiences may be appealed to, their identity must be constituted. Constitution precedes persuasion, but persuasion can still occur. Furthermore, because audience identity usually is presumed and posited, having been constituted on prior occasions, the process of constitution is not apparent

in much public address. Thus, retrospectively, constitution can be treated as a genre: The critic seeking to account for constitution will usually focus on texts such as constitutions, proclamations, declarations, and manifestos, as well as on the rhetoric of mobilization, movements, and war, for as Kenneth Burke notes, extreme division gives rise to extreme identification as well.

The theory of constitutive rhetoric has antecedents in rhetorical theory and criticism, most notably in Edwin Black's "The Second Persona" (*Quarterly Journal of Speech* 56, 1970, pp. 109–119) and Michael McGee's (1975) study of the rhetoric of collectivization. Black's discussion of the second persona did not explore the formal process of constitution per se, but rather called attention to the manner in which ideological rhetoric articulates a worldview or *ēthos* that its audience must adopt prior to any other persuasion. As such, Black placed the subject at the center of ideology and argued that its critical study required an interpretation of that subject's *ēthos.* In doing so, Black offered a hermeneutic of the subject of ideology. McGee, on the other hand, examined the significance of the collective subject. McGee studied the rhetorical invocation and constitution of the "people." He argued that the "people" only exist as individuals are collectivized through rhetorical appeals. Once collectivized, they constitute a reservoir of power that can defend or challenge legitimate authority.

The compatibility between the theory of constitutive rhetoric and the practice of rhetorical criticism is furthermore a consequence of the important place that narrative plays in constitutive rhetoric. Narrative is fundamental to the rhetoric of constitution because narratives open *diagetic* spaces, story spaces, which are meaningful because they produce identification with a point of view. Narratives constitute subjects, protagonists, and antagonists. Rhetorical narratives claim to tell a story about a real rather than a fictive world. They seek to naturalize their diagetic space. Narratives are thus open to hermeneutic analysis. The theory of constitutive rhetoric directs the critic toward an interpretation of narratives serving as allegories or as examples.

Such narratives are based, however, upon a paradox: they must presume an audience that is already consubstantial with the very identity they seek to prove. Although constitution can be understood as a genre of rhetoric, more significant is this very dynamic of the paradox of address. The theory of constitutive rhetoric is fundamentally concerned with what Kenneth Burke described as a "paradox of substance" pertaining to the ontological status of categories immanent to discourse. Audiences are addressed as if their identity existed prior to or served as the "container" of their political community. Furthermore, because address is fundamental to all rhetorical discourse, the paradox of constitution is always latently present as well. Rhetorical address implicitly (and often explicitly) cites or replays the moment of an original constitutive act. To address an audience is always to posit a "subject position," a place from which the audience is called upon to judge and act. The paradox of constitution is imminent to the pragmatics of rhetorical address itself. Attentive to this paradox, the theory of constitutive rhetoric is *deconstructive,* because it renders problematic the categorical distinction between speech and audience upon which rhetoric understood as persuasion is founded.

This paradox of constitution is explored by Jacques Derrida through the categories of speech–act theory. In his analysis of the American *Declaration of Independence,* Derrida observes that no legitimate representatives of the people could exist to sign that document until after the signing itself, out of which the "people" was born. As Derrida observes, constitution is an illocutionary speech act that must deny its illocutionary character, and claim authority by posing as a constative. Thus, as Derrida shows, the *Declaration* must invoke God as witness, for only he can authorize this moment of creation. Derrida's concern with the authority of utterances highlights the relationship of constitutive rhetoric to law. God is, after all, the supreme lawgiver. Constitutive rhetoric will not necessarily require a deity, but will require its proxy, figured as the laws of history or of nature. Constitutive rhetoric asserts a normative principle from what would be ostensibly an empirical claim. As Althusser (1971) observes, the interpellation of subjects requires a Subject, a totality, who stands as law and ultimate principle of authority.

James Boyd White (1987) developed the relationship between constitutive rhetoric and law when arguing that rhetoric constitutes legal communities and establishes the terms for their continued existence. In doing so, White echoes Burke's observation that constitutions are fundamentally rhetorical. The drafters of constitutions not only establish a political order, but issue a command regarding how those in the future shall live. In White's understanding, constitutive rhetoric is addressed not to a populace as members of a people, but to lawmakers. Constitutive rhetoric establishes both the framework for political constitutions, and establishes the parameters for their judicial interpretation. As such, constitutive rhetoric depends not only upon persuasion, but upon the grammar and metaphysics of law and obligation. Furthermore, rhetorical constitution becomes sedimented in institutionalized practices that render such constitution "material," more than only ideas or meaning.

Too, White considered the creative potential of constitutive rhetoric as enabling something new to enter the world. Political community becomes possible. However, viewed through a hermeneutics of suspicion, constitutive rhetoric operates as ideology, understood as the naturalized representation of cultural categories that legitimate institutions of power. With its focus on ideology and its critique of received categories, the theory of constitutive rhetoric is part of what has come to be known as "critical rhetoric," an orientation to rhetorical studies influenced by ideological theory as developed by the Frankfurt School and by French poststructuralism seeking to account for the discursive construction of power. Critical rhetoric calls attention to what public discourse posits and takes for granted and also examines the ways in which the relationship between communicants is one of power. Both ideological theory and poststructuralism call attention to the importance of subjectivity to ideology and the processes by which subjectivity itself is constructed in discourse. The theory of constitutive rhetoric is consequently fundamentally skeptical, because it refuses to take identity, which is the basis of both nationalism and "identity politics," as given. Rather, constitutive rhetoric calls attention to the historically contingent character of identity and its dependence upon discourse. It leads to the charting of mechanisms of power.

Ultimately, constitution, akin to persuasion, is one of rhetoric's functions. It is an element in the process through which language renders possible political community, action, and judgment. While rhetoric may be considered epistemic, because it can contribute to practical or social knowledge, the theory of constitutive rhetoric reminds us that rhetoric is also fundamentally ontological, establishing the very foundations of the political life-world.

[*See also overview article on* Audience; Communication; *and* Social knowledge.]

BIBLIOGRAPHY

Althusser, Louis. *Lenin and Philosophy and other Essays.* London, 1971. The essay "Ideology and the Ideological State Apparatuses" offers a groundbreaking integration of the Marxist theory of ideology with the poststructuralist theory of the subject. Transforms "interpellation" into a powerful concept of subject positioning and ideological production.

Arendt, Hannah. *Between Past and Future.* New York, 1968.

Burke, Kenneth. *A Grammar of Motives.* Berkeley, 1969. First published 1945. Introduces and develops the concept of the paradox of substance through a discussion of words belonging to the "stance" family. The section, "The Dialectic of Constitutions" considers the American Constitution as a "representative anecdote" for the rhetorical and paradoxical nature of acts of founding. Considers how constitutions require an extraconstitutional scene.

Burke, Kenneth. *A Rhetoric of Motives.* Berkeley, 1969. First published 1950. Brilliant and dense discussion of the relationship of persuasion to identification through the organizing principle of "motives."

Charland, Maurice. "Constitutive Rhetoric: 'The Case of the *Peuple Québécois.*'" *Quarterly Journal of Speech* 73 (1987), pp. 133–150. Offers a symptomatic reading of the 1980 rhetoric of the Quebec sovereignty movement in order to articulate the theory of constitutive rhetoric.

Coward, Rosalind, and John Ellis. *Language and Materialism: Developments in Semiology and the Theory of the Subject.* Boston, 1977. Offers a complete, although now somewhat dated, grand synthesis of psychoanalytic theory, Marxism, and poststructuralist semiotics in relation to the concept of the subject.

Derrida, Jacques. "Declarations of Independence." *New Political Science* 15 (1986), pp. 7–15. Considers the paradox of authorization and legitimacy as a tension between constantive and performative speech acts. Brilliant in its demonstration of how authority necessarily depends upon paradox and its dissimulation.

Greene, Ronald Walter. "Another Materialist Rhetoric." *Critical Studies in Mass Communication* 15 (1998), pp. 21–40. Discusses the limits of the theory of constitutive rhetoric as a materialist theory.

McGee, Michael Calvin. "In Search of the 'People': A Rhetorical Alternative." *Quarterly Journal of Speech* 61 (1975), pp. 235–249. Groundbreaking as it develops a materialist theory of rhetoric based in an understanding of the "people" as a rhetorical construct that serves both an ideological justification of political authority and as a human collectivity capable of acting as a force in history.

White, James Boyd. *When Words lose their Meaning: Constitutions and Reconstitutions of Language, Character, and Community.* Chicago, 1987. Offers a model of reading both literature and law as constitutive of community. Provides an exemplary exegesis of American constitutional documents and their judicial interpretation.

—MAURICE CHARLAND

Critical rhetoric

From the time of Plato (c.428–c.347 BCE) the Idealist tradition of Western rhetoric has privileged appeals to a universalized sense of reason at the expense of an appreciation of context and contingency. The critical rhetoric perspective moves in a contrary direction, acknowledging the role of reason but also recognizing that other forces may take center stage in the formation of a discursively constructed reality. The perspective is useful both for the political speaker, as heuristic in composing discourse, and for the rhetorical critic or audience member responding to that discourse.

Two forms of critical analysis comprise the practice of critical rhetoric. A critique of domination has as its aim an emancipatory purpose and can best be styled as a "freedom from" that which otherwise limits its potentiality. A critique of freedom has as its aim a reflexivity that grounds its actions in a constant reflection on the contingency of human relations and can best be styled as a "freedom to" move toward new relations with others (McKerrow, 1991). In the former stance, the recognition of power in its repressive role is paramount; in the latter, the recognition of power as productive is paramount. These two approaches should be characterized as "two sides of the same coin" (Ono and Sloop, 1992, p. 50), rather than mutually-exclusive approaches to critical analysis, especially since both emerge from a concept of freedom. In both instances, the critique is free to move beyond criticism alone and question the assumptions on which critical analysis is based. Thus, if one is working within the constructs of a democratic stage, the assumptions that ground democracy are as open to critique as are the actions that emanate from that state.

Employing either form of analysis, the goal of the critic or *rhētōr* is a commitment to change. "Whether the critique establishes a social judgment about 'what to do' as a result of the analysis, it must nonetheless serve to identify the possibilities of future action available to the participants" (McKerrow, 1989, p. 92). As Ono and Sloop have argued, the critique of freedom carries with it a goal of specific change in the individual moment of advocacy. Once matters have been altered, and relationships have been constructed along new lines, the commitment returns to ask if this is the best option available.

The practice of critical rhetoric works from inquiry rather than from a specific method or means of analysis. Thus, it operates in the tradition of Kenneth Burke (1897–1993), wherein the aim is not to advance a critical terminology or highlight a specific vocabulary, but rather to use such in the service of argument about the manner in which discursive formations are constituted (cf. Foucault, 1972). As a consequence, pointing to a particular piece of criticism as exemplary of critical practice is difficult, for to do so may run the risk of identifying the method as the only useful one. As a practice, critical rhetoric resists the kind of focus often accorded "close textual reading" or a "pentadic analysis." Further, it seeks to reverse the traditional "public address" approach, which presumes a speaker/audience situation, in favor of an approach that focuses on what McGee (1990) has refined as an inventional approach toward critical practice.

In broadening the scope of the critical act, the inventional approach does not seek to discredit the speaker/critic as one who seeks change, nor does it undermine the possibility of enacting a critique in the role of critical agent. Rather, it offers a perspective that contextualizes the role of the agent, whether speaker or critic, as a product of contingent forces that interact with the subject in producing discursive acts. [*See* Ēthos.] That one's voice may count in remaking social relations is evidence of the force a speaker or critic possesses. That force, however, is not the original construction of the speaking subject but rather one that "gives expression to its 'I' and thereby enacts the self. The 'I' implicates itself in both its past and future history as a contingently derived self" (McKerrow, 1993, p. 64). Assuming the position of a critical *rhētōr* is to place critical action within the context of a contingently derived future that is itself open to alteration in an unspecified manner.

Principles of Critical Practice. Eight principles of critical practice have been advanced, with the proviso that these were not meant to be exhaustive. The first incorporates the inventional perspective suggested above in noting that "*Ideologiekritik* is in fact not a method but a *practice*" (McGee, 1984, p. 49). As such, the practice encourages a creativity unencumbered by specific or privileged methodological considerations. In the same sense that Foucault's archaeology or later "genealogy" is not a "method" but a practice, it would be inaccurate to claim that dismissing method therefore dismisses a methodical approach. What is dismissed is allegiance to a specific manner of inquiry in favor of that which fits the context or situation as a methodical means of conducting an analysis.

The second principle underscores the materiality of discourse. What this principle acknowledges is that discourse potentially makes a difference in the social relations that exist, or may exist, among a people. Underscoring materiality of discourse in a relativized world does not remove the possibility of critique. To preclude universal standards is not tantamount to embracing irrationality, any more than it is tantamount to disparaging the possibility of staking a claim to a better future (for an alternate perspective, see Cloud, 1994).

The third principle, that rhetoric centers on opinion (*doxa*) rather than knowledge (*epistēmē*), follows from the second, in highlighting the contingent rather than certain nature of the formations that are created in and through discourse. The focus of this principle is not on what is true or false in the discourse, but on what the symbols used actually do in constructing particular visions of the world—what forms of power are embraced or implicated in the discourse, and what produces *this* discourse rather than other possible discourses. The implication of *doxa* is consistent with Aristotle's (384–322 BCE) original purpose in highlighting rhetoric's contingent nature; it serves to underscore the idea that informed opinion constitutes a "way of knowing" (a weak form of *epistēmē*), while recognizing that what is thereby known is neither absolute nor immune to the forces of time. [*See* Contingency and probability.]

The next principle, that naming is central, follows from the opinion-centered nature of rhetorical discourse. Naming, according to Burke, is not a final act of assessment but an interpretation of what is at any given moment perceived to "be." Being, in this instance, is neither final nor absolute in its own construction, but rather subject to multiple future possibilities. But in naming, one at least momentarily concretizes that which is so named, and thereby confers and confirms one's own relation to the object or person named. Power is a concomitant of naming as well, because it enacts one's relationship within (as well as potential resistance to) what the names conjure. As names change, so does the power relation that inheres within the name employed.

The fifth principle implicates power in a more direct way than through naming, as it suggests that influence does not implicate causation. Rather, it serves to suggest that the forces that bring discourse into being may well be present and purposeful, but are not reducible to simple claims of causality. To limit rhetorical history to causal implications is to frame the production of rhetoric itself in an outmoded linear fashion. The range of possibilities would be likewise limited with respect to an analysis of what brings a discourse forward. History would be seen a continuous, rather than discontinuous. As Foucault took pains to illustrate, this is a far too limited view of how things have come to be in the world.

Once *influence* is conceptualized from a perspectival position, the sixth principle follows naturally: absence may be as influential as presence in constituting the nature of a specific reality. That which is not said or seen can be as important in shaping future courses of action as what is in fact claimed or observed. [*See* Tacit dimension, the.]

If naming is critical, so too is the seventh principle. Polysemic interpretation becomes a key to understanding the relative or contingent nature of claims on belief or action. Ideological critique is not intended to form one and only one view of the universe of discourse; that others might focus on matters differently means that critics or rhetors must defend themselves with sound argument. That others lay claim to their own view of reality does not mean that all are "right" or that no one is "wrong" in some sense. Rather, it means that differing views of what exists or should exist must engage one another as competing rationales for advocacy or for criticism. To say of an act "it seemed a good idea at the time" is to at once suggest that one had sound reasons for engaging in the act and that the soundness of those very reasons may be suspect or challenged. Actions are defensible, just as ideas are open to challenge. Rather than paralyzing advocacy or criticism, critical rhetoric requires making the best case possible for the moment in which one finds oneself, realizing that one may well, in the future, find one's rationale weakened by new information or new insights.

In the eighth principle is the realization that if rhetorical acts are performances, so too are the criticisms that accompany those acts. To take the role of a critic is to be performer in the world—to seek to enact change in the moment, with the full realization that such change may well make things worse rather than better, and that once implemented, new power relations will stand open to further reflection and possible revision. As a performer, the critic or rhetor is imbricated within an ethic of "care of the self" that forecloses the possibility of an unremitting arrogance. The rhetor is neither faceless nor vacant as a performing self. One is identified as an agent for change, whether as a speaker addressing an audience or as one engaged in a critique of the discourse of others. While one may well serve the ends of a "critical servant" in the Isocratean sense (Clark, 1996), one does not do so from a position of the arrogance of one who has "got it right." To do so would contravene adherence to the preceding principles and make a mockery of the difference a critical rhetoric makes.

In sum, to assume the stance afforded by a critical rhetoric is to adopt an attitude that acknowledges the possibility of error in one's attempts to seek an understanding of how the world has been formed in and through the power relations of discourse. The potential to be more open than we are is realized through the twin critiques of domination and freedom.

BIBLIOGRAPHY

NB: What has become known as the "critical rhetoric project" began with the publication of the essay "Critical Rhetoric: Theory and Praxis" (McKerrow, 1989). The essay drew on a conversation among scholars that had been going on for over a decade. Work by Wander (1983), McGee (1975, 1980), Charland (1987), Hariman (1986), and Condit (1987), among others, figured importantly in the synthesis.

Burke, Kenneth. *The Philosophy of Literary Form.* Baton Rouge, La., 1941.

Charland, Maurice. "Constitutive Rhetoric: The Case of the *Peuple Quebecois.*" *Quarterly Journal of Speech* 73 (1987), pp. 133–150.

Clark, N. "The Critical Servant: An Isocratean Contribution to Critical Rhetoric." *Quarterly Journal of Speech* 82 (1996), pp. 111–124.

Cloud, D. "The Materiality of Discourse as Oxymoron: A Challenge to Critical Rhetoric." *Western Journal of Communication* 58 (1994), pp. 141–163.

Condit, Celeste. "Democracy and Civil Rights: The Universalizing Influence of Public Argumentation." *Communication Monographs* 54 (1987), pp. 1–18.

Foucault, Michel. *The Archaeology of Knowledge.* Translated by A. M. Sheridan Smith. New York, 1972.

Hariman, Robert. "Status, Marginality and Rhetorical Theory." *Quarterly Journal of Speech* 72 (1986), pp. 38–54.

McGee, Michael C. "In Search of the 'People': A Rhetorical Alternative." *Quarterly Journal of Speech* 61 (1975), pp. 235–249.

McGee, Michael C. "The 'Ideograph': A Link between Rhetoric and Ideology." *Quarterly Journal of Speech* 66 (1980), pp. 1–16.

McGee, Michael C. "Another Philippic: Notes on the Ideological Turn in Criticism." *Central States Speech Journal* 35 (1984), pp. 43–50.

McGee, Michael C. "Text, Context, and the Fragmentation of Contemporary Culture." *Western Journal of Speech Communication* 54 (1990), pp. 274–289.

McKerrow, Raymie E. "Critical Rhetoric: Theory and Praxis." *Communication Monographs* 56 (1989), pp. 91–111.

McKerrow, Raymie E. "Critical Rhetoric in a Postmodern World." *Quarterly Journal of Speech* 77 (1991), pp. 75–78.

McKerrow, Raymie E. "Critical Rhetoric and the Possibility of the Subject." In *The Critical Turn: Rhetoric & Philosophy in Postmodern Discourse.* Edited by Ian Angus and Lenore Langsdorf, pp. 51–67. Carbondale, Ill., 1993.

Ono, Kent A., and John M. Sloop. "Commitment to *Telos*—A Sustained Critical Rhetoric." *Communication Monographs* 59 (1992), pp. 48–60.

Wander, Philip. "The Ideological Turn in Modern Criticism." *Central States Speech Journal* 34 (1983), pp. 1–18.

—RAYMIE E. McKERROW

Rhetoric and legitimation

To address rhetoric and legitimation is to confront two contested ideas. Legitimation is the process by which political orders and their governing ideas, policies, institutions, and representatives gain acceptability by meeting criteria of normative soundness. Discussions of political legitimacy often include broader arguments about justice, ethics, and the good which, unsurprisingly, yield substantively different normative grounds for political legitimation (MacIntyre, 1988). Since rhetoric itself is a contested term whose relation to justice and the good has been disputed since Plato (c.428–c.347 BCE), there are different perspectives on its relation to legitimation.

From one perspective, political orders are legitimate if those subject to their power believe them to be so. This was the German sociologist Max Weber's position, and his writings remain the classic twentieth-century treatment of legitimation. Weber identified three "ideal types" of political legitimacy, or grounds for establishing the requisite belief by a population: traditional, charismatic, and rational-legal. Though Weber did not make the connection, one can identify each type with rhetorical modes of address. Traditional legitimation rests on "established belief in the sanctity of immemorial traditions and the legitimacy of those exercising authority under them" (1968, p. 215). Ritual address, epideictic, and other rhetorical processes that amplify customary values, draw upon established community *doxa,* and maintain inherited structures of power all contribute to traditional legitimation. [*See* Epideictic genre.] Charismatic legitimation meanwhile rests on "devotion to the exceptional sanctity, heroism or exemplary character of an individual person, and of the normative patterns or order revealed or ordained by him." Charisma points toward *ēthos,* the perceived character of a *rhētōr,* as a legitimating force (Garver, 1994, esp. pp. 188–193). Charisma also accords with a romantic understanding of rhetoric as a daemonic force, which the great orator harnesses to move or remake the world (e.g., Emerson, 1870). Finally, legal–rational legitimation operates through "the belief in the legality of enacted rules and the right of those elevated to authority under such rules to issue commands" (Weber, p. 215). Though Weber identified this type of legitimacy with modern bureaucratic states and their written directives, one can arguably see it at work in the rule-governed procedures guided by deliberative and forensic rhetoric. [*See* Deliberative genre; *and* Forensic genre.]

More strongly normative theories of legitimation would criticize Weber for identifying legitimacy with (mere) recognition by a subject population. Platonic, Aristotelian, and Judeo-Christian philosophical traditions have typically operated with overarching, substantive, often metaphysically grounded conceptions of the good; legitimation is then a process of bringing the political world into alignment with these independent and absolute moral ends. Rhetoric is sometimes disparaged in these traditions, but it also finds a place as that which transmits higher truths to human communities. As such, rhetoric does not itself establish political legitimacy but rather reveals it to a population who might then find it compelling (e.g., Weaver, 1953).

Instead of positing a metaphysical realm of the good, modern theories, driven by liberal and democratic ideologies, have typically located the grounds for legitimation in "the public" and processes of open communication. In a constellation of thought whose key figures include Immanuel Kant (1724–1804), John Stuart Mill (1806–1873), John Dewey (1859–1952), John Rawls (1921–),

and Jürgen Habermas (1929–), legitimacy is generated through real or imagined deliberative procedures that define what is fair and just in political life.

Habermas's theory is especially important. In the mid-1970s, during the so-called crisis of confidence in the industrialized world, Habermas wrote the most important explicit account of legitimation since Weber's. Building upon his earlier *Structural Transformation of the Public Sphere* (1989a), Habermas examined the "legitimation crisis" of modern capitalist states. Moving toward his subsequent work on communicative action and discourse ethics, Habermas argued that legitimacy meant that the norms governing collective action "express generalizable interests [and] are based on a *rational consensus* (or they would find such consensus if practical discourse could take place)" (1975, p. 111). As he has made clear in more recent work, legitimacy is based upon the consensus that might ideally emerge from the rational argumentation of all those affected by a policy or a political system.

Like Rawls and other deliberative political theorists, Habermas posits standards of legitimation that are, strictly speaking, independent of concrete rhetorical practice. As opposed to a more sociological account like Weber's, which sees legitimacy wherever there is popular belief in a regime or policy, Habermas offers a regulative ideal which might be used to guide and assess political decision making and exercises of power. Since all those affected by a policy can never *actually* argue together (the problem of large-scale political societies), Habermasian legitimation is closer to philosophical ideal than rhetorical practice.

Insofar as it is tied to notions of the public sphere, however, legitimation has rhetorical components. For Habermas, the public sphere is the domain of social life where citizens deal with matters of general interest without being subject to coercion, where anyone in principle may take part, and where opinions are freely expressed and criticized. Described this way, the public sphere has a clear history; it emerged during the Enlightenment, when a citizen-public successfully confronted state power, and was eclipsed in the twentieth century by the influence of mass media, large-scale organizations, and market-driven thinking. But some form of publicness is part of all forms of political life, and this domain has long been the province of rhetoric. It can be argued, then, that rhetoric is the vehicle that keeps the promise of a Habermasian public sphere alive (Farrell, 1993, p. 199), one which thus serves to move political orders closer to justice and true legitimacy.

Among Habermas's many critics, some have rejected the ideal of rational consensus, which underlies his account of legitimation. Jean-François Lyotard, for example, has attacked consensus as "an outmoded and suspect value" (1984, p. 66) and championed dissensus, plurality, and agonistic communicative practices instead. Lyotard's social theory can be read as part of a broader postmodernist revival of sophistic rhetoric (e.g., Poulakos, 1995) that substitutes discursive heterogeneity, provocation, and playfulness for the rule-governed argumentation that deliberative theorists like Habermas defend. For postmodernist thinkers like Lyotard, political legitimacy can only emerge as a provisional, contested, and perhaps suspect rhetorical resting point in a world whose basic and fundamental pluralism should be respected and maintained.

BIBLIOGRAPHY

Barker, Rodney. *Political Legitimacy and the State.* Oxford, 1990. A good introduction to the concept of legitimacy and its literature.

Calhoun, Craig, ed. *Habermas and the Public Sphere.* Cambridge, Mass., 1992. Calhoun's introduction is a useful road map to Habermas's theory of the public sphere.

Emerson, Ralph Waldo. "Eloquence." In *The Complete Works of Ralph Waldo Emerson,* vol. 7, pp. 61–100. Boston, 1870.

Farrell, Thomas B. *Norms of Rhetorical Culture.* New Haven, 1993. A philosophically sophisticated marriage of Habermas to Aristotelian rhetorical theory, which examines the prospects for public reason in modern times.

Garver, Eugene. *Aristotle's Rhetoric: An Art of Character.* Chicago, 1994.

Habermas, Jürgen. *Legitimation Crisis.* Translated by Thomas McCarthy. Boston, 1975. Examination of the systemic legitimation problems of late-capitalist nation states.

Habermas, Jürgen. "Legitimation Problems in the Modern State." In *Communication and the Evolution of So-*

ciety. Translated by Thomas McCarthy. Boston, 1979. A 1974 lecture that includes the essentials of *Legitimation Crisis.*

Habermas, Jürgen. *Structural Transformation of the Public Sphere.* Translated by Thomas Burger. Cambridge, Mass., 1989a. First published 1962.

Habermas, Jürgen. "The Public Sphere." In *Jürgen Habermas on Society and Politics: A Reader.* Edited by Steven Seidman, pp. 231–236. Boston, 1989b. Great six-page synopsis of *Structural Transformation of the Public Sphere.*

Habermas, Jürgen. *The Inclusion of the Other: Studies in Political Theory.* Edited and translated by Ciaran Cronin and Pablo De Greif. Cambridge, Mass., 1998. Collection of Habermas's more recent work in discourse ethics and politics, which includes a good introduction by the editors and sections detailing Habermas's view of his differences with John Rawls.

Hariman, Robert. *Political Style: The Artistry of Power.* Chicago, 1995. A provocative mix of rhetorical and political theory that explores the stylistic repertoires that contribute to power, persuasion, and by extension, legitimacy.

Lyotard, Jean-François. *The Postmodern Condition: A Report on Knowledge.* Translated by Geoff Bennington. Minneapolis, 1984. Seminal postmodernist challenge of modernity's legitimation narratives.

MacIntyre, Alasdair. *Whose Justice? Which Rationality?* Notre Dame, Ind., 1988. A criticism of liberal, Enlightenment ideals of justice and reminder of historical disagreements about the normative underpinning of political legitimation.

Poulakos, John. *Sophistical Rhetoric in Ancient Greece.* Columbia, S.C., 1995.

Simonson, Peter. "Mediated Sources of Public Confidence." *Journal of Communication* 49.2 (1999), pp. 109–122. An attempt to theorize the part played by media in legitimation and public confidence.

Weaver, Richard. *The Ethics of Rhetoric.* Chicago, 1953.

Weber, Max. *Economy and Society.* 3 vols. Edited and translated by Guenther Roth and Claus Wittich. New York, 1968. Volumes 1 and 3 include extended treatments of Weber's three ideal types of legitimacy, composed in the ten years before his death in 1920.

— PETER SIMONSON

Rhetoric and power

Politics, rhetoric, and *power* form a constellation of closely linked terms. The word *politics* is virtually synonymous with *power,* while *word* and *strategy* are the sinews of governance. Since the invention of writing, social control, communal myth, and message construction have been the bricks with which we have built the human *polis*. The earliest Greek Sophists forged the links between rhetoric and political mastery. Plato (c.428–c.347 BCE) attempted to break these links with an educational system that appeared to separate eloquence from wisdom. The union of persuasive language and community power was reaffirmed by Cicero (106–43 BCE) only to be lost with the decline of the Western city in 476 CE. [*See* Classical rhetoric.]

The Early Modern power theorist, Niccolò Machiavelli (1469–1527) designed a rhetoric of terror and mystification as a weapon for rulers. [*See overview article on* Renaissance rhetoric.] John Locke (1632–1704) and America's founding leaders rejected both Machiavelli's *Prince* and Hobbes's *Leviathan* (1651), which they eschewed because of its amoral individualism. In the former example, executive and legislative power were divided and the prince was tamed. The eighteenth-century fear of the union of centralized power and demagogic appeal still informs our ideals of governance. [*See* Eighteenth-century rhetoric.] Contemporary democracy positions civic discourse within a community of limited power spheres, countervailing power blocks, and rulers who must be accountable.

Given the vitality of this tradition, it is not surprising that many of the gravest issues in the study of political discourse are issues of power. Vast technological changes and the expansion of mass media have made possible the rapid mobilization of whole populations and have transformed the relationship between the citizen and government. The dominant themes of modern scholars (legitimacy, accountability, media access, political myth, technical discourse, and so forth) deal with the impact of vastly expanded power on the forms, values, and traditions of civic discourse. A few of these issues will be considered here.

Legitimacy. Germany's modern theorist of politics, Jürgen Habermas was one of the first to call attention to the crisis of governing institutions in Europe and North America (1979). Habermas asserted that because the current citizenry had not participated in the genesis and development of these institutions, it might experience a deep separation from these institutions and little responsibility when their performance is poor. He concluded that communication practices must be modified to give the citizen a sense of meaningful participation. Others have extended this work to the study of technical discourse. They argue that the rise of professionalism has allowed experts to claim proprietary power over one area of expertise after another and thus remove it from discussions in the public sphere. This means that decisions that affect land use, resource allocation, and transport are seldom made by the locals who are directly affected by them. Rather they are made by unaccountable experts in distant places.

Political Myth. Despite Marxism's failure as a viable economic system, it has inspired many rhetorical scholars. Foremost among these was Kenneth Burke (1897–1993), who extended Karl Marx's concepts of political mystification. One of Burke's major contributions to rhetorical studies is his view of political discourse as the evocation of political myth. According to Burke, myths are repositories of beliefs that lie just below the surface of conscious thought. Examples of politically useful myths are the triumph of character over circumstance, the inevitability of material progress, and faith in a constantly accelerating science. These myths are evoked in the coded language of power-seeking politicians.

Media Access. The contemporary rhetorician and cultural theorist Mark P. Orbe is one of the foremost representatives of the "muted group" school of political discourse. Orbe asserts that the privileged members of every society formulate and maintain a set of communication practices that present *their* experiences and perspective as the only important experiences and denigrate, conceal, and silence those of marginal groups (1998, p. 11). Other scholars, such as Cal Logue have developed the idea of *speaker status*, noting that the powerful enjoy media access, communal deference, and expanded opportunities to promote their interest-based agendas (Logue and Miller, 1995, p. 20). Although the origin of the term is in dispute, the *subaltern voice* expresses the belief that powerless people speak largely through a form of ventriloquism. The powerless may move their lips but the words they speak belong to the powerful. Like Logue, Orbe has resurrected the idea of the compensation of the powerless. He argues that the marginal person enjoys a double perspective that often results in a more original and deeper understanding of political discourse (p. 29).

Empowerment. In the study of political discourse, empowerment has become almost a shibboleth. Kathleen Jamieson and David Birdsell (1988) lament the decline of rational discourse in presidential rhetoric. The mass of lurid imagery and empty slogans amuse, astonish, and often stupify large portions of the electorate but leave them uninformed. Jamieson and Birdwell recommend a return to rhetorical forms that present rigorous argument on several sides of an issue in order to empower ordinary citizens to make informed and responsible decisions. Feminist scholars such as Carol Buzzanell have dealt with the covert effects of power on conventions of discourse and norms of political expression (1995, pp. 330–332).

Frame Theory. An increasing number of scholars have studied the concepts of divided power and countervailing power through the lens of frame theory. Jim Kuypers's (1997) study of the Clinton administration's foreign policy, which describes a battle of rival frames between the executive branch and the press, is a paradigm example of this sort of research. Kuypers demonstrated that the executive's loss of the potent cold war frame allowed the press to exercise a rival power of definition in framing the meaning of post-cold-war events. The work of Raymond Gozzi (1999), on the mass media's vast enhancement of the power of metaphor as a cognitive model in political discourse, represents another sort of political frame study. The work of the feminist scholar Lorraine Code (1995) has been influential here. Code's idea of the interest-based invention of ideas has been used to explain the power of conventional wisdom, and male-dominated norms of political discourse (p. 69).

Leadership and Elites. Hans Gerth and C. Wright Mills popularized the idea of "vocabularies of motive" in the 1950s. This was a style of discourse in which a self-serving goal was concealed by a rhetoric of communal service and altruistic idealism. Their studies anticipated our contemporary studies of networks of influence, power grids in which closely-knit groups maintain political power by keeping it hidden and therefore acceptable. There has been a return of interest in charismatic leadership represented by the work of J. Michael Hogan and Glen Williams (2000). Their inspiration arises from the pioneering work of Irvine Schiffer (1977), who located the power of charisma in messages rather than in situations or events. This perspective allowed Hogan and Williams to discover the ways in which spokespersons actually helped construct the crisis that brought them to power (Schiffer, pp. 262–265).

Information. The power of political information has not been neglected. A path-breaking study by Richard D. Brown (1989) revealed the historic link between civic culture and the imperative of information seeking (i.e., the public's need to know). The rhetoric of information control is expanding daily with such innovations as economic profiling.

In sum, many studies of political discourse arise from issues of power. The effect of the expansion of power upon norms of discourse, on the quality of participation by citizens, and on the survival of democracy itself, now form a considerable part of the scholarly agenda.

BIBLIOGRAPHY

Brown, Richard D. *Knowledge is Power: The Diffusion of Information in Early America.* New York, 1989.

Burke, Kenneth. *A Rhetoric of Motives.* New York, 1950.

Buzzanell, Patrice M. "Reframing the Glass Ceiling as a Socially Constructed Process: Implications for Understanding and Change." *Communication Monographs* 62 (1995), pp. 327–354.

Code, Lorraine. *Rhetorical Spaces.* New York, 1995.

Gerth, Hans, and C. Wright Mills. *Character and Social Structure.* New York, 1952.

Gozzi, Raymond. *The Power of Metaphor in the Age of Electronic Media.* Cresskill, N.Y., 1999.

Gross, Alan G. "The Roles of Rhetoric in the Public Understanding of Science." *Public Understanding of Science* 3 (1994), pp. 3–23.

Habermas, Jürgen. *Communication and the Evolution of Society.* Translated by Thomas McCarthy. Boston, 1979.

Hogan, J. Michael, and Glen Williams. "Republican Charisma and the American Revolution: The Textual Persona of Thomas Paines' *Common Sense.*" *Quarterly Journal of Speech* 86 (2000), pp. 1–18.

Jamieson, Kathleen Hall, and David S. Birdsell. *Presidential Debate: The Challenge of Creating An Informed Electorate*. New York, 1988.

Kuypers, Jim A. *Presidential Crisis Rhetoric and the Press in the Post Cold War World*. New York, 1997.

Logue, Cal, and Eugene F. Miller. "Rhetorical Status: A Study of Its Origins, Functions, and Consequences." *The Quarterly Journal of Speech* 81 (1995), pp. 20–47.

Orbe, Mark P. *Constructing Co-cultural Theory: An Explication of Culture, Power and Communication*. Thousand Oaks, Calif., 1998.

Schiffer, Irvine. *Charisma: A Psychoanalytic Look at Mass Society*. New York, 1977.

—ANDREW A. KING

The third face of power

The success of a political argument in a mass democracy is largely dependent on traditional methods of rhetorical argumentation. The ability to exercise skill in selecting, organizing, and presenting rhetorical proofs is the first face of power. From the time of the Sophists until the advent of mass media, rhetorical contests were seen almost entirely in this context. Ordinarily, the rhetor with the most refined rhetorical skills was, and still is, expected to win the debate.

The development of mass societies and mass media has introduced a problem not fully anticipated by classical rhetoric. In addition to an effective argument, a rhetor now also needs to gain access to the channels of mass communication in order to reach the mass audience. Communication researchers in the 1960s and 1970s identified control over the channels of mass communication as a second face of power, which they called agenda setting (Bachrach and Baratz, 1963; Macombs and Shaw, 1972). Agenda setting involves the exercise of control over what goes in the newspaper or over the airwaves by editors and producers. It is a higher level exercise of power than creating a rhetorical argument, because someone with control over the agenda for a channel of mass communication can frame the rhetorical argument in ways that are helpful or hurtful or even eliminate the argument altogether by denying access to the mass audience. Thus, compared to the citizen who authors a political message, someone with control over the agenda of public discussion has greater potential to influence the outcome of public debate.

Moreover, the ongoing struggle to negotiate messages through the channels of mass communication led to the discovery that both traditional argumentation and agenda setting can be subjugated by yet another, even higher exercise of power. This third face of power is the ability to manipulate the very rules of discourse, not simply to gain access to the channels of mass communication but often to make the rhetorical situation more favorable for one argument or less favorable for another. [*See* Rhetorical situation.]

Unlike agenda setting, which is essentially limited to processes of mass communication, the third face of power affects the entire range of rhetorical situations. The discourse produced by the engagement of rhetoric and politics is uniquely vulnerable because it takes place in a public forum, it is limited to matters of public interest, and its methods are bound by prescriptive tradition and proscriptive laws. Newspaper editorials and news stories, speeches, campaign advertising, opinion surveys, even song lyrics and novels all may be forms of political rhetoric if they participate in public debate over matters of public interest. All aspects of the genesis and articulation of these forms of rhetorical argument that are governed by perceived or actual rules are subject to third-face-of-power manipulation.

While third-face-of-power strategy may be applied at all levels of discourse, its greatest impact on political rhetoric is as a means of manipulating media gatekeepers. Journalists and other professional communicators are particularly vulnerable to the third face of power because the rules of professional journalism, beyond those to be described below, govern the way in which they communicate. Thus, third-face-of-power arguments are a means by which the individual can attempt to counterbalance the seemingly indomitable power held by proprietors of the very channels of mass communication.

Significant use was made of third-face-of-power strategies in the twentieth century. In "The Man with the Muckrake" (1906) speech, President Theodore Roosevelt cited mainly social rules requiring truthfulness and fairness in order to urge journalists to be more objective. "Honesty," he says, challenging journalists to be not just honest but also unbiased, "can be no respecter of persons." In 1969, Vice President Spiro Agnew claimed that a television commentator who was critical of President Richard Nixon had made a "partisan assault" that "had the apparent dignity of an objective statement." In both cases, the implied rule is that journalists should be objective, a reference that in these contexts not only curbs potential criticism from other journalists but also makes the public more skeptical of what journalists themselves say. Similarly, the 1987 presidential hopeful Gary Hart, in response to the Donna Rice scandal, and the 1988 presidential candidate George Bush, in a live CBS interview on the Iran-contra affair, cited professional journalistic rules governing the selection, research, and presentation of news. Both claimed that journalists had no business covering either matter.

It is generally believed that a journalist selects a topic for a news story because it is of public, not private, interest. Readers expect the story to be researched fairly, typically by interviewing spokespersons on opposite sides of an issue. The story should be written objectively, and there may be an expectation that where the story is placed in the newspaper will reflect its importance compared to other news. A third-face-of-power strategy that seeks to discredit a news story could cite any or all of these rules and claim that they are not followed. One could say that the reporter selected the topic because of a personal agenda, that important arguments were not included, that the writing was slanted or biased, and that the story's placement in the newspaper either overemphasized or underemphasized its importance.

Rules in the form of laws are another frequent focus of third-face-of-power arguments. In the United States, the public sphere is protected by the First Amendment to the Constitution and by rulings in which the Supreme Court refers to the marketplace of ideas. A focus of law in Western democracies has been not to guide the exercise of free speech but to prohibit actions that might inhibit it. The right of free speech is preeminent, since it is through political public communication—that is, through the public sphere—that public institutions like the U.S. government are created and legitimized. Citizens who claim their

legal right to free speech is being violated are in effect making third-face-of-power arguments. Conversely, someone in a position of authority who argues for secrecy is also using the third face of power. (The exercise of the third face of power in this legal context was anticipated by Cicero, 106–43 BCE, in his fourth category of *stasis*.) [*See* Stasis.]

A significant use of the third face of power outside the domain of mass media occurred in the 1991 U.S. Senate confirmation hearings for Associate Justice of the Supreme Court Clarence Thomas, who was appointed by President George Bush. Anita Hill, formerly employed by a government department headed by Thomas, claimed that he had sexually harassed her. She initially made the charges in a closed-door session that was not part of the public hearings; however, one of the senators leaked Hill's story to the news media. In response to intense public interest stimulated by the leak, the Senate interviewed Hill in live televised hearings, and it appeared for a time that Thomas might not be confirmed. Thomas countered with a speech to the Senate in which he accused senators of, among other things, violating Senate rules and confirmation precedent, by leaking Hill's story and then allowing her to testify. The focus of the debate in the confirmation hearings subsequently shifted from Hill's testimony to the confirmation process itself. As a result of this third face of power strategy, the senators and the confirmation process, not Thomas's seemingly indefensible behavior toward Hill, became the subject of public scrutiny. Thomas was ultimately confirmed by a narrow margin.

Most of the rules that govern contemporary rhetoric come not from laws (or mediation processes) but from acculturation and rhetorical tradition. Some rules are unspoken, and some are the result of argumentation and debate. Tacit social rules may require that a rhetor be sincere or objective. The rhetorical tradition itself is replete with warnings about arguments based on empty emotional appeals and faulty logic. In this sense, Aristotle, Cicero, and Quintilian (first century CE) all exercised a kind of third face of power when they authored prescriptive rhetorics. Obviously, third-face-of-power strategy does not guarantee rhetorical success. Yet it is a powerful weapon in the arsenal of political rhetoric, one that deserves closer tactical and ethical examination. [*See* Classical rhetoric.]

[*See also* Expository rhetoric and journalism.]

BIBLIOGRAPHY

Bachrach, Peter, and Morton S. Baratz. "The Two Faces of Power." *American Political Science Review* 56 (1963), pp. 947–952.

Bitzer, Lloyd F. "Political rhetoric." In *Landmark Essays On Contemporary Rhetoric,* edited by Thomas B. Farrell, pp. 1–22. Mahwah, N.J., 1998. Bitzer defines political rhetoric and explores the notion of prescriptive rhetorics.

Bush, George. "CBS Nightly News." Interview by Dan Rather. CBS, 25 January 1988. The transcript of this eight-minute interview is a *tour de force* of third-face-of-power strategy.

Farrell, Thomas B. *Norms of Rhetorical Culture.* New Haven, 1993. While he does not address the third face of power, Farrell reveals rhetoric as a broad cultural process in which rules manipulation may operate.

Goldstein, Tom, ed. *Killing The Messenger: 100 Years of Media Criticism.* New York, 1989. Contains Roosevelt's "Man with the Muckrake" speech and all three of Spiro Agnew's speeches attacking the news media.

Hallin, Daniel C. "The American News Media: A Critical Perspective." In *Critical Theory and Public Life,* edited by J. Forester, pp. 121–146. Cambridge, U.K., 1985. Discusses the relationship between news media rules and legitimacy; this is also one of the first references to a third face of power.

Macombs, Maxwell E., and Donald L. Shaw. "The Agenda-Setting Function of Mass Media." *Public Opinion Quarterly* 36 (1972), pp. 176–187.

Molotch, Harvey L., and Deirdre Boden. "Talking Social Structure: Discourse, Domination and the Watergate Hearings." *American Sociological Review* 50 (June 1985), pp. 273–288. Although applied in a forensic setting, this is the first explication of the third face of power as rules-manipulation strategy.

Simons, Herbert W. "'Going Meta': Definition and Political Applications." *Quarterly Journal of Speech* 80 (November 1994), pp. 468–481. Simons explicates the rhetorical strategy of making the rules of political discourse the subject of political discourse and uses the 1991 Thomas confirmation hearings to the Supreme Court as an example.

—THOMAS JESSE ROACH

The personal, technical, and public spheres of argument

"Sphere" refers to certain expectations that have accumulated over time and provide contexts for argumentative discourse. To talk of a sphere of argument is to recognize that any act of communication can be shaped to assume the form of address typical of its setting or situation. In a pluralistic society, three broad spheres of argument are recognized.

The personal sphere includes contexts developed as shared experiences with ordinary conversations among family, friends, and familiar others. Ideally, the exchanges occur as dialogue, an earnest discussion wherein views are articulated with an interest in developing one's sense of self and the other as well. In such engagements, the rules for arguing are implicit. For example, interlocutors have a sense of turn taking, of propriety in response, when addressing an intimate other. There is no need to look up rules for our conversations; the ability to communicate comes from mastering the rules while maturing. Because not everyone shares exactly the same preferences for dealing with disagreement, sometimes the rules of argument themselves become part of the disagreement, and thus, developing norms for acceptable argument becomes hinged to successful interactions that share agreement on the principles of how to argue.

The personal sphere develops a language based on relationships and varying with the role a person plays, as, for example, father, spouse, lifelong or casual friend. Each discussion puts at issue the relationship among its interlocutors as much as it aims at determining a decision, giving vent to feelings, or coming to terms with values. Relationships develop or decay over time. They tend to become renewed from significant meetings such as observing the rituals of birth, weddings, anniversaries, and deaths. There is a uniqueness to relational development in these moments that cannot be replaced. Being there for and with another at these special times makes an argument of sorts in itself. So does absence.

The autonomy of the personal sphere rests on its privacy. Arguments carry weight precisely because of the relationship with an interlocutor; and it is in the relationship that we discover how far we must go in disclosing our reasons or in justifying argumentative positions to the other. Memory is the chief mode of preserving these arguments. The absence of written records contributes to the richness of the personal sphere as a field of invention. [*See* Invention.] So, the question of consubstantiality—the identity-forming basic agreement on what has transpired between us—therefore is always open and at risk in personal argument. Statements attributing consensus based on past experience can suggest whether we view things the same way. The ends of personal argument are open to renewal and development, so long as interlocutors try to keep intact a common meeting ground that transcends differences of views, time, and place, and the question of what a relationship between two people—one's self and another—can become.

The technical sphere contains, by contrast, certain austere requirements that frame another context for argument. Unlike the personal sphere where credentials are loosely formed through life experience, to argue as an expert is to carry the weight of specialized knowledge based on the rigor of formal training. Personal argument assumes a right to be heard—even within a formal caste system—based on one's common identity as a human being. There is no such expectation in the technical sphere. Rather, a technical context is entered through the door of expertise alone.

Expertise requires mastery of special codes that form the tools of state-of-the-art decision making. To become an expert is to enter into a hermeneutic process where a specialized language creates the basis for systematic claims to authority. [*See* Ēthos.] A technical language is standardized. To master its terms is to embrace a style of reasoning that is backed by the warrants of a field. Although there are often differences among practitioners in a field—especially a lag between researchers and those applying the knowledge—it can be assumed in principle that a valid consensus among specialists can be formed that, when applied in individual cases, differentiates better from worse decisions.

The paradigm for the realm of the expert is the experiment, strategically configured so as to produce measurable results in a carefully controlled sequence of events. The experimenter exercises strict record keeping, and the record of research that has led to current results is open to new questions, the formulation of new hypotheses, the manipulation of different variables, and additional interpretations of outcomes. Should any part of the procedure be weak, the flaw is passed on from part to part. Correct procedural form certifies, but does not guarantee, that technical arguments have the potential of achieving valid conclusions. [*See* Technical communication.]

Not all specialized fields perform experiments. In the field of law, for example, the trial is a paradigm case of communication. The trial and the experiment each have different procedural assumptions because of differences in the ends of each. Nevertheless, the preference for systematization, standardization, regulated timing, specialized codes, and language use yoke legal and experimental argument in ways that are far more specialized than the personal argument. Both paradigms, moreover, emphasize peer review, which is itself a hallmark of the technical sphere. Such regulation of practice assumes that professional identity is constructed in a way that renders the practitioner's decision testable by another, similarly-credentialled expert.

Whereas the ends of personal argument are open, and its qualities are informal and experientially based, professional ends result in state-of-the-art decisions that are recorded, formal, and procedurally based. For the personal sphere, the mode of identification that is at the base of enacting the self is consubstantiality: one discovers who he or she is through acts of communication. For the technical sphere, experts enter into a procedural relationship with claims and evidence.

The public sphere has at its base certain generalizable interests that cannot be handled either by a logic of intimacy or by expert discourse. Public matters extend beyond the personal and technical spheres, and center on issues that affect the community at large. Often these issues are addressed in traditional public assemblies, where representatives of the people gather. Usually matters of legislation, taxation, war and peace, ways and means become debated. Conventional public argument turns upon which side better represents positions vital to holding power. While each public forum may develop its own language and procedures, the norms of public participation require that the terms of debate be transparent enough to be generally accessible. This is especially true of democracies, wherein the discourses of public leadership are tried at election time.

Public discourse tends to employ the deliberative genre. [*See* Deliberative genre.] Audiences are invited to participate through recollection of tradition and admonition to honor abstract values in the pursuit of greater social justice. Performances of public discourse may reenforce standard styles of deliberation along a range of predictable issues or they may innovate patterns of communication through novel challenges to established patterns of argument. Public argument encompasses a politics of issue and of character as spokespersons claim the authority of representing problems and solutions for the public sphere. The time of the public sphere, like that of the personal sphere, is durational, as generations, in this case, influenced by the chief issues of their day, come into power and pass on.

[*See also* Argument fields; *and* Rhetorical situation.]

BIBLIOGRAPHY

Beard, Charles A., and William Beard. *The American Leviathan: the Republic in the Machine Age.* New York, 1930.

Bitzer, Lloyd. "Rhetoric and Public Knowledge." In *Rhetoric, Philosophy, and Literature: an Exploration.* Edited by Don. M. Burks, pp. 67–93. West Lafayette, Ind., 1978. A thorough discussion of the relations among knowledge, rhetoric, and the public.

Dewey, John. *The Public and Its Problems.* Chicago, 1927. The classic pragmatic reading of the prospects for public life in postwar America.

Farrell, Thomas B., and G. Thomas Goodnight. "Accidental Rhetoric: The Root Metaphors of Three-Mile Island." *Communication Monographs* 48 (December 1981), pp. 272–300. A study of the volatile relationship between technological crisis and public rhetoric.

Gregg, Richard B., and Gerard H. Hauser. "Richard Nixon's April 30, 1970 Address on Cambodia: The 'Ceremony' of Confrontation." *Communication Monographs* 40 (1973), pp. 167–181.

Langer, Susan. *Philosophy in a New Key: A Study of Reason, Rite, and Art.* Boston, 1978.

Lasch, Christopher. *The Culture of Narcissism: American Life in an Age of Diminishing Expectations.* New York, 1978.

O'Keefe, Daniel J. "Two Concepts of Argument." *Journal of the American Forensic Association* 14 (1978), pp. 121–128.

Sennett, Richard. *The Fall of Public Man: on the Social Psychology of Capitalism.* New York, 1977.

Toulmin, Stephen. *Human Understanding: the Collective Use and Evolution of Concepts.* Princeton, 1972.

Willard, Charles Arthur. "Argument Fields and Theories of Logical Types." *Journal of the American Forensic Association* 17 (1981), pp. 129–145.

—G. THOMAS GOODNIGHT

POLYSYNDETON (Lat. *accervatio*), which Puttenham (*The Arte of English Poesie,* 1589) calls "cople-clause," is an isotaxeme that connects clauses or single words by the repetitive use of the same conjunction. It slows down the rhythm of speech, thus producing various effects; for example, in combining logically related elements, it renders authoritative dignity: "My sheep hear my voice, *and* I know them, *and* they follow me: *And* I give unto them eternal life" (*Jn.* 10.27–28). In coupling disparate members, the result may be comic surprise: "When shepherds pipe on oaten straws/ . . . When turtles tread, *and* rooks, *and* daws / *And* maidens bleach their summer smocks" (Shakespeare, *Love's Labours Lost* 5. 2. 903–906). Its opposite is *asyndeton.*

[*See also* Figures of Speech; *and* Asyndeton.]

—ANDREA GRÜN-OESTERREICH

POSTMODERN RHETORIC. See Contingency and probability; *and* Sublime, the.

PRACTICAL WISDOM. The relationship between eloquence and good sense is fundamental in the art of rhetoric. Long before principles of the speaker's art were formalized in Greece during the fifth and fourth centuries BCE, Homer recognized the essential connection between oratory and sagacious judgment and the importance of that connection for sound communal deliberation and decision making. Odysseus, a man of considerable shrewdness and cunning, is often characterized as "the equal of Zeus in wise counsel," and in the debates among the Greeks, he is a most persuasive speaker. Likewise, Nestor— "that grand old man whose counsels are always the best"—was noted for the sweetness of his speech.

Recognition of the fundamental relevance of

"wise counsel" and sound moral sense to persuasive speech persists throughout the history of rhetoric as theory and practice. For theorists throughout that history, the foundation of true eloquence and of art in speaking lies in the capacity to discern the good and prudent course of action in a realm of uncertainty and contingent possibility. The Sophists of the fifth and fourth centuries BCE, for example, offered instruction in the arts of citizenship, emphasizing both skill in speaking and, at least in some cases, practical and political sagacity. "From me," Plato has Protagoras say, "[the student] will learn . . . the proper care of his personal affairs, so that he may best manage his own household, and also of the state's affairs, so as to become a real power in the city, both as speaker and man of action" (*Protagoras* 318e). Likewise, so that his students might develop skill in managing public affairs and be properly equipped to provide good advice in the public assembly, the teacher Isocrates required them to study "philosophy" before they could learn the art of persuasion. He advocated a program of mental training that emphasized political and ethical topics in order to foster the development in the would-be statesman of practical knowledge and political wisdom.

Following the Isocratean model of the citizen-speaker, both Cicero (106–43 BCE) and Quintilian (a little over a century later) advocated a conception of rhetoric in which wisdom and eloquence were united in the "perfect orator." As Cicero remarked, "wisdom without eloquence does too little for the good of states, but . . . eloquence without wisdom is generally highly disadvantageous and is never helpful." In his *De oratore* (55 BCE), Cicero's main concern is the proper training of the statesman-orator, and he emphasizes both instruction in the art of eloquence and a broad education in philosophy, politics, history, and law. Such an education, Cicero believed, would enable the orator to acquire the wisdom necessary for giving prudent guidance to the commonwealth. Quintilian, in the *Institutio oratoria* carried on the Isocratean–Ciceronian tradition of broadly educating the citizen-orator so that eloquence might be guided by practical wisdom (*prudentia*) in service of the public good.

During the Middle Ages, the classical model of civic life and public deliberation was eclipsed by a preoccupation with the "city of God" and the dissemination of Christian teachings, and rhetorical skill was devoted more to the explication of Scripture and the art of preaching than to the determination of wise political decision and action. Practical wisdom as a prerequisite of eloquence reemerged, however, with the advent of Renaissance humanism in the fifteenth and sixteenth centuries, and it has retained a connection with rhetoric and eloquence into our own time. Giambattista Vico, in his *On the Study Methods of Our Time* (1709), observes that "young people are to be educated in common sense, . . . [and] common sense, besides being the criterion of practical judgment, is also the guiding standard of eloquence."

While Enlightenment and nineteenth-century treatises on rhetoric and oratory often emphasized scientific over practical reasoning and focused on the technical rather than the philosophical aspects of persuasive speech, a number of twentieth-century theorists have sought to recover the connection between rhetoric and practical judgment. Chaim Perelman's *The New Rhetoric* (1969) and Stephen Toulmin's *The Uses of Argument* (1969) investigate how arguments function in reasoning about practical matters. More recently, Jürgen Habermas's writings on communicative competence (1975, 1984, 1987), Walter Fisher's "narrative paradigm" (1987), and Thomas Farrell's "rhetorical culture" (1993) ground rhetorical efficacy in various conceptions of practical reason. Farrell, in particular, embraces an understanding of practical wisdom and civic rhetoric rooted in the classical tradition.

Any understanding of practical wisdom must take account of this tradition. The classical conception of practical wisdom (Gk. *phronēsis*) finds its fullest expression in the writings of Aristotle and his followers, where it is identified with the capacity to reason well about matters that are probable rather than certain, and that require decisions about actions to be taken. Moreover, this conception is intimately linked to rhetoric, the art of civic discourse by which such decisions are reached collectively.

The *Nicomachean Ethics* is generally regarded as the authoritative exposition of Aristotle's moral philosophy. His inquiry originates in the question, "What is the Supreme Good for a human being?" or "What makes a person's life happy and lacking in nothing?" Aristotle reasons that, since the "good" or "best" state of any particular thing lies in the fulfillment of its proper function, the good for the human being must lie in activity in which our proper function is fulfilled (1094a–1097b). Now, since humans share with all life-forms the power of "nutrition and growth," and with "animals of all kinds" a "sentient life" by which pleasures and pains are experienced, what must be unique to humans is "the practical life that accords with or implies a rational principle [*logos*]" (1097b–1098a). Thus, the proper function of a human being is "a kind of life" where the activities of the soul accord with a rational principle, and the "good life" for a human is one in which these activities are performed with virtue or excellence.

This idea of excellence is central to Aristotle's conception of virtue in general, and particularly to his understanding of the various kinds of virtue. He concludes the foregoing discussion by stating, "the good for the human being is an activity of the soul in accordance with virtue, or if there are multiple virtues, in accordance with the best and most complete" (1098a16–1098a18). There are, indeed, several kinds of virtue in Aristotle's view, each being the excellence of an activity that is proper to one element of the soul. The soul, he tells us, is part irrational and part rational. The irrational part is further subdivided between a vegetative ("the cause of nutrition and growth") and an appetitive element (which we share with all sentient creatures). The latter is the source of desire and concerns pleasure and pain. Unlike the vegetative element, whose proper excellence lies in the maintenance of bodily health and normal growth, the appetitive or desiring element is in a sense "receptive of reason; at any rate in the continent person it is obedient to reason, and . . . [in the temperate and in the brave person] it is in complete harmony with the rational principle" (1102b26–1102b29). Because the appetitive element in the soul can be "in some way persuaded by reason," its proper excellence is receptivity to the guidance of reason in forming desires and in choosing actions. This is Aristotle's conception of *moral* virtue, which he defines as a "disposition" or "state of character" leading one to choose actions that are intermediate between excess and deficiency. Virtuous action lies in a

mean between two extremes. Thus, for example, Courage lies between rashness and cowardice, Temperance between licentiousness and "anaesthesia." These and the other Moral Virtues are excellences of the appetitive element, and they consist in the Appetite's willingness to submit to the guidance of reason in choosing actions. This guidance, as it happens, originates in the *logos* of the prudent person; for the Mean in any given situation is "determined by the rational principle by which the prudent person would determine it" (1107a).

Thus, we come to the remaining element in the soul, which is "rational in the proper sense of the word." It is the *logos* or "rational principle" in the human psyche, the element that for Aristotle constitutes our distinctive nature and whose activity constitutes our proper function. This activity consists in reasoning and thinking, and its forms of excellence constitute the Intellectual Virtues—including Philosophic Wisdom (*sophia*) and Prudence or Practical Wisdom (*phronēsis*). Now, the general aim of the intellect is grasping "truth," but Aristotle distinguishes between two realms of truth and thus between two kinds of wisdom. One excellence of the rational soul involves contemplating "those things whose first principles are invariable," truths that are unchanging and absolute: the realm of science and mathematics. This is the virtue of the Scientific Intellect, and it culminates in a contemplation that yields Philosophic Wisdom. The other form of intellectual excellence involves understanding "things that are variable," the realm of the contingent and particular, the changing and probable. This is the sphere of practical action, and it is the domain of the Practical or Calculative Intellect (the "logistical" mind). The virtue of this form of reason is practical wisdom, and it involves the ability to deliberate well about "what is good and advantageous" for oneself and for humans generally. Practical wisdom, in sum, is the capacity to perceive in particular circumstances the good that can be achieved through action and to determine the best means for attaining that good. It incorporates a number of important philosophical commitments: (1) in the sphere of choice and action, "truth" is contingent on circumstances that are mutable and dynamic; as these change, so may the practical truths they generate; (2) we can attain only probable knowledge of this kind of truth; (3) such practical truths—"truth about right action"—are relative to the individual or group that apprehends them (the Mean is "relative to *us*"); and (4) practical truth is attained through a process of deliberation, of weighing opposing reasons justifying alternative potential courses of conduct.

This conception of practical wisdom informs Aristotle's thinking about rhetoric in several ways. First, in order to be persuasive, speakers must show themselves to be "a certain kind of person," namely, as possessing practical wisdom, a morally virtuous character, and good will (*Rhetoric* 1378a). The persuasive effects of this *ēthos* derive from the tendency of audiences to believe prudent, virtuous, fair-minded people "to a greater extent and more quickly" than they do others. [*See* Ēthos.] Second, inasmuch as it functions to affect judgments concerning matters about which we deliberate, and insofar as it aims at facilitating *reasoned* decisions about such matters, rhetoric is an exercise of the practical intellect, and *phronēsis* is its proper excellence. In this sense, good rhetoric manifests practical wisdom. Third, since practical deliberation itself involves a notable exercise of rhetorical skills—that is, inasmuch as deliberation is a process of assessing the justifications for and objections to alternative courses of conduct in particular situations—the "rational principle" of prudence is essentially rhetorical: it is the standard by which one judges the soundness of reasons that can be advanced in favor of or opposing proposed courses of action. Finally, practical wisdom is a prerequisite for the proper practice of rhetoric in the civic arena; for if speakers lack practical sense "they do not form opinions rightly," and so they are apt to mislead audiences and to give bad advice.

In these ways, then, the intellectual virtue of practical wisdom was intertwined for Aristotle with the art and sound practice of rhetoric in civic life. Moreover, when rhetoric is viewed as fundamentally an art of civic discourse—as it has been by Isocrates, Aristotle, Cicero, Vico, and others—this link between wisdom and eloquence is essential.

[*See also* Logos; Phronēsis; *and* Prudence.]

BIBLIOGRAPHY

Aristotle. *Nicomachean Ethics.* Translated by H. Rackham. Loeb Classical Library. Cambridge, Mass., 1934. Aristotle's principal work in moral theory, representing his mature thought; based on his lecture courses.

Aristotle. *Eudemian Ethics.* Translated by H. Rackham. Loeb Classical Library. Cambridge, Mass., 1992. Somewhat shorter than the *Nicomachean Ethics,* this work shares three chapters with the larger work and is sometimes fuller in expression.

Aristotle. *Magna Moralia.* Translated by G. Cyril Armstrong. Loeb Classical Library. Cambridge, Mass., 1977. Probably a later Peripatetic synopsis of Aristotle's ethical doctrines.

Aristotle. *"Art" of Rhetoric.* Translated by J. H. Freese. Loeb Classical Library. Cambridge, Mass., 1975.

Farrell, Thomas B. *Norms of Rhetorical Culture.* New Haven, 1993. A rehabilitation of the classical ideal of rhetoric as an art of practical reason and civic action.

Fisher, Walter. *Human Communication as Narration: Toward a Philosophy of Reason, Value, and Action.* Columbia, S. C. 1987.

Garver, Eugene. *Aristotle's Rhetoric: An Art of Character.* Chicago, 1994. A densely written study, but full of insight.

Grimaldi, William M. A. *Studies in the Philosophy of Aristotle's "Rhetoric."* Wiesbaden, Germany, 1975. A rich examination of the philosophical contexts of the *Rhetoric* that emphasizes its links with practical reasoning.

Habermas, J. *Legitimation Crisis.* Translated by Thomas McCarthy. Boston, 1975.

Habermas, J. *The Theory of Communicative Action,* vols. 1 and 2. Translated by Thomas McCarthy. Boston, 1984 and 1987.

Hardie, W. F. R. *Aristotle's Ethical Theory.* Oxford, 1968. An invaluable companion to the *Ethics* that considers most of the principal ideas with great insight.

Johnstone, Christopher Lyle. "An Aristotelian Trilogy: Ethics, Rhetoric, Politics, and the Search for Moral Truth." *Philosophy and Rhetoric* 13 (1980), pp. 1–24. Argues that the three works must be read as elements in a comprehensive theory of the complete human life.

Rowe, C. J. *The Eudemian and Nicomachean Ethics: A Study in the Development of Aristotle's Thought,* Proceedings of the Cambridge Philological Society, suppl. 3. Cambridge, U.K., 1971.

Self, Lois S. "Rhetoric and Phronesis: The Aristotelian Ideal." *Philosophy and Rhetoric* 12 (1979), pp. 130–145. A useful examination of the idea of *phronēsis* as the key connection between rhetoric and ethics in Aristotle's thought.

—CHRISTOPHER LYLE JOHNSTONE

PRAETERITIO (Gk. *paralepsis;* Lat. also *occultatio*), called by Puttenham (*The Arte of English Poesie,* 1589, p. 232) "the Passager," is a seemingly hurried reference to material under the pretense of sparing the listener tedious details. This reluctance can be motivated by the speaker's wish to pass quickly over inconvenient circumstances of his case, as when in *Tristram Shandy* (1760–1767), Sterne's narrator drops several subjects and playfully leaves a character "to recover, and get home from *Marseilles* as he can" (6.20). *Praeteritio* is a strategy of ironic dissimulation, disingenuously enumerating details that tact forbids to dwell on. "Why should I mention his decrees, his acts of plunder, his acquisition . . . ?" (Cicero, 2 *Philippica* 25.62).

[*See also* Figures of speech.]

—HEINER PETERS

PRAGMATICS. *See* Linguistics.

PREACHING. *See* Homiletics; Religion; *and* Renaissance rhetoric, *overview article and article on* Rhetoric in the age of Reformation and Counter-Reformation.

PROBABILITY. *See* Contingency and probability.

PROBLEMATOLOGY. Based on the foundational role of questioning for thinking and reasoning at large, problematology is a new approach to language and rhetoric. Rhetoric has been characterized in many ways: by stressing the impact on the audience, as in the manipulative conception held by Plato; by stressing the figures of speech, as found in the Imperial rhetoric of the Roman World and in the seventeenth-century French (and royal) baroque rhetoric; by stressing the role of *bene dicendi* or eloquence as in the Republican rhetoric where the character and virtues of the orator were so important; and by stressing

the role of arguments as found in such contemporary views as those held by Perelman and Toulmin. All those definitions have emphasized the *pathos,* the *ēthos,* or the *logos,* the audience, the orator, or the speech, subordinating the other dimensions of rhetoric to the one privileged. [*See* Ēthos; Logos; *and* Pathos.] In the numerous discrepant definitions of rhetoric we find in the history of the field, all neglect Aristotle's original placement of *ēthos, pathos,* and *logos* on an equal footing. [*See* Classical rhetoric.] If rhetoric is a discursive (*logos*) relationship between advocate and audience (*pathos*), it has also an object or a cause. If that relationship arises, it is because there is a question or a problem that divides protagonists, a problem for which, by the way, some agreement is not necessarily sought. Rhetoric can therefore be defined in the most comprehensive way as the negotiation of a difference between individuals on a given question. This question gives the measure of that difference, of the gap between the locutors, that is, between the *ēthos* (or orator) and the *pathos* (or the one to whom discourse is addressed).

The problematological view of *ēthos, pathos,* and *logos* can now be briefly summarized. The *ēthos* is the stopping point of a questioning process that, in principle, could be infinite, as we all know from three-year-old children who relentlessly ask "why," just to test their parents' authority and vindicate the trust they put in them. *Ēthos* is that resource of trust: we must have the right character, the expertise, the authority to answer. *Pathos* is receptivity: it is where the questions originate. As for *logos,* it is meant to express questions and answers alike, given that their difference must somehow be expressed through the opposition of the explicit and the implicit.

The question view of rhetoric enables us to address a very old problem concerning the distinction between rhetoric and dialectic. [*See* Dialectic.] The distinction amounts to the emphasis put on the questions or on their answers. There are two possible approaches to the resolution of a given problem. The first consists in putting that problem in the open, where explicit alternatives are debated. The second approach tackles the problem as if it did not arise any longer, and that approach therefore focuses on the answer, as if it were *the* answer. By offering a solution through rhetorical means, the *rhētōr* proceeds as if the corresponding question ceased to pose any problem. Style, eloquence, an attractive way of putting words and phrases together all enable the rhetor to perform as if he or she had the solution. The problematic seems to be eliminated or solved, thanks to rendering, sometimes fictionally, problematic the unproblematic by merely formal means. Rhetoric has been condemned because of that illusion. And yet politicians as well as publicists have often resorted to that approach in order to face their problems. They present those problems as solved when they are simply pushed into the realm of the implicit and shoved under the carpet. Recourse to amplification, so common to rhetoric, is meant to emphasize the solving aspects of a given discourse that, otherwise, could appear as highly suspect by recalling the questions to which it purports to provide an answer. [*See* Amplification.]

Finally, a problematological view of literary rhetoric also begins with *ēthos, pathos,* and *logos,* as the basic compositional elements of any rhetorical form. They also lie at the core of the literary genres, as well as at the heart of the literary response defined by reception theory and hermeneutics, where meaning is at stake. [*See* Hermeneutics; *and* Reception theory.] *Ēthos, pathos,* and *logos* have given rise, respectively, to literary genres based on the expression of the self, and on its relationships to the other and to the world. Literature emerged from the metaphorization of the old mythological affirmations: although once considered truths, they became considered as metaphors, that is, as fictions, and were transformed into mythology and parables. For *ēthos,* this process of fictionalization gave rise to lyric poetry, where the metaphors are the expression of the self; for *pathos,* it gave rise to tragedy and drama; for *logos,* where the world is the object of fictionalization, verses were meant to be those of an epic in which some state of affairs is expressed. Later, the form changed and instead of verse, prose developed as a response to the need to have a new literality to replace the sheer metaphorization of the old mythos. And this explains why the lyric expression of the self gave way to the prosaic form of romance (and ultimately, to the novel), while the epic gave way to history, and tragedy was followed by the reign of comedies,

usually written in prose. When history came to be considered as factual rather than literary, the novel filled the vacancy, covering both the narration of the self and the fictionalization of events.

With history accelerating, the unproblematic values of heroic deeds became more questionable, before being replaced in turn. Epic and drama lost their importance, but so did lyric poetry. History became factual, poetry ceased to be merely lyrical, and the novel ceased to be simply descriptive of matter-of-fact episodes. The novel became a major form of fiction, expressing the contingency of the world, of the self, of our relationship to the others. Figuration, then, meant increased problematicity, asking the reader to supplement a meaning the novel could no longer provide. As a consequence, it emerged that the meaning of literature is the question it raises to its readers (Kafka and Borges are striking examples of such enigmatic fictions). The only answer to such questions turned out to be questioning itself. Contemporary rhetoric, when dealing with literature, faces the rhetoric of figurative speech as the voice of the enigmatic.

[*See also* Questioning.]

BIBLIOGRAPHY

Golden, James, and David Jamison. "Meyer's Theory of Problematology." *Revue Internationale de Philosophie* 205 (1990), pp. 329–335.

Meyer, Michel. *Meaning and Reading.* Amsterdam, 1983.

Meyer, Michel. *Rhetoric, Language and Reason.* University Park, Pa., 1994.

Meyer, Michel. *Of Problematology.* Chicago, 1995.

Meyer, Michel. "From Grammatology to Problematology." In *Derrida,* a special issue of the *Revue Internationale de Philosophie* 3 (1998), pp. 359–365.

Perelman, Chaim, and L. Olbrechts-Tyteca. *The New Rhetoric.* Translated by John Wilkinson and Purcell Weaver. Notre Dame, Ind., 1969. First published 1958.

Toulmin, Stephen. *The Uses of Argument.* Cambridge, U.K., 1958.

Yarbrough, Stephen. *After Rhetoric.* Carbondale, Ill., 1999.

—MICHEL MEYER

PROLĒPSIS (Lat. *anticipatio adiectivi*) is a permutative metataxeme. It anticipates the logical relations of consequences in a sentence (which are the result of the predicate) by means of an attributive adjective or participle that functionally represents an assumed consecutive clause or gerund. The correct logical reconstruction of "To break within the bloody house of life" (Shakespeare, *King John,* 4.2.210) is "To break within the house of life [the body] and make it bloody [for example by a dagger]." Since this figure of speech creates by syntactic permutation a rather bold image, it also has a strong semantic dimension.

[*See also* Figures of speech.]

—ANDREA GRÜN-OESTERREICH

PROOF. *See* Classical rhetoric; *and* Law.

PROPARALĒPSIS (also called *paragoge*) belongs to the figures of words (*figurae verborum*) or more precisely to the class of metaphonemes. It describes a deviant linguistic unit that is generated by the addition of a sound or syllable to a word, as in "wingèd" for "winged", "hasten" for "haste," "vasty" for "vast," or "climature" for "climate" (Shakespeare); in Latin, "admittier" for "admitti" (Virgil); in Italian, "fue" for "fù" (Dante); in Spanish, "infelice" for "infeliz"; in French, "avecque" for "avec" (Molière).

[*See also* Figures of speech.]

—HEINRICH F. PLETT

PROPOSITION. *See* Classical rhetoric.

PROPRIETY. *See* Decorum.

PROSŌPOPOEIA. Under the term *prosōpopoeia* (Lat. *fictio personae, sermocinatio*), as can be inferred etymologically from the Greek and Latin appelations, authors use the device of introducing in discourse a feigned presentation of characters or personified things, that is, things feigned *sub specie personae.* The usual form of this presentation is through the attribution of human properties or qualities, especially those of speaking or of listening (the terms *dialogismos* and *sermocinatio* refer to this property). The device must be

properly regulated by the literary norms of stylistic decorum.

The majority of authors usually distinguish between two modalities in attributing the device to characters or personified things: (1) "direct discourse" (*prosōpopoeia recta*) or (2) "indirect discourse" (*prosōpopoeia obliqua*). The most elaborated doctrine concerning this figure of speech, as is the case with *ēthopoeia,* appeared in ancient Greek handbooks for rhetorical exercises (*progymnasmata*), in which both appear tightly linked.

[*See also* Decorum; Ēthopoeia; Figures of speech; *and* Poetry.]

BIBLIOGRAPHY

Lanham, R. A. *A Handlist of Rhetorical Terms.* Berkeley, 1991.

Lausberg, H. *Handbuch der literarischen Rhetorik.* Pp. 820–829. Munich, 1960.

Mayoral, J. A. *Figuras retóricas.* Pp. 278–284. Madrid, 1994.

Morier, H. *Dictionnaire de poétique et de rhétorique.* Paris, 1981.

—JOSÉ ANTONIO MAYORAL
Translated by A. Ballesteros

PROSTHESIS (Lat. *appositio*), called by Thomas Wilson (*The Arte of Rhetoric,* 1560, p. 177) "addition at the first," the metaplasm of a word that results from the addition of a letter or syllable to its beginning, as a prefix. Often it is an archaic or dialect variant of a word or word form, like "y-clad" for "clothed" or "adown" for "down." Its phonaesthetic quality is put to use mostly in poetic diction, as in Byron's line (1817) "So we'll go no more a-roving."

[*See also* Figures of speech.]

—HEINER PETERS

PRUDENCE. From classical antiquity to the Renaissance, the intellectual and moral virtue of prudence, or practical reasoning, was assumed to be part of the education and training of the orator, the politician, and the prince. Devalued, and stripped of both its ethical and intellectual qualities in the years of the European Enlightenment, prudence has resurfaced as one of the most sought after virtues for restoration in modern times. Modern ideas of prudence connote caution, shrewdness, and the proposal of policies that reflect calculated self-interest, thus removing it from the sphere of ethics and situating it in politics. Recent scholarship in the fields of rhetoric, political science, education, and intellectual history has sought to recover the ethical, intellectual, and practical dimensions of prudence (Gk. *phronēsis;* Lat. *prudentia*) by returning to its earlier use in Greek philosophy and by the Renaissance humanists. [*See* Classical rhetoric; *and overview article on* Renaissance rhetoric.] Recovering this premodern conception of prudence is the key, some claim, to restoring ethics and reason to rhetoric and to reinstating rhetoric as a valid intellectual practice.

The history of prudence in Western philosophy and rhetoric begins with Aristotle (384–322 BCE), but the practices of prudent men are already emphasized in the earliest Greek literature. In the *Iliad,* Nestor and Odysseus are highly regarded as men of prudence (*phronimoi*), experienced leaders who command their own men and counsel the leading Greek general, Agamemnon. Aristotle recognizes the importance of prudential practice at the outset of his seminal discussion of *phronēsis* in *Nicomachean Ethics,* Book 6. He says, "We may discover what *phronēsis* is by observing those whom we call *phronimoi*" (6.5.1140a24). The prudent person (*phronimos*) possesses the ability to deliberate well about what is good and bad, not only for himself, but for the community as a whole. *Phronēsis* requires wisdom, which is knowledge about the origins of things, but Aristotle distinguishes it from theoretical wisdom because it is concerned with what is observable. He also distinguishes it from craft knowledge, which is concerned with producing things. Thus, *phronēsis,* though based on an understanding of the universal, involves deliberation about particular, contingent matters, and is realized in action, not in knowledge about an absolute truth or in production. Since it relies upon practical experience and is concerned with both deliberation and contingent affairs, *phronēsis* is most like political science. Moreover, the prudent person is naturally virtuous and works toward the supreme good, happiness (*eudaimonia*). His ability to deliberate well allows him to act or offer counsel in ways that are conducive to *eudaimonia* in whatever specific circumstances may arise. Thus, for Aristotle, pru-

dence participates in and mediates among the spheres of ethics, politics, and rhetoric.

A stronger link between prudence and rhetoric was forged by the Roman orator and statesman, Marcus Tullius Cicero (106–43 BCE), whose notion of the inseparability of prudence and rhetoric was transmitted to the Renaissance. There is no evidence that Aristotle's articulation of the qualities of prudence influenced the pre-Ciceronian, native Roman concept of *prudentia*, which emphasized legal expertise and commonsense experience. Cicero, perhaps under the influence of Aristotle, elevated the native Roman concept of *prudentia* to parity with a concept of wisdom, *sapientia,* tinged by Greek philosophy, which was popular among the Roman upper classes in his day. Unlike Aristotle, however, Cicero did not articulate the qualities of prudence in the abstract, but modeled a form of prudential practice through the characters in his dialogues, especially *De oratore, De re publica, Brutus,* and *De officiis.*

Cicero's three books of *De oratore* are central to the development of a model of prudential practice. Through the give-and-take and sometimes disorderly nature of friendly discussion, he redefines native Roman *prudentia* as a practical wisdom based on experience in Roman cultural institutions combined with an interest in and exposure to theoretical learning, such as Greek philosophy. Cicero situates prudential reasoning and practice at the core of the perfect orator's experience and training. The goal of this prudence is to determine and deliver the best arguments, style, and modes of persuasion in any particular situation. It is assumed that the orator is a good man, so it follows that he advocates not only what is in the best interests of his client or himself, but also what is in the best interests of the state.

The decision to redefine the scope and importance of *prudentia* in a dialogue rather than in a philosophical treatise was no doubt conditioned by the negative attitude Romans had toward philosophical precepts and the positive value they placed on historical examples (and even at that, Cicero's dialogue is a brilliant innovation in Latin literature), but it proved an especially appropriate mode of discussing and displaying prudential reasoning and practice. In *De oratore,* men who are prudent have experience in public affairs, are seen to be interested in learning, able to discuss philosophical and quasi-philosophical topics, arguing both sides of an issue, being witty and urbane, laughing at themselves, and encouraging cooperation and harmony among individuals and political factions. They understand that one becomes a better orator by becoming a better person, so the goal of the orator is not only to master the technical details of rhetoric, but to master himself.

Cicero developed a similar model of prudence and the statesman in *De re publica,* but it has been less influential since all but a fraction of it was unknown before the early nineteenth century. Nevertheless, building upon the demonstration in *De oratore,* Cicero's later accounts, especially *Brutus* and *De officiis,* were important for portraying a model of prudential practice for both orator and statesman. In *Brutus,* Cicero states, "No one is able to speak well if he does not reason prudently; wherefore, he who devotes himself to true eloquence, devotes himself to prudence" (23), and promptly commences to list all the great (and some mediocre) statesmen and orators in Rome's history.

The prudential model of the orator and statesman espoused by Cicero was already an attempt, in part, to recover a deliberative and experiential model of civic participation in the face of a movement toward dictatorship. It comes as no surprise that the features of prudence that Cicero promoted—deliberation, the advice and participation in government of men who had extensive experience in public life—were not emphasized by the dictator Julius Caesar (100–44 BCE) and his successor, Augustus (63 BCE–14 CE), the first Roman emperor. This accounts for the eclipse of prudence as a political ideal in the Roman empire, and suggests why emperors emphasized prudence's sister virtue, providence (*providentia,* from which *prudentia* derived in early Latin), or divine foresight. The later development of Christianity further diminished the status of prudence in the moral sphere, since it substituted the notion of an ethical ultimate end that could be deliberated and would vary due to particular circumstances with a divinely sanctioned moral code and an ultimate end that was knowledge of God himself. The medieval tradition comes to a close with Saint Thomas Aquinas (1225–1274), who recov-

ered the Ciceronian and Aristotelian moral and intellectual virtues of prudence, and allowed the possibility of reason within the framework of faith.

The high point of the influence of prudence on rhetoric and politics occurred under the humanists of the fifteenth and sixteenth centuries, in the wake of newly recovered texts by Cicero and of translations of Aristotle into Latin and the vernaculars. The humanists adopted the Ciceronian dialogue form to discuss philosophy and politics, and used writing as a political medium to gain influence. Several of the leading humanists, including Coluccio Salutati (1331–1406), Leonardo Bruni (c.1370–1444), and Giovanni Pontano (c.1426–1503), wrote treatises or dialogues to educate their readers in the virtue of prudence. Prudence was associated with rhetorical style and functioned as the embodiment of stylistic decorum in action. It was associated strongly with the *vita activa* and emphasized the practical benefits of deliberation *in utramque partem* (on both sides). The humanists' methods of using argument and specific examples of prudential action achieved a true synthesis of the two main forms of writing about prudence, the philosophical, abstract Aristotelian mode and the practical, exemplar tradition of Cicero.

In addition to promoting the development of prudence and rhetorical ability in others, such as statesmen and princes, the humanists (often leading statesmen themselves) came to see their own writing, and the activity of reading, as forms of prudential practice. The act of writing, particularly dialogue, had been understood as prudential deliberation and reasoning from the time of Cicero. As Kahn shows, the humanists transferred this idea to the act of reading as well, infusing it with the ability to help the reader make moral judgments that lead to proper action.

The high valuation of prudence as a standard of judgment leading to right moral action was not shared equally by all humanists, even when they used prudential modes of expression to challenge it. Lorenzo Valla (1407–1457), one of the most brilliant of the humanists, and a harsh critic, disputed the priority of prudence over faith as conducive to moral action in a universe governed by God and partly, at least, unknowable by man. Desiderius Erasmus (1466–1536) was the embodiment of prudential practice and an advocate of prudential reasoning, but in Kahn's assessment of *The Praise of Folly* (*Moriae encomium,* 1511), Erasmus also comes to point out the inherent paradox of prudence in a Christian context by making Jesus "an example that cannot be imitated" (p. 114).

The importance of prudential deliberation and reasoning was greatly diminished after the Renaissance as the notion of contingent truth and the utility of deliberation from experience were devalued. Although the early Thomas Hobbes (1588–1679) used history as a lesson book for contemporary ills, as was done by Cicero, Pontano, and especially Niccolò Machiavelli (1469–1527) in *Discourses on the First Ten Books of Livy* (*Discorsi sopra la prima deca di Tito Livio,* 1521), his later work exhibits a major shift away from prudential reasoning to reliance on an objective Truth and subservience to a single authority. Finally, Immanuel Kant (1724–1804) struck a decisive blow against prudence by separating it from morality, associating it with maximizing self-interest, and distinguishing between a reason that is based on sense experience and "pure reason" that aims at what is universal and transcendent.

The modern notion of prudence as calculating self-interest has lately been considered too narrow and removed from the fields of rhetoric and ethics. Thus, recent scholarship has been concerned with returning to an Aristotelian formulation of *phronēsis,* emphasizing rational deliberation, its ultimate goal of happiness for the larger community, and its eternal ability to adapt to contingent circumstances. The works of Ronald Beiner, of Robert Hariman and Francis A. Beer in political science, of Joseph Dunne in education, Thomas B. Farrell in rhetoric, Thomas O. Sloane in composition, and Douglas J. Den Uyl in philosophy and ethics are united in their concern to reintroduce intellectual and ethical reasoning into their respective fields. These and other works are also attempting to regain the synthesis of the philosophic and practical modes of presentation, and recognize that to restore prudence we must recover the conditions that enabled it. Much of this work, however, does not seem to realize that scholarly discourse will not change the underlying political, ethical, or rhetorical culture. There is still, perhaps, too much emphasis on Aristotle and a bias for locating the roots of philosophical

issues in ancient Greek thought. If we are to succeed in recovering prudence in practice and the social–intellectual conditions that underly it, we need to emphasize modeling specific *cultural* examples of prudential deliberation and action, following the Ciceronian tradition, but going one better by addressing the common person. Nevertheless, with the current climate of intellectual relativism and skepticism, augmented by renewed religious fundamentalism and political conservatism, the conditions may exist for recovering a new version of prudence for our times and achieving a synthesis of prudential reasoning and rhetorical–political practice.

[*See also* Contingency and probability; Decorum; Phronēsis; *overview article on* Politics; *and* Practical wisdom.]

BIBLIOGRAPHY

Beiner, Ronald. *Political Judgment.* Chicago, 1983.

Cape, Robert W., Jr. "Cicero and the Development of Prudential Practice at Rome." In *Discourses of Prudence,* edited by Robert Hariman, forthcoming.

Den Uyl, Douglas J. *The Virtue of Prudence.* New York, 1991.

Dunne, Joseph. *Back to the Rough Ground: "Phronesis" and "Techne" in Modern Philosophy and in Aristotle.* Notre Dame, Ind., 1993.

Farrell, Thomas B. *Norms of Rhetorical Culture.* New Haven, 1993.

Garver, Eugene. *Machiavelli and the History of Prudence.* Madison, Wis., 1987.

Hariman, Robert. *Discourses of Prudence.* Forthcoming.

Hariman, Robert, and Francis A. Beer, "What Would be Prudent? Forms of Reasoning in World Politics." *Rhetoric and Public Affairs* 1 (1998), pp. 299–330.

Kahn, Victoria. *Rhetoric, Prudence, and Skepticism in the Renaissance.* Ithaca, N.Y., 1985.

Reeve, C. D. C. *Practices of Reason: Aristotle's Nicomachean Ethics.* Oxford, 1992.

Sloane, Thomas O. *On the Contrary: The Protocol of Traditional Rhetoric.* Washington, D.C., 1997.

—ROBERT W. CAPE, JR.

PUBLIC SPEAKING. Before the twentieth century, public speakers were customarily referred to as orators and their discourses as orations. In the oral cultures of the ancient world, speech was the only medium through which to reach a mass audience. Oratory was prized both as a mode of social influence and as a means of artistic expression. [*See* Oratory.] Even after the development of print, the orator continued to be apotheosized as a heroic figure who stood at the crossroads of history and helped shape the destiny of nations. Oratory was seen as an indispensable element of statecraft, and training in rhetoric occupied a central place in the curriculum. In Great Britain, the eighteenth and nineteenth centuries produced a level of oratorical excellence rivaling that of classical Greece and Rome. The United States experienced its own golden age of oratory during the years 1820 to 1860. The power and prestige of the orator on both sides of the Atlantic was captured well by Ralph Waldo Emerson. "The highest bribes of society are at the feet of the successful orator," he exclaimed. "All other fames must hush before his. He is the true potentate" (*Complete Works,* Boston, 1903).

Yet even before the end of the nineteenth century, both the nature of public speech and the perception of the speaker had departed from the neoclassical model of oratory. As the patrician world that undergirded that model succumbed to an increasingly democratic and industrialized society, the older traditions of civic rhetoric began to give way as well. Language became more colloquial and speech delivery became more conversational. Women, who had been barred from the public platform until the 1830s, began to exercise the rights of political speech that men had long enjoyed. [*See* Feminist rhetoric.] As more and more citizens of ordinary means took to the rostrum, audiences no longer regarded the orator as a larger-than-life figure to be regarded with awe and deference. The oratorical set piece that had been the metier of such titans as Edmund Burke (1729–1797) and William Pitt (1708–1788), Daniel Webster (1782–1852) and Henry Clay (1777–1852), gave way to shorter, less elaborate addresses. So sweeping were these transformations that U.S. Senator Albert Beveridge, himself an acclaimed speaker, declared in 1900 that the great orators of the past "would not be tolerated now." Unmoved by grandiloquence, modern listeners favored "a simple, quiet, and direct address, a straightforward, unartificial, honest manner, without tricks of oratory" (Reed, 1900–1903).

Given the swollen passages of Beveridge's own speeches, it is difficult, from the perspective of the twenty-first century, to think of him as a champion of the plain style. Yet his observations about the changing consuetudes of public address were echoed by many of his contemporaries, including the editor of the Everyman's Library collection of historical British speeches, who noted that in England, "We talk now, we hardly make orations" (*British Historical and Political Orations,* London, 1915). These permutations in rhetorical practice were reflected in pedagogy. By the 1920s, most college courses in elocution and oratory had been retitled "Public Speaking" and emphasized the conversational mode of presentation. [*See* Speech.] Most influential in this regard was James Winans's landmark *Public Speaking* (New York, 1916), the first modern textbook on its subject. According to Winans, speechmaking was "a perfectly natural act" that called for "no strange, artificial methods, but only for an extension and development of that most familiar act, conversation." The aim, he said, was to prepare one's speech thoroughly but to talk in a lively, direct, spontaneous fashion that epitomized "enlarged conversation."

The shift from oratory to public speaking was reflected in and, to some extent, engendered by the emergence of the business speech as a major genre of public discourse. As the editors of the 1923 edition of *Modern Eloquence,* explained, not only was effective speech a vehicle for selling one's ideas and products and for communicating with other members of one's company, but business had come to realize that the subjects of national debate were often economic in nature. Rather than leaving this debate to politicians, business leaders had "become highly skilled in addressing the public," and their words were "exercising a powerful influence upon the American people." But no matter what the forum, business speakers prided themselves on eschewing oratory in favor of straightforward, unadorned speech. As Dale Carnegie stated in his best-selling *Public Speaking and Influencing Men in Business* (New York, 1926), "A modern audience wants the speaker to talk just as directly as he would in a chat, and in the same general manner that he would in talking to them in conversation." Carnegie's formula for personal success through public speaking took the business world by storm and reinforced the conversational mode as the dominant paradigm of public address.

So, too, did the microphone, which came into widespread use by the 1930s. From Demosthenes (384–322 BCE) to Webster, the great orators had been known for their powerful voices, which allowed them to be heard by audiences of up to several thousand people without the aid of electronic amplification. It was said of the elder William Pitt, for example, that his voice "rose like the swell of the organ of a cathedral" (Jamieson, 1988), while the American abolitionist Frederick Douglass (1817–1895) was typically described as speaking in "thunderous" tones. With the advent of amplified sound, however, it became possible for even the most subdued speaker to be heard in almost any setting. Freed of the need to project to the farthest reaches of an auditorium or amphitheater, public speakers could now modulate their delivery in ways that more closely approximated the inflections of everyday conversation. The stentorian tones of traditional oratory were unnecessary, and often incongruous, in the more intimate vocal relationship between speaker and listener made possible by electronic amplification.

While the microphone enabled a speaker to be heard by a large crowd, the advent of radio made it possible for that same speaker to reach hundreds of thousands, even millions, of people far removed from the physical location of the speech. It is no exaggeration to say that radio revolutionized public speaking in its day as profoundly as television would later. Not only did it dramatically increase the potential size of a speaker's audience—a development of particular importance for political communication—but it transformed the nature of the relationship between speaker and audience. Gone were the nonverbal cues conveyed by gesture, physical appearance, and eye contact that helped listeners assess a speaker's meaning and gauge his or her credibility. [See Credibility.] The message was now carried entirely by the speaker's voice. As the *Saturday Evening Post* noted in August 1924, "Somehow the spread-eagle sort of thing and all the familiar phrases and resources of the spellbinder sound very flat and stale over the air." No one grasped this better than Franklin D. Roosevelt (1882–1945), whose mastery of radio was central to his presidential leadership during the Great Depression and World War II. It is not by chance that his most famous group of speeches are known as the "Fireside Chats"—informal talks with the American people in the privacy of their homes.

Like radio, television is highly conducive to a more intimate, conversational style of public speaking. The vehement and histrionic delivery of classical oratory is far too intense for what Marshall McLuhan dubbed the "cool" medium of television (*Understanding Media*, New York, 1964). In addition, television accentuates the visual, drawing attention to every nuance of a speaker's appearance, gestures, and facial expression. The ability to speak to the television camera is a special skill that no modern democratic leader can afford to ignore. It is no accident that the only United States presidents to serve two full terms between 1960 and 2000—Ronald Reagan and Bill Clinton—were masters of the personal, conversational style and were able to exploit the medium of television as adroitly as Roosevelt had employed radio. Indeed, so ubiquitous is the presence of television that it has affected public speaking in almost every walk of life. From the boardroom to the classroom, the pulpit to the protest rally, speakers face audiences predisposed to the conversational mode and attuned to the power of visual images.

The dominance of the conversational mode, however, does not mean that public speaking has become so casual and colloquial as to be little more than an adjunct to everyday conversation. Public speaking is more highly structured than daily conversation. It usually imposes strict time limits on the speaker and does not allow listeners to interrupt with questions or commentary. Public speaking also requires more formal language than ordinary conversation. Slang, obscenity, and bad grammar have little place in public speeches. Most listeners react negatively to speakers who do not organize their remarks and polish their language when addressing an audience. Nor do listeners expect a speech to be delivered in the same manner as routine conversation. When conversing informally, most people talk quietly, adopt a casual posture, and inject vocalized pauses when searching for the next word or idea. Effective public speakers, however, adjust their voices to be heard clearly throughout the audience, assume a more erect posture, and avoid distracting mannerisms and vocal habits.

Rather than resulting from spontaneity and

artlessness, the conversational mode of public speaking reflects a calculated rhetorical choice designed to enhance the audience's perception of the speaker and acceptance of his or her ideas by incorporating into the speech stylistic and nonverbal attributes associated with conversational discourse. The aim of the speaker is to establish strong eye contact with the audience, to gesture naturally, to use readily intelligible language, and to concentrate on communicating with the audience rather than declaiming to them. [*See overview article on* Audience; *and* Decorum.] All of this can be achieved in a talk that is delivered off the cuff, but the best modern speeches, like those of traditional oratory, grow out of serious thought, extensive preparation, and a substantial dose of rhetorical creativity. [*See* Delivery.]

The shift from oratory to public speaking that crystallized during the twentieth century dramatically changed the tone and texture of oral discourse, but it did not, contrary to the predictions of some critics, produce a wholesale decline in either the quality or importance of that discourse. Every age tends to judge its public speech as inferior to that of the past. Lamentations about the deterioration of the spoken word are endemic throughout Western history, even during times that, in retrospect, are celebrated for their eloquence. At the apogee of America's golden age of oratory, for example, the January 1841 *North American Review* lambasted the "wretched babble" of most public speakers. Edward T. Channing, Boylston Professor of Rhetoric and Oratory at Harvard, noted that "oratory, now, is said to be almost a lost art. We hear constantly that it has fallen from its old supremacy" (*Lectures,* Boston, 1856). No matter the time and place, for every rhetorical jewel there are countless sophistic baubles. Eventually, however, the dross fades into obscurity while posterity extols the exceptional. With the perspective afforded by time, it is clear that the twentieth century produced its full share of eloquent, expressive, and historically significant speeches.

In the United States, a nationwide survey of communication scholars was conducted to determine the top one hundred American speeches of the twentieth century based on the criteria of impact and rhetorical artistry. Given the historical affinity between rhetoric and politics, it is not sur-

prising that the overwhelming majority were delivered in the political arena. [*See overview article on* Politics.] The largest group—fully a quarter of the whole—focused on issues of war and peace, national defense, and foreign policy. Roughly twenty dealt primarily with the rights of labor, women, or African Americans, while almost as many were campaign discourses of one type or another— stump speeches, nominating addresses, keynote presentations, and the like. Several sought to console the nation in the wake of political assassinations or other national tragedies. Still others revolved around such matters as impeachment, McCarthyism, AIDS, poverty, birth control, and the role of the press in a democratic society. All of this suggests that there remains an essential measure of truth in Chauncey Depew's observation that "Eloquence is the master element in politics" (*Library of Oratory,* New York, 1902).

Unlike the nineteenth century, however, when national attention was riveted on the great orators in Congress, the president occupied center stage during most of the twentieth century, a development that reflected the emergence of what has become known as the rhetorical presidency (Tulis, *Rhetorical Presidency,* Princeton, 1987). Before Theodore Roosevelt (1858–1919) transformed the office into a "bully pulpit," chief executives usually deferred to the legislative prerogatives of Congress and seldom took to the hustings in behalf of specific policy initiatives, domestic or foreign. Even presidential candidates eschewed the extensive speech making associated with current campaigns. In keeping with the maxim that the office should seek the man rather than the man seeking the office, they usually remained silent while surrogate speakers stumped in their behalf. After Roosevelt, the president increasingly became the dominant voice in American political discourse. The rhetorical power of the office was augmented by radio and television, which allowed the president to go over the heads of Congress and speak directly to the entire nation. Of the top one hundred American speeches of the twentieth century, thirty-five—more than one-third—were delivered by sitting presidents, while only four were presented by a senator or representative in the course of congressional debate. In contrast, of the eighty-three American speeches from the nineteenth century published in the volumes devoted to political oratory in the 1900 edition of *Modern Eloquence,* thirty-nine were delivered on the floor of the United States Congress, but only six came from a sitting president.

Equally striking, the editors of *Modern Eloquence* did not publish any addresses by women or African Americans in their volumes on political oratory—despite the fact that nineteenth-century speakers such as Frederick Douglass, Sojourner Truth, Booker T. Washington, Susan B. Anthony, and Elizabeth Cady Stanton had produced works of incontestable power and artistry. In contrast, twenty-three of the top one hundred speeches of the twentieth century—almost one quarter—were by women, including suffrage leaders Anna Howard Shaw and Carrie Chapman Catt, birth control advocate Margaret Sanger, anarchist Emma Goldman, AIDS activists Mary Fisher and Elizabeth Glaser, and first ladies Eleanor Roosevelt, Barbara Bush, and Hillary Rodham Clinton. By the end of the twentieth century, women had become so prominent on the public platform that both Bush and Clinton outpolled their husbands in the top one hundred survey and five of the survey's seven speeches from the 1990s were by women. The survey also included thirteen speeches by African Americans. Martin Luther King's "I Have a Dream" (1963) was deemed the finest speech of the century, while Barbara Jordan's keynote address at the 1976 Democratic National Convention and Malcolm X's "The Ballot or the Bullet" were also mentioned in the top ten. Other African-American speakers in the top one hundred were Jesse Jackson, Stokely Carmichael, Mary Church Terrell, Anita Hill, and Shirley Chisholm. In addition to manifesting the rich oral tradition of the black community and the historical significance of the quest for racial justice, the presence of such speakers reminds us that public speaking remains the single most important mode of expression for people seeking to broaden the lines of power and privilege in American society. [*See overview article on* African-American rhetoric.]

Although a comparable survey was not conducted for speeches outside the United States, there can be no doubting the consequence of public speaking in other parts of the globe during the twentieth century. No adequate history of Great Britain can be written without regard to the public addresses of prime ministers such as David Lloyd George, Stanley Baldwin, Neville Chamberlain, and Margaret Thatcher, or of parliamentary speakers such as Keir Hardie, Aneurin Bevin, Leo Amery, Iain Macleod, and Neil Kinnock. None, however, matched the rhetorical achievements of Winston Churchill (1874–1965). First elected to the House of Commons in 1900, Churchill was either a member of Parliament or a cabinet minister for the better part of the next six decades. His crowning achievement came as prime minister during World War II, when he rallied the British people through the darkest days of the conflict with some of the most memorable speeches in history. As broadcaster Edward R. Murrow remarked, Churchill "mobilized the English language and sent it into battle" (*In Search of Light,* New York, 1967). Other British speeches of note during the twentieth century included Emmeline Pankhurst's addresses in behalf of woman suffrage, Roger Casement's speech from the dock after his conviction for high treason in 1916, Edward VIII's broadcast to the nation twenty years later upon abdicating the throne, Bertrand Russell's pleas for nuclear disarmament during the 1950s and 1960s, and the Earl of Spencer's eulogy at the funeral of his sister Diana, Princess of Wales, in 1997.

No speaker of the twentieth century was more universally admired than Mahatma (Mohandas K.) Gandhi (1869–1948). Despite suffering such severe stage fright as a young man that he withdrew from his first case as a lawyer because he could not bring himself to address the court, Gandhi became a champion of the downtrodden who used the moral force of his discourse, in combination with the political tactics of nonviolence and noncooperation, to bring an end to British rule in India. [*See* Indian rhetoric.] His most able compatriot, Jawaharlal Nehru, was an equally talented speaker and became India's first prime minister after independence. Irish nationalists Patrick Pearse and Éamon de Valera were no less eloquent in behalf of their cause. Pearse's fiery speeches helped fuel the Easter Uprising of 1916 and expressed the aspirations that led to creation of the Irish Free State. A riveting speaker who was at the center of Irish politics for sixty years, de Valera helped lead the quest for independence and subsequently served both as prime minister and head of state. Indeed, all the major political revolutions of the twentieth century were fueled in substantial measure by the spoken word, whether expressed by a dominant leader such as Vladimir Lenin in Russia, Mao Tse-Tung in China, or Fidel Castro in Cuba, or by the multitude of lesser-known speakers who worked tirelessly at the local level. Just as Gandhi, de Valera, and Castro (among others) gained moral force as speakers because they were imprisoned by the dominant regime for what they said, so have more recent figures such as Burmese democracy advocate Aung San Suu Kyi and South African leader Nelson Mandela. Their affirmation of the ideals of justice and free expression, coupled with their steadfast commitment to those ideals in the face of oppression, places them in a rhetorical tradition that stretches back more than two millennia to classical orators such as Demosthenes and Cicero. The spoken word was utilized throughout the twentieth century, as it has been since time immemorial, as the primary means of persuasion for religious proselytizers and spiritual leaders the world over. [*See* Homiletics; *and* Religion.]

Unfortunately, public speaking has not always been employed for ennobling purposes. It has been a tool of visionaries and reformers, but also of dictators and demagogues. It has been used to advance the causes of political liberation and personal dignity, but also to promote repression and totalitarianism, religious hatred and racial persecution, genocide and ethnic cleansing. Perhaps the most magnetic speaker of the twentieth century—and certainly its most malevolent—was Adolf Hitler (1889–1945). "The power which has always started the greatest religious and political avalanches in history rolling," he declared in *Mein Kampf*, "has from time immemorial been the magic power of the spoken word, and that alone" (translated by Ralph Manheim, Boston, 1943). Almost hypnotic in his effect on listeners, Hitler galvanized the German people into following one set of ideals and one leader. Yet his aims were barbarous and his tactics despicable. His passionate appeals to the pent-up furies of German nationalism touched off the most destructive war in history, while his venomous doctrines of anti-Semitism and Aryan supremacy precipitated the horrors of the Holocaust. He remains to this day the ultimate example of why the power of the spoken word needs to be guided by a strong sense of ethical integrity.

Contrary to the claims of some critics, however, the fact that speech can be put to evil purposes is not a reason to condemn public speaking in general. Rhetoric is inherently neither moral nor immoral. There is no doubt that it has been abused by unscrupulous speakers for detestable causes, but it has been employed no less often by honorable speakers for noble causes. The ideal of public speaking, as the Roman rhetorician Quintilian declared two millennia ago in his *Institutio oratoria* (12.1.1), is the good person speaking well. To denounce public speaking because it can be misused is as foolhardy as forswearing medicine or science because they can be misused. The best antidote for unethical speech is to combat it with more persuasive ethical speech. In contrast to this view, it has been argued that some ideas are so dangerous, so misguided, or so offensive that society has a duty to suppress them. But who is to determine which ideas are too dangerous, misguided, or offensive to be uttered? Who is to decide which speakers are to be heard and which are to be silenced? No matter how well intentioned they may be, efforts to protect society by restricting free speech usually end up repressing minority viewpoints and unpopular opinions. In the long run, there is no better way to maintain liberty than to protect the right of free and open expression.

Public speaking has historically been the most democratic mode of civic communication. One need not own a newspaper or a television station or radio station to express his or her ideas through public speech. There is, moreover, a special chemistry in the immediacy of the relationship between speaker and listener that is not present in print or even in the same speech mediated through television. Throughout the twentieth century, various observers predicted that the mass media—first newspapers, then radio, and finally television—would destroy the vitality of public speaking as a mode of social influence. Yet while the forms and conventions of public speaking have changed with the emergence of new media and technologies, the ability to express one's ideas to an audience through oral discourse is no less important in our age of instant global communication than it was before. Every day of the year, millions of people around the world depend on public speaking to communicate their ideas and to receive ideas from other people—politicians and citizens, of course, but also lawyers and teachers, ministers and missionaries, engineers and architects, scientists and stockbrokers, developers and preservationists, corporate presidents and sales representatives, union leaders and military personnel, health professionals and community planners. Motivational speaking has become a $1 billion global industry, and there are thousands of professional speakers devoted solely to high-tech issues. As the world becomes ever more complex, the demand for speakers who can translate that complexity into comprehensible, even comforting, terms will continue to grow.

So, too, will the need for informed instruction in public speaking. The oldest known handbook on effective speech was written on papyrus in Egypt more than four millennia ago, and eloquence was highly prized in ancient India, Africa, and China, as well as among the Greeks and Romans. Taught more or less continuously in Western civilization for the past twenty-five hundred years, the art of public speaking has engaged the energies of thinkers such as Aristotle, Plato, Isocrates, Cicero, Quintilian, Saint Augustine, Francis Bacon (1568–1626), Hugh Blair (1718–1800), and Richard Whately (1787–1863). In the popular conception, however, it is too often seen chiefly as a matter of spellbinding delivery or of cultivating a winning personality. Learning to speak clearly and convincingly is a skill—as is learning to write clearly and convincingly—but the most important part of speaking, as of writing, is having something important to say. Given the inextricable relationship between thought and language, cognition and expression, there can be no gainsaying the intellectual substance of a well-taught course in public speaking. As one learns how to choose and develop topics, how to organize and support claims, how to assess evidence and reasoning, and how to employ language clearly and concisely, he or she is, at the same time, dealing with the invention of discourse, the structure of thought, the validity of claims, and the meaning of ideas. [See Argumentation; Arrangement, *article on* Traditional arrangement; *and* Invention.] In the process of learning how to construct speeches with accu-

racy, order, and rigor, students become more adept at thinking with accuracy, order, and rigor. As the ancient rhetoricians understood, training in public speaking involves the education of the entire person. Although the world of the classical orator is irretrievably gone, it is still true today that the process of becoming a capable, responsible speaker entails becoming a capable, responsible thinker. In this respect, public speaking remains, as it has been through much of Western civilization, a vital part of humanistic education and democratic citizenship.

BIBLIOGRAPHY

Andrews, James R., and David Zarefsky. *Contemporary American Voices: Significant Speeches in American History, 1945–Present.* New York, 1992. The most comprehensive anthology of U.S. political speeches from the second half of the twentieth century.

Baskerville, Barnet. *The People's Voice: The Orator in American Society.* Lexington, Ky., 1979. The best cultural history of public speaking in the United States.

Branham, Robert James, and W. Barnett Pearce. "The Conversational Frame in Public Address." *Communication Quarterly* 44 (1996), pp. 423–439. Explores the emergence of the conversational mode as a strategic response to the rhetorical needs faced by public speakers.

Campbell, John Angus. "Oratory, Democracy, and the Classroom." In *Democracy, Education, and the Schools.* Edited by Roger Seder, pp. 211–243. San Francisco, 1996. Elucidates the relationship between public speaking instruction and democratic values and practices.

Campbell, Karlyn Kohrs, ed. *Women Public Speakers in the United States, 1925–1993: A Bio-Critical Sourcebook.* Westport, Conn., 1994. An instructive set of essays on the public-speaking activities of thirty-two American women activists of the twentieth century.

Duffy, Bernard K., and Halford R. Ryan. *American Orators of the Twentieth Century: Critical Studies and Sources.* New York, 1987. Consists of brief essays on fifty-eight major U.S. speakers. Although uneven in quality, a useful source of basic information.

Great American Speeches: 80 Years of Political Oratory. Films for the Humanities and Sciences. Princeton, 1995. A splendid set of six videotapes on political speechmaking from Theodore Roosevelt to Ronald Reagan. Includes excerpts from close to three-dozen speeches.

Great Speeches. Educational Video Group. Greenwood, Ind., 1985– . The best source for video footage of major public addresses. The fifteen volumes produced to date contain seventy-nine speeches, almost all of which are presented in their entirety.

Jamieson, Kathleen Hall. *Eloquence in an Electronic Age: The Transformation of Political Speechmaking.* New York, 1988. Perceptively explicates the differences between classical oratory and political speaking in the modern world.

Kimball, Bruce. *Orators and Philosophers: A History of the Idea of Liberal Education.* Expanded ed. New York, 1995. A prize-winning study that explores the historical relationship between oratory and liberal education.

Lucas, Stephen E. *The Art of Public Speaking.* 7th ed. New York, 2001. Combines classical rhetorical principles with contemporary communication research.

MacArthur, Brian, ed. *The Penguin Book of Twentieth-Century Speeches.* London, 1992. A stellar anthology of works from political speakers the world over.

Reed, Thomas B., ed. *Modern Eloquence.* 15 vols. Philadelphia, 1900–1903. A comprehensive collection of speeches from antiquity onward. The introductory essays to various volumes reveal much about the changing norms of public speaking early in the twentieth century. Subsequent editions were published in 1923, 1932, and 1948.

Safire, William, ed. *Lend Me Your Ears: Great Speeches in History.* New York, 1992. A rich collection that includes more than one hundred speeches from the twentieth century, though most are excerpted.

Straub, Deborah Gillan, ed. *Voices of Multicultural America: Notable Speeches Delivered by African, Asian, Hispanic, and Native Americans, 1790–1995.* Detroit, 1996. Reprints addresses from 133 speakers, two-thirds of whom were active during the twentieth century.

"The Top 100 American Speeches of the Twentieth Century." *http://www.news.wisc.edu/misc/speeches.* December, 1999. Maintained by the University of Wisconsin Office of News and Public Affairs. Presents the results of a nationwide survey of 137 communication scholars conducted by Stephen E. Lucas and Martin J. Medhurst. Also appeared in *USA Today,* 30 December, 1999, p. 8D.

Winans, James. *Public Speaking.* New York, 1916. The first modern textbook on its subject; notable both for its advocacy of the conversational mode and for its use of the psychology of attention as the basis for effective speechmaking.

—STEPHEN E. LUCAS

PUN. *See* Paronomasia.

Q

QUADRIVIUM. *See* Medieval rhetoric, *article on* Medieval grammar; *and* Trivium.

QUEER RHETORIC. The idea of a queer rhetoric emerged in the mid-1990s as rhetoric studies became aware of the impact of the gay and lesbian civil rights movement on the ecology of public deliberation in postmodern democracies.

The annual convention of the National Communication Association, the main international communication and rhetoric professional organization, has held special sessions on gay and lesbian rhetoric and communication since the mid-1990s. From the scholarly point of view, queer rhetoric saw its first formal presentation at the 1997 convention of the International Society for the History of Rhetoric. The establishment of queer rhetoric founded a field of research into rhetorical modes of expression of the gay and lesbian civil rights movement, distinct both from the gay cultural studies or "discourse" of the late 1970s, that grew out of a poststructuralist theory of culture (for example, *QLG. A Journal of Lesbian and Gay Studies* or the *Harvard Gay & Lesbian Review*), and from the ethnography of gay speech (epitomized in the annual "lavender linguistics" convention at American University, Washington, D.C.; see Leap, 1996).

The adjective *queer* was accepted in the mid-1990s as the generic term to designate "gay," "lesbian," "transgendered," or "bisexual" phenomena. The term was first coined in the activist vocabulary of the Queer Nation radical movement in 1990. Although the adjective *queer* has become somewhat interchangeable with "gay and lesbian" (sometimes with the addition of "bisexual" and "transgendered"), in relation to the field of rhetoric it nevertheless implies that the gay and lesbian civil rights movement, as it entered a new phase of consciousness, could be held accountable for having developed a specific rhetorical practice in the public sphere.

By contrast with its two civil rights predecessors, black protest in America and the women's movement in America and Europe in the 1960s and the 1970s, the gay and lesbian, later queer, movement had to develop its own rhetorical forms, without drawing on rhetorical traditions that were either culturally bound, such as African-American pulpit oratory, or of recent acquisition, such as the protest oratory of the late 1960s. By and large, queer rhetoric has unfolded in a postmodern age, marked by the acceptance of capitalism and democracy, the rise of identity and community micropolitics, the pragmatics of conflict resolution, and the decay of cultural and sexual separatism, although rhetorical forms of censure (such as "outing") repeat adversarial tactics from the days of black protest and the 1970s women's movement. Like them, it developed mainly in Western democracies. Unlike them, it is supported by a wide network of media, mainly print, that gives its rhetorical shapes form and function and accounts for their impact or persuasiveness in terms of penal law reforms, constitutional gains, and social acceptability. These print media, most of which are unknown to the general public, are numerous, closely fitting their readership's concerns, community-bound while outward looking. They form a massive communication system where queer rhetoric refines its tools before entering the larger "straight" (i.e., non-queer) readership domain. They support and help create a queer "interpretive community." Law, engagement in the public arena, and shaping of values are the three areas where rhetoric is traditionally operative. Queer rhetoric has impacted all three and, as a result, has brought an original contribution to the building of what is sometimes called "rhetorical democracy." This article charts the sources and methods of queer rhetoric as an interpretive community engaged in public deliberation.

Topics. In terms of its stock of topics or places of rhetorical *inventio,* queer rhetoric first developed them, beginning in the late 1970s, in a wide range of print media (leaflets, tabloids, community notices, bulletins of support groups, mainly for gay men), some of which then grew into full-fledged periodicals or regular magazines serving the growing gay and lesbian readership and community. In the United States, *The Advocate* was founded in 1967 as a tabloid; *The Washington Blade* was founded in 1969; *New York Native* (1980–1996); *The Guide* was founded in 1980; in Britain, *Gay Times* was founded in 1974; in France, *3 Keller* was founded in 1980; in the Netherlands, *De Gay Krant* was founded in 1979. These numerous leaflets and bulletins, many of them ephemeral, some steadily reaching larger circulation and evolving into near magazines (*HX,* founded in 1990, *HOTspots!,* founded in 1986), were coeval with the unfolding of the gay and lesbian civil rights movement in its postmodern phase (since the 1980s) and its concerted effort toward visibility. Before the advent of the Internet, and after which in synergy with Web sites, this variety of print media nurtured and fashioned a series of rhetorical topics apposite to the wishes and values of the gay (and to a lesser extent, lesbian) community. At the same time, the deregulation of air waves in the European Community, later Union, led to the establishment of gay radio (such as Radio Frequence Gay, in France) and gay television (in Britain), while American mainstream TV networks (ABC, NBC, HBO, PBS) no longer shunned gay-themed movies. These media are largely responsible for having transformed the queer community into an interpretive community. They practice persuasive advocacy, a rhetorical form that is even present in sexual-encounter leaflets. They represent an excellent observation site for the unfolding of a queer rhetoric. [*See* Invention; *and* Topics.]

The topics of queer rhetoric fall into four categories: sex, leisure, culture, icons. All four advocate gay and lesbian visibility, try to carve out a space within the public sphere, and aim to mainstream the queer lifestyle.

Sex and sexual opportunities were predomi-nant features of some earlier media. *The Advocate* noticeably shed its sexual-encounter classifieds in 1990, when it transformed itself into a gay and lesbian national news magazine, the popular insert becoming a separate magazine in 1997 retitled *Unzipped.* By contrast, and in relation to a smaller market, Australian *Outrage* still combines news and editorial with sexually explicit, male-oriented classifieds. However, rhetorically, sexual-encounter advertising helped create awareness of larger issues affecting what soon became a community. Sheets of classified advertisements often carried deliberative pieces on gay issues, with regular reporting on legal advances and social rights victories, or directly entering political electioneering at ballot time.

The topic of sex, in turn, opened an avenue onto the advocacy of specific leisure activities as visibility expanded, marked by the appearance in the 1980s of specialized queer travel and leisure magazines, catering to a specialized customer base (this was in addition to older listings of gay places of encounter such as the venerable *Spartacus* guide). These publications, together with the later "resource directories" (professional listings), powerfully argued for enhanced self-perceptions and consolidated communal identity awareness. For example, there were *The Guide, New York Metrosource,* founded in 1989, *The Lesbian & Gay Pink Pages* (Florida), founded in 1991, *Gay Pages* (South Africa), founded in 1995, *De Regenboodsggids* (Dutch), founded in 1996, *Gay Guide of Canada,* founded in 1997.

Cultural events offer a further topic for the deployment of gay and lesbian awareness. *Oblivion* (California) in fact labels such a topic "queer" and detaches it from the topics of sex and leisure. Cultural opportunities, as presented in editorials and stories, either highlight the gay and lesbian content of seemingly mainstream "straight" events, or enhance the high quality of gay and lesbian performers (*Out,* founded 1993) or "queer" events and "queer spaces" over other similar mainstream events (*Circuit Noize,* founded in 1995, although directed at the "queer planet" is the model for all rave magazines). By positing related subtopics of time (the queer calendar enforces different festive days, marked for instance by "white, blue, black parties," "coming-out days," "queer pride weeks") and of space (the queer planet has its own resorts, cruises, package tours, circuit of libraries and theaters, and in many cities, gay tourists are taken on tours of historical queer places that use the time-honored rhetorical tactic *laus civitatis,* the praise of a city, "in a different light"), queer rhetoric finally rests on the reinforcement of icons.

The topic of icons sees the deeds and words of certain personalities as embodying the queer interpretive community. Whether or not they themselves are gay (male or female) or queer (a word straights still have difficulty in using because they do not belong to the queer interpretive community), the common denominator of these icons is their role in advocating queer rhetoric itself: in 1996, *The Advocate* ran on its covers a "gallery" of gay icons, singers, politicians writers, and film stars. *The Advocate* used its thirtieth anniversary issue, in October 1997, to take stock of the queer nation's icons and give them literally the function of queer orators who described in their own words the past thirty years of queer civil rights activism and projected their vision of the next thirty years. In 1995, the British *Gay Times* celebrated its 200th issue with a gallery of "Britain's top 200 gay men and lesbians." "Lambda" book awards belong to the same strategy. "Role models" and "heroes," a terminology by and large frowned upon in other domains of public deliberation, have been adopted and retooled by queer rhetoric.

The AIDS controversy that in the first decade of the pandemic still pitted the queer community against reactionary communities (essentially religious), in a conflict of interpretation and deliberation on its causes, certainly operated as a catalyst for these topics. Once assembled, these topics form the basis for public argumentation.

Queer Argumentation. Queer rhetoric argues publicly for the interpretive community it gives voice to. In postmodern distrust toward ideology, public advocacy is closely assimilated to and accepted as a form of social authority. In this light, the print media are again the best entry into an understanding of the rhetorical stakes of the queer interpretive community. Besides, the development of the Internet expands the sites for public debate (apart from chat rooms, *www.*

queernet.org feeds many community and local tabloids with news items from around the world, enhancing solidarity and globalization of identity). [*See* Argumentation.]

Queer argumentation may be divided into three preferred argumentative techniques: the rule of reciprocity and arguments of transitivity; relations of coexistence; examples and models.

Rule of reciprocity and arguments of transitivity. As an agent in a civil rights battle, queer rhetoric makes ample use of the argument of reciprocity, which is systematically employed by queer communicators. The core of the debate around gays in the military in the United States and Britain and in registered partnerships in the European Union is based on the argument of reciprocity: the same treatment must be applied to two identical situations. Similarly, since the inception of registration of same-gender partnerships (1998), the Dutch *De Gay Krant* runs a "newly wed" page, while British *Oi!* makes subversive use of the argument of reciprocity by entitling its 1997 Christmas issue "Seasons bleatings, Tis the season of goodwill to all men . . . bollocks." South African queer magazines (*OUTright,* 1994), *Esteem* (1993–1994) and *Exit* (1980) use the "rainbow nation" concept of postapartheid society to give gay-inspired semantics a fresh twist of reciprocity. So do Canadian (and noticeably French-speaking Canadian) queer media in close keeping with that country's and province's very advanced charter on civil rights and diversity politics (*MTL Attitude,* 1993, "The Journal of the Queer Confederacy," the aptly named Quebecois *Divers Cité,* 1995, *Homo Sapiens,* 1994).

Arguments of transitivity are also particularly active in queer rhetoric because they allow for aligning gay and lesbian concerns, seemingly opposed, into common "queer" objectives. This is the editorial policy of the French glossy *Têtu* (founded in 1997) and of the French self-explanatory *Tribus* (founded in 1994), which both combine the intellectual style of the 1970s French homosexual revolutionary Front (FHAR) with the advocacy of a queer "tribe" (*tribu*) distinct from the rest of society. Similarly, *American Genre* (founded in 1991) argues for unity of objectives between gay men and women within diversity, for instance on the issue of breast cancer. Besides, with generational change, and as the queer community gains legal acceptance in the public sphere, transitivity arguments allow for diversification within the community, while retaining the generic qualities (British *Attitude* moved in 1997 from advocating "real men" to "where the boys are," in keeping with the new phenomenon of generational awareness, here British "laddism"). By implication, queer rhetoric now engages in yet another area of social deliberation long cast aside by mainstream debate, that of *posteritas,* in this case a studied argumentation about "senior gays," "founders," and "our sons and daughters": as a rhetorical tactic, *posteritas* allows for transitivity in terms of appreciating social and political gains and integrating generations within a single purview, a social compact long lost in the "straight" community.

Reciprocity and transitivity can be seen as the argumentative basis for gay and lesbian "pride," the mark of having argued successfully for a place in the ecology of public debate.

Relations of coexistence. Arguments based on coexistence are typically those that relate or equate a person, group, or community to their actions. Queer rhetoric places massive emphasis on evaluating public persons, whether queer or not, in relation to how they behave toward the queer nation or how they talk about it. In sum, the traditional question of *ēthos* is regularly put into play to evaluate who may or may not be a spokeperson, an orator, for the community.

The Advocate routinely charts levels of discrimination in the United States and in the world with the help of maps and statistics, which allow readers to position themselves and visualize relations of coexistence between, for instance, a holiday resort in Costa Rica and the level of discrimination in the country where it is located. "Sissy of the Year" is awarded by the same magazine to homophobes. Colombia's *Acénto* tries to respond to a beleaguered but well-to-do mainly gay community by drawing almost exclusively on American and European models, while Argentina's *NX* emulates *The Advocate* in the Spanish-speaking domain, including Spain. Such policies help queer readers to position themselves as members of an international community, outside the often prevalent oppression of their home environment. A queer *ēthos* thus takes shape beyond political

boundaries and rhetorically formulates what is and what is not acceptable for queer citizens.

Examples and models. Because arguing by example (or *exemplum*) implies regularity or even rules, queer rhetoric is particularly active in this area. [*See* Exemplum.] For instance, cases of gay bashing are systematically used to illustrate intolerance and oppression, whereas the growing number of judicial cases regarding adoption rights is instrumental in pushing forward the unifying agenda of a unified queer community. These examples serve to illustrate and to reinforce mottos such as "we are family," "we are brothers and sisters," "the queer nation," along with iconic symbols such as the equality (or *ex æquo* =) sign launched by the Human Rights Campaign in the United States and replicated in France. The underlying, systematically used argument is that "an injury to one is an injury to all." Thus, the example often functions rhetorically as an argument of division, a synecdochē, where the part speaks for the whole. [*See* Synecdochē.]

Argumentation by models takes two main forms. To begin with, queer rhetoric is rich in having sustained a stock of social narratives that operate like so many behavioral models. They include: the Stonewall riots in New York (1969), whose "imagined community" spirit is kept alive in the *Stonewall News,* the "gay money" theme ("pink pound," "pink dollar") and, typical of 1990s queer public sphere, the party "circuit," the Gay Games (every four years, since 1982, sometimes larger than the Olympic games). There are the EuroPride and national Gay pride events, as well as national "coming out" days (emblematized, in 1998 for its tenth anniversary, by a famous Keith Haring painting), and the Sydney, Australia Gay and Lesbian Mardi Gras. They are now being supplemented by the celebration and recounting of gay Holocaust survivors and the incipient formation of gay Holocaust memorials and narratives. These rituals of identity function, first, as regulated and regulating models for social and personal behavior, even as pedagogic models for younger queers. Second, models operate also as a celebration of queer life devoid of political instability, offering the image of a life well regulated, without impediments or constraints, public life directed by internalized, reasonable choices and not simply through responding to external pressures, apposite to the newer generation of queers (as evident in *TWN,* the new *Attitude*). Public argumentation in turn forms the basis for understanding a specific conflict within queer rhetoric, a conflict of aims.

A Conflict of Aims. Queer rhetoric has given the gay and lesbian civil rights movement instruments, in terms of *inventio* and *argumentatio,* for deliberating on social issues and reclaiming full citizenship rights, at least in Western-style postmodern democracies, while expanding and enriching the scope of public deliberation in such societies. However, the main point of contention between queer agents concerns the relation between given aims and guiding aims, a tension caused by attempting successfully to convince the imagined community and outsiders or friends, while applying available means of persuasion in order to make an argument. Queer rhetoric strikingly illustrates, especially in a postmodern "rhetorical democracy" framework, a tension between these aims. This tension is seen at work in two specific areas, outing and gay marriages. [*See* Deliberative genre.]

Outing, a tactic used since the 1990s by the radical ACT UP, but now on the decline, a measure of its success, consists in making public the homosexuality of a public figure whose public actions are seen as detrimental to the queer civil rights movement. Those who oppose outing contend that privacy ought to be respected (a guiding aim), although they do not disapprove of the given aim, namely to persuade the outed person to be true to himself or herself. Those in favor of the tactic argue for another guiding aim, that a public persona should be entirely public and accountable to his or her community. Regardless of the value of the arguments exchanged, the rhetorical crucible they illustrate is a weighing of a given aim against a guiding aim—to brazenly censure by outing and beyond that, to better integrate identity politics within the public ecology of deliberation. The result has often been a series of public admissions of homosexuality by public figures, regardless of whether their politics afterward were indeed actively supportive of gay and lesbian rights. This phenomenon is quite unique to queer rhetoric.

As for gay marriages, the debate revolves around the definition of what constitutes citizenship in a democratic society. Contrary to the usual identity and community politics (here, mainly religious values that see the family and not the individual as being central to the social compact), the debate maintains not only that it is the individual who has sole rights but also that he or she has the ability to argue for their reality as *universal* rights as they are proposed in any democracy. Thus, queer rhetoric sheds light on the postmodern conflict regarding citizenship rights between the guiding aim of democratic deliberation, by which the individual is a sovereign and free agent, making reasonable choices, as an individual, and its given aim (how to convince *democratic* subjects that holding *family* rights is a contradiction). There is no other domain of public deliberation that better illustrates this tension within a postmodern rhetorical democracy. It is this vivacity of queer rhetoric in arguing for common values that accounts for its largely epideictic strain.

Creating Values. Queer rhetoric is largely epideictic inasmuch as, stemming from a rebuttal of traditional censure, it offered itself as a "celebration" of gay and lesbian culture. Symbolically, at a time when expressions of national pride are at their lowest ebb in Western democracies, the queer movement harnessed to its aims a social style of deliberation that, taken in the wider framework of postmodern societies, is an oddity. The theme of "pride" is multifarious: the word itself (by contrast "national pride" no longer forms part of standard political vocabulary), the waving of rainbow flags (at a time when national flags have nearly lost all appeal to *pathos* and *ēthos* in Western democracies), the constant celebration of queer exemplary lives, the visible presence in the streets of the queer nation, the holding of festivals and rituals that attract mainstream "straight" attention and participation. [*See* Ēthos; *and* Pathos.] All these are elements of a certain style. More profoundly, they are also elements of the reemergence, in postmodern societies diffident toward such expressions of communal fervor, of what might be termed a *rhetorical link.* [*See* Epideictic genre.]

This link is largely celebratory, epideictic. It is based upon the sharing of common values and their public recitation. The end of the first generation of queer activists (to be "visible") has turned into a method of social integration. It relies on an *ēthos*, exemplary figures of authority, often invented after the fact. It relies heavily on appeals to *pathos*, the emotions specifically linked to the upholding of democratic and secular values, of which queers see themselves as the last true defenders in the face of a perceived general apathy. It sustains a remarkably strong and innovative *logos*, a system of public argumentation.

The commodification and commercialization of queer culture act further as powerful agents for the dissemination of such values and such rhetorical strategies, beyond elite-making rhetoric, to the extent that mainstream communicators have adopted queer images to market their products: appeal has now passed onto once frowned-upon images. Such commodification and commercialization have also fostered within the extended queer community (parents, friends, coworkers) and the 1990s straight generation (which was less impacted upon by prejudices regarding gender) a sense of "rhetorical tradition" (that is, rhetorical turns that are habitually used as norms for social verbal or iconic interaction). The cosmetic appeal integral to queer "desire" rhetoric must not be underestimated (Browning 1993). [*See* Logos.]

Finally, queers have successfully argued for being one of the most active agents in the full integration of values still abstractly dormant in postmodern democracies, namely full equality and secularization, by correlating the sovereignty of individuals to the effectiveness of an interpretive community.

BIBLIOGRAPHY

Primary sources of queer rhetoric remain tabloids, newspapers, and community bulletins, as well as magazines and periodicals. Several of the most significant are mentioned in the preceding essay. These are at best only a sampling, but they underscore the necessity of exploring transient materials for this evolving subject.

Among secondary sources, the following are important:

Browning, Frank. *The Culture of Desire.* New York, 1993.
Chesebro, James W., ed. *Gayspeak: Gay Male and Lesbian Communication.* New York, 1981.
Edelman, Lee. *Homographesis: Essays in Gay Literary and Cultural Theory.* New York, 1994.
Herdt, Gilbert, ed. *Gay Culture in America: Essays from the Field.* Boston, 1993.

Leap, William L. *Word's Out: Gay Men's English.* Minneapolis, 1996.
Ringer, Jeffrey. *Queer Words, Queer Images: Communication and the Construction of Homosexuality.* New York, 1994.
Smith, Ralph R., and Russel R. Windes. "The Progay and Antigay Issue Culture: Interpretation, Influence and Dissent." *Quarterly Journal of Speech* 83.1 (1997), pp. 28–48. An excellent bibliography.
　　　　　　　　　　　—PHILIPPE-JOSEPH SALAZAR

QUESTIONING. Rhetoric has always been conceived as dealing with propositions or theses. With such a definition, rhetoric could only be considered as the weak child of Reason, if not as its handicapped one. Science, and logic at large, are much better suited to establish the validity of a thesis or the acceptability of a proposition; but does rhetoric really debate propositions rather than alternatives, answers rather than questions or problems? Careful analysis shows that the subject matter of rhetoric is actually a problem or a question. The alternatives embedded in such questions often give rise to debate as well as to misunderstandings, to a plurality of readings as well as to the indeterminacy of the "right" answer, exclusive of all other possible ones.

One might object that unproblematic assertions, such as "John is now married to Rebecca," have nothing to do with questioning. But no one would ever proffer such a phrase without having the question of John's (or Rebecca's) status in mind. Moreover, that statement presupposes that *who* John is, *who* Rebecca is, and *what* marriage is are already known and out of the question. All those *when, where, who, what* (usually called the *wh*-interrogatives) are treated as answered by the very fact that noun-terms are used in order to condense those answers and eliminate thereby all problematicity. All questioning seems absent from such assertions: *who* John is, is presented as unproblematic, even if he is the one *who* is this or that. If someone did not understand the sentence, the locutor might then say, for example, "John is the one *who* did this and that, *who* is the son of Arthur." This explains why those *wh*-words are referential and are therefore meaningful. The consequence is that the meaning of the terms employed can be defined with the help of those interrogative clauses without altering the truth-value of the whole statement: "John is the husband of Rebecca" is then logically and semantically equivalent to "John is the man *who* got married to Rebecca," or is equivalent to "Arthur's son is married to Rebecca," since John (is the one *who*) is Arthur's son.

The terms we use in language are the results of answering processes that disappear when the original questions are solved, because those questions have ceased to be questions, enabling us thereby to condense propositions that specify their meaning. Those propositions are answers that do not stipulate in which respect they are answers. To know the meaning of a proposition is to know *what* is in question with the proposition, to what it is an answer. Questions that refer to the terms employed in a proposition can arise when meaning is at stake: "Who is John?" is a question that requires a relative clause that is an answer that takes up the question as being solved: "Oh, you didn't know? But John is the person *who* did this or that, or *who* is this or that." If the locutor did not resort to those clauses, it is because she thought that those questions did not arise in the mind of her interlocutor, because she thought they were solved in his mind.

Thus, all assertions are in effect answers: they refer back to questions, to those they solve as well as to those they raise. Interpretations, dialogues, reading, persuasion, communication, all rest upon this phenomenon. Rhetoric begins when some answer, instead of solving a problem, raises it, rendering the offered answer questionable and sometimes even denying the validity of that answer, by implying the opposite solution as in the case of a Freudian denial. Suppose there is a presidential election in some country and Mr. X is one of the candidates. If I say "Mr. X is a good candidate," there is no rhetoric implied in my statement since the latter is uttered as a reply to what is obviously an existing problem. Now, if I or his opponent, for instance, claim that "Mr. X is an honest person," then the situation is totally different, because nobody asked whether X was honest. My statement raises the question of X's honesty, casting a possible doubt on him. That is where rhetoric begins, because my statement is understood as a question, that is, as an object for possible debate.

As to the rhetorical feature of what is called denial or denegation, it cannot be analyzed without reference to questioning. If I say "I have nothing against you," I imply that the question of my hostility toward you does not exist at the same time as I raise that very question, namely by giving it an answer. This answer destroys itself in the contradiction, and the only one that remains is the alternative, "I have something against you." Other contexts exist in everyday life where rhetoric prevails, for instance when someone wants her interlocutor to infer the answer without affirming it bluntly. Such a strategy is adopted in order to lead the interlocutor to adhere to a conclusion that *he or she* will draw, rather than impose that conclusion which could induce questioning if it were put explicitly on the table. If my son feels that I could express negative dispositions toward his girlfriend, he could say, for instance, that "She is not only beautiful but even clever." The reinforcement of the positive attributes is meant to foster a positive reply on my part; and rather than requiring it explicitly from me, my son prefers to let me attain that answer by myself, in order to make such a conclusion *mine* rather than his.

Rhetoric, in contrast to other arts of discourse, deals with the questions that are implicit in a given context or that remain posed in spite of the answer offered. Explicit disagreement can arise or silent acceptance can ensue, depending on the rhetorical skillfulness of the locutor. One can approve of an answer and think that the question is solved thereby. One can find it pleasant because it is well said. One can also reject it and problematize it afresh with new arguments. All those responses pertain to what is called rhetoric, as much as those figurative and speech devices that are intended to keep (as much as possible) all problematization in the background.

[*See also* Invention; *and* Problematology.]

—MICHEL MEYER

R

READER RESPONSE. *See* Reception theory.

REBUTTAL. *See* Invention.

RECEPTION THEORY. The term *reception theory* is commonly used to designate a direction in literary criticism developed by professors and students at the University of Constance in West Germany during the late 1960s and early 1970s. In general, the members of the Constance School advocated turning to the reading and reception of literary texts instead of to traditional methods that emphasize the production of texts or a close examination of texts themselves. Their approach is therefore related to reader response criticism in the United States, although advocates of reception theory were for a time much more homogeneous in their theoretical presuppositions and general outlook than their American counterparts. Reception theory, sometimes referred to as "the aesthetics of reception" or "reception aesthetics" (*Rezeptionsästhetik*), dominated literary theory in Germany for about a decade. It was virtually unknown in the English-speaking world until around 1980, when it was made more readily accessible by the translation of the most seminal works. Hans Robert Jauss and Wolfgang Iser are the two most original theorists of the Constance School, although several of Jauss's students, among them Rainer Warning, Hans Ulrich Gumbrecht, and Karlheinz Stierle, also made important contributions to this branch of theory. In response to the writings of Jauss and Iser, scholars from the German Democratic Republic (GDR) such as Robert Weimann, Manfred Naumann, and Rita Schober raised objections to some propositions and suggested Marxist alternatives, leading to the most productive East–West dialogue in postwar Germany. In the 1980s, prominent American critics responded to reception theory as well.

The rise of reception theory to preeminence in the Federal Republic has to do with a number of societal and institutional factors, chief among which were the turbulence and subsequent restructuring of higher education in West Germany during the late 1960s and early 1970s. Reception theory comes out of a climate of change and reform and is itself a signal of a decisive shift in direction in postwar German critical methods. Indeed, the history of literary criticism in postwar Germany can be divided into two major phases, with a turning point occurring in 1967 when reception theory burst onto the scene. For the first two decades of the postwar era, most scholars adhered to traditional forms of research informed by the positivistic, historicist, or existential–phenomenological heritage. The most popular introductory works to the study of literature were staunchly conservative, and, like New Criticism, extolled texts for their linguistic perfections or as self-contained works of art. By the midsixties, however, the demand for change had become apparent. On the one hand, external pressures emanating from the student movement called into question traditional values and methods, and this more general radicalization of the universities had a significant effect on scholarly methods. The reevaluation of the canon, the demand for a critical approach that had relevance beyond the walls of academia, and the politicization of literature itself during these years seemed to evoke an altered view of literary theory. On the other hand, scholars themselves, having sufficiently recovered from their anti-ideological reaction to the National Socialist perversion of the university, began to reexamine their role as mediators of knowledge. And in doing so, they started to recognize the inadequacy of the dominant practices in their discipline, especially the popular notion that close reading and a careful attention to textual details were the most fundamentally sound procedures for dealing with works of literature.

An inaugural address at the University of Constance in April 1967 marks the beginning of reception theory. This lecture was delivered by the newly-appointed scholar of Romance languages, Hans Robert Jauss, and the title echoed another famous inaugural essay, one held on the eve of the French Revolution at the University of Jena by the playwright, theorist, and historian Friedrich Schiller. Schiller had spoken on the topic: "Was heisst und zu welchem Ende studiert man Universalgeschichte" (What is and for what purpose does one study universal history?). Jauss modified this title by substituting the word *Literatur-* (literary) for *Universal,* but this slight alteration did not diminish the revolutionary impact at all. Jauss suggested, as Schiller had in 1789, that the present age needed to restore vital links between the artifacts of the past and the concerns of the present. For literary scholarship and instruction, such a connection can be established only if literary history is no longer relegated to the periphery of the discipline, Jauss maintained. He therefore sought to prod his colleagues into a new era of historical criticism, and the revised title to this lecture when it was published as the lead essay in the volume (1970) that bears the same name, "Literaturgeschichte als Provokation der Literaturwissenschaft" (Literary History as a Provocation to Literary Scholarship), captures the innovative challenge that Jauss desired.

The approach to literary texts that Jauss outlined in his lecture became known as *Rezeptionsästhetik.* It should be understood as an attempt to overcome what Jauss viewed as limitations in two important and putatively opposed literary theories: Marxist Criticism and Formalism. For Jauss, Marxism represented an outmoded approach to literature, related to an older positivist paradigm. Yet Jauss also recognized in this body of criticism, especially in the writings of less orthodox Marxists like Werner Krauss, Roger Garaudy, and Karel Kosík, a fundamentally correct concern with the historicity of literature. The Formalists, on the other hand, are credited with introducing aesthetic perception as a theoretical tool for exploring literary works. However, Jauss also detected in their works the tendency to isolate art from its historical context, a *l'art-pour-l'art* aesthetics that valorizes the synchronic over the diachronic. The task for a new literary history, therefore, becomes one of successfully merging the best qualities of Marxism and Formalism. This merger can be accomplished by satisfying the Marxist demand for historical mediation while retaining the Formalist advances in the realm of aesthetic perception.

Rezeptionsästhetik proposed to do this by altering the perspective from which we normally interpret literary texts. Traditional literary histories were composed from the perspective of the producers of texts; Jauss proposed that we can truly understand literature as a process by recognizing the constitutive role of the consuming or reading subject. The interaction between author and public replaces literary biography as the basis for literary historiography. Thus Jauss meets the Marxist demand for historical mediation by situating literature in the larger continuum of events; he retains the Formalist achievements by placing the perceiving consciousness at the center of his concerns. History and aesthetics, which seemed to be irreconcilable, are united in his theory. The historical significance of a work is not established by qualities of the work or by the genius of its author, but by the chain of receptions from generation to generation. In terms of literary history, Jauss thus envisioned a historiography that will play a conscious, mediating role between past and present. The historian of literary reception is called upon to rethink continuously the works of the canon in light of how they have affected, and are affected by, current conditions and events. Past meanings are understood as part of the prehistory of present experiencing.

The integration of history and aesthetics is to be accomplished largely by examining what Jauss called the *Erwartungshorizont* (horizon of expectation). This methodological centerpiece of his theory is an obvious adaptation of the notion of *Horizont* (horizon), found most prominently in the hermeneutic theory of Jauss's teacher, Hans-Georg Gadamer. For Gadamer, the horizon is a fundamental tenet for the hermeneutical situation. It refers primarily to our situatedness in the world, our necessarily perspectival and limited purview. Jauss's use of the term is slightly different. For him, it denotes an intersubjective system or structure of expectations, a pattern of references, or a mind-set that a hypothetical individual brings to a given text. All works are read against some horizon of expectation; indeed, certain types of texts—parody is the best example—intentionally foreground this horizon. The task of the literary scholar, Jauss suggests, is to "objectify" the horizon, so that we may evaluate the artistic character of the work of art. This assessment is most readily accomplished when the work in question thematizes its horizon. But even works whose horizon is less obvious can be examined with this method. Generic, literary, and linguistic aspects of the work in question can be used to construct a probable horizon of expectation.

After establishing the horizon of expectation, the critic can then proceed to determine the artistic merit of a given work by measuring the distance between the work and the horizon. Jauss employs a fundamentally deviationist model: the aesthetic value of a text is seen as a function of its departure from a given norm. If the expectations of a reader are not "disappointed" or violated, then the text will approach the culinary; if, on the other hand, it breaks through the horizon, then it will be a work of high art. Sometimes a work may break its horizon of expectation and yet remain unrecognized as a great work of art in its own epoch. This case poses no problems for Jauss's theory. The first experience of disrupted expectations will almost invariably evoke strong negative responses from its initial audience, but the original negativity will disappear for later readers. The reason for this delay is that in a later age the horizon has changed, so that the work in question no longer ruptures expectations, or at least not to the same extent. Instead, it may be recognized as a classic, that is, as a work that itself has contributed in an essential way to the establishment of a new horizon of expectation.

Jauss's historical approach to understanding literary works was complemented by Wolfgang Iser's examination of the interaction between reader and text. Like Jauss, Iser attracted a great deal of attention with his inaugural lecture at Constance, but his theory is perhaps best represented in his book *Der Akt des Lesens* (The Act of Reading, 1976/1978). What has interested Iser from the outset is the question of how and under what conditions a text has meaning for a reader. In contrast to traditional interpretation, which sought to elucidate a hidden meaning in the text, he wanted to see meaning as the result of an in-

teraction between text and reader, as an effect that is experienced, not an object that must be found. Roman Ingarden's conception of the literary work of art thus provided him with a useful framework for investigation. According to Ingarden, the aesthetic object is constituted only through an act of cognition on the part of the reader. Adopting this fundamental precept from Ingarden, Iser thus switched the focus from the text as object to the text as potential, from the results of a reading to the act of reading itself.

To examine the interaction between text and reader, Iser looks at those qualities in the text that make it readable or that influence our reading, and at those features of the reading process that are essential for understanding the text. Particularly in his early work he adopted the term *implied reader* to encompass both of these functions; it is at once textual structure and structured act. Later, depending more heavily on Ingarden's terminology, he distinguished between the text, its concretization, and the work of art. The first is the artistic aspect, what is placed there for us to read by the author, and it may be conceived best as a potential waiting to be realized. Concretization, by contrast, refers to the product of our own productive activity; it is the realization of the text in the mind of the reader, accomplished by the filling in of *Leerstellen* (blanks or gaps) to eliminate indeterminacy. Finally, the work of art is neither text nor concretization, but something in between. It occurs at the point of convergence of text and reader, a point that can never be completely defined.

The work of art is characterized by its virtual nature and is constituted by various overlapping procedures. One of these involves the dialectic of *protention* and *retention,* two terms borrowed from the phenomenological theory of Edmund Husserl (1859–1938). Iser applies them to our activity in reading successive sentences. In confronting a text, we continuously project expectations that may be fulfilled or disappointed; at the same time our reading is conditioned by foregoing sentences and concretizations. Because our reading is determined by this dialectic, it acquires the status of an event and can give us the impression of a real occurrence. If this is so, however, our interaction with texts must compel us to endow our concretizations with a degree of consistency—

or at least as much consistency as we admit to reality. This involvement with the text is seen as a type of entanglement in which the foreign is grasped and assimilated. Iser's point is that the reader's activity is similar to actual experience. Although Iser distinguishes between *Wahrnehmung* (perception) and *Vorstellung* (ideation), structurally these two processes are identical. According to Iser, reading therefore temporarily eliminates the traditional subject–object dichotomy. At the same time, however, the subject is compelled to split into two parts, one that undertakes the concretization and another that merges with the author, or at least the constructed image of the author. Ultimately, the reading process involves a dialectical process of self-realization and change: by filling in the gaps in the text, we simultaneously reconstruct ourselves. Our encounters with literature are part of an enlightenment process in which we come to understand others and ourselves more completely.

Iser's model of reading has been productively supplemented in the work of Karlheinz Stierle, the most incisive second-generation theorist from the Constance School during the seventies. Stierle proceeded from Iser's contention that the formation of illusions and images is essential for the reading process, and labeled this level of reading "quasi-pragmatic," a designation that distinguishes it from the reception of nonfictional texts ("pragmatic reception"). While Iser seemed to remain on this plane in his studies, Stierle suggested that a quasi-pragmatic reading must be supplemented with higher forms of reception capable of doing justice to the peculiarities of fiction. He argued for a pseudoreferential use of language, an application located between its usage in simple reference and its autoreferential function. What distinguishes narrative fiction is this pseudoreferentiality, which may be considered autoreferentiality in the guise of referential forms. Fiction is self-referential, although it appears to be referential. What Stierle suggested, therefore, is an additional reflexive level of understanding in our encounter with literary texts.

The critics of the Constance School from the German Democratic Republic approached the accomplishments of reception theory from a somewhat different stance. Robert Weimann and Man-

fred Naumann were not so interested in the reading process outlined by Iser and Stierle as they were in the literary historiography developed by Jauss. Their objections to his theory were threefold. First, they complained of one-sidedness, claiming that reception theory had gone too far in emphasizing the response to a work of art. While they admitted that reception is an important aspect—and one that had perhaps been downplayed somewhat in the Marxist tradition—Jauss and his colleagues, in positing reception as the sole criterion for a revitalization of literary history, destroy the dialectic of production and reception. Second, Marxist critics detected a danger in the totally subjective apprehension of art and the resultant relativizing of literary history. The problem here is that if we follow Jauss (and Gadamer) in relinquishing all objective notions of the work of art, then our access to history would seem to be completely arbitrary, because it is ceaselessly changing. Finally, the Constance School model of reception theory provided scant sociological grounding for the reader who supposedly stands at the center of its concerns. Scholars from the GDR found a general failure to link literary history with larger concerns. The reader in the reception theory of Jauss and Iser, they claimed, is conceived as an idealized individual, rather than as a social entity with political and ideological, as well as aesthetic dimensions.

The theories of Jauss and Iser have experienced a quite different reception from critics in the United States. Although Iser has been generally admired in the Anglophone world, his work was subjected to truculent criticism by Stanley Fish (1981), who objected to the opposition determinacy/indeterminacy. Fish questioned the status of the blanks that are constitutive, according to Iser, of the reader's activity. While Iser suggests that blanks exist objectively in the text and independent of the reader, Fish contends that they do not exist before a prior act of interpretation. For Fish, our interactions with texts are always conventional, and therefore, blanks cannot be conceived as given entities. What we see or understand is always already informed by a prior perspective or framework that enables the very seeing and understanding. Thus, there are no determinate objects for interpretation but only interpreted objects that are erroneously called determinate. Fish, however, does not validate a totally arbitrary, subjective indeterminacy; indeed, he disputes the notion of indeterminacy on the same grounds that he rejected determinacy. Because we are always operating inside of an interpretive framework, and have no access to a subjectivity unconstrained by conventions, indeterminacy, considered as the locus of the individual contribution to the meaning of a text, is impossible. While Fish argues, on the one hand, that there is nothing in the text that is given or determinate, and that everything is supplied, he also maintains that nothing is supplied and everything is given. The paradox dissolves once one recognizes that he has simply viewed the problem of reading texts from the perspective of a code or convention that informs and determines individual response. Iser's theory may be an efficient machine for producing interpretations, but every component in such an account is itself the consequence of a particular interpretive strategy that only possesses validity within a particular system of intelligibility.

The reception of Jauss's work by the deconstructionist critic Paul de Man is of a somewhat different nature. What de Man finds lacking about the aesthetics of reception is its inattentiveness to language, manifested in its illicit equating of the phenomenal and the linguistic realm. The hermeneutics of experience, the arena in which Jauss operates, and the hermeneutics of reading are not necessarily compatible. De Man is particularly concerned that the notion of a "horizon of expectation" is not applicable to linguistic phenomena. Jauss's deficiency can be attributed to his neglect of theorists who are attentive to the stability of signification and the determinacy of the signifier. De Man chastises Jauss for failing to integrate the insights of French poststructuralist theorists, in particular for ignoring the linguistically unavoidable ambiguities accompanying any text. Another way to understand de Man's objection involves the claim that Jauss suppresses the potentially destructive force of rhetoric in order to complete his unification of poetics and hermeneutics unaffected by the disruption of the letter. De Man argues that the inclusion of a horizon of expectation as the focal point for *Rezeptionsästh-*

etik makes it a "conservative" enterprise. With respect to the oppositions classical/modern and mimetic/allegorical, Jauss always identifies with the former terms. The use of the horizon metaphor for understanding suggests perception, and understanding is brought into the proximity of the sensory. Jauss is guilty of an illicit identification of word and world that linguistically-sensitive critics carefully avoid. For de Man, the aesthetics of reception, despite its significant insights, appears as a method that fails to break with familiar and conservative presuppositions about the nature of literary texts.

Jauss and Iser have defended their positions against these and other objections in polemical rejoinders during the seventies and eighties. They have also modified and refined theoretical positions based on criticism. But the cost of these corrections has been a loss of the original excitement that had surrounded the emergence of reception theory in the late sixties and early seventies. Both Jauss and Iser subsequently took directions that depart somewhat from their most influential work. Increasingly, Iser concerned himself with the notions of the imaginary in fiction; most recently, he has turned his attention to the anthropological dimension of literature. As early as 1972, Jauss revised his theory significantly: his magnum opus, *Ästhetische Erfahrung und literarische Hermeneutik* (Aesthetic Experience and Literary Hermeneutics, 1977 and 1982); developed a more differentiated notion of response to texts, situating the primarily deviationist model of the "Provocation" essay as one alternative among many. This work, however, has enjoyed a comparatively smaller impact on critical circles in Germany, and one could argue that reception theory as a unified approach to literature ceased to exist by the early eighties. The Constance School, on the other hand, survived the demise of its most important theoretical product by virtue of the personalities of its members and the biannual scholarly colloquia held there. Throughout the 1980s and 1990s, the meetings of the group "Poetik und Hermeneutik," so important for the advent of reception theory, continued to produce some of the most exciting contributions of literary, cultural, and philosophical criticism in Germany.

[*See also* Criticism; *and* Hermeneutics.]

BIBLIOGRAPHY

Primary Sources

Gumbrecht, Hans Ulrich. "Konsequenzen der Rezeptionsästhetik oder Literaturwissenschaft als Kommunikationssoziologie." *Poetica* 7 (1975); pp. 388–413.

Iser, Wolfgang. *Die Appellstruktur der Texte: Unbestimmtheit als Wirkungsbedingung literarischer Prosa.* Konstanz, 1970; "Indeterminacy and the Reader's Response in Prose Fiction." In *Aspects of Narrative: Selected Papers from the English Institute,* edited by J. Hillis Miller, pp. 1–45. New York, 1971.

Iser, Wolfgang. *Der implizite Leser: Kommunikationsformen des Romans von Bunyan bis Beckett.* Munich, 1972; *The Implied Reader: Patterns of Communication in Prose Fiction from Bunyan to Beckett.* Baltimore, 1974.

Iser, Wolfgang. "The Current Situation of Literary Theory: Key Concepts and the Imaginary." *New Literary History* 11 (1979), pp. 1–20.

Jauss, Hans Robert. "Paradigmawechsel in der Literaturwissenschaft." *Linguistische Berichte* 3 (1969), pp. 44–56.

Jauss, Hans Robert. *Kleine Apologie der ästhetischer Erfahrung.* Konstanzer Universitätsreden 59. Constance, Germany, 1972.

Jauss, Hans Robert. *Toward an Aesthetic of Reception.* Theory and History of Literature 2. Minneapolis, 1982.

Naumann, Manfred. "Das Dilemma der 'Rezeptionsästhetik.'" *Poetica* 8 (1976), pp. 451–466.

Naumann, Manfred et al. *Gesellschaft-Literatur-Lesen:Literaturrezeption in theoretischer Sicht.* Weimar, Germany, 1973.

Schober, Rita. *Abbild, Sinnbild, Wertung: Aufsätze zur Theorie und Prais literarischer Kommunikation.* Berlin, 1982.

Stierle, Karlheinz. *Text als Handlung: Perspektiven einer systematischen Literaturwissenschaft.* Munich, 1975.

Stierle, Karlheinz. "Was heisst Rezeption bei fiktionalen Texten?" *Poetica* 7 (1975), pp. 345–387; English (abbreviated): "The Reading of Fictional Texts." *In The Reader in the Text: Essays on Audience and Interpretation,* edited by Susan R. Suleiman and Inge Crosman, pp. 83–105. Princeton, 1980.

Warning, Rainer, ed. *Rezeptionsästhetik: Theorie und Praxis.* Munich, 1975.

Weimann, Robert. "'Rezeptionsästhetik' und die Krise der Literaturgeschichte: Zur Kritik einer neuen Strömung in der bürgerlichen Literaturwissenschaft." *Weimarer Beiträge* 19.8 (1973), pp. 5–33; "'Reception Aesthetics' and the Crisis of Literary History." *Clio* 5 (1975), pp. 3–33.

Weimann, Robert. "'Rezeptionsästhetik' oder das Ungenügen an der bürgerlichen Bildung: Zur Kritik einer Theorie literarischer Kommunikation." *Kunstensemble und Öffentlichkeit,* edited by Robert Weimann, pp. 85–133. Halle-Leipzig, Germany, 1982.

Weinrich, Harald. "Für eine Literaturgeschichte des Lesers." *Merkur* 21 (1967), pp. 1026–1038.

Supplementary List

Bürger, Peter. "Probleme der Rezeptionsforschung." *Poetica* 9 (1977), pp. 446–471.

Fish, Stanley. "Why No One's Afraid of Wolfgang Iser." *Diacritics* 11.1 (1981), pp. 2–13.

Fokkema, D. W., and Elrud Kunne-Ibsch. "The Reception of Literature: Theory and Practice of 'Rezeptionsästhetik.'" In *Theories of Literature in the Twentieth Century,* edited by D. W. Fokkema and E. Kunne-Ibsch, pp. 136–164. New York, 1977.

Grimm, Gunter. *Rezeptionsgeschichte: Grundlegung einer Theorie.* Munich, 1977.

Hohendahl, Peter Uwe, ed. *Sozialgeschichte und Wirkungsästhetik: Dokumente zur empirischen und marxistischen Rezeptionsforschung.* Frankfurt, 1974.

Holub, Robert C. *Reception Theory: A Critical Introduction.* London, 1984.

Link, Hannelore. "'Die Appellstruktur der Texte' und 'ein Paradigmawechsel in der Literaturwissenschaft.'" *Jarhbuch der deutschen Schillergesellschaft* 17 (1973), pp. 532–583.

Solms, Wilhelm, and Norbert Schöll. "Rezeptionsästhetik." *Literturwissenschaft heute,* edited by Friedrich Nemec and Wilhlem Solms, pp. 154–196. Munich, 1979.

Zimmermann, Bernhard. *Literturrezeption im historischen Prozess: Zur Theorie einer Rezeptionsgeschichte der Literatur.* Munich, 1977.

—ROBERT C. HOLUB

RELIGION. All religious systems are rhetorical, states a modern theory, because they strive to communicate truth. It argues for a distinctive rhetoric of religion, based on authoritative proclamation, not rational persuasion, with the speaker's character as dominant. It appeals to a concept of the sacred text, defined as annunciative and revelatory, not demonstrative and inferential, that is immediate and imaginative, absolute and urgent in demanding assent. The theory depends on the conviction that Greek rhetoric conceptualized a universal communicative habit, which historically and culturally exhibited only minor variations of arrangement or style. This essentialist definition falters not only on professional rejection by classical philosophy but also on disagreement about the nature of religion, whether it is indeed systematic and whether its end is truth. It further elides the distinction between revelation and theology. The plurality and diversity of religious manifestations and beliefs, through centuries and across cultures, recommends an investigation of the particular.

Scripture. Sayings of Buddha (c.563–c.483 BCE) and Confucius (c.551–c.479 BCE) evidence rhetorical method in ancient China and India, but it was never developed as a theoretical discipline. The origins of the primary Western religions—Judaism, Christianity, and Islam—are also oral. The foundational discourse is only preserved in writing, however, with its orality continued in communal readings. The sacred texts of Judaism and Christianity are collected in the Bible, whose canon comprises the Hebrew Scriptures and the New Testament. Islam reveres the Qur'ān. Although medieval Arabic scholars developed for it a stylistic hermeneutics, their treatises were not influential beyond Islam, and Qur'ān remains the province of specialists. [*See* Arabic rhetoric; Chinese rhetoric; *and* Indian rhetoric.]

The Hebrew Scriptures were not composed or edited as the product of a deliberate rhetorical culture that understood them as artful persuasion in the classical sense. Yet, even prior to Hellenism, there is evidence dating to the fifth century BCE of a formulaic rhetoric utilizing topics in Israelite military orations by priests. Formal training is suggested by the schools of writing and speaking under the prophets. The biblical invention of narrative, against the epic of other ancient religions, has been represented as construing the divine actions as rhetorical, imitating them by its choice of genre, and prescribing the texts for ritual use, so that it is subject to rhetorical interpretation. The complex cultural exchange of Hellenization was reflected religiously in the historiography of the late biblical *2 Maccabees,* in apocalyptic–pseudepigraphic and wisdom literatures, and in the Dead Sea scrolls. Classical rhetorical forms have been discerned in later Jewish exegesis, in rabbinical principles, and in commentaries, or midrashim. The rabbi Hillel's introduction of Greek hermeneutical terms and rules to Pharasaic circles decisively organized and stimulated mishraic inquiry. Methods of Alexandrian *rhētors* also influenced the treatment of Jewish legal texts. Parallels between Pharasiac and Tannaitic literature and Hellenistic texts are prominent in genres associated with sages, such as anecdotes, consolations, and gnomes, and in pedagogical themes. Such coincidences reflect the intensifying familiarity of urban elites, particularly rabbis, with Greek language and Hellenistic culture, whose literature they adapted, while developing their own inheritance. Acculturation was approved in midrashim on Noah's blessing for the sons who had covered his nakedness (*Gn.* 9.27). [*See* Hebrew rhetoric.]

The reverse impact of Jewish rhetoric on Greco-Roman theory and practice, the rabbinic development of an alternative, is barely under investigation. Jewish rhetoric generally awaits critical attention. There is no tradition of a rhetorical interpretation of the Hebrew Scriptures as argumentative; any criticism has been stylistic. Although Jewish exegetical methods do not explicate a rhetorical theory, they do display strategic purposes that are intrinsically worthwhile and that were influential on early Christian hermeneutics. The contemporary classical treatise *De sublimitate* cited *Genesis* as exemplary, and many Christian authors examined the "Old Testament" for tropes and figures. The earliest extant work on the rhetoric of the Hebrew Scriptures, Judah Messer Leon's *The Book of the Honeycomb's Flow* (fifteenth century), dates only to the Renaissance.

Christianity defined itself both against and within its contextual cultures, Jewish and Greek. The New Testament authors contrasted the novelty of their speech with classical rhetoric, egregiously in Paul's antitheses of human persuasion and divine power, eloquent wisdom and foolish crucifixion. Nevertheless, they abundantly employed not only its customary figures but also its argumentative patterns. The appropriation of Greek literary conventions had been initiated by Egyptian Jews, notably Philo, who recast the biblical narrative in a classical mold through drama, historiography, poetry, and philosophy. Yet a distinction between a Hellenized Diaspora and a Jewish Palestine is untenable, since the prevalence of the Greek language in first-century Palestine conveyed the very ideas and imagery of

Hellenism. It is probable that Jesus spoke Greek, as did native early Christians. In first-century Palestine rhetoric was the sole subject of secondary education. Although the New Testament authors may not have studied it formally, they were exposed to it in oral and written forms, from official documents to private correspondence, in public courts and celebratory assemblies, and in poetic and prosaic literature. The tradition of Christian exegesis, patristic through early modern, recognized this dependence by reading the New Testament through classical rhetoric.

Although the citation of classical texts is rare, similarities abound—if inferior to the standards. Rhetorical units have been identified in the Jesus traditions: the common source (Q) of sayings for the gospels of *Matthew* and *Luke,* and the pronouncement stories prior to *Mark.* The message, or *kērygma,* was proclaimed as religiously authoritative, not rationally persuasive. This distinctive material, neither mythological nor theological, emphasized the authority of Jesus as unique and decisive by his own declaration. The Pauline epistles, *kerygmatically* addressed to the congregations of the Christ, represented a different rhetoric. The issue of authority diverged from that of Jesus as master to that of the apostle as preacher. The gospels merged the affirmations of authority by conferring a plot on teaching to create a narrative of the ministry and passion of Jesus the Christ. This progression beyond classical rhetoric, which lacked a theory of narrative, is as yet inadequately described in its purpose and method. However, the arrangement of the gospels is rhetorical: proem, early narrative, exposition of teaching, account of crucifixion, and epilogue. Stylistically *Matthew* is forceful; *Mark,* plain; *Luke,* elegant; *John,* elevated. Matthew applied rhetoric most broadly, by arranging the gospel into distinct parts with specific functions, by establishing the *ēthos* of Jesus' authority and the *pathos* of his suffering, and by offering probable reasons. Mark asserted absolute claims to authoritative proof without argument. Luke, an educated speaker of Greek who alone among the evangelists knew classical genre, presented an orderly narrative with precise details, exploiting classical *prosōpopoeia* and biography for Jesus' infancy. John employed logical argument to turn and reiterate his topics theologically. [*See* Ēthos; Pathos; *and* Prosōpopoeia.]

The *kērygma* was gradually supported by rhetorical reasoning, the enthymeme. [*See* Enthymeme.] New Testament rhetoric is sharply polemical, addressing two audiences simultaneously to achieve social definition by comparison and contrast. The speaker's character and credibility, or *ēthos* in classical theory, is fundamental. Authority dominates, as leaders compete for the right to speak by appealing to external guarantors of their beliefs, ultimately God. This stratagem distinguishes Christian from classical rhetoric, which relied on convention without extraordinary authorization. Arguments are classifiable into the rhetorical species: forensic (*2 Cor.*); deliberative, for the Sermon on the Mount (*Mt.* 5–7); and epideictic, for the Magnificat (*Lk.* 1.46–55), Jesus' consolation to his disciples (*Jn.* 14–17), and the peerless poem to love (*1 Cor.* 13). [*See* Deliberative genre; Epideictic genre; *and* Forensic genre.] Such assignments are determined with difficulty, since the Christian rhetorical situation did not correspond to the classical occasions. The epistle to the *Galatians,* the first book subjected to modern rhetorical criticism, is contested as either juridical or deliberative. New Testament authors manipulated and altered the conventional proofs and traditional topics, by substitution and creation, to promote the new society and its symbols. Characteristic is the profusion of tropes and figures. For lack of historical behavioral examples, a particularly malleable proof is analogy, from normal to odd. Invention to confer and strengthen Jesus' authority, based on external proofs, is both documentary and eyewitness: scriptural citations, such as prophecies; wondrous signs; and witnesses' names. In the modes of artistic proof, *ēthos* is, again, salient. *Pathos,* or affective response, most commonly involves reward and punishment. *Logos,* or probable argument, is largely replaced by divine authorization. Inductive argument employs examples from Jewish history or from daily life and nature, as in the parables. Deductive argument employs enthymemes, as in the beatitudes (*Mt.* 5.42–48). *Stasis* theory, or the issue of the case, appears in all of its types; so do all common types of topics, the places for a subject. The New Testament also displays practical school exercises in invention: the parable, corresponding to mythos; *chreia,* or the anecdote; the comparison; prosōpopoeia, the speech displaying character; and *ekphrasis,* the vivid portrayal of a scene. [*See* Descriptio; Logos; Stasis; *and* Topics.]

Criticism of the Pauline epistles has identified units—chapter to letter—and analyzed their usage of scriptural citation, epistolary formula, topical argumentation, antithesis, hyperbolē, rhetorical questions, themes of boasting and imitation, and lexical choice. The evidence for Paul's rhetorical education varies, but it may have included handbooks, since he is conversant in the Greek idiom of his audience and with epistolary conventions, and since he also refers to classical literature. The situation of his epistles in the context of communicative practices, oral and scribal, discloses a dynamic relationship between author and receivers, a fact augmented by their very preservation in a sect that multiplied. It grounds the formation of Christian doctrine in specific communal situations, against systematic theological attempts to identify general concepts and dogmas. The speeches in *Acts* by the evangelist Luke, skillfully written and inserted into the narrative, also dramatize Christian formation. Beyond method to doctrine: the very concept of faith (*pistis*) has been associated on semantic, historical, and analytical grounds with the concept of persuasion (*pistis*) that defined rhetoric. The model of trust, assent, and knowledge in faith corresponds to *ēthos, pathos,* and *logos.*

Tradition. Biblical texts were transmitted orally in liturgy, homily, *catēchēsis,* and private reading. Rhetoric powerfully shaped the early Church, identifying it within the environment of Judaic or Roman beliefs, and eventually constructing a Christian empire. The failure of the world to end necessitated an accommodation. Rhetoric was feared as encouraging personal ambition for fame and pride in success. It was decried as amoral and indecent, politically expedient, opinionated, mendacious—the source of heresy. The crucial religious objection was that it celebrated the pagan gods. Rhetoric and paganism appeared inseparable, since belief in the gods of state was intrinsic to the texts of the schools. Christians were deeply conflicted about rhetoric, vacillating between its temptation and promise. Rhetoric bristled with their broad tension of hostility to and sympathy for all secular disciplines. In theory these were vehemently denounced, in practice tolerantly adopted. The famous night-

mare of Jerome, editor of the Vulgate Bible, which damned him as a Ciceronian, did not scare many Christians from reading pagan literature under the covers. Rhetoric was inescapable: speakers and audiences, both educated in it, required and expected its art. Many theologians had been rhetors before their conversion and were unable to discard its habits, even if so consciously desired.

Their uneasy compromise was to convert rhetoric for Christian doctrine: to reject its idolatry but accept its inquiry. Church fathers compared their expediency luridly to sexual intercourse with female booty or to a cure extracted from poisonous snakes, or more mildly to handy baggage for life's journey. While renouncing oratorical puffery, the Greek fathers were devoted to the beauty of their language and cultivated a sophistic style. Gregory of Nazianzus (c.330–389) called the devil a Sophist but obeyed sophistic rules for excellence in its eloquence, structure, and motifs. [*See* Sophists.] The first Latin apologist, Tertullian (c.155–after 220 CE), theoretically opposed classical culture to Christian faith in a motto about Athens against Jerusalem; but practically he integrated them. His arguments were structured by invention and disposition and developed topically, and his exegesis was contextual. [*See* Arrangement, *article on* Traditional arrangement; Invention; *and* Style.] Ambivalence became the checkered career of rhetoric. A wary piety preferred the evangelical simplicity of a plain style, while eloquently transgressing its humility. The patristic accommodation of rhetoric was a synthesis without a theory. There was no unequivocal justification for acculturation, only a transferal of pagan customs to Christian values, as the human pleasures of rhetoric were subsumed to the divine praises.

Augustine (354–430 CE) is the most admired and honored of patristic authors, for his contribution in *De doctrina christiana* of a rhetorical rationale with principles for preaching. Yet this is an apologetics of pabulum. It set the style for the clerical resort to rhetoric as a sop to the laity. With intellectualist bias, Augustine reduced Scripture, already lamented as crude, to divine baby talk. All imagery, even religious, was carnal fiction, prone to deception, capable merely of verisimilitude. In his opposition of fable and doctrine, even Jesus was suspect as a liar for speaking in parables. Augustine repudiated his own education in pagan mythology to sin in imitation of the gods, Zeus the seducer, by mistaking imagery for reality. In vigorously sexual language Augustine related fiction and fornication. Sin regressed to the cultural valuation of rhetoric in the service of social necessity.

Augustine's answer elevated the tendency of rhetoric from concupiscence to charity by dredging from its flux signs of truths. The theological task became the maturation of Scripture by translating its rhetorical images into philosophical ideas. His notorious solution to unbelief was not rhetorical persuasion but political coercion. Augustine was ultimately, profoundly antirhetorical. Ignorant of Greek, he influentially promoted the primordial Speech (*logos*) as Word (*verbum*) (*Jn.* 1.1). Its analogy was not oral discourse but intellectual concept. Augustine displaced the scriptural norm with the contemplative ideal, the temporality of linguistic convention with the eternity of mental covenant, the multiplicity of words with the unity of truth. Rhetoric was a condescension to the flesh, to motivate persons from the corporeal to the spiritual. Its metaphor of service was female and pejorative, a breast-feeding mother (contemplation was male and chaste). Ciceronian precepts were her toys. Truth was apprehended by contemplation, which ascended to the Word beyond words: to silence.

Augustine's submission of rhetoric to philosophy prepared for its subordination in medieval scholasticism. Although rhetoric as a propaedeutic prevailed in exegesis, logic regulated theology into a comprehensive discipline of univocal meaning and constructed abstraction. Theology was a major subject in universities; rhetoric was not. Although rhetoric was thus religiously marginalized, it was appropriated for the distinctive medieval genres of letter writing and preaching. The art of applying Ciceronian rhetoric to letter writing was a monastic invention and it flourished in the cloisters and in chanceries for official ecclesiastical business. Papal letters ranked first as a model in all of the manuals, while the New Testament epistles were ignored. Moral subjects surfaced in familiar letters. Preaching was established on the example and mandate of Christ but it was undeveloped preceptively, save for *De doctrina christiana,* before the thematic treatises of the thirteenth century. This popular new genre

lent a rhetorical art to scriptural proof, glosses, examples, bibliographical aids, and sermonic collections. Other genres were the liturgy and hymn, synodal and conciliar speech, pastoral manual, devotional treatise, scriptural commentary, ecclesiastical history, and hagiography. In theology Nicholas of Cusa (1401–1464 CE) experimentally sealed the mathematical and metaphorical reasoning of *De docta ignorantia* with an argument for Christ as the concept of concepts, composed in deliberative rhetoric and punctuated with epideictic bursts. [*See overview article on* Medieval rhetoric.]

The breakthrough in religious rhetoric was Dante's (1265–1321) singular invention of the poet as theologian. There was a classical tradition of the poet as the messenger of the gods or priest of the Muses. Yet, fearful of this inspiration, shy of even the Holy Spirit (cf. *Mk.* 13.11), early Christians had been poetasters. Dante's source of inspiration for his *Commedia* (c.1310–1321) as the sight of Beatrice is hardly transparent. Research has systematized his theological doctrine, rather than explored his theological method. Nevertheless, Dante's intention to speak a new art with a new voice can be inferred from even a detail of its *Paradiso.* There he surpasses the scholastic Thomas Aquinas (c.1225–1274 CE), dully speaking, and even the monastic Bernard of Clairvaux (1090–1153), spiritually counseling. Dante ascends to God singing, just as he defined poetry in *De vulgare eloquentia* (1304–1305): a rhetorical invention musically composed. Petrarch's (1304–1374) donning of the poetic mantle was more clearly articulated in a concept of genius divinely endowed, an illuminative conflation of Apollo and Christ. Petrarch assumed a prophetic vocation toward the civic destiny to incite patriotic zeal, by his epic *Africa* (1396), to move the papacy from its Babylonian captivity to Rome. Yet, although this intention failed politically, his vernacular *Canzionere* (1360, 1375) indeed displayed a genius, which dared to defy asceticism by poetizing in the face of an Augustinian straw man. The heritage was perfected in the sixteenth century in Juan de la Cruz's sublime "Cántico espiritual," which hymned the ontological union of the soul with God in the erotic pursuit of beauty. He explained its composition as no rational exposition but a figurative effusion of mysterious spiritual experience. This experience radically reversed the human apprehension of the divine that was a common rhetorical intention. Juan's canticle poetized the rare divine apprehension of the human. Rhetoric transcended persuasion to revelation in an art distinguished by the holy authority of inspiration. John Milton intended in *Paradise Lost* (1667, 1674) to justify divinity to humanity by a hybrid biblical epic, another serious leap over poetic bounds into theology.

Philology, the linguistic science of renaissance humanism, established the most important Christian theory of rhetoric. Erasmus (c.1466–1536), editor of the first Greek New Testament (1516, 1519), significantly corrected the Vulgate mistranslation of the paradigmatic *Logos* (*Jn.* 1.1), "in the beginning was the Word (*verbum*)." From philological knowledge, historical evidence, and liturgical practice, Erasmus proclaimed "in the beginning was the Speech (*sermo*)." Although he preferred *oratio*, its feminine gender deterred its association with Jesus, while *sermo* had authority as the original translation. Erasmus argued for this Speech as the perfect paradigm, because the incomprehensible Father disclosed himself through the Son, like a speaker through his speech. The eternal generation and the temporal incarnation of the Son as this paternal discourse was imaged in the creation of humans and in their gift of imitative revelation through speech. Human discourse revealed the divine image and indwelling in a bond of filiation, repeating the eternal Speech in temporal speech, as a sign of understanding, a reflection of character, and a mark of virtue.

Because the divine paradigm was not a terse word but the sufficient and copious medium of revelation, it was an ideal of amplitude, reflected in his *De copia* (1512, 1526, 1534). Erasmus envisioned a society constituted by Scripture, reformed from scholastic barbarism by education in rhetoric and operative on its principles. The particular vocation of theology was eloquent and wise oratory toward personal and social conversion. Its speech was to be invented from Christ as the ultimate commonplace. Its method, established more in dispositions than syllogisms, valued life above disputation, inspiration above erudition, and transformation above reason. No longer elitist and professional, theology extended to everyone's ordinary conversation, coincident with the very meaning of *sermo*. Because the divine paradigm was not a single Word in isolation but a complete Speech to an audience, its imitation was to reconcile individual relationships toward social concord. [*See* Copia.]

The religious conflict of rhetoric with grammar and logic was publicized in Erasmus's dispute with Luther concerning freedom of choice toward grace. Lacking a consensus on the unclarity of Scripture, Erasmus argued the disputed question in *De libero arbitrio* (1524), composed in the deliberative genre of a *diatribe sive collatio*. This exegetical comparison was established in Skeptic epistemology, which debated on both sides of a question toward a probable enough opinion. As the first pacifist on record, Erasmus relinquished the weaponry that had classically trained rhetorical agonism. Luther retorted in the forensic genre with *De servo arbitrio* (1525) to assert the clarity of Scripture and to prosecute rhetoric itself. His argument was established in Stoic epistemology, which defined the criterion of truth as the kataleptic impression, which grasps its object with intrinsic certitude. Scripture both coerced and guaranteed such assent. Luther's culture was fundamentally grammatical, producing an antihermeneutics of Scripture as manifest and a univocal logic of predication, secured in a God of absolute necessity. Erasmus's culture was generously rhetorical, fostering a hermeneutics of Scripture as interpretable and an equivocal logic of predication, figured in the ambiguity of Christ as Folly. The classical metaphor of the clenched fist of logic against the open palm of rhetoric sprang into action. The historic choice was the certitude of the assertive word versus the reasonableness of persuasive discourse.

Erasmus's *sermo* was displaced in the Luther-Bibel (1534) with *Wort* and dismissed by the Tridentine sanction of the Vulgate (1546). But it survived, through John Calvin's approval, in Théodore de Bèze's translation, and also in Milton's *De doctrina christiana* (c.1650, first published 1825). Although textbooks report Calvin's achievement as systematic theology, *Institutio christianae religionis* (1536, 1556) is a rhetorical disposition (*institutio*), in the service of *institutio* as the legal term for inheritance, the adoption of believers into Christ's Sonship. This restructuring of theology on the

Roman civil law of property upset Augustine's contemplative ideal, which was based on a facultative psychology. Yet, although Calvin is recognized for his contribution to French style, his theological alliance of rhetoric and law has just been introduced. Erasmus concluded his reform with *Ecclesiastes* (1535), the first comprehensive rhetoric since antiquity and the first ever on preaching. Its subject presaged the rise of theory to the pulpit in subsequent centuries, although the practice of religious rhetoric in other genres is unsurveyed.

The skepticism of René Descartes (1596–1650), philosopher and mathematician, conceived rationalism, which would prevail as the modern doctrine. Descartes's rational inquiry about God as not a deceiver rendered the deity a guarantor of absolute certainty. Rationalism banished rhetoric, with its acknowledgment of contingency, as a threat to that certainty. Giambattista Vico (1668–1744) advocated rhetoric but, although he traced the imaginative linguistic structuring of reality to myths, he did not consider religion. Major philosophers who did—John Locke (1632–1704), George Berkeley (1685–1753), David Hume (1711–1776), and Immanuel Kant (1724–1804)—exalted empiricism as superior to the communal sense and wisdom of rhetorical method. For its subjectivity, rhetoric was typed as deceitful, even erroneous, thus dismissed as illusory. In the nineteenth century some dissent was voiced by John Henry Newman (1801–1890), who pressed rhetoric to inductive, epistemic, and transformative ends, proposing informal inference for particular reasoning about behavioral choice and action.

Contemporary Issues. A rationalist development in the twentieth century rendered language the central issue in the philosophy of religion. The focus of traditional theology on the nature or acts of God yielded in the modern era to the question of the existence of God, then to language about God. The tradition in the Eastern churches and rites of a negative theology and the presence in the Western churches of a negative mode of reasoning had undercut basic analogical discourse. The new philosophy, however, did not repeat the ancient truth about the ineffability of God. Rather, it radicalized language about God beyond theological intelligibility to question the very reality of faith. The contemporary issue became the correspondence of language to the reality called God-talk.

Suspicion about language as descriptive of experience was raised initially in the nineteenth century by Karl Marx (1818–1883) politically and Sigmund Freud (1856–1939) psychoanalytically. Both asserted its distortion of reality through disguise or rationalization and both challenged the veracity of religious language. The decisive criticism issued philosophically in the twentieth century from logical positivism, which intended to clarify philosophical discourse itself. It altered the issue from the truth of to the meaning of religious claims. A. J. Ayer, in *Language, Truth, and Logic* (London, 1936), posited the principle of verification to distinguish between meaningful and meaningless assertions. Meaningful meant capable of being demonstrated as either true or false. Its criteria were tautologies and empirical facts. Religious language failed to be verifiable, and so was rejected as meaningless. Philosophy of religion and philosophical theology became preoccupied with demonstrating that God-talk met the criteria of meaning. It was argued as verified in the personal encounters of believers with God in mystical experience or at least in the afterlife. The status of the principle of verification was itself challenged. Verification was displaced by Ludwig Wittgenstein's location of meaning in the functional sentence rather than the referential word. Although in his *Tractatus logico-philosophicus* (London, 1922) he found nothing meaningful about God, his later identification of language games provided a concept that religious apologists explored. Language became a pervasive problem in contemporary thought. Apologists strove to articulate the function of religious and theological language: how it, too, was a language game. Various proposals identified religious language with moral language (a predilection since Kant) or acknowledged it as odd, with the insistence that it corresponded to the oddity of discernment and commitment in ordinary life and so was regulated. J. L. Austin's theory of performatives in *How to Do Things with Words* (Oxford, 1955), inspired explanations of religious language as active, particularly in ritual formulas. The theory of speech-action was also applied to the notion of God himself speaking; the claim that God performs illocutionary actions was argued as coherent and entailing no falsehoods. [*See* Speech acts, utterances as.]

Other theory related religious language to ordinary experience by identifying secular analogues of transcendence and mystery. As talk about the ultimate and the sacred within the ordinary experience of the contingent and the relative, religious language was declared symbolic. Examples were the experiences of limitation, confidence, and growth; a desire for order, the character of humor and of joy, a sense of hope, moral outrage and courage, creativity, liberty, guilt, and acceptance. Another response located meaning in the text—not beyond it in reality or experience, so that the word *God* meant only how the word operated within a religion to shape reality and experience. Feminists focused on gender: some argued for an inclusive language that honored the female experience of God; others pronounced the gender of God unimportant, since religious language referred not to a divine being but to human ideals and values. "Thealogians" suggested that women could explore their own ideals and values through the language of the Goddess.

Other responses severed theology from philosophy. Theology made non-sense because it spoke the unspeakable, and so was irreducible to philosophy. Another response considered rhetoric the original language, prophetic and revelatory in its metaphors, the basis for rational and argumentative speech. A related claim was that devotional language required no philosophical justification because, as mythical, it was prior to and fundamental to rational language. Another emphasis recognized that language constructed or created a relation to reality. It was not semantic, as signifying mental experience, but syntactic, as giving thought a social and cultural communication. This linguistic construction of reality required theology to construct its own meaning of this mediation in a poetic expression of the creation, since God is a poetic being. Yet another reaction to rationalism emphasized that speech about God does not assert truths or values but expresses him in irreducible metaphors.

A major response to logical positivism was the process metaphysics of Alfred North Whitehead (1861–1947), another philosopher and mathematician. He thought that all language, as grounded in the discernment and projection of analogies, had metaphysical claims, so that this dimension of religious discourse was not problematical. It was established in a fundamental prelinguistic experience, which it structured in intuitive, exemplificatory, and explanatory ways. Its assertions had both cognitive significance—as based on experience, rather than authority—and affective power. This allowed for the possibility of faith as knowledge. Although there has been some attention to Whitehead on religious language, there has been none on his potential contribution to a rhetoric of religion. This is his belief in a God of persuasion. It was not fortuitous that he regarded as the greatest theologians Origen (c.185–c.254 CE) and Erasmus, both rhetoricians.

The challenge to rationalism and empiricism in the twentieth century also ushered in a rhetorical revival. Chaim Perelman's and Lucie Olbrecht-Tyteca's *The New Rhetoric* (Notre Dame, Ind., 1969, first published 1958) diverged from the Cartesian tradition by restoring Aristotelian dialectical proofs for deliberation. Perelman's alternative discovery of the rhetorical tradition has been associated with his recovery of his Jewish identity, following the antisemitism of World War II. His rhetoric reflects his religious heritage of Talmudic habits of argument as a medium between Enlightenment metaphysics and extreme postmodernism. Another major rhetorical theorist, Kenneth Burke (1897–1993), defined humans as symbol-using animals and employed religious language, a persuasive mode toward action, as a heuristic for language itself. *The Rhetoric of Religion* (Boston, 1961) interpreted verbal action in Augustine's *Confessions* and conceptual order in *Genesis* 1–3 as paradigms, in order to rupture the sacral–secular dichotomy. However, its premise of the analogy between words and the Word depends on the mistranslation *verbum*. And its premise of a supernatural realm, analogous to a natural one, misconstrues the theological term *supernatural* as a state or condition, whereas it is a mode of action; moreover, *supernatural* is a scholastic term, anachronistic to the biblical and patristic texts Burke interpreted. Thus the initial major effort at conceptualization was a literary criticism seriously flawed by a deficiency of theological knowledge.

The difficulty of attaining even a basic competence in both disciplines, rhetoric and religion, marked the beginnings of their new collaboration in the late twentieth century as tentative, if promising. Rhetorical criticism of specific religious texts has been more illuminating than has general theorizing about the rhetoric of religion. In religious studies the academic recognition has been for the interpretation of biblical and patristic literature. The curriculum in theology and church history treats doctrine and institution, not method. Moreover, it regularly skips the Renaissance, thus dismissing the major achievements of the Christian rhetorical tradition. This neglect is compounded by mislocating in the modern era the discovery of historicity, whereas it was an invention of Renaissance humanism, so that the discussion is disoriented. Although the historicity of rhetoric is theoretically invoked, ignorance of the history of rhetoric is practically manifest. The result is gross caricature of the rhetoric for a millennium and a half between Augustine and Perelman as ornamental, rather than argumentative. The interpretation of Christian rhetoric has not yet been shouldered within the field of religion but by rhetorical and literary critics and by intellectual and cultural historians.

Biblical scholars have succeeded in articulating and debating some issues, largely because they practice the interpretation of texts. Exegesis has traditionally been rhetorical, sustained by the educational role of rhetoric in the liberal arts. Yet this tradition was obscured late in the nineteenth century by the methods of scientific exegesis and historical criticism, from which lapse it was only recovering in the last quarter of the twentieth. The impetus for the revival of rhetoric was dissatisfaction with biblical form criticism, which identifies standardized genres, and with literary New Criticism, which interprets texts stylistically and ahistorically and denies authorial intention. The new movement thus proceeds, not only beyond theological or ethical readings but also beyond literary or aesthetic readings. Any reinstatement of an alliance between exegesis and rhetoric by stylistics is severely denounced. The authority of Perelman and Olbrechts-Tyteca on rhetoric as argumentation rules. A retort to the rejection of style in biblical criticism has called for the integration of pragmatic or strategic functions in modern stylistics. (The rejection also disregards the epistemic function of classical aesthetics that

identified beauty with ontology: style could be argumentative.) The preference, nevertheless, is clearly for argumentation. Rhetorical criticism is applied to exhibit not the biblical sources, either for aesthetic value or propositional content, but their social purposes. The epistemic function of rhetoric is approved as not only transmitting or promoting truth but also as creating and constructing it by social interaction. Rhetoric thus becomes a method for discerning the dynamics of early Christian movements. The power of biblical rhetoric is at issue, hence the power of rhetorical criticism within biblical scholarship, to shift the authority from theological claims to social evaluation. As a critical discipline, rhetoric challenges traditional hermeneutics.

Classical rhetorical theory is applied to discern patterns of communication, especially in the New Testament. The method involves reconstruction of the rhetorical situation, identification of the issue, and disclosure of the designs of the author on his readers. Emphasis is on the social and cultural situation of texts as revealing the communicative, rather than significative, function of language. The traditional emphasis on the religious message changes to the formation of communal values. The primary task is identification of the rhetorical situation that invites the utterance, in order to discover the premises conditioning the attitude of the writers and readers. The theory of rhetoric as a universal phenomenon conceptualizing innate ideas has received some adherence and application. More prevalent is a circumspect revival that attempts to learn from the history of rhetoric, while appreciating its historicity. It has even been proposed that rhetoric is historicity, defined by the association between text and context.

A nonsystematic, interdisciplinary approach seeks to provide an orientation to the Bible through imaginative criticism. In contrast, feminist and liberationist theology exhorts scholars to their public responsibility to liberate the Bible from ecclesiastical control and academic science by political interpretation. This practice recommends a hermeneutics of suspicion about critical epistemological discourses, so as to correct ideological distortions. Classical rhetoric is denounced as serving powerful relations of domination and exclusion, and is thus rejected as an antiquarian and conservative method of interpretation. The authority of the Bible is held to be determined by communal assent; thus the theological task becomes persuasion to thought and action for human transformation.

Classicists early contributed valuable cultural analyses of patristic rhetoric, but interest within religious studies has since dwindled to categories. Popular in the examination of imaginative language as a basis for conceptual language is the metaphor, with some recognition of hyperbole. Imaginative language has been advocated more generally as relieving the problems of idolatry (literalism) and irrelevance in religious language. For religious theory, attention has been diverted from the Christian tradition to Aristotle in order to redefine theology as persuasive argument. Rhetoric is acknowledged as an analysis of persuasive discourse, related to logic and poetics. Its social and cultural situation as public discourse commends it to theology, a discipline by definition communal. A major impetus for this Aristotelian turn is dissatisfaction with the abstraction of propositional logic, in recognition of the radical contingency and uncertainty of language about God. Theology is reconceived as humanly constructed argumentation, not divinely inspired assertion. Rhetoric is advocated as a method because of its epistemic function. Although rhetoric is acknowledged to blend rational and affective proofs, emphasis is on rhetoric as knowledge. The Aristotelian conversion thus begs the question whether the end of religion is knowledge. Historically theologians employed rhetoric to challenge such an intellectual imposition on the gospel—to encourage its commandment of love toward the vitality of human communion and divine union.

Linguistic sophistication and hermeneutical consciousness also commend rhetoric. Because rhetoric is respected as metalanguage, a translator among alternative discourses, it has been thought useful to ecumenism, or dialogue among Christian denominations, and to pluralism, or dialogue with other faiths. Discontinuity of doctrine within the Christian tradition can thus be legitimated as a creative process of criticism and development. The diversity, even conflict, among religious traditions also becomes capable of appreciation and tolerance. Rhetoric has also been advocated as a critique of ideology. Feminist criticism has exposed the connection between the marginalization of rhetoric and of women.

Rhetorical analysis, in sum, is considered clarifying for biblical exegesis, ecclesiastical history, and doctrinal formulation. Practicality is its valued recommendation: rhetoric shares with theology a belief in the efficacy of speech to generate action. The universal and self-evident arguments of logic, which prescind from the authority of the speaker and the condition of the audience, are discardable. The communal character of argumentation is emphasized, and the role of reception by the audience is recognized as forming the tradition. This audience is not only composed of individuals but also constitutes a community participating in practices, such as worship and study. In study, rhetoric has provided an alternative paradigm to the instrumental and transmissional models of teaching religion in the university, by establishing a dialogical, local, and practical art. Contemporary theory seeks to mend the historical fragmentation of rhetoric into argumentation and ornamentation. A wider gap between theory and practice more urgently needs a bridge. A beginning would be made by discovering through history the authority and inspiration of rhetoric in the traditions and by understanding rhetorical theory through practicing rhetorical criticism.

[*See also* Criticism; Hermeneutics; *and* Homiletics.]

BIBLIOGRAPHY

Scripture
Useful for nonlinguists are interlinear bibles, which print the English translation above the Hebrew or Greek word or phrase. The preferred English translation for scholarly use is the Revised Standard Version, although its paragraphing has been criticized as inaccurate for rhetorical analysis. Some important historical bibles are:

(Authorized English Version, or King James Bible). *The Holy Bible.* Facsimile reprint of the 1611 edition. Oxford, 1911.

Biblia sacra: iuxta Vulgatam versionem. Translated by Jerome et al.; edited by Boniface Fischer et al. 2 vols. Stuttgart, 1994.

Deutsche Bibel. Translated by Martin Luther. 12 vols. Weimar, Germany, 1906– .

Novum instrumentum. Edited and translated by Erasmus of Rotterdam. Vol. 7 of his *Opera omnia;* edited by Johannes Clericus. 11 vols. Leiden, 1703–1706.

Tradition

Translations should be avoided as frequently unreliable and even tendentious. For patristic and medieval texts, to be consulted only as a last resort are *Patrologia graeca* and *Patrologia latina,* edited by J.-P. Migne, 161 and 221 vols. (Paris, 1800–1912). The following series of critical editions are recommended instead:

Corpus christianorum. Series graeca. Series latina. Continuatio medievalis. Turnhout, Belgium, 1954– .

Sources chretiennes. Series grecque. Series latin. Paris, 1941– .

Critical editions of individual works are also available. Some significant later authors are:

Alighieri, Dante. *La "Commedia" secondo l'antica vulgata,* edited by Giorgio Petrocchi. 4 vols. Milan, Italy, 1966–1968.

Calvin, John. *Opera quae supersunt omnia,* edited by Eduard Reuss, Eduard Cunitz, and Johann Wilhelm Baum. Corpus reformatorum, 29–87. 59 vols. in 26. Brunswick, Germany, 1863–1900. A new critical edition is in progress in Geneva at Droz, with some volumes available.

Cruz, Juan de la. *Obra completa,* edited by Luce López Baralt and Eulogio Pacho. 2 vols. Madrid, 1991.

Erasmus of Rotterdam. *Opera omnia,* edited by Leon-E. Halkin et al. Amsterdam, 1971– . In progress, with many volumes published.

Leon, Judah Messer. *The Book of the Honeycomb's Flow: Sepher Nopheth Suphim,* edited and translated by Isaac Rabinowitz. Ithaca, N.Y., 1983.

Luther, Martin. *De servo arbitrio.* In *Luthers Werke in Auswahl,* vol. 4. Edited by Otto Clemen, pp. 94–293. 6 vols. Berlin, 1950.

Milton, John. *The Works of John Milton,* edited by Frank A. Patterson et al. 18 vols. New York, 1931–1938.

Petrarca, Francesco. *Canzoniere,* edited by Gianfranco Contini. Turin, 1964.

Contemporary Issues

Rhetorical criticism of the Bible is published regularly in the supplements of the *Journal for the Study of the Old Testament* (JSOT) and *Journal for the Study of the New Testament* (JSNT). For the current discipline see:

Wuellner, Wilhelm. "Biblical Exegesis in the Light of the History and Historicity of Rhetoric and the Nature of the Rhetoric of Religion." In *Rhetoric and the New Testament: Essays from the 1992 Heidelberg Conference,* edited by S. E. Porter and Thomas H. Olbricht, pp. 492–513. JSNT supplements, 90. Sheffield, U.K., 1993.

A forum for the rhetoric of religion is the *Journal of the American Academy of Religion;* for the philosophy of religious language, see *Religious Studies* and the *International Journal for the Philosophy of Religion.* A monograph series, Theology and Rhetoric, is being published by the State University of New York Press. Relevant subject categories for research are: rhetoric—religious aspects; rhetoric and theology; language and languages—religious aspects. For a theoretical and critical sampler see:

Rhetorical Invention and Religious Inquiry, edited by Walter Jost and Wendy Olmstead, New Haven, 2000.

—MARJORIE O'ROURKE BOYLE

RENAISSANCE RHETORIC. [*This entry comprises four articles.*

An overview
Rederijkers
Rhetoric in Renaissance language and literature
Rhetoric in the age of Reformation and Counter-Reformation

The first article outlines the revival of classical rhetoric in the countries of Europe emphasizing its impact on the arts and sciences as well as on social development in the general history of culture. The second article is a consideration of the Dutch rhetoric chambers as important social institutions. The third article gives a general overview of Ciceronianism and Anti-Ciceronianism, rhetorical mannerism in Renaissance Europe, and the rhetoric of science. The last article, on Rhetoric in the age of Reformation and Counter-Reformation, discusses Luther's and Melanchthon's reformation of rhetoric, Protestant theories of preaching, and Jesuit preaching and education.]

An overview

The Renaissance represents a decisive climax in the history of Western rhetoric. Renaissance rhetoric, however, does not emerge as an abrupt cultural turn but gradually develops in several stages of imitation and innovation. It reached its telos in the seventeenth century in a widely-diversified range of persuasive activities, both in theory and practice. It continued to exert its influence through the end of the eighteenth century, when the cultural periods of *Sturm und Drang* and Romanticism witnessed its gradual decline.

Renaissance Rhetoric and the Renascences of Rhetoric. Renascences of rhetoric recur at almost regular intervals in the history of Western culture. They are preceded and followed by almost equally-regular periods of rhetorical decline caused either by neglect or by deliberate suppression. Renascences of rhetoric were initiated by Cicero at the end of the Roman Republic; by Saint Augustine (354–430 CE) and other Church Fathers in late antiquity; by Alcuin during the reign of Charlemagne; by Hugh Blair, George Campbell, and Lord Kames during the eighteenth-century Scottish Renaissance; and by linguists, theorists of style, semioticians, and literary historians in the 1960s and 1970s. In contrast to these renascences, rhetoric regained an importance in the time span from about the middle of the fourteenth to about the middle of the seventeenth century, which it did not possess before and after. Many iconographical representations furnish evidence of this. One instance can be found in Gregor Reisch's encyclopedic work *Margarita Philosophica* (The Philosophical Pearl, 1507). In it, a woodcut depicts Rhetorica, personified as a sovereign queen clad in splendid garb, with a sword; a lily is issuing from her mouth, she is seated on a royal throne, and she is surrounded by the ancient authorities of natural and moral philosophy (Aristotle, Seneca), of poetry (Virgil), historiography (Sallust), and law (Justinian) (Stolt, 1974; Plett, 1975). [*See* Iconography.] In the eyes of the Humanists, rhetoric is equivalent to culture as such, man's greatest ontological privilege. Renaissance rhetoric was, however, not confined to the cultural elite of the Humanists but became a substantial factor in a broad cultural movement that had its impact on the educational system of the humanities and encompassed increasingly more social groups and strata. It was not limited to Italy, from whence it took its origin, but spread north, west, and east into Europe and from there to overseas colonies in the Americas, Asia, Africa, and Oceania.

Rhetoric Rediscovered: The Academic (Humanist) Strain. Renaissance rhetoric originated as a result of the rediscovery of the manuscripts of classical rhetoric: two speeches of Cicero and his correspondence with Atticus, by Petrarch (1304–1374); Cicero's *Familiar Epistles,* by Coluccio Salutati (1331–1406); the complete text of Cicero's *De oratore* in a manuscript also containing his *Brutus,* as well as *Orator,* by Gerardo Landriani, bishop of Lodi, in 1421; and the integral text of Quintilian's *Institutio oratoria,* by Poggio Bracciolini (1380–1459), a papal secretary, at the monastery of Saint Gall on his way to the Council of Constance in 1416. Though as a rhetorician Cicero was not unknown in the Middle Ages, his fame derived mainly from the rather unimaginative technical treatise *De inventione* and the spurious *Rhetorica ad Herennium* attributed to him. Now his image changed, and he became known as the witty writer of charming conversations composed in an elegant Latin style. Moreover, he now emerged both as the author of theoretical writings on rhetoric and simultaneously as its practitioner as a lawyer and statesman, thus uniting the qualities of both *vita contemplativa* and *vita activa.*

A further stage in the revival of rhetoric occurred when rediscovered Latin and Greek manuscripts were printed, thus opening the possibility of disseminating their knowledge throughout Europe. Thus, Cicero's *De oratore* was published as a single edition at Subiaco (c.1465), Rome (1468), Venice (c.1470), Naples (1475), Milan (1477), and went through at least eighteen more editions through the 1696 Oxford edition (Murphy, 1981, p. 79). The important collection of *Rhetores graeci* appeared at the Aldine press at Venice from 1508 to 1509 in two folio volumes that contain, according to its Latin table of contents, the following works:

> *Aphthonii Sophistae progymnasmata: Hermogenes ars rhetorica; Aristotelis rhetoricorum ad Theodecten libri tres; Eiusdem rhetorice ad Alexandrum; Eiusdem ars poetica; Sopatri Rhetoris quaestiones de comp[on]endis declamationibus in causis praecipuae judicialibus; Cyri Sophistae differentiae statum; Dionysii Alicamesei ars rhetorica; Demetri Phaleri de interpretatione; Alexanderi Sophistae de figuris sensus et dictionis; Adnotationis innominati de figuris rhetoricis; Menandri Rhetoris divisio causarum in genere demonstrativo; Aristeidus de civili oratione; Eiusdem de simplici oratione; Apsini de arte rhetorica praecepta.* (Murphy 1981, pp. 254–255).

The Progymnasmata by Aphthonius: The Art of Rhetoric by Hermogenes; Three Books of Rhetoric by Aristotle Addressed to Theodectes; The Rhetoric Addressed to Alexander by the Same; The Art of Poetry by the Same; Questions Concerning the Composition of Declamations, Especially in Judicial Causes, by Sopater Rhetor; The Differences of Statutes by Cyrus the Sophist; The Art of Rhetoric by Dionysius of Halicarnassus; On Interpretation by Demetrius of Phaleron; On the Figures of Sense and Diction by Alexander the Sophist; Annotations on the Figures of Rhetoric by an Anonymous Author; The Division of Causes in the Demonstrative Genre by Menander Rhetor; On the Civil Oration by Aristeides; On a Simple Oration by the Same: Precepts on the Art of Rhetoric by Apsinus [i.e. Apsines].

The sheer quantity of these texts of Greek authors, who for the greater part are hardly known to present-day specialists, displays the immense interest and even enthusiasm aroused by the rediscovery of this cultural terra incognita.

Lack of linguistic competence led to another stage of rhetorical revival: the translating of the classical texts into the vernacular to render them accessible to those readers who, as in Ben Jonson's famous dictum about his rival Shakespeare, knew "little Latine & lesse Greeke." First, the poor knowledge of Greek among Humanists raised the necessity of having the relevant Greek texts translated into Latin, the language of the learned international community called the *respublica literaria*. Thus, Aristotle's *Rhetoric* was translated into Latin by Georgius Trapezuntius (Paris, 1475?; Lyons, 1541). Italian translations of Aristotle's *Rhetoric* and *Poetics* were produced by Bernardo Segni in 1549 under the title *Retorica, et poetica d'Aristotile. Tradotte . . . di greco in lingua vulgare fiorentino da Bernardo Segni.* A notable English specimen is Thomas Wilson's translation of *The Three Orations in Favour of the Olynthians* by Demosthenes, whom Wilson calls "chiefe orator among the Grecians" (London, 1570).

A third stage of the rhetorical revival of the classics was the hermeneutic procedure of producing annotations and commentaries. Of foremost importance are the glosses and commentaries on Cicero's rhetorical works, which in their turn show several stages of erudition and complexity (Ward, 1983).

Rhetoric Reinvented: From Imitation to Emulation. In the wake of the Humanist rediscovery and interpretation of the classical treatises of rhetoric, new treatises were composed by the Humanists themselves, some of these in a close imitation of their ancient models, others freely adapted to adjust them to the exigencies of the time. As bibliographical research has shown

(Murphy, 1983; Plett, 1995), Renaissance rhetoricians sometimes wrote several treatises which they published in different forms—as a textbook, as part of an anthology of treatises, as extensively annotated folios or quartos, as well as in epitomized versions or *tabulae,* first in Neo-Latin and later in vernacular translations. It seems possible that by 1650 their total number ran into several thousands.

An illustrative example of how a Humanist wrote and revised a rhetorical work are the three treatises of the *praeceptor Germaniae* Philipp Melanchthon (i.e., Schwartzerdt, 1497–1560), an ardent supporter and propagator of the Reformation (Knape, 1993). His rhetoric first appeared in 1519 at Wittenberg under the title *Philippi Melanchtho-/nis de Rhetorica / libri Tres.* It follows the classical (Ciceronian) schema of the five arts (*officia*) of the orator: *inventio, dispositio, elocutio, memoria, actio,* of which the latter two receive no full treatment. But it also includes, as innovative additions, some chapters on hermeneutics (*De enarratorio genere* [On the genre of expounding]), *De commentandi ratione* [On the method of commenting]), and sermons (*De sacris concionibus*). A characteristic feature that pervades the whole of this rhetoric is the emphasis placed on dialectic, the study of which its author recommends to his students time and again. This treatise was composed as a textbook at the University of Tübingen, where Melanchthon taught as one of the first professors of rhetoric. It is therefore no small wonder that a second version of the same textbook bears the programmatic title *Institutiones rhetoricae* (Rhetorical Instructions, 1521). Smaller in size than its predecessor, indeed consisting only of a few leaves, it is confined to precise terminological definitions of the rhetorical categories and short illustrative examples that can easily be memorized. Its overall disposition is, with minor alterations, patterned on *de Rhetorica,* but by contrast, the section on *elocutio* is enlarged (from 11 percent up to 56.5 percent), thus illustrating the importance Humanists attached to style. The same practice is observed in the last revision of the original work, the *Elementa rhetorices* of 1542, with the difference that it is divided into two books, the first dealing with *inventio* and *dispositio,* the second with *elocutio* alone. Here, as in his first version, Melanchthon emphasizes the relevance of dialectic and now refers to his own work. The *Elementa rhetorices* were immensely popular in their day, as is documented by the large number of editions, a total of thirty-three by Melanchthon's death in 1560. The popularity of Melanchthon's rhetorical concept is also evident by its skeletonized summary in the *tabulae* of Petrus Mosellanus (i.e., Peter Schade), who was one of the great epitomizers of the time. His *In Philippi Melanchthonis rhetorica tabulae* appeared shortly after the publication of the *Institutiones rhetoricae* and went through several editions. On the whole, the three versions of Melanchthon's rhetorical concept, together with their numerous editions, as well as Mosellanus's *Tabulae,* amply demonstrate the wide dissemination of Neo-Latin rhetoric in Renaissance Europe, particularly when it was associated with a general practical purpose, in this case with Protestant education at grammar schools and universities. Nonetheless, Melanchthon's rhetoric has not been made generally accessible in a popular vernacular translation.

Rhetoric Differentiated: The Rhetorical Genres. The growing complexity of social life in the Renaissance required the availability of diversified rhetorical manuals supplying for each profession and occasion practical and suitable techniques of persuasion. The printed manuals still partly adhered to the classical *exempla,* which they imitated more or less closely, but they gradually detached themselves from their normative constraints and gained in independence and contemporariness. From the generic point of view, the most prolific and versatile author of specialized treatises on rhetoric is Erasmus (c.1466–1536), and in this he was often imitated (Schoeck, 1993). A generic classification of Renaissance rhetoric presents the following eight types:

The rhetoric of five arts ("quinque partes artis"). Renaissance manuals of this type are patterned on such classical archetypes as Cicero's treatises on rhetoric and Quintilian's *Institutio oratoria.* Humanists with a predilection for this rhetoric of "the five great arts" (Howell, 1956) aimed at completeness; hence, their books were often voluminous and contain learned glosses and commentaries as well as detailed tables of contents and indices of names and subjects. One of the first Renaissance rhetoricians to compose such a comprehensive work was Georgius Trape-

zuntius (George of Trebizond, c.1395–c.1493) in his *Rhetoricorum libri V* (Venice, 1433/1434), "the only large-scale secular rhetoric produced by an Italian humanist in the fifteenth century" (Monfasani, 1976). The same model served as the basis of Melanchthon's didactic concept of rhetoric, though this was realized on a smaller scale. The Englishman Leonard Cox, a schoolmaster in Reading, made use of a pirated copy of Melanchthon's *de Rhetorica,* published in Cologne in 1521, for his translation *The arte or crafte of Rhethoryke* (London, c.1535), which is, however, limited to invention, the first part of the rhetorical discipline, described by him as the procedure that is hardest to master. Cox's rhetoric is thus an incomplete and unfinished version of the Ciceronian five-part rhetoric. It does not raise a claim to originality but rather promises to impart "the ryght pleasaunt and persuadyble arte of Rhetoryke" to "all suche as wyll eyther be aduocates and proctoures in the lawe or els apte to be sente in theyr prynces Ambassades or to be techars of goddes worde in suche maner as maye be moste sensible and accepte to their audience." The uses of rhetoric in law, statecraft, church service, and on numerous social occasions are also proclaimed in Thomas Wilson's *Arte of Rhetorique* (1553); with a total of eight editions, it was an Elizabethan bestseller. This work further underscores its usefulness by filling the classical structure with practical English illustrations, as in "To aduise one, to study the lawes of Englande," "Saincte George what he signified," and "Priestes mariage." Neo-Latin rhetorics of the comprehensive kind continued to appear. Thomas Farnaby's *Index Rhetoricvs, Scholis & institutioni tenerioris aetatis accommodatus* (A Rhetorical Index, apt for schools and the instruction of those of tender age, 1625) is, as its title indicates, a textbook for classroom teaching. It makes this purpose visible by arranging its content in systematic dichotomies, which facilitate its memorization. On the other hand, the author of this compact little treatise boasts of his erudition by adding to his text numerous marginal glosses. Among these glosses, references are to be found to the *Eloquentiae sacrae et humanae parallela* (Parallels of Divine and Secular Eloquence), which is a large work of sixteen books composed by the French Jesuit Nicolaus Caussinus, professor of rhetoric and confessor of King Louis XIII, to whom this rhetoric is dedicated. First published in Paris in 1619, it was many times reprinted, the last time in Cologne in 1681. Because of its complexity and learning, this rhetorical manual won international acclaim and, though an outstanding product of the Counter-Reformation, it transgressed the boundaries of religious creeds. Book 4 begins with an introduction to the traditional five arts of rhetoric and gives an explanation of *inventio;* the other arts are successively dealt with in books 6 (*dispositio*), 7 (*elocutio*), and 9 (*actio/ pronuntiatio*). Other important aspects of rhetoric treated in separate books are *amplificatio* (5), the affections (8), the demonstrative genre (10, 11), civil eloquence (12, 13), and homiletics (14). This broad treatment of the complete rhetorical system is typical of the Baroque era and has many parallels in vernacular treatises of the seventeenth century (Barner, 1970). [*See* Arrangement, *article on* Traditional arrangement; *and* Inventory.]

The Ars concionandi (Art of preaching). The fourth book of Augustine's *De doctrina Christiana* legitimizes Ciceronian rhetoric for the preaching of the gospel and hence achieves a synthesis of Christian doctrine and pagan rhetoric. One of the most important sixteenth-century humanist attempts to adopt it is Erasmus's *Ecclesiastes sive de ratione concionandi* (The Preacher, or On the Method of Preaching, 1535), whose structure follows the system of the five arts of the rhetorical discipline. In the post-Erasmian era, the theories of preaching branched out according to the denomination of their authors, Roman Catholic or Protestant, and in their turn, are distinguished by the kind of orthodox or liberal stance taken within each Christian denomination. Andreas Gerhard Hyperius, a moderate Protestant, who lived in England between 1536 and 1540, and in 1542 became professor of theology at Marburg, wrote a Latin treatise *De formandis concionibus sacris* (On the Formation of Sacred Sermons; Marburg, 1553) in two books, which were translated into English as *The Practise of Preaching, otherwise called the Pathway to the Pulpet: Conteyning an excellent Method how to frame divine sermons, & to interpret the Holy Scriptures according to the capacitie of the vulgar people. First written in Latin by the learned pastor of Christes Church, D. Andreas Hyperius: and now lately (to the profit of the same Church) Englished by Iohn Ludham, vicar of Weth-* erfield (London, 1577). This treatise, then, serves not only the purpose of providing rhetorical techniques for producing sermons but also for the reverse process of textual hermeneutics. In doing so, it expressly refers to classical rhetoric and its Christian legitimation by Augustine:

> That many thinges are common to the Preacher with the Orator, Sainct Augustine in his fourth booke of Christian doctrine, doth copiously declare. Therfore, the partes of an Orator, whiche are accounted of some to be, *Inuention, Disposition, Elocution, Memory,* and *Pronunciation,* may rightlye be called also the partes of the Preacher. Yea and these three: *to Teache, Delight, to Turne:* Likewise againe the three kyndes of speakyng, *Loftye, Base, Meane:* Moreouer, the whole craft of varienge the Oration by Schemes and Tropes, pertaineth indifferently to the Preacher and Orator, as Sainct Augustine in the same booke doth wittily confesse and learnedly proue.

The equation of pagan orator and Protestant preacher is to the Christian humanist not a contradiction in terms but a self-evident cultural phenomenon. When he utters reservations, for instance against invention, memory, and the three genres of causes, it is not for ideological reasons but because of their professional practicality. On the one hand, Hyperius modifies the rhetorical concept of the affections in that its importance for the preacher is secondary compared to the moving power of the divine word; but on the other hand, the impact of the classical canon with which he has become acquainted at Paris University is so strong that in chapter 16 he gives a broad outline of the Stoical doctrine of the affections. Different in character is the homiletic theory of the prominent Cambridge theologian William Perkins (1558–1602), which was published in Latin as *Prophetica, sive de sacra et vnica ratione Concionandi* (1592) and in an English translation by Thomas Tuke as *The arte of prophecying or a treatise concerning the sacred and onely true maner and methode of Preaching* (1607), each of them extant in several reissues, which propagated its doctrine not only in the British Isles but also in North America. The treatise concludes with an enumeration of the numerous authorities Perkins confesses to rely on: "Augustine, Hemingius, Hyperius, Erasmus, Illyricus, Wigandus, Iacobus Matthias, Theodorus Beza, Franciscus Iunius."

Eclectic though this work seems to be, it is nonetheless firmly rooted in the theological axioms of the Puritan (or Calvinist) creed. This is evident from Perkins's preface "To the Faithfvll Ministers of the Gospell," whom he admonishes that "Prophecy . . . serveth to collect the Church, and to accomplish the number of the Elect." He curtails the five offices of the discipline by dismissing "Artificiall Memorye" altogether; for according to him, "the animation of the image, which is the key of memorie, is impious; because it requireth absurd, insolent and prodigious cogitations, and those especially which set an edge upon and kindle the most corrupt affections of the flesh." This mental iconoclasm and antiemotional bias was in accordance with a demand for "a speech both simple and perspicuous, fit both for the peoples understanding and to expresse the Majestie of the Spirit." Perkins's postulate of the *sermo humilis* (humble speech) or plain style is a basic axiom of many Protestant theories of preaching and marks the practice of those of a more moderate orientation (e.g., George Herbert). In England, it was also paralleled by the stylistic concepts of the Baconians and members of the Royal Society. Whereas a moderate or a radical rhetorical reductionism was typical of many Protestant manuals of preaching, the Roman Catholic (mostly Jesuit) treatises were distinguished by their thorough activation of all available means of persuasion of the classical tradition in order to achieve, at their best, the propagandistic aims of the Counter-Reformation. Hence, these manuals emphatically stressed the sensuality of the rhetorical effect and the concept of the affections. A famous Austrian preacher who illustrated this baroque exuberance in rhetoric was Abraham a Santa Clara (1644–1709); his French counterpart was Jacques-Bénigne Bossuet (1627–1704). [*See* Homiletics; *and* Religion.]

Ars epistolica (Epistolary rhetoric). In the Middle Ages, the art of speaking well had been transformed by Alberich of Montecassino and others into an art of writing well, in order to meet the practical exigencies of state and church administration. In the Renaissance, however, the rediscovery of Cicero's letters by Italian Humanists led to appreciation of their stylistic merits and admiration for their author. They were used for the teaching of Latin in secondary schools in an edi-

tion with a commentary by the Strasbourg humanist Johannes Sturm (1507–1589). The new manuals of letter writing, which replaced the medieval *artes dictaminis,* often had an additional section on the personal letter (*epistola familiaris*). This kind of letter became a fashionable means of communication among Humanists who used it for the exchange and circulation of ideas in the *respublica literaria;* but there was also a notable increase of private correspondence among the literate members of the middle classes. The most important neo-Latin epistolary manuals such as *De conscribendis epistolis* (On Writing Letters, 1522) by Erasmus, *Methodus conficiendarum epistolarum* (A Method of Producing Epistles), published posthumously, 1537) by Conradus (or Konrad) Celtes (1459–1508), and *De ratione scribendi* (On the Method of Writing, 1545) by Aurelius Lippus Brandolinus (c.1454–c.1497) used the structural pattern of the classical rhetorical genres for the classification of the official letter, which, according to Angel Day's *The English Secretorie* (1588), took place "vnder foure especial heads, that is to saie, *Demonstratiue, Deliberatiue, Iudiciall,* and *Familiar Letters*" (1599 ed.). These epistolary genres were again divided into several subclasses, for instance "the *Deliberatiue* kinde into *Hortatorie, Dehortatorie, Swasorie* and *Disswasorie, Commendatorie, Monitorie,* or *Reprehensorie.*" Not only was the structure of the classical oration adopted for the letter, but also the traditional five-part schema for its production, with the exception of memory and delivery, which the medium of writing renders superfluous. Thus, the majority of the Renaissance epistolary treatises postulate traditional categories, procedures and structures of oral rhetoric for a different medium. A notable exception to this rule was Justus Lipsius (1547–1606), who refused the rhetoricization of the letter, since in his opinion it was generally confined to the familiar letter. In the mainstream of epistolary rhetoric, some treatises put a particular emphasis on style, which can be illustrated by the fact that from the 1592 edition of his treatise *The English Secretorie,* A. Day added a second part to it: "With a declaration of such / Tropes, Figures or Schemes, as are fittest / for Ornament." In books on epistolography, the illustrations often exceed the prescriptions in number and length. Their importance is also underlined by the existence of numerous collections of sample letters, which offer themselves for a broad range of occasions and purposes of writing. Thus, a collection of English love letters was published in London about 1633 under the title *Cupid's Messenger or A trusty Friend stored with sundry sorts of serious, witty, pleasaunt, amorous, and delightfull Letters*. Anthologies of this kind are *exempla* of practical rhetoric and resemble in form and function the genre of the commonplace book. [*See* Ars dictaminis; *and* Epistolary rhetoric.]

Formulary rhetoric. This genre of rhetoric does not consist of precepts but of examples, models for imitation. It manifests itself in collections of proverbs, aphorisms, and *sententiae,* compendia of sample letters, poetic anthologies, and dictionaries of quotations. It is usually published in commonplace books because they have become the common property of speakers and writers. This is due to the fact that their content consists of notable sayings or excerpts from outstanding works by classical authors or contemporary works that are regarded as modern classics. The material assembled here has been used and offers itself for reuse in imitative or secondary inventions. Thus, a commonplace book can be interpreted as frozen *inventio* or *memoria*. It represents a printed inventory, which renders superfluous the often complicated and time-consuming labor of the inventive quest by means of formal *topoi* or places. The matter stored up in these treasure houses of printed memory has the advantage of being "authorized" by the *auctoritas* of famous historical works and personalities. This kind of practical rhetoric enjoyed an immense popularity in the Renaissance. It became a reservoir of virtual discourses or excerpts from discourses, often arranged in alphabetical order or according to criteria supplied by philosophical concepts, theological doctrines, and educational curricula. Many encyclopedic works of the seventeenth century testify to this guideline. The outstanding collector and compiler of such commonplaces was Erasmus, whose *Adagia* (1500), according to bibliographical evidence, was many times augmented, reissued, and translated into vernacular languages and thus became one of the most popular books all over Europe. [*See* Commonplaces and commonplace books; *and* Imitation.]

The rhetoric of figures. There is a long tradition of the rhetoric of figures that is represented by treatises and short compilations of late antiquity and continued by the medieval *poetriae novae,* which are little else but compendia of schemes and tropes. Humanism, with its rediscovery of the elegance of Cicero's style and its awareness of the linguistic inadequacy of contemporary writings, endeavored to enlarge and refine the resources of language by collecting the vocabulary and phraseology of the best classical authorities. By far the most influential stylistic rhetoric to serve the purpose of augmenting and refining the resources of language is Erasmus's *De duplici copia verborum ac rerum* (On the Twofold Copiousness of Words and Things, 1512). Originally commissioned by John Colet for Saint Paul's School, London, it quickly found its way into most countries of Renaissance Europe, above all in conjunction with the learned commentary of M. Veltkirchius, but also in Mosellanus's abbreviated version, *Tabulae de schematibus et tropis* (Tables of Schemes and Tropes, 1536). Consisting of detailed explications of the figures of speech, as well as rich illustrations, it occupies an intermediate position between a rhetorical treatise of precepts and a practical compendium of examples. Like Erasmus's *De copia,* many figurative treatises were conceived as textbooks for stylistically elegant composition. But for pupils, an earlier opportunity to become acquainted with the figures offered itself in the grammars, which, like those of Johannes Despauterius (c.1460–1520) or William Lily (c.1468–1522), contained large sections on the figures (Green, 1999). Most of the figurative rhetorics were composed for secondary education. Their structure is almost always the same. A brief, general outline of the virtues of style and its three levels (high, middle, low) is followed by a broad treatment of the figures, which are divided into schemes involving a change in form, and into tropes consisting of a change in the meaning of words (metaphor, metonymy, synecdochē, irony) or sentences (allegory, similitude, fable, emblem). Their principal aim was not to supply poets with stylistic techniques. Instead of being a kind of stylistic poetics, they served thoroughly pragmatic uses, as is shown by Henry Peacham's *The Garden of Eloquence* (1577; 1593, 2d ed.), which, despite its florid title, was written by a clergyman for clergymen. A dramatic change in the condition and status of figurative rhetoric took place with the Ramist reform that allocated invention and disposition to dialectic and left only elocution and delivery to rhetoric. The identification of rhetoric with style led to the misconception of a curtailed rhetoric, a misconceptin that is still alive today. Ramist rhetoricians dissected the corpus of figures into neat dichotomies and arranged them in logically-conclusive hierarchical stemmata that facilitated their memorization. A remarkable feature of the Ramist treatises is their employment of literary examples for illustration. The most famous works of antiquity are quoted, but also, in an English adaptation like Abraham Fraunce's treatise, *The Arcadian Rhetorike* (c.1588), outstanding works of such contemporary authors as Tasso, Sidney, Spenser, Du Bartas, Boscan, and Garcilasso are mentioned. The importance of the figures of speech for the constitution and interpretation of poetry is even more evident from the fact that a special book is reserved for them in some Renaissance poetics. Thus, the fourth book of the *Poetices Libri Septem* (1569) by Julius Caesar Scaliger contains, besides a description of the characters of style, an extensive chapter on the *figurae*. In *The Arte of English Poesie* (1589), George Puttenham differs from Scaliger in the treatment of the figures in that he emphasizes their affective and social functions. The third book of his poetic theory, which bears the title "Of Ornament," contains English translations of the figures such as *Meiosis*, "the Disabler"; *Sententia* "the Sage Sayer"; *Gnome,* "The Directour"; *Hipallage,* "the Changeling"; *Ironia,* "the drie mock"; and so on. The identification of *Allegoria* with "the Courtier" reveals the royal court or, more generally, courtly society, as the adequate social ambient of this kind of rhetorical poetics (Rölli Alkemper, 1995). [*See* Copia; Figures of speech; *and* Style.]

Ars memorativa (Memory). The fourth phase of the constitution of a speech or of any oral discourse, *Ars Memorativa* (Memory), became increasingly detached from the five-part system of rhetoric and achieved an autonomous status. This is manifested by independent treatises such as *Congestorium Artificiose Memorie* (A Compendium of Artificial Memory, 1533) by the Dominican Johannes Host de Romberch (fl. 1485–1533), who addressed himself especially to preachers, or

Thesaurus Artificiosae Memoriae (The Treasure House of Artificial Memory, 1579) by Cosmas Rossellius (died 1578), whose large compendium looks for a wider range of possible recipients: preachers, philosophers, physicians, lawyers, and procurators. The English theologian John Willis (died c.1628) wrote a Latin treatise, *Mnemonica* (1618), which was translated into English. In it, he extended and modified the traditional visual concept considerably; for he included not only pictorial but also verbal representations and such hybrid phenomena as emblems. On the whole, the Renaissance witnessed a change in memory architecture. The Roman villa of Ciceronian rhetoric is converted to a theater, or occasionally the medieval structure of a cathedral or a monastery. Radical Protestant reformers like William Perkins (1558–1602) abhorred the classical art of memory as inflicting damage on the human soul through its appeal to fantasy and the emotions. Though the printing press had created a new medium that produced a new type of memory of greater objectivity, the classical *ars memorativa* was not rendered altogether superfluous but acquired new aesthetic functions in the sister arts of poetry and painting. Whereas sixteenth-century treatises combined the classical theory with medical prescriptions for the preservation of a good memory, it became the structural basis for numerous encyclopedias in the next century (Schmidt-Biggemann, 1993). [*See* Memory.]

Delivery (actio/pronuntiatio). The fourth art in the five-part schema, Delivery (Actio/Pronuntiatio) received some attention in the most extensive type of rhetorical manual and also in Ramist rhetoric, but was rarely published in a separate book. John Bulwer's *Chironomia: Or, The Art of Manual Rhetorique* (1644) specializes in the persuasive faculties of hands and fingers, which he represents by a number of "canons" where he links certain positions and movements of hands and fingers to certain affections. In Canon 9, this relationship is represented as follows: "The palm (the fingers all joined together) turned up, and by the return of the wrist, in one motion, spread and turned about with the hand, is an action convenient for *admiration.*" Or in Canon 21: "To shake the hand, with bended brows, doth *abhor, deny, dislike, refuse,* and disallow." These verbal prescriptions are accompanied by chirogrammatic plates, which contain visual representations of the rhetorical gestures and, as a whole, form a general sign system that can be transferred to creations in the visual arts. [*See* Delivery.]

Intermedial rhetoric. During the Renaissance, rhetoric expanded its range of applications and served as a semiotic model for theory and practice in the nonverbal media. As R. W. Lee demonstrates in *Ut Pictura Poesis* (1940; reprinted 1962), such concepts as decorum and invention were transferred from rhetoric to pictorial theory (Leon Battista Alberti, Leonardo da Vinci) and also served the purpose of raising the former *ars mechanica* to an *ars liberalis.* [*See* Art.] In musical theory and practice, an analogous transfer of rhetorical categories took place, of which Joachim Burmeister's *Musica Poetica* (1600) provides good testimony. This tradition of rhetoricizing music continued well into the eighteenth century, where the "Klangrede" (musical eloquence) was still practiced by such outstanding composers as Johann Sebastian Bach and George Frideric Handel. [*See* Music.]

Practicalities of Renaissance Rhetoric. During the Renaissance, rhetoric was not confined to a single human occupation but in fact, comprised a broad range of theoretical and practical activities. It likewise affected the contemplative lives of scholars and philosophers and the active lives of statesmen and ministers of the church. Some of the fields in which rhetoric played a major part included scholarship, politics, education, culture, science, and literature.

Renaissance rhetoricians were initially Humanist scholars whose primary task was the retrieval of texts long lost. But apart from this kind of text archaeology, they considered it equally necessary to establish linguistically- and historically-correct printed editions of their rediscovered treasures. Thus, critical editions of the standard works of Aristotle, Cicero, Hermogenes, and Quintilian were issued, often furnished with learned annotations and commentaries. When scholars began composing rhetorical treatises of their own, they tried to emulate the ancients, demonstrating their erudition by numerous references to the entire classical canon as well as to select modern authorities. Excellent examples of this learned philological practice are the works of the Strasbourg humanist and pedagogue Johan-

nes Sturm (1507–1589) and, later on, of the Leiden humanist Gerardus Joannes Vossius (1577–1649); for example, in his *De rhetorices natura ac constitutione* (On the Nature and Constitution of Rhetoric, 1622).

The Humanists were not only ardent lovers of classical rhetoric and excellent scholars but also practical-minded men whose professions were often those of a lawyer, notary or secretary, and as such they pursued public careers. In Italy, Coluccio Salutati became chancellor of the Republic of Florence; in England, Thomas Wilson was appointed secretary of state; in France, Nicolaus Caussinus was entrusted with the functions of an adviser and confessor to the king. Rhetoricians, as a rule, had ambitions of entering a diplomatic career as ambassadors of their government. A notorious example of a politician turned rhetorician is Niccolò Machiavelli (1469–1527), who in his treatise *Il principe* (The Prince, 1513) developed a theory of statesmanship recommending that the ruler imitate not the strong lion but the crafty fox in his speaking and acting, a *virtù* (capability) that makes him outwit even superior enemies. Shakespeare's plays contain a whole range of Machiavellian villains (Richard III, Proteus in *Two Gentlemen of Verona,* Don John in *Much Ado About Nothing,* Edmund in *King Lear,* Iago in *Othello*) who commit their crimes through an insinuating, hypocritical rhetoric. In contrast to Machiavelli's concept of a utilitarian rhetoric devoid of any moral scruples, *The Book Named the Governor* (1531) by Sir Thomas Elyot (c.1490–1546) offers the picture of an exemplary Christian ruler who embodies both moral principles and practical eloquence.

Education. Many Humanists were not content with academic scholarship but endeavored to disseminate its intellectual substance among a wider public. Desiderius Erasmus and the Spaniard Juan Luis Vives (1492–1540), like Erasmus a cosmopolitan, sought to establish rhetoric in school curricula in order to make it the property of every educated citizen. Pedagogues of lesser talent but equal enthusiasm followed their examples and wrote rhetorical textbooks and educational treatises, such as *The Schoolmaster* (1570) by Roger Ascham (1515–1568) or *Ludus Literarius* (1612) by John Brinsley (fl. 1633).

Rhetoric became a determining factor in the

creation of a Humanist cultural consciousness. Its core was the Ciceronian belief that through eloquence (*eloquentia*), wisdom (*sapientia*) can be achieved. This belief led to a theory of the origin of culture by means of the eloquent word. Cultural heroes of antiquity were adduced as authorities, like Hercules Gallicus, who by the golden chains of his eloquence tamed the barbarous Gauls and changed them from primitive to civilized men; or like the orator, poet, and musician Orpheus, who tamed wild animals (i.e., men) and, in another version of the myth, made the cosmos rise out of primeval chaos. Thus, the magical force of rhetoric combined with music was believed to create, maintain, and restore harmony and order in all spheres of the universe. For this reason, rulers preferred being as celebrated as Hercules Gallicus or Orpheus, which meant that they were considered preservers of peace and civil harmony. When this ideology was refuted by the reality of events and Humanist culture declined, rhetoric established itself, but in a different way, as the basis of courtly culture. First formulated by Baldassare Castiglione's *Il Cortegiano* (1528; English translation by Sir Thomas Hoby: *The Courtier*, 1561), it is no longer regarded appropriate to exhibit art, including the art of persuasion, but rather to conceal it. This concealment of art, which in Italian is termed *sprezzatura* and appears comparable to "understatement" in English, is considered the utmost achievement of art and is identified with an *altera natura* or a second nature. *Altera natura* is art so skillfully hidden that it can no longer be recognized as such but has the appearance of artless nature; however, not of a nature in its original primitive state but of one domesticated by art. In *The Arte of English Poesie* (1589), George Puttenham equates *allegoria*, the basic trope of courtly rhetoric, with both "the figure of fair semblant" and "the figure of false semblant," which illustrates the delicate balance of courtly culture between appearance and reality or between falsehood and truth. Hence, it is only a small step from the aesthetics of artful artlessness to Machiavelli's amoral rhetoric of deceit. When the middle classes rose to prosperity and social power, they at first sought to compete with the aristocracy by adopting its cultural code; this sometimes proved to be a ri-

diculous failure, as it is wittily shown in Molière's comedy *Le Bourgeois gentilhomme* (1670). With the "crisis of aristocracy" (Stone, 1965), however, the courtly concept of culture was increasingly criticized by the one-dimensional mentality of the middle classes, who regarded it as expressive of decadence and decay. As a consequence, the figurative style of ornamentation was replaced by the artless plain style that turned out to be the new verbal expression of the prototype of bourgeois literature, the novel.

A specific rhetoric of the New Science (Moss, 1993; Nate, 2000) does not exist. Its axioms must rather be deduced from its critique of the counterposition of Ciceronian emphasis on linguistic resourcefulness (*copia*). In his *History of the Royal Society of London* (1667), Thomas Sprat formulates the oft-quoted "constant Resolution" of the Society, "to reject all the amplifications, digressions, and swellings of style; to return back to the primitive purity, and shortness, when men deliver'd so many *things*, almost in equal number of *words*." The direct verbal access to the referential object demanded a plain style with perspicuity as its principal feature. The rejection of the artificiality of rhetoric led to a kind of antirhetoric that is still visible, for example, in John Locke's *An Essay Concerning Human Understanding* (1690): "All the arts of rhetoric . . . are for nothing else but to insinuate wrong ideas, move the passions. and therby mislead the judgment, and indeed are perfect cheats" (3.10.251).

The rhetoricizing of literature produced such features as: figurative ornamentation; generic and structural hybridity: the intermingling of rhetorical and traditional poetical concepts; affectivity: the engendering of moderate affections and violent passions; *enargeia* (vividness): producing the illusion of immediate presence and even of reality. With the rise of the plain style and the prose narrative, these features were not entirely abandoned but remained characteristic of poetry of all kinds.

[*See also* Classical rhetoric; *and* Humanism.]

BIBLIOGRAPHY

Adolph, Robert. *The Rise of Modern Prose Style*. Cambridge, Mass., 1968.

Artaza, Elena, ed. *Antología de textos retóricos espa. oles del siglo XVI*. Bilbao, 1997. A collection of sixteenth-century Spanish texts on rhetoric arranged according to the five *partes artis*.

Ashley, L. R. N. "Research Opportunities in English Homiletics and Rhetoric." *Literary Research Newsletter* 6 (1981), pp. 143–169; 7 (1982), pp. 12–29.

Barner, Wilfried. *Barockrhetorik: Untersuchungen zu ihren geschichtlichen Grundlagen.* Tübingen, 1970.

Bauer, Barbara. *Jesuitische "ars rhetorica" im Zeitalter der Glaubenskämpfe.* Frankfurt a.M., 1986.

Castelli, Enrico, ed. *Retorica e Barocco.* Rome, 1955.

Cave, Terence. *The Cornucopian Text: Problems of Writing in the French Renaissance.* Oxford, 1979.

Fumaroli, Marc. *L'Age de l'éloquence: Rhétorique et "res literaria" de la Renaissance au seuil de l'époque classique.* Geneva, 1980.

García Berrio, Antonio. *Formación de la teoría literaria moderna.* 2 vols. Madrid, 1977–1980.

Grafton, Anthony, and Lisa Jardine. *From Humanism to the Humanities: Education and the Liberal Arts in Fifteenth- and Sixteenth-Century Europe.* Cambridge, Mass., 1986.

Graham, Kenneth. *The Performance of Conviction: Plainness and Rhetoric in the Early English Renaissance.* New York, 1992.

Grassi, Ernesto. *Rhetoric as Philosophy: The Humanist Tradition.* University Park, Pa., 1980.

Green, Lawrence D. "*Grammatica movet:* Grammar Books and *Elocutio.*" In *Rhetorica Movet: Studies in Historical and Modern Rhetoric in Honour of Heinrich F. Plett,* edited by Peter L. Oesterreich and Thomas O. Sloane, pp. 73–115. Leiden, 1999.

Hardison, O. B., Jr. *The Enduring Monument: A Study of the Idea of Praise in Renaissance Literary Theory and Practice.* Chapel Hill, N.C., 1962; reprint, Westport, Conn., 1973.

Hinz, Manfred. *Rhetorische Strategien des Hofmannes: Studien zu den italienischen Hofmannstraktaten des 16. und 17. Jahrhunderts.* Stuttgart, 1992. A study of the rhetorical strategies used and propagated in Italian courtesy treatises and conduct books.

Howell, Wilbur Samuel. *Logic and Rhetoric in England, 1500–1700.* Princeton, 1956; reprint, New York, 1961.

Javitch, Daniel. *Poetry and Courtliness in Renaissance England.* Princeton, 1978.

Kibédi Varga, Á. *Rhétorique et littérature: Études de structures classiques.* Paris, 1970.

Knape, Joachim. *Philipp Melanchthons "Rhetorik."* Tübingen, 1993.

Mack, Peter, ed. *Renaissance Rhetoric.* Basingstoke, U.K., 1994.

Meerhoff, Kees. *Rhétorique et poétique au XVIe siècle en France: Du Bellay, Ramus, et les autres.* Leiden, 1986.

Monfasani, John. *George of Trebizond: A Biography and a Study of His Rhetoric and Logic.* Leiden, 1976.

Moss, Jean Dietz. *Novelties in the Heavens: Rhetoric and Science in the Copernican Controversy.* Chicago, 1993.

Murphy, James J. *Renaissance Rhetoric: A Short-Title Catalogue on Rhetorical Theory from the Beginning of Printing to A.D.1700, with Special Attention to the Holdings of the Bodleian Library, Oxford. With a Select Basic Bibliography of Secondary Works of Renaissance Rhetoric.* New York, 1981. An alphabetically arranged bibliography of rhetorical source-texts in Renaissance Europe.

Murphy, James J., ed. *Renaissance Eloquence: Studies in the Theory and Practice of Renaissance Rhetoric.* Berkeley, 1983. A collection of essays on diverse subject areas: bibliographical research, ethics, politics, theology, style, literature.

Nate, Richard. *Wissenschaft und Literatur im England der frühen Neuzeit.* Munich, 2000.

O'Malley, John W. *Praise and Blame in Renaissance Rome: Rhetoric, Doctrine, and Reform in the Sacred Orators of the Papal Court, c. 1450–1521.* Durham, N.C., 1979.

Ong, Walter J. *Ramus, Method, and the Decay of Dialogue: From the Art of Discourse to the Art of Reason.* Cambridge, Mass., 1958. Reprinted, 1983.

Plett, Heinrich F. *Rhetorik der Affekte: Englische Wirkungsästhetik im Zeitalter der Renaissance.* Tübingen, 1975. A study of *pathos* and affectivity in English and Neo-Latin rhetoric and poetics and rhetorically-influenced treatises (music, painting, conduct books) of the Renaissance.

Plett, Heinrich F. *English Renaissance Rhetoric and Poetics: A Systematic Bibliography of Primary and Secondary Sources.* Leiden, 1995. A classified bibliography of rhetorical and poetological source texts that were of importance for England but also for the European Renaissance in general, with transcriptions of the title pages of each *editio princeps,* including the registration of the library and the call number of the copy used; also a comprehensive bibliography of twentieth-century criticism arranged in a systematic sequence of topics.

Plett, Heinrich F., ed. *Renaissance-Rhetorik / Renaissance Rhetoric.* Berlin, 1993. A trilingual collection of interdisciplinary essays by an international group of scholars on the relations between rhetoric and philosophy, literature, painting, music, acting, medicine, religion, society, and politics in various countries of Renaissance Europe.

Rabil, Albert, ed. *Renaissance Humanism: Foundations, Forms, and Legacy.* 3 vols. Philadelphia, 1988.

Rebhorn, Wayne A. *The Emperor of Men's Minds: Literature and the Renaissance Discourse of Rhetoric.* Ithaca, N.Y., 1995.

Rhodes, Neil. *The Power of Eloquence and English Renaissance Literature.* New York, 1992.

Rölli Alkemper, Dorothee. *Höfische Poetik in der englischen Renaissance: George Puttenhams "The Arte of English Poesie."* Munich, 1995. A study of rhetorical poetics in the context of courtly culture, with special emphasis on George Puttenham.

Schmidt-Biggemann, Wilhelm. *Topica Universalis: Eine Modellgeschichte humanistischer und barocker Wissenschaft.* Hamburg, 1983. A comprehensive study of encyclopedic literature in the seventeenth century from a philosophical point of view.

Schoeck, Richard J. "'Going for the Throat': Erasmus' Rhetorical Theory and Practice." In *Renaissance-Rhetorik / Renaissance Rhetoric,* edited by Heinrich F. Plett, pp. 43–58. Berlin, 1993.

Seigel, J. E. *Rhetoric and Philosophy in Renaissance Humanism: The Union of Eloquence and Wisdom, Petrarca to Valla.* Princeton, 1968.

Sloane, Thomas O., and Raymond B. Waddington, eds. *The Rhetoric of Renaissance Poetry.* Berkeley, 1974. A collection of interpretative essays.

Sonnino, Lee A. *A Handbook to Sixteenth-Century Rhetoric.* London, 1968.

Stolt, Birgit. *Wortkampf: Frühneuhochdeutsche Beispiele zur rhetorischen Praxis.* Frankfurt a.M., 1974. Rhetorical essays on German literature of the Early Modern Age.

Stone, Lawrence. *The Crisis of Aristocracy, 1558–1641.* Oxford, 1965.

Struever, Nancy S. *The Language of History in the Renaissance: Rhetoric and Historical Consciousness in Florentine Humanism.* Princeton, 1970.

Tateo, Francesco. *Retorica e poetica fra Medioevo e Rinascimento.* Bari, 1960.

Vasoli, Cesare. *La dialettica e la retorica dell'Umanesimo: "Invenzione" e "metodo" nella cultura del XV e XVI secolo.* Milan, Italy, 1968.

Vickers, Brian. *In Defence of Rhetoric.* Oxford, 1988. Chapter 3 deals with Renaissance rhetoric under the programmatic title: "Renaissance Reintegration."

Ward, John O. "Renaissance Commentators on Ciceronian Rhetoric." In *Renaissance Eloquence,* edited by James J. Murphy, pp. 126–173. Berkeley, 1983.
— HEINRICH F. PLETT

Rederijkers

The Dutch so-called *rederijker* movement originated in the first half of the fifteenth century when, succeeding the *puys* in northern France, similar literary corporations were also founded in the Netherlands. Organized in "chambers," they were situated in the cities of French- and Dutch-speaking Flanders and Brabant (now in Belgium) and of Zeeland and Holland (now the Netherlands)—a territory that largely corresponds to the fifteenth-to-sixteenth-century duchy of Burgundy. The latter phenomenon may explain the relation with their French counterparts. Also, they called themselves *rethorikers* or *rethoricienen* (the *h* placed in the medieval way after the *t,* instead of the *r*), French derivates, with *rederijkers* a late sixteenth-century puristic neologism.

Unlike the *puys,* however, their scope was not mainly religious. Although they were sometimes named after religious symbols or saints, as The Holy Ghost (Bruges), The Book (Brussels), and Saint Catherine (Ophasselt), far more often they bore the names of plants or flowers, like the Amsterdam *Eglentier* (Eglantine), possibly derived from the rhetorical *colores* with which they ornamented their poetry. [*See* Color.] Their writings, moreover, were not exclusively religious. Besides exercising the poetical talents of their members, and in doing so, furthering joy and friendship among them, they played an important role in the maintenance of the town's internal and external public relations. Indications of both civic functions may be found in the statutes that were granted to them by the city magistrates and sometimes by the dukes themselves, as was the case with the chamber The *Fonteine* (Fountain) of Ghent, one of the oldest in the country, granted in 1448 by the aldermen and council and in 1476 by Duke Charles the Bold.

Their poetry was characterized by an abundance of rhymes and elaborate lyrical forms, that is to say, by features of the *ars versificatoria,* the *seconde rhétorique* of the French *rhétoriqueurs.* The most important lyric genre was the *refrein,* consisting mostly of four or five stanzas, each ending on the same line, the last stanza being explicitly addressed to the chamber's *Prince* (head). The content could be religious or didactic, amorous or comic. *Refrein* contests were held, both among the chambers, as well as within each chamber separately, in which the last repetitive line had to conclude with an answer to a given question or was prescribed beforehand. Sometimes these *refreinen* were followed, or even intersected by the stanzas of a song on the same, or a comparable, subject. From the second half of the sixteenth century onward, the *refreinen* and songs presented at these contests were often published afterward. Songs were also written on special festive days, as, for example, the New Year's songs of which a whole series, written by members of the Amsterdam chamber *De Eglentier,* has come to us.

The public function was especially realized in the performance by the chamber's members of *zinnespelen* and *esbatementen* (moralities and comic plays) in the market square or some other public place. These plays were written by the chamber's poet in charge, the factor. But the collections compiled by some chambers—for example, the Haarlem chamber's very important one, *De Pellicanisten* (Pellicanists), better known by its device *Trou Moet Blijcken* (loyalty has to be proved)—indicate that plays from elsewhere were performed as well. Theatrical contests among the chambers were also held from time to time, although not so often as the *refrein* contests. The plays presented on those occasions were, of course, written by the respective factors themselves.

Very important were the series of contests organized in the duchy of Brabant, called *Het landjuweel* (the nation's jewel). The first series took place in the last quarter of the fifteenth century; the second, consisting of seven contests in as many different cities, between 1515 and 1561. The chamber that won the first prize at one of these contests had to organize the following one. The final one was held in Antwerp in 1561, organized by the painters' chamber *De Violieren* (Stock-gillyflower) on the theme "What best leads mankind to the arts." It was an enormous event, to which visitors came even from far away Leyden. It started with an impressive and colorful entry of the participants, the Princes on horseback, accompanied by their chambers' trumpeters and all the members, including the fools. During the whole month of August, there were almost daily performances and parties. It was the last time such an gigantic event took place. The insurrection against the King of Spain, who as heir to the dukes of Burgundy was Lord of the Netherlands, swept over the country to develop into the Eighty Years War that would separate the Roman Catholic southern provinces and the officially Protestant northern ones.

In the northern Netherlands—from 1579 on, the Dutch Republic—the contests were less impressive, but up to the second decade of the seventeenth century remained major events in a city's life. Here, they often served to raise money for some charity, as for instance the 1596 Leyden contest, organized by the town secretary Jan van Hout to promote a lottery in favor of a new hospice. But soon they were surpassed in importance by the *tableaux vivants* erected to honor the Prince of Orange or some visiting foreign royalty, or to celebrate a peace treaty. These activities, too, fell traditionally under the responsibility of the chambers.

In the meantime, however, classical rhetoric—known to the French as *première rhétorique* (first rhetoric) as opposed to the *seconde rhétorique* of the *ars versificatoria*—had long since made its entry into the Latin schools. Matthys de Castelein, who wrote the only Dutch theoretical tract on the art of the *rethoricians,* entitled *Const van Rhetoriken* (1555), made an impressive effort to combine the *rethoricians'* poetical principles with the more general principles of Cicero's *De oratore* and Quintilian's *Institutio oratoria,* as well as Horace's *Ars poetica.* But in the field of Dutch vernacular poetry also, the new Renaissance movement took over. From the 1580s on, the younger generation of Dutch poets looked with dismay upon the rhymes of the traditional *rethoricians,* who, they believed, had usurped the term but didn't even know what real rhetoric was about.

The Amsterdam chamber *De Eglentier* went gradually along with the new developments, in the 1580s publishing a grammar, a dialectic, and a small rhetoric in Dutch. From the late 1590s on, the chamber performed the first modern tragedies, written by its most gifted young member, P. C. Hooft, while other members wrote epigrams, paradoxes, and sonnets, instead of *refreinen* and the like. In the realm of the city's public relations, however, even in Amsterdam the chambers continued their traditional activities for some time. Elsewhere, the *rethoricians* continued the rhyming *zinnespelen* and *refreinen,* for quite some time; although these genres were increasingly looked down on in social terms, and regarded with contempt by "real" poets, they formed a vital creative force among the lower middle-class population through the first half of the seventeenth century.

BIBLIOGRAPHY

Coigneau, Dirk. "De Const van Rhetoriken, Drama and Delivery." *Rhetoric-Rhétoriqueurs-Rederijkers*, edited by

Jelle Koopmans, Mark A. Meadow, Kees Meerhoff and Marijke Spies, pp. 123–140. Amsterdam, 1995. The only existing article on the relation between the poetry of the French *puys* and the Dutch *rethoricians*.

Hummelen, W. M. H. *Repertorium van het Rederijkers- drama 1500–ca. 1620.* Assen, 1968. Extensively an- noted bibliography of dramatic texts.

Koppenol, Johan. *Leids Heelal. Het Loterijspel (1596) van Jan van Hout.* Hilversum, the Netherlands, 1998. Re- cent and important study on de Leyden contest of 1596, with an exhaustive bibliography on all aspects of the Dutch *rethoricians* and early Renaissance poetry.

Pleij, Herman. "The Despisers of Rhetoric. Origins and Significance of Attacks on the Art of the Rhetoricians (Rederijkers) in the Sixteenth Century." *Rhetoric- Rhétoriqueurs-Rederijkers,* edited by Jelle Koopmans, Mark A. Meadow, Kees Meerhoff, and Marijke Spies, pp. 157–174. Amsterdam, 1995. On the opposition especially by street poets toward the *rethoricians'* arrogance.

Serebrennikov, N. E. "'Dwelck den Mensche, alder- meest tot Consten verwect.' The Artist's Perspec- tive." *Rhetoric-Rhétoriqueurs-Rederijkers,* edited by Jelle Koopmans, Mark A. Meadow, Kees Meerhoff, and Marijke Spies, pp. 219–246. Amsterdam, 1995. On the *rethoricians'* contest in Antwerp, 1561.

Spel in de Verte. Tekst, structuur en opvoeringspraktijk van het rederijkerstoneel, edited by B. A. M. Ramakers. Ghent, Belgium, 1994 . Special issue of *Jaarboek De Fonteine* 41–42 (1991–1992), the leading scholarly periodical on *rederijker* literature, with contributions on the poetical and structural aspects aa well as the staging of *rederijker* drama.

Spies, Marijke. "The Amsterdam Chamber De Eglentier and the Ideals of Erasmian Humanism." In *From Re- volt to Riches. Culture and History of the Low Countries 1500–1700. International and Interdisciplinary Perspec- tives,* edited by Theo Hermans and Reinier Salverda pp. 109–118. (London, 1993).

Spies, Marijke. "Between Ornament and Argumenta- tion: Developments in 16th-century Dutch Poetics." In *Rhetoric-Rhétoriqueurs-Rederijkers,* edited by Jelle Koopmans, Mark A. Meadow, Kees Meerhoff, and Marijke Spies, pp. 117–112. Amsterdam, 1995. Small introductory article on the transition from *rederijker* to Renaissance poetry.

Spies, Marijke. "Developments in Sixteenth-Century Dutch Poetics. From 'Rhetoric' to 'Renaissance'." *Re- naissance-Rhetorik. Renaissance Rhetoric,* edited by Heinrich F. Plett, pp. 72–91. Berlin, 1993. Analysis of the poetical developments in *rederijker*-texts in the sixteenth century.

— MARIJKE SPIES

Rhetoric in Renaissance language and literature

The emergence of the Renaissance in Italy brought with it a revival of interest in classical rhetoric and a desire to emulate the eloquence of its great- est orator, Cicero (106–43 BCE). Burgeoning com- mercial ventures and expansion of the political power of the papacy and of government in the city-states of Italy, had increased the opportuni- ties for employment of secretaries or chancellors, men skilled in speaking and writing, cognizant of protocol yet assertive in argument, and clear in their expression of ideas. Such men were edu- cated in the medieval form of rhetoric, particu- larly in its offshoots, the art of letter writing and the notarial art. [*See* Ars dictaminis.] Newly in- spired by the recently recovered mature rhetori- cal works of Cicero, his orations, and his letters, they sought to publicize his conception of rheto- ric: a union of wisdom and eloquence (*res et verba*) in the service of the state. At the same time, a widening wave of literacy extended beyond the church and the court to include a secular public: merchants, bankers, lawyers, artisans, and others of the middle class. The ease of communicating with this enlarged audience meant that rhetoric was pressed into the growing arguments about religion and science, two areas where formerly other types of discourse were the rule. [*See* Reli- gion; *and* Science.] Thus, the province of rhetor- ical argument gradually increased, although in- fluential philosophers deplored its extension into their areas. Not surprisingly, rhetorical aims and concepts also dominated the emerging art of po- etics. By the end of the Renaissance, the reaction against rhetoric, coupled with a surfeit of artful expression, served to turn the fashion in elo- quence from elaborate and ornamented sen- tences to plain style. [*See* Style.]

The Legacy of the Middle Ages. The Middle Ages bequeathed to the early Renaissance the trivium of basic language studies: grammar, logic, and rhetoric, but the latter had lost its classical function as civic persuasion. [*See overview article a* Medieval rhetoric; *and* Trivium.] That role had waned with the repression of representative gov- ernment during the Roman Empire, and did not stir again until the thirteenth century. Further, in the late Middle Ages, dialectic overshadowed rhetoric in importance and created confusion in the status and scope of the arts that would continue to vex Renaissance pedagogues. [*See* Dialectic.] Rhetoric in the view of philosophers was only a pale imitation of dialectic, for while rhetoric also used probable reasoning and a version of the topics or commonplaces, these were meant to deal with particular cases not the grand universal questions. Students in the Scholastic system of education were exercised rigorously in dialectic, learning how to make distinctions and apply them to often insoluble academic questions. The tedious, repetitive method so bored many students and teachers alike that the Scholastic curriculum came under attack in the Renaissance.

The Effect of Recovery of the Classics. The Renaissance owed much of its energy to the discoveries of Greek and Roman manuscripts, which excited great interest among scholars and turned their minds to new possibilities for research, oratory, prose, poetry, history, and education. Petrarch's (1303–1374) recovery in 1345 of Cicero's informal letters to his friends, inspired the Italian scholar to write in imitation of these on subjects of perennial interest. His letters, were very different from the rigid, formulaic letters of *ars dictaminis*. By the sixteenth century, this version had been transmuted into the essay by Michel de Montaigne (1533–1592) and Francis Bacon (1561–1626). The recovery of other Ciceronian works was, similarly, to have far-reaching effects. Cicero's dialogue *De oratore* was not widely available before. Its reemergence, coupled with the recovery of his orations, revitalized the concept of the citizen orator, which men like Coluccio Salutati (1331–1406), Leonardo Bruni (c.1370–1444), and Poggio Bracciolini (1380–1459) epitomized in their roles as chancellors of Florence and papal secretaries. Poggio was himself responsible for the recovery of the complete manuscript of Quintilian's *Institutes* as well as two of Cicero's speeches.

The recovery of Greek manuscripts revived the fortunes of both Plato (c.428–c.347 BCE) and Aristotle (384–322 BCE). Plato's dialogues disclosed his criticisms of rhetoric and gave a fuller picture of the context of sophistic rhetoric. Aristotle's *Rhetoric*, recovered in the twelfth century, gained increased attention as new translations and numerous commentaries were written in the sixteenth century. In addition, the rhetorical theories of Isocrates and Hermogenes were conveyed to the West in a synthetic text by George of Trebizond (Trapezuntius; 1395–c.1493), which combined the teachings of both Greek and Roman rhetoric.

The development of the printing press quickly disseminated this trove of Greek and Latin manuscripts. The old standbys of the medieval trivium, *De inventione* and the *Ad Herennium*, were among the first works to be printed, preserving their influence. The summary effect for rhetoric of these recoveries was to reinvigorate in the real world of Renaissance life the practice of argument *in utramque partem* (on both sides). A plethora of issues were open for debate on salient topics in politics, science, and religion. The luminosity, fervor, variety, and wit demonstrated by Cicero's writings provided a model of persuasive *virtu* (excellence) desperately sought after by many a Renaissance orator and writer. Classical genres such as the epistle and the dialogue offered new avenues of persuasion. The medieval disputation was transformed into a humanized version in which rigorous arguments were interwoven with oratorical appeals and presented—often as dialogue—to general as well as academic readers or hearers. Too, the epideictic oration of praise or blame found a multitude of new uses from book dedications to academic inaugurals and sermons. [*See* Epideictic genre.]

Ciceronianism and Imitation. Humanist education was expected to supply the means to rhetorical excellence. Its philological and antiquarian explorations led teachers to excoriate Scholastic Latin and recommend imitation of the more elegant Latin of the Augustan period, especially Cicero's prose. Lamenting the low state to which Latin had fallen in the medieval period, Lorenzo Valla (1407–1457) wrote his *De elegantia linguae latinae* (printed in 1471) in an attempt to rectify the problem.

Teachers hoped that the tropes and figures, used so effortlessly by Cicero, would become so familiar to their students that using them would become second nature and would even have the appearance of artlessness (*sprezzatura*) recommended by Baldassare Castiglione (1478–1529) in *Il Cortegiano* (The Courtier; 1514). Figures could furnish both emotional force and develop meaning more vividly than ordinary language.

Although many new textbooks published in the Renaissance covered all five canons of rhetoric, others were devoted to style alone, and still others to invention. Erasmus's *De copia* (1511), one of the first to emphasize style, suggested ways of uniting wisdom and eloquence through alternate means of expression and amplification. [*See* Copia.] Cicero is referenced repeatedly as the touchstone of apt and incisive expression, even though Erasmus was later to deplore excessive imitation of his style. Imitation had been urged by teachers of rhetoric since the Sophists. [*See* Imitation.] Students were perennially instructed to model their writing and speaking on that of preeminent authors. In the Renaissance, Cicero was the most celebrated, although Seneca, Livy, Sallust, Quintilian, and Pliny were also often recommended. The most influential Ciceronian was probably Gasparino Barzizza (c.1360–1431). He is reputed to be the first who successfully returned his language and expression to the Ciceronian standard. He did so through careful study and analysis of the Roman's writings. So enamored were some scholars of Cicero's Latin, however, that they sought to imitate not only the style of his writings, but even his very words. Pietro Bembo (1470–1547) was chief among its advocates, urging his followers to immerse themselves in nothing but Cicero, the best and most beautiful *auctoritas*. Christophe de Longueil (Longolius, 1488–1522), influenced by Bembo, sought to cast his writings solely in Ciceronian language and style, even when writing religious polemics against Luther. This adulation soon bred a critical reaction.

Anti-Ciceronianism. Valla was one of the first to declare that he preferred another model for his Latin prose, Quintilian. Angelo Ambrogini da Poliziano (Politian; 1454–1494), also an early critic of Ciceronianism, stated that he himself followed no one in particular but found many classical authors to be excellent stylists. He defended his own eclectic use of language against two of his correspondents, Bartolomeo Scala and Paolo Cortesi, and deplored the lack of individuality produced by slavish devotion to Cicero. Cortesi declared that assiduous imitation should not produce inferior apes of Cicero, but rather sons who, though resembling their father had their own individuality. Gianfrancesco Pico (1469–1533), nephew of the philosopher Giovanni Pico

della Mirandola, took Bembo to task for not recognizing the weaknesses of Cicero as well as his strengths.

Erasmus was perhaps the most influential critic of the cult. In his satire *Ciceronianus* (1528), he ridiculed the excesses of imitation in general, and many readers thought caricatured Longolius in particular through the pedant Nosoponus. His dialogue generated much ill will: a flurry of letters by Ciceronians offended at being named or not named in the dialogue, two impassioned orations attacking Erasmus by Julius Caesar Scaliger (1484–1558), and a dialogue by Etienne Dolet (1509–1546).

The Ciceronian controversy continued for many years. It flared again when a lexicon and phrase-book drawn from Cicero by Mario Nizzoli with commentaries by Dolet were published. M. Antoine Muret (Muretus; 1526–1585) and other prominent scholars attacked the servile imitation these fostered. Peter Ramus (1515–1572) joined the fray against the pedants in France with his *Ciceronianus* (1557). In England, Gabriel Harvey (c.1545–c.1630) argued in his own *Ciceronianus* (1576) for the emulation of modern authors such as Ramus and Omer Talon (c.1510–1562), whose reforms of rhetoric are described below.

Mannerism. As Latin increasingly gave way to the vernaculars in the sixteenth century, a number of authors attempted to emulate classical style by incorporating Latin terms and sentence structure. In addition, fascination with the possibilities of the fecundity of expression furnished through the figures sometimes led to tedious dilation. John Lyly's *Euphues, the Anatomy of Wit* (1578) and *Euphues and His England* (1580), exemplify this trend. His writings made *euphuism* a term of opprobrium among those who preferred the sparer style of Demosthenes or Seneca. The same kind of elaborate stylistic experimentation, termed *mannerism,* was endemic to poets in Spain and Italy. Luis de Gongora y Argote (1561–1627) wrote in an abstruse and convoluted style, derided as Gongorism by his critics. He liberally used Latinisms of diction and syntax, often amplifying by means of strained conceits. Similarly, Giambattista Marino (1569–1625), in what came to be called contemptuously "Marinism," also carried conceits and metaphors to extremes. In the next century, the rise of a new scientific style increased the perception that artful embellishment was an antiquated, unnecessary practice.

Rhetoric and Poetics. In the early sixteenth century, scholars began to separate poetics from grammar and accord it status as one of three discursive arts—grammar, poetics, and rhetoric. From the outset, poetic's theoretical development was dominated by rhetoric, partly because of the propensity of scholars in the period to classify the arts by means of systems inherited from Scholastic teachers. Most saw rhetoric and poetics as conjoined, and not simply because of their mutual concern with style and the figures. Following Averröes (1126–1198), the medieval commentator on Aristotle's works, rhetoric and poetics were classed with the rational sciences of Aristotle's *Organon*. In that vein, early in the sixteenth century Bartolomeo Lombardi noted that rhetoric and poetics are both faculties, concerned with all kinds of subject matter. Both employ a popular form of reasoning in the example and the enthymeme, and both treat political matters. Francesco Robortello (1516–1567), following the Scholastics, saw the discursive arts on a continuum from certain to false, with demonstration concerned with certain knowledge, dialectic with the probable, rhetoric with the persuasive, sophistic with the seemingly probable, and poetics with the false or fabulous.

By the mid-sixteenth century, other scholars tended to emphasize another classification in which rhetoric and poetics were brought under the umbrella of the architectonic science of politics. Alessandro Piccolomini (1508–1578) in his commentaries on the *Rhetoric* and *Poetics* explains that both are instrumental arts sharing the aim of civic utility. In this view, the poet shares the office with Cicero's *orator perfectus*.

For later scholars such as Giovanni Battista Guarini (1538–1612), pleasure not politics is the end of poetics, and its means is imitation. Guarini argued that Aristotle never subordinated poetics to politics, and, moreover, said that the poet takes his cues from rhetoric not moral philosophy. Rhetoric offers the poet guidance in developing character, argument, and in appealing to audiences. Antonio Riccoboni (1541–1599), writing his widely known translations and commentaries on the *Rhetoric* and *Poetics* near the end of the century, underscores the Aristotelian sense of the

dependence of poetics upon rhetoric in the earlier mentioned areas of composition, and the notion of poetics as an independent study. The aims of poetics he noted are pleasure and utility, which it shares with rhetoric.

Scholastic teachers stressed rhetorical concerns—audience, the poet's character, and the poem's message. Ciceronians spoke of invention, arrangement, and style. [*See* Arrangement, *article on* Traditional arrangement; *and* Invention.] They embraced also the teachings of Quintilian and Horace, repeating their advice about the need to revise, to think of the poem as a unit, and to be cognizant of appropriateness. Horace's *Ars poetica* (first century BCE) had long been viewed as a rhetorical text, reinforcing the linkage of the arts. In addition, the common concern with the tropes and figures of speech in the teaching of rhetoric and poetics imbued poetics with the elements of emotion and character so important to rhetorical persuasion. [*See* Figures of speech.] Learning the tropes and the figures provided still another means of invention for both poet and orator.

Reforms of Rhetoric. Coming first in the order of teaching rhetoric, invention was the focus of educational reformers frustrated with the traditional Scholastic curriculum and yet convinced that attention to the invention of arguments was still necessary. The *studia humanitatis*, begun in the last half of the fifteenth century, had included rhetoric as a prominent part of its new program of studies: grammar, poetry, rhetoric, history, and moral philosophy; but it omitted logic. Rudolfus Agricola (1444–1485) a Dutch Humanist, whose commentaries on Apthonius's *Progymnasmata* helped popularize those ancient exercises in Northern Europe, wrote *De inventione dialectica*. In this text (published in 1515), he simplified the teaching of argument by folding rhetorical invention into dialectic. He believed these combined commonplaces sufficient for questions of any kind. Rhetoric's task, he thought, was to supply ornamentation and emotional color.

Peter Ramus, a professor at the Collège de Presles in Paris, followed in Agricola's footsteps, but more rigorously divided and simplified the two arts. An iconoclast, he attacked all the major figures in rhetorical history—Aristotle, Cicero, and Quintilian. Believing redundancy dissolute, his text *Dialecticae institutiones* (Training in Dialectic;

1543) assigned invention, arrangement, and memory to dialectic, leaving to rhetoric style and delivery. [*See* Delivery; Dialectic; *and* Memory.] Ramus's view of rhetoric was conveyed through his colleague Omer Talon. Their influence, strong in Northern Europe, furthered the belief that style was something added to thought. Other prominent reformers of the rhetorical tradition whose writings were also popular were Philipp Melanchthon (1497–1560) and Bartholomeus Keckermann (1571–1609).

In Spain and Italy, the Scholastic and Humanistic strains were often joined. The Spanish Jesuit Cipriano Soares (1524–1593) authored a rhetorical textbook that drew on the classical tradition, ignoring the reconfigurations of the reformers. His text on rhetoric of 1562 was adopted at the Jesuit Collegio Romano, established ten years earlier, and was used throughout the Jesuit system as it spread throughout the world. The Humanist scholar Riccoboni, who taught at the University of Padua during Galileo's time, in commenting on Aristotle's *Rhetoric* pointed out that rhetoric deals with what is persuasible, dialectic with what is probable.

Aristotelian rhetoric with a humanist slant was preserved also in Northern Europe during the early seventeenth century by Gerardus Johannes Vossius (Gerrit Jansz Vos, 1577–1649). Vossius provided a full treatment of Aristotelian argument with its elements of character, proof, and emotion, and he included the teachings of Cicero and Hermogenes as well.

Renaissance Rhetoric and Science. Science in the Aristotelian sense, regnant throughout the Middle Ages and most of the Renaissance, meant perfect knowledge, the kind guaranteed if a necessary demonstration were forthcoming, where certain principles or causes allowed one to arrive at a certain conclusion. Rhetoric had no purchase in this enterprise. Dialectical reasoning, however, could be employed to look for the basic principles of a demonstration. The rise of Humanist studies, the influence of Agricolan and Ramean dialectic, and the enlargement of the scientific audience eroded the traditional boundaries between science and rhetoric.

In England, the philosophy of Francis Bacon (1561–1626) served to further dissolve the boundaries. In his *On the Advancement of Learning* (1605),

Bacon described rhetoric as the servant of knowledge and the stimulant of emotion and of the will. Seeing rhetoric as an agent of transmission rather than a maker of knowledge, he dispensed with the traditional five-part art. He argued that rhetorical (and dialectical) invention does not really invent anything, only recalls what is already in the memory. What it finds it puts in the form of deductive arguments. True invention belongs to science and its method is induction.

Thomas Sprat in his *History of the Royal Society* (1667) took up Bacon's ideas and announced that scientific writing should eshew figures of speech and use only a clear, plain style to get across its discoveries. The tilt away from conscious rhetorical expression was aided by René Descartes (1596–1650), who deplored the use of rhetoric and extolled the mathematical model of reasoning.

While Humanists had exploited a liberated dialectical rhetoric to move its larger audiences, the rise of a new scientific style gave scientific argument a Scholastic cast. Argument, shorn of the topics, rested on observation and experiment. For Bacon, the individual instance, repeatedly observed, yielded trustworthy inductive evidence. This in turn would eventually lead to deductions of scientific principles and a convincing argument.

Perhaps Bernard Lamy (1640–1715), in his *Art de parler* (1675), best illustrates the divorce of rhetoric from argument proper. For him, the most legitimate form of proof is self-evident truth. To impart it to those who are not immediately open to it, one must play upon auditors' emotions and impress them with one's reputable character. Rhetoric sways an audience through the passions. Although the process Lamy describes appears to invoke Aristotelian *ēthos*, *pathos*, and *logos*, the three appeals do not coalesce as Aristotle conceived them. [*See* Ēthos; Logos; *and* Pathos.] Rhetorical proof has become certain demonstration, not persuasible argument. The idea of looking at both sides of an argument, explicit in the Sophists, in Aristotle, Cicero, and Quintilian, has been lost.

[*See also* Classical rhetoric; *and* Humanism.]

BIBLIOGRAPHY

Conley, Thomas. *Rhetoric in the European Tradition*. Chicago, 1990.

Fumaroli, Marc. *L'age de l'éloquence: rhétorique et "res lit-*

eraria" de la Renaissance au seuil de l'époque classique. Geneva, 1980.

Howell, Wilbur S. *Logic and Rhetoric in England. 1500–1700.* New York, 1956.

Jardine, Lisa. *Francis Bacon: Discovery and the Art of Discourse.* London, 1974.

Joseph, Sister Miriam. *Rhetoric in Shakespeare's Time: Literary Theory of Renaissance England.* New York, 1962. First published 1947.

Kristeller, Paul Oskar. *Renaissance Thought: The Classic, Scholastic, and Humanist Strains.* New York, 1961.

Mack, Peter, ed. *Renaissance Rhetoric.* New York, 1994.

Mack, Peter. *Renaissance Argument.* Leiden, 1993.

Moss, Jean Dietz. *Novelties in the Heavens: Rhetoric and Science in the Copernican Controversy.* Chicago, 1993.

Murphy, James J., ed. *Renaissance Eloquence: Studies in the Theory and Practice of Renaissance Rhetoric.* Berkeley, 1983.

Ong, Walter J. *Ramus: Method and the Decay of Dialogue.* Cambridge, Mass., 1958.

Seigel, Jerrold E. *Rhetoric and Philosophy in Renaissance Humanism.* Princeton, 1968.

Sloane, Thomas O. *On the Contrary: The Protocol of Traditional Rhetoric.* Washington, D.C., 1997.

Struever, Nancy. *The Language of History in the Renaissance: Rhetoric and Historical Consciousness in Florentine Humanism.* Princeton, 1970.

Vasoli, Cesare. *La dialettica e la retorica dell'Umanesimo: "Invenzione" e "metodo" nella cultura del XV e XVI secolo.* Milan, 1968.

—JEAN DIETZ MOSS

Rhetoric in the age of Reformation and Counter-Reformation

The Reformation influenced the Renaissance rhetorical tradition primarily by calling for a renewed emphasis on the Word of God. This emphasis led to (1) new theories and practices of preaching; (2) reevaluations of the written text of scripture and types of verbal style; and (3) debates about the very possibility of Christian eloquence given the Reformation's theological attack on the Humanist rhetoric's core assumptions about divine truths and human nature.

Post-Reformation Preaching. Like earlier proponents of church reform, Martin Luther (1483–1546) denounced the overrational, Scholastic preaching of previous generations. His belief in the priesthood of all believers implied that all Christians, if taught clearly, could understand basic doctrines. This emphasis on teaching re-mained constant in Reformation discussions of preaching, but from the onset, reformers stressed the need for listeners to have an affective response to the Word preached: either fear and shame at hearing the Law or love and comfort at hearing the Gospel. Thus, Protestants contrasted a "feeling faith" (wrought in the believer's heart by the Holy Spirit) with a "historical faith" (based on the knowledge of credible facts). This dual rhetorical imperative—to teach doctrine and to stir emotions—was revived from Augustine's seminal *De doctrina christiana* and exemplified by Luther's sermons, which sought to instruct and exhort in simple but passionate language and were modeled on the deliberative speeches described by Quintilian (first century CE).

The two most influential theorists of sermon rhetoric during the first decades of the Reformation were Luther's colleague Philipp Melanchthon (1497–1560) and Desiderius Erasmus (c.1466–1536). Melanchthon wrote elementary rhetorical textbooks, speeches on sacred eloquence, and a classical defense of Christian rhetoric (cast as a response to the Italian Humanist Giovanni Pico della Mirandola's 1486 Platonizing attack against it) that identifies Humanist rhetoric and passionate preaching as weapons for combating the errors of the Roman Church. Erasmus published numerous rhetorical treatises, editions of scriptural and patristic texts, and, most importantly, his *Ecclesiastes* (1535), a comprehensive and influential sermon manual that stresses the dignity of preaching, catalogs frequently discussed topics, and adapts for the pulpit various principles from the classical rhetorical tradition—the types of oratory, the parts of a speech, the goals of rhetoric, the levels of style, the figures and tropes. Erasmus's *Ecclesiastes* would become a primary source for future texts on preaching and Christian eloquence, including Andreas Hyperius's *De formandis concionibus sacris* (1553; translated by John Ludham as *The Practis of Preaching,* 1577); Bartholomew Keckermann's *De rhetorica ecclesiastica* (1600); Gerardus Vossius's *Commentariorum rhetoricorum* (1603/6); and Johann-Heinrich Alsted's *Orator* (1612).

Rhetoricians in Reformation England studied and borrowed from these Neo-Latin rhetorical treatises, but they also produced a variety of vernacular treatises on Christian rhetoric, most influenced by Calvinist theology and Ramist dialectic. The most important of these was *The Art of Prophesying* (Lat. version 1592, Engl. version 1607) by the Puritan divine William Perkins (1558–1602). Generations of Puritan preachers in England and America followed Perkins's guidelines for interpreting a scriptural text and "dividing" it into two segments: a statement of sound doctrine and an application of this doctrine to the spiritual lives of audience members. In addition to this "Doctrine-Use" sermon structure, Perkins advocates a plain, simple, and direct style and adopts from Ramist dialectic the methodical use of section headings and divisions to aid the preacher's memory and delivery. More liberal vernacular rhetorics, such as Richard Bernard's *The Faithful Shepherd* (1607 and later expanded editions) and John Prideaux's *Sacred Eloquence* (1659), draw more heavily on continental sources, allow for greater stylistic variation and rhetorical sophistication, and complain that Perkins's conspicuous dialectical method would detract from the sermon's emotional impact. Finally, there were the often-reprinted pastoral handbooks such as Richard Baxter's *Gildas Salvianus* (1656) and John Wilkins's *Ecclesiastes* (1646), which addressed Christian rhetoric via their analyses of the qualifications and character of godly pastors.

The Roman Catholic church responded to internal and external calls for reform at the Council of Trent (1545–1563), where it declared preaching the "chief duty of bishops" (*praecipuum episcoporum munus*) and established clear requirements for the frequency of preaching at all levels of the church hierarchy. Preaching should teach things necessary for salvation, and urge, in brief and plain language, the avoidance of vice and the cultivation of virtue—this latter emphasis on moral action conforming to the Council's doctrine of salvation through works rather than through grace. These conciliar reforms and the patronage of Archbishop Charles Borromeo (1538–1584) sparked the production of numerous ecclesiastical rhetorics between 1570 and 1610, notably Agostino Valiero's *De rhetorica ecclesiastica* (1574), Luis de Granda's *Rhetoricae ecclesiasticae* (1576), and Diego de Estella's *Modus concionandi* (1576). In revolt against the Thomistic Scholasticism of the medieval *ars praedicandi*, many Tridentine rhetorics imitated the structure of Ciceronian rhetorical treatises while increasingly invoking nonclassical models (i.e., scriptural, patristic, and hellenistic) of Christian eloquence. [*See* Medieval rhetoric, *article on* Medieval grammar.] The Roman church discouraged arguing from the pulpit against beliefs it deemed heretical, lest incompetent preachers misrepresent or ignorant audiences misconstrue the church's true teachings; except before the most learned audiences, preachers were to praise, rather than justify, the church's doctrines and traditions. Deliberative rhetoric was the predominant mode, as preachers called listeners to works of repentance and participation in the sacraments. [*See* Deliberative genre.] The Society of Jesus (i.e., the Jesuits) was founded in 1540 and quickly established schools around the world that taught a rigorous curriculum with classical rhetoric at its center. Its members authored numerous, frequently-reprinted rhetorical treatises ranging in complexity from Cyprianus Soarez's elementary *De arte rhetorica* (1557) to Nicholas Caussin's voluminous *De eloquentia sacra et humana* (1617/1619).

Scripture and Style. The early reformers appealed to the authority and intelligibility of Scripture in order to combat what they regarded as the abuses of the Roman church. This appeal incited philologists to seek an authentic text of Scripture and translators to render it into vernacular languages for popular audiences. At times, Protestant Scripturalism ran afoul of the stylistic ideals of the Renaissance rhetorical tradition. The debate over Ciceronianism in the early sixteenth century, for example, pitted zealous Ciceronians, who identified stylistic elegance with Cicero's diction and sentence patterns, against reform-minded opponents who claimed that such an identification precluded the words, images, and message of Scripture. Because reformers championed a literal (as opposed to allegorical) interpretation of God's Word, and because much of scripture (Paul's epistles in particular) failed to conform to the precepts of Ciceronian eloquence, Protestant Scripturalism has historically been associated with the rise of a plainer, more modern English prose style. Yet Paul's epistles contain examples of stylistic features—antithesis, *isocolon*, figures of repetition—typically identified as Ciceronian. Recently, scholars have begun to recognize the huge impact of the vernacular Scripture—particularly William

Tyndale's 1525 translation of the New Testament, which would be the basis of the 1611 King James Bible—on the development of English prose style. Several reformers analyzed the style of Scripture and offered explanations of its rhetorical potency. These include Mathias Flacius Illyricus (1520–1575) in his massive analysis of the language of Scripture, *Clavis scripturae sacrae* (1562); John Calvin (1509–1564) in his numerous scriptural commentaries; and John Smith in his Ramistic *The Mysterie of Rhetorique Unvail'd* (1657), a catalog of tropes and figures of speech with biblical illustrations. [*See* Hermeneutics; *and* Style.]

Although rhetoricians across confessional lines credited the Holy Spirit for accomplishing the goals of sacred rhetoric, they developed different understandings of how the Holy Spirit sanctions various verbal styles. One group argued that the preacher's rhetoric should replicate through rhetorical artistry the wonder, gravity, and mystery of God. The preacher's verbal artistry should cooperate with the Holy Spirit to stir his listeners' affections and reform their morals, just as human works cooperate with divine grace in attaining eternal salvation. Scholars have argued that the Roman Catholic church's sacramental mentality, which sought visible signs of God's invisible grace, allowed its rhetoricians to justify more easily than their Protestant counterparts the use of stylistic ornamentation and imaginative vividness that could verge on the baroque (as in the preaching of Lancelot Andrewes, 1555–1626 in the philo-Catholic Stuart court). Another, opposing group held that human eloquence distorts or inhibits the working of the Holy Spirit, transforming the preacher into a cipher or a conduit of the Holy Spirit. This reasoning explained both the so-called Puritan plain style, in which all the human learning used in preparing a sermon is hidden in its delivery, and radical, enthusiastic preaching. A third, more moderate group viewed the arts of discourse as gifts that, like Egyptian gold in the Exodus story (*Ex.* 3.22, 11.2), were originally pagan but given by the Holy Spirit to the elect church for its sustenance and glorification. For this group, the key distinction between sacred and secular rhetoric is in motivation, not method: preachers and writers can exploit the arts of rhetoric, provided they are humble and

charitable, not proud and self-aggrandizing. This group drew an analogy between the theological doctrine of divine accommodation, which states that Jesus became human (*Jn.* 1.14), and a rhetorical hermeneutics that argues that divine truths are and should be accommodated via Scripture to promote human understanding. Proponents of accommodation, including Erasmus, Melanchthon, and Flacius, thus recognized the relevance of both specific historical circumstances and scripture's *scopus* or central doctrinal messages—Jesus' incarnation, death, and resurrection, the salvation of a faithful elect—for determining the meaning of difficult passages and correcting the perceived abuses of Roman Catholic allegorizing and obscurantism.

The Theological Attack on Rhetoric. While the Reformation's views on preaching and Scripturalism integrated many ideas from the humanist rhetorical tradition, modern scholars have argued that it also undermined this tradition by questioning Humanism's optimistic view of human nature. Luther's belief in the innate depravity of the human will and the corruption of human reason led him, in his famous debate with Erasmus on free will (1524–25), to denounce the Roman church's tendency to think of the individual Christian's relationship to God through an accommodating rhetorical vocabulary of prudence, reason, and merit. In its place, Luther substituted a more severe theological vocabulary of sinfulness, faith, and grace. Luther's doctrinal reforms shook the foundation of Humanism's *theologia rhetorica* and its core trust in the enduring utility of "right reason" in addressing matters of faith and determining doctrinal controversies. Taken to an extreme, this line of argument makes sacred eloquence impossible for the same reason it is necessary: because of their fallen reason, enslaved will, and unreliable senses, Christians simply cannot employ the art of rhetoric without surrendering their faith to sinful excesses of carnal desire, Greco-Roman rationalism, or Judaic legalism. In Sir Philip Sidney's famous formulation, our "erected wit" is compromised by our "infected will." Thus, radical reformers denounced rhetoric and other arts because they tempt believers to worship creations instead of the Creator. Opponents of Christian rhetoric claim that it inevitably misrepresents immutable divine truths; or, using the

Reformation's Pauline vocabulary, rhetoric seduces the sinful, carnal, "outer man" while ignoring the justified, spiritual, "inner man" who gloriously transcends it. Human words distort or defile God's Word.

One response to these antirhetorical views was to insist that only the preacher moved by the Holy Spirit could move his listeners, thus removing the taint of sinful, human motivations by identifying the Holy Spirit as the source of Christian eloquence. Other scholars have qualified this argument by noting that, while many reformers denounced Humanism's *theologia rhetorica*, they also fully appreciated the utility of rhetoric in the worldly church. We must accept divine justification on God's terms, terms that offend reason and human dignity; but the preacher is fully capable of reasoning with and persuading his audience to sound belief and moral action. This distinction, roughly between upward and downward rhetoric, explains why Luther can call reason "a whore" and still deliver instructive sermons that rely on his listeners' reason; it explains why Calvin can systematize Christian doctrine beyond debate and still demonstrate great rhetorical sophistication in his sermons and commentaries on Scripture. This distinction also shaped the controversies that split the English Protestants during and after Elizabeth's reign. English Puritans drew from Paul's epistles clear rhetorical imperatives that hinge not on an anthropological antithesis between the Flesh and the Spirit but on ecclesiastical antitheses between disorder and order, destruction and edification, legalistic rigidity and loving accommodation. Consequently, early Elizabethan Puritans advocated church policies—such as providing more and better educated pastors, preaching sermons versus reading homilies or performing ceremonies, and allowing congregations to elect pastors who most effectively preach to their spiritual needs—that stress Humanist rhetorical principles of decorum and accommodation. Likewise, Perkins distinguishes between types of listeners (e.g., the ignorant and knowledgeable, the proud and humbled, the fallen and the believers) and insists that the pastor identify and accommodate them. Yet this pastoral emphasis was (and is) often clouded by the heated doctrinal debates. [*See* Decorum.]

[*See also* Homiletics; *and* Religion.]

BIBLIOGRAPHY

Bayley, Peter. *French Pulpit Oratory, 1598–1650 : A Study in Themes and Styles, with a Descriptive Catalogue of Printed Texts.* Cambridge, U.K., 1980.

Bouwsma, William. *John Calvin: A Sixteenth-Century Portrait.* Oxford, 1988. Stresses the Humanist milieu of Calvin's work and theology.

Boyle, Marjorie O'Rourke. *Rhetoric and Reform: Erasmus's Civil Dispute with Luther,* Cambridge, Mass., 1983. For a discussion of the *Theologica Rhetorica,* see also Boyle's *Erasmus on Language and Method in Theology.* Toronto, 1977.

Breen, Quirinus. *Christianity and Humanism: Studies in the History of Ideas.* Grand Rapids, Mich., 1968.

Eden, Kathy. *Hermeneutics and the Rhetorical Tradition: Chapters in the Ancient Legacy and Its Humanist Reception.* New Haven, 1997. Contains chapters on Erasmus, Melanchthon, and Flacius.

Erasmus, Desiderius, *Ecclesiastes, sive de ratione concionandi libri quatuor,* edited by Jacques Chomarat. Amsterdam, 1991. Modern edition of Erasmus's important treatise published in Volume 5 of *Opera omnia Desiderii Erasmi Roterodami* (Amsterdam, 1969–) with comprehensive introduction and informative notes by Chomarat.

McGinness, Frederick J. *Right Thinking and Sacred Oratory in Counter-Reformation Rome.* Princeton, 1995.

Mueller, Janel M. *The Native Tongue and the Word: Developments in English Prose Style, 1380–1580.* Chicago, 1984. Detailed study on the impact of Protestant Scripturalism and Christian rhetoric on English prose style.

Nembach, Ulrich. *Predigt des Evangeliums: Luther als Prediger, Pädagoge und Rhetor.* Neukirchen-Vluyn, Germany, 1972. Important study of Luther's sermon rhetoric.

O'Malley, John W., S. J. *Praise and Blame in Renaissance Rome: Rhetoric, Doctrine, and Reform in the Sacred Orators of the Papal Court, c.1450–1521.* Durham, N.C., 1979.

O'Malley, John W., S. J. "Content and Rhetorical Forms in Sixteenth-Century Treatises on Preaching." In *Renaissance Eloquence: Studies in the Theory and Practice of Renaissance Rhetoric,* edited by James J. Murphy, pp. 238–252. Berkeley, 1983.

Shuger, Debora K. *Sacred Rhetoric: The Christian Grand Style in the English Renaissance.* Princeton, 1988. Detailed study of theories of persuasion and emotion in Neo-Latin sermon manuals, their classical sources, and vernacular imitators.

Smith, Hilary Dansey. *Preaching in the Spanish Golden Age: A Study of Some Preachers of the Reign of Philip III.* Oxford, 1978.

Spitz, Lewis W. "Luther and Humanism." In *Luther and*

Learning, edited by Marilyn J. Harran, pp. 69–94. London, 1985. A good introduction to scholarly debates on the impact of Reformation theology on Christian humanism.

— GREGORY KNEIDEL

RHETORICAL SITUATION. Lloyd Bitzer's essay "The Rhetorical Situation" was the lead article in the inaugural issue of the interdisciplinary journal *Philosophy and Rhetoric* in 1968. Since its publication, the essay has been at the center of a lively conversation, especially in the periodical literature in speech communication and communication studies. Three decades after its initial presentation, Bitzer's concept still occupies a significant place in both the rhetoric classroom and scholarly discourse.

Bitzer argues that, just as an answer follows in response to a question, all rhetorical discourse emerges as a response to a rhetorical situation. He writes: "rhetorical discourse comes into existence as a response to a situation, in the same sense that an answer comes into existence in response to a question . . . a rhetorical situation must exist as a necessary condition of rhetorical discourse, just as a question must exist as a necessary condition of an answer" (pp. 5–6). After analogically developing the idea of a rhetorical situation, Bitzer provides the following definition: "Rhetorical situation may be defined as a complex of persons, events, objects, and relations presenting an actual or potential exigence which can be completely or partially removed if discourse, introduced into the situation, can so constrain human decision or action as to bring about the significant modification of the exigence" (p. 6). The three primary constituents to which Bitzer devotes significant attention are exigence, audience, and constraints.

An exigence, Bitzer asserts, is "an imperfection marked by urgency; it is a defect, an obstacle, something waiting to be done, a thing which is other than it should be" (p. 6). An exigence is, in other words, a social ill or significant problem in the world, something to which people must attend. The exigence functions as the "organizing principle" of a situation; situations develop around a "controlling exigence." Not every problem merits the designation rhetorical exigence. Bitzer explains:

An exigence which cannot be modified is not rhetorical; thus, whatever comes about of necessity and cannot be changed—death, winter, and some natural disasters, for instance—are exigencies to be sure, but they are nonrhetorical. An exigence is rhetorical when it is capable of positive modification and when positive modification [either] requires discourse or can be assisted by discourse (pp. 6–7).

Bitzer's account of a rhetorical exigence reflects the traditional Aristotelian idea of contingency. [*See* Contingency and probability.] Like Aristotle (384–322 BCE), Bitzer believes that rhetoric traffics in the realm of the contingent and does not engage issues of necessity.

Note that some rhetorical exigencies require discourse while others might be resolved through the assistance of discourse. Racism is an example of the first type of exigence. Bitzer appears to assume that the only way people will alter behavior that demeans people of a different race is if they are persuaded to do so. Persuasive discourse is therefore required to modify the exigence of racism. As an example of the second type of exigence, Bitzer offers the case of air pollution. "The pollution of air is also a rhetorical exigence because its positive modification—reduction of pollution—strongly invites the assistance of discourse producing public awareness, indignation, and action of the right kind" (p. 7).

This second example can help clarify the relationship between exigence and the stock topics of causality discussed in contemporary argumentation theory. The physical presence of hazardous particles in the air—the phenomenon of air pollution—is an ill, a condition that threatens human health. Discourse, by itself, cannot make air pollution go away. But discourse can assist in the elimination of air pollution when it is used to persuade legislators to pass a new law requiring drastic reductions in the quantity of hazardous emissions from automobiles and other sources of air pollution. The specific exigence in this situation is motivating legislators to take action; that is, the exigence in this case is the problem of policy advocacy, the need to induce a legislative body to take action against the ill of air pollution. Finally, we should note that exigencies have a way of redeveloping, of coming back to life after it appears that they have been eradicated. Consequently, most rhetorical scholars believe that rhetorical exigencies are temporarily *resolved* through deliberation and action; they are rarely, if ever, *solved* or eliminated in an absolute sense. [*See* Deliberative genre.]

Not every collection of individuals who happen to listen to a speech in person, watch one on television, or read an essay in a newspaper or magazine constitute a rhetorical audience. A *rhetorical* audience, Bitzer argues, must meet two conditions: it "consists only of those persons who are capable of being influenced by discourse and of being mediators of change." The first condition of a rhetorical audience is that its members are "capable of being influenced." People who refuse to consider an advocate's arguments and appeals or who are completely closed to alternative perspectives cannot, in Bitzer's judgment, constitute a rhetorical audience. In order for an individual to be part of a rhetorical audience or for a group of people to function as a rhetorical audience, they must evince a certain minimum degree of attention and a willingness to entertain the advocate's arguments or proposals. The second condition of a rhetorical audience is that they can function as "mediators of change." At times, an advocate might need to convince his or her listeners or readers that they possess the capacity to act as agents of change (e.g., African-American abolitionist Henry Garnet's efforts in the nineteenth century to show African slaves that they had the power to modify their condition). At other times, a group of people might not have the power to make the final decision but may possess an ability to influence those with final decision-making power. Bitzer's capacity condition might then be divided into (1) an audience capable of making the final decision and (2) an audience capable of exerting influence on those with ultimate decision-making authority. In short, a rhetorical audience is open to, and interested in, the discourse and possesses the capacity to act as a mediator of change.

Constraints are the third constituent of a rhetorical situation (although in a 1980 supplement Bitzer would introduce the idea of "resources" as a complement to constraints). In an often-quoted passage from "The Eighteenth Brumaire of Louis Bonaparte," Karl Marx (1818–1883) wrote: "Men make their own history, but they do not make it

just as they please; they do not make it under circumstances chosen by themselves, but under circumstances directly encountered, given and transmitted from the past" (*The Eighteenth Brumaire of Louis Bonaparte,* New York, 1994. First published in 1852). To simplify Marx's point a bit and incorporate it into Bitzer's account of the rhetorical situation, people "make history" by confronting exigencies. They craft discourse to help resolve these exigencies. But in doing so, they encounter "circumstances" that they didn't choose, and quite possibly if they had a choice would not have chosen, but with which they must nevertheless contend. These circumstances can include: history (past events, traditions, etc.), people, present events, recognized facts, values and beliefs, discursive conventions, written documents (contracts, letters, etc.), authoritative documents (the Bible, the U.S. Constitution), physical location, and other important economic, social, and cultural factors. Constraints, then, are obstacles that influence or impede an advocate's ability to engage an exigence successfully. A politician's negative image is constraint on his or her effort to run for higher office. Conflicting opinions in the scientific community are a constraint on those who want to use scientific testimony to support a policy position. [*See* Ēthos; *and* Politics, *article on* The personal, technical, and public spheres of argument.] The arguments of the opposition are a constraint hampering any policy initiative. A signed confession is a constraint on a defense attorney. When circumstances provide material that can work to the advocate's advantage, those circumstances are potential resources that the advocate tries to exploit. An advocate's first-hand experiences in a foreign country might serve as a resource in an effort to win approval for a military appropriation on the country's behalf. An advocate's prior history with an audience might be a resource in trying to win their support of a local tax referendum.

In the 1980 supplemental essay, Bitzer also outlines an evolutionary model of rhetorical situations, noting that they do not simply appear out of thin air fully formed; they emerge over time through four developmental stages. The first stage is origin and initial development. In this stage "an exigence comes into existence" and "we assume that someone recognizes it." But during this stage, audience, constraints, and resources are either unclear or have not developed fully. In the second mature stage, "the exigence is present and perceived, often by speaker and audience; the audience is capable of modifying the exigence and can be easily addressed; operative constraints are available. The duration of this stage," Bitzer notes, "may be no more than a moment" or it may continue indefinitely. The third stage is deterioration. During this stage the configuration of constituents "changes in ways that make modification of the exigence significantly more difficult." The fourth and final stage is disintegration. During this stage the configuration of constituents dissolves: the audience disappears, the exigence can no longer be perceived, resources have been exhausted or constraints become overwhelming. An advocate who persists in addressing a disintegrated situation is a lone voice howling in the wilderness. But as the fluctuating careers of issues like health care or the resurgence of feminism in the 1960s demonstrate, no situation must remain dormant forever.

One aspect of Bitzer's situational concept that has attracted considerable attention and criticism is its purported objectivism. In 1968, Bitzer wrote:

> The exigence and the complex of persons, objects, events and relations which generate rhetorical discourse are located in reality, are objective and publicly observable historic facts in the world we experience, are therefore available for scrutiny by an observer or critic who attends to them. To say the situation is objective . . . means that it is real or genuine. . . . Real situations are to be distinguished from sophistic ones in which, for example, a contrived exigence is asserted to be real; from spurious situations in which the existence or alleged existence of constituents is the result of error or ignorance; and from fantasy in which exigence, audience, and constraints may all be the imaginary objects of a mind at play. (p. 11)

Bitzer's claim that the situation is an "objective" phenomenon—that it exists as a real thing apart from human perception, recognition, or interaction—has been attacked by subsequent scholars. In one of the earliest critiques of the situational objectivity thesis, Richard Vatz insists: "No situation can have a nature independent of the per-

ception of its interpreter or independent of the rhetoric with which he chooses to characterize it" (1973, p. 154). For Vatz and many other rhetorical scholars, advocates not only respond to situations, they help to create or define situations. Rhetorical discourse, on this view, is not merely instrumental; it also possesses a constructive or constitutive capacity. [*See* Politics, *article on* Constitutive rhetoric.] When a theorist like Vatz invokes the constructive or constitutive potential of discourse, it does not mean that he believes discourse creates the physical particles that pollute the atmosphere. The constructive or constitutive hypothesis only suggests that physical objects like pollutants, or social objects like crime or poverty, are made intelligible or comprehensible in and through discourse.

While the debates between so-called "objectivists" and adherents of some variety of "constructivism" give the appearance of a mutually exclusive disjunction, this appearance may be misleading. Most rhetorical scholars believe it is not a question of whether discourse either responds to or creates situations; in fact it does both. In a 1979 contribution to the ongoing debate about the nature of rhetorical situations, John Patton notes how "the meaning of rhetorical situations is a dual process, partly a matter of recognition, i.e. clarity and accuracy of perception, and partly a matter of intentional, artistic, human action" (p. 49). In 1980, Bitzer modified the rigid objectivism of his initial formulation by adding human "interests" into the process of exigence formation. He writes: "A rhetorical exigence consists of a factual condition plus a relation to some interest. . . . An exigence exists when a factual condition and an interest are joined" (p. 28). For example, grade school students' test scores are a factual condition; the tests were administered, they were scored, and the raw results can be reported. But this factual condition can only become an exigence, Bitzer acknowledged in his 1980 essay, when connected to human interests. "The addition of interest makes" a factual condition "something other than it should be, a defect, a matter to be altered" (p. 28). Test scores reveal a problem that must be addressed when they are connected to human interests in such things as success, prosperity, and achievement. Low test scores can be perceived as a threat to these interests. When they are so perceived, an exigence comes into existence.

Every situation is, in a sense, unique; the particular cluster of events that constitute a situation do not occur twice in exactly the same way. But situations can have similar structures and characteristics. Bitzer suggested as much in 1968 when he wrote: "From day to day, year to year, comparable situations occur, prompting comparable responses" (p. 13). This observation was an important stimulus in the development of genre theory and criticism in contemporary rhetorical studies. Bitzer's observation might also be extended in another direction. The existence of situational similarities might support the development of a typology of situational exigencies that addresses the question: What are some of the recurrent problems that organize rhetorical situations and to which advocates respond?

One of the first things a rhetorical critic frequently does in approaching a text is to reconstruct the situation in order to identify the relevant exigencies, constraints, resources, and audiences. [See Politics, article on Critical rhetoric.] As Bitzer recognized in 1968, situational analysis is at the center of any effort to understand and assess the instrumental function of rhetorical practice. As long as rhetorical scholars are interested in exploring this dimension of discourse, the concept of the rhetorical situation will play a significant role.

[See also overview article on Audience; Hybrid genres; Invention; and Occasion.]

BIBLIOGRAPHY

Biesecker, Barbara A. "Rethinking the Rhetorical Situation from within the Thematic of *Différance*." *Philosophy and Rhetoric* 22 (1989), pp. 110–130. Joins the debate over the nature of the situation from a poststructuralist perspective.

Bitzer, Lloyd. "Functional Communication: A Situational Perspective." In *Rhetoric in Transition: Studies in the Nature and Uses of Rhetoric*. Edited by Eugene E. White, pp. 21–38. University Park, Pa., 1980. Bitzer's effort to ameliorate his objectivism.

Brinton, Alan. "Situation in the Theory of Rhetoric." *Philosophy and Rhetoric* 14 (1981), pp. 234–248. One of the better analyses of Bitzer's original position.

Consigny, Scott. "Rhetoric and Its Situations." *Philoso-*

phy and Rhetoric 7 (1974), pp. 175–186. An early critique of Bitzer.

Crable, Richard E., and Steven L. Vibbert. "Managing Issues and Influencing Public Policy." *Public Relations Review* 6 (1985), pp. 3–16. Develops the useful distinction between audiences with final authority and those possessing influence.

Gorrell, Donna. "The Rhetorical Situation Again: Linked Components in a Venn Diagram." *Philosophy and Rhetoric* 30 (1997), pp. 395–412. One of the most recent contributions to the ongoing discussion.

Jamieson, Kathleen M. H. "Generic Constraints and the Rhetorical Situation." *Philosophy and Rhetoric* 6 (1973), pp. 162–170. Develops the connection between situations and rhetorical genres.

Jasinski, James. *Key Concepts in Contemporary Rhetorical Studies*. Thousand Oaks, Calif., in press. Develops a typology of exigencies.

Miller, Arthur B. "Rhetorical Exigence." *Philosophy and Rhetoric* 5 (1972), pp. 111–118. Another early critic of Bitzer's objectivism.

Patton, John H. "Causation and Creativity in Rhetorical Situations: Distinctions and Implications." *Quarterly Journal of Speech* 65 (1979), pp. 36–55. Patton looks for a middle ground between Bitzer and his critics.

Vatz, Richard E. "The myth of the rhetorical situation." *Philosophy and Rhetoric* 6 (1973), pp. 154–161. The best-known attack on Bitzer's objectivism.

—JAMES JASINSKI

RHETORICAL VISION. Fantasy theme analysis, which is the line of scholarship that resulted in the development of the symbolic convergence theory, is an empirically based study of the shared imagination. In addition, fantasy theme analysis is a humanistically based study of rhetorical history and criticism and interpretative approaches to the study of interpersonal, small group, organizational, and media communication.

The social scientific basis for symbolic convergence came from small group laboratories. Studies at Harvard and Minnesota discovered the basic process of group fantasy chains, which inspired the development of fantasy theme analysis.

The symbolic convergence theory has evolved out of fantasy theme analysis over the last several decades as part of a general movement in rhetorical and communication studies to recover and stress the importance of imaginative language (and the imagination) in nonverbal and verbal transactions and upon group consciousness. The efforts at finding some accommodation for imagination, feeling, and envisioning on the one hand and rationality on the other have included investigations into subjects then thought to be more appropriate to aesthetics, art, and literature than to rhetoric. In the 1960s and 1970s, these efforts often had to face the barrier of rationality. While rhetoricians paid some attention to the imaginative dimension of rhetoric, their attention tended to focus on the logical. Among those who saw themselves as scholars of communication, the hegemony of rationality promulgated a view of communication that suggested that myths were false, that stories were fictitious, that metaphors were rhetorical adornments, and that anecdotal evidence was suspect.

Symbolic convergence theory is based on studies of communication. Scholars and researchers have tested, verified, and modified the symbolic convergence theory by observational studies and experiments using a technique called *grounded theory*. Symbolic convergence theory works across time and cultures.

To examine both the distinctive and general nature of symbolic convergence theory, we need to understand the grounded theory methodology used in its discovery and development. The developers of symbolic convergence theory merged two lines of research into one overarching formula. The first line was that of Robert F. Bales and his associates at Harvard who were studying the dynamics of groups by making a content analysis of their communication. They developed a coding system they called interaction process analysis. They used the system for observing and coding the groups as they worked. The second line was that of Ernest G. Bormann and his associates at Minnesota (1994) who were studying ongoing groups by using such techniques as content analysis, participant journals, interviews, and voice and video recordings.

Another research approach at Minnesota used rhetorical criticism to examine the communication dynamics in task-oriented groups. The investigators examined the nature and results of the members' use of persuasion techniques, *ēthos*-building efforts, logical argument, and style. [*See* Ēthos; Logic; Persuasion; *and* Style.] At this point in the work at Minnesota, Robert F. Bales pub-

lished the latest findings of the Bales group in his book *Personality and Interpersonal Behavior* (New York, 1970). As the Minnesota group read and discussed the new approach, they realized that the Bales group had founded a form of rhetorical criticism. The Bales group reported that from time to time when a member used imaginative language it triggered an explosion of further imaginative language, accompanied by laughter, excitement, sometimes sadness, and other strong emotions. During these episodes the entire climate of the meeting changed. The discussion groups that were subdued, quiet, and sometimes tense would suddenly change to excited involvement. Bales and his group applied a Freudian approach to their analysis of the content of these moments and characterized them as shared group fantasy themes. They found that the sharing of a fantasy helped the members create group cohesiveness. The Bales group also reported that fantasy chains resulted in the participants coming to share a group fantasy with its associated symbolic common ground, emotional evocations, motivations, and group culture.

Researchers at Minnesota continued their studies using the methods of observation, interviews, and content analysis. An early project was to replicate the Bales group's finding of the process and effect of sharing group fantasies. At Minnesota the investigations began with the careful definition of dramatizing messages. Observers then studied the effect of dramatizing on group members. They found that some dramatizations caused a minor symbolic explosion in the form of a chain reaction. As the members shared the fantasy, the tempo of the conversation would pick up. People grew excited, interrupted one another, laughed, showed emotion, and forgot their self-consciousness. The people who shared the fantasy did so with the appropriate responses. If the storyteller wanted it to be funny, they laughed; if it was supposed to be serious or solemn, they grew serious and solemn. Further studies revealed that on some occasions group members were apathetic and ignored the dramatizing while on others they rejected the fantasies contained in the dramatizations. Scholars at Minnesota then found that the sharing of fantasies also characterized listener and reader responses to a wide range of communication including conversations, public speeches, mass media messages, and Web site and Internet speech and writing, as well as reading books and newspapers.

What struck the Minnesota group was that here was a melding of two modes of scholarship: social science and rhetorical criticism. In 1970, communication scholars were using both methods of research but seldom in conjunction. The Minnesota group viewed shared fantasy themes as the key element in integrating social science with humanism and began to use the idea in studies in rhetorical criticism.

The method did several things: First, in the late 1960s and early 1970s, rhetorical critics and the experts in public speaking and persuasion emphasized the role of logical proofs and argument. Fantasy theme analysis emphasized the function of imaginative language in building collective consciousness, group cohesion, and decision making. Second, fantasy theme analysis brought the audience back into the communication paradigm. That paradigm had once been speaker, speech, audience, and occasion. Over time, the audience had essentially disappeared and the emphasis shifted to the text. Third, fantasy theme analysis was a social approach that studied communication in collectives. Fourth, the fantasy emphasis enabled a more complex analysis of both nonfictitious (the facts) and fictitious imaginative language (the fantasies). These studies led to positive results. One earmark of grounded theory is that replications of the same experiments should yield the same results. The group began to see the shape of a social scientific formula, which they called symbolic convergence theory: "symbolic" because it dealt with language and fantasy, "convergence" since its central theorem revealed that the dynamic process of sharing group fantasies resulted in the convergence of the participants' symbolic worlds. They began to see things in the same way. They were converging their beliefs and opinions. To put it in the vernacular, each knew where the others who shared the fantasy were coming from. They experienced an exhilarating meeting of the minds. They shared the same opinions and emotions.

By now the continuing investigations at Minnesota had found the symbolic convergence process operating in the media, in other audience and speaker situations, in reading texts, and in historical documents. Indeed they found the process in every communication situation they observed. They also learned that using observation techniques and interviews of subjects worked well enough in controlled studies in which the investigators could monitor the communication. For historical studies, and in contexts where direct observations were difficult or impossible, other techniques were required.

As the investigations continued, it became apparent that the process of convergence was too complex to be encompassed by the sole early concept of *fantasy theme*. The first breakthrough came with the recognition of a more general structure than the fantasy theme. The phenomenon was a generalized statement incorporating the plot lines of similar fantasies. To illustrate, a group might share a fantasy theme about the Puritan treatment of women accused of being witches. If convicted, the leaders burned them at the stake. The story portrays the Puritan leaders as the evil ones and the women as victims. Subsequently, this group shares another fantasy theme, this one about a congressional committee investigating communists in the State Department. The story portrays the leaders of the committee as villains and the people accused as being the victims. One member says, "It's like the Salem witch hunts." This triggers a sharing of this drama with Senator McCarthy garbed as a Puritan minister. After that, the group refers to the hearings as witch hunts.

Subsequently, they share a fantasy theme about a right-wing group of Christian conservatives who try to impeach a president. They label the situation as "another witch hunt." They have now created a *fantasy type* with a stock plot that they understand. The fantasy type places most prior shared fantasy themes with similar scenarios into a genre. This witch hunt fantasy type can now serve the members as an analogy to make sense out of disturbing and confusing events which they can characterize as witch hunts. When researchers find fantasy types in archives, records, recollections, letters, and other texts and sources, they can use them as evidence to indicate that participants have shared fantasies without the need for developing and implementing an experiment.

A second sharing phenomenon also provides

evidence of a community having shared a fantasy. Investigators called this finding a *symbolic cue*. A symbolic cue is a cryptic feature of the verbal and nonverbal communication that triggers for the listener a reminder of the original fantasy. The listener then experiences again the response of the group sharing of the fantasy. If the cue is for an inside joke, the response is laughter or smiling. For someone who did not participate in the shared fantasies that created the cue, the response may well be confusion. The insider response is often "you had to be there." Like fantasy types, the inside cues are evidence of fantasies shared in the past.

An additional concept resulted from the research findings, namely, that in some situations when many people come to share a group of fantasy themes and types, they then shape these commonalities into a larger coherent vision of some aspect of their social reality. Investigators called the new idea a *rhetorical vision:* "rhetorical" because the larger symbolic structures were constructed by rhetorical imaginative language triggering shared fantasies. Such a vision is a unified putting together of the various scripts, thereby giving the participants a broader view of things. Usually a rhetorical vision is indexed by a key word (feminism), a slogan (Black Power), or a label (American Dream). Such indexing is a special case of the symbolic cuing phenomenon, but in this instance the cryptic allusion is not just to details of fantasy themes and types but to a total coherent view of an aspect of the participants' social reality.

The final current technical term is that of *Saga*. This does not mean that future investigations will not suggest additional terms. The concept of *Saga* has had more study in, and has emerged from, the area of organizational communication. The need for a new term arose because studies of schools and other organizations revealed that many larger units had groups composed of formal units and informal cliques with differing rhetorical visions. These visions often resulted in conflict and competition among various elements in the organization. Yet on occasion, the members of the organization, including those sharing conflicting rhetorical visions, were committed to the overall organization (company, school, or country). For example, middle management is impos-

sible, bungling, and hasn't a clue, but we are proud to work for IBM. Symbolic convergence studies of such situations revealed that there was a phenomenon like a rhetorical vision writ large to which most or all members of the differing rhetorical communities were committed. The concept of *Saga* was designed to indicate such an umbrella-like rhetorical structure. Sagas often have a founders fantasy type with dramatizations of the beginnings of the country, (founding fathers, Jefferson, Washington) and heroic persona (Lincoln). Once the founders fantasy is shared, the organization may have a founder's day celebration and other icons or events to keep the *Saga* alive. There are often other important historical events, failures as well as successes which may be part of the *Saga*. Mission statements, histories, personas who are heroes and those who are villains may also play an important part in the organizational *Saga*.

The Minnesota group expanded the social science component of the theory by integrating the work of Stephenson in developing Q-methodology. In his book *The Study of Behavior: Q-Technique and Its Methodology* (Chicago, 1953), Stephenson wrote that he created Q-methodology to develop a science of subjectivity from the viewpoint of the subjects' own interpretation of events. Stephenson claimed that the insights of famous novelists have been rejected by scientists because they deal with particular events. He argued that he would like to use the insights of humanists for scientific purposes. The method was that of content analysis. Professor Norman Van Turbergen designed the Quanal computer program to use factor analysis to sort out the various rhetorical communities within a sample audience. Integration of rhetorical criticism with this data took place when the Quanal program revealed the shared fantasies of these communities. The investigators could then use fantasy theme analysis to make a rhetorical criticism of the consciousness of these audiences. In this manner, the two research methods were brought into a symbiotic relationship.

The symbolic convergence theory is intellectually fruitful when used with fantasy theme analysis. Critics who reconstruct the rhetorical visions of communities of people can ask general rhetorical questions in order to analyze the hopes and fears, the emotional tone, and the inner life of the group by examining how the rhetoric deals with basic universal problems. Such insight flows from answers to such questions as these: How well did the communication deal with the problem of creating and celebrating a sense of community? Did it help generate group and individual images that were strong, confident and resilient? How did the rhetoric aid or hinder the community in its adaptation to its physical environment? How did the communication deal with the rhetorical problem of creating a social reality that provides norms for community behavior in terms of the level of violence, exploitation, dominance, and injustice? Did the communication create a panoramic vision that served such mythic functions as providing members with an account of the world, the gods, and fate, and that gave meaning to their community and themselves? How well did the vision aid the people who participated in it to live with people who shared different rhetorical visions?

Because fantasy theme analysis incorporates a general social scientific theory of communication (symbolic convergence), it is based on a carefully defined common set of technical terms. Such common terms imbedded in a coherent theoretical structure enables fantasy theme analysts to compare and integrate the findings of a number of separate studies into generalizations about communication. For example, scholars have accumulated considerable knowledge about political campaigns in the United States by integrating the findings of the large number of studies using fantasy theme analysis and symbolic convergence theory to study the rhetoric of political campaigns. Bormann, Cragan, and Shields, "An Expansion of the Rhetorical Vision Component of the Symbolic Convergence Theory: The Cold War Paradigm Case" (*Communication Monographs*, 64, March, 1996) surveyed and synthesized the results of eighty-seven fantasy theme analysis studies in their analysis of the creation and demise of the Cold War rhetorical vision.

In the early years of the development of symbolic convergence theory, a common complaint was that *fantasy* was a confusing technical term for a method that studied both the logical and imaginative elements of rhetoric. In recent years, the confusion has been cleared up and few people believe that the term refers solely to the fictitious.

As scholars conducted new studies and used their findings to elaborate and make more precise their concepts and assumptions of symbolic convergence theory, much of the negative criticism stopped. This does not mean that there were no more doubters, but as we move into the new century the theory and techniques seem well established. The project is now positioned to continue as a viable method of rhetorical study, criticism, and application.

BIBLIOGRAPHY

Bormann, Ernest G. "Fantasy and Rhetorical Vision: The Rhetorical Criticism of Social Reality." *Quarterly Journal of Speech* 58 (1972), pp. 396–407. The first publication of fantasy theme analysis.

Bormann, Ernest G. *The Force of Fantasy: Restoring the American Dream*. Carbondale, Ill., 1985. A historical study of the role of fantasy sharing in rhetoric in the United States from settlement to the Civil War, that moves from the sacred to the secular.

Bormann, Ernest G., John F. Cragan, and Donald C. Shields. "In Defense of Symbolic Convergence Theory: A Look at the Theory and Its Criticisms after Two Decades." *Communication Theory* 4 (1994), pp. 259–294. The definitive article on symbolic convergence theory pro and con.

Chesebro, J. W., J. F. Cragan, and P. W. McCullough. "The Small Group Techniques of the Radical Revolutionary: A Synthetic Study of Consciousness Raising." *Communication Monographs* 40 (1973), pp. 136–146. An early study of fantasy theme analysis and gay liberation consciousness-raising.

Cragan, J. F., and D. C. Shields. *Symbolic Theories of Applied Communication Research: Bormann, Burke, and Fisher*. Creskill, N.J., 1992. A particularly illuminating analysis of the usefulness of symbolic convergence theory in applied communication research. The analysis is presented in the context of the applied usefulness of the works of two other scholars.

Mohrmann, G. P. "Fantasy Criticism: A Peroration." *Quarterly Journal of Speech* 68 (1982), pp. 306–313.

Swartz, Omar. *The View from On the Road: The Rhetorical Vision of Jack Kerouac*. Carbondale, Ill., 1999. Excellent use of evidence indicating fantasy sharing in a historical context. Good analysis of the pros and cons of the debate about fantasy theme analysis.

—ERNEST G. BORMANN

ROMAN RHETORIC. *See* Classical rhetoric.

S

SCHEMES. *See* Classical rhetoric; Figures of speech; *and* Style.

SCIENCE certainly *had* a rhetorical dimension, at least until *scientist* was coined in English by the cleric-cum-geologist William Whewell in the 1830s to designate someone academically qualified and paid to pursue science on a full-time basis—not a mere inventor or naturalist. Soon thereafter, a rhetoric was spawned, which normally goes under the name of *philosophy of science,* to demarcate genuine scientists from those now deemed "pseudoscientific" practitioners of the profession. However, in previous generations, the latter actually constituted the bulk of those engaged in what we would now recognize as science. Most of the early members of the Royal Society could be numbered among these amateurs, as well as Whewell's younger contemporary, Charles Darwin. They also included such American purveyors of the Enlightenment as Benjamin Franklin and Thomas Jefferson, who regarded scientific pursuits like property ownership, as integral to republican citizenry.

In support of their pursuit of science, these amateurs could cite Aristotle's injunction at the opening of the *Metaphysics* (fourth century BCE), which presented the search for knowledge as the ultimate form of self-actualization, an activity available to anyone enjoying sufficient leisure. In other words, before Whewell's semantic innovation, science was not conceptualized as a technical specialty that would have disqualified public discussion of its means and ends. Of course, such discussion did remain restricted, but only because very few people (men, more precisely) enjoyed the requisite leisure to pursue science, not because the subject matter itself precluded more public involvement. Before the extension of citizenship rights to all adult males in the nineteenth century, *public* and *elite* were perfectly compatible terms, and during

this period "technical" most naturally meant an art closely tied to particular manual skills.

It follows that recent classically informed arguments to the effect that "rhetoric of science" is a contradiction in terms are potentially misdirected. For Aristotle to be convinced that the contemporary scene precludes science from having a rhetorical character, he would need to be shown that what we call "science" is primarily driven by skills that are so contextually specific that only practitioners can say anything sensible about their disposition. But to admit this (according to Aristotle) would be also to deny that what we call "science" has universal cognitive purchase. To be sure, this is something that most sociologists of science today would gladly concede. For their part, philosophers of science generally resolve the Aristotelian tension by conceding that science is now (though perhaps not in the past) an expertise dictated by its specialized subject matter and circumscribed more generally by talk of, say, the hypotheticodeductive method and deductive–nomological explanations. Those wishing to contribute to the discourse of science must first master these technicalities.

Unfortunately, this view tends to be treated mistakenly as *the* rhetoric of science, when in fact it is a rhetoric oriented to science as a full-time pursuit, not something that anyone may pursue at their leisure. From the classical standpoint, it amounts to an *antirhetoric of science*. It therefore remains open to rhetoricians to defend the classical view that scientific discourse must allow public participation to live up to its universalist aspiration. Admittedly, this would be a tall order in the current intellectual climate. But once the classical task is reinvigorated, it would make sense for rhetoricians to demystify scientific jargon and introduce considerations that force scientists to address a wider audience than their discourse would otherwise allow. This task has been already undertaken, but less by people who profess to do research in "rhetoric of science" than by teachers of "technical communication" who are typically engaged in instructing students in natural science, engineering, and medical faculties on how to deal with the increasing need to publicly justify expert judgment.

A good example of the contrast between a robust rhetoric of science and what is effectively an antirhetoric of science may be seen in the responses generated to the resurgence of Creationism in the state school systems of the United States. For example, in a series of celebrated articles, the rhetorician John Angus Campbell has recovered the original rhetorical situation that called forth Darwin's *Origin of the Species* (1859). In particular, the book's structure would be difficult to motivate if Darwin's interest in addressing the precursors of today's "intelligent design theorists" is not presupposed. In contrast, in *Abusing Science* (Cambridge, Mass., 1982), the philosopher Philip Kitcher proceeds antirhetorically to exclude Creationism from public debate by setting up criteria of scientificity that Creationists then unsurprisingly fail to meet.

When evaluating Campbell's and Kitcher's positions, we should remember that the federal nature of the U.S. Constitution not only mandates a separation of church and state but also devolves decisions concerning education to local authorities. This creates the tension that has bred the debate surrounding the teaching of Creationism. For, even granting that religion as such should be excluded from the school system, it does not follow that received scientific wisdom should be taught dogmatically. Indeed, religiously inspired inquirers may be better placed than most to see the flaws in secular scientific accounts, simply because they are motivated by something other than the reward system of the scientific establishment. Of course, this does not ensure the validity of their observations, let alone the religious beliefs that underwrite them, but it does provide a kind of check that scientists who specialize in, say, evolutionary biology might not otherwise encounter.

In the end, perhaps the best way to justify science's rhetorical status is to observe that both the foundational and practical issues concerning science that most frequently enter public debate transcend any given scientist's expertise. While the increased division of intellectual labor in the sciences has often been used to license the antirhetoric of science, in fact it provides an argument for opening up the sphere of deliberation. Because each new specialty tends to be defined in relation to already existing specialties rather than a free-standing social problem, lay ignorance and expert specialization turn out to be rhetorically equivalent positions from which to argue for a democratic approach to science policy argument.

The History of Rhetoric as a Guide to the Rhetoric of Science. Those who see science and rhetoric as inherently antagonistic pursuits generally focus on the different uses to which they put language. A good place to start exploring this intuition is William Fusfield, "To want to prove it . . . is . . . really superfluous" (*Quarterly Journal of Speech* 83, 1997, pp. 133–151). Fusfield examines a distinction that has permeated the entire history of Western rhetoric, namely, between what he calls *demonstrative* and *declarative* rhetoric. From the standpoint of this history, defenders of science's opposition to rhetoric aim to deny the rhetorical character of demonstrative rhetoric and the scientific character of declarative rhetoric. Thus, defenders of demonstrative rhetoric tend to practice the antirhetoric of science. From the Greeks onward, the paradigm of demonstration has been geometry because all of its premises are explicit; it is measured in tone; it aims at consensus. If demonstration is guided by method, declaration is led by wit. Its message is conveyed obliquely, in several registers at once, typically inviting the audience to participate in the completion of the message, which may vary according to the context of utterance. This was the view championed by the Sophists (fifth century BCE), who, much to Socrates' dismay, refused to draw a sharp, principled distinction between science and rhetoric.

While it would not be quite right to cast Fusfield's dichotomy in terms of either classicism versus romanticism or modernism versus postmodernism, nevertheless both oppositions convey the legacy of the original Greek disputes. Fusfield argues that the demonstrative–declarative distinction is grounded in the difference in rhetorical situations where a relatively short and focused speech (demonstrative) versus a complex piece of writing (declarative) is the ideal of rhetorical practice. The former invites an immediacy and explicitness of response that is common to both face-to-face encounters in the public sphere and logical proofs. The speech-based model presupposes that consensus is the goal of communication, either because the appeal to reason is purportedly universal (logic) or because the exigence is common to all within earshot of the speech (politics). However, the writing-based model presupposes that the goals of communication are diverse because audiences are diverse, as symbolized by the different places where people would read a written text—not all gathered in the classroom or the forum. Instead of convergence on a set of propositions or even a common course of action, the goal here is to stimulate the reader positively in many different ways, but perhaps all in opposition to a common orthodoxy. Not surprisingly, equivocation is valued in declarative rhetoric, but despised in demonstrative rhetoric. [See Ambiguity.] Conversely, clarity is often regarded with suspicion by declarativists, whereas demonstrativists take it as necessary for communication.

Thus, a demonstrativist would argue that Darwinian evolution enjoys paradigmatic status in biology because the truth of Darwin's fundamental claims enables their fruitful application in various theoretical and practical settings. A declarativist would reply that Darwin's theory is sufficiently open textured to justify a variety of things said and done. The former would explain early resistance to Darwin in terms of the cognitive deficiencies of either Darwin himself or his audiences, the latter in terms of difficulties audiences had in making the theory do something useful for them. This difference in emphasis points to alternative understandings of the "pragmatic" dimension of language. The demonstrativist alludes to the logical positivists and most analytic philosophers, who argue that the content of Darwin's theory, its "semantics," is fixed prior to the communicative act, itself regarded as an "application" of the theory's content. In contrast, the declarativist treats the content of Darwin's theory more hermeneutically, that is, as only partially formed in the pages of Origin of the Species. The text's reception history then tracks the process by which Darwin's argument is continually constituted and reconstituted by the book's readers.

That the declarativist approach is better suited to empirical studies of the rhetoric of science is illustrated by the massive revisions that Origin underwent from its first to sixth editions (1859–1872), in which only half of the original book remained, largely in response to its critical reception. This pattern characterizes scientific (and even philosophical) works that have enjoyed a wide audience. It suggests that scientific argumentation is very much an ongoing and unfinished affair, even after the master has laid down the foundations. Thus, Newton, Darwin, and Einstein—the three most celebrated scientists of the modern era—benefited from powerful rhetorical intermediaries (Locke, Huxley, and Planck) who not only translated formidable technicalities but also contributed catchy images that epitomized the master's work.

Moreover, the declarativist approach may have already dealt with conceptual problems that demonstrativists have only now come to recognize. A good example is what, after the philosopher W. V. O. Quine (Word and Object, Cambridge, Mass., 1960), has been called the "underdetermination of theory choice" in science. The basic idea is that a given datum can be explained by any number of opposing theories, if the theories' background assumptions are adjusted. It suggests that theories function casuistically, so as to invert their status from targets to tokens in scientific argumentation. [See Casuistry.] While news to demonstrativists, this inversion is commonplace to declarativists, who see rhetoric not as an accretion on the ex ante deliveries of logic and methodology but as something from which logic and methodology are abstracted ex post. In that case, why have philosophers spent more time articulating and formalizing the structure of scientific theories than defining the contexts in which theories need to be chosen and applied? After all, scientists themselves exert relatively little effort on these philosophical pursuits, since theories for them are flexibly interpretable texts that can be adapted as the situation demands.

The rhetorical difference between demonstrativists and declarativists on this score is that the former are inclined to a much higher mythos-to-kairos ratio than the latter. In other words, a higher premium is placed on the internal logic of events recounted in a scientific narrative (mythos) than on why the sequence transpired at the pace and over the length of real time that it did (*kairos*): time versus timing. [*See* Kairos.] Of course, some histories of science have been sensitive to timing, notably Paul Forman's account of the adoption of the indeterminacy interpretation of quantum phenomena by physicists in Weimar Germany, especially given that the crucial ideas had been debated inconclusively for the previous fifty years and no new arguments or experimental findings justified a quick closure to debate. In "Weimar Culture, Causality, and Quantum Theory: 1918–1927" (*Historical Studies in the Physical Sciences* 3, 1971, pp. 1–115), Forman turned to the growing cultural hostility to determinism and materialism that attended Germany's loss in World War I, which threatened the funding of physics research.

Without denying the many long-standing theoretical disputes in the history of science, it has often been unclear what is at stake, rhetorically speaking, aside from a point about the right way to talk about certain phenomena. Not surprisingly, then, these disputes can simmer for long periods, causing little disruption to the business of doing experiments and collecting data. One might be tempted to follow Ian Hacking (*Representing and Intervening,* Cambridge, U.K., 1983) in claiming that the relative autonomy of theoretical disputes demonstrates their relative *lack* of influence on the course of scientific research. Yet, there are times when the dispute reaches a climax—the paradigm is in crisis, a revolution ensues, and closure is finally reached. A demonstrativist would presume that the time for closure is always appropriate and the interesting issue centers on the decisive arguments and evidence. By contrast, the declarativist would ask why does the "moment of decision" occur at this point and not some other? After all, had the moment been a bit earlier or later, the relative standing of the parties to the dispute—not to mention the actual composition of the parties—may have been quite different. A slight change in context, and the weaker argument may have been, indeed, the stronger.

In sum, rhetoric's contribution to our understanding of the history of science may be captured in the following subversive hypothesis: Those defining moments of scientific culture—the great paradigmatic showdowns originally identified by Kuhn (1962)—occur only because science does *not* always follow its own internal trajectory. To borrow a current biological image, external pressures provide the "punctuation" that establishes new internal equilibria for science. Left in dialectic, for any two competing theories, every new argument or piece of evidence can be met by a counter or equivalent piece. [*See* Dialectic.] Yet, eventually matters of dialectic get caught up with public action, the stuff of rhetoric, which force the parties to settle their differences summarily. And those who control *when* the decision is made control *what* decision is made. Knowledge of rhetoric is thus necessary for knowing when to *start* and *stop* arguments that would otherwise continue ad infinitum. However, this critique is nothing more than a reinvention of Renaissance humanism's response to the medieval scholastic reduction of rhetoric to dialectic. [*See* Humanism.]

The Public Understanding of Science as a Rhetorical Problem. The cluster of research and policy issues associated with the public understanding of science marks the point where the rhetoric of science addresses most explicitly the democratization and even what may be called the "secularization" of science in the larger society. Activities oriented toward the public understanding of science are most prominent in nations where the links between science and the state are least secure. Britain leads the way here with its perennial "two cultures" problem, which places the public sphere very much in the control of the "arts" culture. Thus, the most noteworthy tendency in the history of science over the last 350 years is that Britain spawned the original geniuses, but a friendlier institutional climate enabled France, Germany, and the United States to convert their insights into full-fledged research programs and, in many cases, academic disciplines. For their part, British scientists have always had to sell their worth to a skeptical public. The result has been the formation of such influential public relations bodies as the British Association for the Advancement of Science, as well as the world's largest per capita consumption of popular science literature.

Anchored in the citizen–scientist tradition of the Founding Fathers, Americans remained fairly close to the British in their skeptical attitudes toward public support for professional scientific pursuits, that is, until the end of World War II, when science policy was made an integral part of national security. However, the end of the Cold War has witnessed a divestiture of public funding for research and education in science, which has led U.S. scientists to resort to many of the same strategies religions have used when church and state have been formally separated. Thus, there has been a rise of "science evangelism," whereby arguments in support of science are specifically oriented toward the satisfaction of human needs. The most obvious general trend is represented by the shift in intellectual and financial interest from high-energy physics and the space program to the human genome project and new age medicine. Solving 2500-year-old conundra about the nature of matter provides a much less persuasive basis for public science policy than the prospect of eliminating hereditary diseases in one's offspring.

This transition has led to a curious rupture in the meaning of the word *science,* one comparable to the fate of the word *religion* in secular times, when it refers to either a mindlessly repeated set of sectarian rituals or a general sensibility about the meaning of life, set adrift from any sectarian moorings. Thus, *science* sometimes refers to little more than the subject matter that must be mastered to acquire the credentials needed to succeed in life. There is no deep spiritual commitment to such knowledge, only a pragmatic awareness of its function in the processes of social reproduction. Other times, *science* means a generalized worldview that licenses doubt of received scientific opinion when it fails to conform to one's personal sense of the scientific. In that case, some illicit state interference may be suspected. The latter are attracted to works of science popularization that blur the line separating fact from fiction, the concrete from the spiritual, and so forth. The result is to destabilize the meaning of key scientific concepts, most notably "gene," popular characterizations of which as "aggressive," "altruistic," "selfish," and "communal" have unwittingly shaped the research agenda of several branches of biology since 1975.

The first wave of empirical research explicitly concerned with the public understanding of science consisted of surveys commissioned by the United Kingdom's Royal Society in the late 1980s. They were designed to diagnose an apparent decline in public support for the natural sciences, namely, an unwillingness to fund scientific research and formal study of scientific subjects. A fairly direct link was presumed between this lack of support and Britain's decline on the global stage since the end of World War II. These surveys claimed to show that the public's suspicion of science was symptomatic of ignorance of basic scientific facts and principles, which produced the "cognitive deficit model" of the public understanding of science. Thus, the respondent's failure to agree with orthodox scientific opinion was taken to imply ignorance rather than reasoned disagreement. Moreover, no baseline level of scientific competence was set among professional scientists against which to measure the public's level. It was simply assumed that, say, physicists would easily recognize the fundamental principles of evolutionary biology, even if nonscientists do not.

Objections were quickly raised to the Royal Society surveys, mainly from sociologists who argued that nonscientists possess knowledge about issues relevant to their lives that scientists either lack or tend to dismiss as merely anecdotal. Such "lay knowledge" typically consists of the accumulated experience of being, say, a sheep farmer or a cancer patient. To be sure, scientists are reluctant to admit the uncertain or ambiguous policy implications of their own knowledge claims, as that would draw attention to the artificial settings—laboratories, or computer simulations—in which scientific knowledge is typically developed. However, the sociological critics tended to slide from acknowledging the public's epistemic contribution to science policy to uncritical deference to an affected interest group.

Although democracy aims to give voice to traditionally disenfranchised groups, that does not insulate them from criticism, once they have been heard. Democracy makes a virtue of political *process,* which presupposes that *all* parties are open to change in light of collective deliberation. Indeed, democracy may not even be fully realizable unless people are willing to rethink their most cherished beliefs for purposes of coordinated action. In this respect, any nonnegotiable sense of identity tied to a specific form of knowledge is anathema to a democratic rhetoric of science. (The position that takes exception to this conclusion, exemplified in our own time by Paul Feyerabend, argues that state authority needs to be devolved so that each community can act on its preferred knowledge base.) Thus, lay understandings provide a "reality check" on the artificial character of scientific knowledge, but little more than that—especially when policy decisions are taken on behalf of relatively large social units that encompass multiple forms of "local knowledge," as is the case in medical and environmental matters. Here the knowledge claims of both scientists and nonscientists need to be reconstructed within a genuinely democratic process that allows give-and-take on both sides.

The public understanding of science has yet to get beyond the binary thinking that one either knows something for oneself or defers to the expertise of others. The missing middle term, where a democratic rhetoric of science dwells, is epitomized by such experiments in *deliberative democracy* as consensus panels and citizen juries. These experiments consist of structured critical exchanges between various experts and a representative sample of citizens on matters combining public concern and high technical content. The main outcome is a set of citizen-authored policy guidelines, which have provided reasonable bases for science and technology policy, even in countries like Japan that do not have robust democratic political traditions. In the process, people typically come to distance their own personal attitudes from what they believe will best serve the interests of society. Unfortunately, outside of Scandinavia, deliberative democracy remains merely an academic exercise that has failed to feed into the institutionalized processes of governance.

Enunciating the Scientific Voice. What does it mean to communicate in a "scientific voice"? Recent research suggests that answers involve specifying how those absent from a knowledge production site—be it laboratory or field—come to believe the testimony of those at the site. Knowledge producers supposedly capitalize on their similarities with anticipated audiences, as well as any distinctive features of their own pasts (e.g., track record) that would make them especially qualified to offer comment. In all this, scientists are presumed to know exactly whom they address. But arguably this approach only obscures the multiple audiences that are simultaneously addressed: beyond fellow specialists (who must not be offended by one's appropriation of the discipline's collective memory) and more general publics (e.g., lay readers, academic evaluators, and policymakers, who must find surface value in what one says), there are also the elusive interests of posterity, those ultimate arbiters of one's contribution as either a foundation or an obstacle. This last group may well be accorded the most respect because of their putative detachment from the exigencies that cause the other audiences to respond disproportionately to the merits of one's claims.

Clearly, it takes different arguments to persuade these different audiences, yet implicit in the nature of science is that somehow they are all part of the same universal audience of knowledge seekers. How, then, can this actual multiplicity be represented as an ideal unity? Here are six rhetorical strategies for addressing this question.

1. One can adopt the "double truth" doctrine and write so as to convey simultaneously a surface truth to ordinary contemporaries and a deeper truth to a mentally prepared elite (perhaps located in the future). This strategy has been associated with esoteric readings of Plato's *Republic* and, more generally, the survival of radical philosophical inquiry in political and religious captivity. Its characteristic features are understatement and prudent omission. Examples from the history of science include Copernicus's sixteenth-century presentation of the heliocentric universe as a simplification of ancient Ptolemaic astronomy, Darwin's agnosticism on the implications of evolution by natural selection for the divinity of homo sapiens, and Kuhn's failure to apply his theory of paradigms and revolutions to an understanding of contemporary "Big Science."

2. A related strategy observes that, prior to its professionalization, the authors of most of the major works in philosophy of science had been on the losing side of the major scientific arguments of their day (the names of Whewell, Mach, and Duhem spring to mind). Even the logical positivists, who celebrated the revolutionary developments in relativity and quantum theory, were deemed too "philosophical" by the physics faculties that refused to pass their doctoral theses. Indeed, positivist appeals to the "Unity of Science" were already nostalgic by the end of World

War I. For them, the "scientific voice" stood for a normative ideal slipping away from practices that have become increasingly fragmented and compromised by their subservience to a host of strictly nonscientific (e.g., ideological, technological) functions. The continuing appeal of Karl Popper's (1945) vision of science as the "open society" testifies to the robustness of this ideal, despite implying the suboptimality of most "normal science."

3. Multiple voices may be acknowledged in scientific rhetoric without presuming their stratification in "mass" and "elite" registers. The nineteenth century reinforced this point, as increased mass literacy coincided with the emergence of specialist discourses. The major scientific works from this period appealed to both without condescending to either. Darwin's *Origin of the Species* epitomized this tendency. The metaphor of "evolution by natural selection" immediately appealed to bourgeois readers accustomed to "invisible hand" explanations of social life. This gave *Origin* the surface plausibility needed to survive more specialist doubts about Darwin's failure to provide a proper genetic account for the transmission of selected traits to offspring. Indeed, the surface plausibility of Darwin's metaphor kept his theory afloat for seventy years, until geneticists came to believe they could help explain the mechanics of evolution.

4. Contrarily, the scientific voice may be rhetorically constructed by *reducing* multiplicity, say, by presuming that sometimes those who regard themselves as scientists must make an irreversible decision between alternative lines of inquiry. It would be difficult to underestimate the significance of this rhetoric for the history of modern science, without which any linear notion of progress would be impossible. The archetype of this approach is Galileo's *Dialogues Concerning the Two World-Systems* (1632), which made it explicit, much to the Papal Inquisition's dismay, that true scientists had to choose between Copernican astronomy and the Holy Scriptures.

5. The multiplicity of scientific voices may also be organized into movements surrounding the reception of a favored text. This practice probably originated with the "Battle of the Books" that entangled literary intellectuals in seventeenth- and eighteenth-century Europe. The debate officially concerned the interpretation of the classics. The "Ancients" treated them as perfect in original composition, whereas the "Moderns" saw them as imperfectly realized versions of truths still awaiting better expression. This dispute continued into the nineteenth and twentieth centuries as, respectively, the "Arts" and "Sciences" side of what C. P. Snow called the "Two Cultures" (1959), a divide that came to be treated as problematic with the increasing specialization of higher education. Meanwhile, a third paradigm of a text-based movement emerged with the production of highly complex and technical pieces of writing explicitly conceived as providing a framework for follow-up activity, not simply critical acceptance. Newton's *Principia Mathematica* (1687) and Marx's *Das Kapital* (1867) are two very different texts that fall under this category: the former sought completion through the conduct of "normal science," the latter through "revolutionary praxis."

6. Sometimes the scientific voice is constructed from a tension in existing voices. In the first half of the nineteenth century, under the influence of Romanticism, it was common to contrast depth and uniqueness with superficiality and generality. The former corresponded to the rhetoric of the poet (Goethe), the latter to that of the physicist (Newton). Self-styled "sociologists" wishing to capture the human condition with some of the systematicity of the natural sciences negotiated the contrast by wedding depth to generality, albeit striking the balance in rather different ways. For example, Georg Simmel (1858–1918) presumed that one well-chosen case could stand for an entire class of social phenomena, whereas Emile Durkheim (1858–1917) held that statistics could uncover subtle features of social life that eluded a fixation on striking cases. Both perspectives continue as exemplars of "micro" and "macro" approaches to sociology.

But the resolution of multiplicity into unity is not the only problem surrounding the rhetorical construction of a scientific voice. There is also the reverse problem of unity fragmenting into multiplicity that is posed by any act of translation, since there is generally a tradeoff between rendering the conceptual framework and the pragmatic import of a source text in the target language. Subtle turns of phrase that would resonate at multiple registers with German readers, in translation might strike the English reader as pedantic. To convey a comparable richness of meaning in English, one might need to deviate quite substantially from the original German form of words. The problem is exacerbated when the translated author appears originally to have struck just the right balance in his or her native language; for example, Sigmund Freud (1856–1939), who, despite his ostracism from the German academic establishment, managed to find a voice that was rewarded for both its scientific and literary virtues. However, Freud's authorized translator, James Strachey, found it difficult to retain both virtues in English. His translation stressed the scientific side of Freud's meaning, leading to a reification of such psychic processes as ego, superego, and id.

The Legacy of Textualism in Rhetoric of Science Research. Much pioneering work in the self-declared "rhetoric of science" has been done by people with strong literary backgrounds, such as Charles Bazerman (1987) and Alan Gross (1990). These origins have anchored the empirical cast of the field, not least the tendency to take a notable text as the unit of analysis. Yet, whatever may be true of literary cultures, there is little evidence that scientific texts are read with the care to which humanists are accustomed. Indeed, there is little reason to think that the reading practices most valued by humanists are shared by the natural scientists they study. For, while texts are the primary objects of inquiry in the human sciences, they are usually means to other ends in the natural sciences. According to Steven Shapin and Simon Schaffer (*Leviathan and the Air-Pump,* Princeton, 1985), one legacy of the Scientific Revolution has been scientists' impatience toward argument and the other verbal arts as so much time taken from the construction of instruments needed to demonstrate findings specifically designed to *silence* opponents.

Not surprisingly, the history of scientific journal writing exhibits successive innovations to streamline the reading process. Nowadays the scientific text is divided into modules of "theory," "method," "data," and "discussion" to enable scientific readers to appropriate relevant sections for their own purposes, and to ignore (*not* criticize) the rest. Indeed, what would strike the humanist as sheer negligence, namely, to read only selected sections of an article, appears crucial to the con- solidation and cumulative growth that distinguish knowledge in the natural sciences from knowledge in the human sciences. Whereas a highly cited article in the natural sciences is usually exemplary in only one or a few respects, a comparably cited article in the social sciences would be regarded more ambivalently—but also in its entirety.

The historian of twentieth-century literary criticism should appreciate the irony here. At the beginning of the century, Russian formalist critics, those spiritual godfathers of French structuralism, had argued that innovation in elite literary forms came from popular genres. At the end of the century, empirical students of the rhetoric of science have admitted that the production and consumption cycles of texts in the natural sciences are like those of the mass media. From patterns discerned in the *Science Citation Index,* the "harder" the science, the more its research specialties resemble fads in their life cycles. By contrast, research specialties in the "softer" sciences have long half-lives, so that it is unclear when they definitively go out of fashion. This probably reflects the similarities in the size and shape of today's scientific enterprise and the mass media. In both cases, "invisible colleges" and "opinion leaders" structure the reception and appropriation of texts. Whether this should cause the rhetorician to reassess our general value orientation toward different forms of knowledge is an open but important question.

Confronted with the brute character of scientific reading and writing practices, the diehard textualist has three options: First, real readers are replaced by an "ideal reader," someone knowledgeable of the science under discussion but also blessed with a humanist's sense of interpretive sensitivity to tropes, topics, and devices. Unfortunately, such generosity would seem to invite specious forms of historical understanding that question the legitimacy of the rhetoric of science as such. Nevertheless, it is common among rhetoricians of science of a literary bent.

Second, it is conceded that everyone routinely misreads each other's texts. Ever since deconstructionists redefined poetic and philosophical originality as the ability to provide "strong misreadings" of one's distinguished predecessors, this view has been credible. Historians interested in reconstructing a debate from original documents often agree, so as to reduce a Manichaean struggle to a comedy of errors: the great minds would have realized they were not so far apart had they bothered to read each other a little more closely. But then any sense of epistemic progress becomes mysterious. Despite its outlandishness, this line of thought usefully shows what happens when certain taken-for-granted notions of communication are put to a serious empirical test.

Third, it is claimed that science would be better, *if* scientists were to adopt the textual practices of humanists, even though this would go against their professional inclinations. Feyerabend (1979) would be a potential ally for arguing that the political and economic stakes make it impossible for contemporary scientists to treat each other's arguments with the care they deserve: because too much money, and too many people's careers, ride on being right, one is forced *not* to take seriously the possibility of being wrong.

Turning the Tables: Rhetoric As Science. Can rhetoric be a science? If so, what sort of science? Skepticism toward this line of inquiry traditionally stems from the reflexive difficulties of joining classical notions of rhetorical timeliness (*kairos*) to modern scientific aspirations to universal laws (*physis*). [*See* Philosophy, *article on* Perennial topics and terms.] On the one hand, once one accepts the rhetorical point of view, can one believe there is a form of expression appropriate for all times and places? On the other, once one accepts the scientific point of view, how can one treat contingencies of utterance as anything more than epiphenomenal on general principles of human expression? It would seem that either rhetoric would reduce the scientific attitude to a hegemonic ideology or science would reduce the rhetorical attitude to a preoccupation with the marginalia of evolutionary psychology.

The Greek Sophists attempted to square this circle by arguing for the possibility of a *science of situatedness,* that is, general principles governing the indexical character of persuasion and expression, regardless of its specific content. Socrates was famously unmoved by the Sophists' arguments for such a science. [*See* Classical rhetoric; *and* Sophists.] He held that any genuine expertise associated with these principles simply flowed from other technical skills possessed by the rhe-

tor. Thus, a persuasive baker would be someone who shows on demand that she can bake bread, a skill that involves knowledge of bakery not rhetoric. (That most firms today spend more on the advertisement than the production of their goods—and seem satisfied with the results—should lead one to question the validity of this argument.)

Notwithstanding Socrates' misgivings, the desire for a science of the situated has persisted as a subterranean current in philosophy's concern for what John Duns Scotus in the thirteenth century called *haecceitas* ("thisness"), the most scientific development of which has been the sociological school of ethnomethodology. Moreover, Socrates may have missed the original democratic spirit informing the science of situatedness, namely, that in the public sphere the only relevant expertise is the ability to control the flow of argument, since all other skills are of potentially equal significance until proven (by rhetoric) otherwise.

Perhaps the most notable modern strategy for overcoming the conceptual impasse surrounding a "science of rhetoric" stems from the sociology of knowledge, which demystifies the difference between *contingency* and *necessity*—the one traditionally associated with rhetoric, the other with science. Sociologists of knowledge claim that our sense of necessity results from ignorance of the conditions under which we take our most general knowledge claims to apply. That a given knowledge claim is invoked only in some contexts and not others does not normally enter our deliberations. We simply conflate the generality of what the knowledge claim says with the generality of when it applies (i.e., the major and minor premises of the Aristotelian syllogism). [*See* Syllogism.] In that case, rhetoric provides the requisite level of self-consciousness, so as to enable both a critique of the content of general claims and creativity in their future application. In practice, this means that scientific laws come to be treated much like civil laws, in which judicial precedent and case-based reasoning are decisive in specifying the use to which laws are put. This perspective has been implicitly adopted by recent sociology of science, which focuses on the flexibility with which scientists adapt general laws to specific experimental or observational settings.

The above strategy can be epitomized in classical Greek terms by saying that science masks its sense of *kairos* with the *mythos* of presenting our most general claims to knowledge as *physis*, which upon demystification really turn out to be instances of *nomos*. In other words, what were previously thought to be universal laws of nature are revealed to be sustained acts of ventriloquism whereby a subset of our social conventions are imaginatively projected on the larger canvass of reality. However, these conventions, once demystified, may suggest that the pursuit of science does an injustice not only to rhetoric but perhaps even the creative capacity of homo sapiens. After all, the conventions governing science largely pertain to the manipulation of physical objects—including human beings regarded as masses whose motions are subject to constraints imposed by external forces. Those sympathetic to such skepticism would be following the eighteenth-century Neapolitan jurist Giambattista Vico, who ranked rhetoric above science—or, more precisely, declarative over demonstrative rhetoric—for the fuller use to which it put our powers of memory and imagination, which most clearly distinguish humans from lower animals. [*See* Eighteenth-century rhetoric.]

[*See also* Contingency and probability; Invention; Politics, *article on* Personal, technical, and public spheres of argument; *and* Technical communication.]

BIBLIOGRAPHY

Bazerman, Charles. *Shaping Written Knowledge.* Madison, Wis., 1987.

Campbell, John Angus. "Intelligent Design, Darwinism, and the Philosophy of Public Education." *Rhetoric and Public Affairs* 1 (1998), pp. 466–502.

Carley, Kathleen, and David Kaufer. *Communication at a Distance.* Hillsdale, N.J., 1993. A sophisticated treatment of the growth of scientific knowledge by regarding writing as a prosthetic extension of speech.

Collier, James. *Scientific and Technical Communication: Theory, Practice, and Policy.* London, 1997. The textbook that best illustrates the challenge that technical communication courses pose to science's official rhetoric.

Feyerabend, Paul. *Science in a Free Society.* London, 1979.

Fuller, Steve. *Philosophy, Rhetoric, and the End of Knowledge.* Madison, Wis., 1993. A systematic attempt to justify a rhetoric of science that would have pleased the Sophists.

Fuller, Steve. *The Governance of Science: Ideology and the Future of the Open Society.* Milton Keynes, U.K., 1999. Argues for a democratic rhetoric of science, in spite of the scale and scope of contemporary scientific enterprises.

Fuller, Steve. *Thomas Kuhn: A Philosophical History for Our Times.* Chicago, 2000. On the debilitating influence of Kuhn on the rhetoric of science.

Gjertsen, Derek. *The Classics of Science: Twelve Enduring Scientific Works.* New York, 1984. The best source for the reception history of science from Euclid to Darwin.

Gross, Alan. *The Rhetoric of Science.* Cambridge, Mass., 1990.

Gross, Alan, and William Keith, eds. *Rhetorical Hermeneutics: Invention and Interpretation in the Age of Science.* Albany, N.Y., 1997. The most important recent anthology on the rhetoric of science, centered on responses to Dilip Gaonkar's claim that the field is a poor relative of the sociology of science.

Hess, David. *Science in the New Age.* Madison, Wis., 1993.

Howe, Henry, and John Lyne. "Gene Talk in Sociobiology." *Social Epistemology* 6 (1992), pp. 1–54. A seminal collaboration between a rhetorician and a scientist on how popular discourse influences technical disputes.

Irwin, Alan, and Brian Wynne, eds. *Misunderstanding Science? The Public Reconstruction of Science and Technology.* Cambridge, U.K., 1996.

Jonsen, Albert, and Stephen Toulmin. *The Abuse of Casuistry.* Berkeley, 1988.

Krips, Henry, James McGuire, and Trevor Melia, eds. *Science, Reason, and Rhetoric.* Pittsburgh, 1995. An ecumenical attempt to unite philosophers, sociologists, and rhetoricians under the banner of "rhetoric of science."

Kuhn, Thomas S. *The Structure of Scientific Revolutions.* Chicago, 1962.

Lepenies, Wolf. *Between Literature and Science: The Rise of Sociology.* Cambridge, U.K., 1988.

McCloskey, Deirdre N. *The Rhetoric of Economics.* Madison, Wis., 1998. First published in 1985. The first distinguished social scientist to openly acknowledge the rhetorical character of her field.

Montgomery, Scott. *The Scientific Voice.* New York, 1995.

Nelson, J., A. Megill, and D. McCloskey, eds. *The Rhetoric of the Human Sciences.* Madison, Wis., 1987. Still the best social science anthology on the rhetoric of science.

Pera, Marcello, and William Shea, eds. *Persuading Science: The Art of Scientific Rhetoric.* Canton, Mass. 1991. Exhibits the strengths and weaknesses of philosophical forays into the rhetoric of science.

Popper, Karl R. *The Open Society and its Enemies.* London, 1945.

Prelli, Lawrence. *A Rhetoric of Science.* Columbia, S.C.,

1989. A work that remains close to the orientation of classical rhetoric.

Roberts, R. H., and J. M. M. Good, eds. *The Recovery of Rhetoric: Persuasive Discourse and Disciplinarity in the Human Sciences.* Bristol, U.K., 1993. The best British anthology, stressing the role of rhetoric in reconceptualizing psychology.

Snow, C. P. *The Two Cultures and the Scientific Revolution.* New York, 1959.

Taylor, Charles Alan. *Defining Science.* Madison, Wis., 1996. Stakes out rhetoric's claim to the "demarcation problem" between science and pseudoscience.

Woolgar, Steve. *Science: The Very Idea.* London, 1988. A good source for recent sociology of science in a rhetorical key, heavily influenced by ethnomethodology.
— STEVE FULLER

SECULAR PIETY is a phrase that combines the material or physical world of the here and now with a religious or spiritual other worldliness. Either word in the term may be emphasized: if *secular* is stressed, then *this* world is important, as it would be, say, to a scientist who has a religious commitment to work; if *piety* is stressed, then spiritual foundation is valued, as it might be in adapting religious beliefs to scientific findings. When the terms are equally stressed, secular piety joins perspectives that are usually considered incompatible. For example, in the twelfth century in Europe, during the religious crusades, the knight was a secular leader piously carrying out the will of the church. Today, secular piety may take the form of advocating prayer in U.S. public schools.

Secular piety is an ambiguous, paradoxical phrase that characterizes the manner in which people identify with their life experience. It is ambiguous because either abstract aspect of the term may be emphasized. It is paradoxical because the term joins concepts from opposing worldviews. Two rhetorical perspectives, traditional and Burkean, provide further understanding of this phrase and its uses in rhetoric.

Traditional Perspective. Pietism, which started in the 1600s, and secularism, which rose to prominence in the 1800s, provide the root meanings of the terms in the phrase. Because both movements radiated through society, both words have a variety of meanings. The concept of decorum from classical rhetoric offers a traditional perspective on the possible balancing of these meanings.

Pietism was a Protestant reform movement in the late seventeenth century that embraced devotion and a personal relationship with God as the essence of Christianity, rather than dogmatic theological identity through rites of baptism, Eucharist, or confessional. It deemphasized academics and insisted that faith must be supported by works, such as repentance, conversion, and a changed life. It opposed dogmatism in both the Roman Catholic and Protestant churches and supported using the Bible for meditation and spirituality; breaking down the separation between clergy and laity; emphasizing practical, not theological, Christianity; abandoning religious argument; and revitalizing preaching to edify the people.

From 1650 to 1750, pietism was a strong force for religious reawakening in western Europe and in the American colonies. By 1760, pietism was strong in all Protestant churches in Europe and had missions in European colonies in Greenland, the Americas, Egypt, Ceylon, and the Caribbean. In North America, such Puritans as Cotton Mather, Jonathan Edwards, T. J. Freylinguyen, George Whitefield, and Gilbert Tennent all promoted religious revivals that became known as the "Great Awakening," which reached its peak between 1739 and 1744. Today, most Protestant churches deemphasize ritual, making the sermon central, and they stress religious and ethical qualifications over ecclesiastical status. Piety's emphasis on "good works" encourages philanthropy and missionary activity. The pietist influence in North America, through the "Great Awakening" and the dominance of the Puritans, resulted in a long-term pragmatic effect that helped shape British and American evangelicalism.

Secularism, in contrast, was an ethical and antireligious movement with a positive and ethical theory of life, which later promulgated secularization. Secularism was born in the mid-nineteenth century out of the wealthy and influentials' unreasoning opposition to political and religious freedom. It was a protest movement with philosophical roots in the "associationists" school of James Mill (1773–1836) and Jeremy Bentham (1748–1832), and the antitheist strain from Thomas Paine (1737–1809) and Richard Carlile (1790–1843).

In the 1850s, George Jacob Holyoake (1817–1906) and Charles Bradlaugh (1833–1891) coined the term *secularism* to distinguish *antitheistic* from *atheistic* beliefs. Secularism's essential principle is human improvement by material means alone, based on experience tested by reason. Initially, people treated religion and the secular as different worlds, one unknown and the other knowable through experience. Secularization meant the decline of religious influence as reflected through a decrease in religious activities, beliefs, and institutions. In the early nineteenth century, secularization implied a pattern of social development that sociologists like Auguste Comte (1798–1857) recognized, in which religious assumptions were less dominant and social institutions were more independent. Secularization continued throughout the twentieth century, deepening the apprehension of natural order and encouraging detachment in observation and experimentation, leading to the institutionalization of science.

The traditional perspective in rhetoric blends the secular world of the here and now with the other worldliness of piety into a system of beliefs, that is, if not unified, then a kind of usable code. The concept of "propriety" or "decorum" from classical rhetoric explains its possible blending and usefulness. [*See* Decorum.]

Postmodern critics such as Paul Ricoeur have argued that classical rhetoric is no longer useful in today's world because it is filled with contradictions: rhetoric as arguing and pleasing, as speaker- and audience-centered, as typology and practical, and as functional and aesthetic. In response, Michael Leff has responded that "propriety," which emphasizes balance between extremes, is imbedded in classical rhetoric. Then, following the lead of Tzvetan Todorov, Leff presents "decorum," based primarily on Cicero's *Orator,* as the means of resolving and balancing contradictory ideas and demands. Leff indicates that "decorum enters our lives at every point where we render judgment without reference to absolutes, for we say 'this is appropriate' or 'that is appropriate' about everything we express or do, whether the matter is great or trivial" (Leff, 1990, p. 121). He then describes the three main strands of decorum as "accommodation to circumstances," "the mediating link between the form and content," and "an organizing principle governing the internal form of discourse" (p. 121). It is thus through decorum that traditional rhetoric allows for a blending of the contradictions inherent in secular piety.

Burkean Perspective. In Kenneth Burke's rhetorical perspective, dramatism treats the terms in secular piety as incompatible worlds that function dialectically. Three Burkean concepts—"secular prayer," "identification," and "perspective by incongruity"—explain the dramatistic functions of secular piety. [*See* Identification; *and* Perspective by incongruity.]

Burke (1897–1993) discusses both "piety" and "secular" in the context of secular prayer, even though he does not employ the term *secular piety* itself. He presents secular prayer as a moral act of character building that serves as a magical "*coaching of an attitude*" (*Attitudes,* p. 322). Burke associates secular prayer with "word magic" (p. 321). Children in their play engage in secular prayer as they break from reality and name "a block," "a train," "a tree," or "a house." Adults engage in a similar process of play as they interpret and name the events in their experience as "rudeness" and "minority" or even "capitalism" and "class struggle" (pp. 322–323).

All propaganda, and even the "best" persuasion, is secular prayer because it involves "a coaching of an attitude." Burke refers to Vilfredo Pareto (1848–1923) when he discusses the most irritating form of secular prayer—the "strictly scientific" approach that claims the "objectivity and precision of mathematics" (p. 326). Another form of secular prayer is the naming of the "essence" of a complex situation or process as "fascism" or "racism" or "globalism" or "communitarianism," and then the enlisting of others on your side to engage in conflict against those people representing this essence.

Burke's association of both "piety" and "secular" with "secular prayer" makes them function rhetorically as active and positive, rather than passive and negative, in their "coaching of an attitude." He acknowledges religion as piety's source, but then he emphasizes that piety goes further and represents the unified whole growing out of all one's childhood experiences. Finally, he defines piety as a holistic "sense of what properly goes with what" (*Permanence,* p. 74). For Burke, piety is a dynamic concept with characteristics of religiousness, appropriateness, orientation, integration, and interaction. Burke discusses secular within the context of piety, as a Freudian, psychoanalytical process of "non-religious conversion" (p. 125). Because piety is "loyalty to the sources of our being" (p. 71), which Freud assumes are religious in nature, "secular" by contrast is a dramatic reorientation that takes the form of a "non-religious conversion" (p. 125). Burke explains Freud's healing of a patient as reorientation that occurs by shifting thinking from "the system of pieties lying at the roots of the patient's sorrows and bewilderments" into a neutral scientific vocabulary that becomes a "non-religious conversion" (pp. 125–127). The characteristics of the secular, he discusses, are scientific, irreligious, impious, and irreverent.

Secular piety, as an ambiguous, paradoxical term, can characterize how people frame and identify with their life experience. Identity is established through a process that Burke develops and applies in *A Rhetoric of Motives*. Burke explains that "A is not identical with his colleague, B. But insofar as their interests are joined, A is *identified* with B. Or he may identify himself with B even when their interests are not joined, if he assumes that they are, or is persuaded to believe so" (p. 20). Just as decorum in traditional rhetoric blends contradictions, so Burke's identification allows people, by assuming that interests are joined, to stress unity in what might otherwise be perceived as a divisive situation or idea. Through secular piety, people can frame their world and identity as both worldly and spiritual. So the various meanings of secular piety are actually ways for people, rhetorically, to frame and relate to their life experience.

Further, the inherently ambiguous but useful nature of the phrase can also be understood through Burke's "perspective by incongruity," which he coined by drawing on Oswald Spengler's (1880–1936) use of a Nietzschean method of bringing together events at similar stages but at different times in history. Joining incompatible ideas consciously violates the "proprieties" and previous "linkages" of the words by taking them out of context. These new linkages allow people to gain new insights. Burke gives "Arabian Puritanism," "that big dog, the lion," and "ape-God" as examples of perspective by incongruity that are capable of communicating new insights through new linkages (*Permanence*, p. 90). Secular piety too incongruously links the physical and scientific world with the spiritual and religious, resulting in new meanings.

For a deeper understanding of how uniting "secular" and "piety" violates their root meanings, one might understand "magic," "religion" and "science" as metaphors for Western cultural history. When people continually employ a specific conceptual frame for their thinking, it solidifies over time into an orientation. Burke analyzes this process when he discusses Western societal thought as three successive orientations in the "Curve of History" (*Attitudes*, pp. 111–175).

Magic, as a pattern for thought or rationalization, is an attempt to control natural forces of the world by understanding them as activating causes of such phenomena as the seasons, growing of food, and the conception of children. Religion stresses a higher, more arbitrary force, God, who through prayer might be influenced to alter the course of nature and human life. Science stresses control over the productive order, technology, which assumes uniformity and the ability to control by manipulating the laws of rational invention (*Permanence*, pp. 59–66).

Burke then explains how each orientation is in turn replaced by another, and even predicts that science will be succeeded by a "poetic humanism" that is more humanistic, pluralistic, subjective, and spiritual than science (pp. 65–66). This succession of terms emphasizes the manner in which each orientation has very different values and linkages. So when "secular" is taken out of a scientific frame and paired with "piety" from a religious frame, two completely different patterns of thought are dialectically joined creating an ambiguous concept with a multitude of meanings. Further, placing "secular piety" within "poetic humanism" creates even greater possibilities for new, creative meanings, since poetic humanism itself brings together technology from science and a controlling individual spirituality.

BIBLIOGRAPHY

Burke, Kenneth. *Permanence and Change*. Berkeley, 1984. First published 1935.
Burke, Kenneth. *Attitudes toward History*. Boston, 1961. First published 1937.
Burke, Kenneth. *A Rhetoric of Motives*. Berkeley, 1984. First published 1950.

Craig, Edward, ed. *Encyclopedia of Philosophy,* vols. 7, 8. New York, 1998.

Eliade, Mircea, ed. *The Encyclopedia of Religion,* vols. 11, 13. New York, 1987.

Frankel, Marvin E. "Faith and Freedom." In *Faith and Freedom: Religious Liberty in America.* New York, 1994.

Hastings, James. *Encyclopaedia of Religion and Ethics,* vol. 10. New York, 1919.

Leff, Michael. "Decorum and Rhetorical Interpretation: The Latin Humanistic Tradition and Contemporary Critical Theory." *Vichiana* 3d series, 1 (1990), pp. 107–126.

Online Resources

"Code of Ethics and Honor in the Crusades." http://www.umich.edu/~eng415/topics/chivalry/chivalry-article.html. Last modified 20 November 1997; maintained at the University of Michigan, Ann Arbor. Provides links to related sites.

—BERNARD L. BROCK

SEMANTICS. *See* Linguistics.

SERMON. *See* Exhortation; Homiletics; *and* Religion.

SIMILE (Gk. *parabolē,* Lat. *parabola, similitudo*) expresses a relationship of likeness and is indicated by the linguistic markers "as" or "like." An example is the first line of the poem by Robert Burns, "My luve is like a red, red rose." The simile involves a comparison between two objects or concepts that are connected through a shared quality, the *tertium comparationis.* In contrast to the metaphor, which is often defined as a simile in an elliptic form, the simile denotes a relationship of likeness *expressis verbis.* Meeting the demands of perspicuity, it has proven to be a suitable means of instruction. Notable is the use of the simile by Jesus in the New Testament, as in *Mt.* 20.1: "For the kingdom of heaven is like unto a man that is an householder." The simile can be used as a form of rhetorical amplification, as is demonstrated by the "epic simile" of Homer, as well as the epideictic similes in the Bible's *Song of Solomon.*

The simile is an isosememe that denotes an object or an idea through more than one lexical item; transferred to a textual level, it assumes the nature of a parable and changes into an isotexteme. A deletion of its linguistic markers results in a transformation to either metaphor or allegory. Such transformations are generally accompanied by a decrease in perspicuity and an increase in obscurity.

[*See also* Allegory; Figures of speech; *and* Metaphor.]

—RICHARD NATE

SLAVIC RHETORIC. Slavic countries differ from those in western Europe in terms of political, cultural, and religious development, differences that are reflected in traditions of rhetorical schooling and the application of rhetorical principles in public life. Literary, linguistic, and historical research into Slavic cultures must therefore take into account not only the integrating function of rhetoric as a universal code of European, and thus also Slavic, rhetoric but also influences that were unique to the Slavic world when rhetoric was first developed there. Notwithstanding these differences, the Humanist period saw the creation of centers from which rhetorical studies spread, transcending ethnic and state boundaries. Particularly dynamic were the contacts between Czechs and Poles, Poles and Ukrainians, Ukrainians and Russians, and Russians and Serbs, strengthened by the migrations of pupils and teachers as well as by the publication of many teaching manuals and their translation into the languages of the region. Such contacts were a part of that cosmopolitanism of rhetoric studies that were characteristic of all European countries at the time. The development of the Renaissance in Italy, for example, had significant contributions by the southern Slavic countries of Croatia and Slovenia (Francesco Patrizzi-Petris, 1529–1597, the author of an ideal rhetoric constructed in an axiomatic manner, was of Slavic origin).

A fundamental dichotomy in the early history of Slavic rhetoric is based on the impact of two language/cultural areas: the eastern (Byzantine) area, whose influence was the result of the mission of Thessalonican apostles Constantine and Method to the Great Moravia at the end of the ninth century, and their disciples, especially in Bulgaria and Russia; and the western (Latin) area, which from the twelfth century onward produced manuals of epistolary rhetoric and preaching. [*See overview article on* Medieval rhetoric.] The boundary between both areas, however, was rather vague.

In Poland, at the end of the sixteenth century, the universities at Warsaw and Cracow as well as other centers produced commentaries on Hermogenes, Dionysius of Halicarnassos, Pseudo-Demetrius, and others. In Bohemia, Sturm's pupil, Jan Kocín, published Hermogenes' works with commentaries (1570–1571). The rhetorical education in Ukraine and Russia, however, was influenced by Latin schools operating in Poland and Lithuania.

The oldest Slavic manual of rhetoric is a short treatise in Old Slavonic (*O obrazěchЪ*) (On Figures), a part of the so-called Sviatoslav volume from 1073. It is an Old Slavonic adaptation of the Byzantine author Georgos Kherobosk (Greek sources situate his life anywhere between the fourth and the tenth centuries). The translation explains twenty-seven tropes and figures and refers to them consistently by Slavic equivalents of Greek terminology. In the Eastern Slavic area, this document remained unique for a long time. In Slavic West, namely, in Bohemia and Poland, schooling in sermonic and epistolary rhetoric became a part of the syllabus at municipal and church schools, and beginning in 1348, when Charles IV founded the university in Prague, it was also a prerequisite of higher education.

Bohemia. The earliest documents on rhetoric in Bohemia date to the end of the thirteenth century, when a representative of Bolognese rhetoric, Henricus of Isernia, moved to Prague. He established a scribes' school at the Vyšehrad cathedral and became a royal notary. In 1278 he compiled the first rhetoric manual, *Epistolare dictamen,* and a collection of letter-writing models. These continued to exercise their influence during the reign of Charles IV through the activity of Humanist circles, which produced several manuals and commentaries on rhetoric. The most significant among them are the commentaries on Eberhard and Galfred's *Artes poetriae* compiled by Nicolaus Dybin in the latter half of the fourteenth century, who was connected with the schools in Prague and Dresden. The inspiring influence of Humanist rhetoric was taken up by a gradually growing number of students and scholars of Czech origin who came to Bohemia from the schools of Basel, Wittenberg, Cracow, Bologna, Ferrara, Padua, and Strasbourg. Many of them were active members of Humanist circles that were in contact with

leading representatives of European rhetorical culture, such as Erasmus of Rotterdam, Johann Frobenius, Philipp Melanchthon, and Johannes Sturm. [*See overview article on* Renaissance rhetoric.] After having returned to Prague, they did their best to disseminate the ideas of these scholars in their homeland and to emulate them in the content and form of their own works, which were mostly written in Latin, but sometimes also in Czech. Their Latin style, so-called *novitas moderna,* is characterized by imitation of classical authors, richly figurative language, and creation of new literary genres, and by syncretism of religious, scholarly, and artistic views. Elaboration of rhetorical terminology in Czech is distinctive for the Czech–Latin manual *Ars dictandi,* written by the historiographer and professor of the Faculty of Arts in Prague, Procopius Pragensis (c.1400–1482).

Czech Humanism developed from the beginning under the influence of Reformation ideas [*see* Renaissance rhetoric, *article on* Rhetoric in the age of Reformation and Counter-Reformation.] The Czech Reformation, which, because of the political radicalism of the Husites (followers of the Czech church reformer Jan Hus, c.1372–1415) penetrated all strata of Czech society and shaped ethical, educational, critical, and national aspects of Czech Humanism. Yet, Humanism, understood as a rebirth of classical antiquity, and the Reformation, understood as a rebirth of early Christianity, had many features in common. They both stressed the need for careful interpretation of the canonical text, for education and for persuasiveness in verbal expression. In Bohemia, rhetoric was taught in the medieval, Aristotelian spirit, as a theory and practice of argumentation, rather than with the Humanist stress on virtuosity of style. Persuasive speech was typical of university disputations, combative preaching, and especially of the Husite manifestoes, which are considered outstanding examples of early fifteenth-century oratorical prose.

Jan Blahoslav (1523–1571) was a prominent representative of Czech Humanism, and a member of the Utraquist movement known as the Brethren's Union. The philological interests of this student of Melanchthon and Camerarius produced the Brethren's Czech grammar containing many passages on rhetoric and also *The*

Preacher's Errors, a work in Czech that taught good style and sober delivery, in contrast to the exaggerations to be found so often in the sermons of Blahoslav's contemporaries. An unpublished manuscript of Czech rhetoric from the 1580s is the work of Gelenius Sušický, a teacher at a provincial school, who follows the Ramist model of rhetoric in ordering his exposition by means of dichotomies.

The subsequent arrival of the Habsburgs on the Czech throne (1526) and the loss of the state's autonomy (1620) was accompanied by a strong Counter-Reformation movement and led to a mass emigration of Utraquists (a Christian sect), including many intellectuals. The result was the appearance of a body of exile literature. It culminated in the vast educational work of Jan Amos Comenius (Kómenský, 1592–1670). His Neoplatonic concept of *paideia (humanitas, cultura animi)* implies teaching and cultivation of human virtues by means of dialogue; that is, a shared search for answers to questions commonly raised. His *Report and Manual of Preaching,* written in Czech, is an attempt at such a dialogue. The book influenced even Komenský's Jesuit antipode Bohuslav Balbín, the author of two rhetoric manuals (1677, 1688). The long-term loss of national autonomy prompted Josef Jungmann, the representative of Czech national awakening and the author of a rhetoric/poetic manual (*Slovesnost,* 1820, 1845), to state that Bohemia "does not provide an opportunity for forensic and political speeches." Practically the same was true for Slovakia. M. Greguss includes a short chapter on the art of rhetoric in his *Compendium Aestheticae* (1826) (according to him rhetoric must be based exclusively on ethical grounds).

Poland. Cracow University, founded in 1364, is the cradle of rhetoric in Poland. The elaboration of the trivium syllabus at the Faculty of Arts that stressed the study of logic, *ars notaria,* and *ars praedicandi,* is mainly the work of teachers and graduates of the Counter-Reformation bent at Prague's Charles University such as Stanislaus of Skarbimierz, Erasmus of Nysa, Albert of Mlodzow, and Francis of Brzeg, who left Prague during the Husite wars to seek peaceful conditions for their pedagogical and scholarly pursuits. [*See* Trivium.] The department of grammar, poetics, and rhetoric in Cracow was founded in 1406. Rhetoric

there was characterized by two orientations, the first of which was based on Moerbecke's Latin translation of Aristotle's *Rhetoric,* which was considered to be a manual of practical philosophy, applied ethics, and political theory. The second, much stronger stream considered rhetoric in the Ciceronian spirit as the art of speaking ornately and well. Collections of model letters, such as *Liber cancelariae* by the royal scribe S. Ciolek or *Liber formularum* by the scribe Jerzy of Kwiatkowo and others, date to the beginning of the fifteenth century. A testimony of the spread of Ciceronianism is the systematic rhetorical manual attributed to Jan Stoll from Glogow (the surviving copy is from 1435–1442), the praise of rhetoric by John of Ludzisko (around 1450), the treatise *De arte dictaminis* (a collection of diplomatic letters from 1460–1467), as well as numerous commentaries on classical authors' works. Later followers of Ciceronianism at the end of the fifteenth century were Jan Grzymala (*De origine et vi eloquentiae* and Jan Ursyn (*Modus epistolandi,* 1496).

Beginning with Lorenzo Valla's and Erasmus's works, in the early Renaissance, all of Europe experienced modifications in the approach to the Humanist worshiping of the Ciceronian corpus. This also had its impact in Poland, especially in the polemics between Jakub Górski (c.1525–1585) and Benedykt Herbest (1531–1598) concerning the *period* as the unit of speech. Górski's liberal attitude to the topic promoted creative imitation of classic literary models, while Herbest's rigorism—based on Byzantine sources, especially Pseudo-Demetrius—insisted on a purist following of all syntactical, semantic, and prosodic rules of style. Górski's views prevailed, and this cleared the way for many excellent Latin works of the Polish Renaissance and Baroque period. In the seventeenth century, rhetorical schools, especially Jesuit ones, increased in number. Their understanding of the discipline was marked by some Mannerist and Baroque features; distinguished authors included Mikhail Radau of Braniewo, Zygmunt Lauxmin, and Jan Kwiatkiewicz. The work of Bartolomiej Keckermann (*Systema rhetoricae,* 1614) and his disciples Jan Martini and Jan Mochinger is linked to the Calvinist college in Gdaňsk (Danzig).

The work of Maciej Kazimierz Sarbiewski (1595–1640) belongs in a context of Baroque concettism, represented primarily in Spanish Jesuit literature by Baltasar Gracián and based on sophisticated metaphors and modes of argumentation. Sarbiewski was inspired by his admiration of the works of Jan Kochanowski, the supreme product of Polish Baroque poetry. In his works on rhetoric, Sarbiewski concentrates on *acumen,* the key concept of concettism, defined as a conscious transgression of language norms, performed in order to attract the reader's or audience's attention—to cause wonder and stir the emotions. In contrast to the *pathos* of the Baroque style, the Latin rhetorical manual of classical orientation, published by the school reformer Stanislaw Konarski in 1767, promoted, in the spirit of Enlightenment ideas, the necessity for concord between language and ideas.

Ukraine and Russia. The creation and development of rhetoric in the Ukraine and Russia were marked by both contrast and symbiosis of two sources: the Western (Latin) and the Byzantine (Greek). An example of their conflict may be seen in the sharp polemics contained in the correspondence of Czar Ivan the Terrible, as an advocate of unlimited sovereign power, with Count Andrey Kurbskii, in 1563 to 1564 and 1577 to 1579. While the letters of Kurbskii, a member of the old Russian aristocracy, are written in exquisite Ciceronian style, the Czar's Byzantine eloquence mixes literary and vulgar colloquialisms.

The study of rhetoric in Russia developed especially under the influence of the idea of "Moscow as the third Rome," formulated in the epistle of Monk Filofei to Czar Vasilii III in 1516. This concept proclaimed that after the decay of the Byzantine Empire and the end of the Roman control over the Christian world, the leading position in both secular and spiritual matters was to be assigned to Russia. Russian Czars and patriarchs would at the same time achieve a rapprochement with Western Europe with the help of Ukraine and Balkan Slavs in particular. Western influence proceeded especially from Poland, Lithuania, and the Ukraine and intensified after 1564 when Russia, after the victory over Poland, established a union with the Ukraine. To fulfill its new role, Russia had to prepare substantial church reforms.

Advocates of church reforms led by the state,

however, soon met with resistance, especially from the Old Believers, who saw the reforms as a threat to traditional Russian spirituality and established methods of spreading the faith. Protopop Avvakum (c.1620–1682), a prominent spokesman for this opposition, admonished his audience not to chase after either the art of speech or philosophy, for "neither a rhetorician, nor a philosopher can be a Christian." He also condemned the teaching of the trivium, for it supplied only "external wisdom," disguised as "ingeniousness."

The earliest rhetorical manual in Russia dates from 1623 and is attributed to Bishop Makarii. This sixty-six-page book was inspired by Polish models that were written in Latin. Its language is the Russian redaction of Church Slavonic, which was commonly used in the cultural sphere. The Makarii's rhetoric became the basis for several later revised editions.

Russia and Ukraine possessed several rhetorical teaching centers. The Kiev–Mohylian Academy in Kiev and the college in Tshernigow were prominent Jesuit schools. Feofan Prokopovich (1681–1736), an advocate of the reforms introduced by Peter the Great, is a representative of the homiletic, juridical, and didactic literature coming from these circles. His *De arte rhetorica libri X* is the first complete rhetorical manual in Russia, containing detailed exposition of all parts of the discipline and based on profound knowledge of the classical authors. The abbreviated Russian version from 1721 became an official document of the Petrine period, published for the use of preachers, lawyers and diplomats.

Another educational center was the Slavic–Greek–Latin Academy in Moscow. Its syllabus was close to that of Western Latin schools: rhetoric was taught following Caussin, Suarez, and Prokopovich, Fedor Kwetnickii's *Clavis poetica* (1732) was used to introduce the trivium. The style of the time shows a predilection for Baroque ornamentation (in Russian *pletenije sloves,* word weaving), prominent especially in Simeon Polotskii's poetry. A Latin rhetoric written around 1733 by a Ukrainian monk Porfyrii Kraiskii has survived in a handwritten copy once in the possession of the Russian polymath M. V. Lomonosov.

The third center of rhetorical schooling was Greater Novgorod where Ioannikii Golyatovskii's rhetorical manual was written in 1653, thus opening a direct line of rhetorical manuals written in Russian. This culminates in Lomonosov and his numerous followers (e.g., M. M. Speranskii, *Pravila vysshago krasnorechiya* (The Rules of High Eloquence, 1844).

In the eighteenth century, Latin was displaced by French in the schooling of the Russian cultural elites. The use of French is advocated by A. Sumarokov, the representative of Russian classicism, known as the "Russian Boileau," who promoted the idea that Russian literature must accept the classicist rules and by doing so reach the level of French literature. In contrast to that, M. V. Lomonosov (1711–1765) in both short and expanded versions of his fundamental Russian rhetorical manual (1742–1748) found his source of inspiration in Cicero and translated examples from Latin authors. The classicist tendency of this work, though permeated with some Baroque elements, played a significant role, one reason being that Lomonosov was a respected poet in the field of high-style genres.

The Renaissance of Rhetoric in Russian Culture in the Twentieth Century. One consequence of the social role of rhetoric in Russian cultural history is the fact that the first significant step toward the renaissance of the discipline in the twentieth century was made in the early 1920s by members of the Russian formalist school (e.g., V. Shklovskii, B. M. Eikhenbaum, V. M. Brik, V. M. Tomashevskii, J. N. Tynianov, R. Jakobson). The objective of these authors was to formulate the difference between poetic and practical language. Rhetoric provided them with inspiration when looking for the answers to two questions: Which particular means (tropes, figures) participate in creating a text's function and what is their effect on the reader or the audience? They studied the works of Russian futurist poets (Mayakovskii, Krutshenykh, Khlebnikov) as well as other types of discourse. They declared the need to reform the teaching of rhetoric so as to reflect "the current decanonization of rhetorical means," and they showed that the apparent simplicity of Tolstoy's novels or Lenin's political speeches was in fact a result of a sophisticated intention. The active period of the Russian formalist school was short and soon ended as a result of political repression, but its impact is apparent in the works of many scholars, especially those of Mikhail

Bakhtin (1893–1975). His concept of dialogicity or polyphony, as demonstrated in the works of Rabelais and Dostoyevski, grasps the confrontation between a character's points of view, thus reminding us of the rhetorical argumentation *in utramque partem.* Bakhtin's ideas inspired Julia Kristeva and Tzvetan Todorov, contemporary French literary theoreticians of Bulgarian origin, in their works on intertextuality as a key concept of modern rhetoric.

[*See also* Comparative rhetoric.]

BIBLIOGRAPHY

Cracraft, J. "Feofan Prokopovich." In *The Eighteenth Century in Russia,* edited by J. G. Garrard, pp. 75–105. Oxford, 1973.

France, P. "Rhétorique et poétique chez les formalistes russes." *Rhetorica* 6 (1988), pp. 127–136.

Jaffe, S. P. "Nicolaus Dybinus' Declaracio oracionis de Beata Dorothea." In *Studies and Documents in the History of Late Medieval Rhetoric.* Wiesbaden, Germany, 1974.

Kraus, J. *Rétorika v evropské kultuře* (Rhetoric in European culture). Prague, 1998. General history of rhetoric, rich bibliography; see especially pp. 164–167.

Lachmann, R., ed. *Die Makarij-Rhetorik.* In *Rhetorica Slavica,* Vol. 1. Cologne-Vienna, 1980. An edition of *Makarii Rhetoric* from the Undol'skii collection, State Library Moscow, with editor's detailed commentary.

Lachmann, R., ed. *Prokopovič Feofan, De arte rhetorica libri X. Rhetorica Slavica,* Vol. 2. Cologne-Vienna, 1982. Editor's detailed commentary.

Lachmann, R. *Die Zerstörung der schönen Rede, Rhetorische Tradition und Konzepte des poetischen* (Essays on the history of Russian and Polish rhetoric and poetics.) Munich, 1994. A rich bibliography.

Lichański, J. Z. *Retoryka od średniowiecza do baroku.* Warsaw, 1982. The history of Polish rhetoric with an extensive bibliography.

Murav'ev, M. N. *Institutiones rhetoricae,* edited by A. Kahn. Oxford, 1995. The editor presents an instructive exposition of the history of rhetoric in Russia. Rich bibliography.

Piccio, R., and H. Goldblatt, eds. *Aspects of the Slavic Language Question.* 2 vols. New Haven, 1984.

Retoryka v XV stuleciu. Studia nad tradycjami, teoria i praktyką retoryki piętnastowiecznej, edited by M. Frankowska-Terlecka. Warsaw, 1988. History of Polish rhetoric in the fifteenth century, essays with French summary, rich bibliography.

Tříška, J. *Pražská rétorika.* Prague, 1987. Prague rhetoric, with bibliographical data.

—Jiří Krause

SOCIAL KNOWLEDGE. The phrase "social knowledge" encompasses a culture's conventional wisdom, as this is emphasized, invoked, and implicated by the ongoing practices of rhetoric. It is, in other words, the sum and substance of what might be called "rhetorical culture." There are several similar notions that have been identified throughout the ages: *doxa* for the Greeks, *sensus communis* for the Romans, even public opinion, political vision, and moral consciousness for the present time. In fact, this sense of the "common understandings" that are in principle open to all seems to be endemic to both ancient and modern understandings of rhetoric. Of course, conventional wisdom has also shown itself to be fallible, disastrously so. A lingering question for students of rhetoric, therefore, has to do with its status and reliability; in short, the usefulness of social knowledge for the practical arts of deliberation and judgment. This question is addressed through a brief overview of the place of conventional wisdom in the origins of rhetorical practice and then a contemporary overview of some problems and issues related to the use of social knowledge.

Despite recurrent attempts to mystify and universalize the realm of the rhetorical, our most educated guess places the emergence of this realm within a particular period of history. More precisely, rhetoric emerges simultaneously *with* history, as writing, story, and something akin to memory begin to take shape in what we now consider to be "classical" civilizations. When cultural "truths" were encoded within the inviolability of myth or unquestioned authority, and everyone shared the code, a practice such as rhetoric would have been incomprehensible (just as it remains in some cultures to this day). Disagreements, such as they were, occasioned war, ostracism, execution; and these in turn became the materials for subsequent myth and oracular authority.

Rhetoric emerges, in early Sophistic thought, with the arrogant and ironic suspicion that cultural "truths" are conventions, and that they are fallible. Interestingly, the most famous Sophistic rhetoric (Gorgias's *Encomium of Helen*, Protagoras's *Truth*, even Isocrates' *Antidosis*) invoke myth *as convention*, a mode of allegory or illustration. So understood, these newly-secularized myths (widely known, but not entirely believed) become

unlikely precursors to our own notion of social knowledge. [*See* Sophists.]

Rhetoric's original struggle to establish its disciplinary status is notoriously bound up in an ambivalent relationship to cultural conventions, in particular, those of its audiences. The first teachers of rhetoric trumpeted its capacity to overpower an audience's received opinions even in sacrosanct matters; for example, the defenses of Helen. And yet, in order for such a great power to be disciplined and taught to others, there needed to be some reliable manner for engaging the accepted convictions of everyday life. Without the minimal rigor of method, rhetoric itself would never have been able to leave the world of magic and myth, the very world it challenged.

It was the first philosophers in Western tradition who were able to best exploit these tensions between rhetoric and cultural conventions. For as the itinerant and worldly Sophists well understood, the cultural conventions of different city-states were themselves quite different, if not incommensurable. For those seeking a stable, obdurate "truth," such as Socrates (c.470–399 BCE) and Plato (c.428–c.347 BCE), rhetoric would seem to be smoke and mirrors, a sham art, preaching different things to different people, knowing and discovering nothing of value. The question, contested to this day, is whether we may reliably guide, and be guided by, the generalizable convictions our cultures bring to practical questions of choice, avoidance, and collective conduct.

It required that great system builder among philosophers, Aristotle (384–322 BCE), to realize that the aforementioned indictments of rhetoric's integrity were also indictments of even the most educated public's ability to recognize, reflect upon, and learn from its own shared experience. Without such an ability, rhetoric may be powerful, but it is morally empty. Perhaps for this reason, Aristotle recast rhetoric as a grand method of inquiry and influence complementary to that of dialectic. [*See* Dialectic.] In his famous justification of the art of rhetoric, Aristotle seemed to have Plato's indictments very much in mind. To the charge that rhetoric lacked "content," Aristotle responded that it dealt with civic matters about which people bring generally accepted opinions (a sort of "common knowledge" or conventional wisdom). And while he did not reply directly to the charge that conventional wisdom was often wrong, we may infer that part of the task of deliberation was to "validate" conventional wisdom by coming as close to the truth as possible in contentious practical settings. Perhaps most important, Aristotle was able to join forms of *logos* with the materials of conventional wisdom to offer the rhetorician modes of persuasion through inference and judgment. [*See* Classical rhetoric; Inference; Judgment; *and* Logos.]

It is impossible, in this space, to exhaust the myriad of ways that the materiality of the "common" are configured by rhetorical form in Aristotle's *Rhetoric*. A broad sketch would need to include the two principal avenues of *logos* in rhetoric: rhetorical deduction and rhetorical induction, the enthymeme and the exemplum. [*See* Enthymeme; *and* Exemplum.] Both work through common premises taken as acceptable to the audience. The very materials of proof; signs, probabilities, *paradigms* are taken to be persuasive because they meet the test of an audience's ordinary experience. Deliberative discourse is viewed by Aristotle as the highest form of rhetoric, because its audiences were viewed as best capable of judging their own interests. [*See* Deliberative genre.] And perhaps the feature most distinctive to Aristotle's great treatise—the centrality of discovery and Invention—depends largely upon the availability of a generally accepted "received opinion." Through commonplaces, lines of argument, issues in controversy, virtues and vices, maxims of counsel, recognizable emotions, and even figures of speech, Aristotelian rhetoric pushes the envelope of the familiar into uncharted public conduct. To optimists, at least, the results seemed to vindicate rhetoric as both a practical and productive art.

Certainly, part of the legacy of Aristotle's *Rhetoric* amounts to a question and challenge for all subsequent theorists and practitioners. The question is the one introduced at the outset of this essay: How reliable are cultural conventions in guiding public decision and action? This is not simply a question of fact. The very priorities we cede to specialized codes, authorities, rules—as well as the performance measures invoked to assess them—are drawn from these same conventions. Like language itself, the normative horizon

of the lifeworld we inhabit is inescapable; and so too, it has been argued, is rhetoric.

But if rhetoric, of a sort, is inescapable, this still leaves unanswered the issue of its priority and mission where public matters are involved. For instance, in the eighteenth century, the British and Scottish Enlightenment attempted to wed the principles of rhetoric to the emerging "science" of human nature. Rhetoric as theory revived for a time, but its effective practice seemed confined to the pulpit and the House of Lords. And once this science of human nature was discredited, the theory of rhetoric seemed to retreat to elocution and stylistics, the imitative arts of a leisure class. Meanwhile the practitioners of "old rhetoric" waged memorable verbal warfare over the great and still-unsettled issues of the day: war and peace, suffrage, slavery and freedom. [*See* Eighteenth-century rhetoric.]

There are, of course, many possible explanations for the peculiar historical disjunction between rhetoric as academic theory and rhetoric as flourishing civic practice. But one that may hold some promise for the modern revival of rhetoric is the uncertain status and shifting historical position of social knowledge as a civic resource. Where there are shared aspirations, mutual interests, common symbols, and lively issues, rhetorical situations abound. And occasionally, as the great speeches of even the past century testify, these situations are accompanied by eloquence.

Attempts to reunite rhetorical practice with a reliable public knowledge base have been more prominent in recent years. Diverse literatures in ethnography, anthropology, critical theory, argumentation, and of course rhetoric have sought to identify distinctive characteristics of the cultural precepts that collaborate most effectively with civic discourse practice. The very features that help to identify and characterize social knowledge, however, also suggest the formidable obstacles facing a renewal of its prominence in civic rhetoric.

First, social knowledge has been characterized as a sort of consensus attributed to the audiences for rhetoric, but generalizable beyond them. It is what we imagine ourselves to be agreeing to, for the sake of argument. This is a helpful heuristic insofar as it directs our attention to what must be "taken for granted" for any specific rhetorical inferences to be plausible in the first place. This characteristic also helps to underscore a neglected resource of rhetoric as social history, as an index for what earlier cultures *did* in fact take for granted as urgent, important, or exemplary.

However, this same identifiable characteristic of social knowledge also has opened it to attack from two outwardly quite different philosophical positions. To the positivist wing of social science, the fact that social knowledge is a cultural emergent, counterfactual on any empirical grounds, also serves to brand it as an *imaginary* in the less salutary sense of that term. Now it becomes quite easy to reintroduce rhetoric's notorious reputation for sophistry, of appealing to what is comfortable for a public audience to believe. From a far different political direction, a similar charge was leveled by whatever remained of scientific Marxism. This position recognized that the truisms, maxims, and conventions of social knowledge are not only not "materially" true; they also routinely reaffirm the cultural . . . routine. In other words, they become a sort of normative resource for propping up the social system as we know it. This position challenges the rhetorical proponents of social knowledge to show that it is anything other than false consciousness, a convenient *mythos* for the worst predilections of modernity.

There are responses to both positions, not to be explored here. It should be noted, however, that the attacks very rarely have come from rhetoric's academic or philosophical allies. And so, if nothing else, the very diversity and intensity of such indictments help to underscore the endemic relationship of some such knowledge base to rhetoric itself.

A second important, and highly controversial, characteristic of social knowledge involved its purported contrast with another type of knowledge called "technical." The distinction was never supposed to be based on epistemic considerations (i.e., the actual status of social knowledge as "knowledge") but rather on the different functional relationships of types of knowledge to the social system. Technical knowledge was seen to be expertise: specialized, coded, and therefore limited to a trained few. This was a sort of knowledge that did not require an audience's tacit assent in order to be effectively implemented. And,

for better or worse, every social system has tended to require some such expertise. On the other hand, there are social "facts" as well, things generically agreed upon, without which no social system could ever reliably operate: things such as routines of civility, following rules in sports (and life), taking one's turn, and so forth. These are not discovered, but learned; they are also followed or violated; they are sanctioned. For better or worse, every society has tended to require these norms of rhetorical culture as well.

This second set of distinctions has also received a deserved share of indictments, largely on epistemic grounds. Variously, the charges have been that the distinction between social and technical knowledge is much too neat, that either all knowledge is social (science, included) or that it is premature to insulate a particular form of "knowing" from cultural critique, as the distinction purports to do. The distinction also seems to ground technical knowledge in precisely the sort of positivist "realism" that was earlier invoked against rhetoric's "content."

Not surprisingly, there are responses to these indictments also, which will not be pursued here. Of course, the ghost lurking behind all these proceedings was the ominous encroachment of technical expertise on all things social. To generalize, the increasing tendency of twentieth-century "modernized" systems was to see more and more issues as system priorities that were simply too esoteric and complex to be adjudicated by ordinary people. To this extent, those who questioned the social–technical knowledge distinction saw it as a self-sealing definition, a way of somehow legitimating the still-ongoing information gap.

There is another, less pessimistic way of reading these, and many other artificial dualities. They are descriptions of an ongoing tension, a dialectic perhaps, that is endemic to late modernity itself. The technical often is immune to critical social reflection. The realm of social convention often is prematurely dismissed as archaic and unnecessary to effective governance. As controversies, scandals, and political interruptions too numerous to mention help to chronicle, both of these avowals are themselves too neat. The hope of a rhetoric grounded in social knowledge is that civic business is ultimately more humane, principled, and fair when it works with what "everyone knows," than it is with any of the foreseeable alternatives.

[*See also* Invention.]

BIBLIOGRAPHY

Aristotle. *On Rhetoric: A Theory of Civic Discourse.* Translated with commentary by George A. Kennedy. New York, 1991. The first and arguably the most comprehensive treatment of rhetoric's relationship to social knowledge and civic life.

Brown, Richard Harvey. *Society as Text: Essays on Rhetoric, Reason, and Reality.* Chicago, 1987. Brown suggests some of the ways academic disciplines produce knowledge as a resource for civic life.

Farrell, Thomas B. "Knowledge, Consensus, and Rhetorical Theory." *The Quarterly Journal of Speech* 62 (1976), pp. 1–5. This essay first attempted to define social knowledge and characterize its rhetorical functions.

Farrell, Thomas B. *Norms of Rhetorical Culture.* New Haven, 1993. An effort to discover the bases for interpreting and judging public advocacy.

Gitlin, Todd. *The Twilight of Common Dreams: Why America is Wracked by Culture Wars.* New York, 1995. An often eloquent call for the restoration of a sense of the "common" in contemporary politics.

Schaeffer, John D. *Sensus Communis: Vico, Rhetoric, and the Limits of Relativism.* Durham, N.C., 1990. A major exploration of the social knowledge legacy from the Italian post-Renaissance.

Walton, Douglas. *Appeal to Popular Opinion.* Pennsylvania University Park, 1999. A reconsideration of the *ad populum* fallacy from a pragmatic–dialectical perspective.

Winch, Peter. *Trying to Make Sense.* New York, 1987. A fresh and still-fascinating examination of "appearances" as they enter into philosophical paradoxes. Winch was a student of Wittgenstein.

—THOMAS B. FARRELL

SOCIAL MOVEMENTS. Beginning with Rosa Parks's 1955 refusal to sit in the back of a bus, Montgomery, Alabama stands as a symbol today of the courage and determination of ordinary black citizens in their struggle to break the shackles of institutionalized, legalized segregation in the southern United States. It is possible to broaden the context; to see Montgomery as part of the worldwide struggle for human rights, or as continuous with efforts at black emancipation since the days of slavery, or as one small blip in a centuries-long conflict over the very idea of human equality.

All of these perspectives can be useful. But most people who study social movements tend to select a narrower frame—say the period from 1955 to 1970 for the U.S. civil rights movement. Even then the task can be daunting, as Leland Griffin observed when he urged rhetoricians to assemble the materials for full-fledged movement study: not just the transcripts of individual speeches by leading figures, but multiple messages via multiple media to multiple audiences, their differences reflective of changing currents in the life history of the movement (Griffin, "The Rhetoric of Historical Movements." *Quarterly Journal of Speech* 38, 1952, pp. 184–188).

Social movements are cause-oriented collectivities: they exist to promote an ideology (e.g., equal rights) or a program of action (e.g., desegregation). This is their cause, and they promote it over an extended period of time. Moreover, unlike self-help groups such as Weight Watchers, social movements attempt to exert influence outside their own group.

By most definitions, social movements are also *uninstitionalized;* that is, outside the mainstream. In extreme cases, such as the Montgomery bus boycott, the ideas guiding movement activists, their modes of action, and their core organizations (SMOs) are all considered suspect or altogether illegitimate in the larger society of which they are a part. To take an even more extreme example, the hundreds of thousands of Chinese university students who occupied Beijing's Tiananmen Square in the spring of 1989 were treading on hallowed ground—equivalent to American students taking over the mall surrounding the Washington Monument. Formally, then, a social movement is an uninstitutionalized collectivity that operates on a sustained basis to exert external influence in behalf of a cause. The civil rights movement in the United States provides an example.

In the 1960s, the SMOs supporting civil rights for blacks included the Southern Christian Leadership Conference (SCLC), headed by the Reverend Martin Luther King, Jr. (1929–1968); the Southern Nonviolent Coordinating Committee (SNCC); the Congress on Racial Equality (CORE); and the National Association for the Advancement of Colored People (NAACP). [*See* African-American rhetoric, *article on* Black Nationalism.] Not everyone who identified with the movement belonged to one or another of these core organizations, but without them there could not have been a movement. The cause of the civil rights movement was, minimally, the abolition of racial discrimination in law and, beyond that, the elimination of all discriminatory practices.

The civil rights movement of the sixties was uninstitutionalized in all three respects: guiding ideas, modes of action, and core organizations. Its detractors in the South viewed the movement's opposition to segregation as nothing less than an assault on their traditional way of life. Its confrontational tactics, such as sit-ins at segregated lunch counters, were subjected to scorn and disapproval; even many in the North who approved of the movement's goals, deplored these tactics as illegal or unnecessarily provocative. Its SMOs had varying degrees of legitimacy, with the NAACP enjoying a measure of respectability due to its relatively conservative style and long tenure as an organization. By contrast, the SNCC members seemed to revel in their "upstart" status within the white South.

A collectivity may be partially institutionalized and still be a movement. For example, the National Organization for Women (NOW) enjoys a good measure of respectability in the larger society, and it seldom if ever engages in practices considered deviant or outside the mainstream, but its feminist agenda is far from being fully institutionalized. [*See* Feminist rhetoric.] Likewise, the National Rifle Association (NRA) is widely accepted in the larger society, but it also spearheads an anti-gun-control effort that is highly controversial in American society, and in that sense is part of a social movement.

Rhetorical Perspectives on Social Movements. The rhetoric of social movements is principally concerned with the exercise of agency in movement struggles; that is, with what movement actors (and the forces they oppose) say and do to make a difference in the world. If rhetoricians err, it is in the direction of emphasizing planned social change over unplanned social change—the latter a result of structural factors beyond any individual's or group's control. Rhetorical perspectives on social movements, whether by self-proclaimed rhetoricians or by social scientists and historians, tend especially to emphasize symbolic agency over the coercive influences

of violence and economic power. They tend in general to see humans as capable of making a difference by their choice of words and symbolic actions, even to the point of undoing, or at least reconceiving for societies, what had long been understood to be natural, immutable, inevitable. This extends to taken-for-granted notions of family, race, clan, nation—of "we the people." It applies also to evils and enemies, problems and causes, all of which are rhetorical constructions, the stuff of movement ideologies, made real to and for people by acts of persuasion.

By implication, movements as well as the institutions and counter-movements they oppose, are engaged most fundamentally in struggles over meaning (Stewart, Smith, and Denton, 1994). The social scientists and historians who view movement struggles rhetorically, tend to join with self-styled rhetoricians in focusing on the dynamics of meaning making: how movement actors choose from among the available means of persuasion; how these rhetorical resources change over time; how conflicts between opposing forces get played out symbolically; how symbolically reconstituted realities function to achieve other goals; how they also impel and constrain subsequent rhetorical choices (Jasper, 1997).

In their focus on agency, rhetorically oriented movement scholars share the activist's angle of view. It would be hard to imagine a feminist leader, for example, who believed that women's liberation was less a function of feminist rhetoric than of such structural factors as the need for female labor during World War II.

Types of Social Movements. The goals that movements seek to realize vary considerably, and there is great variation in their means for achieving them. *Reformist* movements generally seek passage of particular laws, better enforcement of particular laws, or replacement of corrupt or incompetent officials. The gun control and civil rights movements are examples. *Revolutionary* movements go even further by seeking to replace guiding ideologies, institutions, sometimes entire regimes, based on new governing principles. They are also associated with the threat or use of force (e.g., the American Revolution), but there have been largely peaceful revolutions (e.g., Poland, 1989).

Resistance movements, rather than advocating

change, seek to hold it back and keep the status quo (e.g., the anti-gun-control movement). Given the U.S. Supreme Court's decision in Roe versus Wade (1973), the pro-life movement is generally reformist while pro-choice is a resistance movement. But pro-choice seeks federal funding of abortions for poor women, while pro-life resists such funding. In this respect, pro-choice is reformist, pro-life a resistance movement. *Restorative* movements seek a return to an older and supposedly better way of life. The cause of today's "Christian Identity" movement echoes the rhetoric of hate toward minorities in the United States, preached in earlier days by White Citizens Councils and by the John Birch Society. Marcus Garvey's "Back to Africa" (1919–1926) was also a restorative movement.

Finally, *expressivist* movements try to change individuals, rather than directly trying to change institutions or laws. Evangelical groups such as the Promise Keepers offer examples. Expressivists believe that, just as institutions are people-created, so they can only be changed by changes in people. Themes of personal responsibility are common to expressivist movements.

It is not always easy to classify movements based on this or any other typology because of internal disputes over goals and methods within the movement as well as changes in goals and strategies. For example, sixties-style Marxist activists hit on a decidedly expressivist note in a conference report, detailed in Darnovsky (1995), when they concluded that feminism and environmentalism had demonstrated that large-scale social change is accomplished in face-to-face relations, at the level of personal identity and consciousness, whether or not such change is enunciated in public policy.

Tactics of Social Movements. Movements select from a repertoire of possibilities available to them at any given time and place. Some tactics, such as mass demonstrations against administrative practices, are rare in autocratic societies but common in democracies. Other tactics, such as hangings in effigy, were popular for centuries in England and the United States but have largely gone out of style. Some movements rely on verbal appeals, others on a combination of exhortations and demonstrations; still others add the threat and use of force. Movements have characteristically relied on confrontational tactics to advance their

cause, and this is still the method of choice for street protests. But movements seeking both ideological change and resistance to ideological change are increasingly turning to cultural politics.

Confrontation. Consider the demonstrators at Tiananmen Square in 1989, some of them on hunger strikes, none of them knowing at what point the government would strike back. When it comes to making a statement, there is nothing quite like putting one's body on the line. Conflict theorist Thomas Schelling distinguished in this connection between speech and moves, the latter capable of "altering the game" by demonstrating a willingness to incur costs. Said Schelling, "Talk can be cheap when moves are not" (Schelling, *Strategy of Conflict,* Cambridge, Mass., 1960).

The moves that the protesters at Tiananmen were making were forms of *confrontation.* They were reminiscent of the campus sit-ins and demonstrations at colleges and universities across the United States in the late sixties. Some of the campus confrontations were fairly mild while others were quite disruptive, but all of them sought to perform attention-getting, radicalizing, and delegitimizing functions through actions that combined verbal exhortations and pressure tactics.

The confronters joined in a deliberate violation of the institution's written and unwritten code of conduct, fastening on those taboos that symbolized what the protestors took to be the institution's false ideals and inequitable practices. Their aim was to embarrass the institutions into making concessions. Representatives of these institutions were thus presented with a king-sized dilemma. Suppression of the confrontation would belie the institution's appearance of liberality and feed the flames of protest. Yet permitting violations of the code would, in effect, sanction other violations and undermine the offices of authority and discipline in the institution. And so, after promising a fair hearing and pleading in vain for a return to more moderate tactics, the institution acted to check or suppress the violations and punish the violators, frequently breaking its own rules in the process. In this way, its representatives were able, temporarily, to contain the confrontation, but, in doing so, they unwittingly fulfilled their assigned roles as villains.

Cultural politics. Conflicts between movements and countermovements are not always played out on the streets. For example, groups seeking liberalization of social values (the "cultural left") and others resisting what they see as moral decay ("social conservatives") have in recent years been engaged in what some journalists ballyhooed as the "culture wars." Multiculturalists, Afrocentrists, feminists, and others on the cultural left have sought to influence educational curricula. Social conservatives have formed countermovements of their own, pressing in some cases for textbook censorship, and in others for cutbacks in federal funding of the humanities. Some social conservatives have sought to restore America to what they allege was its former greatness, before school prayer was outlawed, for example, and before abortion was legalized by the Supreme Court.

These ideological battles are fought less in the streets than in behind-the-scenes meetings of museum boards, federal funding agencies, university administrators, mental health professionals, or network newsmanagers, and, more openly via television and in classrooms, movie theaters, churches, mental health centers, and the courts. In one women's studies classroom, for example, a concerted attempt is made to "liberate" students from the intellectual and cultural domination of patriarchal (i.e., male-oriented) ideologies. Across the hall, a socially conservative professor of philosophy declaims against postmodernism, deconstruction, culturalism relativism, and other intellectual challenges to Western culture's traditional faith in logic, objectivity, meaning, and scientific method. These are but skirmishes in today's cultural wars, but they illustrate within an academic setting what is meant by cultural politics. It is an attempt by all sides to influence ideological thought via institutions, such as the schools, that are not often thought of as vehicles for propagandizing. Its methods include not just active proselytyzing but control over what gets put before students in the way of textbooks, television viewers in the way of programming, museumgoers in the way of art exhibits, and so on.

Social Protests and Mass Media. Whereas cultural politics is highly dependent on television entertainment to get its message across, the more traditional confrontational politics of social movements relies principally on news coverage, and especially on television's capacity to reach a wide audience with dramatic, attention-getting footage (Gitlin, *The Whole World is Watching*, Berkeley, 1981). That attention may in turn inspire new adherents to join a movement and prompt sympathizers to provide increased resources and support. The larger the movement, and the bigger and more spectacular its demonstrations, the more media coverage it is likely to get, thus engendering further movement support. In this respect, at least, media attention should benefit social movements.

But the media's power and pervasiveness are also a central problem for contemporary movements, and especially for those movements seeking more than modest reforms. Reformist and revolutionary movements, says Gitlin, must either play by the media's rules or risk rejection or inattention. These rules are also in many respects those of the dominant culture. They require that the core interests of political elites not be threatened, and that its prevailing rules of governance be maintained. Thus, however much the state is implicated when evils are exposed, it must still be looked to for the remediation of those evils.

Leading Social Movements: The "Requirements-Problems-Strategies" (RPS) Approach. The following is a framework for leading social movements or for analyzing their moves and speech as a rhetorical critic. The basic assumptions are that (1) any movement must fulfill the same functional requirements as more institutionalized collectivities. These imperatives constitute *rhetorical requirements* for the leadership of a movement. (2) Conflicts among requirements create *rhetorical problems,* which in turn affect (3) decisions on *rhetorical strategy.* The primary test of a leader, and ultimately of the strategies she employs, is her capacity to fulfill the requirements of her movement by removing or reducing rhetorical problems.

Requirements. The basic functional requirements of a social movement are an ability to mobilize human and material resources, to exert external influence, and to mount resistance to counterpressures. These requirements are not unlike those facing leaders of institutionalized collectivities such as business or government. For example, the managers of General Motors must recruit, hire, train, motivate, and deploy personnel, and they must likewise acquire and deploy material resources for the manufacture of its cars and trucks. Likewise, the leadership of social movements must recruit, motivate, and deploy activists; and it needs also to acquire material resources (e.g., money). Just as General Motors must market its vehicles (exert external influence) and beat back its competition (mount resistance to counterpressures), so must the leaders of social movements promote their movement's cause and deal with opposition from countermovements (e.g., pro-life for pro-choice) and from other groups that may regard the movement as a threat.

Problems. Social movements are severely restricted from fulfilling these requirements by dint of their internal strategies and their positions in relation to the larger society. This is especially true of movements lacking any kind of legitimacy. By comparison to the heads of most formal organizations (e.g., General Motors), the leaders of these social movements can expect minimal internal control and maximal external resistance. Whereas business corporations may induce productivity through tangible rewards and punishments, social movements, as voluntary collectivities, must rely on ideological and social commitments. Existing outside the larger society's conceptions of justice and reality, moreover, movements often threaten and are threatened by the society's sanctions and taboos: its laws, its maxims, its customs governing manners, decorum, and taste, and its insignia of authority. Shorn of the controls that characterize formal organizations, yet required to perform the same internal functions, harassed from without, yet required to gain outside support, the leader of a social movement must constantly balance inherently conflicting demands on her position and on the movement she represents.

Many of the foregoing problems pose dilemmas for leaders. Among the demands on any organization are that its leaders maintain a system of accurate communication up and down the line, that they operate an efficient organization, and that they act in a consistent and therefore predictable manner. But in a social movement, the need to speak truthfully must be balanced against the need to inspire members and to fend off attacks on the movement by outsiders. The need for organizational efficiency must be weighed against

the demands of individual volunteers (few of whom can be coerced or paid) for personal gratification or for promotion of pet projects. The need for ideological consistency must be balanced against the need for pragmatic adaptations.

Movements are as susceptible to fragmentation from within as they are to suppression from without. Within movement organizations, factional conflicts invariably develop over questions of value, strategy, tactics, or implementation. Purists and pragmatists clash over the merits of compromise. Academics and activists debate the necessity of long-range planning. Others enter the campaign with personal grievances or vested interests. Preexisting groups that are known to have divergent ideological positions are nevertheless invited to join or affiliate with the campaign because of the power they can wield.

These and other differences may be reflected at the leadership level as well. Rarely can one campaign leader handle all the leadership roles and tasks of the campaign. Hence the need for a variety of leadership types: theoreticians and propagandists to launch the campaign, political or bureaucratic types to carry it forward. There may also be cleavages between those vested with positions of authority in the campaign, those charismatic figures who have personal followings, those who have special competencies, and those who have private sources of funds or influence outside the campaign.

Strategies. Because any strategy represents an attempt to meet incompatible requirements, none is ever fully satisfactory. Each, moreover, creates new rhetorical problems in the process of resolving old ones.

MODERATES AND MILITANTS. As applied to protests against institutional policies or practices, moderates are the embodiment of reason, civility, decorum. They get angry but do not shout, issue pamphlets but never manifestos, inveigh against social mores but always in the value language of the social order. Their "devil" is a condition or a set of behaviors or an outcast group, never the persons they are seeking to influence. Those persons are assumed to be capable of "listening to reason."

If moderates assume or pretend to assume an ultimate identity of interests between the movement and its antagonists, militant *rhētors* act on the assumption of a fundamental clash of interests. Each can boast support from proud philosophical traditions. The moderate's commitment to friendly persuasion is rooted in the Greco-Roman democratic tradition, in Judeo-Christian conceptions of the brotherhood of man, in Emerson's (1803–1882) faith in human educability, and in John Stuart Mill's (1806–1873) conviction that truth will survive any open competition of ideas. Militants, by contrast, are inclined to be mistrustful of ordinary citizens or to assume that the systems they oppose are likely to be intractable. Like Karl Marx (1818–1883), they are apt to believe that the masses have lost sight of their "real" interests or that those in power are unlikely to surrender it willingly. Although Machiavelli (1469–1527) wrote for princes and not for protesters, the militant is inclined to accept that writer's view of persuasion as an adjunct to force rather than its alternative.

This is not to say that militants offer no appeals to shared values. They do, indeed, but in ways that call into question other widely held values. In general, the militant tends to express greater degrees of dissatisfaction than the moderate. Whereas the moderate tends to ask "how" questions, the militant asks "whether" questions. Whereas the moderate sees "inefficiencies" in existing practices, the militant sees "inequities." Whereas the moderate might regard authority figures as "misguided" though "legitimate," the militant would tend to regard these same figures as "willfully self-serving" and "illegitimate." Whereas both might pay homage to law, the militant is more apt to derogate human laws in the name of "higher" laws. Thus, for example, some antiabortionists have interpreted biblical writ as justification for bombings of abortion clinics.

The actions of militants are not all of a piece by any means. The practice of classic civil disobedience, for example, borders on being intermediate between militancy and moderacy. To test the constitutionality of a law, that law is violated. However, the law in question is violated openly and nonviolently, no other laws are breached in the process, the rights of innocent persons are not interfered with, and, if found guilty, the law violator willingly accepts punishment.

Contrast this strategy with acts that can more clearly be labeled combative in nature: strikes, ri-

ots, political bombings, and kidnappings—all the way to organized guerrilla warfare. By means of verbal polemics and direct action techniques, protesters who practice combative persuasion threaten, harass, cajole, disrupt, provoke, intimidate, and coerce. Although the aim of pressure tactics may be to punish directly (strikes, boycotts), more frequently they are forms of "body rhetoric," designed to dramatize issues, enlist additional sympathizers, delegitimize the established order, and—except in truly revolutionary situations—force reconsideration of existing laws and practices, or pave the way for negotiated settlements.

So different are the rhetorical conceptions of moderate and militant strategists that it strains the imagination to believe both approaches may work. Yet, the decisive changes wrought by militant rhetorics on the left and the right in recent years, give credence to the view that friendly persuasion is not the only alternative. What, then, in general terms are the strengths and limitations of moderate and militant approaches?

1. Militant tactics confer visibility on a movement; moderate tactics gain entry into decision centers.

2. For different reasons, militants and moderates must both be ambivalent about success and failures. Militants thrive on injustice and the ineptitude displayed by their targets. Should the enemy fail to implement the movement's demands, militants find themselves vindicated ideologically, yet frustrated programmatically. Should some of the demands be met, they are in the paradoxical position of having to condemn them as palliatives. Moderates, by contrast, require tangible evidence that the larger structure is tractable in order to hold followers in line; yet too much success belies the movement's reason for being.

3. Militant supporters are easily energized; moderate supporters are more easily controlled. Strong identification by members with the goals of a movement—however necessary to achieve esprit de corps—may foster the conviction that any means are justified and breed impatience with time-consuming tactics. The use of violence and other questionable means may be prompted further by restrictions on legitimate avenues of expression imposed by the larger society. As a result, leaders may be required to mask the movement's true objectives, publicly disclaim the use

of tactics they privately advocate, promise what they cannot deliver, exaggerate the strength of the movement, and so on. A vicious cycle develops in which militant tactics invite further suppression, which spurs the movement on to more extreme methods. Having aroused their following, however, the leaders of a militant movement may become victims of their own creation, unable to contain energies within prescribed limits or to guarantee their own tenure. Leaders of moderate groups frequently complain that their supporters are apathetic, lip-service adherents who cannot be depended upon for the work of the movement.

4. Militants are effective with *power-vulnerables;* moderates are effective with *power-invulnerables;* neither is effective with both. Targets of protest may be labeled as power-vulnerable to the degree to which (a) they have something to lose (for example, property, status, high office); (b) they cannot escape from a source's pressure (unlike suburbanites, for example, who could escape, physically or psychologically, from the ghetto riots of the sixties); (c) they cannot retaliate against a source (either because of normative or physical constraints). Such targets as university presidents, church leaders, and elected government officials are highly vulnerable—especially if they profess to be "high-minded" or "liberal"—compared to the mass of citizens who may lack substantial possessions, be able to escape, or feel no constraints about retaliating. The latter are power-invulnerables.

In choosing between moderate and militant strategies, the protest leader faces a series of dilemmas: neither approach is likely to meet every rhetorical requirement or resolve every rhetorical problem; indeed, the introduction of either approach may create new problems.

So it is that the leadership of a protest movement may attempt to resolve or avoid the aforementioned dilemmas by employing *intermediate* strategies, admittedly a catchall term for those efforts that combine militant and moderate patterns of influence. They may alternate between appeals to common ground and threats of punishment, or speaking softly in private and stridently at mass gatherings. They may form broadly based coalitions that submerge ideological differences or utilize speakers with similar values but contrasting styles. They may stand as "conserva-

tive radicals" or "radical conservatives," espousing extreme demands in the value language of the social order or militant slogans in behalf of moderate proposals. In defense of moderacy, they may portray themselves as brakemen holding back more militant followers.

Intermediacy can be a dangerous game. Calculated to energize supporters, win over neutrals, pressure power-vulnerables, and mollify the opposition, it may end up antagonizing everyone. The turned phrase may easily appear as a devilish trick, the rationale as a rationalization, the tactful comment as an artless dodge. To the extent that strategies of intermediacy require studied ambiguity, insincerity, and even distortion, perhaps the leaders' greatest danger is that others will find out what they really think.

Still, some strategists manage to reconcile differences between militant and moderate approaches and not simply maneuver around them. They seem able to convince the established order that bad-tasting medicine is good for it and seem capable, too, of mobilizing a diverse collectivity within the movement. The key, it would appear, is the leader's capacity to embody a higher wisdom, a more profound sense of justice: to stand above inconsistencies by articulating overarching principles. Few will contest the claim that Martin Luther King, Jr. epitomized this approach. Attracting both militants and moderates to his movement, King could win respect, even from his enemies, by reconciling the seemingly irreconcilable. The heart of the case for intermediacy was succinctly stated by King himself. What is needed, he said, is a combination of power and love.

The Fate of Social Movements. There is considerable variety in the fate of social movement organizations. Some ultimately achieve legitimacy in society; the once militant labor union movement in the United States is now the highly institutionalized AFL-CIO. Some movements are successful at promoting their cause; the more moderate the goal (better enforcement of traffic laws), the better the chances of success. Some movements achieve legitimacy *and* desired gains; some achieve neither. But even among the apparent failures, there are often long-term positive effects.

Often ignored are the effects, both symbolic

and material, of one movement group on another. Militant groups help legitimize more moderate groups; Malcolm X's (1925–1965) Nation of Islam did that for Martin Luther King's SCLC. In other circumstances, distant movements serve as important role models; witness King's debts to Gandhi (1869–1948) and Thoreau (1817–1862). Apparently, the students in Beijing were much influenced by revolutionary developments in Eastern Europe and by the freeing of the press in the Soviet Union. Great movements of the past also live on in legends and myths that are invented anew by successive generations, and in institutions and forms of action that are adapted to changed circumstances.

"Open" and "Closed-Minded" Movements. Featured in this essay has been a group with whom most readers could readily identify: the civil rights protesters. Yet it is important to emphasize that social movements come in a variety of shapes and sizes, and that some are downright ugly and more than a bit scary by most Western standards. Vladimir Lenin (1870–1924) led a social movement; so did Adolph Hitler (1889–1945). Religious cults are social movements; so is the right-wing militia movement. Depending on the examples one picks, then, it is easy enough to glorify social movements or to condemn them roundly. One's political sympathies will inevitably play a role in that as well.

Still, if there is one yardstick that all rhetoricians can apply in their judgment of social movements, it is open- versus closed-mindedness. Closed-minded movement organizations exhibit absolutistic, totalistic, dogmatic thinking. Their ideological claims are offered as revealed truths and are thus presented impersonally and authoritatively. Rather than questioning these "truths," members are expected to swallow them whole and to compensate for gaps in their leaders' logic by supplying missing premises. Groups such as these are insular, xenophobic, and frequently paranoid. The world external to the movement is seen as sinister and threatening. Members, too, are seen as sinners or as prone to ideological backsliding, but there is the promise for members of redemption and salvation through acts of contrition and purification.

Clearly, not all movement groups exhibit these characteristics, not even those we might be tempted to regard as radical or extreme. Whenever we are tempted to condemn all radicals or extremists, it is well to remember who made the American Revolution: moderates, they were not.

[*See also overview article and article on* Constitutive rhetoric *in entry on* Politics.]

BIBLIOGRAPHY

Darnovsky, Marcy, Richard Flacks, and Barbara Epstein, eds. *Cultural Politics and Social Movements.* Philadelphia, 1995.

Gamson, William. *The Strategy of Social Protest.* 2d ed. Belmont, Calif., 1990. A fresh methodological approach to deriving generalizations about what "works," drawn from data on "challenging groups" in the United States since 1800.

Gitlin, Todd. *The Twilight of Common Dreams: Why America is Wracked by Culture Wars.* New York, 1995. An ironic take on the culture wars by a gifted essayist.

Jasper, James M. *The Art of Moral Protest: Culture, Biography, and Creativity in Social Movements.* Chicago, 1997. A rhetorical perspective on social movements by a literate sociologist, one that highlights the creative, innovative, and moral aspects of protest actions.

Klandermans, Bert. *The Social Psychology of Protest.* Oxford, 1997. An engagingly systematic treatment of the factors that impel and constrain movement participation, supported by studies of movements on both sides of the Atlantic.

McAdam, Doug, and David A. Snow. *Social Movements: Readings On Their Emergence, Mobilization, and Dynamics.* Los Angeles, 1997. See especially the essays in Parts 6 and 8.

Simons, Herbert. W. *Persuasion in Society.* Thousand Oaks, Calif., 2001. See especially Chapter 10 on campaign planning and Chapter 14 on leading social movements.

Simons, H. W., E. W. Mechling, and H. N. Schreier. "The Functions of Human Communication in Mobilizing for Action From the Bottom Up: The Rhetoric of Social Movements." In *Handbook of Rhetorical and Communication Theory.* Edited by C. C. Arnold and J. W. Bowers, pp. 792–868. Boston, 1984.

Smith, Ralph R., and Russell R. Windes. *Progay/Antigay: The Rhetorical War Over Sexuality.* Thousand Oaks, Calif., 2000. Movement studies tend to focus on one movement, giving short shrift to its evil twin. This marriage of Burkeian rhetorical theory and interpretive sociology is valuable not just as a contribution to gay and lesbian studies, but in more general terms as a case study in the rhetoric of movements and countermovements.

Stewart, Charles J., Craig A. Smith, and Robert E. Denton. *Persuasion and Social Movements.* 3d ed. Prospect

Heights, Ill., 1994. This textbook features the work of rhetorically oriented communication scholars.
—HERBERT W. SIMONS

SOPHISTS. The Sophists formed part of the intellectual culture of classical Greece during the second half of the fifth century BCE. Best known as professional educators in the Hellenic world, they were regarded in their time as polymaths, men of varied and great learning. In addition to their main focus on rhetoric, they taught many other subjects, including politics, law, sociology, literary theory, grammar, mathematics, and natural science. Their doctrines and practices were instrumental in shifting attention from the cosmological speculations of the pre-Socratics to anthropological investigations with a decidedly practical character. Although not philosophers in the modern sense of the term, they have been inserted into the history of philosophy starting with Hegel's early nineteenth-century *Lectures in the History of Philosophy.*

Much of the information about the lives and works of the most famous Sophists comes to us from second-century BCE doxographers like Diogenes Laertius and Philostratus. But their intellectual portraits are found in Plato's works, most notably the *Protagoras,* the *Gorgias,* the *Hippias Major,* the *Republic* (Book 1), and the *Sophist.* In these works, Plato (c.429–c.347 BCE) takes issue with positions he attributes to various Sophists, showing that their views cannot pass the test of dialectical scrutiny. In effect, Plato critiques the Sophists for privileging appearances over reality, making the weaker argument appear the stronger, preferring the pleasant over the good, favoring opinions over the truth and probability over certainty, and choosing rhetoric over philosophy. In recent times, this unflattering portrayal has been countered with a more sympathetic appraisal of the Sophists' status in antiquity as well as their ideas for modernity. Expressed in the nineteenth century in George Grote's *A History of Greece* and in Friedrich Nietzsche's various works, this appraisal persisted in the work of many twentieth-century scholars.

The Sophists' collective thinking can be stated in terms of several doctrines, the totality of which outlines an orientation of being in the world. According to this orientation, man is the measure of all things; knowledge is grounded in human perception and language; words differ from the things they name; language can represent both that which exists and that which does not; people are capable of and subject to persuasion; social and political arrangements are a function of collective agreements brought about through persuasion; for every issue there are at least two arguments opposing one another; justice in practical affairs is prescribed and regulated by the powerful; the existence of the gods is outside the capabilities of human knowledge; as people understand them, the gods are human creations intended to exercise control over human behavior.

The subject of considerable controversy, these Sophistical doctrines have over time been explained in terms of such diverse philosophies as relativism, pragmatism, utilitarianism, empiricism, subjective idealism, atheism, and agnosticism. In light of the Sophists' doctrines, man is an entity not in himself but in his relations with others in the context of the city-state and its political, legal, and social institutions. Language not only regulates human relations and determines the structure of institutions; it also shapes human thought and directs human action. Truths and values are neither universal nor abiding; rather they are determined situationally, out of human needs and interests, which vary across time, peoples, and circumstances. Politics is an issue of deliberation and debate over the affairs of the city-state. Similarly, ethics is a contested issue over the efficacy of standards of communal and personal behavior.

The main goal of the Sophists' educational program was to turn man into an effective citizen. This program was shaped more by practical demands and less by philosophical investigations. In a predominately oral culture, effective citizenship required the ability to listen critically and speak persuasively on issues of common interest; and an effective citizen was one who could participate in and contribute to the management of the affairs of his community. Typical roles for most citizens ranged from legislator in the assembly, juror, prosecutor or defendant in the courts of law, spectator or speaker in state-sponsored festivals, member or leader of a political clan. All these roles dictated that one be competent in public presentation, deliberation, and debate, decision making, adjudication, and critical judgment. Accordingly, the Sophists promised to equip the interested person with rhetoric, the means par excellence to succeed in the arena of public life.

The Sophists' anthropological investigations contributed to the fifth century BCE debate over *physis* (nature) and *nomos* (convention). Some took the position that man is a creature of the natural order, and as such he and the institutions he creates, such as the city, politics, law, and society, obey the laws of nature. Others took the view that man is superior in intelligence to animals and, therefore, can transcend nature by means of his gift of language and practical wisdom. This debate was revisited in the fourth century BCE by Plato, Isocrates, and Aristotle. All three asserted the superiority of man in creation but raised questions about the Sophists' views on knowledge and the proper uses of rhetoric.

In particular, Plato argued that the Sophists' view of rhetoric was inadequate because first, it did not offer a guide for its ethical use, and second, it was predicated on opinion rather than dialectically-secured truths. In the *Gorgias,* Plato denies rhetoric the status of *technē* (art), treating it instead as an irrational knack acquired by habit. Moreover, he observes that rhetoric seeks to flatter ignorant audiences without instructing them, and to appeal to the masses' emotions without engaging their rational faculties meaningfully. At the same time, he maintains that rhetoric concerns itself with replacing one opinion with another without attending to knowledge, and pursues pleasure and power, all along disregarding goodness and justice. In the *Phaedrus,* however, Plato softens his tone as he makes allowances for a legitimate rhetoric, a rhetoric that instructs and inspires instead of merely persuading. Such a rhetoric, he observes, would have to meet a set of criteria; for example, know the nature of the different types of soul, understand the various kinds of discourse, be able to apply the right kind of discourse to each type of soul, and recognize the right occasion for speaking or keeping silent. This set of criteria issues from Plato's own educational program, which relies on dialectic as a means of acquiring knowledge of truth, goodness, and beauty. [*See* Dialectic.]

The Sophists' views and Plato's opposition to them have shaped in important ways the history of rhetoric. To this day, the conflict between them is an important source of significant insights on issues pertaining to language, ethics, and education.

[*See also* Classical rhetoric; Logos; Occasion; Persona; *and* Philosophy, *article on* Perennial topics and terms.]

BIBLIOGRAPHY

Backman, Mark. *Sophistication: Rhetoric and the Rise of Self-Consciousness.* Woodbridge, Conn., 1991. A reading of the Sophists' doctrines in Greek antiquity and their persistence in contemporary modernity.

Guthrie, W. K. C. *The Sophists.* Cambridge, U.K., 1971. An excellent treatment of the Sophists' lives and theories against the philosophical context of their and subsequent times.

Havelock, Eric, A. *The Liberal Temper in Greek Politics.* New Haven, Conn., 1957. A spirited defense of the Sophists' liberalism against the authoritarian and conservative political thought of Plato and Aristotle.

Jaeger, Werner. *Paideia: The Ideals of Greek Culture,* vol. 1. Translated by Gilbert Highet. New York, 1939. An in-depth discussion of the Sophists' position in the history of culture, their educational theories, and the political crises of their day.

Jarrett, Susan C. *Rereading the Sophists: Classical Rhetoric Refigured.* Carbondale, Ill., 1991. An interpretation of the Sophists' doctrines as historical antecedents of and conceptual grounds for contemporary progressive politics, feminism, and composition pedagogy.

Kerferd, George B. *The Sophistic Movement.* Cambridge, U.K., 1981. A sound investigation of the philological evidence pertaining to the Sophists. A reliable discussion of their doctrines and practices in relation both to earlier Greek thought and to Plato and Aristotle.

Poulakos, John. *Sophistical Rhetoric in Classical Greece.* Columbia, S.C., 1995. An account of the receptions the Sophists and their rhetoric occasioned at the hands of Plato, Isocrates, and Aristotle.

Sprague, Rosamont Kent, ed. *The Older Sophists.* Columbia, S.C., 1972. An English translation of the Sophists' fragments collected in *Die Fragmente der Vorsokratiker* by Hermann Diels and Walther Kranz.

Untersteiner, Mario. *The Sophists.* Translated by Kathleen Freeman. New York, 1954. A lengthy study of the Sophists in the terms of the philosophical vocabulary of phenomenalism and in the context of the thought of Benedetto Croce.

—JOHN POULAKOS

SPEECH. Any discussion of the study of speech as an academic discipline must start by grounding that subject in its rhetorical roots. By defining rhetoric as the junction between thought and speech, its dual nature becomes immediately apparent through twenty-five hundred years of Western civilization. In dealing with rhetoric as thought, emphasis was placed on such matters as composition, but in dealing with rhetoric as speech, emphasis was placed on delivery. [*See overview article on* Composition.]

The legitimacy of both emphases had been acknowledged prior to the fourth century BCE. The greatest influence exerted by rhetoric before the invention of the printing press in 1450 CE made mass distribution of written texts possible lay in its oral form. The Greeks valued the oral tradition in their dramatic presentations, lyric poetry contests, and in the great orations of their fourth-century BCE speakers. Following the Renaissance, with its rediscovery of classical texts, rhetoric became prominent in the universities of Western Europe, and that tradition was in turn transplanted to the United States.

But there has always been a tension between the competing branches of rhetoric, that is to say, between its written and oral components. Midway through the nineteenth century, the study of speech and the study of English became distinct disciplines focusing on these two different components of the rhetorical tradition. [*See* Composition, *article on* History of English departments in the United States.] So distinct had they become by the beginning of the twentieth century, that speech departments began breaking away from English departments. To say that English and speech divided along the thinking and the spoken aspects of rhetoric is at once the grossest kind of simplification and a legitimate means of laying down an easily recognizable dividing line between the two that will help make some of the broader distinctions—if not the more subtle ones—immediately clear.

These newly formed speech departments focused almost exclusively on public speaking during their first two decades of life. [*See* Public speaking.] That public speaking was neglected at universities during the nineteenth century, the great age of American oratory, was puzzling. Before the advent of the electronic media, speeches were the chief form of entertainment at political events, religious functions, and holiday festivities like the Fourth of July. Even as late as the close of the nineteenth century, a speaker like William Jennings Bryan was equally at home making speeches in the courtroom, on the campaign trial, and in the Chautauqua tent. Indeed, so accomplished a speaker was he that he entered each of these three separate arenas with little or no change in his content or style of delivery.

These new public speaking courses focused almost entirely on the practical aspects of giving a speech. Even though the courses were new and pragmatic in nature, they employed the received knowledge set down by such classical philosophers as Aristotle, Cicero, and Quintilian. [*See* Classical rhetoric.] Furthermore, because they were interested in teaching skills that led to employment outside the university, they were not particularly interested in theoretical or speculative questions.

By the decade of the 1920s, graduate courses in speech were on the horizon, and new fields of inquiry were sought that broke with the traditions of passing on only established knowledge and of avoiding unsettled questions. To fill this void, two different schools developed with two very different methodologies and goals. In these early attempts to forge new paths for speech can be seen the seeds of the conflict that would flower in the second half of the century, namely whether the discipline should continue to be viewed as one of the humanities or whether it should more properly be classed as a social science.

The Midwestern School, under the leadership of James O'Neill (1881–1970) and Charles Henry Woolbert (1877–1929), reshaped the discipline to examine speech in all its aspects. To that end its curriculum included speech (still largely public speaking) and also argumentation, acting, voice and diction, oral interpretation, radio, television, and later on, public relations and journalism. That impressive list is not exhaustive; more controversial was the methodology proposed by the group, that the school employ the particular and empirical studies used in each of these disciplines, some of which had collected a large amount of specialized or "scientific" data.

The Cornell School, so named for the university where it was located, rejected the growing notion that science was an appropriate way to study an art like speech (public speaking). The individual is unique, its proponents argued, so piles of data collected under controlled circumstances that test only a few variables at any one time can never give an accurate picture of any part of the communication process. While both of these schools of thought had their limitations and their critics, their viewpoints evolved continuously, and both arguments still exist today in one form or another.

Another problem that the Midwestern School presaged lay in the inescapable truth that all other disciplines at times transmit their subject matter in either an oral or a written fashion. Therefore, many have claimed as their own some parts of the field of rhetoric, borrowing from either its thought or its speech components. For example, linguists, philosophers, sociologists, as well as those studying myth (especially as it relates to the oral tradition); medicine (some medical schools are now offering courses in how doctors should communicate with their patients); history (working in the oral histories tradition as Homer *may* have done); and those with a keen interest in a physiological or acoustic approach, among countless others in the first half of the twentieth century, developed a professional interest in the field of speech.

While these new approaches provided much new ground for investigation at a time when the field was actively searching for new avenues of learning, they also sowed hidden difficulties, which would not be harvested until the second half of the twentieth century. In the 1920s and 1930s, satisfied to turn to speech and its principles for a better understanding of their interface with their own content, some of these disciplines tried to abscond with whole portions of the speech curriculum by century's end. For example, because most managerial or teaching jobs involve extensive portions of speech, efforts were made to move those portions away from the discipline of speech and into those other areas. These kinds of thefts even occurred within universities as some schools of business or education attempted to control all speech-related courses and activities until their various accrediting agencies turned that job back over to the speech professionals. Nevertheless, turf battles continue to plague the field.

Slowly, over the middle decades of the twentieth century, a new way arose of viewing rhetoric in both its contexts (as thought and speech). Variously called the new rhetoric, or the listener/reader/audience response theory, this movement shifted the emphasis away from an analysis of the speaker or author and her or his intention in order to focus interest on the interpretation that the listener, reader, or audience member placed on what was heard. [*See* Reception theory.] The increasing dominance of the electronic media—as radio, motion pictures, and finally television captured the public's fancy—helped to speed this trend along. This change proved more disturbing than might be apparent at first glance. Suddenly the rules set down by the ancient classical philosophers of Greece and Rome were not the only means of judging discourse. But perhaps even more startling than this shift in viewpoint was the discipline's acceptance of many of these new methods and techniques as equally valid a means of judging the truth of a communication as any methodology laid down by Aristotle or Quintilian. Instead of a completely closed system of judging communications, one whose every aspect was known and boxed in by rigid rules, this new method postulated a completely open-ended system, which was as unique as that of each individual who responded to a given text.

During the 1930s and 1940s, a trend developed in some universities to place a heavy emphasis on diction much in the manner of the eighteenth-century English elocutionists. [*See* Eighteenth-century rhetoric.] That stress on diction manifested itself in two ways: First, and least noticeable, an upper-class accent was taught, especially at select Southern universities where the Delsarte system, a system for actors adopted by speech teachers that conveyed each emotion and attitude with a specific gesture, was also very popular for much longer than in other parts of the country. While originally developed to make acting and speaking more natural, the system eventually lost favor because it made them too artifical and predictable. This emphasis on diction reflected broadcasting's emphasis on what the BBC (British Broadcasting Corporation) termed *received pronunciation*. But the more dominant trend, as first radio and then television pervaded American life, was to teach each student the Mid-Atlantic dialect preferred by the broadcast industry. Nothing was so damning to a student's chance to enter this profession as a thick Southern drawl. But as time went by and the discipline recognized that not all students in a basic speech class wanted to enter the broadcast profession, the philosophy changed. An accent makes a person a member of a particular social group, most usually but not always the group in which the person grew up. Because changing the accent helps to separate an individual from that group, little or no attempt was made to change a student's accent in the basic speech class. Those wishing to change their speech habits usually have the option of choosing a phonetics or a voice and diction course to help them do so.

President John F. Kennedy's pledge to put a man on the moon during the decade of the 1960s brought a huge increase in experimentation and a resulting explosion of technological advances, which radically changed the field of speech along with so many other fields of human endeavor. The Nixon–Kennedy debates of 1960 had shown the huge impact television could have not only on American life in general, but also specifically on a presidential election. (Many thought Nixon lost because his "five o'clock shadow" made him appear shifty and untrustworthy on television.)

A Canadian scholar, Marshall McLuhan (1911–1980), was also watching the results of those debates and the case studies done on them. The studies showed that those listening to the debates on radio thought Nixon had won, but those watching on television gave the nod to Kennedy. Obviously any content analysis would have shown that the substance of the debates was the same for each audience—that they each heard the same words. The only difference was the medium. McLuhan deduced that in this case the medium was the message and, from this specific case, he then generalized that the medium must be the message in many other contexts as well, thus oversimplifying his findings and, in the eyes of many of his critics, going much too far. A McLuhan advocate was reported to have said that he didn't care to know what the news was but only the medium over which it had been transmitted. Despite McLuhan's excesses, Golden, Berquist, and Coleman *The Rhetoric of Western Thought*, Dubuque, Iowa, 1984) list four rhetorical implications of McLuhan's philosophy for all serious rhetorical scholars: (1) the extent to which the medium affects the message; (2) speakers' choice of media compatible with their styles; (3) the resurgence of the oral tradition in the age of elec-tronic media; (4) the implications for the restructuring of public discourse to suit the demands of the electronic media (pp. 218–219).

If television did not seem to fit comfortably within the traditional field of speech, then a name change seemed called for. Even prior to 1960, the word *communication* had begun to replace the word *speech* as the name of the discipline, a trend that accelerated throughout the next thirty years. If the reality was that the television camera fit comfortably within this newly created communication context, so did television's three predecessors: the print media, radio, and motion pictures. Nor did the field stop with the inclusion of these three. The term *communication* had, of course, been in use for hundreds of years before it came to replace the term *speech* as the name of a discipline. Even the definition commonly accepted for this more inclusive term was foreseen in a work by I. A. Richards (1924, p. 177):

> Communication . . . takes place when one mind so acts upon its environment that another mind is influenced, and in that other mind an experience occurs which is like the experience in the first mind, and is caused in part by that experience.

Richards goes on to explain that if one person relates something to another about a person the other does not know, the other will be strictly dependent on the first for information. Unless the first is unusually well suited to describing the person in question, the experience in the minds of speaker and listener will correspond only roughly or approximately. Thus by implication, the possibilities for miscommunication are very great—so great, Richards concludes, that the narrator and auditor mentioned above may never succeed in communicating anything and both remain unaware that no communication has taken place.

A significant body of work developed after 1960 to measure how much overlap exists between what the speaker says and what the listener hears. Today's marketers have become increasingly sophisticated in combining the form of a persuasive message drawn from Aristotle, on the one hand, with sophisticated visual images drawn from the virtual realty of modern culture on the other, to ensure as high a correlation as possible between their messages and the audiences' perceptions of those messages.

But while the new term *communication* doubtless invited investigations into many more fields of study than the older more restrictive terms *speech, rhetoric,* or *elocution,* it ultimately refers to elements so diverse as to defy any attempt by its adherents to define a recognized body of knowledge to which it could lay *exclusive* claim. [*See* Communication.] Its adherents have also failed to agree on a set of fundamental tenets that must be mastered by all those wishing to enter the field, leading to charges that today the field lacks both a catholic subject matter and universally agreed upon research methods. Today, the academic community still remains divided as to whether a basic communication course should consist exclusively of public speaking or should, in addition, explore a variety of communication situations. Many areas for inquiry were advanced as pathways for admission into the field: intrapersonal communication; interpersonal communication; small-group communication (communicating with fewer than fifteen people); public speaking (communicating with a larger audience than fifteen people); mass communication (communicating with others through print or electronic means); communication theory (a study of the means through which communication takes place); organizational communication (a study of an organization's internal and external communication practices); and multicultural communication (a study of communication practices within and across different cultures), to name just a few. Nor is the communication canon closed; new areas for exploration of new facets of the discipline are still regularly proposed. In addition, each of the above-mentioned topics breaks down into many smaller fields of inquiry, and almost any subject matter could be singled out for an audit of its communication content.

During the late 1960s and 1970s, political communication developed as a distinct way of looking at the impact of certain kinds of persuasive discourse on voting patterns. As most political candidates, but especially presidential candidates, learned the value of presenting themselves to their best advantage, in true McLuhan fashion

they packaged and repackaged themselves until they found messages and personae that connected with large numbers of the voters. [*See* Campaigns.] The 1980s and 1990s saw the process further refined by having candidates present different communications and faces to focus groups before settling on the proper one to broadcast to a larger audience in whatever settings worked best in the focus groups. They sought to ensure that the message they communicated most closely matched the one already in the minds of voters in a process that totally reverses Richards' definition of communication. Rather than using the message to communicate something new to the voter, the politician today often uses communication to reinforce the voters' view of the world in which they want to live.

The communication research that drives so many of the academic and commercial communication practices in both the university and business environments, while it has greatly increased with the easy availability of electronic data retrieval systems, was not new to the second half of the twentieth century. W. Barnett Pearce, writing in *Speech Communication in the 20th Century* (edited by T. W. Benson, Carbondale, Ill., 1985, pp. 255–281) pays tribute to the work done earlier in the century before turning his attention to the massive amounts of research now available and concluding from that research that the power of the discipline lies in both its diversity (of subject matters) and its disorder (a necessary stage in developing anything worthwhile).

In the 1990s, the term *communication studies* came into the lexicon, and in some places replaced the term *communication.* "Communication Studies," says Liora Salter by way of definition, "explore(s) the ways in which information is given meaning by those who produce, distribute, or interpret it" ("Communication Studies." *Canadian Encyclopedia,* vol. 1, Edmonton, Alberta, 1985, p. 382) While the advent of the term is still too recent to know for certain if its use will coalesce these vast and unwieldy fields of knowledge into a more unified and cohesive unit of study, evidence thus far indicates that the field is still expanding and intensifying rapidly rather than contracting. Nor does it seem from this early vantage point as if the change from *Communication* to communication studies will produce the huge changes in content that were occasioned by the earlier change from *speech*.

BIBLIOGRAPHY

Berger, Charles R., and Steven H. Chaffee. *Handbook of Communication Science*. Newbury Park, Calif., 1989. A collection of essays on the analysis and functions of communication as a science.

Berthoff, Ann E., ed. *Richards on Rhetoric*. New York, 1991. A collection of Richards essays showing how he changed his mind over time about rhetoric.

McCroskey, James C. *An Introduction to Rhetorical Communication*. Engelwood Cliffs, N.J., 1972. A historical treatment of the origin and development of rhetoric.

McLuhan, Marshall. *Understanding Media*. New York, 1964. McLuhan's highly controversial theories in his own words.

Richards. I. A. *Principals of Literary Criticism*. New York, 1924. Richards lays down and defends his famous definition of communication.

Richards, I. A. *Practical Criticism*. New York, 1929. A psychology of poetic criticism.

—Robert A. Gaines

SPEECH ACTS, UTTERANCES AS. Speech acts are primarily or necessarily performed in and by saying something; they include the act of saying something itself and such other acts as *promising, advising, accusing, proposing, ordering, convincing*, and *persuading*. When utterances are regarded as speech acts, attention is properly directed both to the act that produces the utterance and to the product of that act.

Historically, students of grammar, rhetoric, and dialectic have given attention to specific kinds of speech acts. Grammarians and linguists have classified sentences as declaratives, imperatives, and exclamations. Students of dialectic and logic have identified propositions as products of asserting or of commanding. Rhetoricians have traditionally focused on discourse designed to persuade, but in studying the means of persuasion, their attention has been drawn to a variety of other speech acts as well. Major classical rhetorical genres have been identified, in part, by reference to advising, accusing and defending, praising and blaming. [*See* Deliberative genre; Epideictic genre; *and* Fo-

rensic genre.] These inherited *schēmatas* lean to varying degrees on speech acts, but they have focused on the products of those acts, namely, on sentences, assertions, advice, and persuasion, giving comparatively little attention to the speech acts themselves. Nor have the traditional arts of thought and speech attempted a general or systematic inquiry into communicative acts.

Systematic interest in speech acts emerged in the philosophy of language, initiated by the seminal work of J. L. Austin (1911–1960). Putting aside inherited distinctions, Austin's *How to Do Things with Words* (1962) sets out to elucidate the full communicative act in all its complexity and variety as reflected in the language persons ordinarily use to perform and identify their speech acts. Austin's work gives greater precision to interests many contemporary philosophers take in the uses of language and language games. Within the larger act of communicating something, Austin identifies three component speech acts: the *locutionary act*—the act of saying something, in direct or indirect discourse; the *illocutionary act,* the act performed in saying something—acts of proposing, promising, apologizing,; and the *perlocutionary act,* identified primarily in terms of the outcome or consequences of a communicative effort, (e.g., persuading and convincing). Of these three classes, the illocutionary act counts as Austin's great conceptual contribution. Although his characterization of the illocutionary act has been subject to major revision, it is the members of this class which come first to mind at the mention of *speech acts.*

For Austin, the illocutionary act is an essentially overt act, necessarily performed by saying something—an act which, if performed in conformity with the pertinent conventions, has the potential to impact the social and moral order. A good example is making a promise: To make a promise a speaker must say something semantically equivalent to "I will do x," where x is the act the speaker promises to perform. The promisor necessarily speaks with the essentially overt intention of giving the promisee reason to believe that she will do x, if only because she said so. This intention can be, but need not be, made explicit by use of the prefatory expression "I promise that. . . ." By promising to do x, the speaker alters the moral order in that she places herself under an obligation to do *x*. In Austin's view, promising has that capacity because it is constituted by conventions that dictate that when a speaker utters these words with that overt intention, her utterance has the illocutionary force of creating an obligation.

It is on this last point, the idea that illocutionary acts are constituted by conventions, that Austin's thinking has come in for its most profound revision. Austin's conception of the illocutionary act grew out of reflection on performative acts, such as marriage, baptism, or calling someone out in a game, which are constituted by conventional rules. There is a convention in some jurisdictions that if the proper parties each say "I do" in the appropriate circumstances and before the appointed agents, the parties are married. Austin thought that acts like promising and advising are similarly conventional. The doctrine that illocutionary acts are constituted by conventional rules has been widely circulated outside the philosophy of language by John Searle's influential *Speech Acts: An Essay in the Philosophy of Language.*

Important work by Austin's colleagues P. F. Strawson, G. J. Warnoch, and Dennis Stampe challenges the idea that illocutionary acts on the order of promising and advising are fundamentally conventional. Rather, an important array of illocutionary acts can be seen to be constituted by practical calculations utilizing resources available in saying something. H. P. Grice's analysis of utterance-meaning has been instrumental in the development of this view. Grice's analysis provides an outline of what a speaker needs to do in order to say seriously something that she means, and it suggests an account of the basic efficacy of saying things. According to Grice, a speaker manages to say something by producing an utterance, while deliberately and openly making known to her addressee(s) that she wants them to respond in a particular way (e.g., believe what the speaker is saying). These efforts are designed, and in favorable circumstances, serve to provide the addressee(s) with reason to respond as the speaker primarily intends. Rationale for the addressee's response is generated roughly as follows. By openly manifesting her primary intention to secure a response from the addressee, the speaker manifestly takes responsibility for her primary communicative effort. She thereby generates a presumption of veracity (viz., a presumption that

she is sincerely expressing beliefs, the truth of which she has made a reasonable effort to ascertain). After all, her addressee can reason, the speaker would not make herself vulnerable to criticism for mendacity, if she were not making a responsible effort to speak truthfully. This pragmatic account of the locutionary act of meaningfully saying something supports, in turn, a general account of how illocutionary acts work. In making a promise, for example, the speaker says that she will come home at seven, thereby generating a presumption that she is making a reasonable effort to speak the truth. But to further reassure her addressee, the promisor strengthens that presumption by openly giving her addressee reason to believe that she will make this prediction come true, if only because she knows her addressee is counting on her. Or in proposing—a rhetorically interesting illocutionary act—a speaker might say, for example, that she and the addressee should invest in such and such a mutual fund, a proposition that her addressee typically would initially be reluctant to consider. In order to induce at least tentative consideration from her addressee, the proposer augments the presumption of veracity by openly committing herself, not only to having reasons that support the truth of what she says but also to providing those reasons to her addressee in response to whatever questions and objections the addressee might raise. The proposer thereby generates a presumption that what she has to say may prove to be worth serious consideration. It seems that other illocutionary acts may work similarly to induce specific kinds of responses from addressees by generating special presumptions built on the basic presumption of veracity. Such illocutionary acts are constituted by practical calculations that utilize and augment resources inherent in the primary locutionary act of saying and meaning something.

It seems then that an account of speech acts can be expected to cast considerable light on the efficacy of communicative means and so might clarify matters of traditional rhetorical interest. There are, however, some hurdles to be mounted in moving from the account of speech acts as developed in the philosophy of language to concepts useful in rhetorical art. Austin's classification of speech acts is built on grammatical and logical considerations. Except incidentally, it does not reflect concerns traditionally central to rhetoric. His category of perlocutionary acts, which includes the rhetorically central act of persuading, is identified more as a backdrop for differentiating the illocutionary act than as a category of distinct and significant interest. More importantly, speech acts, as investigated by philosophers and linguists, are identified on the basis of distinctions drawn in ordinary day-to-day talk, whereas rhetoric has traditionally focused on discourse in public forums. The latter are products of art; day-to-day conversation is, in a sense, natural. An art of public discourse requires discursive practices that are sustained by the conventions to which audiences have become habituated and that consequently in some measure stand apart from ordinary day-to-day conversation. Nevertheless, since much rhetorical discourse is addressed to lay audiences, whose knowledge of communicative means derives largely from plain conversational practices, our ordinary conceptions of speech acts and an understanding of the basic dynamics of speech acts bear very directly on matters of traditional rhetorical interest.

The most obvious connection between our ordinary understanding of speech acts and the lexicon of rhetorical art is to be found in the development and delineation of rhetorical genre. Some rhetorical genres derive their basic structure directly from corresponding speech acts. When Alexander Hamilton opens the *Federalist Papers* (1787) by proposing the new Constitution to his readers for their careful consideration, he does just what a speaker in ordinary conversation does in proposing something. He openly incurs much the same responsibilities as would be taken on by an ordinary proposer, and although he and his coauthors discharge those duties at an extraordinary level of artistic performance, their argumentation has much the same force one finds in any competent defense of a proposal. Accusing, advising, and praising are among the speech acts for which corresponding rhetorical genres are readily identifiable. In these and similar kinds of rhetorical discourse, a rhetor establishes an initial communicative relationship with her audience by openly incurring a discursive burden. By satisfactorily discharging that obligation, she may generate reasons for her audience to, for example,

carefully consider her proposal, hold the accused answerable, weigh her advice, honor the recipient of her praise.

The pragmatics of speech acts can also be seen to operate in discourses that do not derive their generic structure from corresponding ordinary illocutionary acts. Martin Luther King, Jr.'s (1929–1968) celebrated "I Have a Dream" speech (1963) falls into the genre of epideictic. It answers to a set of audience expectations that include the following duties: (1) the speaker is to articulate the immediate audience's commitment to the cause that brings them together; (2) the speaker is to inspire the immediate audience to exhibit their commitment to that cause; and (3) he is to fulfill those two tasks in a way that exhibits to a larger, often dispersed, audience of onlookers the depth of the immediate audience's commitment to a good and worthy cause. At the outset of his address, after elegantly rehearsing the historical denial of civil rights to black Americans, King *openly* takes on the duties incumbent on an epideictic speaker. To his immediate audience he says, "So we've come here today to dramatize a shameful condition." This explicit statement of intent commits the speaker to a clear set of generically relevant duties. By openly making that commitment, King manifestly exposes himself to criticism should he fail to fulfill those obligations; accordingly, he warrants a presumption supporting the solemnity of his address. King's introductory commitment parallels the structure and function to a nonconventional illocutionary act, though there seems to be no corresponding well-established ordinary speech act. [*See* Hybrid genres.]

The relationships between presumption and burden of proof in argumentative discourse is a second matter illuminated by the pragmatics of speech acts. [*See* Argumentation.] At least since Richard Whately's nineteenth-century *Elements of Rhetoric*, students of argumentation have thought that, just as in courts of law a presumption of innocence imposes a burden of proof on parties bringing a charge of criminal wrongdoing, so too in other argumentative contexts presumptions can be discerned that impose probative responsibilities on one or the other side of the controversy. This important insight illuminates much argumentative rhetoric, but it has resisted adequate formulation. In speech acts such as proposing and accusing, speakers openly take on burdens of proof, and they do so in relation to corresponding presumptions. Careful attention to the dynamics of these speech acts promises to clarify long-standing questions about the genesis of argumentative burdens of proof and about the force of arguments that discharge those burdens.

Understanding the pragmatics of speech acts also casts light on some artistic aspects of the *ēthos* speakers may generate. [*See* Ēthos.] Traditional rhetoric teaches that a speaker's apparent character, as known from her reputation and as artistically manifest through her discourse, serves as a primary source of rhetorical proof. The pragmatics of speech acts show one important way in which speakers can make apparent aspects of their characters that warrant favorable responses from their audiences. By openly making herself vulnerable to criticism should she fail, for example, to speak truthfully, slight her audience's interests and concerns, treat her opponents unfairly, the speaker can exhibit aspects of herself that warrant consideration and acceptance of her utterances.

In short, philosophical study of speech acts directs attention to what speakers do in and by producing utterances, and this attention brings to light practical discursive dynamics of considerable interest to rhetorical art.

BIBLIOGRAPHY

Austin, J. L. *How to do Things with Words.* Edited by J. O. Urmson. Cambridge, Mass., 1962.

Grice, H. P. "Meaning." *Philosophical Review* 62 (1957), pp. 397–388.

Grice, H. P. "Utterer's Meaning and Intention." *Philosophical Review* 78 (1969), pp. 147–177.

Searle, John R. *Speech Acts: An Essay in the Philosophy of Language.* Cambridge, U.K., 1969.

Stampe, Dennis. "Meaning and Truth in the Theory of Speech Acts." In *Speech Acts.* Edited by Peter Cole and Jerry Morgan, pp. 25–38. New York, 1975.

Strawson, P. F. "Intention and Convention in Speech Acts." *Philosophical Review* 73 (1964), pp. 439–460.

Warnock, G. J. "Some Types of Performative Utterance." In *Essays on J. L. Austin,* pp. 69–90. Oxford, 1973.

—FRED J. KAUFFELD

SPIN CONTROL. *See* Expository rhetoric and journalism.

STASIS. The theory of *stasis* (Lat. *status* or *constitutio*) develops a system designed to assist rhetors in identifying the central issues in given controversies, and in finding the appropriate argumentative topics useful in addressing these issues. This function has ensured for *stasis* a central place in the rhetorical theory of invention.

Hermagoras of Temnos (fl. c.150 BCE) is most widely credited with giving the theory of *stasis* its basic form, even though prefigurations of it can be identified in earlier writers. Hermagoras's basic scheme, so far as it can be reconstructed from a variety of sources, focused primarily on controversies arising from the conflict of accusation or claim and defense in court cases. The prosecutor's or plaintiff's assertion (Gk. *kataphasis;* Lat. *affirmatio* or *intentio*) would identify the basis for the charge or claim (Gk. *aition;* Lat. *litis causativum* or *ratio*). If this was answered by the defendant's denial (Gk. *apophasis;* Lat. *negatio* or *depulsio*), based on the grounds for this response (Gk. *synechon;* Lat. *continens* or *firmamentum*), a question to be decided (Gk. *zētēma;* Lat. *quaestio*) would be created, requiring a judgment (Gk. *krinomenon;* Lat. *iudicatio*). The etymology of the Greek term *stasis* is not quite certain, but the most likely explanation is that it marks the position that the two parties in a dispute would take up at its inception; the same term is used for the stance opponents assume at the outset of a fight, and for a state of civil strife.

Having thus analyzed the joining of issue between the contending parties, Hermagoras now arranged four lines of controversy in order of decreasing desirability from the perspective of the defense. If someone is accused of having committed a crime, the most effective defense is to deny the performance of the alleged act; this is the *stasis* of *stochasmos* (Lat. *coniectura*), the issue of fact or conjecture. The question is whether the defendant did or did not perform the act (e.g., took or did not take a sacred object). If this line of defense is questionable, the next available strategy is to concede the act and to raise the issue of definition. The question is whether the act fits into the category of acts described in the relevant normative sources as forbidden (e.g., whether the taking of a sacred object from a private house constitutes "sacrilege"); this is the *stasis* of *horos* (Lat. *definitio*). The third line of defense admits that a prima facie illegal act has been performed, but claims that it was justifiable or excusable on the basis of special circumstances, and thus not (fully) punishable as a matter of law or clemency (e.g., the defendant used the stolen vessel to pour hot oil on enemy soldiers intent on climbing the city wall); this is the issue of quality, the *stasis* of *kata symbebēkos* or *poiotēs* (Lat. *qualitas* or *generalis*). Finally, and least desirably, the defendant may concede that a punishable act has been committed, but raise an issue of procedure, leading to the *stasis* of *metalēpsis* (Lat. *translatio*). The question is whether the present court is authorized to hear the case (e.g., whether a religious rather than a civilian court should decide the matter).

Apart from these four *staseis*, Hermagoras's scheme outlined four issues of legal interpretation identified as *zētēmata* rather than *stases*, even though a later Latin tradition would categorize them as the four *status legales* parallel to the *status rationales* of the four *stases*. The first of these legal interpretive issues addresses the relationship between the letter and the intent of a legal rule (Gk. *kata rhēton kai hupexairesis;* Lat. *scriptum et voluntas*); for example, should an ordinance prohibiting vehicles in the park also be applied to an ambulance? The second deals with contradictory laws (Gk. *antinomia;* Lat. *leges contrariae*); for example, how is the conflict between this ordinance and another one requiring the removal of trash from the park by trucks to be resolved? The third issue concerns cases of ambiguity (Gk. *amphibolia;* Lat. *ambiguum*); for example, does the word *day* in the park ordinance apply to the entire twenty-four-hour day or only to the daylight period? And the final issue focuses on cases of analogy (Gk. *syllogismos,* Lat. *ratiocinatio* or *collectio*); for example, should the ordinance prohibiting "vehicles" in the park also be applied to skateboards?

Prefigurations of Hermagoras's theory of *stases* and *zētēmata* can be found for instance in Aristotle's *Rhetoric* (c.335 BCE). There, he discusses the step from the admission of an alleged act to the legal characterization of the event, and emphasizes the significance of definition in this context. He also points to unwritten law and equity as necessary supplements and correctives to the written law that cannot completely regulate the infinite variety of possible circumstances (1374a–

b). He also provides a rudimentary treatment of the interpretive arguments relating to written and unwritten law or equity, conflicting laws, and ambiguity (1375a–b), as well as parallel arguments pertaining to the interpretation of contracts (1376b). Similar anticipations can be found in the works of Antiphon (especially the *Tetralogies*) in the late fifth century BCE, and in the *Rhetorica ad Alexandrum,* ascribed to Anaximenes, in the mid-fourth century BCE (especially 1422b and 1443a).

It can thus be surmised that Hermagoras systematized and elaborated a fairly rich vein of traditional rhetorical materials, and subsequent writers continued this process by increasingly elaborate subdivisions and occasionally shifting terminologies, as well as some rearrangement of basic categories. Such changes were to some extent encouraged by the permeable boundaries of the basic categories of *stasis;* for instance, by the circumstance that issues of fact are hard to separate from issues of definition, that definition also plays a part in legal interpretation, and that questions of letter and intent recur in discussing the other legal interpretive issues. (For details of these developments, see the bibliography at the end of this article.)

Two important developments occurred in the treatment of the *status rationales* or *generales* in the transition from the Hellenistic rhetoric largely reflected in early Roman works such as the *Rhetorica ad Herennium* and Cicero's *De inventione* (early first century BCE) to the later works of Cicero (mid-first century BCE) and the *Institutio oratoria* of Quintilian (late first century CE). In these later writings, we observe a tendency to eliminate the issue of process (*translatio*) as an analytically separate category, treating it instead as a separate occurrence of issues of fact, definition, and quality relating to the procedural posture of the case (see especially Quintilian 3.6.68–79; and earlier, Cicero, *Orator* 14.45, *Partitiones oratoriae* 101, *Topica* 21.82). This elimination of the more technical legal issue of *translatio* from the basic scheme also facilitates Quintilian's insistence, again following Cicero, that the remaining three *status generales* (conjecture, definition, and quality) apply to all questions in all manner of disputes, not only in the judicial genre, and that the *status legales,* too, can ultimately be subsumed under them (3.6.80–82). In his subsequent discussions of *stasis*, Quintilian actually endeavors repeatedly to validate this claim, showing for instance how basic issues of deliberative oratory fit into the three general *status* (3.8.4–5), but it must be admitted that even he does not carry out this project fully. Later writers do not appear committed to it, focusing more and more on a fairly rigid transmission rather than a continuous rethinking and refinement of the system of *stasis*. This attitude also expresses itself in a decreasing attention to matters of actual oratorical practice in general, and to the relation of *stasis* theory to the forensic practice of legal rhetoric in particular.

After some initial limited efforts to incorporate aspects of Roman legal practice in the works of the author of the *Rhetorica ad Herennium*, Cicero, and Quintilian, later writers tend to withdraw from the courts into their schoolrooms, leaving the development of legal rhetoric to the jurists. The work of these legal experts does in fact show a significant awareness and use of elements of *stasis* theory, especially of some of the interpretive arguments related to the *status legales*, and of justifications and excuses discussed in the context of the *status qualitatis*. Another avenue of influence was opened up by Augustine in his *De doctrina christiana* (early fifth century CE), which adapted elements of the *status legales* for use in biblical interpretation, whence they entered into the development of the medieval scholastic method and thence of canon law. [*See* Medieval rhetoric, *article on* Medieval grammar; *and* Religion.] Through these juristic channels that led to the Middle Ages and beyond, *stasis* theory has to this day exercised important influences on the development of Western law, even if the level of explicit attention to the doctrines of *stasis* in the rhetorical as well as the legal literature has fluctuated greatly.

In the earlier Middle Ages, at a time when juristic sophistication was at a low ebb, the teaching of *stasis* theory transmitted at least rudimentary legal knowledge to succeeding generations. Works such as Martianus Capella's *De nuptiis Philologiae et Mercurii* in the fifth century, Cassiodorus's *Institutiones* in the sixth century, Isidore of Seville's *Etymologia* in the seventh century, Alcuin's *Disputatio de rhetorica et de virtutibus* at the turn of the eigth to the ninth century, and Notker Labeo's *De arte rhetorica* at the turn of the tenth to the eleventh century, exemplify this process. With the revival of the study of Roman law toward the end of the twelfth century, the conceptual categories of dialectic gradually tend to replace *stasis* theory as the preferred conceptual schema for the organization of legal arguments. [*See* Dialectic.] Relatively early works, however, such as Sicard of Cremona's *Summa* and Pilius of Medicina's *Libellus disputatorius* (both from the final decades of the twelfth century) continued to use a scheme for the organization of legal presumptions, a scheme based on the *status rationales* of *coniectura* and *qualitas*. The latter was understood as the legal characterization of facts, thus pointing to the fundamental juristic distinction between questions of fact and of law.

Most works dedicated to the teaching of rhetoric continue to feature *stasis* theory, though somewhat removed from specific contemporary legal applications. But the most extensive discussion of *stasis* in the Renaissance, in George of Trebizond's *Rhetoricorum libri V* (1433), does at least make a gesture in the direction of juristic application by introducing, in addition to more traditional terms, the categories of *quaestio facti, nominis, generis, actionis* for the four *status rationales;* especially the first and fourth of these point to legal terminology. [*See overview article on* Renaissance rhetoric.] In juristic works dedicated in part to the discussion of legal interpretation, we still find during these times occasional references to the four *status legales*. The interest in these is then significantly revived with the rise of a separate genre of works on legal interpretation that begins toward the end of the fifteenth century; examples of this are Stephanus de Federicis *De interpretatione legum* (c.1495), François Hotman's *Iurisconsultus* (1559), and Valentin Wilhelm Forster's *Interpres* (1613). Clear traces of the *status legales* continue to appear later in works such as Hugo Grotius's *De iure belli ac pacis* (1625, revised 1631) and Samuel Pufendorf's *De iure naturae et gentium* (1672).

In the course of the eighteenth century, concerns about the political legitimation and control increasingly led, especially on the European continent, to calls for a science of legal hermeneutics. It was intended that the latter would deemphasize the interplay of opposing interpretations highlighted in the rhetorical tradition of *stasis* in favor of methods claiming to produce uniquely correct interpretations of legal norms. This trend is signaled by works such as Chr. H. Eckhard's *Hermeneuticae iuris libri duo* (1750), A. F. J. Thibaut's *Theorie der Auslegung des römischen Rechts* (2d ed. 1806), and F. C. von Savigny's *System des heutigen römischen Rechts* (vol. 1, 1840). [*See* Eighteenth-century rhetoric; *and* Law.]

Significantly, William Blackstone's *Commentaries on the Laws of England* (1765–1769) are somewhat more receptive to the potential for controversy in legal interpretation, a notion less disturbing in a culture emphasizing judicial independence. Nevertheless, lawyer (and later U.S. president) John Quincey Adams, in *Lectures on Rhetoric and Oratory* (1810) briefly discussed the *status rationales*. The *status legales* were omitted entirely, however. Adams insisted instead that "the administration of justice is in substance a strict logical syllogism, of which the written law forms the major proposition, the verdict of the jury the minor, and the sentence of the court the conclusion" (p. 200). [*See* Syllogism.] This emphasis on the legal syllogism in preference to the rhetorical understanding of legal argumentation largely persisted throughout the nineteenth century, but has come under increasing attack since.

There was a strong revival of interest in rhetoric in general and in *stasis* theory in particular, especially during the second half of the twentieth century. This interest is reflected in the brief bibliography accompanying this article, and in further works to which these references will guide the reader. Apart from historical studies, discussions have focused mainly on the applicability of *stasis* theory to deliberative and forensic argumentation, as well as to general argumentation theory. While these analyses show that *stasis* theory offers promising suggestions for the theory and practice of contemporary argumentation, an assessment of the full extent of this promise, and its realization in a full-scale adaptation of *stasis* theory for contemporary application still awaits work in the twenty-first century. [*See* Argumentation; *and* Deliberative genre.]

[*See also* Casuistry; Classical rhetoric; Forensic genre; Invention; Occasion; *and* Topics.]

BIBLIOGRAPHY

Barwick, Karl. "Zur Erklärung und Geschichte der Staseislehre des Hermagoras von Temnos." *Philologus* 108 (1964), pp. 80–101.

Braet, Antoine C. "Variationen zur Statuslehre von Hermagoras bei Cicero." *Rhetorica* 7 (1989), pp. 239–259.

Braet, Antoine. "The Classical Doctrine of *Status* and the Rhetorical Theory of Argumentation." *Philosophy and Rhetoric* 20 (1987), pp. 79–93.

Braet, Antoine. *De klassieke statusleer in modern perspectief. Een historisch-systematische bijdrage tot de argumentatieleer.* Groningen, The Netherlands, 1984.

Calboli Montefusco, Lucia. *La dottrina degli "status" nella retorica greca e romana.* Hildesheim, 1986.

Heath, Malcolm. "The Substructure of Stasis-Theory from Hermagoras to Hermogenes." *The Classical Quarterly* 44 (1994), pp. 114–129.

Hohmann, Hanns. "Juristische Rhetorik." In *Historisches Wörterbuch der Rhetorik,* edited by Gert Ueding, vol. 4, col. 779–832. Tübingen, 1998.

Hohmann, Hanns. "Classical Rhetoric and Roman Law: Reflections on a Debate." *Jahrbuch Rhetorik* 15 (1996), pp. 15–41.

Hohmann, Hanns. "The Dynamics of Stasis: Classical Rhetorical Theory and Modern Legal Argumentation." *American Journal of Jurisprudence* 34 (1989), pp. 171–197.

Hultzén, Lee S. "Status in Deliberative Analysis." In *The Rhetorical Idiom: Essays in Rhetoric, Oratory, Language, and Drama Presented to Herbert August Wichelns,* edited by Donald C. Bryant, pp. 97–123. New York, 1966.

Leff, Michael. *The Frozen Image: Sulpicius Victor and the Ancient Rhetorical Tradition.* Ph.D. Dissertation: University of California, Los Angeles, 1972.

Matthes, Dieter. "Hermagoras von Temnos 1904–1955." *Lustrum* 3 (1958), pp. 58–214.

Nadeau, Ray. "Hermogenes on 'Stock Issues' in Deliberative Speaking." In *Readings in Argumentation,* edited by J. M. Anderson and P. J. Dovre, pp. 142–151. Boston, 1968.

Nadeau, Ray. "Hermogenes' *On Stases:* A Translation with an Introduction and Notes." *Speech Monographs (Communication Monographs)* 31 (1964), pp. 361–424.

Nadeau, Ray. "Classical Systems of Stases in Greek: Hermagoras to Hermogenes." *Greek, Roman, and Byzantine Studies* 2 (1959), pp. 53–71.

Newman, R. P. "Analysis and Issues—A Study of Doctrine." In *Readings in Argumentation,* edited by J. M. Anderson and P. J. Dovre, pp. 166–181. Boston, 1968.

Stroux, Johannes. *Römische Rechtswissenschaft und Rhetorik.* Potsdam, 1949.

Vonglis, Bernard. *La lettre et l'esprit de la loi dans la juris-prudence classique et la rhétorique.* Paris, 1968.

Wesel, Uwe. *Rhetorische Statuslehre und Gesetzesauslegung der römischen Juristen.* Köln, 1967.
— HANNS HOHMANN

STRUCTURALISM. *See* Linguistics.

STYLE is a central category of rhetoric, which at the same time possesses profound cultural significance. As verbal expression, it is essential to rhetoric, but it is also significantly related to other areas of cultural production such as literature, and it has deep socioaesthetic implications. Style forms the center or core of the traditional five-stage model of text production, the theory of the five duties or arts of rhetoric (*officia oratoris, partes rhetorices*). After the discovery of plausible ideas and arguments in the first phase of the compositional process (*inventio*) and their arrangement or distribution in an effective order in the second phase (*dispositio*), they are expressed in proper language in the third phase (*elocutio*), which is followed by the memorizing of the text as the fourth part of rhetoric (*memoria*), and delivery (*actio*) as the fifth part. Style, or *elocutio,* is crucial in the process of textual composition, since it is responsible for the manifestation of the text as text. It is style that brings the text into linguistic existence. Without style or verbal expression, invention and disposition could have no effect. And it is style that provides the basis for memory and delivery. Quintilian (first century CE) expresses the quintessential nature of style when he says that without *elocutio,* our ideas are as useless as a sword kept concealed within its sheath (*Institutio oratoria* 8, Prooemium, p. 15). In what follows, the concept of style will first be looked at in its strictly rhetorical sense as *elocutio,* the system established in classical antiquity. Then, important developments in the history of the concept and system of *elocutio* will be described from classical times to the twentieth century, which will involve wider aesthetic and cultural issues, since literature and culture were for a long time intimately connected with rhetoric and specifically with *elocutio* as its central part. The dissociation of the concept of style from rhetoric, which occurred in the Romantic period, and the development of new, nonrhetorical ideas of style will also be discussed.

Style and Its Components in Classical Antiquity. A comprehensive and coherent system of *elocutio* and its aspects was developed in classical antiquity. The most influential work in this context is the *Rhetorica ad Herennium* (c.80 BCE), a pseudo-Ciceronian work on which later writers from Quintilian to the Renaissance would base their treatment of *elocutio*. The classical theory presupposes a division of content (*res*) and form (*verba*), which is bridged by style. The speaker makes his arguments effective by presenting them in an appropriate verbal shape. The author of *Ad Herennium* (1.3) defines *elocutio* as "adaptation of suitable words and sentences to the matter devised" (*idoneorum verborum et sententiarum ad inventionem adcommodatio*). A metaphor frequently used in this context is that of style as clothing and ornament (*inventa vestire atque ornare oratione,* Cicero, *De oratore,* 1.142). [*See* Classical rhetoric.]

The theory of the qualities or virtues of style (*virtutes elocutionis*) and their negative counterparts, the vices of style (*vitia*), is an important part of *elocutio,* which was developed by disciples of Aristotle (384–322 BCE) such as Theophrastus and Demetrius and taken over by Cicero (106–43 BCE) and Quintilian. The first virtue mentioned is purity or correctness of language (*latinitas*), which is to a large extent a question of grammar. It concerns the correct choice of words, as well as correctness in word formation and syntax. A permissible deviation from correctness is *metaplasm,* a change of a word for artistic reasons in poetry. Metaplasms belong to the so-called licences (*licentiae*), deviations from the grammatical norm for stylistic reasons. An unpermitted deviation from correct usage is called a vice (*vitium*). The use of inappropriate words such as vulgarisms, archaisms, neologisms, and unpardonable changes in the sound and form of a word are called barbarisms (*barbarismus*); an unpardonable breach of the syntactic construction is a solecism (*soloecismus*).

The second virtue of style is clarity (*perspicuitas*), that is, intelligibility as a requirement for the credibility of the orator's words, the use of clear and unambiguous words and sentences. The opposite of clarity is the vice of obscurity (*obscuritas*). Obscurity may derive from ambiguity, from extreme brevity, or from long-windedness. The third virtue of style—related to clarity—is evidence (Gk. *enargeia,* Lat. *evidentia*), the graphic recounting of real or imaginary events, which makes the hearer a kind of eyewitness (*ante oculos ponere*). While clarity tends to have an effect on the recipient's intellectual faculty (*logos*), evidence tends to arouse the emotions (*pathos*). A stylistic device that is related to *evidentia* and to the more general virtue of vividness and vigorousness of expression (*enargeia*) is amplification (*amplificatio*), the heightening or intensification of the argument by rhetorical devices such as exaggeration (*incrementum*), comparison (*comparatio*), and accumulation of expressions (*congeries*).

The fourth virtue of style is propriety or appropriateness (*aptum*). This quality requires that the orator's words must be appropriate to the subject of the speech, to the person of the speaker, the nature of the audience, and to time and place. Propriety is a category which extends from rhetoric to literature and life and culture in general. For Cicero, *aptum* is of universal importance: "The universal rule, in oratory as in life, is to consider propriety" (*De oratore,* p. 71). A synonym for *aptum* is *decorum,* a term that has a moral connotation. [*See* Decorum.] The moral dimension of the concept of *aptum* is stressed by Quintilian: "It is proper for all men at all times and in all places to act and speak as befits a man of honour" (*Institutio oratoria* 11.1.14).

The fifth virtue of style is ornament or ornateness (*ornatus*). Ornament is the aesthetic principle of elocution (Plett, 1971) and as such is an important prerequisite for producing delight in the recipient (*delectare*). Ornament consists of tropes, rhetorical figures, sound, and rhythm. In classical antiquity, great weight was given to ornament, which was conceived of as much more than mere extraneous addition. As Quintilian notes in the introduction to his treatment of *ornatus,* correctness and clarity are not nearly sufficient to secure an orator's success (8.3.1). Hearers are more likely to be persuaded if the speaker's skillful use of ornament produces delight or even admiration (8.3.5). There is a certain tension between the demands of clarity and ornament. An orator should in his attempt to adorn his speech with ornaments not deviate too much from the virtue of clarity and fall victim to the vice of obscurity.

Tropes and figures or schemes. Classical rhetoric developed a system of describing and classifying categories of style, which, originally devised for persuasion in its primary sense, came to provide the basis for style in literature, too. An essential distinction of classical writing on *elocutio* is that between tropes and figures or schemes. To begin with the former, tropes are constituted by the figurative use of single words (or phrases). The basic principle of the formation of tropes is substitution: the proper term (*verbum proprium*) is replaced by a figurative term (*verbum improprium*). Tropes may be differentiated by the criterion of lesser or greater semantic distance between the proper and the figurative term. There is, in fact, a great variety of semantic relationships in tropes, which ranges from near-identity with the proper term (synonymy) to contrast (antonymy). If I say, "Achilles is a lion in battle," instead of "Achilles is an excellent warrior," there is a semantic of similarity between the proper and the figurative term, which is characteristic of the trope in question, metaphor. However, if I say with reference to a giant, "What a dwarf," there is an obvious semantic difference between the two terms, or, to put it in other words, there is an extreme form of dissimilarity, which characterizes the expression as irony. Tropes have traditionally also been classified with the help of the logical relations that may exist between the two terms involved in tropic substitution such as species versus genre, cause versus effect, or part versus whole. [*See* Figures of speech.]

Rhetoric defines the various types of substitution involved in the formation of tropes. In *periphrasis,* the proper term is replaced by a roundabout expression that usually stands in the service of amplification. Periphrasis has different functions ranging from palliation (euphemism) to definition. An example of periphrasis would be the substitution of expressions such as "to pass away," "to go to a better world," "to kick the bucket" for "to die." A special form of periphrasis with an ironic flavor is *litotēs,* in which something is affirmed by the negation of its contrary, such as, "He is a poet of no ordinary merit." Synecdoche is an expression in which the part stands for the whole, the special for the general, the singular for the plural, and vice versa. An example is, "Three families live under my roof." Kenneth

Burke (*A Grammar of Motives,* 1955, p. 508) compares the "representative" relation of proper term and figurative term in synecdochē with the philosophical relation of macrocosm and microcosm. A special form of synecdochē applied to names is *antonomasia;* for example, "the bard of Avon" (Shakespeare), "Denmark" (the king of Denmark), "a Casanova" (a womanizer).

A figure related to synecdochē is metonymy, which substitutes one word for another with which it stands in a close or contiguous relationship, such as cause-effect, author-work, container-content. Examples are "the press" (newspapers), "the stage" (theater), "the steel" (knife). While metonymy involves contiguity, that is, a real relation between two terms, metaphor expresses one thing in terms of another thing from a different context to which it bears resemblance, as for instance in "the winter of our discontent" (Shakespeare, *Richard III*). Like others, Quintilian believed metaphor to be a truncated simile—"he is a lion" would thus be an abbreviated version of "he is like a lion" (8.6.8)—but simile differs from metaphor, since it is not formed on the principle of substitution. Allegory, as a trope, differs from metaphor by its greater extent. Quintilian calls it "continued metaphor" (9.2.46). In allegory, an idea or complex of ideas is expressed in terms of an analogous image or complex of images (e.g., a sea voyage as an allegory of the vicissitudes of life). Tropes are not always clearly classifiable. The line "She's all States and, all Princes I," from John Donne's *The Sunne Rising,* contains two metaphors, which can be defined as hyperbolē, the substitution of the proper term by an exaggerated expression. With the extension of its metaphor, the line also has an affinity with allegory.

Classical rhetoric frequently makes an important distinction between tropes and figures or schemes. While tropes are formed by a process of substitution that has semantic consequences, figures or schemes do not usually involve a change of meaning. Following Quintilian (9.1.4), Plett (1977) defines the figure as "the smallest deviant language unit." It may be characterized as a change from the ordinary scheme, word order, or combination in a sequence of words (Fuhrmann), which does not affect the meaning of the individual words but may, however, have profound effects on the emotional power and argumentative thrust of the utterance. In a tradition that goes back to classical times, notably Quintilian (1.5.38–39), three categories of deviation are distinguished: addition (*adiectio*), subtraction (*detractio*), and transposition or permutation (*transmutatio*). (Quintilian adds a fourth category, substitution or *immutatio,* which refers to the formation of tropes.) In a modern survey of rhetorical figures, which is based on the classical tradition, Plett (1971) distinguishes between figures of position, figures of repetition, figures of quantity, and figures of appeal.

Figures of repetition are extremely frequent in rhetoric and occur in a great variety of forms, such as *anaphora, epistrophē, anadiplōsis.* An example illustrating the emotional potential of repetition is the famous blank-verse line from *King Lear:* "Never, never, never, never, never." Figures of partial repetition are *polyptōton* (repetition of the same word with different inflectional endings, as in *homo homini lupus*); *paronymy* (derivational change of the word repeated, as in "How should we term your *dealings* to be *just,* / If you *unjustly deal* with those that in your *justice* trust?" from Thomas Kyd's *The Spanish Tragedy*); and *paronomasia* (words similar in sound, but different in meaning and without etymological connection, such as "These times of *woe* afford no time to *woo*" from Shakespeare's *Romeo and Juliet*).

Central among the figures of subtraction is ellipsis, which leaves one or more several words in an utterance to be supplied by the reader, as in "What news?" Further types of subtraction are *aposiōpēsis,* the omission of the end of an utterance; *zeugma,* usually two or more semantically disparate nouns, governed by one verb, as in "Time and her aunt moved slowly" (Jane Austen, *Pride and Prejudice*); and *asyndeton,* the omission of connectives in coordinated words, phrases, or clauses ("He came, he saw, he conquered"). Figures of position are, for instance, inversion, change in the grammatically correct order of the parts of a sentence ("Of man's first disobedience . . . / Sing, Heavenly Muse," Milton, *Paradise Lost*), and *chiasmus,* repetition of words in reverse order ("Fair is foul, and foul is fair," Shakespeare, *Macbeth*). Central among the figures of appeal, which foreground the presence of a hearer or audience, is apostrophe. Other figures of appeal include *interrogatio, permissio,* and *exclamatio.*

The three styles (genera elocutionis, genera dicendi). Classical rhetoric distinguishes three genres (kinds, levels) of style: the low, or plain style (*genus humile*), the middle style (*genus medium*), and the high or grand style (*genus grande/grave/sublime*). This distinction was first made in the *Rhetorica ad Herennium*. The choice of these genres in an oration or a literary work depends mainly on: (1) the speaker's intention, the question whether he or she wants to teach, delight, or move (*docere/probare, delectare, movere*); and (2) the nature of the subject dealt with, which, as a consequence of decorum (*aptum*), demands a certain style. The low or plain style is suitable for instruction (teaching) and proof. It uses current speech and a conversational manner. It is largely devoid of tropes and makes spare use of rhetorical figures. Genres traditionally using the low style are, among others, letter, essay, diary, biography, comedy, satire, didactic literature, and scientific discourse. The middle style is more elevated and refined in diction than the plain style. It avoids colloquial elements. It is rich in ornament, that is, the use of tropes and rhetorical figures, and it may develop a florid manner. Figures of appeal are rare. The intended effect is delight (*delectare*). Genres using the middle style are, among others, pastoral poetry (Virgil's *Georgica*), Petrarch's sonnets, John Lyly's *Euphues,* Shakespeare's comedies. Epideictic rhetoric has a predilection for the middle style. The high style is the elevated, impressive style, which is appropriate to eminent and weighty subject matter. Its function is to move the audience (*movere*) "like to some great torrent that rolls down rocks" (Quintilian 12.10.61). It is well suited to the conclusion of a speech. Genres using the grand style are, above all, the classical epic and tragedy.

Literarization. A phenomenon to be noticed in the development of classical rhetoric, which reemerged in later periods, is the passage of rhetoric from its primary oral context to a secondary literary context. George Kennedy uses the Italian term *letteraturizzazione* ("literarization") to characterize the tendency of rhetoric to shift its focus from oral persuasion to literature. In Quintilian, this tendency can be noticed in the great number of examples of figures and tropes taken from literary texts.

The Middle Ages. All-encompassing and systematic treatments of rhetoric such as Quintilian's *Institutio oratoria* did not exist in the Middle Ages. Brian Vickers speaks of the "medieval fragmentation" of rhetoric. Following a tendency of late classical treatises, rhetoric was practically equated with style. As far as style or *elocutio* is concerned, the *Rhetorica ad Herennium* was persistently influential. *Elocutio* was also dealt with in treatises on grammar (*ars grammatica*) and poetry (*ars poetriae*). The two new branches of rhetorical theory that the Middle Ages produced, the art of letter writing (*ars dictaminis*) and the art of preaching (*ars praedicandi*), did not formulate any new principles of style. The ancient discussion concerning the distinction between figures and tropes was continued by writers such as Isidore of Seville (c.560–636). A medieval innovation is the elaboration of the analogy of painting and rhetoric. The categories of style are called "colors of rhetoric" (*colores rhetorici*) in several treatises. [*See* Color.] They embellish—give "color"—to ordinary language (Murphy, 1974, p. 189). Thus, the term *colors* is added to the traditional metaphors of decoration (*ornatus, exornatio*) and clothing (*vestitus*) by such writers as Onulf of Speyer in 1050, or Matthew of Vendôme in 1175. [*See* overview article on Medieval rhetoric.]

Another medieval phenomenon is the rise of a kind of poetics called *poetriae*, which was based on elements of the rhetorical tradition, among which style took a special place (e.g., Matthew of Vendôme, Geoffrey of Vinsauf, and John of Garland). In the course of the Middle Ages, particularly in the twelfth and thirteenth centuries, rhetoric became an important source for poets. [*See* Poetry.] A new distinction that was developed was the differentiation between two types of style: a more complex type, *ornatus difficilis* (consisting mainly of tropes), and a simpler type, *ornatus facilis* (consisting mainly of rhetorical figures), terms applied by John of Garland (Knape, p. 1040). Geoffrey of Vinsauf uses the terms *ornata difficultas* ("ornamented difficulty") and *ornata facilitas* ("ornamented facility"). These distinctions do not relate to the classical three-style theory, which John of Garland links to the *rota Virgilii* ("the wheel of Virgil"), an elaborate classification of Virgil's main works in terms of the three styles (Faral; Quadlbauer).

The Renaissance. The rediscovery of classical

authors in the Renaissance is a rediscovery of rhetoric.

The turn toward elocutio *in Renaissance rhetoric.* The Renaissance comes to pervade all areas of cultural production, so that the age has rightly been called a period of rhetorical culture (Plett, 1993). Just as classical authors like Quintilian made teaching of rhetoric part of a large-scale educational program, humanists like Erasmus (c.1466–1536) viewed rhetorical competence as a central faculty in the process of raising man to perfect humanity. There may be continuity between the Middle Ages and the Renaissance, so far as the focus on style is concerned, but the rise of rhetoric in the Renaissance is basically the product of a large-scale search for and assimilation and synthesis of classical treatises (Vickers, p. 255), as Murphy's short-title catalog (1981) and Plett's bibliography (1995) demonstrate. And right from the start of the period, it is not *inventio* or *dispositio* but *elocutio* that finds most attention, for instance in Lorenzo Valla's *Elegantiae linguae latinae* (1447) or Agostino Dati's *Elegantiolae* (1470), annotated collections of patterns and precepts of expression that were meant to present accomplished Latin to the reader and give him the grammatical and stylistic basis for perfecting his own Latin. Cicero (106–43 BCE) was admired as the unsurpassable master of style. The aim of this type of literature, in whose tradition Erasmus's *De copia verborum ac rerum* (1512) stands, was to enable its recipients to develop an abundant style (*ornatus et copiosus*). Conduct books like Baldassare Castiglione's *Il Cortegiano* (1528), which cultivate elegant conversation of the most refined manner as an end in itself, belong to the clearest manifestations of the Renaissance preoccupation with style. [*See* Copia; *and overview article and article on* Rhetoric in Renaissance language and literature *in entry on* Renaissance rhetoric.]

The turn toward *elocutio,* which is a significant development in Renaissance rhetoric, manifests itself in the specific nature that rhetoric books assumed in the age. A pioneering work in this context is Philipp Melanchthon's rhetoric (1521), which emphasized *elocutio* at the expense of *inventio* (Knape). His comprehensive and highly differentiated account of the figures of style served as a model for many rhetoric books of the time. The most complete English manual on the figures of style is Henry Peacham's *The Garden of Eloquence* (1577, 1593). Peacham gives much more emphasis to the figures than to the tropes. He accords great weight to the emotional and expressive potential of the figures and classifies them according to their emotional power (Vickers, pp. 326–327). In the introductory "Epistle" to the edition of 1577, he says,

> For by Fygures, as it were by sundry streames, that great & forcible floud of Eloquence, is most plentifully and pleasantly poured forth, . . . by the great might of Figures . . . the Oratour may lead his hearers which way he list, and draw them to what affection he will: he may make them to be angry, to be pleased, to laugh, to weepe, and lament: to loue, to abhorre, and loath. . . .

In his view that figures contribute essentially to the power of rhetoric to move men, he is representative of many Renaissance writers on rhetoric who believed that persuasion works by influencing the emotions (Plett, 1975; Vickers 1988). [*See* Pathos.]

The predilection for elocutio *in Ramism.* Another English rhetoric book that evinces the Renaissance predilection for *elocutio* is Abraham Fraunce's *The Arcadian Rhetorike* (1588), whose title refers to Sir Philip Sidney's novel *Arcadia* (1581), from which his examples for figures of style are taken. *The Arcadian Rhetorike* consists of two parts. The first and much longer part is devoted to the treatment of figures and matters of verse and rhyme. The second part, which is relatively short, deals with delivery (*actio, pronuntiatio*). This division into two parts characterizes the text as belonging to Ramism, a school of rhetoric that originated in the sixteenth century and exerted a powerful influence in the seventeenth century. It is named after its founder, Petrus Ramus (Pierre de la Ramée, 1515–1572), who, together with his friend and adherent Omer Talon (Audomarus Talaeus), taught rhetoric in Paris. Seeing that rhetoric and dialectic dealt for a large part with the same subjects, the Ramists, who were very systematic theorists, tried to redefine the spheres of the two disciplines. They argued that with its concern with invention (*inventio*) and arrangement (*dispositio*), rhetoric was repeating what was already, and better, done by the logicians. So they stripped rhetoric of invention and arrangement, reducing it to style and delivery, and assigned invention and arrangement to the domain of dialectic. With this truncation of rhetoric and the concomitant separation of style and thought, which was a radical breach with the classical tradition, particularly with Aristotle and Cicero, the Ramists codified a tendency that had asserted itself in the course of the sixteenth century, that is, the equation of rhetoric and style.

The rhetorical power of poetic style. The close relationship between rhetoric and literature to be noticed in Fraunce's rhetoric book, which takes examples for figures and tropes from Sidney's *Arcadia,* is a hallmark of the Renaissance. A poetic that can be used to illustrate the characteristic fusion of rhetoric and literature in the age is George Puttenham's *The Arte of English Poesie* (1589), a work that chiefly deals with *elocutio.* Puttenham expressly relates poetry and rhetoric. His claim that "the Poet is of all other the most auncient Orator" is related to the postulate that nothing is more appropriate to the poet than rhetorical ornament: "no doubt there is nothing so fitte for him, as to be furnished with all the figures that be *Rhetoricall,* and as such do most beautifie language with eloquence & sententiousnesse" (p. 196). The reason for his opinion that poets are "the best perswaders" is that poets have a better command of ornament than orators, and since it is ornament that has the greatest power over men's minds and emotions, poets are the better rhetoricians (Müller, 1994, p. 143). Like other theorists of his age, Puttenham argues that verse (meter) is better suited for ornament than prose and thus is more "eloquent and rhetoricall": "because it [speech by meter] is decked and set out with all maner of fresh colours, which maketh that it sooner inuegleth the iudgment of man, and carieth his opinion this way and that, whither soeuer the heart by impression of the eare shalbe most affectionatly bent and directed" (p. 8). Style is at the heart of this rhetorical understanding of poetry. To poetry is accorded greater efficacy than to rhetoric, because poetry is more qualified as a medium for figures and tropes than prose. This may be one reason why Shakespeare, who is as well steeped in Renaissance rhetoric as may be, makes the verse of Antony triumph over the prose of Brutus in the forum scene of *Julius Caesar.*

The social function of style in courtly culture. Another aspect of Puttenham's style-centered poetic must be mentioned. Puttenham's work belongs in the context of courtly culture. His concept of style has a socioaesthetic basis, as is shown in the use he makes of metaphors of clothing. He argues that just as courtly ladies gain acceptable beauty only by richly ornamented garments, so it is stylistic ornament that produces the aesthetic effect of poetry. Puttenham's poetic is designed as a "science" for the court which teaches the art of "beau semblant" (fair appearance), "the chiefe profession aswell of Courting as of poesie" (p. 158). The social foundation of Puttenham's theory of style (Javitch, 1972; Plett, 1982–1983; Whigham, 1984) manifests itself in Puttenham's attempt to find English equivalents for Greek and Latin terms for figures and tropes. In this context, the tropes appear more significant than the figures (which Peacham, and following him, Vickers privileges). Puttenham's terms are frequently *nomina agentis* (nouns of action), which refer to social roles. Thus, hyperbolē is named "the Ouer reacher" or "the loud lyer" (p. 191), metonymy "the misnamer" (p. 180), *tapinōsis* "the Abbaser." It is most significant, of course, that allegory, as the trope that Puttenham ranks most highly in his courtly poetic is given the name of "the Courtier or figure of faire semblant" (p. 299).

Style as the image of the soul versus style as dress. A new development in the history of the term *style* in the Renaissance is the evolution of the concept of style as an index of the soul, a concept that is more or less dissociated from rhetorical *elocutio.* It was in the Renaissance that the term *style* adopted its modern meaning (Müller, 1981). The English word *style* is derived from Latin *stilus,* which meant "pin," "stalk," "an instrument of writing." By metonymic transfer, the word for the instrument of writing came to denote the manner of writing and of speaking (*modus scribendi/dicendi*). Latin authors usually employed the term in a normative sense, relating it, for instance to the three genres of style (*genera dicendi*) or to dramatic genres such as comedy or tragedy, *tragicus stilus, comicus stilus.* There were only traces of an understanding of style as a sign of unmistakable individuality; for instance, in phrases such as *stilus Aesopi* or *stilus Homericus* (Müller, 1999). Style as an index to the personality of the writer was found especially in the genre of the familiar letter, which was defined as an image (or mirror) of the soul. Such uses of the term *style* prevented its total subordination under the rules of rhetoric and the principle of imitation. Thus, the poetic language developed by Guido Gunizelli, Guido Cavalcanti, and others in the thirteenth century from Provençal poetry was approvingly called "dolce stil nuovo." And despite their admiration and imitation of classical models, the Humanists endeavored to develop their own style. The formula "genius and style" (*ingenium et stilus,* "l'ingegno e lo stile") is quite frequent in Petrarch's Latin and Italian works. He believes that style is the adequate expression of genius.

There is thus an opposition in the Renaissance between the traditional elocutionary concept of style as dress of thought (*exornatio*), which is associated with rhetorical decorum, and the modern individualistic concept of style as the incarnation of thought and mind. These two positions may occur side by side in one and the same theoretician and it may be difficult to disentangle them, as is the case in George Puttenham's courtly poetic of 1589 (Müller, 1994), which defines style on the one hand as "exornation"—"ornament is but the good and rather bewtifull habite of language and stile" (p. 143)—and on the other as "the image of man [*mentis character*]" (p. 148). All in all, there seems to be more emphasis in Puttenham on style as dress than on style as man. The metaphor of clothing is in just too spectacular a way applied to the idea of style in *The Arte of English Poesie.* When Puttenham compares the richly ornamented robes of courtly ladies to the stylistic decoration of poetry with figures and tropes, the Renaissance image of Rhetoric (*Rhetorica*) as a magnificently-dressed lady—an image that identifies rhetoric with style—comes to mind. In this respect, Puttenham is a characteristically Renaissance author. On the whole, the individualistic concept of style is rare in the Renaissance, which was to a great extent an age of imitation. It emerges above all in the representatives of the "anti-Ciceronian" school. According to Erasmus's *Dialogus cui titulus Ciceronianus* (1528), the strict imitation of Cicero and the genuine expression of personality exclude each other. He argues that if you write like Cicero, you cannot express your-

self, and if you do not express yourself, your style will be a false image of your personality ("*Si te ipsum non exprimis, mendax speculum tua fuerit oratio,*" (*Opera omnia,* Amsterdam, 1971, 1.2, p. 649). In an even more radical way, Michel Montaigne in his *Essais* (1571–1585) and Robert Burton in his *Anatomy of Melancholy* (1621) argue that the imitation of Cicero and, for that matter, the observation of rhetorical rules of composition in general, prevent true self-expression. They advocate the principle *stylus virum arguit,* "Style argues the man" (Burton, *Anatomy,* London, 1881, p. 8).

The Plea for a Naked Style and the Restoration of the Concept of Style as Dress in the Seventeenth and Early Eighteenth Centuries. Toward the end of the sixteenth and in the seventeenth century, the concept of style as dress was rejected as a consequence of Puritanism, the New Science, the spirit of utilitarianism, and the philosophy of rationalism. The demand for a simple, clear, or "plain" style led to a significant redefinition of the concept (Adolph; Trimpi). To the image of style as the dress of thought, the image of the "nakedness" of style was opposed. The metaphor of nakedness appears, for instance, in "An Epistle to Master John Selden" by Ben Jonson (1572–1637), who exerted a profound influence on the movement toward the ideal of the plain style: "Lesse shall I for the Art of dressing care, / Truth, and the Graces best, when naked are." The same metaphor can be found in a Puritan statement on the style of sermons by William Pemble: "Truth is like our first Parents, most beautiful when naked, twas sinne couered them, tis ignorance hides this. Let perspicuitie and method bee euer the graces of speech" (*A Plea for Grace,* London, 1629, pp. 22–23). The Royal Society, which did not only endeavor to promote the development of science, but also advocated a reform of language and style, pleaded for "a close, naked, natural way of speaking" with "positive expressions," "clear senses," "native easiness," "bringing all things near the Mathematical plainness" (Thomas Sprat. *History of the Royal Society,* 1667, edited by J. I. Cope and H. W. Jones, p. 113. Saint Louis, 1958.). As a consequence of the rejection of the elocutionary concept of style with its emphasis on ornament, the visual image of rhetoric as a richly-dressed lady, of which the Renaissance was so fond, disappeared. [*See* Iconography.] An interesting variation of this image is, however, to be found in F. G. Klopstock's theory of style of the second half of the eighteenth century, which expresses the relation between language and thought with the help of the erotic image of a girl who steps out of the bath with her garment fitting closely to her body (Kretzenbacher, p. 24; Müller 1996, pp. 164–165). In this image, two traditional notions of the theory of style are connected: the idea of the perspicuity of style, which reveals truth "nakedly," and the idea of style as dress. [*See* Renaissance rhetoric, *article on* Rhetoric in the age of Reformation and Counter-Reformation.]

It is interesting that after the massive propagation of the plain and naked style in the seventeenth century, a moderate restoration of the elocutionary idea of style occurred in the age of neoclassicism in the first half of the eighteenth century. In this process, the metaphor of style as dress was revitalized. In *An Essay on Virgil's "Georgics"* (1697), Joseph Addison explicitly opposes the idea of dress to that of nakedness, when he says that the *Georgics* should "not to appear in the natural simplicity and nakedness of its subject, but in the pleasantest dress poetry can bestow on it." Two prominent instances among the ubiquitous definitions of style as dress are the definitions of Alexander Pope: "Expression is the dress of thought" (*Essay on Criticism*, 1/11, 1. 318), and Lord Chesterfield: "Style is the dress of thoughts" (Letter of 24 November 1749). The metaphor of dress is also of crucial importance in Pope's famous definition of wit, which can be understood as a neoclassical poetic in miniature (Müller, 1981, pp. 76–77): "True Wit is Nature to advantage dress'd; / What oft was thought, but ne'er so well express'd" (*Essay on Criticism*, 2. 297–298). It is important to realize that the notion of propriety, or, in other words, the rhetorical category of *aptum,* is inseparably connected with the neoclassical concept of style. This notion is central in Jonathan Swift's definition: "Proper words in proper Places, makes the true Definition of a Stile" (*Irish Tracts 1720–1723,* edited by H. Davis, p. 65. Oxford, 1963). Nor can propriety be dissociated from social decorum. In a letter to Pope of 9 September 1706, William Walsh relates his friend's application of the metaphor of dress to style to the proper dress of women: "As for what

you say of Expression: 'tis indeed the same thing to Wit, as Dress is to Beauty; I have seen many Women overdrest. . . ." Pope himself explicitly expresses the idea of the social decorum of different kinds of style with the aid of the metaphor of dress: "For diff'rent styles with diff'rent subjects sort, / As several garbs with country, town, and court" (*Essay on Criticism,* 2. 322–323). [*See* Eighteenth-century rhetoric.]

Style as the Dress of Thought versus Style as the Incarnation of Thought (from the Neoclassical to the Romantic Position). In the course of the eighteenth century, new ideas about style were developed in a critical discussion of the neoclassical concept of style as dress of thought. In his *Lectures on Rhetoric and Belles Lettres* (1783), Hugh Blair rejected the idea of style as outward ornament and the concomitant separation of words and ideas: "It is a very erroneous idea, which many have of the ornaments of Style, as if they were things detached from the subject, and that could be stuck to it, like lace upon a coat." In his own view, style arises from thought and feeling in a process of imaginative expression: "the real and proper ornaments of Style arise from Sentiment. They flow in the same stream with the current of thought. A writer of genius conceives his subject strongly; his imagination is filled and impressed with it; and pours itself forth in that Figurative Language which Imagination naturally speaks" (Vol. 1, 4th ed., p. 231. London, 1790). This citation evinces crucial elements of the new Romantic poetic such as the expressive and organic nature of literary expression, which M. H. Abrams set forth in his study *The Mirror and the Lamp* (1953), but it does not as yet dispense with the notion of ornaments. This, however, is what happens a little later in William Wordsworth's "Essays upon Epitaphs, II," which rejects the metaphor of dress and ornament in general: "If words be not . . . an incarnation of the thought but only a clothing for it, then surely will they prove an ill gift." What is decisive are expressions "which are not what the garb is to the body but what the body is to the soul, themselves a constituent part and power or function in the thought" (*The Prose Works of William Wordsworth,* ed. by W. J. B. Owen and J. Worthington Smyser, vol. 2, p. 84. Oxford, 1974). With this verdict, which is quoted and reinforced in Thomas De

Quincey's essay *Style* (1840), a position has been reached that was to be held all through the nineteenth century.

Buffon's Dictum "The Style Is the Man" and Its Reinterpretations and Variations in the Nineteenth Century. Theorists with an individualistic concept of style have since the beginning of the nineteenth century quoted the definition of Comte de Buffon in his *Discours sur le style,* which he delivered in 1753 to the Académie Française. Buffon argues that the content of a work—the wealth of knowledge, the uniqueness of the facts communicated, and the novelty of discoveries—does not guarantee man's immortality, but that style, as the true testimony of man's character, is the real mark of the greatness of a work: "Ces choses [contents] sont hors de l'homme, le style est l'homme même" (*Oeuvres philosophiques de Buffon,* edited by J. Piveteau, p. 503. Paris, 1954). This definition accords entirely with the culture of the Age of Reason. It is in its substance not different from Pope's and Chesterfield's neoclassical definitions of style, since like the latter it is based on the separation of content and form. Neither does it express a new idea, for it has many classical ancestors such as *Imago animi sermo est* or *ut vir, sic oratio.* But the conciseness and elegance of the formulation "le style est l'homme," with its identification of man and style, made it easily memorable, and, taken out of its context, it could be interpreted in a subjectivist way. Thus, it happened that since the Romantic period, Buffon's definition of "style as man" has been recognized as the definite formula for a nonrhetorical, individualistic concept of style, according to which style is the image of the mind and the sign of a writer's identity (Müller, 1981). [*See* Nineteenth-century rhetoric.]

Buffon's dictum has also been used as a starting point for definitions that regard style as a kind of physiognomy. Quoting Buffon, Jean Paul (1763–1825) calls style the "second flexible body of the mind" ("der zweite biegsame Leib des Geistes," Vorschule der Ästhetik, 1804). Sully Prudhomme (1839–1907) refers to style as "une seconde physionomie" of the author (*Testament poétique,* 1901). This idea found its most succinct formulation in Schopenhauer's definition: "Style is the physiognomy of the mind. It is more unmistakable than that of the body" ("Der Stil ist die Physiognomie des Geistes. Sie ist untrüglicher als die des Leibes." *Parerga und Paralipomena,* 1892 [first pub. 1851] 4–5.282).

Style as vision. The nineteenth century developed the individualistic concept of style further, and it did so significantly in the field of aesthetic philosophy. A climax in this development is represented by Walter Pater's essay *Style* (1888). Buffon's dictum "le style est l'homme même" is here given a new meaning within the movement of aestheticism. Style is, as frequently in the century, equated with the work of art, which is seen as an exteriorization of the interior—"translation from inward to outward"—in an objective, impersonal shape. Pater rejects "subjectivity" as "the mere caprice of the individual." He relates Buffon's concept of "the style is the man" to the idea of an objective work of art, embodying an individual way of seeing, a personal "sense of the world." The new and, in view of traditional definitions, paradoxical idea is that if style is the man, "in all the colour and intensity of a veritable apprehension, it will be in a real sense 'impersonal.'" By absorbing the idea of impersonality into the category of style, Pater's aesthetics belongs in the context of the Symbolist movement. A further significant element in Pater's theory, which is relevant to modernism, is his concept of style as a way of seeing. With this position, he stands in the tradition of Gustave Flaubert, who had defined style as "tout seule une manière absolue de voir les choses" (Letter to Louise Colet, 16 January 1852), and anticipates Marcel Proust, who defines style as "une qualité de la vision, la révélation de l'univers particulier" (R. Dreyfus. *Souvenirs sur M. Proust,* p. 292. Paris 1926). The literary theory of style here converges with tendencies that are characteristic of the theory and science of visual art in the late nineteenth and the early twentieth century.

Style as Nation; Stylistics. The emergence of the individualistic concept of style in Romanticism and Pre-Romanticism coincides with an understanding of "national style" as the expression of "national character" to be found, for instance, in Wilhelm von Humboldt's treatise *Über den Nationalcharakter der Sprachen* (1822). Edmond Arnould reformulates Buffon's dictum in this sense: "Le style, c'est la nation" (*Essais de théorie et d'histoire littéraires,* p. 39. Paris, 1858). The notion of style as the expression of the individual mind, and the analogous notion that a nation's character is reflected in its language, stand at the beginning of the linguistic discipline of stylistics. Scholars like Karl Vossler and Leo Spitzer, who employed stylistic analysis as a key to the intellectual physiognomy of a writer, applied an analogous procedure to national languages, which they treated as styles.

Style in the Theory of Art—Once More: Style as Vision. The term *style* has had a long history in the theory of the visual arts (Müller, 1999). It was first applied to pictorial art in a treatise by G. P. Lomazzo (1584), where it denotes, synonymously with *maniera,* "the master's personal hand." In the course of the history of art, the related term *manner* increasingly received the negative connotation of subjective arbitrariness, while style was, by H. Poussin and G. P. Bellori and others, used to refer to the artist's genius as the result of the intense study of nature and its ideal forms. Goethe's well-known distinction of *style* and *manner* in his essay *Einfache Nachahmung der Natur, Manier, Stil* (1789)— to which he adds the category of *imitation* ("Nachahmung")—is influenced by his Italian predecessors. Goethe defines imitation as the quiet copying of nature, manner as the subjective elaboration in the representation of nature, and style as the capacity for apprehending the ideal being of things in visual shapes. The normative and absolute quality assigned to the term *style* by Goethe and others was problematic in a time that had discovered individual consciousness and original genius. That is why, in his *Vorlesungen über die Ästhetik* (1835–1838), Hegel added the category of *originality* to the terms *manner* and *style.*

A pronounced tendency toward the normative, nonsubjective concept of style can be observed in one of the most influential theories of style in the history of art criticism that arose at the beginning of the twentieth century, Heinrich Wölfflin's typology of the autonomous forms of seeing ("Sehformen"), published in *Kunstgeschichtliche Grundbegriffe* (1915). This work, which was antagonistic to individualized aesthetic positions, find the origin of style in the individual's power of expression. According to Wölfflin, style is determined by the way of seeing, "the relation of the eye to the world." In a comparative analysis of Renaissance and Baroque art, he works out basic categories such as the opposition of the linear and the painterly, of flatness and depth, of close and open form, and of heterogeneity and homogeneity. Wölfflin's theory was criticized by some art historians, but it had a deep influence, particularly on literary historians such as Oskar Walzel and Fritz Strich, who believed they had found in his categories a key to the formal and aesthetic analysis of literary works. There is an interesting parallel between the redefinition of style as vision in the period of aestheticism (Pater) and Wöfflin's theory of forms of seeing. [*See* Art.]

Style and Philosophy (The Style of Thinking, "Denkstil")—The Style of Scientific Discourse. It has been shown that during its history the term *style* had the tendency to transcend its original rhetorical and literary fields of reference and to pass into nonrhetorical and non-literary contexts. Thus, style has become a central category in aesthetics and in the theory of visual art. Another apparently nonrhetorical concept of style is the so-called style of thinking ("Denkstil"), that is, the style of philosophers, which is seen to be intimately connected with their argument, a phenomenon that has increasingly found attention since the 1940s. Gilbert Ryle (1900–1976), for instance, argues that the real achievement of Bertrand Russell was the introduction of an innovative "style of thinking" as a heuristic instrument ("Bertrand Russell," 1972) One of Ryle's main works, *The Concept of Mind* (1949), has itself been made the object of a rhetorical-stylistic analysis (Oesterreich), which works out the philosopher's argumentative mode of proceeding (modus operandi). Here, rhetoric is recognised as a component of philosophical argument.

In German stylistics, *Denkstil* is a well-established term. A related term in linguistically-oriented narratology is *mind-style,* that is, the distinctive literary rendering of individual consciousness, notably in the form of "stream-of-consciousness" (Fowler, 1977; Leech and Short). The term *Denkstil* ("style of thinking") was coined by German philosophers (Müller, 1999). Sources for the term are the early-twentieth-century *Lebensphilosophie* ("philosophy of life") and Neo-Kantian philosophy. Ferdinand Fellmann, Manfred Frank, and Lambert Wiesing, are philosophers who claim that style is a constitutive element of thinking. Philosophical debate appears in this context almost as a kind of a competition of styles. Just as in philosophy style and rhetoric have assumed a new importance, in the last decades of the twentieth century the crucial role of style was discussed with reference to other forms of scientific and scholarly discourse. In postmodern theory, the boundary between literary and nonliterary discourse has largely been broken down. In view of the stylistic or rhetorical turn in many areas of nonliterary discourse, the three traditional taboos for scientific discourse—the prohibition of the writer's reference to himself (the "I"-taboo), the prohibition of narrative, and the prohibition of metaphor (Kretzenbacher)—seem almost outdated. [*See* Philosophy, *article on* Rhetoric and philosophy.]

A Note on the Concept of Style in Stylistics. In linguistics, the term *style* is notoriously ambiguous. It is, in Enkvist's words, a "notational term" (p. 17) that is, a term that has always to be defined anew, depending on what the respective methods and aims of stylistic analysis are (Esser, 1993, 1.6.168). One common feature of most definitions is, perhaps, that style is constituted by a distinctive or characteristic set of linguistic features (Wales, pp. 435–437), whether of author, text, genre, period, register, and others. To be more precise, style is, in whatever context, a distinctive use of language, a specific selection and combination of "language units" (Plett, 1979). Well-known definitions such as style as choice or style as deviation (Esser, p. 1) can easily be related to classical rhetorical principles.

Stylistic analysis in the first decades of the twentieth century tended to proceed from Buffon's idea of style as man, isolating and interpreting distinctive linguistic features that reveal the author's intellectual physiognomy (Vossler; Spitzer). This method was further developed by Richard Ohmann who defines style as "epistemic choice" and acknowledges a rhetorical or persuasive component in style, and Louis Milic, who speaks of "stylistic options" (style as the man) and "rhetorical choices" (style as persuasion). A recent application of Buffon's dictum to the representation of character in fiction is *Mentalstilistik*. The definition "style is the man" is here changed to "style is the figure" (Nischik). A concept athwart all these positions is Roland Barthes's idea of writing degree zero (*"Le degré zéro" de l'ecriture*, 1953), a neutral or indifferent writing that is characterized by the absence of style. In texts by André Gide and Albert Camus, he finds a style that is paradoxically defined as being no style. The shift to the study of the literary text as an autonomous aesthetic system of multiple semantic relationships, which is evinced in the period of the so-called New Criticism, led to yet another variation of Buffon's dictum, "Style is the work" (A. Müller, 1981, pp. 192–195). A more recent variation is "the style as text" (Schaefer). While older stylistic criticism tended to establish shortcuts between intuitively selected phonetic, morphological, lexical, and syntactic features and the text's meaning, advanced recent work on style acknowledges the importance of pragmatic and context-dependent aspects of text structure (Mair). In the course of this development, the term *style* tends to be replaced by *discourse*. The elocutionary aspect of style has been preserved in a reduced form in works such as Kate Wales's *Dictionary of Stylistics* (1989). Even an introduction like Dennis Freeborn's *Style: Text Analysis and Linguistic Criticism* (1996) devotes a fairly extensive section to "rhetorical style" and "tropes and figures." Tropes and figures have by no means disappeared from stylistics and textual criticism. There is even a tendency to assign literary and cultural significance to individual tropes, for instance, in David Lodge's theory of literary style, which uses metaphor and metonymy as central categories in an attempt to establish a new typology of modern literature, or in Hayden White's analysis of the style of history writing (*Metahistory*, 1973), which links the main forms of European historiography to four tropes (metaphor, metonymy, synecdochē, and irony).

BIBLIOGRAPHY

Adolph, Robert. *The Rise of Modern Prose Style.* Cambridge, Mass., 1968.

Barthes, Roland. *Le degré zéro de l'écriture.* Paris, 1964. First ed. 1953.

Bolgar, R. R. *The Classical Heritage and Its Beneficiaries.* Cambridge, U.K., 1954.

Chatman, Seymour, ed. *Literary Style: A Symposium.* London, 1971.

Enkvist, Nils Erik. *Linguistic Stylistics.* The Hague, 1973.

Esser, Jürgen. *English Linguistic Stylistics.* Tübingen, 1993.

Faral, Edmond. *Les Arts poétiques du XIIᵉ et du XIIIᵉ siècle.* Paris, 1923; reprint, Paris, 1971.

Fowler, Roger. *Linguistics and the Novel.* London 1977.

Fowler, Roger, ed. *Style and Structure in Literature: Essays in the New Stylistics.* London, 1975.

Freeborn, Dennis. *Style: Text Analysis and Linguistic Criticism.* London, 1996.

Freeman, Donald C., ed. *Linguistics and Literary Style.* New York, 1970.

Freeman, Donald C., ed. *Essays in Modern Stylistics.* London, 1981.

Fuhrmann, Manfred. *Die antike Rhetorik.* Munich, 1984.

Hough, Graham. *Style and Stylistics.* London, 1969.

Javitch, Daniel. "Poetry and Court Conduct: Puttenham's *Arte of English Poesie* in the Light of Castiglione's *Cortegiano.*" *Modern Language Notes* 87 (1972), pp. 865–882.

Jones, Richard Foster. *The Seventeenth Century: Studies in the History of English Thought and Literature from Bacon to Pope.* Stanford, Calif., 1951.

Kennedy, George A. *Classical Rhetoric and Its Christian and Secular Tradition from Ancient to Modern Times.* Chapel Hill, N.C. 1980.

Knape, Joachim. "Elocutio." In *Historisches Wörterbuch der Rhetorik,* vol. 2, pp. 1022–1083. Tübingen, 1994.

Kretzenbacher, Heinz L. "Wie durchsichtig ist die Sprache der Wissenschaften?" In *Linguistik der Wissenschaftssprache,* edited by H. L. Kretzenbacher and H. Weinrich, pp. 15–39. Berlin, 1995.

Lanham, Richard A. *A Handlist of Rhetorical Terms: A Guide for Students of English Literature.* Berkeley, 1991.

Lausberg, Heinrich. *Handbuch der literarischen Rhetorik.* Munich, 1960.

Leech, Geoffrey N., and Michael H. Short. *Style in Fiction.* London, 1981.

Leeman, A. D. *Orationis Ratio: The Stylistic Theory and Practice of the Roman Orators, Historians, and Philosophers.* Amsterdam, 1986.

Lodge, David. *The Modes of Modern Writing: Metaphor, Metonymy, and the Typology of Modern Literature.* London, 1977.

Mair, Christian. "Dramatic Dialogue between Linguists and Literary Scholars." *Dialogische Strukturen. Dialogic Structures. Festschrift für Willi Erzgräber,* edited by Thomas Kühn and Ursula Schaefer, pp. 290–307. Tübingen, 1996.

Milic, Louis T. *A Quantitative Approach to the Style of Jonathan Swift.* The Hague, 1967.

Milic, Louis T. "Rhetorical Choice and Stylistic Option: The Conscious and Unconscious Poles." In *Literary Style,* edited by Seymour Chatman, pp. 77–88. The Hague, 1971.

Müller, Arnulf. *Stil: Studien zur Begriffsgeschichte im romanisch-deutschen Sprachraum.* Diss. Erlangen, 1981.

Müller, Wolfgang G. *Topik des Stilbegriffs. Zur Geschichte des Stilverständnisses von der Antike bis zur Gegenwart.* Darmstadt, 1981 [A revised edition will appear in 2001].

Müller, Wolfgang G. "*Ars Rhetorica* und *Ars Poetica.* Zum Verhältnis von Rhetorik und Literatur in der englischen Renaissance." *Renaissance-Rhetorik. Renaissance Rhetoric,* edited by Heinrich F. Plett, pp. 225–243. Berlin, 1993.

Müller, Wolfgang G. "Das Problem des Stils in der Poetik der Renaissance." *Renaissance-Poetik. Renaissance Poetics,* edited by Heinrich F. Plett, pp. 133–146. Berlin, 1994.

Müller, Wolfgang G. "Die traditionelle Rhetorik und einige Stilkonzepte des 20. Jahrhunderts." *Die Aktualität der Rhetorik,* edited by Heinrich F. Plett, pp. 160–175. Munich, 1996.

Müller, Wolfgang G. "Stil." *Historisches Wörterbuch der Philosophie.* X, pp. 150–159. Basel 1999.

Murphy, James J. *Rhetoric in the Middle Ages.* Berkeley, 1974.

Murphy, James J. *Renaissance Rhetoric. A Short-Title Catalogue of Works on Rhetorical Theory from the Beginning of Printing to A.D. 1700.* New York, 1981.

Nischik, Reingard M. *Mentalstilistik: Ein Beitrag zur Stiltheorie und Narrativik, dargestellt am Erzählwerk Margaret Atwoods.* Tübingen, 1991.

Oesterreich, Peter L. *Person und Handlungsstil: Eine rhetorische Metakritik zu Gilbert Ryles "The Concept of Mind."* Essen, 1987.

Ohmann, Richard. 1962. *Shaw: The Style and the Man.* Middletown, 1962.

Plett, Heinrich F. *Einführung in die rhetorische Textanalyse.* Hamburg, 1971.

Plett, Heinrich F. *Rhetorik der Affekte: Englische Wirkungsästhetik im Zeitalter der Renaissance.* Tübingen, 1975.

Plett, Heinrich F. "Die Rhetorik der Figuren. Zur Systematik, Pragmatik und Ästhetik der Elocutio." *Rhetorik. Kritische Positionen zum Stand der Forschung,* edited by Heinrich F. Plett, pp. 125–165. Munich, 1977.

Plett, Heinrich F. "Concepts of Style: A Classification and a Critical Approach." *Language and Style* 12 (1979), pp. 268–281.

Plett, Heinrich F. "Aesthetic Constituents in the Courtly Culture of Renaissance England." *New Literary History* 14 (1982–1983), pp. 597–621.

Plett, Heinrich F., ed. *Renaissance-Rhetorik. Renaissance Rhetoric.* Berlin, 1993.

Plett, Heinrich F. *English Renaissance Rhetoric and Poetics: A Systematic Bibliography of Primary and Secondary Sources.* Leiden, 1995.

Quadlbauer, Franz. *Die antike Theorie der genera dicendi im lateinischen Mittelalter.* Vienna, 1962.

Saisselin, Rémy G. "Buffon, Style, and Gentleman." *The*

Journal of Aesthetics and Art Criticism 16 (1958), pp. 357–361.

Schaefer, Ursula. "Der Stil als Text: Über Ernest Hemingway's Erzählung 'Cat in the Rain'." *Stilfragen,* edited by Willi Erzgräber and Hans-Martin Gauger. [ScriptOralia 38] Tübingen, 1991, pp. 163–181.

Sonnino, Lee A. *A Handbook to Sixteenth-Century Rhetoric.* London, 1968.

Trimpi, Wesley. *Ben Jonson's Poems: A Study of the Plain Style.* Stanford, 1962.

Ullmann, Stephen. "Style and Personality." *A Review of English Literature* 6.2 (1965), pp. 21–31.

Vickers, Brian. *In Defence of Rhetoric.* Oxford, 1988.

Wales, Katie. *A Dictionary of Stylistics.* London, 1989.

Whigham, Frank. *Ambition and Privilege: The Social Tropes of Elizabethan Courtesy Theory.* Berkeley, 1984.
— WOLFGANG G. MÜLLER

SUASORIA. *See* Controversia and suasoria.

SUBLIME, THE. A rhetorical form once thought dead by the end of the nineteenth century, the sublime received renewed attention in the twentieth, much of which focused upon the "postmodern sublime." The phrase evokes such topics as the nonreferentiality of language, the construction of the subject, and the subversion of hegemonic authority. As Jean-François Lyotard maintained in *The Postmodern Condition: A Report on Knowledge* (Minneapolis, 1984), the sublime may serve as a key trope for our times by providing a meeting place for the professional specialties of semiotics, psychology, and politics. This essay explores the origins of the "sublime," some of its elusive characteristics, and some of its implications for contemporary rhetoric.

In general, the sublime may be described as grandiose rhetoric that produces uniquely powerful individual, social, and political effects. It contains two structural components, the linguistic and the affective. The language of the sublime employs such devices as elaborate figures, expansive structures, unconventional arrangements, and flamboyant styles. The affects of sublimity include the intense sensation, subjective awareness, and heightened emotion that result from its forceful impact upon listeners and readers. Over time, theorists have varied their emphasis upon either or both of these two components.

The precise definition of the sublime, however, has eluded finality. It has included nonlinguistic elements, such as the beauty or terror of nature; profound simplicity, as in the first words of *Genesis* in the Hebrew Torah; and persuasive motives, as in the description of heroic deeds to encourage imitation by powerful political figures. Indeed, the unknown author (c.213–273 CE) to whom ancient commentators ascribed the name of *Cassius Longinus,* characterized the sublime as that which transports listeners outside of themselves, a formulation that barely qualifies as a definition at all. One might say that the sublime is an indeterminate form of rhetoric. It is not quite capable of encompassing the phenomenon or effect it is to communicate, yet it connotes states of consciousness far beyond quotidian experience.

The history of the sublime is similarly intermittent and fragmented. After a brief period of interest in the classical era, sublimity was ignored until its revival in the seventeenth century. Subsequently, the conception of the sublime departed from a neoclassical framework and adopted a romanticism which fueled revolutionary economic and political change. In the eighteenth and nineteenth centuries, the sublime was associated with the grandiosity of great oratory and the expansiveness of the natural environment. Although the influence of the concept waned by the 1900s, its development from pragmatics to aesthetics and, recently, to politics has established a contemporary alternative to the dominant ancient inheritance.

The sublime tradition began with "Longinus's" fragmentary treatise, *Peri Hypsos* (*On the Sublime*). Written approximately one century into the common era, it deviated from the dominant Ciceronian and Greek traditions in several ways. [*See* Classical rhetoric.] Over and against the reason-based and inventional approaches of Aristotle (384–322 BCE) and Cicero (106–43 BCE), the sublime is preoccupied with style and emotion. [*See* Pathos; *and* Style.] "Longinus's" treatment also differs by positioning its readership as critics, rather than as producers, of public speeches and literature. Finally, "Longinus" presents a quite different understanding of rhetorical amplification. In contrast to the measuring of degree, of "more and less," we find here an open appeal to the power of imagination and the grandeur of thought. [*See* Amplification; *and* Copia.]

For "Longinus," the sublime existed primarily in the excellence of a speaker's presentation, and secondarily in the extreme dimensions of the audience's response. Yet, like Dionysius of Halicarnassus (first century BCE) and Marcus Fabius Quintilian (c.35–c.100 CE), both of whom linked the grand style of speaking with high emotion, "Longinus" dwelled upon the psychological effect of sublimity (*On the Sublime,* London, 1927): "For the true sublime, by some virtue of its nature, elevates us: uplifted with a sense of proud possession, we are filled with joyful pride, as if we had ourselves produced the very thing we heard" (p. 139).

"Longinus" likened the sublime to a force of nature, sweeping all before it like a fire storm. Yet the author neatly sidestepped the ancient controversy that there is an art that may teach the sublime. Nature, the author held, does not "act" randomly, but according to principles that may be understood. Likewise, passions and impulses need a proper understanding and shrewd guidance. The body of this document examines several sources of sublimity, as well as recurring defects that prevent its accomplishment. Interestingly, the sources of sublimity as well as the defects all seem to depend upon command of language.

Of the five sources of the sublime, "Longinus" listed the first as most important, great and noble conceptions, or "grandeur of thought." These were followed by a vigorous and spirited treatment of the passions, artful use of stylistic figures, an elevated, or dignified tone of expression, and majesty or elevation in the structure and arrangement of speech or literature. [*See* Arrangement, *article on* Traditional arrangement.] "Longinus" actually spurned Aristotle's cathartic emotions of pity and fear, deeming these to be of a lower order and therefore less affecting. The improprieties of style included bombast or *bathos,* puerility, false sentiment, and frigidity. In contrast to Aristotle's stylistic advice (to be clear, proportional, and moderate), "Longinus" seemed to endorse a sense of artful ambiguity commensurate with the grandeur of thought. [*See* Ambiguity.]

"Longinus's" treatise was never famous in its time, perhaps because of these very extravagancies of language, and was forgotten until the beginning of the modern era. The popularization of "Longinus's" concept resulted from the translation of his treatise into French by Nicolas Boileau-Despréaux (1636–1711) and its subsequent dissemination into Germany and England. European theorists of the eighteenth century associated rhetoric not so much with public speaking as with belles lettres and imaginative literature. [*See* Eighteenth-century rhetoric.] They identified the sublime and its companion concepts, the beautiful and the picturesque, with the aesthetic form of a sculpture, painting, or literary description, yet they maintained an emphasis upon the relationship between the object and the receiver's response. Archibald Alison (1757–1839) in *Essays on the Nature and Principles of Taste* (Edinburgh, 1790), and Richard Payne Knight (1750–1824) in *An Analytical Inquiry into the Principles of Taste* (London, 1805), derived their theories of the sublime and picturesque from the associationist principles of psychology popular at the time. In his *Elements of Criticism* (Edinburgh, 1762), Henry Home, Lord Kames (1696–1782) characterized aesthetic taste by applying the principles of the sublime and the beautiful to architectural design and landscape gardening.

In a challenge to the neoclassical principles of the age, Edmund Burke (1729–1797) in *A Philosophical Enquiry Into the Origin of Our Ideas of the Sublime and Beautiful* (London, 1757), claimed that the sublime was not merely an artificial effect but a physiological, and therefore natural, psychological process. For example, he identified the aesthetic concept of beauty with the harmonious, balanced, and tranquil qualities associated with the feminine principle. Sublimity, in contrast, was rough, disproportionate, and therefore masculine. For Burke, the fear and terror resulting from a direct exposure to such overpowering instruments of nature as storms and earthquakes qualified as a sublime response. His contemporaries took issue with this notion, not because of its gendered polarities, but because their formalist aesthetics interposed a safe distance between the observer and the source. Nevertheless, Burke's assertions announced a direct, visceral take on sublimity presaging the Romantic period.

When Immanuel Kant (1724–1804) discussed aesthetics in *The Critique of Judgement* (1790), he completed the transition between the neoclassical and the Romantic sublime. Sublimity no longer rested in the aesthetic object but in the faculties of human consciousness, specifically at the juncture between the transcendental (pure reason) and the metaphysical (practical reason). For Kant, transcendence was manifested by what he termed the "mathematical" sublime. In any number approaching infinity, the accretion of units became too great for the human mind to apprehend; at that point, comprehension of the whole failed, and the mind realized the limits of its own capacities. This version of sublimity was complex and exceedingly abstract, unlike the metaphysical, or "dynamical" sublime. Stated succinctly, the dynamical sublime evoked the exultation of contemplating "the starry sky above and the moral law within." Here, Kant associated practical reason not with persuasion but with aesthetics, the moral law being not a compulsion but a condition of existence.

Kant's organizing of the sublime into a system, even while emphasizing a moral component, produced a widespread reaction throughout the late eighteenth and nineteenth centuries. The Romantic expressionism espoused by Friedrich von Schiller (1759–1805), the optimistic individualism encouraged by Ralph Waldo Emerson (1803–1882), and the wilderness grandeur celebrated by John Ruskin (1819–1900) delineated the Romantic sublime and shaped the national cultures of Western Europe and the United States. By the middle of the nineteenth century the sublime came to designate any event of great emotional or spiritual impact. In *Modern Painters* (London, 1903), Ruskin pronounced that "Anything which elevates the mind is sublime, and elevation of mind is produced by contemplation of greatness of any kind; but chiefly, of course, by the greatness of the noblest things. Sublimity is, therefore, only another word for the effect of greatness upon the feelings" (p. 128).

Following Ruskin, the sublime became generalized and infused with moral and spiritual implications as it was put to the task of characterizing the American experience. Whether expressed in the political discourse of the Golden Age of oratory or in the artistic representations of Western scenery, the sublime evoked patriotic emotional responses and influenced the perception of the American character. Sublimity became the discursive vehicle both for self-aggrandizing nationalism and for environmental consciousness. For example, in the early 1800s, Daniel Webster represented a peculiarly American form of bombastic grandeur in public oratory, while later in the century John Muir generated public support for preserving sublime wilderness in the form of national parks. Applied to such a wide domain of reference, sublimity became increasingly formulaic, and certain terms (*elevation, awe, grandeur, wonder, fear,* and *amazement*) were repeated to the point of cliché. The result was the almost universal popularity of the concept throughout the nineteenth century, as well as its commercial exploitation and ultimate decline as an aesthetic and rhetorical principle.

Given such an atmosphere, it is not surprising that Samuel H. Monk's book *The Sublime: A Study of Critical Theories in Eighteenth-Century England* (New York, 1935) was one of the few examinations of the concept to emerge in the first half of the twentieth century. Written just before the formative period of New Critical literary theory (1940–1965), it privileged the complex and intimate relationship between a unique text and the experience of the individual reader. Consequently it rejected late neoclassical and Romantic literature for their repetitive stylistics and extravagant excesses, both emotional and political. But by purging both its conventionalized structure and its power to elicit strong affect, Monk rarified the sublime far beyond any possible utility. Much like Kant, he characterized literature as eliciting the higher emotions while itself remaining perfect and detached.

Throughout the nineteenth and early twentieth century, theories of the sublime like those of Monk increasingly devalued and finally ignored the rhetorical, affective, and pragmatic in favor of the aesthetic, contemplative, and spiritual. But in practice, the sublime demonstrated its effectiveness through the discourse of mass-media advertising, mass rallies, propaganda, and film. The grand sublimities of the nineteenth-century Romanticists became the stock-in-trade of such twentieth-century cultural hegemonists as Joseph Goebbels (1897–1945), Benito Mussolini (1883–1945), and Mao Zedong (1893–1976). Their transparent demonstrations of the power of the sublime decimated its scholarly reputation, which was submerged until the later twentieth century. At that time, a new version of the tradition developed roughly at the same time as the rebirth of rhetorical studies and the advent of postmodernism.

Of all the postmodernists, Paul de Man consistently pursued both rhetoric and sublimity in such works as *Allegories of Reading: Figural Language in Rousseau, Nietzsche, Rilke and Proust* (New Haven, 1979), *Blindness and Insight: Essays in the Rhetoric of Contemporary Criticism* (Minneapolis, 1983), and *The Resistance to Theory* (Minneapolis, 1986). De Man repositioned the term *rhetoric* to challenge the dual bases of the classical tradition—referential realism and suasory impact—and to align with contemporary views of discourse as decentered, deconstructive, and endlessly ungrounded. Viewing the sublime as a linguistic trope, he recognized how language both figures and performs indeterminacy of meaning. Yet, in the course of his efforts to demystify the sublime, de Man sacrificed its force and power, leaving no space for an effective political praxis.

In contrast, Harold Bloom in The *Anxiety of Influence: A Theory of Poetry* (New York, 1973), and his student Paul Weiskel in *The Romantic Sublime: Studies in the Structure and Psychology of Transcendence* (Baltimore, 1976), delved into the construction of individual subjectivity through psychoanalytic method. For classic Freudianism, the response to the sublime was a neurotic defense against the anxiety produced by unconscious relations within the nuclear family, particularly in its authoritarian, capitalist expression. Yet Bloom and Weiskel also included the anxiety generated by such authorities as literary antecedents, symbolic language, and nature itself as a vision of the cosmic void. In the case of literary rhetoric, the excessive fear of powerful forces was transformed into identification, if not fusion, with those forces. Subjects moved from being influenced or coerced by power to becoming empowered in their own right.

Empowerment of the subject, however, did not automatically entail political and social empowerment. Jean-François Lyotard, Neil Hertz, and Hayden White directly addressed the potential for political action in the postmortem sublime. Lyotard in *The Postmodern Condition* (Minneapolis,

1984), implied that the sublime was a revolutionary aesthetic of the avant-garde that rejected the terror of totality and celebrated the play of diversity. Neil Hertz, in *The End of the Line* (New York, 1985), recognized in the sublime a rhetoric of confrontation in the political realm. And Hayden White, in the essay, "The Politics of Historical Interpretation: Discipline and De-Sublimation," in *The Content of the Form* (Baltimore, 1987), related the sublime to the kind of politicized historical writing that, horrible as it might be, recognized fascism's psychological appeal.

Within these new postmodern rhetorics, the practical power of the sublime, recognized as early as "Longinus's" treatise on public speaking, gains new relevance. In such recent versions as the feminine sublime, the technological sublime, and the "democratic" sublime, sublimity continues to develop as an alternative to the ongoing rhetorical tradition. Once again, the historical tradition of the sublime, fragmented, intermittent, and self-referential, takes on the characteristics of its own master trope.

[*See also* Decorum; *and* Eloquence.]

BIBLIOGRAPHY

Boileau-Despréaux, Nicolas. *Traité du Sublime, ou du Merveilleux dans le Discours, Traduit du Grec de Longin.* In *Oeuvres complètes.* Introduction by Antoine Adam; edited and annotated by Françoise Escal. Paris, 1966. Boileau-Despréaux's translation of "Longinus's" treatise was first published in 1674.

Crowther, Paul. *The Kantian Sublime: From Morality to Art.* Oxford, 1989. A refined, detailed, and exhaustive explication in the context of the *Critique of Judgment.*

Emerson, Ralph Waldo. *Nature.* Introduction by Jaroslav Pelikan. Boston, 1985. A facsimile of the first edition published in 1836.

Freeman, Barbara Claire. *The Feminine Sublime: Gender and Excess in Women's Fiction.* Berkeley, 1995. Feminist scholars attempting to reverse or subvert Burke's pronouncements on the gender of sublimity.

"Longinus." *Aristotle The Poetics. "Longinus" On the Sublime. Demetrius On Style.* Translated by W. Hamilton Fyfe and W. Rhys Roberts. London, 1927. A frequently-used and still serviceable translation.

Longinus. *On the Sublime.* Translated with commentary by James A. Arieti and John M. Crossett. New York, 1985. This most recent and perhaps most lively translation contains extensive annotations.

McDaniel, James P. "Fantasm: The Triumph of Form (An Essay on the Democratic Sublime)." *Quarterly Journal of Speech* 86.1 (2000), pp. 48–66.

McKinsey, Elizabeth R. *Niagra Falls: Icon of the American Sublime.* New York, 1985. An important, controversial reading of the rise and fall of the American sublime in literature and visual arts.

Muir, John. *The Mountains of California.* New York, 1894. Muir's most powerfully written book defined the natural sublime for the American public in the last part of the nineteenth century.

Nye, David E. *The American Technological Sublime.* Cambridge, Mass., 1994. The sublime applied not only to oratory and nature but also to industrial capitalism.

Ruskin, John. *Modern Painters,* parts 1 and 2. In *The Works of John Ruskin.* Edited by E. T. Cook and Alexander Wedderburn, vol. 3. London, 1903. The first part of *Modern Painters* was originally published anonymously in 1843, with parts 2, 3, and 4 following at intervals. *Modern Painters* was published in the United States in 1856.

Schiller, Friedrich von. *Naïve and Sentimental Poetry and On the Sublime.* Translated with introduction and notes by Julius A. Elias. New York, 1966. The original publication date for *Über das Erhabene* is unknown. Estimates range from 1793 to 1801.

—CHRISTINE L. ORAVEC

SYLLĒPSIS (Lat. *conceptio*), called by Puttenham (*The Arte of English Poesie,* 1589, p. 165) "the Double supplie," a figure omitting words while making others serve several purposes. There is some confusion in rhetorical treatises as to whether *syllēpsis* or *zeugma* is the generic term for such elliptical constructions. Syllēpsis applies, however, to cases of syntactic incongruity for the sake of parallelism. "My love is like to ice, and I to fire" (Spenser, *Amoretti,* 1595, no. 30). Syllēpsis can create comic effects if the omission is on the semantic level. Thus, Sterne shows us the Shandy brothers "in deep roads and dissertations alternately upon the advantage of learning and arms" (*Tristram Shandy,* 1760–1767, 4.25).

[*See also* Figures of speech; *and* Zeugma.]

—HEINER PETERS

SYLLOGISM. The syllogism is the basic structure of reasoning in formal logic. Typically, it is a series of three statements—two premises and a conclusion. In a valid syllogism, the premises entail the conclusion: if the premises are true, the conclusion must be true. Whether the premises really are true cannot be determined from the structure itself, but *if* the premises are true it would be logically impossible for the conclusion to be false. A corollary is that the conclusion contains no new information beyond what is in the premises. It may rearrange the information or it may make explicit what had been only implicit, but it adds nothing new.

The syllogism takes three general forms: categorical, conditional (or hypothetical), and disjunctive (or alternative). Categorical syllogisms, the best known, contain statements that relate categories to other categories. The relationships can be universal or partial and they can be inclusive or exclusive. The four possible types of categorical statements are identified with the first four vowels:

A-statement: All dogs are mammals.
E-statement: No dogs are mammals.
I-statement: Some dogs are mammals.
O-statement: Some dogs are not mammals.

The A- and E-statements are universal; the I- and O-statements are partial. The A- and I-statements are positive (they include one category within another) whereas the E- and O-statements are negative (they exclude one category from another). The meaning of "some" in the I- and O-statements is "at least one." There are no gradations such as "few," "many," "most," or "nearly all." The only terms that identify quantity are *all, some,* and *none.* Moreover, the A- and O-statements, and the E- and I-statements, are contradictory. In either pair, one statement represents precisely what is needed to deny the other. There also are technical terms to describe the relationship between A- and E-, I- and O-, A- and I-, and E- and O-statements.

A categorical syllogism is built of categorical statements:

All planets are heavenly bodies.
All life-sustaining surfaces are planets.

All life-sustaining surfaces are heavenly bodies.

This is a valid syllogism, as is apparent either from Venn diagrams (circles that clearly place one category inside another) or from applying the rules of distribution. A term is "distributed" if the statement containing it says something about every member of the category. Subjects of A- and E-statements, and predicates of E- and O-statements, are distributed. Rules of distribution are (1) the terms appearing in the conclusion (end terms) must be distributed either twice or not at all, and (2) the term that appears only in the premises (middle term) must be distributed exactly once. The following syllogism is invalid:

All house pets are friendly creatures.
Some dogs are not house pets.

Some dogs are not friendly creatures.

One would not know how to draw the Venn diagram. The circle for "dogs" only partially intersects that for "house pets," but whether or not it fits entirely within the circle for "friendly creatures" is unknown. In terms of distribution rules, the syllogism is invalid because the middle term ("house pets") is distributed twice. The conclusion of an invalid syllogism might still be true, as it is in this example, but its truth cannot be assured by inference from the premises.

A conditional syllogism begins with an "if–then" statement and takes this form:

If a Republocrat is elected, prices will rise.
A Republocrat is elected.

Prices will rise.

The "if" clause is referred to as the antecedent and the "then" clause as the consequent. Valid forms affirm the antecedent (as in this example) or deny the consequent (if prices do not rise, then—given these premises—we could be certain that a Republocrat has not been elected). On the other hand, denying the antecedent *and* affirming or denying the consequent are invalid forms. The reason is the same: based on these premises, nothing prevents prices from rising even if a Republocrat is not elected. Creating a valid form in this latter case requires an antecedent that begins with "if and only if."

The disjunctive syllogism begins with an "either–or" statement and then selects or rejects one of the options, reaching a conclusion about the other:

Either we will go to the beach or we will
  play cards.
We will not play cards.

We will go to the beach.

Although "or" is often used in ordinary language in the sense of "one or the other but not both," its meaning in logic—unless stated otherwise—is "one or the other or both." Accordingly, if the second premise is a positive statement ("We will go to the beach"), one could not reach a valid conclusion about the other option, since one could both go to the beach and play cards. Only those disjunctive syllogisms in which the options are mutually exclusive permit valid conclusions.

The syllogism has had two quite opposed influences on rhetorical studies. In some respects, it has served as the model for reasoning and inference. [*See* Inference.] On this view, both informal logic and rhetoric are less reliable means of inferring conclusions because they never can obtain the certainty of the syllogism. Aristotle proposed the enthymeme as the rhetorical counterpart of the syllogism. [*See* Enthymeme.] In the enthymeme, at least one of the premises is drawn from the beliefs of the audience, and the conclusion can be seen as following necessarily from the premises *for that audience*.

Alternatively, the syllogism has been dismissed as an inappropriate model for rhetorical reasoning, in part because of its highly atypical nature. Very seldom does anyone actually reason in syllogistic form, because of the inflexibility of the term *some* or because truth and validity cannot be separated so neatly as the syllogism requires. Mostly, however, the "revolt against formalism" that has been dominant in rhetoric, at least since the mid-twentieth century, reflects the conviction that rhetoric is not served by a mode of reasoning in which the conclusion contains no new information. On the contrary, rhetorical reasoning involves enabling an audience to move from what they already know or believe to some new position that the rhetor upholds. On this view, both cognitive psychology and informal logic offer more useful insight than does the study of the syllogism.

[*See also* Thesis and antithesis.]

BIBLIOGRAPHY

Aristotle. *Prior Analytics*. Translated by Robin Smith. Indianapolis, c.1989.

Lukasiewicz, Jan. *Aristotle's Syllogistic from the Standpoint of Modern Formal Logic*. Oxford, 1957.

Rose, Lynn E. *Aristotle's Syllogistic*. Springfield, Ill., 1968.
—DAVID ZAREFSKY

SYMBOL. *See* Allegory; Ambiguity; *and* Iconography.

SYMBOLIC CONVERGENCE THEORY.
See Rhetorical vision.

SYMPLOCĒ (Lat. *complexio*), called by Puttenham (*The Arte of English Poesie*, 1589, p. 199) "the figure of replie," one of several figures characterized by the repetition of morphemes. They are differentiated by such criteria as the position, quantity, frequency, or distributional pattern of what is repeated. *Symplocē*, resulting from a combination of *anaphora* and *epiphora*, gives a sequence of sentences that begin and end by repeating the same words. Besides examples in Brutus's speech in Shakespeare's *Julius Caesar* (3.2.30–35), Ernulphus's "fit forms of swearing" in Sterne's *Tristram Shandy* (1760–1767, 3.11) can be instanced: "May the Father who created man, curse him.—May the Son who suffered for us, curse him."

[*See also* Anaphora; Epiphora; Epistrophē; *and* Figures of speech.]

BIBLIOGRAPHY

Lausberg, Heinrich. *Handbook of Literary Rhetoric: A Foundation for Literary Study*. Translated by Matthew T. Bliss, Annemick Jansen, David E. Orton; edited by David E. Orton and R. Dean Anderson. Leiden, 1998. English translation of *Handbuch der literarischen Rhetorik*, first published 1960.

Plett, Heinrich F. *Systematische Rhetorik*. Munich, 2000.
—HEINER PETERS

SYNCOPĒ (Lat. *consicio* erroneous for *concisio*), called by Thomas Wilson (*The Arte of Rhetoric*, 1560, p. 177) "cutting from the middest," a metaplasm by deletion, in which letters or syllables are cut from the middle of a word or phrase, as "ma'am" for "madam" or "good-bye" for "God be with ye." It is considered a barbarism when due to error or negligence. As poetic license, *syncopē* is employed for reasons of meter or euphony. Until sure of Hamlet's death, Shakespeare's Claudius will feel uneasy, "Howe'er my haps, my joys were ne'er begun" (4.3.69).

[*See also* Figures of speech.]

—HEINER PETERS

SYNECDOCHĒ (Lat. *conceptio, intellectio*) is a metasememe that signifies a relationship of the particular and the general. Like metonymy, it is constituted by a substitution of contiguities. Synecdochē presents either particular things instead of a whole, or a whole instead of something particular. An example of the former case is the expression "Caesar conquered Gallia," in which "Caesar" represents the members of the Roman army; an example of the latter is the sentence, "The Americans have landed on the moon," in which the term *Americans* denotes only the astronauts involved.

If contiguity is taken as the distinguishing characteristic of metonymy, synecdochē may be defined as one of its subclasses (Plett, 2000, pp. 191–192). Accordingly, Lausberg describes synecdochē as a metonymy denoting a "quantitative relationship between the word used and the meaning intended" (1998, section 572). Although Quintilian regards synecdochē as a trope in its own right, he acknowledges the kinship of the two tropes by stating that "it is but a short step from *synecdochē* to *metonymy*" (*Institutio oratoria*, first century CE, 8.6.23).

Several types of synecdochē can be distinguished according to their respective functions of generalization or particularization (Plett, 1991, pp. 71–72). The first type includes substitutions (1) of the whole for a part ("*America* [the American team] succeeded in the Olympic games"); (2) of genus for species ("He was lost on *the waters* [the ocean]"); and (3) of plural for singular ("*We* [I] regret to inform you"). The second comprises substitutions (1) of a part for the whole ("There were some new *faces* [people] in the crowd"); (2) of species for genus ("He had spent his last few *dimes* [money]"); and (3) of singular for plural ("*Columbus* [and his crew] set sail for America").

A special interpretation of synecdochē is given by Kenneth Burke, who, in *A Grammar of Motives* (Berkeley, 1969, pp. 507–508) describes it as one of the "Four Master Tropes," which include metaphor, metonymy, synecdochē, and irony. In Burke's system, synecdochē is connected to the function of representation and signifies relationships that on other occasions have been described as metonymic, namely substitutions of "part for the whole, whole for the part, container for the contained, sign for the thing signified, material for the thing made . . . , cause for effect, effect for cause, genus for species, species for genus, etc." Metonymy, according to Burke, is a "special application of synecdoche." Whereas synecdochic relationships are "convertible" and may function in either direction, metonymical relations are restricted to the substitution of quantities for qualities and are therefore unidirectional. Burke finds a "perfect paradigm or prototype" of synecdochē in the philosophical concept of a correspondence between microcosm and macrocosm, which conceives of man as a "little world." Another instance, also taken by Burke (1969, p. 508) from intellectual history, is Jean-Jacques Rousseau's concept of a *volonté générale*, which is assumed to "represent" the volitions of all the members in a society.

[*See also* Figures of speech; Metonymy; *and* Style.]

BIBLIOGRAPHY

Jakobson, Roman. "Two Aspects of Language and Two Types of Aphasic Disturbances." In *Fundamentals of Language*, by Roman Jakobson and Morris Halle. 2d ed., pp. 67–96. The Hague, 1971.

Lausberg, Heinrich. *Handbook of Literary Rhetoric: A Foundation for Literary Study*. Translated by Matthew C. Bliss, Annemiek Jansen, David E. Orton; edited by David E. Orton and R. Dean Anderson. Leiden, 1998. English translation of *Handbuch der literarischen Rhetorik*, first published in 1960.

Plett, Heinrich F. *Einführung in die rhetorische Textanalyse*. 8th ed. Hamburg, 1991.

Plett, Heinrich F. *Systematische Rhetorik: Konzepte und Analysen*. Munich, 2000.

Ruwet, Nicolas. "Synecdoques et Métonymies." *Poetique* 6 (1975), pp. 371–388.

—RICHARD NATE

SYNTAX. *See* Linguistics.

T

TACIT DIMENSION, THE. We always say less than we mean. Not only do we not say or write everything we mean, we cannot, try as we might. In fact, a good exercise is to try to say or write everything one means even for a simple statement; one quickly finds doing so tedious and frustrating. Tedious, because so much that one will add to be wholly explicit is so trivial and seemingly unnecessary; frustrating because if one works critically, one finds the task daunting.

In speaking or writing, one always assumes a relevancy of some sort to the context of one's statements. "Of some sort"? What sort? What context? Contexts are forever elastic. Everything is the context for anything, but we are constantly thinking of some part of that expansive whole as our particular context. Furthermore, rhetoric is addressed. Since we are speaking to or writing for someone, we repeatedly sense that the other is recalling, (i.e., creating), a context that is somewhat different from what we have in mind and, therefore, that we must add extensions and qualifications. If nothing can be assumed, communication becomes difficult to the extreme of seeming impossible.

What we have stumbled across reflects Michael Polanyi's concept of a "tacit dimension," and it is his expression that heads this article. Human beings understand themselves, others, and their environment to some extent. All understanding has a tacit dimension. Polanyi proceeds in this fashion: human understanding is focused. I understand a *this* or a *that*. Moreover, we are focal beings, that is, our sense organs are receptors of information about our environment, others, and ourselves. We must focus on something in order to understand. If we focus, we omit much that is possible to sense. However, there is not a sharp demarcation between what we sense and do not sense. In short, there is a periphery that we take in, but not focally.

Polanyi illustrates the relationship between focal awareness and peripheral awareness in a myriad of ways. Here is one: Perhaps everyone has had the experience of standing on a bridge over a river, looking down. Often, one has the sense that the bridge is moving while the water is standing still. Then suddenly, the bridge and the viewer stops and the water moves. What has happened? One's peripheral vision has picked up some stationary object on the shore. That object, sensed peripherally, "anchors" the viewer and the water flows normally (or at least, what we take as normal).

Quite conventionally, we recognize that much in the practice of rhetoric, and therefore reflected in its theory, is tacit. If *logos* is primary in rhetoric, then the forms of reasoning that we associate with the concept often contain unstated assumptions. [*See* Logos.] Although Aristotle states that enthymemes are often, not necessarily, incomplete, even if complete, the premises *assumed* useful in terms of the acceptance of the audience remain imbedded in tacit understanding. [*See* Enthymeme.] Further, since rhetoric is often thought of as style, to recognize a metaphor as a metaphor is to recognize that relationships are present but unstated. To explain a metaphor completely, were that possible, would be tedious and would erode its effectiveness.

In suggesting rhetoric-as-practice, I have alluded to, and thus depended on a tacit dimension of understanding, the long-held principle that the theory and teaching of rhetoric is determined by the observation of the communicative experiences we have generally marked by the concept of "persuasion." [*See* Persuasion.] The variations of that term in defining "rhetoric" have a long history that will be detailed under obvious headings in this encyclopedia. The observations about practice have formed treatises for teaching rhetoric over at least twenty-four centuries. These treatises are taken for the theory or theories of rhetoric. What difference will thinking in terms of a tacit dimension of understanding make for the theory of rhetoric and for teaching? If theory should precede teaching, then I shall proceed backwards.

Pedagogy. What conclusion or conclusions should we draw as teachers from the concept of "the tacit dimension" applied to rhetoric? We cannot teach all that we understand, or, conversely, our students cannot reach the understanding they need from what we are able to teach explicitly. That conclusion is clearly shadowed these days in the treatises about and workshops stressing "active learning." Discovering or adapting a concept or practice is different from being able to state the concept or outline the practice.

Here we might draw an analogy with what is described as "expert systems." (The term has grown out of the attempt to conceptualize such systems for the increasing use of computers to carry out tasks or important parts of tasks.) Musical performance is often used as an explanatory device to illustrate such "systems"; that is, the performer gradually internalizes such patterns as scales and modes until he or she can play large patterns rather than note-by-note. Musicians performing in ensembles must listen to one another. Why? So that individuals can adjust to being part of a whole, sensing immediately and adjusting not only obvious changes in tempo and intensity, which can be marked after all, but subtle changes in pitch and timbre, changes that they are not focally aware of needing to make or even having made. The members of an ensemble or a conductor may explain phrasing, for example, but there is always more than can be explained, that is, described precisely as instructions.

Learners of complex tasks are almost always frustrated by their instructors or mentors. And their instructors by the learner's common question: What do you want? To various degrees, the skilled instructor can explain, but only to a point, and that point is often marked with a gesture, sometimes a subtle gesture that the instructor herself is unaware of. Verbally, the teacher may only be able to urge continued trials or give general encouragement, or indications of pleasure when the results are positive.

Above, I said "instructors or mentors," as if the two are different. Are they? They are if one re-

sponded in reading to a tacit dimension, that is, sensed the "more than" I said. The "mentor" is an "exemplar," that is, the setter of instructional examples: the skilled performer performing for the tyro.

I am assuming that all learners, including those who have learned to be skilled instructors, have gone through the frustrations and triumphs of assimilating. As Polanyi puts it, "Every time we assimilate a tool to our body our identity undergoes some change; our person expands into new modes of being" (1959, p. 31). Here we must recognize that concepts and practices, as well as instruments, are tools.

Rhetoric may well be thought of as a set of schemes for producing discourse or for becoming critically aware and being able to explain such practices of production. In either case, pedagogically we are trying to produce skilled performers. In doing so, we must recognize the limits as well as the promises of our systems.

Theory. We may take "theory" in its simplest sense as "explanation" of phenomena. The phenomena in question are those of skilled practice as speakers or writers. Speaking and writing takes place in time and therefore exemplifies sequences to which we give various labels. The ancient tradition suggests *dispositio* as an essential part of rhetoric. In using "part," immediately part/whole relationships are implied. For beginners, specifying patterns for organizing the verbal product tends to become a very early aspect of learning (and teaching). Even in the simplest of these, say, chronology, there are tacit dimensions. To illustrate, take two important rhetorical concepts, "topics" and "metaphor," which will be discussed from other points of view elsewhere in this encyclopedia.

Topics is a difficult, often contested term, because it is both abstract and points so immediately to practice as its milieu that it either does not exist independently from or disappears immediately into practice. [*See* Topics.] A topic is not argument nor a part of an argument, but rather a suggestion for creating argument. The term is bound up in Aristotle's emphatic insistence that "rhetoric" is not "persuasion" but rather a ground from which in specific cases discourse may begin (*Rhetoric* 1.1–2, passim). *Argument,* as he uses the term," is the fundamental function of rhetoric for Aristotle and topics its creative engine.

Although Aristotle seems to give lists that often are taken as topics, I hold that these are a step prior, that a topic cannot occur until one is in a specific argumentative circumstance. Thus, *a fortiori* is not a topic, although often taken as such, but rather a pointer, or place-holder; that is, a concept that sends the *rhētōr* into thoughtful action if she is in a rhetorical situation. Here are possibilities for seeing in the situation the constituents of thought that will lead to specific premises on which arguments may be formed. In short, for the discussion here, topics constitute a tacit dimension of rhetorical practice. That practice forms a productive rhetoric of possible "lines" that rhetoric may take to become specific discourse. Our everyday English use of "topics" unfortunately misleads us. In English, *a fortiori*, a sense of more-and-less simultaneously, is a topic. The mode of thought that arises from an abstract understanding of the concept leads to, but is not itself, the active thought necessary to products: premise, enthymeme, argument, speech.

What is expressed above will be controversial among rhetoricians, and the controversy itself indicates a constant struggle toward more complete understanding, either individually or collectively; such a struggle will, if attended to, constantly reveal dimensions that have been and will become again tacit.

Another difficult, important, and controversial rhetorical concept (one might say "and *therefore* controversial rhetorical concept") is "metaphor." [*See* Metaphor.] The concept can be, and often is, defined inadequately as "clothing thought in language" (a phrase hinging on a tired and unfortunately chosen metaphor). George Lakoff, with several collaborators, has defined "metaphor" as the mapping of the understanding of one domain upon another. Here the metaphor "mapping" is the "hinge" (another metaphor). So closely is metaphor bound with the creative activity we call "thought" that, like topics, it remains in part a tacit dimension continually pointing toward both the creative process and the momentary products of that process. There is a sort of infinite regression bound in any language

that attempts to catch its essence, whether Lakoff's "mapping," or I. A. Richards' pair of "tenor and vehicle." The very "richness" of theory belongs in part at least to a tacit dimension in understanding.

Intellectually. Intellectually? But aren't both rhetorical theory and pedagogy intellectual activities? Yes, they are. The point here is simply that both belong to the larger compass of activities we think of as "intellectual." Therefore we should expect to find in our theories, our teaching, and our own speaking and writing the constant struggle to understand and the ambiguities that go with that struggle. We should both expect and welcome these ambiguities, although we shall be engaged in reducing or fixing those ambiguities in some momentary practice. Living will constantly bring the to-be-explained into focus, and with focus, the tacit dimensions attendant to active thought.

We always say more than we mean, that is, our sayings take us into wider orbits than we intend. Intentions are foci, "targets" as it were of thought. The tacit dimensions are the possibilities of thoughts. Although vital to every focus, they are also further openings into thought. Thus rhetoric is redeemed by our always saying less than we mean and simultaneously more than we mean.

BIBLIOGRAPHY

Booth, Wayne. *Modern Dogma and the Rhetoric of Assent.* South Bend, Ind., 1974.

Lakoff, George, and Mark Johnson. *Metaphors We Live By.* Chicago, 1980.

Lakoff, George, and Mark Turner. *More Than Cool Reason.* Chicago, 1989.

Norton, Robert W. "Conviviality: A Rhetorical Dimension." *Central States Speech Journal* 26 (1975), pp. 164–170.

Polanyi, Michael. *Personal Knowledge: Towards a Post-Critical Philosophy.* New York, 1964. First published 1958.

Polanyi, Michael. *The Study of Man.* Chicago, 1963. First published 1959.

Polanyi, Michael. *The Tacit Dimension.* New York, 1967. First published 1966.

Richards, I. A. *Philosophy of Rhetoric.* New York, 1936.

Scott, Robert L. "The Tacit Dimension and Rhetoric: What It Means to Be Persuading and Persuaded." *Pre/*

Text, An Interdisciplinary Journal of Rhetoric. 2 (1981), pp. 115–125.

Verene, Donald Philip. "On Rhetoric and Imagination as Kinds of Knowledge." Mimeograph, 16th World Congress of Philosophy, Düsseldorf, 27 August–2 September 1978.

—ROBERT L. SCOTT

TECHNICAL COMMUNICATION. One undeniable fact of recent modern history has been the widening gap between those possessing highly specialized competencies and those not equipped in these modes of expertise. Simple dualities and hierarchies no longer suffice to explain such discrepancies. In an increasingly networked and globalized world, the practitioners of specialized communication are as apt to be computer hacks in flannel shirts as scientists in white coats. This essay makes no attempt to encompass the extraordinary diversity of technical communication types; any such attempt would be antiquated long before it reached the printed page. Instead, we begin by examining three important conceptions of the "technological society" as well as their implications for what counts as technical communication. Then we attempt to isolate recurring features of technical communication that seem to be constant across types.

Technē, the Greek root of the word *technical*, implies some sort of precise and systematic code of rules and procedures of "technical" communication, a knowable code. This root also suggests that the realm of the technical is not a modern phenomenon, but as old as systematic speculation itself. Nonetheless, one characteristic of modern and postmodern social critique is the suspicion that the realm of the technical has come to dominate most, if not all, contemporary sites of deliberation and judgment. Accompanying this suspicion is the foreboding sense that the dominance of technical communication is not a good thing.

We take some exception to this critique. But first it is necessary to take proper measure of the critique itself. We place our undertaking within a prior conceptual context through an overview of three rather different views of what technological society *is*. As accounts of the fuller picture we seek, the characterizations themselves have serious weaknesses, but they are nonetheless valuable as historical markers of this still pertinent concept. The following discussion addresses technological society as a way of conducting ourselves in the lifeworld, as a way of thinking, and finally as a mode of being.

Technological Society as Conduct. The manner of conducting ourselves we derive rather loosely from Habermas's appropriation of systems theory (1975). In laying out various sorts of systems prerequisites, Habermas makes a fairly basic distinction between the realms of what he calls outer nature and inner nature. Outer nature includes what we might think of as the earth itself, plants, generally speaking, the environment. And then, usually situated within the lifeworld of social systems, one comes upon *inner* nature: the realm of cultural meanings, derived customs and practices with subjective import, the whole process and productive apparatus of human consciousness. Generally speaking, for Habermas, we are to approach the external nature realm in technical terms and to approach the inner nature realm in social and communicative terms.

The initial distinction is not without controversy, and it is not certain that Habermas subscribes to it anymore. The point is, however, that increasingly the technical interest in efficiency, steering, and control has begun to transform not only the realm of external nature but the lifeworld of inner nature as well. This is Habermas's version of Weber's managerial revolution, replete with iron cage, experts, the hegemony of restricted specialities. Now characteristically, Habermas also wants to transcend and set aside his own systems terminology, obsessed as it is with the root metaphor of steering. He reasons that this prior distinction could only have been made if there were a third interest and approach to the lifeworld. This allows him to reintroduce postulates for competence in an emancipatory interest that will reprioritize the proper spheres for technical and social. But the agenda is finally less important to us than the quite striking characterization. This is a critical theorist's view of a technological society.

Technological Society as Thinking. We might also think of a technological society as being characterized by a common manner of thinking: calculative reason that seeks to operationalize all normative properties as measurable and therefore negotiable commodities. The principal architect of this more sweeping conception was Jacques Ellul, author of *The Technological Society* (1968). Ellul's appraisal is considerably more pessimistic than that of Habermas. Over and against a rather idyllic construal of a communal past (with "quilting bees" and pastoral gatherings), Ellul posits the modern primacy of technique as a pervasive trap, from which there is little chance of escape. Here, reason is reducible to cause, purpose and justification to effect. Here ends efficiently justify means or else there is no justification. Action and conduct are subsumed in the crude panoply of behaviors. This is where the language of life and death, welfare and destruction, is refigured and disfigured in the probability statistics of cost and benefit. And here, above all is where the argument from technical authority and expertise displaces commonsense reflection on generalizable human interests. Suffice it to say, the primary rhetorical function of technical authority is to attenuate critical reflection. In its most extreme form, technical reasoning seems virtually to cancel out the normative contents and forms of judgment.

Technological Society as Mode of Being. Finally, in our series, is the Heideggerian notion of technological society as a mode of being. Heidegger's particular argument is itself highly technical, steeped in the language of European ontology. Stripped of its nuances, Heidegger's argument would agree that technological society gives us a culture that is driven by the priorities and needs of something other than ourselves. In such a climate, persons are typically divorced from their acts. We become less part of the world as participants, and more observers of the world. In one of his clearest commentaries on this subject (from *The Question Concerning Technology*), Heidegger states: "[A] world picture . . . does not mean a picture of the world but the world conceived and grasped as a picture. . . . The world picture does not change from an earlier medieval one into a modern one, but rather the fact that the world becomes picture at all is what distinguishes the essence of the modern age" (1977, p. 130). While human nature is a problematic category for Heidegger, there can be little doubt that the primacy of technology places us in a mode of existence that is alien to our true natures. This mode of existence

reifies value, just as it reduces craft to tool, style to technique, purpose to function. It is, one hardly need add, an inauthentic mode of existence.

Taken together, these ideas of technological society suggest an increasingly artificial and even regimented world, in which efficiency and mass satisfaction are purchased at the cost of real participation. We have distilled these senses of a technological society first, so that we may offer some necessary qualifiers to them, and more specifically, so that we may address their common defining features of technical communication.

But first, our two modest codicils. Regardless of the particular form it takes, totalizing critique should be approached with caution. It is a mistake to regard the movement toward a technological society as one irreversible arc of development. In fact, it is one of the self-serving myths of technical thinking that there is only one logical extension and outcome of historic evolution and so-called social progress. That outcome, conveniently enough, is the increasing technologizing of everything. This point is, at best, debatable.

A second codicil is that it is shortsighted to regard all technologies as equally evil, inauthentic, or destructive. There are, after all, hearing aids, dialysis machines, pacemakers, and the rest. If we think of both history and technology in the plural rather than as speaking in a single voice, we will be further along. The question, though, is whether there is any sense of commonality in these admittedly broad normative construals, and whether these commonalities shed additional light on the characteristics of technical communication. We answer this question in the affirmative.

All three of the perspectives view the realm of the technical as juxtaposed to something else. Habermas makes the traditional distinction between nature and culture, one that is almost identical to the archaic Greek distinction between *physis* and *nomos*. [*See* Sophists.] Prior to the revolution in consciousness provoked by the classical Greek rhetoricians, it was assumed by most that nature was itself animated by the same principles as culture (i.e., the mythic gods). Increasingly, the critical theory tradition has argued, not only nature but culture as well have been viewed as something to be explained, rather than appreciated. Now as a Marxist-influenced philosopher with Kantian leanings, Habermas locates this humanizing normative horizon entirely within the realm of culture; as a Kantian-influenced philosopher with Marxist leanings, he tends to assume that nature is simply there, to be harnessed or transformed. For Ellul and Heiddeger, the sphere of the technical seems to swallow up everything. But even these dispiriting visions are juxtaposed to an earlier, purer form of communication, whether it be dialogical, communal, or participatory.

A second commonality is that the realm of the technical is seen as exclusionary in character and that this feature, as well as others, is regarded as normatively problematic. Habermas envisions the rise of a "new class" of technologists who rule primarily through expertise. Ellul also alludes to the rise of technical authority as an ominous successor to participatory communion. Heidegger sees humankind itself as "ruled out" of its own authentic existence by the pervasive domination of the technical.

Some Common Features of Technical Communication. Taken together, these commonalities help to shed light on the character of technical communication, even as they invite careful qualification. Rather obviously, technical communication may be analogized to the realm of the technical itself. [*See* Politics, *article on* The personal, technical, and public spheres of argument.] It is a manner of interaction that is restricted to a field of expertise. Its mode of expression will be based largely upon the codes and competences characteristic of the field in question. Almost by definition, this mode of communication will be restricted in participation as well. The language of orthopedic surgeons or auto specialists or computer hackers will be nearly unintelligible to those not conversant with the code. Technical communication further insulates itself from critique to the degree that those who are competent within the code develop a shorthand or vernacular for their complex concepts.

But we believe it is also possible to take a more even-handed approach to the normative problems our critics find in the technological sphere, at least when it comes to communication itself. To the extent that technical communication is in direct service of the hegemony and control attributed by Habermas, Ellul, and Heidegger to technological society, this fact is, of course, to be deplored. Yet there is reason to question whether

such a singular characterization is fair, given the complexity and diversity of the technical in our time. During the Tiananmen Square student protests in 1989, for instance, Chinese-American students were able to learn of the ruthless suppression of dissent by state power through a medium earlier decades would have found unimaginable. They followed the tragic events by e-mail.

Yet it seems unlikely to be mere coincidence that three bold and visionary thinkers could come to such similar conclusions about the technical sphere. The very characteristics we have found in technical communication imply that it is, to some degree, asymmetrical. It allows for limited access, restricted focus, and selective expertise. It views only part of a larger picture, and implies a sort of secular hierarchy where power and influence are concerned. Given these characteristics, it is only a modest inference to conclude that the increasing prominence of the technical is somehow threatening to traditional cultural values.

However, we stop short of this inference. What we hope to illustrate are some of the challenging implications of technical communication for the world of rhetorical practice.

Technical Communication as Challenge to Rhetoric. Tarla Rai Peterson's *Sharing the World: the Rhetoric of Sustainable Development* (1997) offers a fitting opening to our illustrations by detailing a number of ecological controversies featuring technical communication. Pivotal to her analysis, and of special interest to the present discussion, is Peterson's intriguing distinction between what she terms "technological discourse" and "creative discourse." Echoing, to some extent, disjunctions between restricted and elaborated codes, perhaps even social and technical knowledge, Peterson is able to identify the first and most conspicuous rhetorical challenge posed by technical communication; namely, its capacity to rationalize the exclusion of those participants in controversy presumed to have *diminished* competencies for the issue in question. In fact, she goes so far as to claim this exclusionary function to be the principal defining trait of technical communication.

Her illustration of this challenge, the wood bison controversy in Canada, offers a team of Canadian land-use experts using their own testimonial evidence to exclude an aboriginal tribe of Canadian Indians from any participation in a controversy over their centuries-old land use. Perhaps it is too much to claim that technical communication does this *by definition*. But it is surely the case that the role of expert testimonial evidence in controversy (traditionally an inartistic proof), places new demands on the responsibilities of audiences. [*See* Classical rhetoric.]

For the remainder of our discussion, we wish to pursue the commonality which implicates the diagnostics of technological society in normative concerns. This is equally true of technical communication. It is not only that the profusion of the technical has been subjected to rhetorical polemics. From a rhetorical standpoint, the persuasive challenge to technical communication is complex and ironic. For those who share its codes and premises, technical communication does not appear to require a rhetorical supplement; its very pretence of objectivity is enough to persuade. Yet this "persuasion" is essentially preaching to the converted; and it begs the more challenging question of how to bring others into the fold.

As we have seen from the aforementioned example, it is not unusual for the purveyors of technical communication to simply exclude other rhetorical advocates from participation on competency grounds. But this will simply not work in more public contexts. It may even be that more public contexts find ordinary audiences actively resisting technical communication because of its very complexity and remoteness (the notorious O. J. Simpson verdict comes to mind). It is rare to find technical communication that effectively persuades popular audiences entirely on its own devices.

In practical terms, this means that technical communication only works within a wider forum when it is supplemented by a more traditional form of rhetoric. This rhetoric need not be overtly expressed; it can lurk behind the scenes as tacit, received convention. But it nearly always takes on a mythic form. Perhaps most traditionally, this phenomenon may be detected in Horkheimer and Adorno's intuitively brilliant observation that throughout its history, the Enlightenment recurringly reverts to myths, such as "progress" (1972). The irony, of course, is that it was precisely the realm of myth that science purported

to demystify. As Georg Simmel (*Philosophie des Geldes*, Leipzig, 1990) observed at the dawn of the last century,

> The illusions in this sphere [i.e., the reception of the technical] are reflected quite clearly in the terminology that is used in it, and in which a mode of thinking proud of its . . . freedom from myth, discloses the direct opposite of these features. To think that we conquer or control nature is a very childish supposition, since all notions of conquest and subjugation have a proper meaning only if an opposing will has been broken. . . . Natural events, as such, are not subject to the alternatives of freedom and coercion. . . . Although . . . this seems to be just a matter of terminology, it does lead astray those who think superficially in the direction of anthropomorphic misinterpretations, and it does show that the mythological mode of thought is also at home within the natural-scientific worldview. (pp. 520–521)

Recent times have only confirmed Simmel's prophetic observation. When Americans first landed a man on the moon, President Richard Nixon famously pronounced the event the most significant seven days since the creation. And when, thirty years later, President Clinton appeared with two rival research teams to announce the first nearly complete map of the human genome, not only the President but the research scientists themselves claimed to have uncovered God's blueprint for the human soul. If our intuitions are correct, such captions are not mere artifice, but rhetorically necessary to place each staggering technical innovation within an acceptable popular frame.

The last and perhaps least examined rhetorical challenge accompanying technical communication emerges from technological society's elusive negative, the failure to control, the unanticipated blip on the societal radar screen: the elusive concept of risk. First, the very language in which technical communication is framed, that of positivism, is uncomfortable with any *negatives* this side of the null hypothesis. Second, risk does not rest comfortably within the realm of fact, positive or negative; rather, it lies in the in-between realm of possibility. Understandably, given its negative connotations, the "mood" encouraged by risk is not comfort at all, but anxiety. Third, risk appears to be the Achilles heel of technical hubris. In direct, if not exact, proportion to the confident prediction and control of technical communication practice is the dread utterance indicative of human error: "How did that happen?" Finally, as the previous reason suggests, risk brings in the problematic question of human agency both as potential harm *and* as potential failure in the mastery of the technical. For each of these reasons, risk presents technical communication with rhetorical challenges.

As if to ward off these rhetorical challenges, social science has given us elaborate variations of technical communication in the forms of probability theory, risk–benefit analysis, and impressive game theory simulation. But this may only complicate the Faustian bargain, rather than ending it. In tacitly promising that nothing can occur in ordinary reality that has not already been anticipated in virtual reality, the burden of compensation simply increases exponentially when something unanticipated actually occurs.

In their study of "Accidental Rhetoric: The Root Metaphors of Three-Mile Island 2" (1981), Thomas Farrell and G. Thomas Goodnight noticed that technical communication cannot be relied upon to assuage anxieties in times of perceived crisis. Whatever the actual harms inflicted by the Three-Mile Island "incident," retreat to the language of technicality only managed to dramatize public alarm. It would take the most trusted public communicator of the day, thememaster Walter Cronkite, to effectively caption the fast-breaking events: "The danger faced by man for tampering with natural forces, a theme familiar from the myths of Prometheus to the story of Frankenstein, moved closer to fact from fancy through the day" (1979). Farrell and Goodnight conclude that moments of contingency, within the sphere of the technical (which we might think of as risk actualized), provide a powerful impetus toward the emergence of some compensatory rhetorical supplement.

Rhetorical Responses to Technical Communication. The characteristics of this supplement are as difficult to encompass as those of technical communication itself; and they continue to evolve. However, we underline three of them for the purposes of this essay: the rhetoric that supplements

technical communication tends to be mythic in scope, apologetic in genre, and heroically stoic in mood.

Mythologies, as we have seen, seem to have a recurring tacit relationship to technical communication. Creation myths were routinely invoked as symbolic support for the moon landing and the genome breakthroughs. The myths of progress and childlike faith in invulnerability are part of the social knowledge that is the background to the great affirmative progress of technology itself. Yet the connection is more complex than this might indicate. The fact, and surely the materialization, of risk return us (as in Cronkite's words, and innumerable science fiction films; Rushing and Frentz, 1995) to symbolic accounts of our *lack* of control, and perhaps of the failure of calculative thinking in general. The ease with which we revert to primordial symbolism and devil terms in technical crises offers strong evidence of this tendency.

What we know as apologia is a complex genre, traditionally involving not only self-defense, but also illocutionary utterances of contrition and remorse. Both features come into play, again when technical communication proves insufficient to account for the failings of technology. When questions of consumer safety, large-scale inconvenience, or corporate neglect are already open to public scrutiny, it does little good to "stonewall," or repeat the same internal communication patterns. The already *human* problem requires a sense of agency (from corporation or institution) sufficient to accommodate its weight.

Beginning in the 1980s, a hybrid rhetorical genre we might label "corporate apologia" began to appear with numbing frequency. [*See* Hybrid genres.] Ford (with its infamous "Pinto"), Exxon, Union Carbide, Continental Airlines, Phillip Morris, and literally dozens of other corporate entities found their own internal communications to be insufficient as accounts of "public" misdeeds. Worse yet, these very communications (in the form of cost–benefit analysis) sometimes became starkly incriminating when disclosed to the public. As if to compensate for such deficiencies, corporate relations experts and increasingly visible chief executive officers were sent forth to the public in an effort to present the collectivity as a responsible agent who cares and is working to repair whatever damage was inflicted and win back consumer confidence.

As rhetoric, these performances offered little to distinguish themselves. Typically, they presented a kind of blanket, all-purpose gesture of confession and remorse to the opinion leaders of the mass society. In the process of doing this, they also managed to present a highly condensed editorial chronology, in which they are laboring heroically to set things right again. However, eloquence was not the point of these utterances, just as it was not their point to reach the real victims in any tangible way. The point was and is to get "out in front" of the sequence of events discursively, to gain initiative so that public news and opinion-leader story lines might shift to other matters. For our purposes, the frequency of these messages also helps to dramatize the limits of technical communication, when grappling with public matters.

A third constituent of rhetorical supplements involves the question of mood. In times of progress on the technical front, with seemingly limitless promise, the mood is of course optimistic and utopian. We have already seen this in evidence with the numerous invocations of myth. But given our frequent encounters with the dark side of technological society, a more accommodating *ēthos* proves to be necessary. [*See* Ēthos.] If we are to live with technological progress (an unquestioned assumption in all of this discourse), then we must also be prepared to live with, to *brave* its costs, even if these costs are sometimes lethal.

The mood we are dubbing "heroic stoicism" suggests a kind of fatalism without total resignation. In a Burkean sense, it redefines "cost," even fatality, as heroic sacrifice demanding a renewal and perfection of commitment to the cause. This mood, we believe, realized its own moment of perfection during the Reagan years.

Arguably the most public technical disaster of modern times was the explosion of the *Challenger* spacecraft in full view of thousands of spectators in January of 1986. The launch had been moved up in time to coincide with President Reagan's scheduled State of the Union speech, and it had additional symbolic significance because one of the astronauts, Christa McAuliffe, was to be NASA's first civilian in space. With the disaster, numerous technical questions emerged as to "what went wrong." But the Reagan regime correctly sensed that technical answers alone (even if they were available) would do little to comfort or satisfy those who witnessed the event.

Instead, that same evening (28 January 1986), the president gravely and memorably invoked the language of heroism, blending the dazzling success of NASA technology (not at its best here, of course) with the gleaming, upright certitude of the seven fallen space travelers themselves. They were likened to pioneers, were relieved of that technological variation of *hamartia* ("human error"), were analogized to explorer Francis Drake and fallen air force heroes who die in the line of duty. But in the midst of all this, our consecration was less to the *Challenger* crew and even to their spirit of discovery, than to their symbolic role as an avant-garde for technological progress. In one passage, which would have been chilling if read literally, the President intoned, "The *Challenger* crew was pulling us into the future; and we will follow them." Perhaps only Ronald Reagan could have effectively mythologized technology's dark side, its romance with death. But this is what we believe Reagan to have done in what remains the finest exemplar of technology's rhetorical supplement.

Reagan's speech accomplished what technical communication routinely succeeds in doing, when it is left unchallenged. It indefinitely deferred questions of guilt, responsibility, complicity. However, it is a fact that such questions are frequently raised when something goes wrong. The prominence of risk (as a sort of negative contingency) has also generated what we believe are two novel forensic questions, or points of *stasis*, in the recurring controversy over wrongdoing in time of technical crisis. [*See* Stasis.]

Issues in Technical Communication Controversy. First, there is what we might consider the ecological negative. In a world of unprecedented interconnectivity, as well as untested technology, what J. Robert Cox has termed the locus of the "irreparable" comes into play. [*See* Irreparable, the.] It may well be the case that some large, or even small-scale technological intrusions into the natural scheme of things yield effects that are irreversible. The ozone layer, the polar icecap, the redwoods, the rainforests all may be seen as a seamless web of animate nature, where damage to one feature leads to irreparable damage to all. What is particularly powerful in this locus of the irreparable is its immunity to refutation in technical communication terms alone. Technical evidence alone can never refute the hypothesis of future irrecoverable damage. And rhetorical anecdotes ("When you've seen one redwood, you've seen them all") do not exactly seem to rise to the magnitude of the occasion.

A second emergent forensic issue seems to exploit an ambiguity in technical communication concerning human agency. The preponderance of the technical suggests a world that may be controlled, while simultaneously rendering human resistance pointless. Within the vortex of any disaster that is not an "act of God," it therefore becomes possible to ask whether *the harm might have been avoided.* Reagan's eloquence shrouded this question in the heroic costuming of grief. But not long after a disaster, the nagging questions return: Why was there no escape hatch in the capsule? Why did the protective seal come loose? Was there a bomb aboard the doomed TWA flight? Was critical data on failed safety inspections concealed? It is also the case that even the realm of so-called "natural" calamity now may be opened to sanction for human negligence. Floods, fires, dustbowls may be blamed on everything from failed irrigation, improper land use, to depleted ozone layers. To the degree that the world has been denatured by the technical, it has paradoxically acquired its own public moment.

The increased interconnectedness of technical communications media gives us no reason for supposing that accompanying anxieties will cease. There are several reasons for this. First, the absence of any consensual base for technological imperatives constrains us either to adapt or be left behind. One might *choose* not to employ e-mail or surf the Internet, for instance; but this could be the modern equivalent of choosing to be a hermit. Second, increased sophistication of technical communication virtually guarantees a knowledge and competency gap between media rich and media impoverished areas. Third, more sophisticated technical communication invites more so-

phisticated technical communication mischief. Hence, viruses, blackouts, and hackers with state secrets would seem to be ongoing byproducts of technical communication.

But for all this, we might still conclude that the apocalyptic prophesies of technological triumph in the last century were wrong in at least one key respect. The increasing prevalence of technical communication did not erase or destroy the realm of responsible human choice and conduct. At least this has not happened during our watch. In this great nonevent, there is also an interesting corollary for rhetoric. The inability of the technical to make good on its threat of total determinacy opens an ongoing, and perhaps enduring, space for the art that thrives on chance.

BIBLIOGRAPHY

Cox, J. Robert. "The Die is Cast: Topical and Ontological Dimensions of the *Locus* of the Irreparable." In *Landmark Essays on Contemporary Rhetoric.* Edited by Thomas B. Farrell, pp. 143–157. Mahwah, N.J., 1998.

Cronkite, Walter. CBS Newscast, 30 March 1979.

Ellul, Jacques. *The Technological Society.* New York, 1964. The most sweeping indictment of technology as a manner of thinking.

Farrell, Thomas B., and G. Thomas Goodnight. "Accidental Rhetoric: The Root metaphors of Three Mile Island." *Communication Monographs* (1981), pp. 271–300. A case study that explores the continuing tensions between technical communication and rhetoric in a controversial setting.

Habermas, Jürgen. *Legitimation Crisis.* Translated by Thomas McCarthy. Boston, 1975. The seminal study of crisis tendencies in late capitalism.

Heidegger, Martin. *The Question Concerning Technology and Other Essays.* Translated by William Lovitt. New York, 1977. Explores the triumph of the technical as a mode of being.

Horkheimer, Max, and Theodor W. Adorno. *The Dialectic of Enlightenment.* Translated by John Cumming. New York, 1972.

Peterson, Tarla Rai. *Sharing the Earth: The Rhetoric of Sustainable Development.* Columbia, S.C., 1997. Offers a provocative treatment of the ways in which technical communication and rhetorical practice are invoked during ecological controversy.

Pool, Robert. *Beyond Engineering: How Society Shapes Technology.* New York, 1997. A strong challenge to the view that technology somehow determines our social existence.

Reagan, Ronald. "The *Challenger* Speech." *CBS Special Report.* 28 January 1986.

Rushing, Janice H., and Thomas S. Frentz, *Projecting the Shadow: the Cyborg Hero in American Film,* Chicago, 1995.

—THOMAS B. FARRELL AND THOMAS JESSE ROACH

THESIS AND ANTITHESIS. Antithesis is a distinct attribute of the earliest rhetorical pieces in the Western tradition. It has no documentable origins. In fact, antithetical thought may be a reflection of the binary nature of human thought, according to Lévi-Strauss, the structural anthropologist. The classical scholars Eduard Norden and John Finley, following Quintilian's lead, find the conceptual origins of contrary modes of expression fully developed in the Homeric poems of the eighth century BCE. They thus backdate antithesis as a distinct mode of expression from the period of the Sophists of the early fifth century BCE, where scholars had located its creation contemporaneous with the first formal rhetoric. [*See* Classical rhetoric; *and* Sophists.] It is with Plato (c.429–c.347 BCE) in the philosophical tradition that thesis and antithesis is formalized as a method of proof. The thesis is the statement of a position requiring proof, which comes about through the ordered expression of its antithesis or antitheses (see, for example, *Republic* 335a on friendship and enmity, seeming and being, each proved by its opposite; and Aristotle, *Prior Analytics* 72a and Cicero, *Topics* 21.79 for simple definitions). From the beginning, however, it is the very fact of contrariness that makes antithesis successful in rhetoric, poetry, or philosophy. Lamy (*De l'Art de parler,* 1675) put it aptly: *contraria juxta se posita, magis elucescunt* ("contraries by being juxtaposed with each other, are illuminated all the more").

It is characteristic of the earliest prose for antithesis to be articulated by isocola. That is, the contraries appear in phrases of balanced length and often of an equal number of words. The measured lengths of antithetical phrasing in these texts appear to be a direct result of the measured expression of early poetry. In its simplest form, two types of antithesis are distinguished in antiquity (Aristotle, *Rhetoric* 3.9 and *Rhetorica ad Alexandrum,* both fourth century BCE, the latter perhaps by Anaximines 1435b): antithesis of words (*lexis*) and antithesis of meaning or thought (*dianoia*). [*See* Antithesis.] Because many of the early texts display

a more complex use than this distinction, which the fourth-century rhetorical handbooks prescribe, more properly we should denote the pair as: (1) syntactic antithesis and (2) semantic antithesis, categories that continue to be useful in rhetorical education. The first includes verbal or clausal antithesis or antithesis of whole arguments and of even larger structures, such as speeches (Quintilian, *Institutio oratoria,* first century CE, 9.3.81), and the second involves the presentation of antithetical ideas that may be expressed without corresponding clearly antithetical words or syntax.

The history of thesis and antithesis follows two paths, one rhetorical, the other philosophical, but they have a common origin. The works of Presocratic thinkers, whether Sophists or philosophers, although fragmentary, regularly exhibit antithetical expression closely connected to the ideas expressed, that is, syntactic and semantic antithesis. These thinkers discuss whether sense perceptions are primary in converting thought to language (a Protagorean view) or whether an absolute knowledge (*logos* or *nous*) that is one and indivisible with being (from Parmenides into Plato) controls words (*logoi*). Heraclitus (fl. 500 BCE) provides examples of both types of antithesis: the more simple syntactic: "the sea is the most pure water and the most polluted, for fish it is drinkable and life-preserving, but for men it is undrinkable and destructive" (Diels and Kranz 1951–1952, Freeman 1956, B.61); and with the antithesis clearly resolved into one: "What is composed is whole and not whole, brought together and brought apart, harmonious and unharmonious; from all things is one and from one, all things" (Diels and Kranz 1951–1952, B10). Thus, antithesis does not require contradiction. Understanding comes from realizing the resolution of the antitheses of both word and object or action (*logos* and *ergon*, the most pervasive antithetical pair in Greek thought). Here already the philosophical path of antithesis has begun to emerge: a thesis and antithesis, each existing in balance, approach a unity, a synthesis.

According to Diogenes Laertius, Empedocles and Zeno (both fl. c.450 BCE) were the first to attempt a philosophical resolution of antithesis by expressing the contraries as premises of argumentation, what Plato, through the form of dramatic dialogue and *elenchus* or argumentation, itself antithetical by nature, would convert to the dialectic method.

But it was for Empedocles' student, Gorgias (c.483–c.376 BCE), to become the recognized master of antithetical expression. He separated himself off from philosophy per se and moved toward *logoi* (words, speech) of a different sort: the art of rhetoric (*technē rhētorikē*). Like other Sophists of the second half of the fifth century (e.g., Protagoras, Prodicus), he shows a preoccupation with what words are and how they function to convey truth or, in some cases what is a semblance (*doxa*) of truth. Gorgianic persuasion emerges from the expression of a thesis together with its antithesis. His antitheses come in profusion and are meant simply by their arrangement to lead to the conclusion. For example, in his Funeral Oration, Gorgias praises the dead in a long series of balanced antitheses and concludes in a complex semantic and syntactic antithesis: the men showed "reverence towards the gods by their justice, piety towards their parents by their care, justice towards their fellow-citizens by their fair dealing, respect towards their friends by keeping faith with them. Therefore, although they are dead, the longing for them has not died with them, but immortal, though in mortal bodies, it [the longing] lives on for those who live no more" (Diels and Kranz 1951–1952, Freeman 1956, 6).

Gorgias's name is so connected with antithesis that in the next century the so-called Gorgianic figures, all of them facilitating antithetical expression, are attributed to him. [*See* Gorgianic figures; *and* Isocolon.] Rhetoric as a means of persuasion that privileges *logoi* (words, arguments) over reality blossoms in the mid to late fifth century. [*See* Logos.] Antithesis itself lies at the heart of the most politically troublesome and paradoxical thesis of the century: Sophists were condemned because they were able to use a well-designed *logos* to make the worse argument appear to be the better and its correlative, the false to become true. The dangers inherent in this kind of argumentation, both for the law courts and for education, were felt universally in Athens and vigorously excoriated in the agon between the true and false *logoi* in Aristophanes' play, *Clouds*, where the principle is attributed erroneously, but comically, to Socrates.

It is, however, an entirely understandable pre-cept among those teaching rhetoric. Instruction in constructing paired speeches of antithetical positions, *dissoi logoi*, is part of the curriculum. Sophistic contests (*agōnes*) in which these *dissoi logoi*, both deliberative and epideictic, are delivered and applauded, were regular occurrences in Athens. The victorious argument depends for its success on the style of presentation, not necessarily on the validity of the position. Our one surviving set of *dissoi logoi* from soon after 404 BCE consists of nine antithetical pairs of speeches on subjects such as good/bad, noble/shameful, just/unjust, truth/falsehood, whether wisdom and honor are teachable or not. The best crafted *dissoi logoi* from the period, however, are actually the several sets of speeches in Thucydides' history of the Peloponnesian War (431–404 BCE). The debate between Cleon and Diodotus over whether or not to kill the Mytilenaeans who have revolted against Athens, (3.37–48) and the speeches by Nicias and Alcibiades on the wisdom of an invasion of Sicily (6.9–18), are famous examples.

Thucydides, the earliest political historian (c.455–396 BCE) brings to the technique a complexity and *variatio* that breaks down the normal tendency toward balance and parallelism. *Variatio* is the technical term for the deliberate avoidance of a too strict balance of clauses or words. Thucydides strives to avoid straightforward "Gorgianic" antithesis, often embedding one member of a set in another set. The complexity of the results strains the Greek as well as at times the powers of scholars to understand. Following are two examples from the Funeral Oration Thucydides puts into the mouth of Pericles. The first involves antithetical thought, and the verbal antithesis is muted: "For we use a form of government that does not copy the laws of our neighbors; in as much as we are a model to some rather than imitators of others" (2.37.1) The second is syntactically and elaborately antithetical: "We are lovers of beauty with economy and lovers of wisdom without softness. Wealth we use more for opportune action than for the boasting of it" (2.40.1).

By the beginning of the fourth century BCE, antithesis as a pronounced aspect of composition is found with less frequency. It is relegated to the body of stylistic tactics. Rhetorical prose has moved away from its poetic influence. There is less parallelism generally, including in the repetition of structure and words. In his criticism of Thucydides, Dionysius of Halicarnassus (*On Lysias* 14) warns against excessive use of antithesis and praises the orator Lysias for his avoidance of it. But Lysias (c.445–c.380 BCE) is fond of balanced cola often with *homoeoteleuton* (words with the same endings), even when there is no semantic antithesis. Isocrates (436–338 BCE), too, at times indulges in antithesis to embellish his more balanced periods even when there is no antithesis of argumentation.

During this century, however, while semantic antithesis moved away from stylized verbal antithesis, there remain the basic utilitarian features of antithesis of thought (*dianoia*). The old presocratic expression of contraries appears in Plato as a method of discussion (dialectic) and argument (*elenchus*). Aristotle, in fact, in the opening of the *Rhetoric* calls rhetoric the counterpart of dialectic. More significantly, although not the first to devise formulae, Aristotle begins to establish the terminology of logic and syllogism as direct outgrowths of the Platonic dialectic. [*See* Dialectic; Logic; *and* Syllogism.] All of these forms of philosophical argumentation and proof involve a dualism either of content or structure. For example, the dialogue format requires at least two participants; *elenchus* requires a thesis and a counter thesis; dialectic requires a thesis to be proved one way or another. Syllogism is a precise (mathematical, perhaps) formulation of argumentation, which owes its origins to the Platonic *elenchus*. In its essentials, the syllogism includes an antithetical pair, sometimes in parallel alignment, sometimes expressing true contraries, that "concludes" (the basic meaning of *syllogizein*) in a unification of the separate *logoi*, in a synthesis. Aristotle finds such antithetical expression pleasant (*hēdeia*): "because contraries are most easily understood and are even more comprehensible if they are balanced, and further, because antithesis is like a syllogism; for the argument (*elenchos*) is a bringing together of antithetical pairs" (*Rhetoric* 3.9.1410a). The parallel between this philosophical track that antithesis directed and the evolution of the periodic structure of sophisticated prose, found specifically in the speeches of Demosthenes, is not lost on Aristotle.

The well-developed period, like the well-constructed syllogism, consists of two antithetical clauses, the second looking back to the first (*antikeimenē lexis*). This also marks the beginning of true subordination (*katestrammenē lexis*)—the folding back of the ideas, not the juxtapositioning of them (Aristotle, *Rhetoric* 1409b–1410a and Demetrius, *On Style* 1.22). A stunning example from Demosthenes (*On the Crown,* 330 BCE) follows. I underline the various antitheses within the subordination:

> Since these things are such in this contest, I <u>ask and implore you all alike to listen to me</u> with a sense of justice as I deliver my defense against the accusations, just as the laws bid, which Solon, in setting them up originally, being well-minded towards you and a supporter of the people, thought had to be validated <u>not only through written enactment, but also by means of an oath from the jury, not distrusting you</u>, as it seems to me, <u>but seeing</u> that the charges and the slanders, by which from the opportunity of <u>speaking first, the prosecutor has an advantage</u>, no <u>defendant can overcome</u>, unless each of you as jurymen who preserve the respect towards the gods, <u>receives with equanimity</u> the case of the <u>second</u> speaker and <u>conducts himself</u> in an impartial and democratic way <u>as he listens to both</u>, thus he will be in a position to draw a conclusion over the entire case. (227)

In particular, one notices how successfully the request for the jury to listen with impartiality at the beginning is reaffirmed at the end in antithetical style, but is arrived at as the legitimate conclusion of a long period that functions as a proof of the premise from the opening. Aristotle's student Theophrastus succinctly unites the stylistic with the philosophical: "antithesis is the predication by opposites of the same thing" (Dionysius, *On Lysias* 14).

The two paths of antithesis persist into the late Roman period. The stylistic form is relegated to poetry in the Middle Ages, functioning as a persuasive art form and as a *topos;* antithesis is generally eschewed by philosophers. In rhetorical or religious pieces, argument from *stasis*, a central principle, and argument by analogy are prominent. [*See* Stasis.] Antithesis is no longer a mode of argumentation. After the rediscovery of Aristotelian logic and rhetoric in the Renaissance, antithesis reappears sporadically in the secular prose tradition, and only as a distinct feature of style in tracts that advertise rhetoric as a means to knowledge and reason. [*See overview article on* Renaissance rhetoric.] Significant in the process in Europe are Fenner, *The Artes of Logicke and Rethorike* (1584), Vossius, *Institutiones Rhetoricae* (1606), Bacon *On the Advancement of Learning* (1605, Latin 1623), and Descartes, *Discourse on Method* (1637). Bacon is most important for clear recognition of the split between rhetoric and logic as two distinct parts of the "art of tradition." Rhetoric and the new philology come to occupy French neoclassicism, however, while the antithesis associated with argument and syllogism appears dominant in serious philosophical discussion in Britain and Germany. Kant actually deepens the rift by making rhetoric a branch of the art of speech along with poetry within the fine arts, away from philosophy and science, *Critique of Judgment* (1790). The types of antithesis are fully segregated, the poetic and rhetorical device from the feature of logical syllogistic and argument.

It is Hegel (1770–1831) who revitalizes the presocratic and Platonic understanding of antithesis as a way to determine conclusions, even cosmic principles, through the expression of paired notions, either in contrast or in balance. For Hegel, the Absolute (Whole, Reality, God) can only be apprehended through dialectic in which the thesis and antithesis arrive at a synthesis, *Science of Logic* (1816), which is in turn the philosophical equivalent of the Absolute or Being, what in his phenomenology of the mind is the equivalent of Being or God.

BIBLIOGRAPHY

Aristotle. *Prior Analytics.* Translated by H. Tredennick. Loeb Classical Library. Cambridge, Mass., 1983. Early discussion of logic and metaphysics; development of syllogism.

Baldwin, C. S. *Ancient Rhetoric and Poetic.* New York, 1924. A general survey of the major developments.

Baldwin, C. S. *Medieval Rhetoric and Poetic.* New York, 1928. History of rhetoric from St. Augustine and the last Roman schools through the Carolingians and into the fourteenth century. He traces the two paths through the medieval period: rhetoric and logic and rhetoric and poetry.

Cole, Thomas. *The Origins of Rhetoric in Ancient Greece.* Baltimore, 1991. An excellent history of rhetoric based on theory and its development as a craft and

integral part of ancient poetry, history, and philosophy.

Conley, Thomas M. *Rhetoric in the European Tradition.* White Plains, N.Y., 1990. A general, concise history, but with some insightful discussions of individual speeches; not specifically on antithesis, but deals with tensions and paired speeches.

Connors, R. J., L. S. Ede, and A. A. Lunsford, eds. *Essays on Classical Rhetoric and Modern Discourse.* Carbondale, Ill., 1984.

Denniston, John D. *Greek Prose Style.* Oxford, 1960. First published 1952. Traces the development of specific attributes of prose from the earliest philosophers and Sophists through the orators and later philosophers.

Diels, Hermann, and Walther Kranz. *Die Fragmente der Vorsokratiker.* Berlin, 1951–1952. The major source for the lives, texts, and fragments of the presocratic philosophers and sophists; see below Freeman and Sprague for translations.

Finley, John Huston Jr. *Three Essays on Thucydides.* Cambridge Mass., 1967. Finds sources of Thucydides' style in the Sophists such as Gorgias and Prodicus.

Freeman, Kathleen. *Ancilla to the pre-Socratic Philosophers.* Cambridge, Mass., 1956. Translation of the texts in Diels and Kranz.

Hegel, Georg W. *The Science of Logic.* Translated by A. V. Miller. London, 1969. Essay in which Hegel outlines the process of thesis/antithesis and synthesis.

Hollingsworth, John Emory. *Antithesis in the Attic Orators from Antiphon to Isaeus.* Menasha, Wis., 1915. Still the best discussion of the subject; shows how each used antithesis of argument and/or antithetical stylistic devices.

Kennedy, George. *The Art of Persuasion in Greece.* Princeton, 1963. General history of Greek rhetoric and oratory from its beginnings into the Hellenistic period. Emphasis on characteristics and theory.

Kennedy, George. *Classical Rhetoric and Its Christian and Secular Tradition from Ancient to Modern Times.* Chapel Hill, N.C., 1980. General approach to the major trends and figures. Covers Homer to the twentieth century.

Kenyan, Grover Cleveland. *Antithesis in the Speeches of the Greek Historians.* Chicago, 1941. Good collection of types of antithesis and representative examples.

Kirk, G. S., and J. E. Raven. *The Presocratic Philosophers.* Cambridge, U.K., 1969. Best introductory discussion of these thinkers and their major contributions.

Lloyd, G. E. R. *Polarity and Analogy: Two Types of Argumentation in Early Greek Thought.* Cambridge, U.K., 1966.

Norden, Eduard. *Die Antike Kunstprosa.* 2 vols. Stuttgart, 1974. First published 1909. Best history of specific elements of ancient prose. Traces the devices back into poetry and the presocratic thinkers.

Sprague, Rosamond K. *The Older Sophists*. Columbia, S.C., 1972. Translations of the fragments of the Sophists from Diels and Kranz, including the *dissoi logoi*.

—JUNE W. ALLISON

THREE STYLES, THEORY OF. *See* Classical rhetoric; *and* Style.

TOPICS. The term *topics*, which derives from a Greek word meaning "having to do with commonplaces," was the title given to classical and medieval collections of generally accepted arguments or set pieces for use in a speech or composition. In the singular, a *topos* signifies either a familiar *place* in a text (and hence the sort of passage that occupies that place) or, in the stricter Aristotelian sense, a kind of *argument* (which might generate a specific passage in a text). The overlap of these meanings is complicated by practice. Aristotle's *Topica* (c.350 BCE) teaches how to argue about probable things, yet despite the influence of this title, Aristotle (384–322 BCE) should not be considered the originator of topical arguments or of the term *topos*. First, Aristotle himself offers ambiguous and even conflicting accounts of *topos* and in addition refers to other experts whose rhetorical *technai* covered this or that *topos*. He was thus intervening in an established Greek sophistic practice and term. [*See* Sophists.] This article will treat Aristotle's *Topica*, the first systematic treatment of the subject of general or reusable arguments, the relation of this text and of *topoi* to Aristotle's developing rhetoric, and the major modifications of the theory; it will also touch on the relation of *topoi* to oratorical usage and literary practice.

Aristotle's *Topica* expounds *dialectical* reasoning, which he contrasts to scientific reasoning (often translated as *demonstration*), which he had treated in the *Posterior Analytics*. [*See* Dialectic.] The *Topica* aims to furnish the philosopher (or the speaker—topical reasoning is a universal theory of what can be affirmed) with the method by which to discuss all probables (*endoxa*). Whereas scientific reasoning demonstrates the proofs of, say, geometry, the *Topica* provides the means for argument about the class of things that can be proved in words. The dialectical method it employs is a process of questioning and strengthening a proposed definition, and unlike scientific reasoning, which requires that its premises be true, dialectic (in this early treatment) is concerned with popular opinions. Aristotle thus presents the way for a speaker to move from generally accepted ideas or norms to some particular end. He sees this as a universal language and persuasion method useful to the training of the mind, to daily encounters, and to philosophical investigations. Clearly, Aristotle's thinking evolved from this early systematic account, and so the *Topica* is usually overshadowed by the discussion of enthymeme in the *Rhetoric* and the discussion of types of predication in the *Categories*. [*See* Enthymeme.] (In the *Topica*, all predications fall into one of four categories: definition, genus, property, and accident.) The *Topica* is perhaps of greatest interest for the historian of philosophy as Aristotle's first vision of a universal argument theory, one whose divisions are then much refined in the *Categories*, as indeed the method is made more universally syllogistic in the *Rhetoric*. Yet the *Topica* is no simple precursor to Aristotle's rhetoric: dialectical reasoning examines the ethical, logical, and physical propositions arising from men's consensus, what is acceptable to a majority of the audience. Aristotle does add that the opinions can be those acceptable to wise men, either all of them, the majority of them, or the most renowned of them. The contradictions in these sets do not concern him, for he allows a generous sweep in the analysis of popular opinions. Probables, however, do not include lies or false reasoning (the work that follows in the *Organon, On Sophistical Refutations*, treats bad reasoning).

Despite the emphasis on opinion, Aristotle describes neither amoral argumentation nor opinion mongering: he examines the substructure of everyday opinion making in the same spirit that led him to assemble laws of different communities—seeking elements common to human nature, and in the case of the *Topica*, seeking the grounds for consensus making. Only thus can philosophy and the *polis* progress. Indeed, the theory implies that all discourse is founded on these principles, for Aristotle imagines that human language is interested always in moving from point *a* to point *c,* where *b* has been unexpressed. In its fully developed stage in the *Rhetoric,* this entails finding the middle piece of an enthymeme. In the *Topica,* the student is learning what general kinds of reasoning underlie all propositions. Once we relate the proposition at hand to these governing structures we can determine if it is probable. And at least here, the probable seems synonymous with the good or the advantageous. To use one of Aristotle's illustrations: Should one do good to one's enemies? Dialectical reasoning leads to the answer no by three steps. First, it is a generally received opinion that we should do good to our friends. Second, we arrive at the contrary (which of course is false or inconsistent): we ought to do good to our enemies. The contradictory of the contrary to a common opinion will be probable; that is, one now negates the contrary and can say, we ought not to do good to our enemies. The reasoner is here employing *topoi* and a logic of opposites so as to test whether the proposition fits a known *topos.* Thus the reasoner does not simply canvas opinions empirically.

Topical argument at this level enlarges the stock of common opinions and general judgments. It also examines instances where there are differences of opinion. Aristotle does not ask why people believe different things: he describes a method that submits predications to tests of their consistency. For example, if a proposition uses the word *clear,* the reasoner must beware since the word has different semantic fields. The linguistic term has one range in respect to color, another for sound. Aristotle especially means that in these two different fields color cannot be subjected to the same *topoi* (there is no intermediate between a clear and an obscure sound whereas gray is an intermediate in respect to color). Aristotle seems to be describing linguistic usage, and much of his treatise is taken up with the close analysis of the language of premises. In another example, a Greek verb that means *to see* but can mean *to have sight* is examined: Aristotle is simply leading his student through the kind of questioning that results not in linguistic research but in the distinctions in consistency of parallel items (and their

contraries). Since premise making proceeds by modeling particulars on generals, we must be careful that the language of our premise is analogous to that of the *topos,* or indeed to another premise that we know to be an instance of a *topos.* An ambiguity in a word may prevent it from being used in a premise. The result of adopting this method should be that the reasoner can detect and craft not only consistent definitions but particular premises that consistently mirror the structure of general premises.

Amid the complex and even tedious rules of Aristotle's *Topica* (the reader may well side with Isocrates [436–338 BCE], who said that general arguments were too difficult to learn), it is easy to miss the method. Dialecticians are to collect probables from written works and elsewhere. These are to be subjected to the rigorous methods described in the *Topica,* but the implication is that the student is to make a copybook of opinions under the headings that are the *topoi* of the *Topica.* [*See* Commonplaces and commonplace books.] Definition, property, genus, and accident are not *topoi* but the heads under which he groups *topoi* (e.g., the propositions that predicate accident are in the second and third books). Beneath the subheading of *topoi* he lists propositions. One *topos,* for example, is that every proposition has necessary consequences. The task of the reasoner is usually that of a negative disputant (so reducing the world of probables to consistent, though not strictly verifiable premises). Here, presented with the proposition that Socrates is a man, one seeks out a consequence that the particular does not have; for example, show that Socrates is not a biped or not capable of learning and he will be proved not a man. Under *topoi* of comparison there is the following *topos:* Should two different predicates be affirmed of the same subject, if one can disprove the more probable of the two, the less probable can also be said to be disproved. A *topos* of the more aphoristic type: Something desirable in itself is better than something desirable for another end. This is the general opinion from which we can prove that happiness is better than wealth since wealth is only valued because of its consequences. Statements of comparison and difference fall under numerous *topoi.* One such topos: if two things are said to be the same, check their derivatives, coordinates, opposites. If someone says courage is the same thing as justice, argue that the courageous man must be identical to the just man. It is little wonder that subsequent theorists reduced the elaborate enumeration of analogic thinking to questions of definition, but Aristotle is interested in exhaustively cataloging what to do should one encounter a statement with the word *same* in it.

Aristotle returned to his subject in the *Rhetoric* (1.4.7–14) where he treats *topoi* of the good and the bad, right and wrong, just and unjust, but more generally, the elaborate account of syllogistic reasoning seems to replace or overlap much of the earlier discussion of dialectical reasoning through *topoi*. Aristotle seems to use *topos* somewhat vaguely (*Rhet.* 2.22). He says praise of Achilles is a *topos* provided one praise him as a man or as one of the group who went to Troy. Here he means little more than that general praise, not tied to the particulars of the most exceptional Greek ever, constitutes a *topos,* but he may well be answering the term as commonly used to mean a set piece or hackneyed treatment. Modern scholarship has sought to define *topos,* since Aristotle does not, by comparison with the *Rhetoric,* which states that the element and the *topos* of an argument are the same (see Pater, 1968, who considers *topos* a logical law or reason; this view was opposed by Stump, 1988, who considers *topos* a strategy).

While influential, the *Topica* should not be taken as the font of Greek and Roman theory and practice. In *Sophistic Refutations,* Aristotle indicates that the Sophists had set their students exercises that were generally reproducible (see also Cicero, *Brutus* 46). The *Topica* remained important because it was in the *Organon,* the Aristotlean logical corpus, and because of its commentators, among the most distinguished of whom were Alexander of Aphrodisias (fl. second century CE), who influenced the Byzantine tradition; the tenth-century Muslim scholar Al-Farabi; and the twelfth-century Ibn Rushd (Averröes). [*See* Arabic rhetoric.]

In the West, the history of medieval logic turns again and again to Boethius's *Topics.* Abelard (died c.1144) used Boethius, not Aristotle, but John of Salisbury in 1159 states that Aristotle's *Topics* had been introduced in his lifetime. Boethius (c.480–c.524 CE) echoes much of Cicero's

treatment (the art of discourse is finding and judging arguments, namely, topics and analytics) but provides clues of the tradition between Aristotle and Cicero (106–43 BCE). There is additional if slim evidence from the commentators, such as Alexander of Aphrodisias in his commentary on Aristotle's *Topica* (2.67; see also Wallies, 1891), which gives Theophrastus's definition of a *topos* as the first principle or element from which we take the first principle of particulars, defined in its outline, undefined as to its applications. [*See overview article on* Medieval rhetoric.]

Cicero maintains that he wrote his *Topica* in seven days, from memory, and while en route from Velia to Rhegium. The work has never pleased students of Aristotle because Cicero treats *topoi* as means of invention rather than as an analytics of argument, and because he mixes in *stasis* theory; finally, he makes such indiscriminate blunders as including an account of the inartificial proofs. [*See* Stasis.] The work is in fact a useful aid to invention and no doubt reflects Hellenistic practice. Boethius follows Cicero in language as well as theory, but also Themistius (c.317–c.388 CE), who, Boethius says, subsumed all *topoi* under definition. Boethius lists as one type of *topos/locus* the maxim: *proposito maxima,* a first principle of proof (Aristotle's axiom), and also follows Cicero in an interest in systematic invention, where *topos/locus* is a seat of argument. Cicero had also described *locus* as the house of proofs (*De oratore* 2.162).

In practice, as the school exercises known as *progymnasmata* make clear, Greeks and Romans would have given the term *topos* or *locus* to a section of a speech that amplified the virtue or vice of the particular subject by reference to some well-known event or person. Here, tradition is in direct violation of Aristotle, who faulted teachers for giving their students products of discourse instead of the method of discourse. No matter, *locus* became a point of meeting for author and audience, a familiar place where an author's difference could be viewed as he rehandled a theme and treatments so well known. Much of Latin literature was to be appreciated in this allusive mode, which prizes inventiveness, the interplay of models, author, and reader, and fosters a layered interpretation.

[*See also* Casuistry; Classical rhetoric; Irreparable, the; Logos; *and* Tacit dimension, the.]

BIBLIOGRAPHY

Cole, Thomas. *The Origins of Rhetoric in Ancient Greece*. Baltimore, 1991. An innovative interpretation of the state of rhetorical theorizing before Aristotle.

Green-Pedersen, Niels J. *The Tradition of the Topica in the Middle Ages*. Munich, 1984. A valuable survey of the Western tradition with a useful digest of scholarship on Boethius.

Pater, W. A. De. "La fonction du lieu et de l'instrument dans les *Topiques*." In *Aristotle on Dialectic. The Topics*, edited by G. E. L. Owen, pp. 165–188. Oxford, 1968. Publication of a series of papers from scholars of ancient philosophy.

Stump, Eleonore, ed. and trans. *Boethius's In Ciceronis Topica*. Ithaca, N.Y., 1988. A useful introduction with full translation and notes.

Wallies, M., ed. *Commentaria in Aristotelem Graeca*, vol. 2, pt. 2. Berlin, 1891. The standard edition of Alexander of Aphrodisias's commentary on Aristotle's *Topica*.

— W. Martin Bloomer

TRIVIUM. The trivium and quadrivium were categories that organized the order and relation of the seven liberal arts throughout the Middle Ages. "Trivium" means three ways, an intersection of three roads, and by extension, a common, public area, as a town square. It was applied, perhaps as late as the eighth century (by the scholar Alcuin), to designate the first three arts, grammar, rhetoric, and dialectic, which pertain to logic and language. The term *quadrivium* means a four-way crossroads: the term was applied early on, probably first in the early sixth century by the Roman scholar and statesman Boethius, to designate the assemblage of the four mathematical sciences (or sciences of measurement), geometry, arithmetic, astronomy, and music. The notion of the seven liberal arts divided into two separate thematic units, remained in place throughout the Middle Ages (and to a lesser degree, into the Renaissance) as a conceptual principle for many curricula, from elementary learning to the higher schools, including even the universities, where its distant influence, if not its immediate presence, was felt.

The grouping of the three arts of the trivium, grammar, rhetoric, and dialectic, originated with the Greek Stoics in the third century BCE. Although the term *trivium* was not to be applied until over one thousand years later, the concept of three arts (fields of knowledge, disciplines, or "sciences," as in Latin, *scientiae*) linked by their pertinence to language and verbal logic was fixed in place with Stoic thought. The Stoics divided "philosophy" (meaning all knowledge) into three branches: logic, ethics, and physics. Within the category of logic (from *logos*, meaning "word," but also "concept" or "reasoning"), they placed the individual sciences of grammar, rhetoric, and dialectic. (Several centuries earlier, the Pythagoreans had first linked together the four arts of mathematical measurement—geometry, arithmetic, astronomy, and music or harmony—in what would, much later, come to be known as the quadrivium.) The Stoic system that linked the three language arts together in this strong position persisted through the Roman and postclassical periods. The first encyclopedist to bring together the arts of the trivium and quadrivium in one comprehensive survey was the scholar and grammarian Varro (116–27 BCE), whose *Disciplinarum libri IX* (Nine books of discipline), which has not been preserved, established a canon of what was to become the liberal arts (Varro included medicine and architecture, which were later dropped from the canon). It was also Varro who mapped out an intellectual program for the study of Latin grammar, adapting and expanding Greek models (*De lingua latina*, partially extant).

The links among the three arts can be clearly understood if we begin by considering how they were taught in relation to one another in the classical Roman schools. Book 1 of Quintilian's *Institutio oratoria* (first century CE) attests to how a Roman curriculum would have understood the relationship between two components of the trivium, grammar and rhetoric. Quintilian gives two long-lived definitions of grammar: it is both the art of speaking correctly (*recte loquendi scientia*) and the art of interpreting the poets (*enarratio poetarum*). In both of these roles, grammar is, for Quintilian, preparatory for the study of rhetoric, which is the art of speaking well. Speaking correctly entailed a knowledge of the Latin grammatical system, which Quintilian sketches out (1.4–7). But *enarratio poetarum* entails not only reading and interpretation, but also exercises in composition, including imitation of literary models, and a beginning mastery of tropes and figures of speech (1.8). [*See* Figures of speech; *and* Imitation.] It is in this area of study, as Quintilian warns defensively (1.9; 2.1; 2.5), that the boundaries between grammar and rhetoric need to be patrolled, lest the inferior teachers, the grammarians, presume too much and step over into the proper domain of the teachers of rhetoric. Thus, while grammar is seen here as preparatory to rhetoric, it also shares considerable territory with the "higher" language art of rhetoric. Of course, such overlapping between the two arts was a problem only for Roman schools, where rhetoric claimed distinction as foremost among the sciences (cf. Cicero, *De oratore* 1.4, and Quintilian 1. Pr. 17–18). In fact, in the medieval schools, in the period when rhetoric had lost its social and political application and thus much of its prestige, the overlapping of the spheres of grammar and rhetoric was beneficial to grammatical study, which could take over many of the compositional and stylistic teachings of rhetoric, and which could later (especially in the early thirteenth century) produce a kind of preceptive rhetoric, the *ars poetriae* (art of poetry), which was highly inflected by grammatical interests in imitation, literary interpretation, and style.

At the opening of his *Rhetoric,* Aristotle (384–322 BCE) pronounces rhetoric and dialectic to be counterparts of one another, and the Roman schools would have accepted this in principle. But with Roman culture's predisposition to give rhetoric pride of place in education, dialectic was both rhetoric's counterpart (at least in name) and its helpful aid. Dialectic and rhetoric shared the study of topics, the seats of argument that serve in the process of discovery or invention of arguments. [*See* Invention; *and* Topics.] Dialectic supplied much of the terminology and many of the devices that rhetoric would adapt to its own purposes. In this respect, dialectic became another preparatory path to rhetoric, of higher intellectual prestige than grammar, to be sure, but not itself the fulfillment of educational ideals (as it had been for Plato; 429–c.347 BCE). Aristotle saw dialectical and rhetorical topics as truly counterparts: the dialectical topics deal with terms within a proposition (predicables), whereas rhetorical topics are concerned with the level of the proposition itself, and rhetorical argument tends to make connections between whole propositions rather than between individual terms. It is clear that Cicero (106–43

BCE) believed that the study of dialectical methods of inference was useful and indeed necessary to the control of rhetorical argumentation. In the *De inventione,* his treatment of topics is less indebted to Aristotle than to the *stasis* theory of the Hellenistic rhetorician Hermagoras of Temnos (a system of topics of argumentation to be found in the circumstances and controversies of a hypothesis). [*See* Stasis.] But in Cicero's later books, the *Topica* (a response to Aristotle's own *Topics*) and the *De oratore,* there is a more explicit interest in bringing dialectic to bear on rhetorical invention. Here he is concerned with more general forms of reasoning and matters of logical relation, tending to blur the boundaries between rhetoric and dialectic, but a blurring in favor of rhetorical interests (see Michael Leff, "The Topics of Argumentative Invention in Latin Rhetorical Theory from Cicero to Boethius," *Rhetorica* 1, 1983, pp. 23–44). The favoring of rhetorical interests in the study of dialectic remained constant through Quintilian. It was only with Boethius's important text *De differentiis topicis* (early sixth century CE) that this relationship was definitively reversed. For Boethius, rhetoric becomes truly subsidiary to dialectic: where dialectic uses the thesis ("Is it good for a man to marry?"), rhetoric works from the circumstantially specific hypothesis ("Shall Cato marry?"). Rhetoric and dialectic may use the same language about discovery of arguments, but rhetoric is now a foil to dialectic.

Thus the trivium originated in a notion of a three-way crossroads of grammar, rhetoric, and dialectic. In Roman education, where rhetoric was at the center of language study, rhetoric in effect separated grammar from dialectic, because the focus was on how rhetoric can negotiate a relationship with each of the other arts on an individual basis. The other curricular elements were seen to revolve around rhetoric. Yet this also created a certain dynamic relationship among the three arts. In late antiquity and the early Middle Ages, in the period of the major encyclopedic compilations, that curricular dynamism tended to be replaced by a rather more intellectualized interrelationship, because the arts were seen to inform one another, but were not vying with one another, as in the Roman schools. The pressure in the early Middle Ages was to conserve as much ancient knowledge as possible, and we sometimes have a sense of rather more reified categories of knowledge.

Martianus Capella's *De nuptiis Philologiae et Mercurii* (Marriage of Philology and Mercury), written probably in the early fifth century CE, became one of the most widely-read textbooks in the Middle Ages. This verse and prose allegory provided the foundation for the medieval trivium and quadrivium. As W. H. Stahl, its English translator, has noted, "it had the salient advantage [over other late antique compendia] of offering a well-proportioned and comprehensive treatment of all the liberal arts in the compass of one comfortable-sized book" (Stahl, Johnson, and Burge, 1971, p. 22). Martianus's book presents an ornate mythological story grafted onto encyclopedic summaries. The story is that Mercury, seeking a wife, is advised to marry the learned girl Philology. The wedding party, consisting of many classical deities, allegorized figures, and even philosophers, assembles in the heavens to celebrate the marriage. At the nuptials, the seven liberal arts, represented allegorically as seven learned sisters, each come forward to discourse on their individual disciplines, with Minerva presiding over this academic–allegorical spectacle. The order in which they present themselves follows that of the trivium and quadrivium, and each art makes her presentation for the length of one book. Martianus was sensitive to the intellectual mutuality of the arts: metrics, for example, could be a concern of both the language art of grammar and the measurement art of music, as medieval students would understand, just as they would know that logic is the link between the linguistic analysis of the trivium and the mathematical measurement of the quadrivium. Martianus even made a bit of a joke out of potential disciplinary overlaps; for example, having Minerva condescendingly cut off Grammar's discourse just as the latter is about to introduce the subject of figures and tropes; Minerva thinks this is beyond the "elementary" concerns of Grammar and more fitting as part of Rhetoric's discourse (here Martianus caught the flavor of the more severe territorial and professional rivalries of earlier Roman education).

In other compendia of the late antique and early medieval periods, the pressure toward conservation was combined with a Christian appropriation of the classical curriculum. Augustine had said that the knowledge of pagan antiquity should be carried forward to the Christian era, just as the Hebrews carried gold out of Egypt, and Christian learning accordingly availed itself of as much pagan teaching on the arts as could be encompassed and preserved. Augustine's *De doctrina christiana* (396–427 CE), while not exactly a compendium, could be said to synthesize the arts of the trivium for a Christian hermeneutical and evangelical purpose: grammar (especially philology) is necessary to an understanding of Scripture; dialectic is implicit in Augustine's treatment of signification, where signs are joined to a theory of meaning; and rhetoric is arguably the subject of the whole treatise, from invention (finding one's material for arguments in Scripture itself, which must be interpreted) to delivery (the subject of Book 4, which concerns the "means of setting forth" that which has been discovered). [*See* Delivery; Hermeneutics; *and* Religion.]

The enormous encyclopedia by Cassiodorus (c.490–c.585), the *Institutiones divinarum et saecularium litterarum,* composed for the instruction of the monks at Vivarium, explicitly sets out a Christian compendium of the arts. The second part of the *Institutiones* treats the liberal arts, using mainly late classical sources for the three trivium arts. In the first half of the work, on divine letters, Cassiodorus lays out an argument for the value of classical (pagan) sciences for interpreting Scripture, thus justifying the digest of the arts in the second half of the work. In Cassiodorus's representation of the trivium, grammar and rhetoric receive relatively perfunctory and truncated treatment, while dialectic receives pride of place as that which "distinguishes true from false" and permits discussion of the largest kinds of epistemological questions (e.g., the difference between speculative and practical sciences, a concern borrowed from Aristotelian thought). With Cassiodorus, we have an early instance of how the Middle Ages would preserve the framework of the three language arts, but at the same time redistribute the emphasis, giving greater weight to dialectic as a science that was more readily translatable into new intellectual milieux. The second half of the *Institutiones,* on the liberal arts, was the more widely disseminated in the Middle Ages. It served as an immediate source for the encyclopedists of the next few centuries, including Isidore of Seville (seventh century), whose *Etymologies* became in turn one of the most popular educational encyclopedias; Alcuin (c.732–804), whose treatises on grammar, rhetoric, and dialectic were among the most important productions of the Carolingian Renaissance; and the monastic writer (and pupil of Alcuin) Rabanus Maurus (c.780–856) whose *Institutio clericorum* set a standard for monastic educational programs.

We have seen that Roman academic culture presented a trivium structure in which rhetoric was the central, pivotal component. The compendia of late antiquity and the early Middle Ages preserved the threefold structure of the language arts, but the commitment to the priority of rhetoric was not necessarily strong, so the weight accorded the various arts was redistributed, and their position within models of scientific classification began to shift. For example, Cassiodorus, as we have seen, gave overwhelming weight to dialectic; Isidore of Seville, however, while treating all of the seven liberal arts, also returned to the Stoic model of dividing "philosophy" into physics, ethics, and logic, and under logic listed only dialectic and rhetoric. What can often be seen in the Middle Ages is that the trivium, as an inherited category, retained rhetoric as a component, but many of rhetoric's functions were actually performed either by grammar (which commonly treats style in conjunction with language, composition, and textual commentary), or by dialectic (which used rhetorical teachings to clarify problems of argumentation). [*See* Style.] Having no direct civic function as it did in Greek and Roman antiquity, the art of rhetoric was preserved as a body of academic doctrine often to be mined by the other two language arts. (In some respects, this situation changed in the later Middle Ages, when rhetoric was called into service to meet the documentary requirements of the urban bureaucracies and was taught as an art of letter writing; in the late Middle Ages, rhetoric was also called upon to serve as the preceptive format for new arts of preaching.) [*See* Ars dictaminis; *and* Homiletics.]

The fortunes of the trivium can be traced in relation to conceptions of its internal intellectual structure, which are reflected in many different schemes for the classification of the sciences. Richard McKeon (1952) has shown that medieval academic discussions typically subordinated rhetoric

to whatever was the primary discipline, most often logic (here in the technical sense of inference, argument, and disputation, of which dialectic would be a branch). Thus, for example, in the thirteenth century, Aquinas classified rhetoric as a subdivision of logic, presenting it as one of the three forms, along with dialectic and poetic, of "inventive logic," a kind of reasoning that led to probable proof. Note that in this scheme, poetic has displaced grammar; this phenomenon descends from an Arabic textual tradition that classifies Aristotle's *Rhetoric* and *Poetics* with his logical texts, thus making rhetoric and poetics part of logic. [*See* Arabic rhetoric.] During the twelfth century, rhetoric was most commonly represented as a subdivision of the scientific category of logic. For example, Hugh of Saint Victor, who wrote a guide for students called the *Didascalicon*, offered two schemes of classification: in one scheme, he divided "verbal logic" into grammar and "rational logic," and then subdivided rational logic into dialectic and rhetoric; in the other scheme, he placed rhetoric and dialectic together under probable reasoning, which was itself a subdivision of "rational examination" (*ratio disserendi*). In the first scheme, grammar was isolated from rhetoric and dialectic; in the second scheme it entirely disappeared. Among other commentators, we find that rhetoric shifts ground. Thierry of Chartres, who wrote a commentary on Cicero's *De inventione* in the mid-twelfth century, called rhetoric a "major part of civil science"; he also distinguished it from dialectic because it used the hypothesis as opposed to the thesis. The latter argument was derived directly from Boethius's treatment of rhetoric and dialectic, and it was clear from the commentary itself and from the academic context of Thierry's commentary that he was far more interested in rhetoric as a foil to dialectic than as an art of civil affairs. Not long after Thierry produced his commentary, a Spanish scholar, Dominicus Gundissalinus, wrote a classification of the sciences (*De divisione philosophiae*) in which he offered two very different schemes: first he placed rhetoric, dialectic, and grammar together as arts of speech in civil affairs (*civilis ratio*), grouping them under the Aristotelian category of practical science, and borrowing Thierry of Chartres's treatment of rhetoric as civil affairs; but then he placed rhetoric and poetic under logic, drawing on the Arabic tradition of classifying rhetoric and poetic with the logical works of Aristotle's *Organon*. Two other twelfth-century commentators, William of Conches (who was probably also associated with the cathedral school of Chartres) and an anonymous author invented a new scientific category altogether, "eloquence," which contains rhetoric, grammar, and dialectic.

In the thirteenth century, under the impress of the recovered Aristotelian science, there were various new attempts to place the trivium under larger epistemological categories. Sometimes rhetoric was attached to the trivium, sometimes it was removed from its traditional framework. In about 1250, an English scholar, Robert Kilwardby, wrote a treatise on scientific classification in which he employed the Aristotelian system of practical and theoretical sciences. Enlarging on the Aristotelian scheme, he created a new category, *artes sermocinales* (arts of discourse), in which he placed the whole trivium. He saw the *artes sermocinales* as related to, although distinct from, practical sciences, because the arts of discourse use speech to produce effects, whereas practical sciences, such as ethics, use actions to produce effects. Yet in the same treatise, he also admitted rhetoric by itself into the category of practical sciences, under ethics and civil science, because rhetoric was used in the negotiation of moral and political affairs. Later in the thirteenth century, two Parisian scholars, John of Dacia and Giles of Rome, divided the human sciences into mechanical and liberal; the liberal sciences they further divided into practical and speculative; for the speculative sciences (those sciences whose end is knowledge or theory, not action), they created an "auxiliary" category of rational sciences, into which they placed the trivium. But in a different context, Giles of Rome separated rhetoric from the trivium, to recognize its application to morals, and determined that it derives from dialectic and politics. In an intellectual system based on Aristotelian science in which dialectic was the key device of knowledge, the old trivium structure was no longer truly useful; yet we see here how late medieval Aristotelian thought tried to preserve a place at least for the conceptual category of the trivium.

As an alliance of three arts, the trivium was successful as a conceptual device. As an abstract category, it served very well to articulate what was thought to be the internal relationship among parts of knowledge. But it is not clear how far into practical, quotidien teaching activities the idea of of the trivium as a coherent group of subjects really carried. Medieval schools were probably more likely to teach *about* the trivium as an alliance of three language arts than to teach all of its components in their entirety. In later medieval Europe (from the twelfth century onward), lower (grammar) schools would certainly have concentrated on grammar, the pathway to acquiring mastery of Latin, and for this subject they used various primers and reading anthologies, the most famous of which, the "Cato Book," contained six classical (or classical-based) texts. Such schools most likely taught rhetoric as part of a program of Latin composition exercises, and here their teaching would have been a synthesis of compositional precept (such as Horace's *Ars poetica*) with elements of style and the study of figures and tropes—in other words, a "rhetoric" in which grammatical concerns still dominated. The higher schools (the cathedral schools of the twelfth century; and from the thirteenth century onward, the universities) tended to focus on logic (especially in northern Europe). Students in the higher schools presumably already knew grammar, and there was comparatively little attention given to grammatical texts in the university curricula of the thirteenth century (the Paris curriculum of 1215 mentions reading Priscian, the early sixth-century grammarian, and the Oxford curriculum of 1268 mentions reading Donatus, the fourth-century grammarian, and Priscian). The better part of the university curricula was given over to logic (the "old logic" of Porphyry and Boethius and the "new logic" of Aristotle). Even at the University of Bologna, where there had been a much stronger presence of rhetoric and grammar than in northern Europe, these subjects were gradually overshadowed by logic and relegated to preparatory status. Only in the middle of the fifteenth century is there evidence, from the Oxford University statutes, of an attempt being made to create a curriculum reflecting the whole system of the seven liberal arts, with attention distributed more or less evenly among all the subjects. Overall, we can say that while the trivium remained a coherent conceptual structure, it was not a single, unified application in any one setting at one time. It was at best a sequence of steps (perhaps often irregular), with lower schools handling the preparatory work of grammar and some rhetoric, and higher schools focusing on dialectic and logic, with varying attention to grammar and rhetoric.

Paul de Man's classic essay "The Resistance to Theory" uses the medieval trivium as paradigmatic of the epistemological tension inherent within any system of "language about language." The trivium is the most general of linguistic models. Grammar offers a system of decoding linguistic usage; dialectic links language with reasoning along rigorously codified lines. But rhetoric is the destabilizing element in the triad, for it expressly engages with what is irreducible in language and resistant to any transparent explanation, either by grammar or dialectic: the tropological dimension of language, the unfixing of linguistic reference, the success of arguments that produce belief over argument that aim at certainty. "Rhetoric," de Man concludes, "by its actively negative relationship to grammar and to logic, certainly undoes the claims of the trivium (and by extension, of language) to be an epistemologically stable construct" (p. 17). For de Man, the tensions within the trivium serve as a pointed analogy with the always-contested status of contemporary literary theory. From antiquity through the Middle Ages, the continuous reassessments of the status of the three arts and of the relation among them suggests that the instability at the center of this intellectual canon was intuited, and that the challenge of resolving the system's indeterminacies was as compelling as the imperative of teaching the system itself.

[*See also* Dialectic; Logic; Logos; *and* Medieval rhetoric.]

BIBLIOGRAPHY

Abelson, Paul. *The Seven Liberal Arts: A Study in Medieval Culture.* New York, 1906.

Arts libéraux et philosophie au moyen âge. Montréal, 1969. This grand collection of authoritative essays (contributions from an international congress on medieval philosophy), in several languages (mainly English and French), is the best single-volume source for research on medieval sciences and learning.

Copeland, Rita. "Lydgate, Hawes, and the Science of Rhetoric in the Late Middle Ages." *Modern Language Quarterly* 53 (1992), pp. 57–82. Contains information and bibliography on classification of the sciences and vernacular poetry.

Dahan, Gilbert. "Notes et textes sur la poétique au moyen âge." *Archives d'histoire doctrinale et littéraire du moyen âge* 47 (1980), pp. 171–239. Very informative, scholarly account of the place of poetics in relation to the trivium.

De Man, Paul. "The Resistance to Theory." *Yale French Studies* 63 (1982), pp. 3–20. A classic essay exemplifying the method of deconstruction in relation to contemporary theory, intellectual history, and the trivium.

Hugh of Saint Victor. *Didascalicon.* Translated and edited by C. H. Buttimer. Washington, D.C., 1939.

Hugh of Saint Victor. *The Didascalicon of Hugh of St. Victor.* Translated by Jerome Taylor. New York, 1961.

Irvine, Martin. *The Making of Textual Culture: "Grammatica" and Literary Theory, 350–1100.* Cambridge, U.K., 1994.

Le Goff, Jacques. *Intellectuals in the Middle Ages.* Translated by Teresa L. Fagan. Oxford, 1993. Sophisticated, highly readable introduction to the culture of medieval universities.

Marrou, Henri. *A History of Education in Antiquity.* Translated by George Lamb. New York, 1956.

McKeon, Richard. "Rhetoric in the Middle Ages." In *Critics and Criticism.* Edited by R. S. Crane, pp. 117–145. Chicago, 1952. This fundamental study, first published 1942, considers the intellectual and philosophical traditions that defined the disciplinary status of rhetoric within the trivium.

Minnis, A. J., A. B. Scott, with David Wallace, eds. and trans. *Medieval Literary Theory and Criticism c.1100–c.1375.* Oxford, 1988. This collection of primary texts is a magnificent resource on medieval learning and the arts.

Murphy, James J. *Rhetoric in the Middle Ages.* Berkeley, 1974. The best study of medieval rhetoric, with extensive information on the relation between grammar, rhetoric, and logic.

Orme, Nicholas. *English Schools in the Middle Ages.* London, 1973. An authoritative study of elementary education in England, including the way the arts were taught.

Quintilian. *Institutio oratoria.* Translated by H. E. Butler. 4 vols. Cambridge, Mass., 1920.

Rajna, P. "Le denominazione Trivium e Quadrivium." *Studi Medievali,* n.s. 1 (1928), pp. 4–36. Rajna argues that the terms *trivium* and *quadrivium* were first used together in the Carolingian era (eighth century) to distinguish the seven liberal arts.

Rashdall, Hastings. *The Universities of Europe in the Middle*

Ages. 3 vols. Edited by F. M. Powicke and A. B. Emden. Oxford, 1987. First published 1936.

Riché, Pierre. *Education and Culture in the Barbarian West.* Translated by John J. Contreni. Columbia, S.C., 1978. This important study covers the transitional period of the sixth through eighth centuries.

Stahl, William Harris, Richard Johnson, with E. L. Burge. *Martianus Capella and the Seven Liberal Arts,* vol. 1, *The Quadrivium of Martianus Capella.* New York, 1971.

Stahl, William Harris, with E. L. Burge, trans. *Martianus Capella and the Seven Liberal Arts,* vol. 2, *The Marriage of Philology and Mercury.* New York, 1977.

Wagner, David L., ed. *The Seven Liberal Arts in the Middle Ages.* Bloomington, Ind., 1983. Survey essays by distinguished scholars on each of the arts and their historical contexts.

—RITA COPELAND

TROPES. *See* Classical rhetoric; Figures of speech; *and* Style.

UVZ

◆

UNIVERSAL AUDIENCE. *See* Argument fields; Audience; *and* Conviction.

UTILITY. The principle of utility advises that whenever we are faced with a moral or political quandary, we ought to choose the course of action that will allow us to maximize happiness and minimize unhappiness. We should try, in other words, to make the world as good a place as possible in which to live.

On its surface, utility appears to be an uncomplicated—even innocuous—standard of judgment. But on closer examination, it raises divisive questions: What is happiness? How is happiness measured? Whose happiness counts? How do we reconcile conflicts between our desire to maximize happiness and our duty to comply with social trusts and promises? From ancient times, thinkers of a particular cast of mind have gravitated toward some form of utility as a standard for justifying and judging personal and public policy. Thus, rhetoric, as the oldest avowedly practical art, has always had an interest in the principle of utility as an argumentative topic. It should be clear, however, that utility is not a single, well-defined *topos*. [*See* Topics.] Rather, as in Cicero's *De officiis* (On moral obligation, c.44 BCE) it is an umbrella term designating a variety of related but often widely divergent rhetorical stances.

One of the earliest and most enduring versions of the principle of utility appears in Aristotle's discussion of the deliberative or political genre of rhetoric. Aristotle (384–322 BCE) observed that when a political assembly considers a policy proposal the standard by which they evaluate the policy is "the advantageous [*sympheron*] and the harmful" (*Rhetoric*, New York, 1991, p. 49). As George Kennedy, a translator of Aristotle, observes, the word *sympheron* is frequently translated as "the expedient," but the literal translation is "whatever 'brings with it' advantage" (Lat. *utilitas*). Aristotle's

sympheron, like all forms of utility, represents a "consequentialist" standard of value; that is, the assembly evaluates the rightness of a policy by its anticipated outcomes (things that "come with it") rather than by qualities intrinsic to the policy itself. So, for example, Aristotle advised the political orator to deemphasize questions of justice and honor and focus instead on the advantages to be gained or lost by implementing or not implementing a legislative proposal.

To make a persuasive case, the political orator needs to know what kinds of outcomes are most strongly desired by members of an assembly. Most people are motivated by a desire for happiness, but "happiness" is, of course, a loaded term. It is not, according to Aristotle, merely a simple feeling or transitory condition, but a complex activity of human flourishing. To flourish, individuals require not just enjoyment, but also health, wealth, security, reputation, friendship, and so forth. Any of these "parts of happiness" might be motivating to members of a political assembly. Which parts are most motivating will vary from one question and one assembly to another. Every person has different preferences, and the decisions that members of the assembly make are relative to their actual desire priorities.

Aristotle described *sympheron* as a "contingent good"; its reliability as a standard for good decisions is not absolute. In the first place, audiences frequently are mistaken in their assumptions about what will make them happy. It is depressingly routine that when even our strongest and most central desires are satisfied, we are no happier than we were before. Indeed, sometimes the satisfaction of our actual desires fuels our feelings of discontent. Further, democratic assemblies sometimes will desire things that are unjust or immoral. Aristotle's attitude appears to have been that, ideally, members of the assembly will possess a virtuous character such that they will tend to prioritize morality and justice as important considerations in the determination of long-term and enlightened advantage. In actual practice, however, democratic assemblies are frequently indifferent to issues of injustice and immorality except in cases where doing right happens to coincide with their narrow interests of the moment.

In the ancient world, the major rival to Aristotle's version of the principle of utility was Epicureanism. Epicurus (c.341–271 BCE) expanded the scope and application of the principle of utility, transforming it into the defining concept in a theory of human motivation and the first principle in a theory of ethics. He maintained that all human action, not just political action, is motivated by our desire for "advantage." The advantage we seek is happiness. Unlike Aristotle, however, Epicurus equated happiness with the simple mental state of pleasure and the absence of pain: "From pleasure we begin every act and avoidance, and to pleasure we return again using the feeling as the standard by which we judge every good" (Epicurus, *The Extant Remains*, 1926, p. 87).

As Torquatus, the spokesman for Epicurus in Cicero's dialogue *De finibus* observed, "The Ends of Goods and Evils themselves, that is, pleasure and pain, are not open to mistake; where people go wrong is in not knowing what things are productive of pleasure and pain" (1931, p. 59). Despite his reputation, Epicurus did not see acceptance of the "pleasure principle" as license for debauchery or "self-destructive pleasure-seeking." To the contrary, he taught that self-discipline is essential to achieving the pleasant life. No pleasure is in itself bad, but "the means which produce some pleasures bring with them disturbances many times greater than the pleasures" (*The Extant Remains*, 1926, p. 87). The pains resulting from such activities as unrestrained feasting, drinking, and lovemaking either cancel the pleasures or leave a balance of pain. Similarly, people who devote their lives to achieving the pleasures that come with power, riches, and fame condemn themselves to hectic and anxious lives, dependent on the opinions and actions of others, and with no sure hope of ever achieving their goals. If pleasure is the only intrinsic good and pain the only intrinsic evil, Epicurus reasoned, the best life is one of ataractic contentment that comes from bodily health and spiritual tranquility. The ideal Epicurean leads a frugal and self-

sufficient life, eschewing luxury and suppressing vain and frenetic desire.

Although Epicurus emphasized the need for wisdom in choosing the pleasures that will contribute to our well-being, appeals to categorical imperatives of duty—"Thou shalts" and "Thou shalt nots"—are conspicuously absent from his moral theory. Moral rules are important insofar as they provide *prima facie* guidelines for achieving the life of pleasure; puritanical devotion to those guidelines is irrational and pernicious. Similarly, he considered notions of "Natural Law" and "Divine Justice" to be the dangerous inventions of false theologians who conspire to enslave ordinary men and women through anxiety and fear. Justice is nothing more than a social contract—a "pledge of mutual advantage"—to prevent us from harming one another. Any law that ceases to lead to agreeable or convenient relations among individuals is no longer a just law.

Epicureanism is, in sum, antimystical, unpuritanical, and, in general, optimistic about the human capacity to achieve happiness. Thus, it is not surprising that during the Middle Ages, Epicurus was condemned (by Dante, among others) as a heretic. Believing that the present lifetime is a period of probation determining man's destination for eternity, the prevailing attitude among medieval Christians was that happiness in the next world, not this, is what matters. Eternal happiness can be achieved, not through hedonistic calculations, but only through pious obedience to God's Law.

The Renaissance displaced medieval notions of human powerlessness in relation to providence and reasserted Classical ideas about human dignity and rationality. In France, a revival of interest in the teachings of Epicurus culminated in the apologetics of Pierre Gassendi (1592–1655). Meanwhile, in England, Gassendi's friend, Thomas Hobbes, wrote *Leviathan* (1651), a work that rests on a distinctively Epicurean premise: People have an interest in promoting happiness in the present life and all social rights and duties are a consequence of this interest. By the eighteenth century, this Epicurean premise found repeated expression in the works of writers ranging from the Marquis de Condorcet and Claude Helvétius to David Hume and Joseph Priestley.

The writer most closely associated in the popular imagination with this modern revival of Epicurean philosophy, is Jeremy Bentham (1748–1832). It was Bentham who gave the "principle of utility" its English name. He was inspired by Hume's use of the word in the *Enquiries Concerning the Principles of Morals* (Oxford, 1975, p. 231), and, apparently, he adopted it with little thought. Later writers would complain that "utility" has misleading connotations, but the word caught on so quickly that there was no opportunity to drop it. As Bentham understood the meaning of "utility," it is a synonym for "benefit," "advantage," "pleasure," "good," and "happiness" (*The Principles of Morals and Legislation,* Buffalo, 1988, p. 2).

Despite the new name, Bentham had no illusions about the originality of "utilitarianism." Like Epicurus, he adopted a consequentialist standard of right and wrong. All actions should be approved or disapproved solely according to their tendency to augment or to diminish the happiness of the persons they affect. Also, like Epicurus, Bentham sought to demystify law and morality. He excelled at providing detailed ideological critiques of the self-serving language and rituals of lawyers, politicians, and theologians. He considered words such as *Providence* and *Higher Law* to be code designed to demand despotic unanimity and to conceal who is helped and who is hurt by the law.

Though they have much in common, Epicureanism and Benthamite utilitarianism differ from one another on an essential point. Epicureanism is a theory of personal morality; it focuses on the promotion of happiness for the individual agent. Modern utilitarianism, by contrast, is a theory of social morality; it focuses on the promotion of the general welfare. Bentham frequently is quoted as having said that the fundamental axiom of utility is "the greatest happiness of the greatest number" (*Works*, Edinburgh, 1843, 1. p. 227). The phrase is problematic, and he quickly abandoned it; nevertheless, it does illustrate the contrast between Epicurean concern for the welfare of the self and Benthamite concern for the welfare of society at large. In this respect, Bentham's "utility" resembles Aristotle's *sympheron*. Bentham expounded utility chiefly as a rationale for social policy and political legislation.

Despite this point of agreement, Bentham and Aristotle were worlds apart on other matters. Most importantly, as we have seen, Aristotle considered happiness to be a complex aggregate of types of human activities. Bentham, by contrast, believed that happiness is simply a sum of pleasures. Seven "circumstances" determine the numerical value assigned to pleasures and pains: intensity, duration, certainty or uncertainty, propinquity or remoteness, fecundity, purity, and number of people affected. Having assigned numerical values to pleasures and pains, Bentham believed those values could be added and subtracted on a single cardinal scale, rather like money, to determine the relative merits of different courses of action.

In the nineteenth century, Bentham's naive scientism was replaced by the more sophisticated account of the principle of utility found in John Stuart Mill's *Utilitarianism* (first published in 1861 and republished in *Collected Works,* Toronto, 1969). More sensitive than his predecessors to the many objections that had been raised against the principle of utility over the centuries, Mill provided careful and deceptively complex responses to those objections. In particular, he was concerned with the complaint that as a matter of psychological fact, not all human action *is* motivated by a desire for pleasure. The dictates of conscience, for example, often function to control and mediate our selfish motives. In attempting to account for this notion of "moral conscience," Mill was drawn into the study of the psychological origins of habit and of the relationship of habit to character formation. Rejecting Bentham's felicific calculus and positioning himself close to Aristotelian virtue ethics, Mill argued that the question of what makes good character takes precedence over the question of what makes an action right. In other words, one cannot judge the rightness of an action without taking into account the character and experiences of the judges themselves.

In the twentieth century, the principle of utility was repeatedly declared a dead idea. "Utilitarianism is destroyed," claimed John Plamenatz (*The English Utilitarians,* Oxford, 1949, p. 145). Twenty-five years later, Bernard Williams declared, "The day cannot be too far off in which we hear no more of it" (*Utilitarianism For and Against,* Cambridge, U.K., 1973, p. 150). Almost thirty years later, the flow of writings on the principle of utility is unceasing. As Geoffrey Scarre wrote, if the principle of utility is wrong, "proving it to be so is taking a remarkable amount of intellectual effort" (*Utilitarianism,* London, 1996, p. 2). The most frequent and persistent indictments of utility have also proven to be indictments of rhetoric. So once again, rhetoric and utility find their camaraderie confirmed.

[*See also* Deliberative genre; *and overview article on* Politics.]

BIBLIOGRAPHY

Allison, Lincoln, ed. *The Utilitarian Response.* London, 1990.

Berger, Fred. *Happiness, Justice, and Freedom.* Los Angeles, 1984. Provides an important corrective to many of the misunderstandings perpetuated by critics of Mill's theory of utility.

Burks, Don M. "Psychological Egoism and the Rhetorical Tradition." *Speech Monographs* 33 (1966), pp. 400–418. An examination of the rhetorical topic of self-interest, especially in eighteenth-century rhetorical theory.

DeWitt, N. W. *Epicurus and his Philosophy.* Minneapolis, 1954.

Glover, Jonathan, ed. *Utilitarianism and its Critics.* New York, 1990.

Griffin, James. *Well-Being: Its Meaning, Measurement and Moral Importance.* Oxford, 1986. One of the best treatments of the principle of utility available; provides a comprehensive summary of the most difficult and complex issues of measurement of utility.

Jones, Howard. *The Epicurean Tradition.* London, 1989.

Quinton, Anthony. *Utilitarian Ethics.* La Salle, Ill., 1989. A brief and accessible survey of the history of utilitarianism and some of the traditional objections to utilitarianism.

Scheffler, Samuel, ed. *Consequentialism and Its Critics.* Oxford, 1988.

Stephen, Leslie. *The English Utilitarians.* London, 1900.

Vaughan, Frederick. *The Tradition of Political Hedonism from Hobbes to J. S. Mill.* New York, 1982.

Wilson, Fred. *Psychological Analysis and the Philosophy of John Stuart Mill.* Toronto, 1990. A dense but insightful examination of the psychological underpinnings of modern utilitarianism.

—KAREN E. WHEDBEE

VIRTUAL AUDIENCES. *See* Audience, *article on* Virtual audiences.

ZEUGMA, both a grammatical and a rhetorical term, describes a linguistic phenomenon that is generated by the deletion of syntactic units in favor of a remaining one used to complete the meaning of two or more congruent words or clauses. George Puttenham anglicizes it as "Single supply" in *The Arte of English Poesie* (1589), "because by one word we serue many clauses of one congruitie, and may be likened to the man that serues two maisters at once, but all of one country or kindred" (pp. 163–164). If placed at the beginning of a clause, it is termed *prozeugma* or "Ringleader"; if at the end, *hypozeugma* or "Rerewarder" (Puttenham). If it is placed at the center of congruent words or clauses, it is named *mesozeugma* or "Middle Marcher" (Puttenham), as in *Psalms* 114.1–4: "When Israel went out of Egypt, the house of Jacob [went out] from a people of strange language; Judah was his sanctuary, and Israel [was] his dominion." When, however, the words or clauses are incongruent, the result is a syntactic figure of speech or, more precisely, a subtractive metataxeme or *syllēpsis.* If only the syntax is affected by such a procedure, it is a *syntactic zeugma,* as in "Nor God, nor I, delights in perjur'd men" (Shakespeare, *Love's Labor's Lost,* 5.2.346), where "God . . . delights" is grammatically correct and "I delights" syntactically deviant. If this metataxeme affects the meaning, it can be termed a semantic zeugma, as in, "Whether the nymph shall break Diana's law / . . . Or lose her heart, or necklace, at a ball" (Pope, *The Rape of the Lock,* 2.105, 109), where "lose" in conjunction with "necklace" has a literal meaning and with "heart" assumes a tropical (metaphorical or ironical) meaning.

[*See also* Figures of speech; *and* Syllēpsis.]

—HEINRICH F. PLETT

Directory of Contributors

◆

Danielle S. Allen
*Assistant Professor of Classical Languages and
Literature, University of Chicago, Illinois*
Gorgianic figures

June W. Allison
*Professor, Department of Greek and Latin, Ohio State
University*
Thesis and antithesis

Frederick J. Antczak
*Professor of Rhetoric, and Associate Dean for Academic
Programs, University of Iowa, Iowa City*
Overview article on Composition

James Arnt Aune
*Associate Professor of Speech Communication,
Pennsylvania State University, University Park*
Perspective by incongruity

Wesley D. Avram
*Clement-Muehl Assistant Professor of Communications,
Yale University Divinity School, New Haven,
Connecticut*
Exhortation

Shadi Bartsch
Professor of Classics, University of Chicago, Illinois
Panegyric

James S. Baumlin
*Professor of English, Southwest Missouri State
University, Springfield*
Ēthos

W. Martin Bloomer
*Associate Professor of Classics, University of Notre
Dame, Indiana*
Controversia and suasoria; Declamation; Topics

Wayne C. Booth
*Professor Emeritus of English, University of Chicago,
Illinois*
Criticism

Ernest G. Bormann
*Professor Emeritus of Speech Communication, University
of Minnesota, Minneapolis*
Rhetorical vision

Marjorie O'Rourke Boyle
Independent Scholar, Toronto, Ontario, Canada
Religion

Bernard L. Brock
*Professor Emeritus of Communication, Wayne State
University, Detroit, Michigan*
Secular piety

Robert E. Brooke
Professor of English, University of Nebraska, Lincoln
Persona

Martin Camargo
Professor of English, University of Missouri at Columbia
Ars dictaminis; Epistolary rhetoric

Karlyn Kohrs Campbell
*Professor of Speech Communication, University of
Minnesota, Minneapolis*
Feminist rhetoric; Modern rhetoric

Robert W. Cape
*Associate Professor of Classics, Austin College, Sherman,
Texas*
Prudence

Maurice Charland
*Associate Professor of Communication, Concordia
University, Montreal, Canada*
Politics, *article on* Constitutive rhetoric

David Cohen
*Chancellor's Professor of Rhetoric and Classics,
University of California, Berkeley*
Oratory

Stephen C. Colvin
*Assistant Professor of Greek, Department of Classics,
Yale University, New Haven, Connecticut*
Atticist–Asianist controversy

Rita Copeland
*Professor of Classical Studies, University of
Pennsylvania, Philadelphia*
Overview article on Medieval rhetoric; Trivium

J. Robert Cox
*Professor of Communication Studies, University of North
Carolina at Chapel Hill*
Irreparable, the

Robert T. Craig
*Associate Professor of Communication, University of
Colorado at Boulder*
Communication

Courtney L. Dillard
Doctoral Candidate, University of Texas at Austin
Deliberative genre

Rosa A. Eberly
Assistant Professor of Rhetoric and Composition,
University of Texas at Austin
Overview article on Composition

Richard Leo Enos
Professor and Holder of the Lillian Radford Chair of
Rhetoric and Composition, Texas Christian University,
Fort Worth
Arrangement, *article on* Traditional arrangement

Jeanne Fahnestock
Professor of English Language and Literature, University
of Maryland, College Park
Arrangement, *article on* Modern arrangement

Elaine Fantham
Giger Professor Emerita of Latin, Princeton University,
New Jersey
Eloquence

Thomas B. Farrell
Professor of Communication Studies, Northwestern
University, Evanston, Illinois
Inference; Social knowledge; Technical
communication

Steve Fuller
Professor of Sociology, University of Warwick, Coventry,
United Kingdom
Science

Robert A. Gaines
Professor of Dramatic Arts, Auburn University,
Montgomery, Alabama
Phronēsis; Speech

Dilip Parameshwar Gaonkar
Associate Professor of Rhetoric and Cultural Studies,
Northwestern University, Evanston, Illinois
Contingency and probability

Mary M. Garrett
Associate Professor of Communication, Wayne State
University, Detroit, Michigan
Chinese rhetoric

G. Thomas Goodnight
Professor of Communication Studies, Northwestern
University, Evanston, Illinois
Controversy; Politics, *article on* The personal,
technical, and public spheres of argument

Peter Goodrich
Professor of Law, Cardozo School of Law, New York
Law

Lawrence D. Green
Professor of English, University of Southern California,
Los Angeles
Pathos

Andrea Grün-Oesterreich
Centre for Rhetoric and Renaissance Studies, University
of Essen, Germany
Alliteration; Anadiplōsis; Anaphora; Aphaeresis;
Apocopē; Aporia; Aposiōpēsis; Assonance;
Asyndeton; Auxēsis; Ellipsis; Epanodos; Epiphora;
Epizeuxis; Polysyndeton; Prolēpsis

Robert Hariman
Professor of Rhetoric and Communication Studies, Drake
University, Des Moines, Iowa
Decorum

Roderick P. Hart
Shivers Chair in Communication and Professor of
Government, University of Texas at Austin
Deliberative genre

Gerard A. Hauser
Professor of Communication, University of Colorado at
Boulder
Overview article on Politics

Robert L. Heath
Professor of Communication, University of Houston,
Texas
Identification

Hanns Hohmann
Associate Professor of Communication Studies, San Jose
State University, California
Stasis

Robert C. Holub
Professor of German, University of California, Berkeley
Reception theory

Michael J. Hyde
Distinguished University Professor of Communication
Ethics, Wake Forest University, Winston-Salem, North
Carolina
Hermeneutics

Kathleen Hall Jamieson
Dean of Communications, University of Pennsylvania,
Philadelphia
Hybrid genres

Sharon E. Jarvis
Assistant Professor in Communication Studies,
University of Texas at Austin
Overview article on Audience

James Jasinski
Associate Professor of Communication and Theatre Arts,
University of Puget Sound, Tacoma, Washington
Rhetorical situation

Nan Johnson
Associate Professor of English, Ohio State University,
Columbus
Nineteenth-century rhetoric

Christopher Lyle Johnstone
Professor of Speech Communication, Pennsylvania State University, University Park
Enthymeme; Philosophy, *article on* Perennial topics and terms; Practical wisdom

James L. Kastely
Associate Professor of English, University of Houston, Texas
Dialectic

Fred J. Kauffeld
Professor of Communication Arts, Edgewood College, Madison, Wisconsin
Speech acts, utterances as

George A. Kennedy
Paddison Professor Emeritus of Classics, University of North Carolina at Chapel Hill
Classical rhetoric; Comparative rhetoric; Imitation

Manfred Kienpointner
Associate Professor, Universität Innsbruck, Austria
Linguistics

Andrew A. King
Chair of the Department of Speech Communication, and Professor of Rhetoric, Louisiana State University, Baton Rouge
Politics, *article on* Rhetoric and power

John T. Kirby
Professor of Classics and Comparative Literature, Purdue University, West Lafayette, Indiana
Occasion

Gregory Kneidel
Instructor, Texas Christian University, Fort Worth
Homiletics; Renaissance rhetoric, *article on* Rhetoric in the age of Reformation and Counter-Reformation

Jiří Kraus
Professor, The Czech Language Institute, Prague, Czech Republic
Slavic rhetoric

N. Krishnaswamy
Professor Emeritus of English, Central Institute of English and Foreign Languages (CIEFL), Hyderabad, India
Indian rhetoric

H. Krones
Professor of Stylistics and Performance Practice, University of Music and Dramatic Arts, Vienna, Austria
Music

Don S. Levi
Professor of Philosophy, University of Oregon, Eugene
Logic

Stephen E. Lucas
Professor of Communication Arts, University of Wisconsin–Madison
Public speaking

Jack R. Lundbom
Fellow of Clare Hall, University of Cambridge, United Kingdom
Hebrew rhetoric

John D. Lyons
Commonwealth Professor of French, University of Virginia, Charlottesville
Exemplum

Peter Mack
Reader, Department of English, University of Warwick, Coventry, United Kingdom
Poetry

José Antonio Mayoral
Professor of Literary Theory, Universidad Complutense de Madrid, Spain
Antithesis; Apostrophē; Chiasmus; Ēthopoeia; Hypallagē; Isocolon; Parallelism; Periphrasis; Prosōpopoeia

Michael Calvin McGee
Professor of Communication Studies, University of Iowa, Iowa City
Ideograph

Raymie E. McKerrow
Professor of Rhetorical Studies, Ohio University, Athens
Politics, *article on* Critical rhetoric

Mark Lawrence McPhail
Professor of Communication, University of Utah, Salt Lake City
African-American rhetoric, *article on* Double-consciousness

Michel Meyer
Professor of Rhetoric, Université Libre de Bruxelles, Belgium
Problematology; Questioning

Thomas P. Miller
Professor of English, University of Arizona, Tucson
Eighteenth-century rhetoric

Terence S. Morrow
Assistant Professor of Communication Studies, Gustavus Adolphus College, Saint Peter, Minnesota
Forensic genre

Ann Moss
Professor of French, University of Durham, United Kingdom
Commonplaces and commonplace books; Copia

Jean Dietz Moss
Professor of English, Catholic University of America, Washington, D.C.
Renaissance rhetoric, *article on* Rhetoric in Renaissance language and literature

Wolfgang G. Müller
*Professor of English, Friedrich-Schiller-Universitat Jena,
Germany*
Style

Muhsin J. al-Musawi
*Professor Emeritus, American University of Sharjah,
United Arab Emirates*
Arabic rhetoric

Gregory Nagy
*Francis Jones Professor of Classical Greek Literature, and
Professor of Comparative Literature, Harvard University,
Cambridge, Massachusetts*
Orality and literacy

Richard Nate
*Professor, Centre for Rhetoric and Renaissance Studies,
University of Essen, Germany*
Allegory; Catachrēsis; Metaphor; Metonymy; Simile;
Synecdochē

Peter L. Oesterreich
*Professor of Philosophy, Augustana Hochschule,
Neuendettelsau, Germany*
Irony

Daniel J. O'Keefe
*Associate Professor of Speech Communication, University
of Illinois at Urbana-Champaign*
Persuasion

Kathryn M. Olson
*Associate Professor of Communication, University of
Wisconsin–Milwaukee*
Ambiguity

Christine L. Oravec
*Professor of Communication, University of Utah, Salt
Lake City*
Sublime, the

Heiner Peters
*Professor of Rhetoric and Renaissance Studies, University
of Essen, Germany*
Anastrophē; Antanaclasis; Antisthecōn; Congeries;
Correctio; Epanalēpsis; Epenthesis; Epistrophē;
Gradatio; Hendiadys; Hyperbaton; Hysteron
prōteron; Litotēs; Praeteritio; Prosthesis; Syllēpsis;
Symplocē; Syncopē

John Durham Peters
*Associate Professor of Communication Studies,
University of Iowa, Iowa City*
Audience, *article on* Mass audiences

Heinrich F. Plett
*Professor of English, and Director of the Center for
Rhetoric and Renaissance Studies, University of Essen,
Germany*
Amplification; Descriptio; Digressio; Enallagē;
Figures of speech; Hyperbolē; Oxymōron; Paradox;
Parenthesis; Paronomasia; Pathopoeia; Pleonasm;
Proparalēpsis; *Overview article on* Renaissance
rhetoric; Zeugma

Mark A. Pollock
*Associate Professor of Communication, Loyola University
Chicago, Illinois*
Judgment

John Poulakos
*Associate Professor of Rhetoric, University of Pittsburgh,
Pennsylvania*
Eristic; Sophists

Irving J. Rein
*Professor of Communication Studies, Northwestern
University, Evanston, Illinois*
Campaigns

Thomas Jesse Roach
*Associate Professor of Communication, Purdue
University Calumet, Hammond, Indiana*
Expository rhetoric and journalism; Politics, *article
on* The third face of power; Technical
communication

Matthew B. Roller
*Assistant Professor of Classics, Johns Hopkins
University, Baltimore, Maryland*
Color

Philippe-Joseph Salazar
*Distinguished Professor in Humane Letters, Centre for
Rhetoric Studies, University of Cape Town, Rondebosch,
South Africa*
Queer rhetoric

Bernhard F. Scholz
*Professor of General and Comparative Literature,
University of Groningen, The Netherlands*
Art

Eckart Schütrumpf
Professor of Classics, University of Colorado at Boulder
Credibility

Robert L. Scott
*Professor Emeritus of Speech Communication, University
of Minnesota, Minneapolis*
Tacit dimension, the

Herbert W. Simons
*Professor of Speech Communication, Temple University,
Philadelphia, Pennsylvania*
Social movements

Peter Simonson
*Assistant Professor of Communication and Rhetoric,
University of Pittsburgh, Pennsylvania*
Politics, *article on* Rhetoric and legitimation

Thomas O. Sloane
*Professor Emeritus of Rhetoric, University of California,
Berkeley*
Humor

Marijke Spies
Professor Emeritus of Dutch, Sixteenth- and Seventeenth-Century Literature, Vrije Universiteit Amsterdam, The Netherlands
Renaissance rhetoric, *article on* Rederijkers

Jennifer Stromer-Galley
Doctoral candidate, University of Pennsylvania, Philadelphia
Hybrid genres

Jane Sutton
Associate Professor of Speech Communication, Pennsylvania State University, York
Kairos

James M. Tallmon
Associate Professor of Rhetoric, South Dakota State University, Brookings
Casuistry

Robert E. Terrill
Assistant Professor, Department of Communication and Culture, Indiana University, Bloomington
African-American rhetoric, *article on* Black Nationalism

Yun Lee Too
Assistant Professor of Classics, Columbia University, New York
Epideictic genre

Claus Uhlig
Professor and Chair of English and American Studies, Philipps-Universität Marburg, Germany
Humanism

Frans H. van Eemeren
Professor of Speech Communication, Argumentation Theory, and Rhetoric, University of Amsterdam, The Netherlands
Fallacies

Brian Vickers
Professor of English Literature, Centre for Renaissance Studies, Eidgenössische Technische Hochschule (ETH) Zürich, Switzerland
Philosophy, *article on* Rhetoric and philosophy

Raymond B. Waddington
Professor of English, University of California, Davis
Iconography

Joseph B. Walther
Associate Professor of Communication, Social Psychology, and Information Technology, Rensselaer Polytechnic Institute, Troy, New York
Audience, *article on* Virtual audiences

Douglas Walton
Professor of Philosophy, University of Winnipeg, Manitoba, Canada
Ad hominem argument

Phillip Wander
Professor of Communication Studies, San Jose State University, California
Expediency

Barbara Warnick
Professor of Speech Communication, University of Washington, Seattle
Conviction; Hypertext

Walter Watson
Professor Emeritus of Philosophy, State University of New York at Stony Brook
Invention

Eric King Watts
Assistant Professor of Communication, Wake Forest University, Winston-Salem, North Carolina
Overview article on African-American rhetoric

Kathleen E. Welch
Professor of English, University of Oklahoma, Norman
Delivery

Susan Wells
Professor of English, Temple University, Philadelphia, Pennsylvania
Logos

William N. West
Assistant Professor of English, University of Nevada, Reno
Memory

Karen E. Whedbee
Assistant Professor of Communication, Purdue University, West Lafayette, Indiana
Utility

Kirt H. Wilson
Assistant Professor of Rhetoric and Communication Studies, University of Minnesota, Minneapolis
African-American rhetoric, *article on* Abolitionist rhetoric

W. Ross Winterowd
Bruce R. McElderry Professor Emeritus of English, University of Southern California, Los Angeles
Composition, *article on* History of English departments in the United States

A. J. Woodman
Professor of Latin, University of Durham, United Kingdom
History

David Zarefsky
Professor of Communication Studies, Northwestern University, Evanston, Illinois
Argumentation; Argument fields; Debate; Syllogism

Jan Ziolkowski
Professor of Medieval Latin and Comparative Literature, Harvard University, Cambridge, Massachusetts
Medieval rhetoric, *article on* Medieval grammar

Synoptic Outline of Contents

◆

The entries in the *Encyclopedia of Rhetoric* pertain to the general conceptual categories listed on this page. The following pages in this section provide a detailed synoptic outline of the contents, organized by conceptual category; some category titles are also entries. Some entries are listed more than once in the synoptic outline because the conceptual categories are not mutually exclusive. Entries in the encyclopedia proper are organized alphabetically.

I. ELEMENTS OF RHETORIC

Two elements comprise the foundation of the rhetorical enterprise: an expansive view of proof and the conceptual prominence of the audience.

A. Modes of Proof

A distinguishing characteristic of rhetoric is its expansive view of proof and, consequently, its use of evidence. In the rhetorical view, three kinds of evidence are considered relevant to establish a case: the perceived character of the speaker or writer (*ēthos*), the argument or thought in the message itself (*logos*), and the emotions the audience is led to experience (*pathos*). These terms were early defined by Aristotle (*Rhetoric* 1.2.2), who considered *ēthos*, *logos,* and *pathos* "artistic" modes of proof because they are largely dependent upon the artistry of the composer in fashioning the discourse itself, rather than from such preexisting proofs as witnesses or contracts.

1. *Ēthos*
    a. Credibility
    b. Persona
2. *Logos*
    a. Argumentation
    b. Argument fields
    c. Contingency and probability
    d. Controversy
    e. Enthymeme
    f. Exemplum
    g. Inference
    h. Practical wisdom
    i. Speech acts, utterances as
3. *Pathos*
    a. Humor

B. Audience

An extended discussion of the audience as a constitutive element of and agency for rhetorical practice. An overview essay leads into these types:

1. Mass audiences
2. Virtual audiences

II. SCHĒMA

The rhetorical creative process as well as the rhetorical act itself are theoretically viewed as comprised of five phenomena (variably called arts, offices, or canons): invention, arrangement, style, delivery, and memory. The first four phenomena are implicit in Aristotle's *Rhetoric,* and all become fully codified by the time of Cicero. The extent to which these five phenomena constitute orderly steps to be taken or, rather, are virtually indistinguishable features of a field of activity has varied in theory through the centuries. Variable, too, has been the amount and kind of emphasis and attention given each.

A. Invention

Invention includes the entire process of initial inquiry into uncertain questions, the reflection upon alternative possibilities of position, proofs, and perspectives. Its modern topics include:

1. Ideograph
2. Imitation
3. Occasion
4. Perspective by incongruity
5. Problematology
6. Questioning
7. Rhetorical situation
8. Rhetorical vision
9. Social knowledge
10. Tacit dimension, the
11. Topics

B. Arrangement

Arrangement concerns the place of form in the composition and analysis of discourse. Both "traditional" and "modern" kinds of form are considered.

C. Style

Often regarded as the whole of rhetoric, style is here considered as a functional part of composition and analysis. The concept of *elocutio* and its components are analyzed as well as tracked throughout the history of western culture.

D. Memory

This part of rhetoric includes memory systems as well as mnemonic architecture (such as the memory theatres of the Renaissance) along with some consideration of *memoria*'s lost or changed prominence.

E. Delivery

Delivery—spoken, printed, or electronically transmitted—is usually regarded as the synthesizing act of rhetorical composition.

III. MAJOR PRINCIPLES

A. Ends

Whether arising from the intentions of the *rhētōr,* or composer, or from the rhetorical act generally, the ends of rhetoric have traditionally been divided into two large categories:

1. Persuasion
   a. Conviction
   b. Exhortation
   c. Identification
   d. Judgment
2. Eloquence
   a. Sublime, the

B. Genres of Rhetoric

Rhetorical types have traditionally been allied with three major occasions, which Aristotle spoke of as species of rhetoric (1.3.1) and Cicero as kinds (*De inventione* 2.3.11): deliberative, such as orations before a policy-determining body; forensic, such as orations at a court of law; and epideictic, such as orations given in commemoration, praise, or blame. Since ancient times, other genres have become attached to rhetoric or have been developed from its traditional species. All are allied with considerations of audience and occasion, and all are indicative of the speaker's or writer's intention.

1. Traditional genres
   There are three traditional kinds of rhetoric, each allied with considerations of audience and occasion, and each indicative of intention. From ancient times, certain issues have become attached to these types, and in modern times certain new issues have been added.
   a. Deliberative genre
      This includes the subtopics:
      (1) Expediency
      (2) Irreparable, the
      (3) Utility
   b. Forensic genre
      This includes the subtopic:
      (1) *Stasis*
   c. Epideictic genre
      This includes the closely related topic:
      (1) Exhortation
2. Nontraditional genres
   Genres of rhetorical practice are

traditionally a direct offshoot of cultural conventions and the institutional formation that makes them accessible. But when these conventions and social formations change, so rhetorical genres themselves are likely to shift in unpredictable ways. Subtopics are genres that are characteristic of cultures and conditions that were largely unanticipated by classical formulations.

a. Campaigns
b. Epistolary rhetoric
c. Expository rhetoric and journalism
d. Hybrid genres
e. Hypertext
f. Social movements
g. Technical communication

IV. RELATED SUBJECTS

There are a host of subjects that are related to rhetoric, its elements, ends, *schēma,* and genres. Selection was based on degree, that is, closeness of relationship.

A. Art

B. African-American Rhetoric

An overview essay leads into these subentries:

1. Abolitionist rhetoric
2. Double-consciousness
3. Black Nationalism

C. Casuistry

D. Communication

E. Comparative Rhetoric

This includes these subtopics:

1. Arabic rhetoric
2. Chinese rhetoric
3. Hebrew rhetoric
4. Indian rhetoric
5. Slavic rhetoric

F. Composition

An overview essay leads into a discussion of the history of English departments in the United States.

Index

◆

Page numbers printed in boldface indicate a major discussion.

A

Abhinavagupta, 385
Abolitionist rhetoric, 7–11
Abraham a Santa Clara, 677
Abrams, M. H., 22
  modern rhetoric, 503
  style, 752
Absalom and Architophel (Dryden), 20
Abuse of Casuistry, The (Toulmin), 83–84, 156
"Accidental Rhetoric: The Root Metaphors of Three-Mile Island" (Farrell and Goodnight), 772
Actio. See Delivery
Adams, Hazard, 274
Adams, John Quincy
  forensic genre, 318
  theory of *stasis*, 744
Adam's Rib (Herschberger), 303
Addison, Joseph
  on composition, 149
  style, 752
Ad hominem argument, **1–4**
Advancement of Learning, The (Bacon), 227, 295–296, 358, 401
Aelius Theon of Alexandria, 105
Aeneid (Virgil), 605
Aeschines
  on eloquence, 245
  oratory works, 542, 543, 545
Aesthetics. *See* Eloquence; Style
AFL-CIO, 730
Africa (Petrarch), 666
African-American rhetoric, **4–18**
  abolitionist rhetoric, 7–11
  black nationalism, 14–18
  double-consciousness, 11–14
African Methodist Episcopal Church, 8
Agnew, Spiro, 628
Agon, 60, 205, 338, 423, 467, 551, 776
Agricola, Rudolphus, 120
  on eloquence, 245

Agricola, Rudolphus, *cont.*
  humanism, 355–356
  logos, 463
  pathos, 564
  poetry and rhetoric, 605
  in Renaissance rhetoric, 688
Agrippa, Henry Cornelius, 19
Ajax and Odysseus (Antisthenes), 254
Ajzen, Icek, 577
Akenside, Mark, 149
Alan of Lille, 477
Alberic of Montecassino
  on *ars dictaminis*, 50
  on eloquence, 244
  medieval rhetoric, 475
  Renaissance rhetoric, 677
Alberti, Leon Battista
  on art, 53–54
  humanism, 354
Albert of Mlodzow, 718
Alciato, Andrea, 371, 373
Alcidamas
  epideictic genre, 254
  occasionality of rhetoric, 530
Alcuin
  forensic genre, 317
  medieval rhetoric, 470
  Renaissance rhetoric, 673
  theory of *stasis*, 743
  trivium, 785
Ælfric, 480
Akt de Lesens, Der (Iser), 659
Alison, Archibald, 758
Allegoresis, 18–20
Allegories of Reading: Figural Language of Rousseau, Nietzsche, Rilke and Proust (de Man), 760
Allegory, **18–20**
  Middle Ages allegorical interpretation, 19
  See also Figures of speech
  See also Style
Allegory of Female Authority, The: Christine de Pizan's "Cité des dames" (Quilligan), 507–508
Allen, Richard, 5

Allen, William G., 8
Alliteration, **20–21**
  See also Figures of speech
  See also Gorgianic figures
Allott, Robert, 123
Alsted, Johann-Heinrich, 690
Althusser, Louis, 617, 618
Ambiguity, **21–25**
  experiential and symbolic, 21–23
  rhetorical strategies, 23–24
  symbolic ambiguity, 22
American Anti-Slavery Association, 8
American Anti-Slavery Society, 8, 10
American Civil War, 338
American Colonization Society, 8, 15
American Muslim Mission, 17
American Public Address: Studies in Honor of Craig Baird (Reid, ed.), 504
American Selection of Lessons in Reading and Speaking, An (Webster), 230
Amery, Leo, 644
Amistad, 318
Amplification, **25–26**
  horizontal application, 25–26
  vertical application, 25
  See also Figures of speech
Anadiplōsis, **26**
  See also Figures of speech
  See also Gorgianic figures
  See also Gradatio
  See also Style
Analogy. *See* Casuistry; Metaphor
Analytical Inquiry into the Principles of Taste, An (Knight), 758
Ānandavardhana, 385
Anaphora, **26**
  in comparative rhetoric, 142
  See also Figures of speech
  See also Poetry
  See also Style
  See also Symplocē

Aristotle, *cont.*
  politics and rhetoric, 613, 616, 621
  practical reason, 632–634
  prudence, 638
  public speaking, 646
  in Renaissance rhetoric, 674, 686
  rhetoric and philosophy, 588–590
  science and rhetoric, 703
  social knowledge, 721–723
  style, 745
  sublime, the, 758
  tacit dimension, the, 765–767
  thesis and antithesis, 775
  third face of power, 628
  Topica, 779–783
  utility, 789
"Aristotle on Habit and Character" (Miller), 267–268
Aristotle, Rhetoric: A Commentary (Grimaldi)
  logos, 458
  modern rhetoric, 507
Aristotle's Rhetoric: An Art of Character (Garver), 507
Arnold, Matthew, 147
Arnould, Edmond, 753
Arrangement, **40–50**
  appropriation of Classical arrangement in Middle Ages and Renaissance, 43
  below the level of the whole text, 48–49
  and functional genres: heuristic approaches to arrangement, 48
  and genre, 47–48
  in Greek rhetoric, 40–41
  Hellenistic and Roman notions of arrangement, 41–43
  modern arrangement, 44–50
  rationale by content, 45
  rationales by acts or effects, 45
  rationales by formal features, 45–46
  traditional arrangement, 40–44
  updating traditional schemes of arrangement, 46–47
  in visual rhetoric, 49
  See also Classical rhetoric
Ars dictaminis, **50–52**
  See also Epistolary rhetoric
  See also Medieval rhetoric: overview
Ars maior (Donatus), 481
Ars notaria (Rainerius of Perugia), 318

Ars poetica (Gervase of Melkley), 474
Ars poetica (Horace), 205–206, 610–611
  medieval rhetoric, 469, 471–472, 474
  in Renaissance rhetoric, 688
Ars rhetorica (Victor), 257
Ars versificatoria (Matthew of Vendôme), 474
Art, **52–57**
  See also Classical rhetoric
Arte of English Poesie, The (Puttenham), 27, 261
  humanism, 357
  hyperbaton, 363–364
  on law and rhetoric, 425
  paradox, 552
  poetry and rhetoric, 611
  in Renaissance rhetoric, 679, 681
  style, 750, 751
  zeugma, 792
Arte of Prophesying, The (Perkins), 348
Arte of Rhetorique, The (Wilson), 18, 270, 356–357
  on composition, 143
  exhortation, 280–281
  forensic genre, 318
  humor, 360
  paradox, 551
  prosthesis, 637
  in Renaissance rhetoric, 675
Artes of Logicke and Retorike (Fenner), 778
Arthashastra (Kautilya), 141
Art of Delivering Written Language, The (Cockin), 230
Art of Persuasion in Greece, The (Kennedy), 506–507
Art of Prophesying, The (Perkins), 691
Art of Rhetoric in the Roman World, 300 B.C.–A.D. 300, The (Kennedy), 266
  modern rhetoric, 507
Art of Rhetoric Made Easy (Holmes), 228–229
Art of Speaking, The (Burgh), 230
Art poétique (Boileau), 383
Ascham, Roger
  humanism, 357
  in Renaissance rhetoric, 680
Askew, Anne, 507
Aspects (Chomsky), 434
Assonance, **57**
  See also Alliteration
Astell, Mary, 235
Astrophil and Stella (Sidney), 605

Asyndeton, **57**
  See also Figures of speech
  See also Polysyndeton
  See also Style
Athenäum (Schlegel), 405
Atticist–Asianist controversy, **57–59**
  See also Classical rhetoric
  See also Style
Attitudes toward History (Burke), 572
Atwill Janet, 458
Aubignac, Abbé d', 533
Audience, **59–75**
  ancient assembled and dispersed audiences, 68–70
  attention to authors and texts, 61
  attention to readers, 60–61
  audience analysis, 66–67
  as centerpiece, 60
  communication models, 64–66
  computer-mediated communication (CMC), 67
  conceptualizing audience as a community, 66
  democracy of public opinion, 66
  evolving terminology, 59–60
  history of audience, 59
  identification and cooperation, 62
  as individuals, 65
  influence during composition process, 62–63
  influence of audience upon the speaker, 62
  as institutions, 65
  intended audience, 63–64
  mass audiences, 68–72
  modern mass audiences, 70–71
  reader-response criticism, 64
  recent communication research, 65–66
  relationship between speaker and audience, 61–62
  rhetorical situation, 63
  technologies, 67
  types of, 61
  virtual audiences, 72–75
Auerbach, Erich
  imitation, 383
  medieval rhetoric, 481
Augustine (Saint)
  on casuistry, 84
  in classical rhetoric, 109
  on eloquence, 243
  on *ēthos*, 263, 269–270
  formulation of Christian eloquence, 243–244

Cicero, *cont.*
  on Atticist–Asianist
    controversy, 57–58
  on casuistry, 84
  in classical rhetoric, 94, 101,
    102–103, 105, 110, 111, 112,
    113
  on color, 115
  in commonplaces and
    commonplace books, 119,
    120
  on composition, 145
  on contingency and
    probability, 160
  on *controversia* and *suasoria*,
    168
  on credibility, 179–180, 184
  on criticism, 186
  on decorum, 199, 204–205,
    207
  on deliberation, 210
  on delivery, 217–219
  on digressio, 225
  on eloquence, 238–242
  epideictic genre, 251, 253, 255
  epistolary rhetoric, 257–258
  on *ēthos*, 263, 268–269
  on exemplum, 278
  forensic genre, 314, 315, 316–
    317
  on history, 342–345
  humanism, 351, 353
  humor, 359
  iconography, 367, 368, 373
  on imitation, 382
  invention, 389–391, 393, 396,
    398, 401
  on law and rhetoric, 420–421,
    423, 425
  logos, 460–461, 463
  medieval rhetoric, 469–470
  on memory, 487
  metaphor, 493
  metonymy, 496
  modern rhetoric, 499
  musical rhetoric, 513
  occasionality of rhetoric, 530
  panegyric, 549, 550
  pathos, 559–562
  poetry and rhetoric, 604, 610
  politics, 625
  practical wisdom, 632
  prudence, 638–639
  public speaking, 644–645, 646
  in Renaissance rhetoric, 673,
    677, 685–687
  rhetoric and philosophy, 590
  style, 745, 746, 749
  theory of *stasis*, 742
  thesis and antithesis, 775

Cicero, *cont.*
  third face of power, 628
  Topica, 781
  trivium, 783
  utility, 789
Ciceronianism. *See* Eloquence;
  Renaissance rhetoric: rhetoric
  in Renaissance language and
  literature *and* rhetoric in the
  age of Reformation and
  Counter-Reformation
Ciolek, S., 718
Cistercian, 477
*Civilization of the Renaissance in
  Italy* (Burckhardt), 358
Civil rights movement, 649, 724
Cixous, Hélène
  feminist rhetoric, 306
  logos, 466
Clarissa (Richardson), 259
Clarke, Edward, 303
Classical rhetoric, **92–115**
  Aristotle, 98–100
  Attic orators, 97–98
  canons of rhetoric, 111
  Cicero's *On Invention* and the
    anonymous *Rhetoric to
    Herennius*, 102, 103
  declamation, 105–107
  definitions of rhetoric, 110
  delivery, 113
  determination of question at
    issue, 110–111
  Greek rhetorical teaching in
    first century BCE, 103–104
  Hellenistic rhetoric, 100–103
  Isocrates, 96–98
  later Greek rhetoric, 109–110
  Latin rhetoric after Quintilian,
    108–109
  memory, 113
  parts of a judicial oration, 111–
    112
  Plato, 98
  progymnasmata, 104–105
  proofs, 112–113
  Quintilian, 107–108
  relevance in modern world,
    113–114
  Rhetoric to Alexander, 100
  Sophists, 95–96
  species of rhetoric, 110
  style, 112–113
  theoretically defined, 110–115
Clavis poetica (Kwetnickii), 719
Clay, Henry
  on deliberation, 211
  public speaking, 641
Cleaver, Eldridge, 506
Clément, Catherine, 466

Clemente da Urbino, 370
Cleon, 541
Clinton, Bill, 771
  campaign of, 79, 80, 81
  public speaking, 642
Clinton, Hillary Rodham, 644
Clouds, The (Aristophanes), 96
Cockin, William, 230
Code, Lorraine, 626
Codes, 132
Coke, Edward, 422, 424
Cole, Thomas, 254
Coleridge, Samuel Taylor, 20
  on composition, 149
Colet, John
  on eloquence, 245–246
  in Renaissance rhetoric, 678
Collingwood, R. G., 341–342
Color, **115–119**
  See also Art
  See also Classical rhetoric
  See also Controversia and
    suasoria
  See also Declamation
Colored Temperance Society of
  Philadelphia, 8
Comenius, Amos Komensky,
  718
Commedia (Dante), 666
*Commentaries on the Laws of
  England* (Blackstone), 408
Commonplaces and
  commonplace books, **119–
  124**
  See also Amplification
  See also Copia
  See also Invention
  See also Renaissance rhetoric:
    overview
  See also Topics
Communication, **125–137**
  codes, media, and channels,
    132
  communication studies, 130–
    131
  communication theory, 126–
    127
  critical tradition, 129–130
  culture trends, 134–135
  current trends, 134–135
  cybernetics, 128
  as discourse, 135
  functions, 131–132
  intrapersonal, 133
  levels and contexts, 133–134
  mass communication, 133
  metadiscourse, theory and
    practice, 135–136
  phenomenology, 127–128
  rhetoric, 127

Howe, Julia Ward, 303
Howell, Wilbur Samuel
on eighteenth-century rhetoric, 227
modern rhetoric, 506
Howl (Ginsberg), 606
How Monkeys See the World (Cheney and Seyfarth), 137–138
How to Do Things with Words (Austin), 501, 666–667, 738
How to Write History (Lucian), 343
Hudson, Richard A., 440, 443
Hufford, Roger, 22–23
Hughes, H. Stuart, 573
Hughes, Langston, 6
Hugh of Saint Victor, 488–489
Humanism, **350–359**
afterlife of, 357–358
historical development of, 353–357
See also Eighteenth-century rhetoric
See also Modern rhetoric
See also Renaissance rhetoric: overview
Human Understanding (Toulmin), 38
Humboldt, Wilhelm von
linguistics and rhetoric, 428, 432, 434, 440
style, 753
Hume, David
eighteenth-century rhetoric, 233
invention, 394
rhetoric and religion, 668
Humor, **359–361**
See also Pathos
Hus, Jan, 717
Husserl, Edmund
on communication, 128
linguistics and rhetoric, 440
reception theory, 659
Hutcheson, Francis, 233
Hybrid genres, **361–363**
See also Deliberative genre
See also Epideictic genre
See also Forensic genre
Hyman, Stanley Edgar, 573
Hymes, Dell, 438
Hypallagē, **363**
See also Figures of speech
Hyperbaton, **363–364**
See also Figures of speech
Hyperbolē, **364**
See also Figures of speech
See also Style
Hyperides, 542

Hyperius, Andreas Gerhard, 676, 690
Hypertext, **364–366**
See also Arrangement: modern arrangement
Hysteron prōteron, **366**
See also Figures of speech

I

Icones Symbolicae (Giarda), 373
Iconography, **367–375**
medals, *imprese,* and emblems, 370–371
medieval and Renaissance personifications, 367–370
Renaissance syncretism: Hermathena; and Hercules, eloquent and silent, 372–374
Ripa's *Iconologia,* 371
Iconologia (Ripa), 371
Idea of History, The (Collingwood), 341
Identification, **375–377**
Identity (Baumeister), 270
Ideograph, **378–381**
See also Identification
See also Invention
See also Politics: overview
See also Rhetorical vision
Il Cortegiano (Castiglione), 681, 686
humor, 359
Iliad
oral tradition, 532–533
oratory, 538
politics and rhetoric, 612
Illyricus, Matthias Flacius
humanism, 357
in Renaissance rhetoric, 692
Imitatio Christi (Thomas à Kempis), 382
Imitation, **381–384**
of classical models in the Renaissance, 382–383
models of speech and writing in antiquity, 381–382
in modern criticism, 383
Plato and Aristotle on mimēsis, 383
See also Copia
See also Criticism
See also Poetry
In a Different Voice: Psychological Theory and Women's Development (Gilligan), 306
In Ciceronis topica (Boethius), 462
Incidents in the Life of a Slave Girl (Jacob), 9
India, 140–141

Indian rhetoric, **384–387**
See also Comparative rhetoric
Induction. *See* Exemplum
Inference, **387–389**
See also Logic
See also Logos
Influence of Rhetoric in the Shaping of Great Britain, The (Oliver), 235
Informal Fallacies (Walton), 300
Ingarden, Roman, 659
Innis, Harold, 132
Inquiry into Human Understanding (Hume), 233
Institutiones grammaticae (Priscian), 480
Institutio oratoria (Quintilian), 239
forensic genre, 317
humor, 359
irony, 404–405
metonymy, 496
poetry and rhetoric, 611
practical wisdom, 632
public speaking, 645
International Phonetic Alphabet (IPA), 441
International Society for the History of Rhetoric, 649
Interpretation. *See* Hermeneutics; Law
Interpretation of Cultures, The (Geertz), 267
"Interpretive Function of the Critic, The" (Nilsen), 505
Introduction to the Art of Reading, An (Rice), 230
Introduction to the Classics (Blackwall), 228
In utramque partem. *See* Classical rhetoric; Law; Persuasion
Invention, **389–404**
character of the speaker, 393–394
character of the speech, 394
in Cicero, 389–392
common persuasions, 395–396
decision, 394
emotions of the audience, 394
finality of the invented whole: arrangement, 398–399
finality of invention itself: style, 397–398
finality of invention: style and arrangement, 397
finality of the medium of invention, 398
finality of the process of invention: delivery, 397
form of invention, 394

Maierthaler, W., 440
Mailloux, Steven, 186, 188–189
Makarii rhetoric, 719
Malcolm X, 6, 7, 16–17, 731
    modern rhetoric, 506
    public speaking, 644
Malinowski, Bronislaw, 139
Man, Paul de
    logos, 465
    poetry and rhetoric, 611
    reception theory, 661
    sublime, the, 760
    trivium, 787
Man Cannot Speak for Her
    (Campbell, ed.), 307
Mandela, Nelson, 644–645
Mandeville, Henry, 522
Mansbridge, Jane, 214
*Man's World, Woman's Place: A
    Study in Social Mythology*
    (Janeway), 305
*Manual of Composition and
    Rhetoric, A* (Hart), 526
Manutius, Aldus, 110
Mao Tse-Tung, 645
Marchettus of Padua, 514
Marcus, Jane, 305–306
Marcus, Rabanus, 785
Margarita Philosophica (Reisch),
    673
Marinism, 687–688
Marino, Giambattista, 687
Marshall, Thurgood, 6
Martine's Sensible Letter-Writer,
    520
Martin of Dacia, 482
Marx, Karl, 272
    on communication, 129
    on identification in rhetoric,
        375
    politics, 625
    rhetoric and religion, 668
*Marxism and the Philosophy of
    Language* (Volosinov), 272
Mason, John, 230
Mass audiences, 68–72
Mass communication, 133
Master Tropes, Four. See Irony;
    Metaphor; Metonymy;
    Synecdochē
*Mathematical Theory of
    Communication, The*
    (Shannon and Weaver),
    126
Mather, Cotton, 713
Mathesius, Wilem, 430
Mattheson, Johannes, 511, 512
Matthew of Vendôme, 474
Maurus, Rabanus, 472
Mauss, Marcel, 268

Maxim, 83, 84, 85, 86, 87, 105,
    161, 169, 176, 194, 197, 199,
    249, 319, 395, 417, 439, 449,
    460, 461, 609, 643, 722, 723,
    781
Maximem und Reflexionen
    (Goethe), 20
May, James M., 111
    on *ēthos,* 268
Mayáns y Siscar, Gregorio, 229
McAuliffe, Christa, 773
McCain, John, campaign of, 78
McCarthy, Joseph, 505
McCarthy, Thomas, 213
McCloskey, D., 465
McGee, Brian R., 13
McGee, Michael, 617, 620
McKeon, Richard
    on composition, 147
    on contingency and
        probability, 160
    on criticism, 182–183, 184,
        185, 186–187
    on invention, 402
    modern rhetoric, 501–502, 505
    trivium, 785
McKerrow, Ray E., 39
McLuhan, Marshall
    on arrangement, 47
    on communication, 132
    iconography, 367
    public speaking, 642
    speech, 736
McPherson, James M., 338
Mead, George Herbert, 499–500
Meaning. *See* Hermeneutics;
    Reception Theory; Religion
*Meaning of Meaning, The: A Study
    of the Influence of Language
    upon Thought and of the
    Science of Symbolism* (Ogden),
    22
    influence of modern rhetoric,
        500
Media, 132
Medieval rhetoric, **469–482**
    major genres: poetics, letter
        writing, preaching, 474–478
    Medieval grammar, 479–482
    overview, 469–478
Megill, A., 465
Melanchthon, Philipp
    in commonplaces and
        commonplace books, 121–
        122
    homiletics, 348
    humanism, 356, 357
    pathos, 565, 566
    in Renaissance rhetoric, 674–
        675, 689, 690

Melanchthon, Philipp, *cont.*
    Slavic rhetoric, 717
    style, 749
Mel'cuk, Igor A., 440, 443
Memory, **482–493**
    after rhetoric, 491–492
    architectural memory of Rome,
        485–488
    grid memory of Middle Ages,
        488–490
    memory before rhetoric, 484–
        485
    "real" memories of the
        Renaissance, 490–491
Menander, 550
Menexenus (Plato), 255
Meno (Plato)
    on dialectic, 222
    on memory, 484
Merleau-Ponty, Maurice, 501
Metadiscourse, 135–136
Metalogicon (John of Salisbury),
    463
Metamorphoses (Ovid), 605
Metaphor, **493–496**
    twentieth-century theories,
        494–495
    See also Figures of speech; Style;
    Tacit dimension, the
Metaphors We Live By (Lakoff and
    Johnson), 448
Metaphysics (Aristotle), 2
    on casuistry, 87
    science and rhetoric, 703
Metonymy, **496–498**
    twentieth-century theories of,
        496–498
    See also Figures of speech
    See also Style
Meun, Jean de, 471
Meyer, Michel, 567–568
Michelet, Jules, 344
Mikhail Radau of Braniewo,
    718
Mill, James, 713
Mill, John Stuart
    on criticism, 182
    on deliberation, 211
    expediency, 286
    fallacies, 296
    feminist rhetoric, 303
    politics and rhetoric, 623
Miller, Arthur B., 267–268
Miller, Diane H., 306
Miller, Keith D., 574
Mills, C. Wright, 626
Milton, John
    on audience, 69
    rhetoric and religion, 667
Mimēsis. *See* Imitation